T0388743

The Palgrave Handbook of European Referendums

Julie Smith
Editor

The Palgrave Handbook of European Referendums

Editor
Julie Smith
Department of Politics and
International Studies
University of Cambridge
Cambridge, UK

ISBN 978-3-030-55802-4   ISBN 978-3-030-55803-1 (eBook)
https://doi.org/10.1007/978-3-030-55803-1

Cover image: Andi Edwards/Alamy Stock Photo

This Palgrave Macmillan imprint is published by the registered company Springer Nature Switzerland AG
The registered company address is: Gewerbestrasse 11, 6330 Cham, Switzerland

ACKNOWLEDGMENTS

Somewhat counter-intuitively, this volume on direct democracy has its genesis in an EU-funded network on parliamentary democracy in Europe: PADEMIA. Over the lifetime of that network, two referendums in particular spurred me to organise academic events. The first was the 2015 Greek referendum on the EU bailout during the Eurozone crisis, which served as the catalyst for a panel at the 2016 Annual Meeting of Pademia. The second was the now all-too-familiar and well-studied UK referendum on membership of the EU, leading to Brexit. Having co-organised with the Trans-European Policy Studies Association (TEPSA) a Pademia Roundtable on referendums in Europe following that momentous event, I was contacted by Jemima Warren at Palgrave, who enquired if I would be interested in editing a Handbook on European *Referenda*. After discussing the idea and agreeing it could the Palgrave Handbook on European *Referendums* in line with the usage by David Butler and others, I agreed to do it. That was in the summer of 2016—it has been a long four years punctuated by further referendums in various countries and two general elections in the UK, not to mention a pandemic.

I am very grateful to the participants at the TEPSA-Pademia Workshop for some very productive brain-storming, which helped shape the Handbook, and to the three 'anonymous' reviewers of the proposal submitted to Palgrave, one of whom was to become a contributor.

Thanks are due to the European Commission, which funded the Pademia network (reference number: 540381-LLP-1-2013-1-DE-ERASMUS-ENW), to TEPSA for organising the Brussels event and to Robinson College and the POLIS Department in Cambridge for grants to allow us to run a Handbook workshop in June 2018. On that occasion Claire Darmé and Julia Vassileva both provided help as assiduous rapporteurs. Léonie de Jonge, in addition to co-authoring a chapter, helped on the editorial side, as did Maria Chiara Vinciguerra. I am grateful to them all.

My greatest debt of gratitude, of course, is to all the contributors who have made this book as fascinating as it is. It would be invidious to single out individual authors, so I shall simply say how much I appreciate the advice given to me at various stages of the process by some great figures in parliamentary and referendum studies. It has been an honour to work with them.

The team at Palgrave has been fantastic throughout—thanks to Jemima Warren, Oliver Foster, Nick Barclay and Rebecca Roberts, who have been patient and professional at all times.

Finally, thank you to all my family and friends for putting up with a tired and grumpy editor.

Cambridge   Julie Smith
July 2020

CONTENTS

NOTES ON CONTRIBUTORS

Alex Andrione-Moylan, Ph.D. Fellow at the Leuven Centre for Global Governance Studies, University of Leuven, Belgium. His research focuses on populism and contestation in the EU and global governance. He has published, inter alia, on the impact of populism in European Political Parties (2018), on the G7 in times of antiglobalism and contestation (2018) and the EU's engagement with informal governance bodies (2019).

Ece Özlem Atikcan is an Associate Professor in Politics and International Studies at the University of Warwick, and a Visiting Senior Research Fellow at the European Institute of University College London in the UK. Her research combines a theoretical focus on political campaigns, issue framing, lobbying, transnational social movements and diffusion with a regional focus on the European Union. Based on over 180 in-depth interviews with campaigners, media content analyses and public opinion data, she studies EU referendum campaigns to understand the impact of campaign argumentation on public opinion. Her work has appeared in the *European Journal of Political Research, Journal of Common Market Studies, Journal of Elections Public Opinion and Parties, Journal of Public Policy, Journal of European Integration*, and as books with Cambridge University Press, Oxford University Press and McGill-Queen's University Press.

Agnes Batory is a Professor at Central European University School of Public Policy, and a Research Fellow of the CEU Center for Policy Studies, Vienna, Austria. Her recent publications deal with populism, participatory and collaborative governance and policy failure and compliance problems in the EU context.

Derek Beach is a Professor of Political Science at the University of Aarhus, Denmark, where he teaches case study methodology and EU politics. He has authored articles, chapters and books on research methodology, referendums and European integration, and co-authored the books *Process-Tracing Methods* and *Causal Case Studies* (both with University of Michigan Press). He has taught qualitative case study methods at ECPR, ICPSR and IPSA summer and winter schools, and numerous workshops and seminars on process tracing methods throughout the world. He is also an academic co-convenor of the ECPR Methods Schools.

Andrew Blick is Reader in Politics and Contemporary History, King's College London, UK. During 2010–2015, he was Research Fellow to the first inquiry conducted by the UK Parliament into whether the UK should adopt a written constitution. He was an assistant at the Prime Minister's Office, No.10 Downing Street, in 1999. He is the author of numerous books, including *People Who Live in the Dark: The History of the Special Adviser in British Politics* (2004); *Beyond Magna Carta: A Constitution for the United Kingdom* (2015); *The Referendum in Britain: A History* (with Lucy Atkinson and Matt Qvortrup, 2020 forthcoming); and *Electrified Democracy: The UK Parliament and the Internet in Historic Perspective* (2021 forthcoming). He is editor, with Roger Mortimore, of *Butler's British Political Facts* (2018).

Clive H. Church is Emeritus Professor of European Studies at the University of Kent, UK. Educated at the University of Exeter and University College London, he has taught at Trinity College, Dublin and the University of Lancaster. He has also been a visiting Fellow in several continental Universities. His interests have moved from French history through European Union Studies to Swiss history and politics. He has been working on these last since the early 1970s and has now produced four books *The Politics and Government of Switzerland* (Palgrave, 2004); *Switzerland and the European Union* (ed.); (Routledge, 2007); *A Concise History of Switzerland* (with Randy Head) (CUP, 2013); and *Political Change in Switzerland* (Routledge/Europa, 2016), along with numerous articles, chapters and reports.

John Curtice is Professor of Politics at Strathclyde University and Senior Research Fellow, NatCen Social Research. He has written extensively about political and social attitudes both across the UK as a whole and in Scotland in particular. He has been a co-editor of the annual British and Scottish Social Attitudes survey series for over twenty years, and is a regular contributor to British and international media coverage of politics and public opinion in Scotland and the UK.

Léonie de Jonge is Assistant Professor of European Politics and Society at the University of Groningen. She holds a Ph.D. in Politics and International Studies from the University of Cambridge. Her research focuses on right-wing populism in Western Europe, with a particular focus in the Benelux region.

Johan A. Elkink University College Dublin, Ireland, specialises in quantitative methods in political science, in particular spatial econometrics, and applications in democratisation and voting behaviour. He co-authored reports on voting behaviour in the Irish referendums on the Lisbon Treaty and co-edited *The Act of Voting* (2017). His work has appeared in the *Journal of Politics*, *Comparative Political Studies*, *European Journal of Political Research* and *Electoral Studies*.

David Farrell, MRIA is Head of Politics and International Relations at University College Dublin, Ireland. A specialist in the study of representation, elections and parties, his most recent books include: *A Conservative Revolution? Electoral Change in Twenty-First Century Ireland* (2017) and *The Post-Crisis Irish Voter: Voting Behaviour in the Irish 2016 General Election* (2018). His current work is focused on constitutional deliberation. To date he has advised and/or researched five government-led deliberative mini-public processes (citizens' assemblies).

John Erik Fossum is Professor at ARENA Centre for European Studies, University of Oslo, Norway. He is project coordinator for the H2020-project EU3D—Differentiation, Dominance, Democracy (2019–2023). Most recent books are: *Squaring the Circle on Brexit—Could the Norway Model Work?* (2018), with Hans Petter Graver; *Diversity and Contestations over Nationalism in Europe and Canada*, (2018), co-edited with Riva Kastoryano and Birte Siim and *Towards a Segmented European Political Order,* co-edited with Jozef Batora (2020). Most recent articles are 'European Federalism: Pitfalls and Possibilities', *European Law Journal*, (2017) 23 (5): 361–379; and 'Norway and the European Union', *Oxford Research Encyclopedia, Politics.*

Andrew Glencross is Senior Lecturer at Aston University, UK, and Co-Director of the Aston Centre for Europe. He is also a Senior Fellow of the Foreign Policy Research Institute (USA) and an Associate Editor at ECPR Press. He holds a Ph.D. from the European University Institute and is a graduate of the University of Cambridge as well as a former Joseph Hodges Choate Fellow at Harvard University. He is the author of several books, including *Why the UK Voted for Brexit: David Cameron's Great Miscalculation* (2016) and has published research articles on many areas of European integration in journals such as the *European Journal of International Relations, International Affairs*, and *International Theory.*

Katy Hayward is Reader in Sociology and a Fellow of the Senator George Mitchell Institute for Global Peace, Security & Justice based at Queen's University Belfast, Ireland. She is a Senior Fellow of the UK in a Changing Europe initiative, funded by the Economic and Social Research Council, for which she is working on the topic of 'The Future and Status of Northern Ireland after Brexit'.

Ersin Kalaycıoğlu is a student of comparative politics at Sabancı University, Istanbul, Turkey. He formerly served as the rector of Isik University, Istanbul. He is a member of the Academy of Science, Turkey and also a member of the Turkish Political Science Association, in both of which he also served as Executive Board member until 2017. He has authored, co-authored or co-edited several books, most recently the *Rising Tide of Conservatism in Turkey*, co-authored with Ali Carkoglu (2009), and has published several political science textbooks and monographs in both English and Turkish. His articles have appeared in such journals as *Comparative Political Studies*, *Legislative Studies Quarterly*, *South European Society and Politics*, *Southeast European and Black Sea Studies* and *Turkish Studies*.

Gülnur Kocapınar obtained her Ph.D. in Political Science from Sabancı University, Istanbul, Turkey in 2019. Her research interests include party politics, political elites and recruitment, political party organisations, legislative politics and Turkish politics. Her co-authored articles have been published in journals such as *Party Politics*, *Parliamentary Affairs*, *Turkish Studies*, and *Political Research Quarterly*.

Brigid Laffan is Director and Professor at the Robert Schuman Centre for Advanced Studies, an interdisciplinary research centre at the European University Institute, Italy. The Centre's mission is to contribute to research on the major issues facing contemporary European society. Previously she was Vice-President of University College Dublin and Principal of the College of Human Sciences from 2004 to 2011. She is also the recipient of numerous awards: in 2005 she was elected Member of the Royal Irish Academy and in 2010 received the Ordre nationale du Mérite from the President of the French Republic. Her scholarship has been recognised by the THESEUS Award for Outstanding Research on European Integration in 2012, and the Lifetime Achievement Award for contribution to the development of European Studies in 2014 by the University Association for Contemporary European Studies (UACES).

Christopher Lord is Professor at ARENA, The Centre for European Studies at the University of Oslo, Norway. He has written numerous books and journal articles on democracy, legitimacy and the European Union, as well as problems of differential integration. His current work includes attempts to rethink the 'indirect legitimacy' of the European Union as a means by which member state democracies deliver their own obligations to their own publics.

Jörg Mathias is Senior Lecturer in Politics and International Relations at Aston University, Birmingham, UK. His current research focuses on regional and local aspects of labour market management and social security provision in West European countries.

Fernando Mendez is a Senior Researcher based at the University of Zürich, Switzerland. Dr Mendez gained his Ph.D. in political science at the European University Institute, Florence, and works in various subfields of Political Science (e.g. comparative politics, political behaviour and political communication). He has published extensively on direct democracy with much of his work being interdisciplinary in nature and drawing on fields such as Comparative Law.

Mario Mendez is a Reader in Law in the Department of Law at Queen Mary University of London where he teaches constitutional law, comparative constitutional law and EU law. His research on referendums includes a co-authored monograph entitled *Referendums and the European Union: A Comparative Inquiry* (CUP, 2014) and a co-authored study prepared for the European Parliament entitled *Referendums on EU Matters* (PE 571.402, 2017).

Laurence Morel is Associate Professor of Political Science at the University of Lille, France, and member of the Centre de Recherches Politiques of Sciences Po Paris (CEVIPOF). She has been Chair and vice-Chair of the IPSA/ISA Research Committee on Political Sociology since 2014. Her publications in English on referendums include: *The Routledge Handbook to Referendums and Direct Democracy*, (2018) (ed. with M. Qvortrup); 'Referendums', in Sajo, A. and Rosenfeld, M. (ed.) *The Oxford Handbook of Comparative Constitutional Law*, (2012) 'Referenda', in Badie, B., Berg-Schlosser, D. and Morlino, L. (ed.) *International Encyclopedia of Political Science* (2011).

Philip Norton (Lord Norton of Louth) is Professor of Government, and Director of the Centre for Legislative Studies, at the University of Hull. He also serves as President of the Study of Parliament Group, Chair of the History of Parliament Trust and Editor of *The Journal of Legislative Studies*. He was elevated to the peerage, as Lord Norton of Louth, in 1998 and was the first Chair of the House of Lords Constitution Committee.

Henrik Oscarsson is a Professor of Political Science, electoral studies, at the Department of Political Science, University of Gothenburg, Sweden. He is research director of the Swedish National Election Studies (SNES).

Lina (Triantafyllia) Papadopoulou is Associate Professor of Constitutional Law at the Λας Σψηοολ οφ τηε Aristotle University of Thessaloniki (AUTh), Greece. She has been a holder of a Jean Monnet Chair for European Constitutional Law and Culture, and she is now the Academic Co-ordinator of the AUTh Jean Monnet Centre of Excellence on 'European Constitutionalism and Religion(s)'.

Ralph Petry is a research specialist at the University of Luxembourg for the National Contact Point Luxembourg in the European Migration Network (EMN Luxembourg). He holds an M.A. in Social and Cultural Anthropology from the University of Vienna and wrote his thesis on the 2015 referendum in Luxembourg.

Matt Qvortrup is Professor of Political Science at Coventry University, UK. Described by the *Financial Times* as 'a world authority on referendums', he predicted the outcome of the Brexit referendum in an academic article published three months before the vote. Professor Qvortrup has written several books on the referendums, including *A Comparative Study of Referendums* (2nd Edition 2005), *Referendums and Ethnic Conflict* (2014) and *Government by Referendum* (2018). Professor Qvortrup earned his doctorate at Brasenose College Oxford. In addition to his work as a scholar, Professor Qvortrup was part of President Obama's Special Envoy Team in Sudan in 2009–2010, and he has been a constitutional advisor for more than 20 governments around the world. He is also joint editor-in-chief of *European Political Science Review.*

Theresa Reidy is Head of the Department of Government and Politics, and a senior lecturer at University College Cork, Ireland. Her research interests lie in the areas of political institutions and electoral behaviour and her recent work has been published in *Electoral Studies, Parliamentary Affairs* and *Politics.* She is co-editor of the *International Political Science Review.*

Alan Renwick is Deputy Director of the Constitution Unit and Associate Professor of British Politics in the Department of Political Science at University College London, UK. He has written widely on electoral systems, referendums and mechanisms of deliberative democracy such as citizens' assemblies. His recent research has focused on the conduct of referendums, and he was Research Director for the Constitution Unit's 2018 Independent Commission on Referendums.

Guri Rosén is Associate Professor at Oslo Metropolitan University (OsloMet) and Researcher at ARENA Center for European Studies, University of Oslo, Norway. Her research focuses on political representation and democracy in the EU, the European Parliament and interinstitutional relations as well as EU external relations. Her work has been published in journals such as *Journal of European Public Policy, West European Politics* and *Journal of European Integration.*

Lise Rye is Professor of Contemporary European History at NTNU Norwegian University of Science and Technology, Norway. Her research focuses on European economic and political integration, with emphasis on EFTA-EC/EU relations, the European Economic Area and Norway's relations with the EU.

Jess Sargeant is a Senior Researcher at the Institute for Government, UK where she conducts research into intergovernmental relations and the UK's exit from the European Union. She was formerly a Research Assistant at the Constitution Unit, University College London where she worked with Dr Alan Renwick on comparative research into the use and conduct of referendums internationally, and on the Independent Commission on Referendums, which was established to review the role and regulation of referendums in the UK.

Uwe Serdült is working as a professor at Ritsumeikan University, Japan, in the College of Information Science and Engineering while keeping some projects as a principal investigator at the Centre for Democracy Studies Aarau (ZDA), University of Zurich, Switzerland. In these dual positions, he teaches and does interdisciplinary research in several domains of e-society. Within digital democracy he is especially interested in internet-based platforms and tools for citizens (e-participation) as well as public administrations (e-government) in order to enhance transparency and deliberation in an information society. Regarding referendums he mainly works on Switzerland but is also interested to learn from most different political systems such as Japan and Peru. At the ZDA Serdült and a small team maintain the international referendum results database www.c2d.ch.

Julie Smith is Reader in European Politics at Cambridge University, UK. As Baroness Smith of Newnham, she sits in the House of Lords, the upper chamber of the British parliament. Her research focuses on democracy in the EU and the UK's relations with the EU, as well as the ever-changing topic of the House of Lords and Brexit. Recent publications include: *The UK's Journeys Into and Out of the EU: Destinations Unknown* (London: Routledge, 2017; paperback edition May 2018).

Claudia Sternberg is Principal Research Fellow at the UCL European Institute, University College London. She is the author of *The Struggle for EU Legitimacy. Public Contestation, 1950–2005* (UACES Best Book, 2014) and, with Kalypso Nicolaidis and Kira Gartzou-Katsouyanni, of *The Greco-German Affair in the Euro Crisis: Mutual Recognition Lost?*

Jane Suiter is Associate Professor in the School of Communications at Dublin City University, Ireland. Jane's expertise lies mainly in the area of the public sphere; and in particular participation and political engagement. Her current research focus is on disinformation and direct and deliberative democracy.

Palle Svensson is Professor Emeritus in the Department of Political Science at Aarhus University, Denmark, and holds a doctorate from the same institution. He has written extensively on comparative politics, democracy and political participation, in particular on referendums, including *Folkets røst. Demokrati og folkeafstemninger i Danmark og andre europæiske lande* (The Voice of the People. Democracy and referendums in Denmark and other European countries) (2003) and contributed to *Direct Democracy: The International IDEA Handbook* (2008).

P. V. Uleri has been lecturer in Political Science at the 'Cesare Alfieri', University of Florence, Italy, where he taught courses on *Political Parties* and on *Democracies and Referenda*. He has been co-editor and co-author of *Democrazie e Referendum* and of *The Referendum Experience in Europe*. He is the author of *Referendum e democrazia*.

Joost van den Akker obtained his Ph.D. degree in 2018 at the University of Twente with a thesis titled *Ruling the Referendum? European Integration Challenged by Direct Democracy*. He holds a Master's degree in Analysing Europe/Europastudien (M.A.) from Maastricht University/RWTH Aachen University (2008) and a Master's degree in European Law School (LL.M.) from Maastricht University (2010).

Jan Wouters is Full Professor of International Law and International Organizations, University of Leuven, Belgium, and Jean Monnet Chair ad personam EU and Global Governance. Founding Director of the Leuven Centre for Global Governance Studies and the Institute for International Law. Prof. Dr Wouters is visiting Professor at Sciences Po (Paris), Luiss University (Rome) and the College of Europe (Bruges) and Adjunct Professor at Columbia. Prof. Wouters is a Member of the Royal Academy of Belgium for Sciences and Arts and practises law as Of Counsel at Linklaters, Brussels. He is Editor of the *International Encyclopedia of Intergovernmental Organizations*, Deputy Director of the *Revue Belge de Droit International*, and an editorial board member in ten other international journals. He has published widely on international and EU law, international organisations, global governance, and corporate and financial law. His most recent publications include *The Commons and a New Global Governance* (2019), *EU Human Rights and Democratization Policies* (2018), *International Law: A European Perspective* (2018), *The G7, Anti-Globalism and the Governance of Globalization* (2018), *The Faces of Human Rights* (2019), *Changing Borders in Europe* (2019), *General Principles of Law and the Coherence of International Law* (2019) and *Parliamentary Cooperation and Diplomacy in EU External Relations* (2019).

LIST OF FIGURES

LIST OF TABLES

CHAPTER 1

Introduction

Julie Smith

1.1 Opening Remarks: A Case in Point

Referendums play an increasingly significant role in European politics at both national and European Union (EU) level. Whether it is joining the EU, amending the EU treaties or even leaving the EU, citizens have repeatedly been invited to give their views on European matters in a significant shift from representative democracy towards direct democracy. On other constitutional and social issues, as well as matters of foreign policy and ratification of international treaties, referendums have come to the fore in recent years, both within EU Member States and would-be Member States, and in non-EU European states, most notably Switzerland. The 2016 UK referendum on whether to stay in the EU in particular raised profound questions, both practical and theoretical, about the nature of direct democracy in the twenty-first century and its relationship with representative democracy.

Referendums and plebiscites may allow citizens to respond to a very specific question which raises few wider concerns for the polity as a whole, for example on prohibition (or abolition) of a particular act of the state or of civil society, or they may take place on a broader canvas where the decisions of voters (the 'people') directly answering one question potentially affects the polity overall and may pit citizens against their chosen representatives. Such tensions can occur whether the referendum has been demanded by the citizens (often

J. Smith (✉)
Department of Politics and International Studies, University of Cambridge,
Cambridge, UK
e-mail: jes42@cam.ac.uk

© The Author(s) 2021
J. Smith (ed.), *The Palgrave Handbook of European Referendums*,
https://doi.org/10.1007/978-3-030-55803-1_1

known as a 'citizens' initiative'), offered by the government (sometimes called a 'plebiscite', depending on the specific context) or has been required by the national constitution. Moreover, such tensions can be exacerbated if there is perceived ambiguity in the question put or about implementing the outcome of the vote and its implications.

In the case of a mandatory poll with binding consequences, the legal framework needs to be clear and implementing its outcomes should generally be uncontroversial. Provision for such a vote is enshrined in the constitution of the polity and the government is expected to implement the express will of the people; failure to do so would have consequences. In the case of optional, advisory referendums, the relationship between the electorate's express wishes and the actions of their elected representatives is far less clear. Legally, neither elected representatives nor the executive are bound to obey 'the will of the people' and opponents of the outcome may argue that there is no reason to implement a decision that has no more status than an opinion poll. Yet failure to do so may cause a public backlash and possibly even legal action.

Such differences of interpretation were highlighted in the wake of the UK's 2016 decision to leave the European Union. Prime Minister Theresa May and her government claimed that they were obeying 'an instruction' from the voters, a somewhat odd concept in a parliamentary democracy which prides itself on the strength of parliamentary sovereignty. Four years on, senior cabinet minister Michael Gove was using the same language as the UK moved towards a new relationship with the EU, stating: 'And it was the instruction from the electorate in the 2016 referendum…' (Gove 2020). It appeared that the tools of direct democracy had trumped the instruments of representative democracy. An optional, non-binding vote had created a critical juncture in British politics and apparently constrained the choices of elected representatives. The executive considered itself bound by the referendum and when MPs refused to accept the deal on departure that the PM had painstakingly negotiated with the other 27 EU Member States she spoke directly to the people. In a non-too-veiled attack on fellow MPs, May used an impromptu television broadcast to set the people against Parliament. Her approach elicited concern and condemnation among those who felt this might herald plebiscitary or dictatorial tendencies. True, the people **had** spoken. Yet when invited to endorse their referendum vote by increasing the government's majority at a snap election in June 2017, they failed to do so. May lost the slim majority her predecessor had secured just two years earlier and in the context of a hung Parliament she found it impossible to secure a majority for any sort of Brexit deal. For May this showed that Parliament was not listening to the people. For those who believed in the traditional concept of Burkean representation, there was a sense of disbelief—parliamentarians as representatives of the people should use their judgement in determining how best to respond to the vote to leave the EU they believed, not obey any 'instruction'.

The interplay of direct and indirect democracy was toxic and the situation was compounded by the fact that, unlike a question on, say, prohibition or fox-hunting on which an unambiguous, narrowly defined and reversible binary choice can be made, the question put to the British electorate in 2016 was one that was open to many interpretations. As is usually the case in referendums, the Brexit vote was framed as a binary choice: Remain/Leave.[1] However, in practice 'Leave' can be seen as a catch-all to cover any one of several possible scenarios for the UK's relationship with the EU. The choice was superficially very clear; in reality, it was anything but. Hence, in part, the difficulty the Prime Minister faced in implementing the decision. This was compounded by a further issue: the closeness of the vote. 52:48 sounds decisive. More than a million votes separated the two sides in a poll where a majority of one would have been sufficient to secure victory. Nonetheless, the majoritarian nature of direct democracy discussed by Lord in Chapter 2 ensured that the seemingly decisive outcome would be contested by those on the losing side. The problem was exacerbated by the fact that turnout, although high in UK terms, was only 72%. Fewer than half of eligible voters had backed the decision to leave. In addition, over three million EU nationals were resident in the UK at the time of the referendum, most of whom were not eligible to vote, while hundreds of thousands of British citizens resident elsewhere in the EU were also disenfranchised. Downplayed at the time of the referendum, the fact that millions of people's lives would be affected by a referendum in which they could play no part raises serious questions about the extent of the franchise in referendums.

There was a considerable backlash and attempts to overturn the results of the referendum. The pro-EU Liberal Democrats fought a very successful campaign in the 2019 European Parliament elections with the slogan 'Stop Brexit'. In the event, a further general election resolved the matter. The Conservatives, now led by Leave-supporter Boris Johnson, won a resounding victory in December 2019 and on 31 January 2020 the UK formally left the European Union. The outcome of the June 2016 referendum had finally been implemented but only after years of post-poll debate during which the arguments and deliberation that should have preceded the vote took place. Because the nature of the key aspect of 'Brexit', the UK's relationship with the European Union once it left was never fully elaborated during the referendum, much time was devoted to exploring the implications *after* people had voted.

In many ways, these difficulties reflect a key problem of all referendums: their majoritarian nature. That Brexit became so contested and its outcome so bitterly resented resulted from the majoritarian nature of referendums. Independence referendums, discussed by Qvortrup and Curtice in Chapters 14 and 15 are also marked by a 'winner takes all' aspect that inevitably leaves a section of the population on the losing side, forced to accept a decision they opposed and which, potentially, they will have no opportunity to reverse. Unlike electing a government when people know they will have a chance to

---

[1] Sweden is an exception, offering multiple options in referendums (see Chapter 7 by Qvortrup).

kick out the incumbents after a few years if they believe they are not doing a good job, a referendum decision is typically assumed to be a one-off decision, not one to be repeated on a regular basis. Since many referendums relate to constitutional issues, this is understandable: the very concept of a constitution implies a degree of stability and continuity that may not be provided by ordinary legislation and frequent amendment is undesirable. Thus, the results of referendums should be durable; however, this also means that it is essential that voters do make the right decision based on deliberation and information.

The 2016 referendum on the UK's membership of the European Union serves as a perfect microcosm of the problems caused by grafting tools of direct democracy onto a representative system and exemplifies the questions that underpin the present volume. But first a word about definitions.

1.2   Referendums, Plebiscites or Citizens' Initiatives

The terms 'plebiscite' and 'referendum' are frequently used interchangeably to imply a form of direct democracy, where citizens rather than parliaments decide on policy. A more accurate reading of the terms sees plebiscites as a form of 'caesarism', as practised by Napoleon in the eighteenth century (see Chapter 7 by Qvortrup) and typically seen in autocracies rather than democracies. Referendums are more usually held in democracies and provide a greater opportunity for citizens to say 'No'. Just as democracy during the Soviet era was frequently dubbed 'façade democracy', so plebiscites offer only a pretence of citizens taking decisions. By contrast to referendums and plebiscites, citizens' initiatives provide bottom-up opportunities for citizens to set the agenda. We use the term 'referendums' rather than 'referenda' in line with the practice established by Butler and Ranney in 1994 and, according to the Former Speaker of the House of Commons, Betty Boothroyd, a term used in Britain for over 150 years and quite appropriate for Parliament, which indeed uses that term (*Hansard* 3 June 1998).

Who calls referendums and why is crucial to understanding their nature and ramifications. Are they democratic devices enabling the people to exercise sovereignty or the tools of dictators? Or are they in fact neutral mechanisms, without inherent strengths and weaknesses? To an extent the answer lies in the above-mentioned distinctions between referendums (typically called by governments, or constitutionally mandated, in a democracy), plebiscites (called by autocratic leaders and in which citizens have no meaningful choice), and citizens' initiatives (bottom-up devices where citizens themselves demand a say on an issue, and which can by definition only occur in democratic systems). In many cases, politicians call referendums to try to resolve differences within their own party (see for example Chapter 26 by Oscarsson). This can be a sensible way of addressing a matter that cuts across social and political cleavages and thus cannot be determined through the existing party system. Yet, the decision to call a referendum may, as critics have long claimed, essentially serve as a device of (would-be) demagogues and dictators. Certainly, the 2017 referendum in Turkey was intended to grant greater powers to the President, while the 2015 referendum in Greece was used by the government as a way to try to exert leverage externally—on the EU. By contrast, in Switzerland optional votes are often pushed by citizens rather than political leaders, as Chapter 10 by Serdült demonstrates. Elsewhere, referendums may be pushed by opposition parties, especially at times of economic difficulty—context can be everything.

1.3 Aims of This Volume

This volume seeks to address a range of perennial theoretical and legal questions that face policy-makers when they offer citizens the chance to take or influence decisions by referendum, not least whether to accept the 'will of the people'. It does so via a series of chapters each of which provides an empirically rich analysis of one or more case studies. Despite the recent growth in the study of referendums, there is no comprehensive work that looks at both the empirical and theoretical aspects of referendums in Europe. There are a small number of works focusing closely on matters of European integration as well as seminal works on referendums around the world, including a recent edited volume by Richard Rose, *How Referendums Challenge European Democracy: Brexit and Beyond* (2020), in addition to myriad individual book and articles about specific referendums. The two main volumes on referendums related to European integration—Sara B. Hobolt's *Europe in Question: Referendums on European Integration* (Oxford: Oxford University Press, 2009) and Fernando Mendez, Mario Mendez and Vasiliki Trigas's (2014) *Referendums and the European Union: A comparative inquiry*—are both limited to EU-related matters and the former is now somewhat dated. While other volumes, notably David Butler and Austin Ranney's edited volume, *Referendums Around the World: The Growing Use of Direct Democracy* (Washington DC: The AEI Press, 1994) and Matt Qvortrup's *Referendums Around the World: The Continued Growth of Direct Democracy* (Basingstoke: Palgrave, 2014), provide a wide, comparative perspective, by definition they do not focus in detail on European referendums and, inevitably, they do not cover a range of recent referendums that have raised crucial constitutional questions. Morel and Qvortrup's comprehensive 2018 volume, the *Routledge Handbook on Referendums and Direct Democracy*, looks at all aspects of direct democracy, not just referendums, addressing not only national but also sub-national practices of direct democracy globally. The present volume complements their work, by focusing more narrowly on referendums within Europe, looking at domestic referendums on constitutional matters and questions of social policy, as well as those centred on EU-related matters.

We are not seeking to cover every referendum held in Europe since 1945—this volume is a Handbook, not an Encyclopaedia, far less Wikipedia. Rather, through rigorous empirical analysis, it seeks to address a range of theoretical and empirical questions across a number of European countries where referendums have played a significant role. The empirical chapters focus only on democracies, so that the tools of direct democracy under discussion are referendums, rather than plebiscites, a distinction discussed at some length by both Qvortrup and Uleri (Chapters 7 and 17, respectively). Thus, it does not include the referendum that led to Crimea joining the Russian Federation in 2014, nor yet the so-called referendum called by Vladimir Putin on 1 July 2020 through which he de facto secured the right to the Russian presidency for life in a vote where the outcome was known even before the polls closed. The usual democratic norms were clearly lacking in both cases, rendering them interesting in their own right but qualitatively different exercises from those explored here.

Nonetheless, as the chapters by Batory, Morel, and Kalaycıoğlu and Kocapınar (Chapters 31, 9 and 19, respectively) all demonstrate, plebiscitary tendencies can appear in the use of referendums even in formally democratic systems. Indeed, they can be used by leaders to try to reinforce their own position, whether within the domestic polity as President Erdogan sought to do in the 2017 referendum (Kalaycıoğlu and Kocapınar), or vis-à-vis third parties, notably the European Union, *pace* Viktor Orbán and Alexis Tsipras opposing the EU's responses the refugee and Eurozone crises, respectively. Yet, as Chapters 30 and 31 by Papadopoulou and Batory show, both premiers lost—Orbán because so few Hungarian voters turned out and Tsipras because his snap referendum and the popular vote resulted in a proposal from the EU that was significantly worse than the offer that was previously available. Such outcomes inevitably lead one to wonder why governments hold referendums when they are not legally obliged to do so. As several chapters demonstrate, the answer often lies in intra-party divisions, particularly within governing parties (see Chapters 21, 22 and 26 by Fossum and Rosén, Smith and Oscarsson).

The regional focus on Europe allows authors to go into significant depth, while the systematic framework deployed in Parts II and III means that the authors address the same topics in a broadly similar way. Contributors were not asked to follow a particular theoretical framework, which would have been almost impossible with forty different authors involved. Unlike Morel and Qvortrup (2018: 6), however, we aspire to go beyond being 'a book about questions, not answers'. All contributors to Parts II and III were asked to reflect on a number of quite specific questions, allowing for common themes to emerge, whether relating to the rules in place for referendums, the way key actors—politicians, journalists or NGOs—campaign, and how far context, political and economic, can impact on the outcomes of referendums.

Thus the democratic quality of referendums, the extent of the franchise, the role of campaigns, the involvement of the media, the importance of financing and, especially, the rules of the game are all explored in specific national contexts. In some cases, the referendums in one country are assessed in more than one chapter and in more than one part. This is true for Ireland, Denmark, the UK and Switzerland, where the frequency of direct democratic engagement and/or the significance of particular issues under consideration, such as abortion or equal marriage, devolution or possible secession, or the blocking of EU treaty reform merit detailed analysis from various perspectives. In addition to the impact these referendums have had domestically, many have also affected other countries and/or the EU as a whole and so have wider significance. For example, the Irish vote to legalise abortion fed into the debate over the issue of legalisation in Northern Ireland, a constituent part of the UK, while the fact that Ireland held a referendum on the Maastricht Treaty in 1992 led to demands for the UK to be permitted to hold a referendum on an EU matter—the start of a long road to the 2016 membership referendum and the UK's eventual departure in 2020 (see Chapter 3 by Glencross). Contributors also consider the impact of referendums on national policies and politics and, where appropriate, their wider effects. This particularly applies to EU-related referendums where there may be knock-on effects for other Member States or would-be Member States, leading to a potential for domino effects and domino strategies, for example in EU enlargement (see Chapters 21, 23 and 24 by Fossum and Rosén, Rye, and Mendez and Mendez) or treaty ratification (see Chapter 28 by Sternberg).

1.4   Outline of the Handbook

Part I puts the theme of referendums into theoretical, historical and legal perspective. In Chapter 2, Christopher Lord considers referendums in the light of democratic theory. Andrew Glencross and Matt Qvortrup (Chapters 3 and 7) put European referendums in historical perspective. Glencross sees referendums in part as a search for solutions to policy, driven by the promise that they can bring a certain kind of closure not available via representative government, albeit one that can also lead to crisis. Qvortrup's synoptic analysis puts referendums into their longer-term perspective looking to their Napoleonic roots and how the practice spread and evolved. In Chapter 4, Alan Renwick and Jess Sargeant focus on the more technical issues of the rules established for referendums, highlighting the best practice proposed by the Venice Commission and indicating the issues policy-makers need to consider when preparing to hold a referendum, notably the 'principles of universal, equal, free, and secret suffrage'. In his chapter, Philip Norton considers the role of parliaments in shaping referendums, including the decision to hold referendums, a thorny question in light of the tension between representative and direct democracy. Meanwhile, in Chapter 6 Ece Özlem Atikcan looks at public opinion and how and why it changes during referendum campaigns, considering the significance of campaigns and the arguments deployed.

The rules and practices of referendums in different polities may differ in a variety of ways. For example, is the referendum mandatory or optional? Will the outcome be binding on the executive or only advisory? Is the question on the ballot paper binary or are voters offered a more complex set of choices?

What rules are in place to ensure fairness and other democratic principles are upheld? Each of the case study chapters addresses a range of such vital questions, which help build up a picture of features of referendums that can contribute to certain outcomes and also feed into a wider analysis of the relationship between direct and representative democracy, which differs markedly across the countries that allow for referendums.

Part II explores a series of national referendums, mostly concerning constitutional matters, including moves towards devolution or independence. The chapters by Morel, Serdült and Uleri (Chapters 9, 10 and 17) consider the extensive referendum experiences, respectively, in France, Switzerland and Italy, each of which have well-established patterns of direct democracy. In Chapters 11, 14 and 15, Mathias, Curtice and Qvortrup all look at votes on the related questions of devolution and independence. Mathias looks at the failed moves towards devolution in Scotland and Wales in 1979 and the more successful changes of 1997, while Curtice picks up the narrative with a chapter on Scotland's 2014 independence referendum. Whereas Scotland's vote was held with the consent of the UK government, the Catalan poll explored by Qvortrup in Chapter 15 was held against the express wishes of the Spanish government and was technically illegal. This case is exceptionally included because the reaction of the Spanish government and the wider issues of independence referendums that the case raises merit consideration. Katy Hayward looks at the twin referendums on the island of Ireland required to settle long-standing disputes over Northern Ireland in Chapter 12. In Chapter 16 Reidy et al. consider two of Ireland's recent referendums on social policy: abortion and equal marriage. A rather less heated, albeit divisive matter, the nature of the electoral system in the UK is analysed by Andrew Blick in his contribution. De Jonge and Petry (Chapter 18) discuss a rare referendum on citizenship issues: the right of non-nationals to vote in national elections in Luxembourg. The chapters by Ersin Kalaycıoğlu and Gülnur Kocapınar and by Alex Andrione-Moylan and Jan Wouters (Chapters 8 and 19) consider questions about governance in Turkey and Belgium, respectively. In Turkey, the 2017 referendum was used by President Ergodan to try to consolidate his power. The vote in Belgium in 1950 was much more specific, about the right of King Leopold III to return as monarch after World War Two. Although the referendum experience has not been repeated in Belgium, as Wouters and Andrione-Moylan show, there are lessons from that poll for the EU.

Part III looks at EU-related referendums. The European Union began life as an elite construction with little scope for citizens to express their views on the process of integration. Over the years, the citizens of all Member States would be enfranchised in the context of elections to the European Parliament as a way of introducing democratic elements to the Union, while citizens in some countries were given the opportunity to express their views about joining the Union or whether it should be reformed. The first wave of enlargement in the 1970s heralded the first referendums on membership (see Chapters 20 and 21 by Svensson and Fossum and Rosén), which swiftly became a pattern (see Chapters 23 by Rye and 24 Mendez and Mendez). They were not all supportive of integration. In 1972, Norway opted to remain outside the Union, a position it reconfirmed in a further referendum in 1994 (see Fossum and Rosén). In addition, in 1983 Greenland voted to leave (see Mendez and Mendez), as did the UK in 2016 (see Chapter 22 by Smith). States voting not to join the Union do not have the same impact at those voting to leave. After all, while preparations may have been undertaken to enable enlargement, pre-accession votes by definition occur before countries have joined the EU and begun to alter it. A vote to leave the EU by contrast affects the EU as well as the withdrawing state, yet the EU-1 does not have a say on whether withdrawal can occur and are thus affected without having a say on the principle of withdrawal, just as citizens of a country where one part wishes to secede are typically not able to vote to hold their state together, e.g. regarding Scotland or more controversially Catalonia, the rest of the UK and Spain, respectively, were not enfranchised during independence votes.

A second set of EU-related referendums relates to treaty reform. Votes against treaty reform in one Member State can have a very significant impact, including on those who are not enfranchised. This can create frustration within other states and demands for referendums elsewhere (see Chapters 3 and 28 by Glencross and Sternberg). For example, calls for referendums on various EU matters arose in the UK in the 1990s after the Irish had held their referendum over Maastricht. This was not even because the Irish had rejected the treaty—on that occasion they did not, although the Danes did say 'No' (see Chapter 25 by Beach). The point was, rather, that Irish voters had been invited to have their say and, if they could, why should British voters not have a similar opportunity? That the UK privileges parliamentary sovereignty over referendums whereas Ireland has a constitutional requirement to hold a referendum on issues with a constitutional impact were not sufficient answers to assuage an unexpected move towards direct democracy in the UK. Such demands are indicative of growing calls for citizens to have a say on European matters, as the practices of representative democracy are challenged.

Referendums on European matters may foster a sense of legitimacy in states that have held successful referendums, for example, on accession. However, there are two deep and persistent problems with referendums among EU Member States: asymmetry and repeated voting. The first problem arises from the fact that there is no provision for EU-wide referendums on treaty reform. Unanimity is required for treaty reform, meaning every government must agree and then secure approval at home, but this does not usually involve citizens directly; in most cases, ratification comes via national parliaments. However, in countries where referendums are offered, citizens can affect the process of integration directly, albeit in a negative way by thwarting moves towards a treaty reform. A 'Yes' vote means moving ahead in line with the will of the national government and, as such, has less impact on the integration process, although it may confer a sense of democratic legitimacy among those who have been enfranchised.

If citizens vote 'No' then, in theory, one might expect the reforms to cease. However, on several occasions, citizens who have given the 'wrong' answer have been asked to think again. Rather than increasing democratic legitimacy, such moves have engendered criticism and contributed to a narrative that 'the EU is not democratic' (Hannan 2016). Danish voters were invited back to the polls to vote again on the same issue (Maastricht) on just one occasion, following the unprecedented 'No' vote in 1992 (see Chapter 25 by Beach). By contrast, the Irish have twice been asked to vote again on treaty reform, following their rejections of the Nice Treaty in 2001 and Lisbon in 2008. Yet, whereas the reaction of Eurosceptics elsewhere was one of opprobrium, in Chapter 27 Laffan shows that in Ireland the reaction was somewhat different. Irish citizens had the opportunity to deliberate. Indeed, both Beach and Laffan show that if voters feel their views have been heard, they may be happy to accept the proposals—perhaps suitably tweaked—at the second time of asking. In some cases a No vote may have little effect, as the case of the Dutch referendum on the EU-Ukraine Association Agreement discussed by van den Akker in Chapter 32 shows. By contrast, it did result in a decision to abandon advisory referendums.

In addition to accession referendums and votes on treaty change, countries may vote on specific aspects of European integration, as the remaining chapters in Part III explore. Such referendums may even occur in non-EU states that do not aspire to membership but are nonetheless closely associated with the EU, as Clive H. Church's Chapter 29 on Swiss European referendums shows. Henrik Oscarsson explores Sweden's 2003 decision to remain outside the Euro, despite being formally committed to enter under the terms of its accession to the EU in 1995, while Palle Svensson looks at Danish opposition to joining two aspects of European integration, membership the Unified Patent Court (2014) and relations to the Union's provisions on Justice and Home Affairs (2015) in Chapter 33. Batory and Papadopoulou look at the rather unusual cases of referendums called by national leaders in order to try to circumvent EU decisions, in the case of Hungary, the EU's provisions for refugee relocation and in Greece the EU's proposals for a bailout during the Eurozone crisis. Each of these cases is significant in its own right for the country concerned but also has wider implications for the process of European integration.

1.5   THE PRACTICE OF REFERENDUMS

1.5.1   Why Hold a Referendum if It Is Not Essential?

Why hold a referendum if it is not essential, is a question addressed by Agnes Batory in her contribution on Hungary's referendum on the EU refugee relocation scheme. The country uses referendums regularly but this was the first

EU-related referendum to take place in a central or east European country post accession. In that particular case, the Prime Minister's ambition was to 'send a message to Brussels' (Batory, Chapter 31). Entrenched internal party divisions can explain the necessity or desirability of holding a referendum. As early as 1962 the Norwegian Parliament, the *Storting*, was discussing the necessity of a referendum on the question of joining the Common Market, in marked contrast to the UK where mainstream politicians were determined that any decision to enter should be taken by conventional parliamentary means (see Chapter 22 by Smith in this volume). In the event, the Norwegians did hold an optional, non-binding referendum on joining, in line with the Danes and Irish for whom a referendum was required by their respective constitutions. In Norway and Denmark, the option of a popular vote ensured that political parties were not split irrevocably on the issue at hand. In Sweden too referendums have been held as a way to avert intra-party conflict (see Chapter 26). By contrast, in the UK, the European issue became a running sore, despite the belated decision to hold a vote on staying in the Community in 1975; a vote to join, by contrast, might have ensured the issue did not come to define British politics.

1.5.2   Rules in Practice

'Healthy political debate must be underpinned by a robust regulatory regime. Such a regime should secure compliance with a common set of rules for all campaigners, allow diverse and sufficient funding of participants, without undue dominance of money, and secure transparency for voters' (Sir John Holmes, Chair of the Electoral Commission, 2017). While Sir John's words set the standard for referendum practice, the various contributions to this volume suggest that such aspirations are rarely met, although unexpected examples of good practice do emerge.

1.5.2.1   Equality and Fairness

In referendums, unlike most elections, every vote counts equally—or they do if there is a single count across the whole of the polity; in systems with double-majorities, the voices of the citizens in smaller states may count more heavily. A vote carries the same weight however much the issue at hand affects the individual citizen. Unlike in elections, there is a single choice to be made, so the standard trade-offs seen when a package of issues is on offer does not apply. Thus, every vote matters and there is an incentive to encourage even those voters with little interest in the matter at hand to turn out—assuming, of course, that campaigners are seeking a valid outcome, which, as mentioned below, is not inevitable.

Do both sides secure equal airtime or other provisions to ensure 'balance'? Here, there is an issue that needs to be resolved. Is it appropriate, necessary or desirable for public service broadcasters to give equal airtime to both sides of an issue? If they have a duty to inform the public, this may not be sufficient. As several authors note, a stopwatch approach may not be the best way of ensuring the public service duties are fulfilled. As the old adage goes, the duty of a journalist is not to report that X says it is raining and Y says it is not, but rather to look out of the window and ascertain which assertion is in fact correct. In Ireland, this has been understood, with the Broadcasting Authority of Ireland calling for balance overall, not a stopwatch approach (see Chapter 16 by Reidy et al. [p. 330]). It is not clear that other broadcasters have realised that giving equal time to the two sides does not provide the sort of impartiality required in an election or referendum, with the BBC coming in for criticism in the Scottish independence referendum of 2014 and the Brexit referendum two years later (see Chapters 14 and 22 by Curtice and Smith respectively).

There are also questions of fairness relating to campaign expenditure, the extent to which the government participates in the campaign, and whether they use taxpayers' money to do so. Note that the Norwegian government was criticised in 1972 for trying to skew the referendum result at a time when funding was asymmetric, in favour of the Yes side, even though the Finance Ministry was hostile (Chapter 21 by Fossum and Rosén). A similar situation pertained in the UK in 1975 when the unprecedented referendum campaign saw the government give public funding to both sides of the campaign, providing balance, which it then undermined by producing its own pamphlet which effectively reinforced the message of the 'Yes' campaign. If the referendum had remained unique in the British experience, this might not have mattered. However, as the practice of holding referendums became established the UK introduced formal rules for their conduct. One key aspect of the framework rules was to provide balance for the two sides of any referendum (the assumption being that any referendum would offer a binary choice). This was particularly focused on the question of funding. Provisions were made to ensure that an umbrella group for each of the two sides was given the same amount of public funding and made subject to legal caps on expenditure. Separate spending caps were introduced for political parties participating in referendums. These moves might have appeared equitable but they did not take into account the possibility that the main political parties might be on the same side of a referendum. Thus, in 2016 the Remain campaign could massively outspend the Leave campaign (see Chapter 22 by Smith). Yet the reality was somewhat different as the government distributed a pamphlet advocating Remain to every household, resulting in a backlash from the Leave side, which felt that the spirit of the law, if not its letter had been broken.

1.5.2.2 Rules for Referendums

The referendum question is a crucial aspect of the practice of this type of direct democracy. In some cases, little thought seems to have been paid to the question posed and the result is a convoluted offer to the voters that may be difficult to comprehend. 'Do you approve the law on X?' is an awkward formulation unlikely to yield considered responses unless the voters are engaged and willing to inform themselves of the issues at hand. Since 2000 the Electoral Commission gives advice on the formulation of questions in UK referendums, endeavouring to ensure no ambiguities or biases emerge. Hungary offers a model approach: the constitution requires that the question be clear for voters and for Parliament to implement. This 'double-clarity rule' (Chapter 31 [p. 656] by Batory) provides a mechanism to avoid post-referendum disputes over how to interpret the outcome in practical terms. Such a device could have saved four years of debate in the UK concerning the meaning of the apparently simple decision to 'leave the EU'.

Are thresholds for turnout or voting desirable and effective? In Switzerland, referendums only pass if a majority of both citizens AND of cantons (the relevant sub-unit in Swiss politics) vote in favour, an essential arrangement in a federal country. Such a double majority system would have ensured that the UK's 2016 referendum did not result in Brexit as two of the four nations voted to Remain. However, since the vote was of the whole UK, the fact that Leave won a majority of the overall votes was sufficient to secure victory. The upshot was an immediate reaction in Scotland that a second independence referendum should be held, with the Scottish First Minister arguing that Scotland was being taken out of the European Union against its will. Similarly, Northern Ireland voted to Remain but was faced with a departure that would create a division on the island of Ireland, creating major complications as the UK government sought to negotiate withdrawal from the Union. A double majority system could have prevented such a situation. Its use, however, is unheard of outside a federal system and, despite significant devolution, the UK is not a federal state.

In a few cases reinforced majorities of other sorts have been required, e.g. in the Scottish devolution vote of 1979, which narrowly failed because the positive vote did not comprise at least 40% of the whole electorate (see Chapter 11 by Mathias). It was not a precedent that the UK chose to repeat as Earl Howe told the House of Lords on 13 February 2020, and is not a frequently used device. Indeed, the Venice Commission advises against the use of such thresholds, which could be seen as attempts to skew the outcome of referendums (see Renwick and Sargeant in Chapter 4). What is more commonplace, and equally ill-advised in the eyes of the Venice Commission, are turnout thresholds. These can have perverse outcomes as opponents of a particular proposition may advise their supporters not to turn out in order to invalidate the outcome. Thus, referendums failed in the Netherlands (see Chapter 32 by van den Akker) and Hungary because the necessary thresholds were not met. In the former case, the outcome of the referendum—not to ratify the EU-Ukraine Association Agreement was not implemented because the EU had already implemented the Agreement. Perhaps more extraordinary was that the Government's reaction was to abolish the provision that allowed an advisory referendum to be called by citizens, in a clear rejection of direct democracy.

Elsewhere the reaction to unwelcome referendum results has been variable. In both Scotland and the UK the response of those who lost the votes in 2014 and 2016, respectively, was to call for further referendums, leading their opponents to note the irony that those keenest on referendums seemed to those who could not win them (*HL Hansard* 13 February 2020). An earlier presumption that referendums would decide the matter at hand for 'a generation' was now under great challenge, as the victors argued that 'the will of the people' had to be enacted. The Norwegian case seems to mirror both the British and Dutch cases. A failed accession referendum in 1972 was respected; Norway did not join the European Community. A generation later, the question was asked again and the voters returned to same answer. Since that referendum in 1994, Norway has not held another referendum on any issue (see Fossum and Rosén in Chapter 21). Since there is no formal provision for referendums in the Norwegian constitution the failure to hold further referendums is less significant than the pro-active Dutch decision to abolish the provision, but it appears indicative of a reluctance to ask citizens directly. Elsewhere, referendum outcomes have at times simply been ignored. Sweden voted to continue driving on the left in 1955, but the government nonetheless introduced driving on the right in 1967, following a vote in the Swedish Parliament to that effect in 1963 but without any further chance for citizens to express their views on the matter.

1.5.2.3   Financial Rules

To what extent does money talk? Robert Dahl, in his 1950s critique of US politics, *On Polyarchy*, stresses the importance of money in politics, particularly in pressing the cause of minority interests. Does it matter in referendums? In Chapter 13, Andrew Blick, citing Matt Qvortrup, suggests that it does not matter too much. Considering the results of the three UK-wide referendums held to date, their funding strictures for the two sides, and the actual expenditure equally suggests that money may not talk. The rules in 1975 and 2016 were different both in terms of the role the Government could play and the balance of expenditure. In the former, the 'No' side was very poorly funded compared with the 'Yes', reflecting the weight of major support the two sides enjoyed but also impacting on the former's ability to promote its own case. By 2016, donations were more evenly balanced, as support for the Eurosceptic cause had grown, including among business leaders, who were now willing to donate to the Leave side. The rules prevented Vote Leave from spending all the money it received in donations, leading to some complex machinations as the organisation gave money to BeLeave, another Leave-supporting organisation, which led to a formal investigation once the referendum was over. The rules did have some impact on the referendum but ultimately no funding-related issues were deemed by the Electoral Commission or Crown Prosecution Service to warrant any re-opening of the poll, however much the Remain side might have wished it.

Some countries, most notably the UK, impose quite rigorous rules on donations and expenditure, with money from overseas sources often deemed inadmissible. Elsewhere, financial rules are noticeably absent, see for example the Turkish case, where the role of government and government spending of taxpayers' money in 2016 was wholly unregulated (see Chapter 19 by Kalaycıoğlu and Kocapınar). It is noticeable that Hungary, which appears to be a model in terms of framing the referendum question, does not have rules on financing referendums, meaning that the government can have an unfair advantage.

It is noteworthy that countries opting to hold referendums for the first time often lack adequate rules, especially regarding finance. This was certainly true of Ireland and Denmark when they held mandatory referendums prior to joining the EU. Both the UK and Norway introduced bespoke legislation for their referendums—to an extent this was necessary in both countries as neither has a constitutional provision for referendums. Yet while there must be bespoke legislation for every referendum in the UK, legislation adopted in 2000 created the framework for running referendums, intended to provide appropriate rules.

1.5.2.4 Timetables

How much time is given for campaigners actually to make their case to the voters and for citizens to inform themselves about the matter at hand? If referendums are intended to allow for deliberation, it is axiomatic that sufficient time must be given for the two (or more) sides to make their cases and for potential voters to make themselves fully informed about the issues. While a long timetable does not guarantee that citizens will deliberate, a truncated referendum period renders deliberation impossible. Whereas the UK Electoral Commission and the Venice Commission both recommend setting the rules well in advance of any referendum, in the case of Greece, the referendum on whether to accept an EU bailout during the Eurozone crisis was held at one week's notice (see Chapter 30 by Papadopoulou). This ensured that citizens could not deliberate fully on the matter at hand—a situation compounded by the fact that the deal on the table when the Greek government called the referendum was no longer on the table when the poll was held. Moreover, the question posed was convoluted, requiring voters to have a detailed knowledge of the (no longer extant) proposals. Deliberation was infeasible—following party cues was thus inevitable. The government secured its preferred outcome, namely rejection of the proposals. The will of the people as expressed at the polls was conveniently close to the will of the government so these ambiguities perhaps did not matter in a case where the referendum was essentially intended to give the government the leverage it sought in EU negotiations, in which it succeeded.

1.5.2.5 The Role of Government

Should governments and/or civil servants be actively involved in referendums? In the UK the concept of political 'purdah' was introduced in the Political Parties, Elections and Referendums Act 2000 (PPERA), meaning that the Government and civil service are formally required to behave in such a way that their actions could not be deemed to influence or seek to influence the outcome of an election or referendum for a set period ahead of the referendum. The law was introduced after the first national UK referendum (on continuing membership of the European Community in 1975) and the Scottish and Welsh devolution votes of 1979 and 1997. It was in place for the two subsequent national referendums (on the Alternative Vote in 2011 and EU membership in 2016; see Chapter 13 by Blick and Chapter 22 by Smith). Whether the changed rules effectively led to a more level playing field or not is, in some ways, unclear. Political parties and their leaders, including the Prime Minister of the day, may all participate in the campaigns—so from the perspective of the public, purdah may have little obvious impact. However, from the perspective of the insurgent or opposition campaigner, the PPERA rules do ensure that the weight of the government machine cannot be deployed on a particular side of the argument in the weeks running up to polling day. In addition to caps on expenditure, purdah does rectify the sorts of asymmetry seen during the 1975 referendum, when the Government and most leading politicians, the media and business were on the 'Yes' side; and put their money where their hearts and heads were. The Government could not legally campaign in the immediate run-up to the 2016 referendum and attempts to persuade the public before the start of purdah backfired, as the opposition reminded taxpayers that it was 'their' money that the Government had spent to try to influence their voting intentions. Other countries see governments play a major role in referendum campaigns, either because there is a lack of serious regulation of the referendum process generally or because the role of the government is not viewed as creating an imbalance as it is in the UK. Thus in 2016, the Hungarian government and its dominant ruling party, Fidesz, played an active role in seeking to 'send a message to the EU', including distributing questionnaires and brochures to households (see Batory, Chapter 31). The party spent €48.6 million of taxpayers' money promoting their cause, while the opposition received no public funding at all.

1.5.2.6   Who Interprets the Rules and Ensures They Are Implemented?

Is there an electoral commission or similar body tasked with ensuring the formal rules of referendums are obeyed and able to censure actors, whether political parties, governments, media or individuals, for breaking the rules? In the case of Ireland, two judicial rulings over EU-related referendums, *McKenna* regarding the Treaty on European Union and *Coughlan* over the Treaty of Amsterdam, affected the subsequent running of all referendums in the country, regardless of substance (see Chapter 16 by Reidy et al.). Ireland is unusual, of course, in having frequent experience of referendums, which has allowed them to become streamlined without becoming so routine that voters no longer bother to turn out of vote. Courts may play a role in determining whether referendums may or must be held, and whether and how their outcomes should be treated.

Thus, the UK courts were invoked by Gina Miller and others who argued that the 2016 Brexit referendum did not directly give the Prime Minister the right to begin the process of taking the UK out of the European Union. Such powers still resided in Parliament, even if the public had made their will clear in the referendum—it was, after all, non-binding and did not confer powers on the executive. This was to be the first of a series of judicial rulings associated with the referendum and an early indication of the interplay between democratic moments and the role of the three pillars of executive, Parliament and the judiciary in their implementation. This can have far wider ramifications than simply the outcome of an individual referendum, as the Irish experience has demonstrated.

There is considerable scope for referendums to lead to the judicialisation of domestic politics, given the significant role played by judges, courts and judicial review in implementation of referendum rules. In Ireland, legal rulings on two EU-related cases (*McKenna* and *Coughlan*) had ramifications for the wider practice of referendums in the country (see Chapter 16). This is not untypical. In the UK, the Electoral Commission's role in overseeing the running of referendums is limited (see Chapters 11, 14 and 22). It may rule on financial matters but does not touch questions of the veracity of claims made by campaigners. There is a question of whether it should have such powers or not. Those who favour granting the Electoral Commission more powers believe that it is important that voters can acquire objective information about the referendum questions—as is provided in Swiss direct democracy where citizens receive booklets that include an objective presentation of the issue(s) at stake. Critics claim that allowing the Electoral Commission to comment on the substance of campaign claims could lead to it becoming politicised. What other options there might be short of judicial review in such cases is a question worthy of consideration.

1.6   The Referendum Experience

1.6.1   Experience of Referendums—This Is an Issue for Both Elites and Citizens

Novelty in the practice of referendums can result in the failure of their advocates, or the advocates of a particular outcome, as could be seen in the Netherlands at the time of the 2005 referendum on the Constitutional Treaty (see Chapter 28 by Sternberg). There may also be problems for voters suddenly faced with a choice on an issue of which they have little prior knowledge. It is noteworthy that the most searched for term on Google the day after the UK voted to leave the European Union was 'What is the EU?' Where, then, do cues for referendums come from? In elections it is usually political parties which provide cues to voters, whether through party allegiance or manifesto promises. Referendums, by contrast, are often held precisely because parties are internally divided on an issue (see Chapters 7, 3 and 26 by

Qvortrup, Glencross and Oscarsson). Thus, the cues available are different and there are questions about who or what potential voters can trust. As Glencross notes on p. 53 in this volume: 'The use of direct democracy, which in theory could obviate concerns associated with delegating decisions to representatives, does not make the problem of political trust disappear.' In the wake of the UK Brexit vote, there were repeated allegations that the victorious Leave side had misled the public. The body responsible for overseeing the rules of elections and referendums in the UK was powerless to act, and indeed felt that it would be inappropriate for it to try to adjudicate on the substance of campaigns (Chapter 22 by Smith). In such cases, how do voters find the information or cues necessary to make informed decisions? This matters in particular in the case of complex questions forced into a binary choice by the constraints of the referendum device. Two countries offer lessons in this regard: Ireland and Switzerland.

Switzerland, like Italy, has a long-established practice of using referendums and other tools of direct democracy (see Chapter 10 by Serdült and Chapter 29 by Church). Over the years, the Swiss practice has become extremely well-honed, with citizens provided with information booklets, including the cases for and against the question at hand (typically to approve or otherwise a draft piece of legislation) as well as objective information to ensure that voters participate from a position of knowledge. Yet, a similar attempt to have an information booklet from the UK Government in 2016 backfired. A formal proposal to require a Government brochure failed in the House of Lords, as opponents believed that it would be seen to undermine the balance given by the overarching referendum legislation. When the Government nonetheless produced a brochure, it proved an own goal as advocates of Brexit could argue that the Government was using taxpayers' money to advance a particular cause—no-one believed that the Government was neutral on the matter (see Chapter 22). Simply mirroring practices used elsewhere may not therefore work unless the approach can be explained and the practice trusted by voters, journalists and campaigners.

Ireland has held numerous referendums on constitutional and policy issues, as well as EU-related matters and has institutionalised a rather sophisticated practice over the years. On two occasions, the government failed to secure its preferred outcome and both the Nice and Lisbon treaties were rejected by the voters at the first time of asking. Concerted campaigns ensured that the results were overturned in each case. However, rather than leave subsequent referendums to chance, a new mechanism was introduced—the citizens' assembly. This allows for controversial issues to be discussed in depth and consensual proposals to come forward prior to any referendum on the matter concerned. Deliberative assemblies were held ahead of the referendums on abortion and equal marriage—both potentially highly divisive issues in traditionally Catholic Ireland. In both instances rather liberal policies were subsequently accepted in referendums (Chapter 16 by Reidy et al.). Part of the reason appears to be that voters are content that all aspects of issues have been considered in the assemblies and are willing to trust the recommendations of those involved in a way that modern electorates are rarely willing to do with politicians.

1.6.2   Where Do Voters Acquire Objective Information?

As already noted, voters in Switzerland all receive a booklet outlining the pro- and anti-side of each referendum question alongside the government's position. In a polity where direct democracy has become a way of life, voters appear to trust this information in a way they are reluctant to do in countries where referendums are less commonly practised. To an extent the decline of deferential politics has also affected voters' willingness to listen to politicians. Thus, voters accepted the UK Government's brochure in the 1975 referendum rather more willingly than they accepted Government cues in 2016. Nor did voters seem minded to accept the views of governing parties in a variety of EU-related referendums in Ireland, France and the Netherlands, either rejecting treaty reform or offering only marginal victories (see Chapters 9, 27, 28 and 32 by Morel, Laffan, Sternberg and van den Akker respectively).

If governments cannot be trusted to provide unbiased information, who is? Traditionally, one might have expected experts to be trusted, yet by 2016 even they were set aside in the UK, as leading Leave advocate, Michael Gove, suggested that 'people have had enough of experts'. While this clearly suited his own position given that the majority of experts were in favour of the UK's ongoing membership of the EU, it raised the prospect that people would no longer have or seek the truth but would, instead, base their decisions more on their own opinions than on facts, or even base their decisions on misleading arguments put forward during the referendum campaign. This was a phenomenon already picked up by Blick in Chapter 13 in the context of the 2011 referendum on changing the British electoral system, in which the 'No' side made misleading claims.

One alternative model that engages citizens and ensures that referendums allow for serious deliberation, meaning that citizens feel they understand the issues under consideration and moving beyond a government/elite steer to the people, is the deliberative or citizens' assembly adopted in Ireland. Labour MP Stella Creasy proposed that such a model could be introduced to the UK as it struggled to implement the outcome of the 2016 referendum. However, the timing was quite wrong—it would, perhaps, have been relevant ahead of a referendum, but to suggest it at a time when the outcome of the referendum was clear, if unpalatable, seemed to imply ignoring the will of the people as expressed on 23 June 2016. Were the UK to consider holding another referendum, a citizens' assembly model could help overcome the ignorance surrounding previous referendum questions and ensure a more deliberative model came into effect.

1.6.3   The Role of the Media and the Rise of Social Media

Formal electoral/referendum rules were in most cases drafted in the analogue age and are not well-suited to the digital age (see Chapter 4 by Renwick and Sargeant). Social media are thus often outwith the formal legislative frameworks in which referendums occur, meaning that it is harder to monitor the activities of campaigners online for both those overseeing the probity of the campaigns and, potentially, for scholars looking at those campaigns. This latter problem is compounded by the fact that much social media campaigning is targeted according to detailed algorithms making advertisements and targeted messages harder to track than more traditional media. Both traditional media coverage and social media can impact voter behaviour, creating 'echo chambers' as people purchase or follow those sources that most closely reflect their pre-existing views. However, this phenomenon is much more significant with social media where people tend to 'follow', 'like' or 'friend' people with similar views to their own. Sophisticated algorithms then ensure that messages can be targeted to reinforce those views further. Such techniques were used to a large extent in the 2016 UK referendum on EU membership, with the two Leave campaigns, Vote Leave and Leave.EU both very active on social media. Targeting was effective and oversight limited. There is a further issue from the campaigners' perspective. Spending too much time listening to one's own side of the argument and focusing on the concerns of 'swing' voters, those citizens whose votes will be crucial if a referendum (or election) is to be won, can result in a rather warped perception of public opinion. Thus, campaigners can be outflanked when they have not realised that large sections of society simply do not share their world view.

1.6.4   Declining Party Cues and the Demise of Deference

In the immediate postwar period, citizens were often content to follow where elites led, whether within the emerging European Communities or in nation states. An elite consensus in favour of accession prevailed in Ireland ahead of accession in 1973 and there was a marked lack of public discourse; scarcely the sort of deliberative model that advocates of referendums might extol. Meanwhile, in 1975 when the UK voted on whether or not to stay in the EC, the fact that the Establishment, the vast majority of politicians, political parties, media and business, were in favour of staying in the Community assisted that cause. Still-deferential voters were willing to listen to what leaders recommended. Forty years later, the fact that the Establishment was advocating Remain had precisely the opposite effect as Leavers sought to secure support for their case by vehemently asserting that the 'Establishment is against us'. That most of those uttering that battle cry could themselves only be considered part of the Establishment, scarcely the ordinary people rising up but well-educated, privileged populists, was irrelevant: the slogan had its effect as citizens, some of whom never normally voted, rejected proposals from party politicians, the media or 'Goldman Sachs', the short-hand for business elites supporting Remain. Deference was diminished, no longer were citizens willing to listen to established leaders or party cues.

Similarly, in Chapter 25 Beach points out that the 1992 Danish referendum on Maastricht saw the Yes side dominate the debate, yet it lost. A similar situation arose in the Luxembourgish *Auslännerwahlrecht* referendum in 2015 when the mainstream parties overwhelmingly advocated a proposal rejected by the citizens (see Chapter 18 by de Jonge and Petry). Irish and Dutch voters also demonstrated a marked unwillingness to accept party cues in votes on the Nice and Lisbon treaties in the case of Ireland and the Constitutional Treaty in the case of the Netherlands (see Chapters 27 and 32 by Laffan and van den Akker respectively). Or again, in Sweden, voters were reluctant to accept politicians' lead on membership of the Euro in 2003 (see Chapter 26 by Oscarsson). In the case of the Netherlands, it appeared that the Government was ill-prepared for the country's first-ever national referendum. Such unfamiliarity with direct democracy was not the reason for opposition to treaty reform in Ireland or the Euro in Sweden, however. In the case of Sweden, Oscarsson notes a loosening of party ties in line with a thawing of Lipset and Rokkan's seminal 'freezing hypothesis', first mooted in the 1960s and apparently valid in much of Western Europe until the turn of the century. While partisan dealignment might contribute to an apparent unwillingness on the part of voters to follow party cues, Beach suggests that partisan cues matter far more when voters are not well-informed about the issue and where is it complex and novel. They matter less, he concludes if voters are very familiar with the issues.

Of course, where referendums veer towards a more plebiscitary practice party or elite cues might be expected to persist. Thus, as Kalaycıoğlu and Kocapınar argue, party identification was significant in voting patterns in the 2017 referendum in Turkey. Similarly in Hungary, supporters of Viktor Orbán's Fidesz party were more likely to support his position in the 2016 referendum. Yet, even here the cues were not wholly effective as the turnout was too low to validate the result (Batory, Chapter 31).

1.6.5   *The Campaigns and the Messages*

1.6.5.1   *Do Campaigns Matter?*

Morel in Chapter 9 notes the fall in support for the Maastricht Treaty during the course of the 1992 French referendum. In her contribution, Atikcan observes a similar phenomenon in several other referendums. Certainly, the No side prevailed in various EU-related referendums advocated by governing parties in polls that they anticipated winning, perhaps even winning handsomely. Why should this be? Is it because the No side has better arguments? Or the Yes side is complacent? Or is the government pushing an inherently unpopular policy? What if the government itself is unpopular, as was the case with Mitterrand in 1992? Are there second-order effects coming into play? A vote against the government can be portrayed in this light (see Chapter 33 by Svensson). Even apparently successful politicians can fall prey to this phenomenon as David Cameron, who had won the previous year's general election, would find in 2016. There was a backlash against the mainstream, which could partly be seen to reflect a second-order dynamic, given the main opposition parties were also in favour of remaining in the EU. However, years of austerity also contributed to some voters' decision to vote to leave the EU— whether or not EU membership caused economic hardship was less significant than a perception of being 'left behind' for whatever reason. The chance to kick the Establishment for years of neglect was too good an opportunity to miss.

1.6.5.2   The Message and Messenger

Both the message and the messenger matter in securing victory in a referendum. Voters may take cues from politicians or they may be more tempted to listen to newly formed campaign groups. This in part depends on how well twenty-first century political parties reflect, or appear to reflect, citizens' concerns. In the UK, the traditional left-right, Labour-Conservative divide was fundamentally divided by the cross-cutting issue of EU membership, allowing an insurgent party, UKIP, to make electoral inroads and help generate the momentum for an ultimately successful (in UKIP's terms) referendum campaign to leave the EU. The leaders of the Leave campaign were politicians, but neither the Leave nor Remain side was fronted by a party leader, although one of the two key faces of Leave, Conservative MP Boris Johnson, would eventually assume the mantle of party leader and Prime Minister, enabling him to deliver the outcome of the referendum.

Voters frequently view referendums as the opportunity to deliver a message to the government—and rarely a positive one—reflecting a second-order element to the vote. In the multi-level European context, some governing parties have opted to hold referendums precisely to send a message to the European Union, even though they form part of the European Council and Council of Ministers which make some of the decisions against which they are reacting. This was certainly the intention of Viktor Orbán and his Fidesz party in 2016 (see Chapter 31) and effectively the approach taken by Greek Prime Minister Tsipras in 2015, when his government hoped to reduce the severity of the measures that the Troika sought to impose in return for the bailout the country required. Here, as in the case of Hungary, the national government's actions backfired, albeit in a different way. Whereas Hungarian voters followed Orbán's cues but in insufficient numbers to grant a popular mandate to his opposition to the EU's plans, in Greece there was overwhelming support for Tsipras's hostility to the bailout proposals. The upshot was not a softening of the conditions facing Greece, as Tsipras had intended, but rather the imposition of an even tougher arrangement. The will of the people was formally delivered; the original deal was not ratified. What they received in its place was far more onerous. Meanwhile, in Norway, the result of the second referendum on EU accession led to a somewhat unexpected outcome. Citizens had clearly rejected membership of the Union and the consequent loss of sovereignty which they perceived it would entail. Yet, the government ensured that Norway remained inside the European Economic Area (EEA), meaning it had to 'pay' and 'obey' but with 'no say' in decisions taken by the EU that would affect the country and its citizens. Whether this was the outcome its citizens actually wanted has never been directly tested at the ballot box but after a quarter of century the arrangement appeared embedded in Norwegian political life. The referendum, by contrast, had fallen into disuse.

1.6.5.3   Circumstances Matter

This might include, for example, the economic circumstances in which a referendum is held. For example, the first UK referendum on remaining in the European Community took place at a time when the British economy was performing poorly, as the seventh worst-performing economy out of nine in the Community, and when world food prices were higher than European prices, creating favourable conditions for a 'Yes to Europe'. By contrast, in 2016, the Leave campaign could argue that the UK was the fifth largest economy in the world, conveying a sense of confidence and enabling voters to believe it would be safe to vote to leave the EU, ignoring the fact that the UK's change in fortunes had come about as part of the EU. Changing economic conditions in Ireland also contribute to explaining differing referendum outcomes in the repeated referendums on the Nice and Lisbon Treaties. At the time of the No votes for each treaty, the Irish economy was buoyant; when citizens were asked to vote again, the conditions had deteriorated, particularly in 2009 when the financial crisis ensured that Ireland was reliant on financial support from the EU. Any danger that a No vote might jeopardise Ireland's place in the Union was thus to be avoided and a Yes vote prevailed (see Chapter 27 by Laffan). By contrast, in Norway, the economic conditions were such that on both occasions when citizens were given the choice to join the European Community/Union they declined; there was little obvious material incentive to sway them towards membership. Of course, absent the counterfactual, one can never know whether British citizens would have opted to join the Community—there is an important distinction between the choice of joining and the choice of remaining. Economic conditions alone may not entirely explain contingent decisions. The Greek referendum of 2015 was held against the background of severe austerity policies imposed as a result of the Eurozone crisis, which affected Greece especially badly. The negative outcome of the referendum may have gone against the wishes of the European Union, but was in line with the aims of the incumbent Greek government, which sought to prove to the EU that its proposals were not acceptable (see Chapter 30 by Papadopoulou). By contrast, in Hungary, it was not an economic crisis that helped set the scene for the 2016 referendum, but a refugee crisis. Despite the EU's proposals of refugee reallocation being framed in a negative light, in a rare example of weakness, Prime Minister

Orbán nonetheless failed to secure the outcome he sought as turnout fell below the requisite 50 per cent needed to for the result to be valid. This highlights a major issue for those designing the rules for referendums: should there be thresholds for turnout or reinforced majorities for a vote to pass; the experience of Hungary and indeed of the Netherlands (see Chapter 32 by van den Akker) seem to demonstrate the problems of turnout thresholds, while Scotland in 1979 highlighted the difficulty of setting a minimum percentage for a referendum to pass (see Chapter 11 by Mathias).

1.6.6   What Does All This Say About the Relationship Between Politicians, Parliaments and People?

1.6.6.1   Elite Cues from Party or Government

How much do party cues matter? Atikcan notes that familiar party cues may be lacking in referendums, if parties do not have clear views. This will inevitably be the case in those referendums that have been called precisely because the governing party is split on the issue being voted on, as was the case on EU membership in Norway (see Chapter 21 by Fossum and Rosén) and the UK (see Chapter 22). Where governing parties have agreed to EU treaty reform, they might be expected to advocate ratification to their citizens if a referendum is required or offered. Yet, in several cases governments proved incapable of persuading voters to endorse the decisions they had made with their EU partners. From the Danes' rejection of the Maastricht Treaty in 1992 (see Chapter 25 by Beach) to Ireland's rejections of the Nice and Lisbon treaties in 2001 and 2008 (see Chapter 27 by Laffan) via the decision of the French and Dutch to oppose the Constitutional Treaty in 2005 (see Chapter 28 by Sternberg), voters ignored the arguments put forward by political leaders. In some cases, governing parties were challenged by opposition politicians, meaning that a No vote could have been explained by party affiliations or even second-order theories. Yet, as various chapters show, there are many examples when there was mainstream party support for treaty reform, which was nonetheless defeated by the No side.

In some cases this may have reflected complacency on the part of governments unused to fighting referendums (the Dutch government could plausibly have argued this in 2005 given that the Netherlands had never previously held a national referendum) and the campaign methods for referendums and elections are inevitably, rather different. Yet, such naivety could not explain the Irish No votes, given that Ireland has long-standing experience of referendums as well as a strong pro-European stance. Why, then, did the government twice fail to persuade the electors of the merits of treaty reform? And why did the voters change their minds when they were asked to vote again?

1.6.6.2   Parliament Versus the People

In a representative democracy, the role of an MP is not to take direct instructions from his/her constituents, it is, in part at least, to exercise their judgement on complex issues. The increasingly frequent use of referendums in representative systems raises a number of philosophical and practical questions about the relationship between 'the people' and their representatives and between the tools of direct and representative democracy. Optional referendums are an opportunity for 'the people' to express their views on a particular question, whether of their own choosing in a citizens' initiative or because political leaders have proposed a poll in the hope either of securing the outcome they desire or to try to deal with a divisive issue on which their party is split. While mandatory referendums are not the result of a political decision, they too can pit the Parliament against the people. Absent the sort of Estonian rules that automatically trigger an election if the government does not secure its preferred outcome, what happens when politicians and the voters disagree on the preferred referendum outcome, particularly if the former seek to ignore the 'will of the people'? After all, members of Parliament are elected by those same people who voted in the referendum in order to represent the very same people. These are the themes explored throughout the present volume.

BIBLIOGRAPHY

Butler, D., & Ranney, A. (Eds.) (1994). *Referendums Around the World: The Growing Use of Direct Democracy*. Washington, DC: The AEI Press.

Gove, M. (2020, June 16). UK-EU Negotiations Update Statement by the Chancellor of the Duchy of Lancaster, *HL Deb*. Col. 685.

Hannan, D. (2016). *Why Vote Leave*. London: Head of Zeus.

Hobolt, S. B. (2009). *Europe in Question: Referendums on European Integration*. Oxford: Oxford University Press.

Holmes, J. (2017). Foreword to The Electoral Commission's March 2017 Report on the Regulation of Campaigners at the Referendum on the UK's Membership of the European Union Held on 23 June 2016. Available at https://www.electoralcommission.org.uk/sites/default/files/pdf_file/Report-on-the-regulation-of-campaigners-at-the-EU-referendum.pdf.

Lipset, S. M., & Rokkan S. (1967). *Party Systems and Voter Alignments: Cross-national Perspectives*. New York: The Free Press.

Mendez, F., Mendez, M., & Trigas, V. (2014). *Referendums and the European Union: A comparative inquiry*. Cambridge: Cambridge University Press.

Morel, L., & Qvortrup, M. (Eds.). (2018). *Routledge Handbook on Referendums and Direct Democracy*. London: Routledge.

Qvortrup, M. (2014). *Referendums Around the World: The Continued Growth of Direct Democracy*. Basingstoke: Palgrave.

Rose, R. (Ed.). (2020). *How Referendums Challenge European Democracy—Brexit and Beyond*. London: Palgrave Macmillan.

Part I

Referendums in Theory and in Practice

CHAPTER 2

Referendums and Democratic Theory

Christopher Lord

The referendum is often thought to be the *enfant terrible* of mass demo-cratic politics. It has no manners. It lacks education. It breaks the rules. It causes others to quarrel and fall out. To put each point in that caricature more seriously, referendums are often said to lack deliberative standards (Chambers 2001: 232); to produce ill-informed decisions (Achen and Bartels 2016: 68–89); to strain norms of how majorities should treat minorities in democratic politics (Haskell 2001: 11) and to divide publics by forcing them to make choices that are needlessly binary and winner-takes-all (Tierney 2012: 39).

Some have even argued that referendums can be more of a danger to democracy than an instrument of it. In the words of one British Prime Minister (Clement Attlee) famously quoted by another (Margaret Thatcher), referen-dums can be 'devices of dictators and demagogues' (House of Commons Debates 11 March 1975: Column 306). Or, as Mark Walker has put it (2003: 117), referendums 'have been particularly popular with authoritarian or authoritarian-minded leaders because of their susceptibility to abuse. Leaders can manipulate a referendum where they have the opportunity to decide whether a vote is called, its subject, the wording, the timing of the vote, and the chance to interpret the results. Thus, the ultimate *vox populis* becomes the *vox caeseris*.' Both Napoleons and Hitler used referendums to close down (proto-) democracy. As those examples suggest, referendums can be the ulti-mate mechanism of democratic self-negation where the people itself decides

C. Lord (✉)
ARENA, The Centre for European Studies, University of Oslo, Oslo, Norway
e-mail: christopher.lord@arena.uio.no

© The Author(s) 2021
J. Smith (ed.), *The Palgrave Handbook of European Referendums*,
https://doi.org/10.1007/978-3-030-55803-1_2

by a supposedly democratic procedure that it would rather be ruled in ways that are not democratic, or at least not liberal democratic.

A slightly different complaint is that referendums can be anti-pluralist and, therefore, anti-politics. Referendums can feed populist, as well as authoritarian, temptations. For populists who believe there is a unique authentic will of the people (Weale 2018), referendums may be a 'no nonsense' way of summoning up that will. Referendums can supposedly provide yes/no answers to single questions without corrupting and confusing forms of compromise and chatter. Jan-Werner Müller explains: 'One needs to be clear what the meaning of a referendum for populists really is. They do not want people to participate continuously in politics. A referendum isn't meant to start an open-ended process of deliberation among actual citizens to generate a range of well-considered popular judgements; rather the referendum serves to ratify what the populist leader has already discerned to be the popular interest' (Müller 2017: 29).

However, misuse of some referendums should not be an argument against all referendums. Their abuse under conditions unfavourable to liberal democracy does not mean referendums can never be compatible with standards of liberal democracy. More concerning are criticisms that, even at their best, referendums are only pseudo-democracy or defective democracy. Many criticisms, as will be seen, can be summarised in the claim that—whilst seemingly amongst the most direct forms of democracy—referendums are really short cuts that often fail to reproduce necessary conditions for liberal democracy. All that is made worse by the majoritarian character of referendums. Not only are most referendums decided by simple majorities, but also referendums may, as we will see, make it easier than the normal representative process for majorities to get their way on a single issue without making compromises on all issues.

Still, it is not hard to see why referendums have been understood as, almost by assumption, better mechanisms of democratic choice than the most obvious alternative: namely, electing representatives to approve law or constitutions (Tierney 2012: 19). One does not need to be a populist to see referendums as direct decisions of the people. There is no 'agency loss' from representatives failing to understand what the people want or from representatives pursuing their own views, rather than those of voters. In place of the alienation of the people's rights of collective self-government to a 'representative' system made 'elite' and even *un*representative by the sheer 'effrontery' (Dunn 2005: 19) of a few people presuming to represent the many, referendums give status and recognition to the democratic citizen. Indeed, referendums can help make democratic citizens.

Moreover, there may be strong arguments of democratic theory and practice for doubting that any democratic system can manage without some provision for referendums. Maybe that is why referendums seem to have become a fact of democratic life in many 'advanced' democracies. Whilst their use in authoritarian systems has fallen—perhaps indicating that, even in those systems, referendums involve risks to those who call them (Qvortrup 2017)—many advanced democracies have now used, or considered using, referendums. Even in Germany, once thought to be well inoculated against referendums, the Basic Law has been amended to allow for a referendum on changes to the Basic Law itself (Art 146) and the Constitutional Court (2009: paras 179 and 263) has argued that there could be a threshold in the development of a 'federal state' at the European level that could only be crossed with 'a decision of the German people beyond the present application of the Basic Law'. (See also Grimm et al. 2019.) Interestingly in the British case there is room for disagreement on how far referendums have become a part of the DNA (see Chapter 14 by Curtice) of British politics even though they are comparatively 'recent additions' (on the UK EU membership referendums see Chapter 22 by Smith).

So, anti-democratic, pseudo-democratic, defectively democratic, ideally democratic, or at least useful mechanisms in the toolbox of any democracy? How might we decide between those alternative assessments of referendums? The obvious place to turn is democratic theory. Democratic theory studies justifications for democracy itself. It, therefore, indicates what standards any one means of making collective choices—such as referendums—should meet if it is to be democratically justified. Linking the study of democratic theory to that of referendums can at least help answer following questions:

1. Are various justifications for democracy more likely to be delivered with referendums or without them?
2. Are referendums more likely to satisfy some democratic standards than others?
3. Can referendums help us better understand the puzzles and predicaments involved in delivering democratic standards?
4. Why do people disagree so much about the desirability of referendums?

There is not space here to answer these questions exhaustively. However, enough can be said to clarify where referendums may be democratically required (Sect. 2.1), democratically problematic (Sect. 2.2) and democratically embedded in other principles and practices of democratic politics in ways that may help secure some of their benefits without too many of their shortcomings (Sect. 2.3). Discussion of those strengths, weaknesses and possibilities will make it easier to sketch some answers to the four questions just asked (Sect. 2.4). First, though, a couple of observations:

As explored in the present volume, there are many over-lapping types of referendum: referendums on constitutions or on the institutional design of political systems; referendums to constitute or change the membership of a *demos* (Tierney 2012: 14); referendums on independence or secession from a polity (see Chapter 3 by Glencross); referendums on (partial) integration into other political systems; referendums on transfers of powers up or down between levels of governments; referendums on proposals for new laws; referendums to contest and repeal existing laws; referendums on ethical questions; referendums that either consult or decide; optional or mandatory referendums; referendums called by elected representatives as a result of manifesto commitments or parliamentary votes and referendums called by popular initiative. (Looking across European democracies, Renwick and Sargeant in Chapter 4 of this volume distinguish five types of actor who can call optional referendums.) Hence referendums are themselves procedurally varied mechanisms that can variously decide questions about polity, demos, policy or single laws. Answers to questions 1–4 above will plainly vary somewhat across types of referendum.

Whilst they have many varieties, there is mostly one alternative against which referendums can be appraised: namely, the normal workings of representative democracy. Yet the relationship between referendums and representation is notoriously complex. Both normatively and practically, referendums and representation can be understood as either competitive or complementary. Many a claim has been made that the one or the other is the 'better' or 'the only real' form of democracy. In contrast, many a claim can be made that the one requires or can be improved by the other. Maybe, though, there is one asymmetry. Although, historically, representative democracy has operated without referendums, it is much less clear that democratic systems can have well-designed referendums without well-designed representative institutions. Perhaps only small or hyper-active democratic systems could decide all matters by referendum. Representative institutions may have such a role in authorising, debating, framing and implementing referendums so that it may be unclear how far their democratic quality is attributable to referendums themselves or the representative politics and political systems in which they take place.

2.1   Benefits of Referendums and Difficulties of Doing Without Them

Stephen Tierney has explored how, as suggested in question 4 above, democratic theory can help us understand why people disagree so much about the value of referendums. As Tierney puts it: 'One's attitude to referendums is likely to be shaped by one's ideological approach to the meaning and purpose of democracy' (2012: 286). Indeed, Tierney argues that the two main schools of democratic thought—the liberal and the republican—have quite different implications for how people are likely to think about referendums. For liberals, democracy is best justified as a form of government that is likely to protect the rights needed for individuals to form private spheres in which they can live their lives without interference. For republicans, democracy is best justified as a form of government in which individuals can participate as equals in those shared decisions that affect their lives. Public, as well as private spheres are needed. (For this understanding of the difference between liberalism and republicanism see Habermas 1994: 2.) Given that difference, liberals might worry about risks of majorities using referendums to take away rights, to dominate minorities or to make decisions that belong to individual and private lives. Republicans, in contrast, might see referendums as opening up new possibilities of civic participation in democratic decision-making that are unavailable through the normal operation of representative politics.

So where might it be better that citizens participate in democratic choice or control through referendums and not just by electing representatives? First, there may be some decisions in a democracy that representatives cannot make on their own, since the legitimacy of those decisions is, in some sense, logically or normatively prior to that of the representative process itself. These may include fundamental decisions about the *polis* and *demos*: about the institutional design and membership of a democracy: about how we should be governed and with whom we should be governed.

For sure, pre-definition by pre-democratic processes of state- and nation-building has allowed most *demoi* to avoid problems of self-definition (Flora et al. 1999). Yet, even contemporary systems may need to decide on whether whole populations are to join or secede from their democracies; or whether their own democracies are to be partially merged and integrated with polities with their own law, procedures for making binding decisions and allocations of values. An important reason why such decisions may need to be endorsed by citizens is that democratic political community is a relationship of shared political obligation between citizens (Miller 2007). It implies considerable responsibility of citizens to one another, not least if they are to share a representative system and co-author their own laws through representatives they jointly choose and control.

Nor can representatives legitimately (re-)define their own powers. If representatives are representatives of others, their powers are not theirs to redefine or to give away without some consent of the represented. As John Locke (1924 [1690]: 189) put it: 'the legislature cannot transfer the power of making laws to any other hands, for it being a delegated power of the people, they who have it cannot pass it over to others'. Of course, publics can endorse fundamental changes to the *polis* or *demos* through elections, but referendums can focus the choice on the constitutional change itself.

Yet, second, referendums may be an important instrument of ordinary, and not just constitutional choice. Even the high priest of parliamentary sovereignty, A. V. Dicey, supported referendums because they 'do away with the absurd... presumption that electors can best answer the question raised, for example, by Home Rule, when it is put together with totally different questions' (quoted in Qvortrup 2006: 61). For sure Irish Home Rule was a constitutional choice. But Dicey's point was a general one that referendums allow citizens to decide single issues in ways that differ from the bundled choices offered by the parties they normally support. Later explored more fully by the Ostrogorski Paradox, the role of mass representative politics in aggregating and bundling choices may mean that—without a referendum to separate out some choices that do not combine so easily with others—publics may end up with many individual policies and laws that are only supported by minorities (Setälä 2006).

Third, there may be some questions representative institutions cannot decide at all, or only decide at great cost to the preconditions or infrastructures of representative democracy itself. Political parties might be deeply split (see Glencross in Chapter 3). As just seen, a particular question might not map well on to the main dimensions of political co-operation and conflict within a political system. Political competition might, in any case, be imperfect or oligopolistic. There might also be blind spots and cognitive biases amongst representatives themselves. Yet drifting on without making decisions might not be acceptable either. Non-decisions may themselves be deeply unfair. They privilege the *status quo* over change in ways that violate political equality between citizens of different opinions.

Moreover, different kinds of referendum can help with different kinds of difficulty in representative systems. Referendums by citizens' initiative can respond to biases, blind spots and blockages in the representative process that make it difficult to put some options that are widely supported by the public on the political agenda. Contestatory referendums—that allow publics to contest and undo policies and laws—may be an answer to any tendencies amongst representatives to create cartel parties (Katz and Mair 1995) or to construct elaborate forms of consensus whose individual elements are shielded from normal standards of contestation (Abromeit 1998). Contestatory referendums can also unblock change in systems with multiple veto points. Referendums that allow representative bodies themselves to hand some decisions back to the people can help where there is no majority within those bodies for a decision, or at least none that does not damage a structure of co-operation and competition between representatives that works well on other issues.

Fourth, referendums can have special democratic authority. Some referendums have brought closure even to deeply contested questions, perhaps by clarifying public opinion where there was previously just enough ambiguity for both sides to keep an argument open. In evidence to the House of Lords, Michael Gallagher mentions the example of the Irish referendum in 1995 on divorce. Although, only approved by a narrow majority, divorce 'ceased overnight to be a political issue; opponents immediately folded their tents in a way they probably would not have done had the decision been made by parliament alone' (Gallagher quoted in House of Lords 2010: 14).

Fifth, as already noted, referendums can help develop democratic citizenship. Daniel Smith (House of Lords 2010: 142) cited research from the US (Smith and Tolbert 2004), Canada and Switzerland that referendums increase 'public knowledge' of politics and policy. In the Swiss case, 'citizens are better informed where they live in cantons with more opportunities for direct political participation' (Benz and Stutzer 2004). Moreover, the role of referendums in building public knowledge, interacts with their role in providing citizens with greater status and recognition by allowing them to decide particular questions directly and not just through representatives. Recognition as having a role in public decisions helps people 'feel at home' in the political world and 'think more carefully' about those decisions (Christiano 2015: 201). Such questions of recognition and respect are forcefully illustrated by the Brexit referendum. In a system whose normal system of representation ruthlessly favours marginal voters in a few marginal seats where those voters live, the Brexit referendum was a rare opportunity for all voters to count equally, including many disadvantaged voters and disadvantaged communities that voted for Brexit. 'Ignoring the referendum would be particularly unfair to them. It would not be consistent with treating them as free and equal persons entitled by the law and constitution of their land to a share in self-government' (Ekins 2016). Given that, if they are held at all, referendums are acts in which citizens recognise one another as equal democratic citizens they can, perhaps, only be legitimately reversed if to persist with them would itself be inconsistent with the equal recognition of citizens. If, for example, those seeking a second referendum were to satisfy exactly the same procedure by which the first referendum was authorised—in the UK case a general election in which the winning party made a manifesto commitment to hold a referendum—then equal recognition of citizens would, indeed, require a second referendum, if supporters of the latter are themselves to have equal opportunities and rights to those under which the first referendum was held.

2.2   Six Problems of Referendums

The previous section suggested why democratic systems cannot altogether do without referendums. But what problems may need to be anticipated if referendums are to be designed to democratic standards? Tierney (2012: 24) identifies three difficulties: risks of manipulation; 'deliberation deficits' and 'majoritarian dangers'. My own suggestion is that we should first identify difficulties referendums pose for (a) aggregative, (b) deliberative and (c) epistemic aspects of democracy. That will then help us better understand why referendums raise concerns about (d) manipulation, (e) political irresponsibility and (f) majority domination. These problems are not unique to referendums. However, referendums and representation encounter them in different ways.

2.2.1   Aggregation

Ideally only votes and voices should determine decisions in a democracy, not the sequencing, separation or bundling of choices, nor procedures for aggregating votes into decisions. There are, however, risks inherent to referendums that outcomes will not just be determined by votes in a referendum, but by decisions to hold a referendum at all and by constraints on the kind of choice that can be made by referendum.

First, is the difficulty of separating out one question from all others to be decided by referendum: of effectively privileging one question so that, of all the thousands of interconnected questions in a democracy, it is to be one of a few that gets to be decided on its own by a referendum. The above argument from the Ostrogorski paradox, only works where some political choices really are separable from others. But what if something I believe on one question depends on how many others are settled? I may find that I do not know—and cannot know—how to vote in a referendum. After all, allocations of value and resources cannot be decided by considering issues singly. Rather they require, reasoned judgements across all issues of trade-offs between rights and values, not to mention trade-offs between limited resources within a budget constraint (see also Haskell 2001: 16). As Tierney puts it, 'siphoning off' one issue to be 'put to the people' may be the opposite of what is needed to make democratic choices. So, for example, syphoning off a proposal to cut or abolish a tax by putting it to referendum allows a public to make yes/no choices over that tax cut, but it does not give them an equal opportunity to deliberate and decide all other possible combinations of taxing, spending and borrowing. It may not even be a very good way of deciding the consequences for all those other matters of the one tax cut on which they are able to vote.

The second difficulty is the binary nature of most referendums. The study of social choice famously demonstrates that—where there are more than two choices (as there usually are)—there is no one way of converting individual votes into collective choices that is neutral and non-arbitrary (Arrow 1950; Sen 2017). That problem can hardly be avoided by treating a complex and multidimensional choice as a binary one. To the contrary, options that are not put to voters in a yes/no referendum choice might have won against those that are (See also Nurmi 1998: 334). There may even be a Condorcet winner—an option that can beat all others—that is suppressed because it never gets to be a part of the referendum choice put to the public. Sometimes it may also be important that second, third or fourth preferences should count in ways that at least require multiple choices or preference votes in referendums. These difficulties are explored in Albert Weale's (2017) criticism of the 2016 Brexit referendum.

Some interesting possibilities could alleviate binariness. Referendums in some Swiss cantons have given voters a choice of (a) a proposal, (b) a counter-proposal and (c) the status quo. Referendums may also be parts of 'repeat games'. Any one referendum may influence subsequent political agendas, choices, referendums or elections. The development of the European Union since the Treaty on European Union (1992) has been profoundly shaped by referendums held on each subsequent round of treaty change. Likewise, John Curtice explains in Chapter 14 how referendums in Scotland since 1979 endogenously shaped the politics of devolution and independence. Hence, there may be some scope for subsequent referendums to correct for overly binary choices in previous ones. However, things can also work the other way. Referendums can create their own path dependence in which the binary effects of one referendum become more binary over time. Referendums on non-binary matters may not just be wrong in principle. They may themselves binarily divide a public in ways that were not inevitable before the referendum itself. So, for example, the Brexit referendum created the very divisions it was supposed to resolve. Before 2016, European Union questions were almost never the most salient issues in UK opinion surveys. Since the 2016 referendum, Brexit has been rated as the most important issue in all YouGov surveys, which also show how few people have since changed their positions. The referendum has left leave and remain as two largely equal and opposite camps with seemingly little openness to the views of the other. Maybe, then, it is because of their binariness that Andrew Glencross remarks in Chapter 3 that referendums and the ways in which those referendums are remembered have profoundly shaped the democracies in which they have been held. (That is also illustrated by the Norwegian case. See Chapter 21 by Fossum and Rosén).

For sure, the election and decisions of representatives are also riddled with difficulties in aggregating individual choices into collective choices. Yet, the impossibility—or at least the implausibility—of a referendum ever being a strictly neutral and non-arbitrary choice is especially disappointing. Referendums are supposed to be the one way of arranging a direct and unambiguous decision of the people. Yet, as Laurence Morel and Matt Qvortrup (2018) observe 'it becomes entirely possible that the final outcome (of a referendum) will not correspond to the will of the majority' where, as seen, 'more than two solutions are feasible'.

2.2.2   Deliberation

Deliberation is often seen as essential to managing the predicaments of living and deciding together with others in a democracy: namely, the difficulties just discussed of finding some neutral and non-arbitrary way of converting individual choices into shared decisions and the harshness of minorities being outvoted by majorities. As Simone Chambers (2001: 231) puts it, opinion formation and justification of decisions must 'precede voting'. Here, she argues, deliberation has 'both individual and collective benefits. It helps individuals decide what they want in the first place: to make informed opinions. It makes collectively binding decisions more tolerable to all by exploring where differences can be removed'. Indeed, Joshua Cohen (1997: 416) argues that hearing the other side and giving reasons to the other side are absolute requirements for the legitimacy of majority decisions (Mill 1972 [1861]: 239). Without those forms of deliberation, even majority decisions may not be legitimate.

So why might substituting referendums for representation produce inferior deliberation? First, representatives may simply be better at deliberation because that is something they are selected to do and specialise in doing. Secondly, referendums do not require voters 'to deliberate their choices' (Eisenberg 2004: 6). Indeed, majorities will lack 'the incentive' to deliberate where they know 'that, regardless of discussion or deliberation their views will prevail at the ballot box' (Chambers 2001: 232). Far from requiring the majority to listen to the other side and make its case to it, referendums—perhaps even more so than elections to representative bodies—can allow majorities to get their way by appealing only to arguments that confirm and reinforce the partisanship of their own voters. Or, as Lawrence Le Duc puts it: 'a deliberative model emphasises the importance of voice, whilst referendums prioritise votes' (2015: 139).

2.2.3   Knowledge and Democracy

In his metaphor of the ship Plato (360 BC [1955]: 249–250) taunts democracy with the absurdity of giving the power to make decisions to those who lack the knowledge needed to make them (the sailors) rather than those who do (the captain and the navigator). Democracy has developed two answers to Plato's taunt (Lord 2017). One, quite simply, is representative democracy itself. Representation is based on a competition for the people's vote (Schumpeter 1976 [1943]: 267). Yet it is also part of a system of government that delegates to experts and organises and develops expertise over time. A second answer to Plato is that democracy may itself have epistemic qualities. Up to a point there is an internal relationship between knowledge and (liberal) democracy. The two require and reinforce one another (Talisse 2009: 121).

In contrast to the access of representatives to specialised knowledge, referendums are often charged with over-burdening citizens (Haskell 2001), requiring them to make judgements for which they cannot possibly have the information. That may introduce an element of inequality to referendums. Given that people with greater 'cognitive resources' are more likely to support referendums (Schuck and De Vreese 2015: 159) they may also be more comfortable participating in them.

But maybe the second answer to Plato can work in ways that alleviate concerns about knowledge; as well, indeed, as some of the earlier worries about deliberation in referendums? Some political theorists (Landemore 2013) have been attracted to the idea that important connections between knowledge and democracy create a 'wisdom of crowds'. So, maybe there is a kind of distributed knowledge which means that even where voters are individually ill-informed they can be collectively well-informed? If so, referendums may even score over representative democracy. Referendums involve a bigger crowd of people: usually, millions instead of a few hundred representatives. They may also draw into decisions and deliberation people with more perspectives, problems and experiences than representatives. However, leaders and opinion formers in referendums are usually themselves from political elites, and, contrary to any hope that the greater number and diversity of views in referendums will allow any wisdom of crowds to function all the more effectively, the empirical evidence seems to be the other way around: shortcomings in individual knowledge can compound more than correct one another in referendums. Christopher Achen and Larry Bartels (2016: 68–89 and 302) document several policy disasters that seem hard to reconcile with some myste-rious wisdom of crowds in referendums. As they put it, it is hard to avoid the conclusion that, in various state-level referendums in the US, 'voter choices made a mess of car insurance, damaged their dental health, and even let homes be burned down'.

2.2.4 Manipulation

Even minor variations in the framing of a question—or in the timing of a referendum and in its sequencing with other decisions—can produce large differences in referendum outcomes. That opens the way to subtle forms of manipulation even in advanced democracies. For example—in a move that may have been intended to pressure doubters—the 1994 referendums on EU accession were sequenced in the order of probability of obtaining a 'yes' vote (Austria, Finland, Sweden and Norway) (Jahn and Storsved 1995). More-over, manipulation and structural limitations on referendums as instruments of choice can compound one another. Risks that interconnections between issues will be ignored where just some are singled out for choice by referendum—or that a binary choice in a referendum will pre-empt other choices—mean that decisions to go to referendum or to pose a binary referendum choice can themselves be ways of manipulating particular outcomes. Note, indeed, that manipulating the choice—so that a multidimensional choice is turned into a falsely binary one—is a different form of manipulation to framing an already binary question in a way more likely to get 'yes' or 'no' as the answer. Yet, conversely, non-manipulation will not guarantee non-arbitrariness. Even in a world of saints—free of any manipulation—it may still be arbitrary to 'syphon off' a choice to put to referendum or to hold referendums where choices are complex or multidimensional.

Referendums can also be manipulated by private forms of power. Peter Kellner (House of Lords 2010: 126) argues that citizens' initiative referen-dums in California have given power to the 'sad, the mad, the bad and the very, very rich'. Rather than allow publics to take back control from elite repre-sentatives, such referendums may only create biases in favour of other elites than those favoured by representative democracy. Modern political systems are, perhaps, at their most vulnerable to being bought by what is, for big money, the risibly small money needed to lobby for a referendum, fund a citi-zens' initiative or contribute lavishly to a (social) media campaign before or during a referendum.

2.2.5 Irresponsibility

Referendums can also create risks of power without responsibility. One such risk is with the voters themselves. Referendums can ask voters to decide ques-tions of fundamental importance to societies and political systems they share with others. Yet, arguably, voters, do not take that responsibility seriously where they do not vote on the question or even the issue. Referendums, as well as elections, can be 'second-order' (Garry et al. 2005), or, in other words, a sub-game of some other game. Supporters of parties of government or opposition often vote differently in referendums. That could be because values in a referendum correlate anyway with those that distinguish parties; or more worryingly, it could be that some people treat referendums as conflicts within and between parties by other means. Hence, as the study of social choice puts it, there may be a problem of ensuring the irrelevance of irrelevant alternatives.

Another problem is one of ensuring sufficient accountability of claims made during referendums (Setälä 2006). For sure, losing referendums can be fatal to political careers, whilst individual 'referendum winners' may, conversely, stick around long enough to be accountable. Yet many claims and expectations may be shaped by whole constellations of actors who form and dissolve with any one referendum. That contrasts with an important feature of 'party responsible' government. Parties have an intertemporal character (White and Ypi 2016). They can be blamed and punished for their mistakes long afterwards.

A final problem of responsibility follows from any indeterminacy in interpreting a referendum result. Again Tierney (2012: 237) puts the point well: 'the significant challenges voters face in a referendum on complex issues becomes all the greater, and arguably unmanageable, when they cannot safely predict what the implications of a particular referendum result will be'. That does not just risk indeterminacy in voting. It also risks arbitrariness in implementation. The more a referendum result requires subsequent interpretation and specification, the greater the risk that those implementing it might use as a mandate for whatever suits them.

2.2.6   Majority Domination

Majorities in referendums may require minorities to live under laws, constitutions and whole political systems or *demoi* they dislike. Moreover, as Arend Lijphart (1977: 31) explains, referendums may be both more majoritarian than any other form of collective choice and less able to organise compromise between majorities and minorities. As he puts it, referendums may be even 'more majoritarian than Westminster-style representative democracy, since elected assemblies offer opportunities for minorities to present their case in unhurried discussion and to bargain for support on matters of vital importance to them by promising their adversaries support on other issues'. By contrast, referendums produce (largely) yes/no decisions that are separated out from others and then frozen in time by any more or less justified constraints on changing referendum results. All that limits several sources of political compromise between majorities and minorities: the creation of exceptions, the formation of complex trade-offs across multiple issues, the revisiting of decisions and the continuous adjustment of majority-minority relations through everyday democratic debate and experience in the implementation of policy, law or institutions.

Indeed, referendums would seem to be more vulnerable than representative democracy to a possible absurdity in democratic decision rules: one person one vote gives equal weight to those whose are only weakly affected by a decision and those whose lives are turned upside down by it. Representative democracies can counter that difficulty by building coalitions across many issues. Where multiple minorities and multiple majorities can trade their votes and vetoes over multiple decisions, everyone can increase their chances of getting what they most want or avoiding what they least want. Referendums, on the other hand, allow intensely affected minorities to be outvoted by weakly affected majorities in single-issue contests that restrict opportunities for offsetting that problem across several issues.

However, referendums may not just restrict scope for compromise between majorities and minorities. Majorities can (ab)use them to alter minority rights. Referendums by citizen initiative pose particular difficulties. The more citizens' initiatives allow free choice in what questions can be posed—unconstrained by any prior feature of the political system—the more they risk being used to put questions affecting minority rights to referendum. Barbara Gamble (1997) estimates that 78% of referendums on civic rights in the US have disadvantaged blacks or hispanics. Sometimes referendum questions have also been manipulated so that their challenge to minority rights are not fully explicit. Avigail Eisenberg (2004: 12) gives the example of what she calls 'English-only' referendums in Alaska. In 1998, Alaska voted by a 69% majority 'that the English language is the common unifying language of the state of Alaska and the United States of America'. A statement of the near-obvious obscured a hidden threat to Inuit language rights in schools. For sure, Eisenberg (2004: 5) also notes that minorities come out better where referendums aim to give them equality rather than special status. Yet, as Will Kymlicka (1995) has argued, minorities may sometimes need special status.

I can now explain why I said earlier that many criticisms of referendums come together in the single claim that referendums can be short cuts that miss out necessary conditions for liberal democracy. Majority voting is a central predicament in liberal democracy. Only simple majority decision-making can deliver political equality in which each vote counts equally in the sense that those who favour change or the *status quo* have equal chances of getting what they want (Bellamy 2007: 227). Yet a simple majority of the people is not the people. It is only a part of the people (Rosanvallon 2008: 11) whose right to outvote others may well require those others to live under unwanted institutions policies or laws. Democracy, then, is a form of domination, even if it is a more legitimate one than most. As John Dunn puts it (2005: 19), democracy commits the ultimate 'effrontery' of coercing the people in the name of the people.

In part, losers accept such an arrangement because they have equal chances to become winners. In part, they accept it if they have been heard and if consequences for them are carefully considered before majorities are formed. Hence, as John Dewey (1927 [1954]: 207) argued, 'the counting of heads' requires *prior* recourse to... discussion, consultation and persuasion'. The majority should get its way in a democracy, but with difficulty. As the various points in this section have demonstrated, referendums may make it just a bit too easy for majorities to get their way with insufficient regard for (a) the aggregation of choices across issues and, therefore, (b) for trade-offs of values and resources; (c) for hearing, deliberating and justifying opinions in relation to other opinions; (d) for expertise; (e) for compromise with minorities; and even sometimes (f) for their rights. All those difficulties, of course, are especially acute where majorities and minorities are fixed.

2.3   EMBEDDING REFERENDUMS

Section 2.1 questioned how far democracies can do without referendums. Section 2.2 showed how referendums can struggle to satisfy core democratic standards. Securing their benefits whilst avoiding their problems may require the double embedding of referendums: first in principles of democratic constitutionalism; and, second, in the very systems of democratic representation that some understand as normative or practical opposites (Sartori 1987) to referendums themselves.

2.3.1   Embedding Referendums in Democratic Constitutionalism

It is often argued that referendums need constitutional regulation (Tierney 2012: 105). Risks that referendums might themselves be sources of arbitrary domination and manipulation rather than democratic choice can be reduced by constitutional specification of how referendums should be used. As Alan Renwick and Jess Sargeant discuss in Chapter 4, the following are questions that may call for fixed rules in the regulation of referendums. Who should decide what should be put to referendum and how (by citizens' initiative, by parliamentary vote, by a winning majority in an election)? Who should frame questions for referendums? How should referendum campaigns be conducted? How long should they be and how should they be financed? What procedures should be followed to change or reverse decisions in previous referendums?

Hence there is a need for rules as well as discretion—for a 'rule of law' and not just a 'rule of persons'—in how referendums are used. However, agreeing rules is not enough. It just begs the question how those rules for regulating referendums should be decided in ways that are themselves democratically principled, non-arbitrary and justified. If referendums are to be regulated and constrained by democratic principles—and only democratic principles—a concept is needed of how democracy can be self-limiting and how, therefore, any one instrument of democratic choice, such as a referendum, can itself be legitimately limited by democratic principle. That can be supplied by democratic constitutionalism (Tierney 2012); or, in other words, the idea that the right of publics to choose and control their own laws and the rights of individuals to speak freely and form their own opinions are co-original and mutually required (Habermas 1996: 104). There can be no individual rights without a democratic form of rule that allows individuals to specify those rights as equals. There can be no shared democratic rule without individual freedoms and rights to speak, to be heard, to receive justifications for decisions (Forst 2007). As Thomas Christiano (2008: 11) puts it, the authority of democracy itself limits what democracy can do. Any one form of choice—such as a referendum—cannot be used to remove key equalities (such as one person, one vote) and freedoms needed for democracy without 'forfeiting' its right to decide'.

However, there is likely to be disagreement on how democratic principles—such as political equality and democratic rights—should be used to regulate referendums. Consider two examples, both of them difficult questions that need to be decided in designing rules for referendums. First, should referendums ever require over-sized majorities? As seen, political equality suggests not. Simple majorities are strictly speaking the only decision rules compatible with treating votes and choices equally. But what about deeply divided societies or polities that need to aim at equality between different political communities, not just equality between individual voters (Lord and Pollak 2013; Bellamy 2019)? Surely citizens of those democracies might want key changes to be decided by something more than a simple majority in a single referendum of the whole polity? Jan Wouters and Alex Andrione-Moylan in Chapter 8 of this volume discuss the example of the Belgian referendum in 1950 when a majority for the return of the King was not sufficient for that to be acceptable to the francophone minority. Second, should some decisions—notably, about fundamental rights—be off limits to any referendum? Whilst minorities may need some protection from any redefinition of their rights through majority decisions in referendums, even the most fundamental rights require decisions on how they should be defined and applied. Putting decisions on the specification and application of rights off limits to majority decision (in a referendum or otherwise) would just be a form of minority rule. What, perhaps, these examples illustrate is that members of any one democracy will need to decide how principles of democratic constitutionalism—such as equality and democratic rights—should be used to regulate referendums in their own democracy.

So how far, then, should referendums be governed by international norms, such as the Council of Europe's guidelines for constitution referendums? At one level international standards can just be extensions of democratic constitutionalism within democracies: one more 'commitment technology' by which democracies can bind themselves to democratic standards and then make those commitments more credible to their own publics (assuming they are serious commitments at all). However, international norms may also be part of a 'globalising normative environment' (Tierney 2012: 287; Zürn 2018); perhaps even of a constitutionalism beyond the state. Democracies need to take positions on the validity of referendums in other polities. Are they going to recognise a secession or even an annexation seemingly endorsed by a referendum? Are there circumstances where the European Union might have to question whether a referendum really satisfies obligations on members to accede or withdraw in line with their own constitutional requirements? Finally, in a world of interconnected democracies, referendums could conceivably impose externalities on other democracies in ways that would make the regulation of any one democracy's referendum the legitimate concern of others. For example, the Dutch referendum in 2014 against ratification of the EU-Ukraine Association—itself distorted by a regulation that only encouraged strategic abstention by requiring a threshold of 30% participation—could be interpreted as having undesirable externalities for stabilisation in Eastern Europe. Indeed, the external effects of internal procedural mishaps meant the Dutch government was itself 'embarrassed' by the result (see Van den Akker in this volume).

2.3.2   *Embedding Referendums in Representative Institutions*

David Butler and Austin Ranney (1994: 19) argue that referendums need pose no greater threat to minorities than representative bodies where the latter need in any case to approve referendums. More broadly, constitutional regulation cannot be enough without also embedding referendums in representative bodies. Only representative bodies—and not constitutional regulation—can supply two needs identified here: for deliberation and for non-arbitrary implementation. The problem in both cases is that referendums are not just votes at single moments. Referendums also take place across time (Armstrong 2017). They need to be designed beforehand and implemented afterwards. (See also Chapter 5 by Philip Norton for a discussion of the role of parliaments in initiating referendums.) Yet, unlike the outcomes of elections to representative bodies, referendums are not intrinsically linked to those responsible for subsequent implementation. Referendums decide. But representative bodies are still needed to oversee implementation of referendums, even though, of course, there is scope to challenge decisions on how referendums have been implemented in later elections or even further referendums.

Perhaps the design question that needs most deliberation prior to a referendum is, as it were, the 'decision to go binary'. As seen, the reduction of a multidimensional choice to a more or less binary one may require thorough justification that more complex forms of compromise have been exhausted and that the binary choice does not wrongly exclude other alternatives. But a need to deliberate the design of a referendum need not undermine any prospect of using referendums as alternatives to established representative institutions. There are other ways of making deliberation on the design of a referendum representative. Randomly selected 'mini-publics'—such as the British Columbia experiment and the Citizens' Assembly used in the Irish referendum on abortion in 2018—can also prepare debate and options, even though their deliberations may not always scale up so well to referendums themselves (Pilon 2010). Turning briefly to implementation, that surely does need embedding in standard institutions of parliamentary representation, given the need for any discretionary judgements or interpretations of the referendum outcome to be made by bodies that are formally responsible to voters.

2.4   Conclusion

This chapter started by observing some disagreements about referendums are not just down to how referendums work out in practice but to what people find valuable in democracy in the first place. But how can that—and everything else that has been said here—help answer the four questions with which the chapter opened.

First is the question of whether justifications of democracy are more likely to be met with referendums than without them? Democracy has either been justified as a form of autonomy (it allows the people to make their own laws) or as a form of non-domination (the idea that the people can control their own laws is utopian but democracy can at least prevent governments dominating the governed). A common argument for referendums is that they get as close as possible to a direct authoring by the people of their own laws. It may, however, be less obvious that referendums give powers of decision to the people (Achen and Bartels 2016: 73) when account is taken of constraints on choice that follow from singling just some questions out for decision by referendum; and from making complex choices into more or less binary ones. Those restrictions on choice can also be sources of arbitrary domination.

Second is the question whether referendums are more likely to meet some democratic standards than others. Much in this chapter supports Anthony McGann's (2006: 128) argument that referendums are better suited to delivering standards of political equality and participation than to securing standards of deliberation: (in a referendum) 'everyone's vote counts for the same…and everyone can participate…but it is the antithesis of deliberative democracy…it is not possible for the voters to negotiate a reasonable solution…The voters are simply presented with alternatives and expected to vote on them'.

Third is the question of whether the study of referendums can add to our understanding of puzzles and predicaments involved in securing democratic standards. Pervasive predicaments of democracy include the absence of neutral and non-arbitrary ways of aggregating individual votes and voices into collective decisions; and, indeed, majority decision itself, given that a majority is not the people, but only a part of it (Rosanvallon 2008: 14 and 118). Referendums can create special problems for the aggregation of choices across issues; for deciding trade-offs of values and resources; for hearing, deliberating and justifying opinions in relation to all others; for compromise with minorities and even their rights.

Yet, referendums can be embedded in forms of democratic constitutionalism and representation in ways that alleviate their problems. So maybe there is an over-arching paradox: perhaps it is polities with the clearest understanding of democratic constitutionalism and the strongest representative systems that can use referendums to the best democratic standards. Referendums would appear not to be alternatives to representation and constitutionalism. Rather referendums are forms of democratic choice that require representation and democratic constitutionalism.

REFERENCES

Abromeit, H. (1998). *Democracy in Europe. Legitimising Politics in a Non-State Polity*. New York: Berghahn Books.

Achen, C., & Bartels, L. (2016). *Democracy for Realists. Why Elections Do Not Produce Responsive Government*. Princeton: Princeton University Press.

Armstrong, K. (2017). *Brexit Time. Leaving the EU. Why, How and When?* Cambridge, UK: Cambridge University Press.

Arrow, K. (1950). A Difficulty in the Concept of Social Welfare. *Journal of Political Economy, 58*(4), 328–346.

Bellamy, R. (2007). *Political Constitutionalism, A Republican Defence of the Constitutionality of Democracy*. Cambridge: Cambridge University Press.

Bellamy, R. (2019). *A Republican Europe of Sovereign States. Cosmopolitan Statism, Republican Intergovernmentalism and Demoicratic Reconnection of the EU*. Cambridge: Cambridge University Press.

Benz, M., & Stutzer, A. (2004). Are Citizens Better Informed When They Have a Larger Say in Politics? Evidence from the European Union and Switzerland. *Public Choice, 19*(1), 32.

Butler, D., & Ranney, A. (1994). Theory. In D. Butler & A. Ranney (Eds.), *Referendums around the World. The Growing use of Direct Democracy*. Washington, DC: AEI Press.

Chambers, S. (2001). Constitutional Referendums and Deliberative Democracy. In M. Mendelsohn & A. Parkin (Eds.), *Referendum Democracy. Citizens, Elites and Deliberation in Referendum Campaigns*. Basingstoke: Palgrave Macmillan.

Christiano, T. (2008). *The Constitution of Equality, Democratic Authority and Its Limits*. Oxford: Oxford University Press.

Christiano, T. (2015). Democracy. In E. Zalta (Ed.), *The Stanford Encylopaedia of Philosophy*. Available at www.plato.stanford.edu/archives/spr2015/entries/democracy. Last consulted 7 June 2018.

Cohen, J. (1997). Deliberation and Democratic Legitimacy. In J. Bohman & W. Rehg (Eds.), *Deliberative Democracy. Essays on Reason in Politics*. Cambridge: MIT Press.

Dewey, J. (1927 [1954]). *The Public and Its Problems*. Athens: Ohio University Press.

Dunn, J. (2005). *Setting the People Free. The Story of Democracy*. London: Atlantic Books.

Eisenberg, A. (2004). When (If Ever) Are Referendums on Minority Rights Fair? In D. Laycock (Ed.), *Representation and Democratic Theory* (pp. 3–22). Vancouver: UBC Press.

Ekins, R. (2016). *The Legitimacy of the Brexit Referendum*. UK Constitutional Law Association Blog. Available at www.ukconstitutionallaw.org/2016/06/29/richard-ekins-the-legitimacy-of-the-brexit-referendum. Last accessed 19 June 2019.

Flora, P., Kuhnle, S., & Urwin, D. (1999). *State Formation, National-Building and Mass Politics in Europe. The Theory of Stein Rokkan*. Oxford: Oxford University Press.

Forst, R. (2007). *Das Recht auf Rechtfertigung. Elemente einer Konstruktivistischen Theorie der Gerechtigkeit*. Frankfurt am Main: Suhrkamp.

Gamble, B. (1997). Putting Civil Rights to a Popular Vote. *American Journal of Political Science, 41*(1), 245–269.

Garry, J., Marsh, M., & Sinnott, R. (2005). "Second-Order" Versus "Issue Voting" Effects in EU Referendums: Evidence from the Irish Nice Treaty. *European Union Politics, 6*(2), 201–221.

German Federal Constitutional Court (GFCC). (2009). *Judgement of the Second Senate of 30 June 2009*. 2 BE 2/08 (Lisbon Treaty). http://www.bundesverfassungsgericht.de/SharedDocs/Entscheidungen/EN/2009/06.

Grimm, D., Wendel, M., & Reinbacher, T. (2019). European Constitutionalism and German Constitutional Law. In A. Albi & S. Badutsky (Eds.), *National Constitutions in European and Global Governance. Democracy, Rights and the Rule of Law*. The Hague: T. M. C. Asse Press.

Habermas, J. (1994). Three Normative Models of Democracy. *Constellations, 1*(1), 1–10.

Habermas, J. (1996). *Between Facts and Norms*. Cambridge: Polity Press.

Haskell, J. (2001). *Direct Democracy or Representative Government? Dispelling the Populist Myth*. Boulder, CO: Westview.

House of Lords. (2010). *Referendums in the United Kingdom. Constitutional Committee 12th Report*. London: House of Lords. Available at https://publications.parliament.uk/pa/ld200910/ldselect/ldconst/99/9904.htm.

Jahn, D., & Storsved, A.-S. (1995). Legitimacy Through Referendum? The Nearly Successful Domino-Strategy of the EU Referendums in Austria, Finland, Sweden and Norway. *West European Politics, 18*(4), 18–37.

Katz, R., & Mair, P. (1995). Changing Models of Party Organisation and Party Democracy: The Emergence of the Cartel Party. *Party Politics, 1*(1), 5–28.

Kymlicka, W. (1995). *Multicultural Citizenship*. Oxford: Oxford University Press.

Landemore, H. (2013). *Democratic Reason: Politics, Collective Intelligence and the Rule of the Many*. Princeton: Princeton University Press.

LeDuc, L. (2015). Referendums and Deliberative Democracy. *Electoral Studies, 38*, 139–148.

Lijphart, A. (1977). *Democracy in Plural Societies. A Comparative Explanation*. New Haven, CT: Yale University Press.

Locke, J. (1924 [1690]). *Two Treatises of Government*. London: Everyman.

Lord, C. (2017). Exploring the Connection Between Knowledge and Democracy. In M. Gora, C. Holst, & M. Warat (Eds.), *Expertisation and Democracy in Europe*. Abingdon: Routledge.

Lord, C., & Pollak, J. (2013). Unequal but Democratic? Equality According to Karlsruhe. *Journal of European Public Policy, 20*(2), 190–205.

McGann, A. (2006). *The Logic of Democracy. Reconciling Equality, Deliberation and Minority Protection*. Ann Arbor: University of Michigan Press.

Mill, J. S. (1972 [1861]). *Utilitarianism, On Liberty and Considerations on Representative Government*. London: Dent.

Miller, D. (2007). *National Responsibility and Global Justice*. Oxford: Oxford University Press.

Morel, L., & Qvortrup, M. (2018). *The Routledge Handbook to Referendums and Direct Democracy*. London: Routledge.

Müller, J.-W. (2017). *What Is Populism?*. Harmondsworth: Penguin Books.

Nurmi, H. (1998). Voting Paradoxes and Referenda. *Social Choice and Welfare, 15*, 333–350.

Pilon, D. (2010). The 2005 and 2009 Referenda on Voting-System Change in British Columbia. *Canadian Political Science Review, 4*(2–3), 73–89.

Plato (1955 [c. 360 BC]). *The Republic*. Harmondsworth: Penguin.

Qvortrup, M. (2006). Democracy by Delegation: The Decision to Hold Referendums in the United Kingdom. *Representation, 42*(1), 59–72.

Qvortrup, M. (2017). The Rise of Referendums. Demystifying Direct Democracy. *Journal of Democracy, 28*(3), 141–152.

Rosanvallon, P. (2008). *La Légitimité Démocratique: Impartialité, Reflexivité, Proximité*. Paris: Seuil.

Sartori, G. (1987). *The Theory of Democracy Revisited*. Chatham, NJ: Chatham House.

Schumpeter, J. (1976 [1942]). *Capitalism, Socialism and Democracy*. London: George Allen and Unwin.

Schuck, A., & De Vreese, C. (2015). Public Support for Referendums in Europe. A Cross-National Comparison in 21 Countries. *Electoral Studies, 38*, 149–158.

Sen, A. (2017). *Collective Choice and Social Welfare. Expanded Edition*. London: Penguin.

Setälä, M. (2006). On the Problems of Responsibility and Accountability in Referendums. *European Journal of Political Research, 45*(4), 699–721.

Smith, D., & Tolbert, C. (2004). *Educated by Initiative. The Effects of Direct Democracy on Citizens and Political Organizations in the United States*. Ann Arbor: University of Michigan Press.

Talisse, R. (2009). *Democracy and Moral Conflict*. Cambridge: Cambridge University Press.

Tierney, S. (2012). *Constitutional Referendums. The Theory and Practice of Republican Deliberation*. Oxford: Oxford University Press.

Walker, M. (2003). *The Strategic Use of Referendums. Power, Legitimacy and Democracy*. Basingstoke: Palgrave Macmillan.

Weale, A. (2017). The Democratic Duty to Oppose Brexit. *Political Quarterly, 88*(2), 170–181.

Weale, A. (2018). *The Will of the People. A Modern Myth*. Cambridge: Polity.

White, J., & Ypi, L. (2016). *The Meaning of Partisanship*. Oxford: Oxford University Press.

Zürn, M. (2018). *A Theory of Global Governance. Authority, Legitimacy and Contestation*. Oxford: Oxford University Press.

CHAPTER 3

History

Andrew Glencross

3.1 Introduction

This chapter frames the history of referendums in modern Europe as a set of three intertwined histories, an approach inspired by Paul Nolte's (2012) thematic history of democracy divided into the following *Leitmotifs*: search, fulfilment and crisis.[1] Such a choice reflects a desire to locate referendums within a history of democracy, rather than relegating them to a discrete subform of democratic practice. The chapter's tripartite organisation is designed to define and explain the role played by referendums in modern European politics, which in turn means eschewing a straightforward chronological periodisation in favour of a conceptual mental map of democracy itself.

The first element of this conceptual framework is the idea of the referendum as a search for something to complement representative democracy (Nolte 2012: 407). According to Nolte (2012: 216), innovation and novelty are inherent to democratic politics as an ever-changing *Lebensform* or life form, which is why the appeal of referendums lies in their ability to provide something distinctive that is considered necessary in a particular time and place. Secondly, there is the history of referendums as a type of historically bounded political event or practice as defined by campaigns and the rhetoric

---

[1] *Suche*, *Erfüllung* and *Krise*, respectively.

A. Glencross (✉)
Aston University, Birmingham, UK
e-mail: a.glencross@aston.ac.uk

© The Author(s) 2021
J. Smith (ed.), *The Palgrave Handbook of European Referendums*,
https://doi.org/10.1007/978-3-030-55803-1_3

contained therein. That corresponds with the *problématique* of how to *fulfil* direct democracy's promise, a dilemma that revolves around considerations of how effectively, or not, a referendum lives up to its potential promise when used. Thirdly, and finally, there is the history of the memory, or legacy, of referendums and how this can impact politics and the political system further down the line. The extent to which referendums resolve problems or create new ones thus matches Nolte's claim that democracy does not advance in a straight line but is profoundly shaped by recurring episodes of crisis and countervailing forces (Nolte 2012: 252).

Of course, there is a potentially darker side to referendums, where the purpose of the popular vote is to alter the legal system by eroding certain checks and balances (as exemplified by the 2017 constitutional reform referendum in Turkey; see Chapter 19 by Kalaycıoğlu and Kocapınar). The focus in this chapter is not on anti-democratic initiatives used to diminish democratic constitutionalism, a practice that dates back to the illiberal plebiscites called by Napoleon or Hitler (Qvortrup 2018). Rather, it is on the way referendums fit into the inherently cyclical tendency to search for new ideas or practices as democracies grapple with policy challenges, old or new (Runciman 2014). Consequently, the history of referendums needs to be studied—much like the development of federalism (Burgess 2006)—in terms of processes as well as outcomes. This is particularly the case given the way the long-term resilience (and economic success) of modern democracy is accompanied by a habit of either ignoring policy problems or overreacting to them. As the political theorist David Runciman points out, 'democracies survive their mistakes … [s]o the mistakes keep coming' (Runciman 2014: 294), which is why referendums can be a way out of a democratic impasse—real or imagined—but they can also be a way of getting trapped anew. That oscillation is precisely the overarching historical-conceptual framework in which the use of referendums in Europe needs to be emplotted and which in some instances brings with it the danger of a 'neverendum', i.e. politics operating under the shadow of a future vote.

3.2   A Search for What?
the Referendum as the History of an Idea

Popular sovereignty is the concept used to describe the belief that the people ought to exercise ultimate control over decisions affecting them collectively. However, the practical problem of making this possible in large communities, where face-to-face interaction between all those affected is impossible, explains why popular sovereignty has been delegated in most democratic systems to elected representatives (Manin 1997). The latter rule on behalf of what the political philosopher Richard Tuck (2015) calls 'the sleeping sovereign', i.e. the execution of government is kept separate from the actual mass of individuals in whose name it is exercised. The act of delegation at the heart of political representation implies a great degree of trust: not only trust in representatives' ability or willingness to rule in the interests of the sleeping sovereign, but also trust in the ability of elections and the parties participating in them to correct deficiencies (real or imagined) in delegation.

The primary appeal of a referendum needs to be understood, therefore, in the context of the democratic search to empower the people of a particular community to govern their own affairs as an active sovereign. This search exists because of the inherent difficulty of fulfilling the promise of democracy, as memorably captured by Abraham Lincoln's definition at the Gettysburg Address in terms of 'government of the people, by the people, for the people'. The election of representatives on a periodic basis has not proved sufficient to satisfy fully this promise, for various reasons and at different times across modern Europe (Judt 2011). Dissatisfaction with the results of representative democracy—whether in terms of the policy outputs or the (un)representativeness of those elected—makes the conceit of letting the people decide for themselves inherently attractive (Webb 2013). Other plausible alternatives include technocracy or versions of authoritarian populism that lack democratic credentials and hence are beyond the scope of this discussion.

The search for an alternative to relying on representation to express popular sovereignty explains why referendums have become part of the history of European democracy. What historical analysis can offer, is reasons why representative democracy was not considered sufficient to empower the people at various points. The starting point for this task lies in assessing the way parties, governments and citizens have justified the use of direct democracy, notably arguments revolving around the nature of the decision at hand, including its novelty or constitutional significance.

In this context, it is particularly fruitful to examine the way democracies have adapted to European integration, a process that has obliged political elites to question the legitimacy of pursuing pooled sovereignty in the name of the people without a direct mandate from voters themselves. Transferring sovereignty is an inherently risky proposition for a government and historically it has involved a delicate balancing act between taking the initiative and seeking public approval. A case in point is the way five countries—in the space of three years—held referendums relating to European integration. France did so in 1972, over whether to accept enlargement of the European Economic Community (EEC), which would dilute French influence in European institutions and bring a more Atlanticist, Anglo-Saxon influence to policy-making (Gilbert 2004). Denmark, Ireland and Norway also held votes in 1972 on whether to join the EEC, after French citizens had approved the idea (see Chapters 20 and 21 by Svensson and by Fossum and Rosen elsewhere in this volume). Finally, in 1975, the UK held a vote on whether to leave the EEC, having joined two years previously. This sequence of referendums held close together in time gives an important insight into the underlying tensions occasioned by European integration as part of the democratic search for solutions to vital policy challenges.

On the one hand, the five EEC referendums demonstrated elites' trust in themselves to take the right decisions on behalf of their people. After all, each referendum only came about as a result of a government-led process of international negotiation, EEC membership applications having begun formally in 1970 after the departure of de Gaulle in France paved the way for enlargement (Wall 2012). Governments in the applicant countries, as well as in France, were united in arguing that pooling sovereignty in Europe was a necessary component of the democratic search for solutions to key economic and political challenges (Milward 1992). On the other hand, elected representatives' confidence that they were taking the right decision for their country coexisted, with varying degrees of uneasiness, with a desire to include the people themselves in this process.

What makes direct democracy particularly attractive when it comes to a transfer of sovereign powers is the concern that representative bodies are seldom comfortable alienating or delegating sovereignty supposedly entrusted to them by the people (Bogdanor 2016). This is a problem memorably identified by the seventeenth-century English political philosopher John Locke, who argued that 'the legislative cannot transfer the power of making laws to any other hands, for it being but a delegated power from the people, they who have it cannot pass it over to others' (Locke 1988: 362). In the course of modern European history, this logic of searching for a method of legitimising significant constitutional change by means other than parliamentary procedure has given rise to the cascade effect of referendum usage in Europe in relation to European integration, especially over EU/EEC/EEA membership (Mendez et al. 2014). A membership referendum has been held every decade since the 1970s, with only two countries that joined the EU since 2004 (Cyprus and Bulgaria) not resorting to a popular vote to confirm the elite decision (see Chapter 24 by Mendez and Mendez).

In this way the referendum has become part of the fabric of European democracy as the nature of interstate relations has changed to accommodate supranationalism. The promise of a new constitutional order—which goes beyond the strictures of the conventional (Stein 1981; Weiler 1991)—for tackling transnational issues has thus been accompanied by a desire to go beyond representative democracy in order to legitimise this change. Fifty referendums on European integration have been held since 1972 (Qvortrup 2016), including in countries such as the United Kingdom and the Netherlands that had never before resorted to direct democracy at the national level. However, the same problem identified by Locke also applies in cases of territorial secession or independence, where what is at stake is equally a potential transfer of the locus of legislative power.

Self-determination referendums have a longer, pre-World-War-Two history stretching back to the sixteenth century, with especially notable examples in the process of Italian reunification during the nineteenth century (Qvortrup 2018). Modern instances of the search for an answer to the question of who should govern a particular territory include independence votes in Scotland in 2014 (see Curtice elsewhere in 14), the contested 2017 vote in Catalonia (called without the consent of Madrid; see the Chapter 15 by Qvortrup elsewhere in this volume),[2] as well as the referendums used to deliver devolution in the United Kingdom in 1979 and again in 1997–1998. The 1998 Good Friday Agreement in fact required two referendums, one in Ireland and one in Northern Ireland, to determine that governance of the latter would no longer be a prerogative of the UK government in Westminster (see Chapter 12 by Hayward). In turn, this document necessitated a change in the Irish constitution to end its long-standing territorial claim to the whole of Ireland (Tonge 2000).

Moral issue referendums, such as those on abortion rights, divorce or gay marriage are another constitutive part of the history of direct democracy in Europe. There is a long history of popular votes on questions of morality and social justice, stretching back to the temperance movement that succeeded in organising a vote on alcohol prohibition in Canada in 1898 (Dostie and Dupré 2012) as well as in Sweden in 1922 (Tomasson 1998). Morality policy is distinct from EU-related issues or self-determination in that a transfer of sovereignty is not at stake. Historically, votes of a moral nature intersected with questions of religious identity and were associated with faith-based political mobilisation (Tomasson 1998). Invoking popular sovereignty as a way to provide clarity over sensitive moral policies brings to the fore the dilemma of whether voters are inherently conservative and cleave to traditional norms as supposed by the British legal theorist A. V. Dicey (Qvortrup 1999). Hence moral issue referendums provide a test for whether appealing to citizens directly is a conservative device for frustrating reform. In this context, direct democracy is part of the history of the search for ways to accelerate or impede societal reform and the record in countries such as Ireland, where referendums on legalising divorce were lost and won within a space of ten years (1986 and 1995), is often mixed (Gallagher 1996).

The use of direct democracy, which in theory could obviate concerns associated with delegating decisions to representatives, does not make the problem of political trust disappear. This is because referendums—part of a democratic search for allowing citizens to take collective control of their destinies—raise fundamental questions of trust in those who call referendums alongside trust in those who get to vote in them. For instance, the 2016 Brexit vote and its aftermath highlighted the question of why such a referendum was proposed in the first place and whether citizens can be trusted to come to the right decision on a matter with such far-reaching legal and economic consequences in the UK and beyond. Both these types of concerns are practical considerations associated with the reasons for resorting to direct democracy and the way in which citizens have responded on such occasions. Hence the next section examines

---

[2]The ruling Popular Party, which has a mono-national conception of the Spanish state, opposed the Catalan vote and succeeded in having the Constitutional Court declare the referendum unconstitutional, unlike in Scotland in 2014 where the UK government gave its consent (Cetrà and Harvey 2018).

the history behind the organisation of referendums in modern Europe to shed light on how far they can fulfil the promise of democratic empowerment.

3.3   Fulfilling Their Promise? The Use of Referendums in Practice

As outlined above, referendums have become one of the most important means whereby ordinary citizens can participate in deciding upon and shaping the contours of major national decisions such as European integration, regional devolution or indeed independence/secession, as well as moral values such as gay marriage. In this way, referendums have a number of potential benefits. They offer, in an EU-context, a chance for citizens to debate big EU issues, including enlargement, decision-making and competences that might otherwise be the purview of inter-elite agreement. At the same time, political leaders and parties have to articulate their preferences and visions regarding integration and where it is heading, something mainstream parties have traditionally neglected to discuss in national politics (Hooghe and Marks 2009). Similarly, domestic referendums on specific policies—often associated with normative social values as in the case of abortion policy or gay marriage—or constitutional reform perform the same function of creating space to debate questions of major societal importance as shown in Part Two of this volume. However, the benefits of making government of the people for the people a reality also need to be counter-balanced by an awareness of the potential limitations of referendums. For these can be deployed less as an objective in their own right than as a means to an end, namely for rendering the 'correct' result or shielding elites from negative repercussions stemming from policy choices. Hence this section examines the range of motivations behind such uses of direct democracy as well as the significance and symbolism of various specific campaigns, especially surrounding EU integration, with a view to demonstrating how far these votes fulfilled their democratic promise of public empowerment.

A mixture of motivations can lie behind the decision to hold a referendum in a modern European democracy (Hug and Schulz 2007; Finke and König 2009). Some votes stem from a constitutional obligation, as in Ireland where they are necessary in order to change the constitution. In France and the UK, legislation was passed seeking to create such a constitutional obligation regarding matters of EU integration. French voters were promised an automatic say on future EU enlargement in a 2005 constitutional amendment (greatly watered down in 2008), while UK law was changed via the 2011 European Union Act to make any EU treaty transferring new competences to Brussels subject to a popular vote. At other times, referendums can be the result of a top-down decision by a leader or government, or else the product of a bottom-up initiative based on popular mobilisation (Qvortrup 2015). Use of national-level popular initiatives is less geographically widespread than mandatory or government-initiated referendums, although they are chiefly found on European statute books (Morel 2017). Countries in Central and Eastern Europe legislated for popular initiatives—which are more commonly associated with Switzerland—as part of the democratisation process after the fall of Communism. Indeed, the origin of the initiative as a form of bottom-up participation to contest government policy or propose more radical change lies in nineteenth-century left-wing political organisation (Bjørklund 2009).

Most referendums on EU treaties have been held when a government has sufficient votes to ratify the treaty via parliament, so it is not a question of bypassing parliament to pass a treaty. Rather, national referendums on EU issues are, in theory, a way of connecting citizens to European integration. Asking citizens to vote provides democratic legitimacy to the process and outcome of integration by making their input count. This is in line with the rhetoric of bringing the EU closer to its citizens and making it more democratic, an ideal that emerged following the introduction of subsidiarity in the Maastricht Treaty (Hooghe and Marks 2009). Democratic legitimacy was also at the heart of the debates surrounding the EU Constitutional Treaty, which is why four countries held referendums on that treaty in 2005. Indeed, six more countries planned to do the same before the treaty's rejection by French and Dutch voters derailed the process (see Chapter 28 by Sternberg).

However, there are also tactical political motives at play in the decision to hold a referendum. The balance of power within a party or ruling coalition is historically a crucial factor, as illustrated by the history of the use of referendums in the UK. Both the 1975 referendum on remaining in the EEC and the 2016 EU membership referendum were the product of internal divisions within a governing party (Glencross 2016; Smith 2017). Putting the issue to a national vote was justified as a way to settle the issue without splitting the party for good, on the proviso that individual MPs and cabinet ministers could take their own position. The devolution referendums in 1979 and the 2011 alternative vote ballot were, by contrast, a consequence of government weakness: regional parties and the Liberal Democrats, respectively, extracted these votes in return for keeping a government in power (Seldon and Snowdon 2015).

Another reason to hold a referendum is for elected representatives to avoid taking decisions that could subsequently hurt them in a national election. This was certainly the case when British Prime Minister Tony Blair announced a plan for a national vote on the EU Constitutional Treaty to parliament in 2004. Originally against a referendum, as the negotiations dragged on Blair realised that with a general election scheduled for 2005 it would be useful to separate the EU Constitution from the election campaign (Dür and Mateo 2011). In a country with many Eurosceptic voters, he did not want his party to suffer electorally by being responsible for ratifying an unpopular treaty. Hence the promise in the 2005 general election manifesto to put the constitutional treaty to the British people in a referendum. A similar logic applied to the French constitutional amendment of 2005 mandating a referendum on future EU enlargement—the political class wanted to avoid being held responsible at a future date for Turkish EU membership (Phinnemore 2006).

In practice, public empowerment to shape policy via referendums is a function of how a campaign is fought, not just the motivation that gave rise to a popular vote in the first place. Campaigning in turn affects turnout, a crucial variable as the use of direct democracy often hinges on the number of votes cast as an expression of the level of enthusiasm for participating in a major policy decision. This explains the use in certain cases of a participation quorum without which the status quo cannot be changed, because 'a low turnout in referendums is seen as a threat to their legitimacy' (Qvortrup 2002: 164). Beyond the question of legitimacy, turnout also matters for the purposes of predictability and hence the associated tactical question of whether to hold such a vote. Variation in turnout is one notable element of the unpredictability surrounding referendums on EU issues, where, unlike with European Parliamentary elections, turnout can be very high, as with the 89% who voted in Norway on EU accession on 1994. Turnout fluctuates more in referendums than in national elections (Leduc 2002) and can be lower, as with the 35% who voted on the Nice Treaty in Ireland in 2001. Associated with this uncertainty over turnout is the possibility of shifts in public opinion over the course of a campaign, which can be larger than with national elections where issues and debates are better known (Leduc 2002). Similar to the 2016 Brexit vote in the UK, the 1972 EEC accession referendum in Norway was initially considered to be a foregone conclusion but ended in failure and brought about the resignation of the Prime Minister (Holst 1975). The potential for a large swing vote is also suggested by the evidence from referendums held to, in effect, overturn an earlier electoral verdict. Irish voters rejected the Nice treaty by 54% in 2001 but adopted it a year later with a 63% majority; the Lisbon Treaty similarly failed the first time after 53% of voters rejected it in 2008 before subsequently receiving the backing of 67% of the population in 2009 (Hodson and Maher 2014; see also Chapter 27 by Laffan).

These kinds of shifts in public opinion are the product of campaigns that invariably move away from the specific treaty at hand to debate the entire gamut of policies and problems associated with European integration. This discrepancy makes such referendum outcomes hard to predict and exposes the potential challenges of allowing the people to decide. For instance, one of the most important characteristics of campaigns surrounding referendums on European integration is the way that these 'shift the initiative to citizens and single-issue groups, and disarm party elites' (Hooghe and Marks 2009: 20). In the context of a 'constraining dissensus' (Hooghe and Marks 2009), mainstream political parties have had, at various times and in several countries, a hard task persuading voters to accept an EU treaty. A striking case in point is the Irish rejection of the Lisbon Treaty in 2008, even though it was supported by parties representing 90% of the seats in the legislature (Phinnemore 2013). Both treaty rejections and acceptances with only very slim winning margins (e.g. 51% in the 1992 French vote on the Maastricht Treaty) reveal a discrepancy between the preferences of political elites (governments and mainstream political parties) and ordinary people over European integration.

The campaigns for the referendums on the EU Constitution and its successor, the Lisbon Treaty, illustrate well this tendency to debate matters far beyond the contents of a particular treaty and in so doing lay bare the state of political trust between governed and governing at a given moment. In the 2005 French referendum, for example, the campaign paid little attention to the actual details of EU institutional reform even if this was one of the central components of the new treaty. Instead, opponents of the treaty managed to bring in other issues such as immigration, the possibility of Turkish accession, and whether the EU charter of fundamental rights compromised French abortion law (Glencross 2009). These policy issues were tangential (or indeed factually incorrect in the case of the fear that French abortion law could be altered) to the actual legal implications of the treaty. Yet the issues revealed voters' general concerns about integration and the direction it was taking.

Trust in elites is another key factor affecting the holding of referendums in practice, as party cues that make up for a lack of detailed political information—at least for EU-related votes (Hobolt 2007)—work to the degree politicians are trusted. Issues of trust in the motives of elites were very apparent during the Irish vote on the Lisbon Treaty. In Ireland, the nationalist party, *Sinn Féin*, alongside a coalition of minor and even ad-hoc parties, led the 2008 campaign against ratification of the Lisbon Treaty (O'Brennan 2009). The opposition camp had two principal arguments: objection to the weakening of Irish power (the result of the loss of a permanent commissioner and fewer national vetoes) and preventing 'the militarization of the EU'. The latter targeted the treaty's provisions for beefing up cooperation on foreign and security policy, seen as the death knell for neutrality by requiring Irish contingents for supposedly dubious EU humanitarian interventions.

Supporters of the Lisbon Treaty, a group including all the main parties except *Sinn Féin*, were slow to respond directly to these claims. Rather, they resorted to the stalwart justification of securing economic prosperity and also tried to establish positive historical precedents for Irish peacekeeping efforts. The primary objective, when engaging with the arguments of the 'No' camp, was thus to convince voters that changes to the *status quo* were not deleterious to Irish influence and neutrality (ibid.). This justificatory strategy sat awkwardly with two important contextual elements of the debate. Firstly, it was difficult to maintain that the treaty changes were so trifling when it was well known that the document was essentially the Constitutional Treaty redux, which the European Council wanted to avoid being subject to a new round of referendums (Phinnemore 2013). Likewise, this argument also appeared in contradiction with the grander claim that the new treaty would finally help reduce the democratic deficit, in particular by strengthening the role of national parliaments and adding an element of direct popular input via the 'citizens' initiative' (Monaghan 2012).

What the Irish referendum on the Lisbon Treaty also revealed was the problematic level of knowledge surrounding the contents of what citizens were voting on. A third of Irish voters incorrectly believed the treaty would involve the amalgamation of the Irish army into an EU army and overturn the country's prohibition on abortion, while over 40 per cent thought that the treaty would compel the Irish government to raise its notoriously low corporation tax rate (O'Brennan 2009). It is not surprising, therefore, that political scientists found evidence that voting 'No' on an EU referendum is associated with less knowledge of how the EU functions (Gabel 1998). This concern about a potential 'knowledge deficit' among voters is a double-edged facet of the practice of referendums. That is, public engagement during a referendum campaign offers a unique possibility for generating political information, while also presenting an occasion where extraneous claims and misuse of evidence can impede the quality of decision-making.

When it comes to EU integration, referendum campaigns can generate far more media coverage than is ordinarily the case in national politics. The use of direct democracy can thus open up a space for political contestation that is not ordinarily present. In this way, referendums can fulfil a good part of their promise to empower citizens by getting information about the EU across to voters and making such votes a reflection of majority preferences towards the distribution of supranational competences and not merely second-order moments of anti-government protest (Hobolt et al. 2009). Yet fulfilling the promise of increasing political knowledge is by no means guaranteed in a referendum campaign.

Voter competence is typically considered on the basis of the extent to which citizens are aware of the facts surrounding a given choice they are confronted with (Lupia 2006). Thus, this concern is less applicable to referendums on moral issues, where factual argumentation is a lesser consideration than collective values. The extent of factual knowledge available to citizens has been a concern in a variety of different referendum scenarios, ranging from EU treaties (Hobolt 2007) to California state-level initiatives (Bowler 2015). However, some referendums by definition do not permit full knowledge of the facts because a change in the constitutional status quo creates future scenarios of varying plausibility rather than guaranteed outcomes. Thus a secession referendum, as in the cases of Scotland and Catalonia in 2014 and 2017, respectively, confronted citizens to choose in the absence of certainty over what the full range of implications would be in the event of independence (Cetrà and Harvey 2018). The 2016 Brexit vote was similarly conducted under a cloud of uncertainty as to the exact outcome entailed by EU withdrawal, with voters' appreciation of the economic risks of leaving itself a reflection of attitude towards salient aspects of integration (Clarke et al. 2017).

Direct democracy thus obliges citizens, for better or worse, to ponder, manage and potentially ignore political consequences directly stemming—unmediated by the vagaries of representative democracy—from their choices. That is why it is important to examine what the result of using referendums has meant in different contexts. The next section explores the sometimes painful or positive legacies surrounding them, including notable moments of political crisis engendered by the use of direct democracy.

3.4 Crisis Moments? Historical Legacies and the Memories of Referendums in Contemporary Europe

Just as referendums are a way of adapting to European integration, so are democracies having to adapt to the use of referendums for EU matters and beyond. Memories of previous referendums, compounded by the spectre of new ones, have helped shape political debate and mobilisation across numerous countries in Europe. There is a clear political logic to this process of remembering and of forgetting, which shapes the development of national narratives as noticed by Ernest Renan already in the nineteenth century (2012 [1882]). In some cases, referendums have had spillover effects well beyond national borders, meaning their legacies matter even outside the places where they were held, as when Ireland voted to legalise abortion in 2018, creating pressure for similar change in Northern Ireland (Shepherd 2018). The use of direct democracy has also triggered major domestic and pan-European crises, such as those surrounding Brexit or the earlier rejection of the EU Constitutional Treaty. In other words, referendums have played a central role in the history of contemporary European democracy, which follows a pattern of recurring crises bringing with them episodes of reform and reaction (Nolte 2012).

The overhanging legacy of referendums can be seen in the way individual leaders are closely associated with the fate of the votes they called. Charles de Gaulle's post-war career was essentially defined by the succession of national referendums he organised, beginning with the 1958 vote to approve the establishment of the French Fifth Republic and ending with the failed referendum on Senate reform in 1969 that brought about his exit from power (Gaffney 2010; see also Chapter 9 by Morel). Following de Gaulle, French Presidents have interpreted referendums as confidence votes in their leadership qualities, thereby leading to greater circumspection about their use (Morel 2017). Indeed, one of the hallmarks of optional referendums is government confidence in winning the vote. David Cameron, for instance, will also be forever defined by the drama of his failed In/Out referendum on EU membership. Yet in 2016 he was perhaps entitled to feel confident about his favoured political tactic of managing domestic challenges by forcing voters to choose between the status quo or an unknown future. He had already won two referendums on this basic premise, defeating supporters of the alternative vote in 2011 as well as partisans of Scottish independence in 2014 (Seldon and Snowdon 2015; Shipman 2016; see also the respective Chapters 22, 13 and 14 by Smith, Blick and Curtice elsewhere in this volume). This confidence, however, seemed to rest on a certain degree of forgetfulness, given that the outcome of the Scottish independence referendum (55% in favour of remaining part of the UK) was much closer than originally expected. Indeed, in the final week of campaigning, the narrowness of the polls forced Westminster to offer a further package of devolution in the event that Scots voted to stay part of the UK.

The ramifications of referendums can extend well beyond the country in which the vote was held. This is particularly true of EU-related referendums because of their potential 'extraterritorial' effect, whereby rejection of a treaty in one country creates a conundrum for others (Mendez et al. 2014). This principle applies even to non-EU member states, as exemplified by the EU-Swiss relationship that was fundamentally shaped by the failed 1992 European Economic Area (EEA) membership referendum. Swiss rejection of the EEA led to the construction of an elaborate sector-by-sector bilateral treaty architecture that turned Switzerland into the most frequent EU-related user of direct democratic instruments as a succession of agreements were put to a popular vote (Trechsel 2007; see also Church elsewhere in Chapter 29). It was one of these referendums, the 2014 'mass immigration initiative' that subsequently up-ended the entire relationship. The crisis even prompted retaliatory action by the European Commission, namely suspending participation in Horizon 2020 research funding, which obliged the Federal Council to limit proposed restrictions on free movement (Schimmelfennig 2019).

Hence it is impossible to understand the historical course of European integration without acknowledging the impact left by referendums as Part Three of this volume addresses. The Norway-EU relationship is another example of the long-lasting consequences of the use of direct democracy, although this time the consequences were mostly felt at home. After Norwegian voters rejected EU membership in a 1994 referendum, Norway pursued a form of quasi-membership via the EEA. This established a process of 'dynamic homogeneity' maintained by highly institutionalised cooperation and domestic political adaptation necessary to limit grievances occasioned by implementing single market rules without a say in their formulation (Fossum and Graver 2018). Differentiation in Member State participation in EU policy-making also reflects the need to adapt to referendum results for years to come. Denmark was offered an opt-out in Justice and Home Affairs after Danish voters initially rejected the Maastricht treaty in 1992, resulting in a process of behind-the-scenes informal cooperation that left Danish policy-makers anxious to opt back in to regain decision-making influence (Adler-Nissen 2009). Yet voters failed to accept the government's argument that it was preferable to participate fully in order to shape EU policy in this area, rejecting an 'opt-in' referendum in 2015.

Reactions to crisis moments caused by referendums can take a more subtle and less institutionalised form, as in the way lessons of the failed Constitutional Treaty were internalised by supporters and opponents of the EU alike. In the aftermath of the decisive French and Dutch rejections of the Constitutional Treaty, EU political elites sought to avoid another flurry of referendums on the subsequent Lisbon Treaty (Phinnemore 2013) as well as on the so-called Fiscal Compact, an international treaty intended to fix economic and monetary union (Beach 2013). Leaders across Europe came to mistrust citizens' reactions to referendums on legal and institutional reform of the EU system. In the face of increased policy salience, they nevertheless sought to insulate such developments from political contestation over what European integration is for and whether it is good for one's country.

The decade following the defenestration of the Constitutional Treaty was marked by a populist Eurosceptic reaction (De Vries 2018). Calling for a referendum to expose fear of democracy by EU elites became a core Eurosceptic tactic. Anti-system parties such as the United Kingdom Independence Party, the *Front National* in France, *Movimento Cinque Stelle* in Italy or *Sverigedemokraterna* in Sweden promoted the use of direct democracy to tackle EU issues. Failure to offer a referendum on the Lisbon Treaty was integrated into an overriding populist narrative that elite-serving institutions act against the interests of the 'real people' (Müller 2017). It was no coincidence, therefore, that the first vote to be held under the popular initiative legislation the Netherlands enacted in 2015 was EU-related. Following a successful signature collection campaign, an advisory referendum was organised in April 2016 on the Association Agreement between the European Union and Ukraine (van den Akker 2017; see also Chapter 32 by van den Akker). Voters' rejection of the treaty then led to the amendment of the treaty to clarify, inter alia, that it was not a prelude to being granted EU candidate status or extending free movement rights to Ukrainians. Little more than two years after the Ukrainian Association Agreement vote, the Dutch government had put forward a law to abolish the consultative referendum procedure that had produced this reverse.

The overlap between the politicisation of integration, exacerbated by the Eurozone sovereign debt crisis, and calls to let the people weigh in on EU constitutional reform came to a head in Greece. Negotiations over the 2011 bailout package nearly broke down when Greek Prime Minister George Papandreou proposed to put the terms of the deal to the people in a referendum. The leaders of France and Germany, the largest Eurozone creditors, successfully pressured the Greek government into accepting the bailout without a vote (Glencross 2014). The idea of making the bailout conditional on the will of the people, however, did not disappear for long. In 2015, the radical-left Syriza government organised a vote on a new set of austerity measures that a near-unanimity of expert opinion suggested was the only way to remain in the Eurozone. The Greek government believed rejection of the EU deal—the final result was a resounding No by a 61% majority—would bring about an opportunity for the Eurogroup to rethink the credit terms, notably by offering debt relief (Boukala and Dimitrakopoulou 2016). These concessions never materialised, forcing the Greek government to accept the original terms of the new bailout without a reduction in debt (see also Chapter 30 by Papadopoulou in this volume).

The way the Greek referendum has entered historical memory, therefore, is as another instance where the preferences of the EU outrank the will of a nation (Rose 2019), akin to previous episodes where rejection of an EU treaty was subsequently overturned by a further referendum. Indeed, Eurosceptics appear to have a long memory when it comes to the use of direct democracy and how the results are interpreted. What was significant in the 2016 UK referendum was the way the previous vote on EEC membership in 1975 was (mis)remembered. A key part of the United Kingdom Independence Party's pro-Brexit narrative was that 'the British people were not getting - and have never got - what we were led to believe we were voting for [in 1975]' (Farage 2012). This message leached into Cameron's own justification that 'democratic consent for Britain's membership has worn wafer thin' (Cameron 2014), thereby suggesting that the 1975 referendum was about voting for a common market and not a political union. Yet the complaints from the anti-EEC side during the 1975 campaign are striking for their similarity with the pro-Brexit message of 2016: the UK pays too much for too few benefits, Europe is too inward-looking, accompanied by an overall feeling that it is fine to participate in an economic arrangement but that Britain must stay aloof from federal blueprints for monetary integration (Wall 2012). Hence the earlier referendum became memorialised politically in a way that deliberately obscured the content of what was discussed at the time.

The irony of the Brexit referendum is that it is highly unlikely to be remembered elsewhere in the EU as the moment when populist Euroscepticism delivered a preferable alternative to supranational integration. Despite certain predictions to the contrary, there was no immediate domino effect of other governments pledging to hold referendums on leaving. The illusion of getting a better deal outside the EU than as a Member State could only remain believable until formal exit talks began. Marine Le Pen's *Front National* had advocated 'Frexit' well before the 2016 UK vote (Ivaldi 2018), which explains the praise she originally heaped on the British government's approach to the EU, going as far as to advocate emulating Cameron's renegotiation and referendum tactic. Her intention was to ride a wave of French Euroscepticism to the *Elysée* Palace by offering a radical break with the pro-EU consensus. But her confused strategy on leaving the EU and/or the Eurozone went down badly with voters during her TV debate with Emmanuel Macron days before the presidential run-off (Michel 2018).

Ultimately, the way referendums are remembered and the legacies they leave is open to contestation, thereby affecting trust in the use of direct democracy. The way a referendum was held, or perhaps avoided, is part of political memory and can have long-lasting consequences. The desire to settle a political dispute can be realised, but is by no means a given; otherwise there would not have been two referendums on divorce in Ireland within the space of a decade. Referendums revisiting or linked to earlier votes illustrate the way direct democracy has become part of the fabric of democratic life in Europe as with the UK's EU membership referendum or Denmark's 'opt-in' vote. More subtly, the attempt to depoliticise EU reform after 2005 by dropping any 'constitutional' trappings when designing the Lisbon Treaty allowed populist parties to advocate greater direct democracy and cast themselves as true supporters of democracy. The common thread here is that while referendums may spark crises, they also contribute a fresh impetus for finding policy solutions to problems made apparent precisely by engaging the people directly in the first place, which is typical of the cycle of democratic practice (Nolte 2012). Judging by the historical record examined above, there is no apparent reason to abandon direct democracy for fear of its consequences: crisis can spur the democratic search for fulfilling the potential of citizen empowerment.

3.5   Conclusion

This chapter surveyed the way modern European democracies have used direct democracy as part of a search for solutions to some of the key political challenges they face: self-determination, European integration, public values. This search is motivated principally by the promise that referendums can bring a certain kind of closure not available via representative government. Yet the ability to fulfil this promise is mixed because problems of political trust, which undermine confidence in representative democracy and create the allure of direct democracy, remain present whenever referendums are used. The use of referendums is endorsed or contested because of the processes involved as well as their specific outcomes. This helps explain why, instead of resolution or catharsis, direct democracy can also result in crisis moments whose effects last long into the future. Examined in this fashion, referendums in modern Europe very much belong to the history of contemporary democracy as sketched by Nolte (2012): they are fundamentally political instruments that can engender hope and fulfil the aspiration for self-government, but also bring about bitterness and disappointment.

Bibliography

Adler-Nissen, R. (2009). Behind the Scenes of Differentiated Integration: Circumventing National Opt-Outs in Justice and Home Affairs. *Journal of European Public Policy, 16*(1), 62–80.

Beach, D. (2013). The Fiscal Compact, Euro-Reforms and the Challenge for the Euro-Outs. *Danish Foreign Policy Yearbook, 2013,* 113–133.

Bjørklund, T. (2009). The Surge of Referendums and the New Politics Approach. *Referendums and Representative Democracy* (pp. 135–154). Abingdon: Routledge.

Bogdanor, V. (2016). Europe and the Sovereignty of the People. *The Political Quarterly, 87*(3), 348–351.

Boukala, S., & Dimitrakopoulou, D. (2016). The Politics of Fear vs. the Politics of Hope: Analysing the 2015 Greek Election and Referendum Campaigns. *Critical Discourse Studies, 14*(1), 39–55.

Bowler, S. (2015). Information Availability and Information Use in Ballot Proposition Contests: Are Voters Over-Burdened? *Electoral Studies, 38,* 183–191.

Burgess, M. (2006). *Comparative Federalism: Theory and Practice.* Abingdon: Routledge.

Cameron, D. (2014, March 15). The EU Is Not Working and We Will Change It. *The Daily Telegraph.* Available from http://www.telegraph.co.uk/news/newsto pics/eureferendum/10700644/David-Cameron-the-EU-is-not-working-and-we-will-change-it.html.

Cetrà, D., & Harvey, M. (2018). Explaining Accommodation and Resistance to Demands for Independence Referendums in the UK and Spain. *Nations and Nationalism*, Early View.

Clarke, H. D., Goodwin, M., & Whiteley, P. (2017). *Brexit: Why Britain Voted to Leave the European Union*. Cambridge: Cambridge University Press.

De Vries, C. E. (2018). *Euroscepticism and the Future of European Integration*. Oxford: Oxford University Press.

Dostie, B., & Dupré, R. (2012). "The People's Will": Canadians and the 1898 Referendum on Alcohol Prohibition. *Explorations in Economic History, 49*(4), 498–515.

Dür, A., & Mateo, G. (2011). To Call or Not to Call? Political Parties and Referendums on the EU's Constitutional Treaty. *Comparative Political Studies, 44*(4), 468–492.

Farage, N. (2012). *A Referendum Stitch-up? How the EU and British Elites Are Plotting to Fix the Result*. London: United Kingdom Independence Party.

Finke, D., & König, T. (2009). Why Risk Popular Ratification Failure? A Comparative Analysis of the Choice of the Ratification Instrument in the 25 Member States of the EU. *Constitutional Political Economy, 20*(3–4), 341–365.

Fossum, J. E., & Graver, H. P. (2018). *Squaring the Circle on Brexit: Could the Norway Model Work?*. Bristol: Policy Press.

Gabel, M. (1998). Public Support for European Integration: An Empirical Test of Five Theories. *The Journal of Politics, 60*(2), 333–354.

Gaffney, J. (2010). *Political Leadership in France: From Charles de Gaulle to Nicolas Sarkozy*. Basingstoke: Springer.

Gallagher, M. (1996). Ireland: The Referendum as a Conservative Device? In M. Gallagher & P. V. Uleri (Eds.), *The Referendum Experience in Europe* (pp. 86–105). London: Palgrave Macmillan.

Gilbert, M. (2004). *Surpassing Realism: The Politics of European Integration Since 1945*. Oxford: Rowman & Littlefield Publishers.

Glencross, A. (2009). The Difficulty of Justifying European Integration as a Consequence of Depoliticization: Evidence from the 2005 French Referendum. *Government and Opposition, 44*(3), 243–261.

Glencross, A. (2014). The Eurozone Crisis as a Challenge to Democracy and Integration in Europe. *Orbis, 58*(1), 55–68.

Glencross, A. (2016). *Why the UK Voted for Brexit: David Cameron's Great Miscalculation*. Basingstoke: Palgrave.

Hobolt, S. B. (2007). Taking Cues on Europe? Voter Competence and Party Endorsements in Referendums on European Integration. *European Journal of Political Research, 46*(2), 151–182.

Hobolt, S. B., Spoon, J. J., & Tilley, J. (2009). A Vote Against Europe? Explaining Defection at the 1999 and 2004 European Parliament Elections. *British Journal of Political Science, 39*(1), 93–115.

Hodson, D., & Maher, I. (2014). British Brinkmanship and Gaelic Games: EU Treaty Ratification in the UK and Ireland from a Two Level Game Perspective. *The British Journal of Politics and International Relations, 16*(4), 645–661.

Holst, J. J. (1975). Norway's EEC Referendum: Lessons and Implications. *The World Today, 31*(3), 114–120.

Hooghe, L., & Marks, G. (2009). A Postfunctionalist Theory of European Integration: From Permissive Consensus to Constraining Dissensus. *British Journal of Political Science, 39*(1), 1–23.

Hug, S., & Schulz, T. (2007). Referendums in the EU's Constitution Building Process. *The Review of International Organizations, 2*(2), 177–218.

Ivaldi, G. (2018). Contesting the EU in Times of Crisis: The Front National and Politics of Euroscepticism in France. *Politics, 38*(3), 278–294.

Judt, T. (2011). *Ill Fares the Land: A Treatise on Our Present Discontents*. London, UK: Penguin.

Leduc, L. (2002). Opinion Change and Voting Behaviour in Referendums. *European Journal of Political Research, 41*(6), 711–732.

Locke, J. (1988). *Two Treatises of Government*, (Ed.) Peter Laslett. Cambridge: Cambridge University Press.

Lupia, A. (2006). How Elitism Undermines the Study of Voter Competence. *Critical Review, 18*(1–3), 217–232.

Manin, B. (1997). *The Principles of Representative Government*. Cambridge: Cambridge University Press.

Mendez, F., Mendez, M., & Triga, V. (2014). *Referendums and the European Union: A Comparative Inquiry*. Cambridge: Cambridge University Press.

Michel, E. (2018). The Front National in the 2017 French Election: An Electoral Impasse? In B. Laffan & L. Cicchi (Eds.), *2017: Europe's Bumper Year of Elections* (pp. 241–255). San Domenico di Fiesole: European University Institute.

Milward, A. (1992). *The European Rescue of the Nation State*. Abingdon: Routledge.

Monaghan, E. (2012). Assessing Participation and Democracy in the EU: The Case of the European Citizens' Initiative. *Perspectives on European Politics and Society, 13*(3), 285–298.

Morel, L. (2017). Types of Referendums, Provisions and Practice at the National Level Worldwide. *The Routledge Handbook to Referendums and Direct Democracy* (pp. 27–59). Abingdon: Routledge.

Müller, J. W. (2017). *What Is Populism?* Philadelphia: University of Pennsylvania Press.

Nolte, P. (2012). *Was ist Demokratie? Geschichte und Gegenwart*. Munich: CH Beck.

O'Brennan, J. (2009). Ireland Says No (Again): The 12 June 2008 Referendum on the Lisbon Treaty. *Parliamentary Affairs, 62*(2), 258–277.

Phinnemore, D. (2006). Beyond 25—The Changing Face of EU Enlargement: Commitment, Conditionality and the Constitutional Treaty. *Journal of Southern Europe and the Balkans, 8*(1), 7–26.

Phinnemore, D. (2013). *The Treaty of Lisbon: Origins and Negotiation*. London: Springer.

Qvortrup, M. (1999). AV Dicey: The Referendum as the People's Veto. *History of Political Thought, 20*(3), 531–546.

Qvortrup, M. (2002). *A Comparative Study of Referendums*. Manchester: Manchester University Press.

Qvortrup, M. (2015). *Direct Democracy: A Comparative Study of the Theory and Practice of Government by the People*. Manchester: Manchester University Press.

Qvortrup, M. (2016). Referendums on Membership and European Integration 1972–2015. *The Political Quarterly, 87*(1), 61–68.

Qvortrup, M. (2018). The History of Referendums and Direct Democracy. In L. Morel & M. Qvortrup (Eds.), *The Routledge Handbook to Referendums and Direct Democracy* (pp. 11–26). Abingdon: Routledge.

Renan, E. (2012). *Qu'est-ce qu'une nation?* République des Lettres.

Rose, R. (2019). Referendum Challenges to the EU's Policy Legitimacy–And How the EU Responds. *Journal of European Public Policy, 26*(2), 207–225.

Runciman, D. (2014). *Confidence Trap.* Princeton: Princeton University Press.

Schimmelfennig, F. (2019). Towards a "Reset" of EU-Swiss Relations? In M. Kaeding, J. Pollak & P. Schmidt (Eds.), *The Future of Europe* (pp. 117–119). Basingstoke: Palgrave Macmillan.

Seldon, A., & Snowdon, P. (2015). *Cameron at 10: The Inside Story, 2010–2015.* London: William Collins.

Shepherd, A. (2018). Fight for Abortion Rights Moves to Northern Ireland. *British Medical Journal, 8155*: 361–365.

Shipman, T. (2016). *All Out War: The Full Story of How Brexit Sank Britain's Political Class.* London: HarperCollins.

Smith, J. (2017). *The UK's Journey's Into and Out of the EU: Destinations Unknown.* Abingdon: Routledge.

Stein, E. (1981). Lawyers, Judges, and the Making of a Transnational Constitution. *American Journal of International Law, 75*(1), 1–27.

Tomasson, R. F. (1998). Alcohol and Alcohol Control in Sweden. *Scandinavian Studies, 70*(4), 477–508.

Tonge, J. (2000). From Sunningdale to the Good Friday Agreement: Creating Devolved Government in Northern Ireland. *Contemporary British History, 14*(3), 39–60.

Trechsel, A. (2007). Direct Democracy and European Integration: A Limited Obstacle? In C. Church (Ed.), *Switzerland and the European Union: A Close, Contradictory, and Misunderstood Relationship* (pp. 56–71). London: Routledge.

Tuck, R. (2015). *The Sleeping Sovereign: The Invention of Modern Democracy.* Cambridge: Cambridge University Press.

van den Akker, J. (2017). The Netherlands: The Dutch EU Referendums on the Constitutional Treaty (2005) and the EU-Ukraine Association Agreement (2016). In *Referendums on EU Matters* (pp. 188–208).

Wall, S. (2012). *The Official History of Britain and the European Community, Volume II: From Rejection to Referendum, 1963–1975.* Abingdon: Routledge.

Webb, P. (2013). Who Is Willing to Participate? Dissatisfied Democrats, Stealth Democrats and Populists in the United Kingdom. *European Journal of Political Research, 52,* 747–772.

Weiler, J. H. (1991). The Transformation of Europe. *Yale Law Journal, 100,* 2403–2483.

CHAPTER 4

The Rules of Referendums

Alan Renwick and Jess Sargeant

Referendums, like any large-scale processes of democratic decision-making, need to take place within a framework of rules. This chapter examines such rules. We survey how referendums are regulated in Europe today and how they ought to be regulated. We find that there are many important gaps in current regulatory frameworks: much more could be done to ensure that referendums play the most positive role they could in the overall democratic system.

Making such judgements clearly requires a framework for evaluation. We are helped towards that by the Venice Commission (formally, the European Commission for Democracy through Law), which is the Council of Europe's constitutional advisory body. In 2007, it published a *Code of Good Practice on Referendums*, which sets out recommendations for many aspects of referendum conduct. This is founded largely on the principles of universal, equal, free and secret suffrage. Equal suffrage implies a requirement for balance and state neutrality in the design of referendum processes. Free suffrage implies not only that voters can freely express their wishes, but also that they can freely form their opinions, without being subjected to undue coercion or campaigns of misinformation, and with access to the information they want from sources

A. Renwick (✉)
University College London, London, UK
e-mail: a.renwick@ucl.ac.uk

J. Sargeant
Institute for Government, London, UK
e-mail: jess.sargeant@instituteforgovernment.org.uk

J. Smith (ed.), *The Palgrave Handbook of European Referendums*, https://doi.org/10.1007/978-3-030-55803-1_4

they trust. The Venice Commission also grounds its recommendations on the principles of protecting human rights and the rule of law.

Beyond these principles, we suggest that referendums should also contribute to the effective functioning of the democratic system as a whole. No democracy beyond the tiniest community can operate without representative institutions. Direct democratic instruments such as referendums must exist alongside these and not undermine them. Furthermore, democracy involves not just voting, but also the processes of listening, discussing, deliberating, bargaining and compromising that must precede any decision. Referendums should not circumvent these processes but should rather be designed to enhance them.[1]

Collectively, these principles imply that we should view referendums holistically, looking not just at the vote itself, but also at the entire process of calling a referendum and conducting the campaign. We identify five key dimensions of referendum regulation that demand attention:

- *when referendums take place*: whether this is decided by rules or is a matter of political choice; who can call a referendum; what topics can be put to a referendum; and what procedures surround a decision on whether to call a referendum
- *the structure of the vote*: who can vote; the nature of the referendum question and process for setting it; and the administration of the vote
- *the status of the result*: whether it is binding or advisory, and whether the outcome is subject to special thresholds
- *the conduct of the campaign*: rules protecting both fairness between the sides and the quality of information available to voters
- *enforcement of the rules*: sanctions for rule breaches; and rules on when a referendum should be partially or fully re-run.

The following sections address these five areas in turn, examining the rules that exist and where there are important deficiencies. Before that, we briefly consider a prior, overarching question: where do the rules governing referendums sit?

4.1   WHERE REFERENDUM RULES SIT

There are four possible locations for the rules on referendums:

---

[1] Our thinking on these matters is informed by our having served, respectively, as Research Director and Research Assistant for the UK's Independent Commission on Referendums (see Independent Commission on Referendums 2018). Alan Renwick has also acted as advisor to the Rapporteur of the Committee on Political Affairs and Democracy of the Parliamentary Assembly of the Council of Europe for an inquiry into referendum rules, and this chapter draws on his work in that role. The views expressed here are, however, our own.

- iń the constitution or other entrenched higher law
- in ordinary legislation that applies to referendums in general
- in legislation specific to a particular referendum
- in executive orders or secondary legislation not subject to full parliamentary scrutiny (see also Chapter 5 by Norton elsewhere in this volume).

In addition, a fifth possibility is that regulations on some aspects of referendum conduct simply do not exist in some countries.

In practice, most European democracies set out certain basic features of referendum conduct—such as the franchise and who can call a referendum—in constitutional law. This conforms to a Venice Commission recommendation that such key matters should not be susceptible to short-term manipulation. There are only a few exceptions. The United Kingdom, lacking entrenched constitutional law, places some basic referendum conduct rules in ordinary standing legislation, though these are far from comprehensive (see also Chapters 13 and 5 by Blick and Norton). The only European democracy that holds national referendums but has no standing rules of any kind is Norway: here, all legal provisions relating to a referendum must be established anew when a referendum is called (see also Chapter 21 by Fossum and Rosén).

Some rules, if they are to exist, must be written in constitutional or standing legislation: rules on when and how a referendum may be called by definition cannot be established by the legislation that calls a referendum. Conversely, some rules are necessarily specific to a particular vote: such as the referendum question (unless it is prescribed by formula) and the date of the vote. Other rules can be located at any level. In practice, even countries with constitutional provisions on referendums typically supplement these through ordinary legislation.

4.2   When Referendums Take Place

Having considered the nature of referendum rules, we turn now to their content. The first set of issues concerns when referendums take place. There are three basic approaches to determining this. First, rules may state that referendums *must* take place in certain conditions. Second, rules might provide that referendums *cannot* take place in certain conditions. Third, whether a referendum is held or not may be left as a matter of choice. We can address the first two of these quickly. The third requires more detailed discussion of who can exercise this choice in what circumstances. In addition, for any of these approaches there is an important question regarding the processes through which a referendum may be called.

4.2.1   Rules Requiring or Banning Referendums

Rules requiring referendums in certain circumstances are common, set out in the country's constitution or ordinary law. They mainly apply to constitutional changes. For example, referendums are required for all constitutional amendments in Ireland (Article 46), Denmark (Section 88) and Romania (Article 151), amendments to certain parts of the constitution in Lithuania (Article 148), Latvia (Article 77), Malta (Article 66) and Iceland (Article 79), and for total constitutional revisions in Austria (Article 44[3]) and Spain (Section 168).[2] Although the UK lacks a codified constitution, ordinary legislation requires referendums before certain key constitutional changes— notably, the abolition of the Scottish Parliament or Welsh Assembly.

At the opposite end of the spectrum, no European country explicitly prohibits referendums altogether. Germany is the only European democracy where no national referendum has been held since the Second World War, but, even here, a referendum would be required for a complete revision of the constitution (Article 146).

Rules restricting the subject matter of referendums are more common. Financial, budgetary and tax laws are often protected from referendums (see Denmark, Section 42[6]; Italy, Article 75; Portugal, Article 115[4]), as is legislation relating to treaties. In Slovakia (Article 93[3]) and Slovenia (Article 90), legislation relating to fundamental freedoms and human rights cannot be put to referendum. Hungary (Article [3]) and Portugal (Article 115[4]) bar referendums on constitutional amendments.

4.2.2   Referendums by Choice: Who, How and on What?

Beyond the requirements set out in the preceding paragraphs, many European democracies allow optional referendums. Legal frameworks set out who can call a referendum, by what mechanisms, on what topics.

Looking across Europe's democracies, we find five types of actor that can call an optional national referendum: the legislature (that is, the majority within the legislature), the executive (or the executive and legislature together), ordinary citizens via petition, a minority of parliamentarians, or regional authorities. Current provisions are summarised in Table 4.1. As discussed below, many of these entitlements to call referendums are restricted to particular topics or circumstances.

In most European democracies, the legislature can call a referendum on any matter within its competency. In some cases, this role is specified in constitutional or other law. Where no explicit provision exists, as in the UK and Norway, the legislature can call a referendum ad hoc by passing primary legislation to enable one.

---

[2]Unless otherwise stated, where an article or section of a law is cited in this chapter, it relates to the relevant country's national constitution.

Table 4.1   Who can call a referendum in Europe's democracies

Country	Mandatory	Majority in legislature	Executive	Executive and legislature	Citizens	Minority of MPs	Regional authorities
Austria	✓	✓				✓	
Belgium		✓					
Bulgaria		✓			✓		
Croatia	✓	✓	✓		✓		
Cyprus		✓					
Czech Republic	✓						
Denmark	✓	✓				✓	
Estonia	✓	✓					
Finland		✓					
France	✓		✓	✓			
Germany	✓						
Greece		✓					
Hungary				✓	✓		
Iceland	✓	✓	✓				
Ireland	✓			✓			
Italy					✓	✓	✓
Latvia	✓	✓	✓		✓		
Lithuania	✓	✓			✓		
Luxembourg		✓			✓	✓	
Malta	✓	✓			✓		
The Netherlands		✓			*		
Norway		✓					
Poland		✓		✓		✓	
Portugal				✓			
Romania	✓			✓			
Slovakia	✓	✓		✓	✓		
Slovenia		✓			✓	✓	
Spain	✓			✓		✓	
Sweden		✓				✓	
Switzerland	✓	✓			✓		✓
Turkey	✓		✓				
UK	✓	✓					

*The Netherlands introduced provision for citizen-initiated referendums in 2015, but this was repealed in 2018. Note: This table does not include indirect procedures allowing citizens to petition parliament to call a referendum. Sources: Authors' compilation from the IDEA Direct Democracy Database (IDEA n.d.) and from national constitutions and other relevant legislation.

The executive may also play a role in calling referendums. In some cases, such as France (Article 11) and Croatia (Article 87), the president can call a referendum without parliamentary support, provided she or he has authorisation from the government. This creates the risk that the executive can subvert parliament and gain a mandate for new provisions through a referendum alone. In France, however, it is possible for parliament to prevent the president from calling a referendum on the advice of the government if it passes a censure motion (Morel 1997: 71). Elsewhere—notably, in Iceland—the president can trigger a referendum by refusing to sign a bill that has passed through the legislature (Article 26). Here the president cannot force a measure through without parliamentary consent but can introduce the possibility of a popular veto of measures that parliament has passed.

In other cases, the executive is empowered to call a referendum upon the recommendation or authorisation of the legislature. In Portugal, the parliament or government submits a draft referendum to the president who then decides whether to call a referendum (Article 115, Section 1). Referendums in Spain are proposed by the prime minister after parliamentary authorisation (Section 92[2], Article 125[2]).

Eleven European countries allow citizens to initiate a referendum by petition on at least some matters, as summarised in Table 4.2.

Provisions for a minority of members of the legislature to trigger a referendum can act as a minority veto. Such provisions are relatively common, particularly on constitutional amendments: a tenth of legislators can call such a referendum in Spain, a quarter in Luxembourg, and a third in Austria or Slovenia. In Italy, a fifth of parliamentarians can request a referendum on a constitutional amendment unless the amendment was approved by two-thirds of the members of each house (Article 138; see also Chapter 17 by Uleri); in Sweden, a third of MPs can request a referendum on a constitutional amendment, provided they do so within fifteen days of the *Riksdag* adopting the proposal (Chapter 8, Article 16). Some countries' constitutions also allow a minority of parliamentarians to trigger referendums on other matters: in Denmark (Section 42[1]), a third of MPs can do so on a bill that is not yet law.

Finally, Italy and Switzerland allow regional authorities to trigger national referendums. In Italy, a referendum takes place on the request of five regional councils (Articles 75 and 138). Eight cantons can trigger a referendum in Switzerland (Article 141).

There are often restrictions on when these actors can call a referendum, and on what subject matter. For example, Switzerland (Article 139) and Latvia (Article 78) are unusual in allowing citizens to propose constitutional amendments directly, meaning that changes to the constitution could be mandated without the consent, and possibly against the wishes, of the legislature.

Elsewhere, a referendum request must pertain to a specific piece of legislation, either that is already in force—as in Italy (Article 75) and Malta (1973 Referenda Act: Article 14)—or that has been passed through the legislature

Table 4.2   Citizen-initiated referendums in European democracies

Country	Signatures required	Scope
Bulgaria	400,000	Any subject except changes to constitution, taxes and other specified exemptions
Croatia	10% of registered electors	Any subject
Hungary	200,000	Any subject except changes to constitution, taxes and other specified exemptions
Italy	500,000	Proposals to repeal a law in whole or part; can repeal constitutional changes in limited circumstances; cannot repeal tax, budget or treaty changes
Latvia	10% of registered electors	Any law suspended by the president or a third of parliament, or any proposal, with exceptions including the budget and taxes
Lithuania	300,000	Any subject
Luxembourg	25,000	A proposed constitutional amendment that has passed for the first time in parliament
Malta	10% of registered electors	Proposals to repeal existing laws; cannot repeal constitution, fiscal legislation or certain other existing laws
Slovakia	350,000	Any subject except changes to constitution, taxes and other specified exemptions
Slovenia	40,000	Proposals to repeal recently passed laws, with exceptions including taxes and treaties
Switzerland	New proposal—100,000	Constitutional amendments
	Existing law—50,000	Repeal of recently passed laws

Source National constitutions

and is awaiting final approval—as in Denmark (Section 42[1] and [2]), Austria (Article 43), Ireland (Article 27), Iceland (Article 26) and Slovenia (Article 90).

Referendums on general principles rather than specific legal texts—so-called 'pre-legislative' referendums—are also widely permitted. That can be because no laws expressly prevent them—as, for example, in the UK and Norway—or because specific laws allow them. In Spain, 'political decisions of special importance' can be put to a consultative referendum (Section 92[1]). The Austrian National Council can also call a referendum 'on a matter of fundamental and overall national importance' by passing a motion containing a question (Article 49b). A 2010 Icelandic law permits parliament to call a referendum on any topic without restriction by parliamentary resolution (Act on the Conduct of Referendums 91/2010: Article 1). Countries such as Bulgaria and Lithuania allow citizen-initiated referendums on almost any subject. Pre-legislative referendums such as these can be problematic. If the proposal put to referendum is unclear, voters may find it difficult to make an informed decision, and political actors will lack a clear instruction as to how to implement the result.

4.2.3   Steps Before Calling a Referendum

A proposal put to a post-legislative referendum goes through the full legislative process before it is referred to voters, creating scope for scrutiny and debate. Indeed, for proposed constitutional amendments, there are often requirements for parliamentary supermajorities or repeated parliamentary votes, ensuring that broad consent among representatives is required. In Romania, for example, a proposed constitutional amendment must secure a two-thirds majority in both chambers of parliament before it goes to voters in a referendum (Article 151). In Denmark, such a proposal must pass through the legislature twice on either side of a general election before a referendum can be called (Section 88).

By contrast, serious preparation for abrogative or pre-legislative referendums is rare, creating a risk that voters are asked to decide on under-developed proposals. We have argued elsewhere that this created serious problems following the UK's 2016 Brexit referendum (Renwick et al. 2018). Proposals for citizen-initiated referendums are often subject to legal or administrative checks to ensure, for example, that they are constitutional or do not raise multiple distinct issues in a single question (see the section on referendum questions below). But scrutiny of the actual desirability of the proposals is much less common. Switzerland offers an exception: several years typically pass between a petition and the popular vote, during which parliament debates the proposal, takes a view on it, and can formulate its own counterproposal (Lutz 2012).

Some European countries have begun to use innovative mechanisms for developing and scrutinising referendum proposals. Most notably, the Irish *Oireachtas* has three times in recent years established deliberative bodies comprising randomly selected citizens—and, in the case of the Constitutional Convention of 2012–2014, parliamentarians—which were tasked with considering a series of constitutional issues and making recommendations. These formed the bases for referendum proposals on same-sex marriage (see Chapter 16 by Reidy et al.) and the minimum age for presidential candidates in 2015 and on abortion and blasphemy in 2018 (McGreevy 2018).

The steps taken before a referendum is called are as important as the campaign and the vote themselves. They determine how the prevailing situation is diagnosed and what proposals appear on the ballot paper; they also help shape how the issues are framed during the campaign. They are thus fundamental in determining whether the referendum addresses the issues that concern voters and whether voters can make a free, informed choice. However, few democracies have given sufficient thought to these steps: this is an area where the law is often silent. Greater attention would be desirable, and innovations such as those seen in Ireland deserve serious consideration.

4.3   The Structure of the Vote

We now turn to the basic structure of the vote itself: the franchise, the referendum question and the administration of the vote.

4.3.1   Who Can Vote

There are two ways to think of how the referendum franchise ought to be determined: one says it should be fixed in advance for all referendums and so protected from political interference; the other proposes that it should be tailored to specific referendums, to accommodate those who will be significantly affected by the result (Independent Commission on Referendums 2018: 69–70). These two approaches are most likely to generate divergent prescriptions in referendums on matters of sovereignty, where the boundaries or powers of 'the people' are at stake. For example, there was debate in the UK before the 2016 referendum on whether EU citizens resident in the UK (as well as 16- and 17-year olds) should be allowed to vote (Scott 2015: 4–7). The Venice Commission comes out firmly for the first approach, saying the franchise should be fixed in advance and not changed in the year preceding a referendum (Venice Commission 2007: II.2.b–c). Most experts would concur: whatever the merits of tailoring the franchise in theory, in practice it would risk political manipulation by those in power.

Almost all European countries follow this approach, specifying, either in the constitution or occasionally in other standing legislation, that the franchise for national referendums is the same as for national parliamentary elections. The exceptions are the UK and Norway, which have no standing franchise for national referendums: who can vote is specified in the primary legislation enabling a referendum.

4.3.2   Setting the Question

Many countries—including Austria (Volksabstimmungsgesetz 1972, 9[2] and [3]), Ireland (Referendum Act 1994: Section 24), and Italy (Law 352 of 25 May 1970: Articles 16 and 27)—specify a fixed format for referendum questions in legislation. This applies when the referendum relates to a specific piece of legislation or a constitutional amendment. In Ireland, for example, the question asks, 'Do you approve of the proposal to amend the Constitution contained in the undermentioned Bill?' and then provides the name of the bill.

In most other circumstances, the question is formulated by the authority proposing the referendum. The danger with this is that the proposal's sponsors may seek to introduce biases. Some countries employ political checks and balances. In Portugal, for example, a proposed citizen-initiated referendum goes to the relevant parliamentary committee, which can request changes that the legislature then votes on (Law no. 15-A/98 of 3 April 1998 [rev.

2016]: Articles 12, 20 and 23). Switzerland's constitution requires the Federal Assembly to declare a referendum initiative invalid if it combines excessively disparate matters (Article 139[3]). Elsewhere, an independent body plays a role in formulating the question. The respective Electoral Commissions advise the national parliament on wording for some referendums in Iceland (Act on the Conduct of Referendums 91/2010 2010: Article 3) and all referendums in the UK (Political Parties, Elections and Referendums Act 2000: Article 104 [2] and [4]).

Such independent mechanisms for ensuring questions are clear and unbiased and do not combine multiple issues in one vote are essential. It is therefore striking that many European democracies lack them. The absence of such provisions can undermine perceived legitimacy and increases the danger that a referendum could deliver a skewed measure of public opinion.

4.3.3   Administration of the Vote

Most democracies have comprehensive rules for the conduct and administration of the poll to ensure the integrity of the ballot; such rules are central to ensuring a free and fair vote. Independent electoral commissions are most commonly responsible for the administration and management of the referendum poll. For example, in Spain the Central Electoral Commission is charged with electoral administration, management of the poll and compliance with electoral and referendum legislation (Organic Law 5/1985, of June 19, of the General Electoral Regime: Article 19). In some cases, however, this is the responsibility of the government: in Italy, for example, the Interior Minister (Ministero Dell'Interno, n.d.), and in Ireland the Department for Housing, Planning and Local Government.

4.4   THE STATUS OF THE RESULT

The next dimension of referendums that we examine is the status of the result. Here there are two important issues. First, are referendum results binding or advisory? Second, what threshold must be met for the proposal put in a referendum to be deemed to have passed?

4.4.1   Binding or Advisory?

A referendum result is legally binding, in the conventional sense, if it prevents the legislature from passing a law contradicting that result, at least for a period of time. To be binding in this sense, provision for a referendum must be set out in a country's higher law, most commonly in its constitution. The UK's uncodified constitution and central constitutional principle of parliamentary sovereignty prevents it from holding referendums that bind parliament.

Similarly, Norway, Belgium and the Netherlands have no provisions for referendums in their constitutions, and so legally binding referendums are not possible.

In Denmark, all referendums specified in the constitution are binding, but advisory referendums have also been held on the basis of ad hoc legislation. A 2011 Icelandic law enabled the holding of consultative referendums, but only those triggered through the procedures laid out in the constitution can be binding.

Broadly speaking, post-legislative referendums—on legal texts that have already passed through the legislature—are binding whereas votes held on general proposals or principles are advisory. For example, in Lithuania, all constitutional and abrogative citizen-initiated referendums are binding, but those in which citizens propose the topic themselves are advisory (Lithuania Law on Referendum 4 June 2002 No IX-929 [rev. 2012]: Article 5). Austria, Croatia, Portugal, Spain and Sweden have explicit provisions for both kinds of referendums. Many countries—including France, Greece, Hungary, Ireland, Italy, Latvia, Poland, Slovenia and Switzerland—provide in their constitutions only for legally binding referendums. In Estonia, if the parliament puts a law to referendum and it is rejected, not only is the law not brought into force but a general election is automatically triggered (Article 105). (Perhaps in consequence, only one national referendum has been held since the current constitution came into force. That was on EU accession, where an affirmative result was not in serious doubt.)

For two reasons, however, the distinction between legally binding and advisory referendums is less stark than it might appear at first blush. The first reason is that there are in fact more than two possible legal statuses for referendums: a referendum result can be 'binding' in a more limited sense than the conventional meaning set out above. In the UK, for example, while a referendum cannot bind parliament, it can bind the executive. The law enabling a 2011 referendum on the voting system provided that, if the referendum passed (which in the end it did not), the responsible minister would have to bring into force sections of that law setting out the new voting rules, though parliament would have been free in law to repeal them had it wished (see also Chapter 13 by Blick elsewhere in this volume). Under the Dutch law on citizen-initiated referendums in force between 2015 and 2018, if voters backed the repeal of a law, a bill providing for this had to be brought forward and debated, but parliament was free not to adopt it (Jacobs 2018; see also Chapter 32 by van den Akker elsewhere in this volume). Switzerland exhibits a different kind of pattern. Referendum results there are binding in theory, but the authorities often have considerable flexibility in deciding how to implement them. Thus, while a 2014 vote required the introduction of immigration quotas, for example, the law that was finally passed to give effect to this provided for measures more limited than quotas (Summermatter and Miserez 2017).

Second, even when they are legally only advisory, referendums are often treated as binding politically. The most noteworthy recent example is the UK's

2016 Brexit referendum. Others include the Norwegian EU accession referendum of 1994 and Sweden's referendum on euro membership in 2003 (see Chapter 26 by Oscarsson elsewhere in this volume). In all these cases, most parliamentarians wanted to take one course, but they conceded when voters chose to go the other way.

The legal status of a referendum is often subject to certain validity requirements, the most common being special thresholds. We discuss these next.

4.4.2   What Threshold Is Required?

Every referendum has a threshold that must be reached for a proposal to win: the default threshold is 50% of valid votes cast plus one. However, some democracies supplement or vary this threshold to place additional validity requirements on a referendum result. There are four main kinds of special threshold: turnout thresholds; electorate thresholds; multiple majority thresholds; and supermajority thresholds.

Supermajority thresholds, which require support for the change option to be higher than 50% plus one, have been used in some Canadian provincial referendums (Fournier et al. 2011: 128). But they are not used in any European democracy, except that Lithuania's electorate thresholds, which we set out below, effectively function also as supermajority thresholds.

A turnout threshold specifies a certain percentage of the eligible voters who must cast their vote in order for a referendum to be valid or binding. Such thresholds are premised on the logic that, if a referendum is to be considered an expression of public will, a certain proportion of the electorate need to participate. The most common requirement is that 50% of eligible voters participate. This is required for all referendums in Lithuania (Law on Referendum 4 June 2002 No IX-929 [rev. 2012], Article 7[1], 8[1]), Slovakia (Article 98), Romania (Law No. 3 22 February 2000 on the Organisation and Conduct of the Referendum: Article 5[2]) and Hungary (Article 8[4]), for abrogative referendums in Italy (Article 75) and Malta (1973 Referenda Act: Article 20[1]), and for constitutional amendments in Slovenia (Article 170). Until it was repealed, the Dutch law on citizen-initiated referendums set a 30% turnout threshold.

Rather than stipulating a percentage of eligible voters, Latvia requires that turnout in a referendum on a law must be at least half the level of the turnout at the previous parliamentary election for the result to be valid (Article 74). For a referendum to be binding in Bulgaria, turnout must be at least as high as at the last election; if this requirement is not met but turnout still reaches 20% of eligible voters, the proposition must be considered in the National Assembly (Direct Citizen Participation in State and Local Government Act 4/12.06.2009: Article 23). Similarly, referendums are only binding in Portugal (Article 115[11]) and Poland (Article 125[3]) if turnout is above 50%. A Greek referendum on a specific law or social issue is binding at 50%

turnout; a referendum on a 'crucial national issue' is binding on a turnout of 40% (Law 4023, Expanding Direct and Participatory Democracy through Referenda: Article 16).

An electorate threshold (sometimes referred to as an 'approval quorum') requires a certain percentage of the eligible electorate to vote for a particular option before it wins. This is intended to prevent an active minority from imposing its will on a passive majority. Four European democracies require such thresholds, two of which require different thresholds for different types of referendums, as summarised in Table 4.3.

Multiple majority thresholds require that a majority vote for a proposition not only nationally, but also in a specified number of geographical areas. Such thresholds are designed to protect minorities and ensure that proposals have broad support rather than support that is concentrated in certain localities. Multiple majority thresholds are typically seen in federal systems. Switzerland is the only European country to use them: most referendums on constitutional amendments and on 'accession to organisations for collective security or to supranational communities' need a majority of votes overall and in a majority of the cantons for the proposals to pass (Article 140).

Multiple majority thresholds can be sensible where they reflect the wider structures of a federal system. By contrast, the Venice Commission (2007: section III.7) argues strongly against turnout and electorate thresholds, believing that the former give campaigners for the less popular option an incentive to invalidate the referendum by trying to suppress turnout, while the latter can block change even if it is accepted by a substantial majority

Table 4.3 Electorate threshold requirements in European democracies

Country	Procedure	Subject matter	Electorate
Denmark	Mandatory	Constitutional amendment	40%
	Mandatory	Lowering the voting age	30%
	Initiated by minority of parliamentarians	Legislation	30%
Ireland	Initiated by Executive and Legislature	Legislation	30%
Lithuania	Mandatory	Amendment Article 1 of the constitution: 'the State of Lithuania shall be a democratic republic'	75%
	Mandatory	Amendment to the constitutional act: 'On Non-Alignment of the Republic of Lithuania to Post-Soviet Eastern Alliances'	75%
	Mandatory	Constitutional amendments	50%
	Citizen-initiated	Law or provision proposed by citizens	1/3
Slovenia	Citizen-initiated	Legislation	20%

of voters. In Denmark in 2009, for example, a constitutional amendment to end gender discrimination in the royal succession had overwhelming public backing, gaining the support of over 85% of those voting; but it almost failed, as low turnout meant that the 40% electorate threshold was only narrowly surpassed.

4.5   CONDUCT OF THE CAMPAIGN (I): FAIRNESS BETWEEN THE SIDES

Our fourth dimension of referendum regulation—relating to the conduct of the campaign—raises many issues that have caused much concern in recent years. For this reason, we divide it into the two aspects that have been most contentious. In this section, we focus on mechanisms for ensuring there is a fair balance between the sides in a referendum campaign. In the following section, we look at the information available to voters as they decide how to cast their ballots.

There is general agreement that fairness between the sides in a referendum campaign matters: if voters are to make a free choice, they must be able to hear both sides of the argument and they must not be subject to any undue interference or pressure (e.g., Chambers 2001: 235; LeDuc 2015: 144). There is less agreement, however, on what exactly fairness requires. One view is that it demands balance between the sides: that each side should have equal voice irrespective of who supports it and how much support it has. Another view is that fairness ought to take account of how popular each side is: if one side is supported only by a small fringe, it could create 'false balance' to give it equal weight with its opposition, misleading voters into thinking widely rejected ideas are credible. In practice, both of these views tend to be manifest in different aspects of referendum campaign regulation.

We focus here on fairness in three domains: the role of government in referendum campaigns; the rules around campaign finance; and media coverage.

4.5.1   The Role of Government

Though ostensibly highly democratic, referendums can become the opposite of that if they are used by powerful figures to cement their authority, particularly if in so doing they bypass checks and balances or subvert the rule of law. As detailed by Batory and Kalaysioğlu & Kocapinar in Chapters 31 and 19 respectively, there have recently been serious concerns about such plebiscitary use of referendums in countries such as Hungary and Turkey, where the resources of the state were deployed overwhelmingly to skew the referendum debate. There are also less egregious cases: in the UK in 2016, for example, there was widespread disquiet when the government spent substantial public funds on a leaflet putting the case for staying in the EU just before the start of the official campaign.

It is rare for governments to be restricted from expressing a view on a referendum question. The Venice Commission acknowledges that, unlike in elections, where the authorities should not support any party or candidate, in referendum campaigns, 'it is legitimate for the different organs of government to convey their viewpoint in the debate' (Venice Commission, 2007: 17). Portugal offers an exception to this, where the referendum law requires strict neutrality (Law no. 15-A/98 of 3 April 1998 [rev. 2016]: Article 45). Elsewhere, by contrast, an opportunity for the government to present its advice to voters is sometimes institutionalised into the referendum process. In Switzerland, for example, the referendum booklet prepared for each ballot and sent to all voters is prepared by the federal government, though it must 'take account of the opinions of significant minorities' (Federal Act on Political Rights, 17 December 1976, amended as of 1 November 2015, Article 11.2). Such provisions reflect the idea that voters have a right to know the perspective of their elected government when making their own choice.

Restrictions on governments tend to focus, rather, on the use of public funds. Ireland has particularly tight rules in this regard. A court case was brought against the government in 1995 for using public funds to encourage a Yes vote in a referendum on divorce. The court ruled that this violated the constitutional rights to equality, freedom of expression and democratic procedure in a referendum (*McKenna v An Taoiseach* [1995] S.C. Nos 361 and 366 of 1995). As a result of the judgement, the Irish government now spends public funds on independent, neutral public information provisions, which we discuss further in the following section. Similarly, in Switzerland, although there is no legislation restricting the role of the federal government in referendum campaigns, the political rights of freedom to form an opinion and the unaltered expression of will have been interpreted to mean that the use of public funds on one side is unconstitutional (Serdült 2010). The UK has a prohibition on the use of state resources in the final four weeks before the vote.

Such provisions fit (to varying degrees) with strong Venice Commission guidance that '[t]he use of public funds by the authorities for campaigning purposes must be prohibited' (section I.3.1.b).

By contrast, some countries—even some long-established democracies— have no restriction on government campaigning in referendums. For example, in France, the government's arguments for the ratification of a constitutional amendment are sent out with the referendum ballot papers (Richard and Pabst 2013). This is the area of the Venice Commission's *Code of Good Practice on Referendums* where compliance among Council of Europe member states is weakest. That has the potential to undermine the fairness—and therefore also the legitimacy—of referendum processes.

4.5.2   Campaign Finance

The 'campaign finance' heading encompasses a number of issues: regulation of or limits on campaign spending; equivalent rules for donations to campaigns; and whether public funding is available for campaigning (cf. Reidy and Suiter 2015: 162).

The last of these flows on from the preceding point about the role of government. The Venice Commission, in line with the requirement for state neutrality mentioned above, says that 'Equality must be ensured in terms of public subsidies and other forms of backing' (Section I.2.2.d). It then goes on, however, to allow for the differing notions of fairness outlined above. While it says 'It is advisable that equality be ensured between the proposal's supporters and opponents', it also allows that 'backing may ... be restricted to supporters and opponents of the proposal who account for a minimum percentage of the electorate', and it also suggests that funding may be distributed to political parties, either equally or proportionally 'to the results achieved in the elections' (Section I.2.2.d). In practice, there is wide variation in state funding between countries.

Some, such as Ireland, provide no funding to campaigners. Others, including the UK and the Netherlands, provide equal funding to the two sides: the UK does so by designating an umbrella organisation on each side of the argument to receive public benefits; in the Netherlands, campaigners apply to the Referendum Commission, which awards grants for activities from two equal funds. Others still, such as Denmark, France and Spain, distribute funds to parties in proportion to their strength. This can lead to very unequal funding if most parliamentary parties line up on one side of the debate: in the year of the Danish euro referendum of 2000, for example, pro-euro parties received almost three times as much state funding as did anti-euro parties (Hobolt 2010).

The Venice Commission says little about other aspects of campaign finance, except that it should be transparent and that spending limits are permissible (Section I.2.2.g–h). Campaign expenses are in fact commonly scrutinised through a requirement to submit audited accounts. In Lithuania (Law on funding of, control over funding of, political parties and political campaigns 23 August 2004—No IX-2428 Vilnius [amended 2011]: Article 21), Spain (Organic Law 5/1985, of June 19, of the General Electoral Regime: Articles 131–134), and Portugal (Financing of Political Parties, Law no 19/2003 of 20 June: Articles 15 and 19), this is required for all political parties and campaigns groups. In Denmark (Hobolt 2010) and France (Decree No. 2005-238 of 17 March 2005 on the campaign for the referendum: Article 10), the law only applies to political parties in receipt of public funding. Denmark, France, and Ireland have no spending limits for referendums. In Lithuania (Law on funding of, control over funding of, political parties and political campaigns 23 August 2004—No IX-2428 Vilnius [amended 2011] Article 17), spending limits are calculated on the basis of the number of electors in the area a group intends to campaign in. In Portugal, the limit is linked to the national minimum wage (Financing of Political Parties, Law no 19/2003 of 20 June, Article 20).

Restrictions on donations from foreign actors are common. Some countries, including Ireland (Standards in Public Office Commission 2016), Spain (Organic Law 8/2007 of 4 July on the funding of political parties, Articles 4–7), Lithuania (No IX-2428, Articles 10 and 11) and Portugal (Law 19/2003, Article 16), also cap the amount any individual or body can donate. In Lithuania, this is linked to average incomes, and in Portugal to the national minimum wage.

Some democracies, such as Austria, Iceland and the Netherlands, have little financial regulation of campaigners in referendums. Perhaps most surprisingly, given its frequent use of referendums, Switzerland has almost no such rules. This may advantage well-financed interest groups, leading some to refer to Swiss popular initiatives as 'purchased democracy' (Kobach 1994: 107)—though others see such a claim as exaggerated (Serdült 2010).

4.5.3 Media Balance

Most European democracies have some kind of balance rule for broadcast coverage of referendum campaigns. French broadcasters are required to apply the principles of 'equality and plurality' to referendum coverage (CSA 2005). Portuguese radio and television stations must give 'equal treatment' to all referendum participants (Law no. 14-A/98 of 3 April 1997 [rev. 2016] Articles 57). Ireland has had strict balance requirements since a court case (*Coughlan v. Broadcasting Complaints Commission*) in 2000. In the UK, broadcasters must show 'due impartiality', with 'special impartiality requirements' for 'matters of political or industrial controversy; and matters relating to public policy' (Communications Act 2003, s.320). In practice this is taken to require balance between the sides, though broadcasters are keen to say that they do not apply a rule of 'stop-clock' balance. Provisions such as these fit with Venice Commission guidelines (2007: Section I.2.2.e–f).

By contrast, there are generally no requirements for balance in print or online media. This reflects the principle of free expression. European media regulation thus seeks to combine two goals: the broadcast media are carved out as a space for balanced, impartial reporting to ensure people can hear the debate in the round; in other media, priority is given to people's ability to express their views on one or other side. This framework is based on the assumptions that broadcast and other media are clearly distinct and that the former constitute a major source of news and important location of national conversation. The rise of the internet, however, is rendering these assumptions outmoded: different media are converging, and broadcast is losing its dominance. This raises serious questions about whether current arrangements remain fit for purpose, and whether they can continue adequately to enable integrated political debate. This leads on to the questions about information that are the subject of the next section.

4.6   Conduct of the Campaign (II): Information Available to Voters

Freedom of opinion formation requires that people be able to access the information they want from sources they trust during the course of a referendum campaign. Multiple elections and referendums have raised concerns about that. The most prominent example is the UK's Brexit referendum, where misinformation was spread by both sides (see Renwick et al. 2018: 546), but serious criticisms have been made in many other countries too.

The question of how to promote quality information and limit misinformation is very difficult. Here we examine four approaches, starting with the most basic: ensuring that who is saying what to whom is transparent.

4.6.1   Transparency of Who Is Saying What to Whom

In contrast to the United States, where the Supreme Court has ruled that anonymous campaign materials are protected by the First Amendment right to free speech (*United States v. Alvarez* 2012), European democracies often uphold the principle that campaigning should be publicly accountable. That is evident in the rules of campaign spending discussed above. It also often applies to campaign materials: in the UK, for example, all printed campaign materials must include an 'imprint' stating who has produced them (Political Parties, Elections and Referendums Act 2000, Section 143).

The transparency principle has come under challenge in recent years, however, from the rise of the internet. In many democracies, campaign regulation has not been updated to respond to the new challenges posed by online campaigning. For example, one issue in the UK is that imprint requirements do not apply online—a gap that could easily be addressed (e.g., Independent Commission on Referendums 2018: 181). Another related concern is the rise of microtargeted 'dark ads': Google, Facebook, Twitter and other online platforms allow users to post advertisements that are visible only to the specific people to whom they are targeted; and online usage data allow such targeting to be increasingly sophisticated. As a result, campaigners could target misleading messages at particular sectors of the electorate who may be particularly susceptible to them, without this ever becoming apparent to the wider community.

The large internet companies began to respond to concerns over this in 2018 by creating open, searchable repositories of political advertising (Renwick and Palese 2019: 54). But this has in turn generated its own concerns over the power of these multinational companies to decide what information voters can see (e.g., House of Commons DCMS Committee 2019: 61; Parliamentary Assembly of the Council of Europe 2019: 20). This was thus an area at the time of writing where law-makers lagged behind developments but were working to catch up.

4.6.2 Confronting Misinformation

The transparency approach merely ensures that campaign materials are visible. But what happens if misinformation is found? Should we rely on the market of ideas to expose this fact and rectify it, or is more direct intervention needed. Concerns that traditional journalism has not always been effective in identifying misinformation have fed the growth of independent 'fact-checking' in recent years. But in some jurisdictions state actors are also involved. In Ireland, the Referendum Commissions, whose function is to promote understanding of the issues in each referendum, have sometimes intervened during campaigns to correct misleading information. In France, legislation was passed in 2018 empowering judges to intervene against false information during election campaigns (Loi no. 2018–1202 du 22 décembre 2018 relative à la lutte contre la manipulation de l'information 2018).

Most democracies have been very cautious about moving in this direction, and with good reason. There are concerns, first, about free speech and, second, about whether such interventions are in any case effective. It would be possible to take legal action only against manifestly false claims, but many misleading statements would not meet this threshold. And an anti-establishment campaign could be helped rather than harmed by state intervention against its arguments.

4.6.3 Provision of Information

More may be achieved, therefore, by seeking to ensure that quality neutral information is available to voters, so voters are not reliant solely on information from campaigners. That might be thought a responsibility of public service broadcasters, but in some countries these are captured by partisan interests and in others they often limit their reporting to 'she said/he said' balance, with little analysis of whether claims are reasonable (Hanretty 2011; Cushion and Lewis 2017).

Several models for neutral information provision do exist. In Denmark and the Netherlands, public funding is available for independent neutral information campaign groups as well as for groups on either side of the debate. In several countries, including France, Spain and Switzerland, the government itself provides information, which must fulfil certain requirements for neutrality, objectivity, or balance. This model is, however, problematic: governments generally have a position in referendums, so cannot be expected to provide genuinely neutral information. Some saw the French government's campaign for the 2005 referendum as biased towards a 'Yes' vote (Richard and Pabst 2013), and there have also been concerns in Switzerland.

The best model may therefore be the creation of an independent public body charged with information provision. In Ireland, a Referendum Commission is established for each referendum. It is chaired by a senior judge and also includes four senior public officials whose regular responsibilities demand them to maintain strict neutrality. It is responsible for disseminating explanations of the referendum proposal, promoting awareness of the vote, and encouraging participation (Referendum Act 2001). The most extensive public information campaigns for referendums have been conducted outside Europe, in New Zealand, where they have been run either by the Electoral Commission or by an ad hoc body established for the purpose.

Such interventions can succeed only if it is possible to create a genuinely independent and neutral public body and if there is public trust in the work of such a body. One or both of these conditions is lacking in many countries. This has contributed to the development of a fourth approach to information in recent years.

4.6.4   Citizen Engagement

Though people's trust in politicians, journalists, and state authorities is generally low, their confidence in their fellow citizens is often higher. This is one among several reasons for the growth in recent years in attempts to include citizens in generating quality information. In several American states—most notably, Oregon—a panel of randomly selected citizens is convened in the early stages of the campaign period to examine a ballot proposition over several days. The members hear from campaigners and experts and deliberate among themselves, before producing a statement that is included in the information pack sent to all voters. This indicates what campaign claims members found more or less convincing and sets out how they see the issues (Gastil et al. 2015).

Though no European country has yet institutionalised such a procedure, the UK's Independent Commission on Referendums (2018: 177–178) recommended that it should be trialled. It could be used not only to set out the panel's perceptions but also to identify questions that people want campaigners to answer.

As discussed above in the section on procedures preceding the decision to call a referendum, mechanisms for deliberative citizen engagement are also now being used at much earlier stages of referendum processes, especially in Ireland.

4.7   ENFORCEMENT

Referendum rules clearly need to be backed up by enforcement mechanisms. Two basic types exist: first, sanctions imposed on those found to have breached the rules; second, provisions allowing a referendum to be re-run in serious cases. The former type is uncontroversial: the only questions that arise relate to the level of sanctions and how they might be determined. The annulment of referendum results, by contrast, may have wider implications and therefore be more contentious: there is a danger that it may be seen by many as undue judicial interference in the democratic process. In practice, annulments are very rare. In 2018, the Slovenian Supreme Court declared a 2017 referendum on a proposed new railway line invalid because the government had used public funds to support its favoured outcome; this led to the prime minister's resignation and early elections (Surk 2018).

4.8   Conclusion

Understanding referendum rules is vital for understanding referendums. By determining when and how referendums can be called and what the results mean, the rules shape who can use the referendum instrument, for what purposes and with what effect. By framing the conduct of referendum campaigns, the rules influence the degree to which the outcome constitutes a balanced reflection of informed and considered public opinion.

Some aspects of referendums are generally well regulated in European countries: most countries, for example, have clear constitutional rules on the franchise and on the status of referendum results. Other aspects deserve further attention. These particularly relate to preparation for referendums and the conduct of referendum campaigns. The process of deciding the options that are put to voters can be as important as the final referendum vote itself; but too little thought has generally been given to how this can best be done. Mechanisms for ensuring a balanced campaign are often lax, and only limited attention has been given to ensuring that voters can access reliable information. Referendum rules—and election rules more broadly—have typically not yet adjusted to the digital age.

At the time of writing, the Venice Commission had begun a process of updating its referendum guidelines (Parliamentary Assembly of the Council of Europe 2019). To ensure the future integrity of referendum processes, individual countries need to attend to their rules too.

References

Chambers, S. (2001). Constitutional Referendums and Deliberative Democracy. In M. Mendelsohn & A. Parkin (Eds.), *Referendum Democracy: Citizens, Elites and Deliberation in Referendum Campaigns* (pp. 231–255). Palgrave: Basingstoke.

CSA [Conseil Supérieur de l'Audiovisuel]. (2005). *Recommandation du 22 mars 2005 en vue du référendum du 29 mai 2005*. Available at http://www.csa.fr/Arb itrer/Espace-juridique/Les-textes-reglementaires-du-CSA/Les-deliberations-et-rec ommandations-du-CSA/Recommandations-du-CSA-en-vue-de-consultations-electo rales-ou-referendaires/Recommandation-du-22-mars-2005-en-vue-du-referendum-du-29-mai-2005. Accessed 24 March 2019.

Cushion, S., & Lewis, J. (2017). Impartiality, Statistical Tit-for-Tats and the Construction of Balance: UK Television News Reporting of the 2016 EU Referendum Campaign. *European Journal of Communication, 32*(3), 208–223.

Fournier, P., van der Kolk, H., Carty, R. K., Blais, A., & Rose, J. (2011). *When Citizens Decide: Lessons from Citizens Assemblies on Electoral Reform.* Oxford: Oxford University Press.

Gastil, J., Knobloch, K., & Richards, R. (2015). *Empowering Voters Through Better Information: Analysis of the Citizens' Initiative Review, 2010–2014.* Report prepared for The Democracy Fund. Available at https://cpb-us-e1.wpmucdn.com/sites.psu.edu/dist/8/23162/files/2015/05/CIR-2010-2014-Full-Report.pdf. Accessed 14 September 2018.

Hanretty, C. (2011). *Public Broadcasting and Political Interference.* London: Routledge.

Hobolt, S. B. (2010). Campaign Financing in Danish Referendums. In K. Gilland Lutz & S. Hug (Eds.), *Financing Referendum Campaigns* (pp. 62–80). Basingstoke: Palgrave Macmillan.

House of Commons. (2019, February 18).*Disinformation and 'Fake News': Final Report.* DCMS [Digital, Culture, Media, and Sport] Committee, Eighth Report of Session 2017–2019. HC 1791. Available at https://publications.parliament.uk/pa/cm201719/cmselect/cmcumeds/1791/1791.pdf. Accessed 20 February 2019.

Independent Commission on Referendums. (2018). *Report of the Independent Commission on Referendums.* London: Constitution Unit, University College London. Available at https://www.ucl.ac.uk/constitution-unit/research/elections-and-referendums/independent-commission-referendums. Accessed 18 March 2019.

Jacobs, K. (2018, July 24). *The Stormy Dutch Referendum Experience: Social Media, Populists and Post-materialists.* Constitution Unit blog. Available at https://constitution-unit.com/2018/07/24/the-stormy-dutch-referendum-experience-social-media-populists-and-post-materialists/. Accessed 7 September 2018.

Kobach, K. W. (1994). Switzerland. In D. Butler & A. Ranney (Eds.), *Referendums Around the World: The Growing Use of Direct Democracy* (pp. 98–153). Washington, DC: The AEI Press.

LeDuc, L. (2015). Referendums and Deliberative Democracy. *Electoral Studies, 38,* 139–148.

Lutz, G. (2012). Switzerland: Citizens' Initiatives as a Measure to Control the Political Agenda. In M. Setälä & T. Schiller (Eds.), *Citizens' Initiatives in Europe: Procedures and Consequences of Agenda-Setting by Citizens.* London: Palgrave Macmillan.

McGreevy, R. (2018, May 27). The Citizens' Assembly—A Canny Move on the Road to Repeal. *Irish Times.*

Ministero Dell'Interno (n.d.). *Direzione centrale dei Servizi elettorali.* Available at http://www.interno.gov.it/it/ministero/dipartimenti/dipartimento-affari-interni-e-territoriali/direzione-centrale-dei-servizi-elettorali.

Morel, L. (1997). France: Towards a Less Controversial Use of the Referendum. In M. Gallagher & P. V. Uleri (Eds.), *The Referendum Experience in Europe* (pp. 66–85). Basingstoke: Macmillan Press.

Parliamentary Assembly of the Council of Europe. (2019, January 7). *Updating Guidelines to Ensure Fair Referendums in Council of Europe Member States.* Report of the Committee on Political Affairs and Democracy; rapporteur: Cheryl Gillan. Doc. 14791. Available at http://semantic-pace.net/tools/pdf.aspx?doc=aHR0cDovL2Fzc2VtYmx5LmNvZS5pbnQvbncveG1sL1hSZWYvWDJILURXLWV4dHI

uYXNwP2ZpbGVpZD0yNTIzMSZsYW5nPUVO&xsl=aHR0cDovL3NlbWFudGljc
GFjZS5uZXQvWHNsdC9QZGYvWFJlZi1XRC1BVC1YTUwyUERGLnhzbA==&
xsltparams=ZmlsZWlkPTI1MjMx. Accessed 24 March 2019.

Reidy, T., & Suiter, J. (2015). 'Do rules matter? Categorizing the Regulation of Referendum Campaigns. *Electoral Studies, 38,* 159–169.

Renwick, A., & M. Palese. (2019). *Doing Democracy Better: How Can Information and Discourse in Election and Referendum Campaigns in the UK Be Improved?* London: Constitution Unit. Available at https://www.ucl.ac.uk/constitution-unit/research/elections-and-referendums/improving-discourse-during-election-and-ref erendum-campaigns. Accessed 24 March 2019.

Renwick, A., Palese, M., & Sargeant, J. (2018, October–December). Discussing Brexit—Could We Do Better? *Political Quarterly, 89*(4), 545–552.

Richard, A., & Pabst, R. (2013). Evaluation of the French Referendum on the EU Constitution, May 2005. *Democracy International.* Available at https://www.dem ocracy-international.org/sites/default/files/PDF/Publications/2013-01-17_france eureferendum.pdf. Accessed 18 March 2019.

Scott, E. (2015, October 8). *European Union Referendum Bill (HL Bill 60 of 2015–16). House of Lords Library Note (LLN 2015/033).* Available at https://researchbriefings.files.parliament.uk/documents/LLN-2015-0033/LLN-2015-0033.pdf. Accessed 18 March 2019.

Serdült, U. (2010). Referendum Campaign Regulations in Switzerland. In K. Gilland Lutz & S. Hug (Eds.), *Financing Referendum Campaigns* (pp. 165–179). Basingstoke: Palgrave Macmillan.

Standards in Public Office Commission. (2016). *Annual Report 2017.* Available at http://www.sipo.ie/en/Reports/Annual-Reports/2016-Annual-Report/Annual Report2016/media/sipoc_ar_2016_english.pdf.

Summermatter, S., & Miserez, M. A. (2017, February 9). Swiss Immigration Quotas: Where Do We Stand? *Swiss Info.* Available at https://www.swissinfo.ch/eng/dir ectdemocracy/explainer_swiss-immigration-quotas-where-do-we-stand/42715214. Accessed 11 September 2018.

Surk, B. (2018, March 15). Slovenian Leader Quits After Court Blocks Key Rail Project. *New York Times.* Available at https://www.nytimes.com/2018/03/15/world/europe/slovenia-prime-minister-miro-cerar-resigns.html. Accessed 14 September 2018.

Venice Commission. (2007). *Code of Good Practice on Referendums.* European Commission for Democracy through Law.

Constitutions

Basic Law of the Federal Republic of Germany 1949 (rev. 2014).

The Constitutional Act of Denmark 1953.

Constitution of the Federal Republic of Austria 1920 (reinst. 1945, rev. 2013).

Constitution of Iceland 1994.

Constitution of Ireland 1937 (rev. 2015).

The Constitution of the Italian Republic 1947 (rev. 2012).

Constitution of the Portuguese Republic 1976 (rev. 2005).

Constitution of Romania.

Federal Constitution of the Swiss Confederation 1999 (rev. 2002).

Latvian Constitution.
Polish Constitution.
Spanish Constitution of 1978 (rev. 2011).

Laws

Direct Citizen Participation in State and Local Government Act 4/12.06.2009, Bulgaria.
Referenda Act, Malta.
Lithuania Law on Referendum 4 June 2002 No IX-929 (rev. 2012).
Law 4023, Expanding Direct and Participatory Democracy through Referenda, Greece.
Law no. 15-A/98 of 3 April 1998 (rev. 2016), article 45, Portugal.
Organic Law 5/1985, of June 19, of the General Electoral Regime, Spain.
Decree No. 2005-238 of 17 March 2005 on the campaign for the referendum, France.
Law on funding of, control over funding of, political parties and political campaigns 23 August 2004 – No IX-2428 Vilnius (amended 2011), Lithuania.
Financing of Political Parties, Law no 19/2003 of 20 June, Portugal.
Organic Law 8/2007 of 4 July on the funding of political parties Spain.
Act on the Conduct of Referendums 91/2010, Iceland.
Entire legal provision for referendum law (Volksabstimmungsgesetz) 1972, Austria.
Law 352 of 25 May 1970, Articles 16 and 27, Italy.
Referendum Act 1994, Ireland.
Organic Law 5/1985, of June 19, of the General Electoral Regime, Article 19, Spain.
Law No. 3 22 February 2000 on the Organisation and Conduct of the Referendum, Romania.

CHAPTER 5

Referendums and Parliaments

Philip Norton

The purpose of this chapter is to consider the holding of referendums from the perspective of parliaments. The relationship is not one that has been a feature of scholarly analyses of referendums. Although there have been analyses of the process of holding referendums in some nations which have included the role of the legislature, there has been little attention to the role of parliaments as such in determining when issues are to be referred to the people through the medium of a referendum. This may reflect a perception that legislatures are not significant actors in triggering referral of issues to the public. As we shall see, there may be some basis for such a perception, though one no longer as valid as it once was.

Parliaments, as legislatures, exist to give assent to law. Proposals of law are drawn up for approval. Those measures that pass are usually those formulated by the executive. The legislature gives assent on behalf of a wider body than that responsible for drawing up the measure (Norton 1990: 1). The constitution may confer power on the legislature alone to consider and assent to law or it may limit that power by enabling others to initiate or block proposals for law. A referendum on a specific issue of public policy may limit the legislature *de jure* by being binding in its outcome or limit it de facto where it is consultative, but where the legislature is or feels politically, though not legally, obliged to comply with the outcome.

P. Norton (✉)
University of Hull, Hull, UK
e-mail: p.norton@hull.ac.uk

© The Author(s) 2021
J. Smith (ed.), *The Palgrave Handbook of European Referendums*,
https://doi.org/10.1007/978-3-030-55803-1_5

In terms of determining when a referendum may be held, the constitution may provide that one can be initiated by a body or by bodies other than the legislature. In such instances, the legislature is subordinate to the body vested with such power, although usually having a role prior and consequent to the referendum.[1] The power may be conferred only on another body or bodies than the legislature or it may be shared, with the legislature also having the capacity to trigger a referendum. Even with shared power, the legislature has no power over the other bodies and can be overridden in conditions where it would not wish one to be held. The legislature is also subordinate to the provisions of the constitution in cases where there is no power, explicitly or implicitly, for a nationwide referendum such as Germany.

Where the constitution neither confers power on another body to initiate a referendum nor prohibits one from being held, then the power to hold a referendum rests solely with the legislature. In such cases, the power is exclusive to the legislature.

The distinction between subordination and exclusive power has relevance in terms of the number of referendums that are held. There are two generalisations that can be made. The first is that referendums are fewer in parliamentary systems where the power to initiate referendums is exclusive than in other political systems. This is intuitive. As Altman (2011: 76) has hypothesised, the higher the number of veto players (i.e. those who each can stop a change from the status quo), the greater the likelihood of referendums being held. In such systems, there are more actors and therefore the potential for conflict is greater than is the case where there are few veto players or only one. If we distinguish parliamentary systems from presidential systems, and do not deploy parliaments as synonyms for legislatures, the likelihood of conflict between executive and legislature is smaller, given that the former is formed as a consequence of the results of elections to the latter. It also derives from the exclusive nature of the power. As Altman (2011: 76) observed, 'In a parliamentary regime, sovereignty lies with the parliament, not in citizens' hands' (ibid). Holding a referendum, in other words handing over the decision to the people, would represent the parliament handing over some of its decision-making power. Even if on occasion a parliament does so, we would expect it to be rarer than occasions when a popular initiative is deployed to trigger a referendum.

This expectation is borne out in practice. As Altman (2011: 84) has shown, referendums are held least often in parliamentary regimes (see also Qvortrup 2000: 821). Furthermore, given the emphasis in Westminster-style systems for strong, usually single-party, government, one would expect enthusiasm for referendums to be markedly low in such systems. This has tended to be the case in former British colonies (Altman 2011: 86). In southern and eastern

---

[1] Only Switzerland and 26 US states allow proposals for law to be put to the people through a popular initiative without any engagement by the legislature (see Butler and Ranney 1994b: 19).

Africa, executive-determined referendums, what have been termed presidential plebiscites, 'which is a referendum without approval of parliament is typical for francophone countries but less usual for Anglophone countries' (Kersting 2018: 219). Among major Commonwealth parliamentary democracies, only Australia and New Zealand have held more nationwide referendums than the United Kingdom. A number, such as India, has never held one. Most, but by no means all, European continental parliamentary democracies outstrip the UK in terms of the number of referendums held, though not always by a significant margin. Ireland is sometimes listed as a Westminster-type political system, but in the use of referendums it is very much in the continental parliamentary tradition.

However, there is another distinction in terms of parliamentary regimes. In Western Europe, there has been something of a historic divide between 'north' and 'south', loosely defined. Parliamentary democracies of northern Europe—comprising the UK, post-war Germany, the Benelux countries and Scandinavia, with mostly established parliamentary systems—have been averse to the use of referendums. They may on occasion have been used, but—as Bogdanor (1994: 36) noted in respect of Scandinavia—their use remains 'a last resort'. Southern Europe—encompassing Switzerland, Austria, Liechtenstein, Portugal and those nations with a Mediterranean coastline—has less embedded parliamentary systems and more authoritarian and populist traditions, with presidential plebiscites and citizens wanting to determine outcomes on a range of contested issues (see Leston-Bandeira 2005). There are exceptions to the rule, most notably Ireland and Denmark, which fall within the 'southern' mode. The distinction, though, has in practice fallen away in the twenty-first century, as parliaments of northern Europe, other than Germany and Belgium, have legislated for referendums. Although the difference between north and south remains in terms of the sheer number of referendums held, this is a consequence of their heavy use by Switzerland, Liechtenstein and Italy; once one controls for that, the distinction tends to fall away. What the change reflects is the move by parliamentary regimes to employing a previously little used mechanism.

Although it is possible to generalise that parliaments show little enthusiasm for holding referendums, they have, then, proved somewhat more willing to hold them in recent decades than was previously the case. The latter half of the twentieth century, especially the 1980s and 1990s, saw an increase in the use of referendums in democratic nations (Altman 2011: 72; Qvortrup 2018c: 264–268). In part, this was attributable to the creation of new states, with referendums being employed to confirm independence or a new constitution (Tierney 2012: 7). However, there was also a notable increase, as we have seen in Western Europe, in referendums initiated by parliaments. Indeed, by the second decade of the twenty-first century, the only major democracies where parliaments had the power to initiate referendums, but had not utilised that power, were India, Japan and Israel.

More frequent use, though, has been accompanied by somewhat less certain outcomes. This has been notable in the case of referendums held on the issue of European integration. Getting the legislature to approve a referendum is necessary but not sufficient for a government to achieve its desired outcome. As a result, it is possible that we may be seeing the parliamentary embrace of referendums waning. At the beginning of 2018, the Dutch parliament voted to abolish provision for advisory referendums, introduced only three years before (see Chapter 32 by van den Akker). The legislature was not seeking to limit its own power, but rather to remove the provision for a referendum if 300,000 citizens petitioned for one. Among those non-European nations with a history of using referendums, some show a similar waning of support. As Qvortrup, Morris and Kobori (2018: 258) noted, 'after the failure of the republic question in 1999, Australian enthusiasm for the referendum seems to have dwindled'. These cases do not prove a trend, but they do indicate that there is no uniform enthusiasm among parliaments for continuing or greater use of referendums.

A waning enthusiasm on the part of some parliaments, however, does not necessarily mean an end to referendums in their jurisdiction. Once a referendum takes place, it sets a precedent. As Lord Hailsham (1978: 176) observed, 'It was never possible that such an arrangement, once tried, should not be repeated'. Parliaments may decline to expand the scope for referendums, but they may not be able to refuse them in fields in which they have been held. Indeed, it is notable that two parliamentary systems that have been especially resistant to the use of referendums—the UK and the Netherlands—have both utilised them more than once in recent years to resolve constitutional issues. Their use limits the political and moral if not the legal authority of the parliament to resist them in the event of further proposed major constitutional change.

5.1   Types of Relationship

In terms of the relationship of parliaments to referendums, we can go beyond the dichotomy between subordinate and exclusive power, the latter lending itself to three distinct categories. We can thus identify four types of relationship: *subordination*, *non-decision-making*, *rejection and utilisation*.

5.1.1   Subordination of Parliaments

Subordination, as we have seen, exists where referendums are required by the constitution to approve a constitutional amendment or may be initiated by a body other than the legislature. In some cases, the power is shared or there is no power to hold a referendum at all.

Legislatures are constrained where the constitution confers power for referendums to be initiated bottom up, that is by the people, either to propose a new law (popular initiative) or to veto a law, be it proposed or in place (abrogative referendums) (Qvortrup 2005: 125–131). With the abrogative referendum, the people hold a veto. In Switzerland, a federal law or certain other binding federal decrees are subject to a referendum if 50,000 electors so demand. In Italy, referendums on laws, both proposed or in force, can be forced on the initiative of 500,000 electors (albeit subject not to Parliamentary approval, but to that of the Constitutional Court). There is also provision for popular initiative in the Bavarian state constitution, requiring a referendum on a proposed law if ten per cent of voters demand one. In such cases, the legislature is subordinate to the wishes of the people.

The holding of referendums may also be prescribed by provisions of the constitution or by the decision of the executive (top-down). In some countries including Austria, Denmark, Ireland, Spain and Switzerland, changes to the constitution have to be approved by popular vote. Elsewhere, such as France, a referendum is one alternative for seeking constitutional change. In some nations, the power to call a referendum rests with the executive. Article 11 of the Constitution of the French Fifth Republic enables the President to by-pass the National Assembly to hold a referendum and, indeed, this power has proved the principal basis for referendums held in France (for more details on the French case, see Chapter 9 by Morel). The top-down and bottom-up categories are not necessarily mutually exclusive. It is not unusual for nations that require referendums for changes to the constitution also to provide for referendums to be held on the petition of a specified number of citizens.

The power to call a referendum may, as we have noted, be shared with the legislature. Article 3 of the French constitution states that the people exercise their sovereignty through their representatives in the legislature and through referendum. In some nations, there is a provision for the legislature, or a specified number or proportion of the members, to intervene and trigger, or request, a referendum. In Denmark, for example, after a bill has been passed, one-third of members of the legislature may, within three weekdays from the final passing of the measure, make a request to the Speaker that the bill be subject to a referendum.

Where referendums are held on the instigation of a body other than the legislature, referendums may be deemed to be above parliaments. In such cases, parliaments are nonetheless involved in the process, although their engagement differs depending on the nature of the referendum and the particular provisions of the constitution. The involvement may encompass setting out the conditions for the referendum, advising voters on whether to approve or reject what is proposed in the referendum, or passing a bill that is then the subject of the referendum. Even in Switzerland, the legislature considers issues put to a referendum and advises voters on whether to accept or reject the proposal and can put forward a counter-proposal.[2] The involvement of the legislature may not be formally determinative, but it may be persuasive.

---

[2] For examples of the different engagement of legislatures, see Independent Commission on Referendums (2018: 28).

Subordination, then, should not be confused with detachment. Legislatures are actors in the process.

In a very small number of countries, referendums are not so much above as beyond parliaments in that the issue of holding a referendum does not arise because there is no legal base for holding one. They are not provided for by the constitution and the legislature has no capacity to trigger one. The USA is the principal major democracy to fall in this category. Although it is common for referendums in one form or another to be held at state and local level in the United States, there is no provision in the US constitution for a nationwide referendum (see Dane Walters 2003). Since early in the twentieth century, there have been attempts to legislate for referendums, but it is not clear that if enacted the measures would be deemed constitutional.

Not all nations that have proved referendum-free are so because of a constitutional prohibition, but because the legislature, or other body vested with the power to call a referendum, has chosen not to exercise the power or not even contemplated exercising it.[3] This brings us on to the other relationships, where the legislature does have the power to legislate for a referendum. These can be illustrated especially by reference to UK experience, where Parliament has gone through three phases with regard to referendums. Some other legislatures have gone through similar stages: non-decision-making; rejection; and utilisation. A number, though, have reached the second stage—referendums being on the political agenda—but not the third, that is, legislating to hold one.

5.1.2   Non-decision-Making

In some nations, referendums have not been held, not because there is no power under the constitution to have one, but because the issue has not been on the parliamentary agenda. A referendum may appear alien to the political culture, so may never have been a matter of conscious consideration. For example, although referendums may be, and are, held at state level in Germany, and the 1949 Basic Law implied that a referendum would be necessary in the event of reunification, there has been a national post-war aversion to their use. The *Plebis phobic der Nachkriegsära* (referendum phobia of the post-war era) has engulfed both the Bundestag and the Bundesrat (Qvortrup 2005: 134).

In the UK, until the latter half of the nineteenth century, the issue of consulting the people through a referendum was not one that engaged the thought or discourse of parliamentarians. The debate, at times quite a fraught debate, was over the franchise for choosing representatives, not consulting the people directly (Hamer 1977; Hanham 1959). Politicians and commentators

---

[3]The closest the US came to have a constitutional amendment to provide for referendums on decisions of war was in the 1930s on the Ludlow amendment. In the event, it was rejected on 10 January 1938, on a discharge petition, by 209 votes to 188.

were aware of referendums—the Swiss experience of using them was known—but generally regarded them as alien and not something to be entertained. The British state was very much conceptualised in terms of parliamentarism, with government operating through Parliament (see Judge 1993).

The extent to which referendums were not on the agenda is reflected in the absence of any reference to them in standard works of the time on the development of the constitution and on the British political system. It is also borne out by their absence from parliamentary debate. There was no consideration of any motion relating to referendums as such until the end of the nineteenth century. On 21 February 1896, Professor Robert Wallace, the Liberal Member of Parliament for Edinburgh East, moved a resolution that 'it was desirable to introduce the principle of the institution known as the Initiative and Referendum, with the view of more fully securing the direct and continuous control of the Legislature by the people'.[4] He spoke in support of his resolution, citing the experience of Switzerland and arguing that the people were as good judges as anyone of the main object of the law. The House then moved to next business, meaning that no further action was taken at that time—a clear non-decision. It was to be more than a decade before the issue was again on the parliamentary agenda.

5.1.3   Rejection

Here, we move beyond non-decision-making to consideration—the issue is on the political agenda—but the legislature has not used its power to initiate a referendum. The category encompasses the legislature either not pursuing the proposal, voting it down or making provision for a referendum but not utilising it.

Nations that fall into this category include the three major democracies that have never held nationwide referendums—India, Japan and Israel. Referendums have been brought onto the agenda in all three—indeed two have made provision for referendums—but none has triggered the holding of one.

India has seen referendums at sub-national level, and experienced demands for nationwide referendums, but with the proposals for nationwide referendums failing to bear fruit. There is no provision in the constitution for holding an all-India referendum, but no prohibition either. The Indian parliament appears reluctant to employ a binary referendum in a highly diverse nation with 22 languages (see Mehar 2016). In Japan, calls for a referendum have been more pronounced, but have not resulted in one being held. Unlike India, Japan has constitutional and statutory provision for a referendum, but amendments have not surmounted the hurdle of two-third majorities in the two Houses and hence have not been put to a referendum. Similarly, in Israel calls for referendums have marked much of its history—David Ben Gurion called for one in 1958 on the electoral system and other proposals were made in

[4] *House of Commons Debates*, 21 February 1896, cols. 873–8.

the 1970s and 1990s. Since then, legislation has been enacted providing for conditions in which a referendum may be held, but without the power being utilised.

Other democracies also fell into this category until relatively recently, most notably the Netherlands and the UK. In the UK, referendums at anything other than local level were alien to constitutional practice until the 1970s, but they were certainly not alien to political debate.

Calls for referendums, or at least referral of certain issues to the people, began to be heard in the latter half of the nineteenth century, and were often associated with Conservative politicians, not least those in the House of Lords, as the UK made the transition from the first category.

The 3rd Marquess of Salisbury, later Prime Minister, developed what has been termed his 'referendal', or referral, theory (Weston 1986: 463). If the House of Commons passed a measure on which the views of the country were not clear, the House of Lords was entitled to 'insist that the nation shall be consulted' (see also Norton 2013: 156).[5] Here, though, the 'referendum' was to take the form of a single-issue general election. It was only towards the end of the century that referendums were advocated as exercises separate from general elections with Professor Wallace's abortive 1896 motion.

Referendums came more prominently onto the political agenda early in the twentieth century. Their principal proponent was constitutional lawyer A. V. Dicey (1973 [1886]), whose vehement opposition to Irish home rule prompted him to pursue novel constitutional means to block home rule. Indeed, opposition to home rule was to underpin stances on House of Lords reform during the constitutional crisis of 1909–1911 (Norton 2012). If the House of Lords was to be deprived of the capacity to block home rule, then referendums may substitute for it as a constitutional longstop. During cross-party talks in 1910 to try to resolve the constitutional crisis, one option advanced by the Conservatives was 'a referendum *ad hoc*' (LeMay 1979: 198; see also Qvortrup elsewhere in Chapter 15 for a discussion of ad hoc referendums). When the Tory leader in the Lords, Lord Lansdowne, pursued the proposal, his Liberal counterpart challenged the Conservatives to commit to one on tariff reform. The Conservative leader, Arthur Balfour, promptly did so: 'I have not the least objection to submitting the principles of Tariff Reform to a Referendum', he declared in a speech at the Royal Albert Hall (see Adams 1999: 44). The commitment was embodied in the party's election manifesto. During passage of the Parliament Bill, the Conservatives used their majority in the Lords to provide that any measure establishing home rule for any part of the United Kingdom, or affecting the Protestant succession, or which, in the view of a joint committee, 'raises an issue of great gravity upon which the judgement of the country has not been sufficiently ascertained', would not

---

[5] *House of Lords Debates*, 17 June 1868, col. 84.

receive Royal Assent unless approved by the electors.[6] The amendment was rejected by the Commons.[7] This was the first occasion that a provision for a referendum had been voted on in Parliament.

The use of referendums also arose in the discussion of the Bryce Conference on the Reform of the Second Chamber. Writing to the Prime Minister in 1918, Lord Bryce reported that referring matters in controversy between the two Houses by means of a referendum or popular vote of all the registered electors had been considered. However, the majority of the conference 'did not approve the plan on the ground (among others) that the use of the Referendum once introduced could not be confined to the cases for which it was in this instance proposed, that it might tend to lower the authority and dignity of Parliament, and that it was unsuited to the conditions of a large country, and especially of the United Kingdom, for different parts of which different legislation is sometimes required' (see LeMay 1964: 158).

The Conservative embrace of the referendum principle failed to make it into law and Balfour's commitment to one on tariff reform was later dropped by his successor, Andrew Bonar Law. Proposals for the use of a referendum occasionally surfaced in other contexts, but they made little progress. Churchill and later Lord Curzon proposed one on female suffrage, essentially as a means of blocking it (Butler and Kitzinger 1976: 10; Qvortrup 2018a: 22). In 1930, Stanley Baldwin advocated one on protection (Qvortrup 2018a: 23), and in 1945 Winston Churchill toyed with having one to decide whether the parties should continue in coalition until the war with Japan was completed (Butler and Kitzinger 1976: 10).

The advocacy of referendums failed to sway either the Liberal Party or the Labour Party. Although some Liberals and socialists saw some merit in referendums, neither party was prepared to go along with what was seen as a conservative device in both senses of the term. If the Conservatives could not block change through the parliamentary process, then a referendum may prove a means of preventing it from getting through. In order to prevent constitutional change of which they disapproved, Conservative leaders were thus prepared to advocate a novel constitutional device, one that could be argued to undermine the role of Parliament, in a way that prefigured the three referendums held on David Cameron's watch (see Blick, Curtice and Smith, respectively in Chapters 13, 14 and 22). Labour leaders were not in favour of any constitutional change, be it electoral reform or the use of referendums, that may hinder a future Labour Government implementing a programme of social reform through a parliamentary majority. Attlee rejected Churchill's call in 1945, deeming referendums to be the instruments of Nazism and Fascism (Bogdanor 1997: 120).

As Bogdanor (1994: 36) noted, 'During the immediate post-war years, however, the referendum disappeared as an issue in British politics.' Other than

---

[6] *House of Lords Debates*, 5 July 1911, cols. 277–80.

[7] *House of Commons Debates*, 8 August 1911, cols. 1105–13.

in 1967 when Conservative MP Harold Gurden sought to introduce a private member's bill to provide 'for a referendum to be held with a general election', it was not considered in Parliament.[8] However, the situation changed in the following decade following conclusion of negotiations in 1971 for the UK to join the European Communities. Calls began to be heard for a referendum on the UK joining the EC. The Solicitor General, Sir Geoffrey Howe, took the view that 'The electorate *had* endorsed the principle of membership [in the 1970 general election]. The final crucial stage could properly be entrusted to Parliament itself' (Howe 1994: 67). Some MPs took a contrary view. A Conservative backbench amendment to the European Communities Bill in April 1972, providing that the Act would not take effect until a consultative advisory referendum had been held, was rejected by 284 votes to 235. Although the Opposition supported it—a reversal of Labour's previous stance on referendums—over 50 Labour MPs abstained from voting.[9] A total of 22 Conservative MPs voted for the amendment, and a further nine abstained from voting (Norton 1975: 435–436).

Although Conservative leaders advocated referendums at the beginning of the century, and Labour opposed them, the positions were thus reversed in the 1970s. Indeed, it was to be a Conservative leader who advanced the principal arguments against their use. Margaret Thatcher, in her first major speech as Leader of the Opposition in 1975, adumbrated the key arguments against. She noted that the Lord President of the Council had argued that holding a referendum did not derogate from the principle of parliamentary sovereignty, but that he had said that it would give the final say to the British people: 'That shows our constitutional difficulty in discussing this subject and in taking decisions before we have thought about them properly and considered all the consequences'.[10] On representative democracy, Parliament comprised a body in which different sides of an argument could be considered, and minorities protected. (For more on minority issues, see also Chapter 2 by Lord elsewhere in this volume.) For MPs, it would—as a number argued—be an abdication of their responsibilities.[11] As John Mackintosh expressed it, 'The fundamental assumption behind the referendum is that this House does not adequately represent the feelings of the country'.[12]

Adherence to these principles underpinned resistance to the use of referendums and carried the day until the 1970s. However, Margaret Thatcher was advancing the argument against in the face of a Labour Government

---

[8] *House of Commons Debates*, 17 July 1967, cols. 1450–4. Gurden's attempt failed at the first hurdle, with leave to bring in the bill being denied.

[9] The party's deputy leader, Roy Jenkins, resigned in opposition to the party's stance.

[10] *House of Commons Debates*, 11 March 1975, col. 305.

[11] Paul Rose, *HC Deb. House of Commons Debates*, 11 March 1975, col. 336.

[12] *House of Commons Debates*, 11 March 1975, col. 414.

committed to holding a referendum on continued membership of the European Communities. Since then, the relationship has moved to the final category.

5.1.4   Utilisation

The final relationship is where parliaments have embraced the use of referendums, though not necessarily enthusiastically or systematically. The UK is not unusual, indeed may now be considered fairly typical, in its occasional ad hoc use of referendums. It has moved from being a nation with no history of employing referendums at national level to one that had by 2018 held three. In 1975, Parliament legislated for a UK-wide referendum on continued membership of the European Communities (Butler and Kitzinger 1975; King 1977). It was to be another 36 years before it legislated for another, though in the interim it had provided for referendums in Scotland, Wales, Northern Ireland, Greater London and the North-East of England. It then legislated for two UK-wide referendums within the same decade.

Other parliaments previously reluctant to hold referendums have also on occasion legislated for them. These have included the Netherlands, the Dutch parliament legislating for one on the proposed European constitution in 2005, the first time the nation had experience of a referendum (on the 2005 case see Chapter 28 by Sternberg). The Parliament then enacted in 2015 an Advisory Referendum Act, referred to above, and under this two referendums were initiated by popular initiative: on the Ukraine-European Union Association in 2016, and on the Dutch Intelligence and Security Services Act in 2018 (see Chapter 32 by van den Akker). The Norwegian *Storting* made provision for referendums on EU membership in 1972 and 1994, as did Finland in 1994 (see, respectively Fossum & Rosén and Rye elsewhere in this volume).

5.1.5   The Decision to Use Referendums

There are thus two dimensions to be explained: the general aversion to the use of referendums by parliaments and their recent occasional ad hoc employment of them. The reason why parliaments have been unwilling or reluctant to utilise them are apparent from the foregoing discussion. Where power is concentrated in a veto player, there is a reluctance to give up, temporarily or permanently, the capacity to determine outcomes. Although in practice the power resides usually with the executive, through its parliamentary majority, its preservation is defended in terms of parliamentary sovereignty. As we have seen, resistance to the use of referendums has been couched, in the UK, in the effect on 'the authority and dignity of Parliament' (Bryce Conference). According to Asquith, it would 'degrade the House of Commons to the level of a talking club' (Emden 1956: 301). Butler and Ranney summarised the argument thus: 'As legislatures lose power they will lose popular respect, and outstanding citizens will be less inclined to seek public office' (Butler and

Ranney 1994b: 37). Although other arguments were deployed against the use of referendums, not least of separating out a question from other issues likely to affect voters' behaviour, the constitutional defence was at the forefront of ensuring that decision-making remained in the hands of the parliamentary majority.

Why, then, the greater use of referendums, albeit from a low base? The relevant point is the nature of legislatures. Parliaments are the sum of their parts rather than monolithic entities (see King 1976). The most important parts are political parties. When parties were able to shape debate and act as efficient aggregators of public opinion, issues were resolved through the parliamentary process, with little elite or public questioning of the process. There may have been calls for referendums from opposition politicians, but governments were traditionally able to resist such calls. However, in recent decades, political parties have not always been able to construct a clear, internally unified stance on issues coming on to the political agenda, especially those affecting the nation's constitutional framework. In the UK, for example, that has been the case especially, but not exclusively, with European integration, the two main political parties changing their stances over time, but also being internally divided on the issue. Referendums have been embraced as a means of resolving conflicts on the issue.

The failure of political parties to fulfil their traditional role of aggregating opinion on issues may also further reinforce the pressure for holding referendums. Partisan dealignment and declining trust in established parties may undermine popular support for existing processes of determining public policy (Qvortrup 2018b: 14–15) as well as wider pressures, not least resulting from globalisation (Tierney 2012: 9). Referendums may not only serve to resolve conflicts, but also enhance the legitimacy of the decision reached. For parliaments, though, this creates a Catch-22 dilemma. If they cannot resolve an issue, or believe popular approval is necessary in order to enhance the authority of a decision, they may refer it to the people for resolution. The more they refer issues, the more they limit their autonomy in decision-making. Also, as we have noted, legislating for a referendum sets a precedent.

Legislatures in this context may be deemed to be the principal losers in the process, insofar as there are losers. Legislatures can play a role in influencing outcomes by taking a stance on an issue, but it is the stance of parties that usually matter more and which shape the debate. Parties tend to be the main actors in mobilising support in referendums (Altman 2011: 49). Referendums also, as Altman (2011: 50) has noted, 'makes the lawmaking process more complicated, longer, and more uncertain'.

Whether referendums are held depends in large measure on who is making the case for holding them. They have tended to be advocated by those who have not been able to get their way, or who believe they will not be able to get their way, through established parliamentary means. Advocacy is thus by the 'out' bodies in politics, in other words, those who are in opposition to the existing regime which enjoys a parliamentary majority. As a result, they are not likely to move beyond the rejection category, as was the case with Conservative leaders in the UK early in the twentieth century when they were in Opposition. Unless it is in the interests of government, referendums are resisted. When backbench MPs variously put down questions asking if the government would hold referendums on particular issues, the answer was usually a blunt 'No, sir'.[13] When an MP pursued a supplementary question in support of referendums with Prime Minister, Clement Attlee, the Prime Minister replied: 'It does not commend itself to me in the circumstances of this country'.[14]

Referendums are likely to be utilised by the 'in' bodies in politics, which means in a parliamentary system the government, deploying its parliamentary majority to provide for referendums. As David Butler told the House of Lords Constitution Committee, referendums in the UK 'are only going to happen when the Government of the day wants it or when it would be too embarrassing (because of past promises) to get out of it'.[15] In practice, and in the UK case it has been a relatively recent practice, the government has used them for the purpose of resolving intra-party or inter-party conflict. Loyalty to party, which determines one's membership of the legislature, thus trumps loyalty to the institution itself and its constitutional supremacy. All three nationwide referendums in the United Kingdom were designed to resolve conflict within government whether inter-party (2011 referendum on the electoral system) or intra-party (the 1975 and 2016 referendums on membership of the EC/EU).

Referendums, then, are legislated by parliaments to resolve or attempt to resolve particular issues. They are in effect one of the tools available to governments enjoying parliamentary support to deal with a contested issue. There is no obvious incentive for parliaments to legislate away their own power to trigger a referendum, through for example a measure providing for the popular initiative. When referendums are considered it is in the context of a specific and almost invariably constitutional issue. Those issues may be more to the fore because of contested policies coming onto to the political agenda in recent years and in the context of partisan dealignment, but it is the specific issues that lead to referendums. A referendum is a tool at the disposal of the legislature, usually the executive-dominated legislature.

The issue-specific nature of referendums legislated for by parliaments is reflected in the instances of their use in the UK. The UK Royal Commission on the Constitution, which reported in 1973, noted that popular interest in a referendum on the UK's entry into the European Communities appeared

---

[13] *House of Commons Debates*, 18 February 1924, col. 1304; 5 March 1925, col. 633; 22 March 1949, col. 203.

[14] *House of Commons Debates*, 22 March 1949, col. 203.

[15] Constitution Committee, House of Lords, *Referendums in the United Kingdom*, 12th Report. Session 2009–10, HL Paper 99, p. 16.

to be 'fairly widespread'.[16] However, it noted, it 'arose out of a particular and transient situation and against the background of referenda [sic] being held in other countries faced with the same decision. It did not appear to be part of a general and continuous demand for referenda on all important issues' (ibid.). Although the demand for referendums on other constitutional issues, including devolution, has since developed, that demand still focuses on specific issues, rather than the principle of referendums, triggered by popular initiative or automatically in the case of an amendment to the constitution. Debate, in short, does not challenge the principle of the sovereignty of the parliament, but rather takes place within the existing constitutional framework.

Where a government has a parliamentary majority, it will normally get a referendum. If other parties also have reason to support holding one, the relevant legislation may be enacted without difficulty. As Butler and Kitzinger (1976: 66–67) noted in their study of the 1975 referendum in the UK, 'Political considerations may explain why the Referendum Bill had in the end such an easy passage... pro-Marketeers were in an overwhelming majority in the House of Commons and they had belatedly realised that the referendum would go their way'. Similarly, in 2016, the European Union (Referendum) Bill was passed without undue delay, arguably because debate was largely over detail rather than principle, and in the House of Lords many peers focused on the arguments to be deployed in the referendum debate rather than on the specific provisions of the Bill (see Chapter 22 by Smith and Smith 2019).

However, when parties are not united, or the government lacks a majority in the legislature, then the passage of the legislation may be difficult and the government may not always control the outcome. The UK Labour Government in 1978 suffered defeats in the House of Commons in seeking to get its legislation through to provide for referendums on devolution in Scotland and Wales. The House passed amendments, against the wishes of ministers, stipulating that if 40% of those entitled to vote failed to vote Yes then orders giving effect to the Act would be repealed.[17] In the consequent referendum in Scotland, although there was a majority Yes vote, it failed to meet the 40% threshold. In Wales, there was a decisive No vote. As a result, powers were not devolved to either nation.

According to Butler and Ranney (1994a: 261) as well as Lijphart (1984: 203) parliaments only trigger referendums when the governments, which introduce the legislation, believe that they are likely to get the outcomes they want; and, until relatively recently, they generally did. The first referendum in the UK, in 1973, was essentially an affirmatory one, or plebiscite, on the Northern Ireland border: more than 590,000 voted to retain the border, against fewer than 6,500 voting against. However, there are occasions when

[16]Royal Commission on the Constitution 1969–1973, *Vol. 1: Report*, Cmnd. 5460 (London: HMSO, 1973), para. 318, p. 98.

[17]*House of Commons Debates*, 25 January 1978, cols. 1541–8; 15 February 1978, cols. 597–606; 19 April 1978, cols. 619–24.

the results are not in line with expectations (Butler and Ranney 1994a: 261), and this has been apparent in recent decades, not least in the context of European integration, with voters in the twenty-first century voting No in the Netherlands (2005, 2016) and the UK (2016), as well as in referendums not triggered by the legislature (France 2005; Ireland 2001, 2008).

Although holding a referendum on a major constitutional issue, not least membership of the European Union, sets a precedent, the outcomes have not been such as to produce enthusiasm on the part of parliaments to extend their use and may engender greater circumspection in contemplating future constitutional change. The expectation of holding a referendum, or even a commitment to one if change is proposed, may deter legislators from bringing forward proposals that they cannot be sure would gain a majority. Parties may seek agreement rather than see a matter put to a referendum, as one non-European case demonstrates: 'More than 70 per cent of Uruguayan legislators consider that the presence of a potential referendum is a sufficient reason to look for a broad consensus within the political parties... Evidence suggests that this potential influence is also robust in other latitudes' (Altman 2011: 49). The commitment of the Blair-Brown Government (1997–2010) in the UK to holding a referendum in the event of a decision to join the European single currency served to deter any such proposal coming forward. The longer the government delayed, the greater the belief that a referendum would result in a No vote.

5.2   Regulating Referendums

Although only some legislatures enjoy exclusive power to initiate referendums, the significance of parliaments in regard to referendums is not confined to those enjoying this first-order power. The power to initiate a referendum is necessary, but not sufficient for the purposes of holding one. As Tierney (2012: 99) has observed, there is 'a second agenda-setting stage, which encompasses question-formation, and process planning including timing issues; and, third, the campaign process itself, embracing the campaign rules, provision of information to voters, funding and expenditure rules etc'. Parliaments exercising power in these second and third stages are greater in number than those with the exclusive power to initiate referrals to the people. The power to determine the regulatory regime for referendums encompasses not only parliaments in those states where ad hoc referendums are determined by act of parliament, but also often in states where they are required by the provisions of the constitution (Tierney 2012: 108).

Rules and processes are not neutral in their effect. Stipulating the rules can be as important as the decision to hold a referendum. As we have seen, the provision in the 1978 legislation in the UK for 40% of eligible voters to vote Yes in the devolution referendum for the result to be implemented resulted in no devolution to Scotland. It was another two decades before there was another referendum, this time with no threshold. Timing may also be crucial, as may the resources available to either side in the campaign. Similarly, with the wording of the question or proposition put.

The importance of rules is reflected in the Venice Commission of the Council of Europe having produced guidelines for holding referendums (see Chapter 4 by Renwick and Sargeant elsewhere in this volume). That it has done so essentially acknowledges the importance of referendums and their extent. It also derives from the fact that there is significant scope for rule-making by legislatures.

Legislatures may thus come into their own in regulating the conduct of referendums. As we have noted, legislatures normally have a role prior to referendums being initiated, even where this is by another body, as well as subsequent to it. They may make generic provisions, governing such matters as campaign financing, as well as specific provision for each referendum, not only triggering one, but also determining such issues as the question. Some nations have generic provisions governing the question to be posed, but in nations where the legislature has exclusive power it will usually be the bill passed that stipulates the question. The UK illustrates the use of the generic and the specific. After the use of referendums in different parts of the UK, the Westminster Parliament enacted the Political Parties, Elections and Referendums Act 2000, making provision to ensure some balance in funding each side of a referendum campaign. Specific provision is then made for each ad hoc referendum, including stipulating the question and whether the outcome will be binding. The Electoral Commission, created under the 2000 Act, is empowered by the Act to advise on the question, a provision reflecting the importance of legislative scrutiny: the power was inserted because of prompting in the House of Lords and not on the initiative of the government.[18] In 2016, on the advice of the Electoral Commission, the Referendum Act stipulated that the electors were to face not a yes/no question, but two mutually exclusive propositions: leave or remain. Although referendums until 2011 were advisory, Parliament provided that the outcome of the referendum on a new electoral system would be binding (see Blick elsewhere in Chapter 13). It did not do so for the 2016 EU referendum.

Legislatures can thus come into their own—or at least the legislative process, usually executive dominated—when it comes to these second and third-order powers. Though they may be constrained in determining whether a referendum is held, the laws they enact can be crucial to the outcome.

---

[18]The Bill as introduced gave no role to the Electoral Commission in relation to the question put in a referendum. The government introduced provision for it in response to an amendment moved by the author of this chapter.

5.3   Conclusion

Legislatures have usually a role to play in referendums, be it in a minority of cases exercising the first-order power of determining whether a referendum is held or, more pervasively, serving a role at pre- or post-referendum stages. Where legislatures have the power to initiate referendums, recent decades have seen them overcome a reluctance to employ them, or initially even consider them, and those that have not used the power are now in a small minority. Where the legislature has exclusive power, UK experience has shown the dynamic of moving from not considering them, to having them on the agenda, to utilising them. UK experience has not been atypical.

For most legislatures, the issue is no longer whether to hold referendums, but when and (generally, even where the legislature does not enjoy exclusive power) under what conditions. Where legislatures have used their power to initiate a referendum, even if reluctantly to resolve a specific conflict, that act sets a precedent. Some legislatures may be reluctant to extend their employment—the Netherlands being a prime example—but rather like King Canute holding back the tide, rolling back their use may be an insuperable task. In the United Kingdom, the issue for Parliament is no longer one of whether to hold referendums. The case for them on fundamental constitutional political change has been conceded. The issue now is considering which measures would fall within the rubric of fundamental.[19]

Bibliography

Adams, R. J. (1999). *Bonar Law*. London: John Murray.

Altman, D. (2011). *Direct Democracy Worldwide*. Cambridge: Cambridge University Press.

Bogdanor, V. (1994). Western Europe. In D. Butler & A. Ranney (Eds.), *Referendums Around the World* (pp. 24–97). Washington, DC: American Enterprise Institute.

Bogdanor, V. (1997). *Power and the People*. London: Victor Gollancz.

Butler, D., & Kitzinger, U. (1976). *The 1975 Referendum*. London: Macmillan.

Butler, D., & Ranney, A. (1994a). Conclusion. In D. Butler & A. Ranney (Eds.), *Referendums Around the World* (pp. 258–264). Washington, DC: American Enterprise Institute.

Butler, D., & Ranney, A. (1994b). Theory. In D. Butler & A. Ranney (Eds.), *Referendums Around the World* (pp. 11–23). Washington, DC: American Enterprise Institute.

Dane Waters, M. (2003). *Initiative and Referendum Almanac*. Durham, NC: Carolina Academic Press.

Dicey, A. V. (1973 [1886]). *England's Case Against Home Rule*. London: Richmond Publishing Co.

Emden, C. S. (1956). *The People and the Constitution* (2nd ed.). Oxford: Oxford University Press.

Hailsham, Lord. (1978). *The Dilemma of Democracy*. London: Collins.

Hamer, D. A. (1977). *The Politics of Electoral Pressure*. Hassocks: Harvester Press.

---

[19] See Constitution Committee, *Referendums in the United Kingdom*, p. 27.

Hanham, H. J. (1959). *Elections and Party Management: Politics in the Time of Disraeli and Gladstone*. London: Longmans.

Howe, G. (1994). *Conflict of Loyalty*. London: Macmillan.

Independent Commission on Referendums. (2018). *Report of the Independent Commission on Referendums*. London: The Constitution Unit UCL.

Judge, D. (1993). *The Parliamentary State*. London: Sage.

Kersting, N. (2018). Africa. In M. Qvortrup (Ed.), *Two Hundred Years of Referendums* (pp. 213–235). Basingstoke: Palgrave Macmillan.

King, A. (1976). Modes of Executive-Legislative Relations: Great Britain, France and West Germany. *Legislative Studies Quarterly, 1*(1), 11–34.

King, A. (1977). *Britain Says Yes*. Washington, DC: American Enterprise Institute.

LeMay, G. H. (1964). *British Government 1914–1963: Select Documents*. London: Methuen.

LeMay, G. H. (1979). *The Victorian Constitution*. London: Duckworth.

Leston-Bandeira, C. (Ed.). (2005). *Southern European Parliaments in Democracy*. London: Routledge.

Lijphart, A. (1984). *Democracies: Patterns of Majoritarian and Consensus Government in Twenty-One Countries*. New Haven, CT: Yale University Press.

Mehar, R. (2016, June 28). *Why Referendums Are a Really, Really Bad Idea for India*. Retrieved from The NEWS Minute https://www.thenewsminute.com/article/why-referendums-are-really-really-bad-idea-india-45574.

Norton, P. (1975). *Dissension in the House of Commons 1945–1974*. London: Macmillan.

Norton, P. (1990). Introduction. In P. Norton (Ed.), *Legislatures* (pp. 1–19). Oxford: Oxford University Press.

Norton, P. (2012). Resisting the Inevitable? The Parliament Act 1911. *Parliamentary History, 31*(3), 444–459.

Norton, P. (2013). Parliament Act 1911 in Its Historical Context. *Law in Politics, Politics in Law* (pp. 155–170). Oxford: Hart Publishing.

Qvortrup, M. (2000). Are Referendums Controlled and Pro-Hegemonic? *Political Studies, 48*(4), 821–826.

Qvortrup, M. (2005). *A Comparative Study of Referendums* (2nd ed.). Manshester: Manchester University Press.

Qvortrup, M. (2018a). *Government by Referendum*. Manchester: Manchester University Press.

Qvortrup, M. (2018b). Introduction: Theory, Practice and History. In M. Qvortrup (Ed.), *Referendums Around the World* (pp. 1–18). Basingstoke: Palgrave Macmillan.

Qvortrup, M. (2018c). Two Hundred Years of Referendums. In M. Qvortrup (Ed.), *Referendums Around the World* (pp. 263–272). Basingstoke: Palgrave Macmillan.

Qvortrup, M., Morris, C., & Masahiro, K. (2018). Australasia. In M. Qvorturp (Ed.), *Referendums Around the World* (pp. 237–262). Basingstoke: Palgrave Macmillan.

Smith, J. (2019). Fighting to "Take Back Control": The House of Lords and Brexit. In T. Christiansen and D. Fromage (Eds.), *Brexit and Democracy: The Role of Parliaments in the UK and the European Union* (pp. 81–103). Cham, Switzerland: Palgrave Macmillan imprint of Springer Nature Ltd.

Tierney, S. (2012). *Constitutional Referendums: The Theory and Practice of Republican Deliberation*. Oxford: Oxford University Press.

Weston, C. C. (1986). Salisbury and the Lords, 1868–1895. In C. Jones & D. Jones (Eds.), *Peers, Politics and Power: The House of Lords 1603–1911* (pp. 461–488). London: The Hambledon Press.

CHAPTER 6

The Shifting Will of the People: The Case of EU Referendums

Ece Özlem Atikcan

Referendums on European integration present an important puzzle for academics, policymakers and the general public. The European Union (EU) is distant from its citizens and has a highly technical decision-making system. Voting on this complex entity is thus a challenging task. Early opinion polls on EU referendum proposals are often unreliable because voters tend to change their mind during the course of the campaign, in contrast to what we observe in most elections. In the recent past, some of these referendums witnessed a considerable shift in public opinion, going from a favourable attitude to outright rejection. On several occasions, voters changed their verdict entirely in a second referendum on the same topic. What is more, EU referendums have a reputation for being more advantageous for the anti-EU side. Pro-EU campaigners fiercely criticize these campaigns for involving 'red herrings' and misinformation, which they find difficult to debunk. As a result, Dinan (2012: 95) describes these referendums as 'a lightning-rod for Eurosceptics and a scourge for EU politicians and officials' because Eurosceptics can easily manipulate them and they are 'notoriously difficult to win'.

The answer to these puzzling aspects lies in the peculiar dynamics of referendum politics and the power of certain kinds of political arguments. Referendum campaigns on unfamiliar subject matters are more influential than those on more familiar questions; the No side in a referendum enjoys a superior agenda-setting power; and negative and emotional arguments shape public opinion more than other kinds of arguments. Below I address each of these

E. Ö. Atikcan (✉)
University of Warwick, Coventry, UK

© The Author(s) 2021
J. Smith (ed.), *The Palgrave Handbook of European Referendums*,
https://doi.org/10.1007/978-3-030-55803-1_6

aspects in turn, before concluding with a brief discussion of the Brexit vote. The analysis in this chapter relies on extensive field research in France, Spain, the Netherlands and Luxembourg in 2008 on the European Constitution referendums, in Denmark and Ireland in 2011 on the Nice, Maastricht and Lisbon Treaty referendums, in Ireland again in 2015 on the Fiscal Compact referendum, and in the UK in 2016–7 on the Brexit referendum.[1]

6.1   WHY DO WE OBSERVE DRASTIC SHIFTS DURING EU REFERENDUM CAMPAIGNS?

Referendums are very different from elections and have been studied as a distinct field in political science (e.g. Altman 2010; Butler and Ranney 1994; Closa 2007; Morel and Qvortrup 2018; Oppermann 2013; Qvortrup 2013). The main difference is the specific nature of the referendum question, which can range from a proposal with which the public is highly familiar to one that is complex and technical. Depending on the nature of the proposal and the circumstances of the referendum, these campaigns take different forms. When a referendum question concerns a familiar issue in a longstanding debate such as devolution, and the positions of the political parties on the issue are well known, voting behaviour conforms to predictable patterns and resembles election campaigns. However, when the issue is unfamiliar to the public, ideological alignments are unclear and parties line up in a non-traditional way, referendum campaigns are more influential than regular election campaigns (LeDuc 2002). This is particularly the case in referendums on complex international treaties or large packages of constitutional provisions, as voters do not have well-formed opinions. Consequently, public opinion shows greater movement during these campaigns, culminating in outcomes that pre-campaign polls are unable to predict. In such cases, campaign arguments and their portrayal through posters and leaflets give voters cues, serving as short-cuts to help them make sense of conflicting information.

Accordingly, there are three types of referendum campaigns: opinion formation, opinion reversal and uphill struggle (LeDuc 2002). Volatility in public opinion is highest in the first kind of referendums because the proposal is unfamiliar, and the partisan or ideological cues are limited. This results in a gradual opinion formation period during the campaign. The Canadian constitutional referendum in 1992, or the 2005 referendums on the European Constitution in France and the Netherlands present important examples of this type, where voters had little knowledge on the complex and unfamiliar proposals and public opinion shifted significantly over the course of the campaigns (e.g. Atikcan 2015a; Hobolt 2009; Johnston et al. 1996). Second, opinion

---

[1] I interviewed around 150 campaigners from all political parties and civil society groups that were active in the campaigns. These interviews were face-to-face and semi-structured, based on opportunity and snowball sampling. A full list of the individuals interviewed and the interview questionnaire are presented in Appendix 6.1 at the end of the chapter.

reversal campaigns can bring a new dimension to a fairly well-known issue and thereby decrease the impact of previous beliefs. The results of the 1986 Irish referendum on divorce, or the 1999 Australian referendum on the monarchy contradicted the pre-campaign predictions, proving that campaigns are able to change existing attitudes (e.g. Darcy and Laver 1990; Highley and McAllister 2002). In the third kind, uphill struggle campaigns, volatility in public opinion is the lowest as the issue is familiar to the public. Public opinion is highly stable with pre-existing beliefs anchoring the outcome. This occurs because one of two things results in strong partisan or ideological cues; the nature of the issue itself or the circumstances of the referendum (LeDuc 2002: 728). The 1993 referendum in New Zealand on the electoral system, the 1997 devolution referendum in Scotland and the 1995 sovereignty referendum in Québec were instances in which a significant part of the voters was already mobilized on the basis of available and familiar cues (e.g. Aimer and Miller 2002; Denver 2002; Pammett and LeDuc 2001). Figure 6.1 demonstrates these three patterns of opinion change during referendum campaigns, plotting how public support for the referendum proposal evolved over time. In the third pattern, there is no drastic shift over the campaign because here the referendum reinforces predispositions based on partisanship or ideology.

The treaties of the European Union are particularly difficult to understand because the EU is highly complex and citizens have a limited understanding of its competences and institutions. Moreover, in EU referendums the government and a majority of the mainstream political parties almost always campaign on the pro-treaty side as Euroscepticism is confined to the extremes of the political spectrum (De Vries 2009; Taggart 1998; Taggart and Szczerbiak 2013). The combination of these ad hoc unconventional political alliances and the technical nature of the EU treaties means that the public often needs the campaign information to make up their minds. Looking at the three patterns above, referendums on EU treaty ratification typically belong to the *opinion formation* pattern. This is largely in line with the findings of the existing literature pointing to the initial positive attitudes towards EU treaties, which decline frequently in the process of referendum campaigns.

To take an example, in 2005, four Member States decided asked their publics to vote on the European Constitution: Spain, France, the Netherlands and Luxembourg. While the referendums in Spain and Luxembourg

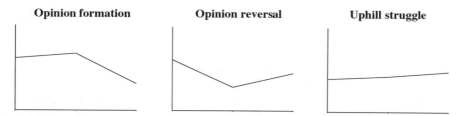

Fig. 6.1 Three patterns of opinion change in referendums (*Source* LeDuc 2002)

approved the treaty, those in France and the Netherlands rejected the Constitution within days of each other. The real puzzle, however, was that in all four votes, polls showed that the voting publics favoured the referendum proposals before the referendum campaigns began but that this initially positive public opinion melted away in two of the cases, culminating in rejections. Why did this occur in some referendum votes but not in others? Detailed studies of the French and Dutch rejections highlight the significance of government unpopularity as well as the role of scepticism towards certain EU policies such as EU enlargement, the EU's market-friendly fiscal policies and the Euro (Aarts and van der Kolk 2005a; Brouard and Sauger 2005; Brouard and Tiberj 2006; Schuck and de Vreese 2008). These factors, which are presented as the cause of rejections, existed at the time of the early polls showing favourable attitudes towards the referendum proposals. Yet these problems were not associated with the reform treaties at the outset. A close look at the campaigns demonstrates that in France and the Netherlands well-organized, strategic anti-Constitution campaigns raised questions in the mind of the public and led to a decrease in the levels of support for the EU Constitution (Atikcan 2015a). In Spain, by contrast, the anti-Constitution campaign lacked resources and remained largely invisible. As a result, the Spanish referendum passed uneventfully, without a heated debate.

Importantly, the negative result of the French and Dutch referendums presented a sudden but *episodic* dip in public opinion. For instance, in France, a post-referendum survey found that 66% of the public wanted France to ask for a new Constitution, which corresponded to 67% of the Yes voters and 66% of the No voters (Atikcan 2015a: 128). In the Netherlands as well, even though there was a sharp decrease in support for 'a' European constitution between the end of 2004 and spring 2005, the post-referendum surveys showed Dutch support for European membership as high as 82% (Dekker and Ederveen 2005: 7; Eurobarometer 2005). These figures highlight the importance of campaigns in referendums on European integration. Although EU citizens may adopt a positive attitude towards the referendum proposals in early polls, it should be kept in mind that this view is often based on a vague support of European integration rather than a specific and firm positive attitude on the EU treaty that is being voted on. The fate of the proposal depends on the mobilization capacity of the pro- and anti-EU campaigners, as discussed in the next sections.

6.2   WHY DO SOME ARGUMENTS GAIN MORE TRACTION THAN OTHERS?

Campaigns are not based on objective statements. Politicians use competing political arguments, to spin and 'frame' the debate, and the way an issue is presented can produce considerable differences in public opinion. Framing is 'a process by which people develop a particular conceptualization of an issue or reorient their thinking about an issue' (Chong and Druckman 2007b: 104). A framing effect occurs when, in describing an issue or event, a speaker's emphasis on a subset of potentially relevant considerations causes individuals to focus on these considerations when forming their opinions. For example, in an American study, when answering whether they would favour or oppose allowing a hate group to hold a political rally, 85% of respondents answer in favour if the question highlighted the importance of free speech, whereas only 45% were in favour when the question emphasized public safety and the risk of violence (Sniderman and Theriault 2004).

Of course, not every argument is equally effective. Why do some arguments resonate and some do not? What are the ingredients of a 'strong' frame? Research on political psychology and social movements shows that individuals should be able to comprehend the content of the frame, in other words, be familiar with its theme and find it applicable to the situation at hand (Benford and Snow 2000; Chong and Druckman 2007b; Snow et al. 1986). Moreover, emotionally interesting, concrete or image-provoking arguments are more easily remembered than those that do not display such characteristics (Brader and Marcus 2013; Ridout and Searles 2011). Emotional appeals project images that are universally valued since they can appeal to everyone regardless of their socioeconomic status or political views (Jerit 2004). Similarly, the media are more likely to cover emotional appeals than sober factual formulations, due to their preference for drama and excitement. Therefore emotional and vivid arguments, especially those evoking fear, anxiety and anger, are expected to be more enduring than those that do not elicit an affective response, all else being equal. People also pay more attention to and are better able to recall negative information (Pfau and Kenski 1990; Soroka 2014). Not only do people weigh negative information more heavily than positive, but also any impressions formed on the basis of negative information are likely to last longer and be resistant to change (Cobb and Kuklinski 1997).

Overall, familiar frames that are presented in an emotional and negative manner are stronger, and are thereby expected to be successful in affecting individuals' opinions by increasing the salience of the particular dimension they emphasize. Importantly, the strength of a frame is not based on its intellectual or moral content, but it is only strong in its appeal to audiences (Chong and Druckman 2007b: 111). What we call 'post-truth' politics is so prevalent today because whether or not a frame is strong does not depend on accuracy, validity or relation to scientific evidence (Chong and Druckman 2007a: 652; Hopkin and Rosamond 2017). Strong frames often rest on symbols, endorsements and links to ideology and may use heuristics rather than direct information on the substance of a policy. For instance, an inaccurate argument on the imminent risk of a major influx of immigrants might lead voters to prioritize such risks in thinking about the upcoming vote. The EU is particularly susceptible to such arguments because the public lacks substantial information concerning how the EU actually works. That is why referendum campaigns on European integration often witnesses misunderstandings of key EU policies, which are not easy to clarify in a heated and short referendum debate.

To go back to the example of the French and Dutch campaigns, in these cases the strategic anti-Constitution campaigns advanced arguments suggesting that the European Constitution would increase immigration, lead to market-friendly reforms, cause rising unemployment, promote decline in the welfare state model and undermine national sovereignty (Atikcan 2015a). On the other hand, the pro-Constitution camp was more hesitant, using broad ideas such as the future and peace or presenting the treaty as an institutional step towards a better Europe. The posters replicated in Fig. 6.2 present these competing campaign strategies.

The first poster was used by the far-left anti-Constitution Socialist Party (SP) in the Dutch referendum. It depicts a map of Europe without the Netherlands. The SP designed it to advance the argument that the Netherlands would lose its sovereignty in a federal Europe, if the EU Constitution passed. The idea that the European Constitution would lead to a European superstate was very influential in the Dutch referendum debate (Aarts and van der Kolk 2005b; Atikcan 2015a). The second poster was used in the French referendum by the far-right anti-Constitution National Front (FN). The poster shows the Turkish Prime Minister signing the European Constitution. Although all the candidate countries were part of the Convention process that drafted the Constitution, the campaigners chose to use this image to imply misleadingly that the Constitution would advance Turkey's accession into the Union. This concrete, vivid message tapped into the fears of the French public regarding immigration. Once again, many voters said they voted against the Constitution because of Turkey's accession into the EU (Atikcan 2015a; Brouard and Sauger 2005). On the pro-Constitution side, as the third and fourth posters demonstrate, the French and Dutch governing parties used the same positive, but also vague and forgettable, message: Europe deserves a Yes. In the French case, the EU flag is reflected in the eyes of the little girl. While the anti-Constitution campaigners emphasized the pressing day-to-day issues,

Fig. 6.2 A selection of campaign posters from the French and Dutch campaigns

mobilizing the existing fear of globalization, the pro-Constitution campaigners were very much tied to the content of the treaty, unable to make the benefits tangible. This is in fact a frequent pattern observed in EU referendums, where the anti-EU arguments prevail over the pro-EU ones, as I discuss next.

6.3   Why Does the No Side Have More Agenda-Setting Power Than the Yes Side?

EU referendums provide a unique opportunity to study voters' attitudes towards a distant level of governance. Scholars have long tried to understand whether EU referendum results reflect domestic (dis)satisfaction with the incumbent governments (Franklin 2002; Reif and Schmitt 1980), voters' identification with political parties (Ray 2003) or actual attitudes towards the EU (Garry et al. 2005; Siune et al. 1994), Finding evidence supporting both domestic and European factors (e.g. Aarts and van der Kolk 2006; Brouard and Tiberj 2006), the recent focus has thus turned to referendum campaigns. In single or comparative studies of EU referendums, scholars convincingly argue that the arguments of Yes and No campaigns on the potential consequences of the vote have an important impact on voting behaviour (Garry 2013, 2014; Hobolt 2009). Put differently, when the public's perceptions of the treaty are aligned with the No campaign, the more they vote No, and vice versa for the Yes campaign (Elkink and Sinnott 2015).

But do the pro-EU and anti-EU sides have equal power in making their case? The broader literature on referendums suggests that No campaigners do not necessarily need to make a coherent and persuasive case against a proposal (Jerit 2004; LeDuc 2005). They need only to raise doubts or link the proposal to other less popular issues. The No side can prevail if it conducts careful research on what parts of the issue voters would not like and make effective posters and slogans playing to these themes (de Vreese and Semetko 2004). Indeed, as the French and Dutch examples show, the anti-treaty campaigns typically argue that the treaty will cause loss of political autonomy in key fields such as social policy, citizenship rules or immigration, even when those themes are not present in the treaty at hand (Hobolt 2009; Mendez et al. 2014).

EU treaty ratification referendums, which involve a clear juxtaposition between pro-treaty (Yes) and anti-treaty (No) campaigns, provide an excellent case to study this asymmetrical advantage (Atikcan 2018). Which are the factors that would make the pro-treaty and anti-treaty campaigns more or less able to exert such leverage? A close study of 11 referendums reveals that the anti-treaty side indeed holds the advantage if it becomes involved in the debate. Nonetheless, the findings also show that this advantage is not unconditional, depending essentially on the availability of arguments. The more multidimensional the topic is, the more campaign material the No side has. When the typical anti-treaty campaigners cannot advance their arguments either because the guarantees from the EU removed their themes from the agenda (in the case of repeat referendums) or because the treaty is a very specific one (Fiscal Compact), this advantage disappears.

The present analysis relies on two kinds of data: first, a series of indicators on campaign characteristics and political setting to serve as controls, followed by interview data from 140 campaigners to study the agenda setting. The 11 EU treaty ratification referendums at hand are shown in Table 6.1. The goal of the indicators presented in Table 6.1 is to compare the various aspects of these referendum campaigns and their political setting to detect any patterns that might correlate with the referendum outcomes.

To begin with, campaign intensity and turnout data help us understand the extent to which there was an active debate between rival campaigns.[2] If the anti-treaty side did not mount a substantive campaign, we would not expect them to have an advantage. Second, the move in the voting intentions over the course of the long campaign shows the extent to which public opinion has potentially been sensitive to campaign information.[3] Similarly, the central themes of the No campaign, based on the interview data and the existing literature, demonstrate whether the anti-treaty campaigners mobilized various attack lines against the EU treaties in an attempt to control the agenda and to drive down the support for these treaties. Next, turning to the political setting, the figures on government popularity, EU support and party consensus (variables closely linked to alternative explanations—second-order, party cues, issue-voting approaches) are important for understanding whether these factors pre-determined the referendum results.[4] Finally, Table 6.1 presents information on the initiator of each referendum.[5]

---

[2] Hobolt (2009: 93) measures campaign intensity (or salience) based on three indicators: the partisan polarization (opposition to the ballot proposal in parliament), the perceived closeness of the race (difference between the two sides in the polls), and the news coverage (number of daily articles monitoring the referendum issue during the three months leading up to the referendum).

[3] This is measured as the difference between the negative voting intentions, due to data availability, six to eight months before the referendum and the percentage of the final No vote. I use the CIS barometers in the Spanish case, the CSA polls in France, the SCP reports in the Netherlands, the TNS-ILRES polls in Luxembourg, and poll figures from secondary sources in the Danish and Irish cases (FitzGibbon 2009, 2013; Sinnott and Elkink 2010; Siune et al. 1994; Svensson 2002).

[4] Government popularity figures are primarily based on national polls in the six months leading up to the vote. The figures on EU support and party consensus are based on the measurement of Mendez et al. (2014). The EU support represents the percentages of those who thought that EU membership was a 'good thing' in the Eurobarometer surveys directly preceding the vote, and party consensus is measured as the absolute difference between the percentage of seats held by political parties in favour of a Yes vote and those that favour a No vote (0 being no consensus and 100 being full consensus). To nuance the party cues point beyond the party consensus measure, the tendency of the government and all the mainstream political parties to campaign on the pro-treaty side (e.g. De Vries 2009) applies to the 11 referendums studied here. Roughly speaking, far right and far left parties are against the EU treaties and the parties in the middle are for them.

[5] This is based on the measurement of Oppermann (2013) to assess whether the triggering mechanism of the referendum correlates with the results, for instance showing a higher

Table 6.1 Campaign characteristics and political setting

	Campaign intensity	Turnout	Yes vote	No vote intention differential	Central themes of the No side	Government popularity (%)	EU support (%)	Party consensus (%)	Initiator
Maastricht Treaty									
Denmark I 1992	11	83.1	**49.3**	+23	Creation of a political 'Union' Loss of sovereignty, citizenship, currency	35	57	61	Mandated by the constitution
Denmark II 1993	9	86.5	56.7	−10	The validity of Danish 'opt-outs'	45	61	61	
Nice Treaty									
Ireland I 2001	4	34.8	**46.1**	+31[2]	Loss of sovereignty, power, social standards Changes in laws on abortion, military neutrality Enlargement	60	72	78	Mandated by the constitution
Ireland II 2002	6	49.5	62.9	+10[3]	The validity of the 'guarantees'	30	78	68	
European Constitution									
Spain 2005	5	42.3	76.7	+13	Loss of social standards Militarization Language recognition (in the regions)	56	72	77	Government
France 2005	12	69.3	**45.3**	+23	Loss of social standards and public services Enlargement, Islam, Turkey's EU membership Militarization	44	56	40	Government

(continued)

Table 6.1 (continued)

	Campaign intensity	Turnout	Yes vote	No vote intention differential	Central themes of the No side	Government popularity (%)	EU support (%)	Party consensus (%)	Initiator
The Netherlands 2005	8	62.8	**38.5**	+50	Loss of sovereignty, power, social standards Euro Enlargement, Islam, Turkey's EU membership Militarization	48	75	67	Opposition
Luxembourg 2005	6	90.4[1]	56.5	+26	Loss of social standards and public services Enlargement, Islam, Turkey's EU membership Militarization	71	85	77	Government
Lisbon Treaty Ireland I 2008	8	53.1	**46.6**	+30	Loss of sovereignty, power, social standards Changes in laws on abortion, military neutrality and corporate tax rate	32	73	73	Mandated by the constitution
Ireland II 2009		59.0	67.1	+5	The validity of the 'guarantees'	10	69	73	
Fiscal Treaty Ireland 2012		50.6	60.3	+5	Negative effects of 'austerity' policies	23	63	61	Mandated by the constitution

Note [1]Rejections in bold, [2]Luxembourg has compulsory voting, [3]Undecided not included

Interview data, in turn, reveals the campaigners' perception of this political advantage. Table 6.2 shows their responses on whether they (or the rival campaign) had an 'advantage' or an 'easier job', and whether they (or the rival campaign) used 'fear' or 'threats' or 'blackmail', which provide direct information on their perception of who controlled the agenda on the negative consequences of the vote choice. More importantly, interview data is helpful

Table 6.2 Perceptions of the agenda-setting advantage

		They had an 'advantage' or 'easier job'	They used 'fear' or 'threats' or 'blackmail'	We had an 'advantage' or 'easier job'	We used 'fear' or 'threats' or 'blackmail'
Maastricht Treaty					
Denmark I	Yes side	X	X		
	No side				
Denmark II	Yes side			X	X
	No side	X	X		
Nice Treaty					
Ireland I	Yes side	X	X		
	No side				
Ireland II	Yes side			X	X
	No side	X	X		
European Constitution					
Spain	Yes side				
	No side	X			
France	Yes side	X	X		
	No side				
The Netherlands	Yes side	X	X		
	No side				
Luxembourg	Yes side	X	X		
	No side				
Lisbon Treaty					
Ireland I	Yes side	X	X		
	No side			X	
Ireland II	Yes side			X	X
	No side	X	X		
Fiscal Treaty					
Ireland	Yes side			X	X
	No side	X	X		

Note Marked cells indicate that a majority of the respondents agreed with the mentioned statement

rejection rate for referendums that were initiated by the opposition. The repeat referendums on the Maastricht, Nice and Lisbon Treaties are more complicated to code than others as they are initiated as a mix of factors, involving the governments, opposition and the EU.

also to understand the reasons behind these perceptions. In explaining their campaigning experience and the challenges they faced, campaigners highlight the factors that cause the political advantage to change hands.

Table 6.1 reveals that government popularity, EU support, party consensus or how the referendum was initiated do not have a systematic relation to the referendum outcomes. On the other hand, the indicators on campaign characteristics (Table 6.1) and the interview data (Table 6.2) tell a meaningful story about how these campaigns unfolded. Where the campaign characteristics indicate high campaign intensity and high volatility in public opinion, campaigners perceive an advantage for the anti-treaty side.

There are two narratives in the interview data. In the first narrative the anti-EU side is perceived to hold the agenda-setting advantage, whereas in the second narrative this advantage changes hands and the pro-EU side is seen as holding this advantage. The first narrative is visible in the European constitution referendums[6] and in the *first referendums* on the Maastricht, Nice and Lisbon treaties. These treaties were hundreds of pages long and multidimensional, arming the anti-treaty side with a wide array of arguments. In the French, Dutch and Luxembourgish campaigns, a majority of the pro-treaty campaigners argue that the anti-treaty side had an advantage and controlled the campaign agenda on the negative consequences of the vote choice. To support their arguments, they suggest that the anti-treaty side brought in (often unrelated) themes to advance the idea that the Constitution would have negative consequences in terms of social benefits, national sovereignty, immigration and militarization. They argue that given the lack of knowledge about the EU, the anti-treaty side could mobilize these themes, which captured the public's mind easily. They explain that it was difficult to counter the multiplicity of anti-treaty arguments while trying to be coherent, and that when they were trying to achieve that they were cornered into a defensive campaign. They similarly add that they could not bring up any negative consequences relating to the rejection of the treaty. The anti-treaty campaigners do not accept that they held an advantage but they do not argue that the pro-treaty side controlled the campaign agenda either. They blame the pro-treaty side for not paying attention to people's existing worries and for discussing Europe only in an abstract manner.

---

[6]Among the european constitution referendums, the Spanish case provides an exception. There has not been a significant campaign against the Constitution, which can be seen in the relatively low campaign intensity and turnout figures as well as the smaller movement of negative public opinion during the campaign in Table 6.1. Campaigners suggested various reasons to explain the lack of the anti-treaty campaign: the lack of a far right movement, the weakness of the far left civil society and the strong association between the EU and democracy. Campaigners from both sides agreed that there was no real debate and that given the lack of anti-treaty arguments, the pro-treaty campaigners were able to tap into what Europe stands for in spain. The pro-treaty side does not hold a majoritarian view on who had an advantage but a majority of the anti-treaty campaigners say that the pro-treaty side had an easier job.

Continuing with the first narrative, the responses in the *first referendums* on the Maastricht, Nice and Lisbon Treaties are in fact surprisingly similar to those in the European Constitution referendums. Like the European Constitution, these treaties provided the anti-treaty side with diverse arguments. A majority of pro-treaty campaigners suggest that the anti-treaty side controlled the agenda on the negative consequences of the vote choice as they mention that the anti-treaty side had an easier job and used fearful arguments. They complain that the anti-treaty side tied the treaties to unpopular themes such as loss of sovereignty, creation of a political Union, interference into national laws and brought in themes unrelated to the EU treaty ('red herrings') such as abortion laws to boost fears. Specifically referring to the public's unfamiliarity with the EU, they add that they had difficulty responding to each and every anti-treaty argument, and that when they were trying to respond to these arguments they were getting into a defensive mode and could not specify their own arguments or the consequences of the rejection of the treaty. The anti-treaty campaigners do not necessarily share this perception but again nor do they say that the pro-treaty side had an advantage in setting the agenda either. They characterize their campaign as superior to the pro-treaty one, arguing that the pro side took the positive result for granted. This first narrative, indicating a perception that the anti-treaty side had a political advantage, is largely paralleled by the high level of movement in negative public opinion in the fifth column of Table 6.1. In short, when the anti-treaty campaign participates actively in the treaty ratification debate and when the referendum proposal is multidimensional, they can control the agenda setting and the pro-treaty side perceives the advantage of the rival campaign clearly.

The second narrative comes from the *second referendums* on the Maastricht, Nice and Lisbon treaties. Here, despite the fact that these treaties offered a multidimensional platform for the anti-treaty campaigners, the guarantees from the EU limited the subject considerably. A majority of both pro- and anti-treaty campaigners agree that this time the pro-treaty side controlled the agenda on the consequences of the vote choice. Campaigners on both sides argue that the EU guarantees removed the controversial first-referendum themes of the anti-treaty camps from the agenda, and that the pro-treaty side presented the second referendum as a vote on EU membership and thereby named clear negative consequences to the rejection of the treaty. In the second referendums, the pro-treaty side could argue that the public no longer needed to fear the themes brought in by the anti-treaty side as the EU had now provided guarantees that they would not materialize. In the face of these assurances, the anti-treaty campaigners could only dispute the validity of the guarantees and lost their earlier advantage, as can also be observed in the change of their central campaign themes in Table 6.1. The pro-treaty campaigners then advanced the idea that a second No vote would mean a rejection of the EU and the loss of membership and economic benefits. In the second Lisbon referendum, in addition to this argument, the pro-treaty campaign also advanced the idea that a Yes vote would be the only solution to the unfolding economic crisis in Ireland. The pro-treaty side could thus control the campaign agenda on the negative consequences when the hands of the anti-treaty side were tied and when they could evoke an argument on economic loss. This second narrative, highlighting the perceived advantage of the pro-treaty side, is also in line with the relatively smaller movement of negative public opinion in the second referendums on Maastricht, Nice and Lisbon treaties shown in the fifth column of Table 6.1.[7] To summarize, the pro-treaty side is perceived to have the advantage in repeat referendums when new guarantees from the EU defeat the arguments of the anti-treaty side and when the pro-treaty side can bring up the economic costs of an exclusion from the EU.

The Fiscal Compact presents an outlier at first glance, however. Table 6.2 shows that a majority of both pro- and anti-treaty campaigners argue that the pro-treaty side had the advantage and controlled the arguments on fear, just as in the repeat referendums, despite this being a single referendum. Irish campaigners from both sides suggest that this is due to the peculiar nature of the fiscal compact. This treaty covered financial issues only and thereby it was not a broad, multidimensional EU treaty like the other ones. Campaigners explain that this limited the role of the usual anti-treaty campaigners in the debate and that the pro-treaty side used the 'fear factor' on the basis of access to European bail out funds. As a result, the pro-treaty side was more able to control the campaign agenda on the consequences of the vote choice. Overall, these findings suggest that although the No side normally has a superior agenda-setting power, under certain conditions the Yes side is also able to attach drastic consequences to a vote against the proposal and play the same game as No campaigners.

6.4   WHY ARE EU REFERENDUM OUTCOMES SOMETIMES REVERSED?

Shifts in attitudes towards referendum proposals have serious policy implications and such swings in public opinion even meant reversal of referendum outcomes. This took place in three instances in the EU, first in Denmark in 1992–1993 on the Maastricht Treaty, then in Ireland in 2002–2003 on the Nice Treaty and once again in Ireland in 2008–2009 on the Lisbon Treaty. In all three cases, the public first rejected the treaty but then approved the same treaty in a second referendum. This section looks into the mechanisms of such reversals and their implications for democratic government. What causes the public to change its mind in a repeat referendum? Does the public vote exactly

---

[7]There is one key difference in the Lisbon referendums. Although sharing the pattern of responses with the other repeated referendums, here, a majority of the anti-treaty campaigners actually accept that they had an advantage in the first referendum campaign. Their argument is that they learned from the Nice referendums that they could ask the public to vote No in the first referendum in order to get a 'better deal' (guarantees) in a not-yet-announced but almost-certain second referendum.

on the same question again? Is the government simply asking the public to vote again because they have given the wrong answer?

Research on the causes of these reversals fall into the camps mentioned earlier, second-order and issue-voting theories (Franklin et al. 1995; Garry et al. 2005; Svensson 2002). The second-order theory argues that the change in the level of government popularity accounts for the switch, suggesting that more popular governments secured positive votes in the second rounds. Yet this explanation is directly challenged by the Irish Lisbon double referendum, as the government was much less popular in the second round that approved the treaty. The issue-voting theory, on the other hand, claims that people's understanding of what the EU treaty meant changed in the second round. Finding more support for the second model, more recent research points to the importance of increasing campaign intensity in the second round of referendums, underlining the vigour, energy and effectiveness of the second-round Yes campaigns (de Vreese 2006; Garry et al. 2005; Hobolt 2005, 2006).

The change in second-round campaigns is highly interesting because it reveals that pro-EU campaigners built a toolkit for overturning the negative verdicts (Atikcan 2015b). As discussed in detail above, in the first rounds in all three instances, as expected, the anti-EU campaign arguments tapped into sensitive subjects for the society. In Denmark, the anti-EU side argued that the Maastricht Treaty would lead to loss of Danish sovereignty in a new United States of Europe, which would overrule Danish currency and citizenship. In Ireland, in both Nice and Lisbon referendums, the anti-EU campaigners repeatedly argued that the treaties would change Irish laws on abortion, cause loss of sovereignty, military neutrality and its permanent EU Commissioner. In the second rounds, the pro-EU campaigners used two new strategies to weaken the anti-EU campaigners. In all cases, after the rejections, the governments sought reassurances from the EU on the controversial themes of the first campaign. This mechanism allowed them to ask the question again. But the fact that the EU agreed to either opt-outs (Denmark) or guarantees (Ireland) meant that the question was not *exactly* the same. Although the treaty at hand was the same, this time the campaigners brought the opt-outs or guarantees onto the agenda and convinced the public that they were voting on a *new aspect* of the original question. This change in the agenda also enabled them to use their second strategy, which was to raise the stakes of a second rejection, with arguments on a potential exclusion from the EU and economic costs. The posters in Fig. 6.3 illustrate this change in the campaign arguments.

A particularly interesting aspect in these double votes is the learning across cases. Interviews with campaigners in these double referendums indicate that Denmark designed these strategies, which the Irish learned and adopted later on. In fact, there is evidence that the anti-EU side learned as well. During the first Lisbon campaign, Irish anti-EU campaigners explicitly stressed that Ireland could get a better deal after a rejection by receiving concessions from the EU. This signals that small states, being unable to pull the plug on the

Fig. 6.3 Campaign Posters in Maastricht, Nice and Lisbon Referendums (*Note* First, third and fifth rows present first-round posters and second, fourth and sixth rows present second-round posters)

EU treaties, developed a method to renegotiate with the Union and get their public on board in a second round.

What are the implications of such strategies for democracy? Are these votes undemocratic? The answers to these questions are ultimately political. Although at first glance such referendums seem to ask the public to change their answer, there are also a few factors that might mitigate such a perception. First, the actual question on the ballot paper might be identical but the existence of a new 'arrangement' between the voting Member State and the Union in the form of opt-outs or guarantees suggests that the vote is on a renewed question with a new set of information. Second, an EU treaty cannot enter into force until all Member States ratify it. Member States can choose between the options of parliamentary ratification and referendum, unless a referendum is constitutionally mandated as in Ireland. Therefore, there is always a potential clash between a decision taken by direct democracy in one Member State and other decisions taken by representative democracy in other Member States. In the treaty ratification process, in contrast with a case such as Brexit, a democratic decision taken in one country, regardless of the method used, could stand in the way of democratic decisions taken in others. This is an inevitable dilemma in a multi-level entity such as the EU.

6.5   THE BREXIT PUZZLE

The Brexit case brings all of these aspects together. A great majority of policymakers, stakeholders, academics as well as the general public expected the British public to vote to remain in the EU. In May 2016, a month before the vote, the British Political Studies Association carried out an expert survey of journalists, academics and pollsters about their predictions of the outcome (Jennings and Fisher 2016). The results, based on the expectations of 596 experts in total, demonstrated that 87% thought the UK would stay in the EU, with only 5% believing that Brexit would be the most likely outcome. But almost 52% of the public voted to leave the EU on 23 June 2016.

A close look at the Brexit campaign reveals important similarities to previous EU referendum campaigns. On the previously discussed continuum (LeDuc 2002), the Brexit referendum would fall between the 'opinion formation' and 'uphill struggle' categories. The Brexit case was not focused on a technical and lengthy EU treaty, which normally leads to opinion formation campaigns. The British public already had an idea of what the EU membership meant to them. However, it also involved a multidimensional referendum question, which allowed the anti-EU side to place any theme they liked on the agenda and redefine the meaning of the vote.

The result was an intense campaign full of emotions. Both the Remain and Leave sides attempted to 'frame' the issue strategically and shape the meaning of the vote for the citizens. Relying on the experience of the previous governments from the 2015 general election and the 2014 Scottish referendum, the Remain camp chose to frame the vote solely as an economic one, emphasizing the economic costs of a departure from the EU. But as the campaign unfolded, the Leave side effectively neutralized these economic arguments and de-risked a departure from the status quo. They discredited 'the experts', proposed their own figures on the economic costs of a Remain vote, famously suggesting that the UK was paying £350 million to the EU budget per week (Atikcan et al. 2020). The Leave side also successfully increased the number of issues in the debate, arguing that there would be other risks relating to remaining in the EU, such as losing control of immigration policy. They vividly urged the public to 'Take Back Control'. These concrete and emotionally compelling arguments immediately struck a familiar chord with voters. Most intriguingly, the Remain side was silent on these issues, without an emotional case to present.

One of the most pressing questions in the wake of the referendum was whether there could be a second referendum on Brexit. Could the Brexit result be reversed in a second referendum much like the Danish and Irish ones? Because the Brexit vote did not concern treaty ratification, which would have blocked the process for all other Member States, there was no such pressure on the British government to renegotiate and reverse the verdict. Nonetheless, during the Brexit campaign the Leave side avoided a conversation on the specific kind of Brexit they advocated. Would it be a soft or a hard Brexit, with or without a deal? These points remained ambiguous. With the actual exit negotiations in progress, there was a real debate on the possible types of Brexit the UK could have emerged. This is why there were calls for a second referendum in order to offer the public a direct say on the ultimate deal. A second referendum as such would have been remarkably similar to the Danish and Irish double votes because there would have been a similar 'new ground', a new arrangement to vote on, which would have made the referendum question necessarily different from the one already asked. The real difficulty would be in designing the referendum question and the ballot paper, however. What could the exact question be and would there simply be two choices, between 'Deal' or 'No deal'? Such a vote would not have contradicted the previous referendum result and would only have been the next step in progressing towards Brexit. Alternatively, as Conservative MP Justine Greening proposed, there could have been three options: 'Remain', 'Deal', 'No deal' (Sabbah and Walker 2018). This three-choice vote would have offered the British public an option to reverse their original decision. That option might not have provided the intended clarity on the topic. Even if a first and second-preference system had been adopted, close percentages on all three choices might have rendered the final decision even more ambiguous.

The Brexit case demonstrates that although each EU referendum takes place in a different context, they share important similarities. The referendum question typically involves a complex and technical aspect, the campaign often takes an emotional tone and shapes the public perception of the vote choice and its consequences, and there is often a discussion of a new vote when there is a negative verdict. Under which conditions referendums are called and how campaigns are organized therefore have crucial implications for the future of European integration and democracy.

APPENDIX 6.1

Interview Questionnaire

1. What were the main issues/arguments raised in your campaign (and second campaign if a repeat referendum)?
2. Why did you specifically choose these issues and arguments?
3. Did your party/organization have a campaigning strategy (and did your party/organization change its campaign strategy in the second referendum if a repeat referendum)?
4. How did you organize your campaign (and was your preparation different for the second referendum if a repeat referendum)?
5. What were the main challenges you faced during your campaign?
6. How well do you think the other side has performed?
7. What would you say were the main challenges the other side faced?

UNITED KINGDOM

- Ryan Coetzee (Director of Strategy of the Remain Campaign)
- James McGrory (Chief Campaign Spokesperson of the Remain Campaign)
- Lord Rose (Chair of the Remain Campaign)
- Alan Johnson (Labour MP, Remain Campaign)
- Matthew Elliott (Chief Executive of the Vote Leave Campaign)
- Gisela Stuart (Labour MP, Chair of the Vote Leave Campaign)
- Richard Tice (Co-founder of Leave.EU Campaign)
- Matthew Ellery (Get Britain Out Campaign)

SCOTLAND

- Blair Jenkins (Chief Executive of the Yes Scotland Campaign)
- Kevin Pringle (Strategic Communications Director of the SNP-Yes Scotland Campaign)
- Robert Shorthouse (Director of Communications of the Better Together Campaign)
- Phil Anderton (Board Member of the Better Together Campaign)

SPAIN

- Juan Fernando López Aguilar (PSOE, MP, Minister of Justice and Interior Affairs)

- Juan Moscoso del Prado Hernández (PSOE, MP)
- Enrique Baron Crespo (PSOE, MEP, the chairman of the Party of European Socialists Group in the EP between 1999 and 2004)
- Orestes Suárez Antón (PSOE, International Secretary)
- Alejando Muñoz Alonso (PP, Senator)
- Ignacio Cosidó Gutiérrez (PP, MP)
- Jordi Xuclà i Costa (CiU, MP)
- José Ramón Beloki Guerra (PNV, MP)
- Carles Llorens I Vila (CDC, International Secretary)
- José Manuel Fernández Fernández (IU, Coordinator of the Parliamentary Group, and mayor of Bustarviejo)
- Joaquim Puig Vilamala and Oriol Duran Torres (ERC, Coordinator, and Spokesperson of the Parliamentary Group)
- Marc Giménez Villahoz (ICV, European Politics Coordinator)
- Mikel Irujo Amezaga (EA, MEP)
- Jaime Pastor (IU, ATTAC, Alternative Space)
- Ricardo Gómez Muñoz (ATTAC)
- Carlos Girbau Costa (Social Forum, IU)
- Luis González Reyes (Ecologists in Action)
- José Ignacio Torreblanca (Senior Analyst for EU Affairs, Elcano Royal Institute for International Affairs)
- Jordi Vaquer i Fanés (Europe Programme Co-ordinator, CIDOB Foundation)

FRANCE

- Olivier Ubéda (UMP, Deputy Director of Communications and European Affairs Delegate)
- Alain Bergounioux (PS, Secretary General of the PS Scientific Council)
- Pierre Kanuty (PS, International and European Affairs Political Assistant)
- Patrick Farbiaz (The Greens, International Secretary)
- Isabelle Sicart (UDF)
- Nicolas Dupont-Aignan (UMP, MP)
- Jacques Myard (UMP, MP)
- Jacques Généreux (PS)
- Francine Bavay (The Greens Executive Committee Member, and the Vice-President of the Regional Council of Île-de-France)
- Daniel Cirera (PCF, International Secretary)
- Dominique Touraine (PCF)
- Alain Krivine (LCR)
- Catherine Salagnac (National Front)
- Yves Salesse (Co-President of Copernic Foundation, Conseil d'État Member, Co-initiator of the Appeal of 200)

- Claude Debons (General Workers' Confederation CGT, Co-initiator of the Appeal of 200)
- Pierre Khalfa (ATTAC, and *Solidarity* Unity Democracy)
- Susan George (ATTAC)
- Aurélie Trouvé (ATTAC)
- Maxime Combes (ATTAC)
- Christophe Beaudouin (Secretary General of the "Group for a Confederation of the States of Europe," campaigned with the MPF)
- Raoul-Marc Jennar (Member of the No Committee)
- Gaëtane Ricard-Nihoul (Secretary General of Notre Europe)

THE NETHERLANDS

- Atzo Nicolaï (VVD, MP, Minister of European Affairs)
- Jan Jacob van Dijk (CDA, MP)
- Marije Laffeber (PvdA, International Secretary)
- Bas Eickhout (GreenLeft, Delegate in the European Green Party)
- Gerben-Jan Gerbrandy (D66, Secretary of the D66 Parliamentary Group)
- Michiel van Hulten (Director of Foundation for a Better Europe)
- Hilde Laffeber (Ministry of Foreign Affairs (MFA), Member of the Yes Campaign Team)
- Delphine Pronk (Ministry of Foreign Affairs (MFA), Head of the EU Communications Unit)
- Marco Pastors (Political Leader of the local party Liveable Rotterdam, Member of the City Council, and deputy mayor of Rotterdam)
- Otto Ter Haar (The Greens, International Secretary)
- Harry van Bommel (SP, MP)
- Renske Leijten (SP, leader of the ROOD, SP's youth organization)
- Hans van Heijningen (SP, Secretary-General)
- Esme Wiegman (CU, MP)
- Mat Herben (LPF, Chairman of the LPF)
- Alexander van Hattem (Young Fortuynists, Youth Organization of the now defunct LPF)
- Willem Bos (President of the ConstitutionNo, and ATTAC Netherlands)
- Erik Wesselius (ConstitutionNo)
- Wim van de Donk (President of the WRR, Scientific Council for Government Policy)
- Monica Sie Dhian Ho (WRR, Scientific Council for Government Policy)
- Patrick van Schie (Director of the Liberal think tank that is related to the VVD)

LUXEMBOURG

- François Biltgen (CSV, MP, Chairman of the CSV and Minister of Labor and Employment)
- Laurent Mosar (CSV, MP)
- Ben Fayot (LSAP, MP, President of the Parliamentary Group)
- Charles Goerens (DP, MP, Minister of Foreign Affairs)
- Abbes Jacoby (The Greens, Secretary General of the Parliamentary Group)
- Dan Michels (The Greens, Parliamentary Attaché)
- Jacques-Yves Henckes (ADR, MP)
- Henri Wehenkel (The Left)
- André Kremer (Coordinator and Leader of the No Committee)
- Pierre Gramegna (Director-General of the Chamber of Commerce)
- Nico Clement (Confederation of Independent Trade Unions of Luxembourg OGBL)
- Nico Wennmacher (President of the Railways Trade Union FNCTTFEL-Landesverband)
- Tom Graas (Director of the national RTL TV News)
- Marc Linster (Director of the national RTL Radio)
- Anne-Marie Berny (ATTAC)
- Adrien Thomas (National Union of Luxembourgish Students UNEL)
- Frédéric Krier (National Union of Luxembourgish Students UNEL)
- Alfred Groff (Luxembourg Social Forum)
- Jürgen Stoldt (Political communication expert and Editor of Forum)
- Thomas Rupp (Organizer of the European No Campaign)

DENMARK

- Uffe Ellemann-Jensen (Minister of Foreign Affairs in 1992 and Leader of the Liberal Party)
- Niels Helveg Petersen (Minister of Foreign Affairs in 1993 and Social Liberal Party MP)
- Mogens Lykketoft (Social Democrat MP)
- Jacob Buksti (Social Democrat MP)
- Charlotte Antonsen (Liberal Party MP)
- Jørgen Ørstrøm Møller (State Secretary, Ministry of Foreign Affairs)
- Holger K. Nielsen (Leader of the Socialist People's Party, MP)
- Steen Gade (Socialist People's Party MP)
- Søren Krarup (Progress Party)
- Kenneth Kristensen Berth (Danish People's Party)
- Ole Krarup (President of the People's Movement against the EU)
- Jens-Peter Bonde (President of the June Movement)
- Erik Boel (President of the European Movement)

IRELAND

- Dick Roche (Fianna Fáil, MP, Minister of European Affairs)
- Timmy Dooley (Fianna Fáil, MP) (2 interviews, in 2011 and 2015)
- David Harmon (Fianna Fáil, Director of Press and Communications)
- Seán Dorgan (Fianna Fáil, General Secretary)
- Lucinda Creighton (Fine Gael, MP)
- Tom Curran (Fine Gael, General Secretary)
- Terry Murphy (Fine Gael, Dublin Director) (2 interviews, in 2011 and 2015)
- Joe Costello (Labour Party, MP) (2 interviews, in 2011 and 2015)
- Thomas Broughan (Labour Party, MP)
- Déirdre de Búrca (Green Party, MP)
- Mary Lou McDonald (Sinn Féin, MP)
- Eoin Ó'Broin (Sinn Féin, Campaign Director) (2 interviews, in 2011 and 2015)
- Killian Forde (Sinn Féin, Director of Strategy in Lisbon1)
- Joe Higgins (Socialist Party, MP)
- Paul Murphy (Socialist Party, MP)
- Padraig Mannion (Workers' Party, Campaign Director)
- Declan Ganley (Libertas, President)
- Naoise Nunn (Libertas, Executive Director)
- John McGuirk (Libertas, Communications Director)
- Scott Schittl (Cóir, Campaign Director)
- Ben Conroy (Iona Institute)
- Anthony Coughlan (National Platform, President) (2 interviews, in 2011 and 2015)
- Peter Lacey (People's Movement)
- Roger Cole (Peace and Neutrality Alliance, President) (2 interviews, in 2011 and 2015)
- Brendan Kiely (Irish Alliance for Europe, Chief Executive)
- Karen White (Irish Alliance for Europe)
- Pat Cox (Ireland for Europe, Campaign Director)
- Brendan Halligan (Ireland for Europe, National Campaign Coordinator) (2 interviews, in 2011 and 2015)
- Brigid Laffan (Ireland for Europe, Chairperson)
- Caroline Erskine (Ireland for Europe, Communications Director)
- Anthony Brown (Ireland for Europe, Director of Research)
- Michelle O'Donnell Keating (Women for Europe, Co-founder)
- Jillian van Turnhout (Ireland for Europe)
- Billie Sparks (Women for Europe)
- Blair Horan (Charter Group) (2 interviews, in 2011 and 2015)
- Dan O'Brien, (Economist, Institute of International and European Affairs)
- Michael Taft (Economist, Unite)

- Andy Storey (University professor and No campaigner)
- Paul Hand (Press Liaison Officer to the Parliamentary Sub-Committee on Fiscal Compact)
- Ciarán Toland (Civil society Yes campaigner in the Nice Treaty referendums)

Bibliography

Aarts, K., & van der Kolk, H. (2005a). Op Weg Naar 1 Juni. In K. Aarts & H. van der Kolk (Eds.), *Nederlanders en Europa: Het Referendum over de Europese Grondwet*. Amsterdam: Utigeverij Bert Bakker.

Aarts, K., & van der Kolk, H. (Eds.). (2005b). *Nederlanders en Europa: Het Referendum over de Europese Grondwet*. Amsterdam: Utigeverij Bert Bakker.

Aarts, K., & van der Kolk, H. (2006). Understanding the Dutch 'No': The Euro, the East, and the Elite. *Political Science and Politics, 39*(2), 243–246.

Aimer, P., & Miller, R. (2002). Partisanship and Principle: Voters and the New Zealand Electoral Referendum of 1993. *European Journal of Political Research, 41*, 795–809.

Altman, D. (2010). *Direct Democracy Worldwide*. Cambridge: Cambridge University Press.

Atikcan, E. O. (2015a). *Framing the European Union: The Power of Political Arguments in Shaping European Integration*. Cambridge: Cambridge University Press.

Atikcan, E. O. (2015b). The Puzzle of Double Referendums in the European Union. *Journal of Common Market Studies, 53*(5), 937–956.

Atikcan, E. O. (2018). Agenda Control in EU Referendum Campaigns: The Power of the Anti-EU Side. *European Journal of Political Research, 57*(1), 93–115.

Atikcan, E. O., Nadeau, R., & Bélanger, É. (2020). *Framing Risky Choices: Brexit and the Dynamics of High-Stakes Referendums*. Montréal: McGill-Queen's University Press.

Benford, R., & Snow, D. (2000). Framing Processes and Social Movements: An Overview and Assessment. *Annual Review of Sociology, 26*(1), 611–639.

Brader, T., & Marcus, G. (2013). Emotions and Political Psychology. In L. Huddy, D. Sears, & J. Levy (Eds.), *The Oxford Handbook of Political Psychology*. Oxford: Oxford University Press.

Brouard, S., & Sauger, N. (2005). Comprendre la Victoire du "Non" : Proximité Partisane, Conjoncture et Attitude à l'égard de l'Europe. In A. Laurent & N. Sauger (Eds.), *Le Référendum de Ratification du Traité Constitutionnel Européen du 29 Mai 2005: Comprendre le "Non" Français*. Paris: CEVIPOF.

Brouard, S., & Tiberj, V. (2006). The French Referendum: The Not So Simple Act of Saying Nay. *Political Science and Politics, 39*(2), 261–268.

Butler, D., & Ranney, A. (Eds.). (1994). *Referendums around the World: The Growing Use of Direct Democracy*. Washington, DC: American Enterprise Institute for Public Policy Research.

Chong, D., & Druckman, J. (2007a). Framing Public Opinion in Competitive Democracies. *American Political Science Review, 101*(4), 637–655.

Chong, D., & Druckman, J. (2007b). Framing Theory. *Annual Review of Political Science, 10,* 103–126.

Closa, C. (2007). Why Convene Referendums? Explaining Choices in EU Constitutional Politics. *Journal of European Public Policy, 14*(8), 1311–1332.

Cobb, M., & Kuklinski, J. (1997). Changing Minds: Political Arguments and Political Persuasion. *American Journal of Political Science, 41*(1), 88–121.

Darcy, R., & Laver, M. (1990). Referendum Dynamics and the Irish Divorce Amendment. *Public Opinion Quarterly, 54*(1), 1–20.

de Vreese, C. (2006). Political Parties in Dire Straits? Consequences of National Referendums for Political Parties. *Party Politics, 12*(5), 581–598.

de Vreese, C., & Semetko, Holli. (2004). *Political Campaigning in Referendums: Framing the Referendum Issue.* Abingdon: Routledge.

De Vries, C. (2009). Taking Europe to Its Extremes: Extremist Parties and Public Euroscepticism. *Party Politics, 15*(1), 5–28.

Dekker, P., & Ederveen, S. (Eds.) (2005). *European Times: Public Opinion on Europe & Working Hours, Compared and Explained.* The Hague: SCP The Netherlands Institute for Social Research, CPB Netherlands Bureau for Economic Policy Analysis.

Denver, D. (2002). Voting in the 1997 Scottish and Welsh Devolution Referendums: Information, Interests and Opinions. *European Journal of Political Research, 41,* 827–843.

Dinan, D. (2012). Governance and Institutions: Impact of the Escalating Crisis. *Journal of Common Market Studies, 50,* 85–98.

Elkink, J., & Sinnott, R. (2015). Political Knowledge and Campaign Effects in the 2008 Irish Referendum on the Lisbon Treaty. *Electoral Studies, 38,* 217–225.

Eurobarometer. (2005). *The European Constitution: Post-referendum Survey in the Netherlands.* Brussels: European Commission.

FitzGibbon, J. (2009). *Ireland's No to Lisbon: Learning the Lessons from the Failure of the Yes and the Success of the No Side* (Sussex European Institute, SEI Working Paper), 110.

FitzGibbon, J. (2013). *The Referendum on the European Fiscal Compact Treaty in the Republic of Ireland, 31 May 2012* (European Parties Elections and Referendums Network, Referendum Briefing Paper), 19.

Franklin, M. (2002). Learning from the Danish Case: A Comment on Palle Svensson's Critique of the Franklin Thesis. *European Journal of Political Research, 41*(6), 751–757.

Franklin, M., van der Eijk, C., & Marsh, M. (1995). Referendum Outcomes and Trust in Government: Public Support for Europe in the Wake of Maastricht. *West European Politics, 18*(3), 101–117.

Garry, J. (2013). Direct Democracy and Regional Integration: Citizens' Perceptions of Treaty Implications and the Irish Reversal on Lisbon. *European Journal of Political Research, 52,* 94–118.

Garry, J. (2014). Emotions and Voting in EU Referendums. *European Union Politics, 15*(2), 235–254.

Garry, J., Marsh, M., & Sinnott, R. (2005). 'Second-order' versus 'Issue-voting' Effects in EU Referendums: Evidence from the Irish Nice Treaty Referendums. *European Union Politics, 6*(2), 201–221.

Highley, J., & McAllister, I. (2002). Elite Division and Voter Confusion: Australia's Republic Referendum in 1999. *European Journal of Political Research, 41,* 845–861.

Hobolt, S. (2005). When Europe Matters: The Impact of Political Information on Voting Behaviour in EU Referendums. *Journal of Elections, Public Opinion and Parties, 15*(1), 85–109.

Hobolt, S. (2006). How Parties Affect Vote Choice in European Integration Referendums. *Party Politics, 12*(5), 623–647.

Hobolt, S. (2009). *Europe in Question: Referendums on European Integration.* New York: Oxford University Press.

Hopkin, J., & Rosamond, B. (2017). Post-truth Politics, Bullshit and Bad Ideas: 'Deficit Fetishism' in the UK. *New Political Economy.* https://doi.org/10.1080/13563467.2017.1373757.

Jennings, W., & Fisher, S. (2016). *Expert Predictions of the 2016 EU Referendum: Political Studies Association.*

Jerit, J. (2004). Survival of the Fittest: Rhetoric During the Course of an Election Campaign. *Political Psychology, 25*(4), 563–575.

Johnston, R., Blais, A., Gidengil, E., & Nevitte, N. (1996). *The Challenge of Direct Democracy: The 1992 Canadian Referendum.* Montreal: McGill—Queen's University Press.

LeDuc, L. (2002). Opinion Change and Voting Behaviour in Referendums. *European Journal of Political Research, 41*(6), 711–732.

LeDuc, L. (2005). Saving the Pound or Voting for Europe? Expectations for Referendums on the Constitution and the Euro. *Journal of Elections, Public Opinion & Parties, 15*(2), 169–196.

Mendez, F., Mendez, M., & Triga, V. (2014). *Referendums and the European Union: A Comparative Inquiry.* Cambridge: Cambridge University Press.

Morel, L., & Qvortrup, M. (2018). *The Routledge Handbook to Referendums and Direct Democracy.* Abingdon: Routledge.

Oppermann, K. (2013). The Politics of Discretionary Government Commitments to European Integration Referendums. *Journal of European Public Policy, 20*(5), 684–701.

Pammett, J., & LeDuc, L. (2001). Sovereignty, Leadership and Voting in the Quebec Referendums. *Electoral Studies, 20,* 265–280.

Pfau, M., & Kenski, H. (1990). *Attack Politics: Strategy and Defense.* New York: Praeger.

Qvortrup, M. (2013). *Direct Democracy: A Comparative Study of the Theory and Practice of Government by the People.* Manchester: Manchester University Press.

Ray, L. (2003). Reconsidering the Link Between Incumbent Support and Pro-EU Opinion. *European Union Politics, 4*(3), 259–279.

Reif, K., & Schmitt, H. (1980). Nine Second-Order National Elections: A Conceptual Framework for the Analysis of European Election Results. *European Journal of Political Research, 8*(1), 3–44.

Ridout, T., & Searles, K. (2011). It's My Campaign I'll Cry If I Want to: How and When Campaigns use Emotional Appeals. *Political Psychology, 32*(3), 439–458.

Sabbah, D., & Walker, P. (2018, June 16). Justine Greening Endorses Second Brexit Referendum, *The Guardian.*

Schuck, A., & de Vreese, C. (2008). The Dutch No to the EU Constitution: Assessing the Role of EU Skepticism and the Campaign. *Journal of Elections, Public Opinion, and Parties, 18*(1), 101–128.

Sinnott, R., & Elkink, J. (2010). Attitudes and Behaviour in the Second Referendum on the Treaty of Lisbon. *Report for the Department of Foreign Affairs.*

Siune, K., Svensson, P., & Tonsgaard, O. (1994). The European Union: The Danes Said "No" in 1992, But "Yes" in 1993: How and Why? *Electoral Studies, 13*(2), 107–116.

Sniderman, P., & Theriault, S. (2004). The Structure of Political Argument and the Logic of Issue Framing. In W. Saris & P. Sniderman (Eds.), *Studies in Public Opinion: Attitudes, Nonattitudes, Measurement Error, and Change*. Princeton: Princeton University Press.

Snow, D., Rochford, E. B., Jr., Worden, S., & Benford, R. (1986). Frame Alignment Processes, Micromobilization, and Movement Participation. *American Sociological Review, 51,* 464–481.

Soroka, S. (2014). *Negativity in Democratic Politics: Causes and Consequences*. Cambridge: Cambridge University Press.

Svensson, P. (2002). Five Danish Referendums on the European Community and European Union: A Critical Assessment of the Franklin Thesis. *European Journal of Political Research, 41*(6), 733–750.

Taggart, P. (1998). A Touchstone of Dissent: Euroscepticism in Contemporary Western European Party Systems. *European Journal of Political Research, 33*(3), 363–388.

Taggart, P., & Szczerbiak, A. (2013). Coming in from the Cold? Euroscepticism, Government Participation and Party Positions on Europe. *Journal of Common Market Studies, 51*(1), 17–37.

CHAPTER 7

Two Hundred Years of Direct Democracy: The Referendum in Europe 1793–2018

Matt Qvortrup

'Our system is one of democracy, but democracy by consent and not by delegation, of the government of the people, for the people, with but not by, the people', wrote L. S. Amery in *Thoughts on the Constitution* (Amery 1947: 21). Three quarters of a century on, it is almost trite to notice the difference. In the aftermath of the 2016 Brexit referendum in the United Kingdom and the 2014 vote on Scottish independence, one is tempted to conclude that 'our system' is *not* one of pure representative government, but a system that is, effectively, 'by the people'. Add to this, the seemingly growing use of referendums in other countries—the Irish referendum on abortion 2018 being a notable example—and one might be tempted to conclude that Amery's observation is outdated; that we live under a system of 'government by referendum'.

Some view this development as a cause for concern. In a recent book on the crisis of democracy, David Runciman (2018: 47) singled out the referendum as one of the causes of the current malaise: 'A referendum', he opined, 'looks democratic but it is not. Spectators get dragged on stage to say a simple yes or no to a proposition they have played no part in devising'. He went on to conclude that the use of this institution, 'shows how easily the popular demand can end up having the opposite effect' (Runciman 2018: 48). This position is not new. Sixty years earlier, the Swedish Prime Minister, Tage Erlander, who served from 1947 to 1969, concluded that 'it becomes much harder to

M. Qvortrup (✉)
Coventry University, Coventry, UK
e-mail: matt.qvortrup@coventry.ac.uk

© The Author(s) 2021
J. Smith (ed.), *The Palgrave Handbook of European Referendums*,
https://doi.org/10.1007/978-3-030-55803-1_7

pursue an effective reform policy if reactionaries are offered the opportunity to appeal to people's natural conservatism' (Erlander quoted in Lewin 1988: 238). Nothing, it seemed, had changed.

These quotes were not were based on historical or empirical evidence. By contrast, this chapter will present an evidence-based overview of the specific use and possible abuse of referendums. It will focus on the historical trends and tendencies of referendums in Europe from Bonaparte to Brexit. The aim of the chapter is to consider, as objectively as possible, the reasons advanced for holding referendums and their political effect but without advancing general theories. The German historian Leopold von Ranke once remarked that the historian 'merely should describe what actually happened' ('*wie es eigentlich gewesen ist*') (Ranke 1824: vi). Thus, the referendums will be described as 'they happened'. Yet, merely reporting their occurrence is in itself of little value. We are not merely interested in what logical positivists call *protokolsätze* (Carnap 1932), namely mere observations. Such social facts are only interesting when they are connected to a larger context. In the words of a more contemporary historian, 'we are not just interested in what actually happened, but also why it happened' (Winkler 2014: 3).

7.1   REFERENDUMS 1793–1900: A FRENCH DEVICE

Leaving aside Switzerland, a *sui generis* case with a total of 584 nationwide referendums between 1848 and 2016, countries in Europe have been modest users of this device (see Qvortrup 2017). It is an addendum and a complement to parliamentary government, not an alternative.

The referendum was initially associated with French politics. Perhaps not surprisingly given the influence of Jean-Jacques Rousseau as 'the author of the French Revolution' (Mercier 1791), all nationwide referendums in Europe in the eighteenth and nineteenth centuries were held in this country (See Table 7.1).[1]

While Rousseau was no doubt a supporter of mechanisms of direct democracy, he contributed little to the practice of referendums and was a good deal more sceptical of popular involvement than most people now appreciate.[2] His contribution was at a higher level of abstraction. This does not mean, however, that the growth of the institution was unrelated to intellectual considerations. Historians of intellectual thought will notice that no less a writer than Nicolas de Condorcet, the father of social choice theory, was the first to develop a rounded argument for having constitutional referendums in the year of the Revolution (de Condorcet 1789). These thoughts were further elaborated

---

[1] Outside Europe there were nationwide referendums in Liberia, Mexico and towards the end of the century in Canada and Australia.

[2] In the *Origin of Inequality* Rousseau was even moderately sceptical of referendums, 'I would not have approved of plebiscites like those of the Romans' (Rousseau 1955: 321). He went on to say that he only wanted referendums as a constitutional safeguard once the issues had been decided by 'the magistrates' (Rousseau, ibid.).

Table 7.1   Nationwide Referendums in Europe 1793–1900

Country	Year	Issue	Turnout (%)	Yes Vote (%)
France	1793	Constitution	13	95
France	1795	Re-elect 2/3 of National Assembly	30	99
France	1795	Constitution	30	99
France	1800	Napoleon as Consul	43	99
France	1802	Napoleon Consul for life	51	99
France	1804	Hereditary rule for Napoleons	43	99
France	1815	Restore empire	18	99
France	1851	Constitutional powers for Napoleon III	79	92
France	1852	Napoleon III as Emperor	79	96
France	1870	Constitution	83	82

Source Qvortrup 2017

in 1793 when Condorcet authored the so-called *Montagnards* Constitution which provided for referendums on constitutional change and even citizen—initiated referendums. While some of these ideas could be traced back to Rousseau and especially to his preface to the *Discourse on Inequality*, it was Condorcet's much more pragmatic and operational ideas that prevailed and were enshrined in the basic law.

This surprisingly liberal 1793 constitution (it enfranchised the Jews and decriminalised homosexuality) enthroned the people as the ultimate sovereign. This did not result in the establishment of pure and participatory democracy. It did mean that the citizens were consulted when Napoleon Bonaparte secured power. Karl Marx summed this up accurately when he observed that the President, through the use of the plebiscite, 'possesses a sort of divine right; he is president by the grace of the people' (Marx 2016: 16). Napoleon Bonaparte organised a total of four referendums. While he could hardly be described as a democrat, it is nevertheless noteworthy that he allowed the Swiss to vote in a referendum on a new constitution in 1802 after he had invaded the country. The opposition to the constitution was (reluctantly) accepted by the French who refrained from imposing their constitution upon their smaller neighbour. The referendum had performed a veto-player function. It is also noteworthy that Napoleon called another referendum after he returned from Elba in 1815. This time on a more liberal constitution drawn up by the philosopher Benjamin Constant.

While the referendum went out of fashion between the Congress of Vienna (1814–1815) and the 1848 revolutions, it was revived by Bonaparte's nephew, Napoleon III, to legitimise his *coup d'état* in 1851. The referendum was also used extensively in Italy to show there was popular support for the *Risorgimento* (the unification of Italy). In the latter country, votes were held in different areas to signify support for unification between 1848 and 1870. Neither of these two referendums were fair, let alone free. The writer George

Sand described Napoleon III's referendums 'as an attack on liberty itself' (Sand 1871: 306). This view is supported by recent scholarship on the French plebiscites (Crook 2015). While, Napoleon III was undoubtedly popular, his regime left nothing to chance. The voting was tightly controlled, and voters were not given a meaningful opportunity to express dissent. While it is a myth that voters were only given the option 'oui', campaigning for a 'non' was non-existent and the Emperor's control over the bureaucracy meant that he could not lose. Similar research on the Italian votes has found that many of the votes were held literally at gunpoint when the—mostly illiterate—Italian voters were asked to support Italian reunification (Beggiato 1999).

Perhaps the best indication that the plebiscite was perceived not as a free choice, but a mechanism of control or repression is provided by literature rather than by historical accounts. Fiction, of course, does not empirically prove theories but it may point to and reflect a deeper and widely shared perception. Giuseppe di Lampedusa's account of the Italian plebiscites in *Il Gattopardo* ('The Leopard') is a case in point. The following exchange about the vote between the protagonist Don Fabrizio and one of his servants Ciccio, says a fair bit about the perceived fairness of the vote:

> You know that everyone in Donnafugata voted 'yes' [said Ciccio]. Don Fabrizio did know this; and that was why his reply merely changed a small enigma into an enigma of history. Before voting many had come to him for advice; all of them had been exhorted sincerely to vote 'yes'. Don Fabrizio, in fact, could not see what else to do...considering the trouble these humble folks might get into if their negative attitude were known. (di Lampedusa 1960: 105)

It is tempting to conclude, therefore, that all the referendums in the nineteenth century were rigged, unfair and undemocratic. This would be inaccurate. Even in France.

French political scientists sometime distinguish between referendums and plebiscites (see, for example, Duval et al. 1970). The former are votes in democracies and can be lost by the proposer. The latter are votes held in more or less autocratic states, votes that tend to be rigged and are almost always won by the incumbent. However, this intrinsically undemocratic nature of the plebiscite does not necessarily mean that the ruler is unpopular. Thus, the plebiscite in 1870 (held shortly before Napoleon was forced from power after the Franco-German War) was regarded by some observers as his desperate attempt to hold on to power. Marx wrote to Engels that 'the referendum is held is the last blow to the empire' (Marx 1974: 516). This assessment seems reasonable in hindsight and before the war. However, at the time, the referendum was actually seen as a stroke of political craftmanship which strengthened the beleaguered Emperor. Louis Napoleon won 82% of the votes. Léon Gambetta, the leader of the opposition, noted in despair, 'We were crushed. The Emperor is more popular than ever' (Gambetta quoted in

Séguin 1990: 370). Emperor Napoleon III did not lose power because he lost the trust of the people but because his army was defeated by Prussia.

Box 7.1

The Referendum Exported
That Louis Napoleon had a fondness for referendums is also evident in his foreign policy. He championed the use of referendums in Italy, and even further afield. France intervened in Mexico, after President Benito Juárez refused to pay his country's debt. Napoleon installed Austrian Archduke Maximilian. But they did not merely act as invaders. Rather, the French insisted on a referendum. This was duly won by 100 per cent! After the French Army withdrew in 1866, the Archduke was captured and executed. Juárez was reinstated and submitted a new constitution to the people. Needless to say, perhaps, this change was also endorsed by 100 per cent of the voters (Duncan 1996).

The referendum went out of fashion in Europe at the end of the nineteenth century. Apart from in Switzerland, there were no nationwide referendums in Europe between 1870 and 1905 when Norway voted to secede from Sweden. Before we leave the nineteenth century, it is helpful to take a quick look at the Helvetic Confederation.

7.2 EXCURSUS: THE REFERENDUM IN SWITZERLAND IN THE NINETEENTH CENTURY

In the late 1840s, Switzerland was in danger of breaking up. Seven Catholic Cantons (*Der Sonderbund*) declared independence in protest against a liberal constitution. War broke out and was won by the seculars after less than a month of fighting. A new constitution was drawn up mainly by the Liberals, the dominant party in the Helvetic Confederation at the time. The Constitution was submitted to the citizens of the new federation and endorsed by 72% of the voters. As a concession, the new Constitution included a provision for referendums in case of constitutional changes. This was considered relatively safe for the Liberals as the confessional parties were split between Calvinists and Catholics who had very little in common.

The *Liberal Party* was the dominant force in Swiss politics until the First World War. The party pursued a twin-track of muscular secularism and free-market, laissez-faire liberalism. Under the majoritarian (first-past-the-post [FPTP]) electoral system the party was able to win a majority of the seats in the *Bundesrat* without winning a majority of the votes. But the party was constrained by the majority in the *Ständerat* (the Second Chamber), which represented the Cantons, and hence allowed the more rurally based periphery to win seats in less populated areas. To change the impasse, the Liberal Party proposed a constitutional revision, which made it possible for the people to challenge ordinary legislation through optional referendums. Their aim was to enact legislation that made education a federal matter and to limit the power of the Catholics. The Liberals expected the Protestants would prevent the Catholics from using the referendum mechanism. It was not a case of turkeys voting for Christmas for the Liberals, rather the party believed another sacrificial animal—in this case the Catholics—would be led to the political slaughter. Idealism was not part of the calculation.

This changed the use of the referendum in Switzerland. The device 'was used by the Catholic conservative opposition to their own advantage and the projects of the radical liberal majority (in the legislature) were shot down as if with a machine gun' (Linder 2008: 103). How did this come about?

To the Liberals' surprise, Catholics and Protestants, their theological disagreements notwithstanding, began to challenge legislation passed by the government through the new referendum mechanism. This resulted in a number of important changes that challenged the Liberals' virtual monopoly on legislative power in the period before the First World War. For example, the rejection of a law on the establishment of the federal ministry of education in 1884, the introduction of the Constitutional initiative in 1891 and the rejection of a more liberal temperance law in 1903 are all examples of how non-liberal groups prevented radical legislation. Thus, through the referendum device, parties in opposition were able to shape public policy. In the view of one observer, 'Strong political minorities were able to threaten and mobilise for an activation of the optional referendum, until they were eventually co-opted into the government'. This tendency became stronger when Switzerland became a multi-party system after the introduction of proportional representation in 1918. At this time, the dominance of the Liberals was over. The rise of the Social Democrats meant that no party was able to dictate policy, and, in any case, any elite compromise could potentially be vetoed by the people.

Overall, the system was not—and is not—one of unfettered direct democracy (see Chapter 10 by Serdült). The people can propose constitutional amendments, but these rarely succeed—fewer than 20% have been successful. In many ways, the system of direct democracy as it is practised in Switzerland today, is close to the ideal envisaged by that country's most famous philosophical son, Jean-Jacques Rousseau: 'the power to propose new laws belong only to the magistrates…the people, for their part, [should] only gave their consent to these laws…if they had time to be convinced' (Rousseau 1955: 321).

7.3   Trends and Tendencies
of European Referendums 1900–1944

'A new political science is needed for a world entirely new', wrote Alexis de Tocqueville in the 1830s (de Tocqueville 2009: 16). The end of the First World War was perceived to have created '*un monde tout nouveau*' in countries that previously had little or no meaningful experience with democracy, let alone referendums. Woodrow Wilson's call to make the 'world safe for democracy' resulted in a greater use of referendums, especially on matters pertaining to sovereignty. The dispute over Schleswig-Holstein between Denmark and Germany, which had caused two wars in the nineteenth century was ultimately resolved with a plebiscite.

Yet, for all his idealism, Wilson was not always true to his word. Indeed, a referendum organised by the council in Tyrol was ignored at the insistence of the French, despite the fact that more than 90% voted for union with Germany (*New York Times*, 11 April 1921). Thus, not all the votes resolved the matters. However, it is worth noting that, has pointed out, 'It was precisely [in] those areas where plebiscites were refused ...that were the subject of revisionist claims by the Nazis in the 1930s'. Tellingly, German revisionist claims were *not* made in areas that were ceded after a referendum, such as Nord Schleswig where there was a large German-speaking minority. This is possibly because 'frontiers that were fixed by plebiscite could not easily be undermined'.

Perhaps, this seismic shift in the tectonic plates of geopolitics necessitated what Tocqueville would have called, '*une science politique nouvelle*'. The political science of the nineteenth century largely saw the plebiscite as a mechanism for granting legitimacy for demagogues with autocratic tendencies (see for example Roshwald 2015). The 'new world' saw a change in this—although, as we shall see, many of the patterns from the previous century persisted.

There were 30 nationwide referendums in Europe between 1900 and the end of the Second World War. During this period there was a slight downward trend towards a more moderate usage of referendums, though not a statistically significant one (see Fig. 7.1). The use of referendums during this period was uneven and characterised by ebbs and flows.

Immediately after the First World War there were many referendums, then a smaller spike in the late 1920s, and a small upsurge in the 1930s. The first referendums were mainly held in democratic countries; the same was broadly true in the late 1920s, but the referendums in the 1930s were in large measure held in non-democratic and even totalitarian countries.

The referendums can be divided between three types of regimes, to wit: democratic countries, competitive authoritarian regimes and dictatorships, as shown in Fig. 7.2. Using the −10 to +10 categorisation used by Polity IV Scores (where the former is the most undemocratic and the latter is the most democratic), we find there were 15 referendums in democratic countries, six in competitive authoritarian regimes and nine in non-democratic states between 1900 and 1944. Notwithstanding the predominance of autocratic leaders at the time, most referendums were held in democratic states, here defined as countries that scored +10 on Polity IV (Fig. 7.2).

While there were referendums on institutional issues, such as the abolition of the Second Chamber in Denmark (1939) and the role of constitutional monarchs (Luxembourg 1919), the most salient issue at the time was prohibition. Norway voted twice on the issue (1919 and 1926), and the issue was

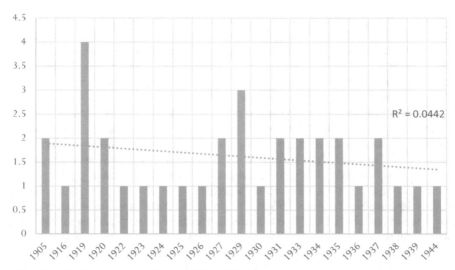

Fig. 7.1 Referendums in Europe 1900–1944

Fig. 7.2 Referendums
by Regime Type
1900–1944 ([N = 30]
Source Qvortrup 2017)

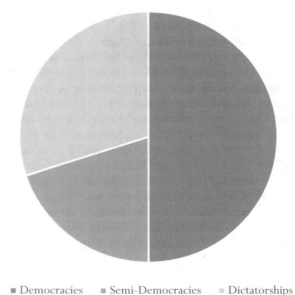

■ Democracies   ■ Semi-Democracies   ■ Dictatorships

submitted to the voters in Sweden (1922) and Finland (1931).[3] There were

---

[3]In the year of this referendum Finland was not a full democracy. Due to the far-right Lapua Movement, which used kidnappings and violent attacks to forward its anti-communist ideology, the country slipped to 4 on Polity IV in 1931 (see Raunio 2004).

also votes in Iceland in 1933 (this country was formally under the Danish Crown until the independence referendum in 1944) and the Faroe Islands (1907).

Why were these referendums held? It seems there was a pattern of sorts. All the votes were a result of split political parties or disagreements between coalition partners. In Sweden prohibition was an issue that divided the bourgeois parties and had to be defused (Ruin 1996). In Finland, the issue 'cut across parties' (Suksi 1996: 52). And, in Norway, 'the parties in the Centre-right bloc had divergent views [on the subject], which made governing difficult. Three governments fell as a result of the disagreement [over the prohibition] issue' (Björklund 2003: 69). There were also similarities in the outcome of the referendums. While Norway voted to introduce prohibition in 1919, this was reversed in 1926. The votes in the Faroe Islands (1907), Sweden (1922), Finland (1931) and Iceland (1933) all yielded victory to the opponents of prohibition.

The referendums in the semi-democratic or outright totalitarian systems had fewer similarities. In Greece, citizens voted to end the monarchy in 1924 as a result of the king's less than skillful handling of the Greco-Turkish war. However, after a military coup precipitated by the economic crisis in the 1930, they voted for the re-establishment of the monarchy in a referendum that was decried as rigged at the time. Greece was not the only country where democratic breakdown was approved via plebiscite. In Estonia, rejection of two proposed constitutional reforms, led to a constitutional initiative sponsored by the far-right Veterans' League in 1932, which 'paved the way for the establishment of authoritarian rule' (Smith 2013: 18). In other semi-democratic states, the trend towards authoritarian rule was averted. Ireland scored a respectable 8 on the Polity IV scale in 1937, the year when Éamon De Valera submitted his constitution to the voters. However, before that in 1927 when the country had scored 10 on this scale, the government had limited the rights to engage in direct democratic participation. Ireland had provisions for citizens' initiatives under the *Irish Free State Constitution Act*. In 1928, the opposition party, *Fianna Fáil*, had collected the 75,000 signatures required to overturn the requirement that members of the *Dáil* swear allegiance to the British Monarch. However, the then Irish Prime Minister, William Thomas Cosgrave, responded not by holding a referendum, but by abolishing the provision before a plebiscite could take place (Gallagher 1996: 16).

7.4   Referendums Under the Frozen Party System 1945–1989

Stein Rokkan and Seymour M. Lipset famously observed that the Western European Party System 'froze' in the mid-1920s (Lipset and Rokkan 1967). For the next half century, the political parties neatly represented particular, often class-based, constituencies and the majority of the voters were in agreement with the later much maligned 'elites'. Yet, much as the party systems were characterised by stability there was, nevertheless, a tendency towards a growing use of referendums. Increasingly, as we shall see, issues that were 'too hot to handle' (Matsusaka 1992: 543) were submitted to the voters (Figs. 7.3 and 7.4).

To explain the growing use of referendums one must be cautious and compare like with like. Above all there is, as Gordon Smith noticed, a fundamental difference between 'controlled' and 'uncontrolled' referendums (Smith 1976). The former are referendums held on the governments' initiative, usually when they think they can win. The latter are referendums that are mandated by the constitution or held as a result of a public petition.

Over the period, the vast plurality of the votes were 'uncontrolled' votes on constitutional changes or amendments. For example, in Denmark (1953), France (1946 and 1958) and on no fewer than eleven occasions in the Republic of Ireland, governments of different colour were forced by the letter of the constitution to submit issues to the voters. In 1959 and 1968, respectively, Prime Ministers Éamon de Valera and Jack Lynch had no choice but to submit the changes of the electoral system to the voters. Both referendums were lost.

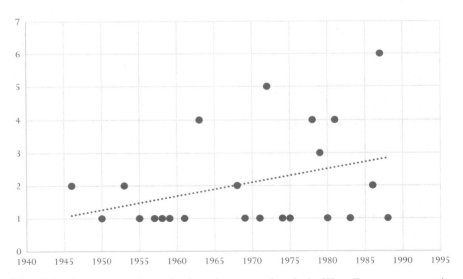

Fig. 7.3 Average number of referendums per decade in West European countries 1945–1990 (*Note* There is a tendency towards more referendums over the period [a correlation of R = .33 [Significant at: p < .01] between the number of votes and years]. Based on Data from C2D and Qvortrup 2017)

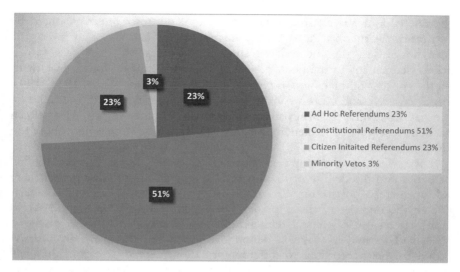

Fig. 7.4 Referendums in Western Europe by Type (N = 50)

During this time the referendum was mostly a 'veto player'; an institutional device, used mainly in countries that had provisions for constitutional referendums, in which certain or all changes to the Basic Laws had to be approved by a majority of the voters. Thus, in this period, there were constitutional referendums in Italy (1946), France (1945, 1946, 1958), Belgium (1950), Denmark (1953, 1961, 1969, 1971, 1978) and Ireland (1959, 1968, 1972, 1979, 1983, 1984, 1986, and 1987). In this period, just over 50% (35 out of 69) of the referendums fell in this category of veto-player.

During the earlier part of this period (1945–1970), referendums were held mainly on controversial issues that divided the political elite. Some of these pertained to fundamental issues of governance, which required endorsement via referendums. For example, the referendums on changing the electoral system from First-Past-the-Post to the Single Transferable Vote in Ireland in 1959 and 1968 (both of which failed) were controversial attempts by *Fianna Fáil* to blatantly gerrymander the constitution to suit their purposes. So too were Charles de Gaulle's referendum in 1958 on the establishment of the Fifth Republic, and his failed attempt to limit the powers of the Senate in 1969. Similarly, the referendums in Italy and Belgium on the monarchy were highly partisan affairs (see Chapter 8 by Wouters and Andrione-Moylan).

By contrast, the Danish referendum on a new constitution in 1953 and the subsequent votes on lowering the voting age were the result of a widespread consensus among the political parties in that country. These referendums were exceptions. Overall, most referendums in the immediate post-World War Two era were held on divisive constitutional issues. The referendum was a constitutional safeguard. Constitutional theorists will notice that this use of the referendum was consistent with the role of the referendum espoused by constitutional theorist A. V. Dicey. According to that Victorian jurist, the referendum was, 'the one available check on party leaders [that] gives formal acknowledgement to the doctrine which lies at the bottom for its enactment on the consent of the nation as represented by its electors' (Dicey 1911: 190). For Dicey, referendums on constitutional changes would guard 'the rights of the nation against the usurpation of national authority of any party which happens to have a Parliamentary majority' (Dicey to Lord Salisbury quoted in Cosgrove 1981:106).

These were not the only referendums held in the period between the fall of Hitler and the demise of the Soviet Union. During the same period there was an increase in the number of ad hoc (or facultative) referendums relative to the number of these in the period leading up to the Second World War. Sixteen out of the 69 referendums in the period fell in this category. It is hard to find a common denominator between them, mainly because they were held according to different provisions. For this reason, they will be treated as distinct cases in this chapter. Fundamentally there is a distinction between referendums called by the executive with the plebiscitary aim of securing popular support (e.g. as in the cases of Charles de Gaulle as discussed in the next section and by Morel in Chapter 9) and referendums called to resolve an intra-coalition or intra-party disagreement (such as the 1975 British referendum on European Economic Community [EEC] membership). We will start with the former.

7.4.1   Ad Hoc Plebiscitary Referendums

Article 11 of the 1958 French Constitution provides that:

> The President of the Republic may, on a recommendation from the Government when Parliament is in session, or on a joint motion of the two Houses, published in the *Journal Officiel*, submit to a referendum any Government Bill which deals with the organization of the public authorities, or with reforms relating to the economic, social or environmental policy of the Nation, and to the public services contributing thereto, or which provides for authorization to ratify a treaty which, although not contrary to the Constitution, would affect the functioning of the institutions.

The aim of the provision was to find a tiebreaker in cases where there was a deadlock between the President and the Parliament. The provision was introduced to institutionalise the mechanism used by Louis Napoleon (see Sect. 7.1) and it was used four times by de Gaulle, twice over Algeria, once to introduce the direct election of the President—although this was ruled unconstitutional by the *Conseil Constitutionnel* and lastly—and fatally—on the issue of Senate and local government reform. The latter vote was lost and precipitated de Gaulle's resignation (see Chapter 9 by Morel). It should be noted here that de Gaulle's resignation was an extremely rare example of a head of government stepping down after a defeat in a referendum. (On this see Appendix 7.1).

Charles de Gaulle was not an accidental referendum-user but a politician who was ideologically committed to using this device as a mechanism of winning approval for controversial issues. As he put it:

> I was convinced that sovereignty belongs to the people, provided they express themselves directly and as a whole. But I refused to accept that [sovereignty] could be parcelled out among the different interests represented by the parties. I found it necessary for the government to derive not from Parliament, in other words the parties but from over and above them, from a leader directly mandated by the nation as a whole (de Gaulle 1971: 6).

From a theoretical perspective it is interesting that this justification for holding a referendum was almost identical with the position espoused by Carl Schmitt. In *Legality and Legitimacy*, the controversial German jurist wrote, 'The institutions of direct democracy, as an unavoidable consequence of democratic thinking, [are] in a superior position to the so-called indirect democracy of the parliamentary state' (Schmitt 1932: 65). As opposed to Parliament—whose powers are but delegated by the people—the people themselves, have an inbuilt legitimacy. Hence, the 'referendum is always a higher form of decision' (Schmitt 1932: 93) as 'plebiscitary legitimacy is the single type of state justification that may be generally acknowledged today as valid' (Schmitt 1932: 64). It is unlikely that de Gaulle would have read the German theorist, but the near identical thinking between the French President and the apologist for the Third Reich does hint at the former's authoritarian-leaning tendencies.

After de Gaulle's departure in 1969, the use of referendums fell considerably. His successor Georges Pompidou held a referendum pursuant of Article 11 to win approval for the UK, Norway, Denmark and Ireland's entry into the EEC (the forerunner of the EU as discussed by Morel and Svensson in Chapters 9 and 20) and François Mitterrand held referendums on the future of New Caledonia in 1988 and on the Maastricht Treaty in 1992. It seems that it took a charismatic leader to make use of Article 11 and that none of his successors had the political gravitas to make use for the provision.

No other West European country has similar provisions for plebiscitary referendums. For this reason, no other countries have had exactly comparable experiences. However, this does not mean that no other West European leaders have used (or attempted to use) the referendum to circumvent opposition from a obstinate opposition. For example, the Danish Prime Minister Poul Schlüter's referendum on the Single European Act in 1986 followed a similar logic. When the *Folketing* voted No to the 'Single Market', Schlüter—the leader of a centre-right minority coalition—submitted the issue to a nonbinding referendum and won a clear majority (Worre 1988). He was not the only one to do so. In 1978, the Conservative *ÖVP* and the *FPÖ*, then in opposition in Austria, were opposed to the opening of the Zwetendorf Nuclear power station. Sensing the issue was controversial with a year to go before the next parliamentary election, Social Democrat Chancellor Bruno Kreisky decided to hold a referendum on the subject (Pelinka 1983). He did not need to do so, as his party had a majority in the *Nationalrat* (the lower house). Kreisky narrowly lost the referendum but he did not resign. Indeed, he won an absolute majority of the vote at the general election the following year and increased his party's representation in the parliament (Nohlen and Stöver 2010: 196).

7.4.2   Policy-Defusing Referendums

While plebiscitary referendums were relatively rare, it became increasingly common to use the referendum as a mechanism to defuse controversial issues. As we saw in Sect. 7.3, votes on prohibition were held in Norway, Finland and Sweden between the Great Wars. The same pattern repeated itself in the post-World War Two era.

Disagreement among the parties in Sweden led to the multi-option referendums on pension plans in 1957 and on nuclear power in 1980. And, disagreement over the issue of EEC membership between the parties in the Norwegian centre-right led to the ill-fated (for the government) referendum on EEC membership in 1972. Indeed, it could even be argued that the Danish referendum on the same issue, resulted from a split among the parties on the left (see Svensson 2020). While the then Danish Prime Minister, Jens-Otto Krag, was a passionate supporter of EEC membership, many members of his own Social Democratic Party were opposed to membership. The same was true for *Socialistisk Folkeparti* (a party, which provided confidence and supply to the minority government). Overall, these referendums were held in an attempt to 'agree to disagree'.

Norwegian political scientist Tor Bjørklund has suggested that for such referendums 'to succeed, two conditions are important: parties which are split and strong commitment on the part of the voters' (Bjørklund 1982: 237). This was true for Sweden in 1957, when 'there was disagreement between the two parties that formed the government, namely the Social Democrats and the Agrarians' (Ruin 1996: 175).

Was this just a Scandinavian phenomenon? Not at all. The same tendencies can be identified in Britain. In the early 1970s, the Labour Party was split over Europe. The parliamentary party was overwhelmingly in favour of Britain's membership of the Common Market (or EEC), but much of the rank and file wanted to leave the newly joined organisation. When Tony Benn, the unofficial leader of Labour's anti-marketeers, first put forward the idea of holding a referendum, the party leadership snubbed his proposal. But, as Jim Callaghan presciently remarked in 1970, the referendum idea was 'a little rubber life raft into which the whole party may one day have to climb' (quoted in Roberts 2015).

So, constitutional necessity, attempts to by-pass the legislature, and the search for a mechanism for 'agreeing to disagree' are all reasons for holding referendums. So, too, are minority vetos (known from Denmark and Slovenia, where a minority in parliament can demand a referendum before a Bill becomes law) and citizen-initiated referendums (a prominent part of the Italian constitution, according to which 500,000 citizens can demand a referendum on any existing law). The latter two require their own distinct treatment as they follow different logics.

The Danish Minority veto, provides that 'one-third of the members of the Folketing may, within three weekdays from the final passing of the Bill, request of the Speaker of the Parliament that the Bill be submitted to a referendum' according to Art. 42 of the Danish Constitution. This provision has only been used once. In 1963 three laws pertaining to town planning issues were rejected by the voters. The vote was prompted by the Danish Social Democrats' attempts to break with the tradition of consensus politics. Having lost the referendum on this relatively mundane issue prompted the Government of Prime Minister Jens-Otto Krag to reach out and make agreements with the opposition. As a Danish scholar has observed, the referendum served as 'minority protection' (Svensson 1996). While the Danish provision has been used only once, the similar provision in the Slovenian constitution has been used extensively, often as a political tactic to obstruct the sitting government. As a result of this the provision was eliminated in a constitutional reform in 2013.

Like the Danish Art. 42 provision, there is something *sui generis* about the use of the referendum in Italy (although a similar provision exists in Uruguay). All the nationwide citizen-initiated referendums in Europe 1945–1990 (with the exception of Switzerland, Liechtenstein and a single initiative in Hungary in 1989) took place in Italy at the end of the period of *La partitocrazia* (Pasquino 1945), the epoch when decisions were taken by the (relatively unaccountable) higher echelons of the Christian Democratic Party (DC).

After 1974, when the Christian Democrats, made the fatal mistake of implementing a dormant clause in the 1946 Constitution allowing for citizen-initiated referendums, the voters were able to call referendums. Yet, while the subsequent referendums were not a result of internal splits in the parties, it is interesting that the original decision to implement the provision in Art. 75 of the 1946 Constitution, was a result of efforts to depoliticise issues that would make a possible government between DC and Enrico Berlinguer's reformed communist party (PCI). Implementing Art. 75 would allow citizens to demand a referendum on divorce, something that, given its ties with the Catholic Church, DC was not in a position to do (Armaroli 1974).

This short-term consideration led to the adoption of a provision which, at least indirectly, led to the demise of the post-war Italian Party system. The old political parties were essentially undermined when laws providing for

Table 7.2   Italian Abrogative Referendums 1974–1990

Year	Issue	Turnout (%)	Yes Vote (%)
1974	Abolish divorce law	87	40
1978	Abolish police powers	81	23
1978	Abolish state funding of parties	81	43
1981	Abolish police anti-terror powers	79	14
1981	Restrict arms licences	79	14
1981	Abortion law	79	32
1981	Liberalise abortion laws	79	11
1985	Wage indexation	77	45
1987	Civil liability for magistrates	65	80
1987	Trial of ministers	65	85
1987	Anti-Nuclear power sites	65	80
1987	Anti-Nuclear power subsidies	65	79
1987	Anti-Nuclear power participation abroad	65	71
1990	European Union mandate	43	88
1990	Prohibit hunting	42	92
1990	Restrict toxins in Food	62	93

Source Qvortrup 2017

party-funding were abrogated in the early 1990s. At this stage, the abrogative referendum had already been used to by-pass the political class in votes to abrogate the ban on abortion in 1979. As Table 7.2 shows, many issues that cut across the traditional left-right divide were submitted to the Italian voters in abrogative referendums (referendums requested by the voters) between 1974 and 1990. In some respects, therefore, it could be argued that the growing use of this type of referendum is a result of the thaw of the frozen party system.

7.4.3   Referendums by Issue

It is one thing to identify the types of referendums held and the reasons for submitting issues to the voters. It is another to specify the issues that were put to a vote. In Western Europe, in the period after the Second World War up to the fall of the Berlin Wall, 42% of the referendums concerned institutional reform (typically reform of the judiciary, parliament, or electoral reform), followed by energy/nuclear power (17%). Behind this we find European integration or membership and new constitutions (both 13%). Only 2% pertained to the economy (such as pension reform in Sweden in 1957). This latter is not surprising, of course, these were issues that were covered by the parties' ideologies (Fig. 7.5).

That institutional or constitutional issues dominate is perhaps an indication that many countries needed to rebuild their political systems after authoritarian rule. This was true for Italy, Germany and to a degree France after the

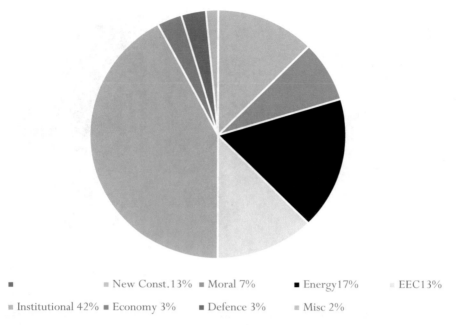

■   ■ New Const.13% ■ Moral 7%   ■ Energy17%   ▫ EEC13%

■ Institutional 42% ■ Economy 3%   ■ Defence 3%   ▫ Misc 2%

Fig. 7.5   Referendums in Western Europe by Issue 1945–1989

Second World War, and Spain and Greece in the 1970s. The other issues such as energy and the EEC were notable for being 'valence' issues that cut across party lines, which were submitted to the voters for fear of alienating voters in the elections. That moral and economic issues were rarely put to a vote reflects the fact that these were core issues, which were consistent with the philosophies of the respective parties. Such issues were only put to a vote when there were coalition governments that disagreed on them (as in the aforementioned Swedish Pension case in 1957).

7.4.4   Referendums 1990–

The fall of the Berlin Wall led to a proliferation of direct democracy in former Communist countries. Most of these states introduced (or re-introduced) provisions of referendums. In some countries, such as Hungary, Latvia, Lithuania and Ukraine provisions for citizens' initiatives were introduced. Most of the countries had provisions for ad hoc referendums and all but Bosnia had provisions for mandatory constitutional referendums. Between 1990 and 2018 a plurality of the referendums in Eastern Europe were ad hoc (a total of 73 or 40%), followed by 34% mandatory constitutional referendums and 26% citizens' initiatives (Fig. 7.6).

During the same period there were 139 referendums in Western Europe. Of these, 27 were ad hoc (such as François Mitterrand's referendum on the

Fig. 7.6 Types of
Referendum in Former
Communist Countries
1990–2018 (N = 202
[Date: C2D –Aarau])

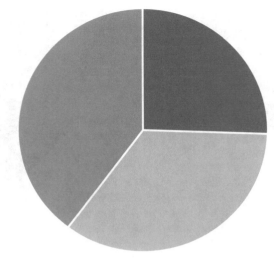

■ Initiatives 26%   ■ Constitutional Ref 34%   ■ Ad Hoc 40%

Maastricht Treaty 1992 and David Cameron's Brexit referendum in 2016), 35 were constitutional referendums (26 of which were in Ireland) and 76 were citizen-initiated referendums, accounting for 55%. All but one of the citizen-initiated referendums were in Italy and tiny Liechtenstein—with the odd one out being a failed citizen-initiated referendum to ban hunting in Malta.

Rather than follow a particular trend, most of the referendums are accounted for by *sui generis* developments in individual countries, such as citizen-initiated referendums in Italy, Slovakia and Slovenia, constitutional referendums in Ireland and, more recently, non-binding constitutional referendums in Iceland. It seems the occurrence of referendums reflects unique circumstance and traditions rather than uniform patterns that can be summarised in recurrent patterns or 'laws'. This begs the question whether there is the same lack of general pattern in the issues that are put to a vote.

Figures 7.7–7.8 show the percental distribution of the issues put to a vote in, respectively, the former Communist countries and West European countries.

There was a total of 84 referendums in the former communist countries in the period 1989–2018. The largest percentage concerned constitutional reform (42% of the total). As in Western Europe during the 1945–1990 period there a high percentage of referendums on new constitutions, although, in Western Europe the figure was only 13 per cent in the previous period. Why were there more constitutional referendums in the former communist countries? Largely, it would appear, because many of the countries had to begin afresh and because many of them had little if any experience with systems of polyarchy. Thus, in Romania (1991), Russia (1993) and Albania (1994) entirely new constitutions were submitted to the voters. In many ways, these

Fig. 7.7 Types of
Referendum in West
European Countries
1990–2018

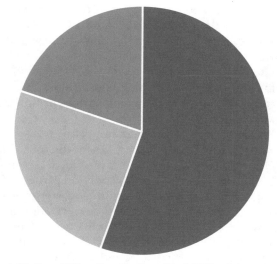

■ Initiatives 55% ■ Constitutional Ref. 25% ■ Ad Hoc20%

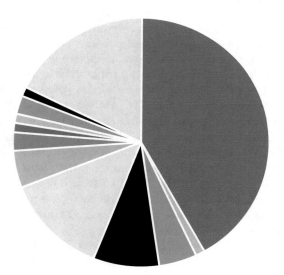

■ Const 42%   ■ Human Rights1%   ■ Energy5%   ■ EU8%
■ Inst13%   ■ Defence5%   ■ Health/Edu2%   ■ Immigration1%
■ Transport1%   ■ Media2%   ■ International2% ■ Economic/Social 1%

Fig. 7.8 Referendums in Eastern Europe by Issue 1990–2018

referendums were strikingly similar to the legitimising referendums held in France and Italy immediately after the Second World War, and the referendums to give the people's blessings to new and democratic constitutions in Spain and Greece in the mid-1970s.

But in many other cases, the referendums pertained to revisions of and amendments to existing constitutions. The latter especially focussed on reforms of the electoral system, such as in Romania (2007), Moldova (2010) and Poland (2015).

In Eastern Europe there was also a large number of referendums on economic issues, constituting 17% of the total. This is different from Western Europe and can probably be explained as a result of institutional factors. Unlike in Western Europe, the political parties in the East were not established along social class issues, which might have prompted new political parties to hold referendums on matters such as taxation in Poland (2015) and pension reform in Slovenia (2011). The parties did not have the solid and reliable support that characterised the class-parties in Western Europe. Rather, the East European parties were cadre-parties, or catch-all-parties (Koole 1996). For these parties, it was essential not to alienate the electorate. Hence controversial issues pertaining to social and economic affairs were submitted to the voters, as they, in Matsusaka's apt phrase, were 'too hot to handle' (1992).

Another issue, which divided political parties in Western Europe in the 1970s and the 1980s was, as we saw above, nuclear power. This issue also led to referendums in former communist countries, albeit with different results. As in Austria in 1978, in 2012 a majority of the voters in Lithuania voted against a nuclear power station (Maj 2018: 159). Yet, not all electorates were as sceptical as the Lithuanians; in Bulgaria 61% of the voters, voted 'yes' to the question, 'Should nuclear energy be developed in Bulgaria through the construction of a new nuclear power plant?' (Peicheva 2018: 65). Though in the latter case, as in so many other referendums, the result was void due to a very low turnout. A mere 20% bothered to turn out to vote in the initiative sponsored by the leftist Bulgarian Socialist Party. Absent a legally binding result, the National Assembly subsequently rejected a motion for developing atomic energy (Peicheva 2018: ibid.).

Things have changed considerably in Western Europe too compared to the earlier period. While there is still a large number of referendums on institutional reform (e.g. electoral reforms in Britain and Italy, and various constitutional amendments in Iceland and Ireland), which account for 34% of the cases, the category of EU referendums has grown to 24% (up from 13% in the previous era). But what is, perhaps, most remarkable is the large number of referendums on economic issues have increased from two to 14% in the period 1990–2018, though the majority of the latter being citizen-initiated referendums in Italy (Fig. 7.9).

Overall, therefore, there seems to have been a convergence of types of issues put to referendums between the former communist countries and countries in Western Europe.

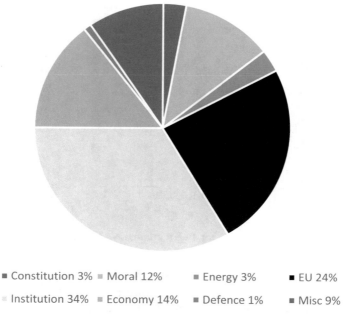

- Constitution 3%   - Moral 12%   - Energy 3%   - EU 24%

- Institution 34%   - Economy 14%   - Defence 1%   - Misc 9%

Fig. 7.9   Referendums in Western Europe by Issue 1990–2018 (*Source* C2D and Qvortrup 2017)

So, what does all this mean for the much-discussed gulf between the voters and their representatives. Are referendums populist tools that allow the people to veto 'sensible' legislation. Do they always say, 'No' as postulated by Tage Erlander? As Fig. 7.10 shows, the average Yes vote has been over 50% in all decades since the Second World War.

Moreover, since 1990, only 33% of all European referendums have seen the governments' positions defeated. This is exactly the same percentage of referendums that were defeated between 1945 and 1990. The proposition that referendums are a recipe for populism gone amok seems difficult to sustain.

7.5   CONCLUSION

'The only really effective weapon of popular control in a democratic regime is the capacity of the electorate to throw a party from power' (Key 1968: 76). Maybe this was broadly true in the 1960s. It no longer is. But that does not mean that our polities have become more direct democratic. Despite the increase in the number of referendums, overall, it has *not* allowed the people to set the agenda. In most cases, the referendum has performed the function of a constitutional safeguard. A. V. Dicey spoke of the referendum as a mechanism 'which by delaying alterations in the constitution, protect[s] the sovereignty of the people' (Dicey 1890: 506).

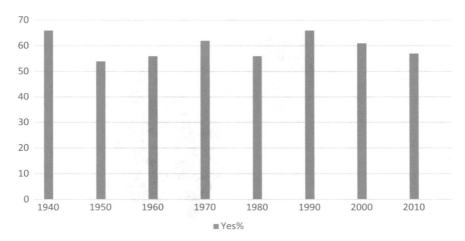

Fig. 7.10 Average Yes Vote (%) for Referendums 1945–2016

There are some indications that the institution has been used in a way that is consistent with this ideal. The many Irish constitutional referendums in recent years, the Italian vote on Matteo Renzi's ill-fated constitution in 2016 and, before that, the Scottish vote on independence were all examples of how the people were able to veto 'alterations in the constitution', or, in the case of Ireland, amendments to the Basic Law.

From a democratic theory point of view, it is noteworthy that most referendums have fallen into the democratic safeguard category. To paraphrase the remark by a democratic theorist at the beginning of the chapter, the 'looks democratic and it is'. Yes, spectators do 'get dragged on stage to say a simple yes or no to a proposition the have played no part in devising' (Runciman 2018: 47), but that is in the nature of things, and arguably a natural consequence of any principal-agent model.

However, this is only true for Western Europe. In Eastern Europe, a plurality of referendums have been ad hoc. Whereas in the former countries, the referendum is a constitutional safeguard, in several former communist countries it is still used as a policy weapon, as it has been in Slovakia and in Romania's recall referendums. Interestingly, the use of the referendum in Britain, explored in several chapters of this volume, is more like in Eastern Europe than in West European democracies.

Of course, some referendums throw up controversial results without showing a massive gulf between the people and the elite. Indeed, it is noteworthy that over sixty per cent of referendums have been 'pro-hegemonic'; the regime won the vote. That this figure has been relatively unchanged over the years, is perhaps an indication that the much-debated chasm between the voters and their representatives is somewhat overstated. Maybe, the referendum is not a populist tool but rather a political safety valve that provides a mechanism for the voters to say that 'enough is enough', that they want a slower pace or a change of direction. Even Viktor Orbán had to concede defeat when his referendum on migration was void due to a boycott in 2016. Even a semi-autocratic leader like the Hungarian Prime Minister was restrained by direct democracy (see Batory in Chapter 31). This provides a glimmer of hope at a time when many are gloomy.

APPENDIX 7.1: DO PRIME MINISTERS AND PRESIDENTS RESIGN WHEN THEY LOSE REFERENDUMS?

David Cameron resigned immediately after he lost the Brexit referendum in 2016. So did Alex Salmond after a majority of the Scottish votes said 'No' to independence in 2014. So, do Prime Ministers resign when they lose? Do presidents? A scholar of French politics famously wrote about 'Presidential suicide by plebiscite" to describe Charles De Gaulle's exit, when the General lost the referendum in April 1969 (Hayward 1969).

However, this is very much the exception to the rule. Apart from the resignation of *Statsminister* Trygve Bratteli after a majority of the Norwegian voters had rejected EEC membership in 1972 (Bjørklund 1997: 39), heads of government have *not* resigned following referendum defeats. Austrian Chancellor Kreisky stayed put, although he, arguably, made the referendum on Zwetendorf into a vote of confidence in himself, yet he duly went on to win the federal election the following year, in 1979. Out of the 275 referendums held in Europe since 1945, prime ministers or presidents only resigned in four cases. This represents a mere 1.4% of the cases.

Though he was no oracle on the subject, Max Weber was broadly correct when he observed:

> A disavowal of the leading officials through a plebiscite which rejects their proposals does not and cannot enforce their resignation, as does a vote of no-confidence in parliamentary states. For the negative vote does not identify its reasons and does not oblige the negatively voting mass, in the way that a parliamentary majority voting against a government does. (Weber 1976: 865, Author's translation)

BIBLIOGRAPHY

Amery, L. S. (1947). *Thoughts on the Constitution*. Oxford: Oxford University Press.
Armaroli, P. (1974). Referendum abrogativo e classe politica. *Italian Political Science Review/Rivista Italiana Di Scienza Politica, 4*(3), 561–587.
Beggiato, E. (1999). *La grande truffa*. Venice: Venice Academic Press.
Bjørklund, T. (1982). The Demand for Referendum: When Does It Arise and When Does It Succeed? *Scandinavian Political Studies, 5*(3), 237–260.
Bjørklund, T. (1997). *Om folkeavstemninger: Norge og Norden 1905–1994*. Universitetsforlaget.

Björklund, T. (2003). *Om Folkeavstemninger*. Oslo: Universitetsforlaget.

Bogdanor, V. (1981). Referendums and Separatism II. In A. Ranney (Ed.), *The Referendum Device* (pp. 143–158). Washington, DC: American Enterprise Institute.

Carnap, R. (1932). Über Protokolsätze. *Erkenntnis, 2*(3), 215–228.

Cosgrove, R. A. (1981). *The Rule of Law: Albert Venn Dicey—Victorian Jurist*. London: Macmillan.

Crook, M. (2015, September). Protest Voting: The Revolutionary Origins of Annotated Ballot Papers cast in French Plebiscites, 1851–1870, *French History, 29*(3), 349–369.

Dicey, A. V. (1890). Ought the Referendum to Be Introduced into England? *Contemporary Review, 57,* 489–494.

Dicey, A. V. (1911). *A Leap in the Dark*. London: John Murrey.

Duncan, R. H. (1996). Political Legitimation and Maximilian's Second Empire in Mexico, 1864–1867. *Mexican Studies/Estudios Mexicanos, 12*(1), 27–66.

Duval, H., George J., & Leblanc-Dechoisay, P. Y. (1970). *Referendum et plébiscite.* FeniXX.

Gallagher, M. (1996). Ireland: The Referendum as a Conservative Device? In M. Gallagher & P.-V. Uleri (Eds.), *The Referendum Experience in Europe* (pp. 86–105). London: Palgrave Macmillan.

de Condorcet, N. (1789). *Sur la nécessité de faire ratifier la Constitution par les citoyens et sur la formation des communautés de campagne*. Paris: P.D. Pierres.

de Gaulle, C. (1971). *Memories of Hope*. London: Weidenfeld and Nicolson.

de Tocqueville, A. (2009 [1848]). *De la Démocratie en Amerique*. Edition bilingue. Indianapolis, IN: Liberty Fund.

di Lampedusa, G. T. (1960). *The Leopard*. New York: Random House.

Hayward, J. E. S. (1969). Presidential Suicide by Plebiscite: De Gaulle's Exit, April 1969. *Parliamentary Affairs, 22,* 289–319.

Key, V. O. (1968). *The Responsible Electorate. Rationality in Presidential Voting 1936–1960*. New York: Vintage Books.

Koole, R. (1996). Cadre, Catch-all or Cartel? A Comment on the Notion of the Cartel Party. *Party Politics, 2*(4), 507–523.

Lewin, L. (1988). *A Century of Swedish Politics*. Cambridge: Cambridge University Press.

Linder, W. (2008). *Swiss Democracy: Possible Solutions to Conflict in Multicultural Societies*. London: Macmillan Press and St. Martin's Press.

Lipset, S. M., & Rokkan, S. (1967). *Party Systems and Voter Alignments: Cross Sectional Perspectives*. Toronto: The Free Press.

Maj, D. (2018). Direct Democracy in Lithuania. In Maria Marczewska-Rytko (Ed.), *Handbook of Direct Democracy in Central-and Eastern Europe* (pp. 146–163). Opladen: Barbara Budrich Publishers.

Marx, K. (1974). Marx and Engels. 18 Mai 1870. In *Marx-Engels Werke*, Vol. 32 (pp. 516–517). Berlin: Dietz Verlag.

Marx, K. (2016) [1852]. *Der achtzehnte Brumaire des Louis Bonaparte*. Berlin: Piper.

Matsusaka, J. (1992). The Economics of Direct Legislation. *The Quarterly Journal of Economics, 107*(2), 541–571.

Mercier, L.-S. (1791). *De Jean-Jacques Rousseau considéré comme l'un des premiers auteurs de la Révolution*. Paris: Buisson.

New York Times. (1921, April 11). French Try to Stop Tyrol Plebiscite: Vote on Annexation to Germany Set for April 24 Strongly Opposed by Paris, A6.

Nohlen, D., & Stöver, P. (2010). *Elections in Europe: A data handbook.* Baden-Baden: Nomos.

Pasquino, G. (1945). *La partitocrazia* (p. 95). Dizionario critico: La politica italiana.

Piecheva, D. (2018). Direct Democracy in Bulgaria. In Maria Marczewska-Rytko (Ed.), *Handbook of Direct Democracy in Central-and Eastern Europe* (pp. 57–68). Opladen: Barbara Budrich Publishers.

Pelinka, A. (1983). The Nuclear Power Referendum in Austria. *Electoral Studies, 2*(3), 253–261.

Qvortrup, M. (2017). *Referendums Around the World.* London: Palgrave.

Ranke, L. von. (1824). *Geschichte der romerischen Volker von 1494 bis 1535.*

Raunio, T. (2004). The Changing Finnish Democracy: Stronger Parliamentary Accountability, Coalescing Political Parties and Weaker External Constraints. *Scandinavian Political Studies, 27*(2), 133–152.

Roberts, R. (2015, January 23). Back to the Future: Britain's 1975 Referendum on Europe. *New Statesman.*

Roshwald, A. (2015). The Daily Plebiscite as Twenty-first-century Reality? *Ethnopolitics, 14*(5), 443–450.

Rousseau, J.-J. (1955 [1755]). Discours sur l'origine et les fondements de l'inégalité parmi les hommes. In J.-J. Rousseau (Ed.), *Oeuvres III.* Paris: Galimard.

Ruin, O. (1996). Sweden: The Referendum as an Instrument for Defusing Political Issues. In M. Gallagher & P.-V. Uleri (Eds.), *The Referendum Experience in Europe* (pp. 171–184). London: Palgrave Macmillan.

Runciman, D. (2018). *How Democracy Ends.* London: Profile Books.

Sand, G. (1871). *Journal d'un Voyageur pendant la guerre.* Paris: Michel Lévy.

Schmitt, C. (1932). *Legalitat und Legitimität.* Berlin: Duncker und Humblot.

Séguin, P. (1990). *Louis Napolén le Grand.* Paris: Bernard Grasset.

Smith, G. (1976). The Functional Properties of the Referendum. *European Journal of Political Research, 4*(1), 1–23.

Smith, D. (2013). *Estonia: Independence and European Integration.* London: Routledge.

Suksi, M. (1996). Finland: The Referendum as a Dormant Issue. In M. Gallagher & P.-V. Uleri (Eds.), *The Referendum Experience in Europe* (pp. 52–65). London: Palgrave Macmillan.

Svensson, P. (1996). Denmark: The Referendum as Minority Protection. In M. Gallagher & P.-V. Uleri (Eds.), *The Referendum Experience in Europe* (pp. 33–51). London: Palgrave Macmillan.

Weber, M. (1976). *Wirtschaft und Gesellschaft* (5th ed.). Tübingen: J.C.B. Mohr.

Winkler, H. A. (2014). *Der lang Weg nach Westen. Deutsche Geschichte vom Ende des alten Reiches bis zum Untergang der Weimarer Republik.* Munich: C.H. Beck.

Worre, T. (1988). Denmark at the Crossroads: The Danish Referendum of 28 February 1986 on the EC Reform Package. *JCMS: Journal of Common Market Studies, 26*(4), 361–388.

Part II

Domestic Referendums

CHAPTER 8

The King Versus the People: Lessons from a Belgian Referendum

Jan Wouters and Alex Andrione-Moylan

8.1   INTRODUCTION

In times of global crisis and uncertainty among voters, the appeal but also the relevance of referendums in the European political landscape appears to have been on the rise in recent years. While they are not new phenomena, referendums have often come to be seen as a quick fix either to inject procedural legitimacy into processes where it is seen as lacking or to resolve complex issues that have at their heart the matter of who can legitimately exercise authority in a multilevel governance system. Belgium is among only five EU Member States (along with Germany, Bulgaria, Cyprus and Portugal) never to have resorted to this tool on any EU-related matter. Belgium is also one of the few countries to lack either the constitutional provisions or the legislation that define the form and remit of referendums. Erik Derycke, a former Belgian Minister of Foreign Affairs, once noted: 'I'm glad that we have no referendums. How for God's sake are you going to explain a complicated thing like the Euro in a yes-and-no question to voters?' (Hobolt 2007: 157). There is, however, one instance in which a referendum was held in this country: on King's Leopold III right to rule (i.e. the *question royale* or 'royal question') in 1950. By examining the 1950 Belgian referendum, this chapter aims to provide some more general insights into the challenges that come with

J. Wouters (✉) · A. Andrione-Moylan
Leuven Centre for Global Governance Studies, KU Leuven, Leuven, Belgium
e-mail: jan.wouters@ggs.kuleuven.be

A. Andrione-Moylan
e-mail: alex.andrione-moylan@kuleuven.be

J. Smith (ed.), *The Palgrave Handbook of European Referendums*,
https://doi.org/10.1007/978-3-030-55803-1_8

165

resorting to this form of direct democracy. The chapter begins by outlining how the Belgian case, despite being something of an outlier in Europe, may in fact point to some important general considerations not only on the perils of majoritarianism in a complex federal system, but also within other Member States and the EU at large. It will then provide an overview of the relevant legal framework surrounding referendums and the debate over their constitutionality in Belgium. The chapter will then focus on the political and historical developments in Belgium and Europe, particularly between 1940 and 1950, followed by a detailed analysis of how the referendum played out, the positioning and role of key actors and the nature and fallout of the outcome. The aim is to draw some conclusions on the impact the Royal question had on Belgian domestic politics, as well as its broader significance.

8.2   REFERENDUMS IN BELGIUM

At first sight it might appear somewhat peculiar to focus on an eminently Belgian crisis in the aftermath of World War II, with the hope of attaining a deeper understanding of the dynamics surrounding referendums. This instance has, however, much to reveal as far as Belgium's enduring aversion to direct democracy is concerned and is also a cautionary tale of sorts on the challenges of direct democracy more generally. In the current debate over rekindling trust among voters, these issues are all the more relevant. Our aim is to bring to light some key issues through this rather unusual case that are worth taking into consideration when making sense of what appears to be a shift in both the quantity and nature of (EU-related) referendums over the past decade. Already in 1999 Maija Setälä noted the consistent rise of referendums since the 1940s, with EU-related votes largely accounting for the shift (Setälä 1999). Even in an era of permissive consensus, the increasingly supranational character of the EU was already perceived to call for such popular assent (Bogdanor 1994). However, it was with the 1992 Maastricht Treaty that politicisation of the European project truly began to emerge, at least partly accounting for the initial rejection of the treaty change in Denmark in June 1992 (see Chapter 25 by Beach). In 2005 referendums in France and the Netherlands rejected the Constitutional Treaty (see Chapter 28 by Sternberg), which was eventually not ratified and was effectively replaced by the Lisbon Treaty in 2007 (Hooghe and Marks 2009).

It could be argued that these referendums were far removed from the 1950 Belgian Royal Question, the latter becoming the manifestation of deep political, economic and cultural divisions, in a country that was facing a deep crisis as it struggled to recover from Nazi occupation. However, particularly since the 2008 economic and financial crisis, the European project and, perhaps more generally the complex social and economic shifts referred to as globalisation, have increasingly come under fire. Political cleavages have been redefined in terms of rather fundamental clashes between cosmopolitan (and pro-European) and nation-focused worldviews, creating fractures that run deep, pushed to the foreground by the salience of emotional issues such as migration (Marchetti 2009). This is particularly the case when examining recent EU-related referendums which, as opposed to the previous prevalence of in-out membership questions and treaty change, increasingly focus also on Union policies (Rose 2018). This has been the case most notably with referendums in Greece (on the bailout agreement, 2015 discussed by Papadopoulou in Chapter 30), the Netherlands (on the EU-Ukraine Association Agreement, 2016; see Chapter 32 by van den Akker) and Hungary (on the relocation mechanism for asylum seekers, 2016; see Batory in Chapter 31). This development, which raises political but also constitutional conundrums, is an indication of how referendums in the future may be resorted to more routinely, requiring a greater awareness of their implications. The United Kingdom's 2016 vote on continued membership of the EU is also relevant in this regard as, although at an elite level the conditions of membership had been renegotiated, this was not deemed enough by a majority of British voters (Glencross 2016).

By delving into the 1950 Belgian referendum, this chapter seeks to draw some broader conclusions on resorting to direct democracy, especially in the context of recent referendums in the EU which appear to contradict the treaty-sanctioned intergovernmental and supranational mechanisms which govern EU-level decision-making processes (Rose 2018). Hence, it is particularly referendums on EU issues that are challenging, by running against the consensus-based approach to the European project and transforming the outcomes of a complex balancing act among various interests and preferences into highly contentious and polarised debates. As will be discussed in some detail below, the extraordinary reliance on a *majoritarian* tool contributed to escalating ethnic tensions, in a system that was held together by strict mechanisms of representative government. There are significant caveats that should be kept in mind when considering this parallel, starting from the particular historical conjuncture in which the Belgian vote took place. Nor does this exercise seek to provide conclusive answers on the debate between direct (majoritarian) and representative (consensus-based) democratic mechanisms: the contrasting views of Lijphart (1989), who saw referendums as empowering minorities, and Sartori (1987), who denounced the dangers of relying on an ill-informed electorate, still echo in today's discussions. The following analysis seeks to contribute to the current reflections on how legitimacy channels may be reassessed both within the nation-state and in supranational institutions such as the EU.

8.3   A REPRESENTATIVE DEMOCRACY BY DESIGN

Prior to delving into the events that surrounded the 1950 referendum, it is essential to provide an overview of the constitutional framework in which the consultation was carried out, as this goes quite a way towards explaining why direct democracy in Belgium has not been resorted to ever since. The

1831 Constitution, which has been amended but is still in force, estab-lished Belgium as a parliamentary monarchy but retained an interpretation of national sovereignty that is rather conservative compared to many post-World War II constitutions. Article 33 (ex Art. 25) stipulates that '[a]ll power emanates from the Nation. This power is exerted in the manner established by the Constitution'. If one reads, for instance, Article 1 of the Italian 1946 Constitution, which asserts that '[s]overeignty belongs to the people and is exercised by the people in the forms and within the limits established by the Constitution', it is immediately apparent that the 1831 Constituent Assembly opted for a wording which, rather than empowering the people, has the *Nation* as emanation of all powers. This has been referred to as the meta-physical foundation of Belgium's Constitution (Lejeune and Regnier 1985). In other words, it is founded on an abstract collectivity which retains exclu-sive sovereignty, while delegating its authority under the terms laid out by the Constitution.

This is far from an insignificant detail, as the implication is that the idea that sovereignty is *of* the people and exercised *by* the people is excluded: the (higher) interests of the Nation are separate from those of the electorate. Hence, the Belgian Parliament formally is not accountable to citizens, but acts independently to uphold the interests of the Nation, even if de facto direct accountability vis-à-vis voters emerged over time (Alen et al. 1992). Some have likened this approach to the ideas of sovereignty and democracy promoted by Emmanuel Sieyès, the French political theorist who played a uniquely crucial role during both Revolutionary France and the Napoleonic Empire (Lejeune and Regnier 1985). In his writings Sieyès noted that '[c]itizens who name representatives renounce and must necessarily renounce directly making laws themselves. They have no particular will to impose' (Baker 1990). In stark opposition to Jean-Jacques Rousseau's *volonté generale* founded on direct democracy, Sieyès stressed that '[w]ithout alienating their rights, [the citizens] commit the exercise of them. It is for the common utility that they name representatives much more capable than themselves of knowing the general interest and of interpreting their own will in this regard' (Baczko 1988: 117). The strong emphasis on representation, the roots of which can be found here, is also related to the consensual dynamics that have long been at the heart of Belgian politics. As per Lijphart's well-known categorisation, Belgium is classed as a consensual democracy, in which politics tends not to be adver-sarial, but rather aimed at ensuring cooperation and stability, a feature which is typical of countries characterised by cultural segmentation, and not unlike the EU itself (Lijphart 1989). It could be argued that if direct democracy in such a context does raise significant issues, then in the EU's Member States making use of referendums on EU-related matters should be considered with great care, as should the prospect of EU-wide referendums. This is a discussion we shall return to later on.

Constitutional referendums are not permitted under the Belgian Consti-tution. Formally there are no explicit provisions on this matter, but there is little doubt among constitutional scholars on whether the mere absence of referendums among the viable methods of constitutional amendment excludes resorting to this instrument as a matter of course. Yves Lejeune and Jacques Regnier note that there are two key factors that prevent this: firstly, derived constituent powers can only be exercised in the manner established by the Constitution (Art. 33, supra); secondly, original constituent powers were only ever exercised by the National Congress, which ran from 1830 to 1831 (Lejeune and Regnier 1985). The involvement of the People in these processes is limited to how the revision of the Constitution can only be carried out by newly elected chambers, i.e. following general elections held for that purpose (Art. 195). To include the electorate in this process beyond such provisions would constitute a fundamental shift in the form and nature of the powers that emanated from the constituent assembly. Although over time a number of proposals have been put forward aimed at allowing the direct consultation of the people on constitutional matters, they have consistently failed to receive the necessary support. One such move was made in 1954 by André Saint-Rémy of the Christian Social Party (PSC): as in other similar instances, shifting the balance in such a way without introducing the momentous changes that re-writing Article 195 (ex-Art. 131) on constitutional revisions would imply, turned out to be impossible (Lejeune and Regnier 1985).

Legislative referendums at a federal level, whether binding or not, have been the object of a perhaps even more intense debate. Article 33 of the Constitution, as discussed above, prevents legislative powers being exercised in any way other than what is set out in the Constitution itself. This has not prevented attempts to introduce even binding legislative referendums, although most have been advisory. The first of these attempts occurred in 1893, within a broader constitutional revision process, and was unique in that it was promoted by the monarch, King Leopold II, himself. It entailed the introduction of a 'King's referendum' (*'referendum royale'*) that would have invested the King with powers to consult with his people on legislative matters, whenever he deemed it necessary (Alen et al. 1992). While the move was made with the support of the incumbent government, parliamentary opposition was unequivocal, especially among the ranks of the Catholic and Liberal parties. The proposal was seen as in marked contrast with the foundations of representative government, in addition to also bringing into play the power balances between the monarchy and the elected chambers. This failed attempt, which would have established a binding ex-post ratification of the King's decision, was followed by several others over the decades, which focused rather on the establishment of consultative referendums (Lejeune and Regnier 1985). While the doctrine on binding referendums has been consistently opposed, advisory referendums have divided opinion a little less. In 1965 a report by the tripartite Commission charged with institutional reform noted that, while binding referendums were unconstitutional and likely to exacerbate animosities among the country's regions, advisory referendums did not contravene, in principle, the strict principles of representative government in Belgium (Delpérée 1985).

In 1985, however, the General Assembly of the Council of State stressed how advisory referendums were de facto binding, hence the implications of such votes were in fact very similar, raising analogous constitutional issues (Raad van State 2003). This would seem to imply that *de jure* admissibility of advisory referendums gives way to the political reality of direct democracy.

Our focus is on national referendums; however, Belgium is characterised by a highly devolved federal system. As a matter of completeness of this brief account, it is worth noting that at the level of the Communities and the Regions, only advisory referendums would not encounter the same constitutional constraints, as all powers related to their competences are left to their regional governments. Municipal authorities, on the other hand, may hold binding referendums on matters under their own authority (Alen et al. 1992).

8.4   An Unconstitutional Referendum?

All that we have discussed above has brought us to the conclusion that, without a major overhaul of the Belgian constitutional foundations, a national referendum could not be held. Why, then, was the 1950 referendum held regardless? Firstly, it should be noted that so momentous and dramatic were the events surrounding the vote, that they are likely to have strengthened positions opposing direct democracy in Belgium. However, as mentioned above, it was exactly that particular conjuncture surrounding the vote that at the time appeared to provide the only way to resolve a complex political deadlock: extraordinary circumstances that called for extraordinary measures. In the following we will endeavour to provide an outline of the arrangements surrounding the referendum, delving then into the political and historical dynamics of *la question Royale*. In fact, the referendum itself stemmed from a constitutional crisis that had at its heart the disagreements that in 1940 arose between the King and his Ministers. At the start of the Second World War, King Leopold III and his Government had hoped to maintain a neutral position in the conflict. When it became apparent that a German invasion was imminent, the Government sought refuge in France, urging Leopold III to do the same, in order to join the Allies and oppose Hitler from abroad (Binion 1969). The King, however, refused to abandon the army and his subjects, leading the Belgian troops in the final defeat against Germany in May 1940, at the Battle of Dunkirk. The exiled Government argued that the King, by surrendering to Hitler, had made a political decision that was in violation of the Constitution: as a consequence, the *impossibilité de régner* (or 'impossibility of reigning') was declared, according to which the King's powers were formally suspended. Following the liberation of Belgium by the Allies in 1944 and the return of the exiled Government from London whence it had fled, Leopold's brother Charles was designated as Regent on 20 September 1944 (Fitzmaurice 1996). Leopold III had been imprisoned in Germany just prior to the liberation and was eventually freed a few months later, with the German capitulation in May 1945. The Government decided that only with the approval of the Chambers of Parliament, could the King retake the throne, therefore he remained in exile in Switzerland. As discussed further below, the mounting tensions between those who supported King Leopold's return (the Christian Democrats and Flanders) and those who were opposed (the Socialists, Liberals and Communists, and Wallonia), finally persuaded the newly formed coalition government of 1949 to approve a proposal for an advisory referendum on whether King Leopold III should exercise once again his constitutional powers (Fitzmaurice 1996). The Law of 11 February 1950 specified that the popular consultation did not put into question the institution of the monarchy itself or relate to the specific events surrounding the Belgian army's surrender in 1940. The vote was held on 12 March 1950. As is the case for Belgian elections, voting was compulsory and voter turnout reached 92.9% (Ministère de l'Intérieur 1950). With 2,933,382 votes (57.68%) in favour of the King's return, the 1940 suspension of Leopold III's powers was formally brought to an end, even though the regency was temporarily bestowed on the crown prince Baudouin (Mabille 2000).

Although some, such as Socialist leader Paul-Henri Spaak, had opposed holding the referendum, it was admitted as a matter of political expediency. One might even say that elected representatives were unable and unwilling to take a decision on the matter and abdicated responsibility (Time 1950). Moreover, the extraordinary nature of the referendum does not appear to overcome its unconstitutionality; quite the contrary. As noted by Jean Rey in a report on the referendum proposal, its unconstitutionality arose, first and foremost, from its 'object' (Lejeune and Regnier 1985). That is to say, the notion itself of a referendum which asks the people to vote on a matter directly related to the Head of State and his position presents clear features of a plebiscite, in stark contrast with the Belgian constitutional foundations discussed above. In many ways this analysis brings us back to the debate that surrounded the proposal to introduce the 'royal referendum', and the concerns that such amendment to the Constitution would bring with it a *caesarist* dimension to the monarchy and hence be unconstitutional. Nevertheless, the vote did take place, even if its result would be overtaken by events meaning that the opposite outcome prevailed in practice.

By remaining in Belgium in 1940, King Leopold III maintained the country's neutral position in the conflict, even requesting the exiled Ministers to sign blank decrees that would allow him to appoint a new government should the armistice with Hitler allow this (Binion 1969). Initially, while Belgians' support for the Government had waned, Leopold's decision not to flee had won him the favour of the people. Nevertheless, his collaborationist tendencies vis-à-vis the Nazi-led New World Order, the extent of which would in fact remain unclear, and the strife that came with the occupation would ultimately turn many—especially in Wallonia—against him. This related most notably to the *Deutsche Vlamenpolitik*, a strategy that entailed ensuring an until-then under-recognised Dutch-speaking community in Belgium a higher status under Nazi rule (Vos 1998). Particularly infamous was Leopold's trip to

Berchtesgaden (Germany) in November 1940, where in a meeting with Hitler the King attempted not only to negotiate the release of war prisoners and increase food rations, but also to secure Belgian independence in the Nazis' 'New Order' (Binion 1969). While an exhaustive account of the events and the debates that surrounded them is beyond the scope of this chapter, there is one other development that is worth mentioning. The King had sought to portray himself as sharing the plight of his people, an image that was shattered when his second marriage in 1941 with a Flemish 'commoner', Liliane Baels, was announced. In 1935 his first wife and Queen of Belgium, Astrid of Sweden, much beloved by the Belgian people, had lost her life in a tragic car accident in the Swiss Alps. This personal matter contributed to further compounding resentment towards the King among the Walloon population (Mabille 2000).

The outcome of the referendum requires closer examination. What the aggregate results presented as a clear-cut response, hid rather deep divisions along ethno-linguistic lines: 72% of voters in Flanders were in favour of the King's return, while 58% of Walloons were opposed, and the Brussels region showed a 50–50% divide (Sinardet 2009). On 22 July 1950, Leopold III returned to Belgium, however, he was greeted by widespread protests and a general strike in the industrial centres of Wallonia (Mabille 2000). With threats of a march on Brussels by the Walloons and following a particularly violent confrontation between protesters and the police in the city of Liège, in which three people died, Leopold finally decided to abdicate in favour of his son Baudouin, who was formally crowned Royal Prince in July 1951. Although the urban–rural divide also constituted a predictor of voter behaviour, with some rural regions in Wallonia voting in favour of the King (e.g. Namur, Luxembourg), the vote effectively played out along the ethno-linguistic divide (Reuchamps 2007). It was the first time these divisions had emerged so starkly, with Walloons successfully opposing the outcome of the referendum, while many in the Flemish-speaking community interpreted the turn of events as a frustration of the popular will, hence contributing to setting the stage for the rise of Flemish nationalism (Vos 1998, Sinardet 2009). This was not so much a consequence of the referendum itself, but perhaps of the inability or unwillingness to maintain a complex political balance at the elite level, as a system which relies on representation and consensus would have required.

8.5   FROM BELGIUM TO THE EUROPEAN UNION

At the start of this analysis of the 1950 Belgian referendum we discussed the influences of the Rousseau-Sieyès debate in shaping the constitutional foundations of Belgium. It is perhaps from here that our broader reflection on what we might draw from the 1950 referendum should begin. Taking into account the influence of these thinkers is far from irrelevant as they reveal the roots of an enduring and indeed deepening tension between majoritarian democracy (and un-mediated forms of government) and, on the other hand, liberal, i.e. strictly representative consensus-based democracy and the focus on individual liberty. It could be argued that the Rousseau-Sieyès debate laid the ground for conceiving democracy—more precisely liberal democracy—as a regime in tension. While majority rule does indeed constitute a basic condition for democracy, *liberalism* implies that pluralism is equally important: the tension arises from the impossibility of reconciling the absolute will of the majority and the complete disaggregation of citizens' preferences and protection of each individual's prerogatives (Plattner 2010). From such a standpoint, it can be argued that representative democracy is, after all, founded on a precarious equilibrium: the will of the people is interpreted by political elites, which entails the potential for perceptions (and the reality) of detachment from citizens' preferences and grievances.

A number of factors come into play in placing a democracy along the consensual-majoritarian spectrum. Lijphart focused on indicators such as the pre-eminence of the executive, the existence of a two-party system, first-past-the-post elections (Lijphart 1989): direct democracy is not necessarily majoritarian, much like representative democracy is not only consensus-based. There is in fact some debate on how referendums fit into this categorisation. There are certainly cases of consensus democracies which rely on direct democracy very frequently. So-called *'uncontrolled referendums'* in Switzerland have led to more inclusive executives and policies, strengthening its consensual nature (Vatter 2009). When it is not the result of a popular initiative, more often than not, it constitutes a majoritarian tool, especially in the hands of elites who seek to strengthen their mandate (plebiscites) or in optional referendums, which are also not constitutionally required and are likely to reveal two different, but often overlapping, dynamics. There are firstly those that Morel identifies as de facto obligatory referendums, in which *'the initiator [is] in practice compelled to organise a referendum as a result of an inescapable pressure – either normative or by external actors – to do so'* (Morel 2007: 1055). Secondly, there are those which Carlos Closa calls *'strategic referendums'*, which reveal party-political dynamics and electoral interests (Closa 2007, p. 200). Admittedly, the line between these types is often blurred, with votes such as the ones on the Greek bailout agreement and Brexit arguably fitting in both categories. The issue then is not whether direct democracy is a good or a bad thing, but rather to reflect on how best to adjust the balance between representative and direct democracy. The *royal question* referendum is, admittedly, a rather unusual case—however, certain Belgian peculiarities might allow us to point to some interesting insights in the context of the EU and its Member States. The first relates to the specific challenges vis-à-vis segmented electorates and legitimacy conundrums in multilevel governance systems and the second touches upon recourse to referendums in the absence of a common public sphere.

The link between the emphasis on representative democracy and the cultural and ethnic dividing lines in Belgium has already been mentioned. Consensual regimes can also arise in the presence of a fragmented electorate, as in the case of Italy or Germany, and not exclusively when there are such clear ethnic distinctions within a country (Lijphart 1989). The case of Belgium is in fact often referred to as a consociational democracy, which requires an inclusive executive that actively counters centrifugal forces, hence beyond proportional regimes that are typical of consensual political systems (Deschouwer 2006). Since the emergence of this category, a significant debate has ensued on the extent to which the EU can be considered a comparable example of consociational democracy (Bogaards and Crepaz 2002). While there is disagreement over the extent to which this classification applies to the EU, the connection is an interesting one in the context of this chapter. The decision-making process in the EU is founded on consensus: bargaining among the Member States and the party groups in the EP ensures that there are no outright winners and losers, but rather compromises seeking to maintain a degree of unity despite the differences (Thomson 2010). As argued by Rose, when dealing with EU-wide policies Member States are *bounded* democracies and when they choose to resort to direct democracy, a conflict emerges between the majoritarian nature of referendums—allowed by many constitutions but rarely required for the ratification of international treaties—and the consensus-based, yet legitimate, EU decision-making process (Rose 2018).

At least to a certain degree, we are comparing apples and oranges, as the EU-related referendums are national referendums, within the broader context of the EU, while the Belgian 1950 vote occurred at a federal level, hence more akin to an EU-wide referendum. Having said this, the crux of the matter is that the *question royale* does show what the consequences of the spread of EU-related referendums could entail, both in a domestic setting and vis-à-vis the EU. Within a segmented system, opposition arising from state-level referendums is likely to lead to divisions similar to those witnessed in Belgium, along economic, social and cultural cleavages. At a domestic level, it might be useful to reflect on how this ethno-cultural segmentation in Belgium compares to the divisions in many of today's Western societies between *cosmopolitans* and *locals* and if similar caution with regard to direct democracy should be exercised, as referendums are likely to deepen mistrust and fragmentation, as can be seen in post-Brexit UK (Marchetti 2009; Corbett 2016).

It should not be forgotten that, at a Member State level, while in a consensus/consociational democracy the *question royale* shows how there is little to be gained with a referendum, in a majoritarian system which allows for referendums with popular initiative, this could in theory lead to a more broadly accepted common position for the executive to upload at the Union level (*uncontrolled referendums*). Shifting to the EU-level context, even in this case there remains the clash of legitimacy between the national provisions for direct democracy and the supranational and legally binding EU decision-making process. The unconstitutionality of the 1950 Belgian referendum, discussed above, relates precisely to the conflict between, on the one hand, a representative system and the specific role played by elites therein and direct democracy on the other. It could be argued that the relationship between the EU supranational decision-making processes and national referendums raise similar questions, as direct democracy generally takes the form of an ex-post contestation of an outcome which is not only legitimate in its own right, but is also the reflection of the complex *interdependence* among Member States (Keohane and Nye 1977).

There is one final consideration that is worth making here. It has been mentioned how in some instances, most notably in Switzerland, direct democracy appears to contribute significantly to the unity of the multilingual country (Stojanović 2006). Why, then, did a similar attempt in Belgium turn out to constitute an utter failure? Some have suggested that perhaps the significance of direct democracy in Switzerland has been overstated and that there are other factors that help to explain the functioning of this federal system (Sinardet 2009). Crucially, national political parties and, as a consequence, a media landscape that is not as fragmented as one might expect, makes for a stark contrast when compared to the fragmentation of the political arena and the media in Belgium. The *question royale* then highlights another key factor: the ethnolinguistic dividing line that emerges from disaggregate results seems to suggest that when there is no common public sphere, referendums can indeed deepen existing divides, enabling an *us vs. them* rhetoric (Sinardet 2009). With this in mind when we consider the EU as a whole, examining the Belgian case allows us to stress the following. The debate on the feasibility and appropriateness of EU-wide referendums, which we cannot delve into here, is a rather longstanding one (Risse and Kleine 2007; Zürn 2016). Of course, pan-European referendums do overcome the legitimacy clash that is apparent in the case of national EU-related referendums, by reflecting cross-Member State interdependence from a bottom-up perspective. However, as emerges in the Belgian *question royale*, the issue is that there is no single public sphere in which referendum campaigns could be conducted. Even though there is a significant increase in the salience of Union-related issues, these tend to be national debates: the many obstacles to an EU-wide public sphere are not easily dealt with, from the enduring language barriers to the segmentation of political arenas (Boomgaarden and de Vreese 2016). It is not inconceivable that socioeconomic and indeed cultural divisions across the EU (e.g. the North-South or East-West divides) would shape and be reinforced by pan-European referendums, in a way that is reminiscent of the Belgian 1950 referendum. Reflecting on how the emerging transnational public sphere might be developed in this direction appears to be a precondition to any discussion on the desirability of EU-wide referendums.

8.6   CONCLUDING REMARKS

The aim of this contribution was to inspire further reflection on the kinds of dynamics that surround recent referendums and the role they might play when it comes to national and European legitimacy and decision-making processes. Looking at these issues through the unusual prism of the Belgian *question royale* highlighted some key elements that require further attention in the debate on referendums in the European Union. The manner in which Belgium is founded upon representative democracy and a consensual/consociational political system allows, with some caveats, the parallels that are drawn here with the EU, a polity that is similarly held together by the consensus built among the Member States. The manner in which the *question royale* played out in an ethnically divided Belgium may offer some insights into the polarising effects of EU-related referendums, both within the Member States—along the cosmopolitans-locals divide—and across different areas of the EU. Moreover, the unconstitutional nature of the Belgian 1950 referendum allows to highlight what has been referred to as the legitimacy clash between exercising direct democracy at a Member State level and the Union's consensual decision-making processes. Finally, the *question royale* is also a cautionary tale when it comes to organising EU-wide referendums in the absence of a common public sphere, likely to increase fragmentation within the EU. As multiple recent crises in the EU have also generated distrust and legitimacy concerns towards the Union, an informed debate on the role direct democracy can and should play in the context of the EU, starting from some of the key issues that have been raised here, is more timely than ever.

Bibliography

Alen, A., Tilleman, B., & Peeters, P. (1992). *Treatise on Belgian Constitutional Law*. Kluwer Law and Taxation Publishers.

Baczko, B. (1988). The Social Contract of the French: Sieyès and Rousseau. *The Journal of Modern History, 60*, S98–S125.

Baker, K. M., (1990). *Inventing the French Revolution: Essays on French Political Culture in the Eighteenth Century*. Cambridge University Press.

Binion, R. (1969). Repeat Performance: A Psychohistorical Study of Leopold III and Belgian Neutrality. *History and Theory, 8*(2), 213–259.

Bogaards, M., & Crepaz, M. M. L. (2002). Consociational Interpretations of the European Union. *European Union Politics, 3*(3), 357–381.

Bogdanor, V. (1994). Western Europe. In D. Butler & A. Ranney (Eds.), *Referendums Around the World: The Growing Use of Direct Democracy*. Washington, DC: Aei Press.

Boomgaarden, H. G. & de Vreese, C. H. (2016). Do European Elections Create a European Public Sphere? In W. van der Brug & C. H. de Vreese (Eds.), *(Un)intended Consequences of EU Parliamentary Elections*. Oxford University Press, 19–35.

Closa, C. (2007). Why Convene Referendums? Explaining Choices in EU Constitutional Politics. *Journal of European Public Policy, 14*(8), 1311–1332.

Corbett, S. (2016). The Social Consequences of Brexit for the UK and Europe: Euroscepticism, Populism, Nationalism, and Societal Division. *The International Journal of Social Quality, 6*(1), 11–31.

Delpérée, F. (1985). *Référendums*. Centre de Recherche et d'Information Socio-Politiques.

Deschouwer, K. (2006). And the Peace Goes On? Consociational Democracy and Belgian Politics in the Twenty-first Century. *West European Politics, 29*(5), 895–911.

Fitzmaurice, J. (1996). *The Politics of Belgium: A Unique Federalism*. Belgium: C. Hurst & Co.

Glencross, A. (2016). *Why the UK Voted for Brexit: David Cameron's Great Miscalculation*. New York, NY: Palgrave Pivot.

Hobolt, S. B. (2007). Taking Cues on Europe? Voter Competence and Party Endorsements in Referendums on European Integration. *European Journal of Political Research, 46*(2), 151–182.

Hooghe, L., & Marks, G. (2009). A Postfunctionalist Theory of European Integration: From Permissive Consensus to Constraining Dissensus. *British Journal of Political Science, 39*(1), 1–23.

Keohane, R. O., & Nye, J. S. (1977). *Power and Interdependence: World Politics in Transition*. Brown: Little.

Lejeune, Y., & Regnier, J. (1985). Belgique. In *Référendums* (pp. 13–78). CRISP: Bruxelles.

Lijphart, A. (1989). Democratic Political Systems: Types, Cases, Causes, and Consequences. *Journal of Theoretical Politics, 1*(1), 33–48.

Mabille, X. (2000). *Histoire politique de la Belgique* (4th ed.). Bruxelles: CRISP.

Marchetti, R. (2009). Mapping Alternative Models of Global Politics. *International Studies Review, 11*(1), 133–156.

Ministère de l'Intérieur. (1950). *Sénat de Belgique—Consultation populaire du 12 mars 1950, au sujet de la Question Royale*.

Morel, L. (2007). The Rise of 'Politically Obligatory' Referendums: The 2005 French Referendum in Comparative Perspective. *West European Politics, 30*, 1041–1067.

Plattner, M. F. (2010). Populism, Pluralism, and Liberal Democracy. *Journal of Democracy, 21*(1), 81–92.

Raad van State, (2003). *ADVIES : Voorstel Van Decreet—van de heren Dirk Holemans, Sven Gatz, Peter De Ridder en André Denys—houdende instelling van een deelstatelijke volksraadpleging kaderend in de procedure van onderzoek*. Vlaams Parlement, No. Stuk 1131 (2001–2002), Nr. 3.

Reuchamps, M. (2007). Cahier—Referendum as a Tool for Building European Identity. The Case of Belgium, Luxembourg, and The Netherlands. *Cahiers de Sciences politiques de l'ULg*, 17.

Risse, T. & Kleine, M. (2007). Assessing the Legitimacy of the EU's Treaty Revision Methods. *JCMS: Journal of Common Market Studies, 45*(1), 69–80.

Rose, R. (2018). Referendum Challenges to the EU's Policy Legitimacy—and How the EU Responds. *Journal of European Public Policy*, 1–19.

Sartori, G. (1987). *The Theory of Democracy Revisited*. Chatham, NJ: Chatham House Publishers.

Setälä, M. (1999). Referendums in Western Europe—A Wave of Direct Democracy? *Scandinavian Political Studies, 22*(4), 327–340.

Sinardet, D. (2009). Direct Democracy as a Tool to Shape a United Public Opinion in a Multilingual Society? Some Reflections Based on the Belgian Case. In D. Sinardet & M. Hooghe (Eds.), *Public Opinion in a Multilingual Society: Institutional Design and Federal Loyalty*. Brussels: Re-Bel Initiative.

Stojanović, N. (2006). Direct Democracy: A Risk or an Opportunity for Multicultural Societies? The Experience of the Four Swiss Multilingual Cantons. *International Journal on Multicultural Societies, 8*(2), 108.

Thomson, R. (2010). The Relative Power of Member States in the Council. In D. Naurin & H. Wallace (Eds.), *Unveiling the Council of the European Union* (pp. 238–258). Basingstoke: Palgrave Macmillan.

Time. (1950). *Belgium: Up in the Air*. Retrieved from: http://content.time.com/time/magazine/article/0,9171,858723,00.html.

Vatter, A. (2009). Lijphart Expanded: Three Dimensions of Democracy in Advanced OECD Countries? *European Political Science Review, 1*(1), 125.

Vos, L. (1998). The Flemish National Question. In K. Deprez & L. Vos (Eds.), *Nationalism in Belgium: Shifting Identities, 1780–1995* (pp. 83–95). London: Palgrave Macmillan UK.

Zürn, M. (2016). Opening Up Europe: Next Steps in Politicisation Research. *West European Politics, 39*(1), 164–182.

CHAPTER 9

The Referendum Experience in France

Laurence Morel

9.1 A Short Long Story
of the Referendum Since the Revolution[1]

It is impossible to understand the current position of the referendum in France without retracing its history, which goes back to the Revolution and the debates in the '*Assemblée Constituante*', where it was claimed and theorised by the Radical Left. Although apparently promised a bright future, in the name of sacrosanct popular sovereignty, what prevailed at the end was fear of the people and the first French Constitution (1791) did not mention the referendum device. Admittedly the second Constitution, two years later, contained generous mechanisms of direct democracy, but it never came into effect because of exceptional circumstances. In the end, the Revolution only introduced the mandatory constitutional referendum in the 1795 Constitution, in accordance with the decree adopted by the Convention at its first meeting that 'there can be no Constitution except that approved by the people'. Both the 1793 and 1795 Constitutions were ratified by universal male suffrage in the first two referendums of French constitutional history. The massive victory and very low turnout (26% in 1793 and 16% in 1795) unequivocally indicate that these referendums were far from meeting democratic requirements; but at least

---

[1] For a complete analysis of the history and current practice of the referendum in France see Morel (2014, 2019).

L. Morel (✉)
University of Lille, Lille, France
e-mail: laurence.morel@univ-lille.fr

© The Author(s) 2021
J. Smith (ed.), *The Palgrave Handbook of European Referendums*,
https://doi.org/10.1007/978-3-030-55803-1_9

they were not deviated as it would soon be under Bonapartism, when their use to demonstrate the confidence of the Nation was pivotal to the regime. Actually, Bonapartist referendums, while pursuing the revolutionary tradition of constitutional referendums, were meant first to provide for approval for the leader. Thus, in 1802 Napoleon asked the French to appoint him Consul for life, and later to approve the hereditary Empire of the Bonaparte lineage (1804)—a question that was again the subject of a referendum in 1852 under the Second Empire, after Louis-Napoleon had sought special constitutional powers following his 'coup d'état' in 1851. In practice all seven Napoleonic referendums mixed, implicitly if not explicitly, constitutional questions and approval of the leader. This enabled them to constitute a powerful mechanism for strengthening the Executive and circumventing the Parliament, which was never involved in the elaboration of the Constitutions, unlike revolutionary Assemblies, and was sometimes downright hostile to the proposed revisions.

While Napoleon I held ad hoc referendums, Napoleon III institutionalised their use by introducing the mandatory constitutional referendum for all constitutional revisions in the Constitutions of 1852 and 1870, and the 'appel au peuple' in the latter (Article 13: 'The Emperor is responsible to the French people, to whom he is always entitled to appeal'). The fall of the Second Empire meant the process was never used, but Napoleon III had enshrined in the Constitution the referendum of confidence invented by his uncle, suggesting he could resign in case of a No victory. He thus anticipated the Gaullist conception of the referendum a century later as an instrument for popular ratification of major decisions and for confirming the people's confidence in the President of the Republic. Napoleonic referendums, with the exception of the last one (1870), which benefited from the relative liberalisation of the regime, were far from meeting democratic standards, as evidenced by their massive approval rate over 90% (only in 1870 was it slightly below 83%). However, compared with the revolutionary referendums these Napoleonic referendums succeeded better in mobilising people (with a turnout around 50% under Napoleon I and 80% under Napoleon III), perhaps because of their strong personal dimension.

The referendum was absent from both constitutional texts and practice during the restoration of monarchy (1815–1848). Its rejection persisted through the short-lived Second Republic (1848–1851) and was confirmed under the Third Republic. Although the 1848 revolution was in the name of universal suffrage, the Constitution of 1848 did not provide for any form of referendum, nor was it submitted to the people. The new elected Assembly was in fact haunted by the twofold fear of social revolution and 'Caesarism', which led to a general agreement for strong representative institutions and against giving the President the power to appeal to the people—a temptation that he could have had all the more since he would be directly elected by the people.

The Third Republic, which was born in the aftermath of the Second Empire and the revolutionary events of the Commune, was even more marked than the Second Republic by the double spectre of Caesarism and social revolution, uniting Monarchists and Republicans in a common rejection of the referendum. The major fact of the period was the definitive breaking up of the Left with direct democracy. The Republicans took a firm stand in favour of pure representative government while the Socialists now focused on the party's leading role in expressing popular will. Like under the Second Republic, the referendum was therefore absent from both constitutional texts and practice of the first stable regime since the Revolution. A proposal to submit the Constitution to popular ratification was rejected in January 1875.

Most lawyers viewed the referendum as not compatible with representative government (e.g. Esmein 1906). Only between the two wars was there a certain rehabilitation of the process as a means of mitigating parliamentary power, which was deemed excessive, such as the promotion of popular initiative by French lawyer Carré de Malberg (1931). Such debate was not unique to France. Much earlier, Briton A. V. Dicey had denounced 'absolute parliamentarism' and 'party dictatorship' in his country and demanded the mandatory referendum on constitutional and sovereignty issues (Dicey 1890). As in France, this plea in favour of the referendum was unsuccessful. By contrast, new inter-war constitutions in several European states gave a large place to the referendum (Mirkine-Guetzévitch 1931)—which meanwhile continued to develop in Switzerland (and the United States) under the impulse of populist movements. In some countries the referendum was also introduced to strengthen the Executive vis-à-vis the Parliament, for example, in the Weimar Constitution under the influence of Max Weber. Similarly in France, former right-wing Prime Minister André Tardieu, known to have had great influence on General de Gaulle (Passelecq 1990), proposed a 'Reform of the State' intended to reduce the power of Parliament, which included the referendum initiated by the President of the Republic at the request of government.

It was de Gaulle, as head of the transitional government established at the Liberation, who reintroduced the referendum. On 21 October 1945, the same day as elections to the National Assembly, the French were asked whether the Assembly they were going to elect should draft a new Constitution, in other words whether or not they wanted to return to the Third Republic. A second question demanded whether, in the event 'Yes' prevailed on the first question, the Assembly should have limited duration and powers; it also provided that the new Constitution would be submitted to a referendum. Officially, these two referendums, as well as the two others held the following year on the Constitution (the first project was rejected), were meant to allow the people to choose their regime and to grant the institutions stronger legitimacy. But tactical motivations were not absent. Bypassing the all-party consultative Assembly set up at the Liberation, de Gaulle hoped to make his institutional preference for a new Constitution with a strong Executive prevail. Parties were divided on whether or not to return to the Third Republic, even though in the end only the Radical party—which was emblematic of the Third Republic—advocated No to the first question. Above all, parties were massively in favour of parliamentarism. Thus, the referendums can be said to have been used by de Gaulle to foster his minority views on the regime. Parties were largely reluctant to hold referendums, since they were hostile both to the process and to the regime that de Gaulle wanted to promote through them. Another concern of the Assembly was that de Gaulle was in fact using the referendum to secure the undisputed legitimacy that he was still lacking in the transitional process of the Liberation.

Although reviving the revolutionary tradition of constitutional referendums, the referendums convened by de Gaulle were also reminiscent of the Bonapartist use of the process to circumvent parliament and legitimise their author—albeit under much more liberal conditions. The result was very mixed: de Gaulle won the referendums but the new Assembly was dominated by the Communists and the Socialists, which were both supporters of strong parliamentarism; and his personal legitimacy acquired through the referendum finally proved to be of little weight compared to that of the victorious parties, which in line with their views proposed a '*régime d'assemblée*', causing de Gaulle to resign in January 1946. Although the Constitution was rejected by the French in May, the second version, which only watered down the first draft, was adopted in October. De Gaulle's only consolation was the poor result (53% of 'Yes' representing only 35% of registered voters), which was insufficient to give a real legitimacy to the Constitution.

9.2   The Decline of the Referendum as a Presidential Weapon Under the Fifth Republic

Although its authors claimed the legacy of the 1793 Jacobine Constitution, the fundamental law of the Fourth Republic, which emerged in 1946, attributed a very limited role to the referendum: it was mandatory on constitutional matters only under certain conditions and explicitly prohibited on legislative matters (Article 3). Indeed, there was never a referendum under this Constitution. It was not until the 1958 Constitution (established this time under the strict control of de Gaulle) that a French Constitution finally granted an important place to the referendum (except for the never-applied Constitutions of 1793 and 1870). Article 3 of the new Constitution now extended it to ordinary legislation, while Article 11 allowed the President of the Republic to submit to the people any draft law 'on the organization of public authorities, entailing the approval of a Community agreement, or for the purpose of authorising the ratification of a treaty which, without being contrary to the Constitution, might affect the functioning of the institutions'. In addition, Article 89 gave the President the power to decide whether a constitutional amendment proposed by him would be submitted to referendum or to Parliament, after having been approved by Parliament at first reading—the referendum being mandatory for revisions initiated by Parliament (see Sect. 9.4). In short, the French President could now circumvent Parliament completely on legislative matters and partially on constitutional matters. Article 11 contributed, alongside other mechanisms such as the early dissolution and the direct election, to forging the direct relationship between the President and the people which was the essence of the regime wanted by de Gaulle.

Until 1962, however, the election of the President was still indirect and the four referendums held by de Gaulle—the last of which to approve the change in the way to elect the President—actually acted as substitutes for the direct election (Morel 2010). Each time de Gaulle explicitly asked for the confidence of the French people and threatened to withdraw in case of a No victory. In 1958, his personal capture of the referendum aimed at verifying that he had the confidence of the Nation in spite of the controversial circumstances of his accession to power, although he had also insisted that the referendum would be mandatory according to the law of 3 June 1958 delegating to government the drafting of the new Constitution—with a view to bypassing the Parliament of the Fourth Republic, which remained very attached to pure parliamentarism. Thus, in the end, de Gaulle's motivations in 1958 resembled much those of 1945. In the following three referendums (on Algeria in January 1961 and April 1962 and on the direct election of the President in October 1962), de Gaulle sought to assert his legitimacy as the real head of government, in spite of Article 20 of the Constitution attributing this role to the Prime Minister. In other words, he wanted the French to approve the de facto 'presidentialisation' of the regime. Admittedly, the primary purpose of those referendums was to serve as a minority weapon for the President, whose *Union pour la Nouvelle République* was the largest party in Parliament but lacked the absolute majority that would have ensured the approval of his Algerian policy, and most of all the direct election of the President, which was unanimously opposed by other parties.

After 1962, the direct election of the President would make the referendum less functional to the regime and the practice declined. The President now draws his legitimacy from this election. Nevertheless, the referendum still served to relegitimise him in the course of a particularly long (seven year) mandate, acting as a sort of mid-term election (Parodi 1973). This was clearly the case of the last referendum called by de Gaulle a year after the crisis of May 1968. This referendum has sometimes been interpreted as a political suicide, the overwhelming victory of the Gaullist party at the early election of June 1968 having demonstrated the confidence of the Nation. But de Gaulle was anxious that such confidence might have concerned more his Prime Minister (Pompidou) than himself. His fear was not totally ungrounded since the French this time voted 'No', triggering de Gaulle's resignation and definitive withdrawal from political life. Similarly, the referendums convened by Pompidou in 1972 and Mitterrand in 1992 can be interpreted as attempts to revitalise their position after a few years in office—although a secondary function was also to divide the opposition (as will be seen in the next section).

The advent of bipolarisation and presidential majorities after 1962 made the minority use of the referendum by the President less necessary. Here the device contributed to its own demise since the bipolarisation started with referendums and was thereafter consolidated by the second round of the direct elections—which a referendum had introduced. After 1962 the referendum became less effective as a presidential weapon. All referendums had a boomerang effect on their initiators either because of a 'No' victory (1969 and 2005), too narrow a 'Yes' victory (1992), or low turnout (1972, 1988, and 2000). This was in part the result of the democratisation of the regime, implying that referendums are less controlled in terms of both outcome and turnout. It was also the consequence of the 'de-plebiscitarisation' of the device, i.e. the fact that de Gaulle's successors carefully avoided taking responsibility—something which played both against participation, suffering from the absence of personalisation, and against the 'Yes', a 'No' victory being no longer considered dangerous for regime stability.

The 2000 reform reducing the presidential term to five years has made the referendum even less functional to the regime. The shortening of the presidential duration in office actually continued what the 1962 reform had initiated, namely the decline of the referendum's legitimising function. In parallel, the minority function of the referendum also lost its purpose as a result of the further presidentialisation of the majority, due to the parliamentary election being now held in the wake of the presidential election—something which sometimes happened in the past but is likely to become systematic. 2017 provides here a masterful illustration with '*La République en marche*', the party that Emmanuel Macron had created from scratch for his election, succeeding in getting a parliamentary majority only one month after its leader becoming President. Finally, the risk of losing the referendum is now increased with the President standing in the front line in place of the Prime Minister, in turn a result of the presidentialisation of the majority. This is likely to be conducive to voters 're-plebiscitarising' the referendum by voting for or against the President, with the result of almost systematic failure in the present context of highly volatile presidential popularity. For all these reasons, the future of the presidential referendum seems quite limited in France, as confirmed by the absence of any new referendum since the failed referendum on the European Constitutional Treaty in 2005 (see Sternberg elsewhere in this volume), even if paradoxically, as will be seen in Sect. 9.5, the referendum has been the object of renewed interest since 2005.

9.3   Referendums in Practice

France has had ten nationwide referendums since 1958 (Table 9.1). The first was held by virtue of the law of 3 June 1958 (mentioned above) while all other referendums were organised on the basis of Article 11 of the 1958 Constitution, with the exception of the one on the reduction to five years of the presidential term, which relied on Article 89. This does not mean that the

Table 9.1   Nationwide referendums in France since 1958

Issue	Date	Legal basis	Field of legislation	Turnout % (including invalid votes)	Yes % (% of votes cast)
Constitution Fifth Republic	28 September 1958	Law June 3 1958	Constitution	80.63	82.60
Self-determination and organisation of public powers in Algeria	8 January 1961	Article 11 (public powers)	Ordinary law	73.75	74.99
Independence of Algeria and extraordinary legislative powers (« Evian Agreements »)	8 April 1962	Article 11 (public powers)	Ordinary law	75.33	90.81
Direct election of President of Republic	28 October 1962	Article 11 (public powers)	Constitution	76.97	62.25
Senate reform and creation of regions	27 April 1969	Article 11 (public powers)	Constitution	80.13	47.59
UK, Denmark, Ireland and Norway to join European Community	23 April 1972	Article 11 (treaties)	Ordinary law	60.24	68.32
Self-determination of New Caledonia (« Matignon agreements »)	6 November 1988	Article 11 (public powers)	Ordinary law	36.89	79.99
Maastricht Treaty	20 September 1992	Article 11 (treaties)	Ordinary law	69.69	51.04
Reducing presidential term to five years	24 September 2000	Article 89	Constitution	30.19	73.21
European Constitutional Treaty	29 May 2005	Article 11 (treaties)	Ordinary law	69.37	45.33

Source: *Digithèque de matériaux politiques et juridiques*, University of Perpignan: http://mjp. univ-perp.fr/france/ref.htm (Numbers include overseas territories)

constitutionality of referendums has been unexceptionable; actually all Gaullist referendums were criticised in this regard, the two on Algeria because self-determination did not unequivocally fall within the scope of 'the organisation of public powers', the latter two because of the use of Article 11 to revise the Constitution. Although there was no proper debate on the subject, the question of the constitutionality of the 1972 referendum was also raised on the grounds that the treaty of adhesion of new countries did not affect the functioning of French institutions (Berlia 1972). To date, only the last three referendums have undeniably belonged to the field of questions provided for by the Constitution, which shows the probably greater concern of a more correct practice of the process.

As shown in Table 9.1, the subjects of referendums have fallen into three broad categories: constitutional matters, colonies and Europe. In the context of Brexit and increasingly numerous referendums on Europe,[2] this chapter will focus on the three referendums held in France on EU matters, which also embody the most recent practice of the process in France (two of the last three referendums held since 1992 having related to Europe).

9.3.1   The 1972 Referendum on the Accession of New Countries

The first of these referendums was initiated by Pompidou. The question was: 'Do you approve, given the new perspectives opening for Europe, the Bill submitted to the French people by the President of the Republic authorising the ratification of the treaty relative to the accession of Great Britain, Denmark, Ireland and Norway to the European Communities?' Europe was not yet an issue for most French people or among parties, only the Communists being opposed to enlargement. The referendum was thus expected to ensure the President a massive victory. Although he insisted in his declaration sent to the electors that he was not asking for an approval of his policies, Pompidou clearly hoped to reinforce his position indirectly through this referendum.

This did not prove a very successful strategy since abstentions (39%) and invalid votes (7%) reached the highest levels ever, roughly double that at previous referendums. This was the combined result of lack of personalisation and dramatisation, the very predictable victory of the 'Yes' side, discontent with the government and, most of all, indifference regarding Europe. In fact, one month before the vote 72% of those polled said they were not or little interested in the referendum,[3] while 22% declared that they did not clearly perceive the consequences of the question asked and another 27% that the entry of new members would have no consequence.[4] Moreover only 51% approved the holding of the referendum.[5]

The very low turnout also resulted from the abstention of half the Socialist electors, in accordance with the Socialist party recommending abstaining (although it was favourable to enlargement), so as to avoid jeopardising the ongoing process of alliance with the Communists. Pompidou also hoped

[2]For a definition, list and detailed analysis of EU-related referendums see Mendez and Mendez (2017).

[3]IFOP (Institut Français d'Opinion Publique) poll, 25–29 March 1972. All IFOP polls are retrieved from *Sondages: revue française de l'opinion publique*. Paris. IFOP.

[4]IFOP, April 1972.

[5]IFOP, March 21, 1972.

the referendum would divide the Left and help him pursue his tactic of extending the Gaullist majority to the very pro-Europe Centrists (Criddle 1972). Here again he failed, since the Socialists and the Communists signed their *'Programme Commun de Gouvernement'* only a few months after the referendum. Moreover, the Left substantially increased its score at the parliamentary election a year later.

The massive abstention of the Socialists also made the victory much smaller than expected. While the 'Yes' scored 89% in the opinion polls shortly after the announcement of the referendum, that had fallen to 68% in the ballot (IFOP). Such a drop was also the result of the defection of part of the electorate of the Centrist party (a minority partner within the majority) and was a blow to Pompidou's political strategy (Criddle 1972: 247). Thus, the President came out weakened from this referendum, not least on the European scene, failing to appear with the enhanced authority he had hoped to gain at the subsequent European Council meeting in Paris (Leigh 1975: 167). As in the Gaullist referendums, the campaign had been dominated by the government, which still fully controlled the audiovisual sector (government control of the radio and the television was progressively reduced from 1974). Only the press had expressed more balanced views.

Until 1969 disloyalty to party recommendations did not really mean that voters were autonomous since it mostly reflected loyalty to de Gaulle. 'Disloyal' voters mostly were electors of parties advocating voting 'No' choosing to vote 'Yes' (to de Gaulle). True disloyalty really started in 1972, though in a rather modest way (Criddle 1972: 247; Leleu 1976: 32). It was mainly about electors opting to abstain rather than following their party stand. Thus 35% of Communist electors abstained but only 5% voted 'Yes' against their party recommendation; while 33% of Centrist electors and 29% of UDR (Gaullist) and RI (*'Républicains indépendants'*) electors abstained and, respectively, 6% and 3% voted 'No' against their party official 'Yes' endorsement. Only Socialist electors proved to some extent more disloyal with half of them going to the polls in spite of their party's call for abstention and a majority of these 'dissidents' voted 'Yes', in line with their party's actual view on the matter. The quarter of Socialist electors who voted 'No' represented a larger contingent of genuinely disloyal voters than in any other party (IFOP).

The impact of the Left-Right divide was also reflected in the territorial distribution of the vote, the 'Yes' being stronger in Right-wing departments and particularly low in Left-wing areas (Leleu 1976: 36). Thus it was highest in the strongholds of the Right in the West (Brittany), the East (Alsace-Lorraine) and the South Centre. And it was lowest in strong Leftist areas: the Paris basin, the Centre and the Mediterranean coast. Notwithstanding the call for abstention by the Socialists, the pattern of participation was also very common, with voters in the North much more mobilised than in the South, suggesting that abstention stemmed more from indifference than from party recommendations. And not surprisingly, the 'Yes' was massive among traditionally most Right-wing social groups, that is, peasants (90%), as well as higher tertiary employees (*cadres supérieurs*) and liberal professions (85%). Turnout was also higher in these groups. Thus 'the electoral behaviour of the French, despite the extent of non-participation which was largely due to the indifference of the electorate towards the European question, remained characteristic of traditional patterns' (Leleu 1976: 46).

Indifference to the issue caused abstention but was also not favourable to issue voting. Thus, although Pompidou had carefully avoided putting his own position or that of his government on the line, only 52% of the electors declared they would actually express their view on EC enlargement, while 13% said they would pronounce on government policy, and 11% on the President of the Republic (IFOP poll, 25–29 March 1972). This was certainly a lesser 'deviation' than at previous Gaullist referendums, but still a major one, showing the somewhat innate plebiscitary bias of the presidential referendum (Parodi 1973).

9.3.2   The 1992 Referendum on the Maastricht Treaty

France was the only country to vote on accession treaties of new countries, but nonetheless proved not to be addicted to EU referendums. The Single European Act was not submitted to popular ratification and Mitterrand's decision in June 1992 to call for a referendum on the Maastricht Treaty under Article 11—which was this time constitutionally irreproachable—came as a surprise. The motives of the President were threefold (Portelli 1992: 5). First, the announcement of the referendum the day after the Danish 'No' to the treaty in June 1992 was a tactical move to prevent the ratification process from being interrupted. Europe was the main axis of Mitterrand's second mandate (1988–1995) and the abandonment of the treaty would have been a serious political setback for him. Second, in line with tradition, the referendum was intended to boost presidential popularity at mid-mandate, through popular approval of a treaty he had effectively co-authored with the German Chancellor Helmut Kohl. Beyond short-term effects, Mitterrand hoped the referendum would help build a new image as European founder for posterity, since he had failed to personify the break with capitalism (Grunberg 2005: 130).

Finally, a third motive was party oriented, in view of the forthcoming parliamentary election due the next year. The Socialist Party had performed dramatically badly in the March 1992 regional elections and could benefit from the internal division of the Right on the treaty. The Gaullist RPR was actually split on the issue, the bulk of its elected officials and party activists being against the treaty in contrast with the leadership, while the Europhile Giscardian UDF was also experiencing internal dissidences. While the Single European Act had been a non-issue, the sleeping consensus of government parties on Europe was reaching its end with the growing hostility of peasants to the common agricultural policy. Moreover, the European currency was controversial, all the more so since the Danes were seemingly unconvinced and the British had secured an opt out. In this context, the Constitutional

Court's ruling in April 1992 declaring unconstitutional the treaty's provisions allowing resident European citizens to vote in local elections and the transfer of monetary powers to Brussels, fuelled party divisions—which further increased during the constitutional review process which immediately followed and culminated after the rejection of the treaty by the Danes.

The referendum proved ineffective except for its first aim, with Ireland ratifying the treaty in June and Luxemburg, Belgium and Greece in July. Admittedly, it also succeeded in shaping Mitterrand as a Father of Europe, but the overly narrow victory was unable to produce the intended authority-enhancing effect. In spite of the overwhelming superiority of the pro-Maastricht side in the official campaign, the 'Yes' actually fell from 65% in voting intentions in early June to 51% in the ballot (Portelli 1992: 9; Criddle 1993: 231–232; Appleton 1992: 7).

This was due to several factors. First, Mitterrand's unpopularity and the lack of conspicuous campaigning by Giscard and Chirac, who did not want to hand a victory to the President and also faced party internal divisions. Second, while the campaign of opponents to the treaty raged and mobilised charismatic tenors during the whole summer, the pro-Maastricht establishment was on holiday. Finally, the supporters of the treaty had obvious difficulties in explaining its merits, while its opponents just relied on the wave of discontent (Criddle 1993: 232; Portelli 1992: 8; Appleton 1992: 7–8). Only thanks to the late mobilisation of the 'Yes' side in September—with Giscard no longer sparing his efforts—and Mitterrand's impressive performance in a debate at the Sorbonne, was the victory ensured despite the 'No' side leading in late August.

The referendum was unable to seriously damage the Right. Although it exacerbated divisions, Chirac was re-endorsed by 95% of his party's National Council soon after the referendum, and the RPR-UDF alliance overwhelmingly won the March 1993 parliamentary election. Nor was the referendum able to rescue the Socialist party, which ended up with half as many votes as in 1988. Ironically, its main impact was rather to split the Socialist party, with the breaking away of the anti-European current led by Jean-Pierre Chevènement.

While in 1972 the referendum had not transgressed the Left-Right cleavage, the Maastricht referendum introduced the European cleavage as we know it today: between pro-European government parties of both Left and Right and the Extreme Right and Extreme Left campaigning for the 'No', albeit on different grounds, the Communists and some Ecologists and dissident Socialists denouncing the 'mercantile and liberal Europe', while the *Front National* (FN) and the Gaullist anti-Maastricht leaders focused their attacks on the infringement of state sovereignty. Party loyalty was strongest among Communist and FN electors (respectively 81 and 92% followed the party line), and was lowest among Gaullist electors (41%). However, the RPR had not given voting instructions, thus the most significant disloyalty was maybe that of the respectively 22 and 39% electors of the PS and the UDF who voted 'No' against their party recommendation, although this may have reflected loyalty to the dissident leaders within these two parties.[6]

The rise of Euroscepticism was well reflected in the geography of the vote, more than half of France having voted 'No' (13 regions out of 22), whereas the 'Yes' had won everywhere in 1972. Nevertheless, the 'Yes' was still highest (over 55%) in the traditional conservative strongholds, especially in Brittany and Alsace, as well as in Paris, which had been divided in 1972. Conversely, the 'No' was still dominant in Left-wing areas and highest (over 55%) in Central France and the Mediterranean coast, where it also benefited FN voters. It also prevailed this time in the North. From a sociological perspective, Eurosceptic voting appeared particularly strong in rural areas and old industrial regions, where it reflected the anxiety of economically fragile and lower educated categories. While peasants had been the strongest supporters of Europe in 1972, there were now its greatest opponents, with 62% of farmers voting 'No'. More in line with their previous vote, 61% of workers rejected the treaty (half of them had voted 'No' in 1972). By contrast, the 'Yes' was urban, rich and like in 1972 it scored highest among high tertiary employees (67%), liberal professions (66%), and most of all intellectual professions (71%) (BVA exit poll, quoted in Portelli 1992: 11). The pro-Maastricht vote was primarily a vote of well-educated categories, with 72% of higher education graduates voting 'Yes' (Habert 1992: 874–876). The influence of the level of education was found in all social groups, quite independently from income, as evidenced by the highest score of 'Yes' among teachers, whether in the primary, secondary or higher education (Criddle 1993: 237).

The 1992 referendum was also for the first time a genuine vote on Europe itself, in sharp contrast with the previous referendum on enlargement and European parliamentary elections. Voting studies show that voters actually focused on the issue at stake. Admittedly, this was less true of 'No' voters, who included a substantial proportion of people expressing dissatisfaction with François Mitterrand and the government (39%) or rejecting the political class (31%). However, 72% of 'Yes' voters said they approved the treaty 'to assure a lasting peace in Europe' and 63% because it was 'indispensable for the building of Europe' (BVA exit poll, multiple responses, quoted in Criddle 1993: 238). Furthermore, 97% of 'No' voters disapproved of the treaty while 88% of 'Yes' voters highly approved it (Habert 1992: 877–880). According to Cautrès (2005: 149–150), the cleavage between 'Sovereignists' and 'Europeanists' was the main explanatory factor of the vote at this referendum. Whereas in 1972 the campaign had been powerless to arouse interest, in 1992 on the contrary people interested in the referendum grew from 58% at the end of June to 67% in early September and 71% on the eve of the vote (Figaro-Sofres poll quoted in Habert 1992: 871; see also Piar and Gerstlé 2005: 44). Moreover, the campaign was paramount for the formation of opinion, with 40% of voters saying they had made their decision in the course of it (Piar and Gerstlé 2005: 144).

[6]BVA exit poll published in daily newspaper *Libération* on 22 September 1992.

9.3.3   The 2005 Referendum on the European Constitutional Treaty

After the political failure of the Maastricht referendum, neither the Treaty of Amsterdam nor the Treaty of Nice were put to a referendum. By contrast, the 2005 referendum on the European Constitutional Treaty was the first 'politically obligatory' referendum under the Fifth Republic, that is, a referendum which was forced on the President (Grunberg 2005; Morel 2007). Chirac's decision to submit the treaty to the people was to a large extent imposed by parties and civil society. Not that tactical considerations were completely absent from Chirac's mind. Such considerations were in a way symmetrical to those of Mitterrand in 1992: a victory could revitalise Chirac's authority mid-term and wipe out the poor results of the Right at recent regional and European elections; it could also enhance the President's image as a true Gaullist and builder of Europe; finally, it was likely to divide the Opposition, especially the Socialist party (e.g. Martin 2005). There is no doubt either that the decision also fitted into a 'logic of appropriateness', that is, Chirac's belief that ratification by the people was particularly appropriate on such an important text.[7] But the fear of a boomerang effect would probably have been stronger, had he not been under heavy pressure from both the Right and the Left. The pressure grew stronger after UK Prime Minister Tony Blair announced in Spring 2004 that he would submit the treaty to the British people. This was followed by the leaders of the Socialist party, François Hollande, and of the UMP, Alain Juppé and Nicolas Sarkozy, officially asking for a referendum. Former President of the Republic Giscard d'Estaing and former President of the European Commission Jacques Delors also declared that a referendum had become 'unavoidable'. At this point, Chirac would have jeopardized the future legitimacy of the Constitution if he had opted for parliamentary ratification. Moreover, he would have passed for a poor democrat, a pseudo-Gaullist afraid of universal suffrage, and been accused of being deaf to the people after the double defeats at the regional and European elections. After lengthy hesitation, he thus announced a referendum to be held on 29 May 2005.

Chirac's fears proved well-founded since, like in 1992, support for the Treaty dramatically dropped, from an initial 65% in favour in January to an actual 45% in the ballot. This was fatal to the treaty since in the aftermath eight countries declared postponing its ratification (Laurent and Sauger 2005: 161; see also Chapter 28 by Sternberg elsewhere in this volume). For the second time since 1958 a referendum had been lost by the President, but unlike de Gaulle, Chirac did not resign—just as he had not resigned in 1997 after his early election failed 'coup' had resulted in the victory of the Left. He just replaced the Prime Minister. Nonetheless, the impact of the defeat was clearly devastating for his image. The main victim of the referendum, however, was François Hollande, who found himself with a severely divided

---

[7]This neo-institutionalist interpretation of the 2005 referendum has been developed in Morel (2007: 1055–1058).

party and lost the primaries for the presidential election a year later. The effects of the referendum were long lasting for the Socialists, since it was the catalyst of the internal rebellion which disrupted the whole Hollande presidency (2012–2017) and culminated with the party's implosion in 2017.

Like with the Maastricht Treaty, the Constitutional Treaty referendum raised a lot of interest and produced a large-scale debate in the country. Turnout at 70% was as high as in 1992 and much above the respectively 66 and 43 percentage levels of participation at the previous year's regional and European elections. As in 1992, the high level of controversy and uncertainty surrounding the outcome stimulated interest, starting with the media. Never before had a campaign proved so volatile. Voting intentions for the 'Yes' side had also shrunk dramatically in 1992, but stabilised at some point, while in 2005 the 'Yes' and 'No' curves crossed three times in nine weeks, and 44% of voters made up their mind during the campaign or in the last days (Piar and Gerstlé 2005: 44–45; Grunberg 2005: 132–135).

The referendum also contributed to redefining the cleavage on Europe: while sovereignty remained the main issue among Right-wing Eurosceptics, anti-capitalism turned into a denunciation of socio-economic drawbacks of the Single Market (such as firm relocation and social dumping) among Left-wing anti-Europeans and to some extent also the *Front national*. This led electors in principle favourable to Europe and who had approved the Maastricht Treaty to vote 'No' this time—not to Europe per se, but to Europe 'as it works today'. These electors, a substantial number of whom were Socialists, made up a third of 'No' voters and greatly contributed to the failure of the treaty (Brouard and Sauger 2005: 135–136; Brouard et al. 2007: 77–116; Cautrès 2005: 151).

As in 1992, the vote reflected the internal situation in the various parties (Brouard and Sauger 2005: 123–125; Grunberg 2005: 135–137). The PS and the Greens being split, so were their electors. Both parties had held internal votes that ended in a close win for 'Yes', which emboldened the minority to campaign openly against the treaty, a situation that was tolerated by the leadership. As a result, 56% of Socialist electors voted 'No' (IPSOS exit poll quoted in Grunberg 2005: 137). Conversely, parties which were united on European matters also saw a united electorate, and the maximum cohesion was found among those advocating the 'No', namely the PC (98% of their electors voting 'No') and the National Front (93% voting 'No'). The pro-'Yes' UDF and the UMP had respectively 76 and 80% of their electors voting for the treaty.

The vote was fairly even across the country, like in 1972, but this time in favour of 'No', which came first everywhere—with the sole exceptions of Paris and the traditionally pro-European strongholds of Brittany and Alsace. The nationalisation of the vote did not preclude however the existence of areas of particular strength for 'No' (over 63%), which were roughly the same as in 1992: the North, the South and the Centre. Again, support for the Treaty was highest in large cities (over 100,000 inhabitants) and in the most privileged areas (typically the richest Parisian arrondissements), while 'No' was leading in the working-class cities of the North, the Parisian belt and in the South East bastions of the *Front national* (Boy and Chiche 2005: 99).

The sociological distribution of the vote clearly pointed to the importance of social and educational factors. As in 1992, the level of education was the key variable, the only categories voting 'Yes' being the 'bac+2' (54%) and 'bac+3' (64%),[8] the high tertiary employees and liberal professions (65%), and the students (54%), as well as people over 60 (57%) (IPSOS exit poll, quoted in Grunberg (2005: 136). Conversely, 72% of those without a diploma voted 'No', and, unsurprisingly, peasants were again massively against the treaty (70%), as were manual workers and the unemployed, whose 'No' increased compared with 1992 (respectively 79% against 61% in 1992, and 71% against 59% in 1992). The main novelty was the hostility to Europe of certain social categories which voted 'Yes' in 1992, namely intermediate professions (53% voting 'No' against 38% in 1992) and public sector employees (64% supporting 'No' compared with 49% in 1992), the latter voting this time against the treaty more than employees in the private sector (56% No against 50% in 1992).

Finally, like in 1992, the vote on the Constitutional Treaty was strongly related to attitudes towards Europe (Brouard and Sauger 2005: 130–135; see also TNS-SOFRES poll of 11–17 May 2005 quoted in Grunberg 2005: 141). Chirac's apprehension of a vote of confidence (or distrust), as expressed in his address of 26 May 2005, was not confirmed.[9] As with the Maastricht Treaty, domestic issues played a role in the rejection of the Constitution (52% of 'No' voters said they had voted thinking more of national problems than Europe), while only marginally affecting its supporters (81% of 'Yes' voters claimed they had thought more of Europe) (CSA exit poll, quoted by Piar and Gerstlé 2005: 60). In the same vein, other surveys show that those who intended to vote 'No' were also the most critical of the government and the President (Brouard and Sauger 2005: 128–129; Ivaldi 2006). The risk that the vote could bear on Turkey's accession—which Chirac had tried to avoid through the adoption of a constitutional amendment requiring a referendum for each new accession—did not happen. Opposition to Turkish membership was not actually a central motivation of opponents to the treaty (Brouard and Sauger 2005: 132). Altogether, it can thus be said that Europe was 'at the top of the head' of electors on 29 May (Grunberg 2005: 142) and that 'electors have decided, as a matter of priority, on the question put to them' (Cautrès 2005: 145).

---

[8] Referring to the number of years post-Baccalaureat University study.

[9] 'We should not mistake the question. The decision before us goes far beyond traditional political cleavages. It is not a matter of saying "Yes" or "No" to the government. It is about your future and that of your children, the future of France and Europe.' Mitterrand had made a similar statement in 1992 and made clear, like Chirac, that he would not resign in the event of a 'No' victory.

9.4   Provisions and Legal Framework of Nationwide Referendums

The various types of nationwide referendums, who can initiate them, their object, the form of the text, approval requirements or the legal impact of the vote, are provided for in Articles 11, 89 and 88 of the French Constitution. These provisions can be changed through an amendment procedure that does not require a referendum and actually have been on some occasions (see below). In addition, the so-called 'shared initiative referendum', which was introduced in Article 11 in 2008 (but has been effective only since 2015 and has never been used), is regulated by a special 'organic' law.[10] This referendum, which can be triggered at the initiative of 20% of MPs, succeeding in a second stage to collect the signatures of at least 10% of the electorate, is not strictly speaking a referendum—although it passes as one—but rather an agenda initiative. A proposal which has reached the number of signatures may actually not be submitted to popular vote by the President of the Republic with the simple requirement that it is scheduled on the agenda of both Chambers within a certain period of time (whatever the outcome of the debate).

This referendum, as well as the presidential referendum, which was the only kind of referendum provided for in Article 11 until 2008, allows the use of a referendum on a large range of issues since its scope was enlarged in 1995 and 2008. It may now deal with any 'draft law on the organisation of public authorities, on reforms relating to the economic, social or environmental policy of the nation and to the public services that contribute to it, or for the purpose of authorising the ratification of a treaty which, without being contrary to the Constitution, might affect the functioning of the institutions'. Concerning the referendum on the initiative of the President of the Republic,[11] it is not clear whether the 'organization of public authorities' may include constitutional matters, in other words if the President of the Republic may bypass the Parliament to revise the Constitution, as de Gaulle actually did in 1962 despite the fierce controversy. Most lawyers believe he may not, arguing that constitutional revision is provided for in Article 89. The fact that it is clearly excluded with regard to the 'shared initiative referendum', whose conformity of the proposal to the Constitution is controlled upstream, also pleads for this interpretation.

Article 89 regulates the revision of the Constitution and provides for an optional referendum on amendments introduced by the President of the Republic (on proposal of the Prime Minister). After the draft has been approved by both Chambers, the President decides either to submit it to the

---

[10] A law on institutional procedures requiring a qualified majority.

[11] Such a referendum is formally required to be proposed to the President by either the Government or the two chambers but this was never an obstacle since all presidents could rely on a Prime Minister freely chosen by them.

people or to the Chambers convened in Versailles, where it needs a majority of three-fifths of the votes cast to be adopted. By contrast, a referendum is mandatory on amendments introduced by Parliament once they have been approved by both Chambers.

Finally, as mentioned above, a provision for a mandatory referendum on treaty accession of new countries to the EU was introduced in 2005 at the initiative of President Chirac, although it was never used (Article 88-5). From being mandatory, such a referendum became optional after the 2008 constitutional revision. In its new version, it states that any bill authorising the ratification of a treaty of accession of a State to the European Union is submitted by the President of the Republic to a referendum, *unless* each Chamber decides by a majority of three-fifths that it will rather be ratified by the two Chambers convened in Versailles with the same majority (as for the constitutional amendments).

All these types of referendums are binding and have a direct legislative effect if approved since they can bear exclusively on draft laws or passed bills. Through Article 11, they may seek to adopt new legislation or to challenge existing legislation—the only restriction being that the law is not less than one year old in the case of a referendum initiated by a joint parliamentary and popular minority.[12] While through Article 89, pending legislation (constitutional revisions passed at first reading by Parliament) is submitted to the people. There is no quorum requirement and voting is not compulsory. Finally, there is no obstacle to the result of a referendum being amended by procedures other than a referendum. For example, the statutes of New Caledonia approved by referendum in 1988 were substantially modified in 1999 by Parliament.

Beyond these basic features, referendum procedures are not laid down in specific legislation and there is a lack of codification. The detailed organisation of referendums is mainly based on five ad hoc presidential decrees, which mostly transpose the rules for elections to the referendum, especially regarding the campaign and the vote. Thus, in a somewhat arguable way, the referendum tends to be treated as an election. The main issue in this respect is the allocation of public resources to parties, in part based on their electoral results in the previous national general elections and number of seats in parliament, rather than to the 'Yes' and 'No' camps. Until 2000 (referendum on presidential mandate duration) this consisted exclusively in speaking time on public airwaves, but in 2005 (referendum on EU Constitutional Treaty) the government decided also to grant public money. Like for elections, campaign funding must be transparent and is controlled by the *Commission nationale des comptes de campagnes et des financements politiques* (CNCCFP), but unlike elections there is no maximum limit on expenditure. The government is not allowed to campaign or to use public resources for propaganda, as was made clear during

---

[12]A restriction that aims to prevent the Parliament being challenged in its role.

the Maastricht campaign, when the President of the *Conseil Supérieur de l'Audiovisuel* (CSA) asked it to give up on its pro-Maastricht spots, and during the 2005 campaign, when the President of the Constitutional Court required a minister to stop campaigning too openly.

Regarding Article 11, the substantial validity of the question asked is completely unregulated, the jurisprudence of the Constitutional Court being the only reference. Thus, recent judgments of the Court, which broke with its traditional refusal to rule on the decrees organising the referendum (see below), put forward the requirement of clarity and correctness ('*loyauté*') of the question. But these notions remain little explained. Correctness could possibly refer to the criteria of unbiasedness and uniqueness of the question (or unity of the subject), commonly used in the legislation of other countries (Roche 2012). Similarly, the control of the substantial validity of the question is not regulated, except for the referendum jointly initiated by a parliamentary and popular minority.

Thus, the judicial control remains very uncertain, insofar as it not explicitly provided for (except for the 'shared initiative referendum') and only works on request by one or several electors. Moreover, with regard to the five decrees calling for the referendum and defining the rules of the campaign and the vote, the Constitutional Court and Council of State's respective competences are neither clearly defined nor clearly distributed. It (the higher administrative Court) is mostly a matter of jurisprudence. Before 2000, the control of these decrees was regarded as falling within the competence of the Council of State; yet it refused to rule on the first decree, which convenes the referendum and states the wording of the question. There was therefore no control over the initiative and the question. Since 2000 (Hauchemaille jurisprudence), the Constitutional Court agreed to rule on all five decrees, including the first. This points indisputably in the direction of increased control of referendums. The Court may dismiss a referendum on procedural grounds or because the question does not respect the requirements of clarity and correctness. It may also reject a referendum whose question clearly does not belong to the referendum domain. It is more arguable whether it would agree, in the case of the referendum initiated by the President of the Republic, to rule on the conformity of the proposed law to the Constitution (Fatin-Rouge Stefanini 2004).[13] In the absence of any formal recourse, it is only required that the Court expresses advice on the decrees, which since 2000 must be published. Finally, it should be stressed that recourses may be examined only before the vote, since the Court has repeatedly reiterated its refusal to rule up on the laws approved by referendum. On the other hand nothing prevents the Council of State or any administrative court from deciding on request on the conformity of the referendum law with treaties or Community law.

---

[13] As said above such a control is obligatory with regard to the 'shared initiative referendum'.

9.5   THE CURRENT DEBATE

Since its intense use by de Gaulle at the beginning of the Fifth Republic, the referendum has been a hot and cold issue in French politics. Very much like in other representative democracies (Svensson 2018), both Left-wing and Right-wing government parties have proved quite hostile to the device, although maybe more so than anywhere else as a result of its Gaullist use reminiscent of Bonapartist methods. Thus, the only use of the referendum has been at the initiative of the President of the Republic, when, for essentially opportunistic reasons, he decided to call one under Article 11 or 89 of the Constitution. This happened once with Pompidou, who actually initiated the series of EU-related referendums. This did not happen with Giscard, perhaps because of a personal reluctance to 'appeal to the people', but was again the case with Mitterrand in 1988—although the referendum on New Caledonia actually arose from a pledge by the Prime Minister to the local separatist leader. The referendum on the Maastricht Treaty (1992) was the only truly 'Mitterrandien' referendum— maybe also the last 'Gaullist style'—and the second EU-related referendum in France. The third EU-related referendum, on the European Constitutional Treaty (2005), which came under the Chirac presidency, five years after the referendum on reducing presidential duration in office, was a turning point in the French experience: for the first time, calls for a referendum came from a large array of parties and personalities, both from the Left and the Right, as well as from civil society. In fact, Chirac was very hesitant to organise this referendum and did so only because of the strong pressure exerted on him (Morel 2007). Thus, 2005 clearly demonstrated that the referendum was no longer a presidential weapon under the Fifth Republic, as conceived and practised by de Gaulle, nor a taboo for parties, but rather increasingly spurred on by growing demands from the society.

The current French paradox is that although absent in practice since 2005, the referendum has been present as never before in the political debate. For sure, this is not yet a major subject. To a large extent it is limited to being discussed at presidential elections. But there was a clear increase in interest from 2007 to 2012 and then again in 2017. The 2007 presidential election was marked by the trauma of 2005 and the referendum was not popular among the two finalists: although she expressed support for a new referendum on European institutions (proposal 91), Ségolène Royal did not mention the mechanism in her cutting-edge programme for participatory democracy, preferring tools such as participatory budgets, citizens' juries, or the agenda initiative (proposal 73); while Nicolas Sarkozy, despite having urged Chirac to hold the referendum on the constitutional treaty while he was UMP General Secretary, had turned around and publicly adopted a very critical tone about the device. Once elected, he failed to submit either the Lisbon treaty or the 2008 constitutional revision to the voters. The introduction as part of this revision of the 'shared initiative referendum' (see Sect. 9.4) was largely imposed on him, although popular initiative figured in his 2007 electoral programme.

And he did not ensure the 'organic' law for implementing this new mechanism was passed during his term in office. This was only done under his Socialist successor Hollande, although the new elected president was far from a supporter of referendums either. Finally, Sarkozy pressed to abolish the mandatory referendum on new EU accessions introduced by Chirac in 2005 (see above), although he was not wholly successful and was only able to make it optional, the decision to hold or not the referendum going to Parliament (see above).

2012 marked the big return of the referendum, as a result of Sarkozy's new turnaround on the matter. The President in office campaigned this time as the 'People's candidate' with the referendum as a flagship proposal of his programme. This allowed him to distinguish himself from François Hollande, who asserted 'the importance of respecting representative democracy' (interview in weekly newspaper *Marianne*, 17 February 2012) and viewed the referendum as an exceptional device, on topics such as institutions and European issues; and on the other side to compete with the referendum-oriented populist candidate Marine le Pen, who advocated referendums on migratory and Islamic issues. Sarkozy remained very vague about which questions should be put to the referendum. He just declared that he would call the French to decide on 'major issues' and 'each time there will be a deadlock', stressing heavily the responsibility of intermediary bodies in blocking reforms. Among the main six presidential candidates, François Bayrou (Centre-Right), who was considered a serious challenger because he came very close to the two leading candidates in 2007, also helped to put the referendum on the campaign agenda. He announced that if elected he would hold a referendum on a package of institutional reforms on June 10th, the same day as the first round of parliamentary elections. This was clearly a tactic intended to help him, as the leader of the small *Mouvement Démocrate* (MODEM), to win a majority at this election. But it contributed to drawing the outlines of a pro-referendum presidency, all the more since Bayrou, although not a Gaullist, had a Gaullist conception of institutions, and was the fiercest critic of Sarkozy's decision not to submit the Lisbon Treaty to the voters. Clearly, one will never know whether Sarkozy would have respected his commitment to referendums if re-elected, but the victory of François Hollande unsurprisingly meant a halt to this referendum momentum. The only exception was the President's support for local referendums following the death of an ecologist activist at a protest against the Sivens dam in 2014. This was followed by his announcement of a local referendum on the project of a new airport near the city of Nantes. But, like his predecessor, the Socialist President did not organise any nationwide referendum.

The Brexit vote, which just preceded the launching of the Republican primaries for the 2017 presidential election, brought the referendum back into the public debate. To a large extent, the question of holding an EU-related referendum became a Left-Right divide as Prime Minister Manuel Valls clearly stated in a speech in the National Assembly in the days following the British vote that a referendum on an amended treaty or a new European project was not a topic for the Executive,[14] while the main Republican candidates, Sarkozy, François Fillon, Alain Juppé and Bruno Le Maire, all advocated a referendum on Europe. Admittedly, only the two latter still had this proposal in their programme for the primaries a few months later—Juppé was in favour of a pan-European referendum and Le Maire a strictly national one. In the meantime most candidates had developed generous proposals for referendums on various subjects: Sarkozy on the reduction in the number of parliamentarians, the interdiction of multiple mandates (just passed in Parliament), restrictions on family reunification for migrants and the preventive internment of people classified as 'dangerous'; François Fillon on making balanced budget equilibrium a constitution requirement, reforming local authorities, ending special pension schemes, introducing immigration quotas and reducing the number of parliamentarians; Bruno Le Maire, in a Bayrou-like tactic, claimed he would hold a referendum the same day as the second round of the legislative elections on a package of institutional reforms so-called of 'moralization of political life'; and the Christian-Democrat Jean-Frédéric Poisson advocated a referendum on the right of foreigners to social assistance. Ultimately, the UK's referendum on EU membership can be said to have been the catalyst of a growing demand for direct democracy reflecting the crisis of confidence towards parties and politicians and the widely shared view that the country was not reformable through 'normal means', leading most candidates to the primaries to advocate the recourse either to the referendum or to decrees.[15]

The referendum became an all-party issue in the weeks prior to the presidential election. Most candidates were now proposing specific referendums and five of the eleven were in favour of popular initiative. On the Right, Fillon stuck to his five above-mentioned referendums to be held under existing constitutional provisions. On the Extreme Right, Marine Le Pen and Nicolas Dupont-Aignan advocated a referendum on 'European refoundation' and the introduction of popular initiative. On the Left, the stronger advocate of the referendum was now Jean-Luc Mélenchon ('*La France insoumise*'), who clearly boosted his direct democracy programme compared with that of 2007, now being in favour of popular initiative and mandatory referendums on all constitutional revisions and new EU treaties (in addition to the recall for any elected representative). But Bruno Hamon (Socialist party) was also not short of ideas with his proposal to introduce the citizen agenda initiative and the veto-referendum on parliamentary laws at the request of 1% of registered voters, and his announcement of referendums on various subjects, such as voting rights to foreigners or counting blank votes in referendum outcomes.

[14]'A referendum cannot be the way to get rid of a problem, let alone a backdoor to solve internal policy problems' (speech of 28 June 2016 about Brexit's consequences).

[15]On this see e.g. https://jean-jaures.org/sites/default/files/lobservatoire_de_la_demo cratie._viavoice_-fondation_jean_jaures-revue_civique_-_france_inter_-_lcp_-_presse_region ale._septembre_2016_-_200916.pdf and http://www.lemonde.fr/societe/article/2016/ 11/17/primaire-de-droite-les-strategies-de-la-reforme_5033032_3224.html.

A major exception to this general infatuation with the referendum was Emmanuel Macron, who carefully remained mute on the subject. It looked as if he had forgotten his post-Brexit commitment to a transnational referendum on a new European project to be held after its discussion by national citizen conventions, when he argued: 'I believe that we must today consult the peoples, ask them their opinion. (…) But this must be done in an appropriate framework, not on the basis of a referendum tomorrow on this Europe, but first by building with the European peoples this new project and then submitting this new roadmap, this new project, to a referendum' (Macron 2016). Like his predecessor, as President Macron rather cooled the referendum frenzy, although he declared in July 2017 in his message to the Congress that he would not hesitate to submit his constitutional reform to the people if necessary (i.e. in case Parliament would not reach the qualified majority). Clearly enough, Macron conceives the referendum as a last resort. In a Pericles-like speech in Athens on 7 September 2017 (Macron 2017), he revived his proposal of democratic conventions, but this time seemingly as an alternative to a referendum:

> I want us to get out of this type of infantile dilemma in which Europe is now plunged, with on the one hand those who want to go and get the people and make them say a "yes" or a "no" that they will manipulate for months, when the referendum becomes the weapon of the populists, the anti-Europeans, and on the other side those who really believe in Europe end up afraid of their peoples and hide behind their own doubts and say to themselves: 'Let's move forward, but let's never change the treaties for fear of returning to a referendum. Let's move forward, but by little steps between us, people will not understand that'. We must choose another path, a third one, the path invented here, the path invented in the very place where we find ourselves, which was not that of demagogy: it was that of democracy, controversy, debate, construction by criticism and dialogue, which consists in returning to the intimacy of each question and its complexity, namely what we want for the common city. That is what I want in the first half of 2018 in all the countries of our continent, of our Europe.

However, the lack of a majority in the Senate to approve the constitutional reform, as well as the Covid crisis, have greatly removed the prospect either of a referendum initiated by Macron or of a reform facilitating the use of the "shared initiative referendum".

REFERENCES

Appleton, A. (1992). Maastricht and the French Party System: Domestic Implications of the Treaty Referendum. *Journal of Comparative Politics, 10*(4), 1–18.

Berlia, G. (1972). Le référendum du 23 avril 1972. *Revue française de droit public, 88*(4), 929–943.

Boy, D., & Chiche, J. (2005). Le référendum français du 29 mai 2005. L'irrésistible nationalisation d'un vote européen. In P. Perrineau (Ed.), *Le vote européen 2004–2005. De l'élargissement au référendum français* (pp. 229–244). Coll. Chroniques électorales. Paris: Presses de Sciences Po.

Brouard, S., & Sauger, N. (2005). Comprendre la victoire du 'Non': proximité partisane, conjoncture et attitude à l'égard de l'Europe. In A. Laurent & N. Sauger (Eds.), *Le référendum de ratification du Traité constitutionnel européen: comprendre le « non » français* (n°42). Paris: Les Cahiers du CEVIPOF.

Brouard, S., Sauger, N., & Grossman, E. (2007). *Les Français contre l'Europe?* (352 pp.). Paris: Presses de Sciences Po.

Carré de Malberg, R. (1931). Considérations théoriques sur la question de la combinaison du référendum avec le parlementarisme. *Annuaire de l'Institut International de Droit Public,* vol. II.

Cautrès, B. (2005). Les clivages socio-politiques sur l'intégration européenne et le vote du 29 mai 2005. In A. Laurent & N. Sauger (Eds.), *Le référendum de ratification du Traité constitutionnel européen: comprendre le « non » français* (n°42). Paris: Les Cahiers du CEVIPOF.

Criddle, B. (1972). Politics by Plebiscite in France. *The World Today, 28*(6), 240–248.

Criddle, B. (1993). The French Referendum on the Maastricht Treaty September 1992. *Parliamentary Affairs, 46*(2), 228–238.

Dicey, A. V. (1890, April). Ought the Referendum to be Introduced into England? *Contemporary Review, 57,* 489–511.

Esmein, A. (1906). *Eléments de droit constitutionnel français et comparé* (1st ed.). Paris: Sirey.

Fatin-Rouge Stefanini, M. (2004) *Le contrôle du référendum par la justice constitutionnelle* (381 pp.). Coll: Droit public positif. Paris: Economica.

Grunberg, G. (2005). Le référendum de ratification du Traité constitutionnel européen. *French Politics Culture and Society, 23*(3), 128–144.

Habert, P. (1992). Le choix de l'Europe et la décision de l'électeur. *Commentaire, 60,* 871–880.

Ivaldi, G. (2006). Beyond France's 2005 Referendum on the European Constitutional Treaty: Second-Order Model, Anti-Establishment Attitudes and the End of the Alternative European Utopia. *West European Politics, 29*(1), 47–69.

Laurent, A., & Sauger, N. (Eds.). (2005). *Le référendum de ratification du Traité constitutionnel européen: comprendre le « non » français* (n°42). Paris: Les Cahiers du CEVIPOF.

Leigh, M. (1975). Linkage Politics: The French Referendum and the Paris Summit of 1972. *Journal of Common Market Studies, 14,* 157–170.

Leleu, C. (1976). The French Referendum of April 23, 1972. *European Journal of Political Research, 4,* 25–46.

Macron, E. (2016, June 25). *Speech at Sciences Po University.* http://www.francetvi nfo.fr/monde/europe/la-grande-bretagne-et-l-ue/brexit-emmanuel-macron-prone-un-nouveau-projet-europeen-et-un-referendum_1517241.html.

Macron, E. (2017). *Speech to Pnyx, Athens*. http://www.elysee.fr/declarations/art icle/discours-du-president-de-la-republique-emmanuel-macron-a-la-pnyx-athenes-le-jeudi-7-septembre-201/.

Marianne. (2012, February 17). Available at https://www.marianne.net/auteur/mag azine-marianne.

Martin, P. (2005). Le choix de Chirac ou pourquoi Jacques Chirac a-t-il choisi la voie référendaire pour la ratification du traité constitutionnel? In A. Laurent & N. Sauger (Eds.), *Le référendum de ratification du Traité constitutionnel européen: comprendre le « non » français* (n°42). Paris: Les Cahiers du CEVIPOF.

Mendez, F., & Mendez, M. (2017). *Referendums on EU Matters*. Brussels: European Parliament. http://www.europarl.europa.eu/supporting-analyses (last view 14 October 2018).

Mirkine-Guetzévitch, B. (1931). Le référendum et le parlementarisme dans les nouvelles constitutions européennes. *Annuaire de l'Institut International de Droit Public*, vol. II.

Morel, L. (2007). The Rise of Politically Obligatory Referendums. The 2005 French Referendum in Comparative Perspective. *West European Politics, 30*(5), 1041–1067.

Morel, L. (2010). La Ve République, le référendum et la démocratie plébiscitaire de Max Weber. *Jus Politicum*, n°4, 55 pp. http://www.juspoliticum.com/La-Ve-Rep ublique-le-referendum-et.html.

Morel, L. (2014, March 12). *The Referendum in the Overall Balance of the Fifth Republic*. Lecture at Collège de France, Paris. http://www.college-de-france.fr/site/en-pierre-rosanvallon/seminar-2014-03-12-10h00.htm, http://www. college-de-france.fr/site/en-pierre-rosanvallon/seminar-2014-03-12-11h00.htm.

Morel, L. (2019). *La question du référendum*. Paris: Presses de Sciences Po. coll. "Nouveaux Débats", 307 pp.

Parodi, J.-L. (1973). *La Cinquième République et le système majoritaire. Le référendum ou l'apparition d'une question de confiance présidentielle*. Institut d'Etudes Politiques de Paris.

Passelecq, O. (1990). De Tardieu à de Gaulle: contribution à l'étude des origines de la Constitution de 1958. *Revue française de droit constitutionnel, 3*, 387–407.

Piar, C., & Gerstlé, J. (2005). Le cadrage du référendum sur la Constitution européenne: la dynamique d'une campagne à rebondissements. In A. Laurent & N. Sauger (Eds.), *Le référendum de ratification du Traité constitutionnel européen: comprendre le « non » français* (n°42). Paris: Les Cahiers du CEVIPOF.

Portelli, H. (1992, September–October). Le référendum sur l'Union Européenne. *Regards sur l'actualité*, pp. 3–12.

Roche, J.-B. (2012). Le contrôle juridictionnel du référendum en France. *Revue Juridique de l'Ouest 2012-1 and 2012-2*.

Svensson, P. (2018). Views on Referendums: Is There a Pattern? In L. Morel & M. Qvortrup (Eds.), *The Routledge Handbook to Referendums and Direct Democracy* (pp. 91–106). Routledge.

CHAPTER 10

The Referendum Experience in Switzerland

Uwe Serdült

In an international comparison over time Switzerland usually stands out as the country with the most frequent and constant application of direct democratic mechanisms such as the referendum and the citizens' initiative. Countries with a low level of referendum practice organise them mainly in order to ratify a new constitution, to sanction an occasional important change in a constitution, or in relation to accession to supra-national bodies such as the European Union (EU). Countries that use them more frequently such as Switzerland tend also to decide important policy matters via popular votes. The different institutional mechanisms triggering referendum votes on all state levels are routinely applied by all political actors whether they are in government or the opposition, whether by political parties, social movements organisations or even individuals.

After a brief historical excursion and explanation of the main institutional rules, this overview emphases the manifold practice of direct democratic votes in Switzerland, citing some well-known and some lesser known but still surprising cases of referendum votes. (Further aspects of EU-related referendums in Switzerland are covered by Clive Church in Chapter 29.) The examples discussed here should make it clear that in Switzerland all politics are influenced by direct democracy. Political issues are therefore not settled

U. Serdült (✉)
Center for Democracy Studies Aarau (ZDA), University of Zurich, Aarau, Switzerland
e-mail: Uwe.Serdult@zda.uzh.ch

Ritsumeikan University, Kyoto, Japan

© The Author(s) 2021
J. Smith (ed.), *The Palgrave Handbook of European Referendums*,
https://doi.org/10.1007/978-3-030-55803-1_10

for good because the people have spoken. All political actors cope with some referendum agenda on a daily basis and with yet another vote on the horizon in mind.

10.1   Historical Development

To gain a better understanding of Swiss constitutional history we must look into the cantonal histories of the nineteenth century. The situation in Switzerland was characterised by an unstable political environment, further exacerbated by an asymmetry among cantons. In the historical development of the Swiss Confederation some cantons gained a certain supremacy over others. Shortly before the revolutionary times the Confederation consisted of 13 cantons and nine allied states as well as some subject territories, governed by a complex set of treaties. Cantonal delegates met and voted according to instructions from their respective governments in a *Diet*. Some allied states were represented in the *Diet*, others were not. Religious conflicts between Protestants and Catholics reappeared throughout the time after the Reformation, leading to several civil wars. Conflicts between city dwellers and inhabitants of the countryside further spurred revolts and disturbances throughout the eighteenth century (Church and Head 2013; Dardanelli 2011: 143; Linder 2007: 18).

During the early part of the nineteenth century the *ideas* of the French Revolution as well as French troops momentarily destroyed the old feudal order through the creation of the unitary Helvetic Republic (from 1802 to 1815). The new republic created national citizenship, representative democracy and freedom of settlement, and equalised all cantons.[1] Opposition to the new order originated mainly from the smaller, predominantly Catholic, rural cantons of central Switzerland. The new regime suffered four coups in three years. However, the pendulum swung back and in the phase of the Restoration (from 1815 to 1830) the older order was brought back. The revolutions of the 1830s subsequently spurred a series of constitutional referendums on the cantonal level (Auer 1996; Church and Head 2013; Dardanelli 2011). Together with the national constitution of 1848 they can be interpreted as the foundations of modern Swiss political history, bringing separation of powers with directly elected parliaments on both cantonal and national levels.

10.2   Referendums as the Cornerstone of the Swiss Political System

Switzerland's political system includes important elements of direct citizen participation for the creation, change and abolition of binding legal norms. The mechanisms and functions of direct democracy are at the core of all

---

[1]Arguably, the full emancipation of formerly subjected territories was only achieved when the Jura split from the Canton of Bern and became a canton of its own right in 1979.

political undertakings (Kriesi 2005; Linder 2007; Papadopoulos 1998; Vatter 2000). Historically, direct democratic institutions developed bottom-up, from the cantonal level to the national level.[2] In the nineteenth century, a consensus emerged among members of constitutional assemblies throughout the country that referendums ought to be held to ratify newly drafted constitutions. With the implantation of direct democratic mechanisms into cantonal constitutions the pressure to extend them to the national level increased as well. However, between 1848 and 1873 only mandatory referendums for constitutional changes and citizens' initiatives aiming at a complete revision of the federal constitution were allowed. The optional legislative referendum was introduced later, in 1874, and the citizens' initiative for amendments of the Swiss constitution in 1891. Mechanisms of direct citizen participation were advocated by the so-called 'democratic movement' (Tornic and Massüger 2013), which was very active in the 1860s and stood in opposition to the dominant political party at the time, the Radicals (themselves the former reformers who had managed to overcome the old feudal order in 1848). During the twentieth century, some additional modifications to direct democratic institutions were made. The referendum for international treaties, introduced in 1921 and extended in 1977, provided for an extension of direct democracy in matters of foreign policy (Marquis and Sciarini 1999). Furthermore, the right of parliament to withdraw its decisions from the referendum procedure through the use of the so-called 'urgency clause' (which was used extensively during the Second World War) was limited in 1949 by the introduction of a mandatory referendum for such cases. Six years after the introduction of women's suffrage at the national level in 1971, the number of required signatures for an optional referendum was raised from 30,000 to 50,000, and for a citizens' initiative from 50,000 to 100,000 (from an electorate of 5.4 million citizens as of February 2019).

On the cantonal level, direct democratic rights have developed considerably since the nineteenth century and can be regarded to be more diversified than on the national level. Mechanisms of direct democracy include legislative initiatives (which are not possible on the national level despite several attempts to introduce them), referendums on administrative acts, as well as referendums on one-time or recurring financial decisions (Auer 2016; Trechsel and Serdült 1999). The most important direct democratic institutions actually in operation on all state levels are thus the mandatory referendum to sanction constitutional change, the optional referendum to challenge legislation that has already been passed, and the citizens' initiative to totally or partially revise the constitution (or laws in the cantons) from outside of parliament. Cantonal level referendums have to conform to national legislation and are subject to judicial review. For national referendums it is parliament that functions as the guarantor of constitutionality not a court (Rothmayr 2001; Tornay 2008).

---

[2]The first country-wide referendum was held in 1802 under Napoleon, establishing the Helvetic Republic.

However, parliament is relatively lax regarding the admission of initiatives. So far only two initiatives have been invalidated (in 1977 and 1995, respectively).

10.3   REFERENDUM VOTES IN PRACTICE

Except for some cases on the local level—usually in relation to municipal mergers—referendum votes are legally binding in Switzerland. All votes taken at the ballots go through parliaments beforehand, including the respective parliamentary committees and pre-parliamentary procedures. That being said it should be noted that referendum votes still represent the exception for legislative processes. More than 90% of Swiss legislation is passed the ordinary way by parliaments rather than the people directly.

In a stark difference to many other polities incorporating elements of direct democracy into their constitutions, the Swiss do not vote on a referendum question, they vote on a parliamentary bill related to a constitutional text, a law or a treaty. Hence the content of the referendum question is less the focus of debate in the Swiss system than in many others. A referendum vote by Swiss citizens is a binding legal act and not a response to a survey question asked by a political authority. In the case of a mandatory referendum citizens are asked whether they are willing to accept a new or changed constitutional article. For optional referendums challenging legislation that has already been passed by a collection of signatures, citizens are asked whether they want to accept or reject the law in question (cited with its name on the ballot sheet, e.g. the energy law). If the majority agrees, the referendum fails and the law can enter into force once the vote is formally validated by parliament. There is a bit more room for debate regarding the wording of the referendum question in the case of a citizens' initiative because the title of the initiative can be selected by the initiative committee within certain limits. The ballot paper would simply ask whether the voter wanted to accept the initiative and the voter can write 'Yes', 'No' or leave the space blank (which counts as an abstention but is taken into account for calculating turnout figures). Any other text on the ballot would invalidate the vote, which is sometimes done on purpose to voice a concern or protest.

Referendum votes can take place up to four times a year (as a rule of thumb) and are often combined votes on all three state levels (national, cantonal, and municipal). Over time the number of votes on the national level has increased. Since direct democratic institutions are also a political weapon for parties opposing majorities or the political opposition in general, an increase in their use may indicate a period of intensified political struggles often related to uncertain or unstable economic or social conditions. Such was the case for example during the 1970s against a background of economic recession and to a lesser degree in the 1980s with cultural unrest and then again during another economic crisis in the 1990s. In these three decades Swiss society and the Swiss economy underwent major transformations. These phases usually go hand in hand with an increase in party competition. A further reason for more

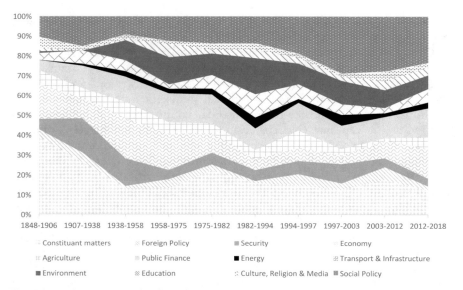

Fig. 10.1 Swiss national referendum topics over time (1848–2018) (*Note* The horizontal axis represents time, slicing up the 640 votes into 10 parts, each comprising an almost equal number of referendum votes. Topic labels read from left to right are represented in the figure from bottom to top (*Source* c2d database [http://c2d.ch]; *N* votes = 640, *n* theme codes = 1040; up to three theme codes allowed per referendum vote])

referendum votes from bottom-up via signature collection is the fact that civil society is nowadays better organised than it used to be.

As Fig. 10.1 shows, there are frequent referendum votes on all possible public matters. Constituent matters putting down the foundations of the state were very important in the nineteenth and early twentieth centuries. Since the 1950s we can observe an increase in votes on environmental issues and social policy but public finance and the economy also seem to be a constant concern in Swiss referendum votes.

10.4   Who Are the People?

Over the centuries Switzerland has gradually expanded the electorate. With the new constitution of 1848 all men, including Jews who had previously been excluded, were enfranchised. Women—and this is probably the darkest stain in Swiss democratic history—had to wait until 1971 for the franchise on the national level. Voting age was lowered from 20 to 18 years in 1991. At the time of writing, a further reduction to 16 years was under discussion at the national level and in some cantons, although only the Canton of Glarus had lowered the voting age for cantonal and local level votes to 16. In 1992 the

Swiss living abroad (roughly 760,000) were granted voting rights. However, barely a quarter of them are registered as potential voters.

Owing to the rather restrictive naturalisation laws, a relatively large part of the adult population in Switzerland is not part of the electorate (Caramani and Strijbis 2013: 399). With a quarter of the population without voting rights, the issues of naturalisation and of political rights for immigrants are two of the hottest potatoes on the political agenda. Voting rights for immigrants are granted at the cantonal (Neuchâtel and Jura) and/or local level (Fribourg, Geneva, Vaud) in all French-speaking cantons to differing degrees. So far only three German-speaking cantons allow their municipalities to decide whether to give voting rights on the local level, Appenzell Ausserrhoden (in three municipalities), Basel City (possible in two municipalities but not implemented) and the Grisons (implemented in a quarter of the communes, typically smaller ones with a lower number of inhabitants). Most of the time voting rights for immigrants were introduced in the form of total revisions of the relevant constitution. However, the Canton of Geneva introduced it via a citizens' initiative. Recent attempts to introduce further voting rights for migrants on the local level elsewhere have failed: Basel-Stadt (2010: 81% No), Bern (2010: 72% No), Luzern (2011: 84% No) and Zürich (2013: 75% No) all rejected respective citizens' initiatives. Political debates on the topic are usually very controversial.

10.5   Mechanisms of Direct Democracy

Since 1848 all modifications of the Swiss national Constitution need to be approved in a referendum vote. Constitutional change—either in the form of a total or partial revision—can originate either from parliament or the citizens themselves. The Constitution of the Canton Schaffhausen became the first in Switzerland that could be totally revised at any time by the will of the people. That principle was introduced in the constitution of 1848 for all cantonal constitutions (as an obligation), as well as the federal one. A successful citizens' initiative for a total revision of the constitution automatically triggers the election of a new parliament which then functions as the body that elaborates the draft constitution. Total revisions are, however, an exceptional undertaking in Switzerland (Biaggini 2011). The constitution is changing on an almost rolling basis via partial revisions. Hence the incentive for a total overhaul is low. After the founding constitution of modern Switzerland in 1848 there was only one substantial additional total revision in 1874 and a more formal one in 1999 which came into force the following year. The total revision of 1999 was announced as a rather technical exercise, attempting to free the 'old lady' of some clumsy and unnecessary baggage she had been carrying through the previous century. The process of total revision was exceptionally long if it was only about tidying up a bit, rephrasing in modern language and getting rid of outdated clauses not being applied anymore. Part of the deadlock during the whole revision process can be explained by the fact that a large part of the political elite either did not see the necessity of a total revision, wanted to pack in too many substantial reforms or was afraid that even a subtle reformulation of constitutional clauses would lead to unwanted consequences. In the remainder of this chapter the main Swiss direct democratic instruments and their use are discussed.

10.5.1 The Mandatory Referendum for Constitutional Changes

A referendum is mandatory for all amendments to the federal Constitution and for membership to some international organisations. A popular vote must be held in such cases and a double majority of the citizens and the cantons is required. In the case of a split cantonal vote (11 and a half out of 23 cantonal votes), the bill does not go through. From 1848 to the end of 2019 197 such automatically triggered referendum votes took place, 149 of which were positive and 48 negative (Table 10.1). This high acceptance rate can also be interpreted as a high governmental approval. On the other hand, the number of No votes shows that there is always a risk of failure at the ballots for a government as well.

Table 10.1 Referendum frequencies by decade, type of legal instrument and success

Decade	Citizens' initiative		Counter-proposal		Mandatory referendum		Optional referendum		Total
	Yes	No	Yes	No	Yes	No	Yes	No	
1848–1859	0	0	0	0	1	0	0	0	1
1860–1869	0	0	0	0	1	8	0	0	9
1870–1879	0	0	0	0	2	1	3	5	11
1880–1889	0	1	0	0	2	1	2	6	12
1890–1899	1	2	0	0	7	3	3	6	22
1900–1909	1	3	1	0	3	1	3	2	14
1910–1919	1	2	0	0	7	0	1	0	11
1920–1929	3	11	1	1	7	2	2	5	32
1930–1939	0	6	3	0	6	0	2	6	23
1940–1949	1	5	1	1	1	1	4	3	17
1950–1959	0	10	2	2	13	7	3	8	45
1960–1969	0	5	0	0	12	1	4	4	26
1970–1979	0	23	4	3	29	9	11	7	86
1980–1989	2	22	5	2	16	5	6	4	62
1990–1999	3	26	2	1	26	5	24	13	100
2000–2009	5	39	1	5	10	3	24	4	91
2010–2019	5	40	5	1	6	1	16	8	82
Subtotal	22	195	25	16	149	48	108	81	
Total	217		41		197		189		644

(*Source* www.c2d.ch)

10.5.2   The Optional Referendum

Citizens can also challenge parliamentary decisions through referendums. Federal laws, generally binding decisions of the Confederation as well as some international treaties are subject to an optional referendum. In these cases, a popular ballot is held if 50,000 citizens or eight cantons request it within 100 days after a decree's publication. It is seen as a veto-instrument against decisions taken by the Federal Parliament and dates back to the total revision of the Federal Constitution in 1874. It was introduced to compensate for the stronger federal centralisation that came with that revision. Nowadays its impact is mostly indirect: the mere possibility of an optional referendum has a strong influence on Swiss law-making and ensures broadly acceptable solutions in early stages of the process. This direct democratic instrument is thus always looming over legislation like the Sword of Damocles (Trechsel and Sciarini 1998; Vatter 2000). In order to increase the chances that a law will not be rejected by the optional referendum a compromise is often sought already before it enters parliament. The optional referendum can only be used on Federal statutes, decrees and international treaties that are foreseen for this referendum vote by the constitution. The vote is always on the bill itself. A simple majority of the citizens will suffice Between 1874 and the end of 2018 189 votes on an optional referendum had taken place, of which 108 were positive and 81 negative (Table 10.1). Positive in this case means that the law passed by parliament was confirmed in the referendum vote challenging the law.

10.5.3   The Citizens' Initiative

An initiative allows citizens to seek a decision on an amendment they want to make to the federal Constitution. Changes to laws or any other government regulations cannot be the subject of a popular initiative at the national level. A popular vote takes place if 100,000 signatures are collected in favour of the initiative within the legal timeframe of 18 months. To be valid a vote requires not only the simple majority of all citizens but also the majority of the 20 full and 6 half cantons (two for each of Appenzell, Basle, and Unterwalden). Thus a proposal for a partial revision must be accepted by the people (the majority of the valid votes cast in the whole country) and by the cantons (voters must accept the proposal in a majority of the cantons). The cantonal score could therefore be a draw of 11½ against 11½ cantons, in which case the vote would not go through even if there was a majority of citizens in favour. Other than the double majority requirement for constitutional changes there are no other thresholds for turnout or the outcome. The citizens' initiative can take two forms: either as a full draft or as a general proposition. The full draft is the more common version; the citizens put forward a full draft of the text of a new article or a new clause. The Federal Assembly cannot change anything in this draft but can put forward an alternative of its own, a counter-proposal.

Since 1988 the double-Yes with a tie-break question is applied. Under these new rules citizens can say Yes to both the initiative and the counter-proposal, hence a separate tie-break question was introduced, only applying in case both proposals gain a majority. In the tie-break question citizens have to answer which option they prefer and the option with more votes would then prevail. Previously, one could only give a vote to either the citizens' initiative or the counter-proposal which were therefore cannibalising each other's votes. Counter proposals are usually less extreme than citizens' initiatives; however, they tend to incorporate some of the demands by the initiators and thus have, in general, a higher chance of passing. At the time of writing, of the 217 votes on a citizens' initiative only 22 had been accepted. With the introduction of the double-Yes procedure chances for passing increased for more recent decades. There have been 41 votes on counter proposals, 25 positive and 16 negative (see Table 10.1).

10.5.4 The Recall

On the subnational level there is also the option to initiate a recall of either parliament or the government or both (Serdült 2015). Currently the recall in Switzerland only exists in a minority of 6 out of 26 cantons and does not exist on the national level. However, indirectly a recall of the national parliament and government can be induced by launching the initiative for a total revision of the Constitution. In the case of a successful recall vote, new elections would be called. So far there were only a couple of attempts and one successful recall vote, namely in the Canton of Aargau in the year 1862. Because of the high accessibility of direct democratic instruments to influence public policies—with on the local and regional level financial matters included—the recall as a mechanism of direct democracy is not used much and can be considered to be dormant.

10.5.5 Finance Referendums

Instruments specifically designed to target financial decisions are only found on the cantonal and local levels, where they play an important role. However, on the national level there is a recent tendency of parliament voluntarily submitting large investments for major national infrastructures or the purchase of new fighter planes to the referendum procedure by including them into a law even if formally it is not necessary. Further, sometimes very specific options for finance referendums in some cantons include instruments targeted at expenses for road construction, debt, issuing bonds, taxes, taking a share in private companies, or real estate transactions (Trechsel and Serdült 1999). As a local level example there is the list of finance referendums which are mandatory in the City of Aarau, capital of the Canton of Aargau, which has a population of 20,000 inhabitants and a budget of 160 million CHF (2014): a mandatory budget referendum held *every* year (on a question like: 'Do you want to accept the budget 2014 for Aarau with a tax level of 94%?'); single expenditures above 6 million CHF; and recurrent expenditures above 400,000 CHF per year. In practice, this means that no school, no major bridge, no football stadium can be built without the explicit approval of citizens in a referendum vote.

10.6   Campaign Financing

One would expect Switzerland, with its longstanding and frequent use of direct democracy institutions to have developed an extensive regulation on referendum campaigns, including rules on campaign financing and on media access. Surprisingly, this is not the case (Braun Binder 2015; Serdült 2010). The referendum at the federal level is governed by provisions of the Federal Constitution and by the Federal Act on Political Rights. None of these contain rules dealing with referendum campaigns in particular. However, several fundamental rights guaranteed by the Federal Constitution have to be considered while examining the legal framework of referendum campaigns. The guarantee of political rights protects the free formation of opinion by the citizens. This provision does not impose strict neutrality on political authorities during the referendum debate. Authorities are allowed to take a position and to recommend the approval or the refusal of a referendum question. However, any kind of political propaganda by political authorities would be contrary to the constitutional guarantee of the political rights, even more so if public funds were to be used for such propaganda. It is also forbidden to grant public funds to private referendum committees. Other fundamental rights guaranteed by the Federal Constitution which ensure that a referendum debate is fair are the freedom of expression and information, the freedom of the media, the freedom of assembly and the freedom of association. However, there is no specific regulation on the financing of referendum campaigns by political parties and other civil society groups. Therefore, while no public funds may be used for political propaganda, campaign spending is not limited, and there is no obligation for campaigners to reveal their donors or the amount of money spent on a referendum campaign. The financing of political parties is not regulated in Switzerland. Political parties do not receive any public funds for their activities. They finance themselves from membership fees, from donations of party members, non-members, private companies and organisations, as well as from contributions from office holders. On the federal level, there are no transparency rules at all. Whereas this is generally also the case at the cantonal level, four cantons have introduced transparency rules. In the cantons of Ticino and Schwyz, donations of more than 10,000 Swiss francs to political parties have to be published. In the cantons of Geneva and Neuchâtel, anonymous donations are forbidden and transparency rules apply not only to political parties but also to other political groups engaged in campaigns. For the time being, such rules are still exceptional and do not exist in other cantons or at the national level. However, a citizens' initiative demanding more transparency on political and campaign financing on the national level managed to gather the necessary signatures and was on its way to a referendum vote at the time of writing.

10.7 FREQUENCY OF REFERENDUM VOTES

Referendum votes can take place up to four times a year (as a rule of thumb) and are often combined votes on all three state levels (national, cantonal, and municipal). Over time the number of votes on the national level has increased. Since direct democratic institutions are also a political weapon for parties contesting majorities or in general the political opposition, an increase in their use can be interpreted as a period of intensified political struggles often related to uncertain or unstable economic or social conditions. Such was, for example, the case during the 1970s with the economic recession and to a lesser degree in the 1980s with cultural unrest and then again during another economic crisis in the 1990s. In these three decades Swiss society and economy underwent major transformations. These phases are usually also marked by an increase in party competition. A further reason for more referendum votes from bottom-up with signature collection involved is the fact that civil society is nowadays better organised than in the past.

The 'participatory age' really started in the 1970s, as we can see in Fig. 10.2, for the national and the cantonal levels (exemplified by the Canton of Aargau). In the addition to elections on all three state levels Swiss citizens are thus coping with roughly ten national, five cantonal and an unknown (due to the lack of data) number of local referendum votes per year.

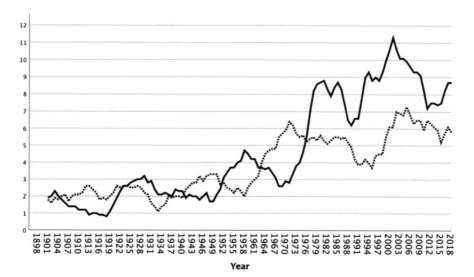

Fig. 10.2 Frequency of referendum votes 1901–2018 (*Source* c2d database [http://c2d.ch])

10.8   TURNOUT

Decreasing turnout rates for referendum votes in Switzerland are frequently deplored by academics as well as policy-makers and debated in the press by political commentators. While the average turnout was approximately 60% just after World War II, this figure had dropped to 40% by the mid-1970s. Turnout for referendum votes in the last few years amounts to 45% on average. Average turnout rates are, however, misleading because they do not measure political participation in an adequate way. Most Swiss citizens do participate occasionally in one or a few referendum votes per year. They might not participate in all the four votes per year but in, let us say, two. In my understanding these citizens had then been politically active in this year and therefore participation in a referendum poll should rather be cumulated over the year and not averaged. Calculated that way the decline in turnout rates would look much less dramatic than they seem and be in addition a better, more valid measurement of political participation. Vote registry analyses show that about 80–90% of the voting population take part in at least one of the many referendum votes within a four-year timeframe, not even counting executive and legislative mandate elections on all three state levels (Goldberg et al. 2018; Serdült 2018). In general, it is worth noting, therefore, that turnout in Switzerland is relatively low on average but fluctuates according to the topic at stake (Sciarini et al. 2016).

10.9   REFERENDUM VOTE EXAMPLES

Due to the high frequency of referendum votes in Switzerland it is not possible to cover them all or in great detail. A selection of cases are presented below in order to demonstrate some of their functions and effects in operation. An overview of topics is presented in Table 10.2 to give a glimpse at most recent referendum activity. What springs to mind is the high rhythm and variety of topics. 'After the referendum is before the referendum', as there is always the next one for which the political elite, the media system and, last but not least, the citizens have to prepare. What also becomes clear in the selection below is the fact that most initiatives fail at the ballot and that they have a higher chance of getting accepted at least partially when they are able to trigger a response by parliament in the form of a counter-proposal. As noted above, in cases where, in the view of the initiative committee, that counter-proposal is close enough to the initiative they might even decide to retract the initiative (and are allowed to do so). In that case only the counter-proposal goes to the stage of a ballot vote.

10.9.1   A Local Level, Cultural Issue: Language Spoken in Kindergarten

In the German-speaking part of Switzerland, the population usually speaks a dialect and only uses German at school or for written text. In the Canton of

Table 10.2   Swiss referendum votes on the national level, 2017–2019

Year	Date	Title	Mechanism	Result
2017	21 May	Energy Act[a]	Optional ref	Yes
	24 September	Food Security[b]	Counter prop	Yes
		Pension reform[c]	Optional ref	No
		VAT increase[d]	Optional ref	No
2018	4 March	Radio and TV licence fee[e]	Initiative	No
		Financial Regulation on Tax[f]	Mandatory ref	Yes
	10 June	Crisis-Proof Money[g]	Initiative	No
		Gambling Law[h]	Optional ref	Yes
	23 September	Food Sovereignty[i]	Initiative	No
		Fair Food[j]	Initiative	No
		Cycle and Hiking Trails[k]	Counter prop	Yes
	25 November	Dignity of Farm Animals[l]	Initiative	No
		Swiss Before International Law[m]	Initiative	No
		Social Welfare Detectives[n]	Optional ref	Yes
2019	10 February	Stop Urban Sprawl[o]	Initiative	No
	19 May	Tax and Pension Reform[p]	Optional ref	Yes
		Firearms Law[q]	Optional ref	Yes

[a]https://tinyurl.com/sp7zsmm, accessed 21 November 2019
[b]https://tinyurl.com/w8ndq79, accessed 21 November 2019
[c]https://tinyurl.com/skqmfhm, accessed 21 November 2019
[d]https://tinyurl.com/qn8k4jz, accessed 21 November 2019
[e]https://tinyurl.com/ybb4s99f, accessed 21 November 2019
[f]https://tinyurl.com/vkpw9hg, accessed 21 November 2019
[g]https://tinyurl.com/rue3sks, accessed 21 November 2019
[h]https://tinyurl.com/w4cmbar, accessed 21 November 2019
[i]https://tinyurl.com/vuo9gqe, accessed 21 November 2019
[j]https://tinyurl.com/ufqubeo, accessed 21 November 2019
[k]https://tinyurl.com/wtaozw5, accessed 21 November 2019
[l]https://tinyurl.com/y7jt9tak, accessed 21 November 2019
[m]https://tinyurl.com/u7apt2f, accessed 21 November 2019
[n]https://tinyurl.com/qrnyagf, accessed 21 November 2019
[o]https://tinyurl.com/v37jrzd, accessed 21 November 2019
[p]https://tinyurl.com/rebjgp6, accessed 21 November 2019
[q]https://tinyurl.com/y5nzwl6w, accessed 21 November 2019

Argovia, children in Kindergarten used to communicate in a Swiss German dialect only. However, since 2008 teachers in Kindergarten are supposed to speak German for about a third of the time in order to prepare the children for what awaits them when they enter elementary school. A smaller right-wing party opposed this recent practice and sought with the help of a citizens' initiative to re-introduce Swiss German as the main language in Kindergarten. The initiative got accepted in 2014 with 121,587 votes in favour and 97,440 against. Practice regarding the language spoken in Kindergarten therefore had to change back to the pre-2008 status. This example shows how the result of a vote can have very direct, immediate consequences.

10.9.2   A National Level Initiative on Work Conditions: Six Weeks of Paid Holidays for Everyone

On 11 March 2012 Swiss citizens decided to reject an initiative entitled '6 Weeks of Holidays for Everyone', with a solid 66.5% against. To the outside observer such behaviour may seem odd. If the opportunity to get some extra weeks of paid work leave is given, why would a majority of voters reject it?

Under current law employees have a right for four weeks of paid holidays. However, many companies already grant more weeks on a voluntary basis. The request to harmonise those rules for all workers and to introduce a minimum of 6 weeks for all was brought up by the workers' union. Among the political parties, only left and green political parties were in favour of the initiative. During the campaign preceding the vote the main topic of the debate was whether the economy would be able to cope with this extra burden or not. According to surveys, many voters did perceive increasing work loads as a problem, however they did not think that more holidays were the solution. To the contrary, 61% of the respondents actually feared that the initiative would lead to additional stress because colleagues on holiday would have to be substituted while they are not at their desks (Greuter et al. 2012). The result of this vote and the arguments supported by the opponents of this citizens' initiative demonstrate that voters need not necessarily behave like short-sighted individuals maximising their personal interests. They seem to be capable of evaluating the direct and indirect consequences of the proposal.

10.9.3   National Level, Social Security and Public Finance, for a Temporary VAT Increase

The mandatory referendum vote of 27 September 2009 dealt with a long-term financial issue, namely the sustainability of the disability insurance (*Invaliden-versicherung*, IV) as one of the social security pillars of the Swiss welfare state.[3] The disability insurance scheme is mainly financed by contributions from the working population in the form of deductions from wages, while employers make at least an equal contribution into the fund. From 1993 the disability insurance fund had constantly run a deficit which had accumulated to a total of 13 billion CHF by 2009. Until that time, the annual deficit was covered by the old age pension fund (*Alters- und Hinterlassenenversicherung*, AHV) with annual contributions of 1.4 billion CHF. These transfer payments put the liquidity of the old age pension fund in danger and could not be sustained in the long run. In order to guarantee the long-term stability of the disability insurance fund, government and parliament suggested temporarily increasing the normal VAT rate from 7.6 to 8% starting in 2011 until the end of 2017. In addition, there would be a last one-off transfer from the old age pension

---

[3]The referendum question asked: Would you like to accept the Federal Act dating from 13 June 2008 regarding temporary additional financing of the disability insurance by raising the VAT rates?

fund to the disability insurance fund in the order of 5 billion CHF. Further reforms would lead to a complete separation of the disability and old age pension funds as well as towards financial stabilisation of the disability insurance scheme. Without additional resources all disability pensions would have had to be cut by 40%—a measure for which neither the government nor the parliament, nor eventually the citizens, wanted to be responsible.

The temporary constitutional clause went through parliament on 12 June 2009 with 114 Yes, 9 No votes and 71 abstentions in the National Council (lower chamber) and through the Council of States (upper chamber) with 34 Yes, 4 No votes and 4 abstentions. Parliament agreed that something needed to be done. As the relatively high number of abstentions in the lower chamber shows, a strong minority did not agree on the suggested measures and would have preferred to increase wage deductions (political left) or not to provide additional finances for the disability insurance at all (political right). However, both the government as well as parliament suggested accepting the proposed solution in the upcoming vote. The Federal Council (the Swiss executive) actually rescheduled the referendum vote, originally foreseen for May 2009, by sending the act back to parliament, fearing that the reform would not go through during an economic recession. Trade associations also asked for more time to implement the necessary administrative changes. The vote eventually took place on the next possible date, which was September 2009.

What should not be forgotten in this case, as for many other referendum votes, is that the main political work, finding a compromise, takes place in parliamentary committees and plenary debates. In order to illustrate this, we can have a look at the parliamentary chronology preceding the referendum vote, which only comes in at the very last stage. The reform bill was prepared by public administration already in 2005. The preparation of the reform already comprises intense pre-parliamentary consultation procedures with the cantons, trade associations, workers' unions and also public administration taking a stance. After committee work the first draft bill entered both parliamentary chambers in 2007, being debated well into 2008. The matter was further complicated by the fifth general revision of the disability insurance scheme, which needed to go through an optional referendum vote in June 2007 first. Without this general revision an increase of the VAT rate would have caused legal problems.

During the campaign the Social Democratic Party and most parties of the right as well as the main business associations were in favour of the proposed solution. The far-right Swiss People's Party and some other smaller right-wing parties opposed the change. For them the solution would have consisted in fighting misuse of the disability insurance. Some opponents also feared that the temporary measure would become permanent. Overall the campaign did not mobilise the masses, turnout for this vote was below the long-term average of 44%.

The cantonal results showed a configuration quite typical for social welfare-related votes in Switzerland: the French-speaking cantons in the West and the

Italian-speaking canton, Ticino, as well as the German-speaking cantons with larger urban centres voted in favour of the VAT increase. More rural cantons in Central and Eastern Switzerland voted against.

The post-referendum VOX analysis (Kuster et al. 2009), which uses a telephone survey among a representative sample of roughly 1000 voters, revealed that political explanatory factors such as the position of a citizen on the left-right axis and party identification were decisive, socio-demographics only played a minor role. On a scale from 0 to 10, the average attributed importance of the vote for the country as a whole among respondents of the survey reached a high value of 7.5. When asked how difficult it was for them to make up their mind most respondents (71%) said they found it rather easy. Respondents to the survey who positioned themselves in the political middle or on the left of the middle clearly supported the temporary VAT increase.

The main argument in favour of the proposed change was straightforward and directly related to the urgent financial needs of the disability insurance. This fact was not much disputed and even opponents of the VAT increase agreed to it in principle (57% agreement to this statement among opponents in the VOX survey). Also largely undisputed was the goal to avoid cuts to the already relatively low payments for disabled people; a financial reform should not lead to lower pensions it was felt. The VAT increase as a measure to sort out the long-term stability of the disability insurance and in addition as a measure to help the old age pension fund as an argument for a Yes vote was more divisive. Only 28% of No voters supported this pro argument whereas 83% of Yes voters accepted it. The main counter-argument to the VAT increase suggested achieving the goal by additional cuts and fighting misuse. Most survey respondents agreed to this argument but also realised that the fight against misuse would not free up enough money to stabilise the disability insurance scheme.

Due to demographic change all social insurance schemes are under financial pressure and are constantly being reformed which in Switzerland automatically involves a referendum vote. Previous major attempts to reform the old age pension for example have failed. For larger social welfare reforms to get adopted all major stakeholders and a large coalition of political parties, especially the Social Democratic Party, need to be on board as a necessary prerequisite. The topic of social insurances will therefore keep Swiss politics as well as Swiss voters busy in the years to come.

10.9.4   National Level, Public Finance, Reduction of Public Debt

On 2 December 2001 in a mandatory referendum 84.7% of Swiss voters and all cantons accepted the introduction of a debt reduction clause into the Constitution aiming to establish a budgetary balance in the long run, while allowing for certain flexibility depending on the economic situation in the short run (entering into force in 2003). With 37.8%, the turnout of voters was lower than the long-term average of 45% but that is not unusual for such a technical and abstract matter. The goal of this new instrument was the reduction and eventual elimination of a structural state deficit on the national level. Spending was made dependent on fiscal income. Deficits are allowed during a recession, however, during an economic uptrend receipts must be used for debt reduction (Linder et al. 2010: 607–608).

The economic world and all bourgeois parties were largely in favour of this new instrument, which was copied by many other European countries; the critical voices were against making parliamentary decisions on the budget dependent on a mathematical formula. After a period of over-spending during the economic boom of the 1980s, households in Switzerland were hit by a real estate crisis, a recession, and relatively high unemployment rates during the 1990s. During this period the state accumulated a debt of roughly 108 billion CHF. Many regional banks, heavily invested in real estate, struggled for survival or went bankrupt. In addition, the whole economy underwent a structural transformation—private firms had to adapt to a globalised market economy. In the light of these events, the citizens realised how important it is to reduce debt and to have the state budgets in order, which explains the outcome of the referendum.

10.9.5 A National Level Referendum on Armed Forces: Abolition

In a thus far unprecedented bold manner, the 'Group for a Switzerland without an Army—GSoA' handed in a citizens' initiative seeking to abolish the Swiss army.[4] The vote took place on 11 November 1989. As a surprise to many, 35.6% of the citizens as well as the two cantons of Geneva and Jura voted in favour of the initiative. The initiators knew from the beginning how unlikely it would be for their claim to be accepted by a majority of the voters. Only political parties from the far left openly supported the initiative. Not even the most daring political commentators expected an acceptance rate of over a third. A first symbolic success of this citizen's initiative was to bring up the topic and engage the people in a public debate about the future of the Swiss army. At 69%, this referendum had among the highest turnout rates in the last decades. Roughly 20% of the voters can be considered to having accepted the initiative because they are pacifists, while a third of Yes voters admitted to having agreed to the initiative just because they wanted to teach the army a lesson. In addition, the authorities at least partially took the initiator's claims into account and started a major reform process as well as a reduction of enlisted men.

---

[4]Further, later attempts at reducing the army via direct democratic mechanisms did not manage to generate political majorities either: 'Saving on army and defense spending' trying to cut the costs for the army in half, on 26 November 2000, saw 62.4% No votes; the initiative 'For a credible security policy and a Switzerland without an army' handed in by the same group 10 years later, 2 December 2001, tried to bring up the topic again but failed, getting only 21.9% Yes votes; on 22 September 2013 the initiative 'Yes to the abolition of compulsory military service' was also rejected with 73.2% No votes.

This initiative is an example for the indirect effects citizens' initiatives can have even when they are eventually lost at the ballot box. According to a thorough legal analysis of all national votes, roughly half of the citizens' initiatives have left some traces in legal texts and public policies (Rohner 2012). Furthermore, they also fulfil the function of activating a political process, serving as a means of political advertising for the initiators, a measure of social protest and a token of negotiation with public authorities.

10.9.6   A National Level Initiative Against Minarets

The citizens' initiative 'Against the construction of minarets' was submitted on 8 July 2008 with 113,540 valid signatures. The initiators' wish was to prohibit the building of minarets in Switzerland. In Switzerland there are four mosques with minarets—in Geneva, Zürich, Winterthur and Wangen. The initiators contend that such constructions symbolise a religious and political claim to power that calls into question the Federal Constitution and the Swiss system of law.

In the view of the Swiss Federal Council, the initiative did not infringe upon the core human rights that are recognised by all states and must be upheld by all. According to the Swiss Federal Council it was nonetheless irreconcilable with various human rights that are guaranteed by the European Convention on Human Rights (ECHR) and by the UN Covenant on Civil and Political Rights (UN Covenant II). In addition, the initiative, which purports to protect social and legal order in Switzerland, contradicted the basic rights and principles that are rooted in the Federal Constitution. The aim of the initiative was to put a stop to the growing influence of Islam in Switzerland and to prevent and combat violence on the part of extremist fundamentalist groups. The Federal Council feared that such a ban would endanger peace between religions and would not help to prevent the spread of fundamentalist Islamic beliefs. It therefore recommended rejecting the initiative without a counter-proposal on 28 August 2008. The initiative went through the National Council with 51 Yes and 132 No votes and through the Council of State with 3 Yes and 39 No votes. The Federal Assembly hence followed the opinion of the Swiss Federal Council and recommended on 12 June 2009 that the initiative should be rejected without submitting a counter-proposal.

The citizen's initiative was submitted to the popular vote on 29 November 2009. The initiative was accepted by 2,709,287 votes with a total turnout of 53.76%. The initiative saw the following constitutional clause added to Article 72 'Church and state' as paragraph 3: The construction of minarets is prohibited. According to the post-initiative VOX analysis (Hirter and Vatter 2010), supporters of left-wing parties rejected the popular initiative with more than 80% opposed, while the right-wing orientated parties decisively accepted it. The voting behaviour of the parties in the centre was essential for the overall result. The Liberals (60% voting Yes) and the Christian Democratic People's Party (54% Yes) were divided but in the end a majority were in favour of the initiative. The end result was surprising as most parties, especially the middle, and left-wing parties were against the popular initiative during the campaign. The post-poll analysis furthermore showed that social characteristics such as access to high education had a high impact on the overall decision of voters. No significant difference could be observed for the male and female citizens. Only 16% of the left-orientated female and 21% of the male voters voted in favour of the initiative. Among supporters of the right-wing parties the proportion of female voters in favour of the initiative was 87% and 71% of the male electorate.

The surprising public vote against minaret construction in Switzerland can be seen as a signal of opposition by voters to the spread of Islam. However, the VOX analysis found that the vote was not against the Muslims or foreigners in principle. After all, about 40% of citizens who favoured equal opportunities between Swiss and foreigners also backed the minaret ban. The authors of the study said that Swiss xenophobia was not the main reason why the ban of minarets was accepted by 57.5% of the voters. The survey further showed that 64% of voters considered Swiss and Muslim lifestyles to be compatible.

For the ban's supporters, it was about making a 'symbolic gesture' against the spread of Islam. Around one in six voters said their decision was a reaction against the discrimination of Christian churches in countries where Islam is strong.

10.10   Concluding Remarks

The final question is maybe why direct democracy seems to work rather well in Switzerland but not necessarily elsewhere. Would it be possible, make sense or even be a 'good' thing to introduce the same or similar mechanisms of direct democracy into another polity? The standard answer to this question would be that in Switzerland the instruments were able to grow over a long period of time from the local to the national level. The standard answer would also assert that institutions cannot be copied, that they need to be adapted to local political culture and context. Contrary to Switzerland, in many countries referendums are the big exception in politics. The very infrequent use—only a vote here and there every decade or so—of direct democracy therefore potentially does more harm than good. The political, administrative and media system does not provide for the action repertoire to deal with such exceptional situations. In Switzerland we find a very, and for some already too frequent, use of referendum votes coupled with a political elite knowing how to cope and make use of the instruments at hand. Direct democracy is not the enemy of political parties, it fulfils—in a balanced way—the functions of power maintenance, power competition and power control at the same time (Leemann 2015; Serdült and Welp 2015), in Switzerland by providing for initiatives as political accelerators and referendums as political brakes. All major parties, as well as those which aim to become major parties, will make use of direct democratic instruments also in a strategic way (Hug and Tsebelis 2002). In case you already have a seat in the executive you have to prove from time to time that you are still able to mobilise citizens for an initiative, gain the necessary support to collect enough signatures and eventually win the referendum vote as well. The same goes for the optional referendum. As soon as a political force, most of the time a political party, is able to block legislation it becomes a serious player not only challenging the parties represented in the governmental coalition but also enabling it to stay in government. Using the optional referendum thus helps to sharpen the profile of a political party.

Last but not least, one can seriously wonder how referendum politics and results in Switzerland do not lead to increased political conflict (Linder 2010). The political elites have learned, maybe ironically had to learn, how to lose a vote and then to make peace again with their political opponents because they might need them as allies for the next referendum vote which might be only three months away. Due to the high frequency of referendums, a political party usually wins and loses several times a year or even on the same weekend when topics on the ballot are bundled.

To the standard answers on why direct democracy works in Switzerland we might add one which is usually omitted: the success of direct democracy in Switzerland should rather be attributed to chance than ingenuity. The Swiss are lucky to live in a political landscape characterised by cross-cutting cleavages. Political conflict does thus not divide the country in two opposing sides but cuts across several large societal divides such as religion (admittedly, less important today but not in the nineteenth century), language, urban-rural, class, international openness and so forth. What we sometimes overlook in our Cartesian quest of finding a logical cause for an effect is that history is contingent. In that sense, the relative success of direct democracy in the Swiss case should rather be understood as a historical coincidence, so to speak a seed that fell on the right soil to grow and could easily be doomed in different, more muddy or arid terrain.

REFERENCES

Auer, A. (1996). *Les origines de la démocratie directe en Suisse – Die Ursprünge der schweizerischen direkten Demokratie*. Basel and Frankfurt: Helbing and Lichtenhahn.
Auer, A. (2016). *Staatsrecht der schweizerischen Kantone*. Bern: Stämpli Verlag.
Biaggini, G. (2011). Switzerland. In O. Dawn & C. Fusaro (Eds.), *How Constitutions Change: A Comparative Study* (pp. 303–327). Hart: Oxford and Portland, OR.
Braun Binder, N. (2015). Financing Popular Initiatives and Referendum Campaigns. In C. Fraenkel-Haeberle, S. Kropp, F. Palermo, & K. P. Sommermann (Eds.), *Citizen Participation in Multi-Level Democracies* (pp. 161–181). Brill: Leiden and Boston.
Caramani, D., & Strijbis, O. (2013). Discrepant Electorates: The Inclusiveness of Electorates and Its Impact on the Representation of Citizens. *Parliamentary Affairs, 66*, 384–404.

Christmann, A., & Danaci, D. (2012). Direct Democracy and Minority Rights: Direct and Indirect Effects on Religious Minorities in Switzerland. *Politics and Religion, 5*(1), 133–160.

Church, C. H., & Head, R. C. (2013). *A Concise History of Switzerland*. Cambridge: Cambridge University Press.

Dardanelli, P. (2011). The Emergence and Evolution of Democracy in Switzerland. In M. F. T. Malone (Ed.), *Achieving Democracy: Democratization in Theory and Practice* (pp. 141–163). New York and London: Continuum.

Goldberg, A. C., Lanz, S., & Sciarini, P. (2018). Mobilizing Different Types of Voters: The Influence of Campaign Intensity on Turnout in Direct Democratic Votes. *Electoral Studies, 57,* 196–222.

Greuter, N., Milic, T., & Widmer, T. (2012). *Analyse der eidgenössischen Abstimmung vom 11. März 2012,* VOX 106, gfs.bern und Institut für Politikwissenschaft, Universität Zürich (https://doi.org/10.5167/uzh-63378. Accessed 28 November 2019).

Hirter, H., & Vatter, A. (2010). *Analyse eidgenössische Abstimmung vom 29. November 2009,* gfs.bern und Institut für Politikwissenschaft, Universität Zürich.

Hug, S., & Tsebelis, G. (2002). Veto Players and Referendums Around the World. *Journal of Theoretical Politics, 14*(4), 465–515.

Kriesi, H. (2005). *Direct Democratic Choice: The Swiss Experience*. Lanham, Boulder, CO, New York, Toronto and Oxford: Lexington Books.

Kriesi, H., & Trechsel, A. H. (2008). *The Politics of Switzerland: Continuity and Change in a Consensus Democracy*. Cambridge: Cambridge University Press.

Kuster, S., Milic, T., & Widmer, T. (2009). *Analyse der eidgenössischen Abstimmung vom 27. September 2009,* gfs.bern und Institut für Politikwissenschaft, Universität Zürich. (https://doi.org/10.5167/uzh-43569, accessed 21 November 2019).

Ladner, A., & Fiechter, J. (2012). The Influence of Direct Democracy on Political Interest, Electoral Turnout and Other Forms of Citizens' Participation in Swiss Municipalities. *Local Government Studies, 38*(4), 437–459.

Leemann, L. (2015). Political Conflict and Direct Democracy: Explaining Initiative Use 1920–2011. *Swiss Political Science Review, 21*(4), 596–616.

Linder, W. (2007). Political Culture. In U. Klöti et al. (Eds.), *Handbook of Swiss Politics* (2nd completely revised version, pp. 13–31). Zürich: Neue Zürcher Zeitung Publishing.

Linder, W. (2010). *Swiss Democracy: Possible Solutions to Conflict in Multicultural Societies* (3rd ed., Revised and Updated). Basingstoke: Palgrave Macmillan.

Linder, W., Bolliger, C., & Rielle, Y. (2010). *Handbuch der eidgenössischen Volksabstimmungen 1848 bis 2007*. Bern, Stuttgart, and Wien: Haupt Verlag.

Lutz, G. (2007). Low Turnout in Direct Democracy. *Electoral Studies, 26,* 624–632.

Lutz, G. (2012). Switzerland: Citizens' Initiatives as a Measure to Control the Political Agenda. In M. Setälä & T. Schiller (Eds.), *Citizens' Initiatives in Europe: Procedures and Consequences of Agenda-Setting by Citizens*. Basingstoke: Palgrave Macmillan.

Marquis, L., & Sciarini, P. (1999). Opinion Formation in Foreign Policy: The Swiss Experience. *Electoral Studies, 18*(4), 453–471.

Papadopoulos, Y. (1998). *Démocratie directe*. Paris: Economica.

Papadopoulos, Y. (2001). How Does Direct Democracy Matter? The Impact of Referendum Votes on Politics and Policy-Making. In J.-E. Lane (Ed.), *The Swiss Labyrinth: Institutions, Outcomes and Redesign*. Frank Cass: London and Portland, OR.

Rohner, G. (2012). *Die Wirksamkeit von Volksinitiativen im Bund 1848–2010*. Zürich: Schulthess.

Rothmayr, C. (2001). Towards the Judicialization of Swiss Politics? *West European Politics, 24*(2), 77–94.

Sciarini, P., Cappelletti, F., Goldberg, A. C., & Lanz, S. (2016). The Underexplored Species: Selective Participation in Direct Democratic Votes. *Swiss Political Science Review, 22*(1), 75–94.

Serdült, U. (2010). Referendum Campaign Regulations in Switzerland. In K. Gilland Lutz & S. Hug (Eds.), *Financing Referendum Campaigns* (pp. 165–179). New York: Palgrave Macmillan.

Serdült, U. (2015). A Dormant Institution – History, Legal Norms and Practice of the Recall in Switzerland. *Representation – Journal of Representative Democracy, 51*(2), 161–172.

Serdült, U. (2018). Switzerland. In M. Qvortrup (Ed.), *Referendums Around the World: The Continued Growth of Direct Democracy* (pp. 47–108). Basingstoke: Palgrave Macmillan.

Serdült, U., & Welp, Y. (2012). Direct Democracy Upside Down. *Taiwan Journal of Democracy, 8*(1), 69–92.

Tornay, B. (2008). *La démocratie directe saisie par le juge: l'empreinte de la jurisprudence sur les droits populaires en Suisse*. Zürich: Schulthess Verlag.

Tornic, A., & Massüger, N. (2013). Constituent Assemblies in Swiss Cantons. In J. Wheatley & F. Mendez (Eds.), *Patterns of Constitutional Design: The Role of Citizens and Elites in Constitution-Making* (pp. 119–144). Farnham: Ashgate.

Trechsel, A., & Sciarini, P. (1998). Direct Democracy in Switzerland: Do Elites Matter? *European Journal of Political Research, 33*, 99–124.

Trechsel, A., & Serdült, U. (1999). *Kaleidoskop Volksrechte: Die Institutionen der direkten Demokratie in den schweizerischen Kantonen 1970–1996*. Basel, Genf, and München: Helbing and Lichtenhahn.

Vatter, A. (2000). Consensus and Direct Democracy: Conceptual and Empirical Linkages. *European Journal of Political Research, 2*, 171–192.

CHAPTER 11

The Scottish and Welsh Devolution Referendums of 1979 and 1997

Jörg Mathias

11.1　The Limited British Experience with Referendums

Referendums were rarely employed as a means of decision-making in British politics up to the end of the twentieth century. Their introduction into the British system came as late as the 1970s, as one way to tackle difficult and heavily contested issues regarding the structure of the system of government. In previous decades the notion of parliamentary sovereignty had reigned supreme, as a rather pure form of representative democracy, with no room for direct-democratic elements. Thus, in the UK there were—and still are—no absolute constitutional or legal requirements to conduct referendums on any political issue. Decisions on all aspects of referendums remain the prerogative of Parliament. For the same reason, referendum results are not absolutely binding and it is Parliament's responsibility to decide on the implementation of any outcome through appropriate legislation. Although acting directly against the expressed will of the electorate would be seen as politically unacceptable, Parliament retains the final say on implementation, with possible adjustments which may not have been known or discussed during referendum campaigns.

In the 1970s, the UK experienced a prolonged period in which economic and political instability reinforced each other, with mounting economic pressures in a still largely nationalised industrial base and an increasingly disenchanted electorate sharply divided regarding the best ways forward.

J. Mathias (✉)
Aston University, Birmingham, UK
e-mail: J.Mathias@aston.ac.uk

© The Author(s) 2021
J. Smith (ed.), *The Palgrave Handbook of European Referendums*,
https://doi.org/10.1007/978-3-030-55803-1_11

Conservative and Labour governments of the day, replacing each other in relatively quick succession, often had to operate with slim or no parliamentary majorities, and found it increasingly difficult to exercise political and economic leadership by traditional means. Therefore, the time was ripe not only to introduce new political directions, but also new political means of determining these directions.

The introduction of referendums was one such new means of decision-making, involving the electorate directly in the process of settling highly controversial issues. The first example of employing a UK-wide referendum—on membership of the European Economic Community—occurred in 1975 and is discussed extensively by Smith in Chapter 22. In this chapter, we will focus on four subsequent referendums which addressed the question of reforming territorial governance within the UK: the two sets of devolution referendums which took place in Scotland and Wales in 1979 and 1997. These referendums were, in chronological order, the next four uses of the referendum device in the UK on a larger territorial scale, and the only ones until the end of the twentieth century other than the Belfast Agreement discussed by Hayward in Chapter 12. Therefore, even by 1997, experience with referendums in the UK remained very limited. The four devolution referendums were not UK-wide referendums. Their inclusion in this volume referendums is nevertheless justified, as they can be seen as national referendums. They were in effect parts of a wider struggle for greater recognition of Scotland and Wales as nations within the multi-national state of the UK, aimed at increasing political self-determination and self-directed economic development. In addition, the central role of Parliament in managing all aspects of the referendum process clearly establishes the link to UK politics (see Chapter 5 by Norton elsewhere in this volume), and as we shall see, the devolution referendums were as much influenced by the interests of the political party leaderships at Westminster as they were by the regional political actors in Scotland and Wales. In 1979, this link was perceived as a problem by some devolution supporters in Scotland. However, a break with the traditional adversarial party politics seen at Westminster became part of the devolution agenda. By 1997, devolution was widely expected to open the door for less adversarial relations between the political parties in both Edinburgh and Cardiff.

Back in the 1970s, the referendum concept was still viewed with a certain degree of scepticism among political observers. In the wake of the EEC referendum, Padfield and Byrne (1987: 373–374) pointed out that: 'the referendum is a device which has consequences affecting (a) Parliamentary sovereignty; (b) collective responsibility; (c) representative Parliament; (d) treaty obligations already entered into […] and (e) subjecting laws to popular vote'. The authors went on to argue that this course of action would amount to a significant change in constitutional practice. Such change should not be undertaken lightly as responsibility for decision-making would shift from the government to the people, undermining ministerial responsibility and introducing an element of uncertainty into the process of government, they believed.

As shown by the continued infrequency of UK-wide referendums in the subsequent decades, such words of warning were well-heeded by parliaments and governments. While local referendums were used occasionally to decide matters of local interest only, the devolution issue remained the only one in which referendums were employed on a larger scale. One key reason for this is the relative disunity within political parties, notably the Labour Party, on how the devolution issue should be handled. As Bogdanor pointed out as early as 1979, 'In Britain, devolution has been seen primarily as a technique to deal with Scottish and Welsh nationalism in the hope that it will lead to better government in Scotland and Wales, and therefore defuse separatist feelings' (Bogdanor 1979: 4). This process would inevitably involve 'demands for an effective transfer of sovereignty or at least a substantial devolution of power in accordance with national sentiment' (Leach and Percy-Smith 2001: 219). Accommodating national sentiment, however, may not necessarily be in the best interest of the people of the other parts of the UK—notably England—and their representatives at Westminster, who would be asked to limit the scope of their own power. Accommodating referendum results also caused some concern about another key component of the Westminster system: binding the freedom of future parliaments, as decisions taken on the basis of a referendum would almost inevitably stand well beyond a single legislative period. While the 1975 EEC referendum confirmed the UK's commitment to an international treaty similar to other international treaties, in domestic politics the acceptance of such binding can be regarded as a new departure in 1979. The issue nevertheless did not feature largely in 1979, as it was assumed that, if necessary, future parliaments would be able to alter the legislation which established devolution. In 1997, devolutionists were more concerned with future-proofing devolution, and establishing new forms of long-term political relationships between the different parts of the UK and the central government became a major part of the devolution debates.

Devolution undoubtedly raised a UK-wide constitutional problem. It also had the potential to place politicians of the same political party on different sides of referendum campaigns. The Labour Party in particular experienced this phenomenon, both in 1979 and in 1997. Overall the party was not fully in favour of devolution but found it necessary to go along with it in order to achieve another goal, namely holding on to power in Westminster (1979) or gaining it (1997). Therefore, in both devolution periods the UK experienced a situation where 'government leaders shift authority for some set of decisions not because they want to rid themselves of responsibility; but because some other concern outweighs their resistance' (Marks 1996: 28).

In these circumstances, the use of referendums provided two key advantages. A referendum would, first of all, be a gauge to measure the actual prevalence of national sentiment within the electorate concerned: to what extent would devolution really be desired? The answer to that question would also indicate the appropriate political response strategy. Even very significant and long-lasting constitutional changes or alterations to territorial governance in the UK would be acceptable in such a situation, as the referendum would have provided the necessary democratic legitimacy.

11.2   The Legal and Regulatory Framework

Not until the twenty-first century, with the introduction of the Political Parties, Elections and Referendums Act 2000 (UK Parliament 2000), did the UK acquire a formal legal framework regulating the conduct of referendums in the UK. In the late twentieth century, Parliament was still entirely free to set both the contents and the procedural rules for any referendum. By and large following the 1975 example, the devolution referendums were governed by ad hoc legislation, providing bespoke devolution contents—separately for Scotland and Wales in 1979, and in a joint Act for both referendums in 1997 (UK Parliament 1997).

In terms of procedures, the governments of the day attempted, as far as practicable, to follow the rules governing local elections, as outlined in the Representation of the People Acts of 1948 and 1983. For instance, while the results were reported by local authority area, for the overall results Scotland and Wales were treated as single constituencies. To be eligible to vote in a referendum, an individual voter had to be at least 18 years of age and be registered on the electoral roll of his or her place of residence, with some exceptions, e.g. for soldiers and students who could register at their place of service or study, respectively. As with local or other second-order elections, citizens of the UK and the Republic of Ireland were able to register without conditions, while citizens of Commonwealth (and by 1997 also EU) countries had to meet specific residency requirements in their local authority area, usually of at least six months duration (UK Parliament 1983: Sec. 4(3)(c)).

The UK also operated an elaborate procedure of updating the electoral register on an annual basis, requiring each household to re-register each autumn. Political parties and referendum campaign organisations gained access to the full electoral register, including names and address data, for political campaigning purposes. An edited version of the register, usually omitting certain categories of Crown employees and persons who object to the publication of their address details, was available for purchase by anyone. Overall, the electoral register for all four referendums can therefore be regarded as highly accurate. However, in 1979 a post-referendum accuracy check of the register was conducted to establish the precise size of the overall electorate on referendum day as this may have had a direct influence on the outcome, at least in Scotland (see below).

As provided by the Representation of the People Acts 1948 and 1983 (UK Parliament 1948, 1983), local authorities were in charge of conducting the referendum, including all technical preparations, and providing local

Returning Officers[1] and other personnel for polling stations and counts. Immediate concerns about technical or procedural improprieties were to be addressed by campaign agents to the Returning Officers, with the possibility of a subsequent judicial review through the Courts system. Outright acts of fraud or other criminal behaviour by anyone associated with the referendum could be reported to the police, triggering a criminal investigation. However, no such cases were publicly reported in the context of the four referendums.

11.3 The Devolution Referendums of 1979

As early as 1969, the Labour party realised that Prime Minister Harold Wilson's 1964 vision of providing a level playing field across the UK economy had not gone very far, and that regional economic diversity remained a constant source of concern. The Local Government Reform of 1968–1969, introducing Metropolitan Regions with some greater local autonomy for urban areas, and the introduction in 1969 of nine Standard Regions for planning purposes in England, had been only small steps to address the issue of regional imbalances. The first practical step towards devolution referred to Wales, not Scotland. In 1969, Labour recommended to the Royal Commission on the Constitution 'that an elected assembly with executive powers be established in Wales' (Wyn Jones and Scully 2012: 17). No such proposal was put forward regarding Scotland, where the Scottish Office, established in 1885, was deemed to fulfil its executive role adequately. Its Welsh counterpart, only established in 1965, had yet to grow fully into a similar role. Labour's defeat in the general election 1970 put these considerations on hold. The Royal Commission on the Constitution, chaired by Lord Crowther from 1969 and by Lord Kilbrandon from 1972, reported in 1973 with recommendations for both legislative and executive devolution for Scotland and Wales. However, the Conservative government led by Prime Minister Edward Heath took no action.

The 1970s were also the decade in which political nationalism, in the form of the Scottish National Party (SNP) and Plaid Cymru—The Party of Wales (PC) saw first their electoral successes, as the established parties seemed unable to improve the economic and social conditions in Scotland and Wales. The Labour Party in particular felt this pressure, as large parts of both nations were traditionally regarded as Labour strongholds, and a number of leading Labour politicians originated from Scottish or Welsh constituencies. The Labour Party at Westminster was therefore well aware that in order to keep Scottish and Welsh nationalism at bay, some political arrangement had to be found to

---

[1] Returning Officers are the leading election officials in each constituency or electoral district. Their role encompasses full supervision of all aspects of the election or poll, from the technical preparations to the certification and publication of the result after the count. The role also includes an initial investigation and decision-making on alleged cases of electoral malpractice.

provide a suitable outlet to express and act upon specific Scottish and Welsh interests.

Devolution, and with it the idea of using referendums, returned to the political agenda in 1974. The February 1974 Labour Manifesto already contained a commitment to Welsh devolution, followed by a similar commitment to Scottish devolution added into that party's manifesto for the October 1974 election. However, these commitments were strongly contested among the party leaders and MPs, and the small majority of just three seats, won in October 1974, allowed Labour MPs opposed to devolution to prevent early progress.

The erosion of this slim majority through by-election defeats forced the new Labour Prime Minister James Callaghan initially to seek support from the Liberals, then led by David Steel.[2] As reported by *The Guardian* at the time (June 1977), among the Liberals' demands for such support was the requirement to use proportional representation in any new assemblies in Scotland and Wales. Following the collapse of this Liberal-Labour partnership in 1978, Callaghan turned to the nationalist parties—the SNP and Plaid Cymru—for support, and consequently the devolution legislation was back on the agenda with some urgency.

The devolution deals on offer were not identical for Scotland and Wales. Two separate bills were drafted, which varied both from each other and from the 1997 devolution proposals. They nevertheless contained features which bear some resemblance to the actual devolution contents which emerged after 1998.

The Scotland Act 1978 contained provisions for a devolved Scottish Assembly, with some primary legislative powers in education, the environment, health, home affairs, legal matters and social services. The Assembly would also share responsibility for agriculture and fisheries with the UK government, while matters related to energy would remain exclusively in the hands of the UK government. The latter is significant insofar as oil and gas deposits had already been discovered in the North Sea off the Scottish coast but were not commercially exploited at that time. Overall, this devolution proposal included taking over significant functions from the Scottish Office, and a promise of financial transfers from the UK government in the form of annual block grants, a more limited package than would be on offer in 1997.

The Wales Act 1978 featured provisions for a devolved Welsh Assembly, without primary legislative powers but devolving a range of functions in the field of education, health housing, planning, managing Welsh public bodies, and various tasks in the fields of culture, heritage, and promoting the Welsh

---

[2]In all, the 1970s saw four UK Prime Ministers, in relatively short succession: Harold Wilson (Labour, serving October 1964–June 1970 and again March 1974–April 1976), Edward Heath (Conservative, serving June 1970–March 1974), James Callaghan (Labour, serving April 1976–May 1979), and Margaret Thatcher (Conservative, serving May 1979–November 1990).

language. The Welsh assembly would take over significant functions of the Welsh Office and would also receive annual block grant financial support.

Neither assembly would have received any tax altering powers. The size for the two nations' block grants would be determined annually, based on which functions had been devolved, and how many people, as a proportion of the overall population of the UK, would be affected by the devolved scheme. The assemblies would nevertheless have been free to set their own spending priorities within the range of their responsibilities. To achieve an orderly financial transition, a temporary arrangement was put in place in 1978 which already based financial expenditure in Scotland and Wales on proportional population size and expected needs—the much-debated Barnett Formula, which, through all the various stages of the devolution process, has survived to the present time, albeit with significant adjustments.[3]

The two Acts were fully completed and approved Acts of Parliament. Therefore, contrary to 1997, there was no room for misrepresentation of the proposals by either side of the campaigns. The voters in the 1979 referendums knew exactly what was on offer if devolution were to go ahead, and the two referendum questions were accordingly phrased in parallel, with the binary YES and NO options provided on the ballot paper:

Scotland: *Do you want the Provisions of the Scotland Act 1978 to be put into effect?*

Wales: *Do you want the Provisions of the Wales Act 1978 to be put into effect?*

(Dewdney 1997: 5)

Depending on the referendum outcomes, Parliament would either put the Acts into effect by means of Statutory Instruments or repeal the Acts.

As it turned out, a late addition to the rules for the referendums had a dramatic effect on the outcome of the referendum in Scotland, but not in Wales: the so-called Cunningham Amendment, proposed by the anti-devolutionist Labour MP George Cunningham (Islington South and Finsbury). In order to succeed, the referendum would not only have to attract a Yes vote from 50% + 1 of the voters turning out, but also from a quorum of 40% of the overall registered electorate.

Thus the scene was set for a short campaign of about of three weeks in February 1979. This seemingly short campaign period was in line with the traditional period of just over three weeks for UK general elections. The campaign culminated in the referendum day of 1 March in both locations.

---

[3]The Barnett Formula is a funding mechanism for public expenditure in Wales, Scotland and Northern Ireland. Used since 1978, it takes into account the relative population size of these three nations compared to England, and factors in specific needs or specific costs in each territory. Initially applied by HM Treasury directly, following the practical devolution in 1999, annual block grants are provided to the respective Parliaments and Assemblies in line with the transfer of functions from UK Government Departments to the appropriate devolved institutions.

Compared to their 1997 counterparts, neither of the two 1979 campaigns was fought very intensively. This low intensity is in part reflected in the relatively low expenditure in the campaigns, which Dewdney (1997: 7) estimates at £0.8 m in Scotland £0.5 m in Wales, less than half the 1997 spending when compared in 1997 prices in both cases. Most of the 1979 expenses were administrative costs, and do not include elaborate government-sponsored information materials. At the time such materials were not provided. This was in sharp contrast to 1997, where the government did incur some significant expenditure in publishing such materials.

In Scotland, the cross-party *Yes for Scotland* campaign was spearheaded by the leader of the SNP, William Wolfe. The Liberals ran the *Alliance for an Assembly*, and there were a number of small and fragmented non-party-political Yes campaign groups in existence. Labour's effort, *Labour Movement Yes*, was led by the then little-known activist Gordon Brown, the future Prime Minister. At the time of the referendum he had not yet entered Parliament and focused his efforts on taking on prominent campaigners for the No side within his own party. These included (future Foreign Secretary) Robin Cook and Tam Dalyell[4] from the *Labour Vote No* campaign. The official *Scotland Says No* campaign was supposedly not party political, while the Conservatives also featured both a very small Yes campaign and a somewhat larger No campaign within their ranks.

A similarly chequered picture of campaign movements was active in Wales. Here too, the nationalists took control of the official, all-party *Yes for Wales* campaign, chaired by PC leader Gwynfor Evans, while the *Labour-Wales TUC Yes* campaign was led by former Labour MP Dafydd Elystan Morgan. On the No side, two different campaigns could again be found. The cross-party *No Assembly Campaign* was strongly influenced by Conservatives from South Wales. For the purpose of the referendum they found themselves on the same side as their fiercest local political rivals, several South Wales Labour MPs who led the *Labour No Assembly Campaign*, including Leo Abse (Pontypool), at the time known for his opposition to Callaghan, and the future party leader Neil Kinnock (Bedwellty).

The Secretary of State for Scotland, Bruce Millan (MP for Glasgow Craigton) remained largely aloof, as did his Welsh counterpart, Secretary of State John Morris (MP for Aberavon), although members of the government were free to campaign as PM Callaghan could not risk a Cabinet revolt over devolution matters. A similar decision to suspend cabinet responsibility had previously been seen in the 1975 EEC referendum.

---

[4]Labour MP Tam Dalyell represented the Scottish constituencies of West Lothian (1962–1983) and Linlithgow (1983–2005). In devolution debates he repeatedly asked the so-called 'West Lothian question' whether after devolution non-English MPs would be able to vote on matters concerning England only, while English MPs would no longer be able to vote on matters which exclusively concerned the devolved territories. From 2001, until his retirement from the House of Commons in 2005, he was the MP with the longest period of continuous service ('Father of the House').

With hindsight it is perhaps not surprising that the campaigning, heavily dominated by political parties, and indeed factions within parties, left the general electorate more confused than enthused. Labour's mixed messages, combined with the still relatively weak voices of the nationalists, were not sufficient to generate a clear pro-devolution movement of the kind seen in 1997 and later. The Conservatives remained fairly steadfast in their opposition to devolution but lacked sufficient electoral support in Scotland and Wales to stifle the devolution idea for long. The Liberals, prior to their transformation into the Liberal Democrats in 1987, also lacked electoral support in both territories, and were only able to make a minor contribution to the pro-devolution cause in Scotland. As the day of the referendum approached, the odds seemed stacked against the proponents of devolution in Scotland, but even more so in Wales (Table 11.1).

The referendums resulted in a rejection of the devolution proposals at the time, but in very different ways. In Wales, the result could not have been more obvious. The devolution supporters were outvoted comprehensively. The margin between Yes and No of about 60% speaks for itself, showing in no uncertain terms that the devolution idea had not genuinely taken hold in the electorate, and there was only very limited demand for a devolved assembly. It appeared that the way forward to address Welsh economic and political problems was seen not in a greater political distance between Cardiff and London, but by further strengthening Welsh influence in UK political decision-making.

The Scottish referendum result requires more careful interpretation. Counting only the votes cast, the devolution idea was approved by a margin of about 3%. Had Scotland voted Yes? In a straightforward contest between the Yes votes and the No votes, this appeared to be the case. However, the referendum result was turned about by the failure to clear the additional hurdle of getting approved by 40% of the overall electorate. Keating (2009: 83) characterised this hurdle as 'a difficult threshold that sabotaged Scottish devolution although the majority of those voting had supported it'. The SNP in particular felt deprived of a victory, yet over time the other political parties appeared to realise too that additional hurdles in referendums have the potential to

Table 11.1 Results of the devolution referendums held in Scotland and Wales, 1979

	Scotland	Wales
Registered electorate	3,747,112 (100%)	2,038,048 (100%)
Turnout	2,384,439 (63.6%)	1,199,378 (58.3%)
YES	1,230,937 (51.6%)	243,048 (20.3%)
NO	1,153,502 (48.4%)	956,330 (79.7%)
40% YES Quorum met?	No (32.9%)	No (11.9%)

Source of figures: Adapted from Dewdney (1997: 11) (Scotland) and 16 (Wales)

become problematic in terms of democratic legitimacy, freedom of choice to abstain deliberately, and accuracy in reflecting the will of the electorate. Later referendums in the UK did not feature any additional hurdles.

Still, under the 1979 referendum rules, the results stood. As planned in the case of No results on the referendums, in late March 1979 Parliament repealed both the Scotland Act 1978 and the Wales Act 1978. Only a few days later, on 28 March 1979, the Callaghan government, no longer supported by other parties, lost a no confidence motion in the House of Commons by one vote, resulting in a slightly early general election. The legislative period would not have ended until October. However, the general election of 3 May 1979 resulted in a loss of power for the Labour Party, which lost 50 seats. The Nationalists did not escape unharmed either: while PC lost one of their previous three seats, the SNP lost nine of their previous 11 seats (UK Political Info 2019). The election brought the Conservatives to power, with the new Prime Minister, Margaret Thatcher, enjoying a quite comfortable majority of 43 seats in the House of Commons. The new government had no interest in devolution and saw its political priorities elsewhere.

11.4   The Devolution Referendums of 1997

The years between 1979 and 1997 saw a prolonged period of Conservative government in the UK, led by Prime Ministers Margaret Thatcher and, from 1990, John Major. Supported by victories in four successive general elections, the Conservatives were able to implement a comprehensive new economic and political strategy, focusing on a reduction of the role of the state in managing the economy. Politically the Conservatives maintained strength and stability of the government through combatting not only the Labour Party but also the Trade Unions. Some strong social consequences of the economic reforms were particularly in evidence in Scotland and Wales, contributing to further differences in the economic experience in different parts of the UK. While some areas, in particular London and the South of England, seemed to benefit from the Conservatives' policies, economic development problems emerged in Scotland, Wales and also the North of England, where many localities underwent major restructuring in industry and mining, with the intended benefits taking 'too long in coming' (Jessop et al. 1988: 84).

Concerning territorial government, the Conservatives maintained a clear unionist stance with no interest in addressing the issue of economic diversity by means of political devolution. The only significant territorial reform which occurred during the Conservative years was the local government reform in Scotland and Wales 1992–1994, which saw the introduction of one-tier Unitary Authorities replacing the previous two-tier structure. This reform was aimed at reducing the cost of local government, but also had the effect of removing alternative sources of political influence, as nearly all of the old local authorities in Scotland and Wales had been controlled by parties other than the Conservatives. In 1986, Margaret Thatcher had already set the example for this strategy by abolishing the Greater London Authority and the Metropolitan County Councils.

The cumulative effect of difficult economic and social conditions, a Conservative-led central government with no electoral support in Scotland and Wales and apparently little interest in territorial politics, and perceived loss of political influence by parties with strong electoral support at the local level resulted in a resurgent interest in nationalism. The nationalists sought alternative ways of political representation, and a lesser degree of dependency on Westminster politics. The devolution question slowly moved back onto the political agenda in the late 1980s and early 1990s.

It can be argued that interest in devolution had never completely disappeared. As early as 1980, a small *Campaign for a Scottish Assembly* had formed out of the defeated referendum campaigns, mostly carried by Labour and SNP supporters. A broader *Scottish Constitutional Convention* was formed in 1989, which comprised not only supporters of political parties (Labour, Liberal Democrats and initially also the SNP), but also representatives of Local Authorities, Churches, Trade Unions, civic community organisations and independent academics. The significant development here was that the devolution issue was taken out of the narrow sphere of party politics and brought into the wider limelight of general civic engagement. The Convention deliberated upon various ideas for devolution, based on historical precedence, the 1979 devolution agenda, and more far-reaching ideas regarding greater political and economic self-determination for Scotland, including a Scottish Parliament. However, the question of Scottish independence was not included in the Convention's proposals, published in 1995 under the title *Scotland's Parliament, Scotland's Right*. By contrast, around this time the SNP began to commit itself to the long-term goal of independence and campaigned accordingly in the 1997 general election (SNP 1997: 6).

In Wales, the devolution idea had been rejected forcefully in 1979. However, during the subsequent two decades Wales experienced similar problems to those in Scotland with regard to economic and social restructuring, coupled with a lack of effective political influence on Westminster politics. Therefore, by 1997 the time had come again for linking economic and social development to the issue of regional autonomy. In Wales this process was driven to a large extent by the political parties, i.e. Labour, PC and the Liberal Democrats, united in their opposition to the Conservatives. The Labour manifesto of 1997 in particular seemed to exemplify a new understanding of the state as an enabling actor for communities, public and private enterprises and the individual. The wide-ranging devolution offers for Scotland and Wales, but also Northern Ireland, London, and possibly the English regions was aimed at wishing 'to see relations between the centre, region and locality based henceforth on collaboration rather than conflict—as with the trade unions and the churches' (Loughlin 2000: 22).

Labour's general election victory in May 1997, winning a majority of 179 seats, was so overwhelming that it did not depend on the Scottish and Welsh results. In Scotland, Labour won 56 of the then 72 seats, in Wales 34 of 40 seats. The SNP won six seats, PC four. The Liberal Democrats won ten of their overall 46 seats in Scotland, and two in Wales. All remaining 165 Conservative MPs represented English constituencies. These results put the pro-devolution parties in a very strong position, and this time the Labour Party managed to retain a united image. Cabinet members and MPs were expected to present a pro-devolution stance.

The referendum promise given by Labour in 1997 was, however, open to more public debate in the period between the election in May and the referendums in September. Labour welcomed suggestions which would help to secure successful outcomes in Scotland and Wales. The Blair government accepted that tailor-made devolution deals had to be offered to satisfy both the need for adequate reform of territorial governance and the need to secure public acceptance of any new arrangements. It was widely understood that the likely outcome would be a system of 'asymmetrical government' (Keating 1998: 195) in the UK, in which the political powers and the degree of autonomy would vary—indeed had to vary—from one constituent part to another. This approach of an open-ended outcome stimulated the public debate in Scotland and Wales, as political, social and economic actors were increasingly challenged to formulate their positions. This situation contrasted sharply with the party-political twisting and scheming behind closed doors which dominated the 1979 preparations.

There was, however, another aspect to this new openness. The government, while remaining generally supportive, was no longer in full control of the process, and local leaders had much more room to launch their own initiatives and to express their ambitions for devolution. In Scotland, the trend was to maximise the scope of devolution, while in Wales a balance needed to be maintained between fulfilling serious devolution ambitions while maintaining public support. In part, this divergence of approaches can be explained by the long shadow cast by the 1979 results. In 1997, in Scotland, a Yes vote seemed assured and the question was how far such a mandate could be stretched. In Wales, however, it was by no means certain that a pro-devolution majority could be obtained at all.

While the political content of debates was characterised by much open-endedness and a multitude of ideas, the formal and legal arrangements were kept to a minimum, which in turn also helped to bring about a Yes vote. This is reflected both in the Referendums (Scotland and Wales) Act, 1997, and in the design of the referendum questions. The Act itself, barely two pages in length, established the fact that the referendums would be held, and fixed the dates: 11 September 1997 for Scotland, and 18 September 1997 for Wales. Contrary to 1979, the Welsh electorate would therefore know the outcome of the Scottish referendum before casting their votes. Again, the then current regulations for local elections were used as the basic procedural reference point, with suitable adaptations where necessary, as outlined in Schedule 3 of the Act (see above).

The design of the referendum questions also reflected the minimalist approach, thus allowing for broad support in principle. In 1979, complete and already approved Acts of Parliament were put to the referendum voters. In 1997, however, not only was there no pre-approved devolution package on offer, the question of devolution itself was avoided. The main questions referred only to a key institutional change in each case, i.e. whether to establish a Scottish Parliament and a Welsh Assembly, respectively. Further details would only be fully worked out and legislated for in the event of a successful referendum. In Scotland, one further specific question was asked: whether a new Scottish Parliament should have the power to vary taxes. There were no additional questions asked in Wales. In all three questions the answer options were phrased in the binary I AGREE/I DO NOT AGREE format, which was translated colloquially by campaigners, voters and the media into YES and NO options. The main question in Scotland was phrased as follows:

I AGREE THAT THERE SHOULD BE A SCOTTISH PARLIAMENT/
I DO NOT AGREE THAT THERE SHOULD BE A SCOTTISH PARLIAMENT.

The secondary question, asked on a separate ballot paper, asked voters to decide between:

I AGREE THAT A SCOTTISH PARLIAMENT SHOULD HAVE TAX VARYING POWERS

and

I DO NOT AGREE THAT A SCOTTISH PARLIAMENT SHOULD HAVE TAX VARYING POWERS

(Referendums (Scotland and Wales) Act 1997, Schedule 1)

However, it was obvious from these phrasings of the questions that the second question would be rendered obsolete in the case of a majority for the I DO NOT AGREE answer on the first question, as the text of the second question presumes the existence of a Scottish Parliament.

In a similar arrangement, voters in Wales were asked (in both English and Welsh) to support one of the following statements:

I AGREE THAT THERE SHOULD BE A WELSH ASSEMBLY

or

I DO NOT AGREE THAT THERE SHOULD BE A WELSH ASSEMBLY

(Referendums (Scotland and Wales) Act 1997, Schedule 2)

In order to provide the necessary link to devolution as a whole, an explanatory statement printed on the ballot paper above the questions referred the voter to the relevant government proposals, on which Parliament had decided to consult the voter. In a single sentence the voters were thus reminded that Parliament was in charge of the process, that the referendum was consultative in nature, and that in order to make an informed decision the voters should refer to the government's proposals, which they should already have received. In Scotland, the government's proposals were sent to all households in the form of leaflets and reminder notes, and by public distribution of an information video. The costs for this exercise were estimated at around £730,000 out of a total public expenditure of around £5 m on conducting the referendum, while the corresponding publicity expenditures in Wales were estimated at around £575,000 out of the total referendum costs of around £3 m (Dewdney 1997: 7). The government's proposals for Wales were brought together in a White Paper, entitled *A Voice for Wales*, which would form the basis of a post-referendum Government of Wales Act. The contents of this White Paper confirmed the focus of the Welsh devolution plans on the executive side, with only secondary legislative powers for a Welsh Assembly but a significant transfer of functions from the Welsh Office. The Assembly would also have extensive flexibility in health and social care matters, education, culture, heritage and the Welsh language. Close legal and economic links to Westminster would, however, be maintained, including the annual funding allocations.

At the time of the referendum, the plans for Scotland were less developed than what would be expected in a White Paper. This allowed the different parties supporting devolution to maintain a united front during the campaign, while the details of a future Scotland Act would be worked out after a successful referendum. Nevertheless, Scottish voters were given a reasonable idea of what to expect, including a clear commitment to both primary and secondary legislative powers for the Scottish Parliament, and, if approved separately, tax-varying powers not exceeding ±3% on the respective tax rate set by Westminster. The issue of independence was deliberately excluded as an issue, although the SNP made no secret of the fact that they saw this devolution only as a first step. Wide-ranging executive devolution was also included, with a corresponding transfer of functions from the Scottish Office and continued appropriate block grant funding (see Keating 2002: 16–19). As in 1979, however, pensions and employment-related social security matters, as well as the North Sea energy resources would remain exclusive matters for the UK government.

Campaigning was in practice a lengthy process, beginning in May 1997, although the 'hot' phase was limited to about four to five weeks from early August to the referendum dates on 11 and 18 September. Campaigning was suspended between 31 August and 6 September due to the death of Diana, Princess of Wales.

Both in Scotland and Wales, the chaos of 1979 with multiple, inconsistent campaigns was largely avoided, although some individual campaigners did not always operate fully in line with their respective official campaigns. However, frequent consultations and joint public appearances between the leaders of the political parties involved in the pro-devolution campaigns provided a clear and united message to the electorate.

In Scotland, the official pro-devolution campaign, *Scotland FORward*, comprised Labour, the SNP, the Liberal Democrats, and the Greens. It was officially headed by the party-politically neutral businessman Nigel Smith, although the leader of the SNP, Alex Salmond, and the then Secretary of State for Scotland and MP for Glasgow Anniesland, Donald Dewar, were by far the more visible figureheads. Overall, this campaign represented an impressive accumulation of support from a wide range of branches of the Scottish civil society, not seen before or since. By contrast, the official anti-devolution campaign, *Think Twice*, was headed by Brian Monteith, a public relations consultant with strong links to the Conservative Party. The member-ship comprised a number of Conservative politicians, including Lord Fraser of Carmyllie, and a number of representatives of the business community, although the business community was by no means united in their scepticism regarding devolution. This campaign suffered from a lack of strength of the Conservative Party in Scotland, and one of their key arguments, a fear of the so-called 'tartan tax' had been effectively undermined by posing the secondary referendum question on that point.

The campaigning in Wales was even more one-sided. Here the official pro-devolution campaign essentially comprised Labour, PC and the Liberal Democrats, with significant support from non-party-political representatives from the business community, academia, cultural organisations and the clergy. There was no overall individual campaign leader, but a wide leadership circle. From Labour this circle included the MPs Ron Davies (Secretary of State for Wales, Caerphilly), Rhodri Morgan (Cardiff West), and Alun Michael (Cardiff South and Penarth); the latter two later becoming First Ministers in Wales. The Liberal Democrat effort was spearheaded Michael (now Lord) German, then leader of the LD group in the Cardiff City Council, along with Kirsty Williams, currently the only LD Assembly Member, and Jenny (now Baroness) Randerson. Plaid Cymru was mainly represented by its President, Dafydd Wigley (MP for Caernarfon; now Lord Wigley), along with Cynof Dafis (MP for Ceredigion).

By contrast, the official anti-devolution campaign, *Just say NO*, was severely under-staffed due to the weakness of the Welsh Conservatives at the time. As the only party to oppose devolution at the time, the lack of Welsh Conservative MPs and the low number of Conservative local councillors and activists in Wales made it impractical to mount a significant campaign effort. However, the No campaign profited from favourable opinion polls, indicating that more than half the electorate remained opposed to devolution or were not interested either way. In addition, there was a shortage of suitable campaign issues. There was no threat of a 'dragon tax' to match the Scottish 'tartan tax' issue, and the government proposals, smaller in scope yet more clearly outlined compared to Scotland, left the No side only the argument of possibly creating a costly extra layer of governmental bureaucracy. The Yes campaign countered this argument by reminding voters that a key problem during the Conservative years was a distinct lack of representation for Welsh political voices.

In the end phase of campaigning in Scotland it was widely expected that the pro-devolution side would succeed, drawing on the combined strength of those who saw devolution as the long-term solution and those who would prefer independence as the long-term outcome. Aggregated opinion polls at the time estimated that these two groups together would encompass about 78% of the electorate (Dardanelli 2005: 122). In Wales, opinion polls continued to predict a fairly narrow outcome, with the likelihood of a Yes victory increasing as referendum day drew near (Table 11.2).

Given these results, the course towards devolution was set in Scotland and Wales, but with different degrees of public expectation. As predicted, the Scottish Parliament had received a clear mandate. On a reasonable turnout of 60%, three-quarters of the voters had approved the establishment of the Scottish Parliament, and almost two-thirds had supported tax-varying powers for it. The pro-devolution alliance parties were therefore expected to take swift action in developing the necessary legislation to enable the new institution to become operational. This was achieved during the following year, with the new Scotland Act receiving Royal Assent on 19 November 1998. Part IV of the Act detailed the practical application of the tax-varying powers. Following the first elections in 1999, the Scottish Parliament was controlled by a Labour-LD coalition government. During this phase the main political efforts concentrated on developing clear and effective relationships with the central government in London, developing strategies for attracting inward investment, and improving Scottish healthcare and transport policies. However,

Table 11.2 Results of the devolution referendums held in Scotland and Wales, 1997	Scotland (11 September)	Wales (18 September)
Registered electorate	3,973,673 (100%)	2,222,533 (100%)
Turnout	2,391,268 (60.2%)	1,112,117 (50.1%)
YES	1,775,045 (74.2%)	559,419 (50.3%)
NO	614,400 (25.7%)	552,698 (49.7%)
Tax varying powers?	Yes 1,512,889 (63.5%)	N/A

Source of figures: Adapted from Dewdney (1997: 12–13) (Scotland) and 17 (Wales)

the new tax-varying powers were not used during the first three legislative periods. Thus, the ways of the parties which had supported a Scottish Parliament during the referendum campaign began to part. While the Labour-LD coalition focussed on the practical implementation of devolution, the SNP, in opposition, maintained its pro-independence stance.

After the SNP took control of the Scottish Parliament from 2012 onwards, the independence issue returned to the agenda, as the SNP saw an opportunity to push forward this political goal (see Chapter 14 by Curtice elsewhere in this volume). By that time the Conservatives, accepting devolution but opposing independence, had returned to power in Westminster. From 2010 to 2015 the Conservatives formed a central government coalition with the Liberal Democrats, who took a similar stance: for devolution but rejecting independence, as did the Labour Party, now in opposition. Devolution was further strengthened by two amended Scotland Acts, one in 2012, before the failed independence referendum of 2014, and the second in 2016, as a response to promises extended by the main parties during the independence referendum campaign.

By contrast, the referendum result in Wales appeared to cast some doubt over the democratic legitimacy of the new National Assembly for Wales. A wafer-thin majority of 50.3%, on a less than impressive 50.1% turnout, meant that the Assembly had received expressed approval by just over a quarter of the electorate. While this result constituted some progress compared to the 1979 Welsh result, it fell clearly short of the resounding mandate received by the Scottish Parliament. However, in 1997 there were no additional hurdles written into the referendum rules. The result stood, although morally the Welsh Conservatives may have felt equally deprived of a victory as the SNP had in Scotland in 1979. Nevertheless, as pledged before the referendum, the Conservatives accepted the outcome and eventually took their seats in the new Assembly. Based on the pre-referendum White Paper, the promised Government of Wales Act received Royal Assent on 31 July 1998. Originally the Act was accompanied by a comprehensive Transfer of Functions Order, emphasising the executive nature of Welsh devolution. Many of those provisions were later included in the Government of Wales Act 2006, and further amendments followed.

Eventually the question arose whether the Assembly should also be given primary legislative powers. This idea clearly exceeded the mandate given by the 1997 referendum. Therefore, an additional referendum was held on 3 March 2011, in which the electorate was asked to respond YES or NO to the question 'Do you want the Assembly now to be able to make laws on **all** matters in the 20 subject areas it has powers for?' [emphasis in bold in the original] (Jennings 2011: 1). The Yes side won with a seemingly clear 63.5%. However, on a rather disappointing turnout of just 35.6%, this translated to just 517,132 Yes votes compared to the original 552,698 Yes votes in 1997 (source of figures: Jennings 2011: 2 and 5). This supports the conclusion that public demand for strengthening devolution remains relatively low on the electorate's agenda in

Wales. Functional efficiency and developing appropriate policy contents in the devolved subject areas appeared more important. All Welsh political parties, including the Conservatives, put considerable effort into this task over the five legislative periods from 1999 to the present time. Since 1999 Labour has remained the strongest party in the Assembly, yet for the most part needing the support of either PC or the Liberal Democrats for a majority. This has harmed PC, who were not able to replicate the success of the SNP. In the most recent election, held on 5 May 2016, the Welsh nationalists fell back to third place behind the resurgent Conservatives. The Liberal Democrats were able to maintain a small presence varying from one to six seats from 1999, and formed a coalition with Labour in the years 2000–2003 and again since 2016. In 2016 UKIP entered the Assembly for the first time, winning seven out of the 60 seats.

Two further Acts, the Wales Act 2014 and the Wales Act 2017, provide routes for further devolution, including tax-varying powers (probably subject to a new referendum), and a new reserved powers model, opening the door for primary legislative powers for a possibly soon to be re-named Welsh Parliament. At the time of writing the trend was to widen the scope of responsibilities and functions to eventually mirror the state of devolution in Scotland, without embarking on a course for independence.

11.5   Conclusions

The devolution referendums of 1979 and 1997 can be regarded as milestones in the establishment of referendums as a tool for political decision-making in the UK. There is now a wide acceptance among the political parties as well as large sections of the electorate concerning the use of referendums in critical decision-making on constitutional matters and matters of territorial politics.

The four referendums provided invaluable practical experience in terms of formalising and organising referendums in the UK. Many of these lessons were absorbed and found their legislative expression in the Political Parties, Elections and Referendums Act 2000, which would be in place for the Scottish independence referendum of 2014 and the UK-EU referendum of 2016 (see Chapters 14 and 22 by Curtice and Smith respectively in this volume). The same applies to the Electoral Commission, an independent body which now oversees the administration of elections and national referendums in the UK. The Commission was also set up in 2000, based on recommendations by the Committee on Standards in Public Life. The Act put referendums procedurally on an equal footing with elections, while on the other hand retaining the UK Parliament's wide-ranging flexibility in terms of scope and contents of referendums. Earlier concerns about undermining parliamentary sovereignty and governmental responsibility have been diminished. Calling a referendum remains a voluntary decision on the part of the Parliament, to be used sparingly and only when necessary to decide a fundamental question. The elected politicians retain full responsibility both for shaping the political contents, and for a publicly acceptable implementation of its outcome. On the procedural side, however, the work of the Electoral Commission provides stability and consistency. Lengthy procedural debates on the ways and means of conducting a referendum, as seen both in 1979 and 1997, can now largely be avoided. It is also unlikely that additional qualification hurdles will feature in future referendums. The lesson from Scotland 1979 had already been taken on-board in 1997 and was indirectly repeated by the 1997 Welsh referendum. Public concern about the apparently low positive support for the Welsh Assembly was less vociferous than the concern expressed about the apparent 1979 Scottish reversal of the referendum result by means of an added clause. Equally valuable was the respect shown in Wales and Scotland for the limitations of a referendum result. When the original terms of the 1997 referendum were clearly exceeded in 2011, it was time to obtain a fresh mandate from the electorate in Wales. The 1997 Scottish referendum did not include a mandate for independence, hence when independence became a viable option a new referendum became necessary in 2014. However, some questions remain regarding the longevity of referendum results. It is understandable that activists and voters on the losing side would seek some redress or even a reversal of the decision. However, in the British context there is some serious danger that the power and effectiveness of a referendum as a political tool can be damaged if an outcome can be easily ignored, subverted or overturned. Recent calls for swift new referendums on Scottish independence and the UK's membership of the EU serve as a warning. The interval between 1979 and 1997 was an adequate time span for significant political developments and demographic changes to have occurred. In this sense the four referendums have set a good example.

Party politics in the UK has also profited from the referendums. Avoiding the fragmentation of campaigns and engaging in co-operation when interests genuinely coincide has been a valuable experience. Stepping away from the strictly adversarial approach prevalent in Westminster had been a declared goal of the devolution campaigns in 1997, and this has been achieved in abundance in both the Scottish Parliament and the Welsh Assembly. Choosing the Additional Member System as a compromise between the familiar First Past the Post and a strict proportional representation system has worked for both the larger and the smaller political parties. Periods of single-party rule have been rare, and some form of coalition government was in place both in the Scottish Parliament and the Welsh Assembly for the majority of the time since 1999. Labour and the SNP have been able to implement much of their political agendas. PC and the Liberal Democrats, while of somewhat lower political profile, also obtained opportunities of experiencing governmental responsibility. The Conservatives have not yet been able to form governments in Scotland or Wales, but the years of providing practical opposition both in Edinburgh and Cardiff have helped to dissipate their original anti-devolution stance.

Overall, referendums have contributed to some major transformation in the political landscape of the UK since 1979, and are now established direct-democratic elements in the constitutional system. At present, referendums are strong political tools and are likely to remain so if not overused or undermined by failures to implement results. By the same token, political activists on all sides in Scotland and Wales can take significant pride in having helped the referendum concept on its way into mainstream UK politics.

References

Bogdanor, V. (1979). *Devolution*. Oxford, London, and Glasgow: Oxford University Press.

Dardanelli, P. (2005). *Between Two Unions: Europeanisation and Scottish Devolution*. Manchester: Manchester University Press.

Dewdney, R. (1997). *Results of Devolution Referendums (1979 & 1997)* (Research Paper No. 97/113). London: House of Commons Library.

Jennings, M. (2011). *Results of the National Assembly for Wales Referendum 2011* (NAW Members' Research Service Paper No. 11/017). Cardiff: National Assembly for Wales.

Jessop, B., Bonnett, K., Ling, T. & Bromley, S. (1988). *Thatcherism. A Tale of Two Nations*. Cambridge, Oxford, and New York: Polity Press.

Keating, M. (1998). What's Wrong with Asymmetrical Government? *Regional and Federal Studies, 8*(1), 195–218.

Keating, M. (2002). Devolution and Public Policy in the United Kingdom: Divergence or Convergence? In J. Adams & P. Robinson (Eds.), *Devolution in Practice. Public Policy Differences Within the UK*. London: Institute for Public Policy Research.

Keating, M. (2009). *The Independence of Scotland. Self-government and the Shifting Politics of Union*. Oxford and New York: Oxford University Press.

Leach, R., & Percy-Smith, J. (2001). *Local Governance in Britain*. Basingstoke and New York: Palgrave.

Loughlin, J. (2000). Regional Autonomy and State Paradigm Shifts in Western Europe. *Regional and Federal Studies, 10*(2), 10–34.

Marks, G. (1996). An Actor-Centred Approach to Multi-Level Governance. *Regional and Federal Studies, 6*(2), 20–38.

Padfield, C., & Byrne, T. (1987). *British Constitution Made Simple* (7th revised ed.). Oxford, London, and Melbourne: Made Simple Books.

Scottish Constitutional Convention (Eds.). (1995). *Scotland's Parliament, Scotland's Right*. Edinburgh: Convention of Scottish Local Authorities. Available at https://paulcairney.files.wordpress.com/2015/09/scc-1995.pdf.

Scottish National Party. (1997). *Yes We Can Win the Best for Scotland. The SNP General Election Manifesto 1997*. Edinburgh: SNP. Available at http://www.politicsresources.net/area/uk/ge97/man/snp97.pdf.

The Guardian. (1977, June 28). David Steel Names His Price for Lib-Lab Pact. *The Guardian*. Available at: http://www.theguardian.com/politics/2017/jun/28/lib-lab-pact-liberals-labour-party-1977.

UK Government (Eds.). (1997). *A Voice for Wales. The Government's Proposals for a Welsh Assembly, Cm 3781*. London: HMSO.

UK Parliament. (1948). *Representation of the People Act 1948*. London: HMSO. Available at https://www.legislation.gov.uk/ukpga/1948/65/enacted.

UK Parliament. (1983). *Representation of the People Act 1983*. London: HMSO. Available at https://www.legislation.gov.uk/ukpga/1983/2.

UK Parliament. (1997). *Referendums (Scotland and Wales) Act 1997*. London: HMSO. Available at https://www.legislation.gov.uk/ukpga/1997/61/enacted.

UK Parliament. (1998a). *Government of Wales Act 1998*. London: HMSO. Available at https://www.legislation.gov.uk/ukpga/1998/38/.

UK Parliament. (1998b). *Scotland Act 1998*. London: HMSO. Available at https://www.legislation.gov.uk/ukpga/1998/46/.

UK Parliament. (2000). *Political Parties, Elections and Referendums Act 2000*. London: HMSO. Available at https://www.legislation.gov.uk/ukpga/2000/41/.

UK Political Info (Eds.). (2019). *1979 General Election Results Summary*. Available at http://www.ukpolitical.info/1979.htm.

Wyn Jones, R., & Scully, R. (2012). *Wales Says Yes: Devolution and the 2011 Welsh Referendum*. Cardiff: University of Wales.

CHAPTER 12

The 1998 Good Friday (Belfast) Agreement Referendums in Northern Ireland and the Republic of Ireland

Katy Hayward

The referendums on 22 May 1998 in both Northern Ireland and the Republic of Ireland were on the new British-Irish Agreement to replace the 1985 Anglo-Irish Agreement. The 1998 Agreement consists of two elements: the agreement reached in the multi-party talks (known as the 'Good Friday' or 'Belfast' Agreement) and the agreement between the British and Irish governments enabling it. The Agreement was reached at the end of a series of multi-party talks in Northern Ireland that sought to end the 30 years of violent conflict known as 'The Troubles'. The talks were supported by the British and Irish governments, both of which had carefully created the context for these negotiations through building a close inter-governmental relationship in the years beforehand (Arthur 2000; Coakley and Todd 2020). This relationship was vital, particularly because the conflict centred on a dispute about competing British and Irish claims for sovereignty over part of the island of Ireland (i.e. Northern Ireland).

A critical juncture in developing a constructive British-Irish relationship had been realised in the Downing Street Declaration of December 1993. In their joint declaration, the British Prime Minister John Major and the Irish *Taoiseach* (Prime Minister) Albert Reynolds established the principle of consent for the peace process (Walker and Weaver 1994). It established that any change to the constitutional status of Northern Ireland would have to be approved by a majority of people there and by a majority of people in the

K. Hayward (✉)
Queen's University Belfast, Belfast, Northern Ireland, UK
e-mail: k.hayward@qub.ac.uk

© The Author(s) 2021
J. Smith (ed.), *The Palgrave Handbook of European Referendums*,
https://doi.org/10.1007/978-3-030-55803-1_12

247

Republic of Ireland. Building on from this principle, the Framework Documents of February 1995 stated: 'Both Governments intend that the outcome of these [multi-party] negotiations will be submitted for democratic ratification through referendums, North and South' (Paragraph 55). Thus, over a year before the multi-party talks began, it was known that any decision would be put to concurrent referendums in both jurisdictions on the island of Ireland. If each referendum returned a positive result, it would constitute a momentous change in the history and constitution of both the UK and Ireland.

The 1998 Agreement is a complicated document, a 'hybrid of domestic and international law' (Campbell et al. 2003). It contains five key elements, each of which are very complex in themselves and, moreover, the impact of which could not be predicted or determined at the time of the referendum. These are: (1) a formalised Irish dimension to Northern Ireland (meaning it could no longer be treated as a purely domestic concern of the UK); (2) constitutional change (devolution for Northern Ireland, the revision to the Irish constitution); (3) new institutions of government (within Northern Ireland, cross-border in Ireland and British-Irish); (4) an equality agenda (advanced rights protections, non-discrimination rules and safeguards); (5) and security-related provisions (including the release of paramilitary prisoners, policing reform and decommissioning) (Doyle 2018). The priority was to set up a new Assembly following elections under the Northern Ireland (Elections) Act. The speed at which this legislation was passed was quite remarkable. The Good Friday Agreement was concluded on 10 April 1998. The Northern Ireland (Elections) Act only completed its Commons stages on 22 April 1998 and ended its passage through the Lords on 7 May 1998. The referendum was held on 22 May and the subsequent elections on the 25 June 1998. Northern Ireland was never to be the same again.

12.1   THE USE OF A REFERENDUM

12.1.1   Previous Experience

The decision to put the Agreement to the people in Northern Ireland via referendum was atypical. Until this point, only two referendums had been held in Northern Ireland. The first was a 'border poll' that took place in March 1973.[1] This was intended to test the desire for Irish unification in the six counties of Northern Ireland. It was called by the British government to demonstrate that such Irish nationalist aspirations were only held by a minority in Northern Ireland (Mac Ginty 2003). The anticipation was that, having shown this to be

[1] The second referendum in Northern Ireland was as part of the UK-wide referendum on staying in the European Community in June 1975 (see Chapter 22 by Smith elsewhere in this volume). The vote in Northern Ireland was 52.1% to remain in the EC, on a turnout of 47.4%. In terms of both turnout and Yes vote, this was by far the lowest of all the component regions/nations of the UK.

the case, government of the region could continue to operate on the assumption that unionism remained the preference of the majority. Aware of this, Catholics boycotted the poll, which returned a vote of 98.9% in favour of remaining part of the United Kingdom, on a turnout of 58.6%.

The close intertwining of the fortunes of the constituent parts of the United Kingdom was also evident nearly a quarter of a century later in referendums not on independence but on devolution. The push for decentralisation within the UK that came soon after the electoral victory of the Labour Party in 1997 was a new way of managing the rise of nationalist movements across the UK. While Scotland and Wales held referendums on devolution in 1997 (see Chapter 11 by Mathias), Northern Ireland was in no position to hold such a referendum. It was clear that devolution alone would not be sufficient to succour the unique demands of Irish nationalists in Northern Ireland, which were not for independence but for Irish unification. Nonetheless, the principle of devolution played a vital part in the Agreement that emerged from the multi-party talks on Good Friday 10 April 1998. Powers were devolved from Westminster to a new Northern Ireland Assembly and Executive, which were designed to ensure power is shared between the two main political traditions of unionism and nationalism. This devolved administration sitting in Stormont, Belfast, was at the first level of new institutions established to govern post-Agreement Northern Ireland. There was also a second level of cross-border bodies for cooperation between Northern Ireland and Ireland, across a range of areas of common interest, such as trade, waterways and food safety. And a third level of governance worked to put it in the broader context of British-Irish relations. Northern Ireland's referendum in 1998 was therefore much more than a straightforward vote on devolution: it was a vote on a peace accord, for multilevel institutions, and for provision for a future referendum.

12.1.2   The Requirement of a Referendum

As anticipated in the Downing Street Declaration, the referendum on the 1998 Agreement was written into the Agreement itself (using the technical parliamentary term of 'Command paper 3883' [the technical term for the Good Friday/Belfast Agreement]—language that was also used in the question posed on the ballot paper). Under the section 'Validation, Implementation and Review', the Agreement set out the requirement and date for a referendum in both Northern Ireland and the Republic of Ireland:

> 2. Each Government will organise a referendum on 22 May 1998. Subject to Parliamentary approval, a consultative referendum in Northern Ireland, organised under the terms of the Northern Ireland (Entry to Negotiations, etc.) Act 1996, will address the question: "Do you support the agreement reached in the multi-party talks on Northern Ireland and set out in Command Paper 3883?". ...

3. If majorities of those voting in each of the referendums support this agreement, the Governments will then introduce and support, in their respective Parliaments, such legislation as may be necessary to give effect to all aspects of this agreement, and will take whatever ancillary steps as may be required including the holding of elections on 25 June…

The primary legislation for the referendum already existed in the NI (Entry to Negotiations, etc.) Act 1996. Two weeks after the Agreement, on 24 April 1998, the Secretary of State Mo Mowlam made an Order under section 4(1)—the NI Negotiations (Referendum) Order 1998—which set the date of the referendum (22 May), the form of the ballot paper and the hours of polling (7 am to 10 pm) (Elliott 1999). This meant that there was just five weeks between the Agreement being voted on and elections being held to the new devolved Assembly (although it officially remained in shadow form until the full devolution of powers from Westminster in December 1999).

It was inevitable that there would be a referendum in the Republic of Ireland relating to the Agreement as it entailed a direct change to *Bunreacht na hÉireann*, the constitution of the Irish state (Chubb 1991). The referendum in the Republic was on the nineteenth amendment to the constitution, which allowed the State 'to consent to be bound' by the Agreement and provided that further amendments, substantively to Articles 2 and 3, would come into effect when that Agreement entered into force. It was the eighteenth referendum held in the state (and the sixth referendum in five years). The key focus of the amendment was Article 2 (which defined the national territory as the island of Ireland) and Article 3 (which stated the 'right of the government and parliament… to exercise jurisdiction over the whole territory'). The revised wording for these articles was included in the 1998 Agreement itself. The constitution would now define the Irish nation in terms of people (i.e. Irish citizens) rather than territory and express a 'firm will' of the nation for Irish unity but qualifying this with the principle of 'consent of a majority of people, democratically expressed, in both jurisdictions in the island' (quotation from the new Articles; see Ruane and Todd 2003; Ó Dochartaigh 2017 for further analysis).

12.2   Notable Characteristics of the 1998 Northern Ireland Referendum

12.2.1   Simultaneous Referendums in Two Jurisdictions

There are several distinctive features about the referendums on the 1998 Agreement. First is the fact that there were two referendums on the same Agreement held on the same day in two different jurisdictions: Northern Ireland and the Republic of Ireland. In the case of the former, it was a regional referendum rather than state-wide across the UK. This is in part a manifestation of the principle of consent (noted above) together with the principle of 'self-determination for the people of the island of Ireland alone, without external interference' both of which are affirmed in the 1998 Agreement itself. The reason why unionists in Northern Ireland (those wanting to remain part of the United Kingdom) were willing to accept this formulation is partly because of long-standing (but rarely articulated) doubt that there would be overwhelming popular support in Great Britain for retaining Northern Ireland within the UK.[2] In the mid-1990s, Northern Ireland was inextricably associated in the minds of many in the British public with economic dependence and security risk. More to the point, the Good Friday (Belfast) Agreement changed the constitution of the United Kingdom only to the extent that it related to Northern Ireland and it could be argued that there was no pressing need for wider UK public approval for an Agreement that only had a direct effect on the two jurisdictions on the island of Ireland.

On the other hand, any amendment to the Irish constitution requires ratification via referendum (as noted above). Since it was first drawn up in 1937, the 2nd and 3rd articles of the Irish constitution laid claim over the territory of Northern Ireland. In 1921, partition was an act by the British government to retain control of six counties of Ireland that was fiercely resisted by Irish nationalists across the island. The constitutional claim over the territory of Northern Ireland in Articles 2 and 3 had given succour to Irish nationalists over the ensuing six decades, but it also served to exacerbate unionist fear and wariness of the Irish Republic. By the 1990s, it was clear to successive Irish *Taoisigh* (Prime Ministers) that the Articles would need to be revised in order to assure unionists of a new relationship of trust and respect between the Republic and Northern Ireland (Hayward 2009). The rescinding of Ireland's irredentist claim over Northern Ireland meant a revision to the wording of Articles 2 and 3—as set out in the 1998 Agreement—and this was required to be put to referendum in the Republic.

12.2.2   Approving a Peace Accord

That the referendums were on an Agreement that came at the end of such a process of peace negotiations is the second distinctive feature here. The Agreement had been achieved in the context of, as Zartman (2001) puts it, 'mutually hurting stalemate', with all sides wishing to see an end to the violent conflict that had been centred in Northern Ireland (but with horrific impact in the Republic of Ireland and Great Britain too). There was a weariness with the Troubles that had continued for thirty years and this was the first point at which the people had been asked to approve by plebiscite an effort to settle it by peaceful means.

---

[2]This was illustrated in the results of the Lord Ashcroft poll (2018) on 'Brexit, the Border and the Union'. Asked in Spring 2018 whether or not Northern Ireland should remain part of the UK, a majority (57%) of voters in England, Scotland and Wales answered that it was for the people of Northern Ireland to decide. And, in the event of Northern Ireland voting to leave the UK, more than six in ten said they 'wouldn't mind either way'.

12.2.3   Majority Approval for Non-majoritarianism

Thirdly—and somewhat ironically—the 1998 referendum in Northern Ireland sought to find majority support for an Agreement which was premised on the notion that majoritarianism does not work in Northern Ireland. The Agreement was introducing multilevel institutionalism and consociationalism in an effort to progress democratic representation in the region beyond the zero-sum calculations that had stymied politics in Northern Ireland for so long. Power-sharing and consensus was to be the new norm in order to move beyond the imposition of majority will on a staunchly resistant minority. And the Agreement itself went a long way from the brutality of the act of partition itself, in which the Irish border was drawn in such a way as to secure a majority Protestant and unionist population in Northern Ireland. In contrast, the Agreement recognised the parity and validity of Irish nationalist aspirations for a united Ireland alongside those of British unionist ones. Such a careful balance is best managed when it is not tested by crude assessments of the 'popular will' of Northern Ireland in the form of a majority. Despite the success of consensus-building and non-majoritarian decision-making experiments in deliberation organised by some civic sector bodies in Northern Ireland (Hayward 2014), there was no effort to consider alternative types of referendum for approving the Agreement that might have been more appropriate than that of a simple binary choice.

12.2.4   Provision for a Future Referendum

Finally, and related to the above point, the Agreement itself contains the promise of future referendums in Northern Ireland and the Republic of Ireland in order to see a change in the constitutional status of Northern Ireland. The Agreement includes draft clauses for incorporation into British legislation (which became the Northern Ireland Act 1998) which declares that Northern Ireland would only cease to be part of the UK if there were a vote for Irish unification in a referendum. This is remarkable, because it means that the very first article and section of the Northern Ireland Act (1998) allows that a referendum in the region could change the constitutional status of Northern Ireland and, thus, the constitution of the United Kingdom—not to mention that of Ireland:

(1) It is hereby declared that Northern Ireland in its entirety remains part of the United Kingdom and shall not cease to be so without the consent of a majority of the people of Northern Ireland voting in a poll held for the purposes of this section in accordance with Schedule 1.

(2) But if the wish expressed by a majority in such a poll is that Northern Ireland should cease to be part of the United Kingdom and form part of a united Ireland, the Secretary of State shall lay before Parliament such proposals to give effect to that wish as may be agreed between Her

Majesty's Government in the United Kingdom and the Government of Ireland. (Northern Ireland Act 1998, section 1)

As such, Schedule 1 of the Northern Ireland Act (1998) also provides for the holding of such a referendum in Northern Ireland 'if at any time it appears likely to him [sic] that a majority of those voting would express a wish that Northern Ireland should cease to be part of the United Kingdom and form part of a united Ireland'. Then, in the event of such a vote, the Secretary of State for Northern Ireland would see a bill before Parliament to enact Irish unification in accordance with an agreement between the British and Irish governments.

The spectre of this so-called 'border poll' haunts Northern Ireland politics. To some degree, it reflects an assumption that 'resolution' of the conflict in Northern Ireland will (only) come through the reversal of the act of partition that created it in 1921. What it means is that, regardless of the consociational, power-sharing mechanisms established by the Agreement, it is the quest to maintain (in the case of unionism) or gather (in the case of nationalism) a majority within Northern Ireland that is still seen as the political ambition of prime importance for the respective sides of the debate. Writing a border poll into the 1998 Agreement helped nationalist parties sell it to their supporters (Mac Ginty 2003). It also helped sweeten the pill of retracting the claim over the territory of Northern Ireland for nationalists in the Republic of Ireland (Ó Dochartaigh 2017). Its importance was downplayed by unionists, who pointed to the low levels of support for Irish unification in opinion surveys and who argued that making a success of the Agreement would erode the demands for a border poll itself. Again, the assumption is that this would be a binary-choice referendum, seeking a simple majority for the change. We return to the irony of this point later on in this chapter.

12.2.5   Differences in Rules

It is worth noting that there are some differences in the conditions for referendums between Northern Ireland and the Republic of Ireland that were pertinent in the case of the 1998 referendums. The Agreement recognises the birthright of those born in Northern Ireland to be 'British, Irish or both'. What this means in terms of voting rights, however, varies according to jurisdiction. In Northern Ireland (and across the UK as a whole), British, Irish and Commonwealth citizens can vote in a referendum (and all elections). In the Republic of Ireland, British citizens can vote in local and national elections, but they are unable to vote in referendums. There are other significant differences in the conduct of referendums between Ireland and the UK. Many of these differences arise from the simple fact that there have been so many more referendums in Ireland (averaging one a year since 1998), and hence there have been legal cases and institutional developments to accommodate them (see Chapter 16 by Reidy et al.). In the UK, however, there was not even an Electoral Commission until the Political Parties, Elections and Referendums Act 2000—over two years too late for the Good Friday Agreement referendum.

The 1998 referendums also revealed very different positions of the British and Irish governments. The Irish government (specifically the governing *Fianna Fáil* party) was able to be supportive of a Yes vote—it had worked hard to realise the Agreement itself. It was free to do so because of the role of the Referendum Commission, which had been established in 1998 in time to manage the Irish referendum on the EU's Amsterdam Treaty and thus, coincidentally, the Good Friday Agreement. The Commission's existence meant that responsibility for giving information, encouraging turnout, stimulating public engagement and ensuring balance was not resting directly with the government. The British government was also heavily invested in the peace talks and in support for the referendum proposals. But it was hamstrung in the campaign itself because there was no body with equivalent powers to Ireland's Referendum Commission, and because the strength of feeling in Northern Ireland both for and against the Agreement was very intense. As noted below, the fact that the government resorted to more surreptitious activity only exacerbated suspicion rather than re-assuring naysayers. Such activity was to have a problematic legacy when it came to implementing the terms of the Agreement itself and attempting to establish stable government in Northern Ireland.

12.3   The Wording of the Question

12.3.1   Northern Ireland

The referendum was held on 22 May 1998—under six weeks from the day the Agreement itself was concluded. The questions on the ballot papers in the referendums in Northern Ireland and the Republic of Ireland were quite different. In Northern Ireland, the question was: 'Do you support the Agreement reached at the multi-party talks on Northern Ireland and set out in Command Paper 3883?' It was assumed that everyone would have read the Agreement itself; a copy was posted through the door of each household and the front page of the document merely had the title 'The Agreement', followed by the sentence 'This agreement is about your future. Please read it carefully'. The ballot paper question took quite an unusual form, on the one hand asking whether the voter would offer their 'support' to the Agreement whilst at the same time referencing a 'command paper' of which few people would have heard. There was no cover note or summary with the Agreement. According to the Northern Ireland Election and Referendum Survey (Curtice et al. 2006), 72% of respondents said that they had read the Agreement prior to voting. However, when pressed further on this, only 28% of those who had read it said that they had read the whole text in detail (Fig. 12.1). Although the most common response was to have read 'parts of it in detail', the choice

If you read the Agreement prior to voting, how much did you read?	%
All of it in detail	28
Parts of it in detail	39
Just skimmed through it	33

Fig. 12.1 Percentage of supporters of the Agreement who had read it (*Source* Curtice et al. 2006)

posed in the referendum, of course, was not to parts of the Agreement but a simple Yes/No as to whether they supported it as a whole.

12.3.2 Ireland

In the Republic, the question took the standard form used for such referendums on changes to the Irish constitution: 'Do you approve of the proposal to amend the Constitution contained in the undermentioned Bill? (Nineteenth Amendment of the Constitution Bill, 1998)'. There was a genuine concern among Irish officials that the referendum might not pass in Northern Ireland and that there was therefore a risk that Ireland could change its constitution and so give up its claim over the territory of Northern Ireland with nothing to show for it on the other side. This was addressed by careful legal drafting. The amendment to the constitution thus includes the phrase:

> If the Government declare that the State has become obliged, pursuant to the Agreement, to give effect to the amendment of this Constitution referred to therein, then, notwithstanding Article 46 hereof, this Constitution shall be amended as follows...

This wording meant that the state would not be bound to alter the constitution in a scenario in which the referendum in Northern Ireland rejected the Agreement. The Article 46 referred to gives the *Oireachtas* (Irish houses of parliament) the duty of formulating proposals for amendment of the constitution but provides that these can be vetoed by the Irish electorate via referendum.

It is significant that this question was not the only one posed to voters in the Irish Republic that day. The referendum on the 1998 Agreement took place at the same time as the referendum on the Amsterdam Treaty, which was to form the eighteenth amendment to the Irish constitution. There was thus some suspicion that the Irish government was hoping that goodwill for the 1998 Agreement would have a positive influence on the support for the Amsterdam Treaty. This misgiving was stated quite clearly by some of those who campaigned against the Amsterdam Treaty. It is difficult to determine what difference, if any, including two referendum questions on the one paper made to either result. The Amsterdam Treaty was passed with a Yes vote of

61.7% (O'Mahony 2009)—some distance short of the 94.4% in favour of the 1998 Agreement.

12.4   The Campaigns

12.4.1   Common Features of the Pre-referendum Campaign

Quite a lot of preparation had already been done in advance insofar as acclimatising the public in both jurisdictions as to what the Agreement would entail (Somerville and Kirby 2012). The negotiations were long and arduous, and daily press statements and media interviews over the course of the talks meant that parties had many opportunities to raise key achievements and stumbling blocks to their supporters. Of course, this being part of a negotiated peace Agreement, the achievements of one party were the stumbling blocks for another. The trick for securing and selling the Agreement was to be able to frame the achievements on all sides as outweighing the sacrifices. This is always difficult in a peace process but it took on a particularly challenging form given the anticipated referendum. The recognition that the Agreement would have to have support from across different parties and communities in Northern Ireland in order to pass meant that there had to be some moderation and consideration of the 'other side' in the way that all pro-Agreement parties presented it, even to their own bases.

12.4.2   Ireland

The referendum campaigns took place in two very different contexts under quite different procedures. In the Republic of Ireland, following the Supreme Court judgement in the *McKenna* Case of 1995 (see Reidy et al. in Chapter 16), the Irish government could no longer use public money to campaign for an outcome that it supported. This led, as noted above, to the Referendum Act, passed by the *Oireachtas* early in 1998, which provided for a Referendum Commission to oversee the use of public money and to ensure that the public was provided with clear information on the referendum proposal. This was well-timed for the referendum on the Good Friday Agreement, and resulted in the dissemination of clear information to the public. An active awareness-raising campaign was initiated by the Commission, which went alongside keen efforts to provide information on the Agreement and the constitutional amendment specifically. In the interests of balance, the Commission had to present some of the arguments made by critics of the 1998 Agreement—who were few in number in the Republic of Ireland and who were not associated with mainstream political discourse (Mansergh 1999).

All the main political parties in the Republic were in favour of the 1998 Agreement and the revision of Articles 2 and 3—including those parties (such as Sinn Féin and the Green Party) which opposed the Treaty of Amsterdam. The most formal opposition to the Agreement came in the form of a case brought by Riordan, arguing that the changes to Articles 2 and 3 conflicted with Article 46 (Mansergh 1999). The only real voices of dissent were hardline republicans who were already marginalised in public debate in the Republic. They emphasised the sacrifice being made by the Irish nationalist cause in effectively recognising the legitimacy of unionism and, more particularly, British rule in the six counties of Northern Ireland. The principle of consent and the act of devolution, for such critics, gave recognition to the very existence of Northern Ireland—something which Sinn Féin had traditionally resisted. In the minds of voters in the Republic, however, the priority was peace on the island of Ireland—and the amendment of two constitutional articles—to revise an irredentist claim that few saw as anything other than symbolic and wholly aspirational (Ivory 1999)—was seen as a reasonable price to pay.

12.4.3   Northern Ireland

The campaign in Northern Ireland was much more contentious and closely fought. Only one in four people claimed to have read the Agreement text in full by the time it came to the referendum (see Fig. 12.1). Much of people's reaction to the Agreement was, therefore, dependent on the lead from political parties and from media coverage. The campaign was extraordinarily intense. The very fact of there being a referendum had served to quell some of the unease about the process of the talks when they were underway. There are other examples of attempts to negotiate a settlement in Northern Ireland that had established some high level British-Irish inter-governmental agreement but which had given rise to serious public disorder, particularly insofar as there appeared to be little effort to include 'ordinary' people. The Ulster Workers' Council Strike which followed the Sunningdale Agreement (1973) was so vigorous and effective that it resulted in the collapse of the Executive and Council of Ireland that had been agreed. The unionist response to the Anglo-Irish Agreement (1985) was also very antagonistic and there had been enormous public protests but they did not result in such civic unrest. That said, some 14 months after the Anglo-Irish Agreement was concluded, a 400,000 signature petition was presented calling for a referendum on the topic.

What this meant was that peace talks tended to be seen as ones in which deals were done in closed negotiations and those on the wrong side of the closed doors were expected merely to accept the outcome. This had bred much resentment in 1974 and 1985, particularly among unionists. The prospect of a referendum made a difference to the support for the multi-party talks, but it also put the main unionist party, the Ulster Unionist Party, under pressure to keep its supporters on board throughout the process. It also meant that the campaigns for and against the Agreement started a long time before the actual text itself was concluded.

There were very public unionist divisions about the talks process (which had been marked by boycotts and protests from the Democratic Unionist Party) and the Agreement. The biggest sticking points for unionist parties about the Agreement tended to focus on security matters. Certainly these are the issues (policing reform, release of prisoners, decommissioning) that caused the Assembly and Executive to run into difficulty fairly soon after they were established. Indeed, the Assembly was suspended after just 19 months of being set up by the then-Secretary of State, Peter Mandelson, over the contentious issue of the decommissioning (and verification of the same) of paramilitary weapons. However, a broader analysis would suggest that the Agreement was overall a 'harder sell' for unionism. Whereas it was clear what nationalists were gaining from the Agreement—cross-border bodies, recognition of the legitimacy of Irish citizenship, identity and political aspirations, promise of a border poll, laws against discrimination—for many unionists, it was all too easy to focus on what was being given away or compromised on (Farrington 2006). This is inevitable in a peace process that attempts to rebalance power in a contested polity; unionists had held a disproportionate amount of power and a fairer balance in that inevitably meant a reduction of that power. More specifically, the very principle of power-sharing—especially sharing power with Sinn Féin, the political party closely associated with the IRA paramilitary organisation—was objected to by many unionists on moral grounds.

There is an interesting dynamic to the campaign in Northern Ireland arising from the nature of the Agreement itself. The unionist and nationalist parties in the region, in principle, broadly hold allegiance to the British and to the Irish states, respectively. The Agreement formally recognises the legitimacy of British and Irish identities, citizenship and aspirations among those born in Northern Ireland. In practice, of course, parties are not uncritical of the governments of the states that they identify most strongly with. In the campaign for the Agreement, the cross-party consensus in the Republic of Ireland certainly helped to assuage some concerns among Irish nationalists in the north about the Agreement—particularly the retraction of the Irish state's claim over the six counties of Northern Ireland. If parties in the Republic saw this as something that could be counterbalanced by other elements in the Agreement—such as the cross-border institutions and the commitment to holding a border poll if the majority will changed in Northern Ireland—then this was some reassurance to northern nationalist parties.

The relationship between unionist parties and the British government and political parties is quite different, however. Unionism is a traditionally conservative, pro-business, political ideology, and unionist parties in Northern Ireland have typically had some natural affiliation to the Conservative Party in Britain. John Major's Conservative government had relied on the support of the Ulster Unionist Party in the early 1990s and this served to strengthen their relationship. Moreover, the Good Friday (Belfast) Agreement talks concluded under a Labour Party government—after Tony Blair's landslide electoral success in 1997—which automatically meant an increased level of distrust for the British government from unionist parties. Although Blair and Mo Mowlam, as the Secretary of State for Northern Ireland, gained a certain amount of respect from across the political spectrum, it was inevitable that it would be harder to bring unionist supporters on board under Labour leadership.

12.4.4   Incentivising Support

Whereas there were rules in the Republic of Ireland about the role of government and limits on public spending in elections, these were less clear in the case of the referendum in Northern Ireland. Given unionist factions and vocal unionist opposition to the talks and to the Agreement—even the very principle of an agreement with the likes of Sinn Féin—the British government had some concerns that the referendum might be difficult to pass. More realistically, even if it got a simple majority, if it did not receive the support of a majority of unionist voters then the Agreement would also be severely hamstrung from the start. The government therefore resorted to surreptitious means of encouraging voter turnout and constructive media debate. Atkinson and Blick (2017) note the embarrassment caused to the Northern Ireland Office of the British government when an internal memo was leaked, revealing its behind-the-scenes efforts to secure a Yes vote.

Some of the British government's endeavours to encourage support for the Agreement were less subtle. The announcement of a £135 m investment plan for Northern Ireland in the week of the vote was an interesting use of public money—although ministers stressed that the money was not dependent on a Yes vote (Atkinson and Blick 2017).

Another type of 'bling' and dazzle for the Agreement was found in the form of a Belfast concert by U2, the go-to rockstars for stirring up good-feeling about Irish initiatives on the international stage. Bringing the somewhat awkward political leaders David Trimble and John Hume on stage with Bono may not have convinced any sceptical unionist stalwarts, but it sought to encourage the younger generation to come out to vote. What happened to these voters after the referendum is an interesting question. There has been a growth in the proportion of the population identifying as 'neither unionist nor nationalist' (Hayward and McManus 2019). Many of these are in the age group 38–45 today, who would have been voting for the first time in the 1998 referendum. There is some evidence of particularly entrenched political apathy among this group—a consequence of the decline in enthusiasm that tends to happen in the years after a 'revolution' such as the 1998 Agreement was felt by many to be (Hayward and McManus 2019).

12.5   Afterwards

12.5.1   The Results

The intensity of feeling around the 1998 Agreement meant that there was lively debate all the way up to polling day in Northern Ireland. The unpredictability of the result was evident in the referendum study (Curtice et al. 2006) which showed how many people only decided which way to vote in the last days of the campaign (see Fig. 12.2). This was particularly true of Protestant (typically unionist) voters, of whom an incredible 42% made their minds up in the last week of the referendum.

In Northern Ireland, the Yes vote was 71.12% on a record turnout of 81.1%. While almost all Catholics (who typically support nationalist parties) voted in support of the Agreement, only 57% of Protestants did so (Hayes and McAllister 2001). That said, the levels of voting across all constituencies in Northern Ireland was consistently high, so there were no large geographical variations that could explain the vote. More particularly, what happened in the referendum was that around 150,000 people voted who never usually did so. This reflects the exceptional nature of the subject of the Agreement and the fact that it was viewed as a once-in-a-lifetime vote for many.

In the Republic of Ireland, the recorded Yes vote was 94.39%, which was the second highest Yes vote ever given in an Irish referendum. Turnout, however, was far lower than that in Northern Ireland, at 55.6%. Just as there was little geographical variation in the vote in Northern Ireland, there were no significant constituency differences in the referendum in the Republic of

%	Catholic	Protestant	No religion
The day the Agreement was signed	51	30	42
After Good Friday but before the last week of the campaign	30	26	27
In the last week of the campaign	12	30	15
On referendum day itself	3	12	14
Don't know	3	3	2

Fig. 12.2 When voters made their minds up in the referendum on the 1998 Agreement (*Source* Curtice et al. 2006)

Ireland—the gap between the largest and the smallest Yes vote was no more than 3.5%. Interestingly, one of the highest votes in favour of Yes (Cork East) neighboured the constituency of one of the lowest Yes votes (Cork North Central). Donegal, which borders the north-west of Northern Ireland, was one of the lowest votes in support of the amendment.

12.5.2 *The Fallout*

There was a strong sense in the Republic of Ireland that the vote to change Articles 2 and 3 was a vote to conclude 'the Troubles'. It was seen as a marker of the end of an era, rather than the start of a new one. Reflecting this, when the democratic institutions and power-sharing began to run into trouble, there was an overwhelming sense of frustration and disbelief among commentators in the south.

In Northern Ireland, there could be no getting away from the fact that the Agreement was the beginning rather than an end. This was evident with the election to the new Assembly, which occurred within four weeks of the referendum. The tight deadline for the election of the new Members of the Legislative Assembly (MLAs) meant that there was a lot of continuity between the campaigning for the Agreement and campaigning for election. The sharp decline in voter turnout is striking. What appears to have happened is that the 'middle ground' unionist voter who came out in support of the Agreement retreated back to a position of abstention. For, by the time of the Assembly election on 25 June 1998, there was a 50/50 split in the unionist vote between pro-Agreement and anti-Agreement parties.

What had not been expected at all after the 1998 Agreement was another terror attack from Irish republicans, but this is what happened on 15 August 1998—not even three months after the referendum. The bomb in Omagh was one of the most costly and devastating acts of terrorism in all Northern Ireland's ghastly experience—29 people died and up to 300 people were injured. The bomb was brought across the border by so-called dissident Irish republicans who opposed the Agreement. The persistence of the terrorist threat was to cast a shadow over the decisions and activities of politicians in Northern Ireland, most particularly in the extent to which they felt able to compromise on their political principles to the same degree they had in the multi-party talks.

12.6 Looking Ahead

One of the most interesting points in the Agreement for the purposes of this chapter is the fact that it contains provision for a future referendum on Irish unification—sometimes colloquially known as a 'border poll'. The text of the Agreement on such a future referendum was translated into the Northern Ireland Act (1998) in the following form:

1. The Secretary of State may by order direct the holding of a poll for the purposes of section 1 on a date specified in the order.

2. Subject to paragraph 3, the Secretary of State shall exercise the power under paragraph 1 if at any time it appears likely to him that a majority of those voting would express a wish that Northern Ireland should cease to be part of the United Kingdom and form part of a united Ireland.

3. The Secretary of State shall not make an order under paragraph 1 earlier than seven years after the holding of a previous poll under this Schedule.

What this means is that the Secretary of State for Northern Ireland is obliged to hold a referendum if the indications are that there is a majority preference for Irish unification. There is no sense of where these indications would be drawn from. Would it give an overwhelming significance to public opinion polls, for example, or would it focus on the vote/seats held by nationalist parties to the NI Assembly (Whysall 2019)? Notably, the question here is anticipated to be a binary one, with a clear Yes/No regarding leaving the UK and uniting with the Republic of Ireland. This is a matter that is at the root of the conflict in Northern Ireland and it is the point that fundamentally divides nationalists and unionists. The spectre of a border poll throws a shadow over most electoral politics in the region. It means that the efforts to create a new form of consociational, power-sharing politics are made against a background in which it is clear that a shift in a majority—a loss for unionism or a gain for nationalism—can completely transform the constitutional status of Northern Ireland.

In many ways, this prospective border poll has been the most decisively enduring feature of the 1998 Agreement itself. For what has happened in the elections since the referendum has effectively determined the interpretation and impact of the Agreement. Since the point of the June 1998 Assembly elections onwards, there has been a steady polarisation of the vote, with the hardline parties (Sinn Féin on the nationalist side and the DUP on the unionist side) becoming the largest parties in 2003. The operation of power-sharing in an Executive dominated by those two parties took on quite a different form to that anticipated when the Agreement was drawn up, when the moderate SDLP and Ulster Unionist Party were in the majority.

At the same time as the polarisation of voting there has been a reduction in voter turnout (reaching a low of 54.9% in 2016, until the 'bounce' of the snap General Election of 2017). It appears that the Agreement might have helped create a moderate middle ground but that this is not reflected in voting patterns. The greatest fear of people who vote for the DUP would be a situation in which Sinn Féin had a majority which then translates into a popular majority for Irish unification. On the other side, the fear of those who vote for Sinn Féin is that the DUP could use a position of power to chip away at the achievements of the Agreement, most particularly in relation to parity of esteem. And so the parties seek to secure their voting bases—at opposite ends of the spectrum—in anticipation that a change in majority preference demonstrated by referendum would inevitably mean a change to the constitutional status of Northern Ireland. The expectation is that such a border poll would also require a concurrent referendum in the Republic of Ireland given that it would require consent and constitutional change in that jurisdiction (Doyle and Kenny 2020). As with the referendums on the 1998 Agreement and the referendum on Scottish independence in 2014, there is no anticipation of there being a UK-wide referendum to approve what would be a fundamental alteration to the constitution of the United Kingdom itself.

12.7 Conclusion

A referendum on a document like the Belfast Agreement is always going to be the start of a process rather than the end. In many ways, the campaign in both Northern Ireland and the Republic of Ireland raised issues and trends that have continued to feature in domestic politics in the subsequent decades. According to Atkinson and Blick (2017), the multiplicity of the issues incorporated into the Agreement itself mean that the repercussions of the Agreement referendums are still being disputed today. It is largely true that the issues that were contentious during the campaign—parity of esteem, dealing with the legacy of the past—have continued to be divisive long into the post-Agreement era. Those matters that did not draw too much political ire (albeit that there were significant and hard-won achievements in the negotiation itself), such as the cross-border bodies and the principle of consent, still stand as solid pillars of the peace process. This suggests that referendum campaigns can sometimes give an accurate indication of the problematic areas for implementation even when something is passed by a convincing majority.

It is worth noting that the implementation of the Agreement soon ran into such trouble that the Assembly and Executive it established were suspended for a few years. This reflected the fact that the quest for a majority was not sufficiently mollified by the proportional, power-sharing measures of the Agreement; instead, its provision for a referendum on Irish unification—despite the anticipation that it would be some considerable time before it might be used—served to encourage binary thinking and to incentivise quests to shore-up a majority. The growing support for parties at either end of the unionist-nationalist spectrum made the legislative bodies less workable. Only with the modification of the 1998 Agreement would the DUP share power with Sinn Féin. Such modification—in the form of the St Andrews Agreement (October 2006)—further weakened some of the measures intended to build a cross-community 'middle ground' in Northern Ireland. This could not have been foreseen by the provision for a referendum in 1998 but it does suggest that the experience of that referendum showed to critics of the Agreement the importance of finding a strong and resolute support base long in advance of the referendum itself. It also made them ready to exploit any wavering among voters in the post-referendum fallout, when the really difficult task of enacting the 'will of the people' began. This will need to be borne in mind by actors on both sides of the Irish Sea and Irish border in light of the prospect of future referendums on Irish unification.

REFERENCES

Arthur, P. (2000). *Special Relationships: Britain, Ireland and the Northern Ireland Problem*. Belfast: Blackstaff Press.

Ashcroft, M. (2018). *Brexit, Border and the Union*. https://lordashcroftpolls.com/2018/06/brexit-the-border-and-the-union/. Accessed on 7 May 2020.

Atkinson, L., & Blick, A. (2017) *Referendums and the Constitution* (Research Paper). London: The Constitution Society. https://consoc.org.uk/wp-content/uploads/2017/02/Web-version-Referendums-paper.pdf. Accessed on 7 May 2020.

Campbell, C., Ní Aoláin, F., & Harvey, C. (2003). The Frontiers of Legal Analysis: Reframing the Transition in Northern Ireland. *Modern Law Review, 66*(3), 317–345.

Chubb, B. (1991). *The Politics of the Irish Constitution*. Dublin: Institute for Public Administration.

Coakley, J., & Todd, J. (2020). *Negotiating a Settlement in Northern Ireland, 1969–2019*. Oxford: Oxford University Press.

Curtice, J. K., Hayes, B., Evans, G., & Dowds, L. (2006, August). *Northern Ireland Referendum and Election Survey, 1998 [computer file]*. Colchester, Essex: UK Data Archive [Distributor]. SN: 5442. http://dx.doi.org/10.5255/UKDA-SN-5442-1. Accessed on 7 May 2020.

Doyle, J. (2018). Reflecting on the Northern Ireland Conflict and Peace Process: 20 Years Since the Good Friday Agreement. *Irish Studies in International Affairs, 29*, 1–16.

Doyle, O., & Kenny, D. (2020). *Models of Irish Unification Processes* (SSRN Working Paper). http://dx.doi.org/10.2139/ssrn.3552375. Accessed on 7 May 2020.

Elliott, S. (1999). The Referendum and Assembly Elections in Northern Ireland. *Irish Political Studies, 14*(1), 138–149.

Farrington, C. (2006). Unionism and the Peace Process in Northern Ireland. *British Journal of Politics and International Relations, 8*(2), 277–294.

Framework Documents. (1995, February 22). *The Framework Documents: A New Framework for Agreement. A Shared Understanding Between the British and Irish Governments to Assist Discussion and Negotiation Involving the Northern Ireland Parties.*

Hayes, B., & McAllister, I. (2001). Who Voted for Peace? Public Support for the 1998 Northern Ireland Agreement. *Irish Political Studies, 16*(1), 73–93.

Hayward, K. (2009). *Irish Nationalism and European Integration: The Official Redefinition of the Island of Ireland*. Manchester: Manchester University Press.

Hayward, K. (2014). Deliberative Democracy in Northern Ireland: Opportunities and Challenges for Consensus in a Consociational System. In E. Ugarriza & D. Caluwaerts (Eds.), *Democratic Deliberation in Deeply Divided Societies: From Conflict to Common Ground* (pp. 11–34). London: Palgrave Macmillan.

Hayward, K., & McManus, C. (2019). Neither/Nor: The Rejection of Unionist and Nationalist Identities in Post-Agreement Northern Ireland. *Capital & Class, 43*(1), 139–155.

Ivory, G. (1999). Revisions in Nationalist Discourse Among Irish Political Parties. *Irish Political Studies, 14*(1), 84–103.

Mac Ginty, R. (2003). Constitutional Referendums and Ethnonational Conflict: The Case of Northern Ireland. *Nationalism and Ethnic Politics, 9*(2), 1–22.

Mansergh, L. (1999). Two Referendums and the Referendum Commission: The 1998 Experience. *Irish Political Studies, 14*(1), 123–131.

Northern Ireland Act. (1998) https://www.legislation.gov.uk/ukpga/1998/47/section/1. Accessed on 7 May 2020.

Ó Dochartaigh, N. (2017). State, Nation, Island: The Politics of Territory in Ireland. In N. Ó Dochartaigh, K. Hayward, & E. Meehan (Eds.), *Dynamics of Political Change in Ireland: Making and Breaking a Divided Island* (pp. 15–28). London: Routledge.

O'Mahony, J. (2009). Ireland's EU Referendum Experience. *Irish Political Studies, 24*(4), 429–446.

Ruane, J., & Todd, J. (2003). A Changed Irish Nationalism? The Significance of the Good Friday Agreement of 1998. In J. Ruane, J. Todd, & A. Mandeville (Eds.), *Europe's Old States in The New World Order* (pp. 121–145). Dublin: UCD Press.

Somerville, I., & Kirby, S. (2012). Public Relations and the Northern Ireland Peace Process: Dissemination, Reconciliation and the 'Good Friday Agreement' Referendum Campaign. *Public Relations Inquiry, 1*(3), 231–255.

The Agreement. (1998, April 10). *The Agreement reached in the Multiparty Negotiations.* https://www.gov.uk/government/publications/the-belfast-agreement. Accessed on 7 May 2020.

Walker, C., & Weaver, R. L. (1994). A Peace Deal for Northern Ireland? The Downing Street Declaration of 1993. *Emory International Law Review, 8,* 817–844.

Whysall, A. (2019). *A Northern Ireland Border Poll.* London: The Constitution Unit, University College London. https://www.ucl.ac.uk/constitution-unit/sites/constitution-unit/files/185_a_northern_ireland_border_poll.pdf. Accessed on 7 May 2020.

Zartman, I. W. (2001). The Timing of Peace Initiatives: Hurting Stalemates and Ripe Moments. *The Global Review of Ethnopolitics, 1*(1), 8–18.

CHAPTER 13

The United Kingdom Parliamentary Voting System Referendum of 2011

Andrew Blick

13.1 The Experience of Referendums in the United Kingdom

On 5 May 2011, voters across the United Kingdom (UK) took part in a referendum that posed the question: 'At present, the UK uses the "first past the post" system to elect MPs to the House of Commons. Should the "alternative vote" system be used instead?' Of a total electorate of 45,684,501, 19,165,730 took part, a turnout of 42%. They were required to answer 'Yes' or 'No'. The 'No' option won, by 19,165,730 (67.9% of those voting) to 13,013,123 (32.1%) (Mortimore and Blick 2018: 448). This episode was significant for a number of reasons. It was important from the point of view of the establishment and operation of the Conservative-Liberal Democrat coalition formed the previous May (Adonis 2013; Bogdanor 2011; Laws 2010; Seldon and Snowden 2016). It signified a rejection of a proposal to move from a plurality to a preferential voting system for the pre-eminent elected body in the UK, the House of Commons (Whiteley et al. 2011: 319). It also represented another instalment in the sporadic history of the referendum in the UK (Atkinson et al. 2020; Bogdanor 1981).

Accounts of the use of referendums in the United Kingdom tend to focus on the period from 1973 onwards (Independent Commission on Referendums 2018: 31–39). It was in that year, on 8 March, that the so-called 'Border Poll' was held in Northern Ireland (Mortimore and Blick 2018: 451). However,

A. Blick (✉)
King's College London, London, UK
e-mail: andrew.blick@kcl.ac.uk

© The Author(s) 2021
J. Smith (ed.), *The Palgrave Handbook of European Referendums*,
https://doi.org/10.1007/978-3-030-55803-1_13

there is a longer history that should be taken into account (Alderson 1975; Goodhart 1971). From the 1880s onwards, a number of prominent political and constitutional commentators and actors advocated the introduction of the referendum to the UK (Blick 2019; Dicey 1890; Qvortrup 1999). Often influenced by their observation of the use of this mechanism in Switzerland, supporters of this form of decision-taking have come from across the political spectrum—as have its opponents (Hobson 1974; Strachey 1924). A chief objection has been that, as a device of direct democracy, the referendum is supposedly not compatible with the representative, parliamentary system of the UK (House of Lords 2010b: 13–20; see Norton elsewhere in this volume). Alongside this recurring debate, referendums of some kind have been in practical use at local level at least since the nineteenth century in the UK, over such matters as the establishment of public libraries, Sunday opening for cinemas, and licensing laws (Alderson 1975). The first national referendum (in the sense of a vote held across the whole of one of the nations of the UK) took place in 1961. In accordance with the Licensing Act of that year, voters across Wales were asked whether public houses should open on Sunday. Votes were aggregated and the different results implemented at county level, not for the whole of Wales; following this vote, Sunday opening was authorised in areas covering 72% of the population of Wales. Referendums continue to be a factor in local politics, under such legislation as the *Local Government Act 2000*, section 27 of which provided for public votes on the introduction of directly elected mayors (Atkinson et al. 2020).

Above local level, that is, across the whole UK, or in Wales, Scotland, Northern Ireland or in the English regions, referendums have not been as frequent. At the time of writing there have been only 13. They have taken place during three main phases. The first came during 1973–1979, when four were held (Northern Ireland in 1973; throughout the UK on Europe in 1975 [see Smith on UK European referendums in Chapter 22]; and in Scotland and Wales in 1979 [see Chapter 11 by Mathias]). After a gap of 18 years that coincided with a prolonged period of Conservative government, their use revived between 1997 and 2004, with five such popular votes occurring (Scotland and Wales in 1997 [see Mathias, Chapter 11]; Northern Ireland [see Chapter 12 by Hayward] and Greater London in 1998; and the North East of England in 2004). After a shorter gap, the referendum returned in 2011, and over the following five years four were held (in Wales and across the UK on the voting system, both in 2011; Scotland in 2014 [see Curtice in Chapter 14]; and throughout the UK on Europe in 2016 [see Smith op cit.]). Referendums in which voters across the whole UK participated, as they did for the AV vote, have been less frequent than those held in sub-UK territories. Only three have taken place, two on Europe (1975 and 2016); and the referendum on the voting system of 2011 (Atkinson et al. 2020; Mortimore and Blick 2018: 447–452).

What of the subject matter of the 2011 electoral system referendum? Internationally, referendums on voting systems 'are extremely rare' (Qvortrup 2012: 115); and the 2011 vote is the only one to have been held on this issue to date in the UK. Referendums have been held in the UK on the membership (or otherwise) of a particular territory within the UK (Northern Ireland in 1973; Scotland in 2014); the formation of sub-UK tiers of governance (Scotland in 1979 and 1997; Wales in 1979 and 1997; Greater London in 1998; the North East of England in 2004); the extension of devolution (Wales in 2011); and continued participation in European integration (1975 and 2016). All of these referendums can be seen as involving possible transfers of sovereignty. The vote that is the subject of the present chapter, however, did not: it pertained to the system by which members of the House of Commons are elected. Yet, it might be held that the AV referendum, like the other votes, dealt with a constitutional issue (Independent Commission on Referendums 2018: 41).

Parliamentary committees in both Houses were supportive in principle of the idea of the use of a referendum over this subject. In 2010, before the General Election of that year, the House of Lords Select Committee on the Constitution had considered the question of what constituted appropriate subject matter for referendums in its report *Referendums in the United Kingdom*. It argued that the most suitable use for referendums was for taking constitutional decisions. The Committee tentatively listed a series of issues of this nature which might appropriately be made the subject of a popular vote, one of which was the voting system used for elections to the House of Commons (House of Lords 2010b: 27). When the coalition government that took office in May 2010 brought forward legislation providing for the 2011 AV referendum, the Lords committee reconfirmed its previously expressed view that the prospect of a change in the voting system used for the House of Commons was of sufficient constitutional significance to make the holding of a referendum proper (House of Lords 2010a). The House of Commons Political and Constitutional Reform Committee also concluded that the holding of a referendum on this issue was apt. Yet it noted that the government of the day was committed to various other reforms of a constitutional nature on which it was not holding referendums. The Committee argued that there was a problematic absence of certainty over the issue of when referendums did and did not need to take place in the UK; and that in theory at some point in the future, another administration could seek to change the electoral system without resort to direct popular authorisation (House of Commons 2010a: 8).

Some observers have speculated about the emergence of a constitutional convention requiring any change in the electoral system used for elections to the House of Commons to be authorised by referendum (Curtice 2013: 222; Qvortrup 2012: 108). But conventions are by their nature vague and difficult to enforce (Blick 2012). The UK lacks what is sometimes called a 'written' constitution—by which is meant a text setting out the fundamental rules of the political system, legally enforceable and subject to alteration only if a specified amendment procedure is followed. Such a text might set out the circumstances in which referendums were necessary (and perhaps some rules about their use, although it could not resolve all possible questions) (Blick 2015). In the absence of a UK 'written' constitution, there is, therefore, no firm constitutional requirement as such for the holding of referendums in the UK, nor prohibitions on their taking place (Marshall 1997; see also Chapter 4 by Renwick and Sargeant). Yet there has been legislation prescribing that certain possible future courses of action must be subject to approval in a referendum. The 2011 Welsh referendum was held in accordance with the *Government of Wales Act 2006*. Section 103 of the Act provided that an extension in the powers of the National Assembly for Wales for which the 2006 Act itself allowed could take place only following approval through a Welsh referendum (see Mathias in Chapter 11). The *European Union Act 2011* set out a wide range of possible transfers of powers to the EU that in future would necessitate consent through a popular vote in the UK. Section 1 of the *Northern Ireland Act 1998* requires the UK government to introduce into a Parliament a bill providing for Northern Ireland to separate from the UK and join the Republic of Ireland, if—and only if—a referendum is held in this territory producing a result in favour of this course of action. Under the *Scotland Act 2016* and *Wales Act 2017*, the devolved parliaments in these respective territories can only be abolished following referendums held within them approving such an action (Independent Commission on Referendums 2018: 39). Beyond these examples of standing requirements, other referendums have been provided for directly, rather than as a possible event that will facilitate or necessitate a given further course of action. The 2011 referendum on the voting system fell into the latter category. It arose from the coalition agreement between the Conservative Party and Liberal Democrats of May 2010 (HM Government 2011: 26–27). Its statutory basis was the *Parliamentary Constituencies and Voting System Act 2011* (PCVSA), Section 1 of which stated that a referendum had to take place before 31 October 2011—and that it would take place precisely on 5 May 2011 unless specified otherwise by order.

The provenance of this referendum was a decision at elite level reached by participants in negotiations aimed at forming a government, following a General Election that—unusually for the UK in the post-1945 era—had not produced a single-party majority (Curtice 2013: 216–217). This means of bringing about a referendum—a government initiative, put into effect by Parliament, is standard. There is no formal means by which members of the public can trigger a referendum (though they can express support for one via petitions to Parliament or government), and there was little evidence of an overwhelming popular desire for this particular vote (Vowles 2013: 255). If a referendum is to take place, it is because a UK government wants it to, or for some reason feels that to do so is politically expedient or necessary (Qvortrup 2006; Chapter 5 by Norton). Having made this judgement, a UK administration can use its parliamentary base—the government normally possesses a majority in the pre-eminent Chamber, the House of Commons—to pass the legislation that is required (in the case of the Scottish independence referendum of 2014, the Scottish Parliament passed the relevant primary legislation, under powers delegated to it within the terms of an Act of the UK Parliament) (Independent Commission on Referendums 2018: 38). While backbenchers in Parliament have sometimes sought to promote the holding of referendums through introducing their own bills, in the UK system the central government dominates the legislative process and its support or compliance is necessary to the success of a given measure (Blick 2019).

13.2   The Legal Framework

The general legal framework for referendums in the UK is provided by the *Political Parties, Elections and Referendums Act 2000* (PPERA). It does not deal with matters such as the subjects over which referendums are required, whether thresholds or supermajorities should be applied, or whether their results should be regarded as binding or advisory (Blick 2019). It addresses instead issues that—while significant—are more practical and of second order constitutional importance. Part 7 of PPERA covers matters including the appointing of a Chief Counting Officer and other counting officers; regulations pertaining to the administration of referendums; rules applying to campaigning and related activities; and spending limits for organisations that are registered to take part in the referendum. PPERA also established the Electoral Commission, which has an oversight role in relation to referendums. Referendums held in the UK above local level before PPERA came into force each had their own specific statutory basis (Commission on the Conduct of Referendum 1996; Committee on Standards in Public Life 1998). The 2011 AV referendum was the first UK-wide vote to take place since PPERA had come into force, though there had been votes in the North East of England (2004) (Electoral Commission 2005) and in Wales (2011). While PPERA now provides the general basis for popular votes, it is supplemented by further primary legislation introduced for each referendum; and further secondary legislation is issued to handle some of the specific details. In the case of the 2011 vote, the *Parliamentary Constituencies and Voting System Act 2011* (PCVSA) provided the required statutory provisions specific to this particular vote. It dealt with the timing of the referendum; the question; the franchise; financial and campaign regulations; and administrative matters. It provided for the new AV electoral system that would come into force in the event of a 'Yes' result. It also stipulated changes pertaining to the number and distribution of parliamentary constituencies that were not tied to the referendum result, as per the coalition agreement (HM Government 2011: 27). Further secondary legislation supplemented PPERA and PCVSA: two ministerial orders dealing with counting officers' expenses and Welsh language material; and regulations issued by the Electoral Commission involving payments to counting officers (Electoral Commission 2011: 26–27).

The referendum question was drafted by the government, but PPERA requires the Electoral Commission to report, or be consulted, on the wording. The question used for the 2011 referendum was included in the PCVSA, and therefore subject to parliamentary scrutiny as part of the legislative process. Initially the government included the following wording in its Bill: 'Do you want the United Kingdom to adopt the "alternative vote" system instead of the current "first past the post" system for electing Members of Parliament to the House of Commons?' However, after conducting various consultations and extensive opinion research, the Electoral Commission recommended that the wording be changed. It found that some people struggled to understand what was meant by terms including 'first past the post' and 'alternative vote'; and judged that the question was too long. The alternative wording it proposed was accepted by the government, adopted into the legislation, and used in the referendum (Electoral Commission 2011: 40–43).

Under PPERA the Electoral Commission also had responsibility for the referendum campaign. It monitored compliance with funding rules and oversaw the system of registered campaign groups in the referendum as well as the selection of lead campaign groups for either side in the vote. It carried out publicity activities to promote awareness of the referendum. It reported on the referendum after it had taken place, and received reports from the registered campaigners. It had investigatory powers and the ability to impose fines (Electoral Commission 2012b, c). The stated objective of the Electoral Commission in its approach to the AV referendum (and other referendums) was that it should concentrate 'on voters and on putting their interests first'. The realisation of this goal, as the Commission perceived it, involved ensuring that those voting were able without difficulty to comprehend the question being put to them and what it implied; that they were aware of the potential consequences and could 'easily understand the campaign arguments'; that those who were 'eligible' to take part could 'register to vote'; that they were reassured 'that campaign funding is transparent'; that the allocation of any public assistance to campaigns and their 'access to media' was equitable; that violation of the rules would 'be dealt with'; that the referendum should be well-administered and 'easy to take part in'; and that the result of the referendum and what it meant should 'be clear and understood' (Electoral Commission 2011: 20).

The so-called 'referendum period', as defined by PPERA, began in the case of the AV referendum on 16 February 2011, when PVSCA received Royal Assent. From this point, organisations had 28 days during which to apply for 'lead campaign' status. The Electoral Commission appointed one 'lead campaign' group for either side in the referendum respectively, in line with PPERA provisions. Those provided with this status were entitled to referendum broadcasts and a free mailshot to voters. Each 'lead campaign' also had up to £380,000 in public funding made available to it by the Commission. They both claimed slightly under £150,000: 'No to AV'—£147,479; 'Yes to Fairer Votes'—£140,457. The absolute limit on their expenditure during the campaign period was £5,000,0000. Political parties were also permitted to register as campaigners in the referendum. Both the Conservatives and Liberal Democrats did so, while Labour did not. They were subject to a ceiling on expenditure worked out in relation to the percentage of votes they received at the previous General Election. For the Conservatives, the figure arrived at was £5,000,000; for the Liberal Democrats £4,000,000. Aside from the 'lead campaign' groups and parties, other organisations wishing to spend in excess of £10,000 during the campaign period were also required to register with the Commission. They were subject to a cap on their spending at £500,000 (Electoral Commission 2011: 86–100). Responding to an earlier recommendation by the Electoral Commission, PVSCA introduced a new rule intended to prevent circumvention of the law by stipulating that spending by groups operating 'in concert' with one-another would be treated as entailing a single total (Electoral Commission 2011: 100–102).

While the Electoral Commission had powers in relation to expenditure it could not regulate the content of referendum material for its veracity (though there was a rule that publications had to state the name of the organisation that produced them) (Electoral Commission 2011: 106). The lack of a role for the Commission in this area was remarked upon in commentary on the 2011 referendum. Observers of and participants in the campaign complained about the deliberate promotion of misinformation by both sides (though they focused more on activities of the 'No' campaign). Jack Vowles (2013) has described how the former Labour minister and 'No' supporter, David Blunkett, subsequently admitted, as covered in the press, that an assertion that the adoption of AV would carry with it a cost of £250 million was 'made up'. Vowles notes that in a parliamentary election, an untruthful claim regarding the character of another candidate can, under the *Representation of the People Act 1983*, lead to the forfeiting of a seat in the House of Commons. Yet the Electoral Commission was not able to deal with objections to this and various other communications during the 2011 referendum. The Commission presented a more positive interpretation of the campaign. It stated that '[e]vidence from public opinion research suggests that most people knew enough about these polls and had adequate information to make an informed decision on how to vote in them'. It based this argument on the fact that, in a survey it commissioned, 73% of those asked 'said they had enough information to make an informed decision on how to vote in the referendum', while 65% 'said that they knew enough on what the referendum was about' (Electoral Commission 2011: 6). Yet if the information on which they were basing their decision was flawed, the value of the referendum as a process in informed decision-making was arguably undermined (Vowles 2013: 253–254). It is of course possible that both interpretations were correct, that is that voters had sufficient information to reach an informed decision but were also presented with misleading claims.

Although complaints were made during the campaign, the Commission was reluctant to become involved in correcting any such defect. It subsequently insisted that, not only was it unable to intervene, but that: '[w]e do not think that any role in policing the truthfulness of referendum campaign arguments would be appropriate for the Commission. It would be very likely to draw the Commission into political debate, significantly affecting the perception of our independent role, and posing substantial operational and reputational risks' (Electoral Commission 2011: 106). Other means of challenging the referendum were limited. While PVSCA referred to the possibility of judicial challenge (Schedule 1, 23), proceedings had to be brought within six weeks, and they had to involve specifically the counting of votes. The complaints the Commission had received were on different grounds altogether.

13.3   The Rules in Place

The referendum was not mandatory in the sense that it only came about because the government of the day, in accordance with the coalition agreement upon which it rested, had adopted it as a policy for which Parliament provided statutory expression (Curtice 2013: 222). However, once legislation was passed requiring that a referendum take place either on 5 May 2011 or else by the end of October of that year, the referendum became mandatory. The result of the vote, moreover, was, under PVSCA, binding. The legislation that provided for the referendum to be held also provided for the new voting system to be used at the subsequent General Election if there were a 'Yes' outcome, or not if the result was in the opposite direction. In theory, given its 'sovereign' status within the UK constitution, Parliament could have abolished the requirement to act upon the referendum result after the vote had taken place, although clearly doing so would have been highly controversial and could well have involved the collapse of the coalition. That the AV referendum was made binding was unusual for the UK in that most referendums in the UK have been only advisory in nature, even if there is clearly a powerful political imperative to act upon the result (Bogdanor 2009: 173; on the UK-EU referendums see Chapter 22 by Smith). The clearest exception, other than the 2011 AV vote, was the Welsh vote, also in 2011. In an historic analysis of their use, Matt Qvortrup (2006: 70) had previously argued that referendums in the UK could be divided into a variety of categories: 'decision solving', 'legislative', 'strategic', 'legitimation' and 'politically obligatory'. Perhaps the 2011 electoral system vote falls most readily into the 'legislative' category, into which Qvortrup also placed the two devolution votes of 1979.

Section 2 of PVSCA determined that the franchise used for the AV referendum was largely the same as that for a UK General Election: that is, people aged 18 years or over who were British or Irish citizens, and Commonwealth citizens. Members of the House of Lords, who could not vote in elections to the House of Commons, were also allowed to take part. Most European

Union citizens, who could not vote in general elections but could vote in local authority elections, could not take part in the referendum. No threshold or supermajority was used. A simple majority of whoever took part was deemed sufficient (Independent Commission on Referendums 2018: 111; Gay and Horton 2011).

Since 2000, legal restrictions apply to the involvement of the government in referendums. Section 125 of PPERA provides for a period of 28 days leading up to the day of the vote itself in which public—or publicly-funded—bodies from central government down to local level are prohibited from publishing material related to the referendum. For this particular referendum, the government did not have a specific outcome it wished to promote, given that the two coalition partners differed in their preferred outcome. Indeed, it was a notable feature of the AV referendum that Cabinet members publicly took opposing sides over the issue. Under the UK system, the principle of collective responsibility means that Cabinet members discuss issues frankly in private in order to reach agreed positions around which they publicly unite (Blick 2016: 134–135). Before 2010, the only exceptions to this rule in which Cabinet reached an 'agreement to differ' came from 1932 (when the National government could not reach a unified position over tariff reform); at the time of the EEC referendum of 1975; and over direct elections to the European Parliament in 1977–1978, when there were disagreements within the Labour Cabinet both over the introduction of the elections and over the electoral system to be used in them (Everett 2016). Maintaining collective responsibility during the 2010–2015 coalition government, given the differences and competition between the two parties that composed it, proved difficult. The Coalition Agreement implied that there could be opt-outs from this rule (HM Government 2011). During the 2011 referendum campaign, the Conservative component of the government supported 'No', while the Liberal Democrat portion backed 'Yes'. Understandably, observers have noted the similarity between the first and second UK-wide referendums in that both involved ministers being authorised to disagree with each other (Curtice 2013: 219). A similar suspension applied to the EU referendum of 2016. But the 2011 arrangement was distinct from other suspensions of collective responsibility. On the previous occasions (and again in 2016) Cabinet had adopted a policy from which members were allowed to dissent. In 2011 there was no specific recommendation from the Cabinet or government over which way the public should vote, given the fundamental disagreement between the two Coalition partners (Blick 2015: 161).

13.4   THE REFERENDUM IN PRACTICE

The electoral system used for the House of Commons is a longstanding subject of controversy, dating as far back as the nineteenth century and the emergence of the mass franchise (Blick 2019; Bogdanor 1981). Commonly voiced criticisms of the existing single-member plurality or 'First-Past-the-Post' (FPTP) system include that it produces a balance of representation in the Commons that does not reflect overall votes cast in the General Election; broadly tends to favour two main parties; and leads to wasted votes. Some opponents of FPTP have supported a shift towards a more proportionate system such as the Single Transferable Vote (STV); or the Additional Member System (AMS). Others have supported AV. It is not a more proportionate system, but ensures through preferential voting that every candidate elected has assembled a majority of votes in the constituency concerned, if necessary through taking into account subordinate preferences of voters (Baston and Ritchie 2011: 1–20). The Liberal Democrats, and its predecessor parties, had long opposed the FPTP system, under which the number of parliamentary seats they won at General Elections was consistently disproportionately small relative to the total votes they received. They advocated a more proportionate replacement for FPTP, although the party was inclined towards STV (Liberal Democrats 2010: 87–88).

At the 1997 General Election, the Labour Party—in accordance with a joint agreement it had reached with the Liberal Democrats over a number of constitutional issues—pledged to hold a referendum on electoral reform. The Labour government that took office instigated the Jenkins Commission, which recommended a hybrid of AV with a regional top-up to ensure greater but not complete proportionality (Gay 1998). Labour did not hold a referendum, however, although it did introduce different and more proportionate electoral systems at other levels (Ministry of Justice 2008). At the 2010 General Election, at which it lost power, Labour pledged to hold a referendum specifically on AV (Labour Party 2010: 9:2). Curiously, this policy was implemented, yet not by Labour, but by a coalition comprising two parties that had not made this proposal in their manifestos.

The Conservative Party, alongside Labour, was one of two longstanding beneficiaries of FPTP (though it had been excluded from power for thirteen years from 1997) and was firmly committed to the system (Conservative Party 2010: 67). Following the General Election of 2010, the arithmetic of the Commons suggested that some kind of deal between the Conservatives and Liberal Democrats would be the most practical basis for the formation of a government. The discrepancy of opinion between the two parties over the voting system was one of the challenges that had to be overcome if an arrangement was to be attained. The referendum was the means of doing so (Curtice 2013: 216–217; Qvortrup 2012: 108–109). A vote on a proportionate system such as STV was unacceptable to the Conservative Party. Even the arrangement to which the Conservative leadership eventually agreed, namely allowing a referendum for electoral reform but supporting the cause of full change, proved to be controversial among its own ranks. There is some doubt around the circumstances in which this deal was reached. The Liberal Democrats held parallel talks with Labour that it used to apply leverage to the Conservatives (Laws 2010: 122; Adonis 2013: 76). But it is not clear precisely what Labour offered the Liberal Democrats with respect to electoral reform (Bogdanor 2011: 29–30; though see also Laws 2010: 120 and Appendix 5: 309). Yet however it came about, the agreement on a referendum was reached and was fundamental to the formation of the coalition (Quinn et al. 2011: 301).

A judgement regarding which side was the more successful in the coalition negotiations should partly take into account the result of the referendum (Quinn et al. 2011: 306). From this point of view, the Liberal Democrats did not secure a gain from this aspect of the coalition agreement. But, even had it been successful in the vote of May 2011, how much the Liberal Democrats would have benefited from the introduction of AV is questionable. There is some evidence that the Liberal Democrats might have tended to win more seats under AV than FPTP, but the party still would not have secured results proportionate to its support (Sanders et al. 2010; Curtice 2013: 217–218). In the words of John Curtice (2013: 218), the AV proposal 'gave the Liberal Democrats something, but from the Conservative's perspective at least, not too much'. As Qvortrup put it (2012: 108), AV 'never had many fans or devotees', not even the Liberal Democrats who had long fought for electoral reform; it was, in fact, a fairly similar system to FPTP (Curtice 2013: 219). Such a compromise was not necessarily a strong basis on which to fight for change in a referendum. There was no prior sign of public clamour for AV; and it was not the favoured option of many supporters of electoral reform, within and beyond the Liberal Democrats (Vowles 2013: 255).

The referendum campaign and its outcome were a subject of subsequent academic interest (Laycock et al. 2013). A central preoccupation of such work was in explaining the decisive 'No' result, an opposite outcome to that suggested by earlier polling (Baston and Ritchie 2011). One clear area of inequity was in the expenditure of the two campaigns during the campaign. The designated lead 'Yes' campaign group spent £2,100,000, with a further £70,000 spent by other 'yes' groups. (The principal non-public donors on this side were the Joseph Rowntree Reform Trust and Electoral Reform Society). The figure for the lead 'No' group was £2,600,000; with additional 'No' spending during the campaign reaching £900,000, as derived mainly from sources that also supported the Conservative Party (Baston and Ritchie 2011: 34–35; Electoral Commission 2012a: 34; Vowles 2013: 255). In total, then, 'No' outspent 'Yes' by well over £1,000,000. From a campaigning perspective, this discrepancy placed 'No' at a considerable advantage in resource terms. If the purpose of a referendum is to achieve a balanced contest, for which the legislative framework seeks to provide, then it was in this respect compromised. The precise difference in practice to the outcome is a matter of debate, however. For instance, drawing on a consideration of international evidence, in his discussion of the AV referendum, Qvortrup holds that there is no clear evidence of a correlation between relative spending and chances of success for either side in a referendum campaign (Qvortrup 2012: 113).

Another notable feature of the referendum was the turnout. The 42% figure seemed relatively low. The previous General Election in the UK had generated a turnout of 65%; as had the only prior UK-wide referendum, on continued participation in European integration, in 1975. The referendum was held at the same time as other elections (at devolved level in Wales, Northern Ireland and Scotland; and at local level in Northern Ireland and England; as well five mayoral elections, a mayoral referendum, and a parliamentary by-election in Leicester South). But there does not seem to have been a significant boost in participation as a consequence. As Bowler and Donovan (2013: 266) note, the previous local elections, which did not have the benefit coinciding with a referendum, had only a slightly lower turnout of 39%. Research commissioned by the Electoral Commission sought to discern why people did or did not take part. Over half of non-voters attributed their non-participation to 'circumstances', the most common variant on which was having been 'too busy'. Those who did participate described themselves as motivated by a 'duty' that compelled them to take part (46%); as well as 'wanting to have their say' (28%). 18% stated that they always used the opportunity to vote (Electoral Commission 2011: 64). The low rate of participation achieved in 2011 might be interpreted as suggesting 'that the issue of electoral reform...mattered more to Britain's political elites than it did to most British voters' (Bowler and Donovan 2013: 266). But did the turnout level favour 'No'? Another group of authors, analysing opinion data, have argued that a higher level of participation would not have altered the result (Whiteley et al. 2011: 317).

Again on a basis of comparative analysis, Qvortrup questions any possible received wisdom that the status quo position enjoys an inbuilt advantage in referendums, at least in as far as they involve electoral reform (Qvortrup 2012: 110–111). Nonetheless, the 'Yes' campaign faced challenges that the 'No' side did not in explaining the new system that was on offer to voters. In the Electoral Commission's information leaflet, the description of AV was nearly eight times the length of the account given of FPTP (Vowles 2013: 255). Indeed, the nature of the information presented to voters and the overall quality of the debate became a subject of criticism. Some analysis of the nature of the campaigns has found that suspect assertions were made on both sides, but that the 'No' cause made more extensive use of misleading messaging (Baston and Ritchie 2011: 33; Qvortrup 2012: 111–112; Vowles 2013: 256). As Vowles (2013: 255) notes, official attempts to provide an impartial account of the issues were minimal. There was an advertisement on television to inform voters that the referendum was taking place; and a referendum leaflet from the Electoral Commission intended for delivery to every household in the UK. In practice the latter may have come to the attention of less than half of voters (ibid.).

The task of supplying the public with information about the referendum fell mainly to the campaigns. Both were provided with two slots for television broadcasts. Their messages also reached voters via coverage in broadcast and print media (including paid-for advertisements and other content); and online. As already noted, the referendum took place at the same time as other elections—local and devolved—across the UK. The Electoral Commission carried out media analysis suggesting that, in areas where devolved elections were taking place they received more attention than the referendum. Across the entire UK, 211 election items appeared in those outlets being monitored, compared with 416 covering the referendum. But the referendum tended not to receive lead status (Electoral Commission 2011: 50–51). Alan Renwick and Michael Lamb (2013: 303) found that the volume of press coverage of the referendum was comparable to that of other referendums on voting systems internationally, but that it was at a significantly lesser level than that provided at the time of the 1975 European referendum in the UK. While the quantity of coverage provided to each side was relatively even, overall the press tended to present 'No' more favourably than 'Yes'. This tendency was heightened when the circulation of papers was taken into account. Particular titles tended to support a specific side rather than presenting differing opinions. For instance, the *Guardian*, *Independent* and *Daily Mirror* supported AV, while the *Daily Telegraph*, *Daily Mail* and *Sun* opposed it. Renwick and Lamb (2013) also found that only 12% of articles advocating particular sides 'were backed up by both a reason and an argument linking a reason to the position'. On this analysis, not only was there an overall press pre-disposition towards 'No', but the coverage largely failed to contribute to reasoned debate.

Both campaigns, Vowles notes, presented themselves as furthering the cause of democracy. The 'Yes' side emphasised the idea of fairness in the electoral system and sought to motivate feelings of hostility towards politicians in support of its cause, seeking in particular to play upon public perceptions prompted by the then relatively recent MPs' expenses scandal of 2009. While 'Yes' campaigners sought to convey the simplicity of the AV system, their opponents set out to depict it as complex. The 'No' campaign argued that AV compromised the principle of 'one person one vote'. It also warned that AV would entail more frequent coalition governments, making the implementation of single sets of manifesto pledges less likely, an accountability issue (Vowles 2013: 256). It is an irony that the three of the four most recent elections in the UK (2010, 2015 and 2017) have produced only small or no single-party majorities and that the referendum on the voting system was itself the consequence of a coalition agreement, and it was a policy to which neither of the parties in the government had pledged themselves in their manifestos. The Conservative Party that campaigned firmly for 'No' had returned to power specifically as a participant in a coalition. The formation of this government had required the abandonment of aspects of its policy programme and the adoption of elements to which it had not previously committed itself. Indeed, in cases including the AV referendum, it had expressly opposed some of the policies that found their way into the coalition programme.

Party-political factors were significant to the campaign. The Liberal Democrats clearly backed 'Yes', while not being as enthusiastic as they might have been had a proportional system, such as STV, the party's policy—been on offer. Indeed, Nick Clegg, the Liberal Democrat Leader and Deputy Prime Minister, had described AV as a 'miserable little compromise' in advance of the

2010 General Election, despite conceding that it would represent 'a baby step in the right direction' (Bogdanor 2011: 91). Labour was in internal disagreement over the question; and the Conservatives were overwhelmingly opposed to AV. The 'No' campaign utilised politicians, including Labour opponents of the proposed change; and the Conservative Prime Minister, David Cameron, also took part in the campaign (Baston and Ritchie 2011, 30–34; Vowles 2013: 255–256). The 'No' side also sought to exploit the perceived poor public perception of Nick Clegg, the Liberal Democrat leader and Deputy Prime Minister, and of the Liberal Democrat Party itself (Qvortrup 2012: 111–112). The 'Yes' campaign avoided deploying politicians, and indeed sought to play to a current in public opinion sometimes labelled 'anti-politics' (Vowles 2013: 255–256). Yet this sentiment may also have been a source of reluctance to participate in political processes (Bowler and Donovan 2013: 272), and therefore may have been a weak basis for motivating voting on any side in the referendum. According to opinion research, levels of support for 'Yes' by party preference were: Conservative, 14%; Labour 37%; Liberal Democrat 58% (Curtice 2013: 222). These figures demonstrate that the activities of parties and the partisan orientation of voters were significant. But they also show that other influences were at work. Curtice therefore concludes that the 'arguments' made during the campaign were of significance (Curtice 2013: 222). Particularly powerful parts of the 'No' case in this regard were the claims that AV entailed some votes counting for more than others; that the referendum itself was 'a waste of money'; and that the existing voting system was desirable because of its propensity to deliver 'strong government'. Key 'Yes' arguments that did not achieve the same impact were that AV could 'restore trust in politicians'; that it would avoid 'wasted votes'; that it would allow voters to back the party that they preferred; and that each MP would need to secure over half of votes cast in their constituencies. One battleground where 'Yes' seemingly did not fare as badly in persuading voters was over how difficult or easy it was for voters to comprehend the AV system relative to FPTP (Curtice 2013: 221).

Whiteley et al., having considered a variety of explicatory models, suggest that a combination of factors was decisive in determining the outcome. They find that: 'Evaluations of the advantages and disadvantages of a change in the electoral system had large effects on referendum voting decisions' (2011: 316–317). They also hold that perceptions of leaders and party alignment were important. Those who were closely interested in the subject were more prone to vote 'Yes'. Being contacted by campaigns had some effect, though it was limited. There was no striking territorial variation in voting patterns such as would occur in the European referendum of 2016 (Blick 2019). However, it is possible to profile voters on each side to some extent. Opinion polling suggested that the younger people were and the higher the level to which they had received formal education, the more likely they were to vote 'Yes' (Curtice 2013: 222).

13.5   The Referendum and Domestic Politics

The vote itself was not seriously questioned. Public confidence in the integrity of the electoral process was high. Research by the Electoral Commission (2011: 77–78) found that just over three-quarters of those questioned were confident that abuse or fraud had not taken place; while slightly under three-quarters judged the process to have been well-administered. Since AV was rejected, there was nothing to implement and therefore no further action was required. It was a path not taken. In recent decades, especially since 1997, the UK has been subject to extensive constitutional change. Important measures have included the *Human Rights Act 1998*; the removal under the *House of Lords Act 1999* of most hereditary peers; alterations to the judicial system through the *Constitutional Reform Act 2005*; and the introduction of devolution to various parts of the UK (often following referendums) (Bogdanor 2009). During the coalition era (2010–2015), further systemic alterations took place, including the *Fixed-term Parliaments Act 2011* and the *European Union Act 2011*. However, two further key changes were foreshadowed in the coalition agreement but never implemented: the introduction of AV and for the House of Lords to be made at least mainly elected (HM Government 2011: 27). Both proposals were inserted into the coalition document on the insistence of the Liberal Democrats. Had they been achieved they would between them have represented a radical alteration in the way that Parliament was composed. Ultimately, the Conservative part of the coalition withdrew support for Lords reform, partly as a consequence of resistance from its own backbenchers.

Supporters of FPTP had secured a significant victory. They were able to claim that their system had been endorsed, and that the demands for change—whether a shift to AV or another more proportionate system—should now cease. Opponents of FPTP had clearly suffered a major setback. Even if they preferred a system other than AV—for instance, STV—it was difficult for them to reopen the issue immediately. The public might not appreciate the distinction between such systems anyway. Thus, as one group of writers concluded:

> The decisive outcome of the AV referendum has settled the issue and the question of electoral reform is unlikely to be re-opened for many years. If attempts are made to raise the issue again in the near future, opponents of reform will be able to say that the people have spoken and the question should no longer be up for discussion. Had the vote been closer, then supporters of STV or a fully proportional electoral system might be able to argue that this should be on the agenda in coalition negotiations if a future general election proves as inconclusive as the last one. However, the strength of opposition to change in the electoral system manifest in the 2011 AV referendum makes this unlikely. (Whiteley et al. 2011: 319)

Yet the features that opponents of FPTP found objectionable continued to be a part of the system, and agitation for reform was unlikely to disappear altogether. But any campaign for reform in future would have to deal with the claim that the issue had been settled by the public in 2011, regardless of the relatively low turnout and that only AV—in comparison to, say, STV, a similar system to FPTP—had been on offer (Curtice 2013: 219). Moreover, making this issue subject to a referendum had set a precedent. Some would insist that it was necessary that this mechanism be used in any effort to address the same subject in future. From this point of view, the potential of the referendum to act as a conservative mechanism, blocking systemic change, had manifested itself; as it had similarly in 2004 when the North East voted against establishing a directly elected regional tier of government.

Of a total of 440 voting areas all but 10 voted 'No'. The areas producing a 'Yes' result were the London boroughs of Camden, Hackney, Haringey, Islington, Lambeth and Southwark; the Scottish urban areas of Edinburgh Central and Glasgow Kelvin; and the two ancient university cities of Cambridge and Oxford (Electoral Commission 2011: 16–17). Behind the overall 'No' majority of 67.9%, while all of Wales, Scotland, Northern Ireland and England produced clear 'No' majorities, the exact percentages varied significantly. The figure for England was 69.14%; for Wales 65.45; for Scotland 63.64; and for Northern Ireland 56.43. There was also variation in turnout. It was significantly higher for Northern Ireland (55.8%) and Scotland (50.7%) than it was for Wales (41.7%) and England (41%).

While the referendum on AV was devised as a means of enabling the Conservatives and Liberal Democrats to form a coalition, that actual event itself was the most serious test for the unity of the government up to that point (Seldon and Snowden 2016). Inevitably, the two parties were campaigning on different sides was a source of tension. There were reportedly complaints from Liberal Democrats within Cabinet about the hostile nature of the 'No' campaign and its personalised attacks on Clegg. In some accounts, the atmosphere within the coalition soured permanently at this point. Nonetheless, the 2011 vote was perhaps from the point of view of the Conservative Prime Minister, David Cameron, a success. It was the first of three referendums—AV, Scottish independence, and Brexit—that helped to define his premiership (the fourth referendum, on Welsh devolution, was inherited from the Labour government and not directly linked to the Prime Minister). Cameron might have viewed the experience in a positive light. He had negotiated the Conservative Party back into power after thirteen years of opposition, and himself into No.10, partly through conceding the possibility of change in the voting system that never materialised. Even had AV been implemented, it likely that it would not have had as negative an effect on Conservative electoral performance as a more proportionate system. However, the next two such votes to which he consented would prove less agreeable.

The 2011 referendum may have provided a political example that Cameron attempted to replicate. But as Curtice (2013: 222) put it '[t]he UK's second ever statewide referendum is unlikely ever to be widely regarded as a model of democratic practice that other states should follow'. A number of the assessments discussed in this chapter were critical of the process. For instance, as Whiteley et al. (2011: 318) argue, 'because of the low turnout it is difficult to escape the conclusion that the AV referendum was a decidedly unsuccessful and unhelpful exercise in direct democracy'. Moreover, in the view of these authors, neither side in the contest was effective at providing useful information to the public or engaging them in the issues. They note that opinion research suggested that the public viewed the quality of the campaign unfavourably. Yet, from the contemporary perspective, in some senses, the 2011 electoral reform referendum adhered to what might be regarded as good practice (Independent Commission on Referendums 2018). It was held on a precisely defined proposition, set out in an Act of Parliament passed in advance of the vote—though there were objections to the speed with which it was moved through Parliament and brought onto the statute book (House of Commons 2010a, b). The referendum result was made legally binding. The differences between the approach taken in 2011 and that used for the EU referendum in 2016 are striking. In the latter instance, the meaning of the 'Leave' result was difficult to discern (and lacked legal force). Unlike in 2016, in 2011, the nature of the decision that faced voters was knowable. The problems lay elsewhere. First, the choice was structured in a limited way, as a consequence of the party-political negotiation in which it arose. Second, while it was possible to be aware of the issues at stake, the way in which the campaign was conducted was not conducive to ensuring the fullest public understanding of them. Any attempts at improvements in referendum processes in future should take into account the importance of this wider political environment. Decisions presented to voters should be as meaningful as possible, as should the debate surrounding them during the campaign. Whether the political system is equipped to facilitate these requirements is another question.

References

Adonis, A. (2013). *5 Days in May: The Coalition and Beyond*. London: Biteback.

Alderson, S. (1975). *Yea or Nay?: Referenda in the United Kingdom*. London: Cassell.

Atkinson, L., Blick, A., & Qvortrup, M. (2020). *The Referendum in Britain: A History*. Oxford: Oxford University Press.

Baston, L., & Ritchie, K. (2011). *Don't Take No for an Answer*. London: Biteback.

Blick, A. (2012). The Cabinet Manual and the Codification of Conventions. *Parliamentary Affairs, 67*(1), 191–208.

Blick, A. (2015). *Beyond Magna Carta: A Constitution for the United Kingdom*. Oxford: Bloomsbury/Hart.

Blick, A. (2016). *The Codes of the Constitution*. Oxford: Bloomsbury/Hart.

Blick, A. (2019). *Stretching the Constitution: The Brexit Shock in Historic Perspective*. Oxford: Bloomsbury/Hart.

Bogdanor, V. (1981). *The People and the Party System: The Referendum and Electoral Reform in British Politics*. Cambridge: Cambridge University Press.

Bogdanor, V. (2009). *The New British Constitution*. Oxford: Bloomsbury/Hart.

Bogdanor, V. (2011). *The Coalition and the Constitution*. Oxford: Bloomsbury/Hart.

Bowler, S., & Donovan, T. (2013). Civic Duty and Turnout in the UK Referendum on AV: What Shapes the Duty to Vote? *Electoral Studies, 32*(2), 265–273.

Commission on the Conduct of Referendums. (1996). *Report of the Commission on the Conduct of Referendums*. London: Constitution Society/Electoral Reform Society.

Committee on Standards in Public Life. (1998). *The Funding of Political Parties in the United Kingdom: Volume I, Report*. London: Stationery Office.

Conservative Party. (2010). *Invitation to Join the Government of Britain: The Conservative Manifesto 2010*. London: Conservative Party.

Curtice, J. (2013). Politicians, Voters and Democracy: The 2011 UK Referendum on the Alternative Vote. *Electoral Studies, 32*(2), 215–223.

Dicey, A. V. (1890). Ought the Referendum to Be Introduced into England? *The Contemporary Review, 1866–1900, 57*, 489–511.

Electoral Commission. (2005). *The 2004 North East Regional Assembly and Local Government Referendums*. London: Electoral Commission.

Electoral Commission. (2011). *Referendum on the Voting System for UK Parliamentary Elections*. London: Electoral Commission.

Electoral Commission. (2012a). *Costs of the May 2011 Referendum on the UK Parliamentary Voting System*. London: Electoral Commission.

Electoral Commission. (2012b). *Offences and Proposed Sanctions*. London: Electoral Commission. https://www.electoralcommission.org.uk/__data/assets/pdf_file/0006/106737/Table-of-offences-and-sanctions_for_EP.pdf. Last accessed 12 October 2018.

Electoral Commission. (2012c). *Use of New Investigatory Powers and Civil Sanctions*. London: Electoral Commission.

Everett, M. (2016). *Collective Responsibility*. London: House of Commons Library.

Gay, O. (1998). *Voting Systems: The Jenkins Report*. London: House of Commons Library.

Gay, O., & Horton, L. (2011). *Thresholds in Referendums*. London: House of Commons Library Standard Note SN/PC/02809.

Goodhart, P. (1971). *Referendum*. London: Tom Stacey Ltd.

HM Government. (2011). *The Coalition: Our Programme for Government*. London: Cabinet Office.

Hobson, J. A. (1974). *The Crisis of Liberalism: New Issues of Democracy*. Hemel Hempsted: Harvester.

House of Commons. (2010a). Political and Constitutional Reform Committee. In *Parliamentary Voting System and Constituencies Bill*. London: Stationery Office.

House of Commons. (2010b). Political and Constitutional Reform Committee. In *Parliamentary Voting System and Constituencies Bill: Report for Second Reading*. London: Stationery Office.

House of Lords (2010a). Select Committee on the Constitution. In *Parliamentary Voting System and Constituencies Bill*. London: Stationery Office.

House of Lords. (2010b). Select Committee on the Constitution. In *Referendums in the United Kingdom*. London: Stationery Office.

Independent Commission on Referendums. (2018). *Report of the Independent Commission on Referendums*. London: Constitution Unit.

Labour Party. (2010). *Manifesto 2010: A Future Fair for All*. London: Labour Party.

Laws, D. (2010). *22 Days in May: The Birth of the Lib Dem-Conservative Coalition*. London: Biteback.

Laycock, S., Renwick, A., Stevens, D., & Vowles, J. (2013). The UK's Electoral Reform Referendum of May 2011. *Electoral Studies, 32*(2), 211–214.

Liberal Democrats. (2010). *Manifesto 2010: Change That Works for You: Building a Fairer Britain*. London: Liberal Democrats.

Marshall, G. (1997). The Referendum: What, When and How? *Parliamentary Affairs, 50*(2), 307–314.

Ministry of Justice. (2008). *Review of Voting Systems: The Experience of New Voting Systems in the United Kingdom Since 1997*. London: Ministry of Justice.

Mortimore, R., & Blick, A. (Eds.). (2018). *Butler's British Political Facts*. Basingstoke: Palgrave.

Quinn, T., Bara, J., & Bartle, J. (2011). The UK Coalition Agreement of 2010: Who Won? *Journal of Elections, Public Opinion and Parties, 21*(2), 295–312.

Qvortrup, M. (1999). AV Dicey: The Referendum as the People's Veto. *History of Political Thought, 20*(3), 531–546.

Qvortrup, M. (2006). Democracy by Delegation: The Decision to Hold Referendums in the United Kingdom. *Representation, 42*(1), 59–72.

Qvortrup, M. (2012). Voting on Electoral Reform: A Comparative Perspective on the Alternative Vote Referendum in the United Kingdom. *The Political Quarterly, 83*(1), 108–116.

Renwick, A., & Lamb, M. (2013). The Quality of Referendum Debate: The UK's Electoral System Referendum in the Print Media. *Electoral Studies, 32*(2), 294–304.

Sanders, D., Clarke, H. D., Stewart, M. C., & Whiteley, P. (2010). Simulating the Effects of the Alternative Vote in the 2010 UK General Election. *Parliamentary Affairs, 64*(1), 5–23.

Seldon, A., & Snowdon, P. (2016). *Cameron at 10: The Verdict*. London: William Collins.

Strachey, J. (1924). *The Referendum*. London: T. Fisher Unwin.

Vowles, J. (2013). Campaign Claims, Partisan Cues, and Media Effects in the 2011 British Electoral System Referendum. *Electoral Studies, 32*(2), 253–264.

Whiteley, P., Clarke, H. D., Sanders, D., & Stewart, M. C. (2011). Britain Says No: Voting in the AV Ballot Referendum. *Parliamentary Affairs, 65*(2), 301–322.

CHAPTER 14

The Scottish Independence Referendum of 2014

John Curtice

14.1 Introduction

Scotland joined the United Kingdom in 1707. Hitherto it had been a separate kingdom, one indeed that had on occasion been at war with England—although in 1603 James VI of Scotland had inherited the crown of England and thus, though still distinct, the two jurisdictions already shared the same head of state. Following a severe financial crash in the wake of a failed attempt to create a Scottish colony in what is now Panama, the Scottish Parliament voted in 1706 to unite with its English counterpart. Under the so-called Acts of Union passed by the English as well as the Scottish Parliament, Scotland was now to send representatives to the parliament in London from whence it would be governed alongside England and Wales. It would also form a monetary and customs union with England, although the country's distinct legal and educational systems as well as its different religious settlement were to be preserved.

Thus, Scotland was no longer an independent state, but could still be regarded as a distinct nation. In forming the union with England (and Wales), it secured access to the commercial activity and power that were to flow from the advent of the British Empire in the eighteenth and nineteenth centuries, an enterprise in which the country was a full participant (Devine 2006). At the same time, a sense of 'British' identity developed throughout much of the island of Great Britain, thereby providing a common emotional

J. Curtice (✉)
University of Strathclyde, Glasgow, Scotland, UK
e-mail: j.curtice@strath.ac.uk

© The Author(s) 2021
J. Smith (ed.), *The Palgrave Handbook of European Referendums*,
https://doi.org/10.1007/978-3-030-55803-1_14

glue with England that overlay people's distinct sense of 'Scottish' identity (Colley 2009). Scotland became strongly wedded economically, militarily and psychologically to the British state.

However, the picture was not a wholly undisturbed one. Ireland, which had become part of the United Kingdom a century after Scotland, was never as successfully integrated into the British state as Scotland had been. In the second half of the nineteenth century whether or not Ireland should be granted 'Home Rule' became one of the most divisive issues in British politics, and inevitably raised the issue of whether Scotland should enjoy a measure of devolution too. In 1885, a Scottish Office headed by a Secretary of State for Scotland was established for the first time, thereby affording the country a measure of administrative devolution. Meanwhile, the following year a cross-party Scottish Home Rule movement was founded. However, an attempt instigated in 1913 to establish a devolved parliament came to a halt following the outbreak of the First World War.

For much of the ensuing sixty years, the question of Scotland's constitutional status remained little more than a fringe political issue. The country might be suffering disproportionately from the UK's relative economic decline, but an expansion of the role of the government during this period, most notably in respect of providing welfare and running a set of national-ised industries that had a major presence in Scotland, meant that the country became, if anything, even more strongly integrated into the British state. True, the Scottish National Party (SNP)—itself a union of two predecessor parties that had been formed a few years earlier—had been founded in 1934 and backed Scottish independence, but apart from winning a by-election against limited opposition just as the Second World War was drawing to a close, it had failed to create even the smallest of ripples on Scotland's political waters.

Then, in the late 1960s substantial quantities of oil were discovered in the North Sea, just at a time when the UK economy was floundering and the capacity of British governments to manage it effectively was beginning to be questioned. This conjunction of events seemed to open up the prospect that Scotland might be better off economically as an independent state. In any event, after making its first electoral breakthrough in a shock by-election victory in Hamilton in 1967, by October 1974, the SNP was able to win as much as 30% of the general election vote in Scotland, following a campaign that declared, 'It's Scotland's Oil'. Scotland's constitutional status now became a central issue, not just in Scottish but also in British politics, and although initial attempts in the 1970s to create a devolved Scottish Parliament ultimately failed to bear fruit, as Chapter 11 by Jörg Mathias elsewhere in this volume explains, a referendum in 1997 eventually paved the way for the creation of a new devolved parliament in Edinburgh together with a devolved Scottish Government that took on most of the responsibilities that were formerly exercised by the Scottish Office.

14.2   Devolution

Both the initial failed attempt to create a devolved parliament in the 1970s and the subsequent successful effort in 1999 were introduced by centre-left UK Labour governments. It could be argued that in doing so the Labour party was finally fulfilling a commitment that it had first made in the 1920s, albeit one that it had subsequently put aside. But whatever the merits of the idea, the party certainly had a clear political motivation for establishing the Scottish Parliament. Labour had come to dominate Scotland's political representation in the UK Parliament. Any SNP electoral success, let alone independence, threatened a hegemony that seemed crucial to the party's ability to win overall majorities in the UK House of Commons as a whole (Curtice 2006). The creation of the Scottish Parliament would demonstrate that the UK could accommodate Scotland's distinct sense of identity, political preferences and needs, thereby undermining the case—and thus support for—independence. As the one-time Labour Shadow Secretary of State for Scotland, George (now Lord) Robertson put it, devolution would 'kill nationalism stone dead'.

Yet, rather than killing the SNP stone dead, devolution provided the party with a life line. Voters proved more willing to vote for the party in Scottish Parliament elections than they had usually been—and continued to be—in elections to the UK House of Commons. In four UK-wide general elections held between 1997 and 2010, the party won on average 20% of the votes cast in Scotland. But in the three elections to the Scottish Parliament held during that period the party won as much as 29% of the vote.[1] Meanwhile, whereas elections to the House of Commons were held under a single member plurality system that made it difficult for a party of the size of the SNP to turn its geographically evenly distributed vote into seats, elections to the Scottish Parliament were held under a mixed member proportional electoral system that ensured that whatever votes the SNP won were more or less reflected in its overall level of representation in the parliament. Indeed, thanks also to a sharp decline in the fortunes of the centre-right Conservative party in the years immediately before the creation of the Parliament, the SNP's performance was enough to establish it as Scotland's second largest party for the first time since the party's foundation in the 1930s—and thus potentially poised to win power in the new devolved parliament.

That objective was soon achieved. In its first eight years of life the devolved Scottish Government was run by a coalition of Labour and the (centrist, socially liberal) Liberal Democrats. But at the third Scottish Parliament election in 2007, the SNP, with just under a third of the vote and only a slightly bigger tally than Labour, emerged as the largest party in the Scottish Parliament by just one seat. Although it was as much as 18 seats short of an overall

---

[1] Elections to the Scottish Parliament are held under a system whereby voters cast two votes, one for an individual constituency MSP and one for a party list. The figure quoted here is for the constituency vote, where the structure of the ballot is similar to that in election to the House of Commons.

majority and was unable to persuade the Liberal Democrats to join it in a coalition, the other parties allowed the SNP to form a minority administration. In eight short years, devolution had proven to be the SNP's pathway to its first ever taste of power.

Among the commitments that the SNP had made in the 2007 election was that a referendum should be held on whether Scotland should become an independent country—a stance that the party had adopted in the late 1990s in the hope that separating the question of independence from that of winning an election would help it win over the support in elections of those opposed to independence. In so doing the party was reflecting a wider change in the zeitgeist of constitutional thinking about referendums in the UK. Traditionally, referendums had been regarded as incompatible with the notion of parliamentary sovereignty, though this had not stopped many a local referendum being held as long ago as the early years of the twentieth century, including on prohibition in Scotland (Bogdanor 1981). But in 1973 a referendum had been held in Northern Ireland on whether it should remain part of the UK, in 1975 a UK-wide referendum had been held on the UK's membership of the Common Market (see Chapter 22 by Smith), and then in 1979 ballots in Scotland and Wales on devolution (see Chapter 11 by Mathias). Meanwhile, by the 1990s Labour were proposing not only a second round of referendums on devolution in Scotland and Wales, but also on devolution for London and, perhaps too, the regions of England. At the same time, in 1998 another referendum was held in Northern Ireland on the Good Friday Agreement (see Chapter 12 by Hayward). As a result, there was by now something of a convention that significant change to the governance of any part of the UK could not take place unless it had first been endorsed by voters in a referendum.

However, as very much a minority government, the SNP found itself faced in 2007 with a parliament in which a majority were opposed to Scotland becoming an independent country. It was also far from clear that the powers that had been devolved to the Scottish Parliament gave it the legal authority to call a referendum on independence even if it wished to do so. In practice, the party used its four years in office to promote the idea of holding a referendum while not attempting to legislate for one. In 2007, it launched a 'National Conversation' about not only how an independence referendum might be held, but also on the relative substantive merits of both independence and maximum devolution as part of the UK as compared with maintaining the status quo (Scottish Government 2007). Two years later, after the Conversation had concluded, the SNP government promised to bring forward legislation on holding a referendum. In the event it simply instigated another consultation, this time on a draft bill which might have allowed for a vote on maximum devolution as well as independence (Scottish Government 2010). The bill never found its way into the parliamentary chamber, far less the statute book.

14.3   Onset

Then, however, the SNP struck gold. Following an inept election campaign by Labour, the party suddenly and unexpectedly found itself swept to an overall majority in the Scottish Parliament election of 2011—despite winning no more than 45% of the vote. As discussed further below, it is far from clear that this success reflected any change of public mood on the merits of independence (see also Curtice 2011; Johns et al. 2013). Nevertheless, it meant that there was now a majority of MPs in the Scottish Parliament in favour of independence. As a result, the SNP government was now more or less guaranteed to be able to secure the passage of legislation on an independence referendum through the Scottish Parliament. However, that still left the question of whether that parliament formally had the right to pass such legislation in the first place.

At this point, politicians in what was now a Conservative-Liberal Democrat coalition government in London, together with the Labour opposition, decided to bow to the seemingly inevitable. Although they insisted that the SNP's victory had not secured it the legal right to hold a referendum, they accepted that the fact that the party had won an overall majority on the back of an election manifesto that had promised an independence referendum meant that it did now have the moral right to do so. There followed many months of haggling between the UK and Scottish Governments about some of the detail of the referendum process. However, in October 2012 the UK Prime Minister, David Cameron, and the Scottish First Minister, Alex Salmond, signed the so-called 'Edinburgh Agreement' (HM Government and Scottish Government 2012). The UK Parliament would pass secondary legislation that would give the Scottish Parliament the legal authority to hold a referendum on independence at some point before the end of 2014. The one condition was that the referendum could only be about independence, and not also about maximum devolution within the framework of the UK. That said, while the Scottish Government was otherwise free to determine the rules under which the referendum would be held, including on who would be eligible to vote, there was an expectation that those rules would follow the general legislative framework on referendums that, in recognition of the growing use of such ballots, had been passed by the UK Parliament in 2000 (formally known as the Political Parties, Elections and Referendums Act [PPERA] 2000). Above all, however, both governments committed themselves to respecting the outcome of what would technically be no more than an advisory ballot. If Scotland voted No to independence, then the Scottish Government would accept that it could no longer hope to pursue independence. If the country voted in favour (and, unlike in 1979, irrespective of the level of turnout or the size of the majority) negotiations would take place between the two governments with a view to giving effect to that decision. There would be no further ballot on the outcome of the negotiations before Scotland became an independent country.

In truth, both sides had decided it was in their interests to play poker. The UK government was well aware (see further below) that opinion polls and surveys suggested that only a minority of voters in Scotland backed Scottish independence at that time. By holding a Yes/No ballot on just independence, it anticipated that it would be able to inflict a serious defeat on the SNP, thereby removing from the heads of the rest of the UK the sword of Damocles that the 'threat' that Scottish independence had become. Meanwhile, by ruling out any vote on some form of maximum devolution there was no chance that the SNP might emerge with a consolation prize for which it could take the credit. Equally, from the SNP's point of view, there was no risk that voters would vote for maximum devolution rather than the perhaps seemingly more risky option of independence. Meanwhile, by ruling out the prospect of a second referendum on the outcome of any independence negotiations, the UK government hoped to dissuade voters from voting for independence in order to see what the subsequent negotiations might turn up, while the SNP feared that voters who had voted for the principle of independence first time around might draw back in a second ballot because they disliked some of the details. In short, both sides regarded it as in their interest to polarise the issue around a single-shot, single question referendum.

14.4   Rules

Once the Edinburgh Agreement was in place, the Scottish Government could set about writing the rules for the referendum. Because it was following the framework already set out in UK Parliament legislation, much of what it proposed was relatively uncontroversial—but not entirely so. One area where there was certainly a degree of controversy was over who should be entitled to vote. There were two issues—the age at which people could vote and the criteria that someone would have to satisfy in order to be able to vote.

Since 1969 the minimum age for voting in the UK has been 18. However, the SNP had long been in favour of the enfranchisement of 16 and 17 year olds, whose future would certainly be affected by the outcome of the referendum and who were also thought to be more favourable to independence than voters in Scotland in general. Their enfranchisement might thus be thought to the SNP's advantage, though in truth the probability that a body of some 100,000 young voters would tip the outcome in an electorate of 4 million was very low. In any event, the Scottish Government duly gave 16 and 17 year olds the vote in the referendum, though in so doing it had to establish a separate, special administrative procedure in order to ensure that they were duly registered.

In the UK, the franchise for elections to the House of Commons and that for local elections are somewhat different from each other. British, Irish and Commonwealth citizens resident in the UK are eligible to vote in both types of contest—the provision for Irish citizens is a legacy of Ireland's membership of the UK before 1922 while that for Commonwealth citizens is a relic of empire.

British citizens who have lived abroad for not more than 15 years are also eligible to vote in UK parliamentary elections. However, they cannot do so in local elections. Conversely, in line with European Union legislation, European Union citizens (who are not also Irish or Commonwealth ones) can vote in local (and, indeed, European Parliament) elections, but not in UK parliamentary contests. Scottish Parliament elections are classified as local elections, and thus, unsurprisingly, the Scottish Government proposed that the same local government franchise be used in the independence referendum. This meant that those of Scottish origin living elsewhere in the UK as well as those living abroad would not be able to vote. However, use of the UK parliamentary franchise would not have enabled 'Scots' living elsewhere in the UK to vote in the referendum either. Who does and does not have the right to Scottish citizenship, and thus might have a potential right to vote in Scottish elections even though living elsewhere, would only ever be determined if and when Scotland became independent, but not before. The Scottish Government thus probably had little option other than to make the choice that it did, albeit it was one that in any event accorded with the SNP's civic rather than ethnic conception of who should be regarded as Scottish.

There was some controversy too about the wording of the question that should appear on the ballot paper. The Scottish Government proposed that the question should be, 'Do you agree that Scotland should be an independent country?' In accordance with the UK framework legislation, this proposal was then passed to the non-partisan Electoral Commission to be tested with voters, on the basis of which it could either approved by the Commission or an alternative recommended. In practice, the Commission had previously indicated that questions that began 'Do you agree' tended to be regarded by voters as 'leading' (Electoral Commission 2011). Thus, it was not surprising that the Commission argued that the question should read instead, 'Should Scotland be an independent country?' to which voters would respond 'Yes' or 'No', a recommendation that the Scottish Government accepted (Electoral Commission 2013). This, however, upset some on the unionist side of the argument who felt that the SNP might derive an advantage by being associated with the positivity of 'Yes' rather than the negativity of 'No'. However, as the Commission itself noted, the question of Scottish independence was one with which most voters were already very familiar, and thus were unlikely to be swayed by the nuances of question wording.

Given the provisions of the UK framework legislation, the Electoral Commission might also have been expected to be responsible for running the ballot itself. However, in 2011, those responsible for running elections in each local authority area (known as returning officers) had formed a Scotland-wide body, the Electoral Management Board for Scotland, that had responsibility for co-ordinating electoral administration across the country. Unsurprisingly, a nationalist government preferred to give responsibility to this Scottish organisation rather than a UK-wide one. However, the Electoral Commission did still play the role to which it had become accustomed in referendums of recommending the rules for, and subsequently ensuring adherence to, the rules on campaign expenditure. In line with what had become regular UK practice, the Commission had to determine which two organisations should be regarded as the lead campaigners for the 'Yes' and the 'No' campaigns and be entitled to a relatively generous spending limit of £1.5 m during the last 16 weeks of the campaign (though unlike other recent referendums in the UK they were not to be entitled to any public funding beyond the free delivery of a campaign leaflet), and also set limits on the amount of money that other organisations, including political parties, could spend.

In the event the first decision proved to be relatively easy—only two applications, one for the Yes side and one for the No, were made to be a lead organisation. The Yes campaign was known as 'Yes Scotland'. It was formally separate from the SNP; its chair was a former Labour MP and subsequently Independent MSP, Dennis Canavan, while its Chief Executive, Blair Jenkins, was a sometime television executive who did not belong to any party and who in practice often acted as the organisation's media spokesperson. While the body also had representatives from the Scottish Greens and the Scottish Socialist Party, inevitably it was the SNP and, above all, Alex Salmond and his Deputy, Nicola Sturgeon, that called most of the shots when it came to campaigning and campaign strategy. The No campaign, meanwhile, was dubbed 'Better Together', which came to seem not only a reference to its message that Scotland would be better off as part of the UK but also the fact that it encompassed under one roof three unionist parties, the Conservatives, Labour and the Liberal Democrats, which were normally in competition with each other. As the largest of these three parties, Labour provided the leading personnel, including the Chair and leading spokesperson, Alistair Darling, who had been Chancellor of Exchequer in the most recent UK Labour government, but, inevitably, the organisation had to liaise closely with leading Conservatives and Liberal Democrats in the UK government, including not least the Prime Minister, David Cameron.

The more difficult decision facing the Electoral Commission was to set spending limits for the political parties that were seen to be fair. The Yes side comprised one large party, one minnow and one that did not have any MPs or MSPs at all. The No side, in contrast, comprised three substantial parties albeit one (the Liberal Democrats) that had suffered a drubbing in the most recent Scottish Parliament election. There was a risk that the rules would allow the three substantial No parties to outgun the one and a bit parties on the Yes side. In the event, however, the Commission found a formula that linked the amount of money that each party could spend to its share of the vote in the last Scottish Parliament election in such a way that in combination those parties backing Yes could between them spend roughly the same amount (just under £1.5 m) as those backing No. The solution also had the advantage that the financial muscle on both sides was shared almost equally between the lead organisations and the political parties. All other organisations that wished to campaign were subject to a spending limit of £150,000. In the event 19 organisations registered, with slightly more arguing for a No than for a Yes vote. The Commission reported that just over £3.5 m was spent by registered campaigners in favour of Yes and just over £3.1 m by those arguing for No (Electoral Commission 2015).

However, this was not simply a referendum that was fought by various campaigning organisations on the two sides of the argument. It was also—and most unusually—a battle between two governments both of whom, apart from the last four weeks before polling day, had access to the resources of their respective civil service machines. Both governments made extensive use of this facility. On the one hand, beginning as early as February 2013, the UK government issued a series of nearly 20 'analysis' papers (including a summary paper, HM Government 2014) on topics ranging from defence and international relations to the economic and currency, each one setting out the UK government's case as to why Scotland would be better off remaining part of the UK and pointing up what it regarded as some of the disadvantageous implications of independence. Meanwhile, in November 2013 the Scottish Government published a 670 page long white paper, *Scotland's Future: Your Guide to Scotland's Future* (Scottish Government 2013), which effectively acted as the prospectus for its vision of independence and thereby helped set the agenda of much the campaign.

14.5 CAMPAIGN

For all intents and purposes, the referendum campaign was up and running as soon as the ink was dry on the Edinburgh Agreement. Indeed, the two lead campaigns, Yes Scotland and Better Together, had already been launched the previous summer. The referendum was thus preceded by some two years of debate and discussion before the country eventually went to the polls on 18 September 2014. Unsurprisingly, given the importance of the issues at stake and its length, the campaign was a wide ranging one, but focussed for the most part on six key issues:

1. Sovereignty. Ultimately the case for independence rested on the claim that, as a distinct nation, Scotland had the right to govern itself, and that, despite devolution, Scotland was still at risk of finding some of its affairs being run by a Conservative-led government whose Commons majority rested entirely on votes cast south of the border. However, rather than just pursuing this essentialist case, the SNP and the Yes campaign also argued that independence would result in better government—because decisions would be taken by those who live in the country and thus have the greatest stake in its future.

2. Economics of independence. Almost inevitably, the two sides disagreed fundamentally on the economic implications of independence. On the Yes side, it was argued that access to the full fiscal levers of independence

would enable the Scottish Government to steer the country's economy more effectively, rather than being linked to decisions that serve primarily the needs and interests of London and the South East of England. The No side countered that, as part of the UK, Scotland enjoyed unfettered access to a large domestic market as well as the stability that came from access to the fiscal resources of the UK as a whole, including a higher level of public expenditure per head than in the rest of the UK. As it happened, while Scotland's fiscal position had in the recent past been a little better than that of the UK as a whole (and had been much better in the 1980s) once (but only once) an estimate of Scotland's share of North Sea Oil revenues was taken into account (Johnson and Phillips 2012), declining revenues from that now diminishing source meant that the position was just about to be reversed. Inevitably this meant that both sides were able selectively to identify statistics that supported their particular view.

3. Currency and banking. One of the fiercest debates was over the currency an independent Scotland should and would use. The Scottish Government envisaged that an independent Scotland should form a currency union with the rest of the UK and thus continue to use the pound, one of a number of proposals (along with retaining access to the BBC, being part of the Common Travel Area currently enjoyed by the UK, Ireland, the Isle of Man and the Channel Islands, and keeping the Queen as Head of State) designed to minimise the everyday impact of becoming independent. However, though perhaps unsurprisingly given the difficulties that had recently been faced by the Eurozone, in a dramatic intervention in February 2014 the UK coalition government, in tandem with the opposition Labour party, set its face against that proposal and thereafter insisted that the Scottish Government should unveil its 'Plan B'. The SNP retorted that the UK government was bluffing. Meanwhile it was also argued that an independent Scotland would have lacked the resources to rescue the two Scottish banks, the Royal Bank of Scotland and the Bank of Scotland, that had come close to collapse at the height of the financial crisis, though given that it was also clear that neither would be domiciled in the country if Scotland were to become independent, the relevance of this history was debatable.

4. Defence. The UK's nuclear weapons facility is based on the estuary of the River Clyde on the west coast of Scotland. This in itself meant that the prospect of Scottish independence presented the rest of the UK with the potential difficulty that a key feature of its defence infrastructure would be located outside its territory. Moreover, the SNP had long been opposed to the possession of nuclear weapons and thus should it at least be running an independent Scottish Government (of which, of course, there was no guarantee) it would be wanting the rest of the UK to move its nuclear weapons facility—and there was little argument that nowhere in England and Wales could be as suitable a base as the River Clyde.

Inevitably, there were arguments too about the merits of an independent Scotland—located as it is on the access to the sea route between Russia and the Atlantic—having a much more limited defence capability than it enjoys as part of the UK.

5. European Union. The SNP envisaged that an independent Scotland should be part of the European Union. That, however, left the question of whether Scotland would automatically qualify for membership or whether it would have to apply as a new state. If the latter were the case, not only might there be a gap between becoming independent and being part of the EU, but Scotland might be required to sign up to the Euro, a step that the SNP did not envisage it should take, while it would neither have access to the various opt-outs that the UK had negotiated, nor would it benefit from any rebate on its contribution to the EU budget of the kind that the UK enjoyed. The No campaign argued that the latter position would pertain and, indeed, suggested that given Spain's sensitivity to the potential parallels between Scotland and Catalonia (see Chapter 15 by Qvortrup) any application from Scotland to join the EU might well be blocked. The Yes side suggested that as Scotland was already fully compliant with the EU 'acquis', it was inconceivable that the country would be denied automatic membership.

6. Equality. The weakness of the Conservative party north of the border helped give rise to the claim that voters in Scotland were more egalitarian in outlook than their counterparts south of the border. The SNP and the Yes campaign suggested that an independent Scotland would be free to pursue policies that helped achieve that objective (Scottish Government 2013). Labour, in contrast, argued that it would be easier to achieve greater equality if Scotland continued to have access to the much larger fiscal resources of the UK as a whole rather than trying to do so on its own more limited tax base.

None of the numerous claims and counter-claims that were made about what would happen if Scotland were to become an independent country was subject to any regulatory check on their accuracy—indeed, that would have been a difficult task given that claims about what will happen in future as a result of a particular course of action are difficult to verify one way or the other. External scrutiny thus came primarily from the media who, in any event, were the principal mechanism through which people were exposed to the arguments that were being promulgated. The broadcast media in Britain have long been required to be politically impartial, including giving equal air time to the principal participants during the official period of the campaign. However, the campaign posed particular difficulties for the BBC which, as a UK-wide institution, would inevitably be affected by any decision by Scotland to become independent. Because of this status, the organisation was viewed with a degree of suspicion by many in the nationalist camp, in contrast to the principal provider of commercial television in most of Scotland, STV, which was a distinctly Scottish company albeit heavily reliant on material emanating from the main commercial channel in England and Wales, ITV. Aware of the sensitivity of the referendum, the broadcasters attempted to demonstrate their impartiality by monitoring the balance of the coverage given to the two sides throughout the 16 week period during which spending was controlled rather than, as in a general election, just during the four week period when neither government had access to its civil service machine. Yet this did not stop the BBC, in particular, from getting into hot water with the Yes camp, not least because, as the campaign came to a conclusion, some of its London based correspondents with few contacts or ties with the Scottish political world became involved in its coverage. For example, a substantial protest was held by supporters of independence outside the BBC's Scottish headquarters in Glasgow following an incident in which the broadcaster's London-based Political Editor (the most senior position among BBC politics journalists) suggested that the SNP First Minister had failed to answer a question about the reported possibility that the headquarters of the Royal Bank of Scotland would be moved from Edinburgh to London in the event of a Yes vote. Still, none of this stopped the BBC from playing host to one of the two 'presidential style' live TV debates between Alex Salmond and Alistair Darling that were the centrepiece of the televised coverage, and were watched, at least in part, by 60% of voters, with the other being hosted by STV.

In truth, whatever unfairness the Yes side felt it suffered from the broadcast coverage of the campaign paled into insignificance compared with the treatment it received from the newspapers, who were not required to be impartial at all. Many of the newspapers that circulate in Scotland are London-based newspapers that in their Scottish editions to varying degrees contain some Scotland specific coverage. Not only did all of these papers advocate a No vote, so also did most of the papers that are wholly produced in Scotland. There was just one exception—the Sunday edition of *The Herald* newspaper based in Glasgow. Interestingly, the impact of that decision on the Sunday *Herald*'s circulation persuaded the newspaper's owners immediately after the referendum to launch a new daily paper, *The National*, with an avowedly pro-independence outlook. Meanwhile, independence supporters were more active digitally than unionists during the campaign, and this ensured that the Yes side won the battle for sentiment on social media (Shephard and Quinlan 2015).

Whatever its limitations, however, the referendum engaged the electorate. As many as 62% reported to TNS-BMRB that they had talked about the referendum with friends and family—while nearly one in five told Survation that they had fallen out with friends or family over the referendum. The ultimate evidence that most voters in Scotland were motivated by the subject came from the fact that, at 84.6%, turnout expressed as a proportion of the registered electorate was higher than in any previous democratic ballot in Scotland since the advent of the mass franchise at the end of the First World War. Against what had been a backdrop of falling turnouts in UK general elections and even lower turnouts in Scottish Parliament elections, this was a truly remarkable level of participation.

14.6 OUTCOME

The result of the ballot failed to give satisfaction to either side in the debate. True, Scotland voted by 55.3–44.7% against the proposition that it should become an independent country, and to that extent victory clearly went to the advocates of the Union. However, this was not the decisive result that David Cameron had anticipated when he had originally agreed that the referendum should be held. Between 2007 and 2012 the annual Scottish Social Attitudes survey had found on average that only 26% supported independence whether inside or outside the EU, a figure that was actually down somewhat on the average figure of 30% recorded by the same survey between 1999 and 2006. Having the SNP in power in Edinburgh had, ironically, seemingly served to diminish somewhat the level of support for leaving the UK, perhaps because the party was regarded as more effective than the Labour/Liberal Democrat coalition at using office to defend Scotland's interests within the framework of the UK. However, the referendum campaign gradually saw support for independence increase. A rolling average of the polls of referendum voting intention published during the campaign suggests that, leaving aside those who said they did not know how they would vote, there was as much as a nine-point swing of support in favour of independence over the course of the final twelve months of the campaign (Curtice 2014a). Indeed, the gradual narrowing of the No lead and the publication in particular of one opinion poll ten days before polling day that actually put the Yes side narrowly ahead (BBC 2014) sparked considerable concern among those campaigning for a No vote. In an attempt to head off the apparent but hitherto largely unanticipated risk that they might lose, all parties to the Better Together campaign, were persuaded by the former Labour Prime Minister (and Scottish MP), Gordon Brown, to sign up to a 'vow' whose central promise was that, in the event of a No vote, a commission would immediately be established to develop proposals for further devolution that would then be put into law by whichever party formed the next UK government (Clegg 2014). The UK government might have originally insisted that more devolution should not be on the ballot paper, but by the end of the campaign voters were being told by the unionist camp that a No vote was a vote for more devolution!

It might be thought surprising that there was a substantial movement in the balance of opinion on an issue that presumably touched on voters' (relatively stable) sense of national identity. Yet, although when forced to choose a single national identity 65% of respondents to the 2014 Scottish Social Attitudes survey said that they were Scottish, while only 23% indicated that they were British (a very different picture from just 40 years previously (Curtice et al. 2009), a clear majority of voters in Scotland acknowledge both identities, albeit that their Scottish identity is usually the more strongly felt. When the same survey gave respondents the opportunity to say so, some 62% indicated they were some combination of both British and Scottish. Thus, although the more strongly someone felt Scottish, the more likely they were to back independence (Curtice 2014b), the fact that many voters had mixed loyalties meant that for many their sense of national identity alone was not necessarily decisive in deciding how they were going to vote. Instrumental considerations mattered too.

No instrumental consideration was more closely associated with support for independence than voters' perceptions of the economic consequences of independence (Curtice 2014b). Moreover, as Table 14.1 shows, this link only seemed to strengthen as the campaign progressed. For example, back in 2011, 78% of those who thought that Scotland's economy would be a lot better as a result of independence were in favour of leaving the UK, compared with just 4% of those who thought the economy would be a lot worse. By shortly before the referendum in 2014, however, the former figure had increased to 88%, while the latter remained just as low as ever. Meanwhile, there was a particularly marked increase in support for independence from 46 to 81% among those who thought the country's economy would be 'a little better' if it left the UK.

It is hardly surprising then that the rise in support for independence during the referendum campaign was accompanied by an increase in the proportion who thought that leaving the UK would be economically beneficial. In three polls undertaken by YouGov in 2011 and 2012, just 26% felt that Scotland would be economically better off if it left the UK, while no less than 49% felt it would be worse off. In contrast, in three polls that the same company conducted shortly before polling day, as many as 37% felt that the country would be better off, while 45% believed it would be worse off. Similarly, whereas in September 2013 ICM found that just 31% thought that independence would be good for the Scottish economy, while 48% reckoned it would be bad, twelve months later the figures were 38% and 45% respectively. Meanwhile, it also appears that whereas voters who during the course of the

Table 14.1 Support for independence by perceptions of the economic consequences of independence 2011–2014

% support independence	2011	2012	2013	2014
As a result of independence, Scotland's economy would be:				
A lot better	78	73	88	88
A little better	46	45	62	81
No difference	32	20	23	35
A little worse	10	4	7	11
A lot worse	4	3	5	3

Source Scottish Social Attitudes

campaign were persuaded that independence would be economically advantageous were indeed quite willing to switch their voting preference in favour of independence, those who came to the opposite conclusion did not necessarily switch in favour of No—they were often already No supporters whose inclination to back the Union was simply reinforced by the view to which they had come about the economic consequences of leaving (Curtice 2015).

In part, then, the referendum was an asymmetric contest in which those who were newly persuaded of the merits of independence changed sides, whereas those who felt that being in the UK would be better were simply reinforced in their existing views. However, it was also an asymmetric contest in that those who felt that independence would not make much difference either way economically did not split evenly between Yes and No. Rather, as Table 14.1 shows, they were mostly disinclined to back leaving the UK. Given that, according to ICM's polls, around a half of voters reckoned that leaving the UK would represent a substantial risk, it is perhaps not surprising that voters largely had to be persuaded that there would definitely be an upside to independence before they reckoned that it was a risk worth taking.

This then was no 'second order' referendum in which voters were distracted by issues of little relevance to the question on the ballot paper (Heath and Taylor 1999). Rather it was one where people's choice reflected their views about the issues at stake, and one where the referendum campaign itself served to crystallise that link. Moreover, although the Yes campaign apparently made some progress in persuading voters that independence would be economically beneficial, the fact that, nevertheless, by polling day those who upheld that view were still no more than a minority meant that it was more or less inevitable that a majority voted in favour of remaining part of the UK.

14.7 Fallout

Even so, this was hardly a vote without consequences. As a result of the 'vow' that had been made shortly before polling day, the UK government had an immediate obligation to convene the commission on further devolution that had been promised. Representatives from all of Scotland's parties, including the SNP, convened under the neutral chairmanship of a prominent businessman and peer, Lord Smith of Kelvin, charged with the task of producing a report and recommendations by the end of November 2014. That report duly proposed a considerable extension of the powers of the devolved Scottish Parliament, most notably in two areas where it had previously had little or no responsibility, taxation and welfare (Smith of Kelvin 2014). The Commission's proposals were enacted in legislation in 2016 and, as a result, there is now hardly any area of domestic policy in Scotland where the devolved institutions do not at least have some policy levers.

The waves created by the independence referendum did not simply break on Scotland's shores. As soon as the result of the independence referendum had been announced, the UK Prime Minister, David Cameron, was standing outside 10 Downing St promising that discussions would also begin on extending devolution elsewhere in the UK. Those discussions eventually led not only to all party agreement on further powers for the National Assembly for Wales, most notably in respect of energy projects (HM Government 2015), but also set in train a more controversial change to the procedures in the House of Commons whereby laws that only apply to England have to be approved by a majority of MPs representing English constituencies as well as by the Commons as a whole (Cabinet Office 2015).

The referendum not only led to significant constitutional change across the UK, but also to major upheaval in the politics of Scotland. The SNP might have been on the losing side in the referendum, but it found itself on the winning side politically as those who had voted Yes looked for ways of affirming the support for independence that they had expressed in the referendum. The party's membership increased four-fold to over 100,000 (Audickas et al. 2018), while opinion polls registered a marked increase in reported willingness to support the party. As noted earlier, success in elections to the House of Commons had hitherto largely eluded the party. But, with a UK election scheduled to be held in May 2015, there suddenly seemed to be the possibility of a SNP breakthrough. And that indeed is what happened. With the party winning almost exactly half of all votes cast, the even geographical spread of its support now worked to its advantage and the SNP secured no fewer than 56 of the country's 59 Commons seats. Scotland might still be part of the UK, but Labour's hopes that the country would continue to bolster the party's prospects of winning power in London lay in tatters.

Central to the SNP's success in 2015 was the fact that no less than 85% of those who supported independence voted for the SNP, well above the 55% who had done so on the occasion of the previous House of Commons election in 2010 (Curtice 2017). Moreover, the body of people who supported independence was now much bigger than before. The Scottish Social Attitudes survey, which had put support for independence on average at just 26% between 2007 and 2011, found as many as 39% in favour in 2015 and no less than 46% and 45% respectively in 2016 and 2017 (Curtice and Montagu 2018). Meanwhile, polls of how people would vote in another referendum in response to the question that was posed in 2014 found that support for independence was holding up at around the 45% mark. The gains the Yes side secured during the referendum campaign had proven to be permanent.

Thus, the September 2014 referendum left in its wake a much higher level of support for independence than had ever previously been in evidence, albeit less than the 50% needed to win a referendum. It left nationalists hoping that, with one more heave, they might deliver their dream in a second ballot, and unionists wondering whether they might be right. Unsurprisingly, therefore, the SNP went into the 2016 Scottish Parliament election leaving their options open on calling a second referendum, simply saying that they might do so if there were a 'material change' of circumstance. In fact, the party lost its overall majority at that election, but the combined strength of the SNP and the Greens still represented a pro-independence majority in the Edinburgh institution. Meanwhile a change of circumstance soon came along—in the form of the outcome of another referendum, the ballot in June 2016 on the UK's membership of the EU. Sixty-two per cent of voters in Scotland backed remaining in the EU, only to find their preference overturned by a 52% vote in favour of leaving across the UK as a whole. Given the debate that had occurred during the independence referendum about what leaving the UK might mean for Scotland's membership of the EU, the irony of the situation was not difficult to discern. Meanwhile from a nationalist perspective the outcome appeared to be the clearest possible demonstration that an independent Scotland was always at risk of having its wishes overturned thanks to the different outlook of voters in England.

Indeed, after it had become clear that the UK government was embarking on a vision of Brexit that found little favour with the Scottish Government, in March 2017 the Scottish Parliament voted to request from the UK Parliament the legal authority to hold another independence ballot. However, even by this stage it was clear that the UK's decision to leave the EU was not necessarily the game changer that the SNP anticipated. In contrast to the position in 2011, the UK government was strongly opposed to the idea. Meanwhile, around one in three of those who supported independence had in fact voted to Leave the EU (Curtice and Montagu 2018). Consequently, while the outcome of the EU referendum persuaded some to switch from No to Yes, there were others that moved in the opposite direction, leaving support for independence at still around the 45% mark. Meanwhile, in a snap UK general election held in June 2017 the SNP lost 21 of their 56 MPs, not least as a result of a loss of support among those who had voted Leave (Curtice and Montagu 2018). That outcome persuaded the Scottish Government to put its request for the authority to hold another independence referendum on hold. Yet thereafter the fallout from the decision to leave the EU did begin to have an impact on the balance of public opinion. While during the course of 2019 the UK Parliament furiously debated the merits of the Brexit agreement that had been negotiated with the EU, in Scotland support for independence in the polls rose to nearly 50%, an increase that occurred entirely among those who had voted to remain in the EU (Curtice and Montagu 2020). That increase, which was followed in another UK general election by a reversal of many of the losses the SNP had suffered in 2017, encouraged the SNP to renew its demand for another referendum. The coronavirus pandemic the following year brought any such prospect to a halt—but also witnessed polls that for the first time were consistently recording majority support for independence. Scotland's constitutional debate clearly remains unresolved.

14.8   Conclusion

There are many ways in which the Scottish independence referendum of 2014 has to be regarded as a success. An issue that often leads to bloodshed—a dispute between those with different national identities about who should have sovereignty over piece a territory—was put to the ballot box rather than the bullet. Moreover, voters recognised the importance of the issues at stake not only by turning out in unprecedented numbers but also by assessing and debating the issues at stake among themselves beforehand. Inevitably, there are arguments about the fairness of some aspects of the process, but in many respects the referendum was a fine example of democracy in action.

However, the exercise failed to resolve the substantive issue at stake. Those wanting Scotland to stay in the Union failed to win the decisive victory that they had originally anticipated and which they hoped would end the debate about Scotland's constitutional status for at least the foreseeable future. Moreover, the SNP emerged as electorally stronger than at any time in its history, wresting from Labour the dominance of the country's representation at Westminster that Labour had tried so hard to preserve. In truth, Scotland's continued membership of the Union now looks more problematic than at any point since it joined in 1707. Yet while, five years on from the referendum, no other party seemed able to challenge the SNP's continued tenure as the provider of Scotland's devolved government, the challenges that lay between the party and achieving independence still seemed formidable. Even the political disruption caused by another referendum—on Britain's membership of the EU—had not taken the SNP to a point where independence looked like an immediate prospect. The debate about Scotland's constitutional status, however, seemed set to continue.

References

Audickas, L., Dempsey, N., & Keen, R. (2018). *Membership of UK Political Parties* (SN05125). London: House of Commons Library. Available at https://researchb riefings.parliament.uk/ResearchBriefing/Summary/SN05125.

BBC. (2014, September 7). Scottish Independence: Vote "Will Go to the Wire". Posted at https://www.bbc.co.uk/news/uk-scotland-29096458.

Bogdanor, V. (1981). *The People and the Party System*. Cambridge: Cambridge University Press.

Cabinet Office. (2015). *English Votes for English Laws: Revised Proposed Changes to the Standing Orders of the House of Commons and Explanatory Memorandum*. London: Cabinet Office. Available at https://assets.publishing.service.gov.uk/government/uploads/system/uploads/attachment_data/file/445062/English_Votes_for_Eng lish_Laws_-_Revised_Proposed_Changes_to_Standing_Orders_Accessible.pdf.

Clegg, D. (2014, September 15). David Cameron, Ed Miliband and Nick Clegg Sign Joint Historic Promise Which Guarantees More Devolved Powers for Scotland and Protection of NHS If We Vote No. *Daily Record*. Available at https://www.dailyr ecord.co.uk/news/politics/david-cameron-ed-miliband-nick-4265992.

Colley, L. (2009). *Britons: Forging the Nation 1707–1837* (Revised ed.). New Haven: Yale University Press.

Curtice, J. (2006). Forecasting and Evaluating the Consequences of Electoral Change: Scotland and Wales. *Acta Politica, 41*(3), 300–314.

Curtice, J. (2011). The 2011 Scottish Election: Records Tumble, Barriers Breached. *Scottish Affairs, 76,* 51–73.

Curtice, J. (2014a). *Poll of Polls: 17 September FINAL.* Posted at http://blog.whatsc otlandthinks.org/2014/09/poll-polls-17-september-final/.

Curtice, J. (2014b). Scottish Independence: A Question of Identity, Economics or Inequality? In A. Park, J. Curtice, & C. Bryson (Eds.), *British Social Attitudes: The 31st Report.* London: NatCen Social Research. Available at http://www.bsa.natcen.ac.uk/latest-report/british-social-attitudes-31/independe nce-referendum/introduction.aspx.

Curtice, J. (2015). *Did Yes Win the Referendum Campaign?* Edinburgh: AqMen. Available at http://www.research.aqmen.ac.uk/files/2017/07/PostGE2015Scotl and_Referendum-Impact.pdf.

Curtice, J. (2017). The Party and the Electorate. In G. Hassan & S. Barrow (Eds.), *A Nation Changed? The SNP and Scotland Ten Years On.* Edinburgh: Luath Press.

Curtice, J., & Montagu, I. (2018). Scotland: How Brexit Has Created a New Divide in the Nationalist Movement. In D. Phillips, J. Curtice, & M. Phillips, & J. Perry (Eds.), *British Social Attitudes: The 35th Report.* London: NatCen Social Research. Available at http://www.bsa.natcen.ac.uk/latest-report/british-social-attitudes-35/ scotland.aspx.

Curtice, J., & Montagu, I. (2020). Is Brexit Fuelling Support for Independence? London: NatCen Social Research. Available at https://whatscotlandthinks.org/ana lysis/is-brexit-fuelling-support-for-independence.

Curtice, J., McCrone, D., McEwen, N., Marsh, M., & Ormston, R. (2009). *Revolution or Evolution: The 2007 Scottish Elections.* Edinburgh: Edinburgh University Press.

Devine, T. (2006). *The Scottish Nation 1700–2007.* London: Penguin.

Electoral Commission. (2011). *Referendum on Law-Making Powers for the National Assembly for Wales: Report of the Views of the Electoral Commission on the Proposed Referendum Question.* London: Electoral Commission. Available at https://www. electoralcommission.org.uk/_media/response-submission/commission-responses- to-external-consultations/Question-assessment-report-English-FINAL-no-embargo. pdf.

Electoral Commission. (2013). *Referendum on Independence for Scotland: Advice of the Electoral Commission on the Proposed Referendum Question.* Edinburgh: Electoral Commission. Available at https://www.electoralcommission.org.uk/__data/assets/ pdf_file/0007/153691/Referendum-on-independence-for-Scotland-our-advice-on- referendum-question.pdf.

Electoral Commission. (2015). *Scottish Independence Referendum: Report on the Regulation of Campaigners at the Independence Referendum Held on 18 September 2014.* Edinburgh: Electoral Commission. Available at https://www.electoralcommission. org.uk/__data/assets/pdf_file/0018/190521/Casework-and-spending-report.pdf.

Heath, A., & Taylor, B. (1999). Were the Welsh and Scottish Referendums Second-Order Elections? In B. Taylor & K. Thomson (Eds.), *Scotland and Wales: Nations Again?* Cardiff: University of Wales Press.

HM Government. (2014). *United Kingdom, United Future: Conclusions of the Scotland Analysis Programme* (Cm 8869). London: HM Government. Available at https://assets.publishing.service.gov.uk/government/uploads/system/uploads/ attachment_data/file/321369/2902216_ScotlandAnalysis_Conclusion_acc2.pdf.

HM Government. (2015). *Powers for a Purpose: Towards a Lasting Devolution Settlement for Wales* (Cm 9020). London: HM Government. Available at https://assets.publishing.service.gov.uk/government/uploads/system/uploads/attachment_data/file/408587/47683_CM9020_ENGLISH.pdf.

HM Government and Scottish Government. (2012). *Agreement Between the United Kingdom Government and the Scottish Government on a Referendum on Independence for Scotland*. Edinburgh: Scottish Government. Available at https://www.gov.scot/resource/0040/00404789.pdf.

Johns, R., Carman, C. J., & Mitchell, J. (2013). Constitution or Competence?: The SNP's Re-election in 2011. *Political Studies, 61*(S1), 158–178.

Johnson, P., & Phillips, D. (2012). *Scottish Independence: The Fiscal Context*. London: Institute for Fiscal Studies. Available at https://www.ifs.org.uk/bns/bn135.pdf.

Scottish Government. (2007). *Choosing Scotland's Future: A National Conversation: Independence and Responsibility in the Modern World*. Edinburgh: Scottish Government. Available at https://www.gov.scot/Publications/2007/08/13103747/0.

Scottish Government. (2010). *Scotland's Future: Draft Referendum (Scotland) Bill Consultation Paper*. Edinburgh: Scottish Government. Available at https://www.gov.scot/Publications/2010/02/22120157/0.

Scottish Government. (2013). *Scotland's Future: Your Guide to an independent Scotland*. Edinburgh: Scottish Government. Available at https://www.gov.scot/resource/0043/00439021.pdf.

Shephard, M., & Quinlan, S. (2015). Social Media and the Scottish Independence Referendum: Events and the Generation of Enthusiasm for Yes. In A. Bruns, G. Enli, E. Skogerbø, A. Larsson, & C. Christensen (Eds.), *The Routledge Companion to Social Media and Politics* (pp. 488–502). Oxford: Routledge.

Smith of Kelvin, Lord (chmn.). (2014). *The Smith Commission: Report of the Smith Commission for further devolution of powers to the Scottish Parliament*. Edinburgh: Smith Commission. Available at http://webarchive.nationalarchives.gov.uk/20151202171029/http://www.smith-commission.scot/wp-content/uploads/2014/11/The_Smith_Commission_Report-1.pdf.

CHAPTER 15

The 2017 Catalan Referendum in Comparative Perspective

Matt Qvortrup

In 2017 a majority of the voters in Catalonia, a Spanish *comunidad autónoma*, voted overwhelmingly for independence in what supporters called a referendum—but which opponents called an illegal and unconstitutional act. The figures seemed impressive. Over 92% voted for independence and just over seven per cent voted against the proposition, 'Do you want Catalonia to become an independent state in the form of a republic?' (Guidi and Casula 2019: 183).

This result was—on the face of it—reminiscent of the 1944 referendum in Iceland and the vote in Norway in 1905 when similar majorities voted for independence from, respectively, Denmark and Sweden. With one exception, that is. The turnout in these referendums was considerably higher. In both Iceland and Norway more than 90% participated. In Catalonia, by contrast, only 43% of the voters turned out to vote (Guidi and Casula 2019: 183).

The aim of this chapter is to analyse the Catalan referendum in the light of more general tendencies in similar referendums in a comparative perspective. Thus, in addition to presenting the background to and the context of the 2017 referendum, the chapter will point out contrasts and similarities with the over sixty referendums that have been held on independence in the past 160 years (see Sect. 15.2 below). Before we turn to this analysis, it is important to understand something about the background to the vote.

M. Qvortrup (✉)
Coventry University, Coventry, UK
e-mail: matt.qvortrup@coventry.ac.uk

© The Author(s) 2021
J. Smith (ed.), *The Palgrave Handbook of European Referendums*,
https://doi.org/10.1007/978-3-030-55803-1_15

15.1   Catalonia the Briefest of Histories

To write about Catalan history is an impossible act. Historians have always aspired to write unbiased chronicles of the past. In the words of Lord Acton,

> Our Waterloo must be one that satisfies French and English, German and Dutch alike; that nobody can tell, without examining the list of authors where the Bishop of Oxford laid down the pen, and whether Fairburn or Gasquet, Lieberman or Harrison took it up. (Acton 1906: 318)

But most believe this to be an impossibility. To be sure many will in principle agree with Mr Gradgrind, the Schoolmaster in Charles Dickens's *Hard Times*, who said, 'Now what I want is facts. Teach these boys and girls nothing but facts. Facts alone are wanted in life' (Dickens 1854: 13). While it is equally important not to fall into the trap of relativism, it is important to forewarn the reader of the difficulty of objective analysis. Hence, before delving into a controversial subject dealing with the past it is advisable to heed the advice of the historian E. H. Carr, who noted, 'The facts, [that is] what the historian [and the political scientist] catches will depend partly on chance, but mainly on what part of the ocean he [or she] chooses to fish in and what tackle [she or] he chooses to use' (Carr 1961: 18).

Unlike Scotland and Serbia, Catalonia (like Norway or Iceland) was never an entirely independent state, in the sense that it had a sovereign government with diplomatic representation abroad. Charlemagne had created *Marca Hispànica* in 795 AD as a buffer-zone against invasion from the south. A large part of this was the Principality of Catalonia, which merged with Aragon (today another Spanish *comunidad autónoma*) to create the Court of Aragon. This was an important regional power in the twelfth and thirteenth centuries. After Ferdinand II of Aragon married Queen Isabella I of Castile in 1469, the two domains gradually merged into one. Though, like in Scotland and England under James VI and I, there were initially separate institutions and separate courts. In a sense the first Spanish King—he was named *el Católico*—was a Catalan. But this meant little politically.

According to Elie Kedouri, '*Nationalism* is a doctrine *invented* in Europe at the beginning of the *19th century*' (Kedouri 1960: 1). In the case of Catalonia, this might be a bit of an exaggeration. Certainly, there was a developed sense of cultural and even political distinctiveness, which led to the Reapers War (also known as Catalan Revolt in the 1640s) and thus some level of political awareness. Politically this was suppressed. While the area which is now Catalonia and Aragon was formally separate until the end of the seventeenth century, this changed. The two were amalgamated into Spain after the *Decretos de Nueva Planta* in the first two decades of the eighteenth century, in response to what the Castile King Philip V saw as the betrayal of the Aragonese during the War of the Spanish Succession (1701–1714). Like the *Act of Union* in the newly minted United Kingdom 1707, Aragon was now—like Scotland—ruled from the imperial capital.

Catalonia prospered economically; again, much like Scotland. In another parallel, there was a romantic revival of Catalan culture. In Scotland in and around the beginning of the nineteenth century the poetry of Ossian and Burns led to a renewed interest in the past. In Catalonia, the so-called *Renaixença* was characterised by a new awareness of Catalan cultural heritage. One of the products of this revival was the architect Antoni Gaudí (Guibernau 2000b).

Politically, Catalonia was still part of a united kingdom. Some desired more autonomy, but mostly as part of a federal structure. The fall of the short-lived *First Spanish Republic* (1873–1974), and the restoration of the Bourbon Monarchy further strengthened Catalan demands for autonomy. Uprisings by anarchists in 1909—in protest against the call-up of reservists to quell an uprising in Morocco—led to a general strike and an uprising, which was brutally suppressed by the authorities. With a death toll of more than a hundred, what the Catalans call *la Setmana Tràgica* ('the tragic week'), gave a boost to demands for further autonomy (Sirvent 2009).

The negative reactions and condemnation by other European states prompted the monarchy to grant the four Catalan provinces the right to create *Mancomunitat*. Formally a commonwealth, but one without political powers. This was disbanded during the Dictatorship of Primo de Rivera (1923–1931).

Timing is of the essence in history. A few hours before the establishment of the Second Spanish Republic in 1931, the leading Catalan politician Francesc Macià declared Catalonia a republic, 'expecting that the other peoples of Spain would constitute themselves as republics, in order to establish an Iberian Confederation' (Macià quoted in Santos 2009: 31). It is telling that he did not speak of complete independence from Spain, but a 'confederation' within it. This declaration and the establishment of the Republic, as we shall see below, led to a referendum and a statute of autonomy.

Under the left-wing government of Macià, Catalonia followed a policy of radical reform with socialist overtones. These were halted in 1934. Following a general strike, the short-lived rightist government in Madrid, elected the previous year, imposed direct rule and suspended Catalan autonomy. However, this was restored in 1936 when the left returned to power. During the Civil War (1936–1939), Catalonia was firmly in the republican camp.

During the one-party rule of the *Falange Española Tradicionalista y de las Juntas de Ofensiva Nacional Sindicalista*, following the victory of Franco, the Catalan language and culture were suppressed. It was not surprising, therefore, that the revival of the autonomy for the province was a key demand after the restoration of democracy in 1976. One of the first demands was for a referendum on a new law—or *Estado* as these statutes are often called in the specialist literature. Before we explore those demands, we need to look at the history of referendums on independence.

15.2   THE BRIEF HISTORY
OF INDEPENDENCE REFERENDUMS

Independence referendums have a long history. In many ways, these were the original referendums. As far back as the fourteenth century, votes were held in present-day France to escape the domination of the Holy Roman Empire. Thus in 1307, Lyonnais (in present-day South Eastern France) voted for independence in the first instance of what we might call a referendum (Mattern 1921: 37). Under similar circumstances, male property-owning citizens in Burgundy voted in 1527 to nullify the Treaty of Madrid, according to which the territory would be ceded to Spain. The vote was a tactical masterstroke by the French King Francis I, who—having read Erasmus of Rotterdam—thought that he could undo the accord he had signed when he was in a weaker position (Wambaugh 1919: xxiii).

While political theorists from John Locke through to Hugo Grotius were in principle in favour of letting people decide whether they wanted to be ruled by one King or another (Qvortrup 2015: 549), it was not until the eighteenth century that this form of consultation began to resemble what we today would consider to be a democratic method of voting.

Modern democracy was not, of course, an American invention, but the new republic in North America shaped the practice of democracy, especially as regards direct citizen involvement. Consequently, it is not surprising that the referendum was used there to determine issues pertaining to sovereignty. Thus, the first referendum in America was held in 1788 in Rhode Island, when voters were consulted on whether they wanted to give up their independence and join the newly minted United States. As it happened, they voted 'No', but—in what some will find to be an interesting parallel—they were eventually forced to join the Federation (Herndon and Murray 2018).

These early experiences were continued in France, though here with a clearer ideological commitment to the sovereignty of the people as originally developed by Rousseau. The 'French revolution proclaimed as the fundamental principle of all government the principle of popular sovereignty' (Mattern 1921: 24). Hence it was natural that after the occupation by the French the Swiss were allowed to vote—and, remarkable, that the French (now governed by Napoleon Bonaparte)—albeit grudgingly accepted the result. However, the referendum as a means of determining sovereignty fell into disuse after Waterloo in 1815, and it only began to be used again in the years after 1848, when there were several votes in Italy and France. For example, Nice voted in a sovereignty referendum to join France, and the process of Italian reunification was codified by popular votes—though it was sometimes difficult to determine the fairness of these.

The first referendums on independence were held in the Confederate states in America in the early 1860s. At this stage the referendum was already a deep-seated part of political life in the United States. By the mid-1850s it had become commonplace to consult the citizens on major issues of constitutional importance. It was natural, therefore, that Texas, Virginia, and Tennessee submitted the decision to secede from the Union to the voters in 1860. What is perhaps interesting is that the support for secession was not unanimous. In Tennessee, for example, 104,019 voted for secession while 47,238 voted against, and in Texas the figures were 34,794 for and 11,235 against. (We do not have figures for Virginia.) These were not endorsements of epic proportions. The less than unanimous support perhaps suggested the Dixie voters did not support the nuclear option favoured by the confederate elites. After the American Civil War referendums on independence were almost forgotten. To be sure, there were debates about plebiscites to resolve the border dispute between Denmark and Germany, but these came to naught.

It took a full 45 years before the next referendum on independence was held. In this case a vote on whether Norway should secede from Sweden (more than 99% supported the proposition) in a referendum in 1905. In the Norwegian case the referendum was the brainchild of Norwegian Prime Minister Christian Michelsen, who wrong-footed the Swedish Unionist elite by calling a surprise referendum after the Swedish king had refused to appoint a government that had a majority in the *Stortinget* (the Norwegian legislature).

Although the principle of self-determination of the people was much espoused in the wake of the First World War—especially by US President Woodrow Wilson who had campaigned for the use of more referendums in America while he was governor of New Jersey—no referendums were held on independence for the newly established countries (e.g. Czechoslovakia or Yugoslavia) or the secession of states from established ones (e.g. Hungary and Finland). To be sure, there were several referendums on the drawing of borders in Europe, e.g. in Schleswig and in Tyrol in 1920. But referendums on outright independence were not held, and the leading scholars of international law were generally sceptical of them. L. F. L. Oppenheim, arguably the most prominent international legal mind at the time, concluded, 'it is doubtful whether the law of nations will ever make it a condition of every cession that it must be ratified by a plebiscite' (Oppenheim cited in Mattern 1921: 195).

In the period between the two World Wars, only two independence referendums were held. One in 1933, on whether Western Australia should secede from Australia, another in 1935, on whether the Philippines should become independent from the United States. In the former, a majority voted for independence, but as the *National Party*, which campaigned for independence, lost the election held on the same day, nothing came of it. In the latter case, a successful referendum was held on a new independence constitution after the Philippine Congress had rejected the US Congress's *Hare-Hawes-Cutting Act*, which granted independence for the erstwhile overseas dependency. However, it was not until after the Second World War that referendums began to be used consistently. This happened when areas seceded from their parent states. Of the over 60 referendums on independence since 1860, 54 have been held after 1944, the vast majority of these—41 in total—after 1990 in Europe.

Table 15.1 Secession referendums 1944–1980

Parent country	Seceding country	Year	Turnout (%)	Yes (%)
Denmark	Iceland	1944	98	99
China	Mongolia	1945	98	64
Denmark	Faroe Islands	1946	50	64
UK	Newfoundland	1948	52	88
France	Cambodia	1955	100	–
France	Guinea	1958	97	95
New Zealand	Western Samoa	1961	86	77
West Ind Fed	Jamaica	1961	46	60
France	Algeria	1962	99	75
Malaysia	Singapore	1962	71	90
UK	Malta	1964	50	80
USA	Micronesia	1975	52	59
Canada	Quebec	1980	85	41

Source www.c2d.ch. Accessed 2 October 2019

As Shown in Table 15.1, There Were Only 13 Independence Referendums in the Four Decades After the Second World War.

One would perhaps have suspected that these referendums would have pertained to decolonisation; that the independence movements would have sought popular approval of their newly gained or espoused freedom. This was not the case. The elites who fought for and won independence were not, in most cases, willing to risk the political victories gained in negotiations or wars by submitting declarations of independence to an unpredictable electorate. Indeed, the only colonies to submit the declarations of independence to referendum were Cambodia, Western Samoa and Guinea. In the first two cases, the votes were held at the instigation of the parent states, which wanted to show that there was popular support for abandoning the territories. The Guinean referendum was somewhat different. Held on the same day as eleven other referendums in other French colonies, on whether to take part in the newly established *Communauté française*, established by Charles de Gaulle, the Guineans, led by the independence leader Ahmed Sékou Touré, defied Paris and voted to become independent. 95% voted in support of independence. France retaliated by withdrawing all aid. However, within two years Mali, Niger, Upper Volta (now Burkina Faso), Côte d'Ivoire, Chad, the Central African Republic, the Republic of Congo and Gabon became independent states. All territories that had returned huge majorities for maintaining links with France in the referendum in 1958 but none of the new states submitted the decision to become independent to the voters. It was almost as if referendums on independence were anathema to the independence movements.

Generally, the reasons for holding referendums in the aftermath of the Second World War were varied. In the case of Mongolia, the vote was held for geopolitical reasons at the instigation of Stalin; the vote in Algeria was held after a lengthy war of independence and negotiations. Overall it would be difficult to find a general pattern of *when* referendums were held after the Second World War.

In the 1970s there was only one referendum on independence: the decision of the Trust Territory of the Pacific Islands to become independent from the United States under the name of the Federated States of Micronesia in 1975. In the 1980s there was a similar paucity of plebiscites. The only one in the latter decade being the 1980 vote in the Francophone Canadian province of Quebec, in which, on a 85% turnout, 59% rejected the secessionist *Parti Québécois's* proposal for 'sovereignty association'—a veiled description of independence.

It was only after the fall of Communism in Europe starting in 1989 and after the collapse of the Soviet Union in 1991 that the floodgates of independence referendums opened. Again, the reasons seem to have been varied. In many cases, referendums were held because the international community—especially the major European powers—insisted upon referendums in order to recognise the new states. Especially the *Badinter Commission*—set up by the European Communities (soon to become the EU)—stressed that referendums were a *conditio sine qua non* for recognizing new states. There is historical and anecdotal evidence to suggest that it was this requirement that prompted a large number of successor-states to hold referendums especially in the Former Yugoslavia (Radan 2000: 47).

The referendum was also in many cases a kind of symbolic national manifestation of a newly found freedom. By voting, often almost unanimously, in an independence referendum, the new state made the plebiscite a symbolic representation of the nation itself: a mirror image of the *demos* and the *ethnos* merged into one indivisible unity. Ernest Renan's often cited remark, that a 'nation is a daily plebiscite' is perhaps an accurate description of these referendums (Renan quoted in Roshwald 2015: 443).

As this author has argued at length elsewhere, the referendums were also held for more prosaic reasons, namely when a new elite was under threat from external and internal powers and wanted to prove that it had popular support and the requisite legitimacy to govern (Qvortrup 2014). Not all of the states, of course were recognized, and not all of the referendums were conducted in accordance with the internally recognized standards of free and fair voting. In addition to referendums in former Soviet and Yugoslav entities, a proliferation of plebiscites was held in sub-national territories such as, for example, Abkhazia in Georgia and Krajina in Bosnia, where minorities sought to win approval for independence from recently declared independent states. None of these sub-national referendums—while the majorities were large—resulted in the establishment of new states.

While most referendums in this period were held in former Communist countries, a few polls were held in western democracies. In 1995 the voters in Quebec again rejected independence, this time by a whisker, and so did voters in Puerto Rico in a multi-option referendum in 1993. And in 1998, the voters in Nevis, failed to meet the required threshold of 66% necessary to secede from the Federation of St Kitts and Nevis. Interestingly, the only unsuccessful referendums on independence have been held in countries with established democratic traditions, prompting a scholar (and later politician to conclude that 'secessions are...difficult in established democracies' (Dion 1996: 269) (Table 15.2).

Table 15.2 Secession referendums 1991–2019

Parent country	Seceding country	Year	Turnout	Yes vote
USSR	Lithuania	1991	91	84
USSR	Estonia	1991	77	83
USSR	Latvia	1991	74	88
USSR	Georgia	1991	98	90
USSR	Ukraine	1991	70	85
Georgia	South Ossetia	1991	98	90
Georgia	Abkhasia	1991	99	58
Yugoslavia	Croatia	1991	98	83
Croatia	Serbs	1991	98	83
Yugoslavia	Macedonia	1991	70	75
USSR	Armenia	1991	95	90
Bosnia	Serbs	1991	90	–
Serbia	Sandjak	1991	96	67
Serbia	Kosovo	1991	99	87
USSR	Turkmenistan	1991	94	97
USSR	Karabagh	1991	NA	NA
USSR	Uzbekistan	1991	98	94
Macedonia	Albanians	1991	99	93
Moldova	Transnistie	1991	100	NA
Yugoslavia	Bosnia	1992	99	64
Yugoslavia	Montenegro	1992	96	44
Georgia	South Ossetia	1992	NA	NA
Bosnia	Krajina	1992	99	64
Ethiopia	Eritrea	1993	99	98
Bosnia	Serbs	1993	96	92
USA	Puerto Rico	1993	48	73
USA	Palau	1993	64	68
Georgia	Abkhasia	1995	96	52
Quebec	Cris	1995	95	75
Canada	Quebec	1995	49	94

(continued)

Table 15.2   (continued)

Parent country	Seceding country	Year	Turnout	Yes vote
St Kitts and Nevis	Nevis	1998	57	61
USA	Porto Rico	1998	50	71
Indonesia	East Timor	1999	78	94
Somalia	Somaliland	2001	–	97
New Zealand	Tokelau	2006		95
Yugoslavia	Montenegro	2006	55	86
South Sudan	South Sudan	2011	97	98
Scotland	Britain	2014	83	44
Kurdistan	Iraq	2017	72	92
Catalonia	Spain	2017	43	92
New Caledonia	France	2018	81	43
Bougainville	PNG	2019	87	98

Source www.c2d.ch. Accessed 2 December 2019

During this period, referendums came in different forms and not all followed legal procedures—or indeed any at all. Some referendums were held under legally agreed rules, such as the ones in Scotland (2014), New Caledonia (2018) and Bougainville (2019), others like the vote in Kurdistan and Catalonia (both 2017) were legally speaking *ultra vires*, not held in accordance with established and codified legal principles. In many cases—Catalonia, New Caledonia and Scotland among them—the vote took place in a political culture that was shaped by the precedents of previous referendums. Thus, as we shall see shortly, Catalonia has a track-record of referendums on territorial matters which makes the province unique. What was new in 2017 was that the vote was about outright independence, something which never previously had been a stated goal for the Catalans.

15.3   THE REFERENDUM IN SPANISH POLITICAL HISTORY

The referendum has a chequered history in Spain. In the 1947 and again in 1966 the dictatorship under Francisco Franco employed the plebiscite (here defined as a rigged referendum) to secure approval of, respectively, the establishment of a Monarchy after the death of the general and an organic law. Both these referendums were endorsed by well over 90% and were democratically speaking farcical.

The same could not be said of the referendums held after the death of Franco in 1975.

Juan Carlos—the King—was clear that he did not wish to reign as an absolute monarch. The option of *Franquismo sin Franco*—Francoism without Franco—was not attractive to many. Spearheaded by Adolfo Suárez (a former Franco loyalist appointed Prime Minister by the King), negotiations began to secure a *reforma pactada*—a gradual reform towards a democratic state. This was in part inspired by similar developments in Greece a few years before, and—like in the Greek case—the process was ratified by a referendum (Tzortzis 2016). Thus, in 1976, in the first democratically held nationwide referendum in Spanish history, 97% of the voters approved the transition. The agreement based on a pact between the outgoing regime and the democratic parties (including the Socialists and the Communist Party) paved the way for elections in 1977, which were won by Suárez's new democratic party *Unión de Centro Democrático*, which went on to negotiate a proposal for a new constitution.

One of the main issues facing Suárez and his colleagues was how to ensure unity of the realm, while at the same time accommodating desire for independence or further autonomy in 'nations'. The constitution of 1978—endorsed by 91% of the voters in a referendum of the same year—established a semi-federal structure, but one where there were provisions for 'three historic nations—Catalonia, Galicia, and the Basque Country—to acquire regional governments with legislative powers' (Rourke et al. 1992: 116).

As is often the case, the Constitution was a compromise, and as a result Art II, which dealt with the Autonomias, was rather vague. It reads:

> The Constitution is based on the indissoluble unity of the Spanish Nation, the common and indivisible homeland of all Spaniards; it recognizes and guarantees the right to self-government of the nationalities and regions of which it is composed and the solidarity among them all.

But it was not clear how exactly the 'nationalities' and 'regions', could get more power. Apparently as an afterthought, the new constitution allowed regional leaders to call referendums if they desired more self-government. This led to a demand from several regions, including Andalucía, which were not considered 'nations'.

The historic nations (Catalonia, Galicia and the Basque Country) had a constitutionally guaranteed 'fast route'. Historically Spanish nationalism had been very weak (Haywood 1995: 14). As the noted social philosopher José Ortega y Gasset, observed in a famous analysis, the loyalty of many in the Basque Country and Catalonia was to the province rather than to the state (Ortega y Gasset 1967). This was especially pronounced in Catalonia. In 1913, a referendum had been held in the municipalities of the province, which led to the endorsement for setting up a deliberative body called *Mancomunitat de Catalunya* (Balcells 2015). At this stage the King had already endorsed a plan for Catalan autonomy, partly in response to the outrage caused by *la Setmana Tràgica*, which as we have seen only led to cosmetic changes.

Some wanted to go further. Thus, the assembly in 1919 proposed the so-called *Projecte d'Estatut d'Autonomia de Catalunya de 1919*. This was largely in response to US President Woodrow Wilson's apparent endorsement of the principle of self-determination of the people. The appeal came to naught. It was rejected by the Cortes, and shortly thereafter Spain became a dictatorship. The aspirations of the Catalans resurfaced again after the establishment of the Second Republic in 1931.

It is a little-known fact, outside the ranks of specialists that there were early referendums on the transfer of powers to the autonomies in the 1930s. The 1931 Constitution of Spain provided that historical nations could hold referendums on further autonomy (Constitución española de 1931, Art 12). Pursuant to this, referendums were held in Catalonia in 1931, in the Basque Country in 1933, and in Galicia in 1936. In all cases the statutes were approved by close to a hundred per cent of the voters and the turnout was around 75%. Thus, there was a clear precedent for the referendums in Catalonia, the Basque Country and Galicia that were held in 1979 and 1980. These referendums resulted in massive support for re-establishing the autonomies, albeit the turnout in these votes was relatively low (Guibernau 2000a) (Table 15.3).

After this relatively little happened until the early 2000s. There was a violent terrorist campaign in the Basque Country, where the separatist terrorist organisation Euskadi Ta Askatasuna (ETA) killed dozens of citizens every year (Pastor 2011). In Catalonia, by contrast, demands for outright independence were non-existent, and there were no examples of terrorist attacks, let alone fatalities.

Several nationalist parties had supported various governments in Madrid and had been able to exert concessions from the governments from the right. For example, between 1996 and 2000, the centre-right Catalan nationalist party *Convergència i Unió*, supported the Conservative prime minister José María Aznar. After the Socialists (PSOE) or *Partido Socialista Obrero Español* returned to power in 2004 tensions rose between the Popular Party (PP) and its erstwhile Catalan allies. The new Prime Minister Rodríguez Zapatero had publicly promised to support a new statute of autonomy for Catalonia. Hence, a vote for the so-called *Estatut d'Autonomia de Catalunya* was held in 2006. The new statute included references to a national anthem, but also—so claimed critics—impacted on the arrangement of transfers between

Table 15.3 Referendums in historic nations of Spain 1979–1980	Area	Date	Yes (%)	Turnout (%)
	Catalonia	25 October 1979	91	59
	Basque Country	25 October 1979	94	58
	Galicia	21 December 1980	78	28

Source: Departament de Polítiques Digitals i Administració Pública 1980

Catalonia and other less prosperous provinces. Second only to the richer Basque Country (GDP per capita €33,000), Catalonia is more prosperous than the average Spanish *Autonomia*. The average GDP per capita in Spain in €26,000. In Catalonia the figure is €31,000, just below the EU average of €32,000 (https://www.statista.com/statistics/327120/gdp-per-capita-in-catalonia-spain-and-eurozone/, Accessed 21 April 2020). The plan had been endorsed by all parties in the Cortes—with the exception of the centre-right *Partido Popular* which was opposed to further decentralisation, and by the Catalan republican party *Esquerra Republicana de Catalunya*, for the very opposite reasons. This was to prove fatal.

Demands for more autonomy were not limited to Catalonia. The following year, on 18 February 2007, a vote was held in Andalucía (supported by 90% on a 35% turnout). This, however, was less controversial. The same could not be said for the developments in the Basque Country.

A vote had been scheduled in the richest province of Spain for 2008 on a statute that—according to critics—amounted to de facto independence. The Basque premier Juan Ibarretxe, who was also the leader of the moderate Basque national party *Euzko Alderdi Jeltzalea* sought to fireproof himself against more radical elements of Basque nationalism. A referendum would showcase Ibarretxe's credentials as a defender of the Basque Country, especially in the eyes of those who wanted to go a good deal further than more devolution. In this case, facing something that amounted to what in Scotland is called 'Devolution Max', the referendum was denounced by both the Socialist Party and the conservative Popular Party. The two parties appealed to the high court against the decision to hold the referendum (*El Tribunal Constitucional de España*), which found in their favour. Judgement No. 103/2008 held that the Basque Parliament had acted *ultra vires* and declared 'the unconstitutionality and subsequent invalidity of the Basque Parliament Law 9/2008 of 27 June'. Mr Ibarretxe declared he respected the court ruling, while adding that the court was 'acting for political reasons disguised in a legal veneer'. The Basque leader appealed the decision to the *European Court of Human Rights*, which also found against him (*El Pais* 2010).

The focus was now on Catalonia. While the *Estatut* was endorsed by just under 74% of those voting in the referendum in 2006, the turnout was paltry, just under 50% (*El Mundo* 2006: 2). The result, like in the case of the Basque Country, was appealed in the courts, in what was becoming a pattern. The courts took their time. Finally, after four years of deliberations, *El Tribunal* ruled the Statute unconstitutional by a narrow 6-4 majority, and substantially rewrote it (see *Tribunal Constitucional* 16 June 2010). This marked a turning point. When the Partido Popular formed a government in the following year, neither side had any incentive to reach a compromise. With little support in Catalonia, Mariano Rajoy, the new Conservative Prime Minister could use the showdown with Artur Mas, the premier of Catalonia to 'solidify his base', as the term is among political consultants. Likewise, Mas, the leader of the largest Catalan party, the previously relatively moderate *Convergència Democràtica de*

Catalunya, became radicalised, not least as Rajoy's stance hardened opinion among Catalan nationalists. An estimated one million Catalans joined a protest in 2012.

When Mas failed to win a majority in the Provincial election, he was forced to rely on support from the more left-wing *Esquerra Republicana de Catalunya* (ERC). While *Convergència* and ERC had only won 44% of the vote, the disproportionality of the electoral system meant that they had a narrow parliamentary majority. They used this to organise a vote in 2014. This was declared illegal by the *Tribunal Constitucional* in October 2014. Mas instead organised a 'consultation', which went ahead despite another ruling by the highest court. On 14 November 2014, 80% of those taking part supported independence, though the turnout (which was never officially provided by the provincial government) was below 41%.

As a result of the political instability that followed, Mas established the overtly separatist party *Junts pel Sí*. However, once again the courts got involved. Mas was charged with misuse of public funds. In 2015 was found guilty and barred from holding public office for ten years. Mas's successor Carles Puigdemont swiftly moved to call yet another referendum on 9 June 2017. Seeking external support, he appealed to the European Parliament. He told the parliamentarians in Strasbourg that the Catalans aimed at 'achieving independence peacefully, in a civic way, and armed exclusively with democracy'. He also stressed that the Catalans were willing to compromise but that if the Spanish government would not give way, he would 'hold it anyway' (Puigdemont quoted in Guidi and Casula 2019: 185). Thus, while claiming to be committed to a compromise, he did not open the possibility of anything short for this, for example, reinstating the original 2006 Statute, or the possibility of a constitutional amendment that could legalise an *a fortiori* vote on independence under a new constitutional framework. Not everyone was happy with this strategy. The escalation of tensions *within* Catalan government led to the sacking of Jordi Baiget on 3 July. The minister of enterprise, and a moderate, had opposed Puigdemont's confrontational approach. Three days later, a further three ministers, were shown the proverbial door for questioning the sagacity of demanding a referendum on independence. Of greater concern, perhaps, the other European countries sided with Madrid.

The referendum was, once again, declared illegal by the Courts. But the Madrid government also used other techniques, not all of which were welcomed by international opinion. Ten days before the referendum, an estimated 10 million ballot papers were seized by *Guardia Civil*. And on the same day, 20 September, fourteen public officials including Josep Maria Jové, the Finance Secretary of Catalonia, were arrested. In a show of force that appeared heavy handed, the Madrid government deployed 16,000 police officers to interrupt the vote.

This notwithstanding, the referendum went ahead on 1 November 2017. As we saw in the introduction, the vast majority voted 'Yes'. A few weeks later the Catalan Parliament declared independence. In response, the Spanish government imposed direct rule. Puigdemont fled to Belgium and the Spanish government refused negotiations. The Spanish government received support from other capitals, while several ministers were charged with sedition. This notwithstanding, the separatist parties won a slim majority of parliamentary seats (70 out of 135 seats) in the Catalan election on 21 December 2017. But they fell short of a majority in the popular vote by securing only 47.6%. Both sides claimed a mandate and the stalemate continued.

15.4   THE LEGAL POSITION

Independence referendums are not a solid part of international law, let alone constitutional jurisprudence. As Yves Beigbeder has observed, 'The crucial requirement for self-determination plebiscites or referenda is the political will or consent of the countries concerned, their conviction that populations should not be treated as mere chattels and pawns in the game, but that their free vote should be the basis for territorial and sovereignty allocations' (Beigbeder 1994: 160).

To take the example of Scotland, although the SNP won a majority of the vote in 2011, the party was 'clearly aware that it would be democratically perverse, as well as politically and legally impossible, to try to override the legal legitimacy of the [Scotland] Act [1998] by way of an extra-constitutional referendum' (Tierney 2012: 147). This situation is not so different from the situation in Catalonia where the regionalist party *Convergencia i Unió* and its allies won an election to the *Parlament de Catalunya* on a similar pledge in November 2012—or even in more recent elections.

Hence, the situation in Catalonia mirrors patterns elsewhere. But in one sense it was unique for the exceptionally prominent role played by the courts. To be sure, in other countries too, legal arguments were prominent—not least in Canada (see below). But the recourse to the courts was exceptional. How does this aspect compare and was the Madrid government correct in following this path?

Fundamentally, very few countries have freely accepted that referendums on independence take place. The Soviet Union did not accept the secession of Latvia, Lithuania and Estonia through referendums. And the break-up of Yugoslavia, which was preceded by popular votes, was likewise rejected by Belgrade. True, neither Yugoslavia nor the Soviet Union were democratic states and might not be expected to be committed to the 'self-determination' of the peoples.

But opposition to the secession through referendums is not confined to authoritarian states. For example, in 1944 the Danish government did not accept the outcome of a referendum on independence for Iceland. And two years later, the Faroe Islands' vote for independence was rejected. After negotiations, the Danes accepted that the Faroese kept their MPs in Copenhagen but were granted legislative power in all areas except foreign affairs and defence. This deal was sealed when the Unionist Parties won the hastily organised general election to the *Lagtinget* (the Faroese legislature) shortly after the referendum (Sølvará 2003: 156).

To hold a referendum is not just a political act. It is a legal one. As such it must be held under legally accepted rules. Generally speaking, it has become an accepted norm in international relations that erstwhile colonies should be granted independence after referendums (UN Secretary-General, SG/SM/11568, GA/COL/3171). This was not always the case and this change represents a break with earlier epochs, when 'the rules governing the intercourse of states neither demand[ed] nor recognize[ed] the application of the plebiscite in the determination of sovereignty' (Mattern 1921: 171).

While referendums on independence have become more common, the overall legal position is simple, 'there is no unilateral right to secede based merely on a majority vote of the population of a given sub-division or territory' (Crawford 2006: 417). Or, as it was stated in an *obiter dicta* in a case about the legality or otherwise of Kosovo's secession from Yugoslavia, the *International Court of Justice* (ICJ), opined that 'a radically or ethnically distinct group within a state, even if it qualifies as a people for the purposes of self-determination, does not have the right to unilateral self-determination simply because it wishes to create its own separate state' (Re Kosovo 2010).

For an entity to hold a referendum on independence it must follow the established rules. The general rule is that referendums have to be held in accordance with existing constitutions (such a provision exists, for example, in Art 39(3) of the Ethiopian constitution) or following an agreement between the area that seeks secession and the larger state of which it is part (this is what happened in the very different cases of Scotland, 2014, and South Sudan, 2011). Following this logic, it was illegal for Catalonia to hold a referendum. Admittedly, the Catalans might have claimed that they were allowed the right to hold a referendum because other avenues were closed. As a legal scholar has put it:

> When the central authorities of a sovereign State persistently refuse to grant participatory rights to a religious or racial group, grossly and systematically trample upon their fundamental rights, and deny them the possibility of reaching a peaceful settlement within the framework of the State structure…a group may secede – thus exercising the most radical form of external self-determination – once it is clear that all attempts to achieve internal self-determination have failed or are destined to fail. (Cassese 1995: 119–120)

In the Catalan case, as we have seen, Puigdemont was not willing to negotiate a constitutional change. His offer of negotiation was solely about an independence referendum (Guidi and Casula 2019: 185). Hence, given that Spain is a democratic state (it scores a top-ranking One on Freedom House, for example), the rule summed up by Cassese hardly covered Catalonia. Was the referendum in the Spanish *Autonomia* consequently illegal? The answer is in the affirmative.

While the reaction of Madrid was heavy handed (and a public relations disaster), it took place within the confines of a democratic state. Legally, the Rajoy government was within its constitutional right to follow the course it chose. But it also exacerbated the situation and—speaking as an outsider—it was not conducive to solving the issue. The Madrid government was inflexible. A bit of forbearance could have solved the conflict. The *Royal Canadian Supreme Court's* judgement in the famous Re Quebec case could serve as an inspiration. The Court held that while the 'secession of Quebec from Canada cannot be accomplished...unilaterally' a referendum itself was not unconstitutional but a mechanism of gauging the will of the francophone province. Consequently, a referendum, provided it resulted in a 'clear majority', 'would confer legitimacy on the efforts of the Quebec government' (Re Quebec 1998: 385). In other words, a result in favour of secession would require the rest of Canada to negotiate with Quebec. Needless to say, this ruling does not apply in Catalonia, however the Canadian example suggests that other countries' courts have shown flexibility and appreciation of nuances that is conducive to compromises.

15.5   Conclusion

Demands for Catalan independence is a recent phenomenon. Previously, the demand had been for greater autonomy. This is what Catalan nationalists demanded (and got) after the referendum in 1931, again in 1980, and, indeed, in 2006. However, the opposition from the Popular Party hardened opinion. Playing to the anti-Catalan feeling in many parts of Spain, the PP deliberately played hard-ball, and the Catalan governments—also seeking to gain support—followed the same strategy. The Catalan referendum in 2017 is an example of how populism may stand in the way of a pragmatic solution.

Referendums are about politics as well as about law. Winning a plebiscite does not give a territory the right to establish an independent state. For that matter, winning a majority in an election is not sufficient to be entitled to hold a referendum. Yet such reasoning can become stale and legalistic, especially when it is being pursued inflexibly and with political motives—as was arguably the case when Mariano Rajoy used force to prevent the referendum and employed the law in pursuit of his goals, which (so it seems) above all was to strengthen his political party. On the other side, there was a similar lack of flexibility. Confrontation suited both sides politically. But, as far as finding a solution, the referendum on independence was not conducive to this. The closing remarks in George Orwell's *Homage to Catalonia* are apt: 'in such circumstances there can be no argument; the necessary minimum of agreement cannot be reached' (Orwell 2000: 247).

REFERENCES

Acton, Lord John Dalberg-Acton. (1906). *Lectures on Modern History*. London: Macmillan.

Balcells, A. (Ed.). (2015). *La Mancomunitat de Catalunya (1914); centennial symposium (in Catalan)*. Barcelona: Institut d'Estudis Catalans.

Beigbeder, Y. (1994). *International Monitoring of Plebiscites, Referenda and National Elections: Self-determination and Transition to Democracy*. Dordrecht: Martinus Nijhoff.

Carr, E. H. (1961). *What Is History?* London: Macmillan.

Cassese, A. (1995). *Self-Determination of the Peoples: A Legal Reappraisal*. Cambridge: Cambridge University Press.

Crawford, J. (2006). *The Creation of States in International Law* (2nd ed.). Cambridge: Cambridge University Press.

Dickens, C. (1854). *Hard Times*. New York: Harper.

Dion, S. (1996). Why Is Secession Difficult in Well-Established Democracies? Lessons from Quebec. *British Journal of Political Science, 26*(2), 269–283.

El Mundo. (2006, June 19). El Estatut sale adelante con el 74% del voto, pero la participación no llega al 50%, p. A2.

El Pais. (2010, February 23). Estrasburgo no admite el recurso del PNV sobre la anulación de la consulta soberanista, p. A1.

Guibernau, M. (2000a). Spain: Catalonia and the Basque Country. *Parliamentary Affairs, 53*(1), 55–68.

Guibernau, M. (2000b). Nationalism and Intellectuals in Nations Without States: The Catalan Case. *Political Studies, 48*(5), 989–1005.

Guidi, M., & Casula, M. (2019). The Europeanization of the Catalan Debate. In C. Closa, C. Margiotta, & G. Martinico (Eds.), *Between Democracy and Law: The Amorality of Secession* (pp. 173–192). Routledge.

Haywood, P. (1995). *The Government and Politics of Spain*. London: St Martin.

Herndon, R. W., & Murray, J. E. (2018). An Economic Interpretation of Rhode Island's 1788 Referendum on the Constitution. In J. Hall & M. Witcher (Eds.), *Public Choice Analyses of American Economic History* (Vol. 1, pp. 117–135). Berlin: Springer.

Kedouri, E. (1960). *Nationalism*. Oxford: Blackwell.

Maine, H. S. (1982 [1897]). *Popular Government*. Indianapolis: Liberty Fund.

Mattern, J. (1921). *The Employment of the Plebiscite in the Determination of Sovereignty*. Baltimore, MD: Johns Hopkins University.

Ortega y Gasset, J. (1967). *La redención de las provincias*. Madrid: Alianza Editorial.

Orwell, G. (2000). *Homage to Catalonia*. London: Penguin.

Pastor, A., & Manuel, J. (2011). El nacionalismo vasco y la deriva terrorista de ETA. In A. Pastor & J. Manuel (Eds.), *Sociedad del bienestar, vanguardias artísticas, terrorismo y contracultura* (pp. 220–221). Madrid: Dykinson.

Qvortrup, M. (2014). *Referendums and Ethnic Conflict*. Pittsburgh: University of Pennsylvania Press.

Qvortrup, M. (2015). A Brief History of Self-Determination Referendums Before 1920. *Ethnopolitics, 14*(5), 547–554.

Radan, P. (2000). Post-Secession International Borders: A Critical Analysis of the Opinions of Badinter. *Melbourne Law Review, 50*(1).

Roshwald, A. (2015). The Daily Plebiscite as Twenty-First-Century Reality? *Ethnopolitics*, *14*(5), 443–450.

Rourke, J. T., Hiskes, R. P., & Zirakzadeh, C. E. (1992). *Direct Democracy and International Politics: Deciding International Issues Through Referendums*. Boulder: Lynne Rienner.

Santos, J. (2009). *La Constitución de 1931*. Madrid: Lustel.

Sirvent, P. G. (2009). La Setmana Tràgica: una revolta política? *L'Avenç: Revista de història i cultura* (348), 32–41.

Sølvará, H. A. (2003). Færøernes Statsretlige Stilling i Historisk Belysning – Mellem selvstyre og Selvbestemmelse. *Faroese Law Review, 3*(3), 156–173.

Tierney, S. (2012). *Constitutional Referendums: The Theory and Practice of Republican Deliberation*. Oxford: Oxford University Press.

Tzortzis, I. (2016). Mirror Images: The Greek (1973) and the Spanish (1977) Reformas Pactadas in Comparison. *Journal of Contemporary European Studies, 24*(1), 101–116.

Wambaugh, S. (1919). *The Doctrine of Self-Determination: A Study of the Theory and Practice of Plebiscites* (Vol. I). Oxford: Oxford University Press.

WEBSITE

https://www.statista.com/statistics/327120/gdp-per-capita-in-catalonia-spain-and-eurozone/.

LEGISLATION

Constitución española de 1931, Art 12.

LEGAL CASES

Sentencia 31/2010, de 28 de junio de 2010 Tribunal Constitucional Pleno, BOE núm. 172, de 16 de julio de 2010.

Re Kosovo. (2010). ICJ Advisory Opinion, per Yusuf, International Law Materials, p. 1410.

Re Quebec. (1998). 161 DLR (4th) p. 385.

DIPLOMATIC SOURCES

Secretary-General, SG/SM/11568, GA/COL/3171.

CHAPTER 16

The Irish Referendums on Marriage Equality and Abortion

Theresa Reidy, Jane Suiter, Johan A. Elkink, and David Farrell

The Republic of Ireland (hereafter Ireland) is among a small group of countries which make increasing use of referendums. The state has an extensive written constitution (*Bunreacht na hÉireann*) which can only be changed by a national referendum vote. In its original draft, the constitution contained detailed clauses on the legal and political architecture of the state, social policies informed by conservative Catholic social thinking, a notional claim to the territory of Northern Ireland and an expansive interpretation of sovereignty. As elements of the constitution became outdated, referendums were necessitated to modernise the document; here Ireland's membership of the European Union is especially noteworthy in requiring a large number of referendums since 1973 (see Chapters 33, 27 and 24 by Svensson, Laffan and

T. Reidy
Department of Government and Politics, University College Cork, Cork, Ireland
e-mail: T.Reidy@ucc.ie

J. Suiter
School of Communications, Dublin City University, Dublin, Ireland
e-mail: jane.suiter@dcu.ie

J. A. Elkink · D. Farrell (✉)
School of Politics and International Relations, University College Dublin, Dublin, Ireland
e-mail: David.Farrell@ucd.ie

J. A. Elkink
e-mail: jos.elkink@ucd.ie

© The Author(s) 2021
J. Smith (ed.), *The Palgrave Handbook of European Referendums*,
https://doi.org/10.1007/978-3-030-55803-1_16

Mendez and Mendez elsewhere in this volume). Broadly, referendums fall into three categories: moral and social policy issues; international treaties affecting sovereignty; and aspects of political and legal design (Sinnott 2002). There is no provision for citizen-initiated votes. A small number of plebiscites have taken place at local level dealing with issues of local administration but these are infrequent and not legally binding.

The focus of this chapter is on constitutional referendums in Ireland. It utilises two recent referendums from the social-moral category to highlight key issues and implications in the conduct of referendum votes. The marriage referendum introduced marriage equality in 2015 and in 2018 the abortion referendum liberalised the provision of abortion services. Section 16.1 details the historical and legal background to all referendum votes. Outlining the process through which issues proceed to a referendum vote, it also documents some important changes, most especially since the 1990s. The section also includes details on the regulations and procedures relating to voting rules and provides a brief overview of the outcome of referendum votes since 1937. Section 16.2 turns to the votes on marriage and abortion and details the deliberative turn in referendum practice which was especially notable for these two votes. Section 16.3 looks at the parliamentary politics of marriage and abortion and the activities of the main campaign actors. Voting patterns in the two referendums were underpinned by value positions on the conservative-liberal cleavage in Irish politics and these dynamics are unpacked in Sect. 16.4. Collectively, these sections also highlight the ways in which campaign regulations shape public discourse at referendums and identify some regulation lacunae that have become apparent at recent votes. Finally, the chapter concludes with some reflections on the Irish referendum experience and the impact of referendum votes on the wider politics of the Irish state.

16.1   THE HISTORICAL, LEGAL AND POLITICAL FRAMEWORK FOR REFERENDUMS

Bunreacht na hÉireann was adopted by plebiscite in 1937 and there have been 40 national constitutional referendums since that date. Twenty-nine referendum proposals have been successful and eleven have been defeated. Data on the distribution of referendums across the decades are included in Fig. 16.1. The legal framework for the conduct of referendums is set out in the constitution and in a number of electoral and referendum laws. The right of initiative lies with the government which introduces a bill in parliament to trigger a referendum vote. Once the bill is passed by parliament the issue proceeds to a national vote, the outcome of which is binding. A common set of laws and regulations apply at all referendums. The referendum acts set out the specific rules governing the wording of the referendum question, the design of the ballot papers and the conduct of the voting and counting.

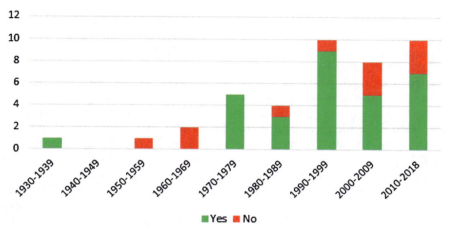

Fig. 16.1 Referendum votes in Ireland, 1937–2018 (*Source* Department of Housing, Planning and Local Government [2018])

The referendum question on the ballot paper must reference the title of the bill proposing to amend the constitution: thus voters are asked to vote Yes/No if they approve/do not approve of the XXth Amendment of the Constitution Bill, 20XX. In the past, the legalistic nature of the question wording has been criticised for being vague and obtuse and posing a challenge for voters (MacCarthaigh and Martin 2015). This may have led to the greater effort expended at recent referendums by media outlets and the government to present images of the ballot paper and describe its content in more explicit detail during news events and debates. Ballot papers are bilingual: the content is included in Irish and English.

The extent of contestation surrounding the naming of referendum proposals in public discourse varies very considerably. Some referendums simply follow the name of the international treaty under consideration (Lisbon, Nice, International Criminal Court) or the aspect of the political or legal system being amended (*Oireachtas* [parliamentary] Inquiries, Court of Appeal). However, the naming of referendums on moral and social issues has been contentious on occasion. To give an example, in 1983 the anti-abortion constitutional amendment was commonly known as the pro-life amendment, a name given to it by conservative campaign groups, and used widely in a sign of their political strength and dominance in debates. The amendment retained this epitaph in public discussions for more than three decades (Gallagher 2018; Reidy 2019). Reflecting the shift in social values, liberal groups claimed the naming rights at the 2018 referendum which sought to liberalise abortion provision and the referendum became widely known as the Repeal referendum (referring to the repeal of the clause entered into the Constitution in 1983).

The franchise at referendums is restrictive relative to most other elections: only Irish citizens, aged 18 and over who are listed on the electoral register are entitled to cast their ballots. The electoral register is updated annually but there is widespread acceptance that this process is inadequate and the register may be overestimated by as many as 500,000 voters (see O'Malley 2001). There have been calls for this role to be taken over by an electoral commission which would be in a position to give priority to voter registration. There are no provisions for out-of-country voting (except for members of the defence forces and civil servants posted abroad) but voters intending to return to reside in Ireland within 18 months may return to Ireland and cast their vote legally (Department of Foreign Affairs, n.d.). The effectiveness of this specific provision has been called into question at both the marriage and abortion referendums when there were media reports of large numbers of emigrant voters returning to Ireland to cast ballots (see Kenny 2018). As many of the electoral registers are out of date, it is possible that voters may continue to appear on the lists many years after emigrating and voters are not required to making any declaration about their entitlement to vote at polling stations.

A simple majority is required for a constitutional referendum to pass and there are no turnout requirements. Average turnout at referendums stands at 52% and has ranged from a high of 75% for the first vote (officially a plebiscite) in 1937 to a low of 29% for the vote on adoption in 1978. The overall pattern is captured in Fig. 16.2. There was a sharp increase in participation at the referendums on marriage (2015) and abortion (2018) but turnout fell again at a second referendum on the removal of the offence of blasphemy from the constitution in October 2018.

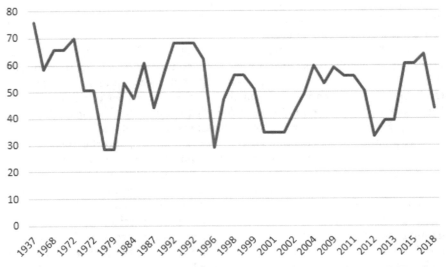

Fig. 16.2 Turnout at referendums in Ireland (*Source* Department of Housing, Planning and Local Government [2018])

The Referendum Campaign Regulation Index (Reidy and Suiter 2015) identified twenty campaign regulations relating to the role of public agencies, campaign finance and campaign communications at referendums and it applied this index to OECD countries which held referendums. Overall, Ireland was placed at the midpoint of the index in terms of the number of campaign regulations that are in place. The remainder of this section will follow the broad parameters set out in the index to identify key aspects of the regulation of referendums.

The practice of establishing a temporary Referendum Commission for each vote was initiated in 1998. It is given responsibility for providing information on the referendum question and also for promoting participation in voting. Its remit was updated in 2001 so that it now provides information on the question being decided but it does not include arguments for and against the proposal as it did in its earlier iteration. Typically, a commission is established about two months before a referendum: it sends an information notice to each household, and uses traditional and social media to share information and promote voting; in addition, the chair of the commission (a member of the judiciary) engages in media interviews. Trust in the commission is very high and it is an influential actor in each referendum campaign (Suiter and Reidy 2013). The commission has no role in resolving disputes. Legal challenges to referendum results are adjudicated by the High Court or the Supreme Court before they make their way into law. Indeed, legal challenges to referendum results have resulted in a number of very important judgements which have shaped Irish referendum law and practice: specifically, the McKenna and Coughlan judgements.[1]

The McKenna judgement arose following the 1992 Maastricht campaign when the incumbent government utilised public funds in order to campaign for a Yes vote. Opponents of the treaty criticised a decision by the state broadcaster *Raidió Teilifís Éireann* (*RTÉ*) to show a special government television appeal for a Yes vote without allowing equal airtime to the opposition campaign. A Green Party MEP, Patricia McKenna, took the case through to the Supreme Court which delivered a judgement that the government was not entitled to use public money to put forward only one side of the case. This case led to the establishment of the Referendum Commission for each future referendum.

A further judgement which has materially impacted the running of campaigns arose from a case taken by Trinity College Dublin academic Anthony Coughlan, a long-standing EU critic and participant in EU referendum campaigns. Coughlan took a case in advance of the Amsterdam Treaty referendum in 1998. The High Court found that *RTÉ*'s allocation of airtime in proportion to electoral support resulted in 'unconstitutional unfairness'

---

[1] In addition, the McCrystal judgement arose from a case taken after the Children's Rights referendum and the Supreme Court found that the government's information campaign in the referendum breached the Constitution (O'Mahony 2016).

which would be mitigated had the principle been to afford equality to each side of the argument (Carney 1998). The decision which was confirmed by the Supreme Court in 2000 has meant that in all subsequent referendums *RTÉ* and other broadcasters have allotted equal airtime to both groups, even in the face of confirmation from the Broadcasting Authority of Ireland which has stressed that a strict 'stopwatch' approach is not required, rather a broad balance. The BAI has ruled that 'fairness, objectivity and impartiality can be achieved during programming by including referendum interests from both sides of the debate. It may also be achieved effectively by input from the programme presenter playing the role of devil's advocate' (Broadcasting Authority of Ireland 2018). The BAI also stipulates that 'every broadcaster shall ensure that all news broadcast by the broadcaster is reported and presented in an objective and impartial manner and without any expression of the broadcaster's own views'. Collectively, these judgements have considerably altered the way all Irish referendums have since been conducted.

Beyond the requirement that the government may not spend public funds on one side of a campaign, there are few financial regulations pertaining to referendums. The Standards in Public Office Commission (SIPOC) is responsible for registering Third Parties (groups/persons other than political parties) at referendums that receive political donations. There are donation limits which apply at all electoral events and foreign donations are prohibited. There are no spending limits at referendums and no public funds for campaign groups.

In many jurisdictions, the funding of campaigns at referendums is controversial and this is indeed also the case in Ireland. Foreign funding of referendum activities was in the spotlight ahead of the 2018 abortion referendum. Amnesty International (Ireland) was ordered to return grant funding received from the Soros Open Society Foundation for its 'My Body My Rights' campaign in 2016 (Gleeson 2018). Amnesty contested the decision on the grounds that the grant was not used for electoral purposes and the decision was quashed by the High Court. However, the incident highlighted uncertainties in the law and prompted the EU Fundamental Rights Agency (FRA) to raise concerns about the provisions arguing that it could potentially constitute a 'blanket ban on foreign funding' of civil society groups, something which they argue is incompatible with international human rights law (ICCL 2018). Concerns were also raised that foreign funding of the pro-life campaign was quite likely (O'Loughlin 2018). It is unclear if, and/or how much funding came from US sources but there were media reports that one of the No side's strongest supporters in the US was the National Organisation for Marriage (NOM). In a letter to supporters around the world, it urged evangelical Christians to visit keepmarriage.org, which was campaigning for a No vote.

Turning to campaign communication regulations, political advertising by campaign groups and political parties in broadcast media is prohibited in Ireland. SIPOC also has the role of defining what is 'political' in terms of advertising. However, the legislation setting out the details predates the digital age and does not apply to online media. This is a significant shortcoming in the regulatory framework and one that has been highlighted by SIPOC on a number of occasions (Finn 2018). Online political advertising has been growing strongly at recent referendums, most controversially during the 2018 abortion referendum (O'Brien 2018; Field 2018). The Referendum Commission following the abortion referendum called for advertisements and posters to be regulated and to also fall under the remit of the Advertising Standards Authority (Finn 2018).

There is some argument that the broad scope of the broadcast advertising ban inhibits public engagement with policy, which means that civil society and campaign groups are often left without redress when illegitimate groups spend money to undermine their position. Specifically, under the current legislation there are few sanctions for misleading campaign messages. The government initiated a wide-ranging review of the regulation of online political advertising at the end of 2018. Reflecting the fragmented nature of the institutional oversight of elections and referendums, there were also renewed calls for the establishment of a permanent electoral commission which could subsume the roles of the referendum commission, SIPOC and the broadcasting authority and provide a more coherent, integrated framework to manage referendums.

In terms of formal referendum rules, Ireland fits the pattern in which most 'occasional to frequent' users of the referendum had a mandatory or optional constitutional referendum in their laws (Lijphart 1984: 206). The Irish constitution distinguishes between the mandatory constitutional referendum and the 'ordinary referendum' (somewhat similar to an abrogative referendum), which may be initiated by both houses of parliament on certain government bills, but only with the consent of the President of Ireland. An ordinary referendum has never taken place, but change in the composition of the *Seanad* could give this power to minorities (Bulsara and Kissane 2009). As such each of the referendums discussed in detail below was a mandatory referendum. Furthermore, the Irish constitution serves as a higher law binding on parliament—a law which cannot be changed by parliamentary majorities. And thus all referendum outcomes are binding; although the state does not always introduce legislative provisions to give them force. For example, the seventh amendment to the constitution extended voting rights to graduates of all Irish universities in the upper house of parliament (*Seanad Éireann*) but this has still not been given legislative force and only graduates of the University of Dublin and the National University of Ireland continue to have voting rights (*Oireachtas* 2015).

In many ways Irish referendum practice and regulation have changed only moderately over the last several decades. The franchise is tightly defined, referendums are mandatory to change the constitution, they are binding and can only be initiated by government. These provisions are permanent. But judgements from the courts have led to important changes in relation to balance in the allocation of broadcast airtime and determined that governments cannot spend public money on one side of a campaign. Provision for the establishment of a referendum commission and some financial regulations have delivered a partial regulatory framework, in which the gaps are becoming increasingly evident as digital technologies assume a more central role in campaigns. Perhaps the most significant evolution in referendum practice has been the deliberative turn which started in 2012.

16.2   THE DELIBERATIVE TURN IN REFERENDUM PRACTICE: MARRIAGE AND ABORTION

The marriage referendum took place in 2015 and the abortion vote occurred in 2018. The two referendums are included in the moral-social category as they both draw from fundamental values that voters hold about individual rights and social organisation. The referendums draw from a deep conservative-liberal cleavage in Irish politics which emerged from the 1960s, became a major fault line in Irish politics by the 1980s, and has tended to be intensely contested and often divisive (Elkink et al. 2017). Furthermore, social and moral referendums have tended to be politically polarising (Girvin 1993; 1994; O'Carroll 1991).

Deliberative assemblies, which were primarily made up of randomly selected citizens, started to become a feature of Irish referendums after 2012 when Irish governments began to institute formal decision-making processes into the procedures for constitutional change. The first deliberative assembly, the Constitutional Convention, was established in 2012 and considered ten issues, most notably marriage equality (for more see Farrell et al. 2017; Suiter et al. 2016). The Convention was made up of 66 randomly selected citizens and 33 politicians, the latter in proportion to their parties' representation in the parliament. There was also an independent chairman. The work programme of the convention included parliamentary reform, suffrage reform and marriage equality. Marriage equality was its most controversial topic. The convention concluded its work in March 2014.

In 2016 the government initiated a second assembly which was named the Citizens' Assembly of Ireland, this time made up of 99 randomly selected citizens (cf. Farrell et al. 2018). The assembly had a list of topics to review but most prominent among them was abortion provision. In both instances, marriage and abortion, the assemblies took a liberal position and recommended referendums be held to decide the issues. In the case of marriage equality the recommendation was accepted and agreed by the government, passed by parliament and the issue put to the people. In the case of abortion, the report of the assembly was further considered by an all-party parliamentary committee which made additional recommendations on the specifics of the abortion proposals which should be put to the people in a referendum (Elkink et al. 2020; Field 2018). The parliamentary committee also voted by a large majority in favour of a referendum to remove the ban on abortion from the constitution while also supporting significant liberalising of legislation (Suiter 2018). Thus, a noteworthy feature of both these referendums is that their pathway to the ballot paper involved a deliberative phase in a forum established by government, instituting an additional deliberative institution between the parliament and the vote (Farrell et al. 2018).

The reason for the referral of the issues to deliberative fora is unclear. But its roots lie in the Great Recession and the period of political crisis which followed the economic crash and the Troika (European Commission, European Central Bank and International Monetary Fund) bailout of Ireland at the end of the noughties. The government was keen to find ways to rebuild trust and to integrate citizens more effectively into the political process (Farrell et al. 2013). The potential of deliberative approaches to policy-making to deliver political engagement and enhance democratic politics were identified by a number of political parties, several of which included deliberative proposals in their election manifestos in 2011 (Suiter and Farrell 2011) and ultimately, the proposal for the Constitutional Convention was included in the 2011–2016 Programme for Government. The successful treatment of marriage by the Constitutional Convention and its subsequent approval in a referendum no doubt influenced the decision to replicate the deliberative phase for the abortion referendum.

The use of a deliberative phase at both referendums had both party political and electoral advantages. From a political party standpoint, both issues had the potential to wreak internal division among elected representatives. The abortion vote in 2018 was the sixth referendum question put before the people on the issue over nearly four decades, demonstrating the intractability of abortion as a political issue. Furthermore, when legislating for a minor change to the restrictive provision of abortion services in 2013, internal division within the largest party *Fine Gael* led to the expulsion of several of its TDs (MPs) and senators from the party after the representatives failed to support the legislative measure in parliament. A number of the expelled *Fine Gael* TDs and senators went on to form a new anti-abortion party, 'Renua' (although all its members would lose their seats at the next general election). The government was thus predisposed to engage in extensive consultation and deliberation as it responded to widespread calls for a referendum on abortion. Deliberation held the potential to minimise further internal division within the party and indeed, it was supported across parliament for similar reasons in other parties. Including deliberation provided an additional set piece which the media covered in advance of the referendum thus potentially it also elongated debate and discussion time on the issues involved for the public.

16.3   Parliamentary Politics and Campaign Agitation

Coalition politics played an important supporting role in the decisions to hold the marriage and abortion referendums. The Irish Labour Party has a long track record of holding progressive positions on social issues and it became a champion of change on marriage rights in the lead-up to the 2011 general election. The party leader, Eamon Gilmore, held that marriage equality was the 'civil rights issue of our time' and that the coalition government had to address the issue over its term in office. Consequently, marriage equality was included in the Programme for Government of the *Fine Gael*/Labour coalition which came to power in 2011. Government formation negotiations were also instrumental in the pathway to the ballot for the abortion referendum. Katherine Zappone, a non-party TD elected to parliament in 2016 required that abortion provision be dealt with during the term of the new minority government as a condition of her support for the government and her participation as a minister in that government. Her involvement certainly accelerated the political impetus to engage with the issue of abortion (Doyle 2016).[2] More generally, there was a sharp change in the ideological composition of the parliament in 2011. Left-leaning parties saw their support levels increase quite significantly and the new representatives were much more supportive of progressive constitutional and policy change.

Changes within parliament created an environment more conducive to movement on the issues of marriage and abortion but progress on both issues also had substantive roots in civil society campaigns conducted outside parliament. In the case of marriage equality, a quiet but sustained campaign group had worked on the issue for more than a decade and had already managed to have legislative provision for civil partnerships introduced in 2010.

Abortion had been on the agenda for women's groups since the original campaign in 1983 to have the anti-abortion clause included in the constitution. The debate on abortion during the 1983 referendum had been especially divisive and the campaign was largely conducted in the political territory of conservative campaigners, with slogans like 'Abortion is murder' predominant in the discourse. The discourse evolved markedly from the early 1990s when a series of grave legal and medical cases pushed abortion onto the political agenda once more. A child rape case where the victim requested an abortion led to a Supreme Court ruling that abortion was legal in very restricted life-endangering circumstances including the threat of suicide by the woman. Later cases would involve women with cancer, brain injury and fatal foetal abnormality. The absolutism so prevalent in 1983 came unstuck as the complexities of the issue became ever more evident in public debates. This is perhaps best encapsulated by the description of the debate at the 2002 referendum as a 'series of moral conundrums' (Kennedy 2002).

Campaign groups representing a variety of positions on abortion were established and became active in the subsequent campaigns. Thus while campaigns can vary on a spectrum from those that are intensive political episodes and mobilise large sections of the electorate to lack-lustre affairs

---

[2]This is not the first occasion in which non-party TDs were instrumental in pushing decisions on abortion. In 1997, a number of conservative non-party TDs required that a referendum be held to make abortion provision even more restrictive as a condition for their support for the minority government (see Kennedy 2002; Reidy 2020).

which mobilise only the most active and interested voters, both of these referendums were mobilising, engaging political parties, civil society groups and politically active individuals in rolling coalitions.

One piece of evidence which supports the active engagement of voters with the issues is the conclusion that both referendums involved first-order decision-making processes by voters (Elkink et al. 2017; Suiter and Reidy 2019). At both referendums, voters had high levels of knowledge on the issues involved, felt informed about their decisions and these two factors were positively associated with voting Yes (Elkink et al. 2017; 2020). Perhaps more persuasively, as voters' objective knowledge and understanding of the substantive issues increased, so did the propensity for voters to cast a ballot which was consistent with their fundamental values (Suiter and Reidy 2019). Those satisfied with the government were also more likely to have voted Yes in the abortion referendum than those not satisfied.

Both referendums also garnered relatively high degrees of support among the political parties and their elected representatives at national level. As noted above, referendums are triggered by government decision in Ireland and a majority vote in parliament is required to initiate a referendum. In both cases, a large majority of TDs supported the holding of the referendums, although it must be mentioned that the majority was significantly higher in the case of the marriage referendum. There was little public dissent within political parties on the marriage vote and all the main parties supported the referendum proposition to introduce marriage equality, although some were more enthusiastic in their campaigning than others. *Fianna Fáil*, the main opposition party, was criticised both by members and by some campaign groups for not being sufficiently active during the marriage campaign (Murphy 2016).

The abortion vote was more difficult and the centre-right parties of *Fine Gael* and *Fianna Fáil* in particular experienced greater internal division. This was managed successfully by both parties which lifted the party whip for votes and the campaign. The abortion referendum was supported strongly by parties of the left. Left-wing parties had a long history of liberal agitation. The Labour Party had campaigned against the pro-life amendment back in 1983 and was a strong advocate for change but it was parties of the far left (Anti Austerity Alliance-People Before Profit and non-party socialist TDs) that were most forceful in advocating for change in parliament in the last decade and they were also at the forefront of the Yes campaign. Nevertheless, parties did not lead either campaign. The Yes campaign was led by an umbrella campaign group which came together for the specific vote. In the marriage campaign, on the Yes side, the group was called Yes Equality, while for the abortion campaign, Together for Yes led the campaign. At the marriage referendum, the No side was more fragmented and the groups included Catholic lay organisations and the institutional Catholic Church. There was a high degree of overlap among the groups and individuals involved in both campaigns, particularly on the No (conservative) side.

At the marriage referendum, there was a strong focus on voter registration by the Yes campaign and up to 60,000 new voters were added to the register, while the campaigns also organised a mass canvass of voters in every constituency in the country. Canvassing of voters is quite typical at elections but more variable at referendums and the scale of the ground canvass for marriage equality was quite different to previous votes (Sinnott 1995; Elkink et al. 2017). A significant amount of campaign paraphernalia such as badges and stickers and t-shirts were evident during the marriage referendum and this approach was also adopted during the abortion referendum with a 'REPEAL' sweatshirt becoming ubiquitous among Yes canvassers and supporters in the closing days of the campaign (Elkink et al. 2017; 2020). Canvassing was also a prominent part of the Yes campaign for abortion.

The No side in both campaigns was more disparate. During the equal marriage campaign, only a very small number of non-party public representatives advocated a No vote. Opposition to the abortion referendum was much more organised, better funded and more active both in the pre-campaign period and during the campaign itself. There were two main groups on the No side at the abortion referendum, Love Both and Save the 8th. The public representative group included a majority of *Fianna Fáil* TDs and a small number from other parties and from the non-party group advocating for a No vote. But in general, the mainstay of the No campaigns at both referendums came from conservative lay groups. It was striking that the Catholic Church as an institution has played a much more low-key role at moral-social referendums in the twenty-first century. A multiplicity of child rape and human rights scandals have significantly eroded its position within the state and Catholic lay groups have taken a more prominent leadership position in public debates as a consequence. Interestingly, there is a sense that lay groups adopt more extreme positions than the institutional church (Scriven 2019).

The ban on broadcast advertising for all campaign groups ensures that the media continue to play a key role with much focus on national television, local and national radio and opinion pieces in the local and national media. As noted above, while political advertising is banned in mainstream legacy media, there are no such restrictions on social media. All of the political parties and the campaign groups made widespread use of social media, not only with their own accounts but also through the adoption of viral hashtags. A global heatmap of the #marref hashtag showed there was considerable international interest in the referendum, while other get out the vote messages also trended including #hometovote. This hashtag was often accompanied with pictures of voters travelling from occasionally far-flung destinations to cast their ballots. It was used approximately 72,000 times during the referendum. As already pointed out, emigrant voting is very restricted in Ireland and the enthusiasm with which citizens abroad engaged in both referendums has added additional impetus to the campaign to develop more generous and effective emigrant voting provisions. Organisations campaigning for a No also engaged on social media although they faced an uphill battle and did not garner the same attention (Murphy 2016). There were also a large number of advertisements on social media channels including Google and YouTube.

The role of ads on social media became particularly sensitive during the abortion referendum. The Transparent Referendum Initiative harvested ads from volunteers' Facebook profiles which revealed that many ads were not transparent about who had paid for them or indeed from which country the payments had originated (TRI, n.d.). Foreign donations or funding of campaigns is illegal in the referendum code. Against the backdrop of scandals surrounding the Brexit referendum and the 2016 Trump presidential election, several social media companies including Facebook and Twitter took the decision to halt or severely limit political advertising on their platforms for the duration of the abortion referendum in Ireland. In media debates, this was deemed to have had the potential to impact more significantly on the No side (Weckler 2018).

Both referendums served to neutralise long connected and contentious issues in Irish politics. Both were notable for the fact that only one electoral constituency voted against either proposal, albeit a different one in each case but both located in the western periphery, an area long associated with conservative values and traditional voting patterns. The referendums also continued an important pattern in the politics of referendums, insulating party politics from some of the most polarising effects of the conservative-liberal cleavage. Campaigns on moral and social issues have always been led by civil society groups with parties playing more low-key roles. The main political parties of *Fianna Fáil* and *Fine Gael* experienced significant internal division, especially on abortion and divorce and allowing free votes in parliament and playing supporting, rather than leading roles in campaigns, were self-preservation strategies designed to minimise splits (Sinnott 1995; Gallagher 2011).

16.3.1 Who Voted Yes?

An examination of the campaign dynamics at the marriage and abortion referendums reveals a number of important aspects. The deliberative phases in both were embraced because of the capacity to deliver consensus positions on major social issues. They also delivered longer, more informed campaigns and campaign groups had opportunities to develop and adapt their messages as the referendum campaigns drew closer. The outcome at both referendums was progressive change delivered by informed voters and the highest levels of referendum mobilisation in more than thirty years.

The evidence points to a significant liberalisation of voter values on marriage and abortion over the last four decades. What was notable about both referendums is that almost every demographic and region voted in favour, even if by small margins. There were also strong generational effects (Elkink et al. 2017). Support for both marriage equality and abortion was strongest in the youngest age cohorts and declined in the older age cohorts. There was majority support for the marriage proposal in each age cohort although at lower levels in the 65 + age group (Elkink et al. 2017). In the case of abortion, only the 65+ age cohort exhibited a conservative majority while just under 90% of those in the 18–24 age cohort voted Yes (see Elkink et al. 2020).

Religiosity is an important factor underpinning the No vote at both referendums with those who attended regular religious services more likely to have voted No to both equal marriage and abortion (Elkink et al. 2017; 2020). Finally, partisan voting patterns align with expectations. *Fianna Fáil* voters are among the most conservative and have displayed a higher tendency to vote No at both referendums. Indeed, the 2018 *RTÉ*-Universities exit poll showed that a majority of *Fianna Fáil* supporters voted against the liberalisation of abortion provision at the referendum (*RTÉ*-Universities Exit Poll, 2018). The most liberal voters are to be found among the parties of the left and the far left, although three-quarters of *Fine Gael* (centre-right) voters also voted Yes (for a more extended discussion see Elkink et al. 2020).

16.4   REFLECTIONS ON THE IRISH REFERENDUM EXPERIENCE

In 2018 the Irish state held a number of events to mark the decriminalisation of homosexuality in Ireland 25 years earlier, culminating in a formal apology issued by the *Taoiseach* (Prime Minister) in parliament. The distance that Ireland had travelled in just 25 years is striking. From having had criminal prosecution of gay men up to the early 1990s, Ireland became the first country to introduce equal marriage in a national referendum vote in 2015. Turnout at the referendum exceeded 60% and reversed a decline in interest in social and moral referendums which had been in train for nearly a decade and a half. The vote passed by a wide margin and a majority voted in favour of the proposal in all but one of the state's forty electoral constituencies.

Abortion remained a deeply divisive issue in the decades after the 1983 referendum inserted the constitutional prohibition on abortion. Again pressure for progressive reform had been building over the intervening decades, although the scale of the referendum support for liberalisation took many commentators and indeed campaigners by surprise. Polls had been pointing towards increasingly liberal views for at least a decade but there was uncertainty about whether this position would be maintained in the heat of what was expected to be a divisive campaign. Ultimately, the abortion referendum allowed the populace to give voice to a changing set of values.

The combination of the two votes suggests that the conservative predisposition so long attributed to Irish voters is no longer real or relevant. Conservative Ireland has been in retreat for some time. Not only do voters now in middle age vote in the same liberal way as they did when they were young, there has also been a move towards more liberal values among rural and working-class voters. The Catholic Church which had been a dominant institutional power broker from the foundation of the state in 1921 experienced some decline in influence from the 1960s driven by economic growth and social change. But domestic and international abuse scandals in the church contributed to the collapse in its authority from the 1990s, leaving it a marginal player in the moral-social campaigns of the early twenty-first century.

Both referendums are notable for the important role that a deliberative assembly made up of randomly selected citizens played in guiding the two issues towards referendums. The evidence collected after both votes indicates that the Constitutional Convention at the marriage referendum and the Citizens' Assembly at the abortion referendum mattered. In both cases those who were aware of, and knowledgeable about, the assemblies were more likely to vote in favour of the proposition and they also likely improved the information environment.

Referendum votes are part of the democratic process in Ireland. The campaigns feature active civil society involvement but the process requires that votes are initiated in parliament and political parties are involved in debates, often on both sides. In this sense, direct democracy votes are a complement to Ireland's representative democracy. The results of recent votes suggest that direct democracy does not always have to be divisive or deliver a tyranny of the majority which restricts rights. The cases presented here demonstrate that referendums can be structured to provide adequate information for voters, to allow time for deliberation and reflection and can deliver outcomes which are expansive, liberal and progressive.

In terms of the impact on domestic politics, these referendums served to reposition *Fine Gael* as a progressive party, moving it away from its conservative roots. During the marriage referendum, the current prime minister, Leo Varadkar, came out as gay on live radio. Prior to that he had in fact expressed doubt about progressive policies such as marriage equality and abortion. When he later took over as leader of the party the focus was firmly on a new leader of a changing country, in the mould of Emmanuel Macron or Justin Trudeau. As noted above, the party had previously lost a number of its TDs when introducing a very minimal change to abortion availability by legislation in 2013. In 2018, when proposing a referendum to introduce a significant liberalisation of abortion provision, *Fine Gael* only lost one TD. Finally, the regulatory framework at referendums is an evolutionary system. It has developed in an ad hoc manner with the impetus for change often stemming from problems identified at a previous vote. Once more the framework is in flux with changes expected to manage challenges presented by digital technologies. The framework is flexible and adaptive, but it has mostly delivered political conditions which are fair and crucially which are accepted as equitable by the vast majority of voters. Consequently, it is best to conclude that there is no ideal set of regulations but that the rules within which referendums are conducted need to be adaptable and subject to regular review and revision.

BIBLIOGRAPHY

Broadcasting Authority of Ireland. (2018). *Updated Guidelines on Referenda Coverage*. http://www.bai.ie/en/bai-publishes-updated-guidelines-on-referenda-coverage/. Accessed 21 October 2018.

Bulsara, H., & Kissane, B. (2009). Arend Lijphart and the Transformation of Irish Democracy. *West European Politics, 32*(1), 172–195.

Carney, J. (1998). *High Court Judicial Review No. 1997 209 "Anthony Coughlan vs Broadcasting Complaints Commission, RTE and the Attorney General"*.

Department of Foreign Affairs. (n.d.). *Voting in General Elections and Referendums*. Guidance. https://www.dfa.ie/global-irish/support-overseas/voting-in-referendums/. Accessed 21 October 2018.

Department of Housing, Planning and Local Government. (2018). *Referendum Results 1937–2018*. Dublin: Department of Housing, Planning and Local Government.

Doyle, K. (2016). Kenny Risks Independent Support With Abortion Plan. *Irish Independent*. https://www.pressreader.com/ireland/irish-independent/20160412/283128543016466.

Elkink, J. A., Farrell, D. M., Marien, S., Reidy, T., & Suiter, J. (2020). The Death of Conservative Ireland? The 2018 Abortion Referendum. *Electoral Studies*. 65, 102–142.

Elkink, J. A., Farrell, D. M., Reidy, T., & Suiter, J. (2017). Understanding the 2015 Marriage Referendum in Ireland: Context, Campaign, and Conservative Ireland. *Irish Political Studies, 32*(3), 361–381.

Farrell, D., Harris, C., & Suiter, J. (2017). Bringing People Into the Heart of Constitutional Design: The Irish Constitutional Convention of 2012–14. In X. Contiades & A. Fotiadou (Eds.), *Participatory Constitutional Change: The People as Amenders of the Constitution*. London: Routledge.

Farrell, D. M., O'Malley, E., & Suiter, J. (2013). Deliberative Democracy in Action Irish-Style: The 2011 We the Citizens Pilot Citizens' Assembly. *Irish Political Studies, 28*(1), 99–113.

Farrell, D. M., Suiter, J., & Harris, C., (2018). 'Systematizing' Constitutional Deliberation: The 2016–18 Citizens' Assembly in Ireland. *Irish Political Studies, 34*(1), 113–123.

Field, L. (2018). The Abortion Referendum of 2018 and a Timeline of Abortion Politics in Ireland to Date. *Irish Political Studies, 33*(4), 608–628.

Finn, C. (2018). Social Media Ad Regulations Should be Drawn Up for Future Referendums, Commission. *The Journal*. https://www.thejournal.ie/referendum-adverts-4338077-Nov2018/?utm_source=twitter_short. Accessed 14 November 2018.

Gallagher, M. (2011). Parties and Referendums in Ireland 1937–2011. *Irish Political Studies, 26*(4), 535–544.

Gallagher, M. (2018). *On the Second 8th Amendment Referendum, May 2018*. https://politicalreform.ie/author/mgallag7/. Accessed 24 July 2019.

Girvin, B. (1993). The Referendums on Abortion 1992. *Irish Political Studies, 8*(1), 118–124.

Girvin, B. (1994). Moral Politics and the Irish Abortion Referendums, 1992. *Parliamentary Affairs, 47*(2), 203–221.

Gleeson, C. (2018). Amnesty Insists Soros Funding Not For Use in Referendum Campaign. *The Irish Times*. https://www.irishtimes.com/news/social-affairs/

amnesty-insists-soros-funding-not-for-use-in-referendum-campaign-1.3457104. Accessed 19 November 2018.

Irish Council for Civil Liberties. (2018). *Electoral Act Stifling NGOs Says EU Rights Agency.* https://www.iccl.ie/human-rights/civil-society/electoral-act-stifling-ngos-says-eu-rights-agency/. Accessed 18 October 2018.

Kennedy, F. (2002). Report—Abortion Referendum 2002. *Irish Political Studies, 17*(1), 114–128.

Kenny, C. (2018). Why Must Emigrants Still Come Home to Vote? *The Irish Times.* https://www.irishtimes.com/life-and-style/abroad/why-must-emigrants-still-come-home-to-vote-1.3513919. Accessed 24 July 2019.

Lijphart, A. (1984). *Democracies: Patterns of Majoritarian and Consensus Government in Twenty-One Countries.* New Haven, CT and London: Yale University Press.

MacCarthaigh, M., & Martin, S. (2015). Bicameralism in the Republic of Ireland: The Seanad Abolition Referendum. *Irish Political Studies, 30*(1), 121–131.

Murphy, Y. (2016). The Marriage Equality Referendum 2015. *Irish Political Studies, 31*(2), 315–330.

O'Brien, C. (2018). Facebook Bans Foreign Ads for Eighth Amendment Referendum. *The Irish Times.* https://www.irishtimes.com/business/technology/facebook-bans-foreign-ads-for-eighth-amendment-referendum-1.3487895. Accessed 19 November 2018.

O'Carroll, J. P. (1991). Bishops, Knights—and Pawns? Traditional Thought and the Irish Abortion Referendum Debate of 1983. *Irish Political Studies, 6*(1), 53–71.

O'Loughlin, E. (2018). As Irish Abortion Vote Nears, Fears of Foreign Influence Rise. *New York Times.* https://www.nytimes.com/2018/03/26/world/europe/ireland-us-abortion-referendum.html. Accessed 19 November 201.

O'Mahony, C. (2016). Falling Short of Expectations: The 2012 Children Amendment, From Drafting to Referendum. *Irish Political Studies, 31*(2), 252–281.

O'Malley, E. (2001). Apathy or Error? Questioning the Irish Register of Electors. *Irish Political Studies, 16*(1), 215–224.

Oireachtas. (2015). *Report of the Oireachtas Working Group on Seanad Reform.* https://merrionstreet.ie/en/ImageLibrary/20150413SeanadReformFinal1.pdf#page=7. Accessed 14 November 2018.

Reidy, T. (2019). Abortion 2018: Over Before It Began. In K. Browne & S. Calkin (Eds.), *After Repeal: Rethinking Abortion Politics.* London: Zed Books.

Reidy, T., & Suiter, J. (2015). Do Rules Matter? Categorizing the Regulation of Referendum Campaigns. *Electoral Studies, 38*(2), 159–169.

Scriven, R. (2019). Placing the Catholic Church: The Moral Landscape of Repealing the 8th. In S. Calkin & K. Browne (Eds.), *After Repeal: Reflections and Futures.* London: Zed Books.

Sinnott, R. (1995). *Irish Voters Decide.* London: Manchester University Press.

Sinnott, R. (2002). Cleavages, Parties and Referendums: Relationships Between Representative and Direct Democracy in the Republic of Ireland. *European Journal of Political Research, 41*(6), 811–826.

Suiter, J. (2018). Deliberation in Action–Ireland's Abortion Referendum. *Political Insight, 9*(3), 30–32.

Suiter, J., & Farrell, D. M. (2011). The Parties' Manifestos. In *How Ireland Voted* (pp. 29–46). London: Palgrave Macmillan.

Suiter, J., & Reidy, T. (2013). It's the Campaign Learning Stupid: An Examination of a Volatile Irish Referendum. *Parliamentary Affairs, 68*(1), 182–202.

Suiter, J., & Reidy, T. (2019). Deliberation Meets Direct Democracy: Evidence From Irish Referendum Votes. *Representation*, 1–19.

Suiter, J., Farrell, D. M., & Harris, C. (2016). The Irish Constitutional Convention: A case of 'high legitimacy'? In M. Reuchamps & J. Suiter (Eds.), *Constitutional Deliberative Democracy in Europe* (pp. 33–54). Colchester, Essex: ECPR Press.

Transparent Referendum Initiative. (n.d.). http://tref.ie/. Accessed 14 November 2018.

Weckler, A. (2018). Google Ad Ban 'Is an Attempt to Rig Vote', Claim No Campaigners. *Irish Independent*. https://www.independent.ie/irish-news/abortion-referendum/google-ad-ban-is-an-attempt-to-rig-vote-claim-no-campaigners-36892220.html. Accessed: 24 July 2019.

CHAPTER 17

Referenda and Constitutional Change in Italy—The Failed Change

P. V. Uleri

Out of the crooked timber of humanity, no straight thing was ever made
  (Immanuel Kant)

17.1   REFERENDA WITHIN A LIBERAL-CONSTITUTIONAL DEMOCRACY[1]

17.1.1   'Reform' of the Constitution: An Ancient Debate and the Other Side the Medal

On 1 January 2020 the Italian Constitution turned 72. The main theme of this chapter is the referendum of 4 December 2016 on the constitutional revision approved by the Italian Parliament in April 2016 and clearly rejected by the majority of the voters (59.1% voting No on a turnout of 65.5%).

[1] In line with Ackerman (2019: 12), Sartori (1987: 112), Sundquist (1986: 233), I use the term referenda rather than referendums to designate in a generic way the variety of the Italian experience constituted by a multiplicity of popular votes, promoted with different procedures by different actors; pace Butler and Ranney (1978: 4–5).

In memoriam of Hans Daalder and Peter Mair.

P. V. Uleri (✉)
University of Florence (formerly), Firenze FI, Italy

J. Smith (ed.), *The Palgrave Handbook of European Referendums*,
https://doi.org/10.1007/978-3-030-55803-1_17

The constitutional law was the culmination of attempts to revise the Constitution which lasted around forty years (Fusaro 2015; Sicardi 2015; Volpi 2015; Sobrino 2017). The main stages were three bicameral commissions for institutional reforms: Bozzi (1983–1985), De Mita-Iotti (1992–1994) and D'Alema (1997–1998). The next steps were constitutional changes ('reforms') approved by centre-left (2001 and 2016) and centre-right (2005) majorities and the related facultative referenda (2001, 2006 and 2016). A fourth referendum to revise the constitution took place on 20–21 September 2020.

The 2016 constitutional referendum was a 'non-arrival' point in a long and gruelling political debate and confrontation which remained open and unsolved after almost forty years (Bartolini 1982; Lombardo 1984).[2] 'Constitutional reform', 'electoral law', 'transition', 'referendum' among others were the recurring words and themes of the debate (Pasquino 2000, 2010).[3] The magic word of those political events was *transition*. After decades of debates and attempts starting in 1980, we can say that the endless 'transition' is not over yet; the popular vote of December 2016 was a 'missed transition' (Gentiloni Silveri 2019: 293–337).

Parallel and closely related to the debates on institutional reforms were changes to the electoral laws aiming to reduce party fragmentation in order to increase the stability of government coalitions (Amato 1980; Barbera 1991; Luciani and Volpi 1992, 1995; Pasquino 1980, 1982, 1985; Regalia 2015; Fusaro 2016: 83–95). The intertwining of the events relating to institutional-constitutional reforms and the change in electoral laws constitutes an inextricable tangle: Gordio's knot has not yet been resolved.

In 1991 the electors voted on a referendum question to repeal multiple preference voting at Chamber of Deputies elections (Barbera and Morrone 2003: 115–131). The previous year, the non-campaign for voting on three ecological abrogation initiatives to limit hunting was successful: the voter *quorum* was not met and the voting results declared invalid. In 1991 things went differently. Turnout was 62.5%; the favourable votes were 95.6%. The issue of multiple preferences was relatively secondary to the more general issue of changing electoral laws, but had taken on a symbolic value; the 'plebiscitary' outcome was a surprise for both promoters and opponents.[4] In 1993 an abrogative *initiative* brought about an important change in the electoral laws for the Chamber of Deputies and for the Senate (with the shift from a proportional system to a mixed-plurality system). It was a crucial political event in Italian political history and in particular in the debate and political

---

[2]Despite the date of publication, Bartolini's article is still extremely helpful in understanding the origins of the topic and the logic of institutional reforms; see his distinction between three types of reforms: *restorative, adaptive and transformative* (p. 204 and following); also very helpful is Lombardo's book, which provides a broad theoretical analysis.

[3]Pasquino's book is an essential dictionary of Italian politics.

[4]For further detail, see Barbera and Morrone (2003: 115–169), Pasquino (2000, new ed. 2010: 171–178), Uleri (1994: 410–417), Uleri (1996: 115–117).

experience related to institutional and constitutional reforms. The referendum of December 2016 did not concern the electoral laws for Parliament. 'It would however be unreasonable to deny that there is a precise, conscious and deliberately pursued link between constitutional reform and electoral law'; in fact, the electoral laws of 1993 were not '... supported by consistent contextual constitutional revisions' (Fusaro 2016: 83–84).

After the 1993 referendum, while Parliament discussed the new electoral laws, the President of the Republic Oscar Luigi Scalfaro said that Parliament had to pass the new laws 'under dictation' of the referendum vote. Was the intervention of the President legitimate? How significant was the President's intervention on Parliament's decisions regarding the new electoral laws? In 1993, citizens voted on eight repeal questions, all of which they approved. One question related to a part of the state party funding law. The Yes to the repeal won with 90% (turnout 77%). Parliament passed a new law that circumvented the outcome of the popular vote (Barbera and Morrone 2003: 141–146). The President of the Republic did not pronounce himself and neither did the Constitutional Court.

In 1999 and 2000, two further repeal referenda were held to change the electoral law passed after the 1993 vote. The aim was to repeal the residual part of the proportional formula to switch to a uninominal majority system. On both occasions, albeit in rather different circumstances, the quorum was not achieved.[5] The outcome of those votes had significant repercussions on the political events that concluded with the vote of December 2016 on the constitutional reform. Between 1993 and 2018 four electoral laws were passed by Parliament for the election of the Parliament (Chiaramonte and D'Alimonte 2018), of which two were declared unconstitutional by the Constitutional Court.[6] Between 1990 and 2009 there were seventeen requests for abrogative referenda on electoral laws. Electors voted on eight abrogative requests, the last time in 2009. (By way of comparison and evaluation, we may remember that in Switzerland, three 'popular initiatives' in twenty years [1900, 1910 and 1918] were enough for the Socialist Party to obtain the adoption of a proportional electoral law for the election of the members of the National Council).

[5]The 1999 vote deserves special mention. In 1999, the quorum was not reached by a few tens of thousands of votes. In the weeks following the vote, the organizing committee raised the problem of non-updated electoral rolls, notably in the municipalities of southern Italy, especially as regards persons who had emigrated decades ago and, in the meanwhile, almost certainly died. Moreover, many of those people had not been sent the electoral certificates necessary to be allowed to vote.

[6]The two laws passed in 2005 and 2015 were declared partially unconstitutional in January 2014 and in February 2017, respectively. The parliament (2013–2018) that approved the constitutional law in 2016 had itself been elected under the 2005 electoral law, declared unconstitutional in January 2014. Opponents of the constitutional law passed in 2016 believed that Parliament was not entitled to discuss and approve a constitutional reform law.

According to some constitutionalists, the holding of the 1993 referendum and the subsequent approval of the new electoral laws (1993) for the Chamber and the Senate constituted a *vulnus* to the Constitution conceived and based on the principle of proportional representation (Luciani and Volpi 1995). According to this interpretation, Art. 138 had been conceived to protect minorities and presupposes a parliament elected with proportional laws (Zagrebelsky 1996: 246–247). This explains the lack of a *quorum* of voters (and of any other type) for the validity of the vote in the referenda called pursuant to Art. 138, unlike the provisions of Art. 75 for repealing referenda.

17.1.2   The Political Context, Parties and Party System: From the 'Golden Age' of Party Democracy to the 'Apocalypse' of Democracy

It is necessary at least to outline a minimum framework of the Italian political events that occurred between 1989 and 1994, and then the electoral cycle for the Italian Parliament (2013–2018) and that for the European Parliament (2014–2019). Republican democracy is born and grows as a 'Republic of the parties' (Scoppola 1997); for about half a century (1943–1992) the parties were the central and undisputed protagonists of the working of the Italian democracy (Cotta 2015; Mershon 2015; Ignazi 2018). What had been the 'Republic of the Parties' collapses and disappears in the short span of a few years. In the early 1990s, the main parties that founded republican democracy and its party system disappear. For this reason, that change is often inappropriately identified as the birth of the so-called 'Second Republic', even though the written Constitution has remained the same.

A plurality of factors determines the collapse of that political regime. First, in time but also in importance, the collapse of the Berlin Wall and of the communist regimes in the Soviet Union and in the countries of Central and Eastern Europe. It is worth mentioning the presence and political, social and cultural strength of the Italian Communist Party; in none of the other European democracies was there in those years a communist party comparable to the Italian one. After the collapse of the Berlin Wall and the communist regimes, the two parties of the left, socialist and communist, were unable to close the divide that occurred in January 1921 on the occasion of the 17th Congress of the Socialist Party (Colarizi and Gervasoni 2005).

Excluding the specific situation of the Federal Republic of Germany, in no European democracy did the events following the collapse of the Berlin Wall trigger political processes similar to the Italian ones (Gentiloni Silveri 2019: 247–292). As Di Nolfo (1996: 15), one of the most authoritative Italian scholars in the history of international relations, wrote '… until the mid-eighties, the international structure became the reference point to which many explanations of Italian domestic life must be traced'.

As for internal affairs, corruption events known as 'Tangentopoli' and 'Clean Hands' (Rhodes 2015) must be mentioned; those events were characterized by waves of judicial and popular Jacobinism. It is also necessary to underline the change in the power relations between politics and the judiciary. According to Guarnieri (2015: 129): '...since the 1980s, the conflict between the courts and the institutions in Italy – that is, goverment and parliament – has been a permanent trait of the political landascape'. The origins of those conflicts went back in time, before the 1980s. With reference to the events of 'Tangentopoli' and 'Clean Hands', Violante (2018) wrote: 'The public prosecutor's offices determined, with a high arbitrariness rate, the winners, the survivors and the defeated ....'.[7] According to Gentiloni Silveri (2019: 257) those events determined a '... general climate [which] calls into question the basic foundations of the rule of law'. The conclusions of an authoritative exponent of the judiciary are somewhat different. In fact, Bruti Liberati (2018: 331–334) writes about '... some excesses (in particular in the use of pre-trial detention in prison) .... (of) ... painful and tragic personal events. But the story of clean hands is not a story of excesses and errors'; the legacy of those events is positive despite negative aspects such as '...corporate closure ... and judicial populism [which] can be devastating ...'.

Finally, we must remember the bloody challenge against the state, by the mafia and other criminal organizations, symbolized by the assassinations of magistrates [8] and law enforcement women and men, and attacks on symbolic places in some of the main cities (Paoli 2015). In a volume on *Fifty years of the Italian Republic* (Neppi Modona 1996), Violante (1996: 145) in a short article entitled: *Italy of illegal powers*, concludes the first short paragraph, *Facts and figures*, with these words: 'Italy is the modern homeland of political murder', in advanced and developed countries.

The 2016 referendum is a constituent part of political processes that marked Italian politics with the 2013 and 2018 elections. Those two elections ended the political system that had formed since the 1994/1996 elections. The campaign for the referendum vote is part of the political conflicts and electoral competitions held between 2013 and 2018. Those two elections shocked Italian political life like earthquakes (Diamanti et al. 2013; Chiaramonte and De Sio 2014; Fondazione di Ricerca Istituto Carlo Cattaneo 2018; Chiaramonte and De Sio 2019).[9] Those elections were interpreted as the *apocalypse* of Italian democracy, in the sense of unveiling the crisis of authority of the parties that governed from 1994 until the economic and financial crises of

---

[7] Quoted in Gentiloni Silveri (2019: 257–258). Violante, an authoritative personality in Italian political life, has been a magistrate, university professor, deputy from 1979 to 2008, President of the Chamber of Deputies (1996–2001); initially elected on the lists of the Communist Party and then of the center-left alliances. He contributed to the debate on constitutional reforms with a proposal, the so-called 'Lodo Violante', and supported the 2016 constitutional reform.

[8] Rosario Livatino, Francesca Morvillo, Paolo Borsellino and Giovanni Falcone.

[9] The copyright of the expression 'electoral earthquake' belongs to Celso Ghini (1976), an official of the Communist party and head of the PCI Electoral Office; after the regional elections of 1975 and parliamentary elections of 1976 in which the PCI had reported significant successes, in 1976 he published a book entitled *Il Terremoto del 15 giugno* (*The earthquake of 15 June*).

2008 and 2011–2012 (Schadee et al. 2019). According to Chiaramonte and Emanuele (2019: 263–264): 'That of the period 2013–2018 is … a change comparable … to what happened in the historical passage between the First and Second Republic'. Chiaramonte and Emanuele refer to political events which took place in the years 1991–1996: two abrogative referendums on electoral laws (1991 and 1993), the approval in Parliament of the new electoral laws and the elections of 1994 and 1996.

The debate on reforms began between the late 1970s and early 1980s. A word absent from Pasquino's two volumes is 'crisis' (Graziano and Tarrow 1979); a word and a concept, perhaps abused, but recurring: '*Republican Italy in the crisis of the 1970s*' is the title of an authoritative four-volume work.[10] With reference to the political events of the 1970s, it is necessary to mention the kidnapping and assassination, between 16 March and 9 May 1978, by a terrorist group called 'Red Brigades', of Aldo Moro, leader of the DC. A tragic story that leaves a profound mark on civil and political life. 'With Moro's death, a page of Italian history is definitively closed' (Craveri 1995: 775).[11]

17.1.3   Democratizations and Referenda Experiences

The democratization processes that affected Europe at different times during the twentieth century gave rise to political-institutional contexts favourable to the institutionalization of the referenda phenomenon. According to a hypothesis based on the democratization thresholds proposed by Rokkan, the institutionalization of referenda in Italian republican democracy can be interpreted as the product of pressures from above and from within the system; that is, from conflicts between elites and from conflicts within the dominant coalition founding the democratic regime (Uleri 1994: 403–406; 1996: 110–111; 2003: 21–55).

From the 1970s, the Italian national referendum experience was probably the most significant, in the context of European democracies, particularly those of an older and more stable consolidation, apart from Switzerland and Liechtenstein, of course,[12] both for the number of issues voted on and for the fact that electors can sign requests to activate referenda procedures. The canvas of republican representative democracy favoured this referenda experience.

[10]Ministero per i Beni e le Attività Culturali (2003, 2003a, 2003b) in the third and fourth volumes (respectively dedicated to '*Parties and mass organizations*' and '*Political system and institutions*') the deep roots of the 'crisis' that manifested itself in the early-1990s are analyzed.

[11]A long previous chapter is entitled 'First serious symptoms of involution of the political-institutional system' (Craveri 1995: 489–633); 'The funeral of the Republic' is the title of the chapter dedicated to those events in Gentiloni Silveri (2019: 155–200).

[12]For further details on national referenda, see Barbera and Morrone 2003; Uleri (1996, 2002, 2012); on regional and municipal referenda experience, Uleri (2008); and on municipal referenda Uleri (2010).

Institutions such as Parliament, the Constitutional Court[13] and Presidency of the Republic, parties and movements wove the fabric of liberal-constitutional democracy in which referendum events have intertwined.[14]

Between 1970 and 2019, electors were called to the polls seventeen times: twice between 1970 and 1979; three times between 1980 and 1989; six times between 1990 and 1999; six times between 2000 and 2019 (see Table 17.1). Seventy issues have been voted on by electors: 67 took the form of abrogative referenda on ordinary laws (ex Article 75 Const.), while only three were referenda to ratify or reject constitutional changes already passed by Parliament but not yet entered into force (ex art. 138 Const.). The first popular vote to abrogate a law was requested in 1971 and held in 1974, the most recent one was held in Spring 2016. The first referendum on a constitutional law took place in 2001; the other two votes took place in 2006 and 2016.[15]

Constitutional referenda in Italy are facultative and refer only to constitutional laws approved by Parliament without achieving a qualified majority. Requests for such referenda must be submitted within three months of the date of approval in Parliament.[16] The popular vote of December 2016 to ratify or reject the amended parts of the Constitution was more hotly contested than the two previous constitutional votes (Table 17.2).

17.1.4   Types of Initiatives and Referendums

Referenda may be classified into two general classes: *decision-controlling* and *decision-promoting*. The referenda foreseen by articles 75 and 138 of the Constitution are both of the first type, but with a difference. Referenda pursuant to art. 75 repeal laws already in force; referenda pursuant to art. 138 decide whether a constitutional law approved by Parliament without a qualified majority will enter into force or not.

I draw a distinction between the terms *initiative* and *referendum* to reflect whether the popular vote is called for by the voters or institutional actors. Those votes arising from the signatures of the voters are termed *initiatives* and those asked by institutional actors *referendums*. This differs from mainstream use, but it is more corresponding to the elementary rules of classification, if

[13]The Constitutional Court is an important player in the *abrogative referenda game*. A constitutional law (1953) established that all requests for abrogative referenda must be examined by the Court to determine whether they are admissible or not. The Court has declared about half of the requests for repeal referenda as inadmissible (Luciani 2005: 322–524; Guarnieri 2015: 128–129).

[14]To better frame the issues that I mention in the chapter, allow me to point out two reference texts for politics in Italy: Cotta and Verzichelli (2007), Jones and Pasquino (2015); plus a text devoted to constitutional change in comparative perspective, Oliver and Fusaro (2011).

[15]A fourth constitutional referendum which should have taken place in March 2020 was postponed because of the Coronavirus crisis (see 17.3.4).

[16]For a legal analysis of the institution envisaged by Art. 138 see Fontana (2012) who also briefly illustrates the cases of the referenda of 2001 and 2006.

Table 17.1 Constitutional referenda held according to Art. 138 of the Italian Constitution (1948–2020)

Date	7 October 2001	25 June 2006	4 December 2016	20–21 September 2020
Question	Do you approve the text of the constitutional law concerning 'Amendments to Title V of the second part of the Constitution' approved by Parliament…?	'Do you approve the text of the Constitutional Law concerning "Amendments to Part II of the Constitution" approved by Parliament…?'	'Do you approve the text of the constitutional law concerning "Provisions for overcoming the equal bicameralism, the reduction of the number of parliamentarians, the containment of the operating costs of the institutions, the suppression of the CNEL and the revision of the title V of part II of the Constitution" approved by Parliament…?'	"Do you approve the text of the constitutional law concerning "Amendments to articles 56, 57 and 59 of the Constitution regarding the reduction of the number of parliamentarians", approved by Parliament and published in the Official Gazette of the Italian Republic n.240 of 12 October 2019?"
Electors (1)	49,462,222	49,772,506	50,773,284	50,953,114
Electors (2)		47,120776	46,720,943	49,462,222
People voting No. (turnout %) (1)	16,843,420 (34.05%)	26,110,925 (52.46%)	33,244,258 (65.48%)	16,843,420 (34.05%)
Valid votes (1)	16,250,101	25,753,782	32,852,112	16,250,101
Non valid votes (1)	593,319	357,143	392,146	593,319
Yes (1)	10,433,574 (64.21%)	9,970,513 (38.71%)	13,431,087 (40.88%)	10,433,574 (64.21%)
No (1)	5,816,527 (35.79%)	15,783,269 (61.29%)	19,421,025 (59.12%)	5,816,527 (35.79%)

(1) In Italy and abroad; (2) In Italy. *Source* Processing by the Author on data from Ministry of the Interior on-line Archive

we choose the *promoter* of the referenda procedure as *fundamentum divisionis* of the classification itself.

Another type of popular vote, the *plebiscite*, is also part of modern and contemporary history of the referendum phenomenon. Some 'plebiscites' played a role in the mid-nineteenth century in events relating to the construction of Italian national state (Danelon Vasoli 1968; Fimiani 2010,

2017; Fruci 2005, 2007, 2010). The fascist regime also resorted to two electoral-plebiscitary hybrid votes.

I refer to the Italian referenda institutes in a minimum typology of four types, both *initiatives* and *referendums*. The Constitution provides procedures that can be activated both with requests signed by at least 500,000 voters, and procedures activated by institutional actors such as regional Councils and Members of Parliament. The scheme aims to frame the Italian referendum experience in a perspective of comparative analysis; it could be much more complex considering further criteria of analysis and classification (Figs. 17.1 and 17.2).

According to Butler and Ranney (1978: 23–24, emphasis added): 'there are several different species of the genus "referendum" and ...they vary from one another mainly in the degree to which they remove control over the making of laws *from elected representatives and transfer it to ordinary electors*'. It is a fundamental criterion for the classification and typology of referenda that I have kept in mind since my first work. It goes without saying that this 'removal of the control' can only be conceived in political systems based on representative government, or in contexts of political transition towards the establishment of representative democratic regimes. European liberal-constitutional representative democracies constitute the horizon of the comparison of the referenda phenomenon in Italy Figs. 17.1 and 17.2.

The basic scheme in Fig. 17.1 is part of a taxonomy (Fig. 17.2) formulated and illustrated in detail in previous publications from 1981 onwards (Uleri 1981: 67; 1985: 217). Both schemes are designed for the analysis of referendum experiences in countries that can be classified as consolidated constitutional liberal democracies; these experiences must be clearly separated from experiences that take place in countries that cannot be classified as democratic.[17] In the latter countries, the use of the term *plebiscite* is more appropriate for popular votes (both 'electoral' and 'referenda' types) which take place without effective, free and fair competition among a plurality of political groups and independent sources of information and with the exercise of intimidation and violence among opponents.

The modern use of the term *plebiscite* cannot be separated from the historical and political analysis of the entire French experience, from the Revolution to the present day. From the votes in France in 1793 and 1795 until 1870 and beyond in Germany and Italy in the first half of the twentieth century, there are two centuries of history and events, political and human, which should be

---

[17] *Pace* Butler and Ranney (1978: 227) and others.

Table 17.2   Abrogative referenda in Italy (1948–2020)

Abrogative initiatives and referendums	1970–1979 N°	1980–1989[a] N°	1990–1999[b] N°	2000–2009 N°	2010–2019 N°	1970–2020 N°
Abrogation requests promoted	10	27	92	12	15	156
Abrogation requests judged by the Constitutional Court	10	27	90	12	15	154
Request for abrogation allowed by the Constitutional Court	6	17	42	7	6	78
Abrogation requests deemed inadmissible by the Constitutional Court	4	10	48	5	9	76
Abrogation requests decided by Parliament before the popular vote	3	3	6	0	1	12
Abrogation requests voted by electors	3	11	32	16	5	67
Abrogation requests approved by electors	0	5	14	0	4	23
Abrogation requests rejected by electors	3	6	7	0	0	16

(continued)

Table 17.2   (continued)

Abrogative initiatives and referendums	1970–1979 N°	1980–1989ᵃ N°	1990–1999ᵇ N°	2000–2009 N°	2010–2019 N°	1970–2020 N°
Votes declared invalid due to lack of quorum (50% + 1) of the members on the electoral roll	0	0	11	16	1	28

Source Author's elaboration; ᵃ3 requests were voted in 1990; ᵇ9 requests were voted in 2000

given adequate consideration and respect.[18] Plebiscites have been an instrument for mobilizing the consensus of the masses in the context of a modern political phenomenon such as Bonapartism.[19]

Bonapartism is characterized by an illiberal and authoritarian conception of democracy. As Grimm (2012: 119) notes: 'The various Napoleonic constitutions preserved the form of constitutional rule, but were not intended to limit the power of the ruler. ......With the Napoleonic constitutions France departed from the liberal-democratic path'. Meanwhile, Rosanvallon (1992: 302) observed: 'The same anti-liberal thread - in the strict philosophical meaning of rejection of pluralism ... crosses the various fields of French culture. The spirit of spring 1848 remains ... faithful to that of Jacobinism'.

Plebiscites are expressions of non liberal-constitutional democratic political regimes[20]; Desző (2001: 265) clearly grasps the problem, while Trechsel and Esposito (2011) miss it. I consider the generalized use of the term *plebiscite* for all 'top-down' referenda in the context of democratic liberal-constitutional regimes to be a conceptual error, source of wrong analysis, perhaps arising

---

[18]The notion of 'plebiscite' as well as the distinction between plebiscite and referendum is as controversial as it is interesting. With reference to the French experience, the fine work by Denquin (1976) seems to me fundamental; Bortoli (1965) does not use the term plebiscite in his quite interesting study of the referenda from 1945 to 1962. The literature is very rich, see for example Bluche (2000). A quite interesting historical and comparative perspective for the European experience is that proposed by Fimiani (2017). Johnson (1981: 20) makes both concise and insightful considerations on the distinction between plebiscite and referendum. I wrote just a short note, Uleri (2000).

[19]The French experience is crucial for the comparative study of referenda. I dedicated two chapters to it (Uleri 2003: 143–201).

[20]A confirmation is found in the work of Altman (2011: 88–109) who extensively uses the term plebiscite in the chapter entitled 'Direct Democracy within nondemocratic Regimes'. The title of the chapter is a perfect example of *contradictio in adiecto*.

Types of decisional procedure: a) to control a decision b) to promote a decision / The actors who start the procedure	Decision-controlling procedure (X ≠ Y)* The actors who start the procedure for a popular vote intend to reject or repeal a law (decision) taken by a different actor (generally a representative assembly)	Decision-promoting procedure (X = Y)* The actor who initiates the procedure for a popular vote, at the same time formulates the proposal that will be submitted to the popular vote for the adoption of a 'law or a political decision'
Electors (by collecting signatures of at least 500,000 electors)	**Controlling-initiative** a) To confirm or repeal 'a decision' (statute) (art. 75 Const., request subscribed by 500,000 electors) – *Quoruom* 50% + 1 registered electors. b) To confirm or reject 'a decision' (constitutional law) not yet enforced (art. 138 Const., request subscribed by 500,000 electors) – No *Quorum*	**Promoting-initiative** To adopt 'a decision' (statute) ex-novo (Constitutional reform proposal under discussion in Parliament, 2019-20)
Institutional actors (a minority of Regional Councils – a minority of Members of Parliament)	**Controlling-referendum** a) To confirm or repeal 'a decision' (statute) (art. 75 Const., request subscribed by 5 Regional Councils) – *Quorum* 50% + 1 registered electors b) To confirm or reject 'a decision' (constitutional law) not yet enforced (art. 138 Const., request subscribed by MPs) – No *Quorum*	**Promoting-referendum** To adopt 'a decision' ex-novo (only one case, *ad hoc*, ex constitutional law, 1989)

Fig. 17.1 Basic scheme for a typology of Italian referenda *A crucial element in my classification system is the role of two 'actors': X, the actor who promotes the referenda decision-making process (electors or institutional actors?); Y, the actor author of the 'object' ('decision', 'law', 'decree') on which the electors (or possibly Parliament) will cast their vote. If X = Y then the referenda decision-making process is of the *decision-promoting type*. If X ≠ Y then the referenda decision-making process is of the *decision-controlling type* (Uleri 1981: 77; 1985: 223; 2003: 98–101). With reference to the referenda provided for by art. 75, it should be noted that, before the popular vote takes place, Parliament may intervene with its own decision to accept the abrogation request; in this case the popular vote does not take place (law n° 352/1970, art. 39). Parliament may eventually approve a new law on the same subject as the repealed law. The new law must respect the principles inspiring the request for repeal. In theory, all requests for repeal could be decided by a parliamentary vote in favour of the request for repeal, *pace* Altman (2011: 42). It should be emphasized that for the validity of the vote of the referenda pursuant to art. 138, unlike Art. 75, no type of *quorum* is envisaged, *pace* Altman (2011: 21)

from ideological prejudices.[21] The two referendums, of 2 June 1946 for the institutional choice between Monarchy and Republic, and of 4 December 2016 on constitutional reform, cannot be identified as 'plebiscites', as briefly discussed in Sect. 17.2 below. Referenda may be part of the representative government but do not establish any type of 'direct democracy'.

---

[21] *Pace* Altman (2011: 10) and Kaufman and Waters (2004: xix) quoted in Altman.

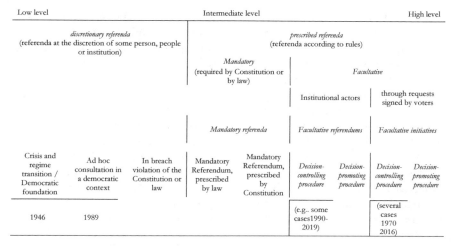

Fig. 17.2 Levels of removal of the control over political decisions operated by different types of referenda (Italian experience, 1946–2020) (*Source* Uleri [1985: 246; 2003: 107–108]. I am indebted to Johnson [1981: 21–22] for the distinction between *prescribed referenda* [referenda according to rules] and *discretionary referenda* [referenda at the discretion of some person or institution] [Uleri 1985: 13])

17.2   WHAT THE 1946 INSTITUTIONAL AND THE 2016 CONSTITUTIONAL REFERENDA WERE NOT: NEITHER 'PLEBISCITE' NOR 'DIRECT DEMOCRACY'

17.2.1   Plebiscites?

Around the middle of the nineteenth century, the history of the Italian Risorgimento for the unity and independence of the peninsula recorded the holding, in some cities, provinces and larger territories, of a dozen popular votes which were called 'plebiscites' (Ballini 1988: 243–244; Fimiani 2017: 364–367). Those plebiscites for Italian nation-building are a matter for historiography, interesting and useful for political science as well.

In Italy, in the liberal age, between the nineteenth and twentieth centuries, there was a rich 'debate on the referendum' (Basile 1992, 1994). There were academic studies on referendum experiences in Switzerland and in the States of the Union (USA) and on the debate in the United Kingdom in the early twentieth century. In Parliament there were political debates on proposals to insert referenda institutes in the Italian political-administrative system.[22] Before the

---

[22]A few bibliographical references testify to those debates: Rensi (1902, 1995), Klein (1905, Regio Istituto di scienze sociali Cesare Alfieri in Firenze); Perassi (1911), Grassi (1913). Both Perassi and Grassi were member of the Constituent Assembly elected in June 1946; Grassi was also Minister of Justice (1947–1950). In his work of 1913 (p. 15), Grassi affirmed the opportunity to 'graft participatory branches' on the 'representative trunk' (Luciani 2005: 82).

outbreak of the First World War, according to a national law, in a good number of cities, including the most important ones such as Milan and Rome, dozens of municipal referenda were held to ratify or reject the decisions of the administrations that set up municipal companies for the provision of public services (Basile 1994; Gaspari 1998).

Subsequently, the fascist regime mobilized popular support (De Felice 1974) with two 'electoral plebiscites'. The electors expressed their 'choice' with a Yes or a No vote on the single national list of fascist candidates for the Chamber of Deputies. The lists were approved in 1929 and 1934, respectively with 98.4% and 99.9% of Yes votes. Voting was mandatory; non-participation was considered an expression of opposition to the fascist regime; turnout was, respectively 89.6 and 96.5%. Before the 1929 vote, Mussolini stated that: '... The people will vote perfectly free. I just need to remember, however, that a revolution can be consecrated by a plebiscite, never reversed ...'; there were 135,761 No and 8,519,559 Yes votes (De Felice 1968: 438; Fimiani 2002).

Can we interpret the votes of June 1946 and December 2016 as plebiscites?— 2 June is the national holiday for the birth of the Republic. On 2 June 1946, women and men who had turned 21 voted to elect the members of the *Assemblea Costituente* (Constituent Assembly), which was charged with writing the first Constitution of Italy.[23] On the same day, an ad hoc institutional referendum was also held to decide whether Italy would continue to be a monarchy or would become a republic (Paladin 2004: 19–71). The decision to put the institutional choice to the people was highly contested (Ragionieri 1976). Despite all the great difficulties of the context, it was by no means a plebiscite.[24] The decision to put the institutional choice to the vote was strongly contested among the parties of the coalition founding the new political regime. In particular, socialists and communists were strongly opposed to the popular vote; the Christian Democrats were divided among themselves. The Christian Democracy party held a referendum among party members who mostly opted for the Republic. It was above all the Christian Democrat leader, Alcide De Gasperi, who more firmly opted for the referendum (Craveri 2006: 171–266). In this way he neutralized a series of conflicts (within his party but above all with the Catholic Church (Sale 2003) and with the British and US governments) that would have been potentially devastating for the stability of the coalition of parties that were about to re-establish democracy (Ricci 1996, 2001: 165–216; Formigoni 2016: 23–85; Gentiloni Silveri 2019: 22–34).

Regarding the constitutional referendum of December 2016, Altman (2019: 119, emphasis added) writes of 'Matteo Renzi's *obligatory* referendum', which he calls a 'plebiscite' (Altman 2019: 84). Altman draws on *Direct Democracy—The International IDEA Handbook* (2008) but that volume does not contain a clear definition of the term 'plebiscite' despite using the term

---

[23]Spreafico (1987) in Presidenza del Consiglio dei Ministri (1987).

[24]*Pace* Altman (2019: 75).

many times, mostly associated with experiences of authoritarian regimes. Thus, it states:

> Referendums conducted by the government, for example, have sometimes been called plebiscites. ...On occasion, referendums or 'plebiscites' have also been employed by authoritarian rulers, either to create a veneer of democratic legitimacy for their actions or to counter domestic political opposition (p. 24).

Such a 'definition' can give rise to a number of *cat-dogs*. According to Sartori (2011: 220–221), the *cat-dog* is an animal that is the fruit of wrong classifications and typologies that violate the rules of classificatory logic. Indeed, in the political science literature on the referendum phenomenon it is easy to come across so-called 'classifications' and 'typologies' full of *cat-dogs*. As Marradi writes: '...many of the classifications actually proposed in the social sciences suffer from a faulty definition of the *fundamentum divisionis*...' (1990: 3). Actually, in some of the so-called 'classifications and typologies' of referenda, there is no trace of any *fundamentum divisionis*: in fact, they are simply lists of *cat-dogs*.

However we define it, the 2016 referendum cannot be seen as plebiscitary. As said, there is no mandatory procedure in Art. 138 of the Italian Constitution (Uleri 1996: 108). Therefore, contrary to what Altman wrote, the procedure was not mandatory, but facultative; moreover the procedure was de facto both 'top-down' and 'bottom-up'.[25] So, according to Altman's criteria, the Italian vote of December 2016 was a 'mandatory plebiscite' 'required by Constitution (or Law)' (Altman 2011: 11). This type of referendum vote seems, logically, somewhat contradictory.[26] Can a liberal-democratic Constitution provide for a plebiscite? The use of the term 'plebiscite' referring to the Italian votes (June 1946 and December 2016) misunderstands the political-institutional culture and the context in which they took place and to which we now turn.

17.3 THE POPULAR VOTE OF DECEMBER 2016 ON THE CONSTITUTION'S CHANGE: THE FAILED 'TRANSITION'

17.3.1 As a Premise

In Italy, the 'constitutional issue' is a historical question in the political–cultural debate (Pombeni 2016). The Constituent Assembly (June 1946—December 1947) was the first national one elected in the history of united

---

[25]The so-called 'direct-democracy', at least in the Italian experience, is a little bit *'crooked'*, see 17.3.2.

[26]Definitions of concepts, classifications and types in the analysis of institutions and referenda experiences are not resolved with simple jokes; in any case, even the classification of '*Bos taurus*' (Linnaeus 1758) requires analytical and classification logic skills, *pace* Altman (2011: 8).

Italy (Bernardini et al. 2017). The Constitution which came into force on 1 January 1948 is the first Italian constitution (Amato 2015: 71–81). There was no popular vote to ratify it. In the Constituent Assembly, 'distrust' for referendum institutions was strong and widespread, especially among the leftist, socialist and communist political groups. There was no request 'from below' for the adoption of referenda-type institutes. However, that Constitution provides for procedural referenda which can be activated with requests signed by the electors (as well as by members of Parliament and by regional Councils) (Luciani 2005: 141–211). In the Constituent Assembly, the adoption of referendum institutes in the Constitution was sought above all by the Christian Democrats and some liberals and democrats as a defensive tool against possible abuse of social-communist majorities (Uleri 1994, 1996). The positions of the main parties reversed after the elections of April 18, 1948; the communists, however, maintained a predominantly hostile attitude (Armaroli 1974).

It was not obvious that democracy would succeed. The extraordinary victory of the DC in the elections of 18 April 1948 (92.2% turnout, over 48% of the votes, giving them an absolute majority of seats in both the Chamber of Deputies and the Senate) and the exceptional quality of the Christian Democrat leader, Alcide De Gasperi, were essential factors for the re-foundation of democracy in Italy. This does not mean underestimating the role of the other leaders and parties present on the National Liberation Committee—CLN, in the Constituent Assembly and then in Parliament; without doubt, between 1943 and 1948, the relationship between the DC and the PCI and their leaders, De Gasperi and Togliatti, was crucial (Ventrone 2008). The international political context, with the accession of Italy to NATO and participation in the European Union, was also of great importance for the democratic consolidation (De Siervo et al. 2004, vol I, pp. 155–219; Formigoni 2016: 223–227; Ministero per i Beni e le Attività Culturali (2003a)).

The Italian Constitution is 'only partly self-executing; when the constitution was adopted (in December 1947) it was expected that it would be implemented gradually by legislation. In fact this has taken a very long time' (Fusaro 2011: 449). This was the case, for example, with Articles 71, 75 and 138 and Title V relating to the regional institutional set-up. The debates and related political events concerning: (a) the implementation of the Constitution; (b) the 'institutional reforms' and (c) the 'constitutional reforms' cover a long period of time. According to Fusaro (2011: 231): 'Whatever definition we give to the notion of "constitution" the Italian Constitution has changed greatly since it entered in force ....The Italian Constitution of 2010 is not the Constitution of 1948.' Other constitutionalists over the decades have expressed different if not opposed views.

When the Constitution came into force it consisted of one hundred and thirty-nine articles. In the meantime five articles were repealed (Constitution Law No. 3 of 2001), although the numbering of the articles remained unchanged; some articles have been modified one or more times. From 1963 to 2019, sixteen constitutional laws were approved (Fusaro 2015; Pasquino 2019).

The execution of the Constitution has been a slow and difficult political process. It was the result of profound political conflicts between the parties in general, between the majority parties and opposition parties, especially of the left, above all the Communist Party (PCI), for many years the second party in electoral terms after the Christian Democrats. There have also been conflicts within the government coalitions that have occurred over the decades. As the constitutionalist and former member of the Constitutional Court Enzo Cheli wrote in the early 1970s:

> If during the first legislature [1948–'53] the Constitution formally manages to survive, this happens only to the extent that the constitutional implementation policy is frozen: the non-implementation and non-observance of the constitution, at this stage, is the price that must be paid to the survival of the 1948 Constitution (Cheli 1978: 60).[27]

The history of the implementation of the Constitution, of institutional and constitutional changes, is the very tortuous and difficult history of the (re-)construction of the new Italian democracy.[28] Indeed, it has been said that the question of institutional reforms begins on 1 January 1948, the very day the Constitution entered into force (Fusaro 2016: 51). The complexity of the subject is constituted by the fact that the execution is intertwined with the changes, the so-called constitutional 'reforms'. A complex plot has been formed in which it is not always possible to distinguish and clearly separate the threads of execution from the threads of 'reforms'. In the decades after the entry into force of the Constitution, the political conflicts were among those who tried to slow down the implementation of the Constitution, those who supported the need for 'full implementation' and the maintenance of the Constitution, and those who considered changes necessary to ensure the stability of governments and the effectiveness of their action.

By October 1990, Giuliano Amato wondered:

> ... In the persistence of the stalemate everyone wants reforms and no reform is made. So it takes a factor to get out of the stalemate. *Who is our general De Gaulle? The electoral body*: luckily for us or bad luck, it depends on the point of view, we do not have a general De Gaulle who cuts the Gordian knot. We can only entrust our Gordian knot to the electoral body. This is why the *proposed referendum serves, but only as a one-off institution* .... (Amato 1992: 214–215, emphasis added)[29]

---

[27] On the first republican legislature, see De Siervo et al. (2004).

[28] In fact, it is a long and complex history reconstructed in a rich essay by Fusaro (2015).

[29] French political events have been the subject of debates, in-depth analyzes and conflicting evaluations, also with reference to the hypotheses of institutional reforms in Italy: Volpi

Since the early 1990s, institutional and constitutional reform has been a recurring theme in the reflections of some Presidents of the Republic (Lippolis and Salerno 2016: 215–246). Indirectly, a reply to Giuliano Amato would arrive a few months later, on 26 June 1991, with the 'Message to the Chambers' of the Christian Democrat President of the Republic, Francesco Cossiga (1991; Chessa and Savona 2014). The message dealt with the issue of institutional reforms and envisaged procedures to deal with the stalemate mentioned by Amato.

President Cossiga's message remained, in fact, a dead letter. The Democratic Party called for the impeachment of the President (Gentiloni Silveri 2019: 251–253).[30] In fact, the President understood that the end of that system was coming, whereas the parties, short-sighted and deaf, no, did not understand it. In an interview with the newspaper *La Stampa*, 13 December 1991, the President will declare his preference for the French semi-presidential system (Galavotti 2018: 351). In any case, no de Gaulle arrived, but Silvio Berlusconi, with *his* system of three TV channels and *his* Forza Italia party (Poli 2001; Donovan and Gilbert 2015). According to Orsina (2015: 249): 'As an ideology, Berlusconism was an "emulsion" of right-wing liberalism and populism'. A confirmation of the weakness of political liberalism as an "organized action" in Italy.

Twenty years later, on the occasion of his second election to the presidency of the Republic in April 2013, the first time in the history of the Republic that a president had been re-elected, the President of the Republic Giorgio Napolitano (2013) denounced the 'fatal deadlock' in which he felt Italian political life found itself (Pons 2018). The President has exercised a constant moral suasion to induce parties and Parliament to carry out, with a large majority resulting from agreements between majority and minority parties, reforms to the constitution and the electoral law as well as of a law on political parties to implement Art. 49 of the Constitution. However, the law on constitutional reform was approved without the qualified majority required by Art. 138 if a referendum was to be averted; a new electoral law was also passed (2015) without a broad agreement between majority and minorities (Lippolis and Salerno 2016: 215–246). As mentioned, the electoral law was declared partially unconstitutional in 2017.

17.3.2   *Constitutional Law*

In December 2016, the object of the popular vote was a constitutional law passed by Parliament in April 2016 after two years of debates; the law modified

---

(1979), Volpi (2014), Bartolini (1981), Quagliariello (2003, 2012), Pasquino and Ventura (2010).

[30]On President Cossiga, see Galavotti (2018: 325–363), Cassese et al. (2018, vol. 2), Gentiloni Silveri, http://www.treccani.it/enciclopedia/francesco-cossiga_(Dizionario-Biografico)/.

some parts of the Constitution. The popular vote had been requested by MPs both favourable to and against the constitutional law. The Democratic Party (PD), the main supporter of the constitutional law in Parliament, had also promoted a popular request signed by over 500,000 electors. The ballot asked electors to answer the following question:

> Do you approve the text of the constitutional law concerning "**Provisions for overcoming the equal bicameralism,** the reduction of the number of parliamentarians, the containment of the operating costs of the institutions, the suppression of the CNEL and **the revision of the title V of part II of the Constitution**" approved by Parliament and published in the Official Gazette no. 88 of 15 April 2016?' (In bold the two central themes of the constitutional law, *emphasis added*)

As the question on the ballot paper made clear, there were two central themes addressed in the constitutional law: 'equal bicameralism', in particular the role of the Senate, and 'revision of the title V of part II of the Constitution'.

The Government must obtain a vote of confidence from both the Chamber of Deputies and the Senate; both Chambers discuss and approve all laws passed by Parliament. The Senate has the same direct legitimation and exactly the same functions as those of the lower house. The Chamber is elected by people over 18 years old, whereas the Senate Chamber is elected by people over 25. Title V of Part II of the Constitution concerns 'regions, provinces, municipalities' and had already been the main objective of the constitutional law approved by Parliament and then ratified by electors in 2001. The law approved in 2001 did not solve all the knots of the 'institutional-constitutional question', but created new ones.

The 2016 constitutional law significantly modified the institutional architecture of the Republic. The revision involved 47 of the 134 articles that make up the Constitution: two articles were repealed, 45 modified (Cavino et alii. 2017). Many authoritative scholars of constitutional law and other academic disciplines have expressed their views for or against the constitutional law, both personally and by signing multiple appeals.[31]

Reasons contrary to and favourable to the law revising the Constitution were expressed, before the vote, respectively in Zagrebelsky (2016) and Crainz and Fusaro (2016).[32] According to Zagrebelsky[33] (2016: 79), the actual

---

[31]A severe judgment of the constitutional law of 2016 as well as of those of 2001 and 2005 is that expressed by Domenico Fisichella (2018a: 103–125; 2018b: 251–253), who was Professor of Political Science in the Universities of Florence and Rome, a Senator for four legislatures (1994–2008) and Vice-President of the Senate (1996–2006). The crucial issue indicated by Fisichella is that of unity of Italy as an essential prerequisite for maintaining a political system of representative democracy.

[32]Indeed, some books and numerous articles have been published; see Vassallo (2017) in favour and Pasquino (2017) contrary.

[33]Professor of constitutional law, he was a member and president of the Constitutional Court.

common goal of constitutional reform and electoral law ... was to shift the 'institutional axis in favor of the executive' to create 'a form of government focused on one man in command. That is to say, not a democracy, but an elective autarchy'. According to Fusaro[34] (2016: 133–134), the reform would have produced 'no Palingenesis', nor 'one man in command' nor 'another Constitution', not to mention an 'authoritarian verticalization of power'. The reform would instead have produced '... with a good degree of probability, political institutions (a little) more reactive and efficient, governments (a little) more stable and more capable of carrying out their program ...., in perspective, a (somehow) more credible institutional system'. Advocates of reform, in seeking a figure like de Gaulle (Amato 1992; Pasquino 2017: 176), indicate one element of the events relating to attempts at institutional reforms in Italy: the lack of leaders suitable for the objective of institutional–constitutional reforms.[35]

A few of the articles of the constitutional law rejected in December 2016 concerned referenda and political participation institutions. Article 11 of the constitutional law was dedicated to the 'Legislative Initiative'; it modified Art. 71 of the Constitution. The number of signatures necessary to promote a popular law increased from 50,000 to 150,000 signatures. As a secondary matter, the constitutional reform provided for the adoption of a new *decision-promoting initiative* for statute laws. In Art. 11 reference was made, in general terms, to promoting-decision type referenda as well as other forms of consultation. Article 15 of the constitutional law amended article 75 of the Constitution providing for the replacement of the *quorum* of 50% + 1 of the voters with 'the majority of the electors in the last elections to the Chamber of Deputies' for requests promoted by 800,000 electors. They were proposals that would strengthen popular participation institutions. What possible objection could there be to those proposals? Parts of the constitutional law (including Article 71) were formulated in such a way that new laws would have to be passed to implement the reform; all this would certainly have taken a number of years (Zagrebelsky 2016: 78).

17.3.3   Parties, Party System and Referendum Popular Vote

As mentioned at the beginning of the chapter, there have been significant changes in the political framework characterized by the parties and the dynamics of the party system. Between 1991 and 1994, the party system that had ruled republican democracy since 1945 left the scene. After the financial

---

[34] Professor of Electoral and Parliamentary Law.

[35] A comparative historiography analysis is carried out by Quagliariello (2012: 11–45). Synthetic comparisons of the Italian leaders are those of Agosti (2015) dedicated to De Gasperi (DC) and Togliatti (PCI), of Bernardi (2015) dedicated to Moro (DC) and Berlinguer (PCI), of Varsori (2015) dedicated to Craxi (PSI) and Andreotti (DC) and, finally, by Donovan and Gilbert (2015) dedicated to Berlusconi (Forza Italy) and Prodi (the Olive Tree).

Table 17.3 Italian (Chamber) and European parliamentary elections (2013–2018, main parties)

Elections Parties	Italian Parliament (Chamber) 2013		European Parliament 2014		Italian Parliament (Chamber) 2018		European Parliament 2019	
Turnout:	No.	%	No.	%	No.	%	No.	%
	35,270,926	75.20	28,908,004	58.69	33,923,321	72.94	27,652,929	56.09
Non-valid votes	1,265,171		1,536,257		1,082,296		989,967	
Partito Democratico - PD	8,646,034	25.43	11,172,861	40.82	6,161,896	18.76	6,050,351	22.69
Movimento 5 Stelle	8,691,406	25.56	5,792,865	21.16	10,732,066	32.68	4.,52,527	17.07
Il popolo della libertà/Forza Italia	7,332,134	21.56	4,605,331	16.83	4,596,956	14.00	2,344,465	8.79
Lega Nord	1,390,534	4.09	1,686,556	6.16	5,698,687	17.35	9,153,638	34.33
Fratelli d'Italia	666,765	1.96	1,004,037	3.67	1,429,550	4.35	1,723,232	6.46

Source processing by the author on data from Ministry of the Interior on-line Archive; parties selected by the author

and economic crises of 2008 and 2011–2012, the elections of 2013 and 2018 wiped out the system started with the two elections of the years 1994–1996. That party system (1994–2008) was, however, fragmented with unstable majorities and ineffective governments (Calise 2015: 95–106; Mershon 2015: 144–158). For at least twenty five years the 'party system' has been unstable, increasingly after the 2013 and 2018 elections, which were both characterized by a strong volatility as great as or greater than that recorded in 1994 (Schadee et al. 2019: 35 ss). The constitutional referendum of 2016 took place about halfway between those two elections (Table 17.3).

'Electoral earthquake' is the recurring expression used to describe the 2013 and 2018 elections. From those elections a third pole seems to have emerged with the electoral successes of the 5 Star Movement (M5S): the largest party after the 2018 elections, opposed to Parliament and representative democracy in the name of a digital 'direct democracy' through the 'Rousseau digital platform'.[36] The dynamics of 'right-left' bipolarism (*Popolo della libertà/Forza Italia* vs. *Partito Democratico*) seem to be replaced by 'tripolar' dynamics.

The elections for the European Parliament in 2019 recorded a retreat of the M5S and the victory of the far-right '*Lega—Lega Salvini premier*' party (Passarelli and Tuorto 2018). Polls and partial (regional) elections attested to the good electoral health of *Fratelli d'Italia*, a right-wing party, a subsidiary of the dissolved *Alleanza Nazionale* (heir of the *Movimento Sociale Italiano*, 1946–1995, a neo-fascist party) and affiliated in the European Parliament

[36]The platform is located at: https://vote.rousseau.movimento5stelle.it/.

to the European Conservatives and Reformists Group. These three political groups, which have the majority of seats in Parliament, share anti-liberal and anti-European Union attitudes; *Lega* and *Fratelli d'Italia* also show (neo-) nationalist attitudes.

The referendum vote of December 2016 is an integral part of this political context. The 2016 constitutional referendum was the event '... which most affected the 2018 [electoral] earthquake ... was therefore a turning point in the process that led millions of electors to reward the League and strengthen the M5S' (Schadee et al. 2019: 153).

Just a few words need to be spent on the king-maker of the constitutional reform rejected by the electors in December 2016. Since his time in local politics Matteo Renzi challenged the local and national establishment of the PD.[37] He had defied the leadership of the PD in the name of 'scrapping' the party's old elites; scrapping in Italian (*rottamazione*) indicates the disposal of old cars, thus earning him the nickname '*rottamatore*'. In December 2013, Renzi, the then 38-year old mayor of Florence, won the 'primary' elections for the position of secretary of the PD. At the end of February 2014 he replaced his party companion Enrico Letta at the head of the government. The bright success of the European elections came at the end of May 2014: in those elections the Democratic Party (PD) obtained the best result of its electoral history in percentage terms, with 40% of valid votes. This fact could have led Renzi and the PD to underestimate the difficulties of the economic, social and political state of affairs, in particular for the primary objective that the President of the Republic had 'pointed out': institutional reforms and electoral law. Indeed, humility is not among the main virtues of the Florentine politician.

The severe crisis of 2011–2012 and the difficult situation resulting from the 2013 elections, indicated the need for personalities capable of bringing together human and political resources for stable and effective government action. Especially in view of the constitutional reform that the government was called to carry out. An initial agreement between Renzi and Silvio Berlusconi, the so-called '*Patto del Nazzareno*' (Pact of the Nazarene),[38] had favoured for some months the debate and the formulation of the main proposals for the revision of the Constitution. The election of the new President of the Republic, Sergio Mattarella, seems to have been the reason for Berlusconi's decision to end that pact (Dau Novelli 2018). In July 1990, Mattarella, together with four other Christian Democrat ministers, had resigned from the post of Minister of Education in order to oppose the vote of confidence, requested by the government to which he belonged, for the approval of the so-called '*Legge Mammì*' which granted a privileged position to the television system of Silvio Berlusconi.

---

[37] Renzi had been President of the Province of Florence, 2004–2009, then he was elected Mayor of Florence, June 2009, with circa 60% of the votes.

[38] The national headquarters of the Democratic Party in Rome is located in Via del Nazzareno where there was a meeting between Renzi and Berlusconi.

Renzi's government, in particular through the work of the Minister for constitutional reforms and relations with Parliament, Maria Elena Boschi, had been a strenuous promoter of the proposed constitutional law. After the approval of the reform in Parliament, in view of the campaign for the referendum, Renzi put his own job on the line, stating he would stand down if the referendum were lost. For this reason he was accused of transforming the constitutional referendum into a 'plebiscite' (that is to say, more properly, into a vote of confidence), even before the constitutional law was definitively approved and the campaign for the referendum vote began.[39] Afterwards, Renzi's attempt to step back was not very convincing and in any case was unsuccessful.

During the discussion of the constitutional reform in Parliament, some authoritative members of the PD's previous leadership group, opposed to the contents of the constitutional revision, left the party, voted against the reform in Parliament and, on the occasion of the referendum vote, participated in the campaign for the No to the ratification of the law.[40] Together with other leftist groups they made up a political group called *Liberi ed Eguali* which in the 2018 elections obtained 3.4% of the vote.

The main opposition parties (M5S, Lega and Fratelli d'Italia) interpreted the campaign for the referendum vote as a '*plebiscite*' against Renzi' government. As soon as the victory for No was unequivocal, Renzi announced his resignation. The rejection by the voters of the Constitution reform law will probably remain in the years to come as a significant event, a turning point in Italian political history. In September 2019 Renzi left the PD to form a political group called '*Italia Viva*' (IV).

Turnout in December 2016 was significant (65.48%) in comparison with the two previous constitutional referenda, with the 2014 and 2019 European elections, and also with the repeal referenda after 1995. For some, the level of participation was 'unexpected' (Pedrazzoni and Pinto 2017: 75–92). Unexpected, perhaps, for those who in previous decades had not observed and taken due account of the numerous campaigns to abstain from voting. In fact, unlike what happened in the two previous constitutional referenda, during the 2016 vote there was a genuine campaign for mobilization on both sides. By contrast, the abrogative referendum held in mid-April 2016 was characterized by a large campaign for non-participation; an effective campaign considering that the turnout was around 32%. In fact, with the exception of the 2011 vote, the last genuine mobilization campaigns for the referendum vote were those of 1993 and 1995 (Uleri 2002).

---

[39] See, Eugenio Scalfari, founder and editor of *Repubblica* (Scalfari 2016); see also Enrico De Mita (2016).

[40] The best known and authoritative leaders were Pier Luigi Bersani and Massimo D'Alema, both with a long career that began as members of the PCI and continued in all subsequent transformations of that party until the formation of the Democratic Party.

In 2011, the decision of the PD to mobilize participation in the vote in favour of repeal in the four referenda questions (a 'Yes' vote), was decisive in achieving the quorum of electors (57%). The decision of the PD to mobilize participation came only after the successes, a few weeks earlier, in the municipal elections that had seen the victories of candidates and lists of the PD or supported by it, in elections that in some cases had required a second round of voting. The PD, initially in favour of abstention in the referendum because it was opposed to the abrogations, changed its opinion and transformed the referenda vote into a sort of third round, to its advantage. Both the municipal elections and the referenda votes actually constituted a defeat for Silvio Berlusconi and his government which, mainly under the weight of the economic crisis, would fall five months later.

A dynamic similar to that of 2011 occurred in 2016. In June there were administrative elections that involved over 15,000,000 voters, including those from major cities such as Turin, Milan, Rome and Naples. The M5S had conquered Rome and Turin, configuring itself as a sort of catch-all party, 'the true' party of the nation; '... the result of the M5S cannot be attributed only to local factors' (Emanuele and Maggini 2017: 120).

In December 2016, the geography of voting participation mirrored traditional patterns. Participation was higher in the central-northern regions (between 72 and 77% approximately) with the exception of Liguria (69.7%). In the remaining central-southern regions and in the two islands, Sicily and Sardinia, where the M5S got the highest percentages of votes in the 2013 and 2018 elections, participation ranged between about 69% in Lazio and about 54% in Calabria. 'Yes' only won in three regions: Trentino Alto Adige, Emilia Romagna and Tuscany. 'No' prevailed in the two islands (over 71%) and the central-southern regions (between 61 and 68.5%); the 'No' side won with over 60% in the Northern Regions (Veneto and Friuli Venezia Giulia) where the League is strongest.

As said, the vote was held on a Sunday in early December. An unusual period for a vote in Italian electoral history. In fact, in general, elections and referenda usually take place on a spring Sunday; repeal referenda must take place, by law, on a Sunday between 15 April and 15 June. As with the two earlier constitutional referenda, that of 2016 took place about seven months after the definitive approval of the law in Parliament. In the intervening months, events of a political and and/or economic nature not related to the contents of the law subject to the vote may influence the choices of the electors. On this occasion, opinion polls over the course of about a year, between the final months of the debate and the approval of the constitutional law in Parliament up to a few weeks before the vote, highlighted the progressive loss of support on the law and the growth of contrary attitudes. In February 2016, just before the definitive approval of the law in Parliament, there seemed to be a majority in favour—68% supporting 'Yes' against 32% for 'No'. In particular, 85% of PD voters supported 'Yes' at that time, along with 78% of Forza Italia voters, 71% of supporters of the League and 66% of M5S voters (Bordignon et al. 2017: 127–148).

Between June and September, the 'Yes' was still obtaining 55–56% of the voting intentions, before falling to 47% in October and 42% in November and down to 40% in the vote in early December. In particular, in the two surveys made in October and November before the vote, the voting intentions according to the political self-placement of the interviewees gave these results: among the left-oriented electors 'No' prevailed (53%); among self-placed electors on the centre-left, 'Yes' obtained 68%; 'No' prevailed among the self-placed electors in the centre (59%), on the centre-right (73%), on the right (77%). Finally, among the electors who do not self-locate along the right–left axis (most of these electors were likely to be voter-oriented for the M5S), 'No' prevails with 71% (Bordignon et al. 2017: 127–148).

In referendum voting, the alignments of supporters on the two sides are often somewhat composite, bringing together 'strange bed-fellows'. The electors followed the cues of their reference parties, in a 'match' in which two 'poles', the centre-right/right one comprising *Forza Italia, Lega and Fratelli d'Italia* alongside the populist M5S lined up for 'No', against the 'Yes'-supporting centre-left/centre. In the central and southern regions, the broad support for 'No' was probably also the result of a protest against a government deemed incapable of effective responses for the difficult social and economic conditions of large sections of the population (Regalia and Tronconi 2017: 93–111). For 59% of the interviewees the vote had above all a meaning in favour or against 'Renzi and his government'; only for 26% was the meaning of the vote '… to maintain or modify the Constitution' (Bordignon et al. 2017: 141). Among 'Yes'-oriented electors, 88% believed that the reform would improve the functioning of Italian democracy; on the contrary, 66% of electors oriented to vote 'No' thought that the reform constituted a danger for Italian democracy (Bordignon et al. 2017: 140).

The PD and the groups or parties that supported the constitutional law in Parliament (generally centre-right and centre-left) lined up for 'Yes'. Behind the 'No' there were disparate groups and personalities of the left, while most of the electoral support, decisive to defeating the 'Yes' vote, was composed of electors mobilized to vote 'No' by movements and parties of the populist matrix, ('neo-sovereign') nationalism, former secessionist, xenophobic, plus assorted minor far-right groups. In addition to the M5S, which cannot be placed in a one-dimensional political space of the right-left type, opposition came from centre-right and right-wing parties and groups such as Berlusconi's *Forza Italia* (*Popolo delle Libertà*), Salvini's *Lega* and Giorgia Meloni's *Fratelli d'Italia*, and sundry groups and parties of both left and extreme left and small groups of radical far right of clear fascist inspiration.

The 'No' was not merely a vote of 'no confidence' on Renzi and his government. Yet, it seems reasonable to assume that a plurality of political choices that characterized the Renzi government's action contributed, to some extent, to the victory of the 'No' in constitutional reform: the electoral law; labour market reform, the so-called 'Jobs Act'; the election of Sergio Mattarella as President of the Republic; the school reform; the public administration reform; the reform of the financial system relating to popular banks and banking foundations, not to mention the law on civil unions; the unsuccessful attempt to approve 'step-child adoption'; and the persistent issue of illegal immigration. Strong opposition crystallized on each of those choices of the Renzi government and became manifest in the constitutional referendum.[41] However, if it is true that, between the 2013 and 2018 elections, we witnessed the apocalypse of Italian democracy (Schadee et al. 2019), then the vote in December 2016 was also and above all the result of attitudes against parties and representative democracy. According to (Schadee et al. 2019: 134–139), three types of political attitudes characterize the M5S voters: (a) parties do not serve democracy; (b) compromise in politics is negative; (c) it is better that the 'citizens' (a word dear to the rhetoric of the M5S) decide for themselves.

17.3.4   The Transition That Failed

The 'transition' processes hypothesized and attempted after the new electoral laws of 1993 proved to be an infinite and inconclusive process. These were marked by bitter conflicts between proponents and opponents who faced each other on the proposals for reforms. At the turn of the century, two scholars concluded their analysis of the 2001 elections: '…however precarious the [electoral] law, however fragmented the party system is, the Italian path towards bipolarism seems clearly traced. *And it can hardly be called into question*' (Diamanti and Lazar 2002: 75, emphasis added). Similarly, at the end of a book on the Italian referenda experience, Barbera and Morrone wrote: 'The referenda, both … for their binary logic, and for the specific electoral questions, have contributed to bipolarizing the political system: their purpose seems to run out of function' (Barbera and Morrone 2003: 249).

The idea that referenda were a tool to transform the Italian party system into 'bipartitism' (not 'bipolarism') was an original idea of the abrogative initiatives' politics of the Radical Party, conceived in the late 1960s and early 1970s (Teodori et al. 1977; Orsina 2015; Teodori 2015). To deem the function of the abrogative referenda to be exhausted because the party system would have bi-polarized is naive, perhaps the result of a distorted, one might say *partycratic*, view of a constitutional institute.

Vassallo and Ceccanti (2004: 30) who were very committed to institutional changes, noted that the change in electoral laws had been 'the only major reform' that had been approved. Those scholars expressed the belief that until then:: '… most of the political actors and electors have now internalized the

---

[41] For a summary of the political framework that preceded the holding of the referendum vote, see Chiaramonte and Wilson (2017); for an illustration of the individual issues mentioned, reference to the annual volumes of the Research Foundation Istituto Carlo Cattaneo, *Politica in Italia*, in particular the 2015, 2016 and 2017 editions, is a must.

basic logic of majority democracy ... For this reason, an agreement that stabilizes and rationalizes in new balances through targeted adaptations of the constitutional design could now become practicable' (Vassallo and Ceccanti 2004: 16). In short, Vassallo and Ceccanti, along with many others, believed that, however difficult and contested, the conditions were in place to implement a constitutional revision that would allow the transition from consensual democracy to majority democracy, according to Lijphart's terminology. By early January 2016 it seemed that 'The transition is (almost) over' (Ceccanti 2016). On 4 December, the voters decided to postpone it.

According to Gianfranco Pasquino (2019: 205–206)—a former member of Parliament[42] and of the first bicameral commission for institutional reforms (Bozzi, 1983–1985), and one of the most prolific scholars on reform issues, who strongly opposed the 'Renzi-Boschi' constitutional law—the Constitution of 1948:

> ...has been frequently called in question and criticized, especially by the centre-right. Many attempts have been made to introduce significant changes into the Italian Constitution, some of them potentially leading to disequilibria. ..... Recently, even some foreign observers have joined the now rather crowded Italian choir criticizing some post-World War Two Constitutions (more precisely, those in Italy, Portugal and Spain) for being 'Socialist'.

Pasquino does not explicitly say who or what he is referring to. Perhaps the first to propose a 'different' republic, so to speak, between the late-1960s and early-1970s, were Randolfo Pacciardi and Edgardo Sogno, two somewhat 'eccentric personalities' with respect to the current regime (Craveri 1995: 35–43, 453–480; Lupo 2004; Orsina 2015). Edgardo Sogno (1974) probably has the copyright of the expression 'Second Republic', since in 1974 he published a book entitled 'The Second Republic'. Pacciardi (1972) had, two years earlier, published *The Presidential Republic explained to the people*. In the 1960s, the French events, with the establishment of the 5th Republic, had been welcomed with great favour by the far right, who evoked the need for the establishment, even in Italy, of a 'presidential republic' in Italy (Craveri 1995: 36–37; Lupo 2004: 232–234; Pasquino and Ventura 2010; Volpi 2014).

In the Constituent Assembly, the proposal for a presidential republic was formulated, among others, by the jurist Piero Calamandrei (Merlini 2007) exponent of the Action Party, a group of democratic-radical inspiration. The American presidential republic was evoked, in generic terms, as an institutional reference model by Marco Pannella, leader of the Radical Party (Teodori 1992).

We might think that in the matter of changing the constitution there was a conflict between the right that proposed the change and the left, which opposed it, or vice versa. That would be too simplistic a hypothesis. Indeed,

---

[42] Parliamentary terms: 1983–1987; 1987–1992; 1994–1996.

Pasquino (2019: 205–206) states that, 'The most insidious attempt to make disjointed and destabilizing changes – made by Matteo Renzi, the secretary of Democratic Party, and his centre-left government – was defeated in a popular referendum held on 4 December 2016.'

From the socialist proposal of a 'Great Reform' in September 1979 to the popular vote in December 2016, something seems to have 'gone the wrong way' (Amato 1980; Pasquino 1980, 1982, 1985).

17.3.5   The Populist Change

On October 12, 2019, Parliament passed a constitutional law to reduce the number of members of Parliament (Clementi 2019). The law was promoted and effectively imposed by the Five Star Movement with the main motivation of reducing the costs of political life. A constitutional referendum, to confirm or reject it, called for 29 March 2020, was postponed due to the crisis caused by the spread of Coronavirus. M5S proposed another constitutional law on the so-called 'referendum propositivo' (decision-promoting initiative); but at the time of writing it had not been definitively approved in Parliament.

According to some, the arguments used by M5S in advocating these constitutional laws delegitimize Parliament and representative democracy (Carnevale 2020; Luciani 2018, 2019). M5S proclaims strong rhetoric in favour of 'direct democracy'; 'Democracy must be re-founded' said Gianroberto Casaleggio, founder of the M5S, demanding 'A new contract between citizens and elected officials: referendum to distrust parliamentarians' (Corriere della Sera, June 26, 2013).'"One is worth one" is the foundation of direct and participatory democracy. Great social changes can only happen by involving everyone through participation in the first person and not by proxy', affirms his son, Davide Casaleggio (2018), who replaced his father after his death. The M5S deserves to be known for what, as a political organization, it is and what it represented until the beginning of 2020 (Vittori 2019). It is necessary to be aware of and carefully evaluate the risks it represents for Italian democracy. The most critical analyzes suggest we would be in the presence of 'fascism disguised as direct democracy' (Dal Lago 2017: 125–159).

Despite the M5S's rhetoric on 'direct democracy', it should be emphasized that the movement/non-party, in about a dozen years of life, has not made any particular effort to promote requests for abrogative initiatives. There is no trace, until 2020, of a single repeal initiative promoted by the M5S and voted on by electors. The constitutional law for the reduction of the number of parliamentarians, strongly desired by the M5S and approved in Parliament, was voted on (20–21 September 2020) in a referendum ex Art. 138 which had not been promoted by them. The vote, was held simultaneously with administrative and regional elections in some areas. The grouping of elections and referenda on the same date is rather unusual; it favoured a good turnout, which the M5S were very interested in. The turnout was 51.1% and the 'Yes' votes were 69.9% of valid votes.

The issue of electoral law is still unresolved (Regalia 2015). As said in the first pages, between 1993 and 2018, four laws were passed regarding the election of the Parliament, of which two were declared unconstitutional by the Constitutional Court. In October 2019, the party *Lega with Salvini* managed to promote an abrogative referendum (under Art. 75 Const.) to change the electoral law on the basis of which the March 2018 parliamentary elections were held. The stated goal was to obtain a law based on the *first-past-the-post* majority principle. The request was promoted by eight regional councils with centre-right majorities. In January 2020, the Constitutional Court declared the request as inadmissible.

17.4 Final Considerations

'*Nomina si nescis, perit et cognitio rerum*' ('If the names are unknown, knowledge of the things also perishes') (Carl Nilsson Linnaeus quoted by Sartori (1975) in his article 'The Tower of Babel'). Scholars of referenda also have their own Tower of Babel regarding concepts, classifications, typologies and strategies of comparative analysis.

Norberto Bobbio (1975) in an article entitled 'Which alternatives to representative democracy?' dedicated a paragraph to the theme 'The fetish of direct democracy'. After stressing 'the serious limits in which the Rousseauian ideal is practicable', Bobbio nonetheless affirms the possibility of integrating referendum institutions into representative democracy.

The use of the verbal expression 'direct democracy' with reference to the referenda is mainstream, and is indeed used by the editor of the present volume.[43] It is a misleading expression for the analysis and empirical theory of the referenda phenomenon. Indeed, there is no experience of democracies based essentially on a continuous and direct exercise of government by voters. With some superficiality, the expression has unfortunately entered the current language of academics, commentators, journalists. It is therefore not surprising that civic and political movements claim 'direct democracy'.

According to Auer (2001: 347; Auer and Bützer 2001): 'direct democracy does not mean sovereignty of the people. Vox populi is not vox dei'. A Swiss juridical definition states that: 'Ce qui est donc direct, en démocratie directe, ce ne pas tant l'exercice du pouvoir par le peuple mais le fait que ce dernier a le droit de déclencer les mécanismes de légitimation du pouvoir' (Auer et al. 2000: 191).

---

[43] Luciani (2005) dedicated an entire chapter to the notion of 'direct democracy' (Chapter 1, *The Referendum and "direct democracy"*, pp. 1–140); it is a comparative critical review of juridical and political science literature unique in its kind, on the theme indicated by the title. In my studies on the referenda phenomenon I have never found (not only in Italian, but also in English, French and Spanish) an essay that is remotely comparable, in terms of breadth and depth. Indeed it is an essay that deserves to be published separately, both in Italian and in other languages. See also Luciani (2019).

Both the question 'Let the people rule?' (Ruth et al. 2017) and the answer 'Let the People Rule' (Matsusaka 2020) are rhetorical artifices that do not go far beyond the title of an academic article or a book. According to Ruth et al. (2017: 218), 'Switzerland, Uruguay and other jurisdictions all display some very longstanding and creditable records of direct democracy success'. Yet, according to Linder (2010: 204–206): 'The Swiss case .... is not an ideal model but a historical experience'; it is not a model suitable for export. The question remains then, how should we measure the success or failure of 'direct democracy'?

Altman (2019: 16) has no doubts that 'direct and representative rules can coexist without undue difficulty' and that 'Citizen-initiated mechanisms of direct democracy democratize democracies' (Altman 2019: 166). Although unintentionally, this statement sounds like an old slogan that populists could endorse without any difficulty. In any case, according to Welp (2014: 261): 'Recall could only function properly in contexts in which democratic institutions operate', and, apart from Europe, according to Rial (2016: 100), in Latin American countries: 'Attempts to create mechanisms of direct democracy and the development of new institutions have not always strengthened democracy'. It seems to me that analyses of other important experiences also raise doubts and questions about the merits of direct democracy (see Gerber 1999; Magleby 1984, 1994a, b; Sabato et al. 2001).

According to Budge (1996: 39–40) political parties, 'the great political invention of the last two centuries', are indispensable for both representative democracy and 'direct democracy'. Budge (1996: 35) believes that 'we can characterize direct democracy in the abstract as a regime in which the adult citizens as a whole debate and vote on the most important political decisions, and where their vote determines the action to be taken'. How many are the 'most important' decisions? Budge (1996: 188) suggested: 'A fair estimate of the number of policy votes required in a year might thus be about fifty'. Approximately one decision per week for the whole year. Is it technologically feasible? In years to come, maybe yes. It is desirable? Absolutely not. One should be aware that 'citizen-initiated mechanisms of direct democracy' could disrupt democracy. Does 'more democracy' ensure better democracy? Does more quantity imply more quality? Not at all, I don't think so.

The new frontier of 'direct democracy' is electronic democracy. Morozov (2011) has already warned of the internet's risks to freedom. A crucial point remains that of the effective, not oligopolistic, plurality of all sources of information and their quality in an era in which disinformation and misinformation seem unstoppable. At the same time it is necessary to monitor and take into account the ability citizens have to use the available information.[44]

---

[44] Fusaro (2018) mentions a conference on 'Misinformation in referenda' which took place in August 2018, promoted by the Faculté de droit, des sciences criminelles et d'administration publique—Center de droit public—University of Lausanne; a publication Baume et al. (2020), came out in summer 2020.

How concrete is the risk of disrupting democratic processes? In particular, do democracies run a risk of 'digital disruption'? (Pew Research Center [2020]; Bertelsmann Foundation [2017, 2018]).

In the early 1980s, K. D. Bracher (1984a: 238–239, 1984b) wrote that, 'Defining the plebiscitarian component of representative democracy and limiting its possible distortions therefore remains a central problem for any modern theory of democracy'. Bracher (1984: 325–341) with reference to the strong criticisms against the social-liberal democracies of the 1960s, recalls 'the right-left totalitarian front against the Weimar Republic (1932)' and states that 'The glorification of direct democratic action and the totalitarian participation that followed is the reawakening of the ancient dispute between idea and reality.' He drew attention to a left and right anti-parliamentarism present in those years, recalled the totalitarian right-left front against the Weimar Republic, and warned of affinities 'which binds certain far-left theorists today to criticism of the democracy of a Carl Schmitt, who fought democracy because he did not see it ideally realized, and theorized a right-wing dictatorship' (Bracher 1984: 341).

Ackerman (2019: 12) rises the question: 'Is it possible to design the referendum process so that it can be triggered by broadly based movements but not by special interests?'.[45] At least as regards the Swiss referendum experience, Kriesi (2005: 239) trusts in the pluralism of the elites in conflict with each other, arguing: 'As long as the elite speak with many voices, as long as there is a conflict among the elite, as long as the elite form clearly structured coalitions and provide a diversity of arguments for the diverging points of view, the direct-democratic process does not risk falling into the populist trap'.

In the 1970s, Ralf Dahrendorf (1974: 673–701) warned against the 'paradox of the total citizen', asserting: 'Nothing favours the deprivation of liberty as the exercise of total participation'; at the same time he urged European liberals to take up the challenge of participation. Half a century later, Dahrendorf's exhortation seemed to have remained a dead letter. However, the anchor point remained stable, as Dahrendorf himself reiterated: 'My central thesis remains this: representative, parliamentary, democracy is threatened by various tendencies, but has not lost nor its strength nor its right. It is worth revitalizing and strengthening it' (2005: 325, emphasis added).

... *it* ... the liberal, constitutional, representative, parliamentary democracy, that is to say, the only sovereign democracy of which a limited part of the inhabitants of the earth have still experience. Referenda do not institute any kind of 'direct democracy'. The theme, therefore, remains how we define *democracy,* and what citizens think is meant by 'democracy' (Ferrin and Kriesi 2016).[46] Paradoxical as it may seem, it is necessary that constitutional-liberal-representative democracy live so that citizens can participate in the government

---

[45]There is a need for empirical and comparative analysis in sufficiently homogeneous political systems of the sort provided by Hollander (2019).

[46]Data can be found in: http://www.europeansocialsurvey.org/.

of the *Res Publica,* also through a limited and wise use of initiatives and referendums.

After 72 years, what was established by the Constitution regarding referendum institutes in the Regions and Municipalities has remained largely dead letter in the printed paper of the laws of the State, of the regional and municipal statutes. The Italian experience is characterized by the significant dimensions of the national referendums and by the irrelevance of the phenomenon in the Municipalities and Regions. Parties and institutions, as soon as they learned the national lesson, worked effectively to block the spread of the referenda in the Regions and Municipalities. Making the provisions of the Constitution effective on this matter is a task that liberal-constitutional-democratic reformers have so far ignored.

REFERENCES

Ackerman, B. (2019). *Revolutionary Constitutions Charismatic Leadership and the Rule of the Law.* Cambridge, MA: The Belknap Press of Harvard University Press.

Agosti, A. (2015). Alcide De Gasperi and Palmiro Togliatti. In: Jones and Pasquino (Eds.) (pp. 341–357).

Altman, D. (2011). *Direct Democracy Worldwide.* New York: Cambridge University Press.

Altman, D. (2019). *Citizenship and Contemporary Direct Democracy.* Cambridge: Cambridge University Press.

Amato, G. (1980). Una Repubblica da Riformare—Il dibattito sulle istituzioni in Italia dal 1975 a oggi. Bologna: il Mulino.

Amato, G. (1992). Discussione. In Luciani & Volpi (Eds.) (pp. 189–193, 212–215).

Amato, G. (2015). The Constitution. In Jones & Pasquino (Eds.) (pp. 71–81).

Armaroli, P. (1974). Referendum abrogativo e classe politica. *Rivista Italiana Di Scienza Politica, 3,* 561–586.

Auer, A. (2001). Conclusions. In Auer & Bützer (Eds.) (pp. 345–355).

Auer, A., & Bützer, M. (Eds.). (2001). *Direct Democracy: The Eastern and Central European Experience.* Aldershot: Ashgate.

Auer, A., Malinverni, G., & Hottelier, M. (2000). *Droit constitutionnel suisse,* 2 vols. Berne: Stämpfli.

Ballini, P. (1988). *Le elezioni nella storia d'Italia, dall'Unità al fascismo—Profilo storico-statistico.* Bologna: il Mulino.

Barbera, A. (1991). Una riforma per la Repubblica. Roma: Editori Riuniti.

Barbera, A., & Morrone, A. (2003). *La Repubblica dei referendum.* Bologna: il Mulino.

Bartolini, S. (1981). *Riforma Istituzionale e Sistema Politico—La Francia gollista.* Bologna: il Mulino.

Bartolini, S. (1982). The Politics of Institutional Reform in Italy. *West European Politics, 5*(3), 203–221.

Basile, S. (1992). *Il dibattito sul referendum in età liberale (1862–1926).* Firenze: Università degli Studi di Firenze—Facoltà di Scienze Politiche—"C. Alfieri", *edizione provvisoria.*

Basile, S. (1994). Il referendum nell'Italia liberale. Dibattiti ed esperienze. In Caciagli & Uleri (Eds.) (pp. 287–315).

Baume, S., Boillet, V., & Martenet, V. (Eds.). (2020). *Misinformation in Referenda.* London: Routledge.

Bernardi, E. (2015). Aldo Moro and Enrico Berlinguer. In: Jones and Pasquino (Eds.) (pp. 369–377).

Bernardini, G., Cau, M., D'Ottavio, G., & Nubola, C. (Eds.) (2017). *L'età costituente. Italia 1945–1948.* Bologna: il Mulino.

Bertelsmann Foundation (2017). *Disrupting Democracy—Point, Click, Transform.* https://www.bfna.org/project/disrupting-democracy/.

Bertelsmann Foundation (2018), *Disrupting Democracy—Point, Click, Transform— vol. II.* https://www.bfna.org/project/disrupting-democracy/.

Bluche, F. (Ed.). (2000). *Le Prince, le peuple et le Droit. Autour des plébiscites del 1851 et 1852.* Paris: Presses Universitaires de France.

Bobbio, N. (1975). Quali alternative alla democrazia rappresentativa? In Mondoperaio (10); reprinted in Il marxismo e lo Stato—Il dibattito aperto nella sinistra italiana sulle tesi di Norberto Bobbio. Pref. Federico Coen (1976); Eng. tr. Telos, (1978) 35 (pp.17–30). Roma: Mondoperaio (pp. 19–37).

Bordignon, F., Ceccarini, L., & Diamanti, I. (2017). L'Italia del Sì e l'Italia del No. Evoluzione e profilo del voto referendario. In Pritoni, Valbruzzi and Vignati (Eds.) (pp. 127–135).

Bortoli, G. (1965). *Sociologie du Référendum dans la France Moderne.* Paris: LGDJ-Pichon-Durand-Auzias.

Bracher, K. D. (1984a). *Zeit der Ideologien,* Stuttgart: Deutsche Verlag (1982), tr. it., *Il Novecento Secolo delle Ideologie.* Roma-Bari: Laterza.

Bracher, K. D. (1984b). *The Age of Ideologies: A History of Political Thought in the Twentieth Centur.* London: Weidenfeld and Nicolson.

Bruti Liberati, E. (2018). *Magistratura e società nell'Italia repubblicana.* Bari-Roma: Editori Laterza.

Budge, I. (1996). *The New Challenge of Direct Democracy.* Cambridge: Polity Press.

Butler, D., & Ranney, A. (Eds.) (1978). *Referendums. A Comparative Study of Practice and Theory.* Washington, DC: American Enterprise Institute for Public Policy Research.

Butler, D., & Ranney, A. (Eds.). (1994). *Referendums around the World. The Growing Use of Direct Democracy.* Houndmills, Basingstoke: The MacMillan Press.

Caciagli, M., & Uleri P. V. (Eds.). *Democrazie e Referendum.* Roma-Bari: Editori Laterza.

Calise, M. (2015). Government and Prime Minnster. In Jones & Pasquino (Eds.) (pp. 95–106).

Carnevale, P. (2020). I Rischi dell'Utopia della c.d. Democrazia Diretta. Per una rilettura critica della storia e della cronaca dei rapporti tra democrazia partecipativa e rappresentativa. *Nomos. Le Attualità Del Diritto, 1,* 1–28.

Cartabia, M. (2007). The Ratification of the European Constitutional Treaty in Italy. In A. Albi & J. Ziller (Eds.), *The European Constitution and National Constitutions: Ratification and Beyond* (pp. 39–44). Kluwr Law International: Alphen aan den Rijn.

Casaleggio, D. (2018). L'intervista integrale di Davide Casaleggio a La Verità. *il Blog Delle Stelle.* Available at: https://www.ilblogdellestelle.it/2018/07/lintervista_int egrale_di_davide_casaleggio_a_la_verita.html. Last accessed on 31 May 2020.

Cassese, S., Galasso, G., & Melloni, A. (Eds.). (2018). *I Presidenti della Repubblica. Il Capo dello Stato e il Quirinale nella storia della democrazia italiana*, 2 vols. Bologna: il Mulino,

Cavino, M. et alii. (2017). *La riforma respinta (2014–2016)—Riflessioni sul d.d.l. costituzionale Renzi-Boschi*. Bologna: il Mulino.

Ceccanti, S. (2016). *La transizione è (quasi) finita. Come risolvere nel 2016 i problemi aperti 70 anni prima. Verso il referendum costituzionale*. Torino: Giappichelli.

Cheli, E. (1978). *Costituzione e sviluppo delle istituzioni in Italia*. Bologna: il Mulino.

Chessa, P., & Savona, P. (Eds.). (2014). *La Grande Riforma mancata—Il Messaggio alle camere del 1991 di Francesco Cossiga*. Soveria Mannelli: Rubbettino.

Chiaramonte, A., & De Sio, L. (Eds.). (2014). *Terremoto elettorale. Le elezioni politiche del 2013*. Bologna: il Mulino.

Chiaramonte, A., & De Sio, L. (Eds.). (2019). *Il voto del cambiamento. Le elezioni politiche del 2018*. Bologna: il Mulino.

Chiaramonte, A., & D'Alimonte, R. (2018). The New Italian Electoral System and Its Effects on Strategic Coordination and Disproportionality. *Italian Political Science, 13*(1), 8–18.

Chiaramonte, A., & Emanuele, V. (2019). La stabilità perduta r non (ancora) ritrovata. Il sistema partitico italiano dopo le elezioni del 2018. In Chiaramonte and De Sio, pp. 263–264.

Chiaramonte, A., & Wilson, A. (2017). Introduzione. L'anno della «grande riforma» che non fu. In Fondazione di Ricerca Istituto Carlo Cattaneo (pp. 29–40).

Clementi, F. (2019). Sulla proposta di riduzione del numero di parlamentari: non sempre «less is more». *Osservatoriosullefonti.it, IX*(2), 1–31. http://www.Osservatoriosullefonti.it.

Colarizi, S., & Gervasoni, M. (2005). *La cruna dell'ago. Craxi, il partito socialista e la crisi della Repubblica*. Roma-Bari: Editori Laterza.

Corriere della Sera. (23/06/2013). *La democrazia va rifondata*. Available at: http://lettura.corriere.it/la-democrazia-va-rifondata/. Last accessed on 31 May 2020.

Cossiga, F. (1991). Messaggio alle Camere del Presidente della Repubblic. In Chessa & Savona (Eds.) (2014), *La Grande Riforma mancata—Il Messaggio alle camere del 1991 di Francesco Cossiga* (pp. 7–87). Soveria Mannelli: Rubbettino.

Cotta, M. (2015). Partitocracy: Parties and their Critics in Italian Political Life. In Jones and Pasquino (Eds.) (pp. 41–52).

Cotta, M., & Verzichelli, L. (2007). *Political Institutions in Italy*. Oxford: Oxford University Press.

Crainz, G., & Fusaro, C. (2016). *Aggiornare la Costituzione. Storia e ragioni di una riforma*. Roma: Donzelli Editore.

Craveri, P. (1995). *La Repubblica dal 1958 al 1992*. Torino: UTET.

Craveri, P. (2006). *De Gasperi*. Bologna: il Mulino.

Dahrendorf, R. (1974). Citizenship and Beyond: The Social Dynamics of an Idea. *Social Research, 41*(4), 673–701, tr. It., Cittadini e partecipazione al di là della democrazia rappresentativa?, In Sartori, Giovanni & Ralf Dahrendorf (1977). *Il Cittadino Totale. Partecipazione eguaglianza e libertà nelle democrazie d'oggi*, Torino: Quaderni di Biblioteca della Libertà, (3), pp. 33–59.

Dahrendorf, R. (2005). *Der Wiederbeginn der Geschichte. Vom Fall der Mauer zum Krieg in Irak*, München (2004), tr. It., *La società riaperta. Dal crollo del muro alla guerra in Iraq*, Roma-Bari: Laterza.

Dal Lago, A. (2017). *Populismo digitale. La crisi, la rete e la nuova destra*. Milano: Raffaello Cortina Editore.

Danelon Vasoli, N. (1968). *Il plebiscito in Toscana nel 1860*. Firenze: Leo S. Olschki.

Dau Novelli, C. (2018). Sergio Mattarella. In Cassese, Galasso and Melloni (Eds.), pp. 477–517.

De Felice, R. (1968). *Mussolini il fascista. II—L'organizzazione dello Stato fascista 1925–1929*. Torino: Giulio Einaudi editore.

De Felice, R. (1974). *Mussolini il duce. 1. Gli anni del consenso—1929–1936*. Torino: Giulio Einaudi editore.

De Mita, E. (2016). Un plebiscito improprio sul Governo. *il Sole 24 Ore*, 28 maggio. https://st.ilsole24ore.com/art/notizie/2016-05-28/un-plebiscito-improprio-governo-081414.shtml?uuid=AD7oSaR.

De Siervo, U., Guerrieri, S., & Varsori, A. (Eds.) (2004). *La prima legislatura repubblicana. Continuità e discontinuità nell'azione delle istituzioni—Atti del Convegno—Roma, 17–18 ottobre 202*, 2 vols. Roma: Carocci.

Denquin, J.-M. (1976). *Référendum et plébiscite*. Paris: Librairie générale de droit et de jurisprudence, Pichon et Durand-Auzias.

Deszõ, M. (2001). Plebiscites and Referendums. In Auer & Bützer (Eds.) (pp. 264–270).

Di Nolfo, E. (1996). *La Repubblica delle Speranze e degli Inganni. L'italia dalla caduta del fascismo al crollo della Democrazia Cristiana*. Firenze: Ponte alle Grazie.

Diamanti, I., & Lazar, M. (2002). Le elezioni del 13 maggio 2001. Cronaca di una vittoria annunciata... sin troppo presto. In Istituto Carlo Cattaneo, *Politica in Italia. I fatti dellanno e le interpretazioni—Edizione 2002*, P. Bellucci & M. Bull (Eds.) (pp. 57–77). Bologna: il Mulino.

Diamanti, I. with Fabio Bordignon and Luigi Ceccarini (2013). *Un salto nel voto. Ritratto politico dell'Italia di oggi*. Roma-Bari: Editori Laterza.

Donovan, M., & Gilbert, M. (2015). Silvio Berlusconi and Romano Prodi. In Jones and Pasquino (Eds.) (pp. 394–406).

Emanuele, V., & Maggini N. (2017). Le Elezioni amministrative di giugno. In Fondazione di Ricerca Istituto Carlo Cattaneo (2017). *Politica in Italia—I fatti dell'anno e le interpretazioni—Edizine 2017*. Chiaramonte, A. & A. Wilson (Eds.) (pp.103–122). Bologna: il Mulino.

Ferrin, M., & K, H. (Eds.). (2016). *How Europeans View and Evaluate Democracy*. Oxford: Oxford University Press.

Fimiani, E. (2002). "Raggiungi Cento per Cento!" : mobilitazione, adesione e coercizione nei plebisciti fascisti (1929–1934). In Ballini P. L. & Ridolfi M. (Eds.), *Storia delle campagne elettorali in Italia* (pp. 168–192). Milano: Paravia Bruno Mondadori Editori.

Fimiani, E. (Ed.) (2010). *Vox Populi? Pratiche plebiscitarie in Francia Italia Germania (secoli XVIII–XX)*. Bologna: CLUEB.

Fimiani, E. (2017). *«L'unanimità più uno». Plebisciti e potere, una storia europea (secoli XVIII–XX)*. Milano: Le Monnier—Mondadori Education.

Fisichella, D. (2018a). *Ascesa e Declino dell'Unità d'Italia*. Roma: Pagine.

Fisichella, D. (2018b). Fondazione di Ricerca Istituto Carlo Cattaneo. *Il Vicolo Cieco. Le elezioni del 4 marzo 2018*. In Marco Valbruzzi & Rinaldo Vignati (Eds.). Bologna: il Munino.

Fondazione di Ricerca Istituto Carlo Cattaneo. (2015). Politica in Italia. I fatti dell'anno e le interpretazioni. C. Hanretty & S. Profeti (Eds.). Bologna: il Mulino.

Fondazione di Ricerca Istituto Carlo Cattaneo. (2016). Politica in Italia. I fatti dell'anno e le interpretazioni. Edizione 2016. M. Carbone & S. Piattoni (Eds.). Bologna: il Mulino.

Fondazione di Ricerca Istituto Carlo Cattaneo. (2017). *Politica in Italia. I fatti e le interpretazioni—Edizione 2017*. A. Chiaramonte & A. Wilson (Eds.). Bologna: il Mulino.

Fondazione di Ricerca Istituto Carlo Cattaneo. (2018). *Il Vicolo Cieco. Le elezioni del 4 marzo 2018*. M. Valbruzzi e R. Vignati (Eds.). Bologna: il Munino.

Fontana, G. (2012). *Il Referendum Costituzionale nei Processi di Riforma della Repubblica*. Napoli: Editoriale Scientifica.

Formigoni, G. (2016). *Storia d'Italia nella Guerra Fredda*. Bologna: il Mulino.

Fruci, G. L. (2005). Il «suffragio nazionale». Discorsi e rappresentazioni del voto universale nel 1848 italiano. Contemporanea, VIII (4), 597–620.

Fruci, G. L. (2007). Il sacramento dell'unità nazionale. Linguaggi, iconografia e pratiche dei plebisciti risorgimentali (1848–1870). In Alberto M. Banti & P. Ginsborg (Eds.), *Storia d'Italia. Il Risorgimento,* Annali (22) (pp. 567–606). Torino: Einaudi.

Fruci, G. L. (2010). Alle origini del movimento plebiscitario risorgimentale. I liberi voti di ratifica costituzionale e gli appelli al popolo nell'Italia rivoluzionaria e napoleonica (1797–1805). In Fimiani (Ed.) (pp. 87–143).

Fusaro, C. (2011). Italy. In Oliver and Fusaro (Eds.) (pp. 211–234).

Fusaro, C. (2015). Per una storia delle riforme istituzionali. *Rivista Trimestrale Di Diritto Pubblico, 2,* 431–555.

Fusaro, C. (2016). Le ragioni di una riforma. In G. Crainz & C. Fusaro (Eds.) *Aggiornare la Costituzione. Storia e ragioni di una riforma* (pp. 47–137). Roma: Donzelli Editore.

Fusaro, C. (2017). L'ennesima riforma costituzionale mancata. In Fondazione di Ricerca Istituto Carlo Cattaneo (2017), pp. 123–42.

Fusaro, C. (2018). Contributo scritto all'istruttoria legislativa relativa alle proposte di legge cost. nn. 726 Ceccanti e 1173 D'Uva recanti modifiche all'art. 71 Cost. in materia di iniziativa legislativa popolare. *Commissione Affari costituzionali della Camera dei deputati,* (5 dicembre), Roma: Camera dei deputati.

Galavotti, E. (2018). Francesco Cossiga. In Cassese, Galasso and Melloni (Eds.) (pp. 325–363).

Gaspari, Oscar. (1998). *L'Italia dei municipi: il movimento comunale in età liberale (1879–1906)*. Roma: Donzelli Editore.

Gentiloni Silveri, U. (2019). *Storia dell'Italia contemporanea, 1943–2019*. Bologna: il Mulino.

Gerber, E. R. (1999). *The Populist Paradox. Interest Group Influence and the Promise of Direct Legislation*. Princeton: Princeton University Press.

Ghini, C. (1976). *Il Terremoto del 15 Giugno*. Milano: Feltrinelli.

Grassi, G. (1913). *Il Referendum nel governo di Gabinetto*. Roma: Eredi Befani.

Graziano, L., & Tarrow, S. (Eds.) (1979). *La Crisi Italiana,* vol. I, *Formazionedel regime repubblicano e società civile*; vol. II, *Sistema politico e istituzioni*. Torino: Giulio Einaudi.

Grimm, D. (2012). Types of Constitutions. In M. Rosenfed & A. Sajó (Eds.), *The Oxford Handbook of Comparative Constitutional Law* (pp. 98–132). Oxford: Oxford University Press.

Guarnieri, C. (2015). The Courts. In Jones & Pasquino (Eds.) (pp. 120–131).

Hollander, S. (2019). *The Politics of Referendum Use in European Democracies*. Cham, Switzerland: Palgrave Macmillan.

Ignazi, P. (2018). *I partiti in Italia dal 1945 al 2018*. Bologna: il Mulino.

International IDEA. (2008). *Direct Democracy—The International IDEA Handbook*. Stockholm: International IDEA.

Johnson, N. (1981). Types of Referendum: Discussion. In Ranney (Ed.) (pp. 19–45).

Jones, E., & Pasquino, Gianfranco (Eds.). (2015). *The Oxford Handbook of Italian Politics*. Oxford: Oxford University Press.

Kant, I. (1784). *Idee zu einer allgemainen Geschichte in weltbürgerlicher Absicht*.

Kaufman, B., & D. Waters (Eds.). (2004). *Direct Democracy in Europe: A Comprehensive Reference Guide to the Initiative and Referendum Process in Europe*. Durham: Carolina Academic Press.

Klein, G. B. (1905). *Il Referendum Legislativo: Studio Sulla Democrazia elvetica*. Firenze: Tipografia Galileiana.

Kriesi, H. (2005). *Direct Democratic Choice—The Swiss Experience*. Lanham: Lexington Books.

Linder, W. (2010). *Swiss Democracy. Possible Solutions to Conflict in Multicultural Societies*. Basingstoke: Palgrave-Macmillan.

Linnaeus, C. N. (1758). *Systema Naturae Per Regna Tria Naturae, Secundum Classes, Ordines, Genera, Species, Cum Characteribus, Differentiis, Synonymis, Locis* (10th ed.). Salvius: Stockholm.

Lippolis, V., & Salerno, G. M. (2016). *La presidenza più lunga. I poteri del capo dello Stato e la Costituzione*. Bologna: il Mulino.

Lombardo, A. (1984). *La Grande Riforma. Governo, istituzioni, partiti*. Milano: SugarCo Edizioni.

Luciani, M. (2005). *Art. 75: La formazione delle leggi. To. 1. 2, il referendum abrogativo*. Bologna: Zanichelli; Roma: Soc. Ed. Del Foro italiano.

Luciani, M. (2018). Audizione del Prof. Massimo Luciani. *Commissione Affari costituzionali della Camera dei deputati*, (4 dicembre). Roma: Camera dei deputati.

Luciani, M. (2019). «Iniziativa legislativa e referendum, le proposte di revisione costituzionale», intervento alla Tavola Rotonda AIC, Roma, 1° marzo 2019. *Osservatorio Costituzionale*, *1–2*, 200–209.

Luciani, M., & Volpi, M. (Eds.). (1992). *Referendum. Problemi teorici ed esperienze costituzionali*. Roma-Bari: Laterza.

Luciani, M., & Volpi, M. (Eds.). (1995). *Riforme Elettorali*. Roma-Bari: Laterza.

Lupo, N. (2004). *Partito e Antipartito—Una storia politica della prima Repubblica (1946–1978)*. Roma: Donzelli Editore.

Magleby, D. (1984). *Direct Legislation: Voting on Ballot Propositions*. Baltimore: Johns Hopkins University Press.

Magleby, D. (1994a). I problematici sviluppi della recente esperienza statunitense. In Caciagli & Uleri (Eds.) (pp. 79–99).

Magleby, D. (1994b). Direct Legislation in American States. In Butler & Ranney (Eds.) (pp. 218–257).

Marradi, A. (1990). Classification, Typology, Taxonomy. *Quality and Quantity*, *XXIV*(2), 129–157.

Matsusaka, J. G. (2020). *Let the People Rule. How Direct Democracy can Meet the Populist Challenge*. Princeton and Oxford: Princeton University Press.

Merlini, S. (2007). La forma di governo della nuova Costituzione. La 'questione sociale', le norme programmatiche e la proposta della Repubblica presidenziale. In

Merlini (Ed.), *Piero Calamandrei e la costruzione dello Stato democratico, 1944–1948.* Roma-Bari: Editori Laterza.

Mershon, C. (2015). Party Systems in Post-World War II Italy. In Jones and Pasquino (Eds.) (pp. 144–158).

Ministero per i Beni e le Attività Culturali. (2003). *L'Italia Repubblicana nella crisi degli anni settanta*—vol. IV, *Sistema politico e istituzioni*, G. De Rosa & G. Monina (Eds.). Soveria Mannelli: Rubbettino

Ministero per i Beni e le Attività Culturali. (2003a). L'Italia Repubblicana nella crisi degli anni settanta—vol. I, Tra guerra fredda e distensione, A. Giovagnoli & S. Pons (Eds.). Rubbettino: Soveria Mannelli.

Ministero per i Beni e le Attività Culturali. (2003b). L'Italia Repubblicana nella crisi degli anni settanta—vol.III, Partiti e organizzazioni di massa, F. Malgeri & L. Paggi (Eds.). Rubbettino: Soveria Mannelli

Ministero per i Beni e le Attività Culturali. (2003c). L'Italia Repubblicana nella crisi degli anni settanta—vol. IV, Sistema politico e istituzioni, G. De Rosa & G. Monina (Eds.). Soveria Mannelli: Rubbettino.

Morozov, E. (2011). *The Net Delusion: The Dark Side of Internet Freedom.* New York: PublicAffairs.

Napolitano, G. (2013). *Messaggio del Presidente della Repubblica Giorgio Napolitano al Parlamento nel giorno del giuramento.* Roma: Aula della Camera dei Deputati, 22 aprile, http://presidenti.quirinale.it/elementi/Continua.aspx?tipo=Discorso&key=2688.

Neppi Modona, G. (Ed.). (1996). *Cinquant'anni di Repubblica italiana.* Torino: Einaudi.

Oliver, D., & Fusaro, C. (Eds.). (2011). *How Constitutions Change. A Comparative Study.* Oxford and Portland: Hart.

Orsina, G. (2015). *Liberalism and Liberals.* In Jones and Pasquino (Eds.) (pp. 240–252).

Pacciardi, R. (1972). La Repubblica presidenziale spiegata al popolo. Roma: Edizioni "Nuova Repubblica".

Paladin, L. (2004). *Per una storia costituzionale dell'Italia repubblicana.* Bologna: il Mulino.

Paoli, L. (2015). *Mafia, Camorra, and 'Ndrangheta.* In Jones and Pasquino (Eds.) (pp. 668–681).

Pasquino, G. (1980). Crisi dei partiti e governabilità. Bologna: il Mulino.

Pasquino, G. (1982). Degenerazioni dei partiti e riforme istituzionali. Roma-Bari: Laterza.

Pasquino, G. (1985). Restituire lo scettro al principe. Proposte di riforma istituzionale. Roma-Bari: Laterza.

Pasquino, G. (2000). *La transizione a parole.* Bologna: il Mulino.

Pasquino, G. (2010), Le parole della politica. Bologna: il Mulino.

Pasquino, G. (2017). Le ragioni del No e il futuro della transizione italiana. In Pritoni, Valbruzzi & Vignati (pp. 161–177).

Pasquino, G. (2019). *Italian Democracy. How it works.* London: Routledge.

Pasquino, G., & Ventura, S. (Eds.). (2010). *Una splendida cinquantenne: la quinta Repubblica francese.* Bologna: il Mulino.

Passarelli, G., & Tuorto, D. (2018). *La Lega di Salvini—Estrema destra di governo.* Bologna: il Mulino.

Pedrazzoni, A., & Pinto, L. (2017). Il ritorno alle urne: anatomia di una partecipazione inaspettata. In Pritoni, Valbruzzi & Vignati (Eds.) (pp. 75–92).

Perassi, T. (1911). *Il referendum: la dottrina giuridica. Appendice: Il referendum nel diritto pubblico italiano, note alla legge 29 marzo 1903 sulla municipalizzazione dei pubblici servizi.* Di Fabio: Roma.

Pew Research Center—Anderson Janna and Lee Rainie (2020). *Many Tech Experts Say Digital Disruption Will Hurt Democracy.* https://www.pewresearch.org/internet/2020/02/21/many-tech-experts-say-digital-disruption-will-hurt-democracy/.

Poli, E. (2001). *Forza italia. Strutture, leadership e radicamento territoriale.* Bologna: il Mulino.

Pombeni, P. (2016). *La questione costituzionale in Italia.* Bologna: il Mulino.

Pons, S. (2018). Giorgio Napolitano. In Cassese, Galasso & Melloni (Eds) (pp. 439–476).

Presidenza del Consiglio dei Ministri. Comitato per le celebrazioni del 40° anniversario della Repubblica. (1987). *La nascita della Repubblica. Atti del Convegno di Studi Storici, 4–5–6 giugno 1987*, 2 vols., Roma: Archivio Centrale dello Stato.

Quagliariello, G. (2003). *De Gaulle e il gollismo.* Bologna: il Mulino.

Quagliariello, G. (2012). *De Gaulle.* Soveria Mannelli: Rubbettino.

Ragionieri, E. (1976). La storia politica e sociale. In R. Ruggiero & C. Vivanti (Eds.), *Storia d'Italia—IV: dall'Unità a oggi* (pp. 1665–2774). Torno: Einaudi.

Regalia, M. (2015). Electoral Systems. In Jones and Pasquino (Eds.) (pp. 132–143).

Regalia, M., & Tronconi, F. (2017). Il no in cerca di spiegazioni: fattori politici e sociali nella distribuzione territoriale del voto. In V. Pritoni & Vignati (Eds.) (pp. 93–111).

Rensi, G. (1902). *Gli "Anciens Régimes" e la democrazia diretta.* Bellinzona: Colombi.

Rensi, G. (1995). *La Democrazia Diretta.* Milano: Adelphi.

Rhodes, M. (2015). *Tangentopoli*—More than 20 Years On. In E. Jones & G. Pasquino (Eds.), pp. 309–324.

Rial, J. (2016). Postscript: The Quality of Democracy. *International IDEA—LUISS, The Quality of Democracies in Latin America* (pp. 97–109). International Institute for Democracy and Electoral Assistance: Stockholm.

Ricci, A. G. (1996). *Aspettando la Repubblica—I governi della transizione 1943–1946.* Roma: Donzelli Editore.

Ricci, A. G. (2001). *La Repubblica.* Bologna: il Mulino.

Rosanvallon, P. (1992). *Le sacre du citoyen. Du suffrage universel en France*, Paris: Gallimard, tr. It., *La Rivoluzione dell'uguaglianza. Storia del suffragio universale in Francia*, Milano: Anabasi, 1994.

Ruth, S. P., Welp, Y., & Whitehead, L. (Eds.). (2017). *Let the People Rule? Direct Democracy in the Twenty-First Century.* London: Rowman & Littlefield International.

Sabato, L. J., Ernst, H. R., & Larson, B. A. (Eds.). (2001). *Dangerous Democracy? The Battle over the Ballot—Initiatives in America.* Lanham: Rowman & Littlefield.

Sale, G. (2003). *Dalla Monarchia alla Repubblica.* Santa Sede, Cattolici Italiani e Referendum, Milano: Jaca Book.

Sartori, G. (1975). The Tower of Babel. In G. Sartori, F. W. Riggs & H. Teune (Eds.), *Tower of Babel: On the Definition and Analysis of Concepts in the Social Sciences*, International Studies Association, Occasional Paper n. 6, University of Pittsburg 1975, pp. 7–37, tr. It., in: Sartori (2011), pp. 91–142.

Sartori, G. (1987). *The Theory of Democracy Revisited*. Chatham, New Jersey: Chatham House Publishers.

Sartori, G. (2011). *Logica, metodo e linguaggio nelle scienze sociali*. Bologna: il Mulino.

Scalfari, E. (2016). Il plebiscito senza quorum nel paese dove regna Don Chisciotte. *la Repubblica*, 3 gennaio. https://www.repubblica.it/politica/2016/01/03/news/il_plebiscito_senza_quorum_nel_paese_dove_regna_don_chisciotte-130539249/.

Schadee, H., Segatti, P., & Vezzoni, C. (2019). *L'Apocalisse della Democrazia Italiana. Alle origini di due terremoti elettorali*. Bologna: il Mulino.

Scoppola, P. (1997). *La repubblica dei partiti. Evoluzione e crisi di un sistema politico 1945–1996*. Bologna: il Mulino.

Sicardi, S. (2015). Costituzione, potere costituente e revisione costituzionale alla prova dell'ultimo ventennio. In S. Sicardi, M. Cavino & L. Imarisio (Eds.), *Vent'anni di Costituzione (1993–2013)—Dibattiti e riforme nell'Italia tra due secoli* (pp. 9–61). Bologna: il Mulino.

Sobrino, G. (2017). Il percorso delle riforme costituzionali. In M. Cavino et al. (Eds.), *La riforma respinta (2014–2016). Riflessioni sul d.d.l. costituzionale Renzi-Boschi* (pp. 15–38). Bologna: il Mulino.

Sogno, E. (1974). La Seconda Repubblica. Firenze: Sansoni.

Spreafico, A. (1987). La competizione elettorale e gli esiti del voto. *Presidenza del Consiglio dei Ministri—Comitato per le Celebrazioni del 40° Anniversario della Repubblica, La Nascita della Repubblica—Atti del Convegno di Studi Storici—Archivio Centrale dello Stato—Roma, 4-5-6 giugno 1987* (pp. 181–238). Quaderni di Vita Italiana: Roma.

Sundquist, J. L. (1986). *Constitutional Reform and Effective Government*. Washington, D.C: The Brookings Institution.

Teodori, M. (1992). *Costituzione Italian e Modello Americano*. Milano: Sperling & Kupfer Editori.

Teodori, M. (2015). The Laity. In Jones and Pasquino (Eds.) (pp. 453–461).

Teodori, M., Ignazi, P., & Panebianco, A. (1977). *I Nuovi Radicali. Storia e sociologia di un movimento politico*. Milano: Arnoldo Mondadori Editore.

Trechsel, A. H., & Esposito, F. (2011). Why Plebiscite? A Critique of a Nebulous Concept. In Auer and Bützer (Eds.) (pp. 185–208).

Uleri, P. V. (1981). 'Le forme di consultazione diretta. *Uno Schema Di Classificazione Per L'analisi Comparata'*, *Rivista Italiana Di Scienza Politica*, XI, 1, 47–90.

Uleri, P. V. (1985). Le forme di consultazione popolare nelle democrazie: una tipologia. *Rivista Italiana Di Scienza Politica*, XV, 2, 205–254.

Uleri, P. V. (1994). Dall'instaurazione alla crisi democratica. Un'analisi in chiave comparata del fenomeno referendario in Italia (1946–1993). In Caciagli and Uleri (Eds.) (pp. 390–429).

Uleri, P. V. (1996). Italy: Referendum and Initiatives from the Origins to the Crisis of a Democratic Regime. In Gallagher & Uleri (Eds.) (pp. 106–125).

Uleri, P. V. (2000). Plebiscites and Plebiscitary Politics. In Richard Rose (Ed.), *International Enciclopedia of Elections* (pp. 199–202). Washington, D.C: CQ Press.

Uleri, P. V. (2002). On Referendum Voting in Italy: Yes, No or Non-vote? How Italian Parties Learned to Control Referenda. In L. LeDuc & P. Svensson (Eds.), *Interests, Information and Voting in Referendums, European Journal of Political Research*, (41), 863–883.

Uleri, P. V. (2003). *Referendum e Democrazia. Una prospettiva comparata*. Bologna: il Mulino.

Uleri, P. V. (2007a). Referendum e iniziative popolari. In G. Pasquino (Ed.), *Strumenti della Democrazia* (pp. 39–73). Bologna: il Mulino.

Uleri, P. V. (2007b, March 14–15). Initiatives and Referendums in Italian Democracy. Imperfect Forms, and Hard-Won Institutionalisation. *International Conference on Direct Democracy in Latin America*, Buenos Aires, pp. 1–44 (unpublished manuscript).

Uleri, P. V. (2008). The Institutionalisation of the Referendum in the Italian Political System: From the Nnational to Regional and Local Levels. In T. Schiller (Ed.), *Local Direct Democracy in Europe* (pp. 75–112). Wiesbaden: VS Verlag.

Uleri, P. V. (2010). Referendum comunali in Italia: la "partecipazione" che non piace. Introduzione elementare a forme ed esperienze. In Annuario di politica & Günther Pallaver (Ed.) (pp. 93–128). Bolzano. Raetia.

Uleri, P. V. (2010b). Referendum comunali in Italia: la "partecipazione" che non piace. *Politika, 10,* 93–128.

Uleri, P. V. (2011). The Institutionalisation of the Referendum in the Italian Political System: From the National to Regional and Local Levels. In Schiller (Ed.) (pp. 75–112).

Uleri, P. V. (2012). Institutions of Citizens' Political Participation in Italy: Crooked Forms, Hindered Institutionalization. In Setälä & Schiller (Eds.) (pp. 71–88).

Varsori, A. (2015). Bettino Craxi and Giulio Andreotti. In Jones and Pasquino (Eds.) (pp. 378–393).

Vassallo, S. (2017). Gli effetti del No. La logica dei veti, lo scettro ai giudici e il gioco dell'oca. In V. Pritoni & Vignati (Eds.) (pp. 149–160).

Vassallo, S., & Ceccanti, S. (2004). Il sistema politico italiano tra cambiamento, apprendimento, e adattamento. In S. Ceccanti & S. Vassallo (Eds.), *Come chiudere la transizione. Cambiamento, apprendimento e adattamento nel sistema politico italiano* (pp. 15–68). Bologna: il Mulino.

Ventrone, A. (2008). *La cittadinanza repubblicana. Come cattolici e comunisti hanno costruito la democrazia italiana* (1943–1948). Bologna: il Mulino.

Violante, L. (1996). L'Italia dei poteri illegali. In G. Neppi Modona (Ed.), Cinquant'anni di Repubblica Italiana (pp. 143–158). Torino: Einaudi.

Violante, L. (2018). Il ruolo della magistratura. (The role of the judiciary). Report for a conference entitled '1992–1993. Uno spartiacque nella storia dell'Italia conteporanea' ('1992–1993. A watershed in the history of contemporary Italy') (Ancona, 30 November–1 December 2018).

Vittori, D. (2019). *Il valore di uno. Il Movimento 5 Stelle e l'esperimento della democrazia diretta*. Roma: Luiss University Press.

Volpi, M. (1979). *La democrazia autoritaria. Forma di governo bonapartsta e V Repubblica francese*. Bologna: il Mulino.

Volpi, M. (2014). Il semipresidenzialismo tra teoria e realtà. Bologna: il Mulino.

Volpi, M. (Ed.). (2015). *Istituzioni e Sistema Politico in Italia: Bilancio di un Ventennio*. Bologna: il Mulino.

Welp, Y. (2014). De venenos y fármacos: la regulación y prácticas de la revocatoria del mandato en Suiza y las Américas. In Yanina Welp & Uwe Serdült (Eds.), *La dosis hace el veneno – Análisis de la revocatoria del mandato en América Larina*. Estados Unidos y Suiza, Quito: Instituto de la Democracia.

Zagrebelsky, G. (1996). Verso una iperdemocrazia plebiscitaria? In N. Modona (Ed.), pp. 245–257.

Zagrebelsky, G. (2016). *Loro Diranno, Noi diciamo. Vademecum sulle riforme istituzionali.* with Francesco Pallante. Roma-Bari: Laterza.

CHAPTER 18

Luxembourg: The 2015 Referendum on Voting Rights for Foreign Residents

Léonie de Jonge and Ralph Petry

18.1   INTRODUCTION

On 7 June 2015, the Grand Duchy of Luxembourg held a consultative referendum in the context of a broader constitutional reform project that had been
launched in 2004 (*Gouvernement du Grand-Duché du Luxembourg* 2013: 6).[1]
Voters were asked to voice their opinion on three issues, namely: (1) lowering
the legal voting age from eighteen to sixteen; (2) extending voting rights
to non-citizen residents; and (3) imposing ten-year term limits on government mandates.[2] This chapter focuses specifically on the second referendum
question on 'foreigner voting rights' (the so-called *Auslännerwahlrecht*).

---

[1]In the aftermath of the 2004 general election, the incoming government
announced its ambition to revise the Constitution. In April 2009, the revision
proposal N°6030 to amend and redraft the Constitution was introduced in Parliament
(*Chambre des Députés du Gouvernement du Luxembourg* 2009).

[2]A fourth question on the State's obligations to provide salaries and pensions for
priests was announced but eventually abandoned following an agreement between the
government and religious representatives in January 2015.

L. de Jonge (✉)
University of Groningen, Groningen, The Netherlands
e-mail: leonie.de.jonge@rug.nl

R. Petry
University of Luxembourg, Luxembourg City, Luxembourg
e-mail: ralph.petry@uni.lu

© The Author(s) 2021
J. Smith (ed.), *The Palgrave Handbook of European Referendums*,
https://doi.org/10.1007/978-3-030-55803-1_18

As in most countries, voting rights in Luxembourg are seen as a corollary of nationality.[3] In practice, only people with Luxembourgish nationality can participate in national legislative elections. Given that Luxembourg has by far the highest proportion of foreign residents in the European Union (EU), as nearly half of the population (47.4% of the 626,000 inhabitants) do not hold citizenship (Statec 2020), the Grand Duchy is confronted with an imminent democratic deficit. In the legislative elections held in October 2013, only 57% of the residents of Luxembourg over the age of eighteen had the right to vote (Zahlen and Thill 2013). In the centre electoral district (one of four electoral districts) comprising Luxembourg City, only 45.4% of the total adult population could participate in the general election, and nearly one-third of those voters were aged sixty or older (Zahlen and Thill 2013). By January 2015, 54.5% of the total adult population had the right to vote (Allegrezza et al. 2015), and in the most recent general election held in October 2018, only 47.2% of residents aged eighteen and older had voting rights (*Paperjam* 2018). Thus, nearly half of the resident population in Luxembourg does not have voting rights.

In light of these socio-demographic developments, the referendum question on voting rights for non-citizens is particularly pertinent for the state of democracy in the Grand Duchy and will therefore be discussed in greater detail in this chapter. The broader aim of the *Auslännerwahlrecht* was to enfranchise non-national residents to address the looming democratic deficit. Under the proposal put forward by the three governing parties at the time (i.e. Greens, Social Democrats and Liberals), non-citizens would have been allowed to participate in national legislative elections provided they had resided in the country for at least a decade *and* had previously participated in communal or European elections. The specific wording of the question was as follows:

> Do you approve of the idea that residents without Luxembourgish nationality should have the right to optionally register on electoral lists to participate as voters in Chamber of Deputies [i.e. parliamentary] elections, on the double condition they have resided in Luxembourg for at least ten years, and that they have previously taken part in European or municipal elections in Luxembourg? (*Gouvernement du Grand-Duché de Luxembourg* 2015a).[4]

In a country otherwise known for its stability, the referendum result resembled a political earthquake as all three questions initiated by the governing parties were rejected by a landslide: 80.87% of the electorate objected to extending voting rights to citizens between the age of sixteen and eighteen; 69.93% was opposed to introducing governmental term limits; and 78.02% of the Luxembourgish electorate said 'No' to enfranchising non-citizens (*Gouvernement du*

---

[3]There are some exceptions where foreign residents can acquire voting rights, including New Zealand and some South American countries (e.g. Chile and Uruguay).

[4]Where appropriate, quotations have been translated by the authors.

Grand Duché de Luxembourg 2015b). The vehement rejection of the *Auslän-nerwahlrecht* left a mark on the Grand Duchy in the sense that it brought issues pertaining to identity politics to the centre of the political debate. Prior to discussing the campaign and legacy of the 2015 referendum, it is helpful to explain the particularities of the Luxembourgish case. The remainder of this introduction therefore provides a brief history of referendums in the Grand Duchy as well as an overview of the legal framework.

Referendums in Luxembourg are relatively rare; unlike Switzerland or Liechtenstein, the Grand Duchy does not have a particularly long-standing tradition of employing direct democratic instruments.[5] The 2015 referendum was only the fourth in the history of the Grand Duchy. Earlier referendums include: (1) the 1919 (double) vote on the preferred head of state and the possibility of entering into an economic union with France or Belgium; (2) the 1937 referendum on the dissolution of the Communist Party; and (3) the 2005 referendum on the European Constitutional Treaty (Fayot 2006; *Gouvernement du Grand-Duché de Luxembourg* 2015a).[6] Referendums in Luxembourg are generally consultative and thus not legally binding.[7] However, in the run-up to the 2015 referendum, the government announced it would adhere to the result, no matter what the outcome would be (*Gouvernement du Grand-Duché de Luxembourg* 2015a).

Contrary to most European countries, voting in Luxembourg is mandatory. Specifically, all Luxembourgish citizens between the ages of eighteen and seventy-five who are registered on the electoral lists and who are residing in Luxembourg are required by law to participate in local, national and European elections.[8] This rule also applies to referendums; voters inscribed on the electoral roll for legislative elections on the day of the referendum are required to participate.[9] Since compulsory voting guarantees a relatively high turnout, there is no need for a participation quorum. In the 2015 referendum, 87% of the electorate turned out to vote (*Gouvernement du Grand Duché de Luxembourg* 2015b).

From a procedural perspective, Article 51(7) of the Luxembourgish Constitution stipulates that Parliament is required to pass a specific law in order to hold a national referendum. This law regulates the conditions of the vote, in accordance with the amended law of 4 February 2005 on national referendums. The draft bill for the referendum of 7 June 2015 was introduced on

---

[5]In recent years, the country has witnessed several consultative referendums at the local level, notably asking residents to decide whether their communes should merge into one.

[6]The 2005 referendum result was surprisingly close for a country that is generally very Europhile: only 56.52% of the voters were in favour of the ratification of the European Union Constitutional Treaty (see Blau 2005: 95ff).

[7]The extent to which referendums in Luxembourg are legally binding is actually subject to debate (see Heuschling 2015).

[8]Luxembourgish citizens living abroad can register by applying for a postal vote.

[9]In case of an unjustified abstention, sanctions can include penalties ranging from €100 to €1000.

4 November 2014 by three parliamentarians of the then governing parties.[10] The explanatory statement of the draft bill referred to the referendum as a 'consultative referendum' on 'controversial questions in relation to the Constitution' (*Chambre des Députés du Gouvernement du Luxembourg* 2014: 5). With regards to the *Auslännerwahlrecht* question, the explanatory statement made reference to the demographic situation of Luxembourg (mentioned above): '[I]n the short run, the Luxembourgish electorate will represent a minority of the people living in the country. The positive experiences of the local and European elections make it possible to envisage this opening of political rights to new categories of citizens' (*Chambre des Députés du Gouvernement du Luxembourg* 2014: 5). The draft bill was adopted on 24 February 2015 with a majority of thirty-four out of sixty votes.

Turning from the formal arrangements to the empirics, the following section discusses the reasons behind the 2015 referendum on voting rights for non-citizens. It does so by providing relevant background information and analysing the campaigns leading up to the referendum. As shown below, the *Auslännerwahlrecht* question proved highly controversial. This became evident in the public debates in the run-up to the vote. Because of their prominent position in these debates, we focus particularly on the role of civil society actors and the media. The conclusion considers the Luxembourgish referendum in cross-national comparative perspective and discusses the legacy of the *Auslännerwahlrecht* vote for the Grand Duchy. The 2015 referendum proved divisive in the sense that it stirred up nationalist sentiments and ultimately failed to resolve the lingering democratic deficit it was meant to address.

18.2   THE *AUSLÄNNERWAHLRECHT*: EXTENDING VOTING RIGHTS TO NON-NATIONALS?

18.2.1   The Political Debate

The idea of extending voting rights to non-citizens was by no means new; indeed, given the looming democratic deficit resulting from the demographic realities of the country, debates on the *Auslännerwahlrecht* date back to the 1980s (see Forum 1981; Petry 2016: 36–42). These debates were primarily launched and steered by migrant worker representatives in Luxembourgish trade unions as well as various non-governmental organisations (NGOs). Two NGOs are particularly worth mentioning in this context, namely the Association for the Support of Immigrant Workers (*Association de Soutien aux Travailleurs Immigrés*; ASTI) and the Liaison Committee of Foreign Associations (*Comité de Liaison des Associations d'Étrangers*; CLAE). ASTI was established in 1979 with the main purpose of enfranchising foreign residents

[10]Parliamentary document N°6738 (see *Chambre des Députés du Gouvernement du Luxembourg* 2014).

(Kollwelter and Zuccoli 2010: 26). CLAE was founded by ASTI in 1985, but now operates as an independent non-profit organisation that serves as a platform for smaller migrant associations (see Petry 2016: 37). The broader aim of these organisations was to lobby for the social and political inclusion of foreign residents in Luxembourgish society.

Since the 1990s, foreigners residing in Luxembourg enjoy extensive voting rights for European and local elections. Following the ratification of the Maastricht Treaty in 1992, EU citizens residing in Luxembourg were given the right to participate in these elections.[11] In 1999, non-national EU citizens were also allowed to stand in local elections, provided they were able to prove six years of residency (CEFIS 2014). In 2003, the Luxembourgish government went one step further by granting *all* non-national residents (including those from non-EU countries) the right to vote in communal elections, provided they had resided in the country for a minimum of five years (Fetzer 2011: 98). Since 2011, non-EU citizens are also allowed to stand for communal elections. In addition, since that year, non-national residents can also run for the posts of mayor and deputy mayor (CEFIS 2014). Thus, the *Auslännerwahlrecht* question had been raised and discussed prior to the 2015 vote.

While the referendum can be seen as the culmination of a long-standing debate, the timing of the vote was the product of national political developments. As mentioned earlier, the referendum was initiated by the three governing parties at the time: the liberal Democratic Party (*Demokratesch Partei*; DP); the centre-left Luxembourgish Socialist Workers' Party (*Lëtzebuerger Sozialistesch Aarbechterpartei*; LSAP); and the Greens (*déi Gréng*). From December 2013, the Luxembourgish government had been headed by Prime Minister Xavier Bettel, leader of the DP.

In fact, 2013 marked a tumultuous year in Luxembourgish politics. Early elections were held in October, after Jean Claude Juncker's coalition government between the conservative Christian Social People's Party (*Chrëschtlech-Sozial Vollekspartei*; CSV) and the LSAP was brought down by a series of scandals involving the Luxembourgish intelligence service (Dumont and Kies 2014). Although the CSV remained the largest party with twenty-three seats out of sixty parliamentary seats (by securing 34.1% of the vote), the party was excluded from forming a government when the LSAP (thirteen seats), the DP (thirteen seats) and the Greens (six seats) decided to form a coalition. The formation of the so-called 'Gambia Coalition' (so-called because the colours

[11]In 1994, in the context of the negotiations on the European directives outlining the procedures for the local and European voting rights, Luxembourg obtained a derogation; since more than 20% of the population was composed of non-citizens, the country was allowed to implement additional restrictions (i.e. a longer residence requirement). However, these additional restrictions were eased gradually (Fetzer 2011: 98). The required period of residence to be able to participate in European elections was initially set at ten years, but then lowered to five years for the 2004 elections and two years for the 2009 elections. Since 2014, EU citizens no longer have to prove any duration of residency to participate in European elections (CEFIS 2014).

associated with the governing parties match those of the Gambian flag) marked the first time in the post-war history of Luxembourg that the country was led by a coalition of three political parties, and only the second time that the CSV played the role of the opposition (*Luxemburger Wort* 2013). The CSV was joined in opposition by the radical Left (*déi Lénk*), which held two seats, and the nationalist Alternative Democratic Reform Party (*Alternativ Demokratesch Reformpartei*; ADR), which held three seats (Dumont and Kies 2014).

Upon taking office, the Gambia Coalition announced its ambition to modernise the political institutions of the country by advocating increased participatory democracy and strengthening the political rights of residents who did not have Luxembourgish nationality:

> We want more participation, which means actively involving people in polit-ical decision-making processes [...]. We are looking to establish a constructive dialogue with them and are therefore willing to strengthen their rights. More-over, we also want to ask citizens directly to voice their opinions by means of referendums. Important reforms should not be made from the top down. (Service Information et Presse 2014: 86)

In line with this announcement, the Prime Minister framed the referendum as an opportunity to boost the democratic credentials of the country. During his annual state-of-the-nation address held on 5 May 2015, Mr. Bettel pledged to introduce a 'resident suffrage' (*Awunnerwahlrecht*), arguing that Luxem-bourg could become a reference country for other European states.[12] Mr. Bettel explained that '[the referendum] is an opportunity for Luxembourg to stand out as a country that is not only characterized by diversity and multilin-gualism, but as a country where people with different nationalities are welcome and invited to participate', and that 'participation should not be limited to people who have a Luxembourgish passport, but should be extended to those who live, work and reside here' (*Chambre des Députés du Gouvernement du Luxembourg* 2015a).

As mentioned earlier, voting rights in national elections in the Grand Duchy have traditionally been reserved for Luxembourgish nationals. Thus, the only way to acquire voting rights is via citizenship. In the past, the acquisition of Luxembourgish citizenship was guaranteed primarily via *jus sanguinis*, but important modifications on the Nationality Law passed in 2008 saw the reintroduction of the *jus soli*; children born in Luxembourg to non-Luxembourgish parents could now receive citizenship, as long as one of their parents was also born in the Grand Duchy (Scuto 2012). At the time of the 2015 referendum, anyone having resided in the country for seven consecutive years could apply for Luxembourgish nationality, provided that they could

---

[12]The term *Awunnerwahlrecht* translates into 'resident voting rights' and was used by proponents of enfranchising non-citizens. In comparison to *Ausländerwahlrecht* ('foreigner voting rights'), the term *Awunnerwahrecht* is considered more inclusive (see also Petry 2016: 86–87).

demonstrate active and passive command of at least one of the three official languages (i.e. Luxembourgish, French and German); basic knowledge of Luxembourgish (i.e. the sole *national* language); as well as 'a sufficient degree of integration' into Luxembourgish society (Finck 2015: 83). Since 2008, the Grand Duchy accepts dual citizenship (Scuto 2012). It should be mentioned that the Luxembourgish Government already planned to facilitate access to citizenship in 2013, in addition to preparing the referendum (*Gouvernement du Grand-Duché du Luxembourg* 2013: 6).

It is worth noting that the *Auslännerwahlrecht* question did not appear to be particularly controversial at the time. Initially, Luxembourgish voters seemed relatively open to the prospect of extending voting rights to non-citizens. A poll from 2012 suggested that 63% of the population (albeit just half of the Luxembourgish residents compared to 80% of foreign residents) were favourable to the idea of extending voting rights to non-national residents (TNS ILRES 2012). In the run-up to the referendum, public opinion shifted towards the 'No' side. However, later surveys merely suggested that the referendum outcome was going to be close, with a slight majority opposed to the enfranchisement of foreign residents. Indeed, no poll came close to predicting the landslide victory of the 'No' camp. According to a poll conducted between April and May 2015 (just a couple of months before the actual vote), 40% of the voters were still in favour of the *Auslännerwahlrecht*, while 53% were opposed and 7% remained undecided (RTL 2015a). Yet, on the day of the referendum, nearly 80% of the electorate voted against the *Auslännerwahlrecht*. To understand this outcome, it is useful to analyse the political debate in the run-up to the 2015 referendum.

18.2.2   The 'Yes' Camp

The official campaign leading up to the referendum was remarkably one-sided. Indeed, the 'Yes' camp in favour of the *Auslännerwahlrecht* seemed relatively strong. At the forefront of the campaign were the three governing parties: DP, LSAP and the Greens. They argued that voting rights in Luxembourg should be seen as a corollary of residency rather than citizenship. Their main arguments in favour of the introduction of the 'resident suffrage' revolved around democratic modernisation and political renewal. The LSAP pointed out that the further enfranchisement of foreign residents was a logical progression of participation in local elections. The Greens and the DP went even further by arguing that the revised dual citizenship law was insufficient to address the democratic deficit given that many other countries refused to grant it, thus forcing residents to renounce their original nationality even though they may still feel connected with their native countries (see Petry 2016: 47–48). Besides the three governing parties, the smallest opposition party (*déi Lénk*) was also in favour of the initiative as a way of strengthening the voice of the 'demos' (Petry 2016: 57–58).

392 L. DE JONGE AND R. PETRY

The 'Yes' camp was backed by four youth parties as well as an eclectic mix of civil society actors. In April 2015, the youth wings of the four main parties (Social Democrats, Greens, Liberals and Conservatives) published a joint statement to express their support for the *Auslännerwahlrecht* and even went one step further by demanding less restrictive prerequisites to enfranchise foreign residents (*Luxemburger Wort* 2015). In an open letter published later that month, a group of some fifty prominent Luxembourgish writers and artists also pledged their support for the initiative, urging voters to say 'Yes' because 'Luxembourg is a multilingual and multicultural country' and 'this diversity should become a driving force for democracy, cultural dialogue and politics, through which a society of "inclusion" emerges' (*Tageblatt* 2015). In June 2015, a group of leading business representatives followed suit by publishing and signing a full-page ad in the printed press: 'We say [...] YES, because we are convinced that this choice is important for our democracy and right for our country' (RTL 2015b). Two of the main trade unions, the socialist-oriented OGBL as well as the Christian-conservative LCGB, also expressed their support for the *Auslännerwahlrecht* by joining the Migration and Integration platform MINTÉ (*Plateforme Migrations et Intégration*), a group composed of nineteen associations representing foreign workers' rights in the Grand Duchy (see *Luxembourg Times* 2015; OGBL 2015).

MINTÉ was established in 2007 in the context of a proposed reform of the Nationality Law (described above) and presented itself as a platform for discussion on the challenges posed by immigration and integration (see Petry 2016: 64). One of the most prominent players within MINTÉ was ASTI, the pro-immigrant NGO described earlier. In the run-up to the 2015 referendum, MINTÉ and ASTI took a lead role in the promotion of voting rights for foreign residents. In the months leading up to the referendum, they organised numerous events and distributed leaflets to inform citizens about the benefits of the *Awunnerwahlrecht*. They argued that 'voting is a basic democratic right', and that 'our democratic principles require that all citizens who are subjected to a given public order should be allowed to influence the political debates and decisions that affect that public order' (MINTÉ 2015: 3). Furthermore, ASTI and MINTÉ maintained that naturalisations alone would be insufficient to address the looming democratic deficit, and that enfranchising non-citizens would generate a more accurate reflection of the demographic realities of the country—especially given that Luxembourg owes large portions of its social and economic wealth to the contributions of non-national residents and cross-border workers from France, Belgium and Germany.[13] Finally, the proponents of the *Awunnerwahlrecht* emphasised that Luxembourgish identity is rooted in multilingualism; in other words, the use of different languages in everyday life is a core characteristic of the Grand Duchy (Petry 2016: 65).

[13]In 2017, cross-border workers made up 45% of the salaried workforce in Luxembourg (ADEM 2018: 6).

Besides these civil society actors, the print media were also generally supportive of the *Auslännerwahlrecht*. Prior to outlining the arguments put forward in and by the press, it is useful to understand the specificities of the Luxembourgish media. The Luxembourgish media landscape is characterized by a remarkable variety of news outlets: next to several radio stations as well as a national television channel, there are over a dozen weekly and monthly print publications and no fewer than five daily newspapers. The surprising amount of print publications can be attributed to two factors. First, there is a generous public funding scheme in place for print publications, which is intended to safeguard media pluralism (see de Jonge 2019; Hirsch 2007). A second particularity of the Luxembourgish media landscape is the persistence of the partisan press. Unlike most European countries, where the media gained independence from political parties in the 1960s, there are only very few truly independent (print) publications in Luxembourg.

In light of these partisan ties, the five daily newspapers published in the Grand Duchy in 2015 could primarily be differentiated by their political and ideological leanings as opposed to their area of specialisation. Indeed, virtually all paid daily newspapers have historic affiliations with political parties. For example, the *Luxemburger Wort* or *Wort* (the oldest and largest daily newspaper in the Grand Duchy), which is read daily by nearly 31% of the population (TNS ILRES 2018), is published by the *Imprimerie Saint-Paul* or IPS. Until 2020, IPS belonged to the Roman Catholic Archdiocese of Luxembourg,[14] and the *Wort* is generally associated with the Christian democratic party (CSV). The *Tageblatt* (the second largest newspaper) is published by *Groupe Editpress*, which is partly owned by the socialist-oriented trade union (OGBL) and maintains ties to the social democratic party (LSAP) (Barth and Hemmer 2008: 210). While partisan links are fading, they continue to influence the overall structure of the Luxembourgish media landscape.

Because of the country's small size, there is a high degree of familiarity between journalists and politicians. Indeed, it is relatively common for media practitioners to maintain personal relationships with key actors in politics and civil society (see Barth and Bucher 2003: 11). This high degree of familiarity in combination with government subsidies and partisan ties make for a relatively moderate media landscape. Given that the Luxembourgish media is not very commercialised, there is very little evidence of 'sensationalism' in the Luxembourgish press; in comparison to other countries, topics such as immigration are not very politicised in the media (de Jonge 2019).

In Luxembourg, there is a general consensus at the elite level that immigration and diversity have contributed to the country's wealth (see de Jonge 2019). This became ever more obvious in the debates leading up to the 2015 referendum. As mentioned earlier, the Luxembourgish press was generally

---

[14]In April 2020. Mediahuis NV acquired the media group Saint-Paul Luxembourg S.A., leaving the Roman Catholic Archdiocese of Luxembourg with a minority stake in Mediahuis (Mediahuis 2020).

quite favourable to the idea of extending voting rights to foreign residents. In an article entitled 'If the "*Wort*" could vote' published just one month before the referendum, the editors of the *Luxemburger Wort* expressed their support for the *Ausländerwahlrecht*:

> The editors of the '*Luxemburger Wort*' are willing to open the right to vote (not, however, the right to be elected) to foreigners having resided in Luxembourg for more than ten years, on the basis of their noticeable integration into everyday-life. We don't see it as a threat to the political order nor to the Luxembourgish language, which we perceive to be more alive than ever. (Siweck 2015)

This statement was surprising insofar as the newspaper is generally considered to be more conservative, given that it was owned by the Catholic Church at the time and maintains ties to the CSV.[15] Thus, the position taken by the editors of the newspaper deviated from the stance of the party (see below).

Apart from the *Wort*, the independent weekly newspaper *Woxx* was also in favour of the *Ausländerwahlrecht*.[16] However, their endorsement was less surprising; unlike the *Wort*, the *Woxx* had long been in favour of extending voting rights to foreign residents (Petry 2016: 77). To the editors of the *Woxx*, the *Ausländerwahlrecht* was a matter of principle. Indeed, their argumentation went beyond sheer demographic considerations. In an editorial published ten days before the referendum, the *Woxx* team argued that political participation should not be linked to citizenship or the ability to speak a certain language: 'the right to vote should not be a privilege reserved for a shrinking caste of "true Luxembourgers" [given that] it is the very essence of a democracy to be able to decide over the laws that one is obliged to follow afterwards' (*Woxx* 2015).

Thus, the *Ausländerwahlrecht* was supported by most of the established political parties as well as media practitioners and prominent civil society actors, who felt that enfranchising the large foreign population in Luxembourg was important for both demographic and moral considerations. Their views were opposed by the CSV, the ADR, and, above all, a grassroots movement called *Nee2015* (i.e. 'No2015').

18.2.3   The 'No' Camp

Opposition to the reforms proposed by the 2015 referendum through established channels was comparatively weak. Only two of the six political parties

[15]This is not to say that the coverage in the *Luxemburger Wort* on the referendum was one-sided; the newspaper also published several columns and letters by people who were opposed to the initiative.

[16]While the *Woxx* grew out of the Green movement in the 1980s, the newspaper has since gained independence (see Graf 2014).

that held seats in parliament at the time voiced concerns over the *Ausländer-wahlrecht*.[17] First, the conservative Christian democratic party (CSV) assumed its role as opposition party by objecting to the *Ausländerwahlrecht* initiative proposed by the governing parties. As mentioned earlier, the party was opposed to holding the referendum in the first place given that it considered referendums an important political instrument that ought to be reserved for essential questions only, notably a final and decisive vote on revising the Constitution (as opposed to letting the people decide directly on specific matters *within* the Constitution). Furthermore, the CSV highlighted the importance of generating a consensus, explaining that a simple 'Yes' or 'No' vote on complex issues such as the *Ausländerwahlrecht* might risk polarising society (see Petry 2016: 53).

In the campaign leading up to the 2015 referendum, the CSV argued against the *Ausländerwahlrecht* on the basis that (1) 'participation in national elections and citizenship are very closely intertwined'; (2) 'nationality is a more effective tool for integration than optional voting rights'; and (3) 'no other European country separates voting rights from citizenship' (CSV 2015). Thus, the CSV was not opposed to the enfranchisement of foreign residents per se. Indeed, over the course of the campaign, the party made it very clear that it shared many of the objectives pursued by the proponents of the *Ausländerwahlrecht*, namely the promotion of social cohesion as well as increased political participation for foreign residents (Petry 2016: 53–54). However, the CSV had different views on how these goals were to be achieved. Specifically, the party suggested alternative routes to ensure the political integration of foreign residents in the future, notably by facilitating access to citizenship.[18] In line with this rather complicated stance, the party's campaign slogan for the referendum was somewhat ambiguous. Indeed, the CSV's campaign posters did not explicitly say 'No' to the referendum question(s), but merely urged voters to inform themselves before casting their ballots (CSV 2015).

In light of the ambivalent position of the CSV, the main partisan opposition came from the nationalist ADR. While Luxembourg does not have an electorally significant far-right equivalent to the French *Front National* or the Dutch Freedom Party, the Luxembourgish ADR can be located on the right end of the Grand Duchy's political spectrum. While the ADR characterises itself as 'a populist party that is neither right nor left' (Dumont et al. 2011: 1059), observers have described it as 'the soft version of right-wing populism' (Blau 2005: 89; see also Mudde 2007: 306). In any case, the ADR is undoubtedly the main political party in Luxembourg most critical towards immigration

---

[17]Besides the six parties in parliament, there were also three smaller political parties active at the time: (1) the Pirate Party, which was in favour of the *Ausländerwahlrecht*; (2) the Communist Party (KPL), which was opposed; and (3) the Party for Integral Democracy (PID), which did not take an official stance (see Petry 2016: 58–62).

[18]To this end, the CSV introduced its own proposal for a reform of the Nationality Law on 24 February 2015 (Parliamentary document N°6781), i.e. several months before the official campaign (see *Chambre des Députés du Gouvernement du Luxembourg* 2015b).

(Fetzer 2011: 15), as demonstrated by the party's promotion of more restrictive citizenship laws (ADR 2013), its advocacy of immigrants' greater use of the Luxembourgish language (ADR 2014), and its staunch opposition to granting non-national residents the right to vote in legislative elections (ADR 2015c).

In comparison to the CSV, the ADR was vocally and explicitly opposed to granting foreigners the right to participate in general elections, arguing that 'the pseudo-referendum' was likely to stoke xenophobic sentiments, and that such an initiative would only lead other countries 'to shake their heads' at Luxembourg (ADR 2015a). Similar to the CSV, the ADR was also opposed to organising the referendum in the first place, but went further by calling the vote unconstitutional (see ADR 2015d: 21).

In the run-up to the 2015 referendum, the ADR put forward a host of reasons to oppose the *Auslännerwahlrecht* (see ADR 2015d; Petry 2016: 55–56). For example, the party argued that voting rights entitle voters to have a say on questions related to national sovereignty, and that the right to vote should therefore remain coupled to Luxembourgish citizenship. The ADR also highlighted the fact that Luxembourg already offers many opportunities for political participation to foreign citizens, and that the country already accepts dual citizenship. Furthermore, the party warned that instituting voting rights for foreign nationals would be irreversible, and that even though the referendum question only concerned active voting rights (i.e. the right to vote in elections), it would likely eventually lead to passive voting rights (i.e. the right to stand in elections). Throughout the campaign, the party relied heavily on emotional arguments by evoking feelings of *Überfremdung* and warning voters that the introduction of the *Auslännerwahlrecht* could indicate that Luxembourgish voters might soon become a minority in their own country, thereby risking being outvoted in the future by foreign residents (ADR 2015b).[19]

Alongside the CSV and the ADR, the civil servants' trade union (CGFP) was also opposed to granting voting rights to non-Luxembourgish citizens, arguing that Luxembourg already grants dual citizenship, which allows non-nationals to acquire voting rights via Luxembourgish citizenship (see Petry 2016: 71–72). Overall, however, the opposition to the *Auslännerwahlrecht* from established political and civil society actors appeared quite weak—especially in comparison to the enthusiastic 'Yes' campaign described above.

Given this half-hearted political response as well as the general lack of space in the media, it is perhaps not surprising that the 'No' campaign for the 2015 referendum largely emerged in virtual forums. Since there was only

---

[19]This claim is likely to be exaggerated; according to a report published by Luxembourg's official statistics agency (STATEC), as of January 2015, a maximum of 105,000 foreign residents (compared to 245,092 nationals) could participate in legislative elections—provided they would all sign up for local elections first (Allegrezza et al. 2015). If foreign residents (who fulfil both prerequisites) had been able to participate in the next legislative election, they would have represented 27.6% of the votes at most.

very little resistance from established parties, two Luxembourgish citizens decided to take matters into their own hands by launching a website entitled 'Nee2015.lu' (i.e. 'No2015.lu'). On their site, Fred Keup and Steve Kodesch presented themselves as 'the political middle' and listed various arguments to persuade readers to say 'No' to the *Ausländerwahlrecht* (Keup and Kodesch 2015; see also Petry 2016: 65–67). Similar to the position of the ADR, the main argument of the *Nee 2015* movement rested on the premise that voting rights should be reserved for Luxembourgish nationals. The movement maintained that 'granting foreign residents access to legislative elections would pose a threat to Luxembourgish sovereignty, language and culture' (Keup and Kodesch, 2015) and that granting voting rights to foreigners might be a disincentive to them acquiring citizenship, which, in turn, would impede their integration into Luxembourgish society. Specifically, they argued that every foreign national can acquire Luxembourgish nationality, and applying for citizenship would signal their willingness to learn the Luxembourgish language, thus preserving the nation's identity. Furthermore, they argued that by extending voting rights to non-nationals, Luxembourgers would 'give up their own sovereignty', which could be 'the beginning of the end of "our" nation' as it would lead to 'the increasing disappearance of "our" language' [i.e. the Luxembourgish language] (Keup and Kodesch 2015).

The website attracted thousands of supporters via social media and eventually became the main voice of opposition to the governmental initiative. Fred Keup, who was the main spokesperson of the movement, soon became the figurehead of the 'No' camp. A geography teacher by profession, he consistently presented himself as 'the voice of the ordinary Luxembourgish people' (Angel 2016). In the run-up to the 2015 referendum, he launched a social media campaign, wrote letters to newspapers, distributed leaflets and participated in various public debates. The success of the 'No' camp can largely be attributed to Keup's political activism. More generally, the *Nee 2015* movement played an influential role in the outcome of the referendum.

18.3   Conclusion

While referendums were originally intended to give voters more of a say in political decision-making, they now seem to be increasingly used as an instrument of political demarcation, where comparatively few voters are deciding over the fates of people who do not have a say because they lack political rights (e.g. the 2016 Brexit vote; the 2016 Hungarian referendum on restricting immigration; and the 2016 Dutch referendum on the EU's association agreements with Ukraine). The Luxembourgish referendum stands out in the sense that the initiative was *intended* as a means of political integration. In other words, unlike many other referendum questions discussed in this volume, the *Ausländerwahlrecht* initiative was meant to enfranchise foreign residents rather than curbing their political rights.

However, the referendum did not achieve its intended outcome. Instead, the Gambia coalition suffered a serious blow in 2015 with the vehement rejection of all three referendum questions. The 'No' campaign proved highly effective as nearly 80% of the electorate voted against the *Auslännerwahlrecht*. It is worth mentioning that although all communes were ultimately opposed to enfranchising foreign residents, voters living in urban, cosmopolitan areas were generally more favourable to the *Auslännerwahlrecht* than those living in the rural regions of the Grand Duchy. The voters in Luxembourg City were most favourable to the idea, with 32.99% supporting the initiative, followed by voters in the surrounding communes of Niederanven (29.26%), Kopstal (28.92%), Strassen (28.56%) and Walferdange (28.32%). On the other hand, opposition to the *Auslännerwahlrecht* was strongest in rural communes located in the east and the north of the country (Reisdorf, Wincrange and Kiischpelt), where only between 12.71 and 12.91% of the electorate voted 'Yes' (*Gouvernement du Grand-Duché de Luxembourg* 2015b).

The reasons behind the clear 'No' vote are complex and the exact motivations of the electorate are difficult to entangle. In any case, the sobering response of the Luxembourgish electorate had two immediate consequences for the government's broader Constitutional reform project. First, the three issues raised in the 2015 referendum—lowering the legal voting age; the *Auslännerwahlrecht*; and term limits for government mandates—will not be included in the proposal for the new Constitution. Second, the referendum put the finalisation of the Constitutional reform project on hold.[20]

While the reform project was postponed, the legacy of the 2015 referendum dragged on. The *Auslännerwahlrecht* debate brought to the fore new dividing lines in Luxembourgish society. Above all, it introduced an 'us versus them' discourse (on the basis of the '80 versus 20 per cent' referendum result) and propelled identity politics to the centre of the political debate. Following the 2015 referendum, issues pertaining to the preservation of the Luxembourgish language have gained traction. In 2016, for instance, a petition asking to make Luxembourgish the country's principal language received a record-breaking 15,000 signatures. This played into the hands of the right-wing nationalist ADR, a party that has long sought to halt the 'Francophonisation' of the country by raising the status of the Luxembourgish language. In response to these concerns, the Gambia coalition adopted an 'Action Plan for the Luxembourgish language' containing forty measures aimed at the promotion of the national language in 2017 (*Gouvernement du Grand-Duché du Luxembourg* 2017). In 2018, a law on the promotion of the Luxembourgish language was adopted unanimously in parliament.

---

[20]While the work on the new Constitution was finalised in June 2018, it will be up to the newly elected 'Chamber of Deputies' to decide when to proceed. The new Constitution must be first approved by the Parliament and the second vote should be replaced by a national referendum (Chambre des Députés du Grand-Duché du Luxembourg 2018).

The ripples of the 2015 referendum were clearly noticeable in the run-up to the 2018 general elections. After the referendum, the 'Nee2015' movement changed its name to 'Wee2050' ('Way' or 'Path' 2050), and in March 2018, the ADR announced that it would join forces with the Wee2050 movement in preparation for the 2018 general elections by reserving eight of the sixty places on its electoral list for Fred Keup and his team (*Tageblatt* 2018).[21] The electoral campaign was dominated by nationalist themes, including concerns over rapid population growth and related fears over the alleged demise of the Luxembourgish language and identity. These themes, which had gained salience in the run-up to the 2015 referendum, were reintroduced by the ADR/Wee2050 in 2018 and co-opted by many of the other political parties. For instance, the liberal Democratic Party ran on the campaign slogan '*Zukunft op Lëtzebuergesch*' ('Future in Luxembourgish'), while the social democratic LSAP opted for '*Lëtz* speak about politics' (in English), with 'Lëtz' being the first syllable of *Lëtzebuergesch,* which is the Luxembourgish term for the local language. This cooptation strategy appears to have borne fruit; the ADR/Wee2050 was unable to capitalise on the alleged rising nationalist sentiments and only managed to increase its vote share by 1.64% (to 8.28% total), while the Gambia coalition parties (i.e. DP, LSAP and Greens) were able to maintain their majority in parliament (despite minor losses for the DP and LSAP).

Although identity politics played a central role in the run-up to the 2018 general elections, the *Auslännerwahlrecht* itself did not form a major topic of debate. While the referendum clearly left a mark on the Grand Duchy, it failed to resolve the looming democratic deficit it set out to address. Although the prospect of introducing voting rights for non-citizens seemed elusive after the 2015 referendum, the question was certainly not off the table—especially given that the proportion of foreign residents in Luxembourg continued to rise (see Bumb 2018). In the meantime, however, the issue will all but disappeared from the agenda of the three coalition parties who had initiated the referendum. How the Grand Duchy will tackle its 'democratic deficit' remains to be seen.

BIBLIOGRAPHY

ADEM. (2018). *Rapport Annuel 2017.* http://adem.public.lu/fr/publications/adem/2018/rapport-annuel-succinct/Annual-report-2017.pdf. Accessed 20 October 2018.

ADR. (2013, February 1). *De Fernand Kartheiser zur Reform vum Nationalitéitegesetz* [Video]. http://www.adr.lu/de-fernand-kartheiser-zur-reform-vum-nationalitei tegesetz-video/. Accessed 7 October 2018.

---

[21]In the end, six members of the Wee2050 movement stood as candidates in the 2018 general elections; however, none of them made it into the Chamber of Deputies (*Luxemburger Wort* 2018).

ADR. (2014, December 4). *17 Argumenter fir d'Lëtzebuerger Sprooch* [Video]. http://www.adr.lu/17-argumenter-fir-dletzebuerger-sprooch-video/. Accessed 7 October 2018.

ADR. (2015a). *3x Nee am Wort vum 23. Mee 2015.* http://adr.lu/wp-content/upl oads/2015/05/wort_2015_05_22_web.pdf. Accessed 7 October 2018.

ADR. (2015b). *Auslännerwalrecht: d'Lëtzebuerger eng Minoritéit?* http://adr.lu/aus laennerwalrecht-dletzebuerger-eng-minoriteit/. Accessed 7 October 2018.

ADR. (2015c, April 13). *Auslännerwalrecht: Objektivitéit an Neutralitéit w.e.g.!* http://www.adr.lu/auslannerwalrecht-wou-bleift-dneutraliteit-vun-der-regier ung/. Accessed 7 October 2018.

ADR. (2015d, April). *Nee Nee Nee: Argumenter.* https://adr.lu/wp-content/upl oads/2015/04/Nee-Nee-Nee.pdf. Accessed 7 October 2018.

Allegrezza, S., Thill, G., & Peltier, F. (2015). *Regards 07—sur les électeurs poten-tiels (STATEC).* http://www.statistiques.public.lu/catalogue-publications/regards/ 2015/PDF-07-2015.pdf. Accessed 7 October 2018.

Angel, D. (2016, December 22). Fred Keup: Der Biedermann. *Woxx.* http://www. woxx.lu/fred-keup-der-biedermann/. Accessed 10 October 2018.

Barth, C., & Bucher, H.-J. (2003). Forschungsbericht und Entwurf eines Verhaltenskodex für Funkmedien des Großherzogtums Luxemburg. *Public research paper.* https://gouvernement.lu/dam-assets/fr/actualites/communiques/ 2005/07/05rapport_CNP/Gesamtbericht_Funkmedien.pdf. Accessed 6 October 2018.

Barth, C., & Hemmer, M. (2008). Medien und Medienpolitik. In W. H. Lorig & M. Hirsch (Eds.), *Das politische System Luxemburgs: Eine Einführung* (pp. 208–230). Wiesbaden: VS Verlag für Sozialwissenschaften.

Blau, L. (2005). *Histoire de l'extrême-droite au Grand-Duché de Luxembourg au XXe siècle.* Esch-sur-Alzette: Le Phare.

Bumb, C. (2018, May 7). Das (fast) vergessene Demokratiedefizit. *Reporter.* https:// www.reporter.lu/luxemburg-auslaenderwahlrecht-das-fast-vergessene-demokratiede fizit/. Accessed 10 October 2018.

CEFIS. (2014). *Centre d'étude et de formation interculturelles et sociales: La partic-ipation électorale.* http://www.cefis.lu/page8/page16/page16.html. Accessed 6 October 2018.

Chambre des Députés du Gouvernement du Luxembourg. (2009, May 15). *Proposition de révision N°6030 portant modification et nouvel ordonnancement de la Constitu-tion.* https://www.chd.lu/wps/PA_RoleDesAffaires/FTSByteServingServletImpl? path=3AD13468897E07C5800887103372B772142DD04A59FCD6E1EE0472 76C75B49DB40155ED83EBC25AE46069E6C721C71F3$9E078DC1A1AA7E1 FE4CDF9DE282AF57B. Accessed 30 September 2018.

Chambre des Députés du Gouvernement du Luxembourg. (2014, November 18). *Proposition de loi N°6738 portant organisation d'un référendum national sur différentes questions en relation avec l'élaboration d'une nouvelle Constitution.* https://www.chd.lu/wps/PA_RoleDesAffaires/FTSByteServingServletImpl?path= 7C8D7CE8790855CCAB5CE1D53D9BDFE55FF4422F22EF5FD9846E75DB0 F450BB035A05E16C13F105F5309EF1B3AFFDE4B$03D4EBBECA1581AF43 0BDAF0A831BA73. Accessed 30 September 2018.

Chambre des Députés du Gouvernement du Luxembourg. (2015a, May 5). *Décla-ration de politique générale sur l'état de la nation de Monsieur Xavier*

Bettel, Premier Ministre, Ministre d'Etat. https://www.chd.lu/ArchivePlayer/video/1482/sequence/65371.html. Accessed 12 August 2018.

Chambre des Députés du Gouvernement du Luxembourg. (2015b, February 24). *Proposition de loi N°6781 portant modification de la loi modifiée du 23 octobre 2008 sur la nationalité luxembourgeoise.* https://www.chd.lu/wps/portal/public/Accueil/TravailALaChambre/Recherche/RoleDesAffaires?action=doDocpaDetails&id=6781. Accessed 10 October 2018.

Chambre des Députés du Gouvernement du Luxembourg. (2018). *Le texte pour la future Constitution est prêt.* https://www.chd.lu/wps/portal/public/Accueil/Actualite/DossiersThematiques/!ut/p/z1/lVHLboMwEPyWHHIMXoxJyZFHmpKqGPEIgQsyYBIkHmmB8vsFVKmNVNF2b7M7OzNeowidUVSz9-LCuqKpWTniMNrGBjZOjkkwHE5UA2ztCdF9RQIAFMwEuCsVNADr4_hAMYr-v_9d6W_7C4RoWT5A0b0F3btbwJItqY6LRw75JCw98TeTcAz5ED8_6bqICVjUpI-gHo-m4TggUVFC7qQR6C-xbaJQnIDujadfQ9rUHa-7Vrj1SVmkQnrNhLJfg-tthmH4gupGTbuelUXH2xkaTdsW_K31rrwaP_O1n_o6tbyfJpNh3caLGeM5HrtwgSuQZNNlmCjvMqIkOWN5Lu9klohAuIhCjG6V75-hsKtKkSp1tfoANhJvOw!!/?1dmy&current=true&urile=wcm%3apath%3a%2Fcontents.public.chd.lu%2Fst-www.chd.lu%2Fsa-actualites%2Fsa-dossiersthematiques%2Fconstitution. Accessed 21 October 2018.

CSV. (2015). *Referendum 2015.* https://referendum.csv.lu/. Accessed 7 October 2018.

de Jonge, L. (2019). The Populist Radical Right and the Media in the Benelux: Friend or Foe? *The International Journal of Press/Politics, 24*(2), 189–209.

Dumont, P., & Kies, R. (2014). Luxembourg. *European Journal of Political Research Political Data Yearbook, 53*(1), 211–221.

Dumont, P., Kies, R., & Poirier, P. (2011). Luxembourg. *European Journal of Political Research, 50*(78), 1058–1064.

Fayot, B. (2006). *Les quatre référendums du Grand-Duché de Luxembourg.* Luxembourg: Editions de la Petite Amérique.

Fetzer, J. S. (2011). *Luxembourg as an Immigration Success Story: The Grand Duchy in Pan-European Perspective.* Maryland: Lexington Books.

Finck, M. (2015). Towards an Ever Closer Union Between? On the Possible Extension of Voting Rights to Foreign Residents in Luxembourg. *European Constitutional Law Review, 11*, 78–98.

Forum. (1981, April). Le droit de vote aux immigrés. *Nr. 47.* https://www.forum.lu/issue/le-droit-de-vote-aux-immigres/. Accessed 7 October 2018.

Gouvernement du Grand-Duché du Luxembourg. (2013). Programme gouvernementale. *The Official Portal of the Government of the Grand Duchy of Luxembourg.* https://gouvernement.lu/dam-assets/fr/dossiers/gouv-2013/assermentation/programme-gouvernemental.pdf. Accessed 30 September 2018.

Gouvernement du Grand-Duché du Luxembourg. (2015a, May 22). Everything is Ready for the Major Referendum on 7 June. *The Official Portal of the Grand Duchy of Luxembourg.* http://luxembourg.public.lu/en/actualites/2015/05/22-referendum/index.html. Accessed 7 August 2018.

Gouvernement du Grand-Duché du Luxembourg. (2015b, June 8). Résultats officieux: Référendum du 7 juin 2015. *The Official Portal of the Grand Duchy of Luxembourg.* https://elections.public.lu/fr/referendum/2015/resultats.html. Accessed 7 August 2018.

Gouvernement du Grand-Duché du Luxembourg. (2017, March 9). *Une stratégie pour promouvoir la langue luxembourgeoise*. https://gouvernement.lu/dam-assets/fr/act ualites/articles/2017/03-mars/09-promotioun-sprooch/langue-sp.pdf.   Accessed 21 October 2018.

Graf, R. (2014). Die 'woxx': Ein Projekt, das es eigentlich nicht geben sollte. *Ons Stad*, 107, 50–51. http://onsstad.vdl.lu/uploads/media/ons_stad_107-2014_50-51.pdf. Accessed 20 October 2018.

Heuschling, L. 2015. Le discours sur la valeur consultative du référendum (art. 51 § 7 Const.). Une déconstruction historique. *Recueil Trimestriel de la Jurisprudence Luxembourgeoise—Pasicrisie Luxembourgeoise*, 1–49.

Hirsch, M. (2007). The Luxembourgian Media Landscape. In G. Terzis (Ed.), *European Media Governance: National and Regional Dimensions* (pp. 134–144). Bristol: Intellect Books.

TNS ILRES. (2012). *Sondage TNS ILRES—Partie 4: Le droit de vote*. http://www.2030.lu/fileadmin/user_upload/documents/2030.lu_TNS_ILRES_Droit_de_vote_FR_28032013.pdf. Accessed 10 August 2018.

TNS ILRES. (2018). Etude TNS ILRES Plurimedia Luxembourg 2018.I. https://www.tns-ilres.com/media/1635/communique_de_presse_etudeplurimedia_2018i.pdf. Accessed 6 October 2018.

Keup, F., & Kodesch, S. (2015). *Auslännerwahlrecht? NEE Merci*. http://www.nee 2015.lu/index.php/argumenter.html. Accessed 20 August 2018.

Kollwelter, S., & Zuccoli, L. (2010). Chronique de l'ASTI 1979–2010. In M. Pauly (Ed.), *ASTI: 30 +: 30 ans de migrations, 30 ans de recherches, 30 ans d'engagements* (pp. 24–59). Luxembourg: Éditions Guy Binsfeld.

Luxembourg Times. (2015, February 2). *Luxembourg Times Campaigners Push for Yes Vote on Foreigner Voting Rights*. https://luxtimes.lu/archives/13315-campaigners-push-for-yes-vote-on-foreigner-voting-rights. Accessed 20 August 2018.

Luxemburger Wort. 2013. *Three-Way 'Gambia Coalition': A First for Luxembourg*. http://www.wort.lu/en/luxembourg/three-way-gambia-coalition-a-first-for-luxembourg-52668327e4b0ff388169e7db. Accessed 20 August 2018.

Luxemburger Wort. 2015. *Jugendparteien vereinen sich*. http://www.wort.lu/de/pol itik/zwei-mal-ja-beim-referendum-jugendparteien-vereinen-sich-551e53930c88b46 a8ce56b77. Accessed 20 August 2018.

Luxemburger Wort. 2018. *ADR präsentiert ihre Kandidaten*. https://www.wort.lu/de/politik/adr-praesentiert-ihre-kandidaten-5b1148f6c1097cee25b8a694. Accessed 20 October 2018.

Mediahuis. 2020. *Mediahuis acquires Luxembourg media group Saint-Paul Luxembourg*.   https://www.mediahuis.be/en/mediahuis-acquires-luxembourg-media-group-saint-paul-luxembourg/. Accessed on 28 June 2020.

MINTÉ. 2015. *Fir d'Wahlrecht vun alle Residenten am Grand-Duché*. [Leaflet].

Mudde, C. (2007). *Populist Radical Right Parties in Europe*. Cambridge: Cambridge University Press.

OGBL. (2015). *D'Fro vum Auslännerwalrecht beim Referendum vum 7. Juni: Wee mat "Jo" stëmmt stäerkt Lëtzebuerg ingesamt*. http://www.ogbl.lu/blog/wee-mat-jo-stemmt-staerkt-letzebuerg-insgesamt/. Accessed 7 October 2018.

Paperjam. 2018. Déficit démocratique. http://services.paperjam.lu/chiffre/deficit-democratique. Accessed 7 July 2019.

Petry, R. (2016). *Voting Rights for Non-Citizen Residents in Luxembourg: An Anthropological Study of a Political Public Debate*. Saarbrücken: AV Akademikerverlag.

RTL. (2015a). *Beim Referendum gesäit et tendenziell no dräimol Nee aus.* http://www.rtl.lu/themen/referendum/630440.html. Accessed 22 September 2018.

RTL. (2015b). *Vertrieder aus ë.a. der Wirtschaft positionéiere sech zum JO.* http://www.rtl.lu/letzebuerg/638079.html. Accessed 7 October 2018.

Scuto, D. (2012). *La nationalité luxembourgeoise (XIXe-XXIe siècles).* Bruxelles: Editions de l'Université de Bruxelles.

Service Information et Presse. 2014. *Bulletin: Édition spéciale - Élections législatives 2013.* https://sip.gouvernement.lu/dam-assets/publications/bulletin/2013/BID_2013_elections/BID_elections_2013.pdf. Accessed 21 August 2018.

Siweck, J.-L. (2015, May 23). Wenn das "Wort" wählen dürfte. *Luxemburger Wort,* 3.

Statec. (2020, January 1). Etat de la population: Population par sexe et par nationalité au 1er janvier (x 1 000) 1981, 1991, 2001–2020. *Statistics Portal Grand Duchy of Luxembourg.* https://statistiques.public.lu/stat/TableViewer/tableView.aspx?ReportId=12853&IF_Language=fra&MainTheme=2&FldrName=1. Accessed 28 June 2020.

Tageblatt. (2015). *Künstler sagen Ja.* http://www.tageblatt.lu/nachrichten/dossier/referendum/story/Kuenstler-sagen-Ja-25444294. Accessed 10 August 2018.

Tageblatt. (2018, March 2). *Fred Keup kandidiert auf ADR-Liste—Kooperation zwischen ADR und Wee2050.* http://www.tageblatt.lu/headlines/fred-keup-kandidiert-auf-adr-liste-kooperation-zwischen-adr-und-wee2050/. Accessed 10 October 2018.

Woxx. 2015. *Prise de position: Natierlech!.* http://www.woxx.lu/prise-de-position-natierlech/. Accessed 6 October 2018.

Zahlen, P., & Thill, G. (2013, October 7). Le profil des électeurs. *STATEC.* http://www.statistiques.public.lu/catalogue-publications/regards/2013/PDF-15-2013.pdf. Accessed 20 August 2018.

CHAPTER 19

Turkey's Constitutional Referendum: The 16 April 2017 Referendum in Historical Perspective

Ersin Kalaycıoğlu and Gülnur Kocapınar

19.1 Introduction: Referendums in Turkey

Turkey's experience of referendums started on 9 July 1961 on the occasion of the adoption of a new written Constitution. This first referendum was intended to enhance the political legitimacy of that document. The second referendum, which was held on 7 November 1982, was also carried out to legitimate the next Constitution. Both constitutional referendums were called for and carried out by military governments that had helped to design and establish the new constitutions. The 1961 referendum on the Constitution was specifically designed as an ad hoc popular vote to demonstrate democratic, popular support for the new Constitution. However, the 1982 Constitution incorporated the referendum device as a general popular vote envisaged in certain circumstances and subject to procedures defined in Articles 67, 175, 177 and temporary Articles 1 and 16.

Turkey has held five more referendums since 1982, including the Constitutional Referendum held on 16 April 2017 (see Table 19.1). There is some ambiguity on the use and translation of the term 'referendum' in the 1982 Constitution; while the term appeared in several articles of the English version of the 1982 Constitution, the Turkish version of the same text mentions the term only once in the newly amended article of 101 (see the Constitution of Turkey 1982). In five articles of the Constitution (Art. 79, 104, 174, 175 and provisional Art. 11) the term 'submitting to the popular vote (*halk oyu*)',

E. Kalaycıoğlu (✉) · G. Kocapınar
Sabancı University, Istanbul, Turkey
e-mail: kalaycie@sabanciuniv.edu

© The Author(s) 2021
J. Smith (ed.), *The Palgrave Handbook of European Referendums*,
https://doi.org/10.1007/978-3-030-55803-1_19

Table 19.1 Referendums in Turkey (1961–2017)

Referendum	Issue	Voter Participation Rate (%)	Yes (%)	No (%)
9 July 1961	New Constitution	81	62	38
7 November 1982	New Constitution	91	91	9
12 July 1987	Constitutional amendment on the restitution of the political rights of the former political elites who had been banned by the military government in1980	94	50.5	49.5
25 September 1988	Constitutional amendment on moving the date of local elections earlier	89	35	65
21 October 2007	Constitutional amendment on the election of the President of Turkey	68	69	31
12 September 2010	Constitutional amendment on a host of other socio-political changes, including a new procedure to appoint the members of the Higher Council of Judges and Prosecutors (HSYK)	74	58	42
16 April 2017	Constitutional amendments to increase the executive powers of the President	85	51.4	48.6

Sources The Supreme Election Council Archives, and Kalaycıoğlu (2013b): 68–69

which probably means referendum, appears among the prerogatives of the President. This complicated legal status of the procedures on general popular votes on constitutional amendments has not prevented pundits of Turkish politics from calling each such exercise a 'referendum'. In this chapter we adopt the same loose terminology as it is generally accepted both in domestic and international politics, journalism, and academic writing. We thus refer to the popular vote on 16 April 2017 as a referendum on constitutional amendments. This seventh and most recent referendum on the Constitution came after a tense, highly polarized and confrontational episode in Turkish politics, following a military uprising in the wake of an attempted coup on 15 July 2016 (see Aydın Düzgit and Balta 2017).

19.2   Legal Stipulations
on the Referendums in Turkey

In Turkey, referendums have primarily been used for extending popular legitimacy to constitutional amendments. The 1982 Constitution stipulated the conditions for the Turkish Grand National Assembly (*Türkiye Büyük Millet Meclisi*, TBMM) to amend the Constitution and other uses of what was referred to as a general popular vote (*halk oyu*—referendum) in Article 175. Referendums may be called for to augment the veto power of the President. Article 175 of the Constitution stipulates that:

> The President of the Republic may send back the laws on the amendments to the Constitution to the Grand National Assembly of Turkey for reconsideration. If the Assembly readopts, by a two-thirds majority of the total number of members, the law sent back by the President of the Republic without any amendment, the President of the Republic may submit the law to referendum [...].

Secondly, Article 175 of the Constitution also states that:

> …If a law on the amendment to the Constitution is adopted by a three-fifths or less than two-thirds majority of the total number of members of the Assembly and is not sent back by the President of the Republic to the Assembly for reconsideration, it shall be published in the Official Gazette and be submitted to referendum…

Additionally, the same article states that 'Entry into force of the laws on the amendment to the Constitution submitted to referendum shall require the affirmative vote of more than half of the valid votes cast'. Finally, the legislature also has the prerogative to decide how the amendment to the Constitution would be voted upon in a referendum: 'The Grand National Assembly of Turkey, in adopting the law on the Constitutional amendment shall also decide on which provisions shall be submitted to referendum together and which shall be submitted individually, in case the law is submitted to referendum' (Art. 175).

The wording of the amendments is composed by the TBMM and its team of legal experts, whose job it is to formulate laws. Given most referendums are highly political, their wording seems to have attracted remarkably little attention in the run-up to referendums or the referendum campaigns as well. Moreover, items presented in a referendum including those more politically critical amendments have not carried equal weight in the eyes of those who voted. For example, it was ironic that whereas in the 2007 referendum, the tenure of the TBMM was decreased from five to four years and presented to the public as an improvement in accountability and democratic representativeness of the political authorities by the governing Justice and Development

Party (*Adalet ve Kalkınma Partisi*, AKP) spokespersons, in the 2017 referendum, the tenure of the legislature was re-extended from four to five years and presented as a symbol of a stable democracy in the country by the same AKP spokespersons. Neither change attracted much public attention or ire.

Referendum procedures have not differed from regular general legislative elections in Turkey and, just like elections, the outcomes of the referendums have also been binding because they changed or failed to change an article of the Constitution. The referendums are also regulated by the judiciary, specifically the Supreme Election Council (*Yüksek Seçim Kurulu*, YSK), a High Court that is composed of high-ranking judges. This practice dates back to the late 1940s, when the leaders of the two main political parties at the time met to negotiate the issue of conducting democratic elections in Turkey. İsmet İnönü as, the leader of the Republican People's Party (*Cumhuriyet Halk Partisi*, CHP), and Celal Bayar, the leader of the opposition Democrat Party (*Demokrat Parti*, DP) agreed that all elections were to be conducted by apolitical, non-executive and non-legislative bureaucracies (i.e. independent judges), and the elections were to be placed under the management and supervision of a fully independent High Court specifically designed for the purpose of administering elections: the YSK was established on 16 February 1950. Referendum procedures are also managed and administered by the YSK and under its authority by the judiciary at each electoral district. Referendums are conducted in accordance with the regulations stipulated by law, Act no: 3376 of 23 May 1987. Art. 3 of Act 3376 authorizes the YSK to make all necessary preparations and decisions to ensure the safety and reliability of the poll, including voting procedures, and the results of all elections. Referendum results can be challenged by individual citizens and every voter has the right to appeal against the results to the YSK, which has the final say on complaints, objections and challenges made to the results or the execution of procedures followed during the voting process.

Voters who are eligible to participate in national legislative elections can also participate in referendums, the outcomes of which have been accepted as binding as the election outcomes by law. Turkish nationals above the age of eighteen are eligible to vote, including citizens who reside abroad. There are no legal thresholds for turnout and the outcome of the referendums. Art. 6 of Act 3376 stipulates that voting in referendums, just like elections since 1983, is mandatory; eligible voters who do not participate and who do not have a legitimate justification are punished by a fine determined by the YSK.

There are some general rules for fundraising in general elections, but there are no specific funding rules for referendums. Although there are no clearly defined spending limits for referendums, there are caps on campaign contributions for the Presidential elections. In the recent referendum the government did not heed the regulation, which it considered not helpful, including the use of public funds and state facilities to promote their propaganda efforts. The news media argued that many state funds not earmarked for use in any elections had been lavishly used in the 16 April 2017 referendum.[1] Political parties can spend their own funds in election campaigns, which include state subsidies to political parties that received more than three per cent of the vote in the previous general elections. However, the mainstream media reported that the governing AKP party used state funds that had been allocated for other purposes in its referendum campaign. The OSCE Report on the 2017 referendum indicated that the government had used various means ranging from media networks to government funds to which the opposition did not have access (OSCE 2017).[2] There were no effective spending limits for the government, not only overspending but also use of the press and the media, and other venues of campaigning as well, while the campaign by the opposition was severely restricted. In a report on the Turkish 16 April 2017 Referendum, the Parliamentary Assembly of the Council of Europe (PACE) also pointed to the dysfunctional influences of the emergency measures (*Olağanüstü Hal*, OHAL) on the democratic integrity of the referendum process in Turkey.[3] The existing rules (including financial regulations) were not applied equally to the three political parties—the governing AKP; the Turkish ethnic nationalist, Nationalist Action Party (*Milliyetçi Hareket Partisi*, MHP); and the ethnic nationalist, Grand Union Party (*Büyük Birlik Partisi*, BBP)—campaigning for the 'Yes' vote versus the opposition parties campaigning for the 'No' vote.

What had started as a mechanism or procedure to provide for popular legitimacy for a brand-new constitution evolved into a popular decision mechanism to settle much more minor disputes in the 1980s. The two referendums conducted on 12 July 1987 and 25 September 1988 were on issues that were not as critical as the legitimacy of a new constitution. The first of those was on re-instating the political rights of the former (pre-1980) political leaders who had been banned from politics by the military junta in 1980. The latter referendum was on moving the date of the local elections at various levels of government from the metropolitan cities to villages so that they could be held on the same day throughout the country. The fifth referendum was held on 21 October 2007. It proposed substantial reforms that would transform Turkey's semi-parliamentary system into a semi-presidential regime. The sixth referendum took place on 12 September 2010, proposed a raft of constitutional changes concerning many articles which had little association and

---

[1]'Örtülü harcama patladı', *Sözcü*, March 16, 2017, https://www.sozcu.com.tr/2017/ekonomi/ortulu-harcama-patladi-1737160/ and 'Örtülü Harcamada Yine Rekor', *Birgün*, https://www.birgun.net/haber-detay/ortulu-harcamada-yine-rekor-165001.html.

[2]https://www.osce.org/odihr/elections/turkey/324816.

[3]The emergency measures (OHAL) severely restricted criticism, freedom of expression, freedom of assembly and the media–press freedom and thus rendered the opposition's campaign almost impossible to be heard and followed by large swaths of the population. For a more thorough explanation of the dysfunctional influences of the OHAL on the integrity of the referendum see 'Turkey referendum: Key reactions' BBC, April 17, 2017, available at: https://www.bbc.com/news/world-europe-39615403.

coherence. However, the crux of that change was about purging the secular-minded judges and prosecutors from the high courts of the country, bringing the judiciary under a strict control of the executive branch of the government, and installing conservative Islamist lawyers, who shared the ideological convictions of the governing conservative Islamist AKP. Finally, the seventh and most recent referendum, which took place on 16 April 2017, involved a far more serious issue of political regime change through 18 constitutional amendments that effectively proposed to change the regime of the country from semi-presidential democracy to an authoritarian regime by increasing the powers of the Turkish President (Anayasa-Der 2017).

19.3   THE CAMPAIGN AND THE VOTE: ISSUES AND THE POLITICAL MILIEU

The 2017 Referendum was initiated by the Turkish nationalist–Islamist coalition of the AKP–MHP and later supported by the ethnic nationalist BBP. However, there were important fissures in the right-wing Turkish nationalist-Islamist camp as the conservative Sunni religious Felicity Party (*Saadet Partisi* – SP) vocally opposed the referendum, as did the other parties of the moderate right. Those politicians who had split from the ranks of the MHP also joined the opposition camp. Thus, the campaign did not seem to look as if it were simply a clash of two irreconcilable 'Images of Good Society' in the strict form of a *Kulturkampf* (see Kalaycıoğlu 2012). Turkish politics seem to be operating under the influence of a deep running *kulturkampf*, which may be defined in the following way:

> …Modern versus traditional, West versus Islam, progress versus going back to the golden ages of the Ottoman grandeur, and other variations of the same theme emerged to divide the Ottoman society into two [….] Those who aspired to be modern and believed in an 'Image of Good Society' built around science versus those who defended the idea of preserving the traditional social order, which inherently possessed an 'Image of Good Society' built around religion as tradition, gained stability and visibility. (Kalaycıoğlu 2005: 20)

Indeed: '…The referendum of 12 September 2010 saw the resurfacing of the main cultural cleavages in Turkish society, resulting in a major *kulturkampf* between the more sociocultural liberal and secular coastal provinces and the more religious conservative hinterland. The AKP and some Islamist and Turkish nationalist fringe parties supported the "yea" vote, the rest of the political parties supported 'nay', and the Kurdish nationalists boycotted the referendum' (Kalaycıoğlu 2012: 1).

Nevertheless, in 2017, above and beyond the ongoing *kulturkampf* it also appeared as if a clash between those who favoured a return to some form of parliamentary democracy and those who supported a rule by popularly elected President with no effective checks and balances occurred (Esen and Gümüşçü

2017: 306–313). This may be considered as a clash of political values or ideologies concerning the basis of sovereign and legitimate political power in Turkey. It seemed as if the 'No' camp valued representative democracy and its core parliamentary institutions, while the 'Yes' camp supported an image of popular sovereignty unhindered by any institution, rights or liberties, except for popular elections (*milli irade, volonté general*). According to the latter view, people would vote for a president who would become their champion and rule with no checking and balancing institutions either of the legislative or of the judicial branch of the government.

The Turkish political system was established through a War of Liberation (WL) under the leadership of a National Assembly (NA), which initially functioned as state and government. As a result, all branches of the government (including the judiciary, which functioned through independence courts— *İstiklal Mahkemeleri*) were embedded in the NA between 1920 and 1924 as committees of that body. The NA also established the army, which fought the WL (1920–1922) under the leadership of the Assembly Government (*Meclis Hükümeti*). Thus, the legitimacy of the Republican Turkish political system rested upon the rule of the people via their representatives in the NA, which constituted the sole organ of the state with the legitimacy to make binding political decisions for a while at the very beginning of the system. Therefore, absent a parliamentary democracy, the Turkish Republic lacked any claim to legitimate political rule, argued one side of the body politic, the nay-sayers.[4]

Meanwhile the AKP and MHP spokespersons argued that the 1982 Constitution was a product of the military government of the 1980s, decrepit, and dysfunctional (Kuzu 2017; Bozlağan 2017). They argued that any kind of presidentialism, especially a rule by a popularly elected President, would be best placed to provide political stability and sustained economic growth (Yıldırım 2017). For example, regarding economic welfare, then Prime Minister Yıldırım mentioned that presidentialism means stability, arguing that it would provide a much faster decision-making process, and that the presidential system would positively affect the Turkish economy.[5] Thus, nationalist/representational versus populist versions of political sovereignty clashed. A campaign based upon post-truth populist politics unfolded and penetrated the mainstream media and the press closely related to the AKP and the MHP.[6] The proponents of parliamentary representative democracy did not

---

[4]For a comprehensive analysis of political legitimacy in the Turkish state, see Kalaycıoğlu (2005), Chapters 1 and 2.

[5]'En büyük yapısal reform: Başkanlık' (The greatest structural reform: Presidentialism) *Hürriyet* (*daily*), October 16, 2016, http://www.hurriyet.com.tr/ekonomi/en-buyuk-yap isal-reform-baskanlik-40250621.

[6]The mainstream media were forced by systematic pressure of AKP governments to change hands from their former proprietors to the cronies of the AKP government. State funds and bank credits by the state-owned banks, such as Ziraat Bank and Halk Bank were utilized to fund the takeover of the mainstream media from 2007 through to 2017. Eventually all of the major networks except for Fox TV and the Halk TV networks of the former mainstream

receive much airtime on the mainstream media. Meanwhile, their messages on social media were targeted by the spokespersons of the governing parties and portrayed as expressions of terror, propaganda or treason (Esen and Gümüşçü 2017: 304). They also did not have much time or opportunity to fact check the many claims of the those advocating Presidentialism, which rested on unsubstantiated claims of many kinds (Anayasa-Der 2017). As a result, facts could now be ignored or presented by the 'Yes' camp as fabrications of heinous forces connected with the terror organizations that were trying to forestall Turkey's political stability and economic welfare (Yıldırım 2017).

On 16 April 2017 voters cast their ballots, and after some debate on the legitimacy of counting non-sealed votes, the 'Yes' camp was pronounced the winner by a narrow margin, garnering 51.4% of the votes (compared to 48.6% for the 'No' side).[7] The opposition parties objected to the results, questioned the legitimacy of the YSK's decision and appealed, which the YSK abruptly turned down. In an unprecedented move, the CHP appealed to the Constitutional Court (*Anayasa Mahkemesi*—AYM). However, the court reasoned that it had no jurisdiction over the decisions of the YSK (Esen and Gümüşçü 2017: 313–314). The CHP then appealed to the European Court of Human Rights (ECHR), with no success. Thus, the 16 April 2017 referendum has now become just like the 1946, 1961 and 1983 general legislative elections, where the results of the elections were not accepted as legitimate by the main opposition party or those who voted 'nay' during the referendum.

The referendum campaign and the vote seemed to be perceived by the average voter as more or less like any legislative election where the government parties and their opponents on both the left and right of the ideological spectrum fought their usual differences. One study argued that, '[…]if political parties choose to treat referenda as elections, voters' predispositions are more likely to be reinforced, and partisan voting is more likely to prevail' (Atikcan and Öge 2012). The 2017 Referendum occurred under such a partisan divide of the governing parties versus all the others; yet other sociocultural factors may also have been in operation as well. In national, legislative elections in Turkey there are numerous other dividing lines, along ethnic lines between

---

media changed hands and became propaganda agencies of the AKP government, as did the Turkish Radio and Television (TRT). The Turkish elections surveys have indicated that most voters follow the TRT and some of the mainstream media for their political news and were thus exposed to 'Yes' campaign claims. These claims included such arguments that the 'Yes' vote would result in a form of Presidentialism that would bring more political stability, an end to the threat from violence, sustained and rapid economic growth and economic development, and a more representative form of government (see Bozdağ 2012; Balta 2015). At the time of writing, none of those claims had been substantiated by facts or any academic research in comparative politics.

[7]See: YSK. 'Yurt İçi, Gümrük Kapısı Ve Yurt Dışı Sandıkları Anayasa Değişikliği Halkoy-laması Sonuç Tutanağı'. Retrieved from: http://www.ysk.gov.tr/ysk/content/conn/YSK UCM/path/Contribution%20Folders/SecmenIslemleri/Secimler/2017HO/2017HO-Ornek135.pdf.

the Kurdish ethnic nationalists and the Turkish ethnic nationalists; confessional cleavages dividing secular voters and Sunnis; sectarian lines dividing the Alevis and the Sunni pious; and economic lines that divide the haves from the have-nots have also been identified as important factors (see Carkoglu and Hinich 2006; Carkoglu 2007; Carkoglu and Kalaycıoğlu 2007; Kalaycıoğlu 2012; Baslevent and Kirmanoglu 2015; Kalaycıoğlu 2018a). However, in the 2017 Referendum, Images of the Good Society were further divided among themselves into supporters of the parliamentary versus the unchecked and uncontrolled executive presidency (Esen and Gümüşçü 2017). Although the 2017 Referendum was fought along mainly partisan lines between the AKP/MHP/BBP Islamist/ethnic Turkish nationalist bloc versus the entire gamut of the opposition parties, there is some evidence that some of the rank-and-file seemed to have split from their former parties which propagated for the 'Yes' vote and seemed to have voted for 'No' (Aytac et al. 2017). Some leaders of the MHP also veered away from the party and eventually established their own political party after the referendum. On the other side of the divide were all the other political parties from religious, conservative right-wing to Marxist—Leninist left that supported a return to parliamentary democracy. There has been some evidence to suggest that the vote was much more based upon partisan identity than the merits of the issue at hand, which the majority voters failed to understand or appreciate; yet especially the AKP was able to rally a majority of its rank-and-file members and supporters, while the MHP failed to replicate such a performance (Aytac et al. 2017).

When the overall geographical distribution of the 'yea' and 'nay' votes is examined, it is clear that North-western, Western, South-western, Southern and South-eastern provinces of the country tended to vote against the Constitutional amendments on the ballot on 16 April 2017 (see Fig. 19.1). The capital city Ankara and the industrialized provinces of Eskişehir and Bilecik in the central part of the country, as well as the North-eastern provinces of Artvin and Ardahan also joined the anti-amendment camp, as did the eastern borderlands, except for Kars (see Fig. 19.1 and Table 19.2). Only the provinces immediately north of Syria (notably Kilis, Şanlıurfa, Gaziantep, Adıyaman, Osmaniye, Kahramanmaraş) broke the chain that connected the South with the South-eastern and Eastern rim of the country. Since they are the provinces most deeply affected by the refugee influx from Syria on the one hand, and the Iraqi-based PKK's terror campaigns coming from the south on the other, they might have still been operating on the assumption that AKP rule would be what they needed to protect themselves from ethnic terror coming from the Kurdish nationalist PKK.[8] However, even in some of those provinces, more than 10 percent of the voters seemed to have shifted their preferences

---

[8] For a more thorough analysis of such an effect in legislative elections see Kibris (2010: 220–247) and Sayarı (2016: 269–270).

Fig. 19.1 Results of 16 April 2017 constitutional referendum in Turkey by region (*Note* The map is coloured in line with the official referendum results retrieved from the official webpage of the YSK [A similar image of this map was originally used by Esen and Gümüşçü [2017]]). *Source* The data are downloaded from the public web site of the YSK [2017]

Table 19.2 Swing voters: changing voting trends in the 'Yes' votes between the 2010 and 2017 referendums in selected cases

Provinces	Yes Votes, 2010 (%)	Yes Votes, 2017 (%)	Change
HAKKARİ	94.27	32.42	61.85
DİYARBAKIR	93.92	32.41	61.51
ŞIRNAK	89.08	28.30	60.78
BATMAN	94.69	36.35	58.34
AĞRI	95.75	43.08	52.67
MARDİN	93.45	40.94	52.51
VAN	94.45	42.73	51.72
SİİRT	95.17	47.81	47.36
MUŞ	92.21	50.56	41.65
BİTLİS	93.07	59.35	33.72
ŞANLIURFA	94.15	70.82	23.33
BİNGÖL	95.26	72.57	22.69
IĞDIR	53.75	34.80	18.95
KARS	65.51	50.95	14.56
ERZURUM	86.86	74.48	12.38
ARDAHAN	55.00	44.27	10.73
ADIYAMAN	80.43	69.76	10.67

Source Official referendum results by province shown by the YSK (2010) and YSK (2017)

away from AKP support, which had been evident in the earlier constitutional amendments of 2010 and 2017 (see Figs. 19.2 and 19.3). Furthermore, when comparing Figs. 19.2 and 19.3 with Fig. 19.1, it appears that there has been a significant change in voting patterns between 2007 and 2010 between 2010 and 2017. Notably, the geographical spread of the 'Yes' vote decreased steadily. In the meantime, the difference between the total number of votes cast in favour of the AKP-sponsored constitutional amendments and those

Fig. 19.2 Results of 12 September 2010 constitutional referendum in Turkey by region (*Note* The map is coloured in line with the official referendum results retrieved from the official webpage of the YSK. *Source* The data are downloaded from the public website of the YSK [2010])

Fig. 19.3 Results of 21 October 2007 Constitutional Referendum in Turkey by region (*Note* The map is coloured in line with the official referendum results retrieved from the official webpage of the YSK. *Source* The data are downloaded from the public website of the YSK [2007])

Table 19.3 Differences between Yes and No Votes in 2007, 2010 and 2017 Referendums

Referendum	Number of Yes Votes	Yes Votes (%)	Number of No Votes	No Votes (%)	Difference between Yes and No Votes (%)
2007	19,403,987	68.95	8,738,794	31.05	37.90
2010	21,667,427	57.86	15,781,873	42.14	15.72
2017	24,325,633	51.18	23,203,316	48.82	2.36

Source Official referendum results by province shown by the YSK 2007, 2010, and 2017

who opposed them dramatically decreased from a high of 38% in 2007 to a low of 2.4% in 2017 (Table 19.3).

By 2017, the country seems to have been divided almost into two equal parts. A mere difference of 2.4% or 1,122,317 votes separated the two blocs. The 'Yes' side was mainly an inner, central and northern Anatolian bloc of voters except for Ankara, Eskişehir, Bilecik, Artvin and Ardahan provinces, and the 'No' camp consisted of the coastal areas on the west and the south, and the southeast and eastern provinces except those provinces neighbouring Syria. All major metropolitan areas of the west and the south, such as İstanbul, İzmir, Adana, Antalya, Mersin, except for Bursa had a majority of 'No' voters on 16 April 2017. It appears that the rural provinces and conservative towns as well as the metropolitan central Anatolian cities as Konya, Erzurum, Kayseri, Sivas voted 'Yes' in large numbers in 2017. The aggregate vote does not seem to indicate that there was an urban–rural divide in the vote. Even the metropolitan population seemed to be divided along different lifestyles. Such a pattern was already visible in an earlier national survey conducted around the time of the 2010 Referendum, whereby a division of the society on the basis of a cultural fault line between different values and lifestyles became evident, which seemed to have been precipitating a value split and struggle in the polity, appeared to be taking hold (Kalaycıoğlu 2012). More specifically, 'The results of the 12 September 2010 referendum indicated that the *kulturkampf* along the religious–secular divide, which is married with left–right ideological orientations, was again effectively at work. The macro-view of the vote also indicated that a geographical divide, with the western "naysayer" provinces versus the rest, emerged to an extent not visible in national or local elections' (Kalaycıoğlu 2012: 17). This 'West versus the Rest' type of cultural division in the 2010 Referendum (Kalaycıoğlu 2012) seemed to have become more complicated as it appeared to reinforce the divide for or against some form of parliamentary democracy across the cosmopolitan West and South, and Southeast, East and Northeast versus the rest by 2017. This is in line with such previous studies as Özen and Kalkan, who concluded in their analysis that since 2015, '[…] electoral competitiveness and concentration mostly stabilized in the Western sub-provinces whereas they are still in flux in the Eastern and Southern regions' (Özen and Kalkan 2017: 358).

There is now a division among voters of Kurdish ethnic origin, as well as the non-Kurdish citizens among themselves, on whether they are for or against some form of democracy. Similarly, secular and Sunni voters also seemed to be split along the same lines of contrasting, irreconcilable images of parliamentary democracy versus presidentialism *alla Turca*. While the central provinces of Konya, Kayseri, Niğde, Nevşehir, Sivas, Yozgat and Çankırı seemed to have voted 'Yes', they had large minorities voting 'No' as well. Big metropolitan coastal areas, where most of the secular voters reside had a large 'No' vote, but they also had large minorities voting 'Yes' as well.

Indeed, rapid social mobilization had led to massive dislocations of the people in Turkish society as peasants and farmers moved from the villages and small towns to cities and metropolitan areas. Particularly in the 1980s and 1990s the populations of large metropolitan areas of İstanbul, Ankara, İzmir, Bursa, Adana and Mersin, Antalya and Diyarbakır more than doubled, with serious political consequences (Kalaycıoğlu 2005). 'Horizontal' social mobility from east to west and northwest of the country simultaneously from villages and small towns to cities and metropolitan areas also provided an opportunity for upward social mobility as access to formal education became enhanced by urbanization (Kalaycıoğlu 2005). The agricultural economy and rural society of Turkey gave way to an industrial economy and urban society by the early 2000s. The services sectors of tourism, education, transportation, banking, communication (media and the press included), municipal administrations and civil society began to emerge as the new job and employment opportunities for the urbanizing, educated and industrial labour. Consequentially, urban metropolitan–cosmopolitan interests versus the rural, small town, traditional and nationalistic or even nativistic interests began to crystallize and clash. What happened was not a simple urban–rural divide, but a more complicated urban–metropolitan and cosmopolitan-global extrovert interests and values versus rural, conservative, traditional, introvert interests and values clashing with each other in determining the agenda of the political economy of the country (for a thorough analysis of this transformation see Keyder 1987; Öniş 1991; Keyder 1994; Öniş and Türem 2001). Therefore, the political behaviour of those closer to one or the other of these camps is not geographically separate and distinct like residing in the metropolitan versus the village areas of the country. They are present in the metropolitan cities as well as the smaller cities and towns. Different lifestyles exist side by side in the metropolitan areas of the country. These people now live in the same city quarters, share the same means of public transport, the same postal codes and even the same polling stations at the time of the elections. Hence, over time, the divisions among voters across the country became murkier, more comprehensive and more intense, especially in the 2017 referendum.

Possible differences may also be observable regarding the educational attainment of the voters on the one hand and their economic voting patterns on the other. For example, as educational attainment of the voters increases, voters tend to vote less for the conservative, ethnic nationalistic and political Islamist agendas and values of the right and far-right and to vote for more liberal, centre, centre-left and social democratic candidates, parties, policies and values in Turkey (Esmer 1999). Similarly, economic interests also lead voters to consider voting for choices that are closer to their economic benefits, values, priorities or those of the country. In practice, such calculations depend on voters' evaluations on the performance of the government of the day. If they make those evaluations retrospectively as some voting behaviour research suggests (Key 1966; Baslevent et al. 2005, 2009; Hazama 2007: 12–13; Carkoglu 2008; Baslevent and Kirmanoglu 2015; Kalaycıoğlu 2015; Kalaycıoğlu 2017), then they would be tempted to support the government with their ballots if the government is considered as having performed well economically, otherwise not. On the contrary, if voters are only concerned about the future prospects of the parties' economic policies, then they will prefer to support the party in power or its opponents according to the promise of their prospective economic policies (Downs 1957). One may argue that if the voters vote on economic interests, those parts of the country that have done well in creating jobs and experiencing less unemployment would be more favourable to the governing party's proposal at the popular vote than others where economic growth had been sagging and unemployment relatively widespread.

Moreover, research on voting behaviour in Turkey has shown that voters have been considerably concerned about security and terror-related incidents in the country, which had been on the rise since the November 2015 elections (Carkoglu and Yildirim 2015; Coskun 2015; Kalaycıoğlu 2017). Therefore, those parts of the country where security had been at increasing risk and terror incidents increased since summer of 2015 would be expected to vote to support the proposal of the governing party, in the hope that the government would take the necessary measures to provide calm, while others who considered the government responsible for the increasing instability would oppose the proposal.

Previous research revealed that 'Views on a presidential system were largely shaped by partisanship, whereby AKP partisans had a positive view and partisans of the opposition parties a negative one' (Aytac et al. 2017: 10), showing that the partisanship variable has an explanatory power on this topic. Similarly, June 2015 and November 2015 party votes may provide useful insights about the influence of party support on the Yes and No votes in the 2017 referendum. Moreover, several independent variables such as parties' vote shares in previous elections, illiteracy, unemployment (Kemahlioglu, 2015), education, religiosity, satisfaction with economy and the perceptions about the most important problem in the form of terror (Aytac et al. 2017: 10), and satisfaction with the government performance of the management of the economy (Kalaycıoğlu 2013a) were employed in previous studies conducted on referendums or national elections. The selection of independent variables in Table 19.4 was done by considering the above-mentioned arguments, the previous research, and by adding other variables which may explain the vote in 2017 referendum in the country. We compiled the referendum data and General Elections data from the official webpage of YSK. Data on our dependent variables regarding population, urban population, (il)literacy, unemployment, migration and energy usage were collected from the official webpage of Turkish Statistical Institute (*Türkiye İstatistik Kurumu*—TUIK), terrorist attacks data from various news sources and gazettes, and the number of mosques data from the official webpage of the Directorate of Religious Affairs (*Diyanet İşleri Başkanlığı*). Hence, regarding the data, we delve into

Table 19.4 Predicting Yes Votes and No Votes in 2017—Linear (OLS) Regression (Provincial Level)

	Model 1		Model 2	
	Yes Votes 2017	*No Votes 2017*	*Yes Votes 2017*	*No Votes 2017*
AKP June 2015 Votes	.7789***(0.072)	−.1552 (0.078)		
CHP June 2015 Votes	.1426 (0.076)	1.088***(0.082)		
MHP June 2015 Votes	.2277 (0.192)	1.288***(0.207)		
HDP June 2015 Votes	−.3804**(0.119)	.6612***(0.129)		
AKP November 2015 Votes			.6447***(0.047)	−.0048 (0.023)
CHP November 2015 Votes			.1249 (0.074)	1.133***(0.036)
MHP November 2015 Votes			.2633 (0.228)	.7909***(0.111)
HDP November 2015 Votes			−.4166***(1236)	.6596***(0.063)
Illiteracy (2016)	4.149***(0.072)	1.322**(0.544)	4.297***(0.453)	1.237***(0.221)
Unemployment Rate (2013)	−7303.5**(2392.4)	−2529.8 (2581)	−6637.9*(2208)	−1021 (1078)
Net Migration (2015–2016)	−2.027 (1.293)	−.8204 (1.395)	−.8260 (1.181)	.5801 (0.576)
Metropolitan Municipality	−4112.01 (22756)	−13193.4 (24566)	−19913.3 (20106)	−8072.1 (9814)
Energy Usage (Industry, 2013)	.0053 (0.007)	−.0072 (0.008)	.0062 (0.006)	−.0003 (0.003)
Number of deaths due to terrorist attacks (2010–2016)	8.893 (45.63)	−41.04 (49.24)	6.353 (41.97)	−6.093 (20.49)
Number of Mosques by Province (2016)	36.19 (27.01)	71.48 (29.15)	7.128 (25.12)	11.40 (12.26)
Constant	15315.6 (22973)	−44895.6 (24791)	21928.6 (21052)	−13284.2 (10276)
Number of Observations	81	81	81	81
R-squared	0.9883	0.9983	0.9903	0.9981

Note Standard errors in parentheses
*$p<0.05$, **$p<0.01$, ***$p<0.001$

and further scrutinize the roles played by the social milieu, urban–rural settlements, social mobility as represented by migration, education, religiosity, performance of the economy in providing growth, development, employment and terror and security on the 'yea' and the 'nay' sayers in the 2017 referendum.

Table 19.4 shows the results of the OLS regression analysis. It indicates that place of residence (metropolitan versus less urban and rural) did not play any role in explaining the vote in the 2017 referendum. Education (measured in terms of the total number of (il)literate people by province), horizontal social mobility (measured in terms of net migration within the country), and unemployment seemed to have some explanatory power, while economic development (measured as energy consumption in industrial areas); total casualties due to terror; and religiosity (measured in terms of total number of mosques per province) did not seem to have an impact. Illiteracy as well as unemployment appear to have boosted the 'Yes' vote. However, partisan affiliation or support levels were the most important predictor for voting behaviour in the 2017 referendum. Specifically, people who had voted for the AKP in 2015 were more likely to support the 'Yes' camp, whereas those who had voted for the CHP, MHP and the Kurdish nationalist Peoples' Democratic Party (*Halkların Demokratik Partisi*, HDP) in 2015 were more likely to support the 'No' camp.

The vote was split almost down the middle in the economically more developed provinces of the country. As the map (Fig. 19.1) indicates, only in a few of the major industrial, metropolitan areas of the country where the average per capita income of the residents and energy consumption are relatively high did a majority vote 'Yes'. In other words, the level of economic development did not have a significant impact on the voting decision in the 2017 Referendum in Turkey. Unemployment was a slightly more useful indicator; in those provinces with higher unemployment levels, the number of 'Yes' voters was slightly lower. Thus, the outcome of the referendum was less a reflection of sociocultural, economic and political (security) conditions, but had much more to do with political preferences.

19.4   The Repercussions of the Referendum: Turkey and Her International Relations

The earlier 2007 and 2010 Turkish referendums were well-received, given that they were considered as significant steps towards the implementation of the Copenhagen criteria for European Union (EU) accession by a candidate country negotiating full membership since 2005 (see Alessandri 2010; Aydın-Düzgit 2010). The 2017 Referendum, however, was received with great anxiety by the same European circles, which were concerned about the future of democracy in Turkey.[9] For example, it was underlined in the European Commission's Turkey Report in 2018 that, in April 2017, Turkey held a referendum on constitutional amendments, which was approved by a close majority and thus introduced a presidential system. '...The amendments were assessed by the Venice Commission as lacking sufficient checks and balances as well as endangering the separation of powers between the executive and the judiciary' (European Commission 2018). Moreover, as *The Guardian* (2017a) noted, '..."The 16 April constitutional referendum took place on an unlevel playing field and the two sides of the campaign did not have equal opportunities," said the preliminary report of the mission, a combined effort of the Parliamentary Assembly of the Council of Europe (PACE) and the Office for Democratic Institutions and Human Rights...'. Additionally, it was mentioned about the 2017 Referendum that '... A spokesman for the European commission president, Jean-Claude Juncker, said claims from neutral observers of election irregularities had been "examined attentively" in Brussels'. Underlining that the referendum irregularities should be investigated by Turkey, '...the commission's spokesman added: "As far as the future is concerned, as President Juncker has said in the past, we encourage Turkey to move closer to the EU again and not to move even further and faster away from us..."' (*The Guardian* 2017b). In fact, developments since the 2010 Referendum, which ended the independence of the judiciary, and the 2017 Referendum, which ended the separation of powers, have rendered the negotiations for full EU membership even more difficult. In accordance with that, then President of the European Commission Jean-Claude Juncker, High Representative for Foreign Affairs and Security Policy/Vice-President of the European Commission Federica Mogherini and Commissioner for European Neighbourhood Policy and Enlargement Negotiations Johannes Hahn underlined in their statement on the 2017 Referendum in Turkey that:

> The constitutional amendments, and especially their practical implementation, will be assessed in light of Turkey's obligations as a European Union candidate country and as a member of the Council of Europe. We encourage Turkey to address the Council of Europe's concerns and recommendations, including with regards to the State of Emergency. In view of the close referendum result and the far-reaching implications of the constitutional amendments, we also call on the Turkish authorities to seek the broadest possible national consensus in their implementation. (EEAS 2017)

This statement may indicate the demand of the EU authorities for elaborating the democratic environment in the country to promote negotiations with the EU.

The AKP government also tightened its grip over the media in the country and increasingly relied on social media to spread its views. The increased

---

[9]For a full report on the perceptions of the 2017 referendum in Europe see: https://www.osce.org/odihr/elections/turkey/324816; see BBC (2017).

nativism, nationalism, chauvinism and xenophobia in the country had made those moves quite acceptable in the eyes and minds of the majority of the Turkish voters, who are deeply suspicious of the United States, Israel, Europe and the EU. Indeed, public threat perceptions in Turkey derived from the pre-election 2007 Turkish Election Study revealed that '… The US became to be perceived by about 80% of the Turkish public as a threat by 2007. It was followed by Israel (67.2%) and Iraq (66.6%), which are in tie for the second place, and third comes the Christian missionaries (60%)…' and additionally the data indicated that '…there is a deeply disturbing perception of being threatened by the world, or a latent form of xenophobia expressed in the responses as well, which was later documented in Carkoglu and Kalaycıoğlu (2009), and again by the Pew Research Center (2017)' (Kalaycıoğlu 2018b: 18–19).

19.5   Conclusion

Referendums have generally functioned as tools for promoting the political agenda of the ruling political parties and authorities in Turkey. They have more often than not been utilized by the political powers that be to bypass established, regular channels and institutions of conducting politics and policy in the country. Political leaders bent upon consolidating power and enhancing their authority to rule despite all the opposition directed at them have resorted to referendums as a way of changing the rules of the political game, while attempting to eliminate the challenges from their opponents and opposition resistance to their political agenda. In the 1987 and 1988 referendums, such moves by the then Prime Minister Turgut Özal and his Motherland Party failed. However, in the 2000s the attempts by the Prime Minister (and later President) Tayyip Erdoğan and his AKP supporters succeeded in changing the character of the semi-parliamentary 1982 Constitution and its political regime first towards a semi-Presidential system in 2007 and then to an unchecked authoritarian Presidency, thanks to the 2010 and 2017 referendums. While the 2007 Referendum ushered in semi-Presidentialism, the 2010 Referendum enabled the AKP government to curtail the independence of the judiciary by installing its supporters and loyalist Islamists in the judiciary in place of the former secular judges. Finally, the 2017 Referendum converted the regime too.

By 16 April 2017, it looked as if Turkey could no longer even go through the motions of free and fair elections or referendums the results of which would be accepted as legitimate by all those parties that take part in them. This development precipitated a constitutional crisis in the country, which not only seems to lack any immediate resolution, but also seemed likely to grow even deeper after constitutional amendments that lacked widespread popular approval came into effect after 24 June 2018 elections.

The 2017 referendum appears to have occurred under bitter polarization, rendering the vote considerably partisan for most party supporters along the lines of the governing AKP party and some ethnic nationalist supporters (Aytac et al. 2017). Using survey data from a nationally representative survey of voting age population, Aytaç et al. (2017) have shown that a huge majority of the AKP loyalists seemed to have continued to support their party and its leader, the President of the country in his 'Yes' vote campaign. However, most supporters of the ethnic nationalist Turkish party MHP seemed not to be so inclined to follow their party and leader in their support of the 'Yes' campaign. The political parties on the far right of the political spectrum championing a highly conservative, Sunni Islamic, ethnic Turkish platform not only initiated the amendments but also won the vote.

Our data analysis has revealed that the vote on 16 April 2017 was influenced most systematically by partisan political orientations, followed by various socio-economic characteristics including the level of literacy, employment and religion. As we had suspected, the urban–rural differences did not seem to play a significant role in the outcome of the 2017 referendum, nor did the impact of terrorist incidents. Net migration into the provinces had some explanatory power, and so had public displays of Sunni religiosity.

In essence, the 16 April 2017 constitutional amendments were about changing the political regime of the country from semi-Presidentialism into a regime of popularly elected, unchecked, unbalanced, and effectively unaccountable executive Presidency. The country was split into two almost equal halves between supporters and opponents of an unchecked presidential system: on the one side were those who demanded to return to a form of parliamentary democracy, whereas on the other, were those who supported to change into a form of unaccountable executive Presidency. The latter seem to have consisted of those who supported conservative Sunni Islamism and ethnic Turkish nationalism, while the former bloc comprised the more secular, democratic leftists, social democrats, socialists and ethnic Kurdish nationalists. This cultural–political division seemed to have been further entrenched by the campaign of the 2017 referendum, building on the ongoing *kulturkampf* of the country. On 16 April 2017, political choices over the character of the country's regime were added on to those politico-cultural fault lines of the country, as all cultural groupings/communities were further divided among themselves into those who supported rule by a form of parliamentary democracy versus those who stood for a form of neo-patrimonial sultanism, whereby the country would be ruled by arbitrary measures and with kin, friends and cronies.

BIBLIOGRAPHY

Alessandri, E. (2010). Democratization and Europeanization in Turkey After the September 12 Referendum. *Insight Turkey, 12*(4), 23–30.

Anayasa-Der. (2017). *Türkiye Cumhuriyeti Anayasası'nda Değişiklik Yapılmasına Dair Kanun* (Üzerine Teknik Bilimsel Rapor). http://anayasader.org/turkiye-cumhur iyeti-anayasasinda-degisikli[k-yapilmasina-dair-kanun-teklifi/.

Atikcan, E. Ö., & Öge, K. (2012). Referendum Campaigns in Polarized Societies: The Case of Turkey. *Turkish Studies, 13*(3), 449–470.

Aydın Düzgit, S. (2010). Constitutional Referendum in Turkey: What Next? *CEPS Commentary*.

Aydın Düzgit, S., & Balta, E. (2017). *Turkey after the July 15ᵗʰ Coup Attempt: When Elites Polarize over Polarization*. Policy Report, Istanbul Policy Center.

Aytac, S. E., Carkoglu, A., & Yıldırım, K. (2017). Taking Sides: Determinants of Support for a Presidential System in Turkey. *South European Society and Politics, 22*(1), 9–16.

Balta, E. (31 March 2015). Başkanlık Sistemi Hakkında Doğru Bilinen Yanlışlar. (What are believed to be right for the Presidential System that are actually wrong) *Birikim* (weekly paper). http://www.birikimdergisi.com/haftalik/1422/baskanlik-sistemi-hakkinda-dogru-bilinen-yanlislar#.XHZ1PPkzYdU.

BBC. (2017, April 17). *Turkey Referendum: Key Reactions*. https://www.bbc.com/news/world-europe-39615403.

Bozdağ, B. (2012). *Başkanlık Sistemini, Siyasal İstikrarın Sürekli Olması İçin İstiyoruz* (We want Presidentialism for sustainable stability). https://www.haberler.com/boz dag-baskanlik-sistemini-siyasal-istikrarin-4114902-haberi/.

Bozlağan, R. (2017). *Interview at Milliyet Newspaper* (daily). http://www.milliyet. com.tr/prof-dr-bozlagan-yeni-anayasa-ve-baskanlik-istanbul-yerelhaber-1250219/.

Baslevent, C., & Kirmanoglu, H. (2015). Economic Voting in Turkey: Perceptions, Expectations, and the Party Choice. *Research and Policy on Turkey, 1*(1), 88–101. https://doi.org/10.1080/23760818.2015.1099784.

Baslevent, C., Kirmanoglu, H., & Senatalar, B. (2005). Empirical Investigation of Party Preferences and Economic Voting in Turkey. *European Journal of Political Research, 44*, 547–562.

Baslevent, C., Kirmanoglu, H., & Senatalar, B. (2009). Party Preferences and Economic Voting in Turkey (Now that the Crisis is Over). *Party Politics, 15*(3), 377–391.

Birgün. Örtülü Harcamada Yine Rekor. https://www.birgun.net/haber-detay/ort ulu-harcamada-yine-rekor-165001.html.

Carkoğlu, A. (2007). The Nature of the Left-Right Ideological Self-Placement in the Turkish Context. *Turkish Studies, 8*(2), 253–271.

Carkoğlu, A. (2008). Ideology or Economic Pragmatism: Profiling Turkish Voters in 2007. *Turkish Studies, 9*(2), 317–344.

Carkoğlu, A., & Hinich, M. J. (2006). A Spatial Analysis of Turkish Party Preferences. *Electoral Studies, 25*, 369–392.

Carkoğlu, A., & Kalaycıoğlu, E. (2007). *Turkish Democracy Today: Elections, Protest and Stability in an Islamic Society*. London: I. B. Tauris.

Carkoğlu, A., & Yildirim, K. (2015). "Election Storm in Turkey: What do the Elections of June and November 2015 Elections tell us?". *Insight Turkey, 27*(4): 57–79.

Coskun, V. (2015). HDP Torn Between Violence and Politics. *Insight Turkey, 17*(4), 47–55.

Downs, A. (1957). *An Economic Theory of Democracy.* New York: Harper.

Esen, B., & Gümüşçü, Ş. (2017). A Small Yes for Presidentialism: The Turkish Constitutional Referendum of April 2017. *South European Society and Politics.* https://doi.org/10.1080/13608746.2017.1384341.

Esmer, Y. (1999). *Devrim, evrim, statüko: Türkiye'de sosyal, siyasal, ekonomik değerler.* İstanbul: TESEV.

EEAS. (2017). Statement on the Referendum in Turkey. *European Union External Action Webpage,* Published on April 16, 2017. Available at https://eeas.europa.eu/headquarters/headquarters-homepage_en/24709/Statement%20on%20the%20referendum%20in%20Turkey.

European Commission. (2018, 17 April). *Turkey 2018 Report.* Retrieved from: https://ec.europa.eu/neighbourhood-enlargement/sites/near/files/20180417-turkey-report.pdf.

Hazama, Y. (2007). *Electoral Volatility in Turkey: Cleavages vs. the Economy.* Tokyo, Japan: I.D.E. (Occasional Papers Series, no. 41).

Hürriyet. (2016, October 16). En büyük yapısal reform: Başkanlık. *Hürriyet.* http://www.hurriyet.com.tr/ekonomi/en-buyuk-yapisal-reform-baskanlik-40250621.

Kalaycıoğlu, E. (2005). *Turkish Dynamics: Bridge Across Troubled Lands.* New York, NY: Palgrave Macmillan.

Kalaycıoğlu, E. (2012). Kulturkampf in Turkey: The Constitutional Referendum of 12 September 2010. *South European Politics and Society, 17*(1), 1–22.

Kalaycıoğlu, E. (2013a). Turkish Party System: Leaders, Vote and Institutionalization. *Southeast European and Black Sea Studies, 13*(4), 483–502.

Kalaycıoğlu, E. (2013b). Türkiye'de Halk Oylamaları: Katılma mı? Yürütme Vesayeti mi? (Referendums in Turkey: Participation or Executive Tutelage?). In İ. G. Şen & B. S. Heinrich (Eds.), *Demokrasi ve Siyasal Katılım* (Democracy and Political Participation) (pp. 68–69). İstanbul: Ezgi Matbaası.

Kalaycıoğlu, E. (2015). Turkish Popular Presidential Elections: Deepening Legitimacy Issues and Looming Regime Change. *South European Society and Politics, 20*(2), 157–179.

Kalaycıoğlu, E. (2017). Two Elections and a Political Regime in Crisis: Turkish Politics at the Crosroads. *Southeast European and Black Sea Studies.* https://doi.org/10.1080/14683857.2017.1379148.

Kalaycıoğlu, E. (2018a). Two Elections and a Political Regime in crisis: Turkish Politics at the Crossroads. *Southeast European and Black Sea Studies, 18*(1), 21–51.

Kalaycıoğlu, E. (2018b, November 15–18). *Domestic Politics, Public Opinion, and Foreign Policy: Case of Turkey,* Paper prepared for presentation at the Middle Eastern Studies Association's (MESA) Annual Conference at San Antonio, Texas, USA.

Kemahlioglu, O. (2015). Winds of Change? The June 2015 Parliamentary Election in Turkey. *South European Society and Politics, 20*(4), 445–464.

Key, V. O. (1966). *The Responsible Electorate: Rationality in Presidential Voting 1936–1960.* Cambridge, MA: Harvard University Press.

Keyder, Ç. (1987). *State and Class in Turkey: A Study in Capitalist Development.* London and New York: Verso.

Keyder, Ç. (1994). The Agrarian Background and the Origins of the Turkish Bourgeoisie. In A. Öncü, Ç. Keyder, & S. E. Ebrahim (Eds.), *Developmentalism and*

Beyond: Society and Politics in Egypt and Turkey. Cairo: American University of Cairo.

Kibris, A. (2010). Funerals and Elections: The Effects of Terrorism on Voting Behavior in Turkey. *Journal of Conflict Resolution, 55*(2), 220–247.

Kuzu, B. (2017). *Interview at Milliyet Newspaper* (daily). http://mekam.org/mekam/anayasa-komisyonu-baskani-burhan-kuzu-ile-baskanlik-sistemi-uzerine.

Öniş, Z. (1991). Political Economy of Turkey in the 1980s: An Anatomy of Unorthodox Liberalism. In M. Heper (Ed.), *Strong State and Economic Interest Groups: The Post-1980 Turkish Experience*. Berlin, New York: Walter de Gruyter.

Öniş, Z., & Türem, U. (2001). Business, Globalization and Democracy: A Comparative Analysis of Turkish Business Associations. *Turkish Studies, 2*(2), 94–120.

Özen, I. C., & Kalkan, K. (2017). Spatial Analysis of Contemporary Turkish Elections: A Comprehensive Approach. *Turkish Studies, 18*(2), 358–377.

Sözcü. (2017, March 16). *Örtülü harcama patladı*. https://www.sozcu.com.tr/2017/ekonomi/ortulu-harcama-patladi-1737160/.

Sayarı, S. (2016). Back to a Predominant Party System: The November 2015 Snap Election in Turkey. *South European Society and Politics, 21*(2), 263–280. https://doi.org/10.1080/13608746.2016.1170254.

The Guardian. (2017a, 17 April). *Turkey vote Curtailed Fundamental Freedoms, say European Observers*. https://www.theguardian.com/world/2017/apr/17/turkey-vote-referendum-curtailed-fundamental-freedoms-european-observers.

The Guardian. (2017b, 18 April). *Turkey Should Investigate Referendum vote 'Irregularities', says EU Commission*. https://www.theguardian.com/world/2017/apr/18/turkey-should-investigate-referendum-vote-irregularities-says-eu-commission.

Yıldırım, B. (2017). *Campaign Speech*. http://www.mynet.com/haber/politika/bas bakan-yildirim-evet-cikacak-teror-orgutleri-bitecek-2914681-1.

OFFICIAL DOCUMENTS AND SOURCES

OSCE. (2017, 22 June). "The republic of Turkey: Constitutional Referendum 16 April 2017" OSCE/ODIHR Limited Referendum Observation Mission Final Report. Poland: Warsaw.

The Supreme Election Council Archives. Available at www.ysk.gov.tr. Last accessed on 3 February 2019.

The Turkish Constitution. (1982). Available at https://global.tbmm.gov.tr/docs/constitution_en.pdf. Last accessed on 3 February 2019.

YSK. (2007, October 30). *İllere göre Anayasa Değişikliği Halkoylaması Sonucu*. Published. Retrieved from: http://www.ysk.gov.tr/doc/dosyalar/docs/2007Referandum/iller/turkiye.pdf.

YSK. (2010, September 22). *İllere göre Anayasa Değişikliği Halkoylaması Sonucu*. Retrieved from: http://www.ysk.gov.tr/doc/dosyalar/docs/2010Referandum/KesinSonuc/IlSonuclari.pdf.

YSK. (2017, April 27). *İllere göre Anayasa Değişikliği Halkoylaması Sonucu*. Retrieved from: http://www.ysk.gov.tr/doc/dosyalar/docs/2017Referandum/2017HO-Ornek134.pdf.

Part III

EU-Related Referendums

CHAPTER 20

The Irish and Danish 1972 Referendums on EC Accession

Palle Svensson

20.1 Introduction

With 40 nationwide referendums in Ireland and 22 in Denmark (2018 figures), these two countries are among the European countries that have most often used referendums to settle major political issues. Only Liechtenstein, Italy and Switzerland have conducted more referendums (Morel 2018: 53).

In both Ireland and Denmark, referendums are mandatory for constitutional amendments. Whereas constitutional amendments, and hence approval by referendum, are always necessary for delegation of sovereignty in Ireland, in Denmark the constitution provides for a particular procedure for delegation of sovereignty of constitutional powers to international authorities: delegation can be adopted by a five-sixths majority in the *Folketing* (the unicameral Danish Parliament), with a referendum required *only* if such a majority is not obtained.

Nine mandatory and legally binding referendums on European Community/Union (EC/EU) matters involving delegation of sovereignty have taken place in Ireland on proposals for constitutional amendments, of which seven were passed—on EC accession in 1972, the Single European Act (SEA) 1987, Maastricht Treaty 1992, Amsterdam Treaty 1998, Nice Treaty 2002, Lisbon Treaty 2009 and the Fiscal Compact 2012, and two were rejected: Nice Treaty

P. Svensson (✉)
Department of Political Science, Aarhus University, Aarhus, Denmark
e-mail: pal@ps.au.dk

© The Author(s) 2021
J. Smith (ed.), *The Palgrave Handbook of European Referendums*,
https://doi.org/10.1007/978-3-030-55803-1_20

2001 and Lisbon Treaty 2008. Such mandatory and legally binding referendums have occurred in Denmark when the qualified majority was not obtained in parliament (three passed—on EC accession, 1972, the Amsterdam Treaty, 1998 and the United Patent Court 2014—while three were rejected: Maastricht Treaty, 1992, adoption of the single currency, 2000, and the Danish opt-out on Justice and Home affairs, 2015).

In Denmark, no fewer than six possibilities for holding referendums are available; five of them are explicitly mentioned in the constitution and some of them have been applied to EU treaties. In addition to the mandatory referendums on constitutional amendments and delegation of sovereignty when a five-sixths majority is not obtained, the constitution provides for a mandatory law referendum on the voting age, an optional rejective law referendum called by a third of the members of the *Folketing*, and an optional rejective law referendum on *Folketing* decisions on foreign policy decisions (Svensson 1996: 34). A final possibility, not mentioned in the constitution, is ad hoc referendums that are formally advisory, whereas the constitutional referendums are legally binding.

In 1986 an ad hoc and advisory referendum was called in Denmark on the SEA (which unlike in Ireland was not considered as delegating constitutional powers). In 1993 a referendum on the Maastricht Treaty and the Edinburgh Agreement was called in the form of an optional rejective law referendum, called by the government even though a five-sixths majority had passed the law in the *Folketing*. The 1993 referendum was a result of the so-called 'National Compromise' on the EC agreed upon by the major political parties in 1992 that all future decisions on EU treaties should be subject to a referendum whether or not a five-sixths majority had been obtained in the *Folketing*.

Constitutional amendments have been rare in Denmark since 1953, when the current constitution was passed. A 2009 act of accession to the Danish throne had constitutional status, resulting in sons losing precedence over daughters in the line of succession, was approved in a referendum. A number of changes of the voting age have a semi-constitutional status as any bill on the voting age has to be approved in a referendum.

In Ireland, constitutional amendments have been more frequent than in Denmark. In addition to the amendments caused by EC/EU membership and treaties, a number of amendments have concerned the voting system as well as moral or religious issues such as abortion and divorce (Gallagher 1996: 56f; Sinnott 2002: 812; Reidy et al. in Chapter 16). A constitutional possibility, under which a majority of senators and a third of the members of the lower house of parliament (the *Dáil*) may petition the President not to sign a bill, but instead submit it to a referendum, has never been used.

20.2   The 1972 Referendums on EC Membership in Ireland and Denmark

20.2.1   The Political Background

Ireland and Denmark had more or less the same economic and political background for joining the European Communities in 1973.[1] *Fianna Fáil's* Seán Lemass became Taoiseach (prime minister) in 1959 and worked for Irish membership (*Oireachtas* no date; Documents on Irish Foreign Policy 1957–1961, as referred to in *The Irish Times*, 13 November 2018). Ireland's first application to join the EC was submitted in 1961, along with applications from the UK, Denmark and Norway. However, it was questioned whether Ireland's economy was sufficiently developed to withstand the potential impact of free trade and competition resulting from EC membership. It was also discussed whether Ireland could join if the UK, its main trading partner, did not join. Moreover, there were concerns regarding Ireland's neutrality and its non-membership of NATO. In 1962, Lemass addressed these concerns directly in a speech to the European Commission and visited the capitals of the six founding states in order to assure them that the issues raised would not be an obstacle to Irish membership. In 1962, the EC Council of Ministers agreed to discuss Ireland's entry to the EC. However, priority was given to the UK and Denmark's applications, and Irish negotiations would not begin until the following year (*Oireachtas* no date).

In the meantime, in January 1963, the UK's application was vetoed by the French President, General de Gaulle, and all four applications were suspended. As a reaction, an Anglo-Irish Free Trade Agreement was agreed in 1965, but the *Fianna Fáil* government continued to push for membership of the EC and worked towards removing trade barriers in order to improve Ireland's economy. In May 1967, the UK made a second application to join the EC, with Ireland's application following closely behind. However, the UK was again blocked by President de Gaulle, and in December 1967, Ireland was informed that its application was also rejected.

De Gaulle resigned in April 1969 and was succeeded by Georges Pompidou, who was more open to EC enlargement. The June 1969 Irish general election saw Patrick Hillary appointed as Minister for External Affairs and he carried out a series of visits to the European Commission and the six capitals in order to assure them that Ireland was ready to undertake the political and economic obligations of membership. To support this, a white paper entitled *Membership of the European Communities—Implications for Ireland* was published in April 1970. It outlined the potential effects that membership of the European Communities could have on Ireland in terms of financial implications, the impact on agriculture, fisheries, and industry, free movement

---

[1] The European Community (EC) comprising the European Coal and Steel Community, the European Economic Community and the European Atomic Energy Community was established by a treaty in 1965.

throughout member states, tax provisions and economic policy, among other things. In January 1972, the final negotiations took place and the Treaty of Accession was signed, permitting Irish membership of the three European Communities.

Denmark's path into the EC followed closely the Irish path. Denmark has traditionally been strongly dependent on foreign trade and Danish exports in the late 1950s were about evenly divided between the EC and the later European Free Trade Area (EFTA) countries. 'A market split in Europe therefore seemed to threaten Danish exports however Denmark reacted to it' (Petersen and Elklit 1973: 198). Understandably, Denmark became a champion of combining the EC countries with other European countries until such a possibility collapsed in 1958. Joining the EFTA (which comprised only industrial products) in 1960 was mainly considered a step towards a more comprehensive European market arrangement, and when the UK applied for EC membership in 1961, Denmark followed suit immediately. In August 1961, the *Folketing* voted in support of the Government decision to apply for membership together with the UK. This was a decision taken by the so-called 'four old parties', *Socialdemokratiet* (the Social Democrats), *Det radikale Venstre* (the Social Liberals), *Det konservative Folkeparti* (the Conservative People's Party) and *Venstre* (the Agrarian Liberals). These parties have since constituted a majority coalition behind Danish market policy, while *Socialistisk Folkeparti* (the Socialist People's Party) formed the parliamentary opposition on this issue (Petersen and Elklit 1973: 199).

The failure of the first negotiation round in 1963 did not affect the Danish 'market' policy, which underwent few changes during the 1960s. When new talks were initiated in 1967, the *Folketing* mandate repeated the 1961 formula of membership together with the UK. This was also the case in May 1970 when the *Folketing* agreed on a mandate for what would be the final round of negotiations. These negotiations with the EC in 1970–1971 were uncontroversial and undramatic as Denmark accepted the full *acquis communautaire* comprising the Rome Treaty and all subsequent decisions of the EC. The only real condition for Danish membership from the Danish perspective was that of British membership (Petersen and Elklit 1973: 199–201; Christensen 1993: 145).

20.2.2   *The Constitutional Provisions*

In both countries, the referendum on EC membership was called by the government after years of negotiating the terms of accession with the governments of the EC countries. In both Ireland and Denmark, the referendums were mandatory and legally binding, but the constitutional circumstances were quite different.

As mentioned, in Ireland EC membership had been an important goal of *Fianna Fáil* administrations since 1961 when Ireland first applied for membership (Murphy and Puirséil 2008: 535). When new opportunities became achievable in 1969, the terms of membership were negotiated and both major parties, *Fianna Fáil* and *Fine Gael*, supported entry (Keatinge and Laffan 1996: 229). The 1972 referendum on membership of the EC was necessary because of the obligations that EC membership would place on Ireland. Such obligations were seen to be in conflict with Article 15 of the Irish Constitution, which states that the sole and exclusive power of making laws for the State is vested in the *Oireachtas*. As legislative authority would no longer be solely vested in the *Oireachtas* and the European Court of Justice would become superior to the Irish Supreme Court it was decided to introduce a general amendment rather than amending each of the affected constitutional articles (Sinnott 1995: 224; Chubb 1992: 51; O'Mahony 2009: 433). Thus, the third Amendment to the Irish Constitution was an addition to Article 29.4 that permitted accession and declared that 'no provision of this Constitution invalidates laws enacted, acts done or measures adopted by the State necessitated by the obligations of membership of the Communities or prevent laws enacted, acts done or measures adopted by the Communities, or institutions thereof, from having the force of law in the State' (article 29.4.3). Article 29.4.3 made Irish entry into the Communities possible but did not incorporate the laws of the Communities into Irish law. That was left to a particular act, the European Communities Act 1972, which provided the legal conduct through which Community law flows into Irish law and thus provides an important part of the Irish framework of government (Chubb 1992: 52).

In Denmark, the *Folketing* decided on 18 May 1971 to subject the EC Membership bill to a referendum, whether the accession bill was passed in the Folketing by a five-sixths majority vote or not. At that time the five-sixths majority seemed to be certain, as all the major political parties, both the Government parties—the Agrarian Liberals, the Conservative and the Social Liberals—as well as the main opposition party, the Social Democrats, were in favour of membership. Thus, there was no constitutional requirement for a referendum. Nevertheless, the Social Democrats demanded a referendum on the issue, undoubtedly because they hoped to keep EC membership out of the approaching election campaign. The Social Democrats—and to some extent the Social Liberals—had by then become internally divided on the EC issue and Social Democrat leaders feared that their party might stand to lose on this issue to the Socialist People's Party and other left-wing parties as the opposition to membership was on the rise both within the Social Democratic Party and the trade unions in the winter of 1971 (Petersen and Elklit 1973: 201f; Nielsen 1993: 86; Svensson 1996: 41). However, in the end a referendum became necessary because twelve Social Democratic members of the *Folketing* (among them ten newly elected in the September 1971 election) broke with the party line and voted against the accession bill resulting in 141 MPs voting in favour of the bill compared with the 150 required for a five-sixths majority (*Folketingsårbog* 1971–1972: 332f). As the passing of the accession bill did not obtain the required majority, a separate bill on holding a referendum on

Danish membership of the EC was passed by the *Folketing*. The law specified that the referendum should follow the rules of the election law and that the referendum should not be conducted on the Faroe Islands as it had been agreed in the negotiations about Danish membership of the EC that the Faroe Islands should not enter unless it was decided by the Faroe Islands home rule government (*Folketingsårbog* 1971–1972: 173f).

In sum, while a constitutional amendment and a law formed the legal basis for accession in Ireland, two laws were needed in Denmark. The Irish referendum was mandatory for a constitutional amendment, while the Danish referendum was mandatory because the requisite five-sixths majority for the accession law was not obtained. Incorporating EC law in the respective national jurisdictions was done in Ireland by a separate law (the European Communities Act), whereas the relevant treaties were enumerated in the Danish accession law.

In both countries, the referendum was conducted under the existing electoral law, under which the vote was to be conducted by secret ballot. No constitutional device or general legal framework with common rules on conducting referendums was in place and applied in 1972.[2] The rules were different in the two countries. In Ireland, a simple majority of votes cast is sufficient to carry an amendment of the Constitution, with no minimum turnout required for the referendum to be considered valid. In Denmark, a constitutional amendment requires a majority of the votes cast in favour of the amendment, and that majority has to comprise 40% of all eligible voters. The rule for a referendum on delegation of sovereignty is less restrictive, as the decision of the *Folketing* stands unless a majority of votes is cast against the decision, and that majority comprises at least 30% of all eligible voters.

In both countries, the right to vote in the EC referendum followed the established rules for conducting elections. In 1972 according to the Irish Constitution (Article 16.1.2): 'Every citizen without distinction of sex who has reached the age of twenty-one years who is not disqualified by law and complies with the provisions of the law relating to the election of members of *Dáil Éireann*, shall have the right to vote at an election for members of *Dáil Éireann*'. The constitution also provided for 'such other persons in the state as may be determined by law' to have the right to vote in parliamentary elections and that such right was (and is) given to British citizens with an ordinary residence in a constituency (Chubb 1992: 319). However, according to Article 47.3 every *citizen* who has the right to vote at elections of the *Dáil Éireann* has the right to vote at a referendum. Thus, while British citizens resident

---

[2] General rules for referendums in Ireland were decided later, in the 1990s, and stemmed directly from two court judgments referred to as the McKenna and Coughlan judgments respectively, O'Mahony (2009: 434f).

in Ireland may vote in general elections, only Irish citizens can participate in referendums.[3]

According to the Danish Constitution (Article 29):

> Any Danish subject whose permanent residence is in the Realm, and who has the age qualification for suffrage provided for in subsection (2) of this section shall have the right to vote at Folketing elections, provided that he has not been declared incapable of conducting his own affairs. It shall be laid down by Statute to what extent conviction and public assistance amounting to poor relief within the meaning of the law shall entail disfranchisement.

No rules on disenfranchisement because of conviction or poor relief were in place in 1972 (nor today) and the voting age had in 1971 been lowered to 20 years.[4]

In both countries, local authorities were responsible for compiling and updating a list of voters in its area. In Ireland, an application is required, while it is done automatically in Denmark based on the population register. In each country, a voter card is sent to registered voters before every election and referendum.

20.2.3   The Campaigns

The campaigns before the EC referendums in Ireland and Denmark shared many similarities. To put it shortly: it was a confrontation pitting the political establishment against the political periphery. The main actors were the political parties, but in both countries 1972 marked a new trend where interest groups and umbrella organisations formed on an ad hoc basis became more important participants. Prior to the Irish referendum held on 10 May 1972, the *Fianna Fáil* government party and the main opposition party, *Fine Gael*, campaigned together for a Yes vote. According to Richard Sinnott (1995: 224), 'the forces ranged on either side of the issue were unevenly matched, at least in term of numbers'. Not only were the two main political parties on the pro-entry side, so were also the powerful farming organisations, the main business and employer's organisations, the Irish Council of the European Movement and all four national newspapers. The opposition to entry was led by the Labour Party and *Sinn Féin*, the trade unions, representatives of some of the smaller farmers, some nationalist cultural organisations and ad hoc groups such as the Common Market Defence Committee. The only newspaper support came from the fortnightly magazine, *Hibernia* (Sinnott 1995: 224; Manning 1978: 207).

[3]In 1972, the voting age in Ireland was 21 years. It was lowered to 18 years by the fourth amendment approved by a referendum on 7 December 1972. This is also the present voting age.

[4]Some years later, in 1978, a referendum approved to lower the voting age to 18 years, which is also the present voting age.

Considering the importance of Irish EC membership it has been argued that the level of the public debate on the subject was 'derisory' (Murphy and Puirséil 2008: 536). Nevertheless, The *Irish Times* Newspaper Archive reveals a number of lively and fairly detailed accounts of arguments for and against Irish membership of the EC, although it hardly amounted to a debate or discourse at the time in the sense of actors exchanging views on the matter.

A main argument for membership among the pro-Marketeers was that Ireland had no real alternative to EC membership. The Government White Paper had underlined that Irish farm products would be excluded from the benefits of the Common Agricultural Policy. This argument, for instance, was expressed by Michael O'Kennedy, Parliamentary Secretary to the Minister of Education, who under the heading 'Say "Yes" or face fight to survive' was reported to say that Ireland could not continue as previously once the enlarged EC came into being: 'Should we elect not to join, it was difficult to see how we could adjust enough to avoid economic collapse' (*The Irish Times*, 6 May 1972). On the same lines, in an editorial on 29 January 1972 the *Irish Times* concluded that 'If Ireland chooses not to join, she will be faced with economic and political problems which neither pro- nor anti-Marketeers have yet imagined'.

It was not only economic arguments that were advanced for Irish EC membership. In a campaign tour through Cork, Tipperary, Laois and Offaly, the *Taoiseach*, Jack Lynch, told meeting after meeting that to vote 'No' would be a wanton abuse of freedom. Turning from the economic issues he stressed that the decision was not whether Ireland should join Europe, but 'whether she should stay with it, helping to realise the aims and ideals which the EEC had set itself and which the Irish people strongly supported' (*The Irish Times*, 8 May 1972).

The pro-marketeers were not, however, completely united. Senator Michael O'Higgins of *Fine Gael* said that although it was the party's intention to launch as full a campaign as possible, the party recognised the risk that if the referendum was carried it might be regarded as a victory for *Fianna Fáil*: 'The fact that *Fianna Fáil* is linked with us in this campaign is an obstacle and not a help' (*The Irish Times*, 26 April 1972.). According to *Fine Gael*, the big hurdle to be crossed in the campaign was in convincing women that membership was necessary. Women had the idea that goods would be dearer in Europe and the big danger was that they did not see their income increasing (*The Irish Times* 26 April 1972).

The campaign against Irish entry into the EC was run mainly by two political parties, Labour and *Sinn Féin*, and the trade unions plus some ad hoc groups. Their main arguments were generally the loss of Irish sovereignty and more specifically the fear of rising prices. The Labour Party on 26 April 1972 launched its anti-EC campaign with the publication of three pamphlets on employment, the cost of living and the alternative to full membership. The leader of the Labour Party, Brendan Corish, argued that Ireland was not ready for membership because of its size, its poverty and its lack of control over its own economy. Instead an association agreement was advocated (*The Irish Times*, April 27, 1972). At a rally in Cork on 5 May, Mr Corish made a strong bid to head the anti-EC forces. He stated that full Common Market membership—with its resulting loss of sovereignty—would involve a denial of the principles enshrined in the 'Declaration' i.e. the 1916 Declaration that the Irish people had the sovereign and indefeasible right to the ownership of Ireland and to unfettered control of Irish destinies. He claimed that Ireland was not yet sufficiently developed for entry, and that instead of undergoing the difficulties of adjusting to the EC he asked: 'Why should this struggle not be devoted to the creation of a new social system, suited to our own needs and traditions, rather than in an anti-social system suited to great industrial giants and international companies' (*The Irish Times*, 6 May 1972).

In order to present an alternative to EC membership, *Sinn Féin* also published a pamphlet advocating a trade or association agreement. According to an article in the *Irish Times*, the pamphlet argued that EC members were committed to political integration with the objective of a United States of Europe with a European Army. Neutrality would go and compulsory military service introduced. Furthermore, the pamphlet claimed that 'farm incomes will be cut drastically, and that money for the higher prices for some farm products will come in the main from the rest of the Irish community' (*The Irish Times*, 18 January 1972).

On the day of voting, 10 May 1972, the *Common Market Defence Committee* ran an advertisement 'To the People of Ireland' which summarised the main point of the anti-marketeers: 'You will decide today whether Ireland is to remain an Independent nation with a Government responsible to the people of Ireland, for the pursuit of legitimate Irish interests ... Or whether we are to become an insignificant off-shore island, craving help from a group of nations who have no knowledge or interest in our problems or any talent for solving them' (*The Irish Times*, 10 May 1972).

According to Murphy and Puirséil, the lack of discourse can mainly be explained by two factors: the first factor is that the public was not alone in its ignorance of the EC issue. While the issue engaged a small number of politicians across the political spectrum, most politicians were not engaged. The second factor is related to the first: there was an elite consensus on the matter. Among the politicians within *Fianna Fáil* and *Fine Gael* who took an interest, there was a belief that entry into the Common Market would be a positive development for Ireland. This meant that even though the issues regarding Ireland's application were debated in the *Dáil*, 'they were of little use for political point-scoring at a more popular level' (Murphy and Puirséil 2008: 536).

In Denmark, the campaign before the referendum held on 2 October 1972 was widely seen as the most extensive political campaign ever undertaken in Denmark. According to Petersen and Elklit, it was also one of the most intensive (1973: 206). In the forefront for the supporting side were the four 'old' parties, operating with varying degrees of effectiveness. The Conservatives and the Agrarian Liberals had practically no internal opposition, while the Social Liberals had some internal opposition. The Social Democratic leadership, on the other hand, had to cope with a broad and vocal opposition within the parliamentary group and among party members. The Social Democratic leaders thus had to tread carefully, which gave their campaign a defensive character. Membership was also supported by the organisations of agriculture, industry and trade as well as the leadership of LO, the top organisation of organised labour. The press was overwhelmingly in favour of EC membership, which was also advocated by the so-called *Committee for Danish Affiliation with the EC* (*Komiteen for dansk tilslutning til EF*) (Petersen and Elklit 1973: 206f).

The Danish opposition to EC membership had many anti-establishment characteristics. Among the political parties, the Socialist People's Party and other left-wing parties were opposing entry, as well as minority groups among the Social Liberals and the Social Democrats. While the Social Democratic anti-marketeers had a separate organisation, *Social Democrats against the EC,* the other opposition groups rallied together in *The People's Movement against the EC* (*Folkebevægelsen mod EF*), an organisation that aimed directly at influencing the mass public. The opposing side was also supported by some of the more influential trade unions, such as the General Workers and the Metal Workers, but had little other organisational support. Its support in the press was also limited (Petersen and Elklit 1973: 206f).

The issues raised in the Danish campaign ranged widely. The supporters in particular stressed the economic question. They argued that the EC was predominantly an economic community and that Denmark could not afford to be excluded from it when the UK became a member. EC membership would, according to the pro-marketeers, prove beneficial for individual sectors (such as agriculture) as well as for Danish society at large (Hansen et al. 1976: 108).

The opponents disputed the claimed economic benefits, especially for the long run, but tended to focus their attention on the political dimension of membership rather than the economic dimension. The main argument against EC membership was the general loss of sovereignty and self-determination entailed in membership. The alleged great power aspirations of the EC, its capitalist image, and its unreceptiveness to others' interests such as those of the developing countries were the main arguments against EC membership. Less ideological and more home-based arguments concentrated on the dangers of the EC to the Danish labour market and on the risk of Denmark being literally 'sold' to foreigners.

The supporters of Danish EC membership were somewhat on the defensive in the political arena. Their main argument was that while membership would undoubtedly reduce national self-determination in some areas, these areas were closely delimited and did not comprise such sensitive fields as social and economic policy. Moreover, 'sitting at the table' would give a small country such as Denmark a disproportionate influence on the community decisions that were important for the country. The fears of the opponents in relation to land purchases and migrant labour were, it was argued, greatly exaggerated. Security policy would remain a NATO and not an EC issue. However, few supporters displayed genuine enthusiasm for a higher degree of integration or anything like a United States of Europe. The Nordic issue, which had been advocated as an alternative a few years earlier, was quite a problem to the supporters of Danish EC membership, especially among the Social Democrats, but they agreed that in economic terms neither Nordic cooperation nor a free-trade agreement would be a viable substitute for EC membership, when Denmark's two main trade partners, the UK and Germany, were members.

In the early 1960s, the cultural aspects of EC membership played a prominent role in the debate. The anti-campaign of that time had distinctly xenophobic (mainly anti-German and anti-Catholic) overtones. In 1972, these aspects were less prominent (Elklit 1974). There were some anti-German and general anti-foreign hints, especially to the debate on land purchases and immigration of labour but, according to Petersen and Elklit, they did not significantly affect the campaign (1973: 207f).

In Ireland, there was no public funding for referendums in 1972 and there were no upper limits on spending. Campaigners had to rely on other means.[5] Much the same was the case in Denmark, where no constitutional or other provisions regulated the financing or funding of referendum campaigns. Nor were there specific legal provisions limiting the spending of parties or other organisations in referendums campaigns or the sources of their funding (Hobolt 2010: 65).

In Ireland no consensus seemed to exist on the role of the mass media, radio and television.

During the campaign, the Labour Party complained that the *Fianna Fáil* party was using taxpayers' money in its EC campaign. Moreover, Foreign Affairs' booklets and pamphlets were being distributed free and advertised on *RTÉ* [*Radio Tellifis Éireann*, a semi-state company and national public service broadcaster] (The *Irish Times*, 27 April 1972). Anti-marketeers complained repeatedly that their viewpoints were either deliberately excluded from national newspapers and by *RTÉ* or cut to such an extent that the points being developed failed to come through (*The Irish Times*, 9 March 1972). Characteristically, towards the end of the campaign the *Common Market Study Group*, which opposed EC membership, criticised the media for not spending enough time, money and energy in investigating important aspects of the EC (*The Irish Times*, 5 May 1972).

In Denmark a variety of programmes were broadcast on television and radio. Supporters and opponents of EC accession were given a fairly even

[5] Regulations of referendum campaigns came later on the basis of Supreme Court rulings that it was not permitted to spend public money on one-sided referendum campaigns and that the public service broadcaster, *RTÉ* was not allowed to give more airtime to one side than the other in referendum campaigns (Lutz 2010: 122–124).

opportunity to present their respective positions. Arranged by the journalists on Denmark's Radio [the state-owned monopoly broadcasting company] these programmes featured both official party spokesmen and experts who debated the issues. All parliamentary parties—as well as those new parties which were allowed to run in the next general election after having collected enough supporting signatures—were given the same amount of time to explain their own views, to answer questions from journalists and to answer questions phoned in by the electorate (Hansen et al. 1976: 117). Thus, the opposition to Danish EC accession had better possibilities to campaign in the audiovisual media than in the printed press.

20.2.4   Public Opinion

In Ireland, little was known about the knowledge and the attitudes of the population on the EC issue (Murphy and Puirséil 2008: 537). By the summer of 1970, the only data available came from a Gallup poll from the previous year. It had found a majority (54%) in favour of membership, with 19% in favour of 'dropping the idea' and 26% responding that they did not know. There was a huge variation in attitudes depending on age, socio-economic group and region. The highest levels of support and lowest levels of 'don't knows' were among the younger, more affluent and the urban, except in political affiliation which saw *Fianna Fáil* with both the highest level of support and highest level of 'don't knows'. Even among Labour supporters, there were more in favour of entry than against (Murphy and Puirséil 2008: 537).

It may be surprising that the percentage of undecided answers was not higher since complaints that the public was not being kept sufficiently informed about the issue were commonplace at the time. Even within *Fianna Fáil*, there were mutterings that the public was being kept in ignorance of the precise nature of the EC. This was the background for the Minister for Foreign Affairs to establish an EC information bureau based in the Department of Foreign Affairs in the autumn of 1970.

The state's failure to provide more information on the membership issue had left a void, which was ably exploited by opponents of membership and by the time the bureau had been established, fears were growing within the 'Yes' camp that the campaign against membership was gaining momentum. Therefore, selling Europe to the people was a delicate project. In the bureau's first effort at producing a series of information booklets 'aimed at the ordinary person' it proved problematic to find the balance between the ideal of a future United States of Europe and Ireland's loss of sovereignty—since loss of sovereignty was one of the primary concerns of the 'No' campaign itself (Murphy and Puirséil 2008: 538).

By June 1971, a journalist hired by the Foreign Office for the campaign was warning of the distinct possibility of EC entry being spoiled because of a variety of factors including the government's failure to persuade voters either factually or ideologically (Murphy and Puirséil 2008: 539). He conceded that the information section in the Foreign Office had been operating since the previous autumn, but that it had to 'make good the diplomatic silence of years. But the level of contribution has, of necessity, been a low one, aimed at easy propagandist targets, and bolstered by a heavy succession of speeches by the Minister which have tended to demonstrate his wish to sidestep serious engagement with those who oppose EEC entry' (Business and Finance, 18 June 1971, here cited from Murphy and Puirséil 2008: 539). Perhaps the officials in the department were playing a long game, trying to ensure that the campaign in favour of entry did not peak too soon so that it would have maximum impact at the time of the referendum. At the same time, it does appear that the department had, to an extent, underestimated the amount of work necessary to bring the Irish public up to speed on the issue (Murphy and Puirséil 2008: 539).

Nevertheless, for the majority of the Irish people entry to the EC was seen as a *fait accompli* in December 1971, as 87% felt that Ireland could not afford to stay out. Even three-quarters of anti-marketeers were agreeing with this point of view and two-thirds of them felt that there was no real alternative. This is hardly surprising since the notion that there 'was no alternative' had been a constant refrain from the Government and one of the foremost themes stressed during the campaign itself (Murphy and Puirséil 2008: 540f).

Those in favour of Irish EC membership were mainly young, middle-class men, and farmers, both large and even small farmers,[6] who were not generally regarded as being beneficiaries of entry. Anti-marketeers were older, less well educated, from the urban working-class, and usually members of a trade union. The uncommitted voters tended to be older than those who had decided on their voting preferences. There was also a relatively higher proportion of working-class people among the undecided (Murphy and Puirséil 2008: 541).

When EC membership became official policy in Denmark in 1961, the public was very much in support. Immediately after the application, it was endorsed by 53% of the public, only eight per cent being against the idea and this initial distribution of attitudes was essentially retained during the 1960s (Petersen and Elklit 1973: 203). Nevertheless, a large proportion of Danish voters who did not know what to vote if a referendum on membership came up characterised the years until 1970. The 'don't know' group comprised around 40% (Petersen and Elklit 1973: 203; Buch and Hansen 2002: 2). Those supporting EC membership usually made up a stable group of between 50 and 60% of the voters, a level apparently unaffected by the failures of the 1961–1963 and 1967 negotiations.

In 1971, this picture underwent a dramatic change. Opposition to EC membership increased to about 30%, where it remained relatively stable until

---

[6]A survey undertaken by *the Irish Farmers' Journal* revealed that over 85% of Irish farmers favoured entry into the Common Market. No significant difference was found between large and small farmers and the overwhelming majority was evenly spread among the provinces (*The Irish Times*, 18 March 1972).

the referendum. At the same time support for membership dropped below the 40% level (Hansen et al. 1976: 103), reaching an all-time low of 35% in June 1971. From then on, another slightly upward trend started, which developed into a landslide immediately before the referendum. The undecided/don't know group continued its slow downward trend during most of the 1971–1972 campaign until a few months before the referendum when it started to drop dramatically. In the referendum, only 10% stayed at home.

For a long period in 1971–1972 there seems to have been a majority against membership among Social Democratic voters, which changed into a slight majority for membership only late in the campaign. Internal disagreements also characterised the Social Liberals, while Conservatives, Agrarian Liberals and People's Socialists followed their official party line more closely (Petersen and Elklit 1973: 204). In general, support was concentrated among farmers (who were the most positive group), self-employed in trade and industry, and the upper white-collar group, while opposition was concentrated among blue-collar workers, students, and to some extent lower white-collar and blue-collar workers.

Even though the latest public opinion polls had clearly predicted the final result there was still some uncertainty about the result of the referendum. This uncertainty was increased by the 'No' in the Norwegian referendum on 24–25 September, just a week before the Danish referendum.[7]

A comparative observation about the campaign and the development of public opinion in Ireland and Denmark indicates that the 'Yes' campaign in Ireland was a campaign run by the state to a larger extent than in Denmark. In both countries it was the establishment against the periphery, but more so in Ireland than in Denmark.[8]

20.2.5   The Referendum Result

The result of the referendum in Ireland was a very clear majority for EC membership with 83.1% of the votes cast for 'Yes' and only 16.9% for 'No'. The turnout was 70.9%—much higher than subsequent referendums on EC/EU-related matters (ranging from 57.3% in 1992 on the Maastricht

---

[7]In Norway, the race between the two sides was closer and the turnout was lower than had been generally expected in Denmark (Petersen and Elklit 1973: 208).

[8]However, in a personal communication to this author, one of the leaders of the 1972 campaign against Danish accession to the EC, and later member of the European Parliament, Jens-Peter Bonde, points to a number of grievances such as the abuse of information by the government and public officials; the denying of the ever closer union; the incorrect translation of 'union' to 'association'; the postponement of the summit in order to conceal the plans for a Union; the denial that Article 235 could be used for new areas; the everlasting guarantee of the right to veto; the capitalisation of agricultural profits; the disproportion of money for campaign purposes; the inconceivable imbalance of the media; the threats on the work place. 'It was not the "Yes"-majority that made us go on, it was the consistent misinformation, which kidnapped me and a generation for years of wasted resistance.'

Treaty to 34.8% in 2001 on the first vote on the Nice Treaty, O'Mahony 2009: 431). The geographic variation was clear, but not overwhelming with a difference at 18.7% between the constituency with lowest support for EC membership (Dublin South West, 73.0% 'Yes') and the constituency with the highest support (Donegal North East, 91.7% 'Yes'). A centre-periphery pattern was obvious, as the urban, Dublin constituencies voted 'Yes' to a lesser degree than rural constituencies of the West and North-West. Yet, in all constituencies a large majority was in favour of accession to the EC.

Two important traits of the referendum result in Denmark were similar to the Irish referendum result, namely a high turnout, actually the highest turnout ever in Danish political history, at 90.1%, and a clear majority in favour of EC membership: 63.3% of the votes cast for 'Yes' and 36.7% for 'No'. However, a number of differences between Ireland and Denmark also stand out. First, the majority for accession was smaller in Denmark than in Ireland (63.3 versus 83.1%); second, the geographical variation between the most pro-EC and most anti-EC constituencies was larger in Denmark than in Ireland, with a 31.5% difference in Denmark between the Ringkøbing constituency (75.3% 'Yes') and a Copenhagen constituency (43.8% 'Yes'); and, third, some constituencies in Denmark had a 'No' majority. On the other hand, the same centre-periphery pattern was notable in the two countries as the urban, Copenhagen constituencies and large towns voted 'Yes' to a lesser degree than rural constituencies of the West with large agricultural and agro- and fishing-industrial interests. Closer analysis has identified that the constituencies of the Greater Copenhagen area were further divided according to their socio-economic demographics. A significantly lower degree of EC support was evident in working-class constituencies than in middle-class constituencies (Borre and Elklit 1972; Petersen and Elklit 1973: 209; Buch and Hansen 2002: 13).

As the main political parties in both Ireland and Denmark were in favour of a joining the EC, there is hardly any reason to believe that the campaign and the voting behaviour should reflect a second-order poll on the government of the day.

In Ireland, no second-order effect can be identified in the 1972 EC referendum. *Fine Gael* Senator Michael O'Higgins had expressed the fear during the campaign that *Fianna Fáil* supporting membership of the EC might endanger the referendum result because *Fine Gael* supporters might register a protest vote against *Fianna Fáil* (*The Irish Times*, 26 April 1972). This fear does not seem to have been well-founded. The effects of party cues were strong. Tom Gavin and Anthony Parker in an ecological analysis have shown that support for Irish membership was strongly correlated with the combined strength of the *Fianna Fáil* and the *Fine Gael* (r = 0.826). Indeed, supporters of the main opposition party, *Fine Gael*, did not use the opportunity to vote 'No' in order to demonstrate opposition to the government of the day, as the correlation between *Fine Gael*'s 1969 parliamentary vote and the 1972 referendum vote was even stronger than the correlation between *Fianna Fáil*'s

1969 parliamentary vote and the 1972 referendum vote (r = 0.743 against r = 0.469) (Gavin and Parker 1972: 37).

In Denmark, the unpopularity among bourgeois voters of the Social Democratic Party, which took office in September 1971, was not enough to make them abandon their beliefs in the desirability of Danish EC membership. Whether or not bourgeois party leaders were tempted to use this opportunity to defeat the Social Democratic government, their voters did not use the referendum as a kind of second-order election to express their critical assessment of the government of the day. A survey analysis has shown that the Conservative and Agrarian Liberal voters closely followed the position of their party and—presumably—their own personal opinion on the issue. 89% of the Conservative voters cast a 'Yes' vote as did 90% of the Agrarian Liberal voters (Svensson 2002: 737f).

20.3   A FRENCH DETOUR

The French referendum on approval of entry into the EC of the UK, Ireland, Norway[9] and Denmark on 23 April 1972 (see Chapter 9 by Morel) was different from the Irish and Danish referendums on several points. First, while the Irish and Danish referendums were mandatory, the French one was not. President Pompidou used Article 11 of the French Constitution according to which the President may submit any bill dealing with, among other things, the ratification of a treaty to a referendum. Second, the constitutionality of the referendum was questionable because according to Article 11 the President may call a referendum 'on the proposal of the government', but this was not the case in 1972, as President Pompidou announced the referendum at a press conference in 16 March 1972 and the government formally proposed it to him only three weeks later (Wright 1978: 154). Furthermore, the treaty of admission of new countries to the EC did not really affect the functioning of the French institutions, which is a condition according to Article 11 (Morel 1996: 74). Third, the referendum was made an issue of confidence by President Pompidou—although perhaps not as demonstratively as General de Gaulle. Maurice Schumann, the Minister of Foreign Affairs said during the campaign that 'if disapproved by the people, it is up to them to designate another president and we shall have another government' (Wright 1978: 158). Thus, it has been argued that there was a certain congruity when President Mitterrand twenty years later called a referendum to ratify the Maastricht Treaty. Both in 1972 and 1992 French presidents were seeking to assert their authority 'through an issue (European integration) assumed to have both a unifying and mobilising potential, while simultaneously exposing the divisions among his political opponents' (Criddle 1993: 228). Fourth, although the vote for

---

[9]In Norway an advisory referendum on whether the country should join the European Community was held on 24–25 September 1972. The 'No' side won with 53.5% of the votes cast.

'yes' was as large as 68.3% of the votes cast, the turnout at 60.2% (Morel 1996: 73) was much lower than in Ireland and Denmark, perhaps indicating a lower level of legitimacy or less salience.

The clear majority for EC membership in Ireland and Denmark meant that the 1972 referendum result was widely accepted in both countries, but it did certainly not end the debate on EC/EU nor settle the issue of European integration once and for all. The debate and voting in 1972 sowed the first seeds of euro-scepticism, which was first and most institutionalised in Denmark with the formation of 'The People's Movement Against the EC' in 1972, a grassroots organisation which from 1979 participated in elections to the European Parliament and was activated whenever a new referendum came onto the agenda. In both countries, this scepticism won majority support in later referendums, in Denmark in the 1992 referendum on the Maastricht Treaty, and in Ireland in the 2001 referendum on the Nice Treaty and the 2008 referendum on the Lisbon Treaty (see Chapters 25 and 27 by Beach and Laffan in this volume).

20.4   Concluding Remarks

The political background for the referendums in Ireland and Denmark in 1972 was quite similar. The referendums were caused by the successful result of four countries' application for membership of the European Communities in 1970–71, and for both countries the UK's central position in the applications process was important, both politically and economically. However, the referendums were regulated by different constitutional rules in Ireland and Denmark, as EC membership required an amendment of the Irish constitution—which required a referendum—whereas the Danish referendum was called because a five-sixths majority for the delegation of sovereignty was not achieved. Nevertheless, similar, intense public debates took place in both countries and the result was a similarly high 'Yes'-vote as well as a high turnout. It goes without saying that few policy decisions have had such profound impact on life in the two countries as EC/EU membership, with regard to both their economic and social development. Furthermore, the 1972 referendums in the two countries marked the first step into a new era with an element of direct democracy about European integration.

Bibliography

Borre, O., & Elklit, J. (1972). Nogle resultater fra TVA's analyse af EF-folkeafstemningen. *Økonomi Og Politik, 46*(3), 256–274.
Buch, R., & Hansen, K. M. (2002). The Danes and Europe: From EC 1972 to Euro 2000—Elections, Referendums and Attitudes. *Scandinavian Political Studies, 25*(1), 1–26.

Christensen, J. (1993). Danmark, Norden og EF 1963–72. In B. N. Thomsen (Ed.), *The Odd Man Out? Danmark og den Europæiske integration 1948–1992* (pp. 135–152) Odense: Odense Universitetsforlag.

Chubb, B. (1992). *The Government and Politics of Ireland* (3rd ed.). London and New York: Longman.

Criddle, B. (1993). The French Referendum on the Maastricht Treaty September 1992. *Parliamentary Affairs, 46*(2), 228–238.

Elklit, J. (1974). Nationalt tilhørsforhold og holdninger til EF. *Sønderjyske Årbøger*, 180–203.

Folketingsårbog 1971–1972, Copenhagen: J. H. Schultz Forlag.

Gallagher, M. (1996). The Constitution. In J. Coakley & M. Gallagher (Eds.), *Politics in the Republic of Ireland* (2nd ed., pp. 49–66). Limerick: PSAI Press.

Gavin, T., & Parker, A. (1972). Party loyalty and Irish Voters: The EEC Referendum as a Case Study. *Economic and Social Review, 4*(1), 35–39.

Hansen, P., Small, M., & Siune, K. (1976). The Structure of the Debate in the Danish EC Campaign: A Study of an Opinion-Policy Relationship. *Journal of Common Market Studies, 15*(2), 93–129.

Hobolt, S. B. (2010). Campaign Funding in Danish Referendums. In K. G. Lutz & S. Hug (Eds.), *Financing Referendum Campaigns* (pp. 62–80). Basingstoke: Palgrave Macmillan.

Keatinge, P. & Laffan, B. (1996). Ireland in International Affairs. In J. Coakley & M. Gallagher (Eds.), *Politics in the Republic of Ireland* (2nd ed., pp. 227–249). Limerick: PSAI Press.

Lutz, K. G. (2010). Referendums and Spending in Ireland. In K. G. Lutz & S. Hug (Eds.), *Financing Referendum Campaigns* (pp. 116–30). Basingstoke: Palgrave Macmillan.

Manning, M. (1978). Ireland. In D. Butler & A. Ranney (Eds.), *Referendums. A Comparative Study of Practice and Theory* (pp. 193–210). Washington, D.C.: American Enterprise Institute for Public Policy Research.

Morel, L. (1996). France: Towards a Less Controversial Use of the Referendum? In M. Gallagher & P. V. Uleri (Eds.), *The Referendum Experience in Europe* (pp. 66–85). Basingstoke and London: Macmillan.

Morel, L. (2018). Types of Referendums, Provisions and Practice at the National Level Worldwide. In L. Morel & M. Qvortrup (Eds.), *The Routledge Handbook to Referendums and Direct Democracy* (pp. 27–59). London and New York: Routledge.

Murphy, G., & Puirséil, N. (2008). "Is it a New Allowance?" Irish Entry to the EEC and Popular Opinion. *Irish Political Studies, 23*(4), 533–553.

Nielsen, H. J. (1993). *EF på valg*. Copenhagen: Columbus.

Oireachtas website. (no date). https://www.oireachtas.ie/en/visit-and-learn/history-and-buildings/historical-documents/ireland-through-the-decades/. Visited 20 March 2019.

O'Mahony, J. (2009). Ireland's EU Referendum Experience. *Irish Political Studies, 24*(4), 429–446.

Petersen, N., & Elklit, J. (1973). Denmark Enters the European Communities. *Scandinavian Political Studies, 8*, 198–213.

Sinnott, R. (1995). *Irish Voters Decide. Voting Behaviour in Elections and Referendums Since 1918*. Manchester and New York: Manchester University Press.

Sinnott, R. (2002). Cleavages, Parties and Referendums: Relationships Between Representative and Direct Democracy in the Republic of Ireland. *European Journal of Political Research, 41,* 811–826.

Svensson, P. (1996). Denmark: The Referendum as a Minority Protection. In M. Gallagher & P. V. Uleri (Eds.), *The Referendum Experience in Europe* (pp. 33–65). Basingstoke and London: Macmillan.

Svensson, P. (2002). Five Danish Referendums on the European Community and European Union: A Critical Assessment of the Franklin Thesis. *European Journal of Political Research, 41,* 733–750.

Wright, V. (1978). France. In D. Butler & A. Ranney (Eds.), *Referendums. A Comparative Study of Practice and Theory* (pp. 139–67). Washington, D.C.: American Enterprise Institute for Public Policy Research.

CHAPTER 21

Referendums: Norway 1972 and 1994

John Erik Fossum and Guri Rosén

21.1 Introduction

Referendums have become more frequent in the last three decades. Politicians have resorted to referendums to help settle a wide range of issues. These range from rather detailed and technical questions such as whether Sweden should join the Euro or whether Norway should ban alcohol to core questions about the nature and status of the polity and its regime. With regard to the latter, Stephen Tierney (2012) presents four circumstances under which referendums are used: (a) as constitutive in connection with the establishment of a new state; (b) as part of constitution-making/change; (c) in the establishment of new forms of sub-state autonomy; and (d) in cases where states transfer sovereign powers to international organisations.

Norway's six national referendums since 1905 cover constitutional issues proper and matters of ordinary legislation. The first referendum was held in 1905 and was of a constitutive character: its positive outcome endorsed the creation of Norway as a new sovereign state. The second referendum, also in 1905, was about a core aspect of Norway's political regime: whether it should be a monarchy or a republic. The third and fourth referendums in 1919 and 1926, were about pieces of legislation, respectively Yes and No to whether Norway should ban a number of types of alcohol (a ban was accepted in 1919

J. E. Fossum (✉) · G. Rosén
Oslo Metropolitan University, Oslo, Norway
e-mail: j.e.fossum@arena.uio.no

G. Rosén
e-mail: gurir@oslomet.no

© The Author(s) 2021
J. Smith (ed.), *The Palgrave Handbook of European Referendums*,
https://doi.org/10.1007/978-3-030-55803-1_21

and abolished in 1926). The two most recent national referendums in 1972 and 1994 were on whether Norway should become an EU member. Thus, out of the six nation-wide referendums that have been organised in Norway in the last 100 years or so four of them have been on constitutional matters, and therefore fall under Tierney's classification listed above.

The focus of this chapter is on Norway's two EU referendums. We have chosen to focus on these referendums, because, firstly, they are the only two national referendums that have taken place after the consolidation of the Norwegian party system[1]; secondly, questions of membership and treaty change are among the most frequent triggers of referendums in Europe[2]; and, thirdly, some argue that the EU referendums in Norway have staked out a new constitutional practice because a potential third referendum would be both 'politically and probably also constitutionally compulsory' (Wyller 2006: 29, authors' translation). We start with some theoretical reflections on referendums in relation to democracy, which helps frame the subsequent assessment of the Norwegian case.

21.2   REFERENDUMS AND DEMOCRACY

Even if their use is contested, there is little doubt that referendums have come to occupy a special role in the modern democratic imagination. Many referendums, as Tierney's overview shows, are associated with fundamental constitutional changes and even moments of constitutive change. Another and perhaps even more telling aspect is that referendums are generally referred to as instances of *direct* democracy, whereas representative democracy is referred to as indirect democracy. The referendum result is a form of popularly mandated instruction to the political system to carry out the popular will. If a referendum is to express the popular will, one vital question is what kind of decision rule is necessary to ensure that 'the people has spoken'? (see Renwick and Sargeant in Chapter 4). Is a mere majority of votes adequate, or should there be additional requirements such as absolute majority or majority of eligible voters or rather some form of supermajority? Multilevel systems, and especially federal ones, bring up the question of governing level: under what circumstances should referendums be held nation-wide and under what circumstances should they be held in sub-unit(s)? Even in Norway, generally understood as a unitary country, albeit with a strong tradition of regional and local democracy, there has been a debate about whether a majority should involve a majority of all the 19 counties.

---

[1]This relates back to the 'freezing hypothesis' which states that: 'the party systems of the 1960s reflect, with few but significant exceptions, the cleavage structures of the 1920s', coupled with the 'party alternatives, and in remarkably many cases the party organizations are older than the majorities of the national electorates' (Lipset and Rokkan 1967: 44).

[2]As many as 46 EU-related referendums have been held since 1972. Source: Beach (2018).

From a normative perspective it is important to underline that all of these decision-making rules are mere approximations to the ideal of the popular will. Constitutional democracy is then also about reconciling popular self-government and the rule of law (Habermas 2001). The question of thresholds appears particularly relevant with regard to constitutional matters, since representative democracies operate with higher thresholds for constitutional changes than for ordinary legislation. The question is what bearing that has on referendums, when they are mandatory and when they are intrinsic parts of a broader set of procedural arrangements for effecting constitutional change.

Another question of particular relevance for today's highly interconnected world with large-scale migration is that of who the subject of the popular will is. EU citizens have rights to access and to operate in other EU Member States, which therefore have ceded control of their membership. Norway is a closely associated non-member that has adopted a large body of EU law. EU citizens who are resident in Norway can influence EU laws with application in Norway, whereas Norwegian citizens cannot because they do not have EU voting rights. In a highly interconnected world, who decides who has the right to vote and what are the criteria for obtaining voting rights is not just an abstract matter. A recent illustration of the question as to who should be included and who should be excluded is the 2016 Brexit referendum, where most EU citizens in the UK were barred from voting, as were UK citizens that had lived more than 15 years outside the UK (see Smith elsewhere in this volume). The deeper problem is that democracy has no *democratic* procedure for determining who forms part of the demos. Popular referendums are at least as vulnerable to this problem as are representative systems, especially since referendums are one-shot decision instances, where the effects of exclusion can be severe.

Finally, there is the question of the execution of the popular will. A referendum result needs to be implemented, which turns the focus to the role of referendums as decision-making devices. The more ambiguity there is surrounding the result (as was the case in the 2016 Brexit referendum where it was not spelled out what kind of future EU relationship a vote to leave would entail), the more difficult it will be for the political system to execute the result of the referendum. Thus, the greater the ambiguity, the more the referendum as a decision procedure will have to rely on inputs from other sources, be they parliaments or executives.

These reflections take as their point of departure that the referendum is binding. There is however an important distinction between binding and non-binding referendums (mandatory or obligatory on the one hand and optional or facultative on the other; see the ACE Electoral Knowledge Network 2020)); thus the formal legal and constitutional status of referendums varies considerably. We will develop this further with reference to the Norwegian case to which we now turn.

21.3   THE LEGAL FRAMEWORK
ON REFERENDUMS IN NORWAY

Referendums are not constitutionally required. In fact the Norwegian constitution does not mention referendums. While this does not exclude the use
of referendums, it does not permit the use of binding referendums because
the parliament—the *Storting*—cannot sign away its decision-making powers,
not even to the people who elected it (Wyller 2006: 28). The government
notes that it considers the *Storting* to have 'constitutional access' to decide
an advisory referendum in all those questions that figure within the *Storting*'s
realm (Ot.prp.nr.79 [1993–1994]). National referendums are either called by
the *Storting* through a plenary vote or through a specific piece of legislation.
There is no provision for other actors or bodies to call national referendums, which follows from the *Storting*'s decision-making prerogatives. EU
referendums represent a potential exception to this pattern, however, as some
argue that a third referendum on EU membership could be considered both
politically and constitutionally obligatory (Wyller 2006: 29).

With regard to the question of EU membership, there has also been some
debate on whether there should be one or two referendums: one to authorise
the government to start the negotiations and one to sanction the result of the
negotiations.[3] The two referendums that were arranged in 1972 and 1994
were both held *after* the accession negotiations had been concluded. When
entering the polling stations, the voters could base their decisions on the type
of negotiated settlement that would be in place. However, it is the *Storting*
that determines not only whether but also when and how the referendum is
to take place (Wyller 2006).

In Norway, since there is no formal referendum requirement, all referendums are optional, and their results are formally speaking advisory. This
situation pertained to each of the two Norwegian EU referendums. Nevertheless, there was disagreement over how the outcome was to be handled
by parliament. An important reason was that the question of EU membership had to be determined by a supermajority in the *Storting* (in 1972 then
Article 93 of the constitution required a three-quarters majority). In 1972, it
appeared as if the opposition to membership could muster a sufficient minority
in the *Storting* to block a decision. But, as Bjørklund (2005: 31) notes, the
number may have been inflated, because some MPs could say that they were

---

[3]For a concrete proposal, see Dok.nr.8:41 (1991–1992). Bjørklund (2005: 16–17) says
that this was a uniquely Norwegian invention. Several of Norway's political parties have
at various times had such a provision in their party programme. Consider for instance
the Progress Party's Principle and Action Programme during the period 2005–2009 (the
party's political platform [FrP 2005]), which states that the two previous popular referendums on EU membership operate as constraints on the procedures guiding Norwegian
EU membership: (a) the decision to apply for EU membership should be preceded by a
popular referendum; (b) Norway should not apply for EU membership unless there are
significant changes in Norwegian public opinion; and (c) the negotiation result should be
subjected to a second referendum.

opposed to EU membership because they knew that there would be a popular referendum. If the referendum ended with a Yes, it was not clear that they would block the result in parliament. In 1994, it was more readily apparent that the opponents could have blocked a Yes majority. Two of the parties would not unconditionally accept a Yes majority and listed a number of additional requirements. The Socialist Left party set as a condition that they would only accept a Yes vote if there was a double majority of citizens and provinces (modelled on the Swiss case). The Centre Party (closely associated with the farming sector) noted that it would consider the result in terms of the size of the majority, the number of votes cast, the geographical distribution of votes, and the election campaign (Bjørklund 2005: 29). The possibility for a parliamentary No minority rejecting a Yes vote in a referendum has led EU supporters to propose that referendums be made binding.

This example shows that it is important to consider how referendums fit into the broader context of procedural arrangements; how the different procedures are configured in relation to each other; and what scope for strategic political action they contain. The different procedures—referendum versus parliamentary vote—cater to different concerns and constituencies and raise different normative expectations. The question is therefore often not one of referendum versus parliamentary sanction but rather one of *how to combine* these procedures so as to ensure a normatively defensible process and outcome.

Each of the two EU referendums was initiated as a result of pieces of bespoke legislation (LOV-1972-04-21-20 and LOV-1994-06-24-42).[4] In both cases the Ministry for Local Government and Labour drafted the proposal, but the Ministry of Foreign Affairs was responsible for the legislative proposal in 1972. The text from 1972 reflects the long history of a connection between the question of Norwegian membership of the EU and a popular referendum. Even back in 1962, a majority of the Foreign Affairs and Constitutional Committee declared that should negotiations lead to full membership of the then European Economic Community (EEC), there would be 'a need to find out how the Norwegian people perceive of the problems such a membership will lead to. It is important that the decision the Storting makes has the support of the people' (Utenriksdepartementet 1971, Ot.prp. 35, 1971–1972, authors' translation). On these grounds, the committee recommended holding an advisory referendum on the matter. Then in 1972, Member of Parliament, Helge Seip, asked the government to confirm that it would propose a law on holding a referendum (ibid.). Such a law was subsequently passed (Justis—og politidepartementet 1972).

The Ministry of Foreign Affairs had debated whether to include the result of the negotiations, and possibly also some conditions for Norwegian membership such as third country membership as part of the topic for the

---

[4]The two first referendums (1905) were determined by the *Storting* in plenary, while the two referendums on the alcohol ban were decided through legislation (Utenriksdepartementet 1971, Ot.prp. 35, 1971–1972).

referendum. It landed, however, on short and succinct answers—Yes or No to membership—a very similar approach to that taken to accession referendums elsewhere. This formula was then repeated in 1994, with the argument that there should be an overlap between the two referendums. However, because referendums are governed according to constitutional practice, the rules can be decided on each occasion. In accordance with electoral law, the *Storting* was given the role of determining the legality of the referendums. Moreover, with regard to disputes, the same rules as for national elections would apply. Thus, everyone who has a right to vote can complain about the preparations and implementation of the referendum. Such complaints had to be presented within eight days of the referendum to the *Storting* (para. 11). Moreover, compared to the law governing the 1972 referendum, the 1994 act included a detailed list of events that could lead to the parliament setting the result aside, provided that it was probable that the error had had an effect on the national results (para. 12).

21.4   For Determining Each Referendum, What Rules Were in Place?

The regulations pertaining to the two referendums in question were adopted from the ordinary rules governing Norwegian elections. With regard to the 1972 EU referendum, Article 2 of the referendum act stated that the referendum should be conducted in accordance with the 10 July 1925 Law on Municipal Elections. Article 3 specified that those permitted to vote were those who had the right to vote according to the Constitution's Article 50 in accordance with how the regulations are when the referendum law takes effect. Accordingly, those entitled to vote were Norwegian citizens who were more than 20 years old. The right to vote was established through a census based on the previous national elections and the national registry.[5]

In 1994, it was underlined that there should be as little discrepancy between the two referendums as possible (Innst.O.nr.69 [1993–1994]). Article 2 of the referendum act states that the preparations and implementation of the referendum shall be governed by the rules that apply to national elections (Valgloven 1985). Based on the constitution and the electoral law, Norwegian citizens who would turn 18 by 31 December 1994 had the right to vote.[6] Citizens who on the day of the referendum resided outside of Norway could vote if they had been listed in the Norwegian national registry (Para. 3). Citizens who had resided in Norway during the 10 years prior to the referendum were automatically included in the census. Other citizens could apply for the

[5]The census was also to include those who turned 20 by 25 September 1972 at the latest, and who had resided in Norway for 5 years.

[6]The law on municipal elections allows for non-citizens to vote, however, this was not considered appropriate for the 1994 referendum by the Ministry (Innst.O.nr.69 [1993–1994]).

right to vote, but citizens who had never been registered as residing in Norway did not have the right to vote (Statistics Norway 1995: 9).

In 1972 there were no rules as to publishing results, however, in 1994, paragraph 7 stated that results could not be published before 9 pm the night of the referendum. This included actual results as well as prognoses based on surveys conducted the day before or on referendum day.

A noteworthy difference between the two referendums is their timing. Whereas the 1972 vote was held before the Danish referendum on EU membership, the 1994 referendum was scheduled after Finland and Sweden had held their positive votes. The government's argument was that the Nordic cooperation would be significantly weakened with Denmark, Finland and Sweden in the EU and Norway outside. It wanted this aspect to be taken into consideration at the time of the vote (Ot.prp.nr.79 [1993–1994]). A majority of the members of the parliamentary committee responsible for the referendum act agreed that the result in Sweden should be known prior to the Norwegian vote (Innst.O.nr.69 [1993–1994]). Jahn and Storsved (2007) have argued that this 'domino-strategy' was successful in most countries, except for Norway (see also Chapter 24 by Mendez and Mendez).

21.5   THE PRACTICE OF THE REFERENDUMS

Turning from the formal arrangements to the practice of the two Norwegian referendums, the *Storting*'s determination to put the membership question to a popular vote was established early in the 1960s. As described above, the parliament repeatedly expressed its preference for an advisory referendum before the *Storting* 'would make its final decision on the question of whether Norway should become a member of the European Community' (Utenriks-departementet 1971, Ot.prp.35 1971–1972: 1, authors' translation). At stake was not only the concern for voters' right to participate, but also party polit-ical considerations. According to Wyller (2004: 195), in 1962, then Prime Minister and leader of the Labour Party Einar Gerhardsen flagged the need for a referendum to signal the expectation that voters would get in line with the government on this issue. Both the Liberal Party and Christian Democrats, it is argued, left the decision to the people in order to overcome disunity within the party (Wyller 2006).

The next time the issue of EU membership arose, in 1992, it was decided to hold another EU referendum.[7] Party divisions were even more pronounced in 1994, especially in the Labour party. The Norwegian Confederation of Trade

---

[7] In the parliamentary debate on 19 November 1992 the following procedure was accepted by a large majority of MPs (104 voted in favour, 55 against): 'The *Storting* gives its consent to Norway applying for European Community membership with the aim that the negotiations be conducted in parallel with the other Nordic states' negotiations and so that the people itself through a referendum is enabled to decide on the result of the negotiations' (Ot.prp.nr.79 [1993–1994, authors' translation]).

Unions (LO), a strong ally of the Labour party, landed on No to membership. In addition, a faction was established within the party calling itself 'Social Democrats against the EU'. This tore the party in two—along a left–right cleavage (Kallset 2009), similar to the situation in Denmark (see Chapter 20 by Svensson). A main difference between the 1972 and 1994 referendums, however, was the 1993 election, which became completely dominated by the membership question (Aardal and Valen 1997). Midtbø and Hines (1998) show how pro-EU parties were punished in eurosceptic electoral districts. The big winner of the election was the Centre Party (Senterpartiet), which went from 11 to 32 representatives in parliament. The Centre Party was the main party political protagonist for a No to membership, and all of its candidates had committed themselves to vote No to membership—regardless of the referendum result. Thus, the Yes and No sides were divided on how to interpret the result of the referendum. The Yes side insisted that the voice of the people had to be respected, knowing that without a qualified majority in parliament (three-quarters), their only chance of success was a positive popular vote. The No side, on the other hand, wanted the referendum to be advisory, knowing that it would have enough votes to block a vote in parliament (Wyller 2006).

Looking at the referendum debates, both were deeply coloured by Norway's historical experiences. Political actors often evoked specific renditions of the past to support their present stances and policies. National sovereignty figured strongly in the debates. A frequent reference was Norway's long experience as variously a junior partner and semi-colony ('*lydrike*') to Denmark (1389–1814) and thereafter in a monarchical union with Sweden (1814–1905). These were historical experiences that cast long shadows on the debates. For this reason, the term 'union' had an odious ring and was evoked to remind people of Norway's subservient relation to Denmark and Sweden. The implicit notion was that were Norway to join the EU, its present status as a sovereign state would be an interregnum as it would effectively move from one union (with Sweden) to another (the European Union), and even that the latter option would be worse.[8]

Further, a close link was drawn to popular sovereignty, where the constitution and parliament figured as vital democratic safeguards. Historically it was well-known that the *Storting* had played a prominent role in wrestling power from the Swedish king, in the long process of forging national independence from Sweden. This historical experience was especially underlined by the No campaign to associate No with preservation of constitutionalism and democracy. The Yes campaign did not refute the importance of these two core concepts but rather sought to redirect the debate to economic issues, and to downplay the constitutional significance of EU membership. The notion that there were somewhat parallel debates is underlined by Bjørklund (2005:

---

[8]Called the 'No queen', leader of Senterpartiet, Anne Enger Lahnstein, stated that membership of the EC would be worse than the union with Sweden (NTB 28 March 1992).

187), who notes that '(t)he same arguments were to a large extent used to support both a yes and a no stance. The debate left the impression that the two parts did not participate in the same war'. An important reason for this was uncertainty about what the future would bring, amplified by ambiguity as to what type of entity the EU was and would become (cf. Saglie 2000). Studies have, however, shown how the No side succeeded in monopolising, and constructing a version of the concept of 'Norway', which was completely incompatible with being in any form of union (Neumann 2001). Easton (2009: 63) draws a distinction between the emotive and rational aspects of the Norwegian debate, arguing that whereas the former was linked to 'culture and a sense of national rural history' and appealed to the No camp, the latter was linked to the 'economy and an urban future' appealing to Yes voters.

History also figured prominently with regard to aspects of social structure. Norway, as Rokkan and Valen (1964) have underlined has long been marked by a significant centre-periphery conflict, which manifested itself in both referendums. A remarkable feature is the sheer continuity between the two referendums. The greater Oslo region, i.e. the provinces surrounding the Oslo-fjord saw a majority in favour of Norwegian EU membership, pitting it against the rest (major cities excepted) of the country, which saw a majority against EU membership. The magnitude of opposition increased with physical distance from the capital city Oslo, and was particularly strong in Northern Norway. Party identification was also a prominent explanatory factor, which is unsurprising given the role of the 1993 national elections (Pettersen et al. 1996).

Another aspect that stands out with regard to the two Norwegian EU referendums is the very prominent role of social movements, especially on the No side, which in 1972 was *Folkebevegelsen mot EU* (People's Movement Against the EU). This was an organisation with 113,025 members, gathering farmers, trade union members and activists, as well as city radicals together. Somewhat paradoxically, it initially gained a foothold in the cities, where the EU opposition was the weakest, and only later where the EU opposition was the strongest, which showed up in massive support. In 1994, the main organisation on the No side was *Nei til EU* [No to EU], with 138,426 members (Bjørklund 2005: 82). There was little direct overlap between the leadership of the two organisations, and in contrast to *Folkebevegelsen mot EU* (1972), *Nei til EU* (1994) struggled to win support in the cities.

A majority of the media in both instances supported the Yes option but there were some news outlets that supported No as well. In 1972, however, the government was heavily criticised for attempts to skew the campaign to its favour. Analysts note that it was accused of distributing information material to argue for its own stance, under the guise of being neutral facts (Wyller 2006). Especially in the 1972 campaign, government officials were also seen as having played an overly strong advocacy role (Gleditsch et al. 1974). On the one hand, it has been argued that civil servants from the Ministry of Finance supported a No, and used their expertise to push for Norway to remain outside the EU (Lie 2015). On the other hand, the government was accused of taking advantage of the bureaucratic apparatus to promote its Yes campaign. In response to this criticism, both the Yes and No organisations received economic support, but this did not compensate for the asymmetrical division of funds that favoured those supporting Norwegian membership of the EU (Wyller 2006). Perhaps as a result of the strong criticism in 1972, funding was more equally distributed during the 1994 campaigns (ibid.).

The question of the role of public administrative officials (the specific category of *embetsmenn* in Norway) in the EU debate was brought up in a debate in the Norwegian parliament 'the *Storting*' where the two representatives from the Progress Party, Carl I. Hagen and Fridtjof Frank Gundersen, proposed a set of guidelines for how public officials should behave. They proposed that public officials in the government ministries should exercise great restraint in terms of participation in EU debates. They argued that the more senior or centrally located the government official, the more restraint he or she should exercise. At the same time, they argued that the leaders of government directorates (expert agencies, which may have considerable independence) should have a duty to express their professionally founded views on the effects of Norwegian EU membership within their respective areas of competence, given that they are best qualified to do so. They stressed that the information thus provided must be based exclusively on professional evaluations and not personal views (Dok.nr.8:70 [1993–1994]). The proposal built on two sets of assumptions: that the institutional affiliation of a government official can be directly associated with the official's ability to act in an exclusively professional capacity, hence the distinction between ministries and directorates, and that the EU issue was of such importance that those with the best professional qualifications should be endowed with a duty to inform the public. The majority of the constitutional committee rejected the proposal and both assumptions, noting that the proposal was tied to a specific issue, and that there was no need to issue specific guidelines for officials' participation in the public debate on the EU (Innst.S.nr.211 [1993–1994]). The debate showed that public officials are generally speaking assumed to balance requirements for loyalty (with the government in power) with neutrality and professional expertise.

The question on the ballot paper in both referendums was whether Norway should become a member of the EC/U or not. There was no ambiguity in the question, but since Norway was already affiliated with the EU, the binary question was not entirely in sync with the underlying options which were actually threefold: first, 'No' to EU membership without the EEA; second, 'No' to EU membership with the EEA; and third, 'Yes' to membership. Symbolically speaking a No vote would suggest the first, whereas substantively the result would be the second. The No vote would preserve the status quo, in other words EEA as a close form of EU affiliation. For the debate, it meant that the Yes side's economic arguments lost quite a bit of their sting, since it was apparent that Norway would have assured access to the EU's internal market regardless of the outcome of the referendum.

In Norway, as elsewhere in Europe, ambiguity and political contestation over the EU's status as a polity spilled over to the referendum debates. We may consider three possible roles for how leaders may be staging such a process:

a. Political leaders may *explicitly express* that the EU referendum is about a matter of the utmost constitutional salience;
b. Political leaders may *actively downplay* the constitutional salience of the EU referendum;
c. Political leaders may *diverge sharply* on the normative salience of the referendum and disagree on the terms of debate.

In Norway, the Yes side often tried to downplay the magnitude of transfer of sovereignty, and therefore tended to depict the EU as an economic institution whose particular historical role was to foster peaceful coexistence in Europe but without abrogating state sovereignty. The No side was far more prone to depict the EU as a fledgling federal state in order to underline that there would be a major transfer of sovereignty to the EU and further that the question of EU membership was of the utmost constitutional importance.[9] The constitutional significance of the underlying issue was thus contested, and that spilled over onto the constitutional status of the referendum instrument itself, which became a matter of political contestation, as noted above. These political assessments have had bearings on the broader effects of the referendums, as we will show below.

21.6   The Effects on Norwegian Politics

Referendums can have direct implications for governing, insofar as government leaders stake their leadership role on a specific referendum outcome. In Norway, the immediate effect of the 1972 referendum was that the Labour party government led by Trygve Bratteli resigned. In August 1972, before the referendum, Bratteli put a vote of confidence to the Norwegian people, stating that he could not continue to govern if the result was a No to membership. As a consequence of his self-imposed withdrawal, a minority coalition headed by Christian Democrat Lars Korvald assumed power. In the second referendum, Prime Minister, Gro Harlem Brundtland, also of the Labour party deliberately did not link her continued role in government to the result.

Another set of more fundamental effects is on societal conflict structures and party constellations. Referendums activate cleavage patterns, often along lines that cut across parties, as was clearly the case in Norway. In the wake of the 1972 referendum, several parties—including the Labour party—took care to nominate both supporters and opponents to Norwegian membership to leadership positions at their ensuing national conventions (Valen

---

[9]For assessments of the implications for sovereignty and constitutionalism, see the contributions in Eriksen and Fossum (2014) and (2015).

1973). Nevertheless, in connection with the 1972 referendum this led to the Liberal Party (*Venstre*) splitting, and the establishment of *Det Nye Folkeparti*. It also precipitated the establishment of the Socialist Left Party (*Sosialistisk Venstreparti*) as a collection of previous organisations on the left.[10]

Referendums have generally tended to reactivate centre-periphery conflicts in Norway (Bjørklund 1997). That was clearly the case in the two EU referendums, and what is also remarkable is the degree of continuity between 1972 and 1994, despite the fact that a very large portion of the voting population had changed between 1972 and 1994. Nevertheless, in addition to this strong continuity, there were three important changes between 1972 and 1994:

1. Voter turnout was quite a bit higher in 1994, at an 'all-time high' for elections in Norway (89%). Mobilisation was especially strong in the No-dominated periphery (Pettersen et al. 1996: 279);[11]
2. In 1994, there was an explicit gender dimension to the result given that a clear majority of women voted against EU membership (Jenssen and Valen 1995);
3. In 1994 there was a more pronounced private–public sector divide than in 1972, in that a larger percentage of public sector workers voted No.

Another effect of the two EU referendums is that their cumulative impact contributed to cement the specifics of Norway's mode of EU affiliation, or what may be referred to as 'the non-membership paradox'. Norway, as was rightly pointed out in the 2012 White Paper (NOU 2012: 2), is both 'in' and 'out'.

The issue of EU membership has been the most conflictual issue in Norway's post-war history, and has led to significant political mobilisations in connection with the referendums, not least through the very influential No-to-EU popular movement, which has a permanent presence. At the same time, neither the political mobilisation nor the tensions that this profoundly divisive issue has generated have been allowed to shape Norway's dynamic EU adaptation, which has proceeded almost without friction (NOU 2012: 2).[12] That is interesting given that the political parties are deeply divided on the EU

[10] *Sosialistisk Folkeparti* (SF) was established in 1961. In the 1972 European Community debate, SF members, EC opponents in the Labour Party, members of the Communist Party (NKP) and politicallly unaffiliated socialists were together in *Folkebevegelsen mot norsk medlemskap i EF*. When the No victory materialised they continued the cooperation under the name *Sosialistisk Valgforbund*. On 16 March 1975 *Sosialistisk Venstreparti* was officially established as a political party in. NKP soon broke from it (SV no date).

[11] However, Midtbø and Hines (1998) argue that the Labour party's inability to mobilise its 'hesitant' voters, contributed to the No outcome.

[12] The EEA Agreement includes a reservation right (Article 102), which allows the EEA states to suspend EU legislation. This is not a veto right because the EEA states have no effect on the status of the legislation within the EU. Thus far, Norway has never used it.

membership issue; and some parties (especially the Labour party) are deeply divided internally as well.

The Norwegian situation post-1994 referendum is almost a mirror-image of the post-2016 UK referendum situation in that the UK situation was marked by politicisation whereas the Norwegian situation has been marked by depoliticisation.

The Norwegian political system is traditionally a consensus-seeking system, which operates on the basis of coalition governments. The EU membership issue, if kept alive, would make consensus politics very difficult. The political parties have accordingly since 1994 sought to limit the political fallout by keeping the contentious EU membership issue off the agenda. In doing so, the Norwegian political system has managed to sustain a very high level of adaptation to the EU that is at the same time depoliticised.

The political system has established a particular mechanism for handling the EU membership question, namely through '*gag rules*'.[13] These are mainly expressed through government declarations or coalition agreements, which specify the government's commitment to maintain the present arrangement with the EU, through the EEA Agreement. Each agreement posits that a political party that seeks to alter the status quo—actively seeking EU membership or revoking the EEA Agreement—will violate the coalition agreement. Especially for the large parties it is a Hobson's choice: if you seek to change the EU membership status quo you will no longer be able to govern. Such agreements have been labelled 'suicide clauses' in the Norwegian media (Fossum 2010).

Gag rules regulate the issue of formal EU membership, *not* the ongoing and dynamic incorporation of EU regulations and directives. If anything, the gag rules have *simplified* the process of active EU adaptation, because they help decouple adaptation from the highly contentious issue of EU membership. For EU opponents, the formal status of non-membership is politically important and provides symbolic reassurance of constitutional democratic sovereignty. The No parties can reassure their voters that they have successfully managed to keep Norway out of the EU. The Yes parties have the assurance that Norway retains access to the EU's internal market and a whole host of other arrangements that they deem necessary for Norway to function in contemporary Europe. Adaptation is dynamic and near-automatic across a very wide range of issues; hence, Norwegian citizens and businesses have access to the EU's internal market and services basically on a par with EU members.

Since 2015 or so we have seen increased controversy over aspects of Norway's EU affiliation, but mainly on issues associated with specific EU directives. By taking attention away from the constitutional aspects of the affiliation, the gag rules have kept the focus on single isolated issues and helped take attention from the *cumulative* effects of Norway's ongoing EU adaptation.

---

[13]For this notion, see Holmes (1995). For an application to Norwegian political parties, see Fossum (2010).

21.6.1   Implications for Executive–Legislative Relations

It is widely asserted that the EU suffers from a democratic deficit and that European integration systematically favours executives over parliaments (Crum and Fossum 2013). From a parliamentary perspective, EU integration has been an ongoing process of trying to catch up with experts and executives that are driving the integration process. The question for Norway is whether Norway's EU relationship exhibits distinctive traits of executive–legislative relations, since Norway incorporates EU legislation without democratic representation at the EU-level. The general impression is that Norway's distinct EU relationship has *amplified* the democratic deficit and rendered parliament more not less subservient to the executive (Fossum 2015). The Norwegian parliament is unable to exert influence over decisions made in the EU; it acts as a glorified rubber-stamper. If the Norwegian government wants any influence on EU decisions, it has to be proactive, thus limiting the scope for public consultation in Norway. Legislative acts are handled in the EEA system after the decision has been reached in the EU, and there is strong pressure to pass them rapidly to ensure legal homogeneity across the 31-member EEA. It follows that Norwegian civil society is one step behind the decision processes; it cannot act as a corrective to a process increasingly determined by external bodies.

21.6.2   Norway's Distinct Europeanisation Paradox

Concerns about how EU integration would alter the Norwegian socio-economic model, not least by public sector downsizing, social dumping, privatisation and welfare cuts figured strongly in the referendums debates. It was frequently noted that the EU's policy style and underlying socio-economic model was quite different from Norway's. But precisely because Norway, through its EEA membership and its many other EU agreements has pursued an active policy of adaptation to the EU since 1994, it has incorporated quite a bit of the EU's socio-economic model. This also includes issue-areas that for political reasons were explicitly excluded from the initial EEA agreement, such as agriculture. Thus, the *scope* of the Europeanised component has increased considerably over time, and so has the scope over which the EU's regulatory style and socio-economic model prevail. Nevertheless, a remarkable feature of Norway is the high level of trust in government (Olsen 2017: 107), which has apparently not declined through adaptation to the EU. The paradox is that the EU-sceptical Norwegian population has been saddled with much of the EU's socio-economic model and regulatory style without any apparent popular endorsement but that has not reduced trust in government.

What may account for this paradox? Norway is a small state and an adaptive non-member, with a history of rapid adaptation to the external world. But that does not tell us much about the high levels of trust. A possible explanation could be that Norway's EU relationship is one of 'virtual representation', which according to Edmund Burke (1792: 23) is 'that in which there is a communion of interests and sympathy in feelings and desires between those who act in the name of any description of people and the people in whose name they act, though the trustees are not actually chosen by them'. Such a communion is certainly found in terms of joint adherence to basic principles such as the rule of law and democracy and shows up in some key issue areas such as the environment, but the Norwegian population remains divided on the basic merits of the EU's socio-economic model and open borders.

Another possible explanation is that the high level of trust relates less to the socio-economic facts on the ground and more to the fact that Norwegians still cling to the standard normative account of state-based constitutional democracy and do so because the EU membership issue is kept off the agenda. That could be exposed as cognitive dissonance unless there were ameliorating socio-economic circumstances. One such might be that the EU has been less of an affront to the Norwegian socio-economic model than initially expected. Perhaps even more importantly, Norway has a comprehensive welfare and public support system that effectively enables it to *compensate for negative effects* of globalisation and EU adaptation (competitive pressures, capital and worker mobility, downward wage pressures, rapid retraining needs, etc.) through a well-functioning state, not least one with a very comprehensive public welfare system and social security net. This encompasses a comprehensive system of regulations and policies to ensure gender equality; and a very substantial fiscal buffer (the large pension fund is a case in point). Norway combines extensive incorporation in the EU's market-oriented socio-economic model with an extensive domestic public presence (public ownership, general welfare provisions). The Norwegian state's role in the process of accumulation has been reduced through privatisations and state corporations operating according to market rules. Nevertheless, Norway has sustained a comprehensive public system of social welfare arrangements that protect and 'compensate' the persons who are the losers in a more open and competitive market. That enables it to sustain a high level of social support and at the same time to avoid the legitimacy fallouts from its lack of influence on the norms and rules that it is subjected to.

Some have argued that whereas the No side won on the day of the referendum it has lost every day since. It is clear that the outcome—Norway is very closely affiliated with the EU despite not being an EU member—is not commensurate with a formal rejection of EU membership. To that must be added two factors, however. The first, as noted, is that Norway was already quite closely affiliated with the EU through the EEA agreement, which had taken effect on 1 January 1994 (the referendum was held on 28 November 1994). The second is that no one at the time could have anticipated how much the EU would integrate in breadth and depth.

21.6.3   How, if at All, Did the Referendum Affect European-Level Politics?

The critical issue is whether a referendum can block or alter the EU's structure and constitutional make-up or policies. In that connection, there is a qualitative difference between the situation of a referendum held in an EU Member State on the one hand and a referendum in a non-member (such as a potentially acceding state) on the other. The former can directly affect the EU, the latter can generally not do so.

Are there circumstances whereby a referendum in a non-member state can affect the EU? In the Norwegian context, it is difficult to claim that the 1994 referendum result could have had any effect on the EU since it did not alter the status quo of Norway's EU affiliation: the EEA agreement came into effect almost a year before the 1994 referendum. On the other hand, if a referendum result serves to lock-in a distinct mode of affiliation, it could be argued that the 1994 referendum result has indirectly affected the EU. For instance, it could be argued that many considered the EEA agreement as a temporary arrangement that was put in place to ease transition to membership. Since Norway's referendum blocked that option, the negative referendum served to solidify this status.

21.7   Concluding Remarks

It is widely held that a popular referendum is an instance of direct democracy whereas representative democracy in parliamentary systems is a form of indirect democracy. In popular parlance and among some scholars 'direct' is associated with proximity to the citizens, whereas 'indirect' is associated with an elected aristocracy. The former is thus considered a superior form of democracy. Such a view has tended to ignore the problems associated with determining who the demos is.[14] It also tends to downplay the problems associated with referendums as decision-making devices. How the referendum result is to be translated into a viable policy stance is often very complicated and requires explicit attention to how the referendum instrument is to be adapted to the other decision procedures in place. We have seen that clearly in the Norwegian case. It is also readily apparent in the UK case. The post-referendum period (2016–) has been marked by a fierce struggle between the government and the parliament (and between parties) over the control of the Brexit process. The struggle is indicative of the need to develop a better understanding of how referendums can and should work in representative democracies. No modern democracy can work without representative bodies, and when there is uncertainty and disagreement over what type of outcome a referendum authorises, parliamentary involvement is necessary to work out a democratically viable outcome. The challenge is to determine the

---

[14]For an incisive account of the difficulties involved see Nasstrom (2007).

best possible arrangement between parliament and referendum as devices for ensuring democratically viable processes and outcomes.

The assumption that it is possible to draw hard and fast distinctions between direct and indirect democracy is overly simplistic. In addition, there are implicit representative assumptions built into the referendum instrument, as well. Since the referendum is assumed to express the popular will, those citizens that do not have the right to vote (especially children but in earlier times a majority of the population) must be assumed to be virtually represented for the notion of popular will to have any meaning. Virtual representation is a form of democratic paternalism; hence the more people are excluded, the greater the paternalistic element.

Finally, the Norway example brings up very clearly the thorny question: How long does a referendum result *last*? The issue is given special credence when the political development (Norway's close and dynamic EU incorporation) is increasingly out of sync with the referendum result (formal rejection of EU membership). Constitutions are understood as 'higher law', and there are therefore higher thresholds for constitutional change than for ordinary legislation. That logic then gives rise to the presumption that the result of a given referendum remains valid until an explicit act is taken to revoke it. And, since referendums are considered constitutionally salient, the presumption is that a result from one referendum can only be revoked by another result in a new referendum. What is generally not included in the equation is a mechanism that monitors the constitutional implications of the results of the previous decision in order for the political system or the populace to consider whether there is a need to reconsider the result and, if so, when and how that should take place.

References

Aardal, B., & Valen, H. (1997). The Storting Elections of 1989 and 1993: Norwegian Politics in Perspective. In K. Strøm & L. Svåsand (Eds.), *Challenges to Political Parties: The Case of Norway* (pp. 61–76). Ann Arbor: University of Michigan Press.

Ace Electoral Knowledge Network. (2020). Available at: http://aceproject.org/ace-en/topics/es/ese/ese08/ese08a/ese08a01. Accessed on 23 November 2019.

Beach, D. (2018). Referendums in the European Union. In *Oxford Research Encyclopedias, Politics*. Available at: http://politics.oxfordre.com/view/10.1093/acrefore/9780190228637.001.0001/acrefore-9780190228637-e-503. Accessed on 22 November 2019.

Bjørklund, T. (1997). Old and New Patterns: The 'No' Majority in the 1972 and 1994 EC/EU Referendums in Norway. *Acta Sociologica, 40*(2), 143–159.

Bjørklund, T. (2005). *Hundre år med folkeavstemninger—Norge og Norden 1905–2005*. Oslo: Universitetsforlaget.

Burke, E. (1792). On the subject of Roman catholics of Ireland, and the propriety of admitting them to the elective franchise, Consistently with the Principles of the Constitution as Established at the Revolution. *A Letter from the Right Hon. Edmund Burke, M.P. in the Kingdom of Great Britain, to Sir Hercules Langrishe,*

Bart. *M.P.* Available at: http://www.econlib.org/library/LFBooks/Burke/brkSWv 4c6.html. Last accessed 21 October 2014.

Crum, B., & Fossum, J. E. (Eds.). (2013). *Practices of Inter-Parliamentary Coordination in International Politics—The European Union and Beyond.* Essex: ECPR Press.

Easton, M. (2009). Emotion, Rationality, and the European Union: A Case Study of the Discursive Framework of the 1994 Norwegian Referendum on EU Membership. *International Social Science Review, 84*(1/2), 44–65.

Eriksen, E. O., & Fossum, J. E. (Eds.). (2014). *Det norske paradoks—Om Norges forhold til Den europeiske union.* Oslo: Universitetsforlaget.

Eriksen, E. O., & Fossum, J. E. (Eds.). (2015). *The European Union's Non-Members: Independence Under Hegemony?.* London: Routledge.

Fossum, J. E. (2010). Norway's European 'Gag Rules'. *European Review, 18*(1), 73–92.

Fossum, J. E. (2015). Representation Under Hegemony? On Norway's Relationship to the EU. In E. O. Eriksen & J. E. Fossum (Eds.), *The European Union's Non-members: Independence Under Hegemony?* (pp. 153–172). London: Routledge.

Gleditsch, N., Østerud, Ø., & Elster, J. (1974). *De utro tjenere: embetsverket i EF-kampen.* Oslo: Pax Forlag.

Habermas, J. (2001). Constitutional Democracy: A Paradoxical Union of Contradictory Principles? *Political Theory, 29*(6), 766–781.

Holmes, S. (1995). *Passions and Constraint.* Chicago: Chicago University Press.

Jahn, D., & Storsved, A. (2007). Legitimacy Through Referendum? The Nearly Successful Domino–Strategy of the EU–Referendums in Austria, Finland, Sweden and Norway. *West European Politics, 18*(4), 18–37.

Jenssen, A. T. og H. V. (1995) *Brussel midt imot. Folkeavstemningen om EU.* Oslo: Gyldendal.

Kallset, K.-E. N. (2009). *Makta midt imot—kampen om EU og Arbeidarpartiets sjel.* Oslo: Manifest Forlag.

Lie, E. (2015). Master and Servants: Economists and Bureaucrats in the Dispute over Norwegian EEC Membership in 1972. *Contemporary European History, 24*(2), 279–300.

Lipset, S. M., & Rokkan, S. (Eds.). (1967). *Party Systems and Voter Alignments: Cross-National Perspectives.* New York: Free Press.

Midtbø, T., & Hines, K. (1998). The Referendum-Election Nexus: An Aggregate Analysis of Norwegian Voting Behaviour. *Electoral Studies, 17*(1), 77–94.

Nasstrom, S. (2007). The Legitimacy of the People. *Political Theory, 35*(5), 624–658.

Olsen, J. P. (2017). *Democratic Accountability, Political Order, and Change.* Oxford: Oxford University Press.

Neumann, I. B. (2001). *Norge—en kritikk. Begrepsmakt i Europa-debatten.* Oslo: Pax. Bok to i Makt—og globaliseringsutredningens serie.

NTB. (1992, March 23). *Lahnstein: EF verre enn Norges union med Sverige.*

Pettersen, P. A., Jenssen, A. T., & Listhaug, O. (1996). The 1994 EU Referendum in Norway: Continuity and Change. *Scandinavian Political Studies, 19*(3), 257–281.

Rokkan, S., & Valen, H. (1964). Regional Contrasts in Norwegian Politics: A Review of Data from Official Statistics and from Sample Surveys. In E. Allardt & Y. Littunen (Eds.), *Cleavages, and Party Systems: Contributions to Comparative Political Sociology.* Helsinki: Transactions of the Westermarck Society.

Saglie, J. (2000). Values, Perceptions and European Integration: The Case of the Norwegian 1994 Referendum. *European Union Politics, 1*(2), 227–249.

SV. (no date). SV sin Historie. Available at: https://www.sv.no/svs-historie/. Accessed on 23 November 2019.

Tierney, S. (2012). *Constitutional Referendums: The Theory and Practice of Republican Deliberation.* Oxford: Oxford University Press.

Valen, H. (1973). Norway: 'No' to EEC. *Scandinavian Political Studies, 8*(A8), 214–226.

Wyller, T. (2004). EU-saken, folkeavstemning og Stortinget. *Nytt Norsk Tidsskrift, 21*(2).

Wyller, T. (2006). *Hvem skal bestemme? Stortinget eller folket?.* Oslo: Vidarforlaget.

PUBLIC DOCUMENTS

Dok.nr.8:41. (1991–1992). Forslag fra stortingsrepresentantene Kåre Gjønnes og Kjell Magne Bondevik om at det avholdes folkeavstemning før eventuell søknad sendes om norsk medlemskap i EF.

Dok.nr.8:70. (1993–1994). Forslag fra Carl I Hagen og Fridtjof Frank Gundersen om at Stortinget skal be Regjeringen legge til grunn at embedsmenn i departementene anmodes om å vise en betydelig tilbakeholdenhet ved den offentlige EU-debatt, men at de øverste ansvarlige embedsmenn for de ytre faglig avgrensede etater inviteres til å klargjøre sitt og etatens syn på virkningene og konsekvensene av et eventuelt norsk EU-medlemskap.

Innst.S.nr.211. (1993–1994). Innstilling fra kontroll—og konstitusjonskomiteen om forslag fra stortingsrepresentantene Carl I Hagen og Fridtjof Frank Gundersen om at Stortinget skal be Regjeringen legge til grunn at embedsmenn i departementene anmodes om å vise en betydelig tilbakeholdenhet ved den offentlige EU-debatt, men at de øverste ansvarlige embedsmenn for de ytre faglig avgrensede etater inviteres til å klargjøre sitt og etatens syn på virkningene og konsekvensene av et eventuelt norsk EU-medlemskap.

Innst.O.nr.69. (1993–1994). Innstilling fra kontroll—og konstitusjonskomiteen om lov om folkeavstemning over spørsmålet om Norge bør bli medlem av Den europeiske union.

Justis—og politidepartementet. (1972). Lov om folkeavstemning over spørsmålet om Norge bør bli medlem av De Europeiske Fellesskap. LOV-1972-04-21-20.

Kommunal og arbeidsdepartementet. (1994). Lov om folkeavstemning over spørsmålet om Norge bør bli medlem av Den europeiske union. LOV-1994-06-24-42 Lov om stortingsvalg, fylkestingsvalg og kommunestyrevalg (Valgloven). (LOV-1985-03-01-3).

NOU 2012:2 [Norwegian Official Report]. (2012). Outside and Inside: Norway's Agreements with the European Union. Report by the EEA Review Committee delivered to the Norwegian Ministry of Foreign Affairs, 17 January. Available at: www.regjeringen.no/no/dokumenter/nou-2012-2/id669368/.

Statistics Norway. (1995). The 1994 Referendum on Norwegian Membership of the EU. Report, *Official Statistics of Norway,* C235.

Utenriksdepartementet. (1971). Om lov om folkeavstemning over spørsmålet om Norge bør bli medlem av De Europeiske Fellesskap. Ot.prp.35 (1971–1972) Available at: www.stortinget.no/no/Saker-og-publikasjoner/Stortingsforhandlinger/Les evisning/?p=1971-72&paid=4&wid=a&psid=DIVL1095.

Utenriksdepartementet. (1993). Om lov om folkeavstemning over spørsmålet om Norge bør bli medlem av Den europeiske union. Ot.prp.nr.79 (1993–1994).

CHAPTER 22

In or Out of 'Europe'? The 1975 and 2016 UK Referendums on Membership

Julie Smith

22.1　Introduction

Harold Wilson's decision to hold a referendum on staying in the European Economic Community (EEC) in 1975 was unprecedented in the UK and unparalleled elsewhere in Europe. It was the first-ever UK-wide referendum[1] and the first time a Member State had voted on the question whether to stay in the Community. By the time David Cameron took a similar course of action in 2016, referendums had become part of the British constitutional order (Bogdanor 2009: 196; see also Curtice in this volume), although the outcome of that vote would in turn be groundbreaking. The UK became the first member state to vote to leave what had now become the European Union (EU).[2] The ramifications for European and, especially, British politics were profound, and the second UK-European referendum raised crucial questions for politicians, citizens and academics, including how long the results of a referendum remain valid and what constitutes the 'will of the people'. Moreover, it left the country deeply divided over the matter it was meant to resolve;

[1] A referendum was held in Northern Ireland in 1973 (see Chapter 12 by Hayward) but no UK-wide referendum had occurred before then.

[2] In 1983, Greenland voted to leave the EEC in a referendum following home-rule from Denmark in 1979, in a decision that had rather less impact on the EC but nonetheless took three years to effect.

J. Smith (✉)
Department of Politics and International Studies, University of Cambridge, Cambridge, UK
e-mail: jes42@cam.ac.uk

© The Author(s) 2021
J. Smith (ed.), *The Palgrave Handbook of European Referendums*,
https://doi.org/10.1007/978-3-030-55803-1_22

Europe had become a salient and divisive issue in British politics. What had changed in the intervening years in European and domestic politics? Why did a country that voted two to one to stay in 1975 narrowly favour leaving four decades later? This chapter looks at the way use of referendums had changed in the UK in the intervening 40 years and considers how far socio-economic and political transformations in the UK as well as institutional change in Europe affected voters' choices. In addition, the chapter highlights a significant degree of continuity in British concerns over European integration juxtaposed with a changing media landscape and a fragmenting party system. Finally, it considers the challenges that direct democracy can bring to parliamentary sovereignty in light of the 2016 referendum and its tempestuous aftermath.

22.2   LEADING OR LEAVING?
THE UK'S EUROPEAN RELATIONS

On 1 January 1973, British Prime Minister Edward Heath took the UK into the European Community (EC) on the basis of a parliamentary vote. This was wholly in line with the UK's long history as a parliamentary democracy, where successive Prime Ministers agreed with Clement Attlee that referendums were best understood as devices of demagogues and dictators. As Enoch Powell put it, 'it is inconsistent with the responsibility of government to Parliament and to the electorate' (Powell quoted by Heath 1998: 540), although Powell himself became an advocate of a referendum precisely because of his concerns that EC membership would damage that very parliamentary sovereignty he prized. Few called for accession to be subject to a popular vote, as occurred in Ireland, Denmark and Norway, which had negotiated membership alongside the UK (see Chapters 20 and 21 by Svensson and Fossum & Rosén respectively). The decision to accede to the EC was thus taken by Parliament on 28 October 1971, by a majority of 356–244 in the House of Commons and 451–458 in the House of Lords (Heath 1998: 380). All but 39 Conservative MPs voted to join and, while Labour imposed a three-line whip against membership, 69 Labour rebels ensured that the vote passed. Legislating what would become the 1972 European Communities Act proved challenging, as the ruling Conservatives' parliamentary majority was compromised by rebel Tory MPs opposed to Community membership with Labour MPs reluctant to offer support to the Government to get its legislation through. However, party loyalty prevailed and Heath secured the legislation required to prepare the UK for entry to the Community—a piece of legislation which later generations of Conservative MPs would campaign to repeal. The Bill received Royal Assent in October 1972.

Heath was not alone in favouring a parliamentary route to ratifying Community membership. As the prime minister who initiated the UK's successful bid to join the Common Market, Labour leader Harold Wilson had also been opposed to a referendum on the European question before the 1970 general election (Heath 1998: 540). However, once out of office, increasing Labour Euroscepticism and party divisions over Europe came to the fore. In the wake of President Pompidou's decision to hold a referendum on EC enlargement, i.e. to let French citizens decide whether the UK along with Ireland, Denmark and Norway should be allowed to join the Common Market (see Chapters 20 by Svensson and Chapter 9 by Morel) the Labour National Executive Committee supported a referendum advocated by Tony Benn, who would become a leading advocate for leaving the Common Market (Heath 1998: 541). Indicative, perhaps, of a minor contagion effect, Wilson changed his mind on the question of a referendum and the Shadow Cabinet adopted a policy of holding a referendum, causing the pro-European referendum-sceptic deputy leader, Roy Jenkins, to resign from the Labour front bench.

In the February 1974 general election, the Labour Party pledged to rene-gotiate the UK's terms of EC membership, dubbed 'Tory terms', and then allow voters to decide either at a general election or by referendum whether they wished to stay in the Common Market, perhaps fitting Salisbury's refer-endal model of a single-issue election (see Chapter 5 by Norton). However, when the outcome of that election was a hung parliament, necessitating a second election in October 1974, Wilson backtracked on the idea of what would have been a third general election within a short space of time, and instead proposed a referendum on membership following the renegotiation the government was undertaking (Wilson 1975; see Smith 1999, 2016).

The resounding decision to stay in the Community—'This is the most crushing victory in British political history. The effects of this thunderous YES will echo down the years' (*Daily Mail* quoted by Beckett 2016)— was expected to end any uncertainty over membership. Those who favoured membership believed their job was done; there was no need for ongoing work to remind people of the benefits of membership. With the apparent resolu-tion of the issue, most mainstream politicians assumed it was safe to move on to more vote-worthy issues—after all, membership of the Community was not highly politically salient, and it was only put to the voters to try to avert splits in the ruling Labour Party. It was a break with convention but one that reaffirmed a decision taken by Parliament, and it did not fundamentally alter the balance between *represented* and *representative*: parties and people were broadly united on the desirability of staying, or so it seemed.[3] Nor did its use immediately appear to alter the UK's constitutional norms; those who sought to leave the EC accepted the result, which was not challenged in parliament, the media or through the courts. The referendum did, however, create a prece-dent that would be used decades later by proponents and opponents of the EU alike.

Over the course of the next thirty-five years, the balance of opinion on European integration would change fundamentally within the two main

---

[3]Such assumptions were quite swiftly dispelled. As Roy Jenkins noted in his memoirs, 'Within two years Tony Benn was campaigning for a reversal of the verdict of the oracle of direct democracy, about which he had spoken so sacerdotally before it had given him the wrong answer; and within six years he had got the whole of the Labour Party committed in this direction' (Jenkins 1991: 418).

political parties, and two new parties—the Referendum Party and the UK Independence Party (UKIP)—would emerge to oppose integration, yet the issue remained one of low public salience. John Major deftly negotiated opt-outs from the major treaty reforms that culminated in December 1991 with the Treaty on European Union (the so-called Maastricht Treaty) and was greeted as a hero by his Conservative parliamentary colleagues when he first returned from Maastricht. However, a decision to delay ratifying the Treaty until after the April 1992 general election proved misguided. Major faced a reduced parliamentary majority of just 21, which gradually ebbed away owing to deaths and 'defections', and he was severely hampered by a significant Eurosceptic tendency among the new intake of MPs. The situation was compounded by his predecessor, Margaret Thatcher, now publicly advocating a referendum from her new place in the House of Lords, arguing that, 'It was wrong to "hand over the people's parliamentary rights on the scale of the Maastricht Treaty without the consent of the people in a referendum". To do so would be "to betray the trust … that they have placed in us"' (Moore 2019: 783 quoting Thatcher's maiden speech in the Lords). The Cabinet too was divided, with some ministers favouring a referendum (Moore 2019: 784). While the treaty was eventually ratified by traditional parliamentary means, the episode marked the first major fissure within the Conservative Party over Europe and would help pave the way for growing Euroscepticism within the party. Like Heath before him, and indeed Thatcher during her own time as PM, Major was determined that ratifying this new European treaty was a matter for Parliament, not the people. British parliamentary sovereignty seemed alive and well. Yet, the legacy of Major's European decisions was profound. The failure to lance what became a running sore within the party, and the reluctance to provide a referendum, contributed to the fateful decision of his successor David Cameron to offer an in/out referendum more than two decades later, as frustration rose among grassroots members who sought to express their increasingly Eurosceptic views.

Although mainstream politicians remained reluctant to turn to referendums, the Maastricht Treaty generated a new demand for direct democracy as voters and the media watched citizens elsewhere voting on it. If the Danes and the Irish could have a say on the treaty, why could the UK not? Thus, a single-issue party, the Referendum Party, founded (and funded) by Sir James Goldsmith was established to make precisely this case.[4] While it did not win any parliamentary seats, and indeed vanished in the late 1990s, the Referendum Party did put the idea of a new referendum firmly on the agenda. Demands for a referendum did not go away, fuelled as they were by the media, notably the Murdoch press, and by a second new political party, the United Kingdom Independence Party. Eventually these demands paid dividends but only after three more EU treaties (of Amsterdam in 1997, of Nice in 2000 and a Constitutional Treaty in 2004) had been negotiated.

---

[4]Goldsmith was a financier and politician, who was elected to the European Parliament on a Eurosceptic ticket in France in 1994.

The three main parties, Labour, Conservative and Liberal Democrat, all committed to holding a referendum prior to any decision to take the UK into the Euro, but since the UK never came near to joining, no such poll was ever held. A referendum finally seemed on the cards when Labour Prime Minister Tony Blair pledged to hold a referendum to ratify the Constitutional Treaty, agreed by the EU in 2004, fearing that the House of Lords would otherwise not accept the Treaty (Blair 2010: 501; Bogdanor 2009: 178). His commitment was a catalyst for France to hold a referendum, which saw the Treaty voted down and ultimately replaced by the Lisbon Treaty before the UK could hold a popular vote (see Sternberg elsewhere in Chapter 28). Since the replacement Lisbon Treaty was not deemed to have the same constitutional implications as the Constitutional Treaty, Blair's successor, Gordon Brown, took the view that a referendum was not necessary. Consequently, following hotly contested debates, Lisbon was ratified by Parliament, not directly by the people, in line with normal UK practice. The Conservatives under David Cameron pledged that if the Treaty had not come into effect by the time they took office (something Cameron hoped but could not predict would happen in the near future) they would hold a referendum on the Treaty. The Liberal Democrat leader, Nick Clegg, went a step further calling for an in/out referendum, on the grounds that no-one under the age of 50 had had a chance to vote in EU membership.[5] Given the UK's long-standing commitment to parliamentary democracy, this line of argument may appear peculiar unless one recalls the precedent set by Wilson—once voters had been asked about an issue once, why not on subsequent occasions? Especially if one's party is divided over the issue at hand, as all the main UK parties have been over the years, the Liberal Democrats included. If questions can be decided by the people, can the people not be given a chance to change their minds and new generations have their say? The fact that the UK does not have a codified constitution ensures that precedent may be relied upon to help determine such issues rather than any mandatory constitutional requirement of the sort that applies in Ireland or Denmark.

In the event, the Lisbon Treaty was ratified by all Member States by November 2009 and came into effect the following month. Thus, when the Conservatives took office in May 2010 in a historic coalition with the Liberal Democrats, it was too late to hold a referendum on the Treaty—much to the chagrin of Conservative Eurosceptics (Lynch 2011: 230). For nearly two decades, leading politicians had been raising the prospect of allowing citizens to vote on the nature of European integration—in effect on further deepening the UK's relations with the Union—yet no vote ever came, leading to some public frustration and much party division. By 2010, the Conservative Party was deeply divided over the issue, and appeared to be haemorrhaging

---

[5]The party launched a petition, stating, 'It's time for a real referendum on Europe' and noting 'It's been over THIRTY YEARS since the British people last had a vote on Britain's membership of the European Union.'

support to the single-issue UKIP which, like the Referendum Party, had been established around the time of the Maastricht Treaty. Unlike, the Referendum Party, however, UKIP proved electorally successful. It began to secure seats in the European Parliament (EP) from 1999 when a system of proportional representation was introduced, coming second in the 2009 EP elections and apparently taking votes from the Conservatives in both European and general elections.

During this time the Conservative Party had become increasingly Eurosceptic, in part reflecting the attitudes of party members who were over-whelmingly elderly and anti-EU, in part as a pragmatic way of trying to steal the sceptics' thunder. Having sought to stop his party 'banging on about Europe', Cameron found the issue dominated his premiership and, thus, on 23 January 2013 he pledged that if re-elected Prime Minister he would seek to reform the EU, renegotiate the terms of the UK's membership of the Union and then hold a referendum on continued membership by the end of 2017. The offer was enough to stem internal party hostilities until the 2015 general election, but not enough to staunch the rise of UKIP, which won the most seats (24) and largest proportion of the votes (26.77%) in the 2014 EP elections (European Parliament, nd). As Cameron returned to No. 10 in May 2015, now leader of a majority Conservative government, the question was not *if* but *when* a *second* referendum on the UK's membership of the EU would be held. Eventually the date was set for 23 June 2016, leaving little time for his proposed renegotiation, the necessary legal provisions for the referendum or, crucially, a campaign to stay in the EU.

22.3   LEGAL FRAMEWORK

Famously lacking a codified constitution, there was no provision or precedent for a nation-wide referendum when the Labour Party pledged to put a rene-gotiated membership deal to voters in their October 1974 manifesto. Such a referendum was neither mandatory nor binding and required bespoke legis-lation, as would all subsequent UK referendums (see Norton in Chapter 5). Thus, in February 1975, the Lord President of the Council and Leader of the House of Commons, Edward (Ted) Short, put proposals to Cabinet for a White Paper outlining options for various key issues such as the framing of the question, the extent of the franchise, funding (or otherwise) for the two sides, information campaigns and the need for a level playing field, including the recommendation that there should be no cap on expenditure (Cabinet 1975). The European Referendum Bill 1975 was introduced on 26 March so that the relevant legislation could be enacted shortly after Easter and a refer-endum held before the summer holidays, the assumption being that Parliament would not delay the passage of the necessary legislation. The Referendum Act 1975 was duly enacted on 8 May 1975 (House of Commons 2015). The detailed arrangements were not, however, in that Act but rather in a Statutory Instrument passed within weeks of the renegotiation being completed and given Royal Assent on 14 May 1975, barely three weeks before the appointed date for the referendum: 5 June. While this may appear a rather last-minute arrangement, it was in line with the normal provisions for a general election at the time: 22 days between the announcement of an election and it being held. The arrangements for this first national referendum were very similar to those for general elections, with the normal parliamentary franchise of citizens over 18 (plus Irish and Commonwealth citizens) with the addition of peers, who are not permitted to vote in elections to the House of Commons. There were limited rights for absentee citizens to vote by proxy or post.

Although the legislation for 2016 was inevitably also bespoke, the Government's actions were this time considerably constrained by the Political Parties, Elections and Referendums Act 2000 (PPERA 2000), which had been introduced by the previous Labour Government. That Act had established the Electoral Commission, which now played a key role in determining the question that would be offered to voters. In 1975, the Government had asked: 'Do you think that the United Kingdom should stay in the European Community (Common Market)?' which could have been construed as unfair or 'leading', despite the government's purported concern to ensure a level playing field. Thus, while the question was accepted at the time, there was some frustration among the No side that it had perhaps unfairly skewed citizens' responses (Smith 1999: 53–54). In the 2016 referendum, the precise wording of the question had been recommended by the Electoral Commission, which had opined that the Government's original wording 'Should the United Kingdom remain a member of the European Union?' could have 'encouraged voters to consider one response more favourably than the other. This could raise concerns about the legitimacy of the result of the referendum' (Electoral Commission 2019a).

When passing the European Union Referendum Act 2015, therefore, parliamentarians accepted, albeit after some debate, the Electoral Commission's recommended wording, 'Should the United Kingdom remain a member of the European Union or leave the European Union'? which it considered 'the most neutral wording from the range of options we considered and tested' following a Private Member's Bill brought by James Wharton in the previous parliament (Electoral Commission 2019a). The question set was binary, with Remain/Leave replacing the more usual Yes/No options.

In both 1975 and 2016 there were two designated umbrella organisations, one associated with each side of the referendum, which were eligible for state funding. However, in 2016 they now came under the clear regulations of PPERA and were subject to clear limits on expenditure, which was not the case in 1975. The European Referendum Act 2015 (Section 25 (2)(b)) raised the spending limits envisaged by PPERA 2000 in line with inflation, resulting in provision for the Remain and Leave umbrella organisations to spend up to a limit of £7 million each. Under that PPERA framework, political parties are also eligible to participate in referendums separately from the two umbrella organisations and may spend up to a limit determined in accordance with their votes in the previous elections, which effectively meant the Conservatives could spend up to £7 million, Labour £5.5 million, UKIP £4 million and the Liberal Democrats £3 million, while the smaller parties, the DUP, Greens, Plaid Cymru and the SNP could each spend up to £700,000 (Electoral Commission 2017: 14). The rules were intended to provide a level playing field but the fact that political parties could spend significant sums of money meant that potentially one side could heavily outspend the other.

Whereas in 1975 there was no regulatory body charged with overseeing the referendum, which was run as far as possible along the lines of a general election, in 2016, the Electoral Commission had the task of overseeing various aspects of the referendum. In particular, it was responsible for determining which umbrella organisations would be 'designated' as the main Remain and Leave bodies and for registering other campaigning bodies. Questions about the probity of funding and spending, including whether donations were permissible, fell under the Commission's purview. Similarly, it sought to ensure that only permitted actors participated in the referendum and enforced 'purdah', the provision that the Government should not be involved in elections or referendums for four weeks before the date of the poll (Section 125, PPERA 2000). The Government sought to set aside this provision for the EU Referendum (House of Commons 2017: para. 33). Introducing the draft legislation in the EU Referendum Bill, Europe Minister David Lidington argued it could 'prevent the Government or any public body from making any comment not necessarily on the referendum question but on an issue that might be discussed in the Council of Ministers meeting or in response to a European Court of Justice judgement…and could make it impossible to explain to the public what the outcome of the renegotiation was and what the Government's view of that result was' (David Lidington, quoted in House of Commons 2017: para. 34). After pressure from Parliament, including defeats on the draft legislation, the Government accepted that it could not circumvent this now-established practice and Section 125 was thus applied. For a period of 28 days before 23 June the Government had to refrain from anything that looked like campaigning. This was a relief for the Leave campaign, which knew that once the controlled period commenced their claims would not be challenged by the weight of the government machine.

The Electoral Commission can ensure that the Government does not breach purdah. It even contacted the Bank of England, which agreed to 'voluntarily observe pre-referendum purdah in the spirit of guidelines issued by the Cabinet Office on 26 May 2016', and also international bodies including the IMF and the OECD to ensure they understood the rules (Electoral Commission 2017: 23), as well as checking that organisations which were not registered or not eligible to participate did not do so. However, there was one significant gap in its powers: it does not have to power to 'regulate the content or design of referendum campaigns' (Electoral Commission 2017: 20). Although citizens and organisations have a right to complain to the Electoral Commission, it has no role in dealing with messages that might be deemed 'misleading'. The Commission itself argued after the fact that 'because of our independent role in running and regulating UK referendums, it would be inappropriate for the Commission to be drawn into political debate by regulating the accuracy and truthfulness of referendum campaign arguments' (Electoral Commission 2017: 42). Thus, unless material breaks the law for example by inciting racial or religious hatred there is no way for sanctions to be imposed on campaign materials. Whether this is a victory for free speech or an unwanted result of the fact that the impact of referendum outcomes might be in the realms of speculation not certainty is an open question.

The one area where the Electoral Commission did have a say was over 'imprints'—the requirement that any printed materials such as posters and leaflets must have a clear indication of who published them. Thus, for example, it tackled Vote Leave over a complaint that they were distributing a leaflet without an imprint (Electoral Commission 2017: 21). Whereas the rules were very clear for printed material, the same was not true of social media, since PPERA largely predates the age of social media, which formed a key part of the 2016 campaigns. The Commission subsequently recommended that imprint information should also be provided for online and electronic material.

22.4   The Rules of the Game

Constitutionally, both referendums were optional—they could scarcely be otherwise, since there is no codified constitution enshrining the referendum device.[6] Legally, both were advisory, yet the letter of the law and the political reality differed somewhat. It is often suggested that Wilson *opted* for a certain course of action, namely, to renegotiate the UK's terms of EC membership and then to offer the citizens a chance to vote on the outcome. Cameron in many ways seemed to be following the same pattern (see Smith 2016). In fact, both leaders were, or believed themselves to be, constrained by the political reality of divisions within their own parties. Wilson's move to support a referendum came only once the NEC had expressed its support, while Cameron came to believe that a referendum was 'inevitable' when he made his Bloomberg Speech on 23 January 2013, 38 years to the day from Wilson's speech in the House of Commons committing his government to a referendum. Certainly, the decision met the concerns of many in his own party, allowing some breathing space during which the European question could be put to one side, as passionate Eurosceptics had finally received the promise they desired. Cameron's Liberal Democrat deputy, Nick Clegg, claims that he was 'non-plussed' when Cameron told him he intended to 'declare his intention, in the event of a Conservative majority government, to hold a referendum', which

---

[6]A partial exception came in the form of the EU Act 2011, enacted under the Conservative-Liberal Democrat Coalition government, which provided for a referendum if significant powers were to be transferred to the EU; it was never triggered.

Clegg saw as 'a wilful elevation of an internal party problem to the level of a national plebiscite' (Clegg 2016: 205).

Moreover, Cameron pledged to abide by the outcome of the referendum he triggered. Whether UK referendums are binding is not straightforward. Conservative leader Margaret Thatcher was one of the first to query whether Labour's 1975 referendum would be binding (Aqui 2019: 7). Legally it would not be—arguably no referendum can be binding in the UK, although the AV Referendum Act 2011 did enshrine in law that the outcome would be binding. Neither the Referendum Act 1975 nor the EU Referendum Act 2015 contained a similar provision, meaning the ensuing polls would technically be only advisory. However, both Wilson and Cameron indicated that the results of the EC/U membership referendums would be respected (Aqui 2019: 6; Supreme Court 2019). Thus, they became *politically* binding even if they could not be enforced legally. The longer the campaigns went on and the more frequently politicians stated they would abide by the results, the tighter they bound themselves. In 1975 this was not a particular problem— the outcome was clear and accepted by both sides, at least initially; the narrow outcome in 2016 would prove controversial, not least as those on the losing Remain side argued that the Leave side had lied and broken various rules.[7] Some Remainers would argue that the referendum was little more than an opinion poll; legally that may have been true but politically it was hard for politicians to resile from their commitment to respect the outcome, difficult though it would prove actually to deliver.

In 2016, as in 1975, the franchise was that used for general elections: UK, Irish and Commonwealth citizens over 18 could vote. In 1975 there was no argument about this provision but in 2016, the situation was somewhat different. As the European Community evolved into the European Union following the 1993 Maastricht Treaty, EU citizens had acquired certain electoral rights, notably to vote in local and EP elections in the country in which they reside. The Scottish independence referendum was fought on the local government franchise; EU nationals resident in Scotland were thus able to vote (see Chapter 14 by Curtice). The right of EU citizens to vote did not apply to general elections, however, so most non-UK European citizens were not able to vote in 2016.[8] While amendments to the proposed legislation were discussed in Parliament the idea of enfranchising EU nationals was never put to the vote. Indeed, there were concerns that anything that might look as if government or parliament were trying to manipulate the franchise could be seen as unfair to one side of the argument—likely to be Leave. Moreover, both the Venice Commission (see Chapter 4 by Renwick and Sargeant) and the Electoral Commission advise against changing the franchise on an ad hoc basis

---

[7]Equally, leading Leave campaigner Priti Patel would send a dossier of materials to the Electoral Commission, seeking to show that the Remain campaign broke the rules.

[8]The exceptions were Irish citizens and citizens of the two other EU-Commonwealth countries: Malta and Cyprus.

or too close to the date of the poll. Such advice notwithstanding, the House of Lords did adopt an amendment to give the vote to 16- and 17-year-olds, as had been the case in Scotland, where it had not caused any difficulty. Although this would have been an ad hoc change to the franchise, peers believed that the decision was of such import and would affect young people's lives so significantly, that they should be able to vote in the referendum. The House of Commons reversed this bid and eventually the franchise used was as for general elections with the addition only of peers and residents of Gibraltar who had the right to vote in EP elections on a UK list. There were generous rules for postal voting (any registered elector could apply for a postal vote) and proxy voting was possible. UK citizens resident outside the UK for more than 15 years were not permitted to vote, thereby disenfranchising many UK civil servants and others who work in the EU institutions. The fact that millions of EU nationals resident in the UK and many UK nationals abroad could not vote despite arguably having a very significant stake in the outcome contributed to the significant backlash the government faced after the referendum when their rights were left uncertain.

There were no thresholds for turnout or any reinforced majority in either membership referendum. A simple majority of those who turned out to vote across the whole UK would suffice to determine the UK's future in Europe. This was in line with Venice Commission guidance—a turnout threshold can create perverse incentives as seen in Scotland in 1979 (see Chapter 11 by Mathias). Yet the decisions not to require a reinforced majority and to have a single UK-wide result would prove controversial after the fact. In 1975 this was uncontroversial because the whole country, all bar two Scottish constituencies, voted 'Yes'—the result was decisive. In 2016, by contrast, the narrowness of the result—Leave winning with just 51.9%, albeit on a high turnout of 72%—was compounded by the fact that two of the four nations, Scotland and Northern Ireland, voted to Remain (as did Gibraltar with a massive 96%). Had a double-majority of nations and of votes been required as is the case in federal Switzerland, Leave would not have prevailed in 2016. A referendum intended to resolve a problem within the Conservative Party now left the country divided and Scotland considering whether to depart one Union in order to stay in the other.

22.5   THE REFERENDUM IN PRACTICE

22.5.1   What Was at Stake?

The issue at stake in both referendums was ostensibly the same: the UK's membership of the European Community/Union. But the stakes were very different. At the time of the first referendum, the UK had been a member of the EC for just two and a half years and the integration process itself was barely a quarter of a century old; the bonds that tied the UK to its European partners were thus not deep and while leaving would inevitably have entailed economic consequences, they would have been relatively limited. In 2016, by contrast, the UK had been a member for over 40 years of a Union that had expanded geographically (with the strong endorsement of the UK), deepened its cooperation and extended to cover myriad policies unthought of in the 1970s. Leaving the EU would necessitate complex legal and financial negotiations, but this was barely discussed in the actual referendum. The stakes were thus much higher in 2016, but the same type of binary question was asked: should the UK remain or leave. Yet neither side had a blueprint for what leaving the EU would look like, as the Leave campaign argued it would be for the government to implement the outcome, while Cameron refused to let the civil service plan for a possible Leave vote, lest it look like it was admitting the possibility of defeat.

The Remain campaign was flawed in many ways, overly focused on narrow economic arguments intended to win over 'minds', while the Leave campaign targeted the 'heart', running an emotive campaign centred on issues of sovereignty and immigration. Cameron had perhaps been lulled into a false sense of security having, he believed, 'won' the 2011 referendum on the Alternative Vote and the 2014 Scottish Independence referendum (see Chapters 13 and 14 by Blick and Curtice respectively). However, in the former case, the issue at stake was neither popular nor salient, with neither main party in favour of electoral reform, whereas in the latter case, a hotly contested referendum was narrowly won thanks to cross-party support from Labour and the Liberal Democrats, with former Prime Minister Gordon Brown playing a strong part in the campaign to 'save the Union'. Moreover, in both instances, as with successive general elections, Cameron and his party had enjoyed overwhelming support from the print media. The situation would be quite different in the 2016 referendum on an issue where the media had become deeply sceptic, and in some instances had been pressing a sceptic case for decades.

Cameron's, and by extension the Remain campaign's, problems were compounded by the precedent of the 1975 experience. Where Wilson could claim to have gained concessions from his European partners, the fact that his achievements were subsequently recast as negligible 'window-dressing' ensured that Brexiteers were on the lookout for any sense that the PM was trying to overstate his achievements. Thus, while Cameron undertook several months of negotiations with the other EU members, focusing on four 'baskets' of issues, including economic governance, competitiveness, sovereignty and immigration, the last of which related to the rights of EU citizens exercising their rights of free movement rather than immigration more widely, the Leave side was unimpressed. The EU believed that they had gone a long way to give the PM what he asked but Leave campaigners swiftly rubbished the deal. UKIP leader Nigel Farage claimed that Cameron had 'asked for little and got less'. This sense that the renegotiation had changed little was compounded by the fact that Cameron and fellow Remainers essentially ignored it throughout the referendum campaign. Wilson's renegotiation allowed him to say that he could now recommend the UK stay in the Community, Cameron sought to take a similar approach, but his attempts fell rather flat. He had asked his MPs to remain neutral on the membership question until after the renegotiation, in order not to jeopardise his leverage. Some had long nailed their colours to the EU or to leaving but many did stay silent until February 2016.

When Cameron concluded his discussions in Brussels on 19 February 2016, he rushed back to a specially convened Cabinet meeting at which he managed to persuade his colleagues to support staying in the EU. That would be the official Government position. However, like Wilson before him, Cameron recognised that seeking to impose a party whip on the issue could be counter-productive. After all, the purpose of the referendum was to allow everyone to have their say on the question that had divided British politics for so long—and that included MPs. Collective responsibility on this one question would thus be lifted for the duration of the referendum. Scarcely had Cameron finished his statement outside No. 10 announcing the 'Government' position when five of his Cabinet colleagues launched their own Leave campaign. Key among them was Michael Gove, hitherto a close personal friend of Cameron, who had indicated to Cameron that even if he decided to vote to leave the EU he would not campaign on the issue, saying '...if I do decide to opt for Brexit, I'll make one speech. That will be it. I'll play no further part in the campaign' (Gove quoted by Cameron 2019: 651). In the event, Gove would become co-chair of the formally designated Leave umbrella organisation, Vote Leave. Any sense that the referendum would take the heat out of internal Conservative Party divisions was immediately dispelled.

22.5.2   The Campaigners

Politicians were the leading figures on both sides of the debate in 1975 and 2016, but cross-party campaigning organisations were established to reflect the binary nature of the referendum question. In 1975 the two umbrella organisations were rather ad hoc. Butler and Kitzinger (1996: 68) argue that they 'were in fact entirely self-appointed federations of activists'. The advocates of 'Yes' came under the umbrella Britain in Europe (BIE) campaign, which brought together leading politicians from across the political spectrum. While Harold Wilson himself took a backseat, long-time pro-Marketeer Roy Jenkins played an active role for Labour alongside Edward Heath and Willie Whitelaw on the Conservative side and Jeremy Thorpe and David Steel for the Liberals (see Heath 1998; Jenkins 1991). Like Wilson, Conservative leader Margaret Thatcher did not play a leading role in the 'Yes' campaign, leaving that to Whitelaw, but she did actively support it. Business and the print media were heavily in favour of staying in the Community. In short, the 'Establishment' was clearly behind 'Yes'. The National Referendum Campaign (NRC) was the umbrella group for 'No', bringing together a number of mostly maverick politicians, including a former pro-Marketeer, Tony Benn, on the left and Enoch Powell on the right as well as the Rev Ian Paisley, leader of the Democratic Unionist Party (DUP). The NRC thus included articulate politicians, but it had little support from business or the trade unions, ensuring that it garnered fewer resources than BIE (see Butler and Kitzinger 1996).

By 2016, the role of umbrella organisations had been formalised under PPERA 2000. The Electoral Commission required that the organisations seeking to be designated as the lead organisations needed to demonstrate cross-party support. On the Remain side, there was little question that Britain Stronger in Europe (BSE), formally registered with the Commission as The In Campaign Ltd, would be the lead organisation—it was the only contender and brought together leading figures from across all the main parties. On the Leave side, three organisations sought the nomination, with the well-funded Leave.EU, closely linked to UKIP, losing out to Vote Leave, which boasted figures from all the main parties—Labour MP Gisela Stuart, former Europe Minister under Tony Blair, became co-chair alongside Gove. However, the person Stuart would spend most of her time campaigning with was the former Mayor of London, Boris Johnson. The two of them were pictured frequently on a red double-decker bus emblazoned with the statement: 'We send £350 million a week to Brussels. Let's fund our NHS instead.' That figure would be hotly contested by Remainers, who argued that actual UK contributions to the EU were about half that amount. Yet, the fact the Remain side was trying to dispute the claims left it constantly on the back foot as Leavers would simply retort: 'It's still a lot of money!'

The Remain side was also challenged by a degree of complacency. 'At the very start we felt like winners-in-waiting. The Remain campaign, named Stronger In, would be headed by Labour (predominantly New Labour) figures such as Peter Mandelson and Jack Straw's son Will, because we knew victory would rest of Labour votes. But it would be steered by Conservatives' (Cameron 2019: 658). What Cameron perhaps failed to understand was the abysmal effect of asking Lord (Stuart) Rose to front the Remain campaign. While all the key figures on the Leave side made passionate cases for withdrawal, Rose's commitment to EU membership appeared at best half-hearted. He could barely remember the name of the organisation he was meant to be leading and had been involved in Business for Britain, a Eurosceptic group that advocated Leave in the referendum.[9] Had David Cameron replaced him once the renegotiation was complete the dynamic might have changed, but in reality the Remain campaign never caught the popular imagination.

22.5.3   The Issues

Funding the National Health Service (NHS) was a key plank of Vote Leave's referendum strategy, reflecting the iconic status the NHS enjoys in the UK. Coupled with the £350 million figure on the side of a red bus (red to bring

---

[9]Tim Shipman (2016: 65–66) claims that Rose was Cameron's preferred choice to run the campaign, and a view was taken that his role could be seen as 'a defection'—unfortunately for the Remain campaign, Rose did not display the zeal often associated with converts.

over Labour supporters, so it was claimed) and the slogan 'Vote Leave – Take Back Control', this helped Vote Leave set the agenda. Taking back control played well, as it could offer voters a menu of issues over which to take back control: 'our laws', 'our money', 'our borders'. Sovereignty, financial matters and immigration could all be woven into Vote Leave's narrative in this way.

By contrast, in 1975 emphasis was placed on 'bread and butter' issues, notably the price of food, as well as concerns over the state of the economy more generally. In the face of the oil price shock and rampant inflation, businesses were keen to alert their workers and consumers to the potential dangers of leaving the Common Market (Saunders 2018) in a way they were more reluctant to do in 2016. Sovereignty was discussed in 1975, particularly by the 'No' side, yet people seemed to have forgotten this in the intervening years. Flawed memories of 1975 had an impact on discourse in the 2016 referendum.[10] One oft-rehearsed assertation from older voters was a variant on 'I voted to join a Common Market', with the wider point that loss of sovereignty had not been highlighted at that time. Such comments were frequently made by people who had voted 'Yes' in 1975 but were committed to leaving by 2016. That no one other than parliamentarians had had a chance to vote on whether to *join* the Common Market seemed to have been forgotten—1975 was essentially a rather delayed 'confirmatory' referendum. That sovereignty had been debated had been forgotten and attempts by Remainers to claim otherwise had little traction. Certainly, the Union of which the UK was a part in 2016 had changed dramatically from the Community of 1975. So too had the UK. The 1975 referendum took place against a background of long-term British economic decline. By 2016, the UK was the fifth largest economy in the world. Leavers could thus argue that the UK was a strong economic player, not needing to rely on the EU; what they neglected to say was that this profound change in the UK's fortunes had occurred while, and largely because, the UK was in the EU. Nor did the Remain side make such an argument effectively.

The economy was the main focus of the BSE/Stronger In campaign in 2016, although many advocates of Remain also sought to stress the importance of the EU in maintaining peace in Europe for over half a century and emphasised the EU's role in security and tackling climate change.[11] The umbrella campaign endeavoured to garner support from a narrow section of the electorate which they believed was crucial to success and whom they assumed would be susceptible to perceived economic benefits or losses from leaving the EU. This logic had worked in Scotland in 2014 and the

---

[10]The historian Robert Saunders (2018: 3) has noted that, 'Neglected by historians and political scientists, 1975 has become the property more of myth than of history'.

[11]Indeed, then Home Secretary Theresa May focused on security issues in the one speech she made during the referendum campaign. Nominally a Remainer, her approach was so low-key that some of Cameron's team called her 'the submarine' and speculated that she was actually a Leaver, a possibility given some credibility by the fact that several of her former staff went on to key roles in the Leave campaign.

Stronger In campaign, with direction from the Conservatives (Cameron 2019: 658), hoped to repeat this tactic in 2016, unaware that for many voters the ideas of sovereignty and 'taking back control' would trump economic concerns. This situation was compounded by the fact that 'Project Fear', as the Leave campaign dubbed the Treasury's attempts to demonstrate the negative economic consequences of departure, would fall flat: such a strategy only works if people feel they will *personally* be worse off. In 2016, the general view was that although the UK economy might suffer people did not believe that they themselves would be affected. Project Fear without the fear was inevitably ineffective, regardless of the accuracy or otherwise of the projections. The Leave campaign could not offer greater credibility on the economics of Brexit, so it did not even try. Rather it focused on another policy area that was more salient and more emotive than EU membership, namely immigration.

Vote Leave tapped into a narrative that had been driven by UKIP ever since the 2010 general election. This was not an EU matter per se, as more than half of immigrants to the UK were from non-EU countries. Nonetheless, Vote Leave effectively elided the two aspects of immigration, arguing that outside the EU the UK would be better able to determine who entered the country, leading opponents of immigration to believe that Brexit would lead to reduced immigration while simultaneously letting many black, Asian and minority ethnic voters believe that it would be easier for them to bring in family members from third countries once the UK no longer participated in European free movement. Such messages were compounded by Vote Leave's claim that Turkey was about to join the EU and hence 76 million Turks would be hoping to move to the UK. The facts that Turkey's slow progress to membership had effectively stalled and that the UK could in any case veto its eventual accession were ignored and even rejected by the Leave campaign, with prominent Leave campaigner Penny Mordaunt flatly denying this on live television (see Cameron 2019: 669). As with the issue of money, the accuracy of the claims seemed to matter less than the force with which they were expressed.

Leave.EU went a step further, featuring a poster of Nigel Farage in front of a line of people and the headline: 'Breaking point'. This poster was swiftly decried as fostering anti-immigrant sentiment, but it highlighted one of the advantages enjoyed by the Leave side: Vote Leave could effectively target more mainstream voters and distance itself from Leave.EU if the latter's approach was deemed offensive, yet the messages nonetheless formed part of a wider Leave narrative. By contrast, BSE did not have an impassioned sister organisation to bolster support on the Remain side and mobilisation was an issue, since the BSE campaign overall was lacklustre. 'Stronger In' as a slogan was not nearly as powerful as 'Vote Leave: take back control'.

Nor was the Remain campaign as robust in its campaigning as the Leave campaign. This in part reflected the Prime Minister's concerns about intra-party divisions. Whereas Cameron was willing to attack Nick Clegg during

the AV referendum—or at least allow those producing the campaign literature to do so, claiming 'Politics is a brutal business. You have to campaign
with all you've got. You have to put long-term interests above immediate
concerns, and your own party and survival above other parties and leaders –
however much you like and get on with them' (Cameron 2019: 293), during
the EU referendum he felt rather differently about attacking his opponents,
precisely because so many came from his own party. In his memoir, Cameron
acknowledged that he had '...pulled my punches. Again and again the option
came to hammer Boris and Gove. "These are now your opponents. They're
killing you", George [Osborne] said. "You've got to destroy their credibility."
Every time I was shown a mocked up poster like the one of Boris in the
pocket of Farage (like Ed Miliband and Alex Salmond in 2015), I vetoed
it' (Cameron 2019: 671). Cameron hoped that Labour's support for EU
membership would carry the day, but he found its commitment lacking: 'Our
cross-party clout relied mostly on Labour, but they were AWOL' (Cameron
2019: 671). The main frustration was with Labour leader Jeremy Corbyn, a
life-long Eurosceptic, who nominally supported Remain but claimed to be '7
out of 10' in favour (BBC 2016): not the most emphatic endorsement but
rather in line with the general approach of the Remain campaign. The Liberal
Democrats, SNP and Plaid Cymru all actively supported Remain (the Scottish and Welsh nationalists having changed their positions fundamentally since
1975 when they had advocated 'No'), but they could not gain traction in
an arena where most attention was paid to an active Leave campaign and a
lacklustre Stronger In campaign.

22.5.4 Funding

In 1975 there was a marked disparity in spending between the 'Yes' and 'No'
sides. Both umbrella organisations received a Government grant of £125,000
but whereas Britain in Europe raised a further £1.7 million, the National
Referendum Campaign only managed another £8,610, meaning they were
vastly outspent by the 'Yes' campaign (Butler and Kitzinger 1996: 86 and
110). In financial terms, as in every other way, the 'No' side was weaker than
'Yes'. The situation would be rather different in 2016, when the Vote Leave
campaign had a very effective fundraising operation, securing £9,858,149 in
donations compared with £12,119,050 for the In Campaign. In total, the
Leave campaigners reported higher donations than Remain: £15,854,432–
£14,859,674 (Electoral Commission 2017: 15). The balance of donations was
51.62% for Leave to 48.38% for Remain, remarkably similar to the percentage
votes received by the two sides: 51.9–48.1% respectively. Leave.EU received
£3.2 million in a donation from Peter Hargreaves and, most significantly, a
loan of £6 million from Aaron Banks. Grassroots Out received £2,312,425
in donations. By far the largest donations came from individuals—Hargreaves
for Leave.EU and Lord Sainsbury for the Remain side, but businesses also
contributed. There were even micro donors to the Leave—schoolchildren

sending money earned from doing a paper round and pensioners sending in loose change. This would not feature in Electoral Commission reports but is indicative of campaigns that reached beyond regular voters including those too young to vote themselves. The Leave campaign also indirectly benefited in some ways from the Prime Minister's decision to circulate a leaflet to every household. The cost, estimated by the Electoral Commission to have been about £9.3 million, and the fact it was publicly funded led some to believe that the campaign was not fair and resulted in some donations to Vote Leave arising from the perceived injustice of Government intervention on the Remain side (source: private information). The leaflets went out just before the start of 'purdah', meaning the spirit, though not the letter, of the law had been broken. The Electoral Commission looked at the Government pamphlet and other government activities in the referendum and concluded that 'the lack of clear and meaningful controls on the activities of governments and other publicly funded bodies (not least the lack of any sanctions for breaches) has the potential to undermine voters' trust in the integrity of referendum controls, and, in the most serious cases, undermine confidence in referendum results' (Electoral Commission 2017: 44). It therefore recommended that Section 125 of PPERA be changed before any future referendums.

Despite the Leavers' success in fundraising, spending was heavily in favour of Remain. The two umbrella organisations reported spending very similar amounts: Vote Leave Ltd £6,742,466 and The In Campaign Ltd (the registered name of BSE) £6,767,584, just under the £7 million cap in each case (Electoral Commission 2017: 14). In total, there were 123 registered groups, 63 on the Remain side and 60 on the Leave side and overall the Remain campaigners spent £19,309,569 to registered Leave campaigns' £13,332,569 (Electoral Commission 2017: 5; Electoral Commission 2019b). This marked disparity in spending can be explained by the role of political parties, which predominantly favoured Remain. The Labour Party spent £4,859,243 and the Liberal Democrats £2,223,901 in support of Remain, with much smaller amounts spent by the Greens, SNP and Plaid Cymru. The Leave side by contrast only secured £1,044,349 from UKIP and £425,622 from the DUP. The Conservative Party opted to remain formally neutral during the referendum owing to the internal party divisions and thus did not register as a campaigner with the Electoral Commission, although a Conservatives In group was registered.

22.5.5   The Media

The media were broadly pro-membership in the 1970s, with the weekly *Spectator* almost the only dissenting voice. It would again advocate departure in the 2016 referendum but by then much of the press concurred. Over the years, the *Express*, *Mail* and the so-called 'Murdoch press' of the *Times*, *Sunday Times*, *Sun* and *News of the World* all articulated sceptical editorial lines, which in part reflected public opinion and in part helped drive anti-European senti-ment.[12] While the *Times* and the *Mail on Sunday* both came out for Remain, alongside *The Guardian* and *Mirror*, the other Murdoch titles, the *Daily Mail* under Paul Dacre's editorship, the *Telegraph* and the *Express* all advocated Leave.[13] There were no constraints on the print media in either referendum, although in 2016 the Electoral Commission recommended that *The Sun* become a registered participant in the referendum such was the extent of that title's proposed activity during the referendum period; it duly did so. While print journalists have the freedom to follow the lines set by their editors or proprietors, the BBC as the country's public service radio and television broad-caster is required to inform and to be impartial. Its attempts at impartiality caused frustration in 2016 as many Remainers felt it gave undue weight to a small number of people with opinions rather than expertise, all in the name of 'balance', while Leavers equally felt poorly served by the public service broad-caster. After the referendum even BBC journalists expressed their frustration at the Corporation's approach to impartiality (Cushion and Lewis 2017: 221–222). One particular concern related to the veracity of statements made in the broadcast media. This was also an issue in the campaigns more generally, as the Electoral Commission had no powers to censure inaccurate or misleading statements. Its role was even more limited in the area of social media, which had become a major component of campaigning by 2016 (Usherwood and Wright 2017; Electoral Commission 2019b). Promoted ads on Facebook and Twitter were an innovation that had not been envisaged by PPERA 2000 and hence there were few rules surrounding their use. In addition to ques-tions about veracity of the message, these new media contributed to an 'echo chamber' effect (Hänska and Bauchowitz 2017), ensuring that rather than the campaigns reaching everyone they were both targeted according to demo-graphics and self-reinforcing. The targeting required the use of micro-data and resulted in significant criticisms of the Leave campaigns, which had spent much of their campaign funds on data from firms in North America, notably Aggregate IQ for Vote Leave (Cadwalladr 2017). Cambridge Analytica, which subsequently went bankrupt following a data scraping scandal using Facebook data, also did work on behalf of Leave.EU and UKIP (Scott 2019). The actual impact of such activity on the outcome of the referendum is destined to remain unclear but the activities of social media and campaign groups in this new field contributed to a situation where the results of the referendum were still viewed with suspicion some years after the event.[14]

---

[12]On the Murdoch press's influence, see Daddow (2012).

[13]For detail on the media's activities during the 2016 referendum, see, Centre for Research in Communication and Culture Loughborough University (2016).

[14]As the House of Commons Select Committee on Digital, Culture, Media and Sports point out, some sanctions were taken for breach separate data protection legislation.

22.5.6   The Outcomes

In 1975 the Establishment's preferred outcome prevailed: deferential citizens dutifully voted two to one to stay in the Common Market, based essentially on cues from the leading politicians of the day. Since most mainstream politicians advocated 'Yes' there was little scope for second-order factors to come into play. Even in Scotland and Wales, where the nationalists were advocating 'No', voters opted heavily to stay. By 2016, any hint of the deferential voter had vanished; people did not want to be told how to vote whether by UK politicians or leaders from elsewhere. Thus, Vote Leave adopted a tactic that would soon enter American and wider UK discourse, an 'us versus them' narrative, implying that 'the Establishment is against "us"'; a distinctly populist approach and one that resonated among certain voters. For some there was a chance to vote against the incumbent Conservative party but for those subsequently dubbed 'the left behind', voting Leave was their chance to be heard. Whereas all parts of the UK supported 'Yes' in 1975, the outcome in 2016 revealed a country deeply divided, between city and town, north and south, with two of the four nations voting to Remain and two to Leave, and tiny Gibraltar voting 96% to Remain. In Scotland, where the dominant SNP had favoured Remain, 62% voted to Remain. Meanwhile, in Northern Ireland, a nation still deeply divided politically, despite twenty years of peace under the Belfast Agreement, the majority view was to Remain, despite the preference of the largest party, the DUP, for leaving. England and Wales both saw a majority voting to Leave but the results were not uniform across the two nations. Large cities tended to see majority support for remaining in the EU—London, Oxford and Cambridge were heavily Remain. Manchester and Liverpool likewise voted to remain although Birmingham bucked the trend, narrowly supporting Leave (see BBC News and for details by area).[15] By contrast, many towns supported Leave, as did rural areas; some coastal towns voted heavily Leave. The disparities seem to reflect socio-economic differences, with many of those who voted Leave being in the more deprived parts of the UK, areas where voters could not discern the benefits of either globalisation or European integration. That these areas had in many cases been significant beneficiaries of EU funding failed to persuade voters; indeed, many would have been hard-pressed to hear about any benefits from the EU, since such funding was rarely highlighted in the UK, in contrast to other Member States. Thus, the allure of 'taking back control' resonated with those who felt the EU had brought them few tangible benefits. The idea of cutting immigration resonated particularly in areas of low immigration, reflecting fears of something that might happen rather than everyday reality. This was not directly an EU-related matter but it did reflect a key strand of the Leave campaign's messaging. Finally, there was an element of voting against the incumbent Conservative Prime Minister, with some Leave-supporting areas being traditional Labour areas, some of which had drifted

[15]See BBC News (n.d.) for a clear summary of results by area; a more detailed account is provided by the Electoral Commission (2019c).

towards UKIP in the EP elections and 2015 general election. Overall, just as in 1975, this was a referendum that focused largely on the key question: in or out of Europe? The result, however, was very different; the status quo had been rejected.

22.6   Consequences for British Politics

During the referendum, David Cameron undertook to deliver the outcome, whether to Remain or Leave. In the event, he resigned on the morning of the result. He sought to justify this apparent change of heart by saying that although he had realised that he would not be personally able to negotiate the UK's departure from the EU he had not wanted the referendum to be about him (Cameron 2019: 681). To an extent this was an effective if disingenuous strategy, although there had been much speculation over his likely successor since he had already stated in the 2015 general election campaign that he would not serve another full term. The outcome of the referendum ensured that his likely successor, George Osborne, a committed Remainer, was no longer a contender and, following a series of unexpected machinations, Home Secretary Theresa May assumed the mantle of Tory leader and Prime Minister. Nominally a Remainer, she coined the mantra 'Brexit means Brexit'. Since Cameron had made no preparations for the eventuality of a Leave vote, she appeared to have *carte blanche*, and set about delivering it with the zeal of the convert. Her original plan was simply to trigger the Article 50 procedure, using prerogative powers and claiming the authority of the referendum; taking back control seemed to mean 'executive control', not a return to parliamentary sovereignty. However, in a case brought by Gina Miller and others, the Supreme Court ruled that there would be domestic implications, which rendered the use of prerogative powers inappropriate. In effect, representative democracy could not simply be countermanded by direct democracy, certainly not in the form of an advisory referendum. Parliament would have to take the decision to invoke Art. 50. While a majority of MPs had voted Remain, they acknowledged the outcome of referendum and Parliament duly passed the EU (Notification of Withdrawal) Act 2017, enabling the PM to write to Donald Tusk as President of the European Council on 29 March 2017 under the Article 50 provisions, thereby starting the clock on the two-year process for leaving the EU.

Despite her oft-repeated commitment to leaving the EU, and indeed her success in negotiating a Withdrawal Agreement with the 27, May was unable to get the Agreement through Parliament, having lost her majority following a misguided snap election held in June 2017. An extension to Article 50 was therefore sought—initially to 12 April and then to 31 October 2019. More than three years after the Referendum, the UK had not left the EU and the divisions that had emerged during the referendum had become increasingly visceral. Ironically, those divisions were seen most profoundly within the very Conservative Party that Cameron had sought to reconcile by putting the issue to the people in the first place. In the 2019 European Parliament elections—elections that the UK was not intended to participate in but were required because of the delay to its departure from the Union—the largest numbers of votes went to the Brexit Party, a newly established party led by former UKIP leader Nigel Farage, pressing for a no-deal Brexit, short-hand for leaving without any negotiated agreement with the EU, and the pro-Remain Liberal Democrats pledging to 'stop Brexit', reflecting the deep divisions in public opinion that had become engrained since the referendum. The two main parties, Labour and the Conservatives saw their support plummet as voters backed the clearest positions on Brexit—for or against. The referendum had transformed domestic politics, without being implemented. In July 2019, May's premiership gave way to an administration led by one of the Conservative faces of Vote Leave: Boris Johnson, who pledged to take the UK out of the EU by 31 October, 'do or die'. However, like May before him, Johnson found an intractable breach with Parliament. The stage was set for a stand-off between Government and the legislature, with the 'parliament versus the people' trope deployed to try to woo citizens to Johnson's cause. Against him was the increasingly outspoken Speaker of the House of Commons, John Bercow, who sought to ensure the rights of parliament were respected until his retirement on 31 October 2019—the day the third Brexit departure date was missed.

Beyond the party political and legislative-executive balance, the referendum and proposed Withdrawal Agreement that Johnson put to Parliament also raised further constitutional challenges, including the spectre of the break-up of the UK. The proposals would put a line down the Irish Sea, to the chagrin of the DUP, and potentially lead to a united Ireland, or so its detractors argued. Meanwhile, the fact that one Remain-voting nation should have a different arrangement from the rest of the UK gave momentum to the SNP's desire for a second independence referendum to complete the job that failed in 2014, a line that was frequently used in the December 2019 general election.

22.7   Consequences for European Politics

A decision not to join the European Union is, by and large, without consequence for the EU—time wasted on negotiating membership, perhaps, but beyond that there is no actual impact on the Union and its institutions, as the Norwegian case has shown twice. The UK's decision to *stay* in 1975 similarly had relatively little impact on the Community, at least in the short-term—an existing, albeit awkward, member was staying so there would be no immediate disruption, even if long-standing disagreements on the Budget led by Margaret Thatcher and the UK's reluctance to engage in deeper integration beyond the single market seemed to impede the ambitions of some European politicians and officials. By contrast, a state seeking to depart inevitably has consequences for the Union as a whole, as the UK's protracted attempts to leave would show. The EU27 expressed regret at the UK's decision but swiftly demonstrated both their commitment to move ahead without the UK and their ability to show a united front. As early as September 2016, the 27 met in Bratislava to discuss the way forward, resulting in the eponymous Bratislava Declaration. The UK's departure could not weaken the European project as some UK Brexiteers had predicted, even hoped for. Moreover, while the UK took several months to decide what it would ask for in the negotiations beyond the simple demand to leave the EU—and even then the country, the political class, and the governing party itself remained divided—the EU27 made their position clear before the Article 50 process was triggered and their resolve endured. Suggestions that the UK would be able to peel off certain countries in bilateral negotiations proved false. The 27 abided by the Union's motto: 'United in Diversity', at least as far as the UK's impeding departure was concerned. While there were divergent interests among the 27, at the time of writing splits remained mostly hypothetical and the prospect of other states seeking to leave the Union had receded, in marked contrast to pre-referendum fears.

22.8 Concluding Remarks

In the wake of the second UK referendum on EU membership, George Brown's 1967 comment appeared to have come true: 'Left versus Right had lost its old meaning' (cited by Pimlott, quoted in Smith 1999: 56); left and right had ceased to matter. The divisions in British politics now appeared to be between Remainers and Leavers. The 1975 referendum had weakened traditional party cohesion (Smith 1999: 56); that of the 2016 seemed to have broken it fundamentally. This situation seemed to be reinforced by the 2019 general election fought and won by the Conservatives with the slogan 'Get Brexit done', which resulted in a parliamentary majority of 80, paving the way for the UK finally to depart the EU on 31 January 2020, albeit with little clarity about the nature of the UK's future relationship with its erstwhile partners.

A precedent set in 1975 ensured that as the integration process in Europe developed and new treaties were agreed by the Member States, the UK would consider holding a referendum to ratify them. Initially party leaders held out against a move towards institutionalised direct democracy—Margaret Thatcher rejected a referendum on the SEA and John Major was clear that the Maastricht Treaty should be ratified by parliamentary means. Yet, by the mid-1990s the pressures for another referendum on an EU topic had become overwhelming; politicians from all parties indicated their willingness to allow voters a say on the Euro, the Constitutional Treaty and finally the Lisbon Treaty. For twenty years such promises went unfulfilled. Cameron's Bloomberg pledge was thus intended as a safety valve, allowing citizens finally to have another say on the UK's place in Europe. The attempt to dampen internal party divisions and steal the ground from UKIP failed. Rather than uniting his party, the referendum had merely magnified divisions in the country. Moreover, the complex nature of 'Brexit'/leaving the European Union ensured that it was not a simple matter to deliver 'the will of the people' as many called the 17.4 million Leave votes cast on 23 June 2016. The legislation to notify the EU of the UK's desire to leave the EU was merely the starting point. The complexity of undoing 43 years of legislative, economic, cultural and social entanglement had been played down during the referendum. And the nature of departure and the final destination could be very different from expectations and promises. The reality left politicians struggling to obey the 'instruction' of the voters as successive prime ministers called it, even if they wished to do so. Crucially, the challenges facing both May and Johnson in delivering Brexit when there was no parliamentary majority for any given outcome demonstrated the dangers of trying to graft elements of direct democracy onto a representative system. 'The will of the people' was expressed at a single point in time: 23 June 2016. MPs elected later—at the snap election held by Theresa May in 2017—were expected to deliver on that decision. It would be undemocratic to do otherwise, the Leavers claimed. Yet in a democracy people are allowed to change their minds. Two abiding questions arise from the UK case: how long does a referendum outcome last and how can it be reconciled with parliamentary elections that arise subsequent to the referendal moment? What was clear was that the 2016 referendum had not resolved the European question in British politics, least of all within the Conservative Party, which Cameron had sought to hold together by triggering it.

Bibliography

Aqui, L. (2019). Government Policy and Propaganda in the 1975 Referendum on European Community Membership. *Contemporary British History*. https://doi. org/10.1080/13619462.2019.1588115. Accessed on 15 September 2019.

BBC. (2016, June 11). Corbyn: I'm "7 out of 10" on EU. Available at: https://www.bbc.co.uk/news/av/uk-politics-eu-referendum-36506163/ corbyn-i-m-seven-out-of-10-on-eu. Accessed on 12 November 2019.

BBC News. (n.d.). *EU Referendum Local Results*. Available at: https://www.bbc.co. uk/news/politics/eu_referendum/results/local/. Accessed on 9 October 2019.

Beckett, A. (2016, June 5). Daily Mail Backs Campaign to remain in Europe...in 1975. *The Guardian*. Available at: https://www.theguardian.com/politics/2016/ jun/05/daily-mail-backs-campaign-to-remain-in-europe-in-1975-eec-eu-refere nfum. Accessed on 10 October 2019.

Blair, T. (2010). *A Journey*. London: Hutchinson.

Bogdanor, V. (2009). *The New British Constitution*. London and Portland, OR: Hart Publishing.

Butler, D., & Kitzinger, U. (1996). *The 1975 Referendum* (2nd ed.). Basingstoke and London: Macmillan Press.

Cabinet. (1975, February 17). *Referendum: Draft White Paper*. Memorandum by the Lord President of the Council, C(75) 19.

Cadwalladr, C. (2017, May 7). The Great British Brexit Robbery: How Our Democracy Was Hijacked. *The Guardian*. Available at: https://theguardian.com/technology/2017/may/07/.... Accessed on 3 November 2019.

Cameron, D. (2019). *For the Record*. London: William Collins.

Centre for Research in Communication and Culture Loughborough University. (2016). *Media Coverage of the EU Referendum* (Report 5). Available at: https://blog.lboro.ac.uk/crcc/eu-referendum/uk-news-coverage-2016-eu-referendum-report-5-6-may-22-june-2016/. Accessed on 12 November 2019.

Clegg, N. (2016). *Politics: Between the Extremes*. London: The Bodley Head.

Cushion, S., & Lewis, J. (2017). Impartiality, Statistical Tit-for-Tats and the Construction of Balance: UK Television News Reporting of the 2016 EU Referendum Campaign. *European Journal of Communication, 32*(3), 208–223.

Daddow, O. (2012). The UK Media and "Europe": From Permissive Consensus to Destructive Dissent. *International Affairs, 88*(6), 1219–1236.

Electoral Commission. (n.d.). *Donations and Loans Received by Campaigners in the European Union Referendum—Fourth Pre-Poll Report: 10 June 2016 to 22 June 2016*. Available at: https://www.electoralcommission.org.uk/sites/default/files/pdf_file/Pre-poll-4-Summary-Document.pdf. Accessed on 1 March 2020.

Electoral Commission. (2017). *The 2016 EU Referendum: Report on the Regulation of Campaigners at the Referendum on the UK's Membership of the European Union held on 23 June 2016*, published March 2017.

Electoral Commission. (2019a). *Testing the EU Referendum Question*. Available at https://www.electoralcommission.org.uk/. Accessed on 17 September 2019.

Electoral Commission. (2019b). *Report: The Regulation of Campaigners at the Referendum on the UK's Membership of the European Union held on 23 June 2016*. Available at https://www.electoralcommission.org.uk/. Accessed on 17 September 2019.

Electoral Commission. (2019c). *Results and Turnout at the EU Referendum*. Available at: https://www.electoralcommission.org.uk/who-we-are-and-what-we-do/elections-and-referendums/past-elections-and-referendums/eu-referendum/results-and-turnout-eu-referendum. Accessed on 25 September 2019.

European Parliament. (n.d.). *Results of the 2014 European Elections*. available at: http://www.europarl.europa.eu/elections2014-results/en/country-results-uk-2014.html. Accessed on 17 September 2019.

European Union Act 2011.

European Union Referendum Act 2015.

Hänska, M., & Bauchowitz, S. (2017). *Title Tweeting for Brexit: How Social Media Influenced the Referendum*. LSE Research Online. http://eprints.lse.ac.uk/84614/.

Heath, E. (1998). *The Course of My Life—My Autobiography*. London: Hodder and Stoughton.

House of Commons. (2015). *The 1974–1975 Renegotiation of EEC Membership and Referendum*. Available at: https://researchbriefings.parliament.uk/ResearchBriefing/Summary/CBP-7253#fullreport. Accessed on 22 September 2019.

House of Commons. (2017). Lessons Learned from the EU Referendum. *12th Report of the Public Administration and Constitutional Affairs Committee 2016–2017 Session*. Available at: https://publications.parliament.uk/pa/cm201617/cmselect/cmpubadm/496/49606.htm. Accessed on 25 September 2019.

Jenkins, R. (1991). *A Life at the Centre*. London & Basingstoke: Macmillan London Ltd.

Lynch, P. (2011). The Con-Lib Agenda for Europe. In S. Lee & M. Beech (Eds.), *The Cameron-Clegg Government—Coalition Politics in an Age of Austerity* (pp. 218–233). Basingstoke: Palgrave Macmillan.

Moore, C. (2019). *Margaret Thatcher—The Authorized Biography Volume Three—Herself Alone*. London: Allen Lane.

Political Parties, Elections and Referendums Act 2000.

Saunders, R. (2018). *Yes to Europe! The 1975 Referendum and Seventies Britain*. Cambridge: Cambridge University Press.

Scott, M. (2019). Cambridge Analytica Did Work for Brexit Groups, Says Ex-Staffer. *POLITICO*. Available at https://www.politico.eu/article/cambridge-analytica-leave-eu-uk…. Accessed on 03 November 2019.

Shipman, T. (2016). *All Out War*. London: William Collins.

Smith, J. (1999). The 1975 Referendum. *Journal of European Integration History*, 5(1), 41–56.

Smith, J. (2016). David Cameron's EU Renegotiation and Referendum Pledge: A Case of Déjà Vu? *British Politics*, 11(3), 324–346.

Supreme Court. (2017). *R (on the Application of Miller and Another) (Respondents) v Secretary of State for Exiting the European Union (Appellant)* etc [Miller 1].

Supreme Court. (2019). *R (on the Application of Miller) (Appellant) v The Prime Minister Respondent* [Miller 2].

Usherwood, S., & Wright, K. (2017). Sticks and Stones: Comparing Twitter Campaigning Strategies in the European Union Referendum. *British Journal of Politics and International Relations*, 19(2), 371–388.

Wilson, H. (1975). Statement by the Prime Minister on 23.1.75. *Hansard*.

CHAPTER 23

The EFTA Enlargement

Lise Rye

In the course of 1994, four countries held national referendums on the question of membership of the European Union (EU). This chapter reviews the course of events in the three countries where the voters came out in favour of joining the EU: Austria, Finland and Sweden.[1] These countries were all members of the European Free Trade Association (EFTA), which had been established with a view to promoting free trade in Western Europe. The 1995 enlargement completed this process. The literature on EFTA has tended to highlight the differences between its members (Robertson 1970). The literature on these countries' referendums argues in contrast that while the referendums display major differences, they also reveal 'astonishing similarities' (Detlef and Storsved 1995: 18). The year 1994 was not the first year that countries conducted referendums on identical issues. The same had happened in 1972, when Norway, Ireland and Denmark put the question of membership of the European Community (EC) to voters. Compared to those referendums, the EU referendums in 1994 stand out for their interlinkage, for the degree of strategic synchronization and for the way issues travelled across borders. The 1994 referendums on EU membership were a watershed, introducing the trans-nationalization of national EU referendums.

---

[1] The fourth country, Norway, is covered by Fossum and Rosén in Chapter 21.

L. Rye (✉)
Department of Historical and Classical Studies, Norwegian University of Science and Technology (NTNU), Trondheim, Norway
e-mail: lise.rye@ntnu.no

© The Author(s) 2021
J. Smith (ed.), *The Palgrave Handbook of European Referendums*,
https://doi.org/10.1007/978-3-030-55803-1_23

495

This chapter is divided into five parts. The first presents the historical context within which the votes took place. The second and third sections introduce the EFTA-countries' experience with referendums and the constitutional provisions for this instrument. The fourth (and main) part focuses on the campaigns in the three countries with an emphasis on the actors, their platforms and main arguments. The concluding section explores voting behaviour in the referendums.

23.1   The Historical Context

The 1995 enlargement of the EU marked the highpoint of a process that started 35 years earlier with the creation of the European Free Trade Association. Austria and Sweden were founding members of this organization, which entered into force in 1960 with the express purpose to bridge the gap to the European Economic Community (EEC) without having to join that organization.[2] Finland joined EFTA as an associate member in 1961 and became a full member in 1986. The new organization brought together a heterogeneous group of countries that included neutral states and NATO allies, rich and poor, countries that remained outside the EEC by choice, and countries that did so by necessity. What united them was an interest in Western European free trade. The members of EFTA viewed their organization as 'a step toward an agreement between all member countries of the Organization for European Economic Co-operation (OEEC)' (EFTA 1959). The idea was that the establishment of an outer free trade area would induce the EEC to engage in new negotiations on an OEEC-wide free trade deal. As a short-term aspiration, this strategy failed. One important reason was that the EFTA project went counter to the interests of the Eisenhower Administration in Washington. For geopolitical and commercial reasons alike, the US government was opposed to a project that would dilute the EEC, strengthen a British-dominated OEEC and increase the discrimination against US exports (Winand 1993: 134). Against this backdrop, the EEC settled for a pragmatic and liberal policy towards third countries that sought to mitigate against unfortunate effects of the creation of the EEC on third countries without a grand scheme (Rye 2015: 6).

From a longer-term perspective, the creation of EFTA led to formalized trade cooperation between the members of this organization and the EC. The EFTA countries completed the dismantling of their internal tariffs by 1967, eighteen months ahead of schedule. A few years later, and in the context of the first enlargement of the EEC (then known as the EC), the existence of this outer free trade area encouraged the EC to conclude bilateral free trade agreements with the non-joining members of EFTA.[3] The decision did not

[2] The other members were Denmark, Norway, Portugal, Switzerland and the United Kingdom.

[3] The EC was established in 1967 as a result of the merger of the institutions of the ECSC, the EEC and the European Atomic Energy Community (Euratom).

only reflect the economic significance of EFTA-EC trade; for the EC, this was also a matter of duties and responsibilities. In order to respect the principles of the Treaty of Rome, the Community had to provide for the maintenance of the degree of free trade that existed between the candidate countries and their EFTA partners (Rye 2017: 199). Brussels signed agreements on free trade in industrial products with each of the remaining EFTA members between July 1972 and October 1973.

Two countries in particular, Austria and Sweden, wanted relations with the EC that went beyond free trade. Both before and after the free trade negotiations, these countries approached the Community with requests for more comprehensive cooperation. More specifically, they asked for a harmonization of policies in areas that included, among others, industrial policy and environmental policy. They asked for procedures for information and consultation and, so far as possible, for procedures that would allow for joint decision-making in areas of cooperation. Unsurprisingly, the EC flatly refused, making it clear that any arrangements that would threaten the Community's decision-making autonomy were out of the question (Rye 2017: 200).

The EFTA Summit in Vienna in May 1977 marked the beginning of a joint approach on the part of the EFTA countries towards the EC. In the context of the global economic downturn following the OPEC oil embargo, the EFTA countries expressed concern with the mushrooming of new protectionist measures that threatened the existing levels of free trade in Western Europe. To protect this trade, they called for extended cooperation with the EC in the form of more frequent exchanges of information, closer consultation on related economic issues and enhanced coordination. After some initial hesitation, the Community decided to develop its cooperation with EFTA in a more pragmatic fashion. Both sides were concerned with the fact that the implementation of their free trade agreements at this point had created a de facto free trade area between them. Their economies had become interwoven and demarcation lines between domestic policies and external relations were no longer wholly clear. Formally, relations between the Community and EFTA remained unchanged until the 1984 Luxembourg Declaration, where they agreed to extend their cooperation beyond the scope of the free trade agreements. Informally, this cooperation had started in the late 1970s. In 1978, the EC drew up a list of items of eligible cooperation. It included rules of origin, technical barriers to trade and state aid. The move from first to second-generation free trade had begun.

The 1992 Agreement on the European Economic Area constituted a new and significant milestone in EFTA-EC relations. The agreement extended cooperation between the two sides to new areas and introduced an institutional structure that enabled the EFTA countries to form part of the EC internal market on equal terms as EU member states. The development of a common market between EFTA and the EU in tandem with the implementation of the EC's Single Market programme had been a declared objective ever since the 1984 Luxembourg Declaration. The follow-up to this declaration had, however, been piecemeal and slow, and failed to keep pace with the ongoing dismantling of non-tariff barriers to trade within the Community. With his January 1989 suggestion for a new and more structured relationship between EFTA and the EC, Commission President Jacques Delors proposed a more efficient approach. He would later describe his proposal as a helping-hand to the EFTA countries, facilitating the transition to full membership of the EU. Contemporary commentators suggested in contrast that the true intention behind the new agreement was to keep prospective new applicants at arm's length in order to enable the EC to concentrate on its internal development.

Austria, Sweden and Finland each applied for full EC membership before the conclusion of the negotiations on the EEA Agreement. Austria's decision to apply was above all motivated by economic incentives. Symptomatically, the first call for full membership in this country came from the Federation of Austrian Industrialists, in May 1987 (Kaiser 1995: 412). More than 60% of Austria's exports went to the EC market. Against the backdrop of the emerging Single Market, the export dependency on the Community consti-tuted an obvious pull-factor (Dupont et al. 1999: 190). Push-factors were also in play. Austria was facing increasing economic problems and these were partic-ularly pressing in the nationalized sectors of the economy. To the governing grand coalition, membership appeared to be a means to facilitate long-overdue domestic economic reforms (Müller 2009: 8). In October 1988, the European Commission made it clear to Alois Mock, the Austrian Minister of Foreign Affairs, that the benefits of the Single Market could only be enjoyed in full by EC Member States (Müller 2009: 10). At the same time, the international law department of the Austrian Foreign Ministry concluded that the country's neutrality was compatible with EC membership. Austrian neutrality had at this point lost its original purpose. Neutrality had nevertheless grown to become an integral part of this country's national identity, and polls had consistently shown that a majority of Austrians would give up the bid for EU membership to maintain it (Fitzmaurice 1995: 228). Four months before the fall of the Berlin wall, Austria submitted its application to the EC in July 1989 on the understanding that it could maintain its status as a neutral country.

Research on Sweden's European policy offers diverging perspectives on this country's October 1990 announcement to seek membership of the EC. The fact that the announcement came in the midst of an acute economic crisis has led some to conclude that it was a crisis management measure, launched to strengthen faith in the Swedish economy. Others argue that it was the realization that the EEA association model would only offer a consultative decision-shaping role that tilted the Swedish government in favour of full membership (Miles 1996: 64). Carl Bildt, the prime minister of the conser-vative government that assumed office a few weeks after the announcement, argued in keeping with the second interpretation. Bildt acknowledged that until 1990 Sweden had discussed its European policy in economic terms. However, he also pointed out that if the Swedish position had remained unchanged, Sweden would have been satisfied with access to the Single Market on the terms provided for by the EEA Agreement. According to Bildt,

Sweden's wish to become a member of the EC had become 'much more than a desire to share in the economic benefits of integration' (Rye 2017: 207).

Finland applied for EC membership in March 1992, three months after the dissolution of the Soviet Union. In contrast to Austria and Sweden's self-imposed neutrality, the credibility of Finland's neutrality had been a political imperative during the Cold War. It was only with the end of the Cold War that Finland could tie itself to the West. Research has interpreted the application as an act of continuity, rather than change, highlighting reasons related to state security. Teija Tiilikainen explains how Finnish political elites initially downplayed the security considerations. She refers to the Finnish President at that time, Mauno Koivisto, who later argued that an explicit security reasoning would have weakened Finland's security in the event that membership had not been achieved. Later on, security policy arguments came to the fore and were exploited by both sides of the EU campaign (Tiilikainen 2006: 77).

23.2   THE REFERENDUM EXPERIENCE

Unlike countries like Ireland or Switzerland, Finland, Austria and Sweden all have limited experience of using national referendums. Bjørklund links Sweden and Finland's decisions to put the issue of EU membership to the voters to the fact that their Nordic neighbours, Denmark and Norway, had already made referendums on EC issues a practice. Therefore, Finnish and Swedish politicians 'were more or less obliged to see that referenda were carried out' (Bjørklund 1996: 12). As for Austria, this country had no choice. The Austrian constitution required a referendum on the issue. The Austrian electorate had expressed itself on the matter of *Anschluss* with Nazi Germany in 1938 (Detlef and Storsved 1995: 20–21). The first national referendum after World War II took place in 1978 on the issue of nuclear power. A majority of 50.5% then cast their votes against the opening of a nuclear power plant in Zwentendorf, a result later interpreted as 'a challenge to the entire political system, expressing much more than mere anxiety about nuclear energy' (Pelinka and Greiderer 1996: 23). In 1994, Austria was the first of the four candidate countries to put the question of EU membership to the voters in a referendum. The Austrian referendum took place in June, when a solid majority of 66.6–33.4% voted in favour of joining the EU. The turnout was 82.3%.

The Finnish referendum on EU membership was only the second national referendum in Finland—a fact that has led researchers to describe the referendum option as 'a dormant feature in Finnish politics' (Suksi 1996: 52). Finland held its first national referendum in 1931 when a clear majority voted for the abolition of Finland's long-term ban on the sale of alcohol. In October 1994, a majority (56.9%) supported the proposal that Finland should join the EU. The turnout in Finland was 74%.

In neighbouring Sweden, the EU referendum was the fifth since this instrument was introduced in 1922. The first took place that year, when a small majority (51%) rejected a proposal to introduce a ban against alcoholic drinks.

Then followed two referendums in the 1950s, on the questions of driving on the right and occupational pensions respectively. In 1955, a majority of 82.9 rejected the proposal that Sweden should move from driving on the left to driving on the right. Eight years later, the Swedish Parliament (*Riksdagen*), nevertheless approved the change, leading the country to introduce driving on the right in 1967. In the 1957 referendum on occupational pensions, the voters had a choice between three different plans, out of which none received a majority. Then followed a referendum on nuclear power in 1980—a divisive issue in many countries at the time, and one that had also been a heated topic in the 1976 general elections in Sweden. Finally, on 13 November 1994, a majority of 53.2% endorsed the proposal that Sweden should become a member of the European Union on a turnout of 83.3%. Since then, Sweden has held one further EU referendum—on whether to adopt of Euro in 2003. On that occasion, a majority of 55.9% voted in favour of keeping the krona (see also the Chapter 26 by Oscarsson elsewhere in this volume).

23.3   The Legal Frameworks

It was only in Austria that a referendum on the issue of membership was constitutionally required. The Austrian constitution includes provisions for optional and mandatory national referendums. In accordance with Article 43 of this constitution, the National Council (*Nationalrat*)—the lower of the two houses of the Austrian Parliament may submit any legislative act to a popular referendum if the *Nationalrat* itself so decides or if a majority of its members demands it. Austria distinguishes between decision-making referendums and consultative referendums according to the nature of the text put to the vote. A referendum on an important issue is consultative, while both constitutional and legislative referendums are legally binding (European Commission for Democracy through Law 2005: 20).

Article 44 of the Austrian constitution provides the legal basis for mandatory referendums. A referendum is mandatory if the legislation in question involves an amendment to or alteration of the constitution's fundamental principles: the democratic principle; the republican principle; the federal principle; and the principle that law binds government activity. The constitution also allows for popular votes on partial revisions of the constitution. One-third of the Members of Parliament can call a national referendum on partial revisions of the constitution. Austria's accession to the EU was considered a total revision of the constitution and was consequently submitted to mandatory referendum (European Commission for Democracy through Law 2005: 11). Every Federal citizen who is qualified to vote for the National Council on the day of the ballot enjoys the right to vote in referendums. The voting age for parliamentary elections in Austria is sixteen.

The governments of the Nordic countries were not legally bound to put the membership question to the electorate. The Swedish constitution provides for two types of optional referendums: consultative referendums and binding

referendums on matters of fundamental law. The possibility of calling consultative referendums has existed since 1922. The introduction of this instrument
reflected a general demand in the inter-war years for more democracy; additional pressure came from the temperance movement, which hoped to achieve
a ban on alcoholic drinks by means of a referendum (Ruin 1996: 172). The
possibility of calling binding referendums on constitutional measures dates
back to 1980. As of 2018, however, no such referendum had taken place.
The Swedish Parliament (the *Riksdag*) is the only authority able to call a
national referendum. The *Riksdag* adopts the decision by means of an act
of law that also determines which question(s) to put on the ballot. When the
Riksdag decides to hold a referendum, it is also usual that it allocates funding
to organizations campaigning for the various alternatives. Finally, it is also the
task of the *Riksdag* to interpret the results of the referendum. As referendums
may offer multiple alternatives, this is not necessarily a straightforward process.
The right to vote in referendums is, unless otherwise decided, identical with
the right to vote in general elections. Swedish citizens who have reached the
age of 18 and who are, or have been, registered resident in Sweden, enjoy
the right to vote. Citizens who do not want to vote for any of the alternatives, have the opportunity to cast a blank vote. In contrast to parliamentary
elections, a blank voting slip in a referendum is valid and tallied.

The Finnish constitution has included provisions on the holding of consultative referendums since 1987. In 2012, Finland introduced a new instrument
of direct democracy, when the country adopted a National Citizens' Initiative
law that enables a minimum of 50,000 citizens to suggest new legislation or
changes to existing legislation. In 2016, the constitutional law committee of
the Finnish Parliament (*Eduskunta*) decided, however, that this initiative was
only applicable to matters under Parliament's purview, not to policies related
to international treaties and obligations. Thus, as is the case in Sweden, only
Parliament has the power to call national referendums in Finland. Furthermore, and in keeping with Swedish practice, the decision to organize a
consultative referendum requires a special Act of Parliament. The Finnish
constitution contains no provisions on the conduct of a referendum. Such
provisions are laid down by bespoke legislation in the special act, which also
contains provisions on the timing of the referendum and on the choices to be
presented to the voters. Every Finnish citizen who has reached eighteen years
of age has the right to vote in national elections and referendums.

23.4   THE CAMPAIGNS

The Austrian government concluded its negotiations with the EU on 1 March
1994 and decided shortly thereafter to hold the mandatory referendum on
12 June. The timing reflected a wish to separate the EU campaign from the
campaign for Austria's federal elections, which were due in October of that
year (Kaiser 1995: 413). The literature on advisory EU referendums argues
that governments predominantly convene such referendums for norm-related

concerns regarding the need to ensure democratic legitimacy or for politically strategic reasons (Beach 2018). In the case of the Nordic countries, both types of motives were in play. In 1994, the practice of asking the people for advice on EU issues was already relatively well established. Of the seven optional referendums on EU issues in the period of 1972–1994, three had taken place in Scandinavia. In Norway's 1972 referendum on EC membership, a majority of the people had gone against the government's advice. The event established the principle that what the people had decided, only the people could dissolve (Bjørklund 1996: 12). Denmark's referendum on EC membership later that same year was constitutionally required. Subsequent Danish governments have, however, since then called advisory referendums on the 1986 Single European Act (SEA) and on the 1993 revised Maastricht Treaty. In the first case, Copenhagen used this instrument to solve a parliamentary deadlock, and as an alternative to calling new elections to the Danish parliament, which had rejected the SEA (Svensson 1996: 42). In the latter case, the decision to refer Maastricht to the people reflected the widespread expectation in the Danish electorate that they should have a say on the new version of an agreement that a majority of the voters had rejected the year before (Beach 2018). Norwegian and Danish practice created expectations that gave politicians in Sweden and Finland little choice but to put the question of EU membership to the people (Bjørklund 1996: 12). Strategic considerations were also prominent. In Finland, the governing coalition was advocating a policy that a clear majority of Prime Minister Esko Aho's Centre Party opposed. Allowing voters to decide the issue thus appeared as the only possible way to settle the matter (Suksi 1996: 56). In Sweden, two small opposition parties—the Left Party and the Environmental Party—first put forward the demand for a referendum. As pointed out by Ruin, they thereby demonstrated the traditional pattern that parties that disagree with the parliamentary majority turn to direct citizen participation (Ruin 1996: 177).

The sequence of the Nordic referendums was the result of a strategic choice. The general assumption was that the outcome of the first referendum would influence the outcome of the subsequent ones. Proposals that the referendums should take place on the same date failed and they eventually took place in the order of most to least likely 'Yes' (Bjørklund 1996: 12–13).

Referendum campaigns differ from election campaigns in important respects. One is that political parties do not necessarily play the lead (Jahn et al. 1998: 61). That was the case in the one 'No'-voting EFTAn state, Norway, where the social movement 'No to the EU' constituted a broad-based and influential umbrella organization with impressive membership and local associations in every municipality. In Austria, Sweden and Finland social movements did not carry the same weight. In these countries, the political parties and prominent politicians were the most important campaign actors. Moreover, in all these countries, anti-establishment parties doubled as anti-EU parties. This aspect constituted another contrast to the situation in Norway, where the established Centre Party was a key player in the anti-membership campaign.

23.4.1 Austria

In 1994, a coalition consisting of the Social Democrats (*Sozialdemokratische Partei Österreichs*; SPÖ) and the People's Party (*Österreichische Volkspartei*; ÖVP) governed Austria. These parties were firmly rooted in the Socialist and Christian Democratic Party camps respectively. Together, they had dominated the Austrian political system since World War Two. Both parties strongly recommended membership. The Freedom Party (*Freiheitliche Partei Österreichs*; FPÖ) and the Greens formed the opposition. The FPÖ originated from the German-nationalists and had a much less coherent ideological base than the governing parties. The Greens had entered parliament for the first time in 1986. They combined a strong environmental commitment with left-wing social and economic policies (Meyer 2011: 203). Initially, only the Greens opposed Austrian entry into the EU. From around 1991–1992, the FPÖ under the leadership of Jörg Haider changed its position, joining the anti-EU camp. In 1993, liberals left the FPÖ and formed the Liberal Forum. Thereafter, the debate on EU membership followed along the same lines as those of party competition, with the SPÖ, ÖVP and the Liberal Forum supporting membership and the FPÖ and the Greens opposing it.

Stable elite consensus on the desirability of membership marked the Austrian EU campaign (Kaiser et al. 1995: 78–79). The pro-membership parties enjoyed the support of Austria's main economic interest groups: the Chambers of Labour; the Trade Union Federation; the Chambers of Agriculture and the Chambers of Commerce. Even the Church spoke out in favour of membership. The campaign intensified in early May, with massive information offensives from both sides. Only the pro-EU side received public funding (Pelinka and Greiderer 1996: 26). In March 1994, Austria's largest circulation daily, the *Kronen Zeitung*, moved from a critical to a more supportive stance. With a coverage rate of approximately 40%, this tabloid was an influential actor in the Austrian debate, with potential to secure widespread public support for accession. In 1994, the majority of the country's media community voiced support for joining the EU. The exceptions were the two powerful mass-circulation newspapers, *Täglich Alles* and *Ganze Woche*, which conducted a massive anti-EU campaign.

The Austrian government named its information campaign '*Wir sind Europa*' ('We are Europe'). The title reflected a longtime campaign on the part of the Austrian political elite to anchor their country in the economic and democratic successful parts of the continent (Luif 1998). Within the grand coalition, the SPÖ focused on content-related arguments such as jobs, export opportunities, security and environment, while the ÖVP adopted a more personalized campaign with photos of Alois Mock, the Foreign Minister, as the 'the hero of Brussels' (Müller 2009: 19). On the 'No' side, the FPÖ's slogan was '*Österreich zuerst*' ('Austria first'), often accompanied by a portrait of Haider. The FPÖ focused on the disadvantages as they saw them for Austria of membership, such as increased unemployment, increased criminality and the loss of the Austrian currency (Müller 2009: 19).

23.4.2   Sweden

In Sweden, the EU membership issue united across the traditional left-right divide. The pro-membership parties were, from left to right on the political spectrum, the Social Democratic Party, the Centre Party, the Liberal Party, the Liberal-Conservative Party (*Moderaterna*), the Christian Democratic Party and the New Democracy. The Left Party and the Greens constituted the anti-EU membership faction. The governing Social Democratic Party's October 1990 announcement that it was in favour of an application for EC membership provoked strong opposition within the party. The internal divisions led the party to postpone a final decision on the matter until June 1994, when 232 delegates voted in favour and 103 against (Jahn et al. 1998: 63). Eventually, 50% of this party's voters cast their votes in support of Swedish accession to the EU. The gap between official party positions and their supporters' voting behaviour was striking in other parties as well. Forty-five per cent of the Centre Party's supporters cast their votes in favour of accession while only 41% of the supporters of the Christian Democratic Party voted in keeping with their party's official stand. In contrast, within the Liberal-Conservative Party, in office from 1991 to 1994, and the Liberal Party, elites and supporters saw eye to eye on the membership issue. The Liberal-Conservative Party and the Liberal Party had been in favour of membership for more than two decades. Eventually, 86 and 81% of their supporters respectively voted in keeping with their parties' official position. Unity also characterized the Left Party and the Green Party. Both these parties campaigned strongly against membership. Nevertheless, between 10 and 15% of their supporters cast their votes against these parties' official positions (Johansson and Raunio 2001: 234).

Two umbrella organizations campaigned in favour of Swedish EU membership. '*Ja till Europa*' ('Yes to Europe') organized hard-core supporters, including the Liberal Party, the Liberal-Conservative Party and the Swedish Employers' Association. 'Network for Europe' brought together the Farmers' Association and the 'Yes' fractions of the Centre Party and the Social Democrats. Meanwhile, opponents joined forces in the 'People's Movement against EU', founded in 1990 by leading politicians of the Green and Left parties. More than thirty organizations linked their campaigns with this movement, among them the 'People's Movement No to EU', party-based initiatives, EU-critical trade unionists and various interest groups connected with the environmental movement and the temperance movement (Schymik 2011: 57). With a membership of 10,000, the 'People's Movement No to EU' did not nearly carry the same weight as its Norwegian counterpart, which had 145,000 members. Overall, campaigning in Sweden was less intense than in Finland and far less hectic than in Norway. The general election on 18 September left time only for a concentrated two-month campaign, and the many actors and stakeholders had difficulties in getting themselves organized and getting their message through in the media (Jahn et al. 1998: 72).

23.4.3   *Finland*

In Finland, the question of EU membership rose to the top of the political agenda 'quite unexpectedly and within a very short time' (Raunio 1999: 143). As had been the case in Sweden, calls for membership came first from industry and commerce, who argued that the EEA-association would leave Finland in a secondary position. Political elites started to debate the issue after the Swedish government's October 1990 announcement (Raunio and Tiilikainen 2003: 24). Public discussion of the membership issue only took off, however, after the dissolution of the Soviet Union. In February 1992, President Koivisto informed Parliament of the government's intention to apply for EU membership. The *Eduskunta* approved the submission of a membership application in March, with 108 votes in favour and 55 against. The membership issue cut across Finland's government at the time, a four-party centre-right coalition headed by Esko Aho of the Centre Party. One of the coalition partners, the Christian People's Party left the government over the issue. Two of the others governing parties, the National Coalition Party (KOK) and the Swedish People's Party (RKP), were unequivocally in favour of accession. Finally, there was the Prime Minister's own party, which depended heavily on agricultural and rural votes. In these communities, opposition to EC membership was considerable because it would entail the loss of national subsidies. While the Centre Party took an official stand in favour of Finnish accession, its policy contradicted the view of the majority of its supporters. In Finland's October 1994 referendum, only 36% of the supporters of the Centre Party cast their votes in favour of Finnish membership. As in Austria and Sweden, the EU question cut across traditional party competition lines. The Social Democratic Party had demanded membership since September 1991. The Left Alliance and the Green League took no official position on the matter, a fact that reflected internal division between members and party leadership (Johansson and Raunio 2001: 234).

The pro-membership campaign brought together actors such as the Central Chamber of Commerce, the Centre for Finnish Business and Policy Studies and the Central Federation of Finnish Employers. Most trade unions also joined the pro-membership campaign which received a major boost when President Mauno Koivisto came out in favour of membership during the opening session of the *Eduskunta* in 1992 (Raunio and Tiilikainen 2003. 28). The pro-EU side in Finland used a diversification strategy where different organizations targeted different groups. In both Sweden and Finland, access to better campaign funding gave the pro-EU movements a decisive advantage.

The Finnish anti-EU movement was the least influential of the Nordic movements (Schymik 2009: 206). Here, organized extra-parliamentary opposition to EU membership only appeared in late 1991, with 'Alternative to the EU' as the most influential actor. At the time of the referendum, this organization comprised 150 local groups and a total membership of 3000–4000.

Anti-membership campaigners eventually joined forces in the umbrella organization called 'Independent Finland – the Best Alternative', which brought together 16 different groups (Jahn et al. 1998: 68). Others continued their individual campaigns including the main social group opposing membership, the Finnish farmers, whose federation did not want to join the national campaign conducted by 'Alternative to the EU' (Schymik 2009: 206). Environmentalists constituted another stronghold against EU membership. Among the public, opposition was stronger among female voters, who feared that membership would lead to the deterioration of social and employment rights (Raunio and Tiilikainen 2003: 28).

23.5   THE ARGUMENTS

In all three countries, the nation-state was the dominating framework for the debate. Concern was with the effects of membership domestically, not with EU visions and the future of European integration. Economic arguments dominated the 'Yes' campaigns (Detlef and Storsved 1995: 32). The predominance of economic issues might come across as puzzling as the EFTA candidates had participated in the EU internal market on equal terms as EU Member States since January 1994. Jahn et al. suggest that this should be seen in light of the EEA Agreement's complexity, which failed to make it a suitable campaign issue; that its effects had yet to be fully recognized; and that the adherents of extensive economic integration had more to gain from EU membership (1998: 79). In this context, it is worth recalling that EFTA countries had always wanted more comprehensive relations with the EU than was provided for in the EEA Agreement. Austria had requested, for instance, a relationship that included agriculture. During the EEA negotiations, the Austrian government also emphasized the importance of full participation in the customs union and EU decision-making (Kaiser 1995: 412).

On a more fundamental level, the prominence of economic arguments reflected the fact that the three membership campaigns took place against the backdrop of an economic downturn. In Austria, nationalized industries had been in a state of deep crisis since the mid-1980s. Unemployment was on the rise and the economic system was perceived to be in need of major structural reform (Kaiser 1995: 412). The Finnish economy fell into deep recession at the end of 1990. Between 1990 and 1993, GDP in Finland dropped by 10.5% and the unemployment rate rose sharply from 3.2 to 16.6%. It was an extreme economic event (Verho 2008: 3). In Sweden, which did not have to deal with the collapse of bilateral trade with USSR, the crisis was less severe. Unemployment in this country nevertheless rose from 2 to 10% in the period 1993–1997. In both countries, the crises were closely related to the financial liberalization in the mid-1980s (Jonung et al. 2009: 21). While economic arguments were also important to membership supporters in Norway, many more Finns and Swedes saw EU membership as an opportunity for improvements in the economy and as a measure that would have positive employment effects.

In all three countries, both sides made frequent use of arguments related to the interrelated concepts of democracy and sovereignty. EU membership opponents argued that membership would entail a loss of national independence through the delegation of sovereignty to the EU and a loss of democracy, as the EU political system suffered from a democratic deficit. In contrast, advocates of accession stressed the fact that only as a member would countries be able to participate in EU decision-making. This argument was prominent in the 'Yes' campaigns in Austria, Sweden and Finland.

Alongside common topics, a series of country-specific arguments made their mark on the debates. National security issues were important for the pro-EU sides in all countries but the closeness to Russia made this aspect particularly relevant in Finland. Here, the concern with security arguably also travelled under the guise of identity arguments. The claim that membership would tie Finland to the block of Western democracies to which it had belonged since 1917 played a central role in the Finnish debate, where it proved to have particular appeal to the younger generation (Arter 1995: 361). The conditions for joining the Common Agricultural Policy (CAP) was another key issue in Finland. The attention given to this topic reflected the internal division between the farmers as a social group on the one hand, and the stand of this group's political representative on the other (Raunio and Tiilikainen 2003: 25). While the vast majority of Finnish farmers were opposed to membership of the EU, the party representing their interests, the Centre Party, was the lead party in the pro-membership coalition government (Arter 1995: 376).

In Austria, opponents of accession responded to the dominating economic discourse with ecological arguments. Such arguments appeared, for instance, in connection with discussions on one of the most challenging topics in Austria's relations with the EU, namely the question of transit traffic through the Tyrol region. The focus on drugs-related concerns constituted, in turn, a characteristic feature of the Swedish debate. This country had a restrictive policy on drugs. While opponents argued that the liberation of border controls would lead to an increase in drugs abuse, proponents argued that membership would enable Sweden to upload its national policies in this field to the European level (Detlef and Storsved 1995: 32).

In all three countries, the debate exposed a split between traditionalists and modernizers. The general assumption was that accession would disadvantage the traditional primary industries together with other sectors dependent on protectionism and state aid. In all three countries, opposition was strongest in rural areas—in the far west of Austria and the northernmost parts of Sweden and Finland. In contrast, modern sectors of the economy were confident in accruing significant benefits from membership. As Fitzmaurice points out, 'In broader terms, this became a debate about ways of life, between urban and rural cultures and rural depopulation' (Fitzmaurice 1995: 229). The 'green' strand in opposition to membership constituted another common denominator. The Green parties in Austria and Sweden were critical of the EU on environmental grounds. They feared a weakening of environmental and social policy standards and doubted that they would be able to mobilize sufficiently against unwanted pieces of Community legislation (Fitzmaurice 1995: 229).

23.5.1   The Results

In Austria, the 'Yes' vote surpassed all expectations. In all the nine *Bundesländer*, a majority of voters came out in favour of membership. Support was lowest in Tyrol, with a 'Yes' rate of 56.7%, and highest in Burgenland, where 74.7% cast their votes in favour of joining. In Tyrol, the voting behaviour reflected the worry that membership would intensify traffic over the Brenner Pass. Burgenland was eligible for funding from the EU's Cohesion Fund for less developed areas. The Governor of Burgenland highlighted the area's status as an Objective 1 area as a key factor when explaining the region's positive stance towards EU membership (Müller 2009: 17). The 'Yes' vote ratio was lowest among farmers (34%), followed by blue-collar workers (49%), students (52%) and professionally inactive housewives (52%). The approval rate was highest among white-collar workers (59%), retirees (59%) and self-employed people (54%). Men were more ready to vote 'Yes' than women, while young people under thirty (aged 18–29) were more likely to vote 'No' than people over fifty (Müller 2009: 17). Overall, 'Yes' voters listed economic advantages, the possibility of obtaining jobs and training abroad, the abolition of borders and the possibility of influencing European level policymaking as their most important reasons for voting to join. Concerns relating to the effects on the agricultural sector, fears of increased unemployment, threats to the status of neutrality, and deterioration in the quality of products and the environment mobilized 'No' voters (Pelinka and Greiderer 1996: 28).

The Finnish referendum offered no real surprises. In keeping with expectations, voters in urban areas cast their votes for accession, while voters in rural areas voted against membership. Women were less supportive (54%) of joining than men (61%) and people with higher education and better incomes were more pro-membership than those at the other end of the education and income scales. While only 6% of Finnish farmers cast their vote in favour of accession, corresponding figures for blue-collar workers, white-collar workers and management were 53, 65 and 73% respectively (Raunio and Tiilikainen 2003: 34). Data collected after the vote found that arguments relating to democracy, independence and neutrality mobilized the 'No' voters, while arguments pertaining to the economy, security, identity and greater influence were the ones that primarily energized pro-EU voters (Suksi 1996: 58–59; Jenssen et al. 1998: 310). The existing research argues that in the Finnish case, identity arguments had security undertones and that this was particularly the case for the older generation (Arter 1995: 383; Jenssen et al. 1998: 310). Economic gains motivated the 'Yes' side in all three countries examined in this chapter. Jenssen et al. point out, however, that it was only after Russian nationalists had made threatening statements about Finland that Finnish public opinion swung decisively in favour of EU membership (Jenssen et al. 1998: 310).

In light of the Swedish establishment's strong support for membership, the fact that nearly half of the voters cast their votes against accession to the EU is remarkable. As was the case in Austria, men, persons over the age of 50 and the professionally active were more likely to vote for membership than were women, younger voters, the unemployed and the retired. As was the case in both Austria and Finland, support for accession was stronger among managers than among blue-collar workers. In Sweden, both supporters and opponents made arguments pertaining to democracy and the economy, issues that were seen as vital in how they voted. Those who voted in favour of Swedish accession stressed how EU membership was a means to gain access to EU-level decision-making, and thereby to increase democratic control with issues that transcended national borders. The opponents argued that Sweden's domestic democracy would suffer from the delegation of authority to Brussels-based institutions, perceived as less democratic. As for the economic arguments, supporters of joining considered entry as a means to improve the conditions for Swedish trade and exports. Opponents, by contrast, feared that it would lead to a weakening of economic growth and increased unemployment (Jungar 2002: 400–401).

23.6   Conclusion

For the Austrian, Finnish and Swedish governments, the 1994 referendums constituted the final chapter in a debate that had been ongoing for 35 years. In the course of this period, their relations with the EU had slowly developed from foreign policy cooperation to deeper economic integration without full Community membership. The experience gained in the course of this process shaped their policies towards the EU and the domestic debates and campaigns in the run-up to the referendums. Ultimately, these three countries all wanted more than the EEA framework provided for. As seen from the perspective of both government and voter, full membership offered better prospects for economic growth, for security, for the nurturing of a western identity and, crucially, a seat at the table in Brussels as an equal partner. While the history of the 1994 referendums is one of continuity, it is also one of ruptures. While the military neutrality of these three countries constituted very different kinds of policy constraints, the end of the Cold War created unexpected space for greater foreign policy flexibility and possibilities for Helsinki, Stockholm and Vienna. The prominence of economic arguments in the referendum debates, while not a real surprise, was given added prominence at a time when domestic and international economic crises were shaping the European policies of each country.

Bibliography

Arter, D. (1995). The EU Referendum in Finland on 16 October 1994: A Vote for the West, not for Maastricht. *Journal of Common Market Studies, 33*(3), 361–387.

Beach, D. (2018). *Referendums in the European Union*, Oxford Research Encyclopedias, Online Publication Date: Feb 2018.

Bjørklund, T. (1996). The Three Nordic 1994 Referenda Concerning Membership in the EU. *Cooperation and Conflict, 31*(1), 11–36.

Detlef, J., & Storsved, A.-S. (1995). Legitimacy Through Referendum? The Nearly Successful Domino-Strategy of the EU Referendums in Austria, Finland, Sweden and Norway. *West European Politics, 18*(4), 18–37.

Dupont, C., Sciarini, P., & Lutterbeck, D. (1999). Catching the EC Train: Austria and Switzerland in Comparative Perspective. *European Journal of International Relations, 5*(2), 189–224.

EFTA. (1959). *Resolution adopted by EFTA* (Stockholm, 20 November 1959). Available at https://www.cvce.eu/. Accessed on 3 July 2019.

European Commission for Democracy through Law (Venice Commission) (2005). *Referendums in Europe—An Analysis of the Legal Rules in European States*. Study No. 287/2004.

Fitzmaurice, J. (1995). The 1994 Referenda on EU Membership in Austria and Scandinavia: A Comparative Analysis. *Electoral Studies, 14*(2), 226–232.

Jahn, D., Pesonen, P., Slaata, T., & Åberg, L. (1998). The Actors and the Campaigns. In A. T. Jenssen, P. Pesonen, & M. Gilljam (Eds.), *To Join or Not to Join: Three Nordic Referendums on Membership in the European Union* (pp. 61–84). Oslo: Scandinavian University Press.

Jenssen, A. T., Gilljam, M., & Pesonen, P. (1998). The Citizens, the Referendums and the European Union. In A. T. Jenssen, P. Pesonen, & M. Gilljam (Eds.), *To Join or Not to Join: Three Nordic Referendums on Membership in the European Union* (pp. 309–326). Oslo: Scandinavian University Press.

Johansson, K. M., & Raunio, T. (2001). Partisan Responses to Europe: Comparing Finnish and Swedish Political Parties. *European Journal of Political Research, 39*, 225–249.

Jonung, L., Kiander, J., & Vartia, P. (2009). The Great Financial Crisis in Finland and Sweden: The Dynamics of Boom, Bust and Recovery 1985–2000. In L. Jonung, J. Kiander, & P. Vartia (Eds.), *The Great Financial Crisis in Finland and Sweden: The Nordic Experience of Financial Liberalization* (pp. 19–70). Northampton: Edward Elgar.

Jungar, A.-C. (2002). Integration by Different Means: Finland and Sweden in the EU. *Scandinavian Studies, 74*(3), 397–426.

Kaiser, W. (1995). Austria in the European Union. *Journal of Common Market Studies, 33*, 411–425.

Kaiser, W., Visuri, P., Malmström, C., & Hjelseth, A. (1995). Die EU-Volkabstimmungen in Österreich, Finland, Schweden und Norwegen: Folgen für die Europäische Union. *Integration, 18*(2), 76–87.

Luif, P. (1998). Austria: Adaptation through Anticipation. In K. Hanf & B. Soetendorp (Eds.), *Adapting to European Integration: Small States and the European Union* (pp. 116–130). London and New York: Longman.

Meyer, S. (2011). Ideas of Europe in Austrian Parliamentarian Discourse. In C. T. Ramos (Ed.), *Ideas of Europe in National Political Discourse* (pp. 199–228). Bologna: il Mulino.

Miles, L. (1996). The Nordic Countries and the Fourth EU Enlargement. In L. Miles (Ed.), *The European Union and the Nordic Countries* (pp. 63–80). London: Routledge.

Müller, M. H. (2009). *Taking Stock of the Austrian Accession to the EU: With Regard to the Arguments of its Referendum Campaign in 1994*. Mémoire présenté pour l'obtention du Master en études européennes, Institut Européen de l'université de Genève, Collection Euryopa Vol. 57-2009.

Pelinka, A., & Greiderer, S. (1996). Austria: The Referendum as an Instrument of Internationalization. In M. Gallagher & P. V. Uleri (Eds.), *The Referendum Experience in Europe* (pp. 20–32). Basingstoke: Macmillan.

Raunio, T. (1999). Facing the European Challenge: Finnish Parties Adjust to the Integration Process. *West European Politics, 22*(1), 138–159.

Raunio, T., & Tiilikainen, T. (2003). *Finland in the European Union*. London: Frank Cass.

Robertson, D. (1970). Effects of EFTA on Member Countries. In H. Corbet & D. Robertson (Eds.), *Europe's Free Trade Area Experiment. E.F.T.A. and Economic Integration* (pp. 79–112). Oxford: Pergamon Press.

Ruin, O. (1996). Sweden: The Referendum as an Instrument for Defusing Political Issues. In M. Gallagher & P. V. Uleri (Eds.), *The Referendum Experience in Europe* (pp. 171–184). Basingstoke: Macmillan.

Rye, L. (2015). EFTA's Quest for Free Trade in Western Europe (1960–1992): Slow train coming. *EFTA Bulletin* (July), 4–17.

Rye, L. (2017). Integration from the Outside: The EC and EFTA from 1960 to the 1995 Enlargement. In H. Ikonomou, A. Andry & R. Byberg (Eds.), *European Enlargement across Rounds and Beyond Borders* (pp. 194–214). London and New York: Routledge.

Schymik, C. (2009). Anti-EU Movements and Nordic Cooperation. In N. Götz & H. Haggrén (Eds.), *Regional Cooperation and International Organizations: The Nordic Model in Transnational Alignment* (pp. 201–215). London and New York: Routledge.

Schymik, C. (2011). European Antifederalists. In H. Høibraaten & J. Hille (Eds.), *Northern Europe and the Future of the EU* (pp. 49–66). Berlin: Berliner Wissenschafts-Verlag.

Suksi, M. (1996). Finland: The Referendum as a Dormant Feature. In M. Gallagher & P. V. Uleri (Eds.), *The Referendum Experience in Europe* (pp. 52–65). Basingstoke: Macmillan.

Svensson, P. (1996). Denmark: The Referendum as Minority Protection. In M. Gallagher & P. V. Uleri (Eds.), *The Referendum Experience in Europe* (pp. 33–51). Basingstoke: Macmillan.

Tiilikainen, T. (2006). Finland—An EU Member with a Small State Identity. *European Integration, 28*(1), 73–87.

Verho, J. (2008). *Scars of Recession: The Long-Term Costs of the Finnish Economic Crisis*, Institute for Labour Market Policy Evaluation (IFAU), (Working Paper 2008: 9).

Winand, P. (1993). *Eisenhower, Kennedy, and the United States of Europe*. New York: St. Martin's Press.

CHAPTER 24

EU Accession Referendums

Fernando Mendez and Mario Mendez

24.1 Introduction

The European Union (EU) itself cannot hold referendums but since 1972 it has been the object of them as states and sub-national entities have held referendums on a range of different matters pertaining to the EU. Over fifty such referendums have been held to date and this has given rise to a rich and growing body of literature across a number of disciplines that has explored questions such as: why they are called and how they can be avoided, how they should be regulated, their outcomes and how campaigning, political parties and turnout affect these outcomes, as well as how voters decide (recent contributions include Auer 2016; Qvortrup 2016; Mendez and Mendez 2017a; Lacey 2017a; Beach 2018). There are various typologies in the literature concerning EU referendums that normally involve between three and five categories of such referendums (e.g. Hobolt 2009; Auer 2016; Mendez and Mendez 2017a; Lacey 2017a; Beach 2018). Membership referendums are typically included as a category that encapsulates both referendums on joining

F. Mendez
University of Zürich, Zurich, Switzerland
e-mail: Fernando.Mendez@zda.uzh.ch

M. Mendez (✉)
School of Law, Queen Mary University of London, London, UK
e-mail: mario.mendez@qmul.ac.uk

J. Smith (ed.), *The Palgrave Handbook of European Referendums*,
https://doi.org/10.1007/978-3-030-55803-1_24

and leaving the political organisation that is now called the EU.[1] This chapter explores those on joining, which we will refer to as EU accession referendums, with reference to other categories of EU referendum were relevant to the analysis.

The core of the chapter will focus on the distinct rounds of enlargement that have given rise to referendums while also mentioning those that avoided referendums as a legitimation device. The aim is to highlight the context and the debates that surrounded these referendums, beginning with the first deployment of the accession referendum in 1972 through to its most recent appearance in 2012. Most European countries have grappled with accession to the EU in their past or are still in the process of negotiating accession. This includes microstates within the core of the EU, such as San Marino, through to the largest of European states such as Turkey on the periphery. The focus of this chapter, however, is on those candidate countries that have actually held referendums on joining the EU. This excludes a number of cases, such as those in Switzerland (see Church in this handbook) or most recently, in San Marino, in which referendums have been held on the domestic issue of pursuing a policy to join the EU.

After presenting the various enlargement rounds and the referendum events generated (or avoided) we take a more panoramic view of the accession referendum. In doing so, we deal with some of the issues raised in the various enlargement rounds at a broader level while answering a specific research question: is there anything distinctive about the accession referendum at the aggregate level? By way of conclusion, the final section summarises some of our key arguments about this particular type of referendum while also touching on its future evolution.

24.2   Enlargement Rounds and Accession Referendums

This section focuses on the enlargement of the EU with a particular emphasis on the enlargement rounds that have led to referendums. Not all enlargements generate accession referendums and understanding the reasons for this is a question of interest in and of itself. As can be seen in Table 24.1, the accession referendum made its first appearance in the 1970s and, with the exception of the 1980s, has been present in every decade since. Before delving into the details of the enlargement rounds, it is appropriate to comment briefly on the absence of the referendum device at the EU's founding, via the two Treaties of Rome of 1957 establishing the original European Communities (EC), which, like the earlier European Coal and Steel Community Treaty of 1951, provided for the would-be founding Members to ratify 'in accordance with

---

[1] Some have used membership referendums as a broader category to include those referendums held by third states on their relationship with the EU (e.g. Hobolt 2009; Mendez et al. 2014).

Table 24.1 Yes votes and turnout in accession referendums

Case	Date	Yes vote (%)	Turnout (%)
Ireland	10-05-1972	83.10	70.88
Norway	26-09-1972	46.49	79.22
Denmark	02-10-1972	63.39	90.14
Austria	12-06-1994	66.58	82.35
Sweden	13-10-1994	52.74	83.32
Finland	16-10-1994	56.89	70.79
Åland Islands	20-11-1994	73.64	49.10
Norway	28-11-1994	47.82	89.04
Malta	08-03-2003	53.64	90.86
Slovenia	23-03-2003	89.64	60.41
Hungary	12-04-2003	83.76	45.62
Lithuania	11-05-2003	91.07	63.37
Slovakia	17-05-2003	93.71	52.15
Poland	08-06-2003	77.45	58.85
Czech Republic	14-06-2003	77.33	55.21
Estonia	14-09-2003	66.83	64.06
Latvia	21-09-2003	66.97	72.53
Romania*	19-10-2003	91.06	55.70
Croatia	22-01-2012	66.27	43.51

*Romania's referendum vote was on a constitutional amendment

their respective constitutional requirements'.[2] That none of the six founding Member States sought to put the issue of membership to popular approval can be explained by a number of factors. Firstly, although these treaties most certainly gave rise to domestic constitutional controversy, their true constitutional import would not become apparent until later. A second and directly related reason is that, with the exception of Belgium, to the extent that the treaties were constitutionally novel they were being accommodated domestically by the presence of new constitutional provisions that legitimised the delegating of powers to international organisations (de Witte 2001). Thirdly, referendum practice was a rare occurrence outside Switzerland prior to the 1960s and rarer still in relation to treaties (for data, see Morel 2018). At least one of the founders, Germany, would have needed a constitutional amendment to permit use of a referendum. As a result, it is unsurprising that the referendum device was not used at the founding of this international organisation. The accession referendum was to emerge at the first realistic juncture for its use, namely when the EC first enlarged.

[2]Article 224 EAEC Treaty; Article 247 EEC Treaty; Article 98 ECSC Treaty.

24.2.1   The First Enlargement Wave and the Birth of the Accession Referendum

The EU's rules on accession (currently outlined in Article 49 TEU) stipulate the requirement for an accession treaty between the applicant state and the Member States that will be submitted for ratification by all the contracting parties in accordance with their respective constitutional requirements. It is thus largely at the constitutional discretion of the accession state, and its internal organisation, as to whether a referendum or referendums (in the event of separate sub-national unit referendums) will be held as a precursor to accession. The cross-referencing to domestic constitutional requirements has always been reiterated in the accession treaties themselves. The first round of enlargement culminated in an accession treaty that was signed in Brussels in January 1972 by the existing six Member States and the 'candidate countries' of Denmark, Ireland, Norway and the UK. By then the constitutional significance of the EU and the limitations on sovereignty that membership entailed had become considerably more pronounced particularly as a result of a number of court-inspired legal developments.[3] Three of the four signatory states duly held referendums on accession.

Ireland was the first to do so (see Chapter 20 by Svensson).[4] The Irish Constitution of 1937, like its 1922 predecessor, contains a constitutional amendment procedure requiring a referendum. The major constitutional ramifications signalled by accession meant that there was never any doubt that a constitutional amendment and thus a referendum was required.[5] Following the passage of the Third Amendment of the Constitution Act by the bicameral Irish parliament in 1972, the Irish people duly voted in May 1972 in favour of membership by an overwhelming majority of 83.1% on a 70.9% turnout (the highest turnout achieved on an Irish constitutional amendment referendum to date). The Yes campaign was supported by the then governing party (*Fianna Fáil*) and the main opposition party (*Fine Gael*), whilst the No campaign had the backing of the then third and fourth largest parties (Labour and *Sinn Feín*) as well as the main trade unions (see Svensson at Chapter 20 of this handbook).

The Norwegian accession referendum was the second accession referendum to be held (see Chapter 21 by Fossum & Rosén. In contrast to the Irish referendum, it was not constitutionally mandatory. Indeed Norway's Constitution had been amended ten years before the 1972 accession referendum to require

---

[3] These included the EU law principles of direct effect, supremacy, and implied powers (see Weiler 1991 for the classic account of such developments).

[4] This was the second EU-related referendum to be held, as France had held the very first EU referendum some weeks earlier on whether the French people approved of the EU enlarging to include these four new Member States (see Chapters 9 and 20 by Morel and Svensson).

[5] The 1970 White Paper on membership expressly stated that accession 'would involve an amendment of the Constitution'.

a super-majority of three-quarters for parliamentary approval to participate in supranational organisations, a provision inserted precisely to accommodate EU accession (Anderson 1965). There was a persuasive case for the need to secure popular endorsement given developments since the Norwegian transfer of powers clause was enacted, which included the deepening of political and legal integration and, crucially, the fact that Norway's Nordic neighbour (Denmark) was holding an accession referendum as well as Ireland. The Norwegian accession referendum was the first example of what the literature has referred to as a 'mediating referendum', that is a referendum convened primarily for healing divisions within a party in government or among a governing coalition (Mendez et al. 2014: 80). Ultimately internal party divisions on EU accession were such that the decision was taken by a minority Labour government to hold a referendum to try and hold the party together (Björklund 1982). There was significant elite level contestation during the campaign with centrist parties opposing membership. Also, while the grassroots 'People's movement against Norwegian Membership of the Common Market' began campaigning against membership as soon as the application was announced, the Yes campaign did not begin until the negotiations were concluded (Sogner and Archer 1995). The No vote that opinion polls had been predicting in the months leading up to this hotly contested referendum emerged with 53% voting against on a 79.2% turnout, despite the minority Labour government having made this an issue of confidence (Sogner and Archer 1995).

The third accession referendum was held by Denmark only a week after its Nordic neighbour had voted against accession. The Danish Constitution also contained a transfer of powers clause drafted with the European integration project in mind. The Danish clause predated the Norwegian variant by nearly a decade and had a higher approval requirement, five-sixths of MPs. In the absence of that hurdle being surmounted but a parliamentary majority being obtained, then the issue is put to a referendum with rejection requiring a majority of at least 30% of the electorate (Danielsen 2010). A referendum would therefore not have been constitutionally mandatory if the five-sixths parliamentary majority had been met.[6] Constitutional issues aside, a political agreement had in any case been reached by the main parties on holding a referendum regardless of the parliamentary vote (Koch 2001: 110). The political ramifications of accession were such that accession could only be legitimated via direct popular approval. As it turned out, the five-sixths parliamentary threshold was not obtained and a referendum thus became constitutionally mandatory (Svensson 2002: 736; see also Chapter 20 by Svensson in this handbook). That vote saw 63.3% vote in favour of membership on a 90.1% turnout.[7]

[6]A constitutional challenge arguing that the constitutional amendment procedures would need to be used for accession, and thus an obligatory referendum held, was rejected (see Danielsen 2010).

[7]As a constituent part of Denmark, Greenland voted overwhelmingly against joining in the 1972 accession referendum. Following the granting of a form of home rule, Greenland voted to withdraw in 1982 by a small majority which duly took place in 1985.

It was telling that the only candidate country not to hold an accession referendum was the United Kingdom (UK). The only state without a codified constitution, one in which a national referendum had never previously been held and where it was thus generally viewed as a constitutionally alien device. Despite this there were in fact calls for a referendum on accession including attempted amendments to require one in the legislation providing the basis for EU accession (Norton 2011: 58, 60). Recourse was also had to the Courts where the argument that accession constituted an irreversible transfer of sovereignty only constitutionally permissible through the adoption of a new constitution consented to by the people was dismissed.[8] Shortly after accession the Labour opposition party committed itself to renegotiating membership and a referendum. This it duly implemented when it came to power in 1974, thus giving birth to the category of 'withdrawal referendums'. This latter referendum on continued membership was held a mere two and a half years after accession and was comfortably won (for detailed discussion of both the 1975 referendum and the repeat referendum in 2016, see Chapter 22 by Smith in this Handbook).

24.2.2   Southern European Enlargement & Avoiding the Accession Referendum

The 1980s saw the EU gain three new Southern European Member States that were all relatively economically underdeveloped, former military dictatorships and for which EU membership signalled an important and symbolic integration into the Western democratic fold. All three avoided the popular approval route to accession.

Greece signed an accession treaty in May 1979, which the Greek Parliament approved the very next month, with Greece joining in January 1981. The Greek Constitution of 1975 contained an express transfer of powers clause with a view to EU accession requiring a three-fifths majority in Parliament, and a limitation of sovereignty clause requiring an absolute majority. The appropriate procedure generated constitutional debate, but the point became moot when the Greek Parliament voted overwhelmingly in favour of accession in June 1979 (Chryssogonos 2001: 141–142). The Constitution empowers a large proportion of parliamentarians (two-fifths of total members) and the cabinet to propose a referendum subject to parliamentary approval. A referendum, however, was not considered by the governing centre-right New Democracy (ND) party. The opposition socialists (PASOK) which obtained more seats in the 1977 elections than expected, albeit short of one-third, had a manifesto commitment to hold a referendum on Greek membership and boycotted the parliamentary approval debate in June 1979 (Verney 2011: 57). As it turns out Greece did not hold a referendum under its 1975 Constitution

---

[8] Blackburn v Attorney General [1971] 1 WLR 1037.

until its recent, notoriously polarising referendum on Greece's bailout in 2015 (see Papadopoulou elsewhere in this handbook).

Greece joined prior to the integrationist steps signalled by the first treaty revision round—the 1986 Single European Act—even being on the agenda. That is one contrast that might be drawn with Spain and Portugal where treaty revision was firmly on the agenda by the time they signed their accession treaty in June 1985. The intergovernmental conference was still some months away and the Single European Act that flowed from it was not signed until a month after Spain and Portugal joined in January 1986. In the Spanish case, the Constitution of 1978 contains a general transfer of powers clause drafted with the EU in mind (Ferreres Comella 2013: 17, 65). It requires an increased quorum—an absolute parliamentary majority in one chamber. It was this option that was pursued for accession, with the treaty receiving unanimous support in the lower house (Lloréns 2003). Spanish public opinion was 'overwhelmingly favourable to adhesion' (López Gómez 2014: 87) and a referendum was never seriously considered. The ruling Socialists were already in the difficult position of upholding a 1982 manifesto commitment on a referendum to leave NATO, which Spain had joined in 1982. The Socialist leader performed a *volte-face* on NATO upon entering government and successfully campaigned to deliver a vote to remain in a referendum deferred until EC accession was assured (Powell 2009). The NATO referendum was Spain's first national referendum under its 1978 Constitution; the only other national referendum was the 2005 Yes vote to the ill-fated Constitutional Treaty (Ferreres Comella 2013: 37–39).

In Portugal the ordinary treaty approval procedure, via a simple parliamentary majority, was used to legitimate accession. Surprisingly, the Portuguese constitutional system then had no delegation of powers clause, one was added prior to the Maastricht Treaty ratification. Portugal, unlike the two other Southern European states that joined in the 1980s, had actually never held a national referendum. So it is perhaps unsurprising that an accession referendum was not seriously contemplated, not least given that the Constitution contained a provision barring treaty-ratification referendums, which was not to be lifted for more than a decade (Moura Ramos 2001).

24.2.3 The Nordic and Austrian Enlargement Round

An accession treaty was signed in 1994 by the EU's existing Member States and Norway, Austria, Finland and Sweden. All four candidate states held accession referendums. It is commonly said that there was a 'domino strategy' whereby the most pro-EU populations would vote first to encourage the others to vote accordingly (Jahn and Storsved 1995: 21; Hobolt 2009: 11). Austria went first with a constitutionally mandatory referendum held in June 1994. The Austrian Constitution requires a referendum for total revisions of the constitution and EU accession was viewed as constituting such a total revision (Stelzer 2013). The Yes campaign in Austria was reported to have received the backing of employer, labour and farming associations along with the conservative parties and social democrats, the No campaign being carried by anti-establishment parties (Jahn and Storsved 1995). The referendum delivered the anticipated strong endorsement of membership: 66.6% in favour on an 82% turnout.

The three Nordic countries came next. Finland's Constitution allowed for the use of an 'exceptive enactment' requiring a two-thirds parliamentary majority where a treaty conflicted with the Constitution as EU accession was considered to do. This was accordingly the procedure used (Ojanen 2013: 105). However, the coalition government decided also to hold a consultative referendum on accession. Undoubtedly a plausible case can be made for its necessity to legitimise such a momentous step, especially in the post-Maastricht era with the deepening of integration particularly in the monetary and foreign policy spheres. But it was also the case that this was only the second referendum ever held in Finland, and the first in over 60 years. It 'helped to rein in a substantial split within the largest government party, the Centre Party, and took an issue off the agenda of inter-party politics which was contested between the coalition parties' (Oppermann 2013: 694). In a setting of a serious economic recession with high unemployment and security concerns vis-à-vis Russia, the Yes campaign was supported by most major political parties (the Greens did not have an official position and the former Communists were against membership) as well as employers' associations (Björklund 1996). On a 74% turnout, the Finnish voted 56.9% in favour of accession. Approval in the relatively autonomous and primarily Swedish-speaking province of the Åland Islands was lower than the national average at 51.9%, as was the turnout at 61.2%, but they were able to hold their own separate consultative referendum a month later in which the Yes vote increased dramatically to 73.6%, albeit on a lower turnout (49.1%) (see Björklund 1996: 17–18; Jahn and Storsved 1995: 26). This is to date the only example of a sub-national accession referendum being held, a sub-national withdrawal referendum having already been held by the Danish province of Greenland in 1982.

Sweden was the third of these candidate states to hold an accession referendum. The Constitution had been amended in 1965 to include a transfer of powers clause partly with a view to eventual EU accession. That clause was no longer viewed as a constitutionally adequate basis for accession in the early 1990s and was amended in 1994 so that accession would require either a three-quarters majority parliamentary approval or use of the constitutional amendment procedures (Griller 2001: 169–170). The latter option was chosen in combination with a consultative referendum. As with the earlier Finnish consultative referendum, a persuasive case could be made for the necessity of popular approval to legitimise accession, nonetheless it is frequently identified as a referendum called to mediate internal party divisions in the governing party (Aylott 2002: 447–450). As with Finland, Sweden was also suffering from an economic recession in the early 1990s, and the Yes vote was supported by business, occupational and professional organisations and all but two of the parties represented in Parliament (the former Communist Party and the Greens, which had only regained parliamentary representation in the months running up to the referendum: Björklund 1996: 15). Nonetheless a relatively close vote followed in which, on an 83.3% turnout, 52.3% voted in favour. It has been suggested that the domino strategy, with Austria and Finland having already approved accession, may have worked for the Swedish case (Jahn and Storsved 1995).

Like the other Nordic candidate states of this accession round, Norway's referendum was not constitutionally mandatory. Norway however was in the very distinct position of having seen a popular rejection of membership two decades earlier, and an accession referendum was thus viewed as the de facto obligatory means to membership of an organisation that had also taken qualitative steps forward in integration since the earlier popular vote. The circumstances were not nearly as propitious as in the two other Nordic countries. Anti-accession parties had a substantial parliamentary presence, including influential political parties in the centre,[9] the No to the EU campaign was already organised on a national basis when the government applied for membership, the Federation of Trade Unions voted to oppose membership (having supported membership in 1972) and farming and most fishery organisations remained against (Sogner and Archer 1995; Björklund 1996). In November 1994 on an 88.8% turnout, 52.3% voted against membership of an organisation to which one Nordic state had long been a member, the Danes having voted to accede after the first Norwegian rejection in 1972, and which another two (Finland and Sweden) would imminently join following the popular approval delivered shortly before the second Norwegian referendum. The much-noted domino strategy (Jahn and Storsved 1995) was thus ultimately unable to bring Norwegian public opinion on board with the EU project.

24.2.4 The 'Big Bang' Enlargement

In May 2003 an accession treaty was signed by the EU's existing Member States and ten states of which all bar the two Mediterranean islands of Cyprus and Malta were post-Communist Central and Eastern European countries. This gave rise to the biggest expansion in terms of number of states and population added to the EU, often dubbed the 'big bang enlargement'. It also gave rise to the largest number of EU accession referendums held, more than all previous enlargement rounds combined as, over a six-month period, nine states put the issue of the accession treaty to popular approval, which it duly received in all nine.

---

[9]According to Hobolt (2009: 148) pro-EU parties made up 65% of the seats in Parliament.

24.2.4.1   Malta

The first referendum was held by Malta in March 2003, its very first national referendum under its 1964 Constitution and one that was a non-constitutionally mandatory consultative referendum (referred to as 'de facto binding' on the incumbent government by Cini 2004: 29). In this two-party system, the opposition Labour party campaigned against EU membership, as did the largest Maltese trade union, while the Yes campaign was supported by the governing Nationalist Party, much of the business community, and certain trade unions (Cini 2004). This gave rise to a heated campaign and a close result with 53.65% voting in favour on what remains the largest turnout ever seen for an EU accession referendum—90.86%—(Denmark in 1972 being the only other country to surpass 90% turnout for an accession referendum). As Cini (2004: 37) pointed out, referendum turnout mirrored the high levels of electoral participation in general elections. A general election called by the governing party immediately followed, which it duly won. The timing of the referendum was potentially strategically driven by a relatively unpopular government wanting to use a positive referendum to boost its chances of securing a further term of office (Cini 2004).

24.2.4.2   Slovenia

Slovenia was the first of the post-Communist states to hold an accession referendum, doing so two weeks after the Maltese referendum. Slovenia's Constitution had been amended earlier that month so that powers could be transferred to international organisations by a two-thirds majority in Parliament, with Parliament able to require a binding referendum before ratification (Albi 2005). A referendum on accession was duly held simultaneously with one on joining NATO. A Yes vote was never in doubt given a particularly congenial environment in which polling in the years and months prior to the referendum had shown consistent majority support for accession. Furthermore, there was a broad consensus in favour of accession among the political elite and all the main political parties. The Slovenian National Party, which was against membership, had less than 5% of the parliamentary seats (Krašovec and Lajh 2004). In March 2003, the then highest Yes vote in an accession referendum—89.64%—was delivered, on an unexpectedly low turnout of 60.4%, the lowest for an accession referendum until then.

24.2.4.3   Hungary

Three weeks after the positive result in Slovenia, popular approval for accession was forthcoming in Hungary with the highest Yes vote share of 83.76% seen in an accession referendum. The positive endorsement was, however, overshadowed by the then lowest turnout by far in an accession referendum, a mere 45.62%. This referendum was mandatory as the Hungarian Constitution had been amended in 2002 to require an accession referendum as well as a delegation of powers clause vis-à-vis the EU that needed two-thirds parliamentary approval (Albi 2005). A Yes result was never really in doubt, with polling leading up to the referendum showing a consistently high majority support for accession, indeed higher than in any of the other Central and Eastern European states set to join in 2004. Also, there was little in the way of contestation with the only parties opposing EU membership being small, non-governing and of the extreme left and right (Fowler 2004). It is because of such high levels of public support for the EU that the Visegrád states (the Czech Republic, Hungary, Poland and Slovakia) are reported to have agreed in 2002 that Hungary should hold its accession referendum first with a view to a 'pro accession cascade effect' (Fowler 2004: 633).

24.2.4.4   Lithuania

Before any further accession referendums by Visegrád states, a Baltic state voted. This was the product of another 'domino strategy' as the Baltic referendums started with the most pro-EU Lithuania (Albi 2005: 154). Although it was concluded that the Lithuanian Constitution did not require a referendum for accession, nor a new constitutional provision on delegating powers, the Parliament opted for a binding referendum (Van Elsuwege 2008: 380–382). There was, however, a high turnout threshold of 50%. The latter helps to explain why law-makers focused energies on encouraging turnout through mechanisms that included extending voting time, making voting permissible over two days, as well as expanding postal voting (Mazylis and Unikaite 2003). Significant turnout concerns aside, it was a favourable setting for a referendum with all major political parties supporting membership (Mazylis and Unikaite 2003). This first Baltic state referendum delivered an unexpectedly high Yes vote of 91% on a 63.37% turnout.

24.2.4.5   Slovakia

Following Lithuania's vote the three remaining Visegrád states voted. Slovakia did so first and delivered the highest Yes vote of any EU referendum ever held at 93.7%, albeit on the then second lowest turnout for an accession referendum (52.15%). While the Yes vote share was certainly impressive and unprecedentedly high, the referendum's validity was only marginally above the 50% turnout requirement. Slovakia's Constitution had been amended in 2001 to include a delegation of powers clause vis-à-vis the EU requiring a three–fifths majority but a referendum was also constitutionally permissible in addition (Kühn 2007). A high Yes vote was expected given the relatively high levels of public support for EU membership. Furthermore, all parliamentary political parties supported EU membership and there was no organised 'No' campaign. Given the high turnout threshold, an abstention strategy may have been followed by opponents with a view to invalidating the referendum (Henderson 2004).

24.2.4.6   Poland

Some three weeks after Slovakia's endorsement of EU accession, the Poles delivered a 77.45% Yes vote on a 58.85% turnout. Poland's new Constitution of 1997, adopted partly with a view to preparing for EU accession, contained a transfer of powers clause requiring a two-thirds majority in both parliamentary chambers while permitting the use of a referendum as an alternative. It was this latter option that the lower chamber selected. Polling in the run-up to the referendum showed consistently high levels of support and there was strong elite consensus in favour of the accession campaign. The government was languishing in the polls but most opposition parties were supportive of a Yes vote (Szczerbiak 2004). Yet, while a majority Yes vote was never in doubt, clearing the high turnout threshold of 50% certainly was. Interestingly, Parliament adopted a law that would allow it to ratify the accession treaty with a super-majority if the 50% threshold was not met in the popular vote (Szczerbiak 2004). As in the case of Lithuania, additional safeguards to help raise turnout were applied such as extending voting over a two-day period. The Yes vote was also assisted by the Polish Pope famously intervening in support of accession, a matter of no small significance in a society where Catholics comprised over 90% of the population (Szczerbiak 2004).

24.2.4.7   Czech Republic
Within days of popular approval in Poland, came popular approval in the Czech Republic. As in Poland, under a newly added transfer of powers clause the Czech Republic's Constitution required a super-majority approval in both houses but this could be substituted by a national referendum (Hanley 2004). In pursuing the referendum route, the Czech Republic's endorsement of accession, at 77.33%, was virtually identical to that of Poland's, albeit on slightly lower turnout of 55.21%. A crucial difference was that in the Czech Republic there was no minimum turnout requirement for the validity of the referendum. At the elite level there was much more polarisation in the Czech Republic than in other Eastern European countries. Indeed, the third largest political party in the lower house, the Communists, campaigned against membership, and a Eurosceptic discourse emanated from the second largest political party albeit without overtly opposing entry. Furthermore, a Eurosceptic President (Václav Klaus) refused to publicly advocate a Yes vote, the only head of an accession state not to do so (Hanley 2004). At the same time, public support for the EU was among the lowest of the Eastern European candidate states. Under such conditions a 77% Yes vote signalled a significant endorsement of accession.

24.2.4.8   Estonia and Latvia
Turning to the remaining Baltic states, Estonia and Latvia, it is noteworthy that the two neighbours organised their votes a week apart in September 2003. No doubt due to the low levels of public enthusiasm for the EU in the Baltic states, there had been high profile proposals to circumvent the accession referendums in all three Baltic states (Albi 2005). In Estonia a constitutional clause precludes treaty-ratification referendums, but an expert commission concluded that it did not preclude an EU accession referendum due to the

national importance of the issue. However, the use of the rigid constitutional amendment procedure with its referendum requirement was bypassed in favour of a supplementing constitutional act on EU accession that needed and received popular approval (Albi 2005). As for Latvia, its Constitution had been amended in 2003 to include a delegation of powers clause that required two-thirds parliamentary approval whilst also requiring a referendum for EU membership albeit on a lower turnout than required for use of the constitutional amendment procedure, namely half the turnout at the previous elections (Albi 2005).

In contrast to neighbouring Lithuania, which delivered the second highest Yes vote in an accession referendum, the Yes votes in Estonia and Latvia were the lowest among the post-Communist states in this accession round at 66.83% and 67% respectively. From a comparative perspective the results nonetheless constitute a strong endorsement of accession, all the more so compared to the other post-Communist states given the higher participation rates in Estonia and Latvia of 64.06% and 72.5% respectively. During the Estonian campaign the opposition Centre Party, which had the greatest parliamentary representation with nearly 30% of the seats, saw a significant part of its leadership campaign for Yes, while the party congress called for a No vote. All other parliamentary parties adopted strongly pro-EU positions (Mikkel and Pridham 2004). In Latvia there was also strong party and elite support for accession. Indeed, in Latvia several parties moved from Eurosceptic to pro-EU positions in the run-up to the referendum, generating virtually complete cross-party consensus (Pridham 2003). While it is possible to talk of high elite consensus in favour of accession, mass opinion in terms of public support for the EU was for these two Baltic states consistently among the lowest of all post-Communist states. Latvia's marginally higher Yes vote than Estonia, might attest to some potential impact of the domino strategy, and certainly the campaign following Estonian approval played on Latvia being left as the isolated Baltic non-EU member state.

24.2.4.9 Cyprus

While the Constitution of the Republic of Cyprus makes no reference to referendums, the referendum is provided for via a legislative Act of 1989. Accession to the EU was pursued without recourse to the referendum, with overwhelming support for joining the EU. The accession treaty was approved with unanimity by the Cypriot Parliament in July 2003 and signed by the President two weeks later. Thus, the Republic of Cyprus would formally join the EU in May 2004 as part of the 2004 enlargement wave. But this is only half the story. Cyprus is a divided island between the Greek side, formally known as the Republic of Cyprus, and the internationally non-recognised Turkish Republic of Northern Cyprus (TRNC). After decades of internationally brokered negotiations, the most significant attempt and historic opportunity to date for the resolution of the Cypriot dispute emerged in the form of the UN-sponsored Annan Plan (Christophorou 2005; Mendez and Triga 2009). The Annan Plan would be put to the people in a referendum on both sides of the island in April 2004, one week before the Republic of Cyprus was due to join the EU. The outcome of the 2004 referendum had significant consequences. If approved by both sides, Cyprus would have joined the EU as a reunified state. The alternative scenario was that the TRNC would be outside the EU since the Republic of Cyprus had already secured accession. In the end, the Greek side failed to endorse the Annan Plan by a significant majority and the EU inherited a divided island. The Annan Plan referendum is therefore indirectly related to accession and helps explain why there was no referendum on accession in Cyprus. Resolution of the so-called Cyprus problem was the only salient issue and joining the EU was part of that solution.

24.2.5   The Post-2004 Enlargement Rounds

Three states joined the EU after 2004, in two accession rounds. The EU's existing Member States signed an accession treaty with two post-Communist states, Bulgaria and Romania, in April 2005 (both countries joined in January 2007). Romania's 1991 Constitution was amended for the first time in 2003 precisely to accommodate EU and NATO accession. This included creating a two-thirds parliamentary majority requirement for accession and future changes to the EU's constitutive treaties. As a constitutional amendment this required popular approval, which it duly received in October 2003 when, on a 55.7% turnout, 91% voted in favour (perhaps unsurprisingly given that Romanian public opinion had been the consistently most pro-EU of the Central and Eastern European countries; Albi 2005: 147). The referendum was thus held contemporaneously with the 2003 wave of enlargement referendums. To be precise it in a sense brought them to a close, coming only weeks after the Latvian referendum. There was never the likelihood of a separate accession referendum in this state, which had commenced accession negotiations along with the other Central and Eastern European states. As a result, this constitutional referendum is frequently categorised as an accession/membership referendum (e.g. Hobolt 2009; Mendez et al. 2014; Qvortrup 2016; Beach 2018) even if it was clearly distinguishable from the accession referendums held on finalised accession treaties. The accession treaty itself was then unanimously approved in 2005 by the bicameral Romanian Parliament (Hoffmeister 2007: 74).

Like Romania, Bulgaria's Constitution was also subject to significant amendments with a view to EU accession, including the addition of a provision permitting ratification of treaties conferring powers on the EU subject to two-thirds parliamentary approval (Hoffmeister 2007: 73–74). This took place in 2005. Unlike the Romanian constitutional amendments, in the case of Bulgaria this did not require popular approval. Popular opinion was highly supportive of membership and while there were calls for an accession referendum, including a Presidential suggestion, the new parliamentary two-thirds approval route was used and delivered near-unanimous approval in the unicameral parliament (Hoffmeister 2007: 73–74). Bulgaria is thus the unique case since 1986 not to have had a referendum that either directly impacted on accession or had the potential to do so indirectly (see earlier discussion on Cyprus).

Croatia signed its accession treaty with the EU's Member States in 2011. A provision in its 1990 Constitution that was drafted with EU accession in mind paradoxically made it difficult to achieve (Rodin and Capeta 2007). This astonishingly rigid provision on 'alliances with other states' required two-thirds parliamentary approval and a referendum with a 50% turnout requirement and a majority of all eligible voters needed to vote in favour. In order to save an accession referendum from failing, the Constitution was amended in 2010 with the support of all the major parties (Butković 2017: 55). Without a constitutional amendment to remove the participation thresholds, the accession may well have failed the turnout requirement and indeed the actual referendum held in 2012 would not have satisfied the previous rules as it only secured a 43.5% turnout, the lowest turnout to date for an accession referendum. While the turnout was poor, the referendum did pass comfortably with a 66.3% vote in favour of membership. The majority of parliamentary parties unreservedly supported EU membership and exhorted citizens to vote for accession, while clear opposition to EU membership was only expressed by one right-wing party with a single parliamentary seat (see Butković 2017: 56).

24.3   Mapping the Accession Referendum

Having dealt with some of the particularities of the individual accession referendums, in this section, we take a broader perspective with a view to mapping some of the aggregate patterns this particular type of referendum has generated. Excluding the case of Romania, which voted on a constitutional amendment to allow for membership of the EU as well as NATO, there have been 18 accession referendums on an actual accession treaty with the EU.

The accession referendum is the most common type of EU-related referendum, accounting for close to 40% of EU referendum activity. In their lengthy treatment of the largest wave of accession referendums, the Eastern enlargement, Szczerbiak and Taggart (2004) suggested that while the accession referendum constituted a specific sub-type it nonetheless allowed for broader generalisation. The question we pose in this section is whether it has any special properties compared to other referendums.

Comparing the accession referendum to all other EU-related referendums allows us to assess whether it constitutes a different species of referendum. Evidently, the accession referendum has a very different subject matter, i.e. that of joining what has now become the EU. But does it differ in other respects such as the degree to which citizens harbour positive attitudes towards the EU, the degree to which they participate or are likely to vote in favour of a pro-EU position? And, in relation to party competition, are there differences

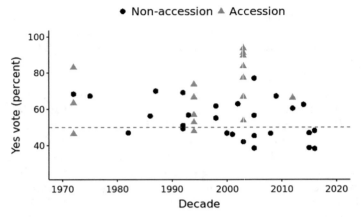

Fig. 24.1   Diffusion of 'accession' referendums over time

with regard to the degree to which parties are polarised on the subject matter of accession? Lastly, does the accession referendum exhibit any particular type of diffusion? This section takes a brief look at these different dimensions. In doing so, it moves the discussion to the aggregate level.

We first focus on the diffusion patterns of the accession referendum. This aspect of the accession referendum has already been covered at length in the preceding section. Figure 24.1 simply shows how the accession referendum is spread over time compared to referendums on EU-related issues other than accession. A clear vertical clustering pattern can be seen at specific points along the *x*-axis, which corresponds to the waves of successive EU enlargement. Figure 24.1 also plots on the *y*-axis the Yes percentage of votes. In the plotted observations, the Yes (per cent) refers to the vote in favour of a pro-EU position (e.g. a Yes vote in favour of a proposed treaty ratification, or Yes vote on an issue of EU integration such as adopting the Euro). The dashed line depicts the 50% threshold for endorsing a positive EU vote. Clearly, there are far fewer observations falling below the threshold among the accession referendums than other referendum types. Indeed, in terms of substantive referendum outcomes, rather than the Yes vote share, accession referendums hardly ever fail—Norway being the sole exception to this empirical regularity. But whether the accession referendum is more positively endorsed than other types of EU referendum is a question we shall probe further below.

We have mentioned a number of putative variables above, with some related to citizens' behaviour or their attitudes and others to party competition. These variables will be the basis for investigating patterns of association by comparing the accession referendums to other types of EU referendum.[10] For citizens there are two key variables that relate to their behaviour, the degree to which

[10] Our data for this analysis are drawn from Mendez and Mendez (2017b).

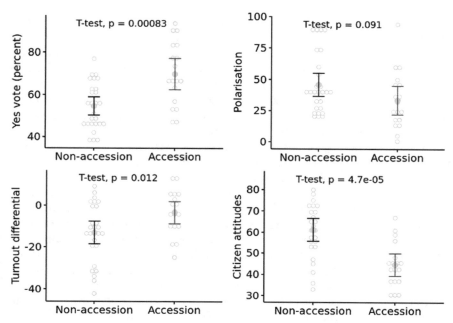

Fig. 24.2 Comparisons of means with 95% confidence intervals for four variables

they endorse a positive EU integration policy and their propensity to participate. The first is straightforward to measure: the Yes vote share. The second raises some issues about how to compare turnout rates. Simply looking at turnout rates across the different countries tells little about whether that level was high or low for a given country. Szczerbiak and Taggart (2004: 770) note that levels of participation at general elections are the crucial determinant and provide a good indicator of the range of turnout to be expected. Thus, to take account of general levels of electoral participation we create a variable that measures the turnout differential compared to the previous parliamentary election. A third citizen-related variable is mass attitudes towards the EU, which can be measured with a standard *Eurobarometer* survey item. The last variable relates to the positions taken by political parties and measures the degree of polarisation among the parties that have gained representation in parliament. A 0 score means complete polarisation while a score of 100 means all parties agree on the pro-EU position.[11]

To examine putative associations we turn to some of the bivariate results. In Fig. 24.2 the four graphs present the group means for the Non-accession versus Accession referendums with 95% confidence intervals. In addition, each plot includes the results of an independent T-test comparison.

---

[11] The score is calculated as the absolute difference in the percentage of parliamentary seats between parties advocating a Yes vote and those advocating a No vote.

Taking the two plots in the top row of Fig. 24.2 first, we inspect the group means for the 'Yes Vote' and the 'Polarization' variables. For the Yes vote share, we notice significant differences in the means between the two groups, 54.9% for non-accession referendums compared to 70.9% for accession. Not surprisingly, given the relatively large difference, the results of the T-test are significant as shown in the graph. For the levels of polarisation we can also see a difference between the two types. The mean level of polarisation index for the accession referendums is 33 compared to 44 for the non-accession referendums. These differences turn out to be statistically significant only if the weaker <0.1 level is used. Further post-hoc inspection reveals that the weakly significant result is driven by the case of Malta (a complete outlier in terms of party polarisation as discussed above). Removing Malta would make the differences in levels of polarisation between accession referendums (low polarisation) and all other EU referendums (higher polarisation) more notable.

Turning to the two graphs in the bottom row of Fig. 24.2 we examine the group means for 'Turnout' and 'Citizen Attitudes' variables. For the turnout differential, we find that on average there is little difference in terms of participation rates for accession referendums and the previous parliamentary election. Specifically, the group mean for accession referendums is only 3.7% less than the most recent parliamentary election. For the non-accession EU referendums there is a much bigger gap between the two electoral events. The group mean for non-accession EU referendums is much lower, 13% less than the most recent parliamentary election.[12] For the last graph in Fig. 24.2, which measures differences in terms of citizens' positive attitudes towards the EU, we also find significant differences between the two types of referendum. Citizens in countries about to hold accession referendums tend to have much lower positive attitudes towards the EU than citizens in those countries that have already joined the EU and hold EU-related referendums.

In sum, accession referendums do seem to exhibit some noteworthy differences when compared to non-accession referendums. They are characterised by lower levels of polarisation among parties and higher Yes vote shares, and smaller difference in levels of turnout when compared to general electoral practices. On the other hand, and somewhat paradoxically, citizens voting in these referendums do not seem to be particularly enthusiastic about the EU.

24.4   CONCLUSION

A first point to underscore is that the EU accession referendum has become the constitutional norm. We have shown that some referendums while not specifically on the accession treaty can be indirectly related to membership (Romania and Cyprus). Leaving the special case of Cyprus aside, only four candidate countries have never sought popular approval for accession (or continuing their membership shortly after joining as was the case for the UK). Three

---

[12]These differences are statistically significant at the <0.5 level.

of those cases were in the Southern enlargement round of the 1980s (Greece, Spain and Portugal) that pre-date the more integrationist steps of the Single European Act. In the post-Maastricht phase only Bulgaria has not held a referendum connected to accession.

Broadly speaking, one can say that accession referendums have been held because they have been constitutionally required or viewed as *de facto* obligatory. This is in stark contrast to other types of EU referendum which have frequently been held for nakedly partisan reasons as indeed was the case for both the UK withdrawal referendums (on the UK specifically see Smith, Chapter 22 in this handbook; for criticism of partisan EU referendums, see Cheneval and Ferrin 2018). In many respects, the referendum cannot be rivalled as a legitimising device as it is the only means of ensuring an express manifestation of the popular will in favour of accession. This also means that a patiently negotiated accession treaty may not be approved, as has twice been the case with Norway. Accession referendums are thus of great benefit to the EU because they reduce the likelihood of states joining without popular, as opposed to parliamentary, support. It is perhaps unsurprising then that some have seen a normative case for them to be made mandatory and for this to be codified in the treaties (Lacey 2017b: 113–114, 226).

We have also shown in this chapter how the accession referendum constitutes a particular sub-species of EU-related referendum. Evidently, its subject matter is very specific, i.e. acceding to the EU. This fact, not surprisingly, appears to have a number of consequences in terms of citizen behaviour, such as notably higher rates of endorsement and higher relative turnout rates than non-accession referendums when both are compared to general levels of electoral participation. It also seems to affect party competition with generally lower levels of polarisation among parties on the referendum issue. Oddly, citizens do not seem to be especially positive about the EU when voting on accession, at least when compared to non-accession EU referendum cases. Yet, candidate states tend to overwhelmingly endorse accession while referendums on European integration held in EU member states more frequently reject the proposals, even in those member states with comparatively high levels of positive EU attitudes. The answer to this conundrum must lie in relation to what is at stake for a candidate country.

Joining the EU is a big issue and has direct and profound consequences for a candidate state. We know from the literature that non-accession referendums can be afflicted by so-called second-order dynamics in which concerns other than the EU issue at stake, such as the popularity of the government of the day, can be a key factor determining a referendum outcome (see Beach 2018 for valuable recent discussion). While there is still some debate as to the continued relevance of the second-order thesis with the EU's growing politicisation, the logic hardly applies to accession referendums given what is at stake during the vote. Indeed, there is no evidence that we are aware of successfully linking second-order voting to accession referendums.

Although this chapter has focused on accession referendums, it is worth highlighting the potential for interaction effects between different types of EU referendum. Having recently held an accession referendum can be used to justify non-recourse to popular approval for other constitutional moments. Many of the big bang enlargement states used this rationale to justify non–recourse to a referendum for legitimising ratification of the Constitutional and Lisbon Treaties (although Poland and the Czech Republic did promise referendums on the Constitutional Treaty) (see Mendez et al 2014, chapter 2). The other side of this coin is that the non-use of an accession referendum can bolster arguments for deployment of other EU referendums as was the case for the UK's continued membership referendum in 1975, and for referendums on important constitutional moments by Member States that had never previously held an EU referendum (as with Luxembourg, the Netherlands and Spain with respect to the Constitutional Treaty).

Finally, given that EU accession referendums have become the constitutional norm, which flows from the demands made by membership of this organisation as well as the growth in recourse to referendums globally to decide on sovereignty-related issues (Mendez and Germann 2018), we can expect them to be deployed for legitimising future accessions. There are currently five candidate countries—Albania, the Republic of North Macedonia, Montenegro, Serbia and Turkey—and Turkey applied to join more than thirty years ago. Not to hold an accession referendum would run against what has become mainstream constitutional practice. Nonetheless, accession referendums are likely to form a diminishing share of EU-related referendums given the small number of foreseeable candidate countries as contrasted with the many types of EU referendums that can be called. Indeed, over the last decade the accession referendum has already come to form a smaller share of total EU referendums given the growth in use of EU policy referendums in particular (see Mendez and Mendez 2017b).

References

Albi, A. (2005). *EU Enlargement and the Constitutions of Central and Eastern Europe.* Cambridge: CUP.

Anderson, S. V. (1965). Supranational Delegation Clauses in Scandinavian Constitutions. *The Western Political Quarterly, 18*(4), 840–847.

Auer, A. (2016). The People Have Spoken: Abide? A Critical View of the EU's Dramatic Referendum (In)experience. *European Constitutional Law Review, 12*(3), 397–408.

Aylott, N. (2002). Let's Discuss This Later: Party Responses to Euro-Division in Scandinavia. *Party Politics, 8*(4), 441–461.

Beach, D. (2018). Referendums in the European Union. In W. R. Thompson (Ed.), *Oxford Research Encyclopedia of Politics.* Oxford: OUP.

Björklund, T. (1982). The Demand For Referendum: When Does It Arise and When Does It Succeed? *Scandinavian Political Studies, 5*(3), 237–259.

Björklund, T. (1996). The Three Nordic 1994 Referenda Concerning Membership in the EU. *Cooperation and Conflict, 31*(1), 11–36.

Butković, H. (2017). The Rise of Direct Democracy in Croatia: Balancing or Challenging Parliamentary Representation. *Croatian International Relations Review, 23*, 38–80.

Cheneval, F., & Ferrin, M. (2018). Referendums in the European Union: Defective by Birth? *Journal of Common Market Studies, 56*(5), 1178–1194.

Chryssogonos, K. (2001). The European Union and the Greek Constitutional Order. In A. E. Kellerman, J. W. de Zwaan, & J. Czuczai (Eds.), *EU Enlargement—The Constitutional Impact at EU and National Level*. The Hague: TMC Asser Institute.

Christophorou, C. (2005). South European Briefing: The Vote for a United Cyprus Deepens Divisions: The 24 April 2004 Referenda in Cyprus. *South European Society and Politics, 10*(1), 85–104.

Cini, M. (2004). Culture, Institutions and Campaign Effects: Explaining the Outcome of Malta's EU Accession Referendum. *West European Politics, 27*(4), 584–602.

Danielsen, J. H. (2010). One of Many National Constraints on European Integration: Section 20 of Danish Constitution. *European Public Law, 16*(2), 181–192.

de Witte, B. (2001). Constitutional Aspects of European Union Membership in the Original Six Member States. In A. E. Kellerman, J. W. de Zwaan, & J. Czuczai (Eds.), *EU Enlargement—The Constitutional Impact at EU and National Level*. The Hague: TMC Asser Institute.

Ferreres Comella, V. (2013). *The Constitution of Spain: A Contextual Analysis*. Oxford: Hart.

Fowler, B. (2004). Hungary: Unpicking the Permissive Consensus. *West European Politics, 27*(4), 624–651.

Griller, S. (2001). Introduction to the Problems in the Austrian, the Finnish, and the Swedish Constitutional Order. In A. E. Kellerman, J. W. de Zwaan, & J. Czuczai (Eds.), *EU Enlargement—The Constitutional Impact at EU and National Level*. The Hague: TMC Asser Institute.

Hanley, S. (2004). A Nation of Sceptics? The Czech EU Accession Referendum of 13–14 June 2003. *West European Politics, 27*(4), 691–715.

Henderson, K. (2004). EU Accession and the New Slovak Consensus. *West European Politics, 27*(4), 652–670.

Hobolt, S. (2009). *Europe in Question: Referendums on European Integration*. Oxford: OUP.

Hoffmeister, F. (2007). Constitutional Implications of EU Membership: A View From the Commission. *Croatian Yearbook of European Law and Policy, 3*, 59–97.

Jahn, D., & Storsved, A.-S. (1995). Legitimacy Through Referendum? The Nearly Successful Domino-Strategy of the EU-Referendums in Austria, Finland, Sweden and Norway. *West European Politics, 18*(3), 18–37.

Koch, H. (2001). The Danish Constitutional Order. In A. E. Kellerman, J. W. de Zwaan, & J. Czuczai (Eds.), *EU Enlargement—The Constitutional Impact at EU and National Level* (pp. 109–116). The Hague: TMC Asser Institute.

Krašovec, A., & Lajh, D. (2004). The Slovenian EU Accession Referendum: A Cat-and-Mouse Game. *West European Politics, 27*(4), 603–623.

Kühn, Z., (2007). Ratification without Debate and Debate without Ratification: The European Constitution in Slovakia and the Czech Republic. In A. Albi & J. Ziller (Eds.), *The European Constitution and National Constitutions: Ratification and Beyond*. Dordrecht: Kluwer.

Lacey, J. (2017a). National Autonomy and Democratic Standardization: Should Popular Votes on European Integration Be Regulated by the European Union? *European Law Journal, 23*(6), 523–535.

Lacey, J. (2017b). *Centripetal Democracy: Democratic Legitimacy and Political Identity in Belgium, Switzerland and the European Union*. Oxford: OUP.

Lloréns, F. B. (2003). Spain: The Emergence of a New Major Actor in the European Arena. In W. Wessels, A. Maurer, & J. Mittag (Eds.), *Fifteen Into One?*. Manchester: Manchester University Press.

López Gómez, C. (2014). Europe as a Symbol: The Struggle for Democracy and the Meaning of European Integration in Post-Franco Spain. *Journal of Contemporary European Research, 10*(1), 74–89.

Mazylis, L. & Unikaite, I. (2003). *The Lithuanian EU Accession Referendum*. 10–11 May 2003, EPERN Referendum Briefing No. 8.

Mendez, F., & Germann, M. (2018). Contested Sovereignty: Mapping Referendums on Sovereignty Over Time and Space. *British Journal of Political Science, 48*(1), 141–165.

Mendez, F., & Mendez, M. (2017a). The Promise and Perils of Direct Democracy for the European Union. *Cambridge Yearbook of European Legal Studies., 19*, 48–85.

Mendez, F., & Mendez, M. (Eds.). (2017b). *Referendums on EU Matters*. Brussels: European Parliament.

Mendez, F., & Triga, V. (2009). Constitution-Making, Constitutional Conventions and Conflict Resolution: Lesson Drawing for Cyprus. *Journal of Balkan and Near Eastern Studies, 11*(4), 363–380.

Mendez, F., et al. (2014). *Referendums and the European Union: A Comparative Inquiry*. Cambridge: CUP.

Mikkel, E., & Pridham, G. (2004). Clinching the 'Return to Europe': The Referendums on EU Accession in Estonia and Latvia. *West European Politics, 27*(4), 716–748.

Morel, L. (2018). Types of Referendums, Provisions and Practice at National Level Worldwide. In L. Morel & M. Qvortrup (Eds.), *The Routledge Handbook to Referendums and Direct Democracy*. London: Routledge.

Moura Ramos, R. M. (2001). The Adaptation of the Portuguese Constitutional Order to Community Law. In A. E. Kellerman, J. W. de Zwaan, & J. Czuczai (Eds.), *EU Enlargement—The Constitutional Impact at EU and National Level* (p. 131). The Hague: TMC Asser Institute.

Norton, P. (2011). Divided Loyalties: The European Communities Act 1972. *Parliamentary History, 30*(1), 53–64.

Ojanen, T. (2013). Constitutional Amendment in Finland. In X. Contiades (Ed.), *Engineering Constitutional Change. A Comparative Perspective on Europe, Canada and the USA*. London and New York: Routledge.

Oppermann, K. (2013). The Politics of Discretionary Government Commitments to European Integration Referendums. *Journal of European Public Policy, 20*(5), 684–701.

Powell, C. (2009). The Long Road to Europe. Spain and the European Community, 1957–1986. In J. Baquero Cruz & C. Closa (Eds.), *European Integration from Rome to Berlin: 1957–2007*. Brussels: Peter Lang.

Pridham, G. (2003). Latvia's EU Accession Referendum. 20 September 2003, *EPERN Referendum Briefing 10*, Sussex European Institute.

Qvortrup, M. (2016). Referendums on Membership and European Integration 1972–2015. *Political Quarterly, 87,* 61–68.

Rodin, S., & Capeta, T. (2007). A View from a Candidate Country: Implications for Croatia of (Non) Ratification of the Treaty Establishing a Constitution for Europe. In A. Albi & J. Ziller (Eds.), *The European Constitution and National Constitutions: Ratifications and Beyond.* Dordrecht: Kluwer.

Sogner, I., & Archer, C. (1995). Norway and Europe: 1972 and Now. *Journal of Common Market Studies, 33*(3), 389–410.

Stelzer, M. (2013). Constitutional Change in Austria. In X. Contiades (Ed.), *Engineering Constitutional Change. A Comparative Perspective on Europe, Canada and the USA.* London and New York: Routledge.

Svensson, P. (2002). Five Danish Referendums on the European Community and Union: A Critical Assessment of the Franklin Thesis. *European Journal of Political Research, 41*(6), 733–750.

Szczerbiak, A. (2004). History Trumps Government Unpopularity: The June 2003 Polish EU Accession Referendum. *West European Politics, 27*(4), 671–690.

Szczerbiak, A., & Taggart, P. (2004). Conclusion: Towards a Model of (European) Referendums. *West European Politics, 27*(4), 749–777.

Van Elsuwege, P. (2008). *From Soviet Republics to EU Member States: A Legal and Political Assessment of the Baltic States' Accession to the EU.* Leiden: Brill.

Verney, S. (2011). An Exceptional Case? Party and Popular Euroscepticism in Greece, 1959–2009. *South European Society and Politics, 16*(1), 51–79.

Weiler, J. H. (1991). The Transformation of Europe. *Yale Law Journal, 100,* 2483.

CHAPTER 25

'If You Can't Join Them…': Explaining No Votes in Danish EU Referendums

Derek Beach

25.1 Introduction

Denmark holds the distinction of being the Member State in which most EU referendums have been rejected (1992, 2000, 2015).[1] The Danish electorate has been asked to vote in referendums related to accession to the EU, treaties amending the EU (e.g. the Treaty of Maastricht) and to remove Danish opt-outs (e.g. euro, Justice and Home Affairs). In all, Danes have voted No in three out of the eight EU referendums held. What can explain why voters reject EU-related propositions that are supported by a large majority of political parties, newspapers and interest organizations?

The chapter first presents a brief history of Danish EU referendums and the rules governing them, followed by an analysis of what can account for the No and Yes votes on basically the same proposition in the two Treaty of Maastricht referendums in 1992 and 1993. This is then followed by an examination of

[1] The term EU is used throughout this chapter to refer to the European Union and the predecessor communities.

The quote 'If you can't join them, beat them' stems from then Foreign Minister Uffe Elleman-Jensen's quip as he met with his EU colleagues immediately after the Danish No vote to Maastricht, in June 1992, linking the No vote to Denmark's recent surprise victory in the European championship in soccer.

D. Beach (✉)
University of Aarhus, Aarhus, Denmark
e-mail: derek@ps.au.dk

© The Author(s) 2021
J. Smith (ed.), *The Palgrave Handbook of European Referendums*,
https://doi.org/10.1007/978-3-030-55803-1_25

why Danes have rejected removing several of the Maastricht opt-outs in subsequent referendums, using the most recent No vote (on Justice and Home Affairs) in December 2015 as a case study. All of the referendums investigated in this chapter were high salience, where there were significant media coverage and partisan debate (Hobolt 2009: 97–98).

25.2   The Danish History of Referendums

There have been eight EU-related referendums in Denmark since 1972 (see Table 25.1). Most EU referendums have been *constitutionally mandated and binding*, based on §20 of the Danish Constitution, which states that ratification of an international treaty that transfers sovereignty to an international organization requires either a five-sixths parliamentary majority (150 out of 189 members), or a majority in a referendum according to §42. The Danish Ministry of Justice determines whether there is a transfer of sovereignty. It defines transfers of sovereignty as provisions that involve the introduction of new EU competences, whereas changing how decisions are taken in a given policy area (e.g. from unanimity to majority voting, or introducing co-decision for the European Parliament) are not. Both the Treaties of Nice and Lisbon were therefore interpreted as not containing any transfers of sovereignty in the areas applicable to Denmark and were therefore ratified as normal laws. *Advisory referendums* are possible but have only been used once (for the

Table 25.1   EU referendums held in Denmark

	Date	Required constitutionally?	Turnout (%)	Yes votes (%)	Ratified
Accession to EU	2 October 1972	Yes	90.1	63.3	Yes
Single European Act	27 February 1986	No (advisory)	75.4	56.2	Yes
Maastricht I	**2 June 1992**	**Yes**	**83.1**	**49.3**	**No**
Maastricht II	**18 May 1993**	**Partially (5/6 majority present, but ratifying law mandated approval by a referendum)**	**86.5**	**56.7**	**Yes**
Amsterdam	28 May 1998	Yes	76.2	55.1	Yes
Euro opt-out	28 September 2000	Yes	87.6	46.8	No
European Patent Court	25 May 2014	Yes	55.9	62.5	Yes
JHA opt-out	**3 December 2015**	**Yes**	**72.0**	**46.9**	**No**

1986 ratification of the Single European Act [SEA]). The 1993 referendum on Maastricht II was a peculiar case because there was a clear transfer of sovereignty, but there was also a 5/6th parliamentary majority present for ratification. For political reasons, it was decided to send the national laws ratifying the Treaty of Maastricht with the Edinburgh clarifications to a binding referendum based on the rules of §42 of the Danish Constitution.

Only Danish citizens eighteen years or older can vote in these types of referendums.[2] §42.5 of the Danish Constitution states that for a referendum motion to pass, it must have a majority of voters approve, representing at least 30% of all eligible voters. There are no specific laws regulating referendum campaigns, but the government has to follow normal Danish practice as regards the use of the civil service, which for instance means that the administration (civil servants or ministers) cannot release non-truthful material (*sandhedspligt*) to the public. Complaints can be lodged to the Danish *ombudsmand* or courts.

25.3   FROM NO TO YES—DENMARK
AND THE TREATY OF MAASTRICHT—1992 AND 1993

The Danes shocked the EU by voting No to the Treaty of Maastricht by a narrow margin on 2 June 1992 (49.3% voted Yes). They then ratified the same treaty with a series of political declarations (Edinburgh Agreement) attached to it on 18 May 1993 (56.7% Yes). Both referendums saw high turnout, meaning that the difference cannot be explained by higher turnout in the second referendum, as happened in the Irish Nice referendums (see Chapter 27 by Laffen). What then can explain why some voters switched from voting No to Yes? Was the difference due to: the change to a more popular Social Democrat-led government, changes in the proposition itself ('Maastricht without thorns'), and/or whether voters viewed the consequences of voting No in the second referendum as being too high? The analysis first describes the situation leading to the referendums and traces the course of the two campaigns. The analysis then assesses whether post-election surveys can shed light on what factors were most important in accounting for the different outcomes.

25.3.1   The Non-ratification of the Treaty of Maastricht in June 1992

At the start of the 1990–1991 intergovernmental conferences (IGCs) that eventually resulted in the Treaty of Maastricht,[3] an agreement was reached between the conservative-led minority government and the opposition Social

---

[2] Resident non-Danish citizens can vote in municipal referendums in Denmark.

[3] There were two parallel IGCs: one on economic and monetary union, the other on political union. They were eventually folded together into a single treaty reform that resulted in the Treaty of Maastricht.

Democrats on what positions the Danish government should take in the negotiations. These positions included a Social Democratic demand to seek an opt-out from a potential common currency.

Concluded in December 1991, the Treaty of Maastricht was undeniably the largest integrative step since the Treaty of Rome. Innovations included the creation of an Economic and Monetary Union (EMU) with a common currency, the increased use of majority voting and upgrading the role of the European Parliament to co-legislator in many areas, and the introduction of the so-called 'Social dimension' in labour market-related policies, along with measures creating the so-called Political Union that included intergovernmental cooperation in foreign and security affairs and justice and home affairs. Thus, it was not difficult for the lawyers in the Ministry of Justice to determine that the Treaty involved a transfer of sovereignty, which meant that it had to be ratified by either a five-sixths parliamentary majority or a referendum. As the vote on the Treaty passed a parliament vote by 130 to 25 (out of 179 total), an obligatory referendum had to be convened to pass the ratifying legislation.

The relatively intense campaign up to the June 1992 referendum was dominated by the pro-ratification Yes side; a position advocated by almost all the major Danish parties, major interest groups and major newspapers. Opposition to the Treaty was found in both far-left and far-right parties in Denmark, and the People's Movement against the EC (see the Chapter 20 by Svensson elsewhere in this volume). The No side had few funds at their disposal (Hobolt 2009: 167).

Arguments from the Yes side focused initially on political aspects in its arguments, while also playing up the costs of voting No. Leading politicians from both the government and Social Democrat opposition argued that a No vote would not result in the mere continuance of the status quo, but would have substantial negative costs for Denmark. Prime Minister Schlüter said that while Denmark probably would not be thrown out of the EC, the other 11 Member States would adopt a modified Maastricht Treaty on their own, excluding Denmark from influence. More bombastic claims were made by Foreign Minister Uffe Elleman-Jensen in Parliament on 12 May 1992, where he stated that a No would be 'barren and negative', and would result in a very uncertain economic future for Denmark, including a flight of capital and a massive increase in interest rates. New opposition leader Poul Nyrup Rasmussen was somewhat milder, stating that in the event of a No vote, Denmark should try to negotiate a deal with the other Member States, but that it would be very difficult to get anything other than Maastricht or exit, and therefore voters should say Yes.

Arguments from the left-wing Socialist People's Party (SF) focused on political union, especially in foreign and defence policy, along with the common currency. Fears were raised about a 'European army' led by French or German generals. The term 'union' was widely used by opponents as a derogatory term, with the slogan coined by the SF chairman Holger K. Nielsen—'Holger and his wife say no to the union'—particularly resonant.[4] The right-wing Progress Party focused its opposition on the 'Social dimension' (labour market policies) and environmental policies. Another major No organization was the People's Movement against the EC, which focused its arguments also on political union, the surrender of sovereignty and the threat to the welfare state posed by further integration.

Debates in the mass media during the campaign concentrated on political issues, with the loss of national sovereignty prominent, along with issues related to foreign and defence policies (Siune et al. 1992: 38–46). While opinion polls were positive for the Yes side at the start of the campaign, almost 40% of voters were undecided (Hobolt 2009: 168). The gap in polls narrowed steadily during the campaign, with a small majority voting against the Treaty on 2 June 1992.

25.3.2 'Maastricht Without Thorns'—The Edinburgh Agreement and the Yes Vote in May 1993

After the No vote, the major Yes parties entered into the so-called 'National compromise',[5] which mandated that the Danish government would ask for certain clarifications related to the common currency, defence cooperation, justice and home affairs and citizenship, along with an attempt to push for more 'openness' and subsidiarity. The UK Presidency—assisted by the Council Secretariat Legal Service—negotiated directly with the Danish government leading to the formulation of the four Danish opt-outs that were accepted at the Edinburgh European Council in December 1992 as the 'Edinburgh Agreement' (EA). Denmark—alongside the UK—had a potential opt-out vis-a-vis the common currency in the Treaty of Maastricht. The protocol stated that Denmark could choose not to join the third phase of EMU (common currency), whereas in the EA the Danish government stated up-front that it would not join the third phase, although it could always reverse this decision later. The EA clarified that there was nothing in the treaties that forced Denmark to join any future supranational cooperation in Justice and Home Affairs (JHA), which of course was re-stating legal facts because all JHA cooperation at the time was intergovernmental, and any change had to be adopted through an IGC by unanimity. Denmark also clarified that it was not obliged

---

[4]It rhymes in Danish—'Holger og konen siger nej til unionen'.

[5]The Yes side now included the Socialist People's Party, who chose to change sides in order to gain influence on the terms of the Danish solution, but also to pave the way for possible participation in a potentially incoming Social Democrat-led government. It was widely expected in the autumn of 1992 that the Conservative government would have to step down after the publication of the findings of an inquiry into the so-called 'Tamil case'. After the very critical report was published in January, Prime Minister Poul Schlüter resigned the same day, leading to a new Social Democrat government led by Poul Nyrup Rasmussen.

to take part in EU military actions, and therefore would stay out of any potential future military cooperation. Finally, the EA made clear that the so-called Union citizenship provisions were not intended to replace national citizenship, which was also re-stating a legal (and political) fact.

Legally, the Treaty of Maastricht with the clarifications in the EA was therefore not different from the proposition rejected in June 1992 (Piris 2006: 24–25). However, the EA signalled to voters that Denmark would not take part in the future in some of the most politically sensitive issues, including the common currency and military cooperation. Therefore, proponents of the deal viewed it as 'Maastricht without thorns', because it weakened the opponents' argument that an out-of-touch pro-EU Danish elite could allow Denmark to continue on a slippery slope towards 'ever closer union'.

After a change of government in early 1993, the new Social Democrat-led government steered a relatively short and ill-tempered campaign towards a Yes vote in May 1993. In April 1992, the Social Democrat party had replaced their leader, Svend Auken, with Poul Nyrup Rasmussen. During the 1992 campaign, the Social Democrats were still reeling after the bitter leadership battle, leading to a disjointed campaign to convince their voters (Hobolt 2006). In contrast, in the spring of 1993 the Social Democrats were united behind their new party leader and now Prime Minister. Another key difference that weakened the No side was the switch of the left-wing Socialist People's Party to supporting a Yes vote. Even though they did not convince their voters to switch, it silenced a left-wing No voice that could have potentially convinced some sceptical Social Democrat voters not to follow their party's recommendation. On the No side, the June Movement had been formed in the aftermath of the 1992 No vote. The June Movement was a more moderate organization than the People's Movement, opposing 'union' but in favour of a continued Danish EC membership that was limited to the Single Market.

The debates in the second referendum centred on whether the Edinburgh Agreement actually changed anything and whether it lived up to the reasons for voting No, together with whether a new No vote for Denmark would lead to an exit from the EU. The Yes side argued that 'Maastricht without thorns' was a significantly new deal that enabled Denmark to opt-out of significant areas. In contrast, the No side claimed that the EA was in effect the 'Emperor's new clothes', meaning that Danish voters were essentially being asked to vote on the same proposition a second time.

Interestingly, whereas many on the Yes side in the first campaign had tried to use scare tactics to frighten voters into voting Yes, these tactics were actually toned down in the second referendum. After the Danes voted No in 1992, the other 11 Member States clearly signalled that if Denmark could not ratify, they would proceed without them. Danish politicians could therefore much more credibly state in 1993 that a second No would not result in the resumption of the status quo but would be some form of exclusion/isolation. This suggests that the key to voter perceptions of the consequences of a second No was not the substance of elite arguments per se, but instead the perceived credibility of significant negative consequences. When elites argued that a No would have extreme costs in 1992, these scare tactics could actually have undermined their credibility, whereas in the second campaign pro-Maastricht campaigners could let the political situation speak for itself. Indeed, it was very evident to most voters that some form of Danish exit from the EU was a probable result in the case of a second No. Given that a large majority of Danes wanted to stay in the Internal Market for economic reasons, this was seen as a potentially very negative consequence of a second No.

Combined with perceptions that Denmark was able to stay outside of the most unwanted areas of more political cooperation, this was sufficient to convince enough voters to switch from No to Yes to ensure a relatively comfortable Yes margin. Denmark was able to ratify the Treaty of Maastricht along with its partners, committing itself to stay outside of the common currency and military cooperation, and pledging to not join potential future supranational JHA cooperation. When areas of JHA were then transferred to the supranational first pillar in the Treaty of Amsterdam, Denmark was able to negotiate a legally binding treaty protocol that kept it out of the new supranational cooperation in areas like the common asylum and immigration policies, thereby creating a real legal opt-out instead of the declaratory EA.

25.3.3   *From a No to a Yes—Explanations of the Different Outcomes*

What factors determine voter choice in EU-related referendums? The core theoretical debate is whether voters decide based on considerations other than the issue itself because they do not believe the proposition is important enough to expend the effort required to understand the issue and how it potentially could affect them (second-order), or they actually decide in relation to the issue being considered (issue-voting).

Many scholars and commentators claim that EU referendums are perceived by ordinary citizens as abstract and relatively unimportant affairs, meaning that we should not expect voters to spend the effort to evaluate the proposition in relation to their underlying attitudes towards European integration—if these even exist at all. Instead, voters can be expected to treat an EU referendum as a *second-order* vote, where they can express their level of satisfaction with the performance of the government by voting Yes or No (Franklin 2002; Franklin et al. 1994; Reif and Schmitt 1980; Ivaldi 2006). A popular government will be able to steer a proposition to ratification because a majority of voters will trust that the government will only endorse it if it is good for the country, and vice versa (Franklin et al. 1994: 102). When going to the polls in European referendums, voters therefore focus on how they feel about national politics rather than how they feel about European integration. Second-order dynamics are particularly dominant in low salience referendums (Franklin 2002). Since the referendums analysed in this chapter are all of high salience, they may not meet the criteria for second-order dynamics (Svensson 2002).

Many scholars claim that voter behaviour in referendums on EU matters is similar to normal elections, where voters decide based upon the issues themselves (Merrill and Grofman 1999; Svensson 1994, 2002; Hobolt 2006, 2009). Early versions of the *issue-voting model* as regards EU referendums argued that voter choice was based upon voters' *general attitudes* towards European integration (Svensson 1994, 2002), whereas more recent formulations focus more explicitly on voter attitudes towards the *specific question* they are posed (e.g. Hobolt 2006, 2009). Hobolt (2006, 2009) has developed a rational choice-based proximity model. In her model, the median voter is theorized to make a choice between the level of EU integration that the voter ideally wants (the 'ideal point') and what is expected to occur in the event of a No vote (aka the 'reversion point').[6] When the proposition is closer to the median voter's ideal point than the reversion point, the voter will vote Yes, and vice versa. While it is usually not made explicit in issue-voting models, it is assumed that these issue-related attitudes reflect voter evaluations of their utility gains in relation to EU integration based upon the socio-economic predispositions of the individual voter, in that those groups that stand to gain the most from integration support it and vice versa, other things being equal (Gabel 1998; Hooghe and Marks 2005).

A potential mediating factor is partisan cues and endorsements (de Vreese 2007; Hobolt 2006). In situations where the issue is novel and very complex, how issues are framed by media and political elites can be very important, shifting public opinion on the issue in the short term in ways that can affect the final outcome. Here voter attitudes are very volatile and malleable because they are not anchored in solid attitudes towards the EU that can be retrieved to help voters make an informed choice based on their underlying attitudes. In contrast, at the other extreme, when voters are very familiar with EU-related issues, campaigns and partisan endorsements merely provide information that enables voters to decide based on their underlying, non-malleable issue attitudes.

What does the evidence suggest in relation to these theories? For both referendums, large post-election surveys were undertaken that enable us to explore the strength of correlations and the differences across the two referendums in attitudes towards national politics, broad EU attitudes, partisan endorsements and/or specific attitudes towards the proposition and voter choice (DDA 1743, 1784).

If the different outcomes can be explained by second-order factors, we would expect that the unpopular government being replaced by a more popular government to explain the difference (Franklin et al. 1994: 120). There is however little evidence supporting this explanation. The two parties

---

[6]While it cannot be reasonably expected that average voters engage in a synoptic evaluation of the proposition in relation to their ideal point and the expected reversion point in the event of a No, voters can utilize heuristics like cues from referent persons to calculate their position 'as if' they had expended the analytical resources to calculate their utility function (Hobolt 2009; Lupia 1992, 1994).

in the incumbent Conservative-led government were actually *more popular* in 1992 than in the most recent election. In the 1990 parliamentary election they had won 31.8% of votes, whereas in the spring of 1992 their net support was around 35% (Svensson 2002: 740). Additionally, if the second-order explanation holds, we would expect differences in trust in politicians in 1992 and 1993. Hobolt (2009: 178) however finds little evidence of an increase in trust of politicians.

Research has found that there were two differences that mattered: changes in perceptions of the costs and benefits of voting Yes, and the more united campaign of the Social Democrats (partisan endorsements). Regarding perceptions of the treaty, the Yes side was arguably successful in framing the second referendum as pulling out the more political 'thorns' of the Treaty of Maastricht. In both post-referendum surveys, voters were quite supportive of more 'economic' issues (Internal Market), whereas they were opposed to integration in areas that can be interpreted as being more 'political'. This is illustrated in Table 25.2, where it can be seen that the areas encompassed by the EA clarifications are all quite unpopular.

More technical statistical analysis has found strong evidence for issue-voting. One way of doing this is to investigate the relative strength of different factors in explaining the outcome (marginal effects). Using this technique, Hobolt found that the EU attitudes of voters had a stronger effect on voter choice than whether a given voter supported a Yes party (partisanship). Taken together, this evidence suggests that the most important driver of the switch in votes from No to Yes was more positive interpretations of the treaty, although the evidence does not enable us to determine whether this is because voters thought the political 'thorns' were removed by the EA, or whether voters feared the negative consequences that a second No vote was widely perceived to have. In all, 52% of voters stated that their motivation for voting Yes was based upon concerns about the costs of No in 1993, with the most common

Table 25.2 Voter approval of EU integration in different issue areas (1992 and 1993)

	June 92	May 93
Internal Market	74	74
Removal of trade barriers	69	65
Economic and Monetary Union	53	42
Reducing economic differences in Europe	49	43
Common foreign policy	38	37
Common currency	34	23
Common defence policy	30	34
United States of Europe	19	21
Union citizenship	13	14

Source Siune et al. (1994)

Table 25.3 Yes vote by current party preference, 1992 and 1993

	Yes vote (%)—1992	Yes vote (%)—1993
Conservatives	88.4	88.9
Liberals	83.0	84.3
Social Democrats	37.0	54.9
Socialist People's Party	7.8	29.8
Progress Party	45.8	20.8

Source Siune et al. (1999, 2001)

answers being 'Denmark cannot survive without the EC', 'avoid isolation of Denmark' and 'we cannot continue to vote no'.

Partisan endorsements did, though, have some effect. In particular, there was a significant shift in voting behaviour amongst voters of the Social Democrats and Socialist People's Party (see Table 25.3). Here we see that almost 20% more voters who identified as Social Democrats and with the Socialist People's Party voted Yes in 1993 than in 1992.

25.4   No Votes in Opt-Out Referendums

Danish voters have rejected removing opt-outs in two referendums: joining the common currency in September 2000, and the JHA opt-out in December 2015. This section focuses on the JHA opt-out referendum in December 2015. After discussing the campaign, it explores contrasting explanations of why a majority of Danes voted No.

25.4.1   Replacing the JHA Opt-Out with a New Opt-In

The Treaty of Lisbon moved the rest of JHA cooperation into the supranational first pillar in December 2014, meaning that Denmark would have to leave cooperation in areas of JHA like police (e.g. Europol) and legal cooperation, in which a broad majority of pro-EU Danish elites wanted to participate. When the Treaty of Lisbon was being negotiated, the Danish government had negotiated a British-style opt-in protocol that would enable a majority in the Danish Parliament to decide on a case-by-case basis whether to join supranational JHA legal acts or remain outside in order to avoid having to leave these areas of cooperation and then negotiate legally and politically difficult 'parallel agreements' that would enable Denmark to participate in an intergovernmental fashion.

However, moving a policy area from intergovernmental to supranational cooperation involved a clear transfer of sovereignty based on the Ministry of Justice's definition. Therefore, to avoid having to engage in a §20 procedure (five-sixths parliamentary majority or a referendum) every time Denmark joined a new supranational JHA act, the protocol was to be ratified domestically in a manner where the full transfer of sovereignty in all areas of JHA would happen only once—i.e. when the protocol itself was ratified. If the opt-in protocol was ratified, the decision to join a supranational JHA act would then only be based on approval by a parliamentary majority.[7]

An agreement was reached in March 2015 between the then Social Democrat/Radical Left government and the other major Yes parties (Conservatives, Liberals and Socialist People's Party), which stated that a referendum should be held in the near future to activate the Lisbon opt-in protocol. At the same time, the parties agreed that Denmark would stay out of existing supranational asylum and immigration legal acts (except the Dublin regulation and Eurodac) and only join new acts in this area if all of the parties agreed to it. In other areas of JHA, it was decided that Denmark would join twenty-two JHA acts and stay out of the rest, and that in the future they would decide on a case-by-case basis as regards new acts. However, the problem with this agreement was that it was not legally binding on future parliaments, meaning that there was always the 'risk' that a future parliamentary majority would decide to opt into JHA areas that were opposed by majorities of voters (e.g. the common asylum and immigration policies).

The JHA opt-out issue was highly salient in Denmark because it was related to one of the four Danish opt-outs that were originally agreed in relation to the Treaty of Maastricht (see above). This meant that it was viewed as part of the core of the Danish special relationship with the EU, making it very sensitive for sovereignty-conscious Danish voters. In addition, while the 22 legal acts that the Yes majority in the Danish parliament stated that it would join if the proposition was ratified were relatively unimportant, the most salient issue for many voters was one that the Yes majority said it would *not* join in the foreseeable future: the common EU asylum and immigration policies. Here the crucial difference between before and after a potential Yes vote was that with the existing opt-out Denmark could only join the common asylum and immigration policy with either a five-sixths parliamentary majority or a referendum, but with the opt-in a mere parliamentary majority could decide to join at a later date without convening a §20 mandated referendum. This difference proved to be a major strategic mistake from the Yes side because it gifted the No side a winning argument: could voters trust the Yes majority in parliament to *not* join the asylum and immigration policy in the future without convening a referendum? Danes were split on the issue of joining the common asylum and immigration policies (44% in favour, 37% opposed, 19% undecided or don't know; Beach 2016), with a majority of left-wing voters in favour and right-wing voters opposed to joining.

---

[7]In practice, given the history of minority governments in Denmark, there is an informal tradition that important EU matters are adopted using consensus amongst the major pro-EU parties.

After a narrow victory in the June 2015 parliamentary election, a new Liberal-led minority government was formed. The new government, with the support of a large majority of pro-EU parties in parliament, decided to call a referendum on 21 August, with the vote to be held on 3 December 2015.

After the campaign had been running over two months, the Danish Prime Minister on 6 October tried to counter the No argument about potentially joining the common asylum and immigration policy in the future by promising that his party would not support joining it without convening an advisory referendum. But this promise was purely political and could not in Danish law be legally binding on future governments, or even his own party in the future. Further, the political promise was not perceived as very credible by many voters in a time of dramatically declining levels of trust of politicians in general (in particular amongst voters with Eurosceptic attitudes). The importance of remaining outside of the common asylum and immigration policy became even more salient for voters as the refugee crisis exploded in August and September of 2015.[8]

The core Yes side argument was that the opt-in model had to be adopted in order for Denmark to remain in Europol after the legal base became community-based. However, when the No side and experts argued that a form of Europol membership was also possible in the event of a No vote because Denmark could negotiate an intergovernmental 'parallel agreement' that would allow participation, the Yes side was left without clear arguments in favour of removing the opt-out.

The actual referendum campaign was surprisingly low key, with political parties and organizations on both sides deploying relatively few resources. A key strategic mistake by the Danish government was that the campaign was occurring at the same time as it was negotiating its first budgetary law. This meant that leading politicians on the Yes side were unable to dedicate time to the referendum campaign until after the budgetary law was passed in mid-November, leaving only two weeks for active campaigning by high-level politicians. As a result, there was little news coverage and few events held prior to the referendum (see Table 25.4). Not surprisingly, there were record levels

Table 25.4 Number of stories in the main newspapers

	September	October	November	December (1st to 3rd)
Referendum issues	108	91	338	105
Budgetary negotiations	170	306	320	

Source Infomedia search of 17 nation-wide daily newspapers

[8]In August and September of 2015, over one million refugees arrived in the EU, many escaping from the Syrian civil war. The refugee crisis led to unprecedented numbers of asylum claims in many countries, and to other countries closing their borders.

of undecided voters until the final weeks of the campaign. Ten days before the referendum, 35% of potential voters were either 'very in doubt' or 'somewhat in doubt' (Beach 2016).

In the final vote on 3 December, the Yes side was only able to win 46.9% of votes, leading to the measure being rejected.

25.4.2 Explaining the No Vote in the JHA Opt-In Referendum[9]

What factors can explain why Danes voted No? Given that there is no published statistical analysis of voter behaviour in this referendum, I will present the data used, followed by an analysis of the relative explanatory power of different factors. The data used is a large post-election survey of voters after the No vote in December 2015 that asked a number of different questions (Beach 2016). To measure voter attitudes towards the EU, a battery of questions was asked about different aspects of the EU. To measure second-order factors, voters were asked about their satisfaction with the incumbent government. To assess the importance of partisan endorsements, voters were asked which party they had voted for in the last parliamentary election. A set of socio-demographic control variables was also included (age, education, income, gender).

Table 25.5 presents the results of a multivariate statistical analysis. As can be seen from the table, all the competing explanations (issue-voting, second-order and partisan endorsements) are statistically significant. However, when we assess their relative effects (marginal effects), the analysis suggests that EU attitudes are the most important driver of voter choice, with second-order factors

Table 25.5 Predicting the No vote in the 2015 JHA referendum

Independent variables	Coefficient	SE
General EU attitudes	.721***	.066
No party endorsement	1.029***	.193
Government satisfaction	.291***	.072
Age	−.314*	.113
Gender	−.454*	.168
Education	.216	.177
Income	−.042	.031
Constant	1.393	.495
Pseudo R^2	.546	
N	502	

Source DK-OPT JHA post-election survey (Beach 2016). *$p <$ .05, **$p <$ .01, ***$p <$ .001

---

[9]This section uses the data from the DKOPT-JHA post-referendum survey designed by the author to investigate voter behaviour (Beach 2016).

having only a minor impact.[10] The results provide evidence that suggests that voting behaviour in the JHA referendum was dominated by issue-voting, with a secondary impact of partisan endorsements. In other words, a majority of Danes voted No because they did not like the proposition (issue-voting).

25.5 Conclusions—Denmark as the Home of Issue-Voting

Given the salience of most EU referendums in Denmark, it is perhaps not surprising that voter behaviour has been dominated by issue-voting. In all three of the cases investigated in this chapter, the dominant explanation for why Danes voted Yes or No is based on their perceptions of the costs and benefits of the proposition in relation to their underlying EU attitudes. There has, though, been one low salience referendum in Denmark: in 2014 when the European Patent Court (EPC) was sent to ratification by a referendum. Given the perceived low salience of the issue, the government decided to hold the ratification at the same time as the May 2014 European Parliament (EP) elections in order to ensure that turnout reached the required threshold for ratification. The EPC issue was not really discussed—with attention focused during the campaign solely on the parallel EP elections. There is strong evidence from the post-election survey (DDA-26709) suggesting that voters merely followed the endorsements of the party they were voting for in the EP elections.

However, when salience is relatively high—as was the case in all other Danish EU referendums, issue-voting dominates. The implication of this is that it is probably very difficult to remove the Danish opt-outs in the future due to issue-voting. While there are strong majorities for continued EU membership in Denmark, many Danes do not want more integration. In the 2015 DK-OPT JHA survey, only 10% of respondents said they wanted to leave the EU, but 38% stated they wanted less EU interference (Beach 2016).[11] This does not mean that EU referendums can never be won, but given that the reversion point in the event of a No vote in an opt-out referendum is the continuation of the opt-out (i.e. status quo), it can be difficult to convince voters that the opt-out situation is so bad that it has to be removed. As was seen in the 2015 referendum, the No side argument that Denmark could stay in popular areas of JHA like Europol through future parallel agreements was a particularly resonant argument.

This contrasts with the situation in the 1992/1993 referendums, where a Yes vote was secured in the second referendum by a combination of removing

---

[10]More technically, a half SD increase in negative EU attitudes increases the probability of voting No by 50%, whereas the impact of partisan endorsements is slightly weaker (37%), and second-order factors matter little for voting intentions.

[11]36% stated they wanted the EU preserved in its current form, 9.5% wanted more integration and 10% wanted a federal Europe.

'thorns' that made the proposition more attractive, and the credibility of the prospect that a second No vote would result in Danish exit from the EU. This meant that even voters with relatively Eurosceptic attitudes preferred voting Yes over what they perceived to be a very harmful reversion point in the event of another No vote (Hobolt 2009).

This difference implies that getting rid of opt-outs in countries like Denmark and Sweden, where there is a significant group of voters with relatively Eurosceptic attitudes, might be almost a 'mission impossible' unless we see major shifts in voter attitudes towards the EU, or if the status quo becomes widely perceived to be so negative that it trumps Eurosceptic voters' predispositions to stick with what they know over the uncertainty of more integration.

REFERENCES

Beach, D. (2016). *Undersøgelse om danskernes holdninger til retsforbeholdet.* Survey implemented by Epinion, Fall 2015.

DDA. Various. *Dansk Data Arkiv* [Danish Data Archive].

de Vreese, C. H. (2007). Context, Elites, Media and Public Opinion in Referendums: Why Campaigns Really Matter. In C. H. de Vreese (Ed.), *The Dynamics of Referendum Campaigns in International Perspective* (pp. 1–20). London: Palgrave.

Franklin, M. N. (2002). Learning from the Danish Case: A Comment on Palle Svensson's Critique on the Franklin Thesis. *European Journal of Political Research, 41*(6), 751–757.

Franklin, M. N., Marsh, M., & Wlezien, C. (1994). Attitudes Towards Europe and Referendum Votes: A Response to Siune and Svensson. *Electoral Studies, 13*(2), 117–121.

Gabel, M. J. (1998). Economic Integration and Mass Politics: Market Liberalization and Public Attitudes in the European Union. *American Journal of Political Science, 42*(3), 936–953.

Hobolt, S. B. (2006). How Parties Affect Vote Choice in European Integration Referendums. *Party Politics, 12*(5), 623–647.

Hobolt, S. B. (2009). *Europe in Question: Referendums on European Integration.* Oxford: Oxford University Press.

Hooghe, L., & Marks, G. (2005). Calculation, Community and Cues: Public Opinion on European Integration. *European Union Politics, 6*(4), 419–444.

Ivaldi, G. (2006). Beyond France's 2005 Referendum on the European Constitutional Treaty: Second-Order Model, Anti-establishment Attitudes and the End of the Alternative European Utopia. *West European Politics, 29*(1), 47–69.

Lupia, A. (1992). Busy Voters, Agenda Control, and the Power of Information. *American Political Science Review, 86*(2), 390–403.

Lupia, A. (1994). Shortcuts Versus Encyclopedias: Information and Voting Behavior in Californian Insurance Reform Elections. *American Political Science Review, 88*(1), 63–76.

Merrill, S. I., & Grofman, B. (1999). *A Unified Theory of Voting.* Cambridge: Cambridge University Press.

Piris, J.-C. (2006). *The Constitution for Europe: A Legal Analysis*. Cambridge: Cambridge University Press.

Reif, K.-H., & Schmitt, H. (1980). Nine Second-Order National Elections: A Conceptual Framework for the Analysis of European Elections Results. *European Journal of Political Research, 8*(1), 3–44.

Siune, K., Svensson, P., & Tonsgaard, O. (1992). *Det blev et nej.* Aarhus: Politica.

Siune, K., Svensson, P., & Tonsgaard, O. (1994). *Fra et nej til et ja.* Aarhus: Politica.

Siune, K., Tonsgaard, O., & Svensson, P. (1999). *Folkeafstemningen om Maastrichtaftalen, 2. juni 1992.* Data set deposited as DDA-1743 1. udgave. Odense, Dansk Data Arkiv [Danish Data Archive].

Siune, K., Tonsgaard, O., & Svensson, P. (2001). *Folkeafstemningen om Edinburghaftalen, 18. maj 1993.* Data set deposited as DDA-1784. Odense, Dansk Data Arkiv [Danish Data Archive].

Svensson, P. (1994). The Danish Yes to Maastricht and Edinburgh. The EC Referendum of May 1993. *Scandinavian Political Studies, 17*(1), 69–82.

Svensson, P. (2002). Five Danish Referendums on the European Community and European Union: A Critical Assessment of the Franklin Thesis. *European Journal of Political Research, 41*(6), 733–750.

CHAPTER 26

The 2003 Swedish Euro Referendum

Henrik Oscarsson

26.1   Introduction

On 29 November 2002, the leaders of the parties in the Swedish Parliament (*Riksdag*) announced an agreement that a national referendum on 'the introduction of the euro as a currency' would be held on the third Sunday of September the following year. They had also decided on the wording of the question that would take the Swedish voters to the polls in September 2003: 'Do you think that Sweden should introduce the euro as its official currency?' In early 2003, the *Riksdag* enacted the law on a national referendum about the euro currency (Government proposition 2002/03:46).

The timing of the announcement was considered by most commentators to be an advantage for the pro-euro side. At that point in time, the Yes side had been ahead in the polls for the previous eighteen months. The large November 2002 poll from *Statistics Sweden* (SCB/PSU) showed a clear five percentage point lead (40–35%) for the Yes side. However, the announcement of the referendum immediately triggered an opinion shift against membership of the

---

This chapter is based on the Swedish National Election Studies' large extensive analyses of the 2003 euro referendum and Oscarsson and Holmberg (2004) as well as similar research anthologies (in Swedish) on previous national referendums: Gilljam and Holmberg (1996); Holmberg and Asp (1984).

H. Oscarsson (✉)
Department of Political Science, University of Gothenburg, Gothenburg, Sweden
e-mail: henrik.oscarsson@pol.gu.se

J. Smith (ed.), *The Palgrave Handbook of European Referendums*,
https://doi.org/10.1007/978-3-030-55803-1_26

euro. During spring 2003 the lead for the No side had grown to around 10 percentage points. Thus, in hindsight, the victory for the No side seems to have been consolidated long before the summer. In spite of a very intense and dramatic campaign, there was no large or decisive aggregated opinion shift after April–May 2003. The referendum on 14 September resulted in a clear win for the No side (55.9%).

This chapter will put the Swedish euro referendum into an historical perspective, discussing when, how and why the institution of national referendums has been used historically in Sweden. The chapter will also briefly discuss the evolution of the referendum device in Sweden and assess the contemporary debate on whether and how national referendums will be arranged in the future.

26.2   THE SWEDISH EXPERIENCE OF NATIONAL REFERENDUMS

The 2003 referendum on membership of the euro currency was the sixth national referendum in Sweden since the democratic breakthrough in 1921. Only the parliament is able to call national referendums, although new rules were adopted in 2009 (Government proposition 2009/10:80) that made it easier for citizens to initiate referendums on local and regional levels. The themes of the national referendums in Sweden are most varied (see Table 26.1).Historically, referendums have been used mainly as tools for settling societal and intra-party conflicts around political issues that the main actors have considered hard to resolve in a regular parliamentary process. In this way, national referendums have often been a method to contain conflicts rather than a method for a unitary political elite to legitimise reforms (Möller 2011).

The possibility of arranging an advisory national referendum was introduced in 1922, and already in the first year a referendum on alcohol prohibition was held, resulting in a slim victory for the No side (51.0%). There exist no special arrangements for constitutional changes. Sweden has never held a national referendum on constitutional changes, although for instance the outcome of the EU membership referendum in 1994 de facto resulted in such changes when Sweden joined the EU in 1995 (see Rye elsewhere in this volume).

Interestingly, in Swedish national referendums, the status quo-alternative has won and the 'change' alternative has lost five times out of six. Sweden did not adopt a law on alcohol prohibition in 1922. Sweden did not vote for switching to driving on the right in 1955—although this switch to right-hand traffic was realised in 1967. A majority of Swedish voters did not vote for the most ambitious and far-stretching reform of the pension system ('Alternative 1') in 1957. Sweden did not vote for a fast closedown of nuclear power plants in 1980 ('Alternative 3'). And Sweden did not introduce the euro as a

Table 26.1   Results in Swedish national referendums 1922–2003

Referendum	Alternatives			Blank vote	Total	Turnout	Turnout in most recent general election	Type of referendum	Outcome
1 Alcohol prohibition 1922	Yes	No							
	49.0	51.0		–	100.0	54.2	54.2 (1921)	Advisory	No prohibition of alcohol; but still a state regulatory monopoly
2 Right-hand driving 1955	Yes	No							
	15.5	82.9		1.6	100.0	53.2	79.1 (1952)	Advisory	Right-hand driving was introduced in 1967
3 Pensions 1957	'Alt. 1'	'Alt. 2'	'Alt. 3'						
	45.8	15.0	35.3	3.9	100.0	72.4	79.8 (1956)	Advisory	Unclear; General Supplementary Pension (ATP) was introduced in 1960
4 Nuclear power 1980	'Alt. 1'	'Alt. 2'	'Alt. 3'						
	18.9	39.1	38.7	3.3	100.0	75.6	90.7 (1979)	Advisory	Unclear; nuclear power was not abolished in 2010, ten reactors remain
5 EU membership 1994	Yes	No							

(continued)

Table 26.1   (continued)

Referendum	Alternatives		Blank vote	Total	Turnout	Turnout in most recent general election	Type of referendum	Outcome
	52.3	46.8	0.9	100.0	83.3	86.8 (1994)	Advisory	Swedish EU membership 1995–
6 Euro currency 2003	Yes	No						
	42.0	55.9	2.1	100.0	82.6	80.1 (2002)	Advisory	No euro currency

Note Results are collated from various sources: Statistics Sweden and the Election Authority (see Oscarsson and Holmberg 2004)

currency in 2003. The only instance of a win for the 'change' option is the EU membership referendum in November 1994.

All national referendums so far have been optional and advisory/consultative. Decisions to arrange national referendums are the result of political judgements from party elites, often as a response to internal and external pressure. The decisions to consult the citizens via a national referendum are most often taken in broad consensus, and in situations when government or the political elites are not advocating any particular outcome. Rather, Swedish national referendums have triggered elite competition, with experts, business, labour market interests and party representatives mobilising behind all the alternatives. Since 1980, new rules make it possible to hold binding referendums on pending decisions for constitutional change: it takes a tenth of the Members of Parliament (35) to initiate such a process and a third of the parliament to decide to hold a referendum. A binding referendum of this sort can only be held in conjunction with a general election, held on fixed dates every four years on the second Sunday of September (2018, 2022, 2026, 2030 and so forth). In these instances—a referendum on constitutional change in conjunction with a general election—only a No majority is binding (Swedish constitution, *Regeringsformen* 8 Chapter §16). No such referendum on constitutional change has been held so far.

Voter turnout in Swedish national referendums has generally been lower than in the most recent general elections. In 1922, the turnout was on par with the turnout in Sweden's first democratic national election in 1921 (54.2%). And in the two EU-related referendums in 1994 and 2003 turnout was close to the levels in the general elections in 1994 and 2002. However, in the referendums on right-hand driving in 1955 and on nuclear power in 1980, the turnout levels were far lower than in national elections at that time (see Table 26.1).

The same basic rules apply for referendums and general elections: all Swedish citizens around the world that have turned 18 years old before the Election Day are eligible to vote. No pre-registration is needed to be able to participate at referendums, since the voter registers are acquired from continually updated population registers. Very generous systems for absentee voting are in place both for citizens living abroad and for voters residing in Sweden (18 days before the election). No quorum rules are in effect in national referendums. Disputes are handled by the Election Review Board (*Valprövningsnämnden*), a committee appointed by the Swedish parliament (Teorell 2012).

Historically, the Tax Authority and the County Administrative Board (*Länsstyrelsen*) have been involved in the practical arrangements of elections and referendums in Sweden. In 2003, the Election Authority (*Valmyndigheten*) was established to take overall responsibility for carrying out all democratic elections and referendums on local, regional, national and EP-level. However, most practical administrative tasks are delegated to Election Boards (*Valnämnder*) in 290 local constituencies. The tallying of the votes on Election Day is highly decentralised: a manual count of the votes is performed at 6000+ polling stations nationwide. A second tallying of all votes takes place in 29 *Länsstyrelser* in the week following the elections. The process of recounting the votes can be monitored in real-time via Valmyndighetens homepage (www.val.se). The final election results are officially declared about a week after the election.

Historically, there has been no official monitoring or even regulation of election campaign financing at Swedish elections or referendums. However, after severe international criticism from NGOs such as The Organization for Security and Co-operation in Europe (OSCE) and Transparency International, since April 2018, political parties are obliged to make all details of their campaign financing publically available. As a consequence, it is now illegal to make larger (more than 2300 SEK) donations anonymously to political parties or their sub-organisations (Government proposition 2018:90). However, it is still quite unclear whether the new law will affect organisations campaigning on either side in a future national or local referendum. A stand-alone campaign organisation without ties to any political party would not be affected by the new laws on party financing.

26.3   The Referendum Campaign 2003

Parties, party leaders and party representatives are the main political actors, including at times of referendums. As for previous national referendums, several new campaign organisations were formed before the euro referendum in 2003, such as *Sweden in Europe*, *Social Democrats pro Euro* and *No to the Euro*, with varying organisational links to the political parties.

The campaign messages from the two sides were characterised by 'heaven and hell' arguments of the potential future consequences of joining or not joining the euro. The Yes campaign emphasised economic arguments for joining, outlining the prospects of more trade, more jobs, a sounder economic competition, lower prices and higher economic growth. Full membership would also give Sweden formal influence on the decisions made by the European Central Bank, they argued.

The No side communicated a larger array of arguments. Joining the euro would cost in terms of national sovereignty over the monetary politics and would also be another step towards a federal superstate in Europe: 'Membership in the EU is fine, but let's not take this further'. The fact that Sweden was better off economically than the Eurozone at the time of the referendum—in terms of interest rates and growth rates—made it possible to push the argument that 'if it's not a problem: don't fix it'. Potential membership of the Eurozone might as well be postponed into the future, and Sweden could join at a later stage.

No purdah for public officials was activated before the referendum. However, some Social Democratic cabinet members who were officially against the euro currency had to promise not to participate actively in the referendum campaign. Their noticeable absence from the campaign coverage became a powerful reminder that there were conflicting opinions on the Euro also within the Social Democratic government. This triggered a debate about whether Prime Minister Göran Persson had put a gag on some of the cabinet members.

Campaign financing was heavily skewed in the euro referendum. According to estimates (see Oscarsson and Holmberg 2004), the Yes side enjoyed the benefits of having almost ten times as much economic resources as the No side. Because of that, in the public debate, the referendum on the euro is often referred to as an illustrative example that money alone cannot buy election results.

According to extensive content analyses of the media coverage (Asp 2004), during the last four weeks of the euro referendum campaign, a full two-thirds of the reporting was devoted to the Yes side. Most of the coverage was game oriented, i.e. oriented towards the actors' strategies of political persuasion and the race between the Yes and No sides, and focused on the representatives of the Yes campaign, mainly on Social Democratic Prime Minister Göran Persson. A majority of this news coverage of the campaign was on the negative side. The negative attention for the actors on the Yes side dominated all media, particularly the television news. On the other hand, the media coverage of the political issue at hand—the euro currency—was predominantly positive. Of all media content during the euro campaign, 30% depicted the euro in a positive manner, 20% in a negative manner and 50% in a neutral manner.

During the final weeks of the campaign, the No side enjoyed the privilege of presenting their preferred arguments from a relatively strong position, as they had a comfortable lead in the opinion polls. The Yes side was, of course, under more pressure and had to be much more active. In the media, the representatives of the No side were predominantly engaged in discussions where they seem to have had the upper hand (sovereignty and macroeconomics), and they therefore avoided appearing in contexts where the euro issue was framed more positively for the Yes side (European cooperation and enterprise).

According to extensive content analyses of the media coverage by Kent Asp (2004), the Yes side was subject to far more scrutiny than the No side in the media during the euro campaign. One explanation is that journalists and the media took it upon themselves to balance out the striking imbalance of resources between Yes and No. The media logic, paired with a general idea of maintaining a democratic equilibrium, had the effect that the Yes side was scrutinised and the No side was portrayed favourably in the media. Ironically, the No side was still perceived as the underdog, although they had been consistently ahead in the polls nine months.

26.4   The Death of Anna Lindh

The Swedish referendum on the euro currency 2003 is still mostly remembered for a traumatic event: the murder of foreign minister Anna Lindh. She was stabbed to death when visiting a shopping mall in Stockholm 10th September, just a few days before Referendum Day. In the final hours of the referendum campaign, the reasons behind the killing were still unknown. Lindh's tragic death was at that time generally considered to be a terrorist attack or a sabotage of the democratic process. As a consequence, all debates and campaign activities were called off, and the referendum campaign came to a halt. The traditional TV debate on prime-time Friday night was cancelled. Instead, a one hour-long conversation about Swedish democracy was broadcast. All party leaders collectively pleaded for national mobilisation to the polls on Election Day.

The tragic event may have had a large impact on many different things in Swedish society. Anna Lindh was one of the most high profile advocates of Swedish euro membership. But according to detailed analyses from the SNES 2003 referendum voter study—designed as a campaign panel study with pre- and post-referendum interviews—the event had limited effect on the outcome of the referendum. Although we can see a dramatic rise of Anna Lindh's already very high personal popularity—the most dramatic short-term change ever recorded with the 11-point dislike-like scale—the effects of this rise in popularity on euro-attitudes was very limited (Oscarsson and Holmberg 2004: 31).

Results from internal party opinion polling that was released only after the referendum show that the Yes side may have had a momentum in the first days of the final week of the campaign, and that this shift may have resulted in a very close race between Yes and No sides. However, the abrupt ending of the campaign on the Thursday meant that all opinion formation processes came to a full stop. Of course, there is no telling how close the referendum might have been without the tragedy.

In any case, most voters did not let Anna Lindh's death, their mourning and their increasing sympathies affect their behaviour. Voters generally resisted letting a murderer or a terrorist sabotage the democratic process. In the case of the Swedish euro referendum, the most dramatic and unexpected campaign events you could possible imagine—the killing of a leading actor during the most intensive last week of the campaign—produced almost no measurable impact on the opinion formation or the referendum outcome, other than an increased propensity to turn out to vote and manifest support for the democratic process.

26.5   Why Sweden Voted No to the Euro

The Swedish No to the euro in 2003 was, according to extensive analyses of standard determinants of voting behaviour, mainly an ideological response: a highly politicised context resulted in extensive ideological voting, early mobilisation of the electorate, and limited short-term campaign effects (Oscarsson 2007). The clear result of the referendum meant that there were no major actors questioning the outcome. The losing side accepted that Swedish euro membership had been postponed for decades.

If the Swedish voters had been more prone to take cues from their own parties' positioning on the issue of euro membership—as they had done at previous referendums—the outcome in 2003 would probably have been a Yes. Especially the Social Democrats and the Christian Democrats were highly divided on the issue both on the elite level as well as among their own sympathisers.

The tendency for party sympathisers to align their vote with the official party line at referendums has weakened substantially over the years (Table 26.2). In the pension fund referendum in 1957, 85% of the voters aligned their vote to the party-sponsored alternative. In the euro referendum of 2003, the corresponding proportion was down to 64%. This development is not surprising as it is parallel to the generally weakening ties between parties and voters and the increasing volatility in the Swedish electorate.

As a direct consequence of the outcome of the euro referendum, a new political party was formed based on the popular movement of the No side in the referendum: the June List. In the European Parliamentary elections of May 2004, only four months after it had been formed, the euro-sceptic *June list* with spokespersons from Swedish banks and businesses coming from outside the political elites received 14.5% of the votes and became Sweden's third largest party with three seats in the European Parliament (Oscarsson and Holmberg 2006). Five years later, the *June List* did not manage to repeat this success, as it fell below the 4% threshold and lost its representation in the European Parliament.

Table 26.2 The proportion of party sympathisers who voted on their own party's sponsored alternative in Swedish referendums

Party sympathy	Pensions 1957 (%)	Nuclear power 1980 (%)	EU membership 1994 (%)	Euro currency 2003 (%)
The Left Party	100	90	89	91
The Green Party	–	–	87	82
Center Party	86	90	43	81
Social Democratic Party	88	74	52	47
Christian Democratic Party	–	77	44	47
Liberal Peoples Party	63	45	80	70
Conservative Party	93	67	86	76
All voters	85	74	67	64

Note Data are from Swedish National Election Studies conducted at national referendums. Results are compiled from the following volumes: Särlvik (1959), Holmberg and Asp (1984), Gilljam and Holmberg (1996) and Oscarsson and Holmberg (2004)

26.6 Concluding Remarks: The Swedish Experience of National Referendums

Sweden's earliest experiences of referendums serve as a deterrent. Anecdotally, in its pre-democratic history Sweden lost two territories as a result of using referendums: the referendum on Swedish colony St Bartholomei's reunion with France in 1877 was lost by 351 colonist votes to 1. The Norwegian referendum to leave the union with Sweden in 1905 was lost by 368,200 votes to 184. And in 1919, 96% of the population in the small island of Åland between Sweden and Finland voted to be reunited with Sweden, but Finland refused to abandon the territory.

Since the introduction of democracy in 1921, the experience of national referendums has also been quite bad. The votes of men and women were counted separately in the first national referendum after the female suffrage (1922); in 1957 and 1980 three hard to interpret alternatives were on offer; meanwhile the outcome of a very clear result (in 1955) was not respected by the political elite. Lastly, in the two most recent national referendums (1994 and 2003) the economic resources to run campaigns were very unevenly distributed between the Yes and No alternatives.

Also at the local level, the use of referendums has clashed with the representative, party-oriented democracy at many occasions. The typical clash happens when local referendums are held on issues where the local constituencies (*communes*) lack political competence concerning things like national regulations of wolf-hunting or large national infrastructure projects. Other clashes arise when referendums are held on very general matters—such as the level of taxes in the local constituency—which one would expect the representative electoral democracy to handle.

The once-in-a-decade pace of national referendums seems now to have come to a halt. Since the euro referendum in 2003, few political actors have pursued the ideas of arranging new national referendums in Sweden. Previous experiences have a bearing on these judgements: The strong polarised and heated debate at the time of the euro referendum and the national trauma following foreign minister Anna Lindh's death in the midst of the campaign has been considered important when explaining the widespread reluctance to engage in new referendums, especially so within the Social Democratic party.

Future national referendums on for example the issue of NATO membership or Sweden leaving the EU (Swexit) sometimes surface in the public debate, but there is still no real movement in that direction. The unstable parliamentary situation following the elections in 2014 and 2018—with electoral gains for the far-right anti-immigration party Sweden Democrats—is putting political parties under strong pressure in much the same ways as the energy and nuclear power debate did in the 1970s. However, the hardening cultural conflicts surrounding migration, globalisation and multiculturalism are considered harder to disarm through the mechanism of a national referendum.

References

Asp, K. (2004). Medierna som beslutsunderlag [The Quality of the Media Coverage]. In H. Oscarsson & S. Holmberg (Eds.), *Kampen om euron* [The Battle Over the Euro]. Göteborgs: Department of Political Science, University of Göteborgs.

Gilljam, M., & Holmberg, S. (1996). *Ett knappt ja till EU. Väljarna och folkomröstningen 1994* [A Yes-Win with a Slim Margin. The Voters and the EU-Referendum 1994] (1. uppl. ed.). Stockholm: Norstedts juridik.

Holmberg, S., & Asp, K. (1984). *Kampen om kärnkraften: en bok om väljare, massmedier och folkomröstningen 1980* [The Battle Over Nuclear Power] (1. uppl. ed.). Stockholm: Liber.

Möller, T. (2011). Folkomröstningar. In O. Petersson & I. Mattson (Eds.), *Svensk författningspolitik* (1. uppl. ed.). Stockholm: SNS förlag.

Oscarsson, H. (2007). The Ideological Response: Why Sweden Said No to the Euro. In C. H. de Vreese (Eds.), *Dynamics of Referendum Campaigns: An International Perspective*. Basingstoke: Palgrave Macmillan.

Oscarsson, H., & Holmberg, S. (2004). *Kampen om euron* [The Battle Over the Euro]. Göteborgs: Department of Political Science, University of Göteborgs.

Oscarsson, H., & Holmberg, S. (2006). *Europaval* [European Elections]. Gothenburg: Department of Political Science, University of Gothenburg.

Särlvik, B. (1959). *Opinionsbildningen vid folkomröstningen 1957*. SOU 1959:10. Stockholm.

Teorell, J. (2012). Omval och andra omtagningar under 300 år. In L. Berg & H. Oscarsson (Eds.), *Omstritt omval*. Göteborgs: SOM-institutet, Göteborgs universitet.

CHAPTER 27

Referendums on EU Treaty Reform: Revisiting the Result in Second Referendums

Brigid Laffan

27.1 Introduction

Eight times since the mid-1980s, the Irish electorate has had to engage in an intense, albeit not always informed debate, on a European treaty. Twice, Irish voters rejected an EU treaty and twice Irish governments, supported by the main opposition parties, went back to the electorate to ask: 'Is this your final answer?' The processes of treaty ratification were lengthy, so the electorate had to confront Europe in ways that the peoples of most of the other member states never experience. Irish voters had to address the realities of interdependence and EU membership. Revision of the Irish constitution requires the consent of the people, which in practice means that EU treaties are subject to referendum in Ireland with the result that Ireland has held more EU-related referendums than any other member state. Each EU treaty must be ratified by every member state before it comes into operation. Thus, when a Member State's electorate vote in a referendum, their vote has consequences not just for them but for the EU as a whole; a domestic political process in one state becomes part of wider EU multilevel politics. The focus in this chapter is on the holding of second referendums, primarily on ratification of the Lisbon Treaty, in order to illustrate the deep connectedness between politics in one country and the EU as a whole.

B. Laffan (✉)
European University Institute, Florence, Italy
e-mail: Brigid.Laffan@eui.eu

© The Author(s) 2021
J. Smith (ed.), *The Palgrave Handbook of European Referendums*,
https://doi.org/10.1007/978-3-030-55803-1_27

27.2   NICE

Prior to the Nice Treaty vote on 4 June 2001, Irish voters had endorsed four EU treaties in succession. When the ballot boxes were opened on Friday 5 June 2001, however, a shock awaited the Irish government, EU institutions and the candidate states. The treaty was defeated by 54–46% with a very low turnout of 34%. Most Irish voters stayed at home. The Nice Treaty was a relatively minor treaty that was part of the preparations for the enlargement of the EU to the East. In the aftermath of the referendum, the government faced a challenging external and domestic environment. It had taken the electorate for granted and Irish voters pushed back. Externally, the government tried to assure the other member states and the candidate countries that it remained committed to the Union and that the defeat of the treaty was not a rejection of enlargement. Given the centrality of the member states to the Union, the government was the central node in managing the multilevel politics of the Union and Ireland's place in the wider EU polity. The executive, which commanded a majority in parliament, began to design a strategy that involved responsiveness at a domestic level ('the people have spoken') and the search for a changing context with partners in the EU.

Domestically, the government sought to create the conditions that would allow it to consider re-running the referendum without being accused of ignoring the will of the Irish people. Its emphasis was on strengthening deliberation on European matters in Irish politics by institution-building and by enhancing existing institutions. The Government, backed by parliament, established a new institutional node called the National Forum on Europe under the Chairmanship of an independent senator. It had two pillars, a political pillar consisting of individuals nominated by the political parties and an observer pillar consisting of representatives of civil society, particularly those on both sides of the EU argument, as well as representatives from local authorities and Northern Ireland. The role of the Forum was to debate salient issues on the EU agenda and to discuss Ireland's place in the Union. Its deliberations widened the societal actors debating Europe in Ireland, raised the salience and knowledge of the EU among Irish politicians and legitimatised the engagement of representatives of partner countries in the Irish debate (O'Brennan 2004; Holmes 2005). In the aftermath of the Nice 1 Referendum, the Forum was a signal of government responsiveness to the voter. The second dimension of the domestic response was to ratchet up parliamentary oversight of European affairs (see for example Barrett 2015).

A general election in May 2002 returned the government to power and provided a mandate to the Prime Minister to go back to the people. *Fianna Fáil* in its manifesto pledged the following: 'If we succeed in negotiating a suitable Declaration, and in the light of the work of the Forum on Europe and proposals to improve the oversight and understanding of our work within the EU, we will submit the Nice Treaty to the people in a referendum to be held this autumn and will campaign strongly for a Yes vote' (*Fianna Fáil*

2002: 19). Before it was returned to the electorate, the government sought to frame the second referendum by seeking and securing at the Seville European Council (21 June 2001) a Declaration on Irish Neutrality, one of the salient campaign points, which clarified the impact of the common foreign and security policy (CFSP) on Ireland. Armed with this clarification, the government, main opposition parties and newly mobilised civil society organisations ran a highly energetic campaign. The second Nice referendum, held on 19 October 2002, was passed by a sizeable majority of 63–37% with a turnout of 49%, significantly higher than Nice I. The second referendum was followed by Ireland's very successful EU Presidency in the first half of 2004 that was marked by both the welcome ceremony for ten new member states and the successful conclusion of the Intergovernmental Conference (IGC) on the Constitutional Treaty, chaired by Bertie Ahern, the Irish Prime Minister. The Irish political elite had sufficient political authority and legitimacy to manage the multilevel political world of EU membership.

27.3   IRISH VOTERS SAY NO AGAIN

During the 2000s, the politicisation of European integration and the rise of Euroscepticism in Europe led to the two 2005 failed referendums in France and The Netherlands (see Chapter 28 by Sternberg). These referendum results did not lead to a second referendum, which begs the question concerning the differential impact on large and small states and newer versus founding states of referendum defeats. Neither the French nor Dutch government showed any desire to re-run the referendums. The Union resorted to problem-solving mode by taking time to reflect and ultimately transformed the Constitutional Treaty into the Lisbon Treaty in 2007.

The official narrative of Ireland's relationship with the EU was tested for a second time in June 2008 when a majority of the Irish electorate voted against the Lisbon Treaty; on a turnout of 53.1%, 53.4% voted No. This was a significant increase in the No vote as a proportion of the electorate, from 18 to 28% (Quinlan 2009) the highest percentage of the electorate that ever voted against an EU treaty in Ireland. This brings the difference between Lisbon I and Nice I, where low turnout was the key factor in the No win, sharply into focus. For a second time within a decade an Irish electorate, with traditionally positive attitudes towards the EU, had voted No to a European treaty. The sense of crisis in the Union was pervasive given that this was the third rejection of a European treaty between 2005 and 2008. Popular discontent with Europe was on the rise.

In June 2008, a new Prime Minister, Brian Cowen, was faced with a complex challenge given the referendum and the onset of the global financial crisis in autumn 2008. Faced with a number of difficult political dilemmas, the government was unsure of its response and did not declare its willingness to have a second referendum until December 2008. Nor was it willing to accept the advice of *Sinn Féin* (SF), the only parliamentary party to oppose the treaty. In June 2018, SF argued:

> The people have now spoken and the Lisbon Treaty is over. The ratification process should now end and the leaders of the EU's 27 Member States must now negotiate a new treaty. (*Sinn Féin* 2008)

Sinn Féin was suggesting to the Irish government that it essentially request an end to the ratification of the treaty, something it was unwilling to do. SF launched a poster campaign showing an arrow through the heart of the Lisbon treaty to increase the pressure on the government.

27.3.1   Buying Time at Home

The new Irish Prime Minister, Brian Cowen, attended his first European Council on 19/20 June 2008. Given the failure of the referendum, he received rather more attention than a new PM might have wanted at his first European Council. The Council Conclusions open with five paragraphs on the treaty. The European Council by its nature is hardwired to understand and respond to events in domestic politics, as its members are the highest political office-holders in their respective member states. The other heads of government agreed with the Irish PM that time was needed to find an agreed way forward but also stressed that the treaty had been ratified by 19 partners and that ratification processes would continue in other member states. This was a reminder to SF that the Treaty of Lisbon was not dead. The Council, which became the key EU level arena to address the issue decided to address the question again at the October European Council (2008a). The Irish government was given time to deal with the domestic consequences of the vote without pressure from the Union.

The reflex response of the government was to underline the role of the *Oireachtas* and to restate the centrality of representative democracy in Irish politics. The main political parties that had campaigned for Lisbon I were supportive of this. A sub-committee of the European Affairs Committee was established by the two houses of parliament that set itself the tasks of:

- analysing the challenges to Ireland following the rejection of the Lisbon Treaty;
- considering Ireland's future in the EU across the key policy areas;
- making recommendations on the role of the *Oireachtas* in EU affairs;
- considering measures to improve public understanding of the EU and its fundamental importance for Ireland's future. (*Oireachtas* 2008)

The sub-committee met in autumn 2008 and heard from a wide array of civil society organisations on both sides of the argument, individual experts, state agencies, Church leaders, a delegation from the German *Bundestag*, journalists, Commissioners and the Secretary-General of the EU Commission (*Oireachtas* 2008). A wide-ranging and serious debate kept the issue of Lisbon in the public mind. The report on *Ireland's future in the European Union: Challenges, Issues and Options* was published in November 2008 and was central to re-framing the debate from a focus on individual and arcane articles of a treaty to the core issue of Ireland's membership of the EU (*Oireachtas* 2008). The report concluded that 'Ireland's decision not to ratify the Lisbon Treaty has made the country's long-term position at the core of the European Union considerably less certain' (*Oireachtas* 2008: 3). It went on to argue 'that Irish sovereignty has flourished in the European Union, and Ireland's role as a fully committed and engaged member state has been vital to the advancement of the country's national interests' (*Oireachtas* 2008: 3). This was linked to a commitment to address the 'concerns' of the Irish people. The political message was clear; Ireland was a committed EU member state but its government and parliament understood that there were issues of concern to the public. The fact that all members of the Committee, apart from two anti-Lisbon parliamentarians, strongly endorsed the report transformed the issue into a national rather than a party political one. The opposition parties were part of the search for an agreed roadmap from the outset. Given the unpopularity of the government, this was a crucial element in the second referendum.

In order to understand the concerns of the voters, the government resorted to research, which became part of the strategic response to managing the tensions and pressures arising from the decision of the Irish electorate and the reaction of Ireland's partners in the Union. The government wanted solid evidence of the concerns so that it could begin to address them. A political research company, Millward and Brown, supported by Ireland's leading public opinion scholar, Professor Richard Sinnott, was asked to conduct a major study on voting behaviour in Lisbon I. The research was conducted in summer 2008 and its results were known by September, which gave the government deep knowledge long before the issue would be revisited at the October European Council. The key conclusions of the research were:

- 23% of voters on both sides were classified as 'soft';
- Opposition to the Treaty was apparent predominantly among 25–34-year olds (59%), the C2 and DE socio-economic groups (63% and 65%) and women (56%). Among the main political parties, 63% of Fianna Fáil supporters voted for the Treaty, 52% of *Fine Gael* supporters also voted in favour of it. Labour and Green party supporters both voted against (61% and 53%, respectively) as did *Sinn Féin* supporters (88%);
- The main reason cited for voting No was 'lack of knowledge/information/understanding' at 42%;
- The main reason for abstention was the lack of knowledge and understanding (46%);

- Knowledge of the EU in general and understanding of the Treaty were reported as significant issues.
- Of specific concern to No voters were erosion of Irish neutrality, the end of control over abortion and conscription to a European army, which were portrayed as part of Lisbon, in addition to the loss of an Irish Commissioner. (Millward and Brown 2008, 1–4)

This gave the government and parliament a very good grasp of voting behaviour in the referendum across different cohorts of the electorate, a set of issues to address and the knowledge that some voters who were open to changing their minds. It also highlighted the role that lack of knowledge played in both voting No and in abstaining. Significantly, the Millward and Brown study found that 60% of respondents believed that Ireland's interests were best pursued by remaining fully involved in the EU; only 18% of electorate believed that Ireland would be well served by opting to be less involved (Millward and Brown Study 2008). This highlighted the underlying commitment to EU membership in the Irish electorate.

27.3.2   The EU Level Strategy

The politics of Lisbon involved not just domestic politics but was an issue in Ireland's relations with its partners. The parliamentary sub-committee ruled out any attempt to ratify the Lisbon Treaty by parliamentary means but hinted at a new deal for Ireland suggesting that the concerns of the Irish electorate 'be accommodated by the other Member States' (*Oireachtas* 2008: 6). The government was the pivotal node in managing the domestic and EU-level deliberations on Lisbon. In the EU arena, the European Council was the key institution in managing the collective response to the Irish referendum. European Council meetings are highly orchestrated and the tip of the iceberg in a complex network of bilateral discussions. The Irish government engaged in intensive talks with the other member states to ensure that by the time it came to a European Council meeting, it achieved its key objectives. The first European Council that formally addressed the way forward was the October 2008 European Council.

The October 2008 European Council signalled the collective desire for a 'common way forward', while the subsequent December meeting established the EU roadmap and time-frame. The French Presidency, under President Sarkozy's chairmanship, was committed to making progress on an Irish deal and without President Sarkozy's commitment a deal may not have emerged. There were three options in the lead-up to December:

1. that the Council would mark time and note progress;
2. that the Council would agree a progress report and identify areas for further work; or
3. that the basis of an agreement would be outlined.

The Irish government and the French Presidency shared a strong preference for the third option as they had little confidence in the incoming Czech Presidency to broker a deal in the first half of 2009. In the event, the Council reaffirmed the importance of the Treaty to the future of the EU and offered Ireland a new deal subject to the ratification of the Lisbon Treaty. A statement from the Irish prime minister outlining the concerns of the Irish people with regard to the Lisbon Treaty appeared as an appendix to the Council conclusions. The broad outline of the new deal included a commitment that:

- the Commission would continue to include one Commissioner per member state;
- the EU would give legal guarantees to Ireland on: (a) taxation, (b) security and defence policy and (c) provisions of the Irish Constitution dealing with the right to life, education and the family and
- the Council would agree A Solemn Declaration on Workers' Rights. (European Council 2008b)

This was a game changer as it allowed the Irish government, if it succeeded in translating this deal into agreed text, to go back to the people. In response, the Irish government committed itself to seeking ratification of the Treaty of Lisbon by the end of the term of the then Commission, in other words to a second referendum in autumn 2009 (European Council 2008b). Agreement within the European Council on the Irish package was difficult. There were many member states, notably the Benelux, which objected to the decision on the number of Commissioners as they were committed to a smaller Commission and there were compelling reasons to reduce the size of the Commission. The question of the legal guarantees proved difficult for the United Kingdom and it required an all-night session brokered by the French Presidency to get Gordon Brown to agree to the text. Prime Minister Brown was concerned about domestic politics in the United Kingdom including pressure from the opposition Conservatives to reopen the UK ratification process.

Following the December European Council, very complex and protracted negotiations were needed to flesh out the outline agreement. The Irish negotiators had to meet every member state government at least twice and many three or four times between January and June to get agreement to the wording of the text. The Council Legal Secretariat was central in drafting a text that would command agreement. On the eve of the June 2009 European Council, the Irish Prime Minister took the decision to write to his counterparts saying that in the absence of legally binding guarantees he was unwilling to hold a referendum. The PM opted to play this very high stakes game on the eve of the Council as the government felt that legal guarantees were the minimum needed to re-run the referendum by demonstrating that the concerns of the Irish electorate had been listened to. In the event, the European Council agreed a Decision of the Heads of State and Government. The outcome could be sold domestically as a new deal for Ireland.

The deal had three elements. First, was the agreement on the retention of a Commissioner per member state. Second, was a set of legal guarantees addressing issues that had been raised in Lisbon 1. Section A of the Decision established that the Irish constitution prevails in relation to the right to life, family and education and that nothing in the Lisbon Treaty affected these articles of the Irish constitution. Section B confirmed that the Lisbon Treaty did not alter the powers of member states in the area of taxation. In other words, Lisbon does not affect Ireland's rate of corporation tax. Section C, a very long section, covered Ireland's traditional policy of military neutrality and the EU's foreign, security and defence policy. It provided clarification and specifically mentioned that the Lisbon Treaty did not provide for the creation of a European army or conscription. This section emphasised that it is up to Ireland to decide on the manner and nature of its engagement with the Union's security policy. This was further underlined by an accompanying Declaration by Ireland on Irish security and defence policy. The third element was a Solemn Declaration by the European Council on workers' rights and social policy as there were issues raised about a number of European Court of Justice cases during the referendum campaign. The value of the guarantees was the clarification they provided concerning elements of the Lisbon Treaty that would make it more difficult for the No campaign to get traction on these issues in a second campaign. The guarantees took potentially contentious issues off the agenda.

The Irish government backed by the Irish parliament and not the other member states drove the political processes associated with Lisbon between June 2008 and 2009. The other member states, however, had made it abundantly clear that they wished to see the Lisbon Treaty ratified. Why did the government and parliament, the core of Ireland's representative democracy, go down this route and not accept the advice of Sinn Féin offered immediately after the referendum? There were three key reasons. First, the Irish government was part of the EU consensus that led to the reform treaty in the first place. The government and the other member state governments spent seven years negotiating treaty reform because they felt that there were systemic reasons for the reform and that it represented an improvement on the pre-existing treaty architecture. Second, asking the Irish electorate to think again was indispensable to Ireland maintaining control over its future relationship with the European Union and its member states. There is an understandable tendency among electorates to think that rejection of a European treaty maintains the status quo as the default mechanism. This is not the case as the rejection itself is a major political event that triggers responses at domestic and EU levels. Third, the economic crisis was felt acutely in Ireland, which altered the context of the referendum. By the end of June 2009, a deeply unpopular government turned its attention to the up-hill battle of winning the second referendum.

27.4   The Second Lisbon Referendum

Having charted the course for a second referendum, the government found itself facing formidable challenges in its efforts to win; the government needed to appeal to more than its core supporters given its standing in the polls (LeDuc 2002: 728). Scholars are divided about the nature of referendums as political events and about voting behaviour in referendums. The literature divides into two schools of thought. The first school regards referendums as 'second order elections' that are dominated by domestic political issues whereby voters are motivated by satisfaction or dissatisfaction with the government (Franklin et al. 1994, 1995). From this perspective, a referendum becomes a plebiscite on the government (Franklin 2002; Garry et al. 2005). The second school of thought considers that voting behaviour in referendums is based on attitudes and beliefs, in this case attitudes and beliefs towards European integration (Svensson 2002). Svensson posits the divide with the following question: do voters 'really address the issues and involve themselves actively in the policy-making process on a vital issue or do they merely vote for or against the current government' (2002: 733). The second Lisbon referendum offered a ready-made test of the second-order or issue-driven hypotheses concerning referendums. In addition, it provided a lens on the role and impact of political parties, political elites and the media on voter behaviour and the outcome of referendums which is of growing interest in the literature (Hobolt 2006). It has been argued that a vigorous campaign may be more significant in referendums than in electoral contests (Garry et al. 2005: 215).

27.4.1   Punishment or Issue on Its Merits

The Irish electorate had an opportunity in the second referendum to punish a deeply unpopular government or to deal with the question before it—the ratification of the Lisbon Treaty. The choice was between treating the referendum as a second-order political contest and opting for punishment or elevating the issue above domestic and partisan considerations. In September 2009, just before the vote, satisfaction with the government was 14% with a staggering 81% expressing dissatisfaction with its performance. Even a majority of supporters of the governing parties were dissatisfied with the government's performance. In response to questions about who they would vote for in a general election, the two governing parties languished at 24% in the polls whereas the main opposition parties were on 56% (*Irish Times*, 26 September 2009). Hence, the outcome of Lisbon II depended not on the ability of the governing parties to deliver their supporters (Crum 2007: 62) but on the commitment of the opposition to support a Yes and campaign actively for it. It also required the active mobilisation of civil society groups to elevate the issue beyond partisan politics. In the end, a significant majority of the Irish electorate was persuaded in Lisbon II that the issue was strategic rather than domestic or partisan.

It was clear to the electorate in December 2008 following the European Council that a second vote on the Lisbon Treaty was highly likely, which meant that there was time to become accustomed to a second ballot. Lisbon was a recurring topic on the political, parliamentary and media agenda throughout the period. By November 2008, polls suggested that there was a small swing back in favour of Lisbon; an *Irish Times*/TNS poll found that 43% would vote Yes, 39% No and 18% remained in the 'don't know' category. Excluding the don't knows, this gave the Yes side 52.5% and the No side 47.5% (*Irish Times*, 17 November 2008). The margin was however narrow: the government was acutely aware the first Lisbon campaign was an 'opinion reversal' campaign as the Yes side was ahead at the outset of the campaign and yet lost (LeDuc 2002: 729). There was a determination that this would not occur again (Laffan 2015).

There was a high level of mobilisation for the second referendum. Support for the treaty was drawn from the government parties, the two main opposition parties, the key economic interest organisations and, especially, civil society groups. A feature of the second campaign was the role played by individual executives such as Michael O'Leary of Ryanair and Jim O'Hara, chief executive of Intel Ireland. Among those opposing the treaty were *Sinn Féin*, the only parliamentary party in the No camp, anti-system parties such as the Socialist Workers party, the Workers' party and the Socialist Party in addition to protest movements such as People Before Profit on the left and *Cóir* on the right. Libertas, led by Declan Ganley, which was very influential in the first Lisbon referendum only re-entered the debate in mid-September 2009 when the campaign was up and running. The No side had decisively won the first campaign; following the 2008 referendum, 67% of those polled felt that the No campaign was the more convincing, with only 15% convinced by the Yes campaign. Those supporting a Yes had to mount a much stronger campaign.

The key components and strategy of the Yes campaign in Lisbon II were therefore mobilisation, research, framing the debate and message and delivering the message through the right messenger. From the outset, there was an understanding that a significant proportion of the electorate had to be persuaded to switch from No to Yes if the Treaty was to be carried. Given the multiplicity of Yes groups, there needed to be a consistency of message and no infighting. After all, one of the reasons for the loss of the Danish Euro referendum was that the Yes campaign stressed different and frequently contradictory reasons for voting Yes (Qvortrup 2001: 193).

27.4.2   Mobilisation

If in the first Lisbon referendum there was weak mobilisation of those supporting Yes, Lisbon II was marked by a very high level of mobilisation. Ireland for Europe mounted a national campaign from a standing start. It began without a name, visual identity, logo, headquarters and, most importantly, money. It was a coalition of the willing, the committed and the available. The group emerged in the aftermath of the Lisbon I rejection of the treaty. Pat Cox, former President of the European Parliament, took on the role of campaign director. Ireland for Europe launched its campaign on the Sunday after the summit that agreed the Irish guarantees in June 2009. A number of highly influential people agreed to act as patrons of Ireland for Europe including The Edge from U2, Robbie Keane, the captain of the Irish football team, Mary Davis, the chief organiser of the Special Olympics, and most notably of all, Seamus Heaney, the Nobel Laureate. Seamus Heaney in a video interview shown at the launch, before reading one of his poems said: 'There are many reasons for ratifying the Lisbon treaty, reasons to do with our political and economic wellbeing, but the poem speaks mainly for our honour and identity as Europeans'. The verse included the line 'Move lips, move minds and make new meanings flare' (*Beacons at Bealtaine*), which became the beacon for the campaign.

The launch of Ireland for Europe received extensive coverage on the main radio and television news and current affairs programmes and was carried by 23 newspapers, national and local. The most widely read national newspaper, the *Irish Independent*, had an editorial praising the launch, stating:

> This is exactly what the Yes campaign needs – and notably lacked last year, when the first Lisbon vote was lost. The support of so many of the country's most attractive and successful personalities will surely have an effect on the apathetic and the wavering. In addition, these personalities and the organizers of the movement possess something that is little in evidence among the members of the Government: communication skills. (*Irish Independent*, 22 June 2009)

Ireland for Europe established itself as a key player, the leading non-party group, from the outset. There were two dimensions to the process of mobilisation: spatial and sectoral. On the ground, the key was to organise local groups throughout Ireland around key nodes of communication, notably, local radio and newspapers and the political constituencies. This stemmed from an understanding that the campaign could not just be Dublin-based but had to become a national movement. In all, Ireland for Europe supported 22 local groups that were separately branded and provided with area-specific literature. The groups tended to have between 20 and 40 volunteers. Each group devised its own strategy depending on resources. The local campaigns involved feet on the street, visibility through posters, billboards, interviews on local radio stations and photographs in local newspapers. Headquarters supplied tailored leaflets, T-shirts, stickers and other campaign material. In the latter stages of the campaign, there was a conference call with the local groups to gather intelligence about what was happening on the ground each day.

Sectoral mobilisation, which was designed to address key niches of the electorate, complemented the spatial mobilisation. The two most significant sectoral groups were 'Generation Yes' and 'Women for Europe' as a majority of young people and women had voted No in the first Lisbon campaign.

Generation Yes shared campaign headquarters with Ireland for Europe but were autonomous in terms of look, message and channels of communication. Generation Yes supplied enormous energy to the campaign, were the main source of volunteers for canvassing and were active on facebook, twitter and blogs. The youth group organised throughout the country, with a particular focus on the universities and institutes of education. Generation Yes was indispensable to the major swing of 21% that was achieved among the 18–24 group.

Women for Europe were not formally part of Ireland for Europe but close relations were maintained. The group worked to enhance women's knowledge of the EU and the treaty; they produced leaflets and maintained an active website. The primary channels of communicating with women were coffee mornings, small meetings and limited canvassing. Ireland for Europe also worked on communicating with women. A special leaflet with an appeal from a high-profile woman was distributed throughout the country and care was taken in news media to appeal to women voters. The tabloids received particular attention as these papers were widely read by women in the C2DE categories who had voted No in the first referendum. In Lisbon II, 66% of women voted Yes in contrast to 44% in Lisbon I.

Whereas young people and women were two of the key demographics, there was extensive mobilisation of other groups under the banner of Ireland for Europe such as Lawyers for Europe, a key group as they could speak with authority on the treaty and the Irish Constitution. A former staff member of the Irish Farmers' Association organised a number of high-profile representatives of the farming community to write for local newspapers and speak at appropriate events. A group of trade unionists known as the Charter Group did extensive work on the issue of workers' rights. Business for Europe, under the auspices of the Irish Business and Employers' Confederation (IBEC), was influential in putting the business and economic argument. A small but influential group, Christians for Europe, was pivotal in bringing the argument to the religious right. Retired army officers were vocal and influential on the European Security and Defence Policy (ESDP).

27.4.3   Research

Research served a political purpose in the unfolding of the Lisbon II referendum. The September 2008 Millward Brown study, cited above, provided the government with a clear set of issues that had to be addressed if there was to be a second referendum. The key message concerning the loss of the first referendum was the lack of information and knowledge. Lack of knowledge, information and understanding was cited by 42% of those who voted No in Lisbon I. Moreover, the study highlighted the key issues that divided the Yes and No voters: neutrality; European regulation; the loss of the Commissioner; workers' rights and retaining control over abortion laws. These issues formed the basis of the search for a new package to put to the Irish electorate.

The Millward Brown research was followed by extensive quantitative and qualitative research undertaken by different campaign groups during the preparatory period. Research was sporadic rather than systematic because of the high cost of extensive fieldwork, but it was sufficient to provide key insights to those designing and managing the campaign. Participants in the focus groups tended to be drawn from the key target groups, women, young people and those of lower socio-economic status. In addition, care was taken to conduct the focus groups throughout the country. The qualitative research probed attitudes to European integration, reasons for the Lisbon treaty and the strength or otherwise of the Yes and No arguments. It became clear why the No campaign had won the first referendum. The No campaign, notwithstanding their anti-system and marginal status, had successfully captured the middle ground. The first Yes campaign was seen to have engaged in parent-to-child communication rather than treating the electorate as adults. Voters felt that the government seemed 'to presume a blind acceptance of their recommendation and put little effort into the campaign', that 'The Yes side didn't really put forward an advantage' and that 'We're waiting on the reasons to vote Yes' (Focus Groups, June/July 2009). The research provided a number of key considerations for those mounting a Yes campaign:

- Address the concerns of the electorate;
- Provide information in a clear and accessible style;
- Mobilise to show that it matters;
- Watch the tone with which messages are delivered;
- Make the campaign about Ireland not the government;
- Make the campaign about Ireland in Europe and not just about the specific treaty;
- Give the electorate reasons to vote Yes.

The research suggested that among 'soft' No voters there was a concern that they may not have voted 'correctly' the first time. Given the coverage of, and reaction to, the first No, many voters were unsure about whether they had really understood what the implications of a No vote were. Among 'soft' No voters a second referendum was not regarded as an imposition; they were willing to think again and there was a strong sense in the focus groups that making the right decision in a second referendum was crucial. Only 'hard' No voters were opposed to a second referendum.

27.4.4   Framing the Debate

The Yes campaign failed to frame the debate in Lisbon I. It was reactive, lacked focus and persuasive power. For Lisbon II the Yes campaign had to become proactive in framing the debate: it needed to develop general overarching arguments that were in tune with more specific arguments. The launch of Ireland for Europe on 21 June 2009, just after the June summit, was strategically important. It enabled the campaign to focus on the New Deal, New Question and New Context. It sought to elevate the debate from the Lisbon Treaty per se to the Lisbon Treaty as part of Ireland's relations with the European Union. It sought to highlight the positive benefits of Lisbon with a credible framing of the costs of a No vote. Central to this endeavour was the distinction between text and context. The first Lisbon referendum involved a series of textual wars about articles of the treaty that succeeded in boring and alienating the voters and giving advantage to the No campaign, notwithstanding the fact that most of their pronouncements on the treaty were inaccurate or exaggerated. The Yes campaign was determined to put context centre stage while having credible text warriors go out and bat on air and in the print media against the No campaign.

The context of the vote was multifaceted. First, was the importance of Ireland's relationship with the EU and in the EU. The benefits of that relationship both in the past and anticipated in the future were central to the narrative. Second, was the multilevel nature of the EU and the importance of Lisbon not just to Ireland but to Ireland's partners in Europe. Third, was the dramatic reversal in Ireland's economic fortunes in the autumn of 2008 arising from the banking crisis, the real economy crisis and the public finance crisis. Fourth, were the unknowable political and economic consequences of a second No. The interaction and intersection of a number of different contingencies enabled the Yes campaign credibly to stress the salience of the vote, the consequences of the vote, the dynamics of interdependence and Lisbon as a necessary, albeit insufficient, platform for recovery. Finally, was the need to ensure that the referendum was not about the government.

The Yes campaign could not ignore the treaty itself as it had been accused during the Lisbon I campaign of being unwilling to discuss the treaty. It had to manage the delicate balance between fighting on the text while preventing text wars taking over with ensuing confusion among voters. The No arguments focused on classical issues of sovereignty, workers' rights, neutrality and the prospects for a better deal. The No campaign also targeted the government and in particular the prime minister.

27.4.5   Framing and Delivering the Message

The need to elevate the debate above partisan politics and a narrow focus on the Lisbon Treaty molded the first wave of posters and messages. Straplines such as 'We are stronger in Europe', 'We are stronger with Europe', 'Vote Yes for Ireland's Future', 'We're better together', 'It's Simple, We need Europe', 'The Choice is Yours', 'Lisbon: We Belong-You Decide' and 'It's Simple: I want a strong voice in Europe' provided a soft introduction to the issues. Many posters included photographs of men and women—the people who had to make the decision. Respect for the autonomy of the voter was underlined by phrases such as 'The choice is yours', and 'You Decide'. The first wave of messages was followed by a number of messages that focused on the economy; 'Vote Yes for Jobs: Our Future Begins with a Yes to Lisbon', 'Yes to Jobs: Yes to Europe', 'Yes to Recovery: Yes to Europe', 'Work with Europe: Work Together', 'Yes for Jobs and Investment' and 'For Growth and innovation in Ireland: stay connected to Europe'. Specific segments of the electorate or specific gains from the new deal were targeted with straplines such as 'Europe has made life better for Women, Workers and Ireland'.

The messaging became sharper as the campaign went into its final phase. Towards the end of the campaign a number of posters carried a stark message of the choice facing the electorate, 'Recovery or Ruin: Put Ireland First'. Attention was also paid to the lies told by the No campaign particularly one on the minimum wage that had a significant impact among the lower socio-economic groups. 'Do not Believe the Lies' became the by-line for a number of very effective posters. The Labour Party in an effort to raise the issue beyond the government in office had a very effective poster, 'Yes: It is That Important'.

27.4.6   Delivering the Message

All of the actors involved in the campaign understood that television, newspapers and radio were the preferred communication channels for the electorate. In Lisbon I, 61% identified television as the major channel, followed by 33% newspapers and 25% radio. The broadcast media in Ireland are subject to stringent coverage requirements during the course of a referendum campaign. The Broadcasting Act and a Supreme Court Judgement (Coughlan vs. BCC) has effectively been interpreted by the national broadcaster, *RTÉ*, as 50:50 airtime for Yes and No. There was however a marked difference between the *RTÉ* coverage of Lisbon I and II. In Lisbon I, a conflict frame, akin to Punch and Judy contests between Yes and No was the main news frame deployed. There was little or no editorial intervention to correct inaccurate claims. During Lisbon II the conflict frame was accompanied by a responsibility frame, i.e. *RTÉ* accepted that the issue was salient and had to be taken seriously. An economic consequences frame, significant in the literature, was also evident with the extensive coverage received by well-known businesspeople (de Vreese 2003: 21–22). The broadcaster used experienced journalists to set out the facts of the case, which served to provide essential context before interactions between Yes and No campaigners. These framing packages played an important educational role.

Local radio has considerable reach in Ireland and hence it was vital to have local actors available to speak on programmes. The print media in Ireland was divided between the Irish-owned press and UK-owned press, which is read by 40% of the Irish electorate. There was a strong editorial support for ratification in all of the Irish-owned newspapers, both broadsheet and tabloid. The UK-based media, particularly the Murdoch-owned press, was hostile to the EU and had adopted a very Eurosceptic line during the first Lisbon referendum.

The *Sunday Times* in particular was strongly opposed to the treaty. The UK-owned press was more muted in its coverage the second time around. Perhaps, sensing the mood swing in Ireland, it did not want to be too out of touch with its readership.

The message was delivered through multiple channels: online, print media, radio and television, outdoor advertising including posters, Bus T-slides, billboards, leaflets and photocalls. Different messengers, national and local, EU specialists, stars and notables were deployed for different media. Ireland for Europe created its own content, held its own events, participated in events created by others, offered spokespeople to major programmes, provided a platform for those outside politics and worked under the radar to make sure that the media was properly briefed on the issues at stake. The electorate was segmented into different groups and communication strategies were developed to address women and men, young and old and the richer and poorer parts of society. The broadsheets responded to key issues whereas the tabloids favoured short snappy pieces accompanied by photographs. There was continuous engagement with the producers of important programmes to ensure that coverage was fair and balanced.

27.5   Winning the Referendum

The mobilisation, framing and messaging worked remarkably well as more Irish people voted for Lisbon the second time around than for any other European treaty (Sinnott and Elkink 2010) Turnout was the highest for any referendum apart from the accession referendum in 1972; second time around the Yes votes grew from 48 to 67% of the electorate. A majority Yes was recorded for all age cohorts, socio-economic groups, men and women, urban and rural. The reasons for voting Yes were largely similar in the two referendums with the notable exception of the economy. In 2008, 9% voted Yes to help the economy; by October 2009, this had grown to 23%. A sense that a Yes was in the best interests of Ireland, that Ireland got considerable benefits from the EU and that a Yes vote would keep Ireland fully engaged in Europe were the dominant reasons for voting Yes. The reasons for voting Yes suggest that the electorate was persuaded that the vote was important to Ireland and that it was related to Ireland's standing in Europe. The changing economic context was crucial to this (see Table 27.1).

The most significant reasons for voting No in 2009 were to protect Irish identity and sovereignty (17%), followed by a lack of trust in politicians (10%), objections to having a second referendum (9%), to safeguard Irish neutrality in security and defence (6%) and to protest against the government's policies (5%) (*Eurobarometer*, September 2009). One of the major reasons for voting No in 2008 was absent; the proportion of those who voted No because they thought they did not know enough about the treaty, fell from 22% to just 4%. This removed a key argument of the No campaign that if you don't know, vote No. The guarantees removed two other themes of the No campaign;

Table 27.1 A tale of two referendums

	Turnout	Yes	No	Swing	Constituencies won
Lisbon 1	53%	46.4%	53.2%		10/45
June 2008		752,451	862,415		
Lisbon 2	59%	67.1%	32.9%	+20.7%	43/45
October 2009		1,214,268	594,606		

Source http://www.nsd.uib.no/european_election_database/election_types/eu_related_referen
dums.html

those voting No because Ireland would lose its Commissioner fell from 6% to just 2% and those wishing to protect the Irish taxation system fell from 6 to 2%. A large number of voters switched from No to Yes and from abstention to Yes between the two campaigns. The main reason for switching was increased information and communication (29%), more engagement in the public debate (21%) and that it would help the Irish economy (25%). The *Irish Times* editorial on Monday 5 October drew attention to the difference between the Lisbon II and Nice II referendums. It said:

> What marks the second Lisbon vote out strikingly from the second Nice vote in 2002 is that, while the latter reversal largely reflected a massive increase in the Yes turnout, this time it is clear that although turnout played a part, the No vote declined by some quarter of a million. In other words, at least a quarter of a million voters changed their vote from no to yes. In part that was clearly due to the new context - the chill winds of recession which would isolate Ireland and the 'guarantees'. Credit is also due to the critically important role played by activists from civic society, among Ireland for Europe, whose arguments made it possible to disconnect the treaty as an issue in the minds of voters from the performance of the Government. (*Irish Times*, 5 October 2009)

The extent of the swing would not have been possible without the bedrock of support there is in Ireland for the EU and EU membership. Diffuse support for European integration was strong enough to legitimise asking the question again, albeit in a different context and with a different package.

27.6 Conclusions

The second Lisbon referendum was salient for both Ireland and the EU. For Ireland, a second No to Lisbon and three rejections of European treaties in less than a decade would have altered Ireland's position in the Union in a myriad of ways. The stakes were no less high for the European Union. The UK Independence Party (UKIP) was active in Ireland during the referendum campaign, sending a highly misleading booklet to every house in the country, and was prepared to play the race card in its effort to derail the Lisbon Treaty. At the hustings, UKIP was joined by Open Europe, a pro-Conservative think

580   B. LAFFAN

tank. Ireland became the battleground for Eurosceptics and was in danger of getting caught up in the slipstream of the British Conservative debate on Lisbon. The bedrock of support for EU membership in Ireland inoculated it somewhat from the virus of UK Euroscepticism.

The experience of revisiting issues in second referendums underlines the dynamic and temporal dimension of democracy. The Irish electorate was open to thinking again about a political issue if they were convinced about the salience of the issue. Moreover, they voted differently when they felt that they had a better grasp of the context and content of the Lisbon Treaty. The dynamic of multilevel politics in the EU underlines the centrality of national governments deploying their political authority to manage the interaction between the pressures of the EU collective and domestic politics. Having opted to ask the Irish electorate again, pro-EU political and social forces ran an effective campaign to deliver the result.

REFERENCES

Barrett, G. (2015). Long Train Running: The Slowly Developed (and Slowly Developing) Role of Ireland's Oireachtas in EU Affairs. In C. Hefftler, C. Neuhold, O. Rozenberg & J. Smith (Eds.), *The Palgrave Handbook of National Parliaments and the European Union* (pp. 290–311). Basingstoke: Palgrave Macmillan.

Crum, B. (2007). Party Stances in the Referendums on the EU Constitution. *European Union Politics, 8*(1), 61–82.

De Vreese, C. (2003). *Communicating Europe.* 'Next Generation Democracy: Legitimacy in Network Europe' project. https://fpc.org.uk/wp-content/uploads/2006/09/89.pdf.

European Council. (2008a). *Conclusions, 19–20 June 2008.* http://www.consilium.europa.eu/ueDocs/cms_Data/docs/pressData/en/ec/101346.pdf.

European Council. (2008b). *Conclusions, 11–12 December 2008.* https://www.consilium.europa.eu/ueDocs/cms_Data/docs/pressData/en/ec/104692.pdf.

European Council. (2009). *Conclusions, 18–19 June 2009.* http://www.consilium.europa.eu/uedocs/cms_data/docs/pressdata/en/ec/108622.pdf.

Fianna Fáil. (2002). Election Manifesto 2002. http://michaelpidgeon.com/manifestos/. Accessed 1 July 2019.

Franklin, M., Marsh, M., & McLaren, L. (1994). Uncorking the Bottle: Popular Opposition to European Unification in the Wake of Maastricht. *Journal of Common Market Studies, 32*(4), 455–472.

Franklin, M., van der Eijk, C., & Marsh, M. (1995). Referendum Outcomes and Trust in Government: Public Support for Europe in the Wake of Maastricht. *West European Politics, 18,* 101–117.

Franklin, M. N. (2002), Learning from the Danish Case: A Comment on Palle Svensson's Ctitique of the Franklin thesis. *European Jounral of Political Research, 41,* 751–757.

Garry, J., Marsh, M., & Sinnott, R. (2005). 'Second-Order' Versus 'Issue-Voting' Effects in EU Referendums. *European Union Politics, 6*(2), 201–221.

Hobolt, S. B. (2006). Direct Democracy and European Integration. *Journal of European Public Policy, 13*(1), 153–166.

Holmes, M. (2005). *Ireland and Europe: Nice Enlargement and the Future of Europe*. Manchester: Manchester University Press.

Laffan, B. (2015). Confronting Europe: The Irish referendums on Lisbon. In J. A. Elkink & D. M. Farrell (Eds.), *The Act of Voting Identities, Institutions and Locale* (pp. 116–134). London: Routledge.

LeDuc, L. (2002). Referendums and Elections: How Do Campaigns Differ? In D. Farrell & R. Schmitt-Beck (Eds.), *Do Political Campaigns Matter? Campaign Effects in Elections and Referendums* (pp. 45–162). London: Routledge.

Millward Brown IMS. (2008, September). *Post Lisbon Treaty Referendum Research Findings*. https://infoeuropa.eurocid.pt/files/database/000041001-000042000/000041516.pdf.

O'Brennan, J. (2004). Ireland's National Forum on Europe: Elite Deliberation Meets Popular Participation. *Journal of European Integration, 26*(2), 171–189.

Oireachtas. (2008). *Ireland's Future in the European Union: Challenges, Issues and Options*. Oireachtas Report. http://www.oireachtas.ie/viewdoc.asp?fn=/documents/committees30thdail/j-europeanaffairs/Sub_Cttee_EU__20081127.doc. Accessed 1 July 2019.

Quinlan, S. (2009). The Lisbon Treaty Referendum 2008. *Irish Political Studies, 24*(1), 107–121.

Qvortrup, M. (2001). How to Lose a Referendum: The Danish Plebiscite on the Euro. *Political Quarterly, 72,* 190–196.

Sinn Féin. (2008). A Better Deal—Sinn Féin Submission. Dublin: Sinn Féin.

Sinnott, R., & Elkink, J. A. (2010). *Attitudes and Behaviour in the Second Referendum on the Treaty of Lisbon*. Report prepared for the Department of Foreign Affairs, Dublin. https://www.ucd.ie/t4cms/Attitudes%20and%20Behaviour%20in%20the%20Second%20Referendum%20on%20the%20Treaty%20of%20Lisbon.pdf.

Svensson, P. (2002). Five Danish Referendums on the European Community and European Union: A Critical Assessment of the Franklin Thesis. *Journal of European Political Research, 41*(6), 733–750.

CHAPTER 28

The French and Dutch Block the Constitutional Treaty

Claudia Sternberg

The 2004 Treaty Establishing a Constitution for Europe was meant to bring the European Union and its institutions 'closer to its citizens' (Laeken Declaration on the future of the European Union, 15 December 2001), to give birth to a constitutive constitutional moment, to European constitutional patriotism, and indeed a European people (see Sternberg 2013; Reh 2009). Ironically, it became the first treaty in the history of European integration to be stopped by popular resistance, expressed in two referendums. On 29 May 2005, 54.7% of French voters rejected its ratification on a 69.7% turnout, and three days later the Dutch followed suit, with 61.5% voting No on an unexpectedly high turnout of 63.3%.

This chapter reviews what happened in France and The Netherlands at the time, and what scholarship knows about why people voted the way they did. It discusses the roles and dynamics of the referendum campaigns, and of domestic and party politics. In doing so it raises the question of how we might know what people's electoral choices may actually have meant to them (see Sternberg 2015a). Of course, the No votes meant No to the draft treaty, but they 'also had multiple other meanings' (Berezin 2009: 193). What considerations may the French and Dutch voters have brought to the exercise of choice on the day, what may they have wished to get across with their votes? This chapter brings together available causal explanations of the votes

C. Sternberg (✉)
UCL European Institute, University College London, London, UK
e-mail: c.sternberg@ucl.ac.uk

© The Author(s) 2021
J. Smith (ed.), *The Palgrave Handbook of European Referendums*,
https://doi.org/10.1007/978-3-030-55803-1_28

with some 'thick descriptions' of the narratives and discursive repertoires available to people at the time (see, for example, Berezin 2009; Glencross 2009; Sternberg 2015a).

What follows is divided into three parts. First, the two referendums' political and discursive backgrounds are introduced. The second section turns to the campaigns and the third discusses explanations of voting behaviour in these referendums. The conclusion closes on what they may be missing.

28.1   BACKGROUND: THE DISCURSIVE AND POLITICAL CONTEXTS

Neither referendum was obligatory and both were technically non-binding. The referendum in The Netherlands was the first since 1797. Yet there had been a long debate in Dutch politics over the introduction of the instrument. The small social liberal party, Democrats 66 (D66), had traditionally advocated greater elements of direct democracy in Dutch politics, making this a condition for joining Jan-Peter Balkenende's Christian Democratic Appeal (CDA)-led coalition in 2003. The political elite overall and the larger political parties especially had traditionally been sceptical, and in 1999 a previous constitutional amendment for a referendum had narrowly been rejected in the Senate. In the end, the 2005 consultative referendum was called as a result of a parliamentary motion by three backbenchers, one each from the three centre-left parties of the incumbent D66 and the opposition Labour (PvDA) and GreenLeft parties (Qvortrup 2006: 90; Startin and Krouwel 2013: 69).

In France, by contrast, referendums are an 'integral part of the constitution of the Fifth Republic', often debated, if less frequently held (Qvortrup 2006: 89). Charles de Gaulle had used the instrument, four times, to by-pass Parliament to pass or legitimate legislation by going directly to the people, and since then four more referendums have been held, in attempts to reinforce the President's power (Qvortrup 2006: 89; see Chapter 9 by Morel). At the time of the constitutional treaty referendum, the unpopular President Jacques Chirac was often accused of using the instrument in this plebiscitary form (see Brouard and Tiberj 2006: 262), as well as tactically, so as to deepen already apparent divisions within the Socialist Party (Crespy 2008), and to pressurise opponents within his own party to campaign alongside him. Effectively, however, the referendum was forced on Chirac. It became 'politically obligatory' given the demands of public opinion, significant cross-party political mobilisation, the UK government's announcement of one, as well as the consideration that a solely parliamentary ratification would have jeopardised the future legitimacy and acceptance of the EU constitution (Morel 2007: 1058–1060; see also Qvortrup 2006: 89; Marthaler 2005: 228).

The results of the Dutch and French referendums came as a shock to many. The *Nee* in The Netherlands conflicted with the traditional '(self) image' of the Dutch as staunch champions of the European integration project (Harmsen 2008). The Dutch 'political elites have consistently supported developments towards closer European co-operation' (Startin and Krouwel 2013: 66). The major political parties—the Christian Democrats (CDA), the Labour Party and the liberal parties, People's Party for Freedom and Democracy (VVD) and Democrats 66—had supported all major EU treaties in parliament, with only the smaller orthodox-Calvinist parties, some smaller left-wing parties and, more recently, the List Pim Fortuyn (LPF) opposing them (Aarts and van der Kolk 2006: 243). The French 'Non', in turn, was at odds with the notion of the French as customary champions of the European cause, despite Charles de Gaulle's 'France First' approach to European integration of the 1960s, or historical opposition from the French Communists. France had, after all, fielded a great number of the key actors driving integration forward, Valéry Giscard d'Estaing, who had chaired the convention that prepared the draft treaty, being only the most recent in an illustrious line including Robert Schuman, Jean Monnet, François Mitterrand and Jacques Delors (Startin and Krouwel 2013: 66).

The Dutch population had, ever since the early 1970s, been even more enthusiastic about the EU than the citizens of the other founding Member States (Aarts and van der Kolk 2006: 243). French popular support for membership, likewise, while lower than in The Netherlands, had similarly been 'consistently positive towards European integration' (Atikcan 2015a: 98). (Remarkably this did not even change with the negative referendums; in the immediate aftermath of the vote, 82% of Dutch and 88% of French citizens considered their country's membership 'a good thing' [*Flash Eurobarometer* 171/June 2005: 22 and *Flash EB* 172/June 2015: 20, respectively].) And yet, both the Dutch and the French electorates rejected the ratification of the EU constitution.

A pervasive reading of the constitutional referendums is that they exposed a gap opening up between the preferences of the two countries' elites, who would have ratified the constitution, and the people, who stopped them (e.g. Startin and Krouwel 2013: 67; Aarts and van der Kolk 2006: 243; Crum 2007: 74). In both countries the (mainstream) political establishment was in favour of ratification, including the respective centre-right coalition governments, the major centre-left opposition parties and overwhelming majorities in Parliament. In The Netherlands the pro-ratification parties held 85% of the seats in the lower house, and in France, 93%, but only 38 and 45%, respectively, of the voters voted Yes to the Treaty (Schuck and de Vreese 2008: 101; Crum 2007: 75). To be sure, the faultline ran much less neatly than this reading may suggest between citizens and elites, but actually ran across both groups (and across parties), as discussed below.

In addition, disagreements regarding the EU had been brewing up for years. To observers of the Dutch and French domestic contexts, the victories of the No sides were no bolt out of the blue (Startin and Krouwel 2013: 67; Taggart 2006: 15). Eurosceptic discourses, public attitudes, as well as parties and politicians had been gaining ground in both countries ever since the early 1990s (see e.g. Harmsen 2008; Sternberg 2013; Schmidt 2007;

Eichenberg and Dalton 2007; Hooghe and Marks 2009; Leruth et al. 2007; Taggart 1998). In addition, broader developments in public and political discourse, public opinion and in domestic politics in the years leading up to the referendum had further helped to prepare the ground for the 2005 outcomes.

28.1.1   The Context in France

In France, the 1992 referendum on the Maastricht Treaty had acted as a 'watershed in terms of raising the profile of Europe as an issue, and more specifically Euroscepticism, in the domestic political arena' (Startin and Krouwel 2013: 67). This referendum passed by a narrow margin (51% in favour), but the campaigns and debate around it had a lasting influence on the discursive landscape against which the EU could be discussed in years to come (Sternberg 2013: 103–128; Schmidt 2007). National republican discourses became part of the public discursive repertoire that confined the exercise of the will of the people, democracy and 'the political' *tout court*, to the confines of the nation. In these discourses, popular sovereignty emerged as inseparable from national sovereignty, and the capacity to control the world, over the forces of the market, was limited to the nation-state—and, importantly, at odds with the European Union (Sternberg 2013: 118–122, 162). Illustrating the resonance of these views, Charles Pasqua's pro-sovereignty Gaullist breakaway *Rassemblement Pour la France* (RPF) outscored the Gaullist party itself in the 1999 European election on such a platform.

Resistance to the Euro, and fears around its economic consequences, furthermore, permanently undermined the central promise justifying European integration, of prosperity and better living conditions (Sternberg 2013). This promise was severely undercut further by successive governments justifying substantial cutbacks to the French welfare state as necessary to help France meet the convergence criteria for monetary union (Hay and Rosamond 2002). The long decade between France's two EU referendums was marked by a series of mass protests against pension reforms, social spending cuts, reforms to education and privatisations (Smith 2004; Atikcan 2015a: 97). Remarkably, in the 1995 'strikes against globalisation' (a formative collective political event), the wider public, unlike the government, did *not* yet generally blame France's economic problems on the EU, but rather on globalisation (Hay and Rosamond 2002).

Anti-globalisation and anti-liberal discourses started taking root in the French public imaginary around that time and had become firmly ingrained by 2005 (see Hay and Rosamond 2002; Schmidt 2007). Originally framed and mobilised by the radical left and a highly active anti-globalisation movement, they affected political discourse across the whole spectrum, not only within the Socialist Party but also forcing governments to respond to public opinion in this regard (Crespy 2008, 2010). Both Gaullist President Jacques Chirac and his Socialist Prime Minister Lionel Jospin wooed the anti-globalisation movement in the run-up to the 2002 election, in tune with the 'clear popular resonance' of 'anti-American, anti-imperialist' and anti-liberal sentiments (Hay and Rosamond 2002: 153). Official discourse under Chirac (as under Mitterrand) held out Europeanisation as a 'shield' against globalisation and a means of rescuing the French welfare state (Schmidt 2002: 187; 2007). However, a competing and accelerating discourse defined Europeanisation and globalisation as 'iterations of the same economic processes', blaming the EU for France's economic malaise and welfare retrenchment (Berezin 2009: 207).

As a result, to picture the EU as a safeguard of collective and individual riches was barely plausible in France on the eve of the constitutional referendum. In autumn 2004, the French public ranked highest among all Member States in mentioning *délocalisations* (the relocation of jobs to countries with lower production costs) among their fears about the building of Europe (*Standard Eurobarometer* 62: 141–144). They ranked high also with regard to the loss of social benefits, difficulties for French farmers and the budget contribution. After years during which the French political elite had raised these issues in relation to European integration, this was no 'coincidence'. Nonetheless, the French public attitude towards the EU remained 'fairly positive' (Atikcan 2015a: 96, 98–99; see above).

By contrast, the French public had been dissatisfied with the *domestic* level of governance in the years before the referendum. Chirac and his Prime Minister Raffarin were unpopular, with confidence levels (44 and 28%, respectively) reaching their lowest in the autumn of 2004 and right before the referendum. Again, socio-economic and welfare-related concerns ranked highest in surveys, with immigration another important source of contention. Raffarin's highly contested plans to reform education, health care, pensions, unemployment benefits and the 35-hour week sparked strikes in 2003 and in 2005, weeks and days before the referendum (Atikcan 2015a: 96; see Marthaler 2005). Chirac's whole second term, moreover, suffered from the 'birth defect' of the 2002 election, when he won in a second round against Jean-Marie Le Pen, with the grudging votes of many of his opponents. Le Pen had run on an explicitly Eurosceptic platform, and his success (17% of the vote in the first round) did 'nothing to bolster the confidence of France's pro-EU political elites', dampening any appetite to submit the 2004 enlargement directly to the people (Startin and Krouwel 2013: 67). That Le Pen reached the second round of a presidential election indicated, and promoted, the normalisation and wide reach of the *Front National*'s ideas regarding Europeanisation, globalisation and immigration—all framed as threats to French society and to national identity, and as processes inextricable from each other (Berezin 2009: 133). Le Pen had linked unemployment and insecurity to illegal immigration, and condemned Islam as inexorably hostile to French republican values (Atikcan 2015a: 98).

In this context, the 'headscarf' controversy formed another important discursive backdrop to the French constitutional debate (see Bowen 2008; Scott 2010; Berezin 2009: 71–72, 168). This debate had been smouldering, with intermittent flareups, ever since 1998, when a head teacher had expelled three school girls for wearing headscarves. In March 2004 the *Assemblé Nationale* voted by a large majority to ban 'conspicuous signs' of religious affiliation in public schools, invoking the principle of *laïcité*, that is, the strict separation of Church and State mandated since 1905 by French law. Combined with a fear of terrorism heightened in 2004 by the Islamist terrorist bombings in Madrid and the threat of attacks on the French railway, the headscarf debate provided starting points for the campaigns on the EU constitution in the form not only of (latent) anti-immigration and anti-Islamist sentiments, but also of the perceived need to defend the constitutive principles and values of French republicanism (Atikcan 2015a: 97).

28.1.2   The Context in The Netherlands

The Netherlands had likewise 'seen a marked shift in the terms of Dutch European discourse' since the early 1990s (Harmsen 2008: 316). In party and governmental documents, as well as the national press and polling data, a 'traditional "federalist" referential was progressively replaced by an elite discourse focused primarily on "national interests" and on defining the "limits of Europe"' (Harmsen 2008: 316). The specific limits discussed were 'substantive', regarding distinctive Dutch institutional forms or policy choices such as the broadcasting system, euthanasia, same sex marriage or the toleration of soft drugs. Concerns were also voiced about the EU's geographical boundaries. The liberal VVD in particular vocally opposed the 2004 enlargement. It split over the issue of a future Turkish accession in 2004, when the high-profile populist Geert Wilders left the part to create his own Party for Freedom (PVV), 'rejecting further integration and the EU accession of Turkey' (Startin and Krouwel 2013: 67).

As in France, criticism of the European integration project moved from the margins of the national political debate to the mainstream around the time of the Maastricht negotiations. Its prominent voice was VVD leader Frits Bolkestein (later a European Commissioner), who demanded that European cooperation be limited to the governance of the internal market and monetary union. From this 'initial epicentre' in the VVD, criticism gradually spread, including to the Christian Democratic CDA and the governing Social Democratic (or Labour) PvDA, which took a 'Eurorealist' position, emphasising subsidiarity from the 2002 election (in which it lost power) onwards (Harmsen 2008: 321–323).

Party positions on Europe were found not to have played a decisive role in electoral competition or as a cleavage dividing Dutch parties at that time (Binnema and Crum 2006), and voters' opinions about European integration were relatively unimportant for vote decisions in national and European elections (Aarts and van der Kolk 2006: 245). Still, the 'two major pro-European parties', PvDA and CDA, 'suffered heavy electoral losses' during the 1990s and in 2002 (Startin and Krouwel 2013: 67). Concurrently, populist political movements that espoused Eurosceptic views enjoyed dramatic electoral successes. On the far right, the charismatic Pim Fortuyn claimed to defend the interests of the people against a 'soulless' EU that served the interests only of national and European elites. On the left, the Socialist Party (SP) 'combined an *altermondialiste* critique of a "neo-liberal" economic project with a strong nationalist discourse, stressing the extent to which The Netherlands was losing the ability to make and sustain distinctive policy choices' (all Harmsen 2008: 321–323).

The years from 2002 in particular were a period of exceptional unrest in domestic politics in The Netherlands (Atikcan 2015a: 131–134, see Roes 2008: 29). Nine days before the 2002 general election, the country was shocked by the political assassination of Pim Fortuyn. His List Pim Fortuyn (LPF) went on to win 17% of the vote and, as the second party in parliament, to enter a coalition with the CDA and the VVD. Headed by Jan Peter Balkenende (CDA), this unstable coalition fell by the end of the year as a result of internal conflicts within the LPF. The second Balkenende government, from 2003, was a coalition of CDA, VVD and D66. It carried out an extensive, and highly unpopular, programme of harsh interventions and serious cutbacks in housing, pensions and social security (Atikcan 2015a: 132–134; see Roes 2008: 30–35). Satisfaction levels with the government and public administration dropped drastically between 2000 (77%) and 2002 (59%), and even further by 2004 (48%; Roes 2008: 132). The 'main reasons' for this dip in government popularity were the economic downturn and welfare state reform, as well as controversy over national identity and immigration (Atikcan 2015a: 132; see *Standard Eurobarometer* 62).

Migration became a salient issue with fears around 'Islamisation' and increasing arrivals particularly from 'non-Western' groups, taken as an opportunity to raise the question of whether The Netherlands was losing its cultural and national identity (Roes 2008: 12–13; Lechner 2008). Such misgivings were further stoked by the murder of Fortuyn, who had declared Islam a 'backward culture' and The Netherlands a 'full country', followed in 2004 by the assassination of film-maker Theo van Gogh, author of a controversial short film on violence against women in Islam. In tune with changing public attitudes, the government had already begun to change its discourse in the 1990s, away from the aspiration of the 1980s to a 'multicultural society', towards emphasising the need for 'integration' into the nation. Now, in response to mounting public pressure, it changed its 'policy on minorities' into an 'integration policy, aimed at curbing the influx of migrants and integrating those (non-Western) ethnic minority groups already present in the Netherlands' (Roes 2008: 14, 32; see Atikcan 2015a: 133–134).

Regardless, the Dutch public's support for EU membership, and the perception of benefitting from it remained well above the EU average. They did have misgivings too, though. Support for the introduction of economic and monetary union and later of the euro had been comparatively high in The Netherlands. In the build-up to the 2005 referendum, however, suddenly public complaints that the common currency had been imposed on the people without their having any say in the matter, and that it had reduced people's buying power flared up retrospectively (Engelen 2007; Atikcan 2015a: 136). Moreover, in autumn 2004, the Dutch ranked highest among all Member States in citing the loss of social benefits as a fear concerning the building of Europe, and high also in fearing the loss of power for smaller member states (*Standard Eurobarometer* 62: 142–144). As in France, all of this, and especially fears around social retrenchment and immigration, provided fertile ground for the 2005 referendum campaigns (Atikcan 2015a: 131).

28.2   THE CAMPAIGNS: ACTORS, DYNAMICS, ISSUES

The actual campaigns in the two countries were similar in many respects but differed greatly in others. The French controversy was drawn out and extremely intense, while the Dutch referendum 'almost seemed like a non-event' (Qvortrup 2006: 92). The campaign in France began as early as October 2004 (see Atikcan 2015a: 103) and attracted 'colossal media interest' (Qvortrup 2006: 92; see Hobolt and Brouard 2010). It penetrated deeply into society; one poll showed that the referendum was the subject of 26% 'of conversations' in January, 48% in March and 83% in May 2005 (Ricard-Nihoul 2005: 3). By contrast, the Dutch campaign began less than a month before the vote. The campaign was highly visible in the news (Schuck and de Vreese 2008: 114–115), and media coverage reached levels previously unseen for European issues, although it was nowhere near as intense as in France and remained 'sporadic' in comparison (Atikcan 2015a: 156–157; Hobolt and Brouard 2010: 313). France, hosting the earliest debate among all the referendums on the EU constitution, greatly influenced the other referendum debates (Atikcan 2015a: 32–33; 2015b).

Above all, the Dutch and French campaigns had in common that the No side managed to set the agenda for the debate and continued to dominate it, putting the Yes campaigns on the defensive and forcing them to play catch-up (Atikcan 2015a, 2018; Marthaler 2005; Mergier 2005: 22; Maatsch 2007). In The Netherlands this was in part due to the effective failure of the Yes camp to 'mount a convincing campaign' (Harmsen 2005: 1, 13), and to timing. 'Perhaps because they had no previous experience with referendums, the government misread the dynamic of a referendum campaign (where voting intentions are often shaped early in the campaign) [...] and left it to the no side to set the agenda' (Qvortrup 2006: 92). Assuming that voters would not decide which way to vote until the last stages, as they tend to do in parliamentary elections, 'all major politicians were on recess' up until two weeks before the referendum (Startin and Krouwel 2013: 69). Besides, there was 'a responsibility crisis concerning who would run the campaign for the Yes side', as the government had been against calling a referendum in the first place (Atikcan 2015a: 137). It further did not help the cause of the Yes side that the other pro-constitution parties were reluctant to share the same platform as the unpopular government (Atikcan 2015a: 137), and that supporters of the constitution hence kept a 'very low profile' (Startin Krouwel 2013: 69).

In the event, the Yes campaign was fronted by the Minister for Europe, supported by the governing CDA, VVD and D66, as well as the Green and Labour parties. It was backed by all trade unions and business federations, which did not, however, launch significant campaigns. The No camp was small in comparison and ideologically diverse, a 'motley crew of far-left and further rightist individuals, groups, and organisations' (Qvortrup 2006: 92). It included right-wing groups LPF and Group Wilders, the fundamentalist Protestant parties and the far-left Socialist Party (SP). The SP quickly emerged as a key player in the No campaign, drawing on its grassroots support and local network as well as supplementing its own financial resources (Atikcan 2015a: 141, 154; Startin and Krouwel 2013: 69; Harmsen 2005; Schuck and de Vreese 2008: 104).

In France, the governing UMP and its junior ally UDF campaigned in favour. Mindful not to share a platform with Chirac (many Socialist Party [PS] voters were still bitter that they had had to vote for him in 2002, Marthaler 2005: 5), the PS nevertheless decided in an internal poll in December 2004 to campaign for ratification (59% in favour). A sizeable left-wing faction, however, spearheaded by former Prime Minister Laurent Fabius, campaigned on the No side, as did the Communist Party, other groups to the left of the PS, and large parts of the (officially pro) Green party. The left-wing No campaign was very united. Anti-ratification parties were joined by civil society in forming a No Committee with exceptional local support and about 900–1000 local committees across the whole country. The anti-globalisation group ATTAC played an important role in bringing diverse social forces together for the No side (Atikcan 2015a: 118–121), using the referendum to 'gain credibility and momentum' for their cause (Marthaler 2005: 236; Sternberg 2015a: 3–4). Civil society mobilisation was exceptional in France, particularly on the No side and at the local level (Atikcan 2015a: 118–121). The right-wing No campaign was less well-integrated than that on the left (Atikcan 2015a: 102–103). Its vocal proponent, traditionalist Eurosceptic Philippe de Villiers (*Mouvement Pour La France*, MPF)—a 'constant presence in the media'—steered clear of the FN and Le Pen, who himself lay low strategically so as not to alienate his opponents from the No by his association, while relying on his supporters' secure preference against ratification (Marthaler 2005: 232; Berezin 2006; Ivaldi 2006: 55–56).

The media in both countries gave a prominent position to arguments in favour of ratification. In The Netherlands, 'practically every newspaper in the country' and all major media outlets supported ratification (Hobolt and Brouard 2010: 313; Aarts and van der Kolk 2006: 243). The tone of the Dutch media coverage was overall positive towards the constitution, and 'higher levels of exposure to referendum news increased the likelihood of voters to switch over to the Yes side' (Schuck and de Vreese 2008: 101). Nonetheless, even if the media gave the Yes campaigners more coverage than the No campaigners, they also evaluated them more negatively and represented them as performing poorly overall (Schuck and de Vreese 2008: 101, 114; Atikcan 2015a: 156–157). The French media were widely perceived as having a 'pro-European bias', and did indeed give more coverage, and specifically television airtime, to the arguments of Yes campaign (Marthaler 2005: 233; Gerstlé 2006). On the other hand, the No campaign made more extensive and effective use of non-traditional media such as blogs, internet forums and chain emails (Marthaler 2005: 233; Sternberg 2015a: 6).

28.2.1   Argumentative and Discursive Strategies

The main reason for the No camps' dominance over the discursive agenda in both cases was that opponents of ratification were more successful than its proponents 'in initiating public debate and in defining the meaning' of the constitutional treaty (Maatsch 2007: 261). Political campaigns can significantly shape voting behaviour and public opinion, and are more likely to do so for referendums than in elections (see Schuck and de Vreese 2008: 104; Hobolt and Brouard 2010: 310; Atikcan 2015a: 15). They work by 'priming' certain issues, that is, placing them on the agenda, making them salient by 'making information about that issue available in people's memories' (Hobolt and Brouard 2010: 310) and defining them as principal dimensions for evaluating the question on the ballot paper. In addition, they work by 'framing' the question at hand in particular ways, delimiting what it is about and orienting people's thinking about the issue in particular ways (see Atikcan 2015a: 16–19). In the case of the two referendums under discussion, the No campaigners were the 'better *framers*' because they managed to connect the EU constitution to certain existing problems and fears in people's minds, and to promote 'vivid, concrete, image-provoking frames that contain negative information', which, research shows, are more likely to affect people's opinions. By contrast, the Yes campaigns, tied to the content of the treaty and unable to make its benefits tangible, 'sounded overly technical and broad, presenting the treaty as an institutional step toward a better Europe' (Atikcan 2015a: 4, 7–8, 13, 32; see Sternberg 2015a).

In France, the anti-ratification camp focused heavily on social and economic issues (Hobolt 2009: 205–206). Strong No frames (as in frames that the public later used in explaining their vote choices) linked the constitution to 'declining social protection, increasing immigration, and the potential Turkish accession' (Atikcan 2015a: 32, 159ff, 165). The No campaign successfully tapped into existing fears of globalisation and anti-liberal sentiments and linked them firmly to the EU and the constitution. Indeed, the constitutional debate marked the 'coming of age' of the anti-globalisation discourses discussed above and their articulation with respect to European integration (Crespy 2008; see Sternberg 2015a: 12–13). It also chimed with the above-mentioned national republican discourses around political voluntarism and the ability to control one's destiny in the face of market constraints. The French debate was structured in part by the binary between a 'social Europe' and a 'liberal Europe' (Sternberg 2015a). The first side of this was equated with a snug, humane world where political will and the French social model triumphed over external constraints. The other side of the binary was that of the inhuman forces of 'the market' and of globalisation, of a dismantled French education and social system, of unemployment. The constitution-liberalism link was underpinned by a corresponding link between the constitution and unemployment, that is, both the relocation of French jobs abroad (omnipresent in the French media) and the influx of cheap East European labour into France (see Cambadélis 2005: 33; Le Gall 2005: 106). The infamous 'Polish plumber' became a symbol of such fears. The No camp successfully associated the constitution with the bugbears of liberalism and employment. Although the Yes camp meekly kept repeating that the constitution was instead the way to 'social Europe', to controlling 'liberalism', the No camp's associations were so deeply anchored that even the mention of the word 'liberalism' tended to trigger a reaction against the constitution (Duhamel 2005). The social-liberal binary structured the French debate so deeply that even supporters of the constitution came to justify it on the grounds of social justice (Glencross 2009).

Dutch No campaigners, in turn, successfully primed culture and identity concerns, and framed the EU constitution in these terms (Hobolt 2009: 205–206). The far right emphasised that the constitution represented a threat to Dutch national sovereignty and culture. Interestingly the left No campaign and the Socialist Party, too, focused on the dangers the draft treaty accordingly represented to Dutch liberal culture and identity, and to what made the Dutch institutional and policy landscape what it was (Hobolt and Brouard 2010: 313). 'As in France, the Dutch No campaign frames effectively linked the public's existing concerns to the European constitution, highlighting the danger of losing social protection and sovereignty in a European "super-state"' as well as increasing immigration (Atikcan 2015a: 32–33). The anti-constitution camp 'successfully struck an already sensitive nerve given unpopular welfare state reforms and recent assassinations of populist politician Pim Fortuyn and the controversial film-maker Theo van Gogh – both related to increasing immigration in the Netherlands' (Atikcan 2015a: 32–33, see 159–165; see Aarts and van der Kolk 2006). At the same time, the 'EU was painted as a distant entity, unable to see people's real concerns, as was the Dutch mainstream political elite' (Atikcan 2015a: 32–33, 159ff., 165). The media coverage of the Dutch campaigns, further, has been shown as preoccupied with procedural issues, including whether the result of the consultative referendum would be respected, and with the French debate (Hobolt and Brouard 2010: 319). Economic and social questions, moreover, came to play in the Dutch debate as well, particularly when the Executive Director of the Dutch Central Bank, Henk Brouwer, admitted that the Dutch guilder had been undervalued when the Euro was created, causing contestation around its introduction to flare up belatedly and consolidating the widely shared perception that it had caused serious damage to The Netherlands and that prices had risen because of it (Atikcan 2015a: 152, 160–161; Engelen 2007).

The prospect of Turkish accession to the EU, finally, was both central and a strong frame in both debates. In The Netherlands, Geert Wilders notably linked his opposition to ratification to the threat of Turkish membership and the erosion of what made The Netherlands what it was under the slogan of 'The Netherlands must remain!' (Aarts and van der Kolk 2006). In France, too, the issue of Turkey turned into a symbol of the people's loss of control over the integration process, of not having been consulted over the 2004 enlargement. The 2005 referendum was hailed as their one chance finally of throwing a spanner into the works of a process that had been racing ahead inexorably beyond their influence. Although Chirac had attempted to disentangle the issue by promising a separate referendum on Turkey, opponents of the constitution insisted that a No vote was the only way to stop Turkey from joining (Sternberg 2015a: 19–20).

28.3   EXPLANATIONS OF THE VOTE

The campaigns, and their framing dynamics, have been identified as 'the key' to the puzzle of a monumental reversal of public opinion on the EU constitution over the course of the campaigns (Atikcan 2015a; Hobolt 2009; Hobolt and Brouard 2010; Schuck and de Vreese 2008). In the autumn of 2004, 73% of the Dutch and 70% of the French said they supported the idea of a constitution for the EU (Standard EB 62: 150). Yet, by May and June the following year many had changed their minds, with only 38.5 and 45.3% voting in favour of ratification, respectively. In fact, public attitudes towards the constitution shifted even more, if changes between individual vote intentions at the beginning of the campaign and final vote choices rather than aggregate figures are considered (Schuck and de Vreese 2008: 113).

Polling data on people's motivations in voting confirms the No campaigns' success in framing the ballot question in terms of social and economic issues in France, and sovereignty, culture and identity concerns in The Netherlands (see *Flash Eurobarometers* 171 and 172; Atikcan 2015a: 162–163). The single most important reason to vote No in France was economic and social concerns, even if they played a more 'marginal' role among voters on the right (Brouard and Tiberj 2006: 266–267; Ivaldi 2006; Hobolt 2009: 224, 215). More specifically, voters named as reasons for their choice their discontent with the current economic situation in France (52%), the risk of making unemployment worse (46%) and that the EU/the constitution were 'too liberal in economic policies' (40%; see Atikcan 2015a: 124–125).

In The Netherlands, in turn, concerns with national power and sovereignty losses ranked highest, and identity concerns were also prominent (see Atikcan 2015a: 162), as were cost–benefit calculations regarding EU membership. The chief motivation cited by No voters was that 'the Netherlands pays too much to the EU' (62%), closely followed by it 'will have less control over its own affairs' (56%), had 'too little influence in comparison with other countries' (55%) and 'will lose its own identity' (53%). Moreover, a 'diffuse sense of European integration having gone "too far, too fast" and the rejection of a European "superstate" found an unexpected resonance with Dutch voters' (Harmsen 2005: 1, see 10). Most importantly, people felt that the costs of European integration were too high and the benefits too low (see Glencross and Trechsel 2011) and that the common market was 'a threat rather than an opportunity'. This perception was fuelled not least by the only now, tardily established notion that the Euro had greatly disadvantaged the Dutch (Aarts and van der Kolk 2006: 246; Engelen 2007).

Turkish accession was an important secondary motivation for French No voters overall (35%), and the most decisive issue for UMP and FN supporters who voted No (Atikcan 2015a: 124–125; Brouard and Sauger 2005: 132–134). In The Netherlands, by contrast, very few voters named Turkey as a reason for voting No (only 1.2% of No voters, see Atikcan 2015a: 162). Yet, the prospect of a Turkish enlargement indirectly intensified negative cost–benefit evaluations as well as sovereignty and identity concerns; for, 'new member states [were] not seen as new markets to be explored, but as expensive reservoirs of cheap labour threatening Dutch jobs', in that it was perceived to mean that 'the power of the Netherlands in the EU will be further watered down, while at the same time Dutch, or Western, values [were] perceived to be in danger' (Aarts and van der Kolk 2006: 246).

At the time, many commentators further explained the French vote on the ground that it was at least in part a sanction vote against the unpopular President, Jacques Chirac, and the centre-right government (see Hainsworth 2006; Ivaldi 2006; Hobolt and Brouard 2010: 316–317). Yet, only 24% of the No voters specified their opposition to Chirac and the government as one of their motivations (see Atikcan 2015a: 124–125). On the whole, opposition to Chirac has been shown to have been important in explaining the No vote among his opponents, and more specifically among right-wing and neither left-nor-right factions, but not among the leftist voters (Brouard and Tiberj 2006: 266). It was, however, the No vote on the left that made all the difference, and that was much stronger than on the centre-right; 94% of far-left (Communist and *Lutte ouvrière*) voters, and 56% of PS voters went for No, against only 20% of UMP voters (see Qvortrup 2006: 94). On this basis a chief cause of the French No has been located in the division of the PS (Crum 2007: 76–77).

In The Netherlands, too, there is 'little statistical evidence' to support a hypothesis that the referendum outcome was a result of the unpopularity of the Balkenende government (Qvortrup 2006: 94). The supporters of both CDA and D66 voted overwhelmingly for ratification (at 76%, respectively), while support was significantly lower among liberal VVD voters (57%). The Dutch result, too, was 'largely due to a split' among the voters of the Labour Party, which persuaded only 42% of its voters to support the treaty (Qvortrup

2006: 94; Harmsen 2005: 12). In fact, in the Dutch case, partisanship was the best predictor of vote choice (Hobolt and Brouard 2010: 316). Yet, whereas in France, the hypothesis that, in common with the 2002 presidential election, the referendum was a vote of distrust and dissatisfaction with political elites is not supported by polls and surveys (Brouard and Tiberj 2006), the No vote in The Netherlands does fit in a 'wider trend of disconnection' and the 'sense of a growing "gap" (*"kloof"*) between the political establishment and Dutch society' (Harmsen 2005: 13). Either way, in both countries the unpopularity of the governments was in part due to unpopular reforms, which had also fostered a general discursive climate defined by a sense of exposure to social and economic decline or cutback, incontrollable forces of globalisation or Europeanisation, all of which, combined with more or less latent fears for a national culture, identity and values, provided abundant campaign material for the No sides (Atikcan 2015a).

Against explanations centred on domestic politics—and mirroring the debate on whether or not EU votes are really 'second-order national elections' (see Crum 2007: 63–64 for an overview)—a number of survey-based studies have concluded that both votes were indeed 'about Europe', or EU-related issues. Whereas some do see a general 'rejection of the European project' at play (Brouard and Sauger 2005: 140), others clarify that vote choices were 'driven by specific issue concerns rather than general dissatisfaction with the European Union or national governments' (Hobolt and Brouard 2010: 309). From this vantage point, the No votes were *not* a vote against Europe as such. Rather, they were dramatic assertions that the voters were re-claiming a say in deciding on their countries', and Europe's, future, including when it came to making choices about its economic and social setup (see Sternberg 2015a).

Interestingly, democracy, or a lack thereof conspicuously does not feature as an important voting motivation. Only 3% of French and 5% of Dutch respondents spontaneously mentioned a lack of democracy as one of several possible reasons for voting No (*Flash Eurobarometer* 171: 17 and 172: 15). The Yes campaigns did prominently justify the constitution in terms of its making the EU more democratic (Maatsch 2007: 272–273; Atikcan 2015a: 139), but with little resonance, even among Yes voters. The No frame that the EU was not democratic enough proved weak even among No voters (see Atikcan 2015a: 161–163; Hobolt 2009: 210).

28.4   CONCLUSION

By way of conclusion, two observations may add additional pieces to the puzzle of what meanings, beyond the literal Yes or No answers to the ballot question, people's vote choices may have carried for them, and what messages they may have wished to get across in them.

Firstly, as mentioned, the literature on political campaigns finds that frames that contain negative information do better than positive ones in influencing public opinion and voting behaviour (Atikcan 2015a: 4). On the other hand, positive news framing has been shown to mobilise *sceptics* rather than supporters of a proposal, by generating a perception of risk among those opposing it (Schuck and de Vreese 2009). Is this mechanism what explains the following discursive dynamic? Perhaps the decisive argumentative move of the French No campaign was that they effectively redefined the question at hand, shifting it from the one on the ballot paper, about whether or not to ratify the constitution, to a rather different, open one, of 'What kind of Europe do we want?' (Sternberg 2015a). This allowed them to exploit a glaring gap between an ideal, brave new Europe and the Europe of the constitution. On top, everyone could define this ideal measuring stick as they liked. Redefining the question also allowed taking on board all those who were fundamentally in favour of integration—the great majority in France. In the redefined picture, a No vote was not an act of obstruction, but an 'act of hope', of ushering in a better Europe.

Secondly, was the issue of democracy really as absent from people's considerations as the relevant literature on public opinion and voting behaviour has it? If one looks at the arguments and narratives on offer in the debates, it did arguably feature—and very prominently—albeit indirectly. The indisputably salient controversies over Turkish accession and over the social and economic makeup of France, The Netherlands and the EU as a whole, were on some level reassertions of popular sovereignty. They importantly asserted a desire to participate in the political will-formation and to hold decision-makers accountable when it came to taking critical decisions in these regards. In France, the most powerful critique of the EU's democratic deficit did not concern institutional or procedural questions. Rather, it took as its emblem the disenfranchisement of the European citizens in the construction of 'Europe' over the previous five decades, including when it came to enlargements and here particularly the 2004 wave, and to momentous economic decisions (see Sternberg 2015a: 18–19). Democracy and 'the political' were re-cast as being essentially about enabling and channelling contestation. The EU constitution of course had been in part an exercise in depoliticising parts of the EU's framework by placing certain rules and principles beyond contestation. If read against important narratives and arguments in the French and Dutch referendum debates, the 2005 votes made a resounding statement against the long-standing 'unwillingness' of Europe's political and administrative elites 'to subject the question of integration to meaningful political contestation in domestic politics' (Glencross 2009: 244; see Sternberg 2013: 210–223). The French and the Dutch were claiming their right to disagree, and to make their voices count. If the legitimacy of European integration was to rest on the delivery of certain outputs (see Sternberg 2015b), then these European citizens were asserting their right to have a say in defining what the EU should be doing and how, and where it should stop.

REFERENCES

Aarts, K., & van der Kolk, H. (2006). Understanding the Dutch "No": The Euro, the East, and the Elite. *PS: Political Science & Politics, 39*(2), 243–246.

Atikcan, E. Ö. (2015a). *Framing the European Union: The Power of Political Arguments in Shaping European Integration*. Cambridge: Cambridge University Press.

Atikcan, E. Ö. (2015b). Diffusion in Referendum Campaigns: The Case of EU Constitutional Referendums. *Journal of European Integration, 37*(4), 451–470.

Atikcan, E. Ö. (2018). Agenda Control in EU Referendum Campaigns: The Power of the Anti-EU Side. *European Journal of Political Research, 57*(1), 93–115.

Berezin, M. (2006). Appropriating the "No": The French National Front, the Vote on the Constitution, and the "New" April 21. *PS: Political Science & Politics, 39,* 269–272.

Berezin, M. (2009). *Illiberal Politics in Neoliberal Times: Culture, Security and Populism in the New Europe*. Cambridge: Cambridge University Press.

Binnema, H., & Crum, B. (2006). Resistance to Europe as a Carrier of Mass-Elite Incongruence: The Case of The Netherlands. In J. Lacroix & R. Coman (Eds.), *Resisting Europe. Euroscepticism and National Civic Culture* (pp. 113–128). Brussels: Université Libre de Bruxelles.

Bowen, J. R. (2008). *Why the French Don't Like Headscarves*. Princeton: Princeton University Press.

Brouard, S., & Sauger, N. (2005). Comprendre la victoire du "Non": proximité partisane, conjoncture et attitude à l'égard de l'Europe. In A. Laurent & N. Sauger (Eds.), *Le référendum de ratification du Traité constitutionnel européen du 29 mai 2005: comprendre le "Non" français* (pp. 121–142). Paris: Cahiers du CEVIPOF.

Brouard, S., & Tiberj, V. (2006). The French Referendum: The Not So Simple Act of Saying Nay. *PS: Political Science & Politics, 39,* 261–268.

Cambadélis, J.-C. (2005). Pourquoi le "non" a été irrésistible. In G. Finchelstein (Ed.), *Le jour où la France a dit non. Comprendre le référendum du 29 mai 2005* (pp. 26–36). Paris: Fondation Jean-Jaurès.

Crespy, A. (2008). Dissent Over the European Constitutional Treaty Within the French Socialist Party: Between Response to Anti-globalization Protest and Intra-Party Tactics. *French Politics, 6,* 23–44.

Crespy, A. (2010). When "Bolkestein" Is Trapped by the French Anti-liberal Discourse: A Discursive-Institutionalist Account of Preference Formation in the Realm of European Union Multi-level Politics. *Journal of European Public Policy, 17*(8), 1253–1270.

Crum, B. (2007). Party Stances in the Referendums on the EU Constitution: Causes and Consequences of Competition and Collusion. *European Union Politics, 8*(1), 61–82.

Duhamel, O. (2005). *Des raisons du "non"*. Paris: Seuil.

Eichenberg, R. C., & Dalton, R. J. (2007). Post-Maastricht Blues: The Transformation of Citizen Support for European Integration, 1973–2004. *Acta Politica, 42,* 128–152.

Engelen, E. R. (2007). *How to Solve the Riddle of Belated Euro Contestation in The Netherlands?* The Hague: WRR (Scientific Council for Government Policy).

Gerstlé, J. (2006). *The Impact of Television on French Referendum Campaign in 2005: From the European Parliamentary Election of 2004 to the French Referendum of 2005.* Paris: Notre Europe.

Glencross, A. (2009). The Difficulty of Justifying European Integration as a Consequence of Depoliticization: Evidence from the 2005 French Referendum. *Government and Opposition, 44,* 243–261.

Glencross, A., & Trechsel, A. (2011). First or Second Order Referendums? Understanding the Votes on the EU Constitutional Treaty in Four EU Member States. *West European Politics, 34*(4), 755–772.

Hainsworth, P. (2006). France Says No: The 29 May 2005 Referendum on the European Constitution. *Parliamentary Affairs, 59,* 98–117.

Harmsen, R. (2005). *The Dutch Referendum on the Ratification of the European Constitutional Treaty* (EPERN Referendum Briefing, No. 13).

Harmsen, R. (2008). The Evolution of Dutch European Discourse: Defining the 'Limits of Europe'. *Perspectives on European Politics and Society, 9*(3), 316–341.

Hay, C., & Rosamond, B. (2002). Globalization, European Integration and the Discursive Construction of Economic Imperatives. *Journal of European Public Policy, 9,* 147–167.

Hobolt, S. B. (2009). *Europe in Question: Referendums on European Integration.* Oxford: Oxford University Press.

Hobolt, S. B., & Brouard, S. (2010). Contesting the European Union? Why the Dutch and the French Rejected the European Constitution. *Political Research Quarterly, 64*(2), 309–322.

Hooghe, L., & Marks, G. (2009). A Postfunctionalist Theory of European Integration: From Permissive Consensus to Constraining Dissensus. *British Journal of Political Science, 39,* 1–23.

Ivaldi, G. (2006). Beyond France's 2005 Referendum on the European Constitutional Treaty: Second-Order Model, Anti-establishment Attitudes and the End of the Alternative European Utopia. *West European Politics, 29*(1), 47–69.

Lechner, F. J. (2008). *The Netherlands: Globalization and National Identity.* London: Routledge.

Le Gall, G. (2005). La démythification d'un "non" tribunitien. In G. Finchelstein (Ed.), *Le jour où la France a dit non. Comprendre le référendum du 29 mai 2005* (pp. 100–123). Paris: Fondation Jean-Jaurès.

Leruth, B., Startin, N., & Usherwood, S. (Eds.). (2017). *The Routledge Handbook of Euroscepticism.* London: Routledge.

Maatsch, S. (2007). The Struggle to Control Meanings: The French Debate on the European Constitution in the Mass Media. *Perspectives on European Politics and Society, 8,* 261–280.

Marthaler, S. (2005). The French Referendum on Ratification of the EU Constitutional Treaty, 29 May 2005. *Representation, 41,* 228–236.

Mergier, A. (2005). Pourquoi le "non" était possible. In G. Finchelstein (Ed.), *Le jour où la France a dit non. Comprendre le référendum du 29 mai 2005* (pp. 14–25). Paris: Fondation Jean-Jaurès.

Morel, L. (2007). The Rise of "Politically Obligatory" Referendums: The 2005 French Referendum in Comparative Perspective. *West European Politics, 30*(5), 1041–1067.

Qvortrup, M. (2006). The Three Referendums on the European Constitution Treaty in 2005. *The Political Quarterly, 77*(1), 89–97.

Reh, C. (2009). The Lisbon Treaty: De-constitutionalizing the European Union? *Journal of Common Market Studies, 47*(3), 625–650.

Ricard-Nihoul, G. (2005). *The French "No" Vote on 29 May 2005: Understanding and Action* (Notre Europe. Etudes & Recherches, No. 44).

Roes, T. H. (2008). *Facts and Figures of The Netherlands: Social and Cultural Trends 1995–2006*. The Hague: Netherlands Institute for Social Research.

Schmidt, V. A. (2002). Does Discourse Matter in the Politics of Welfare State Adjustment? *Comparative Political Studies, 35*(2), 168–193.

Schmidt, V. A. (2007). Trapped by Their Ideas: French Élites' Discourses of European Integration and Globalization. *Journal of European Public Policy, 14*(7), 992–1009.

Schuck, A. R. T., & de Vreese, C. H. (2008). The Dutch No to the EU Constitution: Assessing the Role of EU Skepticism and the Campaign. *Journal of Elections, Public Opinion and Parties, 18*(1), 101–128.

Schuck, A. R. T., & de Vreese, C. H. (2009). Reversed Mobilization in Referendum Campaigns: How Positive News Framing Can Mobilize the Skeptics. *The International Journal of Press/Politics, 14*(1), 40–66.

Scott, J. W. (2010). *The Politics of the Veil*. Princeton: Princeton University Press.

Smith, T. B. (2004). *France in Crisis: Welfare, Inequality, and Globalization Since 1980*. Cambridge: Cambridge University Press.

Startin, N., & Krouwel, A. (2013). Euroscepticism Re-galvanized: The Consequences of the 2005 French and Dutch Rejections of the EU Constitution. *Journal of Common Market Studies, 51*(1), 65–84.

Sternberg, C. S. (2013). *The Struggle for EU Legitimacy*. London: Palgrave Macmillan.

Sternberg, C. (2015a). What Were the French Telling Us by Voting Down the 'EU Constitution'? A Case for Interpretive Research on Referendum Debates. *Comparative European Politics, 16*(2), 145–170.

Sternberg, C. S. (2015b). Political Legitimacy Between Democracy and Effectiveness: Trade-Offs, Interdependencies, and Discursive Constructions by the EU Institutions. *European Political Science Review, 7*(04), 615–638.

Taggart, P. (1998). A Touchstone of Dissent: Euroscepticism in Contemporary Western European Party Systems. *European Journal of Political Research, 33*(3), 363–388.

Taggart, P. (2006). Keynote Article: Questions of Europe—The Domestic Politics of the 2005 French and Dutch Referendums and Their Challenge for the Study of European Integration. *Journal of Common Market Studies, 44*(s1), 7–25.

CHAPTER 29

Swiss Votes on Europe

Clive H. Church

Direct democratic 'votations' are not merely more numerous in Switzerland than anywhere else, but, as Serdült (2013) has shown, they are fundamental to Swiss politics and especially to the Swiss constitution.[1] All Swiss votations matter, irrespective of their subject. Yet it is arguable that those touching on Europe matter more than most. Hence, they deserve special attention. This is not simply because they have more implications and interest for outsiders than more domestically orientated votations. There are other reasons, beginning with the great importance of relations with the European Union (EU) in Swiss politics, which raise questions about prosperity, identity and foreign policy, especially as they have become intertwined with concerns over immigration. Secondly, they matter because they are central to the growing argument among the Swiss over how far their direct democracy can be reconciled with acceptance of international law. Thirdly, they matter because the European question is not just an institutional matter but, as a result of Switzerland's geographical position, something which embraces transport and transit in ways

[1] The term referendum can be misleading in the Swiss context because there it can often mean only specific kinds of direct democratic vote, thus excluding initiatives and some other forms. As a result, this chapter follows the lead of the late Christopher Hughes, the doyen of British students of Swiss politics, and uses the French term *votation* (the equivalents being *votazione* in Italian and *Abstimmung* in German) to mean any kind of public decision-making in Switzerland.

C. H. Church (✉)
University of Kent, Canterbury, UK
e-mail: C.H.Church@kent.ac.uk

© The Author(s) 2021
J. Smith (ed.), *The Palgrave Handbook of European Referendums*,
https://doi.org/10.1007/978-3-030-55803-1_29

not found in other third countries like the UK. In other words, the policy impact of Swiss votations on Europe is very large. Lastly, the European question is also highly sensitive, not to say explosive. Indeed, some votations on Europe can seem to threaten the country's otherwise iron-clad stability.

Despite their significance, such votations have rarely, if ever, been covered systematically in the academic literature. Indeed, some studies of referendums on Europe ignore them (Kobach 1993; Fossedal 2002; Kaufmann 2005; Hobolt 2009). Putting this right, however, requires setting them in context. Understanding how and why the European question has become so salient is an essential preliminary to examining the various votations themselves. Although the relevant votes cover a range of topics, their underlying dynamic has always been changes in Swiss concerns over their independence and nature as a nation.

All the votations studied in this chapter have taken place over the last 30 years, a time of considerable political change in Switzerland, with old-style stability and consensus giving way to more competitive and confrontational politics (Church 2016). It was also a period of striking developments in Switzerland's European relations. In fact, a new era in European relations began in the late 1980s when existing relationships with the then European Community (EC) began to run out of steam; this was intensified in 1992 when the country was called on to vote on entry to the European Economic Area (EEA) and related topics. Then, after the EEA was narrowly rejected, the country went through a new phase, lasting nearly a decade, of seeking and preparing for a new relationship. A third phase began at the turn of the century as the various bilateral arrangements were voted on and implemented.

Thereafter, new questions began to emerge as the country became increasingly polarized. All this has had significant effects on Swiss politics and international relations as Swiss Euroscepticism, properly understood, struggled to contain rising Swiss Europhobia. Although the pragmatists seemed to have the upper hand at the time of writing, it was clear that there were still challenges and uncertainties to be faced and more votations to be called, as 'Europe' continued to be a sensitive and divisive question.

Moreover, not only do votations on Europe embrace most of the forms of direct democracy described by Serdült (in Chapter 10 of this volume) and Goetschel et al. (2005: 37–44) and which allow Swiss citizens a voice on foreign policy, but they have been involved in the extension of its applicability to external questions, something which had been discussed for decades (Meuwly 2018: 110–112). In 1975, the authorities rejected a right-wing call to make all treaties subject to popular approval, but two years later direct democracy was permanently extended to a wider range of treaties. And there was increasing concern about how to handle initiatives in conflict with international law (Tanquerel 1994). The practice which developed was to reject those which clashed with the most basic principles of international law such as the rejection of torture, while allowing the people a free vote on more technical treaties. This was largely codified in the new constitution of 1999 (Haller

2016). Further extensions of direct democracy to treaties were made in 2003. Although no more than 4% have ever been subject to a votation.

29.1   THE EUROPEAN QUESTION IN SWISS POLITICS

The idea of having a policy towards something called 'Europe' is a relatively new concept in Switzerland. In the nineteenth and early twentieth centuries, Europe was essentially a matter of limiting the effect of conflicts among surrounding nations by a policy of strict neutrality. Then, around the time of the First World War, neutrality became not just a means of preserving independence but a way of ensuring that European conflict did not exacerbate differences between the country's linguistic communities. Hence foreign policy was often seen as more of an internal than an external affair.

The rise of Fascism and Nazism presented new challenges, forcing the country back into its shell, and then into difficult, and still controversial, relationships with the combatants in World War II (Kreis 2013). Here the fact that the Swiss view of neutrality was that it was purely political and not economic caused difficulties with the victor powers. It was partly because of the suspicions prevailing outside that Switzerland was very slow to associate itself with new institutional developments after 1945. Thus, it stayed out of the United Nations (UN) and of the Organization for European Economic Cooperation (OEEC), the Council of Europe and the General Agreement on Tariffs and Trade (GATT) (Gabriel and Fischer 2003). The decision of neighbouring states, all now pacific and democratic, to integrate structurally posed especial problems for Switzerland as it saw the Coal and Steel Community and the Common Market as threats.

Only slowly did Switzerland overcome the belief that such bodies were nascent supranational agencies which would threaten national independence, neutrality and economic autonomy. It was instrumental in setting up the European Free Trade Association (EFTA) in 1959 and the government did consider association with the European Economic Community (EEC) in 1961–1962 but the conditions it wanted were unacceptable to the Six. The next year it joined the Council of Europe. Then, when the UK announced that it was seeking EC membership, the Swiss government worked with its other partners in EFTA to improve their market access. This eventually led to the 1972 Free Trade Agreement, signed in parallel with other EFTA states (Dupont and Sciarini 2001).

Accepting the new deal was made the subject of an obligatory votation on 3 December 1972. It was carried by 72.5% of those voting, on a 52.9% turnout. And it won a majority in every canton and half canton. Indeed, only in Obwald and Schwyz did support fall below 60%, while in some cantons, notably in the Suisse Romande, support reached around 80%. Its combination of secure and easier cross-border trade and an absence of supranational threats to institutions won it wide backing. Thus, alongside solid government input, all the main parties supported it, leaving only the far left and the extreme right, opposing it (Linder et al. 2010: 319–321). This opened the way to some 15 years of successful relations with Brussels. Dozens of technical agreements were signed. The government believed it had found a third way between membership and isolation, if not a form of 'quasi-membership'. These were also golden years in another way because there was general domestic consensus about Europe.

This mutually satisfactory arrangement began to unravel in the mid-1980s by when the 1972 agreements, which had by now been extended to Finland, were fully operational, raising the question of how relations between the EFTA states and the Community should develop in future. An initial attempt to increase cooperation and consultation, agreed in Luxembourg in December 1984, proved a disappointment. However, five years later, Jacques Delors offered a new possibility: a European Economic Space runs jointly by the two bodies, thus opening a new phase in relations with the EC, leading to the EEA debacle.

At the same time, a second factor was making it increasingly important for the country to have good relations. This was because the Community had developed a new dynamism, expanding to take in Spain and Portugal, accepting majority voting and setting late-1992 as the deadline for the completion of the Single Market. This moved it away from a mainly economic body towards what many saw as a more supranational political Union, forcing Switzerland to adapt in order to avoid getting sucked in as a government report put it (Federal Council 1988).

All this happened when Swiss politics were changing, with the government's attempt to join the UN causing a mobilization of conservative forces. These not only defeated the proposal but saw the transformation in 1986 of their organizing committee (under the leadership of Swiss People's Party [SVP] MP Christoph Blocher) into a new social movement the Campaign for an Independent and Neutral Switzerland (AUNS from the German abbreviation) which was dedicated to preserving Swiss freedom from outside influences. This meant that the Swiss passive consensus on Europe began to fray.

Negotiations on what became the European Economic Area proved difficult, despite the offer to build a new railway tunnel under the Alps, to be inserted at the base of the mountains. Hence, even the government negotiators were not satisfied with the results, saying that the EEA was not right for a proud and autonomous nation. So, encouraged by opinion polls and votations, the government applied for EU membership in May 1992. This complicated things for the vote on EEA entry, which the government lost.

The defeat of 6 December 1992 opened a new phase in the European question as Switzerland sought to make up for the self-inflicted exclusion from the Single Market. This had to be carried out against a background of a rising tide of environmentalism, focused on transport. Hence for over 12 years the Swiss sought to negotiate bilateral deals that provided some economic compensation. A first set of bilaterals were negotiated and approved at the end of the decade. However, because the EU was by then very aware of the way in which Swiss direct democracy could upset things, it insisted that the seven deals were held together by a tripwire, meaning that if the Swiss tried to 'reverse cherry pick' and drop one deal, all the others would be simultaneously guillotined.

Thereafter, while the government almost immediately set about negotiating further deals, public opinion began to change. Support for membership began to fall, encouraged by government mistakes. Indeed, the very idea of closer relations with Brussels became one of the major dividing lines in an increasingly polarized and fractious country. As a result, by 2006 the government had to downgrade entry from being its main aim to being merely one possibility for the future. This reflected the way the rise of the SVP had led to a series of initiatives which seemed to clash with international law (Skenderovic 2009). Moreover, by then, changes in migration patterns and votations on entry into Schengen had meant that immigration and foreigners had become increasingly part of the European question. All this complicated the task of implementing the bilateral agreements.

Once the bilaterals had been implemented, a new phase opened after 2012 as the new settlement was called into question, initially with the SVP launching an initiative demanding the imposition of ceilings and quotas on foreign workers, knowing that this would mean resiling from many of the bilateral agreements. The initiative went through two years later, leaving the government unsuccessfully trying to square the circle and implement the new constitutional article. This proved impossible and, in the end, in December 2016, the Parliament pushed through a somewhat dubious and evasive formula for giving preference to resident workers, which the EU accepted, and the SVP decided not to challenge. This avoided a new votation on a proposal to excise the 2014 text from the constitution, a simple but constitutionally doubtful action.

However, this pushed the SVP to launch new initiatives seeking to undermine the bilaterals and also to ban free movement. The explosive nature of the Mass Immigration Initiative also helped to stimulate counter-vailing forces which were able to defeat other proposals: on population in November 2014, asylum in 2016 and naturalization in 2017. Meanwhile, the government had been under pressure: the EU was pressing Switzerland to sign a framework agreement which would co-ordinate, regularize and update its relations since it believed that the bilaterals were now past their use-by date, even though some three-quarters of the population believed strongly in them. Negotiations have been going for several years so a rapid and mutually acceptable solution cannot be relied on, even though the EU wanted a decision by July 2019.

All this shows that the European question remains ultra-sensitive and salient, reflecting a division between urban and outward-looking Switzerland and an inward-looking nation, based in the country, small towns and outer suburbs. Such cultural feelings play a major role in Swiss votations on Europe, raising questions about national identity, the overall drift of foreign policy and the nature of Swiss society, as well as technical questions about EU relations and the future of the Swiss economy (Sciarini and Tresch 2009: 459 and 475–476). In other words, Europe is a surrogate for national debate about the very nature of the nation and its future. Moreover, the debate is not a simple matter of 'Euroturbos', as the Swiss call them, against anti-Europeans. It is more complicated than that, often—as already suggested—with somewhat sceptical pragmatists resisting visceral Europhobia (Church 2009). Equally the width of the European question, as revealed by the choice of votations examined here, takes it into unexpected corners of Swiss life. So, clearly, votations on Europe justify special attention.

29.2   THE SELECTION

Given what has been said about the width, complexity and controversial nature of the European question, there is clearly a case for choosing a larger number of votations for study than is conventionally done. Here 17 votations have been singled out, from five thematic groups. Four deal with the key domain of transport and relate to Europe through the fact that the Swiss chose to make alpine transport a key element of their negotiations. Although these are somewhat technical and may seem distant from what are normally considered European questions, in their time they were essential to Swiss negotiations. Had they been rejected, Swiss relations with the EU would have been very different.

Four are more constitutional decisions about the process of decision-making on what should be negotiated with Europe, and how this should be done. This included starting membership applications on the spot, ensuring that ultimate decisions were reserved to the people whether on the policy as a whole, on the way it should be pursued or enforced over international law. A third group of six votations concern the bilateral agreements and their extensions. To this group can be added the vote on biometric passports, the rejection of which would have significantly complicated relations.

This leaves two votations. Firstly, that on Swiss entry to the Bretton Woods institutions which paved the way for the submission of the application for membership and is coupled here with the December 1992 rejection of entry to the EEA, probably the most significant of all the popular votes to date. Secondly, there is the initiative against mass migration. This is included, almost as a group on its own, because, whether deliberately or not, it threatened to cause the renegotiation of virtually all Switzerland's existing agreements with the EU. Overall, the selection gives a good idea of the wide-ranging nature of Swiss relations with the EU. However, further additions are likely to be forthcoming.

1. 17 May 1992	Approval of Swiss entry to the World Bank and the IMF
2. 27 September1992	Approval of New Alpine Base Tunnels
3. 6 December 1992	Rejection of entry to the EEA
4. 20 February 1994	The Alps Initiative on shifting transit from road to rail

5. 8 June 1997	'Let the people decide!'
6. 27 September 1998	Approval of heavy lorry transit charges
7. 29 November 1998	Agreement on state financing of transport Infrastructures
8. 21 May 2000	Approval of the Bilaterals I package
9. 4 March 2001	Defeat of the 'Yes to Europe!' proposal for immediate entry talks
10. 5 June 2005	Acceptance of Schengen and Dublin processes (Bilaterals 2)
11. 25 September 2005	Extension of bilaterals to Bulgaria and Romania
12. 26 November 2006	Approval of cohesion payments to Eastern Europe
13. 8 February 2009	Extension of free movement to Bulgaria and Romania
14. 17 May 2009	Acceptance of the introduction of biometric passports
15. 17 June 2012	Rejection of 'Let the people speak!' on negotiations
16. 9 February 2014	Approval of the 'Stop Mass Immigration' initiative
17. 25 November 2018	Self-Determination Initiative

Technically, the 17 include three types of Swiss direct democratic votes. Nine of them were *challenges*—otherwise known as 'facultative referendums'—to federal legislation, including diplomatic agreements. Such challenges require 50,000 signatures and are decided simply by popular vote. A second group of six arose from *popular initiatives*, which, because they involved changes to the constitution, required cantonal and popular majorities. The third group comprises two *government proposals*. One was the EEA vote, which was seen as an obligatory referendum on a major treaty. The other was the obligatory referendum on infrastructures, which again needed a double majority because it involved a constitutional amendment. Thus, only two did not emerge from popular action, whether positive or negative. In all cases, the results were binding although it is arguable that, as will be seen, the response to the Stop Mass Migration initiative was to treat it as binding only in principle.

Equally, all 17 were opened to decision by ordinary citizens according to general rules. They were also subject to normal age limits of 18. Simple, not fixed majorities sufficed for acceptance or rejection. Spending was not limited and, in all cases, the government was an active participant in the campaigns. However, the motivation for the votations varied as the following analyses show.

29.3   ANALYSES OF INDIVIDUAL VOTATIONS

29.3.1   *Towards the EEA*

After a long period in which there were no votations which really touched on Swiss relations with the European Community, the early 1990s saw a flurry. Chronologically, the first was on membership of the World Bank and the IMF, neither of which were EC bodies, but acceptance was taken as suggesting the electorate was now open to such international involvement. The second, authorizing the construction of the Gotthard base tunnel, was an essential negotiating tactic with the Community. However, while both seemed to pave the way for institutional involvement with the Community, the December 1992 defeat of EEA entry wrote *finis* to passive acceptance of closer EU relations, opening a new and difficult phase for the country.

1. 17 May 1992 Bretton Woods Although this votation was not directed at any European bodies, it deserves inclusion because it opened the way to a more active European policy (Linder et al. 2010: 484–485). It was a twofold affair, involving challenges to a law regulating Swiss participation in the two institutions, including the power to sign accords with and provide finance to the two and to a government decree on approving entry to the World Bank and the IMF. Passed on 4 October 1991, they were then challenged. The first was endorsed by 55.8% to 44.2% on a 38.8% turnout, the second by 56.4% (923,685 votes) to 43.6% (730,553) on a turnout of 38.81%. In both cases, voters in seven full and half cantons, mainly in the German-speaking Alpine areas of central Switzerland, rejected the proposals. The three most westerly French-speaking cantons voted most heavily in favour.

The arguments for entry—put by the government and supported by most parties—were that, in a world where the states of the former Soviet Union had joined these institutions, the country could no longer stand aloof. It needed to join so that its voice could be heard, and it could influence policies which had an increasing influence on Switzerland. As an outsider it could not do this. Joining would also strengthen the country's international position and show solidarity with the developing countries to which the institutions lent money. It was here that the two opposing campaign groups, third-worlders (led by the Berne Declaration movement and the Social Democrats) and enthusiasts for a small state (including the SVP), concentrated their attacks, arguing that the institution simply drove developing countries into debt. The latter also complained about what the allegedly inordinate costs of entry.

Their defeat suggested to the Federal Council that the country would back entry to the EU, encouraging it to ignore the EEA and apply for membership. This happened three days later. The government's view was to prove over optimistic. Approval of IMF and World Bank entry did not mean that the electorate would approve closer European integration, even though membership of the Bretton Woods bodies was to become generally accepted.

2. 27 September 1992 NEAT/NLFA. Gotthard/Lotschberg base tunnels[2] This too was a votation which, while it did not directly mention Europe, played a role in facilitating relations with the Community. Technically the votation was on a challenge to the federal ordinance of 4 October 1991 proposing the new Alpine rail transit which had been crucial in getting the European Community to agree to a new transport deal which offered the Swiss a number of advantages such as new transit levies and bans on night-time working. Without it, Switzerland would not have been able to fulfil its new obligations to the Community (Linder et al. 2010: 492–493). Coming in the run-up to the EEA vote, as it did, it had a further significance as a test of attitudes to Europe. However, the European dimension was played down in the campaign, the government stressing its environmental and economic benefits, notably the protection it would offer the Alps. It would also facilitate goods traffic and halve transit time for all, arguments which commended it to the main parties and most business and economic lobbies. It was opposed by Greens and Social Democrats, organized into three opposition groups. They attacked its grandiose (and anti-ecological) nature, its costs and the damaging trajectory planned for Uri.

The proposal passed by 63.6% (1,305,914) to 36.4% (747, 048) on a 45.9% turnout. However, like the Bretton Woods vote, it did not prove a good guide to popular views on wider European policy. It did help towards developing further transport deals relevant to the EU. Construction commenced in 1999 and the tunnels opened in May 2017.

3. 6 December 1992: Entry to the European Economic Area The 6 December 1992 votation was a far better guide to popular attitudes to European integration than its predecessors (Linder et al. 2010: 499–500). Its effects were significant. Not only did it prevent Swiss entry to the EEA, it also blocked the pending application for EU membership, of May 1992 and, by generally discouraging Europhiles and encouraging the populist opposition, it changed public opinion, altering the country's political balance and tone. Its impact has been compared to that of the Battle of Marignano in 1515 which started Switzerland on the road to neutrality. Consequently, it left the government scratching round for a pragmatic means of filling the gaps left by exclusion from the EEA which it had seen as a new 'Third Way'.

Not surprisingly many think the campaign was of unrivalled intensity. Certainly, it was an extraordinarily narrow defeat (Kriesi et al., 1993). Entry was rejected by 50.3% (1,786,708) to 49.7% (1,762,872) and this on the highest turnout since 1947 of 78.74%, and the fifth highest ever, because many habitual abstainers felt compelled to vote. In No-voting Zug turnout reached 87% and the lowest score (in Yes-voting Basel Stadt) was 'only' 72.37%. Rejection carried 14 full and four half cantons, as against six full and two half cantons which voted Yes. One problem was that save for the two Basel half cantons, all these Yes-voting cantons were French speaking.

---

[2]Die Neue Eisenbahn-Alpentransversale/*Nouvelle ligne ferroviaire à travers les Alpes.*

Moreover, the German-speaking districts of Fribourg and Valais voted 'No'
just as the French-speaking parts of Bern voted 'Yes'. Italian-speaking Ticino
voted against by 62%. If, in Neuchâtel, support for entry reached 80%, in
German-speaking Switzerland it fell as low as 25.21 per cent in Uri. This was
perceived as a damaging linguistic and cultural divide between French and
German speakers, the so-called 'Röstigraben' and led to soul-searching and
new legislation on language use.

The reasons for this striking popular decision were manifold. Much was
due to the way the government and its allies handled the issue. Their communication policies were poor and there was a shortage of leadership in the
campaign, while big business came in too hard and too late (Sally 1993).
Equally, although the official booklet denied that this was the case, the application for membership sowed confusion and left many thinking they were voting
against entry. This confusion did not help the establishment's cause, with
support for entry—in the majority at the time the deal was signed—halving
between August and November.

This abrupt descent into scepticism was caused by the superior campaigning
of Blocher and his forces and the way they were able to play on underlying
fears of conservative Swiss opinion which patriotically valued independence.
The opposition argued that the EEA would mean satellization and the end
of Swiss independence. The EEA was thus seen as especially threatening. Nor
were voters convinced by talk of economic gain because they feared an influx
of foreign workers, along with social dumping. Opponents felt the country
was alright as it was and would not be helped by being tied to an EU which
had its own problems. Some on the left also feared higher rents, lower wages
and environmental damage. There were also worries about the threats to
neutrality and direct democracy, not to mention the likely subordination to
the European Court of Justice (ECJ). This made it one of the most bitter and
passionate campaigns on record. Such views were to persist. All this the EU
much regretted, especially after the message of the railway vote, but left it to a
much-weakened Swiss government to look for replacement arrangements. This
they were to do but the road ahead was to prove long and testing, involving
new transport and political challenges.

29.3.2   Seeking a New Settlement 1993–1999

For years after the 6 December 1992 votation, the government sought to mitigate the legal and economic losses inflicted on it by exclusion from the EEA.
This meant trying to negotiate new economic links. It also meant consolidating transport arrangements, something made harder by an environmental
initiative which threatened all trans-alpine transit. The financial underpinnings
of any new deal had also to run the gauntlet of public opinion. At times, the
government's right to do all this was under threat from the far right, which
wished to use direct democracy to block further integration.

4. The 20 February 1994 Alpine Initiative This came as an unexpected and unwelcome shock to the government. On a day when it was getting approval for extending the life of charges for road use and its powers to charge lorries for other factors than their weight, something it expected to co-ordinate with the EU, the government was confronted with an initiative which both complicated its policy choices and was offered as a model for overall European Transport policy. The initiative, pushed by Alpine communities and environmentalists, mobilized by debate over allowing 40 tonne lorries to circulate in Switzerland, sought to mitigate the negative effects of foreign transit across the Alps, thus preserving the Alpine way of life. To do this it demanded that all foreign goods travelling across the country in transit should, within ten years, all be moved by rail. It also demanded that no roads should be built or extended in Alpine areas.

The government argued that this would be discriminatory, difficult to implement and would not achieve the desired ends (Linder et al. 2010: 529–530). It also threatened to breach the hard-won transit agreement with the EU, raising questions about the country's observance of international law. Economically it could also be harmful, notably to jobs. Such warnings failed to convince. Likewise, the government's talk of foreign retaliation fell on deaf ears. So, the initiative passed by 51.9% (954,491) to 41.8% (884,362) on a turnout of 40.86%. Only six French-speaking cantons, along with Aargau, voted against it, while the main parties and the car lobby opposed the initiative.

The acceptance of the initiative delayed negotiations with the EU which suspended talks until new assurances were received. EU visitors were treated to helicopter flights over the most damaged valleys. Acceptance of the initiative also reinforced both the centrality of transport to the European question and the strength of opposition to establishment wishes in this domain. In the end, the government had to revise the text and make it applicable to domestic as well as foreign transit so as to avoid charges of discrimination. Parliament heard calls from pragmatists to ban such wide-ranging initiatives in future.

5. 8 June 1997: 'EU Membership Negotiations: Let the People Decide' As the government negotiated replacement deals with the EU, the question of how these should be approved rose up the political agenda, adding a new blockage to that created by the Alpine Initiative (Linder et al. 2010: 552–553). In the mid-1990s the Swiss Democrats and the Ticinese League launched an initiative which sought to create a popular veto on negotiations with the EU, proposing a new transitional article in the Constitution which called for the breaking-off of ongoing entry negotiations and demanded a decision by people and cantons before any new negotiations could start. This more restrictive approach, they claimed, would make a reality of commitments to uphold national independence.

The idea was ridiculed and dismissed, only 10 members of the Lower House voting for it, as for once the SVP did not object. The Eidgenössisch-Demokratische Union/Union Démocratique Fédérale (EDU/UDF), which had been sympathetic, retreated. The Federal Council called it illogical, uncon-stitutional and unsuitable. It also pointed out that there were no ongoing entry negotiations to annul. Moreover, the initiative implied that the people did not presently have a voice and also required them to vote without knowing the shape of any deal. Nonetheless, its call for the SD to withdraw the initiative failed.

A pragmatic electorate agreed with the establishment and voted the initia-tive down by 74.1% (1,189,440) to 25.9% (416,720), the initiative failing to win a single canton. There was no real linguistic divide although Ticino was the most supportive canton with 38% in favour. Turnout was 35.44%. This was the first of many occasions on which pragmatic but sceptical Swiss rejected extreme anti-EU proposals, for the initiative was aimed at relations with the EU, not at other votations. Its defeat allowed the government to press on with its bilateral negotiations which, as before, required new land transport legislation.

6. 27 September 1998 Heavy Lorries' Charge This was the first of two votations needed to provide the domestic financial underpinnings for deals with the EU. It came from a challenge by haulage lobby ASTAG to a highly technical law of 19 December 1997 which implemented legislation previously mentioned by shifting taxation from weight to distance and pollution level (on a sliding scale), thereby helping to protect the Alps. This partly reflected the increasing volume of Alpine transit traffic and partly the need to arrive at an acceptable level of charges for the EU. At the same time, by raising the permissible weight of lorries on Swiss roads, it would reduce the number of journeys (because lorries would be able to carry more) and prepare the way for a transport accord with the EU, strengthening the Swiss negotiating position. Without the charge, the government argued, it would be hard to conclude a deal and it would leave Switzerland exposed to uncontrolled traffic (Linder et al. 2010: 562–563).

The charge was the keystone of overall land transport policy as the monies raised would help to improve the nation's roads. ASTAG's view was that the taxes were too high and would cost jobs. The lobby also doubted that the charge would reduce pollution or divert much traffic to rail. Yet neither this, nor the interesting claim that the law was not EU-compatible convinced, and it went down by 57.2% (1,355,735) to 42.8% (1,014,370) on a 51.8% turnout. This left one question open before the transport deal with the EU could be concluded.

7. 29 November 1998 Financing of Public Transport Infrastructures The second question was the financing of the proposed Gotthard base tunnel, which was necessary to strengthen Swiss relations with the EU and link the country more effectively to wider European rail networks. The Swiss had insisted on paying for it themselves, in line with their belief in autonomy of foreign policy, and it was expensive. So, the government was desperate to get it passed. The votation was, moreover, an obligatory one, one the govern-ment had to call. The 20 March *arreté* proposed the financing not only of

NEAT but also a domestic rail modernization programme, known as Rail 2000, connections to the European high-speed network, and work on noise abatement. The financing package ran to 2017 and relied on tolls and the lorry charge (Linder et al. 2010: 566–567).

It was overwhelmingly backed by parliament, with only the SVP and some smaller right-wing parties opposing, along with the Touring Club Suisse, the equivalent of the RAC and AA. The latter argued that it discriminated against drivers. Popular pragmatism meant that the challenge was rejected by 63.5% (1,104,294) to 36.5% (634,714) on a 38.31% turnout. Only Thurgau and the two half cantons of Appenzell rejected the idea. The fact that the package would facilitate the establishment of the Lotschberg link with the western TGV network helped to win over French speakers. Approval cleared the way for the key land transport deal with the EU and hence to the completion of a general arrangement with the EU to make up for exclusion from the EEA.

29.3.3   2000–2009: Installing the Bilaterals

The third phase opened with the approval of the first linked package of sectoral deals with the Union negotiated in the 1990s. A year later this bilateral approach, as it came to be called, was consecrated by a massive rejection of a proposal to start immediate entry negotiations. The approach was then rein-forced by a further set of sectoral arrangements and then, twice, by agreement to extend their effects to new EU Member States. All this was then rein-forced by the approval of agreements, first to make a financial contribution to help the integration of the former Soviet satellites into the western European socio-economic order and second to update the Schengen agreements to take account of technological progress.

8. 21 May 2000: The Bilateral I Agreements This votation was called by the government on its own decree promulgating the seven linked agree-ments with the EU which had been negotiated so painfully through the 1990s, covering free movement, land transport, air transport, technical barriers to trade, public procurement, research and processed agricultural goods (Linder et al. 2010: 589–591). For government and parliament (which gave them full support), they constituted a balanced package which opened EU Member State markets to Swiss people and goods, increasing economic growth and ensuring Switzerland got fair payment for allowing transit. They denied there would be an avalanche of costs, lorries and people. Indeed, it offered flanking measures to protect wages, transit and other social concerns. Nor did it mean membership. Saying 'No' to the package would, moreover, create many difficulties. The granting of free movement was only for seven years.

Opposition came from 11 separate campaign organizing committees which, between them, attracted 66,000 signatures. These had a threefold objection to the package. They saw it not merely as unnecessary but, consequently, as a symbol of a government desire to enter the EU. At the same time, they were fearful of its effects, prophesying an influx of workers and traffic. It would also be harmful to the peasantry. Left-wingers protested against the likely negative effects of the liberalization enshrined in the package. There were also environmental concerns, one committee stressing the threats the package posed to ecology and direct democracy. However, there seems to have been little concern about the trip-wire nature of the deal.

The package got emphatic public backing. It was seen as the best way forward for Switzerland and the majority accepted that it was not a highroad to entry. It was endorsed by 67.2% (1,497,093) against 32.8% (730,980). Only Schwyz and Ticino rejected it, while Vaud approved it by 80%. The turnout was a respectable 48.30%. This provided the basis for the remarkable legitimacy which was to be enjoyed by the bilateral approach.

9. 4 March 2001: The 'Yes to Europe!' initiative This was an emphatic but much misunderstood defeat of an initiative by the Swiss European Movement (NOMES/NEBS) calling for immediate negotiations on EU membership (Linder et al. 2010: 601–602). It had been launched in 1995 to bring clarity to the Swiss stance on Europe. Motivated by the 1992 No, it secured sufficient signatures in 1997. Two years later it was rejected by Parliament although almost a third of National Councillors supported it.

This initiative had been pending for a longish time when it came up for decision. By then circumstances had changed, support for membership had fallen and the bilaterals were popular. Hence the establishment (and many pro-Europeans) brought great pressure on NOMES to withdraw, offering a virtual counter-project to assure proposers that the government's heart was still in the right European place and would ultimately apply. Unwisely, NOMES persevered but, with everybody against the idea, the initiative was calamitously defeated by 76.8% (1,982,549) to 23.2% (597,217) with not a single canton being in favour, and on a healthy turnout of 55.79%.

The initiative proposed altering the constitution's transitional arrangements to state that Switzerland participated in European integration with a view to entering the EU. It then called for membership negotiations to start 'without delay'. It also provided for popular approval of the outcome of the proposed negotiations and enjoined negotiators to ensure that Swiss democracy, federalism and social gains were preserved. This would enable Switzerland to participate effectively and not merely be handed down decisions. However, for the Federal Council the initiative took away its right to decide on treaties and required it to negotiate at the wrong time and in too much of a hurry. The nation clearly agreed, but many outside failed to understand that the government remained committed to entry and that this was not a decision of principle against membership. Thus, it left the government looking weak and somewhat embarrassed, while anti-European forces were encouraged.

10. 5 June 2005: The Schengen Agreement and the Dublin Convention Freed of the necessity to consider immediate entry, the government continued with the second round of bilateral negotiations which it had started almost before the ink was dry on the first batch. In particular, the Swiss wanted entry to the Schengen Agreement and Dublin Convention as they would help tourism and minimize border friction. Although the EU was initially dubious, it agreed when it realized it needed Swiss cooperation on taxation of savings. Talks started in June 2002 and finished two years later (Linder et al. 2010: 656–657).

The new set of bilaterals consisted of nine free-standing agreements: taxation, fraud, Schengen, agricultural products, media, education, pensions, environment and statistics.

Since many of these were technical they were not challenged, as they could have been. Schengen and Dublin, however, were a different matter as they involved the emotive subjects of free movement and internal security. The SVP, AUNS and others made great play of these issues in challenging the agreement, obtaining 85,000 signatures. They argued that signing up to the two accords would mean increased criminality and unemployment. It would also entail subjection to foreign laws, notably on the possession of weapons and a general loss of sovereignty, detractors/opponents asserted. Moreover, it was a step down the slippery slope to membership.

This the government firmly denied. It claimed that signing up would mean enhanced security, partly through access to Schengen databases, plus economic advantages. Joining Dublin would prevent people making dual applications. Signing up provided protection against crime and misuse of asylum. The pragmatic public accepted this by 54.6% (1,477,260) to 45.4% (1,227,042) on a 56.63% turnout, further reinforcing the bilateral strategy.

11. 25 September 2005: Extension of Free Movement to Ten New EU Member States In 2004 the EU expanded to take in Cyprus, Malta, Slovenia and seven former Soviet satellites from Eastern Europe. While most of the bilateral agreements were not affected by this, free movement meant that special arrangements had to be made to extend the right to the new Member States. Switzerland and the EU agreed an addendum to the existing accord. While Cyprus and Malta gained immediate access to the Swiss labour market, that for the other eastern states was to be phased in gradually up to 2011. Safeguard clauses were also included. The Swiss then decided to add extra domestic flanking measures to this, aimed at policing the labour market and avoiding abuse. This all added up to a long and complex federal decree, listing amendments to dozens of existing laws (Linder et al. 2010: 658–660).

The Government Message accompanying the decree was immediately challenged by five campaign committees, mainly from the far right but including socialists. Together they raised 77,000 signatures to support their charge that the extension would inevitably lead to uncontrolled immigration. It was also inimical to prosperity, the social welfare system and the interests of small businesses. It would also mean more illegal labour. The left felt that the flanking measures proposed were insufficient notwithstanding the promise of hundreds of new inspectors to check on possible wage dumping.

Nonetheless, the electorate, like the majority in parliament (SVP, EDU, SD and the Lega excluded), pragmatically followed the government, accepting that, if the Swiss discriminated by rejecting the new eastern members, the EU could cancel all deals. The government was also offering more controls and more protection for Swiss workers. This carried the day by 56.0% (1,458,686) to 44.0% (1,147,140) on a turnout of 54.51%. Opposition was strongest in Central Switzerland although it was highest in Ticino where 63.9% objected. Their opposing arguments were to be heard again in subsequent years.

12. 26 November 2006: Cohesion Contribution Since the Berlin Wall came down in 1989 the Swiss had been providing 200 million CHF annually to a thousand projects in countries in Central Europe and elsewhere, following on previous EFTA help to southern Europe. However, the 2004 expansion of the EU meant more security and prosperity for Europe as a whole, including Switzerland. Hence Brussels felt the Swiss should contribute to the costs of rebuilding its still poor new Member States, leading the government to legislate in March 2006 for payment of 200 CHF annually for five years. The monies would go to projects in the new members chosen by the Swiss themselves. This was seen as a means of consolidating the bilaterals as well as an altruistic act (Linder et al. 2010: 667–668).

This was opposed in parliament by the SVP and outside by three committees (including the Swiss Democrats and AUNS) who obtained 83,500 signatures. Their arguments were mainly financial. Not merely could Switzerland not afford the money but it did not need to pay what was essentially a blank cheque. It would also create debt, unemployment and higher taxes. Out and out opposition to the EU played a minor role although the campaign was very emotional. Nonetheless, a pragmatic and generous electorate accepted the law by 53.4% (1,158,494) to 46.6% (1,010,190) on a 44.98% turnout.

13. 8 February 2009: Extension of free movement to Bulgaria and Romania Once the EU had agreed to accept Bulgaria and Romania, it was axiomatic that Switzerland would eventually have to grant them free movement status. Voters clearly saw the logic and equity in doing this. They accepted that free movement was juridically linked to the bilaterals and that rejection would activate the tripwire for all the first batch of deals. The fact that the enlarged free movement would be phased in and for some years could be controlled by quota in case of problems would have helped. Hence the decision was approved more easily than in 2005, by 59.6% (1,517,132) to 40.4% (1,027,899) on a 51.44% turnout (Federal Chancellery 2009; *Année Politique Suisse* 2009). This was despite the absence of new flanking measures and a decision to make free movement permanent and not time limited, a decision which the authorities had always said would be laid before the people.

The opposition's argument that there were special problems with the two countries, as well as the, often rehearsed, threats to socio-economic stability, failed to convince. Bulgaria and Romania were seen as very poor countries and, as such, likely to generate attractively cheap labour and this worried opponents. Prevalent crime and corruption were also hinted at. Accepting the two would also constitute a precedent for future Balkan enlargements and could mean importing unemployment, lower wages and social costs, opponents argued. Government arguments that to deny access to the two new EU members would be politically risky, given the delicate state of Swiss relations with Brussels, were dismissed by opponents.

14. 17 May 2009: Introduction of biometric passports With no further enlargement in sight, the bilateral approach might have seemed complete. However, a change in EU practice forced one final consolidating votation (Federal Chancellery 2009; *Année Politique Suisse* 2009). This proved to be worryingly close, 'un petit oui' as it was called, even though it easily passed Parliament. This was symbolic of what was to come.

There were two reasons why the government decided to go for biometric (or electronic) passports. One was that, with over 50 states using them (many of which would accept only biometric documents), Swiss travellers would need them if they were not to be banned from going abroad, Hence, they were trialled from 2006. The second was that, in August 2006, the Schengen system required its members to adopt them. Failure to follow suit would jeopardize all free movement arrangements. So, an implementing decree was issued in June 2008. This met objections from centre-right legislators, mainly on independence grounds. It was then challenged by a number of opponents including the Greens, who argued that it made passports very expensive, created an insecure central data storage system—which did not exist anywhere else—and subjected citizens to extreme state surveillance. A desire to hinder relations with the EU may also have motivated some, although personal liberty questions predominated, with one committee wanting them to be purely voluntary.

The combination of libertarianism and anti-Europeanism almost pulled it off. In the event, the idea prevailed by a very few votes. It was accepted by 50.1% (953,173) to 49.9% (947,493) on a turnout of 38.77%. This showed that acceptance of the bilaterals was not complete.

29.3.4   2009–2018 New Questions

Hence, although the bilaterals had been bedded in and generally accepted, debate on Europe continued. In fact, it took a new turn as anti-European pressure increased, with new targets, notably immigration and judicial control. Although a new attempt to subordinate treaty-making to popular decisions failed, the whole bilateral approach was then threatened by the acceptance of an SVP initiative on migration. This was eventually circumvented, while an attempt to subject international law to popular veto was roundly defeated. Nonetheless, the shape of Switzerland's relations with the EU remained unresolved.

15. 17 June 2012: 'International Agreements: let the people speak!' The first sign of this pressure came in a 2009 initiative from AUNS which sought a wide extension of the range of treaties which would have to be approved by the people. The initiative proposed a new constitutional Article 140 which extended the obligatory votation requirement to treaties in (undefined) important domains and led to multilateral unification of law, forced

Switzerland to take on external rules, accept foreign jurisdiction or entailed capital outlays of a billion francs or 100 million francs annually. This requirement was defended as following the example set by the government in 1992 and restoring the old Swiss administrative order after a period when Switzerland had to submit to EU jurisdiction. It was also a means of defending Swiss democracy, independence and prosperity. The stress on the necessity for Swiss law to enjoy priority pointed the way to future SVP initiatives.

For the Federal Council this was unnecessary as the existing direct democratic system worked well and the initiative would have meant far too many votations, given how many treaties the state signed annually. It was also somewhat imprecise. The government urged Parliament to produce a counter-project but its advice was ignored. In the end, despite the SVP spending a million CHF on the campaign, the public emphatically and pragmatically backed the government, rejecting the initiative by 75.3% (1,462,659) to 24.7% (480,173) on a 38.53% turnout. Implicitly the electorate accepted that this was a loaded initiative and not a sincere defence of direct democracy. Nonetheless, the pressure on closer relations with Europe remained.

16. 9 February 2014: The 'Stop Mass Immigration' Initiative In fact, encouraged by the success of its Minarets and other earlier initiatives, the SVP found a means to challenge the status quo, including the bilaterals, by using the sensitive question of immigration. Launched in late July 2011 and obtaining the necessary number of signatures by mid-March 2012, nine months ahead of schedule, the proposal was that, as a general principle, Switzerland should manage its migration policy autonomously. This entailed imposing ceilings on the number of residence-permits provided to foreigners, including asylum-seekers. The state was also given the right to limit family reunification and welfare provisions. Ceilings and quotas were to be fixed in relation to national need which meant privileging nationals. No treaties contrary to this could be signed and, according to a transitional article, any treaties which contradicted these new principles had to be renegotiated within three years. What was to happen if this was not done was not stated, although if there had been no implementation law within three years, the government was to produce provisional regulations.

Although the EU was nowhere mentioned in the text, with the promoters being very coy on the issue (although the government made it clear that acceptance could force Switzerland to renegotiate its bilateral agreements), it was very much evident in the debate (Federal Chancellery 2014; Steinberg 2015: 303–306; Meuwly 2018: 119–20). The SVP view was that, since 2007, when free movement came into full effect, the country had lost control of its borders, as well as suffering high unemployment and growing over population. It expected the government to undertake new negotiations with the EU to remedy this. Conversely, the Federal Council argued not merely that immigration helped prosperity but that to reject free movement would invoke the tripwire and end all the agreements in the first bilaterals package. It also pointed out that asylum was governed by different legislation, implying that the initiative was too wide ranging and too vague.

Nonetheless, the electorate adopted it, probably in the knowledge that it was incompatible with Swiss agreements with the EU, as Brussels made clear. It scraped through by 50.3% (1,463,854) to 49.7% (1,444,552) meaning that some 19,000 (mainly German-speaking areas often without many foreign residents) swung the popular vote. However, the initiative carried 12 full and five half cantons against eight full cantons and one half-canton on a turnout of 56.57%. All the French-speaking Swiss cantons voted against, along with Basel Stadt, Zug and Zurich. Rural areas, suburbs and smaller free-standing towns all voted for it, whereas conurbations opposed it.

The SVP was jubilant, claiming that it would force a sea change in Swiss migration policy and would encourage a Europe-wide shift to tougher asylum policies. Certainly, it created a real crisis in Swiss–EU relations. In fact, the Union, although disappointed, left it to the Swiss to solve. The vote did, however, convince Brussels that a new framework agreement was needed. Despite the text calling on the government to implement the votation 'without delay', this did not happen. Consultation saw government ideas rejected and an impasse followed, until an implementing law was passed in December 2017 by Parliament in what many considered an unconstitutional sleight of hand (Church 2019a). Although the initiative failed to achieve its ends, it had a real impact on Swiss politics, ensuring that the issues it raised would not go away.

17. 25 November 2018: Self-Determination Initiative Out of the SVP's belief in sovereignty and its objection to a 2012 Federal tribunal reference of the proposed deportation of a foreign criminal to the European Court of Human Rights came the 2015 initiative on giving precedence to Swiss law over international. This was a significant proposal and was, unusually, given considerable attention in the British media. Often known as the 'No Foreign Judges' initiative, it was devised by law professor MP Hans-Ueli Vogt and collected 116,428 signatures by June 2016. It was submitted two months later.

The initiative consisted of four amendments to the constitution starting with a firm statement of the supremacy of the Swiss constitution. The second barred the Confederation from contracting any arrangement in conflict with the constitution, with any offending international rule having to be adapted to Swiss norms. The Federal Tribunal was also ordered to obey only international rules approved by referendum. This was to apply to all existing and future treaties.

While this arose out of ECHR rulings, it also had severe implications for agreements with the EU. Indeed, SVP leaders implied that it ruled out the free movement agreement and would prevent the creation of the arbitration tribunal being considered as part of a framework agreement. Hence the government rejected the idea in July 2017. The two houses of parliament turned it down by 129–68 and 38–6, respectively.

MPs' and government objections were that the initiative called 5000 existing treaties into question, making Switzerland an unreliable partner. It was risky and de-stabilizing, potentially threatening the economy, human rights and EU relations. Nonetheless, the government went out to consultation on a proposal to give the people a voice in abrogating treaties, hoping thereby to blunt accusations that the present system was undemocratic. Business was emphatic that the initiative was a danger to prosperity while civil society organizations, including Amnesty, saw it as a major threat to human rights, forcing Switzerland to resile from the European Convention and generally isolating the country. In fact, they made much use of the idea that the initiative was another Trojan horse, following on the 2016 election of Donald Trump in the US and the UK Brexit referendum, designed to allow the persecution of minorities. And self-determination was an illusion.

In contrast, the SVP saw it as a means of preventing sovereignty being denied to the people. It would end a vagueness in the constitution and stop the authorities ignoring votations, as they had with the Alps Initiative and, especially, the 9 February 2014 votation. Blocher saw it as preventing Switzerland becoming an EU satellite (Guillaume 2018). He also argued that the present situation turned Switzerland into a prison and represented a '*coup d'etat*' against the popular will. Moreover, the party argued that very few treaties would actually have to be amended, let alone denounced.

The campaign was an unusual one, with the SVP adopting a more sober tone than in previous votations and increasingly stressing that the initiative was a means of saying 'Yes to direct democracy'. This seems to have been an attempt to get beyond its core vote. Conversely, the opposition in which the liberally minded online political network known as Libero, the *Schutzfaktor M* information campaign on human rights protection and other non-partisan bodies, played a large part, actively targeted a much wider range of voters, using the internet and social media with great efficiency. At the same time, it deployed unusually strident language and images, such as showing the initiative a red card. Social Democratic posters, in fact, equated passing the act to aligning Switzerland with Erdogan, Putin and Trump.

In the event, as the polls predicted, the initiative failed, and quite dramatically (Federal Chancellery 2018). It obtained only 33.8% (807,883) of the vote on a 47% turnout. The No side polled 1,712,999 votes (66.2%), carrying every canton even UrSchweiz, the lowest vote being 53% in the Inner Rhoden of Appenzell. In Vaud and Geneva over 75% of voters opposed it.

This stinging defeat was due, on the one hand, to weaknesses on the SVP side. Its unusually tame campaign meant that it appealed only to the converted. Moreover, the subject was too abstract for many voters. And some of the forces which had helped it in the past, economic downturn and especially rising numbers of migrants, were no longer operative. Even its argument that the initiative was a means of defending direct democracy failed to convince voters who wanted to show confidence in Swiss institutions or were just fed up with SVP extremism.

On the other hand, and perhaps more importantly, the opposition was far more organized. Thanks to the emergence of alliances of civil society organizations, churches and business, it was able to bring concentrated pressure on electors. It did this through a sophisticated and phased media campaign. Opponents also argued that the initiative would actually harm direct democracy because it would force the country to resile from treaties without the people having a say (Schlegel 2018).

In any case, the votation inflicted yet another referendum defeat on the SVP, suggesting to some that its influence, and that of strident nationalism, had peaked. This may be an exaggeration but it does seem to have sowed seeds of doubt in SVP minds. It also dynamized the opposition which began planning an assault on the anti-free movement initiative. So, the votation has implications both for direct democracy and for Swiss European policy.

29.4   DIRECT DEMOCRACY AND SWISS EUROPEAN POLICY RECONSIDERED

While many accounts of direct democracy pay little attention to its implications for foreign affairs, the analyses presented in this chapter make it clear that, in recent years at least, it has come to matter a great deal in Switzerland, even if the significance of its decisions is often hard to interpret (Cheneval and Ferrin 2018). Votations have increasingly become the arena for debate and decision on European relations, revealing a very divided, but cautious, country. Changes in public opinion have played a key role in deciding policy on Europe. Equally the outcome of one votation can influence the holding of another. This is likely to be the case in the future as the new questions of recent years continue to come before the people. Understandably, the EU has become very wary of it (Meuwly 2018: 125).

Many of the votations have been very close, given the depth of divisions over Europe. However, the division is clearly not a simple one between pro- and anti-Europeans. In fact, there has been a sharp decline of pro-Europeanism. Until recently, when there were signs of a new style anti-populist movements, sceptics have been left facing up to the majority of Europhobes. If the majority of votations go the government's way this is usually because pragmatic Eurosceptics/pragmatists block Europhobic propositions which might damage the satisfactory status quo, even though many votes are initiated by the Europhobes for their partisan interests, and in line with their belief in direct democracy as their secret weapon (Amstutz 2017).

Despite losing two significant votations in late 2018, the SVP continued to push its anti-EU line. Thus, it easily and rapidly won sufficient signatures to ensure that its December 2017 Begrenzung or Limitation initiative went before the people. This had emerged from the party's annoyance at the way the 9 February 2014 initiative had been eviscerated by Parliament and attacked free movement head on, requiring the repeal of the 1999 bilateral agreement on free movement. This would have had drastic implications for all Switzerland's relations with the EU. Originally due to be voted on in May 2020, this was postponed to 27 September due to the pandemic. As polls suggested, it was easily defeated, winning only 38.3% of the votes cast against 61.7% for opponents, on a relatively high turnout of 59%. Only the cantons of Appenzell Inner Rhoden, Glarus, Schwyz and Ticino voted in favour. Opposition campaigning proved much more effective than that of the SVP which hardly won any support outside its core vote. Yet, nothing daunted, the party has decided to focus on opposing the signing of the pending Framework Agreement with the EU, which it sees as a frontal assault on Swiss sovereignty and more important than Covid-19. In this it may have support from some on the left who worry about the Agreement's social implications.

In other words, Swiss policy towards the EU is likely to remain contested and uncertain. The SVP is far from finished and its doubts are shared, albeit more mildly, by many others. So, the Agreement, if it ever comes to a vote, could be defeated. This leaves policy largely stuck in the impasse which began in 2008, something which would hardly lower the political temperature. Nonetheless, Europeanization will continue (Linder 2011), as will concern about the relationship between direct democracy and international law (Masmejan 2017). All this could leave direct democracy somewhat exposed, raising difficult questions about process and policy (Blocher 2016; Steinberg 2015).

BIBLIOGRAPHY

Ammann, O. (2018). The European Court of Human Rights and Swiss Politics: How Does the Swiss Judge Fit In? In M. Wind (Ed.), *International Courts and Domestic Politics* (pp. 262–295). Studies on International Courts and Tribunals. Cambridge: Cambridge University Press.

Amstutz, A. (2017, 14 January). *Le cas particulier suisse: l'importance de la démocratie directe*. Available at https://www.udc.ch/actualites/agenda/.

Année Politique Suisse. (2009). Bern: IPW (pp. 60–63).

Blocher, C. (2016, March 1). Blocher will die SVP bei Initiativen bremsen. *Tages Anzeiger*.

Cheneval, F., El-Wakil, A., et al. (2018, May). Debate on Referendums. *Swiss Political Studies Review, 24*(3), 294–358.

Cheneval, F., & Ferrin, M. (2018). Referendums in the European Union: Defective by Birth? *Journal of Common Market Studies, 56*(5), 1178–1194.

Church, C. H. (2009, March 6). Setting Limits to Europhobia?: Recent Developments in Swiss Euroscepticism. In K. Arato & P. Kaniok (Eds.), *Euroscepticism and European Integration/Euroskepticizam i europske integracije* (pp. 217–242). Zagreb: Political Science Research Centre/Forum CPI Library.

Church, C. H. (2016). *Political Change in Switzerland: From Stability to Uncertainty*. Europa Country Perspectives. London: Routledge.

Church, C. H. (2019a). Switzerland: History and Politics. In *Western Europe Handbook 2018*. London: Europa.

Church, C. H. (2019b). Switzerland and European Integration. In F. Laursen (Ed.), *Oxford Encyclopedia of European Union Politics*. Oxford: Oxford University Press. https://www.oxfordre/politics.

Dupont, C., & Sciarini, P. (2001, May). Switzerland and the European Integration Process: Engagement Without Marriage. *West European Politics, 24*(2), 211–232.

Federal Chancellery. (2009). *Results of Votation on Extension of Free Movement*. Available at https://www.bk.admin.ch/ch/f/pore/va/20090208/index.html.

Federal Chancellery. (2014). *Results of Stop Mass Migration Votation*. Available at https://www.bk.admin.ch/ch/f/pore/va/20140209/can580.html.

Federal Chancellery. (2018). *Results of Self Determination Votation*. Available at https://www.bk.admin.ch/.

Federal Council. (1988, August 24). *Rapport sur la position de la Suisse dans le processus d'intégration Européenne*. Berne: Swiss Government: 88.045.

Fossedal, G. A. (2002). *Direct Democracy in Switzerland* (pp. 99–100). London: Transition Books.

Gabriel, J. M., & Fischer, T. (Eds.). (2003). *Swiss Foreign Policy 1945–2002*. Palgrave: Basingstoke.

Germann, R. (1994). La Diplomatie Reféréndaire de la Suisse. In Y. Papadopoulos (Ed.), *Présent et avenir de la démocratie direct* (pp. 111–119). Geneva: Georg.

Goetschel, L., Bernath, M., & Schwarz, D. (2005). *Swiss Foreign Policy: Foundations and Possibilities*. London: Routledge.

Guillaume, M. (2018, October 22). Christoph Blocher: Les juges étrangers sont les baillis modernes. *Le Temps*. Available at https://www.letemps.ch/suisse/christoph-blocher-juges-etrangers-baillis-modernes.

Haller, W. (2016). *The Swiss Constitution in a Comparative Context* (2nd ed.). Zurich: DIKE/Swiss law in a nutshell.

Hobolt, S. B. (2009). *Europe in Question. Referendums on European Integration*. Oxford: Oxford University Press.

Hug, S., & Sciarini, P. (2000). Referendums on European Integration: Do Institutions Matter in the Voter's Decision? *Comparative Political Studies, 33*(1), 3–36.

Hughes, C. (1954). *The Federal Constitution on Switzerland*. Oxford: Clarendon.

Katzenstein, P. J. (1984). *Corporatism and Change: Austria, Switzerland and the Politics of Industry*. Cornell University Press: Ithica, NY.

Kaufmann, B. (2005). *Guidebook to Direct Democracy in Switzerland and Beyond* (pp. 91–92). Amsterdam: IRI.

Kobach, K. (1993). *The Referendum. Direct Democracy in Switzerland*. Aldershot: Dartmouth Press.

Kreis, G. (2013). *Switzerland and the Second World War*. London: Routledge.

Kresi, H. P., Longchamp, C., Passy, F., & Sciarini, P. (1993, February). *Analyse de la votation fédérale du 6 Décembre 1992*. Bern: GfS and Geneva: Département de science politique, Université de Genève.

Kriesi, H. P., Sciarini, P., & Marquis, L. (2000). *Démocratie directe et politique éxterieure: étude de la formation des attitudes en votation Populaire* (NFP 42 Rapport de Synthese 1999). Bern and Geneva: Nationalfonds.

Kuzelewska, E. (2013, January). Do the Swiss Not Want to Join the EU? Swiss Referenda on European Integration. *Researchgate*. https://doi.org/10.14746/pp.2013.18.3.7.

Linder, W. (2011). Europe and Switzerland: Europeanization Without EU Membership. In C. Trampusch & A. Mach (Eds.), *Switzerland in Europe* (pp. 43–60). London: Routledge.

Linder, W., Bolliger, C., & Rielle, Y. (2010). *Handbuch der Eidgenössischen Volksabstimmungen 1848–2007*. Berne: Haupt.

Masmejan, D. (2017). *Démocratie Directe contre la Droit International*. Lausanne: PPUR, Le Savoir Suisse.

Mendez, F., Mendez, M., & Triga, V. (2014). *Referendums and the European Union*. Cambridge Studies in European Law and Policy. Cambridge: Cambridge University Press.

Mendez, F., & Germann, M. (2018). Contested Sovereignty: Mapping Referendums on Sovereignty over Time and Space. *British Journal of Political Science, 48*(1), 141–165.

Meuwly, O. (2018). *Une histoire politique de la démocratie directe en Suisse*. Neuchâtel: Alphil.

Sally, N. (1993). The Basel Chemical Multinationals—Corporate Action Within Structures. *West European Politics, 16*(4), 561–580.

Schlegel, S. (2018, November 19). Die direkte demokratie ist das erste opfer der elbstbestimmungsinitiative. *Neue Zürcher Zeitung*. Available at https://www.nzz.ch/meinung/die-direkte-demokratie-ist-das-erste-opfer-der-selbstbestimmungsinit iative-ld.1437243.

Sciarini, P., & Tresch, A. (2009). Two-Level Analysis of the Determinants of Direct Democratic Choices in European Immigration and Foreign Policy in Switzerland. *European Union Politics, 10*(4), 456–481.

Serdült, U. (2010). Referendum Campaign Regulations in Switzerland. In K. Lutz & S. Hug (Eds.), *Financing Referendum Campaigns* (pp. 165–179). Basingstoke: Palgrave.

Serdült, U. (2013). Referendums in Switzerland. In M. Qvortrup (Ed.), *Referendums Around the World: The Continued Growth of Direct Democracy* (pp. 65–121). Basingstoke: Palgrave Macmillan.

Skenderovic, D. (2009). *The Radical Right in Switzerland: Continuity and Change, 1945–2000*. New York and Oxford: Berghahn Books.

Steinberg, J. (2015). *Why Switzerland?* (3rd ed.). Cambridge: Cambridge University Press.

Tanquerel, T. (1994). Démocratie directe et intégration supranationale. In Y. Papadopoulos (Ed.), *Présent et avenir de la démocratie directe* (pp. 93–110). Geneva: Georg.

CHAPTER 30

The 2015 Greek Referendum on Bailouts

Lina Papadopoulou

30.1 SETTING THE SCENE

30.1.1 *Constitutional History in a Nutshell*

Greece or, to be more precise, what constitutes Greece today, was for many centuries after the end of the Classical and Hellenistic eras merely part of a series of multi-ethnic empires: namely, the Roman, Byzantine and Ottoman Empires. In the nineteenth century, the period which saw the rise of many modern nation-states, the ethnic groups living in the Ottoman Empire each started to develop a national consciousness and to struggle for their own nation-state. Modern Greece as an independent state was formally constituted in 1830 as a product of a revolution—an almost ten-year-long War of Independence—influenced by the European Enlightenment and assisted by military aid provided by the Great Powers of the day (Hatzis 2019). The Kingdom of Greece was then formally established by the London Protocol in August 1832. Greece became an ally and *protégé* of the British Empire. The first revolutionary Constitutions (1822, 1823 and 1827) were exemplarily liberal by the standards of the time. Ioannis Kapodistrias, the first President of the Greek Republic, governed as an authoritarian moderniser but was assassinated shortly after gaining power. Prince Otto from the House of Wittelsbach, Bavaria, was then selected as Greece's first king. He was forced to grant a constitution (*constitution octroyée)* by an insurgency in September 1843 (Hatzis 2019). The Constitution of 1844 established a constitutional monarchy and introduced

L. Papadopoulou (✉)
Law School, Aristotle University of Thessaloniki, Thessaloniki, Greece

© The Author(s) 2021
J. Smith (ed.), *The Palgrave Handbook of European Referendums*,
https://doi.org/10.1007/978-3-030-55803-1_30

almost universal male-only suffrage. Parliamentary democracy was later consolidated by the 1864 Constitution, adopted after King George I had succeeded King Otto. Since then, excluding short periods of dictatorship, Greece has been a parliamentary democracy, with or without (as has been the case since 1974) a king and with a prime-minister-centred system of mainly bipolar party politics.

30.1.2   A Rare and Undemocratic Use of the Referendum

Historically, the institution of the referendum or popular initiative rarely existed in the earlier Greek constitutions. While the proposal in 1921 to introduce a 'genuine' referendum into the Constitution failed, a stipulation was introduced into the 1927 Constitution concerning the possibility of a constitutional revision being approved by the people, a stipulation which was never actually used. Apart from this stipulation, no other provision had been made for a referendum in any Greek constitution until that of 1975 (which is still in force after three revisions).

Nevertheless, and despite the absence of any relevant constitutional provision, referendums have been used as a means of settling the question of whether the country should have a republican or monarchical regime or other questions concerning the monarchy for a century and a half. There were nine such referendums in 1862, 1920, 1924, 1926, 1935, 1946, 1968, 1973 and 1974. More specifically, the referendum in 1862 concerned the election of a new King of Greece. It is noteworthy that the right to vote was given to every Greek male aged at least 20 (even those living abroad, who were permitted to vote in the Greek Consulates). This universal male suffrage was an institutional innovation at the time, although the ballot was nominal (not secret).

Subsequent referendums also referred to the question of the Head of State: that of 22 February 1920 concerned the question of the return of King Constantine, while that of 13 April 1924 was about whether the royal dynasty of the House of Glücksburg should be expelled in favour of a republic. In 1926 an irregular 'pseudo-referendum' (plebiscite) was held in order to elect a President of the Republic. Equally rigged by the government was the referendum of 3 November 1935 on abolishing the republican character of the regime.

The institution of the referendum was also (ab)used on two occasions by the military dictatorship of 1967–1974: first, in 1968 (to approve a 'pseudo-Constitution' which had been drafted by an appointed 20-member-commission); and second, in 1973, with the aim of changing the regime to a 'presidential parliamentary democracy'. Both pseudo-referendums were held under conditions marked by a total lack of political freedom. The only democratically unadulterated referendum, concerning a choice between a republican or monarchical regime, was held on 8 December 1974. It resulted in the consolidation of the Republic.

Evidently, most of these referendums related to specific persons and did not concern substantive decisions. They were thus more akin to elections than referenda. In addition, all of them were held under conditions of political turmoil and there was no constitutional provision for them. Most of them should rather be characterised as a form of 'plebiscitum' (Pantelis 1979: 118), confirming decisions that had already been made. Consequently, this has been the only 'genuine' referendum in Greek history, despite the fact that there was no constitutional provision for it and it was only consolidated in a Special Constitutional Act. In this respect, it can be characterised as a 'constitutive referendum': it had a constitutive character and as such created a 'constitutional moment'. Nevertheless, this exception only proves the rule that referendums have proved to be a rather *undemocratic* instrument in Greek constitutional history.

30.2 The Legal Architecture of the Referendum

30.2.1 *The Constitutional Enshrinement of Referendums*

Since 1975, when the Constitution currently in force was put into effect, Greece has been a parliamentary democracy in the form of a republic, with a president elected by the Parliament, as stipulated in Article 1 para 1 of the Greek Constitution (Const). The representative character of the regime springs both from its attribute as a 'parliamentary' democracy and from the constitutional provisions pertaining to the function of the Parliament, the members of which 'represent the Nation' (Article 51(2) Const). Real political power, though, is vested in the Prime Minister, who presides over a government supported by the majority of the Members of Parliament.

The representative character of the regime is strong although not absolute: referendums are constitutionally provided for in Article 44(2) Const, albeit in a very limited manner, as it provides only for referendums, not popular initiatives. Consequently, it does not undermine or challenge the representative character of the state. The innovative, compared with the content of previous Greek Constitutions, inclusion of this particular provision proves that the Constitution does not opt for a purely and strictly representational form of government, but rather implicitly, yet clearly, acknowledges the possibility of enriching the representative democracy with elements of participatory democracy. Still, these elements are very limited and are subject to the majoritarian character of the political regime.

In its original wording, Article 44 of the 1975 Constitution provided for the proclamation of a referendum as a presidential prerogative. The 1986 constitutional revision curtailed the competences of the President of the Republic, and thus also transformed the institutional shape of the referendum, turning it into a political instrument of the governmental and/or parliamentary majority. Nowadays, the involvement of the President of the Republic is nominal and consists in a circumscribed power. Article 44 para 2 Const now provides for two types of referendum: first, the so-called 'governmental referendum' on crucial national matters; second, the 'legislative referendum'.

The first type, the '*governmental referendum*', is proposed by the government itself and decided upon by the Parliament with an absolute majority of its members (at least 151 of the 300 MPs). By definition, there is no way such a referendum can be held if the government does not want it to be. There is no constitutional or legislative definition of what constitutes a 'crucial national issue'. According to legal theory, this abstract notion refers predominantly but not exclusively to foreign relations and national defence but it is practically the parliamentarian majority who decides in a sovereign manner on its content. This form of referendum is directly bound up with the government's competence to decide upon such issues, hence the name 'governmental referendum'. It is the government that asks the people to consent to a decision principally taken by itself, after the approval of the referendum by Parliament.

Such referendums are considered to be of a consultative character since they do not bear direct legal consequences and cannot be immediately implemented without any intermediation, although they do oblige the government to follow the direction indicated by the people in the result they produce (Spiliotopoulos 1988: 327). Nevertheless, Article 16(3) of L.4023/2011 provides that 'the result of a referendum on a crucial national issue is binding when at least 40% of those enrolled in the electoral roll take part in the vote'.

The second type, the '*legislative referendum*', applies to a bill which regulates a serious social issue (except those of a fiscal nature). A proposal has to be made by at least two-fifths (120) of the Members of Parliament and has to be approved by a reinforced majority of three-fifths (180) of the Members of Parliament. This majority necessarily—politically speaking—comprises at least a certain proportion of the parties supporting the government. This is a referendum of a decisive abrogative kind, through which a bill may be repealed, after it has been passed by the parliament but before it is promulgated and published by the President of the Republic.

According to Article 16 §4 of L.4023/2011, the result of a referendum on a bill regulating a serious social issue is binding when at least 50% of those enrolled in the electoral roll take part in the vote. In this case, the referendum's result is an unmediated one: should the people vote in favour of the bill, the latter is published in the *Government Gazette* (GG). In the opposite case, the bill is dismissed.

Given their institutional architecture, both types could be characterised as *plebiscites*, if the latter term is used to indicate the dominant role of state or majoritarian organs—not the citizens themselves—in the process of proclaiming a referendum. In this sense, it may be considered rational that neither the government nor the parliament would ever opt in favour of sharing their power with the electorate, unless they were certain that it would lead to a ratification of their own decisions (Papadopoulou 2016).

Review of the validity of referendums and the results of their votes falls under the jurisdiction of the Supreme Special Court, a provision made in

Article 100 Const. Objections to the validity of a referendum and the result of its vote are discussed as a matter of priority and in any case within one month of the vote being held. In the case of a legislative referendum, the decision of the Supreme Special Court must be issued within fifteen days of the date of discussion (Article 20(2) of L.4023/2011).

There is no provision for constitutional referendums in the Greek Constitution. The participation of the people in the revision process is only stipulated in an indirect manner, as a second stage of the three-step procedure (first step: three-fifths parliamentary majority, second step: elections, third step: absolute parliamentary majority by the following Parliament—parliamentary majorities are interchangeable).[1]

Nevertheless, this kind of public participation, although considered to be an element of direct participation in constitution-making has no obvious practical significance. Amendment proposals which have already been voted for by one Parliament—and are awaiting approval by the next, newly elected Parliament—only marginally affect the citizens' vote. This is even truer if one considers the fact that a large number of amendments are usually proposed each time, due to the fact that the revision process is very lengthy and difficult to complete.

In 2016 the then Prime Minister Alexis Tsipras, in a speech on the proposed revision of the Constitution, declared the political will to hold a consultative referendum (formally conceived as a governmental one) in order to allow the people to approve the revision which his party, SYRIZA, would soon be proposing in Parliament following the procedure described above. According to prevailing opinion, however, such a referendum is not provided for by the Constitution: the 'national matters' under Article 44 para 1 Const may not be interpreted as including the approval of a revision proposal voted upon by the preceding, proposing Parliament. In the case of the proposed revision just mentioned, the official revisionary process only started over two years later but since then the proposal for a 'constitutional referendum' seems to have been dropped by the governing party (SYRIZA) and its leader.

30.2.2 General Provisions for Holding a Referendum; Law 4023/2011

According to the provisions of the relevant Law (L.) 4023/2011 (it replaced L.350/1976), after it has been decided upon by Parliament, a referendum is proclaimed through a presidential decree, which also needs to be signed by the Cabinet in the case of a 'governmental referendum' or the President of the Parliament in the case of a 'legislative referendum'. Article 3(2) stipulates that '[t]he question or questions and their answers are expressed in a clear and concise manner' and they must be specifically mentioned in the presidential decree. The exact wording of the referendum is approved by Parliament, as stipulated by Article 115 of the Parliament's Standing Orders (PSO), which

---

[1] This procedure took place three times—in 1986, 2011 and 2008—and started again in 2018, with the 2019 Parliament expected to be a revisionary one.

also provides that the question(s) should be clearly expressed and is published in the *Government Gazette*.

In the case of a 'governmental referendum', a parliamentary majority of at least 151 MPs means in a parliamentary system—politically speaking—a governmental majority. Moreover, according to the prevailing view, the President of the Republic does not have any room for manoeuvre either on the matter or on the wording.

Not only political parties (regardless of whether they have seats in the Greek or European Parliament or not) but also scientific or professional NGOs and trade unions are welcome to participate in the dialogue on the question(s) posed in the referendum. Any costs incurred during the pre-referendum period are considered to be related to elections, although no additional state funding is provided to the political parties, while private funding is allowed only by a natural person of Greek nationality up to a total of €5000. Sanctions for breaching these stipulations are provided for (Article 6) as well as in cases where the upper limits on spending are exceeded.

During the period between the presidential decree proclaiming the referendum and the Friday before its execution, public and private radio and TV stations, together with any kind of television service provider, are required to broadcast messages from those participating in the referendum free of charge. The airtime available is allocated equally among those who favour each of the answers to the question or queries posed in the referendum. Political parties, associations of individuals, scientific, professional or trade union organisations and any other civil society organisation may participate in the 'Support Committee' reflecting their views on the issue at stake.

As in the case of parliamentary elections, the vote must be held on a Sunday within thirty days of the publication of the presidential decree announcing the referendum (Article 12). All Greeks above the age of 17 have voting rights, but the voting procedure may only take place within Greek territory.

30.3   THE 2015 REFERENDUM ON THE BAILOUT AGREEMENT

30.3.1   *Contextualisation of the 2015 Referendum*

The revitalisation of referendums, which had not been used since 1974, came about as a result of the notorious and spiralling Greek sovereign debt crisis. Already in 2011, the then Prime Minister George Papandreou had announced his intention to ask the government and Parliament, as authorised by the Constitution, to consent to the holding of a referendum. The question back then would have been connected with the Private Sector Involvement (PSI) scheme, which was agreed upon between Greece and its creditors in 2011. PSI was part of a debt restructuring programme to ensure the recapitalisation of Greek banks and involved a debt exchange with the remaining private creditors of the country in order to reduce its debt burden. This debt restructuring was the largest operation in the history of sovereign defaults, involving securities with a face value of €205 billion (Xafa 2014). Although the planned referendum question was never actually formulated, Papandreou's intention was to ask the Greek people whether they wanted to consent to PSI and also a new bailout programme designed by the European Commission, the European Central Bank and the IMF (the so-called 'troika', which were later renamed 'the institutions' by the SYRIZA-ANEL government).

However, after both external pressure (mainly from French President Nicolas Sarkozy and in a milder way by German Chancellor Angela Merkel) and internal pressure (from members of his own Cabinet and the parliamentary group of the governing PASOK party, which rejected the idea), Papandreou abandoned the idea of a referendum, shelved the plan and, under intense pressure to end the political uncertainty engulfing Greece, formally resigned. He did so under the realisation that not only was Greece's economy at stake, but also the country's EU membership itself. In this way, he paved the way for a tripartite, national unity government, headed by the non-parliamentarian and erstwhile Vice-President of the European Central Bank, Loukas Papadimos (see Venizélos 2017: 558), and the second bailout programme by the EU and International Monetary Fund that included painful new austerity measures. This time, however, the new bailout scheme was also supported by the Conservative party, New Democracy, led by the right-wing Antonis Samaras, which had fiercely opposed the first one. This widened the divisions between the pro- and anti-memorandum political forces. To the former group now belonged the centre-left Socialist Party (PASOK), the right-wing New Democracy (ND) and the far-right Popular Orthodox Rally (LAOS). In the anti-memorandum camp remained mainly the Coalition of the Radical Left (SYRIZA), the Independent Greeks (ANEL, consisting mainly of anti-Memorandum ex-ND members), the Greek Communist Party (KKE) and the neo-Nazi Golden Dawn (Chrysi Avgi).

In this debt-stricken Greece, SYRIZA's electoral victory in January 2015 was almost inevitable. SYRIZA, a party of leftist populists led by the young and charismatic politician Alexis Tsipras, formed a coalition government with the Independent Greeks, a far-right-wing nationalist populist party. What united the two parties was their vehement opposition to the two first bailout programmes (Memoranda of Understanding) between Greece and its creditors, and their populist political ethos combined with a nationalist political rhetoric against the creditors and the EU. This rhetoric intensified the Greeks' anti-EU sentiments and politically legitimised the similar, but bolder rhetoric of Golden Dawn.

The Finance Minister of this government, Yanis Varoufakis, had been criticising the bailout programmes since as early as 2010, and pledged national democracy, meaning that the Greeks should be helped without the imposition of further austerity measures. During the first six months of 2015, Prime Minister Tsipras and Minister of Finance Varoufakis, empowered by their fresh mandate, toured a string of European capitals evasively negotiating (or pretending to negotiate, in a game of brinkmanship) better terms for a new loan for Greece and demanding debt relief in the form of a deep 'haircut' of the Greek sovereign debt. This delay in reaching a new agreement with the 'institutions' caused a deterioration in the country's economic situation (Venizélos 2016: 28). On 30 June 2015 the Master Financial Assistance Facility Agreement (MFFA, as amended by the Amendment Agreement dated 12 December 2012 and the third amendment agreement of 27 February 2015) was due to expire and Greece was obliged to make a €1.6 billion payment to the IMF on that same day.

30.3.2   A Chronicle of the Referendum

As Greece was running out of time, with the deadline of 30 June fast approaching, the government proposed a list of reforms, which included austerity measures amounting to a total of €8 billion, based mainly on higher and wider taxation. Despite Tsipras's retreat, Greece's interlocutors did not accept his proposals and demanded immediate measures, such as VAT rises and pension cuts. On Thursday 25 June an offer by the creditors was available on the negotiating table consisting of two texts, one on 'Reforms for the completion of the Current Program and Beyond', the other named 'Preliminary Debt Sustainability Analysis'. At this standoff in the negotiations, on Friday 26 June the Greek PM left the negotiating table unexpectedly and returned to Greece, backing down from his responsibility to conclude the negotiations (Sotiropoulos 2015). He then (on the evening of 26 June) proposed to his cabinet that a referendum on the bailout conditions offered by Greece's creditors should be held already on Sunday 5 July 2015 and, at midnight, he announced this decision (Shin 2015; Morris 2015). In his emotionally charged message he invoked national sovereignty, unity, history and the dignity of the Greek people (Sygkelos 2015: 2), while at the same time he suggested that the citizens should reject the draft agreement offered by the 'institutions', although it was the product of a six-month negotiation he himself had achieved. The referendum appeared at that point to be the only means the government had at its disposal to avoid the risk of having 'five months of negotiations transformed into a negative-sum game' (Chatzistavrou 2015). In a similar vein, Tsebelis (2016: 31) has suggested that 'the referendum was the excuse to close the banks and introduce the painful deal as the alternative to chaos, in order to achieve the agreement of the party'.

This move led the President of the European Commission, Jean-Claude Juncker, to accuse the Greek government of being guilty of 'egotism, tactical games, populist games' by walking out of the talks and declaring a referendum (Evans-Pritchard 2015). Varoufakis's belief seemed to be that if Greece remained outside a rescue programme, it would create a danger of contagion to other Eurozone member states. This would then persuade Greece's creditors to offer a much improved rescue scheme than the one he and Tsipras had succeeded in obtaining during their five-month-long round of negotiations. Within this context, the referendum was seen either as a tool for

The ballot paper

REFERENDUM of 5th July 2015		ΔΗΜΟΨΗΦΙΣΜΑ της 5ης Ιουλίου 2015	
Should the draft agreement which was submitted by the European Commission, the European Central Bank and the International Monetary Fund to the Eurogroup on 25.06.2015, and which consists of two parts that form their unified proposal, be accepted? The first document is entitled 'Reforms for the Completion of the Current Program and Beyond' (*this is followed by a Greek translation of this title*) and the second 'Preliminary Debt Sustainability Analysis' (*this is followed by a Greek translation of this title*).	NOT APPROVED NO ☐ APPROVED YES ☐	ΠΡΕΠΕΙ ΝΑ ΓΙΝΕΙ ΑΠΟΔΕΚΤΟ ΤΟ ΣΧΕΔΙΟ ΣΥΜΦΩΝΙΑΣ, ΤΟ ΟΠΟΙΟ ΚΑΤΕΘΕΣΑΝ Η ΕΥΡΩΠΑΪΚΗ ΕΠΙΤΡΟΠΗ, Η ΕΥΡΩΠΑΪΚΗ ΚΕΝΤΡΙΚΗ ΤΡΑΠΕΖΑ ΚΑΙ ΤΟ ΔΙΕΘΝΕΣ ΝΟΜΙΣΜΑΤΙΚΟ ΤΑΜΕΙΟ ΣΤΟ EUROGROUP ΤΗΣ 25.06.2015 ΚΑΙ ΑΠΟΤΕΛΕΙΤΑΙ ΑΠΟ ΔΥΟ ΜΕΡΗ, ΤΑ ΟΠΟΙΑ ΣΥΓΚΡΟΤΟΥΝ ΤΗΝ ΕΝΙΑΙΑ ΠΡΟΤΑΣΗ ΤΟΥΣ; ΤΟ ΠΡΩΤΟ ΕΓΓΡΑΦΟ ΤΙΤΛΟΦΟΡΕΙΤΑΙ «REFORMS FOR THE COMPLETION OF THE CURRENT PROGRAM AND BEYOND» («ΜΕΤΑΡΡΥΘΜΙΣΕΙΣ ΓΙΑ ΤΗΝ ΟΛΟΚΛΗΡΩΣΗ ΤΟΥ ΤΡΕΧΟΝΤΟΣ ΠΡΟΓΡΑΜΜΑΤΟΣ ΚΑΙ ΠΕΡΑΝ ΑΥΤΟΥ») ΚΑΙ ΤΟ ΔΕΥΤΕΡΟ «PRELIMINARY DEBT SUSTAINABILITY ANALYSIS» («ΠΡΟΚΑΤΑΡΚΤΙΚΗ ΑΝΑΛΥΣΗ ΒΙΩΣΙΜΟΤΗΤΑΣ ΧΡΕΟΥΣ»).	ΔΕΝ ΕΓΚΡΙΝΕΤΑΙ/ ΟΧΙ ☐ ΕΓΚΡΙΝΕΤΑΙ/ ΝΑΙ ☐

Fig. 30.1   The ballot paper for the 2015 referendum

gaining enhanced leverage in the negotiations (Lakhani 2015: 109) or as a step towards a rupture with the Eurozone, facilitating the transition to a national currency (Hope and Barber 2015).

The referendum was voted upon the following day, Saturday 27 June, by the Parliament in plenary session (176 votes in favour, from SYRIZA, ANEL, and Golden Dawn MPs, and 120 votes against by New Democracy, PASOK, the Communist Party and 'The River', while two MPs were absent).[2] An objection on the grounds of unconstitutionality (Article 100 of the Standing Orders) raised by the MP Evangelos Venizélos, ex-Deputy President of the Papandreou and Samaras governments and a Professor of Constitutional Law, was rejected by the majority. In the meantime, the Ecofin Council had decided—with Varoufakis the only minority voice—not to extend the MFFA, which was due to end on 30 June.

The Parliament's decision and Presidential Decree 38/2015 declaring the referendum were then published in the *Governmental Gazette* (GG A' 62 and 63, respectively) on Sunday 28 June, as stipulated by the Constitution and Article 115 §6 of the Parliament's Standing Orders. The question on the ballot paper concerned the approval or not of the draft agreement offered by the creditors, which was at the time available only in English (Fig. 30.1).

On the same day, Sunday 28 June 2015, an 'Act of Legislative Content' on an 'Emergency Regulation for organising the referendum process' was

---

[2]The Communist Party proposed that Parliament should also vote on two more questions to be added to the referendum ballot paper. These were as follows: '*1. No to the proposals for an agreement made by the EU-IMF-ECB or the Greek Government. 2. Disengagement from the EU – Repeal of the Memoranda and of all anti-grassroots executive legislation*'.

issued (GG 64 A′), which regulated some organisational issues and short-ened the deadlines provided for by L.4023/2011 and Presidential Decree 26/2012 (GG A′ 57, 15.03.2012). More specifically, the deadline for the political parties, NGOs, etc., to form 'Support Committees' was only one day, instead of three days. It thus changed the legal terms of this particular referendum after its proclamation.

The Act also stipulated that, specifically for this referendum, in the event that the formation of a 'Support Committee' was not possible, due to ideolog-ical, political or other disagreements between the parties, the party with most members in Parliament should announce this to the Minister of the Interior and Administrative Reconstruction within one day after the proclamation of the referendum. In this case the Act modified the way in which airtime in the media and places for political advertisements was distributed, so that two-thirds of them were distributed to political parties according to their strength in the Parliament and one third to NGOs, in equal proportion to the 'Yes' and 'No' camps. The Act also specifically provided that the non-formation of Support Committees would not impair the validity of the referendum and that political parties would also have the right to appoint a representative in each electoral centre (not only 'Support Committees').

A 'Yes' Support Committee was formed on Wednesday 1 July, backed by New Democracy, PASOK, 'The River', the 'Movement of Democrats and Socialists', the 'Democratic Left', 'Creation Again' and many other NGOs and professional organisations, while the parties supporting 'No' (SYRIZA, ANEL, Golden Dawn and other minor parties) did not form such a Committee. These last-minute modifications allowed SYRIZA to actively participate in the campaign without the need to sit together with Golden Dawn in the same Support Committee. Notably, the (orthodox) Communist Party urged the Greeks to cast an invalid vote, not wishing to identify itself with either of the two camps.

Due to concerns over a run on the banks provoked by the insecurity caused by the announcement of the referendum, the government, upon a proposal of the Governor of the Bank of Greece, Yannis Stournaras, decided that the Greek banks should be closed and capital controls imposed until the Tuesday after the referendum. The 'Act of Legislative Content' (GG A′ 65 of 28.06.2015 and A′ 66 of 30.06.2015) confirmed the closure of the banks from 28 June until 6 July and a limit for cash withdrawals of €60 per card. This, in turn, forced Greeks to queue up to withdraw money from cash machines. The Prime Minister, Tsipras, in a (quite successful) attempt to demonise Greece's lenders and urge people to vote No,[3] asked the European Council to overturn the Eurogroup's decision and extend the programme that was still running for a few more days. Furthermore, in a public address he asked the Greek people to remain calm and not be cowed by their blackmailing and unjust treatment

---

[3]Prime Minister Tsipras, still very popular at the time, had even implied that he would resign if the 'Yes' vote prevailed.

at the hands of the 'institutions'. In a populist anti-elite crescendo, he tweeted: 'The recent decisions of the Eurogroup & ECB have only one objective: to attempt to stifle the will of the Greek people' (Udland 2015). On the contrary, Antonis Samaras, the leader of the main opposition party, New Democracy, who formally decided to vote Yes, declared that the real question was 'yes or no to Europe, yes or no to the euro' (Makris 2015). The 'Yes' camp employed the declaration 'We remain in Europe' as their main slogan. On the other side, Tsipras insisted, in an address to the Greek people on Wednesday 1 July, that 'No' did not mean a 'GREXIT' from the Eurozone or much less from the EU, but the enhancement of Greece's negotiating power.

On 2 July, the Prime Minister visited the Ministry of National Defence and heard, without any reaction, the Minister of Defence (and head of the junior coalition party, ANEL), Panos Kammenos, say, among other things, that 'the armed forces ensure stability within the country', a statement that sparked strong reactions from the opposition, since the armed forces' goal is to ensure Greece's stability from external threats, not internal ones.

During the one single pre-referendum week, many newspapers, politicians, political parties and organisations in Greece, Europe and elsewhere issued endorsements, either of the 'No' or the 'Yes' vote. In favour of 'No' were Jeremy Corbyn (2015), the UK Labour Party leader, and Bernie Sanders, a US senator and presidential candidate (Marans 2015), as well as populists of all colours, such as the French National Front, the UK Independence Party, the Italian Five Star Movement and Venezuelan President Nicolas Maduro but also Stiglitz (2015) and other economists, such as Sinn, Krugman and Sacks. On the contrary, Jean-Claude Juncker (Holehouse 2015), President of the European Commission, and Martin Schulz, German MEP and President of the European Parliament expressed their preference for the 'Yes' vote (Elliott et al. 2015). While Juncker declared that a 'No' vote would be 'an act of suicide' that would eject Greece from Europe, Angela Merkel, the German Chancellor (Elliott et al. 2015), the French President, François Hollande, and Sigmar Gabriel, Germany's Vice-Chancellor and Social Democrat leader, warned that what was at stake was Greece's exit from the Eurozone (known as 'Grexit') (Evans-Pritchard 2015).

In a context of unprecedented polarisation (Rori 2016: 1333), big rallies were organised by both camps and people participated vociferously in the campaigns, including in the social media, in a way that was more emotional than rational, and with little reference to the content of the agreements in question. Rather, the campaigns were either on the vital question of the Euro (for those in favour of Yes) or against austerity (for those in favour of No, see Mavrozacharakis and Tzagarakis 2015). The Yes camp, however, lacked established organisational structures and expertise in grassroots politics, compared to the No side, with its huge number of supporters from left-wing groups active in universities, labour unions and the civil society and social movement sphere (Aslanidis and Kaltwasser 2016: 1083). Many TV stations, newspapers and new electronic media had backed the anti-memorandum camp and had offered hidden leverage or open support to the SYRIZA-ANEL government during the first few months of its tenure. Now, however, the danger of 'Grexit' made them rally around the 'Yes' camp and they accused SYRIZA of 'blatantly violating the principle of journalistic impartiality' (Tsatsanis and Teperoglou 2016: 436). This stance, however, confirmed, in the eyes of many, the anti-establishment credentials of the populist government (Aslanidis and Kaltwasser 2016: 1084). Although to a large extent the dividing line followed party political divisions, the polarisation also revealed a more fundamental divide in Greek politics between hardline Eurosceptic and leftist anti-austerity Euro-critical groups on the one hand, and pro-European political forces on the other (Tsatsanis and Teperoglou 2016: 436).

Despite the hope fostered by Tsipras and Varoufakis that the mere announcement of the Greek referendum, combined with the expiration of the programme, would cause a mess in global financial markets, the latter remained quite calm and were only slightly and briefly affected before returning to normality. On Tuesday 30 June the second bailout programme expired and Greece failed to pay the €1.5 billion instalment due to the IMF, thus becoming the first developed country to default on its obligations to the IMF. The Greek government asked the ESM to take over Greece's liabilities for a period of two years, combined with a debt restructuring scheme, and a short-term extension of the previous programme, while it would then accept the offer of 25 June and implied that in this case the referendum would be revoked. If this proposal were accepted, Tsipras could present it as a great success story; if it were not, he could still manage to put the blame once more on the creditors, presenting them as unwilling to help Greece and lending weight to the No camp. In the event, the latter happened.

In his last pre-election TV appearance on Friday 3 July, Tsipras called for 'silencing the sirens of scaremongering and disaster' and rephrased the referendum dilemma as 'a move towards the slow death of the economy and impoverishment if we impose more cuts on pensions in order to repay an unsustainable debt unless we strengthen our resolve to put a final end to the five years of disaster' (Antonopoulos 2015). The left- and right-wing populist narrative of the time was that the 'foreigners' wanted to overturn democracy. The people or the multitude could prevent this *coup d'état*, since a patriotic, anti-memorandum government was giving them the opportunity to do so and resist the capitalist neoliberal world order. In this context, it has been claimed that the people took the affair into their own hands and voted 'no' out of indignation, and as a reaction to 'the blatant attempts to blackmail them and manipulate their freedom of expression' (Bartsidis et al. 2015). 'No' in the referendum was compared with, and was reminiscent of, the firm No answer that Greece had given to the Axis forces during the Second World War (Vouloumanos 2015), so it acquired heroic overtones and attracted solidarity and sympathy from all over Europe, if not further afield. On the other hand, the Yes narrative was that a No might bring about a 'Grexit' not only from the Eurozone, but also—as this in itself was not legally possible—from the EU (Jurado et al. 2015; Walter 2015).

30.3.3 The Result and the Outcome

The referendum turnout was 62.52%. A majority of 61.31% rejected the bailout conditions; a majority in all regions was against the bailout. This resounding victory for Prime Minister Tsipras made the referendum look like 'a proxy-election aiming to determine the popularity of the incumbent government' (Sygkelos 2015: 3). The percentage of those voting for Yes was 38.69%, while 5.04% of the votes were invalid and 0.75% of them blank. The pollsters had failed to identify this significant difference and had talked about a marginal win for either side, as people were jumping party lines and were unwilling to reveal their preferences, although they could have been inferred from Google trends (Askitas 2015). Arguably, the great majority of voters in the lower economic and social strata voted No, while the upper-middle class was more in favour of Yes (Andronides 2015; for a detailed analysis see Rontos et al. 2016). In the central squares of many cities, including Athens, there were people celebrating the prevalence of the No vote. However, Tsipras interpreted the vote as a plebiscite empowering him to do what he wanted (Rori 2016: 1335) and declared that the 'No' vote did not mean a rupture with the EU and called all political leaders to meet in Council. Samaras resigned as President of New Democracy, since the party had campaigned in favour of Yes (Kathimerini 2015b).

According to popular understanding, the No vote meant rather a rejection of the Memoranda and the austerity imposed by the creditors in general, rather than simply a rejection of the latest two-document proposal, which very few Greeks, whether in favour or against, had really read, given the circumstances of the referendum. Despite the Greek people's negative answer, the Prime Minister was soon offered and accepted a new deal, not necessarily more advantageous for Greece than the one just rejected. Tsipras secured his political survival by replacing, in a conciliatory move on 6 July, his Finance Minister Varoufakis, who was an opponent of any new deal, with the more emollient Euclid Tsakalotos (Deane 2015; Hodson 2016: 153), although the closure of the banks and capital controls continued. Secret plans designed by Varoufakis—with the PM's consent—for a system of parallel currency in the case of 'Grexit' remained on paper.

The week after the referendum, Tsipras and his government had to choose between a Grexit with unknown consequences and a new austerity-conditioned bailout programme worth approximately €86 billion. Greece's PM appeared before the European Parliament—where he was given a mixed reception—and asked the EU to pay heed to the message that had been delivered by the Greek people, while also reiterating his intention to keep Greece in the Eurozone. The European Council and Eurogroup met again and agreed on a new stability support programme for Greece, comprising a new Memorandum and loan under strict conditionality, on 12 July 2015. The result of the referendum did not seem to play a role in the reaching of this agreement, except for the fact that the whole endeavour had 'undermined the relationship of trust between Greece and the other member states' (Venizélos 2016: 13), which, as Merkel stated, was 'the most important currency' (Erlanger 2015). Merkel, for her part, demonstrated great personal fortitude in the face of numerous attacks by Greek government officials. On the other hand, she maintained a hard line against debt relief, which caused a rift between her and Hollande, the IMF, the US and the Greek people (Lakhani 2015: 131). The euro summit ignored the Greek people's opposition to austerity, as expressed in its referendum, and lost, at least in Greece, more of its legitimacy (Hodson 2016: 164).

What might be viewed as surprising, however, is SYRIZA's victory in the general election of September 2015, after having lost the parliamentary majority and resigning in favour of an official government led by the President of the *Areios Pagos* (the supreme civil and penal court) as acting Prime Minister. A large number of SYRIZA party officials remained faithful to the pre-2015 anti-memoranda line and formed another party, 'Popular Unity', which failed to enter Parliament, as it did not exceed the 3% electoral hurdle. One would have thought that since the people had been asked to participate directly in politics and had celebrated the 'No' outcome, they would have punished SYRIZA for its notorious volte-face: instead, they gave it the greatest share of the vote (35.5%). Once again SYRIZA formed a government with ANEL and managed to remain in power longer than all previous governments had been able to since the crisis originally broke out in 2009. Both coalition partners represented a solid populist base, which had been formed in previous decades, with voters coming from both the left and right of the political spectrum (Pappas 2015).

30.4   The Constitutional and Democratic Deficiencies of the Referendum

30.4.1   An Inappropriate Question

According to Article 3 §2 of L.4023/2011, the question posed in a referendum should be **straightforward,** clear and concise, a requirement that was not met in this case. The question was inappropriate and unreasonable for a number of different reasons. First, the proposal encapsulated in the question to be approved or rejected by the people was not a final one in the form of a demand by the creditors to 'take it or leave it' (Sotirelis 2015). The negotiations were still open and the deal offered on 25 June was still open to amendment when the Prime Minister left Brussels, although by the day the referendum was held (Sunday 5 July) it had become irrelevant, having already expired (Steinhauser et al. 2015). So, in effect, the Greeks were invited to vote on a non-existent agreement. Besides, the content of the agreement was not solely in the hands of the Greek institutions, either in the form of the government, the parliament or the people: it was a matter to be jointly and equally decided by the same institutions of all the Eurozone states (Gerapetritis 2015). The idea that the referendum was to do with the sovereign democratic right of a single people to be independently self-governed, as the Prime Minister sought to present the whole issue, ignored the externalities that such a question involved for other Eurozone member states and their peoples.

Secondly, the question was also illogical. It makes sense if a government wants to sign an agreement and wishes to enhance the legitimacy of its decision: in such a case, it presents its decision to the people and asks them to validate it. It is irrational, however, for a government to present to the people an agreement which it itself disagrees with and which is not an ultimatum. It is enough that the government itself does not sign and carries on negotiating. The devil hidden in this 'detail' is the abuse of the institution of the referendum, an abuse which is often perpetrated by populist political forces.

Thirdly, the question itself was not clear, short and explicit, as stipulated by Article 3 §2 of L.4023/2011. It was lengthy and convoluted, referring as it did to two lengthy texts (running to 26 pages) which were written in difficult economic language, and which voters had to search for elsewhere in order to read. The contents of these texts were not summarised on the ballot paper—although it was unlikely that they could have been summarised at all. They were initially available only in English and were only translated into Greek some days later and uploaded onto the website of the Ministry of the Interior. But even if one had wanted to read them, these texts were very difficult to comprehend, even for MPs and economists, let alone the ordinary citizens who were called upon to vote on them. Thus, the referendum was characterised by 'oracular ambiguity' and 'its answer was incapable of leading to a foreseeable closure' (Contiades and Fotiadou 2015).

Consequently, each citizen interpreted the question in his or her own way. There is a risk in every referendum that the citizens respond to a different question from that actually on the ballot paper, but in this particular case people interpreted the referendum question in different ways because from the outset the drafters of the ballot paper deliberately designed that question to be nonsensical. As if this nonsensical question were not enough, the answer No was placed above the Yes option on the ballot paper—contrary to the logic of the Greek (or any other) language. This can easily be criticised as a bias in favour of the government's choice (Gunter 2015).

30.4.2   Can Fiscal Matters Be Put to the Popular Vote?

Constitutional lawyers, such as Contiades and Fotiadou (2015), and political scientists, such as Dimitris Sotiropoulos (as reported by Euronews 2015), have raised the question of whether a national issue framed in a referendum can concern fiscal matters, given the fact that bills passed by Parliament regulating fiscal matters are excluded from Article 44 §2 Const. Stathopoulos expressed the opinion that putting a fiscal matter in the form of a national issue violates or at least circumvents Article 44 §2 GrConst, since it is irrational to ask the citizens if they like austerity or not, while Contiades also challenged the same issue (quoted by Tsiboukis 2015). It could be argued that by defining as a national issue a question that was predominantly fiscal, the government circumvented the constitutional prohibition on bills on fiscal matters being put to a referendum (Alivizatos 2015).

However, the limitation on fiscal matters concerns only bills which have already been voted on, not the first type of referendum on national matters, which can be social, economic and fiscal at the same time (Gerapetritis 2015). This is due to the different nature of the questions set under the first and second types of referendum in the Greek Constitution. The problem lies in the way in which crucial national matters may be expressed and in the fact they may not involve lengthy texts like bills. Asking the people, for example, to decide between the euro or the drachma (the Greek national currency) does involve a fiscal dimension but is a straightforward question. In the case of the 2015 referendum, however, the people were asked to choose one of two ways forward for the government, which would then have to act on and work out the technical details of implementing that choice. A lengthy bill on fiscal matters is not only likely to be incomprehensible to the majority, it also increases the possibility of being abused as referendum material, since the people cannot be expected to choose austerity or financial burdens.

30.4.3   Too Short a Time Interval

L.4023/2011, by stipulating that a referendum should be held within thirty days of the publication of the presidential decree announcing it, does not actually specify a minimum period; a similar provision, however, for national elections has always been interpreted as meaning an interval close to 30 days. In the case of the 2015 referendum, however, the time interval given to the Greek people to allow them to study the two lengthy texts and discuss the binary answers was too short. On the grounds of reasonableness, allowing only a week for deliberation was clearly against the law and arguably also against the Constitution. Given that campaigns play a vital role in referendum outcomes (Hobolt 2006), this lack of time had a significant effect on the result.

Not surprisingly, the Secretary General of the Council of Europe, Thorbjørn Jagland, told the Associated Press, on the Wednesday before the referendum, that voters needed at least two weeks, and perhaps even more in the case of such a complex issue with potentially far-reaching consequences (Kathimerini 2015a; Parashu 2015: 811). As Sygkelos (2015: 3) notes, such a brief period is unprecedented and calls to mind the referendums held by authoritarian or illegitimate regimes, such as that held on the status of the Crimea (2014), which was held within ten days of being proclaimed by pro-Russian secessionists.

The totally incomprehensible question on the ballot paper and the very limited amount of time in which to research and discuss it reveals that the parliamentary majority itself wanted the people to respond to anything but the real question, thus recognising how nonsensical the latter was. It was a referendum designed to allow for only subjective responses based on individual voters' sentiments, predetermined wishes, fears and expectations formed during the years of the crisis. The divide between the proponents and opponents of the Memoranda, in the form it had already assumed, could now be formally expressed.

30.4.4 Change in the Terms of the Game

The procedures provided for by L.4023/2011, such as the formation of the two opposing Support Committees and the organisation of discussion tables in the media and elsewhere, were impossible to implement within the strict timetable allowed. This was not just a coincidence or a side-effect: the government desperately wanted to avoid being identified with the neo-Nazi Golden Dawn party, with which it would be lumped together in the 'No' camp. The change in the terms of the game after it had already begun has rightly been characterised as an 'institutional aberration' since the government 'has, in fact, placed it in the bloody bed of its small party choices, both by arbitrarily shortening the deadlines and by substituting Committees with parties' (Sotirelis 2015; see also Gerapetritis 2015).

30.4.5 Indefinite Outcome of the Result

The government had not made it clear what would follow a No vote. Although he had declared that a No vote did not mean a Grexit, the PM did not outline a clear plan as to how to proceed. But even the outcome of a Yes vote was not clear, since, as has already been stressed, the draft agreement was not a final text but merely a working document that was in fact no longer under consideration on the day of the referendum. Nevertheless, while the draft agreement reflected the continuation of austerity in the form the Greeks had already experienced, the 'No' vote did not correspond to anything tangible, allowing everybody to attach to it his or her own fears or hopes, ranging from trivial loan cuts to romantic dreams of regaining national sovereignty (see Boukala and Dimitrakopoulou 2017). This lack of equilibrium prevented a levelling of the playing field for the two options.

Arguably, the signing of a third Memorandum and the agreement on a new Support Programme was against the people's will, as expressed in the referendum, and thus the government's and Parliament's actions were ostensibly unconstitutional and contrary to the guidelines of the Venice Commission.[4] Technically speaking, this was not the case, as the new Programme was in its details different from the one rejected by the people. But this 'technical' detail also shows how vacuous the referendum itself was. It would perhaps have made sense to ask the Greek people if they were in favour of a new Programme or against it, which would have meant a bankruptcy with unknown consequences, including exiting the Eurozone, as a bold decision independent of incomprehensible details, which would then have been decided upon by the government in power.

30.5   Concluding Remarks

30.5.1   The Caricatural Nature of the 2015 Referendum

Based on all the above, the referendum was rightly characterised as being unconstitutional, undemocratic and farcical, as it fell short of all democratic and international standards for the conduct of referendums (Contiades and Fotiadou 2015). Both its deficient constitutional design and the governmental choices prevented proper public deliberations of the subject of the referendum and a flawless outcome.

This unique application of Article 44 §2 Const revealed its inadequacies and deficiencies—despite its thorough regulation by L.4023/2011, which nevertheless left the time interval between the proclamation and realisation of a referendum open to manipulation—especially in respect of judicial review ex-ante and the lack of an independent Committee to regulate the process. Having the Supreme Court only review the referendum ex-post is not appropriate, since after the will of the people has been expressed it is hard to suppress it through legal means. Apart from this, such ex-post control is incapable of preventing the institution of the referendum from being abused and usurped, as happened in 2015, when the referendum was only used to empower the government and offer an allure of resistance rather than really allowing people to decide rationally on a crucial issue. For those believing in the usefulness of referendums, a constitutional amendment is necessary that will institutionalise the effective judicial review of referendums. The executive law should also be amended to provide for a minimum time interval of at least four weeks in accordance with the Guidelines of the Parliamentary Committee of the Council of Europe (2018).

The government, for its part, designed the referendum deliberately as a snap poll, held at its own behest, as a political gamble rather than as a democratic device, one that could be easily manipulated by the elites. Initially, the proclamation of the referendum seemed to respond to trends favouring the grassroots political engagement of citizens by unconventional means—trends

[4]See section III.5 of the Venice Commission's guidelines, according to which when the referendum is legally binding, for a certain period of time, a text that has been rejected in a referendum should not be adopted by a procedure that does not include a referendum.

that were, during the crisis, also supported by SYRIZA. The referendum was not meant to function as a meaningful expression of the popular will. The government rather opted to exploit 'a populist and irredentist "no"' (Mavrozacharakis and Tzagarakis 2015) and abused the referendum as a weapon for blackmailing Greece's international creditors and convincing the voters that the government was really struggling for a better outcome in the negotiations.

The Greek bailout referendum of 2015 is a par excellence example of an elite-manipulated referendum (Fotiadou 2015). Although it was presented as being an enhancement of democracy, it was merely a **sham leading to manipulation of the masses and was only a manifestation of constitutional populism in action.** Sotirelis (2015) concluded that the whole endeavour was only a demagogic act of 'democratisation' that was contrary to the spirit of real democracy, and that it was the most extreme and dangerous manifestation of institutional populism. It is thus no exaggeration to characterise it as a 'sham referendum' (Fotiadou 2015), or a constitutional mockery. Eminent constitutional lawyers have expressed their concern: for example, Manitakis (*Proto Thema* 2015a) characterised the referendum as 'divisive' and 'technocratic', and 'grotesque', since the people were called upon to decide on a text that did not actually exist on the day of the referendum itself. Stathopoulos (*Proto Thema* 2015b) found it 'unconstitutional and irrational', while Gerapetritis thought it was contrary to political correctness due to the extreme brevity of the deliberation period, the change in the terms of the game after its proclamation by the legislating government and the inappropriateness of the question (Tsiboukis 2015). However, such criticisms were regarded—in a crescendo of populist feeling—as an attempt to stop the people from expressing—at long last—its authentic political will.

Unlike the Scottish experience where, according to Tierney, the winner was the referendum itself (Tierney 2014), in the Greek paradigm the only winner was populism, with the referendum itself being the big loser. However, the end result of populist responses to what is perceived as a 'democratic deficit' can only be a trivialisation of democracy itself (Antonopoulos 2015). Not only did the SYRIZA-ANEL government exhibit no prudence in the use of referendums, despite their allegedly positive stance towards them, but by spoiling and trivialising the institution as a whole, they gave the opponents of direct democratic instruments the best arguments against them, since they were seen as tools in the hands of autocratic regimes and demagogues. In other words, if one wanted to design a mock referendum, to undermine the institution as a whole, one would create one exactly like the Greek referendum of 2015, which is now often presented as a caricature by the opponents of referendums. Tsipras abused the referendum as 'a strategic negotiating move, designed, in part, to perhaps seek enough vote of confidence from the Greek people' in order to sign an agreement not significantly different to the one they had previously been offered (Lakhani 2015: 109).

However, pre-emptive judicial control of the referendum is not provided for in the Constitution. Consequently, an attempt to have the referendum judicially declared null and void was rejected by the Council of State (the supreme administrative court and High Court of Cassation in Greece). In its Decision of the Plenary 2787/2015 of 03.07.2015, the Council of State declared an application for annulment of Presidential Decree 38/2015 and of the Ministerial Decision of 26.06.2015 to be inadmissible. Based on existing case law on similar types of act (e.g. acts on the dissolution of Parliament or the proclamation of elections), the Court concluded that the contested acts were 'governmental acts' since they concerned the exercise of political power. Thus, according to Article 45 §5 of Presidential Decree 18/89, they lay beyond its judicial control. The only possibility remaining was of ex-post judicial control by the Supreme Special Court, as laid out in Article 100 §1 b Const. However, no one applied for such a ruling since the consequences of the referendum could already be seen to be political and not legal. Thus, there was no point for anyone to seek to annul its (non-existent) legal consequences.

30.6   DRAWING CONCLUSIONS FOR THE FUTURE

Participative legislation, through referendums and popular initiatives— although not a substitute for the necessary upgrading of parliament and the recovery of its lost credibility—can revitalise the citizens' interest in politics and policymaking but they cannot remove the inherent or acquired drawbacks involved in representation, which need to be addressed separately. Citizens' participation could possibly help to counterbalance the majoritarian parliamentary system and offer added legitimacy value to government policies and parliamentary legislation. However, referendums without a proper institutional design, without the necessary procedural and substantive guarantees, are apt to serve as an unmediated link between the people and the executive and become a pseudo-democratic façade. They can thus be easily turned into a manipulative tool in the hands of autocratic regimes, elites, demagogues and populists. The abolition of checks and balances and the power gained from the people's direct legitimation also allow those in power to deal with the outcome as they please, twisting it or interpreting it to serve their own power game. Such political misuse of referendums not only proves to be an undemocratic endeavour but also undermines constitutional democracy in general.

The necessary preconditions that will allow for meaningful deliberation include an independent organising committee, a sufficient amount of time, the formation of opposing camps and judicial review both ex-ante and ex-post of both the question(s) posed in the referendum and the circumstances in which the latter is conducted. Only under these limitations will there not arise a populist, purely procedural, unlimited, pseudo-democracy, a dictatorship of an easily manipulated majority. The lesson to be drawn for the future is that direct democratic institutions should be designed with substantive safeguards against potential abuses. Unfortunately, in the constitutional revision procedure being undertaken at the time of writing, no such proposals had gained support. SYRIZA's proposals aimed at enhancing the direct democratic institutions but without offering the guarantees necessary for such institutions to resist populist manipulation. Greece's political system does not thus seem to have drawn the right conclusions from the referendum adventure of 2015.

REFERENCES[5]

Alivizatos, N. (2015, June 28). Referendum or a [Democratic] Sideslip. *Kathimerini* (in Greek). Available at: http://www.kathimerini.gr/821262/opinion/epikairot hta/politikh/dhmoyhfisma-h-ektroph.

Andronides, S. (2015, July 14). The Class Dimension of the Referendum (Η ταξική διάσταση του δημοψηφίσματος). *To Vima* (in Greek). Available at: https://www. tovima.gr/2015/07/14/opinions/i-taksiki-diastasi-toy-dimopsifismatos/.

Antonopoulos, E. (2015, September 7). *The Greek Referendum: Popular Verdict or Foregone Conclusion?* blogs.lse.ac.uk/eurocrisispress/2015/07/09/the-greek-refere ndum-popular-verdict-or-foregone-conclusion/.

Askitas, N. (2015). *Calling the Greek Referendum on the Nose with Google Trends* (IZA Discussion Paper No. 9569). Institute of Labor Economics. Available at: https:// www.iza.org/.../calling-the-greek-referendum-on-the-nose-with-google-trends.

Aslanidis, P., & Kaltwasser, C. R. (2016). Dealing with Populists in Government: The SYRIZA-ANEL Coalition in Greece. *Democratization, 23*(6), 1077–1091.

Bartsidis, M., Gavriilidis, A., & Lalopoulou, S. (2015, July 8). *July the 5th: How the Multitude Blocked a Post-modern coup d'état in the EU.* Available at: http://www.connessioniprecarie.org/2015/07/08/july-the-5th-how-the-multit ude-blocked-a-post-modern-coup-detat-in-the-eu/.

Boukala, S., & Dimitrakopoulou, D. (2017). The Politics of Fear vs. the Politics of Hope: Analysing the 2015 Greek Election and Referendum Campaigns. *Critical Discourse Studies, 14*(1), 39–55.

Chatzistavrou, F. (2015, July 3). *The 2015 Greek Referendum* (Commentary No. 24). European Policy Institutes Network. Available at: https://www.ceps.eu/publicati ons/2015-greek-referendum.

Contiades, X., & Fotiadou, A. (2015). *The Greek Referendum: Unconstitutional and Undemocratic.* Available at: https://constitutional-change.com/the-greek-ref erendum-unconstitutional-and-undemocratic/.

Corbyn, J. (2015, June 29). A Europe of Domination or of Solidarity? *The Huffington Post.*

Council of Europe, Parliamentary Assembly. (2018, December 11). *Updating Guidelines to Ensure Fair Referendums in Council of Europe Member States, Provisional Version.*

Deane, D. (2015, July 6). Greece's Flamboyant Finance Minister Quits, Decries "Debt Bondage". *The Washington Post.* Available at: https://www.washingtonpost. com/world/greeces-flamboyant-finance-minister-goes-out-in-his-typical-combative-way/2015/07/06/5acc3116-23af-11e5-b72c-2b7d516e1e0e_story.html?noredi rect=on&utm_term=.4afd160bf825.

---

[5]All internet articles were last accessed on 5th January 2019.

Elliott, L., Wearden, G., Watt, N., & Smith, H. (2015, June 29, Monday). Europe's Big Guns Warn Greek Voters That a No Vote Means Euro Exit. *The Guardian*. Available at: https://www.theguardian.com/business/2015/jun/29/greek-crisis-referendum-eurozone-vote-germany-france-italy.

Erlanger S. (2015, July 13). Deal on Greek Debt Crisis Exposes Europe's Deepening Fissures. *The New York Times*. Available at: http://www.nytimes.com/2015/07/14/world/europe/greece-debt-deal.html.

Euronews. (2015, July 2). Greek Referendum Bid for "Reinforcements" Is "Anti-constitutional". Available at: https://www.euronews.com/2015/07/02/greek-referendum-bid-for-reinforcements-is-anti-constitutional.

European Commission for Democracy Through Law (Venice Commission). (2006). Code of Good Practice on Referendums, Adopted by the Council for Democratic Elections at Its 19th Meeting (Venice, 16 December 2006) and the Venice Commission at Its 70th Plenary Session (Venice, 16–17 March 2007), Study no. 371/2006, Cdl-ad(2007)008rev-cor. Available at: https://www.venice.coe.int.

Evans-Pritchard, A. (2015, June 29). Greece Threatens Top Court Action to Block Grexit. *The Telegraph*. Available at: https://www.telegraph.co.uk/finance/economics/11707092/Greece-threatens-top-court-action-to-block-Grexit.html.

Fotiadou, A. (2015, June 29). *A Non-deliberative Snap Referendum: Greece*. Available at: https://constitutional-change.com/a-non-deliberative-snap-referendum-greece/.

Gerapetritis, G. (2015, June 29). Constitutionality and Political Correctness of the Referendum. *Huffington Post* (in Greek). https://www.huffingtonpost.gr/giorgos-gerapetritis/-_626_b_7685248.html.

Gunter, J. (2015, , June 29), The Greek Referendum Question Makes (Almost) No Sense. *BBC*. Available at: https://www.bbc.com/news/world-europe-33311422.

Hatzis, A. (2019). A Political History of Modern Greece (1821–2018). In A. Marciano & G. B. Ramello (Eds.), *Encyclopedia of Law and Economics*. New York: Springer. Available at: https://link.springer.com/referenceworkentry/10.1007/978-1-4614-7883-6_53-1. Accessed 1 June 2019.

Hobolt, S. (2006). How Parties Affect Vote Choice in European Integration Referendums. *Party Politics, 12*(5), 623–647.

Hodson, D. (2016). Eurozone Governance: From the Greek Drama of 2015 to the Five Presidents' Report. *Journal of Common Market Studies, 54*(S1), 150–166.

Holehouse, M. (2015, June 29). Don't Vote for Suicide, 'Betrayed' Jean-Claude Juncker Begs Greeks. *The Daily Telegraph*. London.

Hope, K., & Barber T. (2015, July 24). Syriza's Covert Plot During Crisis Talks to Return to Drachma. *Financial Times*. Available at: https://www.ft.com/content/2a0a1d94-3201-11e5-8873-775ba7c2ea3d.

Jurado, I., Konstantinidis, N., & Walter, S. (2015). *Why Greeks Voted the Way They Did in the Bailout Referendum*. Available at: blogs.lse.ac.uk/europpblog/2015/07/20/why-greeks-voted-the-way-they-did-in-the-bailout-referendum/.

Kathimerini. (2015a, July 1). Council of Europe: Conditions of Greek Referendum Fall Short of International Standards. Available at: http://www.ekathimerini.com/198779/article/ekathimerini/news/council-of-europe-conditions-of-greek-referendum-fall-short-of-international-standards.

Kathimerini. (2015b, July 5). Greek Conservative Opposition Chief Samaras Resigns. Available at: http://www.ekathimerini.com/198993/article/ekathimerini/news/greek-conservative-opposition-chief-samaras-resigns.

Lakhani, A. (2015). David Versus Goliath and Multilateral Diplomatic Negotiations in the 21st Century: How the Greek Debt Crisis Negotiations Marked the Revenge of Goliath. *Cardozo Journal of International and Comparative Law, 24,* 97–151.

Makris, A. (2015, June 29). ND Leader Samaras: The Real Question Is 'Yes' or 'No' to the Euro. *Greek Reporter.* Available at: https://greece.greekreporter.com/2015/06/29/nd-leader-samaras-the-real-question-is-yes-or-no-to-the-euro/.

Marans, D. (2015, July 1). Bernie Sanders Blasts Greece's Creditors. *Huffington Post.* Available at: https://www.huffingtonpost.com/2015/07/01/bernie-sanders-greece_n_7709322.html.

Mavrozacharakis, E., & Tzagarakis, S. (2015, July 21). *The Greek Referendum: An Alternative Approach* (MPRA Paper No. 65738). Available at: https://mpra.ub.uni-muenchen.de/65738/.

Morris, C. (2015, June 27). Greece Debt Crisis: Tsipras Announces Bailout Referendum. *BBC News.* Available at: https://www.bbc.com/news/world-europe-332 96839.

Pantelis, A. (1979). *Les grands problèmes de la nouvelle Constitution Héllenique.* Paris: LGDJ.

Papadopoulou, L. (2016). Institutions of 'Direct Legislation'—With a Special Focus on the Greek Constitution, in: 1st (First) Albanian-Greek symposium organised on July 29–30, 2013 at the Aristotle University of Thessaloniki, Greece, Publication of proceedings (pp 79–103). Tirana: Vllamasi.

Pappas, T. (2015, September 25). *Populist Hegemony in Greece.* Available at: www.opendemocracy.net/can-europe-make-it/takis-s-pappas/populist-hegemony-in-greece.

Parashu, D. (2015). Die Volksabstimmung in der Hellenischen Republik vom 05.07.2015 vor verfassungsrechtlichem und einfachgesetzlichem Hintergrund. *ZÖR, 4,* 801–823.

Proto Thema. (2015a, June 27). Manitakis: The Referendum Is Constitutional, the Question Is Divisive. Available at: https://www.protothema.gr/politics/article/488 241/manitakis-sudagmatiko-to-dimopsifisma-dihastiko-to-erotima/.

Proto Thema. (2015b, June 27). Mich. Stathopoulos: The Referendum Is Unconstitutional and Irrational. Available at: https://www.protothema.gr/politics/article/488 327/mih-stathopoulos-adisudagmatiko-kai-paralogo-to-dimopsifisma/.

Rontos, K., Grigoriadis, E., Sateriano, A., Syrmali, M., Vavouras, I., & Salvati, L. (2016). Lost in Protest, Found in Segregation: Divided Cities in the Light of the 2015 "Oxi" Referendum in Greece. *City, Culture and Society, 7,* 139–148.

Rori, L. (2016). The 2015 Greek Parliamentary Elections: From Great Expectations to No Expectations. *West European Politics, 39*(6), 1323–1343.

Shin, S. (2015, June 29). 'An End to the Blackmail'—Alexis Tsipras Calls Greek Referendum on Troika Bailout Deal. *Verso.* Available at: https://www.versobooks.com/blogs/2070-an-end-to-the-blackmail-alexis-tsipras-calls-greek-referendum-on-troika-bailout-deal.

Sotirelis, G. (2015, June 27). *The Constitutional Parameters of the Referendum. Interview to G. Lakopoulos, on "Anoihto Parathyro"* (in Greek). Available at: https://www.constitutionalism.gr/sotirelis-dimopsifisma/.

Sotiropoulos, D. (2015, July 3). The Greek Referendum of 5 July 2015: A Series of Blunders of Which the Largest and Latest Was Syriza's Blunder. *Heinrich Böll Stiftung.* Available at: https://gr.boell.org/en/2015/07/03/greek-referendum-5-july-2015-series-blunders-which-largest-and-latest-was-syrizas-blunder.

Spiliotopoulos, E. (1988). The Legal Aspect of the Referendum on Article 44 Paragraph 2 of the Constitution. In *A Collection in Honour of F. Vegleris* (Vol. A, pp. 320ff.). Athens and Komotini (in Greek).

Steinhauser, G., Thomas, A., & Dalton, M. (2015, July 6). Greek Debt Crisis: Athens, Creditors Scramble to Find Solution After Vote. *The Wall Street Journal*. Available at: http://www.wsj.com/articles/conditions-not-right-for-new-negotiati ons-on-greek-bailout-germany-says-1436180226.

Stiglitz, J. (2015, June 29). Europe's Attack on Greek Democracy. *Huffington Post*. Available at: https://www.huffingtonpost.com/joseph-e-stiglitz/europes-att ack-greek-democracy_b_7692156.html?guccounter=1.

Sygkelos, Y. (2015). A Critical Analysis of the Greek Referendum of July 2015. *Contemporary Southeastern Europe, 2*(2), 1–6. Available at: http://www.contempor arysee.org/en/sygkelos.

Tierney, S. (2014, September 26). And the Winner Is... the Referendum: Scottish Independence and the Deliberative Participation of Citizens. *International Journal of Constitutional Law*. Available at: http://www.iconnectblog.com/2014/09/and- the-winner-is-the-referendum-scottish-independence-and-the-deliberative-participa tion-of-citizens/.

Tsatsanis, E., & Teperoglou, E. (2016). Realignment Under Stress: The July 2015 Referendum and the September Parliamentary Election in Greece. *South European Society and Politics, 21*(4), 427–450.

Tsebelis, G. (2016). Lessons from the Greek Crisis. *Journal of European Public Policy, 23*(1), 25–41.

Tsiboukis, P. (2015, June 27). Four Academics Divided on the Constitutionality of the Referendum. *Proto Thema* (in Greek). Available at: https://www.protothema. gr/greece/article/488372/dihasmenoi-tesseris-panepistimiakoi-gia-ti-sudagmatikot ita-tou-dimopsifismatos/.

Udland, M. (2015, June 29). Greece's Prime Minister Seeking to Calm Greek Citizens Quotes FDR: "The Only Thing to Fear Is Fear Itself". *Business Insider*. https://www.businessinsider.com.au/alexis-tsipras-quotes-fdr-tries-to-calm- greek-citizens-2015-6.

Walter, S. (2015, July 9). What Were the Greeks Thinking? Here's a Poll Taken Just Before the Referendum. *The Washington Post*. Available at: https://www.washingtonpost.com/blogs/monkey-cage/wp/2015/07/ 09/what-were-the-greeks-thinking-heres-a-poll-taken-just-before-the-referendum/.

Venizélos, E. (2016). *State Transformation and the European Integration Project— Lessons from the Financial Crisis and the Greek Paradigm* (CEPS Special Report No. 130). Available at: https://www.ceps.eu/publications/state-transformation-and-eur opean-integration-project-lessons-financial-crisis-and.

Venizélos, E. (2017). Crise grecque et zone euro. *Commentaire*, N° 159, 555–563.

Vouloumanos, T. (2015, July 2). *Syriza, The EU Institutions & Struggle for Democracy*. http://www.stokokkino.gr/details_en.php?id=1000000000012083/Syr iza-The-EU-Institutions–Struggle-For-Democracy.

Xafa, M. (2014). *Sovereign Debt Crisis Management: Lessons from the 2012 Greek Debt Restructuring*. Available at: https://www.cigionline.org/publications/sov ereign-debt-crisis-management-lessons-2012-greek-debt-restructuring. Accessed 20 November 2018.

CHAPTER 31

Hungary's EU Refugee Relocation Quota Referendum: 'Let's Send a Message to Brussels'

Agnes Batory

31.1 Introduction

Sending a message to Brussels was the main declared objective of Hungary's Fidesz government, which posed the following referendum question to voters on 2 October 2016: 'Do you want the European Union to be entitled to prescribe the mandatory settlement of non-Hungarian citizens in Hungary without the consent of parliament?' Set against the background of the EU's refugee crisis reaching its peak in 2015, the answer, from virtually everyone who cast a valid ballot, was 'No'. This outcome was quite predictable, given that the referendum was preceded by the relentless campaign of the government to portray migrants and refugees crossing Hungary en masse to Western Europe as a threat to the country's culture, traditions and economic interest. However, while the majority of the 'No' votes was taken for granted, turnout was much more uncertain, and in the end failed to reach the required 50% for a valid result. This was widely seen as a failure for the government and Hungary's firebrand prime minister, Viktor Orbán, at least by his critics and opponents both at home and in other EU capitals.

In the context of referendums on the EU, the Hungarian referendum of 2016 offers an interesting case study for several reasons. It is the only EU-related referendum in one of the newer Member States since the accession referendums of 2003, accompanying the EU's 'big bang' enlargement of

A. Batory (✉)
School of Public Policy, Central European University, Vienna, Austria
e-mail: batorya@ceu.edu

2004, apart from the Croatian referendum on membership in 2012.[1] It is also the only one to date in the Central Eastern European (CEE) post-communist Member States concerning (at least ostensibly) whether competencies for dealing with a newly salient policy issue, in this case responding to the challenges posed by a large number of migrants arriving to the EU from the Middle East and North Africa, should be located at the national or the European level. The Hungarian referendum is also a rare example of a government calling a referendum of its own accord on an EU issue, without either legal obligation or political or internal party pressure. Referendums have always been an exception rather than the rule for deciding important EU issues, but especially in the wake of the, from the perspective of David Cameron's divided government, woefully miscalculated Brexit vote (see Chapter 22 by Smith), and in fact since the failed Constitutional Treaty, ruling governments have tended to try and diffuse pressure for putting questions to the electorate (Oppermann 2017). Moreover, the Hungarian referendum is probably exceptional in that an internally united ruling party fought it on a Eurosceptic platform, explicitly aiming to mobilise public sentiment *against* 'Europe'.[2]

Hungary's domestic politics is in itself worthy of attention as the most prominent example of democratic backsliding in the EU, having been governed by a populist Eurosceptic party that gained a large majority in parliament in the 2010, 2014 and 2018 elections. Referendums are a favoured instrument for populists since they seem to give credence to claims of 'power to the people' (Canovan 1999: 2; cf. Qvortrup 2018). The migrant quota referendum, as it is known in Hungary, thus also provides an opportunity for studying the dynamics of populism and direct democracy in the EU context and allows for some conclusions to be drawn as to whether the exercise indeed served to give 'the people' a chance to 'send a message to Brussels', as claimed by the government, or was motivated by partisan goals.

The chapter starts with a brief section on some of the most relevant findings from scholarship on referendums in the EU context, focusing on the relatively limited literature on referendums in the 'new' Member States, which joined in 2004 or later. Sections 31.3, 31.4 and 31.5 provide some essential background to the country case in terms of the political and party system, previous referendum experience and legal regulations pertaining to referendums. Section 31.6 turns to the question why the referendum was called. The bulk of the chapter discusses the referendum campaigns and key actors in Sect. 31.7. Section 31.8 briefly reviews the result. Finally, the implications for Hungarian politics and for the EU are discussed in the conclusion, Sect. 31.9.

---

[1] Although debates took place in several of the 'new' Member States on holding referendums on the failed Constitutional Treaty and in the five countries joining the Euro on adopting the single currency, in the end none of these referendums took place (Batory 2017).

[2] As the British example perhaps most prominently shows, internal divisions in governing parties are a common cause for governments to pledge referendums; see e.g. Smith (2016).

31.2   REFERENDUMS AND EUROPEAN INTEGRATION

Much of the literature on direct democracy generally and on referendums specifically focuses, first, on whether they are normatively superior to representative democracy and, second, on whether they can indeed be considered as the expression of 'the will of the people' (see also Lord in Chapter 2). The former question, going back to Rousseau and John Stuart Mill in political thought, is clearly beyond the scope of this chapter, but the competence question—i.e. whether voters are able to judge complex political questions—is even more pertinent in the European integration context than generally. This is because a full grasp of EU policy and politics is traditionally assumed to require expert knowledge, leaving voters unable or unwilling to form a firm opinion on issues pertaining to it (e.g. Lindberg and Scheingold 1970; cf. Hooghe and Marks 2009).

Consequently, a key question for comparative scholarship on EU referendums is whether outcomes reflect the public's views on the issue at hand, or something else. This question is a reflection of the classic debate on European parliamentary elections, traditionally characterised as 'second order elections' (Reif and Schmitt 1980). Accordingly, since government formation is not at stake, the salience of the elections is thought to be low and voters assumed to use it as an opportunity to send a signal to their national capitals rather than to Brussels or Strasbourg. Referendum outcomes are similarly argued to reflect domestic political factors, primarily government popularity, rather than 'genuine' preferences about European integration or the specific EU issue directly at stake. As Franklin et al. (1994, 1995) have argued, voters cast their ballot following partisan cues and endorse or reject the substantive question of the referendum in line with their evaluations of the government. At the same time, there is considerable evidence that at least in some referendums public attitudes to the EU or even opinion on specific EU issues played a key role (e.g. Svensson 2002; Garry et al. 2005; Hobolt and Brouard 2011; Glencross and Trechsel 2011; Garry 2014). Government popularity emerged as only one of a range of factors that influence the outcome, including public confidence in the main actors, the competitiveness or intensity of the campaigns, political information availability, party unity, and the legal nature of the referendum as binding or consultative (e.g. Schneider and Weitsman 1996; Hobolt 2005, 2006).

The experience of the CEE countries joining the EU in 2004 offers little support for the second-order thesis (see e.g. Szczerbiak and Taggart 2004a, b). The 2003 accession referendums were won in each of the countries, including those proposed by relatively unpopular governments. To varying degrees, all accession referendums were characterised by domestic elite consensus, public support for EU membership and a sense of a historical choice which translated into very high proportions of voters endorsing EU membership. At the same time, turnout was low, and at just 45% lowest in Hungary, largely due to a perception that the outcome was inevitable. However, given the near absence of relevant empirical cases, scholarship on the subject of referendums on EU issues since membership was decided is relatively scarce. The Hungarian migrant quota referendum addressed here is the only such vote.

31.3   THE HUNGARIAN POLITICAL LANDSCAPE

For the first two decades after its democratic transition, Hungary was generally considered as a leading reformer in Central and Eastern Europe and, prior to 2004, a forerunner for EU membership. Governments came and went in a more or less orderly fashion, and while the party system was strongly polarised, relative stability characterised the country's political landscape. From the mid-1990s, elections were fought primarily between two major parties, the Socialist Party on the centre-left, and Fidesz, initially a liberal, then national-conservative, and eventually populist party on the right (see e.g. Mudde 2016; Enyedi 2016; Batory 2016b), alongside a number of smaller competitors.

2010 represents a watershed in Hungarian politics. Following eight years in office, for much of the time in coalition with the small Alliance of Free Democrats, and having struggled with the fallout from the global economic crisis, corruption scandals and a messy prime ministerial succession, the Socialist Party suffered a massive defeat at the polls. Viktor Orbán's Fidesz received 53% of the votes in 2010 which, thanks to the very disproportional electoral system, translated into 68% of the seats in parliament. Since laws of a constitutional nature can be amended by a two-thirds majority in parliament, this election result essentially removed any possibility for the opposition parties to block changes to the country's basic institutional architecture. Losing no time, the new government set about dismantling the existing constitutional order, systematically removing checks and balances in what is now well-known as a textbook example of democratic backsliding (e.g. Ágh 2016; Bánkuti et al. 2012; Closa et al. 2014; Sedelmeier 2014). The 'reforms' included a new, strongly majoritarian electoral system designed to give Fidesz an advantage, which played an important part in its repeated electoral victories in 2014 and 2018, and a new constitution with changes to the legal regulation of direct democracy instruments (further discussed below). The so-called Fundamental Law was formally introduced as a private member's bill and passed in 2011 in Parliament with the support of Fidesz MPs, without a single vote in favour from the opposition and without confirmation by a referendum (Bánkuti et al. 2012).[3]

In the years after Fidesz took office in 2010, the Hungarian party system changed beyond recognition. The party was in a league of its own in terms of popular support, with its earlier main contender, the Socialist Party, having

---

[3]Among many other international bodies, the Venice Commission severely criticised the constitution-making process for lacking transparency, 'shortcomings in the dialogue between the majority and the opposition, the insufficient opportunities for an adequate public debate, and a very tight timeframe' (Council of Europe, European Commission for Democracy Through Law [Venice Commission] 2011: 28).

split up and been in disarray for much of the period. Alongside the Socialists, the Left featured several other small parties, making it too fragmented
to stand a chance for office, particularly given the characteristics of the electoral system. On the Right, Fidesz competed with the extreme-right Jobbik
(short for Movement for a Better Hungary), although, given the latter party's
efforts from the middle of the decade to project a more moderate image, by
2018 it was arguably Fidesz that occupied more radical policy positions. In
terms of the parties' attitudes to the EU, the picture is relatively simple: the
centre-left opposition parties were generally Europhile, while Fidesz shifted
from the soft Eurosceptic position it adopted by around the time of EU accession to an increasingly vocal and radical critique of the EU while in office.[4]
Jobbik, traditionally a hard Eurosceptic party, on the other hand moder-
ated its position on the EU. Nonetheless, from 2010 onwards, populism and
Euroscepticism became a strikingly dominant feature of the party system, with
Fidesz and Jobbik together securing between 65 and 70% of the popular vote
in parliamentary elections. This is despite the fact that public opinion remained
supportive of EU membership, and the fact that Fidesz remained a member
of the centre-right European People's Party.

31.4   Referendum Experience in Hungary

Hungary held seven national referendums in the thirty years after regime
change in 1989, which makes it a 'regular' user of the instrument in international comparison (Qvortrup 2018). The first two, in 1989 and 1990
respectively, settled some of the institutional questions involved in the democratic transition. In 1989, before the first free elections, voters answered
altogether four questions, three to do with the removal of communist era
'remnants', such as banning party cells in workplaces, and one about the
election of the President of the Republic to take place after a new parliament is constituted. The 1990 referendum, probing whether the President
of the Republic—a largely ceremonial office at the time—should be directly or
indirectly elected, attracted little attention and, failing to reach the 50% participation threshold, did not produce a valid result. (The parliamentary parties
eventually settled on indirect election.)

The following two referendums concerned what was widely seen as the
country's 'return to Europe', or to 'the West' more broadly. In 1997, a
referendum confirmed Hungary's NATO membership with an overwhelming
majority (85%) of the votes. Joining the Alliance enjoyed strong cross-party
and public support—which also meant that the referendum was a rather lack-
lustre affair. Anticipating low turnout, the parliamentary parties lowered the
bar for a valid result prior to the vote, with the new legal provision requiring
that at least 25% of all registered voters vote 'Yes'. This proved fortuitous from

---

[4]For the definition of soft and hard Euroscepticism see Taggart and Szczerbiak (2008).

the point of view of those supporting NATO membership, since turnout was only 49%.

This pattern—high support from those voting but with low turnout—was repeated six years later when, in April 2003, Hungarians voted to join the EU. In fact, the Hungarian vote produced the lowest turnout of EU accession referendums among post-communist countries joining the EU in 2004. Only 45% of eligible electors voted, with 84% supporting EU membership. One reason was probably the fact that—unlike in other EU referendums—for voters 'EU accession was not necessarily recognisably the project of the government that called it' but rather 'symbolic celebrations of their countries' achievements' (Szczerbiak and Taggart 2004a: 562). As Fowler (2004: 624) argues, in Hungary low participation was also due to 'low levels of participation in elections in general and referendums in particular, low contestation of EU membership at elite and mass levels, and a low intensity of EU-related preferences'. Indeed, the dominance of political parties and non-governmental bodies calling for a 'Yes' was overwhelming. Among the major parties, Fidesz showed the least enthusiasm for EU membership, with Viktor Orbán as party leader carefully feeding soft Eurosceptic rhetoric into the public debate, although the party nonetheless also formally endorsed membership (Batory 2008: 137–138).

In contrast, the referendums that followed—both pushed by Fidesz—were about hotly contested issues. In both 2004 and 2008, Fidesz was in opposition to a Socialist-Free Democrat government coalition, and on both occasions the party intensively campaigned to undermine the government's position. In 2004, the first question posed in the referendum was to prevent privatisation in healthcare, and the second to introduce a preferential naturalisation procedure for ethnic Hungarians from the neighbouring countries. Voters supported Fidesz's position against privatisation by a large majority (65%) and for preferential naturalisation by a narrow margin (51%) but turnout was too low for the result to be valid. In 2008, however, Fidesz fared better. The party initiated a referendum on three popular (or populist) proposals: one to abolish fees in publicly funded higher education, the second against the planned introduction of small fees in primary healthcare and the third against fees charged during hospital stays. Unsurprisingly, the electorate was keen to endorse these proposals, as seen in an over 80% Yes vote for all three questions, and at 50.5% turnout was also sufficient for a valid outcome. (Fidesz obviously drew some lessons from this: it banned referendums with implications for the central budget in the 2011 Fundamental Law). Party preference played a dominant role in people's orientations to the referendum questions (Enyedi 2009). The result directly contributed to the Free Democrats quitting the deeply unpopular governing coalition and further weakened the Socialist Party, which limped on in office for another year, then, for the final year before the elections, backed a 'technocratic government' led by Gordon Bajnai.

What this overview of referendums over two decades shows is that participation in referendums tended to be rather low: aside the votes in the context of the democratic transition in 1989–1990, there has been only one occasion when participation exceeded 50%, and even then only barely, despite the fact that the questions posed dealt with bread and butter issues. It is also quite evident that, as far as our limited sample of two referendums (2004 and 2008) shows, for the referendums that took place on 'regular' policy issues amidst political contestation, party preference was a key factor in determining the outcome.

31.5   The Legal Framework Governing Referendums

Hungary's first law on referendums was passed in 1989, as part of the country's negotiated transition from communism to multi-party democracy. The law allowed for referendums and popular initiatives to be called on a wide range of issues, but left many procedural questions open. This was remedied by a new law on referendums and the insertion of provisions into the law on electoral procedure in 1998 (Szabó 2017: 6). That legal framework remained in force until the adoption of the new constitution in 2011.

The Fundamental Law, which entered into force on 1 January 2012, allows for direct democracy in exceptional cases—generally, 'power shall be exercised by the people through elected representatives' (Article B). Article 8 stipulates that referendums can only be held on issues within Parliament's competences, and excludes a number of issues from among possible referendum subjects: notably, referendums cannot be held about amending the Fundamental Law itself, electoral laws or about obligations that arise from international treaties. In contrast, there is no subject that requires a referendum to be called—i.e. in contrast with many other European countries, there is no question that belongs to the exclusive competence of referendums (Bakó 2013: 169; see also Norton in Chapter 5). Article 8 of the Fundamental Law also sets a high benchmark for opposition parties or citizens to launch a referendum: referendums have to be called by the National Assembly (parliament) if at least 200,000 voters initiate it (obligatory referendum), and may be called by parliament if initiated by 100,000 voters, the President of the Republic, or the government (optional referendum).[5] Under the Fundamental Law, a referendum is only valid if turnout exceeds 50% (higher than previously), and conclusive if more than half of the valid votes cast give the same answer. In the case of a valid conclusive referendum, the outcome is binding on parliament.

Further important rules are provided by Law CCXXXVIII of 2013 on Initiating referendums, European popular initiatives and referendum procedures. Accordingly, the referendum question has to be formulated in a way that enables voters to understand and answer it clearly, and also creates clarity

[5]The Fundamental Law uses the term 'referendum' for both votes initiated by voters (commonly referred to as 'initiatives' in the literature, see e.g. Uleri 1996 or Morel and Qvortrup 2018), and by other actors such as parliament or the government. In the following referendum refers to both kinds of direct democracy instruments.

for parliament to then act on the referendum outcome by passing the appropriate legislation. Failure to meet any of these formal requirements results in the rejection of the question by the National Electoral Commission, which is also charged with the verification of the signatures submitted in the case of referendums initiated by citizens. Significantly, the 2013 law stipulated a ban on parallel proposals: only one referendum question could be validated by the Commission on the same subject. Consequently, by proposing a question to the Commission for validation, differently framed or worded questions on the same subject could be blocked (as discussed below, this provision became very controversial and was amended in 2016). Finally, a significant omission from the law is regulation of campaign financing: there is no provision made for funding both sides of a debate or imposing spending limits on campaigners, which puts the government at a great advantage given its ability to use public resources for propagating its own position (László 2016: 15).

A few salient points about the legislative framework are worth pointing out. One such noteworthy feature is the absence of a requirement that a constitution or a constitutional amendment should be confirmed by a referendum, which enables a political party or parties that command a qualified majority in parliament to change the foundations of the country's legal and political order at will—an opportunity that Fidesz has used several times, adopting seven amendments to the Fundamental Law by June 2018. Conversely, referendums are banned for a wide range of subjects, and in the remaining areas the double clarity requirement (i.e. that the question is clear for the voter and creates a clear obligation for parliament) leaves wide scope for interpretation by the Electoral Commission, which has the prerogative to validate the question proposed before a referendum can be called. In the interpretation of the Commission, clarity requires that the question is short and simple and can be answered with a Yes or No, but at the same time draws attention to the consequences of the alternatives—which is obviously quite challenging (Bakó 2013: 177). The Commission has the competence to decide about campaign advertising in the public service media and to deal with complaints during campaigns.

The members of the Electoral Commission are nominated by the President of the Republic (since 2012, Janos Áder, formerly a prominent member of Fidesz) and confirmed by two-thirds of the members of the National Assembly, in accordance by the Electoral Procedure Act of 2013 (also adopted by Fidesz). Appeals against the Commission's decision are decided by the Highest Court, the *Kuria*, and citizens affected may also petition the Constitutional Court which, however, had been packed by judges supportive of the governing party's agenda (Hungarian Helsinki Committee 2015). Thus, it is perhaps not surprising that few referendum questions proposed by citizens (and through them, opposition parties) have been validated: 15 out of 274 between January 2014, the entry into force of the 2013 law, and December 2017 (National Election Bureau, 2017). Only one of the validated questions—the quota referendum initiated by the government—was actually put to the voters, often because the organisers failed to collect the required 200,000 signatures from voters supporting the proposal within the available time period.

Two significant initiatives are worth mentioning, even though neither actually resulted in a referendum being held: one to reject a law introduced by Fidesz requiring larger commercial outlets to stay closed on Sundays, which was extremely unpopular with voters, and another—on this occasion a local referendum proposal in Budapest rather than a national one—to reject the government's bid to host the Olympic Games. The referendum proposal on Sunday shopping was especially controversial: when a representative of the Socialist Party, the chief proponent of the referendum, tried to submit their question to the Electoral Bureau for validation, he was physically blocked to allow a competing (presumably Fidesz-sponsored) question to be submitted ahead of his, thereby preventing the opposition party's proposal from going ahead given the prohibition on parallel proposals in the law (László 2016: 21). In both cases, the government eventually backed down and withdrew the legislation and the Olympic bid, respectively, presumably not wishing to take the chance of a humiliating defeat at the polls.

Altogether, it is fair to conclude that the legal regulation of referendums under the Fidesz government considerably weakened the potential for direct democracy—and for opposition parties mobilising voters—to act as a veto players (László 2016; Hug and Tsebelis 2002). Referendum proposals now needed to pass several legal hurdles before they could seriously inconvenience a government in office.

31.6   WHY HOLD A REFERENDUM?

Given the difficulty of launching a referendum for opposition parties or civil society organisations, it is not surprising that the only referendum to take place after Fidesz came to power was initiated by Viktor Orbán himself. The prime minister announced on 24 February 2016 that—bowing to popular pressure—his government was proposing a referendum about the 'migrant quota' prescribed by the EU, since no EU body should be entitled to redraw the cultural and ethnic map of the country, which was what the quota would amount to (*Magyar Nemzet* 2016). The direct cause thus appeared to be a September 2015 Council decision on the mandatory relocation of 120,000 persons who made an application in an EU country for international protection (Council of the European Union 2015), one of the EU's attempts to address the migration crisis.

The question proposed by Orbán (quoted in Sect. 31.1) was whether the EU should be able to 'prescribe the mandatory settlement of non-Hungarian citizens in Hungary without the consent of parliament'. Formally, the question was adopted as a parliamentary resolution with the support of the Fidesz and Jobbik MPs (the other opposition parties boycotted the vote), and quickly approved by the Electoral Commission. The parliamentary resolution and the

Commission's decision were legally challenged by private citizens and opposition parties both in front of the *Kuria* and the Constitutional Court, on the grounds that the question affected an obligation arising from an international treaty (one of the subjects banned by the Fundamental Law); was not clearly formulated; and did not belong to parliament's competences (László 2016). However, the courts did not find these objections convincing and allowed the question to stand.

Why such a question would need to be put to a referendum was indeed quite puzzling. First, it was not clear what precisely Parliament's authorisation would be necessary for, but even had an authorisation been necessary, there was no doubt that the government would be able to secure it. Fidesz had a comfortable majority and its highly disciplined caucus reliably obeyed the leadership's commands. In any case, it was the government itself that was in the best position to defend the country's interests in the EU decision-making process, particularly in the Council. Secondly, the 'non-Hungarian citizens' who were to be relocated to Hungary for the purposes of processing their asylum requests as a consequence of the EU redistribution scheme numbered about 1300 people (Groenendijk and Nagy 2015)—a much smaller number than the (also non-European) beneficiaries of the government's residency bond programme, for instance. Non-European immigration to Hungary had been negligible; the vast majority of asylum-seekers arriving in 2015 simply wanted to cross the country en route to Germany and Scandinavia.

Third, as many of Orbán's opponents both in Hungary and in the EU pointed out, the desired referendum outcome contradicted Hungary's obligations as an EU Member State, since it aimed to overrule a decision of the Council of the European Union. While the 2015 Council decision was hotly debated in the EU, subject to intensive negotiations, and legally challenged by Hungary and Slovakia, in the meantime it was binding on all Member States.[6] Therefore, it was evident that should the referendum return a valid 'No' vote, the government would be put in a position to either disregard the outcome or pursue policies that directly defied the EU's authority—something that Hungary's prime minister was no stranger to (Batory 2016a). Finally, as David Cameron's—and Orbán's own—experience shows, referendums are always a bit of a gamble; it is not uncommon for governments to see an initial poll lead evaporate during campaigns (Renwick 2014). The Hungarian government was under no formal, legal obligation or political pressure to take this kind of political risk.

So why hold a referendum? Part of the answer probably lies in Orbán and his cabinet's ambition to project (more) authority in the EU. The Hungarian government had sought to revive the previously rather lame Visegrád group and position itself as leader of the group, for which the issue presented an

---

[6]Two countries that voted against the decision in the Council, Hungary and Slovakia, legally challenged it at the European Court of Justice which at the time had not reached a verdict (Groenendijk and Nagy 2015).

ideal platform given shared public sentiment against non-European migration in these countries. In all four Visegrád states, Eurosceptics found a new narrative, essentially portraying the migrant relocation scheme as being forced 'to adopt multi-culturalism', which allowed them to raise 'doubts about whether the elites and publics in these countries were still making the same civilizational choices as their West European counterparts', in stark contrast with the accession referendums (Taggart and Szczerbiak 2018: 1208). In fact, framing 'immigration in ethnopluralist and security terms' was a common strategy of populist Eurosceptics in the EU (Pirro et al. 2018). Given that Fidesz was in office, the party could also claim that the referendum would be a vital boost to its authority vis-à-vis the EU institutions, arguing that it would be impossible for 'Europe' to go against the Hungarian government's democratic mandate, and that this mandate was necessary to fight the folly of 'Brussels'—not just for Hungary's sake but for that of Europe itself. As Viktor Orbán said on 12 September 2016 at the opening of the autumn session of parliament, 'Due to this modern-day mass migration, terror and violence have become part of life in Western Europe …. The policies Brussels is pursuing will lead to a civilizational catastrophe' (Orbán 2016).

However, a clearer rationale for the referendum came from domestic politics, and Fidesz's efforts to keep its stranglehold on the political agenda (the government had been the main agenda-setter; Boda and Patkós 2018). In late 2015, Fidesz continued to lead in the polls, but its support dropped, whereas its main competitor, the extreme-right Jobbik was gaining ground (Portfolio.hu 2016). Meanwhile, the Hungarian media was full of coverage of migrants—sometimes several thousand a day in summer 2015—making their way through the country, walking by major roads or sleeping in railway stations. While there were expressions of solidarity with the refugees, public opinion surveys showed that the majority of the Hungarian public held negative attitudes to 'migrants', 'strongly support[ed] anti-illegal migration measures, and while they [were] not against common EU migration policies, they at the same time prefer[red] to have more elbow room at national level' (Sik and Szeitl 2016: 20). By October 2015, 62% of respondents agreed that immigration was out of control and Fidesz and Jobbik sympathisers perceived migration more negatively than the population as a whole (Simonovits 2016: 27, 34). Thus, from a purely partisan point of view, the refugee crisis was a godsend for Fidesz: it offered a perfect opportunity to solidify and broaden its electoral base by outflanking Jobbik.

31.7   THE CAMPAIGNS

Although the Fidesz ticket was principally migration, the government's main campaign message appeared to be 'We must stop Brussels'. From the spring of 2015, Fidesz strategists masterfully fuelled the public's fears of uncontrolled (non-European) mass migration and linked the issue to the EU, moving from criticising the EU for its alleged inability to deal with the refugee crisis to a more systemic critique of the Union as dysfunctional, captured by special interests and/or the interests of the larger member states, and removed from the concerns of ordinary people. The incompetence or ill-will of 'Brussels' was contrasted with the Hungarian government's own measures to protect 'the people', notably the controversial fence along Hungary's southern border with Serbia which was constructed to block the migrants' transit route.

Although the referendum campaign only geared up in summer 2016, the ground was carefully prepared by an anti-immigration campaign starting a year before, featuring warnings ostensibly addressed to 'migrants' on billboards along busy roads, such as 'If you come to Hungary, you cannot take the Hungarians' jobs away'. Fidesz also launched a so-called National consultation on immigration and terrorism. A questionnaire sent to every Hungarian household (approximately 8 million copies in total) ostensibly sought to map the public's views on immigration, terrorism and unemployment in order to inform government policy, but did so in a way that suggested a link among these phenomena. For instance, questions included: 'Do you agree with the government that instead of allocating funds to immigration we should support Hungarian families and those children yet to be born?'; Or 'there are people who believe that welfare immigrants put Hungarian people's jobs and livelihoods at risk. Do you agree with these views?' Reportedly over a million people returned the questionnaire.

The next phase in the party's communication strategy moved to assigning blame to the EU for the situation, with the centre-piece slogan 'Let's send a message to Brussels they can understand'. This was combined with a publicly funded 'governmental information campaign' to communicate some salient points about migration, designed to come across as objective fact. Giant billboards and a direct mail campaign posed questions such as 'Did you know? The Paris attacks were committed by immigrants'; or 'Did you know? Brussels wants to settle a whole city's worth of illegal immigrants in Hungary'. In September, over 4 million copies of booklets were sent to Hungarians at home and abroad to 'explain' the issues at stake, advising voters 'Let's send a message to Brussels so they can understand too! We must stop Brussels!' (Halmai 2016). Reportedly, 'ministry officials were making phone calls on behalf of Fidesz during working hours to voters in rural districts, encouraging them to vote "No"' (Halmai 2016). Finally, in the run-up to the referendum, Viktor Orbán made it clear that the vote was to be a show of strength, of national unity backing the government's position. However, polls in the final days before the referendum indicated that the 50% threshold required for a valid result might not be reached, causing Orbán and his colleagues to back-pedal and try to downplay the importance of high participation.

To what extent did the parliamentary opposition shape the public discourse? The answer is, at least concerning the moderate political forces in parliament, less than they could have done had they been able to make up their minds about a common strategy early on. Fidesz's arguably most effective competitor was Jobbik, which was however neutralised on this issue. The party called for a

'No' in the referendum (the desired answer from the Fidesz perspective), and pointed to the fact that it was in fact Jobbik that first called for a referendum, implying that Fidesz simply appropriated what was originally 'their' issue, but only for show (Jobbik 2016). This message was not strong enough to allow the party to carve out a distinctive position—which was probably one of the main attractions of the question from the Fidesz strategists' perspective. The several parties that made up the fragmented centre-left opposition appeared confused, confusing and divided on the issue. After some hesitation, they settled on boycotting the referendum in recognition of the fact that suppressing turnout was the only plausible way to defeat the government, in that at least the result would not be valid. Only one party, the Liberals, the tiny rump of the defunct Alliance of Free Democrats with insignificant electoral support called for a 'Yes' and tried to explain to the voters that a positive vote would confirm European values.

The centre-left's advice to abstain was substantiated with the argument that, first, the referendum was not necessary, since there was no sinister EU migration ploy to combat, and second, that the vote was not about the resettlement quota or even about migration but 'really' about Hungary's continued EU membership. Former Socialist prime minister Gyurcsány's campaign posters consequently told people to 'Stay home – stay in Europe'. This was based on sound strategic thinking: while anti-immigration sentiments were strong in society, Hungarian voters were, at least in comparison with many other EU countries, relatively pro-EU. In 2016, 62% of respondents thought that their country benefitted from EU membership (European Parliament 2016: 19). Thus, managing to shift the debate from the migration issue to the EU issue was certainly suitable for dampening participation in a referendum that the government explicitly framed as a weapon against 'Brussels'.

The main weakness of the Socialists' and other centre-left opposition parties' campaign was that they had relatively little street-or media-presence, for the simple reason that they could not compete with the massive financial and media resources that the government campaign drew on: Fidesz reportedly spent 5 billion of the tax-payers' Forints (approximately €48.6 million) on the campaign, considerably more than the costs of the Brexit campaign (Halmai 2016). In fact, the most visible counter-campaign came from a group of activists who defined themselves as a 'satirical party' and went by the name of Two-Tailed Dog Party (TTDP). The party became known in the previous election campaign where it ridiculed Orbán's populism, promoting 'electoral pledges' such as the classic 'Long life, free beer, down with taxes'. The TTDP's response to the government's summer 2015 anti-immigration campaign consisted of billboards addressed to the refugees making their way through Hungary, featuring slogans such as 'Sorry about our prime minister' or 'Feel free to come to Hungary, we already work in England' in giant letters.

The TTDP anti-referendum anti-campaign was crowd-funded, and consisted almost entirely of (a few) large commercial billboards and, in bigger cities, masses of small posters on photocopied A4 sheets, making fun of the government slogans in the same irreverent tone. Mirroring the government's 'Did you know' (dis-)information campaign, TTDP posed questions such as 'Did you know? The average Hungarian encounters more UFOs than migrants'; 'Did you know? There is a war in Syria'; or 'Did you know? Since the beginning of the migration crisis, over 300 people took the train in Felcsút [Orbán's hometown]'? The party's advice to voters was to register their disapproval by spoiling their ballot, captured in 'Ask a stupid question, get a stupid answer'.

31.8   The Result

In the end, the 'No' votes were in the overwhelming majority (98%), but, with only 41% valid votes, turnout was well below the required 50%. Turnout was even lower in Budapest, 35% valid votes against 65% spoiled ballots and abstentions, indicating that in the capital proportionally more voters heeded the moderate opposition parties' advice and boycotted the referendum. This corresponds to a well-known urban-rural divide in Hungarian politics: the centre-left tends to receive a higher share of support in Budapest than in the countryside. In this case too, in the Western counties where the government party traditionally enjoyed strong support turnout approached the 50% benchmark. Given how small TTDP was, their impact on the outcome was also remarkable: in Budapest almost 12% and nationally over 6% spoiled their ballot, sending a message not so much to Brussels as the prime minister's office.[7] Polls in the wake of the referendum indicated that participation was strongly structured by partisanship: those identifying themselves as 'left-wing' (i.e. critical of the government) were most likely to abstain but if they turned out (very few did) they mostly also voted 'No' (Századvég 2015).

The low turnout was hailed by the opposition as a vindication of their messages and campaign tactics, and also interpreted as a blow to the government and Orbán personally in much of the international press. In his characteristically confident style, Viktor Orbán however seemed to take no notice. His public statements in the wake of the referendum neglected to mention the participation rate altogether and instead focused on the overwhelming majority of voters supporting his government's position, welcoming the result as a much-needed boost to continue to fight 'Brussels'. Moreover, he announced that his government intended to 'implement the will of the people' by amending the Foundational Law with new provisions reflecting the 'unity' of voters' opinions' (Index 2016a).

Indeed, the vote was almost unanimous: 3,362,224 (98.36%) 'No' votes against just 56,163 (1.64%) 'Yes' in a country of over 8 million voters (National Election Bureau 2018), which requires an explanation. One evident reason was clearly the wording of the question (see generally Rocher and

---

[7]Of course it is difficult to say whether voters acted on the TTDP advice, but the proportion of spoiled ballots in the referendum far exceeded that of earlier referendums.

Lecours 2018). Anyone objecting to any of the major claims in the question (i.e. that the EU could 'prescribe' something; that the 'prescription' would be without parliament's consent; that the prescribed action would 'mandatory'; that the arriving non-Hungarians would be 'settled') would have been in no position to answer anything but 'No' (unless deciding to abstain), even if he or she agreed with the general principle of burden-sharing among EU countries with respect to the resolution of the refugee crisis. The question was also misleading in some respects, e.g. by implying that the 'migrants' would be sent to Hungary to be 'settled' permanently. This kind of (mis-)interpretation was common in the pro-government media, which tended to refer to the vote as the 'referendum against forced resettlement' rather than use the more neutral 'migrant quota referendum'.

The referendum also followed a massive, one-sided and at times misleading 'public information' campaign. If genuinely intended to facilitate an informed vote, a more balanced and comprehensive coverage of issues would have included, for instance potential positive impacts associated with migration and/or messages to invoke compassion with legitimate asylum-seekers fleeing war or persecution. Instead, as a report from the Friedrich Ebert Stiftung and think tank Eötvös Károly Institute (2016: 3) summed up, the 'information campaign' the government ran 'conflated immigration and terrorism; portrayed asylum-seekers as criminals and consistently referred to them as illegal immigrants; and falsely juxtaposed the interests of the EU with the national interest'.

Moreover, the government's campaign used public resources that were not available to the opponents' side. The 'Did you know?' billboards were all displayed, and paid for, as 'government information'. According to the government, almost 7 billion forints were spent on 'information campaigns and political advertising' (Index 2016b), while no public funding was allocated to the opponents. One particularly important channel for the government's position to reach the voters was through the public service television and radio. The former showed news clips and 'public interest advertisements' in the breaks of the then ongoing football championship and Olympic Games, which were keenly followed everywhere in the country (Friedrich Ebert Stiftung—EKINT 2016: 13). Combined with Fidesz's ever tighter hold over the Hungarian media market (see e.g. *Financial Times* 2016), the average voter had little exposure to an open debate that would have enabled him or her to gain a more nuanced understanding of the complex issues at stake. In any case, no significant political actor risked being seen as an open proponent of immigration given the deep unpopularity of such a position with the voters. Instead, the moderate opposition parties uniformly objected to holding a referendum on the government's question. Only after failing to stop it through the available legal channels did they resort to a boycott.

31.9   Conclusion: Consequences
for Hungary and the EU

After what some claim had been the most expensive campaign in Hungarian political history to that date, the 41% valid 'No' vote was clearly a disappointment for Orbán, regardless of the Fidesz spin doctors' and the prime minister's insistence that only the large majority of the 'No' votes mattered. It was one of the very rare occasions since Fidesz's landslide victory in 2010 that Orbán's will did not carry the day: despite the massive propaganda effort, the majority of Hungarians decided not to play along.

Nonetheless, Fidesz leaders had little reason to worry. The party continued to lead the polls by a large margin. The approximately 3.4 million 'No' voters in the referendum numbered some 300,000 more than those who supported Hungary's EU membership in the 2003 referendum, and about a million more than those who supported the Fidesz list in the 2014 elections, suggesting that the government succeeded in reaching people beyond its core base. Consequently, from the Fidesz perspective, the referendum largely achieved its partisan goals. Given, furthermore, the electoral system tailored to the party's needs, the dominance of Fidesz-friendly media outlets and the fragmented mainstream opposition, it was not surprising that Hungary's 2018 elections subsequently returned Fidesz and Viktor Orbán to office for a third consecutive term.

The migrant quota referendum thus did not bring significant changes to the party-political landscape in Hungary. It did, however, have more lasting consequences for attitudes among Hungarian citizens. According to a comparative study, people in Hungary feared migration more than in almost any other EU country in terms of an employment threat, a welfare threat and a cultural threat in 2015 (Messing and Sagvari 2018). Time-series analysis demonstrated that there was a strong connection between high levels of rejection of migration and the government's communication on the issue (Tárki 2016: 3). In spring 2016, amidst the governmental 'information campaign', large majorities agreed with statements such as 'refugees will increase the likelihood of terrorism' (76%) or 'refugees are a burden on our country because they take our jobs and social benefits' (82%) (Pew Global 2016). Irrational as these attitudes may seem in a country which is not a destination for non-European migrants, they were unlikely to fade away, particularly as the Fidesz government used the spectre of mass immigration orchestrated by hostile foreign actors (in government propaganda, chiefly George Soros) as one of its principal campaign messages in the 2018 elections.

The consequences for the EU were no less far reaching, although not primarily in terms of undermining the relocation scheme, which in any case had been subject to severe criticism. Rather, an arguably far more damaging consequence is that a precedent was set: the government of a Member State called a referendum in open defiance to, and with the express intention of undermining the authority of, the Union and its institutions. The EU's legal and political order is dependent on the Member States observing a core norm, the principle of sincere cooperation (embodied in Article 4 TEU). The migration quota referendum indeed sent a message to Brussels, though not necessarily the one that voters associated with it: a strong signal from the Hungarian government that rather than seeking common solutions in cooperation with other EU countries and/or accepting binding decisions arrived at in negotiations in the appropriate EU forums, it was willing, and would perhaps even prefer, to go it alone. In this reading, the referendum thus killed several birds with one stone: it allowed Fidesz to capture electoral ground in domestic politics, asserted Orbán's authority on the European scene and taunted 'Brussels' to react against 'the will of the people'. As in several instances in the past, Orbán's government 'got away with it' (Batory 2016a). It is only a question of time that other EU governments follow suit, reinforcing already strong centrifugal tendencies in the wake of Brexit.

As to scholarship on direct democracy, the quota referendum holds a number of lessons. First, it confirms that not even very popular governing parties campaigning on widely supported issues are fully able to anticipate or 'induce' the desired result. In the Hungarian case, the governmental propaganda machine managed to deliver an overwhelming rejection of 'Brussels' plan', but not high rates of participation convincingly demonstrating that 'the people' stood united behind the government. High rates of abstention and deliberately spoiled ballots in fact showed that 'the nation' is not quite the monolithic entity populists the world over would like to claim. Second, this referendum indicates that shifting the blame for a negatively perceived phenomenon (in this case, fear of non-European mass immigration) to the EU 'sells' even in the 'new' member states—although those staying at home presumably did so primarily because they disagreed with the government's tirades against 'Brussels' rather than because they would welcome the arrival of high numbers of 'migrants' to live in their country. It is also evident that, mobilising public sentiment against the EU is a viable party strategy while remaining formally committed to EU membership. Finally, like the Brexit referendum, the migration relocation quota vote also serves as a cautionary tale: rather than decisively settling an issue and thereby removing it from the political agenda, referendums and particularly the campaigns preceding them may reinforce prejudices, spread misinformation and set the tone and quality of the debate for years or decades to come.

References

Ágh, A. (2016). The Decline of Democracy in East-Central Europe. *Problems of Post-Communism, 63*(5–6), 277–287.

Bakó, B. (2013). How Much About Us Without Us: Direct Democracy in Hungary, Switzerland and Austria (in Hungarian). *Justum Aequum Salutare, IX*(3), 167–185.

Bánkuti, M., Halmai, G., & Scheppele, K. L. (2012). Disabling the Constitution. *Journal of Democracy, 23*(3), 138–146.

Batory, A. (2008). *The Politics of EU Accession: Ideology, Party Strategy and the European Question in Hungary*. Manchester: Manchester University Press.

Batory, A. (2016a). Defying the Commission: Creative Compliance and the Respect for the Rule of Law in the EU. *Public Administration, 94*, 685–699.

Batory, A. (2016b). Populists in Government? Hungary's "System of National Cooperation". *Democratization, 23*(2), 283–303.

Batory, A. (2017). EU Referendums in the "New" Member States: Politicization After a Decade of Support. In B. Leruth, N. Startin, & S. Usherwood (Eds.), *The Routledge Handbook of Euroscepticism* (pp. 256–267). Abingdon: Routledge.

Boda, Z., & Patkós, V. (2018). Driven by Politics: Agenda Setting and Policy-Making in Hungary 2010–2014. *Policy Studies, 39*(4), 402–421.

Canovan, M. (1999). Trust the People! Populism and the Two Faces of Democracy. *Political Studies, 47*, 2–16.

Closa, C., Kochenov, D., & Weiler, J. H. H. (2014). *Reinforcing Rule of Law Oversight in the European Union* (EUI Working Papers, RSCAS 2014/25). Florence: European University Institute.

Council of the European Union. (2015). *Council Decision (EU) 2015/1601 of 22 September 2015 Establishing Provisional Measures in the Area of International Protection for the Benefit of Italy and Greece*. Available at https://eur-lex.europa.eu/legal-content/EN/TXT/PDF/?uri=CELEX:32015D1601&from=EN.

Council of Europe, Venice Commission (European Commission for Democracy Through Law). (2011). *Opinion on the new Constitution of Hungary* (Opinion No 621/2011). Available at http://www.venice.coe.int/webforms/documents/default.aspx?pdffile=CDL-AD(2011)016-e. Last accessed on 13 March 2019.

Enyedi, Zs. (2009). The Logic of Voters' Choice in Light of the Online Research. In Zs. Enyedi (Ed.), *The Dilemmas of the Popular Will* (pp. 17–36). Budapest: DKMKA and Századvég (in Hungarian).

Enyedi, Z. (2016). Paternalist Populism and Illiberal Elitism in Central Europe. *Journal of Political Ideologies, 21*(1), 9–25.

European Parliament. (2016). *Parlemeter 2016: Analytical Overview. Special Eurobarometer of the European Parliament*. Available at http://www.europarl.europa.eu/pdf/eurobarometre/2016/parlemetre/eb86_1_parlemeter_synthesis_en.pdf. Last accessed on 11 March 2019.

Financial Times. (2016, August 16). Orbán Tightens Grip on Hungarian Media. Available at https://www.ft.com/content/50488256-60af-11e6-ae3f-77b aadeb1c93. Last accessed on 13 March 2019.

Fowler, B. (2004). Hungary: Unpicking the Permissive Consensus. *West European Politics, 27*(4), 624–651.

Franklin, M., Marsh, M., & Wlezien, C. (1994). Attitudes Toward Europe and Referendum Votes: A Response to Siune and Svensson. *Electoral Studies, 13*(2), 117–121.

Franklin, M., van der Eijk, C., & Marsh, M. (1995). Referendum Outcomes and Trust in Government: Public Support for Europe in the Wake of Maastricht. *West European Politics, 18*(3), 333–354.

Friedrich Ebert Stiftung and Eötvös Károly Institute. (2016). *Sending a Message to Hungary* (in Hungarian). Available at http://library.fes.de/pdf-files/bueros/bud apest/13067.pdf. Last accessed on 12 March 2018.

Garry, J. (2014). Emotions and Voting in EU Referendums. *European Union Politics, 15*(2), 235–254.

Garry, J., Marsh, M., & Sinnott, R. (2005). "Second-Order" Versus "Issue-Voting" Effects in EU Referendums: Evidence from the Irish Nice Treaty Referendums. *European Union Politics, 6,* 201–221.

Glencross, A., & Trechsel, A. (2011). First or Second Order Referendums? Understanding the Votes on the EU Constitutional Treaty in Four EU Member States. *West European Politics, 34*(4), 755–772.

Groenendijk, K., & Nagy, B. (2015, December 16, Wednesday). Hungary's Appeal Against Relocation to the CJEU: Upfront Attack or Rear Guard Battle? *EU Migration Law Blog.* Available at http://eumigrationlawblog.eu/hungarys-appeal-against-relocation-to-the-cjeu-upfront-attack-or-rear-guard-battle/. Last accessed on 11 March 2019.

Halmai, G. (2016, October 4). The Invalid Anti-migrant Referendum in Hungary. *VerfBlog.* Available at https://verfassungsblog.de/hungarys-anti-european-immigration-laws. Last accessed on 11 March 2019.

Hobolt, S. B. (2005). When Europe Matters: The Impact of Political Information on Voting Behaviour in EU Referendums. *Journal of Elections, Public Opinion and Parties, 15*(1), 85–109.

Hobolt, S. B. (2006). Direct Democracy and European Integration. *Journal of European Public Policy, 13*(1), 153–166.

Hobolt, S. B., & Brouard, S. (2011). Contesting the European Union? Why the Dutch and the French Rejected the European Constitution. *Political Research Quarterly, 64*(2), 309–322.

Hooghe, L., & Marks, G. (2009). A Postfunctionalist Theory of European Integration: From Permissive Consensus to Constraining Dissensus. *British Journal of Political Science, 39*(1), 1–23.

Hug, S., & Tsebelis, G. (2002). Veto Players and Referendums Around the World. *Journal of Theoretical Politics, 14*(4), 465–515.

Hungarian Helsinki Committee. (2015). *Hungary's Government Has Taken Control of the Constitutional Court.* Available at https://www.helsinki.hu/en/hungarys-government-has-taken-control-of-the-constitutional-court/. Last accessed on 11 March 2019.

Index.hu. (2016a). *Orbán Claims New Unity Created on Sunday.* Available at https://index.hu/belfold/2016/10/04/Orbán_viktor_kosa_lajos_fidesz_nepszavazas_sajtotajekoztato/. Last accessed on 11 March 2019.

Index.hu. (2016b). *Government Discloses Costs of Quota Campaign.* Available at https://index.hu/belfold/2016/10/04/elarulta_vegre_a_kormany_mennyibe_kerult_a_kvotakampany/. Last accessed on 11 March 2019.

Jobbik. (2016). *National Campaign Against the Settlement Quota* (in Hungarian). Available at https://www.jobbik.hu/hireink/orszagos-kampany-betelepitesi-kvota-ellen. Last accessed on 11 March 2019.

László, R. (2016). *The Institution of Referendum in Illiberal Hungary.* Budapest: Political Capital and Friedrich Ebert Stiftung (in Hungarian). Available at http://www.valasztasirendszer.hu/wp-content/uploads/PC_FES_Nepszavazas_Tanulmany_160629.pdf. Last accessed on 11 March 2019.

Lindberg, L. N., & Scheingold, S. A. (1970). *Europe's Would-Be Polity: Patterns of Change in the European Community.* Englewood Cliffs: Prentice-Hall.

Magyar Nemzet. (2016). Orbán: There Will Be a Referendum on the Settlement Quota (in Hungarian). Available at https://mno.hu/belfold/Orbán-nepszavazas-lesz-a-betelepitesi-kvotarol-1330246. Last accessed on 11 March 2019.

Messing, V., & Sagvari, B. (2018). *Looking Behind the Culture of Fear: A Cross-National Analysis of Attitudes Towards Migration*. *Fridrich Ebert Stiftung—European Social Survey*. Available at http://library.fes.de/pdf-files/bueros/budapest/14181-20180815.pdf. Last accessed on 11 March 2019.

Morel, L., & Qvortrup, M. (Eds.). (2018). *The Routledge Handbook to Referendums and Direct Democracy*. London: Routledge.

Mudde, C. (2016, November–December). Europe's Populist Surge: A Long Time in the Making. *Foreign Affairs*, 25–30.

National Election Bureau. (2017, December 18). *Statistics on Submitted and Decided Referendum Proposals* (in Hungarian). Available at http://www.valasztas.hu/doc uments/20182/305738/Statisztik%C3%A1k+az+elb%C3%ADr%C3%A1lt+n%C3% A9pszavaz%C3%A1si+kezdem%C3%A9nyez%C3%A9sekr%C5%91l.pdf/a0655454-ecd7-412f-ab08-8a23dc419f5e. Last accessed on 11 March 2019.

National Election Bureau. (2018). *Referendum, 2 October 2016 [Results]* (in Hungarian). Available at http://www.valasztas.hu/20. Last accessed on 11 March 2019.

Oppermann, K. (2017). Derailing the Process of European Integration? EU Referendums and the Politics of Euroscepticism. In B. Leruth, N. Startin, & S. Usherwood (Eds.), *The Routledge Handbook of Euroscepticism* (pp. 243–255). New York: Routledge.

Orbán, V. (2016). *Viktor Orbán's Speech Before the Agenda [in Parliament]* (in Hungarian). Available at http://www.kormany.hu/hu/a-miniszterelnok/beszedek-publikaciok-interjuk/Orbán-viktor-napirend-elotti-felszolalasa-20160912.   Last accessed on 11 March 2019.

Pew Global. (2016). *Many Europeans Concerned with Security, Economic Repercussions of Refugee Crisis*. Available at http://www.pewglobal.org/2016/07/11/europe ans-fear-wave-of-refugees-will-mean-more-terrorism-fewer-jobs/lede-chart-1/. Last accessed on 11 March 2019.

Pirro, A., Taggart, P., & van Kessel, S. (2018). The Populist Politics of Euroscepticism in Times of Crisis: Comparative Conclusions. *Politics, 38*(3), 378–390.

Portfolio.hu. (2016). Parties' Popularity According to Three Polling Institutes (in Hungarian). Available at https://www.portfolio.hu/gazdasag/igy-all-a-partok-nep szerusege-nem-akarmi-tortent-aprilisban.231040.html. Last accessed on 11 March 2019.

Qvortrup, M. (2018). Two Hundred Years of Referendums. In M. Qvortrup (Eds.), *Referendums Around the World*. Basingstoke: Palgrave Macmillan.

Reif, K., & Schmitt, H. (1980). Nine Second Order National Elections: A Conceptual Framework for the Analysis of European Election Results. *European Journal of Political Research, 8*(1), 3–44.

Renwick, A. (2014). Don't Trust Your Poll Lead: How Public Opinion Changes During Referendum Campaigns. In P. Cowley & R. Ford (Eds.), *Sex, Lies and the Ballot Box: 50 Things You Need to Know About British Elections* (pp. 79–84). London: Biteback.

Rocher, F., & Lecours, A. (2018). The Correct Expression of Popular Will: Does the Wording of a Referendum Question Matter? In L. Morel & M. Qvortrup (Eds.), *The Routledge Handbook to Referendums and Direct Democracy* (pp. 227–246). London: Routledge.

Schneider, G., & Weitsman, P. (1996). The Punishment Trap: Integration Referendums as Popularity Contests. *Comparative Political Studies, 28*(4), 582–607.

Sedelmeier, U. (2014). Anchoring Democracy from Above? The European Union and Democratic Backsliding in Hungary and Romania After Accession. *Journal of Common Market Studies, 52*(1), 105–120.

Sik, E., & Szeitl, B. (2016). Some Characteristics of the European Public Opinion on Migrants and Asylum-Seekers. In B. Simonovits & A. Bernat (Eds.), *The Social Aspects of the 2015 Migration Crisis in Hungary.* Budapest: Tárki Social Research Institute.

Simonovits, B. (2016). Migration-Related Fear and Scapegoating: Comparative Approach in the Visegrad Countries. In B. Simonovits & A. Bernat (Eds.), *The Social Aspects of the 2015 Migration Crisis in Hungary.* Budapest: Tárki Social Research Institute.

Smith, J. (2016). David Cameron's EU Renegotiation and Referendum Pledge: A Case of déjà vu? *British Politics, 11*(3), 324–346.

Svensson, P. (2002). Five Danish Referendums on the European Community and the European Union: A Critical Assessment of the Franklin Thesis. *European Journal of Political Research, 41*(6), 733–750.

Szabó, S. (2017). Contributions to the Regulation of the Referendum After 2013 (in Hungarian). *Metszetek* (1), 5–25.

Századvég. (2015). *The Majority Believes It's Brussels' Turn Now: The Afterlife of the Referendum* (in Hungarian). Available at https://Századvég.hu/hu/kutatasok/az-alapitvany-kutatasai/piackutatas-kozvelemeny-kutatas/a-tobbseg-szerint-most-bru sszelen-a-sor-a-nepszavazas-utoelete. Last accessed on 11 March 2019.

Szczerbiak, A., & Taggart, P. (2004a). The Politics of European Referendum Outcomes and Turnout: Two Models. *West European Politics, 27*(4), 557–583.

Szczerbiak, A., & Taggart, P. (2004b). Conclusion: Towards a Model of (European) Referendums. *West European Politics, 27*(4), 749–777.

Taggart, P., & Szczerbiak, A. (Eds.). (2008). *The Comparative Party Politics of Euroscepticism.* Oxford: Oxford University Press.

Taggart, P., & Szczerbiak, A. (2018). Putting Brexit into Perspective: The Effect of the Eurozone and Migration Crises and Brexit on Euroscepticism in European States. *Journal of European Public Policy, 25*(8), 1194–1214.

Tárki Social Research. (2016). *Social Responses to the Migration Crisis. Rejection and Solidarity in Hungary in 2015.* Available at http://old.Tárki.hu/hu/news/2016/kitekint/20160330_pressrelease.pdf. Last accessed on 11 March 2019.

Uleri, P. V. (1996). Introduction. In P. V. Uleri & M. Gallagher (Eds.), *The Referendum Experience in Europe.* Basingstoke: Macmillan.

CHAPTER 32

The Dutch Referendum on the EU-Ukraine Association Agreement

Joost van den Akker

32.1 INTRODUCTION

In April 2016 an EU-related referendum took place in The Netherlands on the ratification bill on the Association Agreement of 2014 between Ukraine, the EU and its Member States. This advisory popular veto was initiated by means of 400,000 signatures, based on the 2015 Advisory Referendum Act (ARA) which just had entered into force. 61% of the voters rejected the agreement, with a turnout of 32.3%. This rendered a valid result, as the 30% turnout threshold was just met. At the same time, the outcome was not binding, although most parties had indicated that the result should be respected in some way. This chapter explores this first nationwide advisory referendum in The Netherlands. The case study explores the earlier experience of referendums in The Netherlands. It briefly outlines the legal framework of referendums and rules in place at the time of the vote. The main part is dedicated to the analysis of the 'Ukraine referendum' and its aftermath. First, it analyses the ways in which citizens and politicians triggered the vote. Second, it reflects on the political actors, citizens, the media and the dominant issues that played a role during the campaign. Third, it analyses to what extent issue voting or second-order considerations were the predominant explanations of the vote. The aftermath of the vote is discussed both from the domestic and the European perspective. At the domestic level a renewed debate on the referendum instrument emerged, while in Brussels the European leaders had to deal with the delay of the ratification of the Association Agreement and the

J. van den Akker (✉)
University of Twente, Enschede, The Netherlands

interpretation of the Dutch referendum result. In the meantime, the Dutch parliament repealed the Advisory Referendum Act, leaving the holding of a referendum with a vacuum at the national level, as discussed in the concluding remarks.

32.2   Referendum Experience in The Netherlands

Until the early 2000s, Dutch law did not provide for (or prohibit) nation-wide referendums, whether binding or consultative. The Dutch Constitution stipulates that the bicameral States-General and government are responsible for law-making, i.e. not the citizens themselves.[1] As such, binding referendums would be unconstitutional. Therefore, consultative referendums are to be regulated ad hoc.

32.2.1   1800: Authoritarian Plebiscites Under French Rule

However, two centuries ago, The Netherlands did experience some author-itarian forms of referendums. The first introduction of referendums in The Netherlands was inspired by the developments of the French Revolution. During the Napoleonic periods, referendums of imperfect democratic decision-making took place, characterised by authoritarian mobilisation and fraud. It provided popular legitimacy to strengthen dictatorship. In the Napoleonic era the *French* authorities held some controlled plebiscites inspired by the treatises of Rousseau (Bogdanor 1994: 48). In 1797, 1798, 1801 and 1805, other authoritarian referendums were held in the Batavian Republic under French rule to legitimise its new draft constitutions.

32.2.2   1900s: Nationwide Referendums Regularly Discussed but Never Held

Throughout the twentieth century, several so-called state committees, commissioned by the Dutch government, discussed the introduction of the referendum. In 1920, the *state committee Ruys de Beerenbrouck* recommended holding a referendum on bills concerning constitutional amendments, and on the future of the Dutch monarchy in the case of the absence of an heir to the throne. However, these suggestions did not obtain serious consideration in the final bills to change the Dutch constitution, which in any case did not receive the required parliamentary majority either (Hendriks et al. 2017: 61–64). The referendum did not obtain serious attention until the 1960s.

The 1968 revolts in Western Europe sought more participatory individu-alism, independent from a political party's cue or from the virtue of social class

---

[1]Dutch Constitution, Art. 81: 'Acts of Parliament shall be enacted jointly by the Government and the States General.'

or religion. The referendum functioned as an alternative participatory mechanism, when citizens became dissatisfied about the perceived malfunctioning of the political system and the way they were represented (Qvortrup 2018: 22). Hence, the (worldwide) use of referendums has increased since the 1960s.

In The Netherlands, these movements resulted into the foundation of the *state committee Cals/Donner*. A majority of the committee advised against the introduction of the referendum and popular initiative. However, it recommended that if the government did introduce the referendum, a majority of the voters rejecting a bill passed by parliament should comprise at least 30% of the electorate. A couple of years later the *state committee Biesheuvel* suggested introducing an optional binding referendum at national and regional level. It proposed holding a binding popular veto in cases where citizens collected 300,000 signatures. Like the Cals/Donner committee, it argued that the outcome of a popular veto should only be valid if a majority rejecting the bill comprised at least 30% of the electorate. However, the committee was divided on the introduction of a plebiscite at national level. Although the government did not explicitly dismiss the plebiscite, neither form of referendum could count on sufficient parliamentary support, particularly from the incumbent conservative-liberal (CDA-VVD) cabinet of Prime Minister Ruud Lubbers.

Despite these earlier attempts, and indeed another study by the *state committee De Koning* suggesting a binding popular veto, it was not until the late 1990s that both bills introducing nationwide binding and consultative referendums received serious attention. The social-liberal coalition of Labour (PvdA), Liberals (VVD) and Democrats (D66) (1994–2002) agreed to introduce a binding ('corrective') referendum. A major difference compared to the suggestions made by several committees in the preceding decades was that the number of citizens calling a referendum was set at 600,000 (Hendriks et al. 2017: 64–69). A bill providing for the necessary constitutional amendment had almost passed both houses of parliament, but the final vote in the Dutch Senate in May 1999 failed to meet the required two-thirds majority by a single vote. Somewhat unexpected, VVD Senator (and former party leader) Hans Wiegel dissented from his party's stance. As a consequence, D66 announced it would leave the government (Elzinga 2005: 98).

Renegotiations after the fall of the government led to the introduction of a Temporary Referendum Act (valid between 2002 and 2005), together with another bill providing for binding referendums by constitutional amendment. The latter was rejected (at second reading) in 2004 by the Second Chamber (*Tweede Kamer*), as the first Balkenende cabinet did not endorse it (Interior Ministry 2002). The Temporary Referendum Act provided for advisory referendums to be called by 600,000 citizens within six weeks and enabled referendums to be held at the local and regional level. Because of the relatively strict requirements (initiators had to submit their signature at their municipality), a referendum was never held. However, at the local (and regional) level, many municipalities and provinces enacted regulations to provide for advisory and consultative referendums (i.e. popular initiatives, popular vetoes and plebiscites initiated by the municipal council). In 2015, about one third of the almost 400 Dutch municipalities, and five of the twelve provinces, provided for a referendum regulation. Between 1906 and 2014, 193 local referendums were organised, in many instances on the amalgamation of municipalities. However, by 2019, no referendums had been held at the provincial level (Van der Krieken 2015: 31–40).

32.2.2.1   2000s: Referendums on the Constitutional Treaty, Ukraine and the Intelligence Services

These developments in the early 2000s, plus the fact that many EU-related referendums took place or were announced across Europe in that period,[2] shaped a broad opinion in parliament that in the case of a European Constitution, the people ought to be directly involved. The Dutch CDA-VVD-D66 government led by Prime Minister Balkenende, however, did not support this—as had become clear through its decision not to endorse the introduction of a binding referendum. As the Dutch Constitution does not explicitly provide for non-binding referendums, a legal base for a consultative referendum on the Constitutional Treaty had to be created by law first. Moreover, the usage of such a referendum required special justification. The Council of State (*Raad van State*) provided in its legal advice that the European Constitution had to contain constitutional elements to justify such a referendum, which ought to be the case (Council of State 2003). The general rule of Art. 91 of the Dutch Constitution that international treaties are to be ratified by parliament eventually remained unchanged (Massüger and Kuoni 2011: 150).

After a first proposal for a consultative referendum on the eventual outcome of the Convention on the Future of Europe by opposition Labour MP (and member of the Convention) Frans Timmermans had failed in 2002, a new bill for an 'Act on the consultative referendum on the European Constitution' proposed by Green, Labour and Liberal-Democratic MPs (Karimi, Dubbelboer and Van der Ham) was finally adopted.[3] Their tripartite proposal was not guaranteed to secure a parliamentary majority in the Senate. The liberal VVD held the key and somewhat surprisingly[4] lent decisive support to the referendum proposal in both the Second and First Chambers (see Table 32.1). Only the confessional parties CDA, CU and SGP voted against the initiative, because they saw it against the spirit of the Dutch Constitution (Aarts and Van der Kolk 2005: 15). The decision-making in the Dutch parliament lasted until February 2005—four months before the referendum was scheduled. The

---

[2]In Denmark and Sweden on the introduction of the Euro, in Ireland on the Nice Treaty and in ten Central and Eastern European candidate member states.

[3]*Wet raadplegend referendum Europese Grondwet van 27 januari 2005. Staatsblad 44/2005.*

[4]Traditionally, the VVD has been against referendums. Its new 'Liberal Manifesto' group leader, and former foreign minister, Jozias van Aartsen endorsed the use of referendums more frequently supplementary to representative democracy.

Table 32.1 Nationwide referendums in The Netherlands (%)

Year	Subject	Yes	No	Turnout
2005	Constitutional Treaty	38.2	61.8	63.0
2016	EU-Ukraine Association Agreement	38.5	61.5	32.3
2018	Act on Intelligence and Security Services	48.5	51.5	51.5

Referendum law itself was principally concerned with the establishment of an independent Referendum Commission. Although this Commission preferred a relatively late date of 29 June 2005, under pressure from the Interior Ministry the referendum was set for 1 June, three days after the scheduled vote on the Constitutional Treaty in France. Compared to referendums on the CT in other Member States, the Commission formulated a somewhat complex question: 'Are you in favour of or against approval by the Netherlands of the Treaty establishing a Constitution for Europe?' (Lucardie and Voerman 2006: 1201).

The establishment of the institutional framework for the referendum was very much a matter of 'learning by doing'. From September 2004 to January 2005, polls had indicated that about 60% of the Dutch were in favour of the Constitutional Treaty. Nevertheless, on 1 June 61.5% of the voters rejected the treaty, following the French who had done the same three days before. This double rejection meant the total failure of the ratification process of the Constitutional Treaty (see also Chapter 28 by Sternberg).

The high turnout contributed to renewed efforts by parliamentarians to settle the referendum instrument in The Netherlands permanently. After the expiration of the Temporary Referendum Act, MPs Niesco Dubbelboer (PvdA), Wijnand Duyvendak (GreenLeft) and Boris van der Ham (D66) submitted two other bills: the Advisory Referendum Bill which was eventually revised and adopted in 2015 (see below), and the Corrective Referendum Bill, which was eventually rejected by the Second Chamber at second reading in 2017, as it did not meet the required two-thirds majority.

It took more than ten years until another nationwide referendum was held: on the Ratification Act on the EU-Ukraine Association Agreement (2014) in 2016. It was followed in 2018 by one on the Act on the Intelligence and Security Services (2017). Both referendums were triggered by more than 300,000 citizens' signatures based on the new Advisory Referendum Act which had entered into force in 2015. Like the 2005 vote on the Constitutional Treaty, the latter two referendums resulted in a loss for the government.

32.3   THE 2015 ADVISORY REFERENDUM ACT

The legal framework enabling the 2016 referendum was the Advisory Referendum Act (2015). Although an original bill[5] was initiated in 2005, it took parliament a decade to enact this successor of the Temporary Referendum Act, which had expired in 2005. The original initiating MPs had all retired from parliament, so it was up to their successors Manon Fokke (PvdA), Gerard Schouw (D66) and Linda Voortman (GreenLeft) to finalise the decision-making process.

An unusual amendment was enforced by the Senate (i.e. the First Chamber).[6] Labour Senator Koole, who was appointed as member of the Referendum Commission after his retirement from the Senate following its 2015 election, demanded a turnout threshold of 30% be included. As the Labour Party's support was indispensable for the adoption of the bill, the initiating MPs submitted a small second bill, including the requested threshold. Although the Council of State concluded in its advice on this bill that the introduction of a turnout threshold would not combine well with the non-binding character of the advisory referendum, the initiators upheld their bill, supported by the favouring parties (Council of State 2014). In the event of a negative vote, and if the turnout threshold of 30% is met, the Act requires the government to propose a law *as soon as possible* that repeals or approves the Act that had been the subject of the vote and that Act itself cannot be the subject of a new referendum (Van der Loo 2016). Hence, the government cannot withdraw the act itself; it can only propose to parliament to do so.

The original bill was adopted in April 2014; it took until January 2015 until both Chambers adopted the second bill, which was published in the Official Journal in March 2015, indicating that the law would enter into force four months later. Hence the Advisory Referendum Act entered into force on 1 July 2015. The combination of a turnout quorum and a non-binding referendum are rather exceptional compared to referendum regulations in other European democracies.

32.3.1   Procedural Issues

The Advisory Referendum Act provides for a referendum to be held on adopted bills or ratification laws of international treaties if at least 300,000 citizens so request within a few months after its adoption, and if the government indicated in a document accompanying the act in the national Official Journal that the law can be put to a referendum. Referendums concerning

---

[5] *Voorstel van wet van de leden Dubbelboer, Duyvendak en Van der Ham, houdende regels inzake het raadgevend referendum (Wet raadgevend referendum). Tweede Kamer, 2005–2006, 30 372, nr. 2.*

[6] As the Dutch Constitution does not permit Senators the right of amendment, the only way the Senate can enforce their demands is by adjourning its adoption and requesting the Second Chamber to adopt a bill revising the law originally adopted.

the monarchy, amending the constitution or the national budget, however, are excluded, as well as those acts arising from international treaty obligations (cf. Passchier and Voermans 2016). As was the case with the referendum on the Constitutional Treaty in 2005, the date, precise question and allocation of campaign subsidies are decided by a Referendum Commission, to be appointed by the government as soon as the law entered into force. The question would include in any case whether the citizen is 'in favour or against the Act [...]'. The date should be set within 85 days of the Electoral Council deciding that the citizens' request for a referendum has met the formal requirements (i.e. more than 300,000 valid signatures collected within a stipulated period of time). This Commission is also entrusted the task of providing information to the citizens on the act which is subject to a referendum. A maximum €2 million public funding is allocated to the Commission to be distributed to 'societal initiatives with the objective to foster the public debate in the Netherlands on the Act which is subject to the referendum' (Art. 90 Advisory Referendum Act). It could equally distribute these means to initiatives supporting a Yes vote, a No vote, or to neutral initiatives promoting the turnout. No provisions regarding additional public spending limits were made, except that unjustified expenditures of the referendum subsidies would be reclaimed by the Referendum Commission.

32.3.2 Rules for the 2016 Referendum

Based on the legal framework in force in 2015, the Ratification Act of the Association Agreement was subject to an optional referendum under the Advisory Referendum Act when 300,000 citizens so demanded. In the event that the turnout threshold of 30% of the electorate was met, the outcome would be advisory to the government. The franchise was as for national elections: persons over 18 years of age holding Dutch citizenship. Dutch citizens living in the overseas islands Bonaire, St. Eustatius and Saba and Dutch EU citizens living abroad were also entitled to vote (hence excluding the other non-European constituent parts of the Kingdom of The Netherlands, i.e. Aruba, Curaçao and St. Maarten).

Except for the rules on the allocation of subsidies to foster public debate (which were capped at a maximum of €50,000 per initiative), there were no legal spending limits. Although the organisation of the referendum was left to the Referendum Commission, the government was free to express its views on the issue. There was no period of purdah during the campaign in which the government was supposed to remain inactive and publication of opinion polls were allowed throughout the campaign.

32.4   The Referendum Analysis

32.4.1   *Triggering the First Nationwide Advisory Referendum*

After the failed referendum on the Constitutional Treaty, Dutch calls for another referendum on the EU had never faded away. As the Dutch parliament ratified the Lisbon Treaty in 2008 without another consultative referendum, some opposition parties viewed the avoidance of a referendum as betrayal. Although there was not sufficient appetite within parliament for another EU referendum on e.g. membership or the fiscal compact, outside parliament citizens demanded more direct influence on EU politics. The 2014 elections for the European Parliament could not fulfil these demands. Turnout in The Netherlands was rather modest (36%) and the outcome meant merely a status quo for the influence of Dutch MEPs. Because the Dutch news agencies were not allowed to publish local results of the EP elections, anti-establishment blog *GeenStijl* recruited volunteers to report the official notification of local results in order to circumvent this ban (called the *GeenPeil* initiative). In the meantime, the newly established NGOs active in the European debate, *Burgercomité EU* and *Forum voor Democratie*, were well aware of the looming referendum laws.

The *Burgercomité* was founded in January 2013 as *Burgerforum-EU*, in reaction to British Prime Minister Cameron's 'Bloomberg speech' in which he pledged a referendum on British EU membership. It started a citizens' initiative demanding that no further national competences would be transferred to the EU, unless citizens could decide on such a transfer by referendum (Van den Dool 2013). However, when the initiative was debated, parliament showed no support for such a referendum. Most parties argued, as did Foreign Minister Timmermans, that no further transfer of sovereignty had occurred since the last treaty revision (Tweede Kamer 2014). The initiative was in vain. Thereafter, the *Burgercomité* launched a citizens' initiative for parliamentary scrutiny on the introduction of the Euro. From April 2014 onwards, it already started to recruit volunteers in order to collect enough signatures as soon as the Advisory Referendum Act had entered into force. In June 2015, they used the 10th anniversary of the Dutch 'No' to the Constitutional Treaty to launch a manifesto calling for a referendum on Dutch EU membership (Burgercomité-EU 2014, 2015). However, because (as in the UK) such a referendum required a separate act of parliament which was not been likely to be adopted in the short term, the NGOs sought recourse to other means to hold 'any' EU referendum.

Their first opportunity was the ratification laws of the so-called mixed Association Agreements between the EU, its Member States, and Ukraine, Georgia and Moldova. The Association Agreement with Ukraine would intensify the cooperation between the EU and Ukraine and mainly dealt with trade (about two-thirds of the treaty articles) and economic cooperation (a quarter of the articles). The remaining articles primarily dealt with democracy, financial cooperation, justice, peace and security. The main objectives of the association agreement were to promote peace and security, to strengthen economic and trade relationships between the EU and Ukraine and to enlarge their cooperation on justice, freedom and security (Hendriks et al. 2017: 25–26).

The Ratification Acts on these Association Agreements were approved by the Second Chamber in April 2015 by a large majority of about 80%, and by the Senate in July 2015, promulgated by the King and published in the national Official Journal. Subsequently, the Foreign Minister announced, according to the Advisory Referendum Act, that all three laws could be subject to a referendum, if, within four weeks, more than 10,000 citizens requested one (the introductory stage). The *Burgercomité* and *Forum voor Democratie* joined forces in reactivating the *GeenPeil* initiative in order to collect enough signatures. In mid-August, the Electoral Council announced that on all three association agreements, introductory requests had been submitted: 14,441 on the association agreement with Ukraine (of which 13,480 were valid requests), and, respectively, 98 and 100 on the agreements with Georgia and Moldova. As only the request on the agreement with Ukraine passed the first threshold, the initiators proceeded to the final stage in which they had to collect 300,000 signatures within six weeks (Ministry of Foreign Affairs 2015). Citizens were hardly aware of the new referendum possibility, let alone the ratification of three association agreements between the EU, its Member States and Ukraine, Moldova and Georgia. Given this lack of awareness and despite the fact that the collection of signatures started during the holidays, the initiators of *Geen-Peil* and their volunteers managed to collect more than 400,000 signatures before the deadline. Robust checks by the standing Electoral Council (*Kiesraad*) eventually estimated that of the 472,849 requests 427,939 were valid and 44,910 requests invalid (Electoral Council 2015). It was now up to the Referendum Commission, appointed by the government, to determine the date of the referendum (within six months of the announcement of the referendum on 14 October 2015) and the wording of the question. The Commission decided that the referendum would be held on 6 April 2016. The question was more straightforward than in 2005: 'Are you in favour or against the Act approving the Association agreement between the European Union and Ukraine?' (Referendum Commission 2015).

There are two main factors which may have contributed to *GeenPeil*'s successful triggering of the referendum. First, the Electoral Council allowed them to design a special website by which citizens could support the initiative. However, the law stipulated that signatures had to be submitted in writing, so *GeenPeil* printed all digital requests and submitted the packages to the bureaus of the Dutch Tax authorities in Heerlen, which would check and process the requests on their validity. This smart digital, easily accessible way to support the request, enabled the initiators to pass the threshold of 300,000 signatures. It turned out to be a game changer (Hendriks et al. 2017: 21–23).

Second, the potential salience in The Netherlands of the situation in Ukraine has to be emphasised: when Ukraine's President Yanukovych refused to sign the draft AA in November 2013, the ensuing demonstrations at the Maidan Square in Kiev triggered Dutch support for the pro-European politicians and protesters: PvdA Foreign Minister Timmermans, MEP Hans Van Baalen and well-known Belgian MEP Guy Verhofstadt visited the Maidan square. The Russian annexation of Crimea in March 2014 triggered a short wave of protest in Dutch politics and the issuing of sanctions and boycotts against Russia. The situation did not calm down, marked by political instability in Kiev and a war in the eastern part of Ukraine. The eventual signing of the Association Agreement in June 2014 did not attract much attention among Dutch public opinion. However, when on 17 July 2014 passenger flight MH17 from Amsterdam to Kuala Lumpur was hit high above the war zone area and almost 300 civilians died, the crisis topped the agenda. The public mourning, the war in Ukraine, the cooperation of local authorities with the Western investigation teams and the discussions in the UN Security Council dominated the Dutch politics and public opinion during the following months.

Hence, the recurring news around the investigation of the crash and the questions of how to handle the tense situation with Russia and Ukraine and what, if any, role the European Union should fulfil in this may have puzzled Dutch citizens in 2015 more than the calm relationship with the smaller countries Georgia and Moldova. By their grassroots campaign for the required 300,000 signatures, *GeenPeil* initiators appealed to this situation by questioning potential future Ukraine EU membership and dismissing the envisaged Association Agreement with a country 'at war' which, they argued, upset Russian President Vladimir Putin.

32.4.2   A Lacklustre Campaign

As the referendum was initiated bottom-up, the political establishment and their parties were neither prepared nor very motivated to run an active campaign. The referendum was not received with great enthusiasm among the great majority of MPs. Already in autumn 2015, it was reported that the Yes camp was 'listless'. Leading CDA and VVD MPs were almost invisible during the campaign. Whereas D66 and GreenLeft organised a modest campaign in favour, the incumbent PvdA and VVD announced that they would participate in (small) debates if requested but did not organise anything themselves. As had been the case with the Constitutional Treaty in 2005 (see Chapter 28 by Sternberg), the politicians had no idea how to defend such a comprehensive, technical agreement in the media.

A dominant argument dividing the Yes camp, was whether proponents of the AA should turn up on the polling day given the turnout threshold of 30%. As the first polls indicated that turnout figures would be about 25–40%, it might well be that the interests of the proponents would be served best if all Yes voters stayed at home, because the No voters would not be able to pass the turnout threshold on their own (Passchier and Voermans 2016). This would make the outcome of the referendum void. Several (former) politicians and public opinion figures therefore recommended not voting.[7] Only as the polls indicated that the turnout threshold could be met indeed, the government and main parties hastily started to call for a Yes vote.

As a result, some ministers did some public interviews during the last weeks before the vote, but they did not take part in any public debate. Prime Minister Rutte was not motivated to campaign for the referendum, as it was not 'an ordinary election campaign'. Problematic for the government was the leaking of a Q&A for ministers in February 2016 on possible questions from the press on the referendum. The spin doctors tried to frame the agreement as an ordinary trade deal, like the EU had concluded with countries such as Chile and Israel, which would provide The Netherlands access to a market of 45 million citizens. The question of what the cabinet would do in case The Netherlands did not ratify the agreement, should be answered as: 'that is uncharted territory'. Ministers were advised not to mention arguments about Russia (Geraedts 2016).

Although the small confessional parties Christian Union (CU) and the Reformed Political Party (SGP) had supported the government's proposal, this did not mean that they would actively support the coalition parties in order to secure a majority for the AA. Both parties merely supported the AA in order to stimulate good relations with the EU's neighbours. Voters of both parties were rather Eurosceptic, however. Too explicit support for the European case could possibly have alienated voters towards the general elections of 2017. This certainly also applied to the Christian Democrats (CDA). Party leader Van Haersma Buma disliked the referendum as such and warned on television that a possible 'No' could pose the Dutch 'enormous problems'. The CDA evolved into a critical proponent of the AA, a stance comparable to its opposition against Romanian and Bulgarian EU membership in 2007 (Otjes 2016: 141–142).

As political parties did not take a clear position, the 'Yes' campaign was led by the foundation *StemVoorNederland* (Vote for The Netherlands), established by former Labour MEP Michiel van Hulten and conservative activist Joshua Livestro. Billionaire George Soros's Open Society Foundation donated €200,000 to *StemVoorNederland* (Dirks and Visser 2016). Van Hulten characterised the first months of the campaign as a 'phoney war', with arguments about campaign subsidies and the number of polling stations as the main disputes (Niemantsverdriet 2016). A large event on the central Dam square in Amsterdam (symbolically called '*Maidam*') organised by the Yes campaign on the Sunday before the vote, attracted only some hundreds of non-partisan supporters and little media attention, despite the prominent speakers such as

[7]Those included D66 Laurens Jan Brinkhorst (former Economic Affairs minister at time of the Constitutional Treaty, who warned that the 'lights went off' in case of a Dutch No), VVD Frits Bolkestein (former European Commissioner for the Internal Market), VVD Hans Wiegel (former party leader and Senator who had always been against referendums), Bas de Gaay Fortman (former ARP, PPR MP) and GreenLeft youth organisation DWARS.

Dutch and Ukrainian ministers, leaders of the main political parties (CDA, D66, PvdA, VVD) and employers' organisation *VNO-NCW*. The employers were only willing to participate in the Yes campaign if this was supported widely by the trade unions and civil society. As the Yes campaign never actually took off, the wide support of civil society was missing.

Instead, the strongest campaign comments came from Brussels. European Commission President Juncker who warned the Dutch population, that a No vote could 'open the door to a large continental crisis' without however clarifying why this would be the case (Alonso 2016). Former European Council President Van Rompuy declared that a 'No' vote would be a 'disgrace for the Dutch government' and would make The Netherlands 'a less reliable partner' on the international scene (Schmidt 2016). As a result, the Yes campaigns were perceived poorly in the media. The context was not only dominated by the upcoming Brexit referendum due in June 2016, but also by events like the publication of the 'Panama papers'[8] two days before the vote, and the miscommunication between Dutch, European and US intelligence agencies after the Brussels terrorist attacks.

Despite limited parliamentary support, the No camp managed to mobilise itself much more effectively. *GeenPeil*, using its *GeenStijl* blog and network as its main outlet, mobilised a 'canvassing army' of 1500 volunteers for a grassroots campaign. *Forum voor Democratie* and *Burgercomité-EU* organised debates, published a manifesto and gave remarkable performances in the media.[9] When parts of the Association Agreement had already provisionally entered into force by January 2016 (particularly the Deep and Comprehensive Free Trade Area between the EU and Ukraine), *Forum voor Democratie* went to court to stop the Dutch implementation of the treaty before a positive outcome of the referendum. However, the District Court in The Hague ruled that the parts falling under EU competences were allowed to be provisionally applied, while indeed the parts falling under national competences could only enter into force after completion of the ratification procedure (Rechtbank Den Haag 2016). However, Geert Wilders's Freedom Party (PVV) copied his successful anti-European strategy of the 2005 referendum. The Socialist Party (SP) and the Party for Animals (PvdD) followed a similar strategy. Whereas the PVV classified a rejection of the Association Agreement as a backlash for the 'elites' in Brussels, the PvdD opposed the agreement because it would lead to a 'race to the bottom' in animal welfare standards.

---

[8]The *Panama Papers* comprise 11.5 million documents that were leaked to the International Consortium of Investigative Journalists who exposed a global pattern of powerful persons using secret hideaways in tax havens.

[9]In an interview one week before the vote, the leading campaigners of *Burgercomité-EU* ostentatiously repeated their argument that they did not care about Ukraine, just the EU. This caused a storm of criticism in the Yes camp (mainly D66), which accused the initiators of calling the referendum on 'fake arguments' (Heck 2016).

32.4.3   Campaign Issues

The debate during the campaign was focused on European integration (notably future EU accession of Ukraine), the performance of the Dutch government, the influence of Russia and whether the turnout quorum would be reached (Jacobs et al. 2018). Apart from these issues the campaign was characterised by debates on the provision of information and the way that the government and parliament would handle the outcome. Arguments in favour of ratification emphasised the moral duty to help Ukraine, like other CEECs previously, to reform into a full-fledged democracy, and to keep it out of Russia's sphere of influence. The Yes parties stressed that the AA would benefit Ukrainian democracy, human rights, its economy and, thus, the Ukrainian citizens (Hollander and Van Kessel 2016). The welfare for both Ukraine and The Netherlands was framed in terms of the advantages of the extended trade agreement, The Netherlands being the second largest investor in Ukraine (Otjes 2016: 135–136).

Two prominent arguments against the AA were that political and economic integration with a corrupt country like Ukraine was undesirable, and that the agreement would be a first step towards Ukrainian EU membership. Moreover, the opponents argued that the AA would lead to a further influx of Ukrainian migrant workers into The Netherlands and a waste of money for development cooperation in terms of culture, environment, justice and anti-terrorism policies. Indeed, the AA did not mention anything about future membership, but up to its conclusion EU leaders had cheered that it was the most far-reaching AA ever concluded by the EU and a third country. This gave impetus to the opponents' argument, that the Agreement would be a first step towards EU membership. The geopolitical conflict between the Europe-oriented Western part of Ukraine and the Russia-oriented Eastern part could be triggered by the AA. In their flyers, *GeenPeil* framed Ukraine as a 'civil war country' and the 'most corrupt European country'.

The limited campaigning failed to foster a well-informed public debate. Up until the last weeks of the campaign, discussions (and even litigation) about the number of voting booths per municipality and the allocation of campaign subsidies hampered a proper debate on the substance of the agreement (Hendriks et al. 2017: 32). Municipalities complained to the national government that the €30 million (initially €20 million) was not sufficient to organise the referendum, as the budget was considerably smaller than for national elections (€42.2 million in 2012). The cabinet answered that it expected lower costs, due to a lower expected turnout (and municipalities anticipated this by installing fewer polling stations) and less complicated vote counting procedures compared to national elections (Engelkes 2016: 145–150). Although the Referendum Commission was obliged to 'provide information to every voter on the referendum issue' (Art. 90 ARA), the Commission did not distribute information separately. It limited its informing actions to its website, without distributing any brochure (digital or in print) to the voters. Voters only received their polling card at home. As a result, voters had to rely completely on information available to them via other channels. The allocated budget of €2 million subsidies to foster the referendum debate was spent on a first-come-first-serve basis. The organisation behind the voting-advice application (VAA)[10] *Referendumwijzer* which was used in 2005, was refused a subsidy this time because the Commission ran out of money (although another VAA, *Kieskompas*, did receive a subsidy). A €48,000 subsidy to a one-person legal entity (notably called *Raspoetin BV*) became the slapstick of the campaign as it was spent to print toilet paper with (partly) misleading arguments against the AA, such as the suggestion that Ukrainians would be allowed to work in the EU without a visa (Hollander and Van Kessel 2016). About €250,000 of allocated subsidies had to be reclaimed due to underspending or insufficient implementation of the sponsored activities (Hendriks et al. 2017: 33).

From the moment it was known that the referendum would take place, questions arose about the way parliament and the government would handle the outcome. Whereas the government did not want to disclose its strategy in case of a No before the vote had actually taken place, a majority of the parties declared that they would consider the outcome as 'binding' and respect it, in case the turnout threshold of 30% was met (*Telegraaf* 2015). Although MPs are constitutionally free to vote however they want in parliament, a scholarly discussion started on whether respecting the outcome *ex ante* by means of a political declaration would constitute an implicit binding referendum, which as such is constitutional (Heringa 2016: 17).

32.4.4   Explaining the Vote

As stated above, the referendum resulted in a large majority rejecting the Association Agreement (61.5%). The overall turnout of 32.3% just passed the 30% threshold. What were the most important motives to vote in a certain way? Survey analyses of polls preceding the vote (by I&O Research in December 2015) show that the level of support for European integration is a much stronger predictor of the vote than government support, albeit that the interaction of these factors shows that if voters were not satisfied with the government, they were also negative on the EU (Rosema et al. 2016: 116). Hence, the vote was not about the government or Russia primarily but about the overarching position of the EU. The National Referendum Study confirms that voters mainly considered the issue at stake rather than second-order considerations. Yes voters wanted to support Ukraine (37.7%) or to foster trade relations (21%) rather than to oppose Russia (7%) (Jacobs 2016). Voters who trusted the EU and Ukraine were far less likely to vote No than voters who did not trust the EU and Ukraine, while voters who did not trust Russia were much more likely to vote Yes (Jacobs et al. 2018: 18). Opponents

---

[10]VAAs purport to provide content-based advice to the voter.

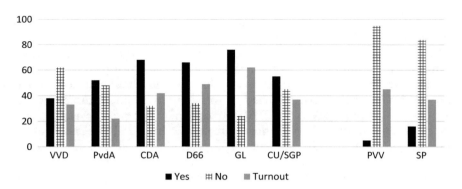

Fig. 32.1 Yes/No votes and turnout per party (%) (*Source* Ipsos Exit Poll, April 2016)

used the (alleged) levels of corruption in Ukraine as the main argument to vote No (34%), or the fear of Ukrainian EU membership (17%) rather than their opposition against the EU in general (8%).

The National Referendum Survey found that the most important reasons to abstain were a lack of information (19%), a lack of interest (13%), the practical inability to vote (13%) and the estimation that voting would not make sense (1%). 11% of the abstaining proponents of the treaty strategically hoped that the turnout threshold would not be met (Van der Kolk 2016: 31–32). Moreover, the Ipsos survey exit polls revealed that many voters abstained because (i) they believed the government would neglect the outcome anyway; (ii) they did not know what to vote; and (iii) they were against this referendum in particular (Ipsos 2016). This third argument was also confirmed in the National Referendum Study, as only 24% of the voters considered the treaty a suitable issue for a referendum. This figure correlates with the relatively large number of respondents (47%) favouring a referendum in general compared to those rejecting a referendum (18%) (Jacobs 2016: 22).

The Yes parties were not able to convince their own voters (indicated on the left side in Fig. 32.1), many of whom abstained (78% of PvdA voters; 51% of D66 voters) or voted contrary to their party's stance (62% of VVD voters). The No parties were much better able to mobilise their voters than the Yes parties: 95% of the 45% PVV voters who turned up voted against the AA; as did 84% of the SP voters of whom 37% turned out (Poort 2016).

32.5   THE AFTERMATH OF THE VOTE

As with the failed Dutch 2005 referendum on the Constitutional Treaty, the Dutch government reacted grumpily on the referendum result. The non-binding result constrained the Dutch government as it could not be sure that the ratification bill would pass anyway. Prime Minister Mark Rutte made clear that the Dutch government had no intention of ignoring popular opinion and 'simply ratify[ing]' the AA by parliamentary means. This was not surprising given the potentially damaging ramifications for the elections of March 2017. The National Referendum Study revealed that 63% of voters argued that the government 'should listen' to the result, while only 18% argued that it could neglect the outcome, because the referendum was non-binding (Jacobs 2016: 26). Although the government had to withdraw or maintain the ratification act '*as soon as* possible' (Art. 11 ARA), parliament accepted that the matter be postponed until after the Brexit vote on 23 June 2016, because of the huge implications of this vote and the opportunities to discuss it within the European Council only then. Two weeks after the Brexit vote, *Forum voor Democratie* went to court again, this time arguing that the government acted unlawfully by not withdrawing the Ratification Act immediately. However, the court ruled that it was not supposed to interfere in the Dutch legislative process, because lawmaking (adopting, implementing and withdrawing acts) is an exclusive competence of parliament. Hence it is up to parliament whether the government has acted in accordance with the ARA and rejected *Forum*'s claims (Rechtbank Den Haag 2017).

The subsequent European Council of 28 June 2016 urged the Council of the EU to seek a solution to address the concerns expressed in the debate preceding the Dutch referendum as soon as possible. The Dutch government did not stop or push through ratification but sought a third 'legally binding' alternative solution by means of a declaration.[11] Hence, other Member States did not hint at any renegotiation but simply pointed at the advisory nature of the referendum and framed it as a Dutch domestic political problem. Since parts of the agreement had already provisionally entered into force, a possible decision of the Dutch government not to ratify the AA would not have the same far-reaching consequences as the Dutch No in 2005 had. However, given the international pressure and image of The Netherlands, not ratifying was not considered a desirable option for the Dutch government. If the agreement could not enter into force, this could further increase the tensions between the EU and Russia. Hence, there was considerable pressure from Brussels not

---

[11] Report on the European Council 28–29 June 2016, by the Dutch government (translated by the author):

> *Dutch referendum on the Association Agreement with Ukraine*. The Prime Minister has outlined the situation resulting from the referendum outcome in the Netherlands on 6 April. He indicated that the agreement cannot simply be ratified. He mentioned some concerns which appeared during the debates preceding the referendum, such as the concern that this Association Agreement implies Ukrainian EU membership in the long run, the concern that it will lead to comprehensive additional financial obligations, and the fear that military cooperation also constitutes a security guarantee for Ukraine. A satisfactory solution needs to be found which addresses these concerns. The Prime Minister has made clear that such a solution should be legally binding. He also emphasised that the Netherlands does not intend to wait very long with this. It is agreed upon in the conclusions that a solution addressing the concerns raised, should be found as soon as possible.

to follow the referendum result straight away, but to look for an alternative interpretation of the vote.

Called upon by parliament to act before November 2016, Prime Minister Rutte asked for some extra time and urged all political parties, 'given the national interest', to look for a solution before 2017. He emphasised the geopolitical context of Ukraine, the civil war taking place and pressure on the country from Russia (Hendriks et al. 2017: 20). The Christian Democrats in the Second Chamber were stubbornly against (despite the fact that they had favoured the AA before the referendum), but some of their senators in the First Chamber (whose support was needed for a majority) seemed willing to cooperate. Keeping that envisaged majority in both houses in mind, the European Council of December 2016 adopted a 'Decision' on the interpretation of some parts of the AA. This decision is legally binding as a matter of international law on the EU Member States—but not on Ukraine—and may only be repealed unanimously. It would take effect once The Netherlands ratified the agreement. If The Netherlands were not to ratify, the Decision would cease to exist. The Decision contains six clauses as common understanding that the Association Agreement:

i. does not (constitute a commitment to) confer on Ukraine the status of candidate member state;
ii. does not contain an obligation for the EU or Member States to provide collective security guarantees or other military aid or assistance to Ukraine;
iii. does not permit EU or Ukrainian citizens to reside and work freely in each other's territories;
iv. does not require additional financial support by the Member States to Ukraine;
v. makes the fight against corruption central to enhancing the relationship between the EU and Ukraine;
vi. puts respect for democratic principles, human rights and fundamental freedoms and respect for the principle of the rule of law as its essential elements (European Council 2016).

Although the decision did not change anything in the AA itself, Prime Minister Rutte hoped to convince a majority in both houses. After the Council of State had confirmed in its advice that the additional declaration was in line with the existing agreement (in May 2017), the Dutch Senate did finally adopt the Association Agreement. Comparing the three adopted referendum acts of 2005, 2015 and 2018, one can observe that the political support for nationwide referendums decreased over time (see in Table 32.3). The 2005 Referendum Act on the Constitutional Treaty received a two-thirds majority. In 2015 the Advisory Referendum Act was adopted by a simple majority. Meanwhile, the 2017 Repeal Act was adopted by the smallest majority of one seat in the lower house (in the Senate 40 versus 35 seats), indicating the strong divisions within parliament on the referendum instrument. The most remarkable changes came from the liberal parties. The VVD supported the referendum in 2003 and 2005 but opposed them from 2015 onwards. D66—one of the staunchest supporters of referendums since its foundation—supported the Repeal Act because as a government party it was bound to the coalition agreement which contained the political agreement that the referendum at national level would be abolished.

On substance, the parliamentary support for the Association Agreement dropped from almost 80% in 2015 to 61% in 2017. As indicated in Table 32.2 the CDA, CU and SGP parties changed sides by arguing that the government should follow the referendum result.

After the ratification of the agreement, the debate on the EU's relationship with Ukraine faded away. The issue had hardly any impact on the general election campaign in 2017, although *Forum for Democracy* transformed itself into in a political party and managed to obtain two seats in the Second Chamber.

Table 32.2 Parliamentary support for ratification of the Association Agreement before and after the 2016 referendum

Party	EU-Ukraine AA 2015 (seats)		EU-Ukraine AA 2017 (seats)	
	For	Against	For	Against
CDA (Christian Democrats)	13			13
CU (Christian Union)	5			5
D66 (Liberal Democrats)	12		12	
GreenLeft	4		4	
LPF (Fortuynists)	–	–		
PvdA (Labour)	36		36	
PvdD (Party for Animals)		2		2
PVV (Freedom Party)		12		12
SP (Socialist Party)		15		15
SGP (State Reform Party)	3			3
VVD (Liberals)	40		40	
50PLUS	1			1
Independents	5	2	1	7
Total (150)	119 (79.3%)	31 (20.7%)	92 (61.3%) (89 present)	58 (38.7%) (55 present)

Source Tweede Kamer (2015, 2017)

GeenPeil also took part in the elections but did not obtain sufficient votes to enter the parliament.

32.5.1 Disappearance of the Advisory Referendum

The first bottom-up referendum experience on an EU matter in a Member State had a remarkable epilogue. Shortly after the vote Interior Minister Plasterk announced an evaluation of the ARA (implying possible modification or abolition of the turnout quorum). However the new coalition agreement between VVD, CDA, D66 and Christian Union was committed in 2017 to repealing the ARA, because it 'has not met expectations' (Dutch Coalition agreement 2017). The Repeal Act included a highly disputed rule that the act itself could not be subject to an advisory referendum itself, which the Dutch Council of State qualified as legally effective, but politically debatable (Dutch Council of State 2017).

Comparing the three adopted referendum acts of 2005, 2015 and 2018, one can observe that the political support for nationwide referendums decreased over time (see in Table 32.3). After a fierce debate in parliament and in the public opinion, the small coalition majority in the Second Chamber repealed the Act in February 2018 and the Senate followed this decision in July 2018. Hence, it appears that the vote in March 2018 on the Act on the Intelligence and Security Services turned out to be the last nationwide referendum as long as no other (ad hoc) referendum laws are provided.

32.6   Concluding Remarks

The Dutch referendum on the EU-Ukraine Association Agreement is exceptional due to its subject matter and non-binding nature, combined with a turnout threshold. The advisory vote proved as a first test to the new Advisory Referendum Act. Parliament and government were taken by surprise that the act was triggered immediately, and many parties were not able or willing to set up an active campaign. In contrast, the societal actors triggering the vote in opposition to the Association Agreement had been seeking a referendum opportunity on 'any' EU matter for some years. They were quite successful and creative in gathering the required signatures, allying with anti-European parties and mobilising sufficient No voters. The set up of the Referendum Committee, the provision of information and allocation of subsidies for campaign activities had to take place in a short time in a country which had relatively little experience in organising nationwide referendums. Despite these constrained campaigning conditions, and debates on procedural issues about the referendum instead of the substance of the treaty itself, many voters based their choice on the issue at stake. Voting arguments were predominantly related to several aspects on the desired relationship between the EU and Ukraine, rather than second-order considerations. The strategic calculus

Table 32.3 Parliamentary support for nationwide referendums in The Netherlands

Party	Consultative Referendum Act European Constitution 2005 (seats)		Advisory Referendum Act 2015 (seats)		Advisory Referendum Repeal Act 2018 (seats)	
	For	Against	For	Against	For	Against
CDA (Christian Democrats)		44		13	19	
CU (Christian Union)		3		5	5	
D66 (Liberal Democrats)	6		12		19	
GreenLeft	8		4			14
LPF (Fortuynists)	8		–	–	–	–
PvdA (Labour)	42		38			9
PvdD (Party for Animals)	–	–	2			5
PVV (Freedom Party)	–	–	15			20
SP (Socialist Party)	9		15			14
SGP (State Reform Party)		2		3	3	
VVD (Liberals)	28			41	33	
50PLUS	–	–	2			4
DENK	–	–	–	–		3
FvD (Forum for Democracy)	–	–	–	–		2
Total (150)	101 (67.3%)	49 (32.7%)	88 (58.7%)	62 (41.3%)	76 (51%)	69 (present of 74) (49%)

Source Tweede Kamer (2003, 2015, 2018)

of some Yes voters to abstain hoping that the turnout quorum would not be met failed as it just passed the 30% mark.

The clear and valid No vote of 61% put the political actors in dire straits. The pressure of domestic and European partners not to retain the status quo by simply ratifying the agreement without any change, and the potential consequences for the EU having concluded an agreement whose ratification was never completed, urged skilful interpretation by means of alternative policies. In fact, the Dutch parliament proved to have the final say on the popular vote which had been initiated by citizens. Although pressure was put on the Dutch government to continue ratification, the European partners also had to give in by providing the Dutch government with a way out to ratify supported by an additional declaration of the European Council. This deal sufficed for the Dutch parliament eventually to support the agreement without ordering a second referendum. The withdrawal of the Advisory Referendum Act after the government's negative experience hints at referendum avoidance in general and fewer opportunities for direct democracy on European matters in The Netherlands, such as on treaty reform or on future accession of prospective member states.

References

Aarts, K., & Van der Kolk, H. (2005). *Nederlanders en Europa; het referendum over de Europese grondwet*. Amsterdam: Bert Bakker.

Alonso, S. (2016, January 9). Juncker: 'Nederlands nee kan leiden tot grote continentale crisis'. *NRC Handelsblad*.

Bogdanor, V. (1994). Western Europe. In D. Butler & A. Ranney (Eds.), *Referendums Around the World: The Growing Use of Direct Democracy*. Washington, DC: American Enterprise Institute for Public Policy Research.

Burgercomité-EU. (2014). *Help mee met een referendum*.

Burgercomité-EU. (2015). *Manifest aan het volk van Nederland*.

Council of State. (2003). *Advice of the Council of State of 14 July 2003*. W04.03.0194/I. Kamerstukken II 2002/03, 28 885, A.

Council of State. (2014). *Advice of the Council of State of 28 May 2014*. W04.14.0143/I. Tweede Kamer, 2013–2014, 33 934, nr. 4.

Dirks, B., & Visser, J. (2016, February 1). De dans om de referendumgelden. *De Volkskrant*.

Dutch Coalition Agreement. (2017). *Confidence in the Future VVD—CDA—D66—Christian Union*.

Dutch Council of State. (2017). *Rapport over voorstel tot intrekking van de Wet raadgevend referendum*.

Electoral Council. (2015). *Announcement 14 October 2015*.

Elzinga, D. J. (2005). Het referenduminstrument. In K. Aarts & H. Van der Kolk (Eds.), *Nederlanders en Europa; het referendum over de Europese grondwet*. Amsterdam: Bert Bakker.

Engelkes, J. (2016). 'Een kostenefficiënt referendum': de beschikbaarstelling van maximaal 35 miljoen euro door het kabinet. In A. W. Heringa (Ed.), *Het eerste raadgevend referendum*. Den Haag: Montesquieu Instituut.

European Council. (2016). *Conclusions 15 December 2016* (EUCO 34/16).

Geraedts, J. (2016, February 18). Strategie uitgelekt: zo promoot het kabinet een 'ja' bij het Oekraïne-referendum. *RTL Nieuws*.

Heck, W. (2016, March 31). Oekraïne kan ons niets schelen. *NRC Handelsblad*.

Hendriks, F., van der Krieken, K., & Wagenaar, C. (2017). *Democratische zegen of vloek? Aantekeningen bij het referendum*. Amsterdam: Amsterdam University Press.

Heringa, A. W. (2016). Het eerste raadgevend referendum in Nederland. In A. W. Heringa (Ed.), *Het eerste raadgevend referendum*. Den Haag: Montesquieu Instituut.

Hollander, S., & Van Kessel, S. (2016, June 20). The Dutch Ukraine-Referendum: Campaign, Results and Aftermath. *EPERN* [Online].

Interior Ministry. (2002). *Letter of the Interior Minister to the Second Chamber, 16 September 2002. Tweede Kamer, 2001–2002, 28.515, nr. 4.*

Jacobs, K. (2016). Attitudes ten aanzien van het akkoord en de uitslag. In K. Jacobs (Ed.), *Het Oekraïne-referendum. Nationaal Referendum Onderzoek 2016.* Nijmegen: Stichting Nationaal KiezersOnderzoek Nederland (SKON).

Jacobs, K., Akkerman, A., & Zaslove, A. (2018). The Voice of Populist People? Referendum Preferences, Practices and Populist Attitudes. *Acta Politica, 53,* 517–541.

Lucardie, P., & Voerman, G. (2006). The Netherlands. *European Journal of Political Research, 45,* 1201–1206.

Massüger, N., & Kuoni, B. (2011). Viel Raum für Politik - die rechtlichen Grundlagen der nationalen EU-Referenden. *Zeitschrift für Staats- und Europawissenschaften, 9,* 131–155.

Ministry of Foreign Affairs. (2015). *Inleidend verzoek referendum over EU-associatieverdrag met Oekraïne toegelaten.*

Niemantsverdriet, T. (2016, March 16). De voorstander is een beetje lui. *NRC Handelsblad.*

Otjes, S. (2016). Stabiliteit en welvaart ter discussie. De posities van Nederlandse politieke partijen over het associatieakkoord met Oekraïne. In A. W. Heringa (Ed.), *Het eerste raadgevend referendum.* Maastricht: Montesquieu Instituut.

Passchier, R., & Voermans, W. (2016). Going Against the Consociational Grain: The Debate on the Dutch Advisory Referendum Act and the Ukraine-EU Association Agreement Referendum. *IConnectBlog* [Online].

Poort, A. (2016, April 8). Boze man tegen? Vooral boze vrouw [Ipsos Exit Poll]. *NRC Handelsblad.*

Qvortrup, M. (2018). The History of Referendums and Direct Democracy. In M. Qvortrup & L. Morel (Eds.), *The Routledge Handbook to Referendums and Direct Democracy.* Abingdon: Routledge.

Rechtbank Den Haag. (2016). *Kort geding. Vordering strekkende tot buitenwerkingstelling van - de Nederlandse participatie in - het Associatieverdrag met Oekraïne afgewezen.*

Rechtbank Den Haag. (2017). *Onrechtmatige overheidsdaad? Rechtbank niet bevoegd te oordelen over de vraag of de regering artikel 11 van de Wet raadgevend referendum heeft geschonden.*

Referendum Commission. (2015). *Press Release.*

Rosema, M., Kanne, P., & Klein Kranenburg, L. (2016). Het 'Oekraïne-referendum' in de ogen van de kiezers. In A. W. Heringa (Ed.), *Het eerste raadgevend referendum.* Den Haag: Montesquieu Instituut.

Schmidt, C. (2016, March 14). Van Rompuy: 'Een nee bij referendum is blamage voor Nederland'. *Trouw.*

Telegraaf. (2015, November 24). Kamer: uitslag Oekraïnereferendum overnemen. *Telegraaf.*

Tweede Kamer. (2003). *Voorstel van wet van de leden Karimi, Dubbelboer en Van der Ham betreffende het houden van een raadplegend referendum over het grondwettelijk verdrag voor de Europese Unie (Wet raadplegend referendum Europese Grondwet).*

Tweede Kamer. (2014). *Handelingen 21 januari 2014: Burgerinitiatief "Geen EU-bevoegdhedenoverdracht zonder referendum".*

Tweede Kamer. (2015). *Goedkeuring van de op 27 juni 2014 te Brussel tot stand gekomen Associatieovereenkomst tussen de Europese Unie en de Europese Gemeenschap voor Atoomenergie en haar lidstaten, enerzijds, en Oekraïne, anderzijds (Trb. 2014, 160)*.

Tweede Kamer. (2017). *Regeling inwerkingtreding van de goedkeuring Associatieovereenkomst tussen de Europese Unie en de Europese Gemeenschap voor Atoomenergie met Oekraïne (Tweede Kamer 2016–2017, 34.669 nr. 2)*.

Tweede Kamer. (2018). *Intrekking van de Wet raadgevend referendum*.

Van den Dool, P. (2013, January 26). Onherroepelijk richting een federale unie. Ook wij eisen een referendum! *NRC Handelsblad*.

Van der Kolk, H. (2016). De opkomst. In K. Jacobs (Ed.), *Het Oekraïne-referendum. Nationaal Referendum Onderzoek 2016*. Nijmegen: Stichting KiezersOnderzoek Nederland (SKON).

Van der Krieken, K. (2015). Het lokale referendum in Nederland. Een verkenning van de lokale referendumpraktijk in Nederla nd en scenario's voor de toekomst. *Rapport in opdracht van het Ministerie van Binnenlandse Zaken en Koninkrijksrelaties*. Tilburg: Tilburg University.

Van der Loo, G. (2016). The Dutch Referendum on the EU-Ukraine Association Agreement: Legal Options for Navigating a Tricky and Awkward Situation. *CEPS* [Online].

CHAPTER 33

Issue Voting in Danish EU Referendums

Palle Svensson

33.1 Introduction

Denmark is (together with Ireland) one of the European countries which has conducted most referendums on European issues. As indicated in Table 33.1 no fewer than eight referendums have been held on these issues in Denmark. Except for the 1986 and 1993 referendums they have all been obligatory and except for the 1986 referendum they have also been legally decisive.[1]

A reason for the large number of EU referendums in Denmark is that the Danish constitution provides for a particular procedure for delegation of sovereignty of constitutional powers to international authorities. No constitutional amendment is required for such delegation, as such delegation can be passed by a five-sixths majority in the *Folketing* (the unicameral Danish Parliament). However, if such a majority is not obtained, a referendum becomes necessary. According to Sects. 20 and 42 of the Constitution of Denmark a majority consisting of at least 30% of the electorate is required to *reject* the decision of the Folketing for delegating constitutional powers to international authorities. Only in 1993 was a five-sixths majority obtained, but as a result of a 'National Compromise' between the government and the opposition it was

---

[1] For an overview of Danish referendums, see Chapters 20 and 25 by Svensson and Beach respectively.

P. Svensson (✉)
Department of Political Science, Aarhus University, Aarhus, Denmark
e-mail: pal@ps.au.dk

Table 33.1   Danish referendums on Europe

	Yes %	No %	Result
1972: Denmark's Accession to the EEC	63.4	36.6	Passed
1986: The Single European Act	56.2	43.8	Passed
1992: The Maastricht Treaty	49.3	50.7	Failed
1993: The Edinburgh Agreement	56.7	43.3	Passed
1998: The Amsterdam Treaty	55.1	44.9	Passed
2000: Denmark's Accession to the Euro	46.8	53.2	Failed
2014: The Unified Patent Court	62.5	37.5	Passed
2015: Opt-Out on Justice and Home Affairs	46.9	53.1	Failed

agreed that a voluntary and legally binding referendum should be conducted, applying a particular constitutional possibility (combining Sects. 42 and 19).[2]

33.2   EXPLAINING REFERENDUM VOTING

Two main schools of thought—the issue-voting approach and the second-order elections approach—confront each other when it comes to explaining how people vote in EU referendums (Hobolt 2015; Garry et al. 2005; Svensson 2007). Whereas the first school assumes that voters' attitudes on the EU are the main determinants of voting in EU referendums, the second school assumes that the voters use referendums for signalling their support, or lack of support, for their domestic political parties and the actual government. The same kind of schools or approach deal with explaining European Parliament elections. Thus, a study of the 2014 European Parliament elections found that 'the degree to which individuals were adversely affected by the [2008 financial] crisis and their discontent with the EU's handling of the crisis are major factors in explaining defection from mainstream pro-European to Eurosceptic parties in these elections. This suggests that far from being second-order national elections concerned only with domestic politics, European issues had a significant impact on vote choices' (Hobolt and de Vries 2016: 504). Other studies have argued that EU issue voting in European Parliament elections is ephemeral and context-dependent, as EU attitudes matter for voting behaviour in contexts where the EU is salient to voters, visible in the media, and where there is meaningful partisan conflict (van Elsas et al. 2019: 341f).

The issue-voting approach to EU referendum behaviour focuses on individual attitudes, values and beliefs. It is argued that voters support or reject EU treaties on the basis of their underlying broad attitudes towards the EU project. Voters who are generally positive towards European integration and the development of the EU will be likely to support an EU treaty and vote

[2] See Chapter 25 by Beach for a more detailed analysis of the 1992 and 1993 referendums.

'Yes'. People who are generally sceptical about integration and the EU 'project' will vote 'No'. Whatever the particular nature of a person's attitude to the EU, the issue-voting approach suggests that it is primarily voters' views on the development of the EU that drive voting in a referendum on an EU treaty (Siune and Svensson 1993; Siune et al. 1994; Svensson 1994; 2002). Overall, the issue-voting approach assumes that views on the EU and on the substance of the treaty are the main determinants of voting behaviour in EU referendums. In general, this theory or approach is in line with the idea of direct democracy: it does makes sense to let the people rule.

The second-order approach to explaining voting behaviour in EU referendums focuses on concerns quite separate from the EU. This explanation is associated with the theory that certain elections are best seen as of a 'second-order' (Reif and Schmitt 1980). Second-order elections are elections such as local elections, European Parliament elections and referendums on EU and other matters that are not perceived by political actors to be as important as first-order elections that have an impact on the formation of the government of the country. According to this theory—also called 'the Franklin thesis'— voting behaviour in second-order electoral contests is heavily influenced by first-order considerations, as voters might be expected to use second-order contests as mechanisms for signalling their support, or lack of support, for their domestic political parties and government (Franklin et al. 1994a, b, 1995; Franklin 2002). Thus, in EU referendums voters who are not satisfied with the performance of the incumbent government may take the opportunity to punish the government by voting against a proposal to endorse a new EU treaty. On the other hand, voters who are satisfied with the performance of the governmental party (or parties) may vote in line with the government's wishes. In this way, an EU referendum may, in fact, be a general election by another name. The people cannot rule, but has to rely on elected representatives.

An analysis of five Danish referendums on the EC/EU from 1972 to 1998 conducted in order to test the validity of the second-order hypothesis concluded that in both the 1998 Amsterdam Treaty referendum and all the earlier referendums on European integration, the second-order thesis was only confirmed when it was weakly tested. The thesis nicely 'explains' the behaviour of Danish voters when there is no conflict between their party loyalty and their own attitudes towards European integration. However, when the test is stronger because of cross pressure between party loyalty and individual attitudes, the thesis does not hold (Svensson 2002).

In a response to this analysis Mark Franklin clarified the second-order hypotheses on voting in referendums. He concluded that the Danish case 'teaches us much about referendum voting that has relevance outside Denmark' (2002: 756). The importance of government standing applies most strongly to issues about which voters have no clear preferences. However, the EU issue may eventually cease to be seen by citizens as a low-salience foreign policy matter: 'So, even without the educative effect of repeated referendums on this issue, we can perhaps expect that any referendum called to decide the nature of European Union structures will increasingly come to resemble the Danish case' (2002: 756).

However, Franklin maintains that on matters of low saliency to voters, a referendum called by the government and opposed by opposition parties should generally be seen as a test of the standing of that government rather than as a test of support for the policy nominally at issue. And even on matters of higher salience, 'the standing of the government could still influence the outcome of a referendum whose result would otherwise have been close' (2002: 756).

Irish voters have, like the Danes, voted several times on EU matters. Perhaps the educative effect of repeated referendums may have given the EU issue higher saliency, so that the Irish rely less on the cues of political parties and more on their own attitudes? In an analysis of the 2001 and 2002 Irish Nice Treaty referendums John Garry, Michael March and Richard Sinnott raised the question: are referendums on EU treaties decided by voters' attitudes to Europe or by their attitudes to their national politics and to the incumbent government (2005: 202). They pointed out the saliency of the referendum issue as a key element, even though they did not distinguish explicitly between salience and importance: 'The more important the election or referendum in question is seen to be, the lower the role that will be played by domestic political (second-order) effects and the higher the role played by citizens' attitudes towards, or views on, the EU and the substantive content of the treaty in question' (2005: 204). Using precise data and regression analysis they showed that in both the Irish referendums on the Nice Treaty, issues were stronger predictors of vote choice than were second-order effects and that issues turned out to be even stronger predictors in the second and more salient referendum (2005: 211–213).

Garry, Marsh and Sinnott concluded that government satisfaction levels and support for political parties are likely to play some role in determining the outcome, 'but this role is presumably much smaller than the role played by "issue effects", that is by attitudes to European integration and to issues arising from the new constitution' (2005: 216). They add, however, that the Irish case indicates that the extent of the impact of European attitudes may depend on 'the vigour and the effectiveness of the referendum campaign'.

This conclusion is in line with the argument put forward by Lawrence LeDuc. He has proposed that the extent to which basic beliefs are linked to a referendum issue in the public debate provide a key starting point for understanding the empirical reality of referendum voting: 'When strongly held predispositions are reinforced by the campaign, referendums begin to take on some of the characteristics of elections, in which factors such as party identification or ideological orientation typically play a crucial role' (2002: 713). However, when parties are internally divided, when ideological alignments are unclear and when an issue is new and unfamiliar to the mass public, voters might be expected to draw more or less of their information from the campaign. Under these circumstances, LeDuc argued that the outcome of the contest becomes 'highly unpredictable' (2002: 713)—presumably because the voters have less consistent attitudes and the quality of the campaign and the actions of the Government may either change or confirm the predispositions of the voters.

It may be hypothesized that if the referendum issue is highly salient for the voters, so that they are interested in and knowledgeable about the subject and have developed consistent attitudes of relevance for their voting, there is a clear case for issue-voting. In this case a large number of voters will have made up their minds about how to vote even before the campaign begins. The campaign in this case is first and foremost important for mobilizing the voters to turn out to vote.

If the referendum issue is less salient for the voters, i.e. they are neither particularly interested in it nor knowledgeable about it, few may have well developed attitudes on the specific issue. In this case it may be hypothesized that the voters may need advice about how to vote and take cues from reference groups such as political parties. If the issue is not very important for the everyday life of the citizens, and if it is complex or completely new, more voters need advice and may turn to the political party they prefer to get a cue. If the parties are united behind a clear standpoint, they may influence the voting in the referendum to a high degree. This is also the case where voters and political parties in opposition to the incumbent government may be tempted to use the referendum as a 'second-order mechanism' to send a message to the government about its lack of popularity, while the government on the other hand appeals for support. However, taking cues from political parties and using a referendum as a second-order mechanism are not the same thing. Opposition parties may—and often do—recommend their voters to vote 'yes' to a government proposal. Whether or not the referendum is used as a second-order mechanism, it is conceivable that more voters under these circumstances make up their mind during the campaign and those who are most in doubt perhaps even as late as on the day of voting.

In sum, the most volatile voting intentions and the best possibilities for the political parties to use referendums as a second-order mechanism may be found when the referendum issue is less salient to the voters, when the result of the referendum is not very important for the daily life of the citizens and when the issue is of a complex nature or completely new to the voters. However, whereas these are necessary conditions for second-order voting, they may not be sufficient. What is required, in addition, is that the government is unpopular and that political actors such as political parties give cues to use the referendum to punish the government (Svensson 2007: 166). The two referendums in Denmark in 2014 and 2015 provide an excellent opportunity to test some aspects of the two theories of referendum voting.

33.3   Two Danish European
Referendums 2014 and 2015

33.3.1   *Unified Patent Court 2014*

On 2 October 2013 the Danish centre-left government (a minority coalition of the Social Democrats, Social Liberals and the Socialist People's Party) presented a bill on Danish membership of the Unified Patent Court (UPC). Previously, on 19 February the same year, Denmark together with other members of the European Union had signed an *Agreement on a Unified Patent Court*. The agreement had to be ratified by 13 states, including France, Germany and the United Kingdom before the agreement could be enforced. Strictly speaking the Court is not an EU institution, as it is established by an intergovernmental treaty. It is, however, open to any Member State of the European Union, but is not available to states outside the EU.

The overall aim of European patent reform was to make it simpler and cheaper to achieve and enforce patents widely in Europe. According to the Danish government that would benefit Danish business and be an important factor in creating a better framework for innovation, growth and job creation. With the introduction of the new European patent a uniform legal effect—the so-called unitary patent—would make it possible to obtain patent protection widely in Europe on the basis of only one application. The unitary patent introduced a new alternative that complemented existing patent protection options. The use of the unitary patent would be voluntary for companies, which could continue to choose to apply for national patents and ordinary European patents. Previously, a patent holder had to act in each European country where the patent holder experienced their patent infringed. The cases had to be brought before the national courts and decided in accordance with the national law of the countries concerned. This took time and was resource-intensive. In addition, there was a risk that the cases might result in different decisions in various countries. With the establishment of a single patent court in Europe, only one action was to be taken in case of a dispute over a European patent or unitary patent before a joint specialized court, which would take decisions on the basis of the same legal basis and common rules of procedure.

The EU Patent Court should have the exclusive right to take decisions on patent disputes and the decision would have a direct effect in the participating EU countries. In particular, small and medium-sized enterprises would benefit, as they could hardly afford to run a number of parallel enforcement cases. On the other hand, the EU Patent Court could also trip a business up if it decided that its patent was not valid. If that happened, the patent would be invalid in all countries, and not just in a single country as previously.

If Denmark acceded to the new European patent reform, a local branch of the Patent Court could be set up in Copenhagen. This would mean that when Danish companies brought cases in Denmark, they would have the opportunity to bring their case in Danish or English, just as there could be a Danish judge present. A unified patent had been a request from companies for a long time, and the Danish government argued that it was important for securing jobs in Denmark. That is also why both trade unions and industry clearly supported a common patent court.

The Danish Ministry of Justice ruled in May 2013 that a five-sixths majority in the Folketing or a referendum was necessary for the government to ratify the agreement due to constitutional requirements on the transfer of sovereignty as was the case with earlier EU treaties.[3]

From the outset the bill on Danish membership of the UPC was supported by all Danish political parties in the Folketing, except the left-wing Unity List and the right-wing, anti-immigrant Danish People's Party (DPP). These two parties are generally European sceptic, opposing any further delegation of Danish sovereignty to the EU, but whereas the Unity List rejected Danish participation in the UPC from the outset, the Danish People's Party initially tried to negotiate some concessions from the government in return for accepting the UPC. Thus, the party demanded that the governing parties should promise to either hold a referendum on the proposed EU Banking Union or increase restrictions on the distribution of welfare benefits to foreign nationals in Denmark. As the party did not feel its demands were met by the government, it announced that it would vote against the bill on the UPC, thus preventing the five-sixths majority necessary for delegation of sovereignty. The government then decided in December 2013 that the referendum should take place on 25 May 2014 alongside the European Parliament elections.

The issue of the UPC cannot be characterized as complex, but it was quite new for most voters. It was not very important to the individual life of most Danes, and it was only salient to the extent that it was presented as an EU issue. As the government was rather unpopular, receiving only a 4.34 support (on a 12 point scale) in average for 2014 in Gallup polls—Social Democratic voters supporting by 7.65 and Social Liberal voters by 6.43, whereas Conservative voters (3.75) and Liberal voters (3.51) were critical and Danish People's Party voters even more critical (2.32)—it might be conceivable that the vote could be of a second-order, because opposition voters might cast a vote against the UPC in order to express their lack of support for the centre-left government. However, this is not very likely as far as the Conservative and Liberal voters are concerned, because their preferred parties were strongly in favour of the UPC, generally pro-EU and did not give any cues to their voters to support a 'No' vote. On the other hand, for the DPP voters a 'No' vote was obvious both because of the issue and the critical view on the government. For them there was no contradiction between issue-voting and second-order voting.

The situation was further complicated as the Socialist People's Party (SPP) left the government in early February 2014 due to a conflict about the Government's decision to sell DONG (Danish Oil and Natural Gas) shares.

[3]On the Danish rules on the delegation of national sovereignty, see Chapter 20 by Svensson.

The minority government lost its coalition member in pushing through parliament an approval for a highly unpopular deal, which would involve selling a share in state-owned energy giant DONG to Goldman Sachs. The development did not make the Danish government collapse, but the remaining two parties had to replace six ministers previously held by SPP members. It is conceivable that SPP voters might have used the UPC referendum to express their dissatisfaction with the government, which their party had just left, but this is hardly likely as their preferred party continued to support the UPC and gave no cues for a No vote.

The referendum was approved with 62.5% of the votes cast, enabling the government to proceed with the ratification of the *Agreement on a Unified Patent Court*, which constitutes the legal basis for the Unified Patent Court. The Court is to be common to several Member States of the EU for proceedings regarding European patents. Ratification of the agreement, which had already been approved by a simple majority of the Folketing, would also render the unitary patent applicable in Denmark.

33.3.2   Opt-Out on Justice and Home Affairs 2015

After the Danes rejected Danish participation in the Maastricht Treaty in a referendum in 1992, a 'National Compromise' agreed between all political parties except the Progress Party formed the basis for the Danish government to negotiate four so-called opt-outs from the Maastricht Treaty in December 1992 in Edinburgh (see Chapter 25 by Beach). These opt-outs outlined in the 'Edinburgh Agreement' were accepted by the Danish voters in a referendum on 18 May 1993. The opt-outs concern the Economic and Monetary Union (EMU), the Common Security and Defence Policy (CSDP), Justice and Home Affairs (JHA) and citizenship of the European Union.

The EMU opt-out means that Denmark is not obliged to replace the Danish krone with the euro. The abolition of the EMU opt-out, also called the euro opt-out, was proposed by the Danish government and put to a referendum in 2000, but was rejected by the Danish voters. The CSDP opt-out means that Denmark does not participate in the European Union's foreign policy where defence is concerned. The JHA opt-out exempts Denmark from certain areas of home affairs. The citizenship opt-out stated that European citizenship did not replace national citizenship. However, this opt-out was rendered meaningless when the Amsterdam Treaty adopted the same wording for all EU Member States.

Under the Lisbon Treaty, Denmark can change it opt-outs from a complete opt-out to the case-by-case opt-in version applying to Ireland and, until 2020 when it formally left, the United Kingdom. A protocol governing this provision stipulates that if Denmark exercises this option, the country will be bound by the Schengen *acquis* under EU law rather than participating on an intergovernmental basis.

In October 2014 the Social Democratic Prime Minister Helle Thorning-Schmidt announced plans to convert the inflexible opt-out on JHA into the more flexible case to case opt-in according to which the Folketing would decide the Danish participation in EU decisions about justice and home affairs. The specific reason for converting the JHA opt-out to an opt-in was that the JHA opt-out would force Denmark to leave the European police cooperation (Europol), as rules surrounding Europol were to change from intergovernmental cooperation to be part of the European Union.

Five pro-EU parties (the Social Democrats, the Social Liberals, the Conservative People's Party, the Socialist People's Party and the Liberals) agreed in December 2014 to hold a referendum after the up-coming general election in order to convert the opt-out on the JHA to a case-by-case opt-in similar to that held by Ireland and the United Kingdom. This was supplemented by an agreement in March 2015 among the same parties that if the referendum were approved, Denmark would join 22 EU regulations that it was not currently able to participate in.

Following the general election in June 2015, the Liberals formed the government with Lars Løkke Rasmussen as Prime Minister. He confirmed the government's intention to hold the referendum on converting the JHA opt-out into an opt-in before Christmas. On 21 August 2015, the Danish government announced that the referendum would be held on 3 December 2015.

During the campaign the five pro-EU political parties supported a 'Yes' while the Danish People's Party, the Unity List and the Liberal Alliance recommended a 'No'.

The main argument for 'Yes' was that the conversion of the opt-out to an opt-in was necessary for continued Danish participation in Europol. According to legal experts, the protocol in the Lisbon Treaty did not allow Denmark to opt-in only on Europol. It was further argued that accepting the 22 existing regulations on legal cooperation was in the Danish interest. And, finally, it was emphasized, in particular by the Liberals, that no EU decisions regarding asylum or refugee policy were to be decided by the Danish Folketing unless a new referendum that included these issues was put to a popular vote.

The main argument for 'No' was that the Europol was a bad excuse for delegating more sovereignty to the EU and in fact give up the JHA opt-out. It was argued—and towards the end of the campaign actually accepted by the foreign minister—that a referendum could have been held solely on the Europol. It was also claimed that an opt-in was unnecessary as it was possible to negotiate a parallel agreement on Danish participation in the Europol. Furthermore, the 'No' side attacked the 22 EU regulations, some of which were very technical and complicated. It was argued that further explanations were required as to why the five pro-EU parties had decided to select precisely these existing regulations and no other regulations. More specifically, the Danish People's Party in particular feared that Denmark would not be able to decide its asylum and refugee policies in the future. This argument further drew on a lack of confidence in the five EU-positive parties. It was argued that by voting 'Yes' in the referendum, Denmark could in the future delegate sovereignty in the many areas covered by EU cooperation on justice and home affairs. It would be up to the ever-present majority in the Folketing to enforce Sect. 20 of the Constitution—that there should be a five-sixths majority in the Folketing or a referendum, if Denmark should delegate sovereignty. As it was not clear what EU regulations in this area would actually imply in the future, a 'Yes' vote was in fact a kind of a blank cheque to the present and future elected representatives of the five EU-positive parties. The people, not the Folketing majority, should decide this kind of issues.

In sum, the issue and the debate on the JHA were extremely complex and salient. The vote involved several quite different things. It was not just specifically about police cooperation and Danish accession to the new Europol, but also more generally about changing one of the Danish opt-outs into an opt-in. Further it legally involved accepting 22 EU regulations with delegation of sovereignty. Finally, in political terms the vote involved confidence, or lack of confidence, in the pro-EU parties in the Folketing to decide Danish participation in future EU policies on judicial and home affairs.

A large number of voters were uncertain about how to vote and many seemed to have changed their mind during the campaign. According to opinion polls about a third of the voters had not made up their mind as late as mid-November. Up to the end of August polls showed a majority for 'Yes', but during the following three months the majority shifted between 'Yes' and 'No', while a majority for 'No' became stable from the end of November at the same time as the number of undecided voters declined.

According to Gallup polls the Liberal government was in 2015 as unpopular (4.4) as the Social Democratic-led government had been the previous year. In particular, the Liberal government was very unpopular among voters for the Unity List (1.0), the Socialist People's Party (1.4), the Social Democrats (2.5) and the newly formed party Alternative (2.6). Thus, it is conceivable that SPP, SD and Alternative voters would cast a No vote in the referendum, even if their party recommended a 'Yes' and did not give any cues for a 'No' vote. If a second-order effect should be at work, it should be found among these voters.

The referendum with a turnout of 72% rejected converting the JHA opt-out to an opt-in, as 53.1% of the participating voters cast a 'No' vote and the 'No' votes comprised 37.5% of all eligible voters.

33.4   Issue-Voting or Second-Order Voting?

In referendums on issues of European integration, it is not only debated how important attitudes towards Europe are for the voters, it is also an open question whether and to what extent these attitudes change during the campaign. In an analysis of the referendum on the Dutch Ukraine–European Union Association Agreement, Andreas C. Goldberg and Claes H. de Vreese (2018) have

Table 33.2   Reported time of vote decision

	UPC referendum 2014		JHA opt-out referendum 2015	
	Yes %	No %	Yes %	No %
Long before the referendum was called	22.1	20.4	19.9	27.3
More than a month before the vote	18.3	13.9	22.8	23.3
Within the last month of the vote	26.0	27.7	18.2	16.3
The last days before the vote	23.2	22.3	24.6	18.7
On the day of the vote	5.9	7.7	8.8	10.6
In the polling room	3.9	6.5	5.7	3.8
Don't know/refuse to answer	0.6	1.5	–	–
Total	100.0	100.0	100.0	100.0

shown significant changes in EU attitudes during the referendum campaign and indicated the relevance of some of these changes for the referendum vote. Dynamic data as applied by Goldberg and de Vreese were not available for this paper, but it could be argued that whereas the Netherlands have had only two EU referendums, Denmark has held several referendums on the EU and for this reason a large number of Danish voters might have well-established and stable views in favour of or against proposals concerning the EU. The more voters have stable EU attitudes, the less the campaign has an impact on the referendum vote, and only a fairly small number of voters make up their mind about how to vote during the last days before the vote.

As shown in Table 33.2,[4] about half of the voters who voted 'No' and about two out of five of those who voted 'Yes' in the 2015 referendum on the JHA opt-out had taken their decision well before the campaign. This indicates that a large number of the voters acted on the basis of their attitudes to the EU without being dependent on cues given by their preferred political party. The issue-voting tendency seems less evident about the UPC referendum in 2014, but it is, nevertheless, remarkable that about a third of the 'No' voters had made up their mind even before the campaign started on this new, but rather practical proposal, which was not even a part of the EU. Apparently, a number of Danish voters have such strong anti-EU feelings that they vote against everything with the slightest relation to the EU.

Turning to the relationship between referendum vote and party vote in the recent national election it should be remembered that five pro-EU parties (the Social Democrats, the Social Liberals, the Conservative People's Party,

[4]This and the following tables have kindly been provided to the author by Professor Derek Beach, Department of Political Science, Aarhus University. The data were collected by Epinion combining web interviews and telephone interviews. In 2014 the data were collected between 28 May and 22 June (n=1.012). In 2015 the data were collected between 4 December 2015 and 5 January 2016 (n=1.005).

the Socialist People's Party and the Liberals) recommended a 'Yes' vote in both referendums.

In 2014 a second-order vote should have motivated Conservatives and Liberals to vote to a lesser extent than the supporters of the governmental parties (the Social Democrats and the Social Liberals) but, as shown in Table 33.3, this was not the case. About or more than 60% voted 'Yes' exactly to the same extent as the Social Democrats and the Social Liberals. Only among Socialist People's Party voters was the 'Yes' vote lower (51%), which might indicate a second-order effect, caused by the recent break-up of the centre-left government. That Danish People's Party voters and Unity List voters voted 'Yes' to a much lesser extent is hardly surprising, both from an issue-voting and a second-order voting point of view. It is, however, remarkable that about a quarter of these voters voted 'Yes', which indicates a kind of opposite second-order voting as the UPC was less salient to the voters, not very important to their daily life, and completely new. Some of the DPP and UL voters did not follow the cues from their party but accepted the practical arguments from the main parties, the media and the business organizations.

The 2015 vote on the JHA opt-out indicates issue-voting rather than second-order voting more clearly than the 2014 vote on the UPC. Second-order effects should be found among the Social Democrats, the Social Liberals and the Socialist People's Party voters, but only among the last mentioned (52.8% 'Yes') could such effects be observed and just to a small extent. The Social Democratic voters in opposition to the centre-right government voted 'Yes' to the same extent as the Conservative voters whose party participated in the government, and the Social Liberal voters in opposition to the government voted 'Yes' to an even larger extent than the Liberal voters whose party was the leading governmental party. Furthermore, the JHA vote was a clearer case of issue-voting than the UPC vote as the DPP and UL voters followed the cues of their party (and presumably their own attitudes) to a stronger extent in the JHA vote than in UPC vote.

Table 33.3 Party vote in most recent national election and referendum vote

Percentage of Yes-voters among those voting for various political parties in 2011/2015	2014 %	2015 %
Social democrats	61.6	59.1
Social liberals	68.4	77.8
Conservatives	58.9	58.6
Socialists people's party	51.0	52.8
Liberal alliance	66.7	54.2
Danish people's party	28.7	18.8
Liberals	69.1	72.7
Unity list	28.6	17.4
Alternative	–	52.3

Closer scrutiny of the figures in Table 33.3 reveals that about two out of five Social Democrats and Conservatives did not follow the cues given by their party leaders whether their party was in government or not. This indicates that a considerable number of Social Democrats and Conservatives hold EU-sceptic views and attitudes. Much the same holds for about half of the voters supporting the Socialist People's Party. In other words, when a conflict arises between the cues given by political party leaders and the voters' own views and attitudes on the issue to be decided many voters do not follow their party leaders. This observation rather points to issue-voting than to second-order voting.

That both Danish referendums discussed here, but the 2015 vote more so than the 2014 vote, were cases of issue-voting is further documented when the focus is shifted more directly to the views and attitudes of the Danish voters. As shown in Table 33.4, those voters who viewed Danish EU membership as more advantageous than disadvantageous voted strongly 'Yes' in both referendums, in particular in 2015, where almost 90% of those who found Danish EU membership clearly more advantageous supported the proposal. That the 2014 referendum was a little less clear as a case of issue-voting is indicated by the higher number of voters who found that Danish EU membership had neither more advantages nor disadvantages (41.9% in 2014 compared to 19.2% in 2015), and that the voters who found Danish EU membership disadvantageous voted 'No' to a higher degree in 2014 than in 2015.

The relationship between views on EU membership and referendum vote was, however, as to be expected from the issue-voting theory, and this relationship is further confirmed when the attitudes to the EU are considered. Table 33.5 presents a scale of attitudes from the most negative (that Denmark should exit the EU) to the most positive (that the EU should over time become the United States of Europe). The table further shows that the 'Yes' vote increased systematically as the attitudes to the EU got more and more positive. The only—small—deviation from the pattern expected from the issue-voting theory is the drop in 2015 from 89% to 84% from the next-most positive to the most positive attitude.

Table 33.4 Views on EU membership and referendum vote

Percentage of Yes voters who agreed with the following views	2014 %	2015 %
Clearly more advantages	81.7	88.5
Mainly more advantages	66.1	68.2
Neither nor	41.9	19.2
Mainly more disadvantages	23.5	11.7
Clearly more disadvantages	14.5	9.0
Don't know	19.2	–

Table 33.5 EU attitudes and referendum vote

Percentage of Yes-voters who agreed with the following statements	2014 %	2015 %
Denmark should exit the EU	19.1	6.7
EU should interfere less in the member states	44.8	26.6
EU should maintain its present form with neither more nor less decisions taken at the EU level	70.7	68.0
The Member States should increasingly entrust decisions to the EU and submit to the community	77.2	89.0
The EU should over time become the United States of Europe	77.4	84.0

Once again, the 2015 referendum proved the clearer case of issue-voting. Not only were the 'Yes' percentages smaller among the EU sceptics and higher among the EU-positive voters than in 2014, but the distance between EU sceptics and EU-positive voters was also larger in 2015 than in 2014 (percentage differences 77.4 − 19.1 = 58.3% in 2014 compared to 84.0 − 6.7 = 77.3% in 2015).

To sum up, both Danish referendums in 2014 and 2015 were characterized by issue-voting, but the 2015 vote more so than the 2014 vote. Second-order effects were few and small. Very few used the opportunity to cast a vote against a government that they disliked. A large number of voters made up their mind well before the campaign started, and those who came in doubt because of the arguments advanced during the campaign ended up following the cues given by their preferred party on the issue to be decided when the cues were not in conflict with their own views and attitudes, but in case of conflict relied on their own views and attitudes on the EU.

33.5   Conclusions

Some years after adopting the 'National Compromise' of 1992 the actual and potential governmental parties in Denmark tried to get rid of the opt-outs to the Maastricht Treaty and subsequent treaties, but failed in 2000 on the Euro and in 2015 on Justice and Home Affairs. It could be argued that the referendum device in this sense has contributed to the legitimacy of democracy in Denmark by maintaining a correspondence between popular opinions and political decisions on the EU and by improving the understanding and information of such policies among the voters. On the other hand, the efficiency of the political authorities in Denmark have been limited or even undermined, as it has become more difficult to formulate policies in relation to the EU and implement such decisions.

As far as issue-voting contra second-order voting is concerned, the case of Denmark may be a special one, because a broad pro-EU consensus exists among the actual and potential governmental parties—a consensus which is not to the same extent shared by the voters for these parties. General elections in Denmark are generally decided on topics other than the EU. Usually it is not the case that a referendum is called by the government and opposed by the opposition parties that constitute an alternative government. Thus, few opportunities are open for the voters to use referendum votes on the EU to express their dislike of the current government because their own party leaders also do their best to convince them to vote for the policy proposed by the government. While second-order voting has difficult conditions to unfold, issue-voting is far better off, which means that results of EU referendums in Denmark can, by and large, be taken as valid expressions of the will of the Danish people and that—differently stated—direct democracy works for EU matters.

References

Franklin, M. N. (2002). Learning From the Danish Case: A Comment on Palle Svensson's Critique of the Franklin Thesis. *European Journal of Political Research, 41*(6), 751–757.

Franklin, M., Marsh, M., & McLaren, L. (1994a). Uncorking the Bottle: Popular Opposition to European Unification in the Wake of Maastricht. *Journal of Common Market Studies, 32,* 455–472.

Franklin, M., Marsh, M., & Wlezien, C. (1994b). Attitudes Toward Europe and Referendum Votes: A Response to Siune and Svensson. *Electoral Studies, 13,* 117–121.

Franklin, M., van der Eijk, C., & Marsh, M. (1995). Referendum Outcomes and Trust in Government: Public Support for Europe in the Wake of Maastricht. *West European Politics, 18*(3), 101–117.

Garry, J., Marsh, M., & Sinnott, R. (2005). 'Second-Order' versus 'Issue-Voting' Effects in EU Referendums: Evidence From the Irish Nice Treaty Referendums. *European Union Politics, 6*(2), 201–221.

Goldberg, A. C., & de Vreese, C. H. (2018). The Dynamics of EU Attitudes and Their Effects on Voting. *Acta Politica, 53*(4), 542–568.

Hobolt, S. B. (2015). The 2014 European Parliament Elections: Divided in Unity? *Journal of Common Market Studies, 53,* 6–21.

Hobolt, S. B., & de Vries, C. (2016). Turning Against the Union? The Impact of the Crisis on the Eurosceptic Vote in the 2014 European Parliament Elections. *Electoral Studies, 44,* 504–514.

LeDuc, L. (2002). Opinion Change and Voting Behaviour in Referendums. *European Journal of Political Research, 41,* 711–732.

Reif, K., & Schmitt, H. (1980). Nine Second Order National Elections: A Conceptual Framework for the Analysis of European Election Results. *European Journal of Political Research, 8,* 3–44.

Siune, K., & Svensson, P. (1993). The Danes and The Maastricht Treaty: The Danish EC Referendum of June 1992. *Electoral Studies, 12*(2), 99–111.

Siune, K., Svensson, P., & Tonsgaard, O. (1994). The European Union: The Danes Said 'No' in 1992 but 'Yes' in 1993: How and Why? *Electoral Studies, 13*(2), 107–116.

Svensson, P. (1994). The Danish Yes to Maastricht and Edinburgh. The EC Referendum of May 1993. *Scandinavian Political Studies, 17*(1), 69–82.

Svensson, P. (2002). Five Danish Referendums on the European Community and European Union: A Critical Assessment of the Franklin Thesis. *European Journal of Political Research, 41*(6), 733–750.

Svensson, P. (2007). Voting Behaviour in the European Constitution Process. In Z. T. Pállinger, B. Kaufmann, W. Marxer, & T. Schiller (Eds.), *Direct Democracy in Europe, Developments and Prospects* (pp. 163–173). Wiesbaden: Verlag für Sozialwissenschaften.

van Elsas, E. J., Goldberg, A. C., & de Vreese, C. H. (2019). EU Issue Voting and the 2014 EP Election Campaign: A Dynamic Perspective. *Journal of Elections, Public Opinion and Parties, 20*(3), 341–360.

INDEX

Printed in the United States
By Bookmasters